THIRD EDITION

BIOINFORMATICS
A Practical Guide to the Analysis of Genes and Proteins

THIRD EDITION

BIOINFORMATICS
A Practical Guide to the Analysis of Genes and Proteins

Edited By

Andreas D. Baxevanis

B. F. Francis Ouellette

WILEY-
INTERSCIENCE

A John Wiley & Sons, Inc., Publication

Published by John Wiley & Sons, Inc., Hoboken, New Jersey.
Published simultaneously in Canada.

For general information on our other products and services please contact our Customer Care Department within the U.S. at 877-762-2974, outside the U.S. at 317-572-3993 or fax 317-572-4002.

Wiley also publishes its books in a variety of electronic formats. Some content that appears in print, however, may not be available in electronic format.

Library of Congress Cataloging-in-Publication Data:

Bioinformatics : a practical guide to the analysis of genes and proteins / edited by Andreas D. Baxevanis, B. F. Francis Ouellette.– 3rd ed.
    p. ; cm.
  Includes bibliographical references and index.
   ISBN 0-471-47878-4 (cloth)
  1. Bioinformatics. I. Baxevanis, Andreas D. II. Ouellette, B. F. Francis. [DNLM: 1. Base Sequence. 2. Sequence Analysis–methods.
3. Computational Biology–methods. 4. Databases, Genetic. QU 58 B61523 2005] I. Baxevanis, Andreas D. II. Ouellette, B. F. Francis.
  QH324.2.B547 2005
  572.8′633′0285–dc22
2004011822

Printed in the United States of America

10 9 8 7 6 5 4 3 2

ADB dedicates this book to his best friend, Tom Young,
in celebration of a friendship full of laughter, loyalty, kindness, and all-around silliness.

BFFO dedicates this book to his daughter, Pascale.
Her smile and joy brings consonance to a complicated world.

Contents in Brief

Contents

Foreword

As we move into the 21st century, we stand at a grand inflection point in biology—how we view and practice biology has forever changed. This inflection point has been catalyzed by a number of events, perhaps the most important of which is the human genome project. It provided a genetics parts list and catalyzed the development of high throughput measurement tools (e.g., the high speed DNA sequences, DNA arrays, high throughput mass spectrometry, etc.) and high throughput measurement strategies (e.g., yeast two-hybrid technique for measuring protein/protein interactions and the genome-wide localization technique for delineating protein/DNA interactions), as well as stimulating the development of powerful new computational tools for acquiring, storing, and analyzing biological information.

The human genome project also changed how we view and practice biology in several other ways. First, it has catalyzed the view that biology is an informational science. There are two fundamental types of biological information, the digital genome and the environmental signals, intracellular, extracellular, or even from outside the organism, that impinge on the genome to facilitate the development of living organisms. These two types of biological information operate across three different time dimensions with regard to the lifetime of individual organisms—evolution, development and physiological responses. There are two major types of genomic (digital) information–the genes encoding proteins, which assemble to create the molecular machines and networks of life, and the cis-control elements that, through interactions with their cognate transcription factors, regulate the expression of their associated genes and establish the linkage relationships and architectures of the gene regulatory networks, those grand integrators of environmental signals, which then transduce the input information to the protein modules or protein networks that mediate the developmental and physiological responses of living organisms. Biological information is also

hierarchical—as one moves from the genomes to ecologies, successively higher levels of biological information are created (DNA, RNA, protein machines, protein and gene regulatory networks, cells, etc). Since environmental signals change the information at each level, in order to understand systems one must collect and integrate information from as many different hierarchical levels as possible.

Second, biology has become increasingly cross-disciplinary as biologists, chemists, computer scientists, engineers, mathematicians, and physicists work together to develop the high throughput technologies and computational/mathematical tools required for this new biology—all driven by the contemporary needs of biology. Finally, all of these changes have enabled the emergence of systems biology—the idea that we can study the interactions of all the elements in a biological system and from these come to understand its systems or emergent properties. Systems approaches have been practiced for many years, but what is unique about today's systems biology is that it can make global measurements (e.g., all mRNA, all proteins, etc.) and can integrate the global measurements from different levels of biological information.

The world of biology is, accordingly, very different from what it was even ten years ago. There are many different categories of scientists that must be educated as to this new world—undergraduate, graduates, practicing biologists, and our cross-disciplinary colleagues. One of the biggest challenges with regard to this education is to bring an awareness and understanding of the central role that mathematics, computer science, and statistics plays in deciphering the complexities of this new world of biology. Indeed, one of the most interesting exercises we at the Institute for Systems Biology have undertaken in the past year is a series of institute-wide discussions concerning ten grand computational and mathematical challenges in biology (Table 1). I will not discuss these challenges here, but will point out that they represent a very broad list focused on deciphering biological information—the digital information of the genome, the three- and four- dimensional information of proteins, the dynamic nature of protein and gene regulatory networks to the metrics and analyses necessary for global data sets—as well as their integration.

TABLE 1: ■ Grand Computational and Mathematical Challenges in Biology

1.	How to fully decipher the (digital) information content of the genome
2.	How to do all-vs.-all comparisons of thousands of genomes
3.	How to extract protein and gene regulatory networks from 1 and 2
4.	How to integrate multiple high-throughput data types dependably
5.	How to visualize and explore large-scale, multi-dimensional data
6.	How to convert static network maps into dynamic mathematical models
7.	How to predict protein structure and function *ab initio*
8.	How to identify signatures for cellular states (e.g., healthy vs. diseased)
9.	How to build hierarchical models across multiple scales of time and space
10.	How to reduce complex multi-dimensional models to underlying principles, e.g., the reduction of information dimensionality

This book attempts to bring this world of computer science and mathematics in biology to the entire spectrum of scientists with an interest in biology—advanced undergraduates, graduates students, practicing biologists, and our cross-disciplinary colleagues. The chapters represent serious attempts to deal with differing aspects of many of the challenges listed in Table 1. This book is particularly important because it represents a readable and concise approach to educating ordinary biologists and equipping them with the fundamental tools necessary for participating in the paradigm changes that have occurred as a consequence of the grand inflection point in biology. To all of you who are new to the worlds of genomics, proteomics, and systems biology—welcome and good reading.

Lee Hood

Preface

In the foreword to the Second Edition of *Bioinformatics*, Eric Lander conveyed the sentiment that modern biology had entered a new era with the official publication of the initial sequence and analysis of the human genome. Since that moment in time, in February of 2001, the impact of having the human sequence in hand has been nothing short of tremendous. In the last few years, we have witnessed the completion of human genome sequencing, the completion of numerous model organism genome sequences, the development of new genomic technologies and approaches, and a proliferation of innumerable databases attempting to catalog all of the information that has been learned about genes, proteins, structures, mutations, polymorphisms, and many other biological features of interest. The advent of the genomic era has also laid a strong foundation for the development of new areas of endeavor, such as proteomics and systems biology, fields that are still in their infancy but that have the potential to have an even greater impact on our understanding of basic biological processes and human disease. What has become obvious in these last few years is that, regardless of one's specific area of endeavor, one of the critical keys to being able to do cutting-edge biological research in this new era lies in the ability to combine both laboratory- and computationally-based approaches in a synergistic manner, allowing the investigator to better-design experiments (based on database searches and the like), as well as facilitating the analysis of larger and larger data sets generated through experimentation. Unfortunately, despite its great power and potential in solving biological problems, the realm of bioinformatics still remains *terra incognita* for many biologists. To address the need for training and education in this area, we have developed a new edition of this book as a resource for our scientific colleagues.

This new edition of *Bioinformatics* follows in the tradition of the last two editions in keeping up with the quick pace of change in this field. In this edition, tried-and-true concepts and approaches that have stood the test of time are featured, as well as new approaches and algorithms that have emerged since the publication of the First and Second Editions. In considering how to refine the focus and content of the book, a questionnaire was sent to a number of professors currently teaching bioinformatics courses, as well as to people who are actively called-upon to lecture on these topics. Based on these responses, published reviews of the Second Edition, and our own experience in the classroom, we have included a number of new features in the Third Edition.

Six chapters have been added on topics that have emerged as being important enough in their own right to warrant distinct and separate discussion: genomic databases, predictive techniques using RNA sequences, sequence polymorphisms, intermolecular (protein-protein) interactions, comparative genomics, and protein identification using proteomic techniques. The chapter on Internet basics has been retired, and the chapter on submitting sequence information to public databases has been folded into the chapter on sequence databases. We have supplemented many of the chapters with text boxes and appendices that highlight basic biological techniques or provide more advanced information that may be of interest to readers or useful to instructors. A more rigorous set of problem sets has been included, and we hope that the reader will work through these examples to reinforce the concepts presented throughout the book. The solutions to these problems are available through the book's Web site, at *http://www.wiley.com/bioinformatics*. We are also pleased that the current edition contains color figures throughout; this is in recognition of the way in which bioinformatic information is presented nowadays by many Web sites, using color much more than before to communicate basic biological information to the user. We are hopeful that the inclusion of all of these features, in response to the valuable feedback we have received, will make this book much more useful both in the classroom and in the laboratory.

There are many people whom we need to thank, on many fronts, for all of their efforts in bringing this Third Edition to press. As always, our thanks go to all of the authors who took time out of their busy schedules to write the individual chapters in this book. Collectively, this stellar group of individuals from around the world has provided the kind of expertise and perspective that is, by far, the most important factor in making the content of this book as robust and insightful as it is. We also thank the authors for bearing with us through revisions, reminders, and a tight production schedule. We've thoroughly enjoyed the scientific discourse and the numerous chats about how to present all of this information in a way that our readers will be able to master it as easily as possible.

We also thank the numerous professors and instructors—whose identity is known to the folks at Wiley but not to us—for taking the time to respond to questionnaires and letting us know how to improve upon previous editions of the book. While we are quite pleased to see the number of course adoptions continue to grow well into the triple digits and translations of the book into languages ranging from Greek to Chinese, this kind of valuable feedback has helped us to continue to live up to our original goal in taking on this project: making bioinformatics accessible and useful to as broad of a group of scientists as possible, presented at a level that can successfully drive biological inquiry forward.

Of course, there are many people behind-the-scenes at Wiley who have worked tirelessly to actually produce the book and get it into our readers' hands. First, we thank our editor, Luna Han, for her continued support and confidence in this project, and we look forward to continuing our professional relationship with her well into the future. We also thank Kristen Hauser for taking care of all of the logistics that go into a project such as this one, a substantial undertaking with the large number of authors involved. Our thanks also go to Danielle Lacourciere and Camille Pecoul Carter for being part of this project once again, helping us with all of the production-related details and making the final product look as professional as it does. We thank Alexandra Anderson, our copyeditor, who has done a wonderful job in painstakingly proofreading the final text. Finally, we wholeheartedly thank Dr. Ann Boyle, our developmental

editor, for joining us on conference calls (and putting up with our banter) week after week, giving us the benefit of her scientific expertise and, more importantly, for helping us achieve our goal of effectively communicating the concepts presented in this book to such a broad audience.

ADB would like to specifically thank Debbie Wilson for her help through rounds of editing, wading through a myriad of proofreading marks along the way, as well as her good-natured moral support during the last two editions of this book. I would also like to thank Drs. Shonda Leonard and Dan Davison, my colleagues at *Current Protocols in Bioinformatics*, for their helpful discussions and critical reading of a number of the chapters in this book. My heartfelt thanks also go to Darryl Leja, whose creativity has led to a very impressive and eye-catching cover design. I would also like to extend special thanks to both Eric Green and Tyra Wolfsberg at NHGRI for being incredibly supportive of this effort, letting me bend their ears on many occasions and providing much-appreciated insight and advice along the way.

BFFO would like to thank his colleagues at the University of British Columbia for their vision and continued support of bioinformatics. I also want to strongly acknowledge the uncompromising support provided by my spouse, Nancy Ryder. Nancy has made it possible for me to work on this book, enduring my long nights of work on this project and never-ending discussions about production issues. Since the last edition, we have been blessed with a new daughter, Pascale, and both she and our first daughter, Maya, have been very understanding of their Papa's spending long hours at the computer. Most of all, Andy Baxevanis is the one I owe the most gratitude to. His project management skills, in addition to his always keeping what was best for the reader first and foremost, has made this book something that I am very honored and proud to be able to share with him.

The field of bioinformatics continues to become more complex and diversified, requiring that all biologists have a firm understanding of the broad array of tools available to them. We truly hope that this book will help provide our students and colleagues with the kind of insight and vision needed for tackling their next big biological question.

Andreas D. Baxevanis
B. F. Francis Ouellette

Contributors

Rolf Apweiler, Ph.D. is Head of the Sequence Database Group at the European Bioinformatics Institute. He is currently a member of the editorial boards of the European Journal of Biochemistry, Proteomics, and Biochimica et Biophysica Acta.

Gary D. Bader, Ph.D. is currently a post-doctoral fellow in the lab of Dr. Chris Sander at the Computational Biology Center at Memorial Sloan-Kettering Cancer Center in New York City. Previously, Dr. Bader completed a Ph.D. in the lab of Dr. Christopher Hogue in the Department of Biochemistry at the University of Toronto and the Program in Proteomics and Bioinformatics at the Samuel Lunenfeld Research Institute at Mount Sinai Hospital in Toronto. His thesis was the development and research use of the Biomolecular Interaction Network Database (BIND).

Geoff Barton, Ph.D. is Professor of Bioinformatics at the School of Life Sciences, University of Dundee, and Co-Director of the Post Genomics and Molecular Interactions Centre. Dr. Barton obtained his doctorate in the Department of Crystallography, Birkbeck College, University of London, and then spent two years as an ICRF Fellow working with Chris Rawlings at the Imperial Cancer Research Fund Labs in London. In 1989 he was awarded a Royal Society University Research Fellowship to work in the Lab of Molecular Biophysics, University of Oxford. Since that time Dr. Barton has held posts as Head of Genome Informatics at the Wellcome Trust Centre for Human Genetics (1995-1997), Research and Development Team Leader at the EMBL European Bioinformatics Institute (1997-2001), and Head of the European Macromolecular Structure Database at EBI (1998-2001) before taking up his present appointments in 2001. Dr. Barton has published over 50 papers about computational protein sequence and structure analysis in refereed journals as well as around 20 book chapters and other contributions. Software developed by his group is widely distributed and in daily use in many research laboratories worldwide.

Andreas D. Baxevanis, Ph.D. is the Deputy Director for Intramural Research and the Director of the Computational Genomics Program at the National Human Genome Research Institute, National Institutes of Health. He is currently the editor-in-chief of Current Protocols in Bioinformatics, senior editor of Molecular Cancer Therapeutics, and associate editor of Proteins: Structure, Function, and Bioinformatics. His involvement in educational activities include teaching bioinformatics at The Johns Hopkins University, serving as adjunct faculty at Boston University, lecturing in numerous courses, and developing materials intended to facilitate the use of genomic sequence data. His current research focuses on better-understanding structure-function relationships in DNA-binding proteins and how mutations in these proteins contribute to human disease. He is the recipient of the Bodossaki Foundation's 2000 Academic Prize in Medicine and Biology, Greece's highest honor for young scientists of Greek heritage throughout the world.

Enrique Blanco is a computer engineer at Universitat Politècnica de Catalunya, Spain, finishing his Ph.D. thesis in the Genome Bioinformatics Laboratory from Institut Municipal d'Investigació Mèdica-Universitat Pompeu Fabra in Barcelona, Spain. He works in the design of new algorithms of sequence alignment for the detection and characterization of the gene promoter regions. He has been involved in many educational activities, including teaching bioinformatics in numerous courses, and developing materials to facilitate the understanding of bioinformatics for undergraduates, graduates, and Ph.D. students from other disciplines.

Gerard G. Bouffard, Ph.D. is the Director of the Bioinformatics Group of the National Institutes of Health Intramural Sequencing Center (NISC) where he oversees data generation, management and analysis for this high-throughput DNA sequencing facility. His graduate work in mapping and sequencing in the *E. coli* genome evolved into post-doctoral research in physical mapping of human chromosome 7 and interest in comparative genomics.

Fiona S. L. Brinkman, Ph.D. is an Assistant Professor in Molecular Biology and Biochemistry at Simon Fraser University. She is also Research Director of the Genome Canada Pathogenomics Project, Coordinator of the Pseudomonas Community Genome Annotation Project, and a Core Faculty for the Canadian Bioinformatics Workshops. She has won numerous career awards for her evolutionary infectious disease and bioinformatics research, including being the only Canadian professor listed as one of the "Top 100 of the World's Young Innovators in Technology" in 2002 by the Massachusetts Institute of Technology, the 2003 Science Council of BC Young Innovator award, and Canada's "Top 40 Under 40" for 2003–2004. She has a strong interest in bioinformatics education through development of both graduate and undergraduate curricula and she developed the first undergraduate bioinformatics joint major program (computing science and molecular biology and biochemistry) in Canada.

Anton J. Enright, Ph.D. is a Research Group Leader at the Wellcome Trust Sanger Institute in Cambridge, United Kingdom. Previously he worked at the Computational Biology Center at Memorial Sloan-Kettering Cancer Center, New York and completed his EMBL and Cambridge University predoctoral fellowship at the European Bioinformatics Institute (EBI) in Cambridge, United Kingdom.

Morgan C. Giddings, Ph.D. is an Assistant Professor in the Departments of Microbiology and Immunology and Biomedical Engineering at the University of North Carolina at Chapel Hill. He is a founding member of the UNC-CH training program in bioinformatics and computational biology, computational advisor to the Michael Hooker Proteomics Core at UNC, and a member of the Carolina Center for Genome Sciences. He is the recipient of an NIH/NHGRI Genome Scholar Career Development award. His research applies both computational and laboratory science to examine how genomes encode proteomic diversity.

Roderic Guigó i Serra, Ph.D. leads the Genome Bioinformatics Laboratory at the Institut Municipal d'Investigació Mèdica in Barcelona. He is also Professor at the Universitat Pompeu Fabra, and coordinates the Bioinformatics and Genomics program within the recently created Center for Genomic Regulation. His research focuses on computational gene prediction. He is author of one of the first general purpose gene finding programs, and he has contributed to the development of standards for the evaluation of the accuracy of gene prediction programs. He has also participated in the analysis consortiums of numerous eukaryotic genomes.

Nancy Fisher Hansen, Ph.D. is a Member of the Bioinformatics group at the National Institutes of Health Intramural Sequencing Center. She designs, implements, and modifies software tools to facilitate the generation and analysis of Ordered and Oriented sequence data. She received her doctorate in physical chemistry from Stanford University, and subsequently worked as a software developer at the Stanford Genome Technology Center.

Mark Holmes is a Bioinformatics Developer in the Department of Microbiology & Immunology at the School of Medicine, University of North Carolina at Chapel Hill. His professional computing experience began in 1974 and includes early work automating his own experimental protocols at the Clinical Center of the U.S. National Institutes of Health. A former art historian and museum registrar, he worked for many years in the private sector as a senior computing consultant before returning to academic life in 2000.

David H. Mathews, M.D., Ph.D. is an Assistant Professor of Biochemistry and Biophysics in the Center for Human Genetics and Molecular Pediatric Disease at the University of Rochester Medical Center. He is the author of RNAstructure, a software package for analyzing RNA secondary structure on Windows.

Tara C. Matise, Ph.D. is Associate Professor in the Department of Genetics at Rutgers University in New Jersey. She runs the Laboratory of Computational Genomics, serves on the editorial board of Genome Research, has previously served on the Board of Scientific Counselors for the National Institute of Biotechnology Information (NCBI), National Institutes of Health (NIH), and was previously a HUGO editor for human chromosome 1.

James C. Mullikin, Ph.D. is an Associate Investigator within the Genome Technology Branch of the National Human Genome Research Institute, National Institutes of Health. Prior to joining NHGRI, Dr. Mullikin served as the Head of production software development from 1988–2002 at the Sanger Institute, where he also served as Acting Director of Informatics in 2002. He has been involved in polymorphism discovery and analysis methods since the beginning of The SNP Consortium project in 1999 while at the Sanger Institute.

Yanay Ofran, Ph.D. is a Research Fellow at Columbia University Bioinformatics Center (CUBIC) in the Department of Molecular Biophysics and Biochemistry. He is the developer of several tools and Web servers for sequence analysis and prediction. His educational activity includes teaching bioinformatics and computational biology at Columbia University. He is the recipient of the 2002 Freund Memorial Prize.

B. F. Francis Ouellette, M.Sc. is Director of the University of British Columbia (UBC) Bioinformatics Centre and Associate Professor in Medical Genetics and the Michael Smith Laboratories at UBC. He is also the Director for the Canadian Genetic Diseases Network (CGDN) Bioinformatics Core Facility, where he coordinates the Canadian Bioinformatics Workshop series. He works in comparative genomics and in building tools and databases for bioinformatics analyses. He has previously served as GenBank coordinator at the National Center for Biotechnology Information (NCBI), National Institutes of Health (NIH).

John Quackenbush, Ph.D. is an Investigator in Functional Genomics and Bioinformatics at The Institute for Genomic Research (TIGR) in Rockville, Maryland. He also holds appointments as Professor of Biochemistry at The George Washington University, as Adjunct Professor of Biostatistics at the Bloomberg School of Public Health at The Johns Hopkins University, and as Adjunct Professor of Chemical Engineering at the University of Maryland. Dr. Quackenbush has organized and taught many workshops and courses on DNA microarray analysis and has authored a book (with Helen Causton and Alvis Brazma) as well as numerous articles in the subject. Among other accomplishments, he and his group build the TIGR Gene Index databases, including RESOURCERER and are responsible for the freely-available, open-source TM4 software package for DNA microarray analysis. He is also actively involved in the Microarray Gene Expression Data society (MGED), which has been developing standards for microarray data reporting.

Kevin R. Ramkissoon, B.Sc. is a doctoral graduate student in the department of Microbiology & Immunology at the University of North Carolina at Chapel Hill. His current research interests include the development proteomic and bioinformatic methods to study viral and prokaryotic evolution with a focus on antimicrobial drug resistance, pathogenicity, and immune response evasion.

Burkhard Rost, Dr. rer. nat. is an Associate Professor in the Department of Biochemistry and Molecular Biophysics at Columbia University. Since obtaining his doctorate at the Institute of Theoretical Physics, Heidelberg, Dr. Rost held posts at EMBL Heidelberg (1990–1994), EBI Cambridge (1995), EMBL Heidelberg (1996–1998), and LION Biosciences (1998) before taking up his present appointment in 1999. His group focuses on methods for predicting protein structure and function from sequence, primarily in the context of entirely sequenced organisms. Dr. Rost has given 93 invited lectures in 16 countries, has had over 100 papers published that have been quoted over 5,000 times, and has been responsible for PredictProtein, one of the first Web servers in molecular biology.

Stephen T. Sherry, Ph.D. is Staff Scientist at the National Center for Biotechnology Information (NCBI), National Library of Medicine (NLM), National Institutes of Health (NIH), where he supervises the dbSNP database of genetic variation and directs the development of open-source software tools for quality assessment of DNA forensic data. He received the Library's Board of Regents Award for Scholarship or Technical Achievement in 2003 for his advisory role in applying computational forensic methods to help identify victims of the September 11, 2001 tragedy of the World Trade Center in New York City.

Lincoln D. Stein, M.D., Ph.D. is an Associate Professor at the Cold Spring Harbor Laboratory, where he works on genome databases. He teaches bioinformatics and genetics at the Watson School for Biomedical Sciences, and was recently awarded the Benjamin Franklin prize for service to bioinformatics.

Pamela Jacques Thomas, Ph.D. is a Member of the Bioinformatics Group at the National Institutes of Health Intramural Sequencing Center (NISC) where she focuses on the assembly and annotation of BAC-derived sequences from multiple vertebrates. She received her doctorate from Case Western Reserve University and previously worked as a GenBank Scientific Data Analyst at the National Center for Biotechnology Information (NCBI), National Institutes of Health (NIH).

Peter S. White, Ph.D. is a Research Assistant Professor in the Department of Pediatrics at the University of Pennsylvania, and in the Division of Oncology, Childrens Hospital of Philadelphia (CHOP). Dr. White holds the David Lawrence Altschuler Endowed Chair in Genomics and Computational Biology at CHOP. He is a member of Penn's Center for Bioinformatics and Penns Genomics Institute, and he is the Faculty Director of CHOP's bioinformatics core facility.

David S. Wishart, Ph.D. is a Professor of Biological Sciences and Computing Science at the University of Alberta. He also holds the Bristol Myers Squibb Chair in protein chemistry and is a Senior Research Officer with the National Institute for Nanotechnology (NINT) in Edmonton. In addition to starting two bioinformatics companies (BioTools and Chenomx) in the 1990's, Dr. Wishart has been actively involved in teaching bioinformatics for nearly a decade, including several undergraduate and graduate courses at the University of Alberta. He has been a principal instructor for numerous week-long training workshops offered through the Canadian Bioinformatics Workshop series (CBW), the Canadian Proteomics Initiative (CPI) and Genome Canada (ACGC).

Tyra G. Wolfsberg, Ph.D. is an Associate Investigator and the Associate Director of the Bioinformatics and Scientific Programming Core at the National Human Genome Research Institute, National Institutes of Health. She lectures and publishes extensively on using bioinformatics tools, especially online genome browsers, to mine genomic sequence information.

Michael Zuker, Ph.D. is a Professor of Mathematical Sciences and Biology at Rensselaer Polytechnic Institute. He works on the development of algorithms to predict folding, hybridization and melting profiles in nucleic acids. His educational activities include developing and teaching his own bioinformatics course at Rensselaer, and participating in both a Chautauqua short course in bioinformatics for college teachers and an intensive bioinformatics course at the University of Michigan.

## PART ONE

BIOLOGICAL DATABASES

Sequence Databases

ROLF APWEILER

Bioinformatics: A Practical Guide to the Analysis of Genes and Proteins, Third Edition, edited by
Andreas D. Baxevanis and B.F. Francis Ouellette.
ISBN 0-471-47878-4 Copyright © 2005 John Wiley & Sons, Inc.

▋ INTRODUCTION

Over the past three decades, there has been a feverish push to understand, at the most elementary of levels, what constitutes the basic "book of life." Biologists (and scientists in general) are driven to understand how the millions or billions of bases in an organism's genome contain all the information needed for the cell to conduct the myriad of metabolic processes necessary for the organism's survival, information that is propagated from generation to generation. To have a basic understanding of how the collection of individual nucleotide bases drives the engine of life, large amounts of sequence data must be collected and stored in a way that these data can be searched and analyzed easily. To this end, much effort has gone into the design and maintenance of biological sequence databases. These databases have had a significant impact on the advancement of our understanding of biology, not just from a computational standpoint, but also through their integrated use alongside studies being performed at the bench.

The history of sequence databases began in the early 1960s, when Margaret Dayhoff and colleagues at the Protein Information Resource (PIR) collected all of the protein sequences known at that time; her group published this collection as a printed work called the *Atlas of Protein Sequence and Structure* (Dayhoff et al., 1978). When a significant number of nucleotide sequences became available, those also were included in the *Atlas*. (It is important to remember that, at this point in the history of biology, the focus was on sequencing *proteins* through traditional techniques such as the Edman degradation, rather than on sequencing DNA.) As the *Atlas* evolved, it included text-based descriptions to accompany the protein sequences, as well as information regarding the evolution of many protein families. This work, in essence, was the first annotated sequence database, even though it was in printed form. By 1972, the amount of data contained in the *Atlas* became unwieldy, and the need for it to be available in electronic format became obvious. The contents of the *Atlas* were distributed electronically by PIR on magnetic tape, and the distribution included some basic programs that could be used to search and evaluate distant evolutionary relationships.

The advent of DNA sequence databases in 1982, initiated by the European Molecular Biology Laboratory (EMBL) and joined shortly thereafter by GenBank, led to the next phase in the history of sequence databases: the veritable explosion in the amount of nucleotide sequence databases available to researchers. Both EMBL (then based in Heidelberg) and the National Center for Biotechnology Information (NCBI, part of the National Library of Medicine at the National Institutes of Health) were contributing to the input activity, which consisted of transcribing and interpreting what was published in print journals to an electronic format more appropriate for use with computers. The DNA Databank of Japan (DDBJ) joined the data-collecting collaboration a few years later. In 1988, after a meeting of these three groups (now referred to as the International Nucleotide Sequence Database Collaboration), there was an agreement to use a common format for data elements within a unit record and to have each database update only the records that were directly submitted to it. Now, all three centers (the National Institute of Genetics in Mishima, Japan; the European Bioinformatics Institute [EBI] in Hinxton, UK; and NCBI in Bethesda, Maryland, USA) are collecting direct submissions (see Box 1.3) and distributing them so that each center has copies of all the sequences, meaning that they each act as a primary distribution center for these sequences. However, each record is managed by the database that created it and can be updated only by that database. DDBJ/EMBL/GenBank records are updated automatically every 24 hours at all three sites; therefore, any and all sequences present in the DDBJ also will be present in the EMBL and GenBank, and so forth (see Figure 1.1).

In a parallel track, the foundations for the Swiss-Prot protein sequence database also were laid in the early 1980s, when Amos Bairoch at the University of Geneva converted PIR's *Atlas* to a format similar to that used by EMBL for its nucleotide database. In this initial release, called PIR+, additional information about each of the proteins was added, increasing its value as a curated, well-annotated source of information on proteins. In the summer of 1986, Bairoch began distributing PIR+ on the US BIONET (a precursor to the Internet), renaming it Swiss-Prot. At that time, it contained the grand sum of 3900 protein sequences; this was seen as an overwhelming amount of data, in stark contrast to today's standards. Because Swiss-Prot and EMBL followed similar formats, a natural collaboration developed between these two European groups; these collaborative efforts strengthened when both EMBL and Swiss-Prot's operations were moved to EMBL's EBI in Hinxton, UK. One of the first collaborative projects undertaken was to create a new supplement to Swiss-Prot. Maintaining the high quality of Swiss-Prot entries is a time-consuming process involving extensive sequence analysis and detailed curation by expert annotators (Apweiler, 2001). So as to allow the quick release of protein sequence data not yet annotated to Swiss-Prot's stringent standards, a new database called TrEMBL (for "translation of EMBL nucleotide sequences") was created. This supplement to Swiss-Prot initially consisted of computationally annotated entries derived from the translation of all coding sequences (CDS) found in DDBJ/EMBL/GenBank, including only data that was not already present in Swiss-Prot.

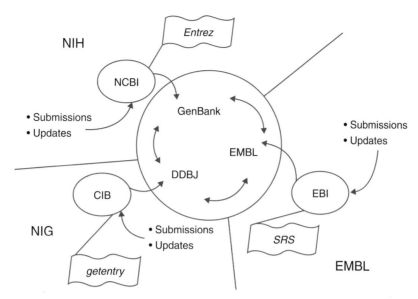

FIGURE 1.1   Data flow for new submissions and updates between the three databases. See text for details.

PRIMARY AND SECONDARY DATABASES

Before undertaking a detailed description of the major sequence databases, it is important to make a distinction between primary (archival) databases and secondary (curated) databases. The most important contribution that sequence databases make to the biological community is making the sequences themselves accessible. The primary databases contain, for the most part, experimental results (with some interpretation), but are not a curated review. Curated reviews are found in what are called secondary databases. The nucleotide sequences in DDBJ/EMBL/GenBank are derived from the sequencing of a biological molecule that exists in a test tube, somewhere in a lab. They do not represent sequences that are a consensus of a population, nor do they represent some other computer-generated string of letters. This framework has consequences in the interpretation of sequence analysis. Each such DNA and RNA sequence will be annotated to describe the analysis from experimental results that indicate why that sequence was determined in the first place. A great majority of the protein sequences available in public databases have not been determined experimentally, which may have downstream implications when analyses are performed. For example, the assignment of a product name or function qualifier based on a subjective interpretation of a similarity analysis (e.g., BLAST; see Chapter 11) can be very useful, but sometimes can be misleading. Therefore, the DNA, RNA, or protein sequences are the "computable" items to be analyzed, and they represent the most valuable component of primary databases.

NUCLEOTIDE SEQUENCE DATABASES

As described above, the major sources of nucleotide sequence data are the databases involved in the International Nucleotide Sequence Database Collaboration: DDBJ, EMBL, and GenBank; again, new or updated data are shared between these three entities once every 24 hours. This transfer is facilitated by the use of common data formats for the kinds of information that is described in detail below.

DDBJ/EMBL/GenBank nucleotide records often are the primary source of sequence and biological information from which records in other databases are derived. Because so many other databases are dependent on the accuracy of DDBJ/EMBL/GenBank records, some important considerations immediately come to the fore:

▶ If a coding sequence is not indicated on a nucleic acid record, it will not lead to the creation of a record in the protein databases. Sequence similarity searches against the protein databases, which are the most sensitive way of doing sequence similarity searches (Chapter 11), therefore may miss important biological relationships.

▶ If a coding feature in a DDBJ/EMBL/GenBank record contains incorrect information about the protein, this incorrect information will be passed on to other databases directly derived from the record; it could even be propagated to other nucleotide and protein records on the basis of sequence similarity.

▶ If important information about a protein is not entered in the appropriate place within a sequence record, any programs that are designed to extract information from these records more than likely will miss the information, meaning that the information will not filter down to other databases.

Database Formats

The elementary format underlying the information held in DDBJ/EMBL/GenBank is the *flatfile*. The correspondence between individual flatfile formats facilitates the exchange of data between each of these databases; in most cases, fields can be mapped on a one-to-one basis from one flatfile format to the other. Over time, various file formats have been adopted and have found contin-

ued, widespread use; others have fallen to the wayside for a variety of reasons. The success of a given format depends on its usefulness in a variety of contexts, as well as its power in effectively containing the types of biological information that need to be archived and communicated to the community.

In its simplest form, a sequence record can be represented as a string of nucleotides with some basic tag or identifier. The most widely used of these simple formats is FASTA, which provides an easy way of handling primary data for both humans and computers. FASTA nucleotide sequence records take the following form:

```
>U54469.1
CGGTTGCTTGGGTTTTATAACATCAGTCAGTGACAGGCATTTCCAGAGTTGCCCTGTTCAACAATCGATA
GCTGCCTTTGGCCACCAAAATCCCAAACTTAATTAAAGAATTAAATAATTCGAATAATAATTAAGCCCAG
TAACCTACGCAGCTTGAGTGCGTAACCGATATCTAGTATACATTTCGATACATCGAAATCATGGTAGTGT
TGGAGACGGAGAAGGTAAGACGATGATAGACGGCGAGCCGCATGGGTTCGATTTGCGCTGAGCCGTGGCA
GGGAACAACAAAAACAGGGTTGTTGCACAAGAGGGGAGGCGATAGTCGAGCGGAAAAGAGTGCAGTTGGC
GTGGCTACATCATCATTGTGTTCACCGATTATTTTTTGCACAATTGCTTAATATTAATTGTACTTGCACG
CTATTGTCTACGTCATAGCTATCGCTCATCTCTGTCTGTCTCTATCAAGCTATCTCTCTTTCGCGGTCAC
TCGTTCTCTTTTTTCTCTCCTTTCGCATTTGCATACGCATACCACACGTTTTCAGTGTTCTCGCTCTCTC
TCTCTTGTCAAGACATCGCGCGCGTGTGTGTGGGTGTGTCTCTAGCACATATACATAAATAGGAGAGCGG
AGAGACAAATATGGAAAGAATGAAAAAGAGTGAATTACTGCAATTAACCAGTCGCGAACAGTTAAATCAT
ATTTTTGTCGGCCATTGCAGTAAATAAACCGTTGGCTTTCCCTCCTTCACTTTCCACCTCCTTTCTTGAC
```

Here, only the first few lines of the sequence are shown, for brevity. In the simplest incarnation of the FASTA format, the greater than character (>) designates the beginning of a new sequence record; this line is referred to as the *definition line* (commonly called the "def line"). An identifier (in this case the *accession number.version number*, U54469.1) is followed

by the DNA sequence, in either uppercase or lowercase letters; usually, there are 60 characters per line. Users and databases then can, if they wish, add a certain degree of complexity to this format. For example, without breaking any of the rules just outlined, one could add more information to the FASTA definition line, making the simple format a bit more informative, as follows:

```
>gb$|$U54469.1$|$DMU54469 Drosophila melanogaster eukaryotic initiation
factor 4E (eIF4E) gene, alternative splice products, complete cds
```

This modified FASTA file now has information on the source database (gb, for GenBank), its accession.version number (U54469.1), a LOCUS name identifier (in GenBank parlance), or entry name identifier (in EMBL

parlance; DMU54469), and a short description of what biological entity the sequence represents.

Similarly, a protein record would be represented as follows:

```
>uniprot$|$P48598$|$IF4E_DROME Eukaryotic translation initiation factor 4E
(eIF4E) (eIF-4E) (mRNA cap-binding protein) (eIF-4F 25 kDa subunit).
MQSDFHRMKNFANPKSMFKTSAPSTEQGRPEPPTSAAAPAEAKDVKPKEDPQETGEPAGN
TATTTAPAGDDAVRTEHLYKHPLMNVWTLWYLENDRSKSWEDMQNEITSFDTVEDFWSLY
NHIKPPSEIKLGSDYSLFKKNIRPMWEDAANKQGGRWVITLNKSSKTDLDNLWLDVLLCL
IGEAFDHSDQICGAVINIRGKSNKISIWTADGNNEEAALEIGHKLRDALRLGRNNSLQYQ
LHKDTMVKQGSNVKSIYTL
```

This record is derived from the nucleotide record shown above. The definition line takes the same form as before, giving the source database (uniprot), its accession number (P48598), a Uni-Prot identifier (IF4E_DROME), and a short description of what biological entity the sequence represents.

NUCLEOTIDE SEQUENCE FLATFILES: A DISSECTION

Since flatfiles represent the elementary unit of information within DDBJ/EMBL/GenBank and facilitate the interchange of information between these databases, it is important to understand what each individual field within the flatfile represents and what kinds of information can be found in various parts of the record. At this time, the DDBJ and GenBank flatfile formats are nearly identical (Appendices 1.1 and 1.2), whereas EMBL uses line-type prefixes; these prefixes indicate the type of information present within each line of the record (Appendix 1.3). Flatfiles can be separated into three major parts: the header, which contains the information (descriptors) that apply to the entire record; the features, which are the annotations on the record; and the nucleotide sequence itself. All major nucleotide database flatfiles end with // on the last line of the record.

The Header

The header is the most database-specific part of the record. Individual databases are not obliged to carry the same information in this part of the record, and minor variations do exist from database to database. Despite this, significant efforts are made to assure that the same information is, indeed, represented across DDBJ/EMBL/GenBank. The first line of all flatfiles is the LOCUS line in DDBJ and GenBank; this is equivalent to the ID line in EMBL:

curators attempted to give useful, intuitive locus/entry names to records; however, to be usable, these locus/entry names needed to be unique within the database. Since virtually all meaningful designators have already been assigned, the locus/entry name really does not serve as a useful format element at this time. They continue to be present in records, though, since many software packages rely on the presence of this locus/entry name.

The second item on the locus line in the DDBJ/GenBank entry is the length of the sequence; this corresponds to the last item on the ID line in the EMBL entry. The third item on the locus/ID line indicates the molecule type—the biological nature of the molecule. The "mol type" is usually DNA or RNA. In this example, the mol type is DNA within the DDBJ/GenBank record, whereas it is listed as genomic DNA within the EMBL record.

The fourth item on the locus/ID line is the division code: three letters, which have either taxonomic inferences or are used for other classification purposes. These codes exist for historical reasons, harking back to the time when the various divisions were used to break up the database files into what was then a more manageable size. The most important point of difference that users should be aware of is the different definition that each database uses for the different organismal divisions (see Table 1.1). Historically, NCBI decided not to update the list of organismal division because it did not think that this three-letter code was appropriate to represent the biological diversity present on the planet. Because of this, NCBI did not create the FUN or HUM divisions (see Table 1.1). New, functionally based divisions have been useful from the standpoint that they represent functional, definable sequence types. Some of the more important functional divisions are described in Box 1.1.

The date on the LOCUS line represents the last date when the record was last made public. If any of the

```
DDBJ/GenBank
LOCUS       DMU54469                 2881 bp    DNA     linear   INV 22-FEB-1998

EMBL
ID   DM54469      standard; genomic DNA; INV; 2881 BP.
```

The locus/ID line first gives an arbitrary name (DM54469), which is the locus name in DDBJ/GenBank terminology or the entry name in EMBL terminology. This element must begin with a letter, and subsequent characters can be either alphabetic or numerical. All letters are uppercase, with the length of the name not exceeding ten characters. In the past, sequence database

features or annotations were updated and the record were rereleased, then the date corresponds to the last release date. Note that the EMBL ID line does not contain date information; instead, the date information is found on separate date lines, and this is one of the line types that is much more clear in EMBL format compared with GenBank/DDBJ formats:

TABLE 1.1 ■ **Organismal Divisions Used by the Three Major DNA Sequence Databases**

Division		DDBJ	EMBL	GenBank
BCT	Bacterial	✓		✓
FUN	Fungal		✓	
HUM	Human	✓	✓	
INV	Invertebrate	✓	✓	✓
MAM	Other mammalian	✓	✓	✓
ORG	Organelle		✓	
PHG	Phage	✓	✓	✓
PLN	Plant[a]	✓	✓	✓
PRI	Primate[b]	✓	✓	✓
PRO	Prokaryotic		✓	
ROD	Rodent	✓	✓	✓
SYN	Synthetic and chimeric	✓	✓	✓
VRL	Viral	✓	✓	✓
VRT	Other vertebrate	✓	✓	✓

[a] Not same data in all; includes all FUN sequences in DDBJ and GenBank.
[b] Not same data in all; includes all HUM sequences in GenBank.

```
DT   19-MAY-1996 (Rel. 47, Created)
DT   04-MAR-2000 (Rel. 63, Last updated, Version 3)
```

The dates supplied on each DT line indicate when the entry was created (first line, above) or last updated (second line, above). The release number in each line indicates the first quarterly release made *after* the entry was created or last updated. The version number for the entry appears on the second line. The purpose of version numbers is to allow users to determine easily whether they are looking at the most up-to-date record for a particular sequence. Version numbers are incremented by one each time the entry is updated, because an entry can be updated several times before its appearance in a quarterly release. If an entry has not been updated since it was created, it will still have two DT lines, and the dates and release numbers on the two lines will be the same. (The concept of versioning is revisited below.)

The next part of the header is the definition lines, which attempt to summarize the biological content of the record. The definition lines take the following form:

DDBJ/GenBank
```
DEFINITION  Drosophila melanogaster eukaryotic initiation factor 4E (eIF4E)
            gene, alternative splice products, complete cds.
```

EMBL
```
DE   Drosophila melanogaster eukaryotic initiation factor 4E (eIF4E) gene,
DE   alternative splice products, complete cds.
```

Much care is taken in the generation of these lines, and, although many of them can be generated automatically from other parts of the record, they are reviewed to assure that consistency and richness of information are maintained. Nonetheless, it is not always possible to capture all of the biology underlying a sequence in a single line of text; users should exploit the wealth of information found in the record as a whole rather than just relying on these summary lines.

Continuing down the record, the accession number represents the primary key used to reference a given record in the database:

DDBJ/GenBank
```
ACCESSION   U54469
```
EMBL
```
AC   U54469
;
```

BOX 1.1   Functional Divisions in Nucleotide Databases

The organization of nucleotide sequence records into discrete functional types provides a way for users to query specific subsets of DDBJ/EMBL/GenBank. In addition, knowledge that a particular sequence is from a given technique-oriented database allows users to interpret the data from the proper biological point of view. Several of the most frequently used divisions are described below.

EST   Expressed Sequence Tags. This division, introduced in 1993, contains short (300–500 bp) single reads from mRNA (cDNA) that are usually produced in large numbers. ESTs represent a snapshot of what is expressed in a given tissue or at a given developmental stage. They represent tags (some coding, others not) of expression for a given cDNA library.

STS   Sequence-Tagged Sites. These are short (200–500 bp), operationally unique sequences that identify the combination of primer pairs used in a PCR assay, generating a reagent that maps to a single position within the genome. The STS division is intended to facilitate cross-comparison of STSs with sequences in other divisions for the purpose of correlating map positions of anonymous sequences with known genes.

GSS   Genome Survey Sequences. This division is similar to the EST division, except that its sequences are genomic in origin. The GSS division contains (but is not limited to) random, single-pass read genome survey sequences, single-pass reads from cosmid/BAC/YAC ends, exon-trapped genomic sequences, and Alu PCR sequences.

HTG   High-Throughput Genome sequences. Unfinished DNA sequences generated by high-throughput sequencing centers, made available in an expedited fashion to the scientific community for homology and similarity searches. Entries in this division contain keywords indicating its phase within the sequencing process. Once finished, HTG sequences are moved into the appropriate DDBJ/EMBL/GenBank taxonomic division. See Chapter 13 for a description of the finishing process and the various finishing phases.

HTC   Unfinished sequences from high-throughput cDNA projects.

WGS   Whole Genome Shotgun sequences. Projects using a whole genome shotgun approach gain large genomic coverage for an organism, the trade-off being the generation of huge amounts of unassembled, unfinished sequences. Such data is made available in the WGS division.

PAT   Patent sequences. This division contains sequence data provided by the American, European, and Japanese patent offices.

CON   Constructed (or "contigged") records of chromosomes, genomes, and other long DNA sequences. This division contains segmented sets as well as all large assemblies. It does not include sequences or annotations; rather, it includes instructions on how to assemble pieces present in other divisions into larger or assembled pieces.

The accession number is the number that should be cited in publications and is always associated with this record; that is, if the sequence is updated (e.g., by changing a single nucleotide), the accession number will not change. At this time, accession numbers exist in one of two formats: the "1 + 5" and "2 + 6" varieties, where 1 + 5 indicates one uppercase letter followed by five digits, and 2 + 6 indicates two letters followed by six digits. Most of the new records now entering the databases are of the latter variety. The vast majority of records only have one accession number, and this number is always referred to as the primary accession number; all others are secondary. In cases where more than one accession number is shown, the first accession number is the primary one.

Returning to the concept of versioning, the next line in DDBJ and GenBank records carries the `VERSION` key, whereas the equivalent information in EMBL is found in the `SV` (sequence version) line:

DDBJ
```
VERSION      U54469.1
```

EMBL
```
SV   U54469.1
```

GenBank
```
VERSION      U54469.1  GI:1322283
```

In these three examples, the version lines take the form `accession.version`. Here, the `accession` part remains stable, but the `version` is incremented each and every time the sequence changes. The GenBank `VERSION` line also contains a gi number (the geninfo identifier). If the sequence changes, the gi will change to the next available integer. These gi numbers are GenBank specific; the accession.version numbers are now the preferred identifier to be used to refer unequivocally to one and only one sequence record in all three databases.

Lines with keywords appear in each of the three databases. The keywords line is a historical relic that is, in many cases, unfortunately misused. Adding keywords to an entry often is not very useful because, over time, submitters have selected words that are not part of a controlled vocabulary or are not applied uniformly to the entire database. Their inclusion in database records is, therefore, of questionable usefulness. For this reason, many of the database curators discourage the use of `KEYWORDS` in the DDBJ/EMBL/GenBank records.

Taxonomy information is found in the SOURCE and ORGANISM lines in DDBJ/GenBank, and in the corresponding OS (organism source) and OC (organism classification) lines in EMBL:

DDBJ/GenBank

```
SOURCE      Drosophila melanogaster (fruit fly)
  ORGANISM  Drosophila melanogaster
            Eukaryota; Metazoa; Arthropoda; Hexapoda; Insecta; Pterygota;
            Neoptera; Endopterygota; Diptera; Brachycera; Muscomorpha;
            Ephydroidea; Drosophilidae; Drosophila.
```

EMBL

```
OS   Drosophila melanogaster (fruit fly)
OC   Eukaryota; Metazoa; Arthropoda; Hexapoda; Insecta; Pterygota; Neoptera;
OC   Endopterygota; Diptera; Brachycera; Muscomorpha; Ephydroidea;
OC   Drosophilidae; Drosophila.
```

The `SOURCE`/`OS` line specifies the preferred scientific name of the organism from which the sequence was derived. In most cases, this is carried out by providing the Latin genus and species, followed (in parentheses) by the preferred English common name, where available. The `ORGANISM`/`OC` lines contain the complete taxonomic classification of the source organism. The classification is listed top-down, as nodes in a taxonomic tree, with the most general grouping given first. The taxonomy is shared by all nucleotide sequence databases, as well as by UniProt (below).

Each DDBJ/EMBL/GenBank record must have at least one reference or citation. These reference blocks offer scientific credit and set a context explaining why this particular sequence was determined. In many cases, the record will have two or more reference blocks, as shown in the appendices to this chapter. The reference blocks take the following form:

DDBJ/GenBank

```
REFERENCE   1 (bases 1 to 2881)
  AUTHORS   Lavoie,C.A., Lachance,P.E., Sonenberg,N. and Lasko,P.
  TITLE     Alternatively spliced transcripts from the Drosophila eIF4E gene
            produce two different Cap-binding proteins
  JOURNAL   J. Biol. Chem. 271 (27), 16393-16398 (1996)
  MEDLINE   96279193
  PUBMED    8663200
REFERENCE   2 (bases 1 to 2881)
```

Continued

```
AUTHORS    Lasko,P.F.
TITLE      Direct Submission
JOURNAL    Submitted (09-APR-1996) Paul F. Lasko, Biology, McGill University,
           1205 Avenue Docteur Penfield, Montreal, QC H3A 1B1, Canada
```

EMBL

```
RN   [1]
RP   1-2881
RX   MEDLINE; 96279193.
RX   PUBMED; 8663200.
RA   Lavoie C.A., Lachance P.E.D., Sonenberg N., Lasko P.;
RT   "Alternatively spliced transcripts from the Drosophila eIF4E gene produce
RT   two different Cap-binding proteins";
RL   J. Biol. Chem. 271(27): 16393-16398(1996).
XX
RN   [2]
RP   1-2881
RA   Lasko P.F.;
RT   ;
RL   Submitted (09-APR-1996) to the EMBL/GenBank/DDBJ databases.
RL   Paul F. Lasko, Biology, McGill University, 1205 Avenue Docteur Penfield,
RL   Montreal, QC H3A 1B1, Canada
```

In this case, there are two references shown, one referring to a published paper, and the other referring to the submission of the sequence record itself. The submission citation gives scientific credit to the people responsible for the work surrounding the submitted sequence; it usually includes the postal address of the first author of the lab where the work was carried out. The date represents the date the record was submitted to the database, but not the date on which the record was first made public, and is therefore irrelevant with respect to claiming first public release. Additional submitter blocks may be added to the record each time the sequence is updated.

In some headers, the optional line type COMMENT (in DDBJ/GenBank) or CC (in EMBL) is found. Comment lines include a great variety of notes and comments (also called *descriptors*) that refer to the entire record. Often, genome centers will use these lines to provide contact information and to confer acknowledgements. Comments also may include information on the history of the sequence. If the sequence of a particular record is updated, the comment will contain a pointer to the previous version of the record. Alternatively, if an earlier version of the record is retrieved, the comment will point forward to the newer version, as well as backward, if there was a still-earlier version.

Finally, EMBL has a line type called DR, for database cross-reference. These lines cross-reference other databases that contain information related to the entry being examined. For example, if the protein translation of a sequence exists in Swiss-Prot, there will be a DR line pointing to that entry.

The Feature Table

The middle segment of the DDBJ/EMBL/GenBank record, the feature table, is the direct representation of the biological information in the record. The format of the feature table is based on a tabular approach, consisting of feature keys (a single word or abbreviation indicating the described biological property), the location information (where within the sequence that the feature is located), and additional qualifiers (auxiliary information about a feature). The online DDBJ/EMBL/GenBank feature table documentation is extensive and describes in great detail what features are allowed and what qualifiers can be used with each individual feature.

Wording within the feature table uses common biological research terminology whenever possible, and is very consistent between DDBJ, EMBL, and GenBank. For example, consider the following portion of a GenBank feature table (taking note that the DDBJ/EMBL/GenBank record here presents three alternative splace variants of this mRNA product that, in turn, encode two different protein products, all of which are identified in this record):

```
CDS                    join(201..224,1550..1920,1986..2085,2317..2404,2466..2629)
                       /gene="eIF4E"
                       /note="Method: conceptual translation with partial peptide sequencing"
                       /product="eukaryotic initiation factor 4E-II"
```

This would be "translated" as follows: the sequence has a coding sequence (CDS) made up of five exons, the first of which begins at base 201 and ends at base 224, then is joined at basepair 1550 until basepair 1920, and so forth. Each comma in this line represents a splicing event, and each ".." represents the string of letters between the two coordinates. The gene product is eukaryotic initiation factor 4E-II, and the gene name is eIF4E. The various ways in which the location of any given feature can be indicated are shown in Table 1.1. Some rules sometimes need to be applied for valid biological representation and are not explicit in the database system here, but only in the respective data models used by the respective databases.

The *source feature* is the only feature that must be present in all DDBJ/EMBL/GenBank entries, because all DNA or RNA sequences come from somewhere. All features have a series of allowed (legal) qualifiers, some of which are mandatory. All DNA sequence records have some origin, even if synthetic (in the extreme case). In most cases, there will be a single source feature, and it must contain the /organism qualifier, indicating the scientific name of the organism from which the sequence was derived. The following is an excerpt from the sequence records in Appendices 1.1-1.3 to this chapter:

DDBJ/GenBank

```
        source         1..2881
                       /organism="Drosophila melanogaster"
                       /mol_type="genomic DNA"
                       /db_xref="taxon:7227"
                       /chromosome="3"
                       /map="67A8-B2"
```

EMBL

```
FT   source            1..2881
FT                     /chromosome="3"
FT                     /db_xref="taxon:7227"
FT                     /mol_type="genomic DNA"
FT                     /organism="Drosophila melanogaster"
FT                     /map="67A8-B2"
```

In this case, additional qualifiers are present that contain information relating to the entire sequence. These include the nature of the molecule sequenced (/mol_type="genomic DNA"), the chromosome mapping, as well as the more specific mapping coordinates (/chromosome="3" and /map="67A8-B2", respectively). In all DDBJ/EMBL/GenBank records, there is always a cross-reference to NCBI's taxonomy database (/db_xref="taxon:7227"). When reading these features, anything that cannot be validated computationally should be disregarded. Tissue source and library origin are only as good as the controls present in the associated publication (if any such publication exists) and only insofar as that type of information is applied uniformly across all sequence records. Unfortunately,

many qualifiers are derived without sufficient uniformity across the database and hence are of lesser value.

Implicit in the source feature and the organism that is assigned to it is the genetic code used to translate the nucleic acid sequence into a protein sequence when the CDS feature is present in the record. The CDS feature contains instructions to the reader on how to join two sequences together or on how to make an amino acid sequence from the indicated coordinates and inferred genetic code. The DNA-centric nature of flatfiles map all features through a DNA sequence coordinate system, not that of amino acid reference points, as illustrated in the example shown in Figure 1.2. The example also illustrates the use of the database cross-reference (db_xref). This controlled qualifier allows

DDBJ

```
CDS             join(201..224,1550..1920,1986..2085,2317..2404,2466..2629)
                /gene="eIF4E"
                /note="Method: conceptual translation with partial peptide
                sequencing"
                /codon_start=1
                /product="eukaryotic initiation factor 4E-II"
                /protein_id="AAC03524.1"
                /db_xref="GI:1322284"
                /translation="MVVLETEKTSAPSTEQGRPEPPTSAAAPAEAKDVKPKEDPQETG
                EPAGNTATTTAPAGDDAVRTEHLYKHPLMNVWTLWYLENDRSKSWEDMQNEITSFDTV
                EDFWSLYNHIKPPSEIKLGSDYSLFKKNIRPMWEDAANKQGGRWVITLNKSSKTDLDN
                LWLDVLLCLIGEAFDHSDQICGAVINIRGKSNKISIWTADGNNEEAALEIGHKLRDAL
                RLGRNNSLQYQLHKDTMVKQGSNVKSIYTL"
CDS             join(1402..1458,1550..1920,1986..2085,2317..2404,
                2466..2629)
                /gene="eIF4E"
                /note="Method: conceptual translation with partial peptide
                sequencing; two alternatively spliced transcripts both
                encode 4E-I"
                /codon_start=1
                /product="eukaryotic initiation factor 4E-I"
                /protein_id="AAC03525.1"
                /db_xref="GI:1322285"
                /translation="MQSDFHRMKNFANPKSMFKTSAPSTEQGRPEPPTSAAAPAEAKD
                VKPKEDPQETGEPAGNTATTTAPAGDDAVRTEHLYKHPLMNVWTLWYLENDRSKSWED
                MQNEITSFDTVEDFWSLYNHIKPPSEIKLGSDYSLFKKNIRPMWEDAANKQGGRWVIT
                LNKSSKTDLDNLWLDVLLCLIGEAFDHSDQICGAVINIRGKSNKISIWTADGNNEEAA
                LEIGHKLRDALRLGRNNSLQYQLHKDTMVKQGSNVKSIYTL"
```

GenBank

```
CDS             join(201..224,1550..1920,1986..2085,2317..2404,2466..2629)
                /gene="eIF4E"
                /note="Method: conceptual translation with partial peptide
                sequencing"
                /codon_start=1
                /product="eukaryotic initiation factor 4E-II"
                /protein_id="AAC03524.1"
                /db_xref="GI:1322284"
                /translation="MVVLETEKTSAPSTEQGRPEPPTSAAAPAEAKDVKPKEDPQETG
                EPAGNTATTTAPAGDDAVRTEHLYKHPLMNVWTLWYLENDRSKSWEDMQNEITSFDTV
                EDFWSLYNHIKPPSEIKLGSDYSLFKKNIRPMWEDAANKQGGRWVITLNKSSKTDLDN
                LWLDVLLCLIGEAFDHSDQICGAVINIRGKSNKISIWTADGNNEEAALEIGHKLRDAL
                RLGRNNSLQYQLHKDTMVKQGSNVKSIYTL"
CDS             join(1402..1458,1550..1920,1986..2085,2317..2404,
                2466..2629)
                /gene="eIF4E"
                /note="Method: conceptual translation with partial peptide
                sequencing; two alternatively spliced transcripts both
                encode 4E-I"
                /codon_start=1
                /product="eukaryotic initiation factor 4E-I"
                /protein_id="AAC03525.1"
                /db_xref="GI:1322285"
                /translation="MQSDFHRMKNFANPKSMFKTSAPSTEQGRPEPPTSAAAPAEAKD
                VKPKEDPQETGEPAGNTATTTAPAGDDAVRTEHLYKHPLMNVWTLWYLENDRSKSWED
                MQNEITSFDTVEDFWSLYNHIKPPSEIKLGSDYSLFKKNIRPMWEDAANKQGGRWVIT
                LNKSSKTDLDNLWLDVLLCLIGEAFDHSDQICGAVINIRGKSNKISIWTADGNNEEAA
                LEIGHKLRDALRLGRNNSLQYQLHKDTMVKQGSNVKSIYTL"
```

FIGURE 1.2   An example of a CDS feature in DDBJ/EMBL/GenBank records illustrating differences in format between the three databases. See text for details.

EMBL

```
FT   CDS             join(201..224,1550..1920,1986..2085,2317..2404,2466..2629)
FT                   /codon_start=1
FT                   /db_xref="FLYBASE:FBgn0015218"
FT                   /db_xref="GOA:P48598"
FT                   /db_xref="Swiss-Prot:P48598"
FT                   /note="Method: conceptual translation with partial peptide
FT                   sequencing."
FT                   /product="eukaryotic initiation factor 4E-II"
FT                   /gene="Eif4E"
FT                   /protein_id="AAC03524.1"
FT                   /translation="MVVLETEKTSAPSTEQGRPEPPTSAAAPAEAKDVKPKEDPQETGE
FT                   PAGNTATTTAPAGDDAVRTEHLYKHPLMNVWTLWYLENDRSKSWEDMQNEITSFDTVED
FT                   FWSLYNHIKPPSEIKLGSDYSLFKKNIRPMWEDAANKQGGRWVITLNKSSKTDLDNLWL
FT                   DVLLCLIGEAFDHSDQICGAVINIRGKSNKISIWTADGNNEEAALEIGHKLRDALRLGR
FT                   NNSLQYQLHKDTMVKQGSNVKSIYTL"
FT   CDS             join(1402..1458,1550..1920,1986..2085,2317..2404,
FT                   2466..2629)
FT                   /codon_start=1
FT                   /db_xref="FLYBASE:FBgn0015218"
FT                   /db_xref="GOA:P48598"
FT                   /db_xref="Swiss-Prot:P48598"
FT                   /note="Method: conceptual translation with partial peptide
FT                   sequencing; two alternatively spliced transcripts both
FT                   encode 4E-I"
FT                   /product="eukaryotic initiation factor 4E-I"
FT                   /gene="Eif4E"
FT                   /protein_id="AAC03525.1"
FT                   /translation="MQSDFHRMKNFANPKSMFKTSAPSTEQGRPEPPTSAAAPAEAKDV
FT                   KPKEDPQETGEPAGNTATTTAPAGDDAVRTEHLYKHPLMNVWTLWYLENDRSKSWEDMQ
FT                   NEITSFDTVEDFWSLYNHIKPPSEIKLGSDYSLFKKNIRPMWEDAANKQGGRWVITLNK
FT                   SSKTDLDNLWLDVLLCLIGEAFDHSDQICGAVINIRGKSNKISIWTADGNNEEAALEIG
FT                   HKLRDALRLGRNNSLQYQLHKDTMVKQGSNVKSIYTL"
```

FIGURE 1.2   (Continued)

databases to cross-reference the sequence under consideration to an external database, using an identifier unique to that external database. The list of allowed db_xref databases is maintained by the International Nucleotide Sequence Database Collaboration. In the example shown in Figure 1.2, there are cross-references to the corresponding entries in FlyBase, Swiss-Prot, and GOA (Camon et al., 2004).

Every CDS in a DDBJ/EMBL/GenBank record also is assigned a protein identifier (/protein_id). These unique identifiers change when the sequence of the translation changes. The identifier is in "3 + 5" format (three letters, followed by five numbers). As with the nucleotide sequence accession number, versions are indicated using a protein_id.version format (e.g., AAC03524.1); when the protein sequence in the record changes, the version is incremented by one. As mentioned above, NCBI also assigns a gi (geneinfo) identifier to all sequences; this means that all translation products also receive a gi number. These gi numbers appear as a gi db_xref (Figure 1.2). When the protein sequence in the record changes, the gi also changes, receiving the next available unique number. As for nucleotide sequences, these gi numbers are kept

for historical purposes, because NCBI used gi numbers before accession.version numbers were implemented, and none of the databases except those from the NCBI had unique identifiers for their sequences. The accession.version now used by all three databases for nucleic and protein sequences makes the use of gi numbers obsolete.

The CDS examples shown in Figure 1.2 contain the /product qualifier. The assignment of a gene product or protein name often is subjective, sometimes being assigned via weak similarities to other, poorly annotated sequences. Because of the potential for the transitive propagation of poor annotations, users are advised to consult *curated* nucleotide and protein sequence databases for the most up-to-date, accurate information regarding the putative function of a given sequence.

Third Party Annotation (TPA)

Until recently, the DDBJ/EMBL/GenBank databases have collected and distributed only primary nucleotide sequence data resulting from direct sequencing of cDNAs, ESTs, genomic DNA, and other defined constructs. In general, these are characterized as "primary data," annotated sequences that have been determined experimentally by a submitter and their team. Primary database entries are owned by the original submitter and the co-authors of the submission publication(s), and owners have privileges to update the data contained in the record.

In response to suggestions from the research community, DDBJ/EMBL/GenBank have created the Third Party Annotation (TPA) dataset. The types of entries in the TPA dataset include reannotations of existing entries, combinations of novel sequence and existing primary entries (i.e., sequences with accession.version numbers), and annotation of trace archive and whole genome shotgun data. TPA submitters are required to provide DDBJ/EMBL/GenBank `accession.version`

numbers and nucleotide locations for all primary entries to which the TPA entry relates. For TPA sequences derived from trace archive data, the trace identifier and corresponding nucleotide locations must be provided. TPA entries are exchanged among the DDBJ/ EMBL/GenBank database collaborators on a daily basis.

TPA entries are easily distinguished from their primary counterparts. The abbreviation `TPA:` appears at the beginning of every definition/description (`DE`) line, and the keywords `THIRD PARTY ANNOTATION` and `TPA` appear in the keyword (`KW`) line. In addition, `primary/assembly` header (`AH`) and assembly (`AS`) lines may appear, as shown in the following example (DDBJ/EMBL/GenBank accession.version number `BN000024.1`):

DDBJ/GenBank

PRIMARY	TPA_SPAN	PRIMARY_IDENTIFIER	PRIMARY_SPAN	COMP
	1-251	BE529226.1	1-251	
	68-450	BE524624.1	1-383	
	394-1086	AJ420881.1	1-693	
	826-1211	AV561543.1	1-386	c

EMBL

AH	TPA_SPAN	PRIMARY_IDENTIFIER	PRIMARY_SPAN	COMP
AS	1-251	BE529226.1	1-251	
AS	68-450	BE524624.1	1-383	
AS	394-1086	AJ420881.1	1-693	
AS	826-1211	AV561543.1	1-386	c

The assembly header line provides column headings for the assembly information. The individual assembly lines provide information on the composition of the TPA sequence listing in the following order: the span of positions in the TPA sequence; the primary sequence identifier for the originating, primary sequence; and the positions from the originating, primary sequences.

RefSeq

Many sequences are represented more than once in DDBJ/EMBL/GenBank, and in certain cases, this leads to huge degrees of redundancy. To address this, NCBI developed the RefSeq collection (Pruitt et al., 2003), a curated secondary database that aims to provide a comprehensive, integrated, nonredundant set of sequences, including genomic DNA (for example, all of the human genome assemblies), transcripts (RNA), and protein products, for selected organisms. Additional information on RefSeq can be found in Box 1.2.

EMBL Genome Reviews

As alluded to above, most of the data in DDBJ/EMBL/GenBank entries cannot be updated, corrected, or amended without the permission of the original submitter. To overcome this, EBI recently released Genome Reviews, a secondary database that provides curated versions of entries representing complete genome sequences in DDBJ/EMBL/GenBank. Each Genome Review is an enhanced version of the original, primary entry, with additional information imported from sources such as the UniProt knowledgebase (Apweiler et al., 2004), the Gene Ontology Annotation (GOA) project (Camon et al., 2004), InterPro (Mulder et al., 2003), and other sources. One of the main goals of the Genome Reviews effort is to standardize annotations that have been used inconsistently among the original, primary submissions, sometimes deleting annotations where coverage is low. The information in Genome Reviews is completely synchronized with UniProt, with evidence tags attached to most feature qualifiers, including the primary source of

BOX 1.2   RefSeq

The first several chapters of this book describe a variety of ways in which sequence data and sequence annotations find their way into public databases. Although the combination of data derived from systematic sequencing projects and individual investigators' laboratories yields a rich and highly valuable set of sequence data, some problems immediately come to the fore. The most important issues in this regard are that a single biological entity may be represented by many different entries in various databases. It also may not be clear whether a given sequence has been experimentally determined or is simply the result of a computational prediction.

To address these issues, NCBI has initiated the RefSeq project, whose major goal is to provide a reference sequence for each molecule in the central dogma (DNA, mRNA, and protein). Since each biological entity is represented once and only once, RefSeq is, by definition, non-redundant. Nucleotide and protein sequences in RefSeq are explicitly linked to one another. Most importantly, RefSeq entries undergo ongoing curation, assuring that the RefSeq entry represents the most up-to-date state of knowledge regarding a particular DNA, mRNA, or protein sequence.

RefSeq entries are distinguished from other entries in GenBank through the use of a distinct accession number

series. RefSeq accession numbers follow a "2 + 6" format: a two-letter code indicating the type of reference sequence, followed by an underscore and a six-digit number. Experimentally determined sequence data are denoted as follows:

NT_123456	Genomic contigs (DNA)
NM_123456	mRNAs
NP_123456	Proteins

Reference sequences derived through genome annotation efforts are denoted as follows:

XM_123456	Model mRNAs
XP_123456	Model proteins

It is important that the reader understand the distinction between the "N" numbers and "X" numbers. The former represent actual, experimentally determined sequences, whereas the latter represent computational predictions derived from the raw DNA sequence.

Additional types of RefSeq entries, along with more information on the RefSeq project, can be found on NCBI's RefSeq Web site.

the information. A sample Genome Reviews record is shown in Appendix 1.4.

PROTEIN SEQUENCE DATABASES

With the availability of hundreds of complete genome sequences from both prokaryotes and eukaryotes, efforts are now focused on the identification and functional

analysis of the proteins encoded by these genomes. The large-scale analysis of these proteins has started to generate huge amounts of data, in large part because of a range of newly developed technologies in protein science. For example, mass spectrometry now is used widely in protein identification and in determining the nature of posttranslational modifications (Chapter 17). These and other methods make it possible to identify large numbers of proteins quickly, to map their interactions

BOX 1.3   Submitting Sequences to the Databases

The DDBJ/EMBL/GenBank sequence databases have a common process for accepting and managing DNA/RNA sequence submissions. Journals reporting newly generated sequences require authors to submit their sequences to either DDBJ, EMBL, or GenBank so that an accession number can appear in the journal article. DNA or RNA submissions and annotations may be made through the Web (in the case of simpler, non-batch mode submissions) or through an application called Sequin (used for more complex cases). At DDBJ, the Web interface is called Sakura, whereas it is called wEBIn at EMBL and BankIt at GenBank. The URLs for each of these, as well as for downloading and using Sequin, can

be found in the list of Internet Resources at the end of this chapter. Regardless of how the sequence is submitted, expert reviewers check all submissions, and accession numbers are issued within 24 hours.

The process for genome centers is somewhat different because of the large amount of data generated by these centers. It is highly recommended that interested parties consult with staff at the target database, so that key factors such as the number of submissions and the frequency of updates can be taken into account. Often, procedures are different for specific types of sequence data, such as those described in Box 1.1.

(Chapter 10), to determine their location within the cell, and to analyze their biological activities. This increasing "information space" reinforces the central role that protein sequence databases play as a resource for storing data generated by these and more conventional efforts, making them freely available to the scientific community.

Because most sequence data in protein databases are derived from the translation of nucleotide sequences, they are, by and large, secondary databases. Universal protein sequence databases cover proteins from all species, whereas specialized data collections concentrate on particular protein families, groups of proteins, or those from a specific organism (Chapter 3). Universal protein databases can be divided further into two broad categories: sequence repositories, where the data is stored with little or no manual intervention, and curated databases, in which experts enhance the original data by adding new information.

GenPept

The most basic example of a protein sequence repository is NCBI's GenPept. Entries in GenPept are derived from translations of the sequences in DDBJ/EMBL/GenBank (the CDS feature) and contain the annotation present in the nucleotide record; the entries are not curated. GenPept does not contain proteins derived through direct amino acid sequencing. Also, each protein may be represented by multiple records, and no attempt is made to group these records into a single database entry, they represent the archive of all sequencing activities.

RefSeq

The NCBI RefSeq project (Pruitt et al., 2003) is, as mentioned above, a curated secondary database that aims to provide a comprehensive, integrated, nonredundant sequence set on both the genomic, transcript, and protein levels for an increasing number of selected organisms (Box 1.2). RefSeq presents an important effort to curate all of the sequences, but it is currently limited in scope and scale because of the labor-intensive activity it represents.

UniProt

Although data repositories are an essential vehicle through which scientists can be provided sequence data as quickly as possible, it is clear that the addition of biological information greatly increases the power of the underlying sequence data. Curated databases enrich the sequence data by providing information validated by expert biologists, ensuring that the data found in these curated collections are highly reliable. One

recent, significant advance in this arena was bringing three long-standing databases (Swiss-Prot, TrEMBL, and PIR-PSD) under a single umbrella, called UniProt (Apweiler et al., 2004). UniProt is comprised of three major components:

▶ the UniProt Archive (UniParc), into which new and updated sequences are loaded on a daily basis;

▶ the UniProt Knowledgebase, extending the work originally done with Swiss-Prot, TrEMBL, and PIR-PSD with the goal of providing an expertly curated database; and

▶ the UniProt nonredundant reference database (UniRef), which provides nonredundant views of the data contained in UniParc and the UniProt Knowledgebase.

The flow of information from primary sources into these components of UniProt is illustrated in Figure 1.3, and each of these UniProt components is described in greater detail below.

UniParc

Although most protein sequence data is derived from the translation of DDBJ/EMBL/GenBank sequences, a large amount of primary protein sequence data resulting from the direct sequencing of proteins was submitted directly to other sources, including Swiss-Prot, TrEMBL, and PIR-PSD; in addition, a large number of protein sequences are found in patent applications, as well as in entries from the Protein Data Bank (PDB; Westbrook et al., 2003; Chapter 9). Given the wide variety of primary sources and variation in the degree and quality of annotation, UniParc (Leinonen et al., 2004) was created; it is designed to capture all available protein sequence data not just from the aforementioned databases, but also from sources such as the International Protein Index (IPI; Kersey et al., 2004), RefSeq, FlyBase (The FlyBase Consortium, 2003; Chapter 3), and WormBase (Harris et al., 2003; Chapter 3). This combination of sources makes UniParc the most comprehensive, publicly accessible, nonredundant protein sequence database available. UniParc represents each protein sequence once and only once, assigning it a unique UniParc identifier. UniParc cross-references the accession numbers of the source databases, providing sequence versions that are incremented in the usual fashion. Status flags are used to indicate the status of the entry in the original, source database, with "active" indicating that the entry is still present in the source database and "obsolete" indicating that the entry no longer exists in the source database. UniParc's intended use is for sequence similarity searches, given that all known protein sequences are represented. UniParc records carry no annotation,

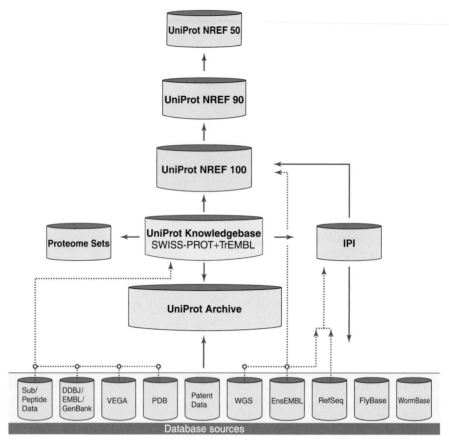

FIGURE 1.3 **The flow of data from primary data sources into the component databases of the Universal Protein Resource. See text for details.**

but this information *can* be found in the UniProt Knowledgebase.

UniProt Knowledgebase

The UniProt Knowledgebase contains two major elements: a section containing manually annotated records, based on information from the literature, and curator-evaluated computational analysis (referred to as Swiss-Prot); and a section containing computationally analyzed records awaiting manual annotation (referred to as TrEMBL). In addition, all suitable PIR-PSD entries not found in Swiss-Prot or TrEMBL are incorporated into the UniProt Knowledgebase. By design, the Knowledgebase is nonredundant, with the goal of representing all known information regarding a particular protein. The definition of non-redundancy here is different from that employed in UniParc: in UniParc, all sequences that are 100% identical over their entire length are merged into a single entry, regardless of species. The UniProt Knowledgebase aims to describe, in a single record, all protein products derived from a certain gene (or genes if

the translation from different genes in a genome leads to indistinguishable proteins) from a certain species and to give not only the whole record an accession number, but to assign to each protein form derived by alternative splicing, proteolytic cleavage, and post-translational modification Isoform identifiers, which are accession numbers for the isoforms. Isoform identifiers have been only introduced for splice isoforms so far. The UniProt Knowledgebase only represents a subset of the sequences found in UniParc, given the labor-intensive nature of the curation process. The UniProt Knowledgebase provides extensive cross-references to external data collections, such as the corresponding nucleotide entries in DDBJ/EMBL/GenBank, 2D-PAGE data, protein structure databases, protein domain and family characterization databases, posttranslational modification databases, species-specific data collections, and disease databases. As a result of this extensive cross-referencing, the Knowledgebase serves as a de facto hub for biomolecular information about any given protein.

Each entry in the Swiss-Prot portion of the UniProt Knowledgebase is analyzed and annotated thoroughly.

Literature-based curation is used to extract experimental data; this experimental knowledge is supplemented by manually confirmed results from various sequence analysis programs. The annotations include a description of the properties of the protein, such as its function, any known posttranslational modifications, domains, catalytic or other sites, secondary and quaternary structure, similarities to other proteins, diseases caused by mutations in the protein, pathways in which the protein is involved, sequence conflicts, and variants. These pieces of information are stored primarily in the description (DE), gene (GN), comment (CC), and keyword (KW) lines, as well as in the feature table (FT). The addition of qualifiers to these lines allows users to distinguish easily between experimentally verified data that has been propagated from a characterized protein based on sequence similarity, in contrast to data for which no experimental evidence currently exists (Junker et al., 1999). Examples of comment keys can be found in Table 1.3. Gene names are standardized through the use of authoritative sources such as the HUGO Gene Nomenclature Committee's Genew project (Wain et al., 2002), FlyBase, and the Mouse Genome Database (MGD; Blake et al., 2003). A sample Swiss-Prot record can be found in Appendix 1.5.

Producing a fully curated Swiss-Prot entry is obviously a highly labor-intensive process, and this rate-limiting human component makes it difficult for Swiss-Prot to keep up with the flow of newly available protein information. To address this, the TrEMBL portion of the UniProt Knowledgebase provides computer-based annotation of entries. The creation of a TrEMBL record begins with the translation of a new coding sequence from DDBJ/EMBL/GenBank, bringing along all annotation from the source nucleotide entry. TrEMBL also uses PDB as a primary source of new protein data, as well as sequences submitted directly to UniProt. UniParc sequences identified as being important by UniProt curators are also included. As soon as the initial data is collected from any of these sources, redundancy is removed through the merging of multiple records (O'Donovan et al., 1999). The automated enhancement of the information content then begins (Apweiler, 2001). An attempt is made to capitalize on information already in Swiss-Prot, assigning TrEMBL entries to defined protein groups (Fleischmann et al., 1998; Kretschmann et al., 2001). Resources used to make these assignments to functional groups or protein families include InterPro (Mulder et al., 2003), PROSITE (Falquet et al., 2002), and Pfam (Bateman et al., 2002), among others; more information on these resources can be found in Chapter 8.

The Anatomy of a UniProt Knowledgebase Flatfile

An example of a complete Swiss-Prot entry can be found in Appendix 1.5, and the important features of a Swiss-Prot flatfile are described here. At a quick glance, the flatfile looks very similar to an EMBL entry, with the characteristic two-letter code at the beginning of each line classifying what type of information is found on that line. As before, some line types may occur multiple times, and some line types may not occur at all. Consider the header of the sample entry:

```
ID   ROA1_HUMAN      STANDARD;      PRT;    371 AA.
AC   P09651;
DT   01-MAR-1989 (Rel. 10, Created)
DT   01-AUG-1990 (Rel. 15, Last sequence update)
DT   15-MAR-2004 (Rel. 43, Last annotation update)
DE   Heterogeneous nuclear ribonucleoprotein A1 (Helix-destabilizing
DE   protein) (Single-strand binding protein) (hnRNP core protein A1).
GN   HNRPA1.
OS   Homo sapiens (Human).
OC   Eukaryota; Metazoa; Chordata; Craniata; Vertebrata; Euteleostomi;
OC   Mammalia; Eutheria; Primates; Catarrhini; Hominidae; Homo.
OX   NCBI_TaxID=9606;
```

Each entry begins with an identification line (ID) containing the name of the entry. The accession number is found on the AC line. In TrEMBL records, the accession number also is used as the entry name. As before, the accession number should be used to refer unequivocally to a specific entry. In some cases, there will be multiple accession numbers on the AC line; in this case, the first one is considered to be the primary accession number, the one that should be cited in any publication or correspondence. Following are three date lines (DT), showing when the entry was created, when the sequence was last updated, and when the most recent annotation was added. The description lines (DE) list all the names under which the protein is or has been known. Thereafter is

TABLE 1.2 ■ Indicating Locations Within the Feature Table

`345`	Single position within the sequence
`345..500`	A continuous range of positions bounded by and including the indicated positions
`<345..500`	A continuous range of positions, in which the exact lower boundary is not known; the feature begins somewhere before position 345 but ends at position 500
`345..>500`	A continuous range of positions in which the exact upper boundary is not known; the feature begins at position 345 but ends somewhere after position 500
`<1..888`	The feature starts before the first sequenced base and continues to position 888
`(102.110)`	The exact location is unknown, but it is one of the positions between 102 and 110, inclusive
`123^124`	A site between positions 123 and 124
`123^177`	A site between two adjacent nucleotides or amino acids anywhere between positions 123 and 177
`join(12..78,134..202)`	Regions 12 to 78 and 134 to 202 are joined to form one contiguous sequence
`complement(4918..5126)`	The sequence complementary to that found from 4918 to 5126 in the sequence record
`J00194:100..202`	Positions 100 to 202, inclusive, in the entry in this database having accession number J00194

the gene name line (GN), listing all known gene symbols for this gene. The organism species (OS) and organism classification (OC) lines provide the scientific name of the source organism, its common name (where available), and the taxonomy of the source organism. Finally, the OX line gives the cross-reference to NCBI's Taxonomy database. In cases where the sequence comes from a particular organelle or extrachromosomal element, an organelle line (OG) line will appear (e.g., an OG line may carry a descriptor such as Chloroplast).

As with DDBJ/EMBL/GenBank entries, Swiss-Prot and TrEMBL records contain reference blocks (Appendix 1.5). In this example, the reference blocks cite not only the sequencing work, but also references to three-dimensional structure determination, mutagenesis, and the detection of posttranslational modifications and isoforms. Reference blocks include information not only from the published literature; information submitted to UniProt may be included, to account for the fact that an increasing amount of sequence information is no longer "published" in the traditional sense.

After this section are a series of lines marked DR, for database cross-reference. Currently, UniProt is linked to more than 50 different databases. The example shown in Appendix 1.5 is linked to 27 different entries in 13 different databases. These cross-links allow users to navigate easily to the other source databases to retrieve additional information about the protein sequence in question.

The most important parts of a UniProt Knowledgebase entry are the comment lines (CC; Table 1.3), keyword lines (KW), and the feature table (FT), because they contain all of the known biological information relating to the sequence, providing a quick overview of the function and structure of this protein to the user. Considering the example shown in Appendix 1.5, note that the comment lines are grouped together so that all information of a particular type is found in one place. The various

kinds of information that can be found in the comment lines are listed in Table 1.2. The keyword lines list relevant keywords that can be used to retrieve specific subsets of protein entries from the database. Finally, the feature table provides detailed information about specific sites or regions within the sequence, such as posttranslational modifications, binding sites, enzyme active sites, regions of secondary structure, signal sequences, transmembrane regions, and other discrete characteristics. The FT lines have a fixed format; each line starts with the key name, describing the kind of biological feature being catalogued on that line. After the key name are the start and stop positions for that particular biological feature. The sequence is numbered from 1 to *n* and is not necessarily the same as that of the sequence from the source database(s). In addition,

▶ If the "from" and "to" specifications are identical, the feature involves just a single amino acid.

▶ If a feature is known to extend beyond the end(s) of the sequenced region, the endpoint specification will be preceded by a < (for features which continue in the N-terminal direction) or a > (for features which continue in the C-terminal direction).

Unknown endpoints are indicated with a question mark. Uncertain endpoints are denoted by a question mark and a position number (e.g., ?42).

The feature line ends with a description containing additional information about the feature. For example, for a posttranslational modification (MOD_RES), the chemical nature of the modification is given; for a sequence variant (VARIANT), the exact nature of the variation is indicated. The record ends with the actual sequence, marked SQ, and the usual // mark indicating the end of the record.

TABLE 1.3 ■ UniProt Comment Keys

Key	Description
Allergen	Information relevant to allergenic proteins
Alternative products	Description of the existence of related protein sequence(s) produced by alternative splicing of the same gene or by the use of alternative initiation codons
Biotechnology	Description of the use of a specific protein in a biotechnological process
Catalytic activity	Description of the reaction(s) catalyzed by an enzyme
Caution	Warning about possible errors and/or grounds for confusion
Cofactor	Description of an enzyme cofactor
Database	Description of a cross-reference to a network database/resource for a specific protein
Developmental stage	Description of the developmentally specific expression of a protein
Disease	Description of the disease(s) associated with a deficiency of a protein
Domain	Description of the domain structure of a protein
Enzyme regulation	Description of an enzyme regulatory mechanism
Function	General description of the function(s) of a protein
Induction	Description of the compound(s) or condition(s) that stimulate the synthesis of a protein
Mass spectrometry	Reports the exact molecular weight of a protein or part of a protein as determined by mass spectrometric methods
Miscellaneous	Any comment that does not belong to any of the other defined topics
Pathway	Description of the metabolic pathway(s) with which a protein is associated
Pharmaceutical	Description of the use of a protein as a pharmaceutical drug
Polymorphism	Description of polymorphism(s)
PTM	Description of a posttranslational modification
RNA Editing	Description of any type of RNA editing that leads to one or more amino acid changes
Similarity	Description of the similaritie(s) (sequence or structural) of a protein with other proteins
Subcellular location	Description of the subcellular location of the mature protein
Subunit	Description of the quaternary structure of a protein
Tissue specificity	Description of the tissue specificity of a protein

The final portion of UniProt consists of the nonredundant reference databases (UniRef), which is based on the same general principles as the UniProt Knowledgebase, but with some significant differences. UniRef merges sequences automatically across different species and also adds some data from UniParc, such as translations from highly unstable gene predictions; merging in the Knowledgebase is restricted to curator-assisted inclusion of reliable and stable sequence data for a single species. UniRef100 is based on all UniProt Knowledgebase records, as well as UniParc records that represent sequences deemed overrepresented in the Knowledgebase, DDBJ/EMBL/GenBank WGS CDS translations, Ensembl protein translations from various organisms, as well as IPI data. The production of UniRef100 begins with the clustering of all records by sequence identity. Identical sequences and subfragments are presented as a single UniRef100 entry, containing the accession numbers of all merged entries, the protein sequence, and a bibliography; links to the corresponding Knowledgebase and archival records are provided, as well as to close sequence neighbors having at least 95% sequence identity.

UniRef90 and UniRef50 are built from UniRef100 and are intended to provide nonredundant sequence collections for the scientific community to use in performing faster homology searches. All records having more than 90% or more than 50% identity are merged together into a single UniRef90 or UniRef50 entry, respectively. The UniRef90 set is approximately 40% smaller than UniRef100, and the UniRef50 set is approximately 65% smaller than UniRef100.

UniProt Proteome Sets and IPI

UniProt constructs complete, nonredundant proteome sets on a biweekly basis; these are available for download through EBI's Proteome Analysis Database (Preuss et al., 2003). Each set is made available shortly after the appearance of a new, complete genome sequence in the nucleotide sequence databases. EBI also produces a third data set for human, mouse, and rat that provides complete coverage of all predicted coding sequences, called the IPI (Kersey et al., 2004). IPI is derived from the UniProt Knowledgebase, Ensembl, and NCBI RefSeq. Each IPI entry represents a cluster of entries from the

BOX 1.4 Assuring the Continued Quality of Data in Public Sequence Databases

Given DDBJ/EMBL/GenBank's role as the archive of all publicly available DNA, RNA, and protein sequences, the continued usefulness of this resource is highly dependent on the quality of the data found within it. Despite the high degree of both manual and automated checking that takes place before a record becoming public, errors still will find their way into the databases. These errors may be trivial and have no biological consequence (e.g., an incorrect postal code), may be misleading (e.g., an organism having the correct genus but wrong species name), or downright incorrect (e.g., a full-length mRNA not having a coding sequence annotated on it). Often times, records will have incorrect reference blocks, preventing researchers from linking to the correct publication describing the sequence. Over time, many have taken an active role in reporting these errors (see Korning et al., 1996), but more often than not, these errors are left uncorrected.

Users are actively encouraged to report any errors found when using the databases in the course of their work. Given below are the E-mail addresses for submitting information regarding errors to the three major sequence databases; recall that, because all the databases share information with each other nightly, the error must be reported only to one of the three members of the consortium. Authors also are actively encouraged to check their own records periodically to assure that the information they submitted previously is still accurate. Even though this charge is discussed in the context of the three major sequence databases, all databases provide a mechanism through which incorrect information can be brought to the attention of the database administrators.

DDBJ	ddbjupdt@ddbj.nig.ac.jp
EMBL	update@ebi.ac.uk
GenBank	update@ncbi.nlm.nih.gov

source databases believed to represent the same protein. In assembling IPU data sets, an automatic and pragmatic approach is used to build clusters, combining knowledge already present in primary data sources (and their cross-references) with the results of protein sequence comparisons. As soon as a cluster is assembled, a master entry is chosen from the cluster members, supplying the IPI entry with its sequence and annotation; an identifier is then chosen for each cluster.

SUMMARY

The rapid pace of discovery in the genomic and proteomic arenas require that databases are built in a way that facilitates not just the storage of these data, but the efficient handling and retrieval of information from these databases. Many lessons have been learned over the past 20 years regarding how to approach critical questions regarding design and content, often the hard way. Thus, the continued development of currently existing databases, as well as the conceptualization and creation of new types of databases, will be a critical focal point for the advancement of biological discovery. As should be obvious from this chapter, keeping databases up-to-date and accurate is a task that requires the active involvement of the entire biological community (Box 1.4).

It is incumbent on these submitters to assure the accuracy of these data in an active fashion, engaging the curators in a continuous dialogue to assure that these widely used resources continue to remain a valuable resource to biologists worldwide.

ACKNOWLEDGMENTS

The author thanks Ilene Mizrachi and B. F. Francis Ouellette for their helpful comments and the use of material from prior editions of this book.

INTERNET RESOURCES

BankIt	http://www.ncbi.nlm.nih.gov/BankIt/
DNA DataBase of Japan	http://www.ddbj.nig.ac.jp/
European Bioinformatics Institute	http://www.ebi.ac.uk/
EMBL Nucleotide sequence database	http://www.ebi.ac.uk/embl/
GenBank	http://www.ncbi.nlm.nih.gov/Web/Genbank/
NAR Database issue	http://www3.oup.co.uk/nar/database/c/
National Center for Biotechnology Information	http://www.ncbi.nlm.nih.gov
National Institute of Genetics	http://www.nig.ac.jp/index-e.html
PIR	http://pir.georgetown.edu/
RefSeq	http://www.ncbi.nlm.nih.gov/RefSeq/
Sakura	http://sakura.ddbj.nig.ac.jp/
Sequin	http://www.ncbi.nlm.nih.gov/Sequin/
Swiss-Prot (ExPASy)	http://www.expasy.org/sprot/
Swiss-Prot (EBI)	http://www.ebi.ac.uk/swissprot
Taxonomy	http://www.ncbi.nlm.nih.gov/Taxonomy/
UniProt	http://www.uniprot.org/
wEBIn	http://www.ebi.ac.uk/embl/Submission/webin.html

FURTHER READING

COOK-DEEGAN, R. (1994). *The Gene Wars . Science, Politics and the Human Genome.* (New York and London: W. W. Norton & Company). For an insightful historical rendering of the beginning of the nucleotide sequence databases.

Each year, the journal Nucleic Acids Research *devotes its first issue to the myriad of sequence databases currently available. The papers listed below provide further information on the major sequence databases discussed in this chapter. The reader is encouraged to refer to these yearly updates to learn about improvements and enhancements to these critical resources.*

BAIROCH, A., AND APWEILER, R. (2000). The SWISS-PROT protein sequence database and its supplement TrEMBL in 2000. *Nucl. Acids Res.* 28, 45–48.

BENSON, D. A., KARSCH-MIZRACHI, I., LIPMAN, D. J., OSTELL, J., AND WHEELER, D. L. (2004). GenBank: update. *Nucl. Acids Res.* 32, D23–D26.

KULIKOVA, T., ALDEBERT, P., ALTHORPE, N., BAKER, W., BATES, K., BROWNE, P., van den BROEK, A., COCHRANE, G., DUGGAN, K., EBERHARDT, R., et al. (2004). The EMBL Nucleotide Sequence Database. *Nucl. Acids Res.* 32, D27–D30.

MIYAZAKI, S., SUGAWARA, H., IKEO, T., GOJOBORI, T., AND TATENO, Y. (2004). DDBJ in the stream of various biological data. *Nucl. Acids Res.* 32, D31–D34.

WU, C. H., YEH, L. S., HUANG, H., ARMINSKI, L., CASTRO-ALVEAR, J., CHEN, Y., HU, Z., KOURTESIS, P., LEDLEY, R. S., SUZEK, B., et al. (2003). The Protein Information Resource. *Nucl. Acids Res.* 31, 345–347.

REFERENCES

APWEILER, R. (2001). Functional information in Swiss-Prot: the basis for large-scale characterisation of protein sequences. *Brief. Bioinf.* 2, 9–18.

APWEILER, R., BAIROCH, A., WU, C. H., BARKER, W. C., BOECKMANN, B., FERRO, F., GASTEIGER, E., HUANG, H., LOPEZ, R., MAGRANE, M., et al. (2004). UniProt: the Universal Protein knowledgebase. *Nucl. Acids Res.* 32, D115–D119.

ATTWOOD, T. K., BLYTHE, M. J., FLOWER, D. R., GAULTON, A., MABEY, J. E., MAUDLING, N., McGREGOR, L., MITCHELL, A. L., MOULTON, G., PAINE, K., and SCORDIS, P. (2002). PRINTS AND PRINTS-S shed light on protein ancestry. *Nucl. Acids Res.* 31, 239–241.

BATEMAN, A., BIRNEY, E., CERRUTI, L., DURBIN, R., ETWILLER, L., EDDY, S. R., GRIFFITHS-JONES, S., HOWE, K. L., MARSHALL, M., AND SONNHAMMER, E. L. L. (2002). The Pfam protein families database. *Nucl. Acids Res.* 30, 276–280.

BLAKE, J. A., RICHARDSON, J. E., BULT, C. J., KADIN, J. A., AND EPPIG, J. T. (2003). MGD: the Mouse Genome Database. *Nucl. Acids Res.* 31, 193–195.

CAMON, E., MAGRANE, M., BARRELL, D., LEE, V., DIMMER, E., MASLEN, J., BINNS, D., HARTE, N., LOPEZ, R., AND APWEILER R. (2004). The Gene Ontology Annotation (GOA) Database: sharing knowledge in UniProt with Gene Ontology. *Nucl. Acids Res.* 32, D262–D266.

DAYHOFF, M. O. (1978). *Atlas of Protein Sequence and Structure.* Vol. 5, Suppl. 3. (Washington, DC: National Biomedical Research Foundation).

FALQUET, L., PAGNI, M., BUCHER, P., HULO, N., SIGRIST, C. J. A., HOFMANN, K., AND BAIROCH, A. (2002). The PROSITE database, its status in 2002. *Nucl. Acids Res.* 30, 235–238.

FLEISCHMANN, W., MOELLER, S., GATEAU, A., AND APWEILER, R. (1998). A novel method for automatic and reliable functional annotation. *Bioinformatics* 15, 228–233.

FLYBASE CONSORTIUM. (2003). The FlyBase database of the Drosophila genome projects and community literature. *Nucl. Acids Res.* 31, 172–175.

HARRIS, T. W., LEE, R., SCHWARZ, E., BRADNAM, K., LAWSON, D., CHEN, W., BLASIER, D., KENNY, E., CUNNINGHAM, F., KISHORE, R., et al. (2003). WormBase: a cross-species database for comparative genomics. *Nucl. Acids Res.* 31, 133–137.

JUNKER, V., APWEILER, R., AND BAIROCH, A. (1999). Representation of functional information in the Swiss-Prot data bank. *Bioinformatics* 15, 1066–1067.

KERSEY, P., DUARTE, J., WILLIAMS A., KARAVIDOPOULOU, Y., BIRNEY, E., AND APWEILER R. (2004). The International Protein Index: an integrated database for proteomics experiments. *Proteomics* In press.

KORNING, P. G., HEBSGAARD, S. M., ROUZE, P., AND BRUNAK, S. (1996). Cleaning the GenBank Arabidopsis thaliana data set. *Nucl. Acids Res.* 24, 316–320.

KRETSCHMANN, E., FLEISCHMANN, W., AND APWEILER, R. (2001). Automatic rule generation for protein annotation with the C4.5 data mining algorithm applied on SWISS-PROT. *Bioinformatics* 17, 920–926.

LEINONEN, R., GARCIA-DIEZ, F., BINNS, D., FLEISCHMANN, W., LOPEZ, R., AND APWEILER, R. (2004). UniProt Archive. *Bioinformatics* In press.

MULDER, N. J., APWEILER, R., ATTWOOD, T. K., BAIROCH, A., Barrell, D., Bateman, A., Binns, D., Biswas, M., Bradley, P., Bork, P., et al. (2003). The InterPro database: 2003 brings increased coverage and new features. *Nucl. Acids Res.* 31, 315–318.

O'DONOVAN, C., MARTIN, M. J., GLEMET, E., CODANI, J., AND APWEILER, R. (1999). Removing redundancy in Swiss-Prot and TrEMBL. *Bioinformatics* 15, 258–259.

PRUESS, M., FLEISCHMANN, W., KANAPIN, K., KARAVIDOPOULOU, Y., KERSEY, P., KRIVENTSEVA, E., MITTARD, V., MULDER, N., PHAN, I., SERVANT, F., AND APWEILER, R. (2003). The Proteome Analysis database: a tool for the *in silico* analysis of whole proteomes. *Nucl. Acids Res.* 31, 414–417.

Pruitt, K. D., Tatusova, T., and Maglott, D. R. (2003). NCBI Reference Sequence Project: update and current status. *Nucl. Acids Res.* 31, 34–37.

Wain, H. M., Lush, M., Ducluzeau, F., and Povey, S. Genew: the human gene nomenclature database. *Nucl. Acids Res.* 30, 169–171.

Westbrook, J., Feng, Z., Chen, L., Yang, H., and Berman, H. M. (2003). The Protein Data Bank and structural genomics. *Nucl. Acids. Res.* 31, 489–491.

KEY TERMS

DDBJ
EMBL
GenBank
PIR
RefSeq
Sequence databases
Swiss-Prot
TrEMBL
UniProt

Mapping Databases

PETER S. WHITE

TARA C. MATISE

Bioinformatics: A Practical Guide to the Analysis of Genes and Proteins, Third Edition, edited by
Andreas D. Baxevanis and B.F. Francis Ouellette.
ISBN 0-471-47878-4 Copyright © 2005 John Wiley & Sons, Inc.

▌INTRODUCTION

Genomic mapping is comprised of two fundamentally different components. The first component is the creation of a representational measurement of a genome or a portion thereof. This measurement can take several forms, depending on how the observations of the genome were collected. Although most people first think of physical maps, such as those constructed from DNA sequence or DNA clones, there are other important ways in which genomic information is collected, including visual information (cytogenetic maps) and genetic information (genetic linkage and haplotype maps). For the genomes of an increasing number of species, the task of equating these scales has been increasingly simplified because of concentrated mapping and DNA sequencing efforts, such that many species will have only one or a few comprehensive maps of each type that are commonly used. However, initial and refined genome exploration through the use of different mapping techniques will continue for many additional species as they are studied more thoroughly.

The second component of genomic mapping is the process of determining where an object of biological interest, such as a gene, a genomic variation, or a disease predisposition locus, lies within a defined genome. This aspect is of extreme importance because it marks a crucial step in equating a molecular signature with a biological outcome. For example, identification of a gene causative for a particular disease, or a polymorphic variant associated with a specific phenotype exhibited by a cell or organism, provides the necessary genomic context in which an underlying biological process, such as a nonfunctional protein, can be defined. Needless to say, identification of these molecular signatures can lead to dramatic advances in the fields of applied biomedicine and agriculture.

Increasingly, the major bioinformatics challenges of genomic mapping are the efficient mining and use of the vast array of genomic data now available. Subsequently, the researcher's burden has shifted from mapping the genome to navigating a vast terra incognita of Web sites and databases. These range from large resources encompassing many types of data from numerous organisms to sites used by smaller laboratories to publish highly detailed maps of specific regions. This chapter is intended as a "map of the maps," a way to guide readers through the maze of publicly available genomic mapping resources (see also Chapter 4). Herein, the different types of markers and methods used for genomic mapping are reviewed, accompanied by a discussion of the inherent complexities in the construction and use of genome maps. Several large, community databases and method-specific mapping projects are discussed in

detail. Last, practical examples of how these tools and resources can be used to aid in specific types of mapping studies such as localizing a new gene or refining a region of interest are provided. A complete description of the mapping resources available for all species would require an entire book. Therefore, this chapter focuses primarily on humans, with some references to resources for other organisms.

▌RELATIONSHIP BETWEEN MAPPING AND SEQUENCING

The distinction between a map and a sequence is not always clear, because in some sense, large, uninterrupted DNA sequence tracts can be thought of as ultra-high–resolution maps. A brief discussion of how to distinguish between the mapping process itself and the genomic elements being mapped is, therefore, in order. For the mapping process, a defined, specific localization in the genome is central (e.g., bp 247 of the PGD gene; between D1S450 and D1S228; 1p36.2). The map elements describe biological attributes of each genomic position (e.g., an anonymous DNA marker, a gene, or a DNA clone). Viewed in this way, a DNA sequence tract can be considered an annotation of the position: as an object that is "placed" onto a map with a defined position. For genomes with complete or partial sequences available, maps and mapping resources commonly integrate available sequence tracts with other mapping information. Often, sequence position is used as the universal scale by which other mapping scales are integrated or aligned. The significance and usefulness of genomic sequence tracts and their associated annotations (e.g., genes and repetitive elements) is dependent on the extent and availability of the sequence. As genome projects progress from mapping to sequencing, sequence position becomes more central to the way in which different mapping scales are aligned. As of March 2004, fewer than 30 eukaryotic genomes had complete sequences, whereas almost 400 had partial sequences available; further, the number of partially sequenced genomes is likely to increase in the future.

Before determination of an entire chromosome's sequence, the types of sequences available can be grouped roughly into marker-based and gene-based tags (e.g., expressed sequence tags [ESTs] and sequence-tagged sites [STSs]; Box 1.1), single gene sequences, prefinished (draft) DNA clone sequences, and completed, continuous genomic sequence tracts. The first two categories provide rich sources of the genomic markers used for mapping, but only the last two categories can order genomic elements reliably. Prefinished genomic sequences, where as much as 95% of the entire sequence is available, but where continuous sequence tracts are relatively short (usually fewer than 100 kb and often fewer than 10 kb), provide high local resolution but little long-range ordering information. Genomic maps can help provide a context for this sequence information. Thus, two or more sequences containing unique genomic markers can be oriented if these markers are ordered on a map. In this way, existing maps serve as a scaffold for orienting, directing, and troubleshooting sequencing projects. Similarly, users first can define a chromosomal region of interest using a traditional map approach, and then can identify relevant DNA sequences to analyze by finding long sequences containing markers mapping within the defined region. Genomic analysis tools such as BLAST (Chapter 11) and electronic polymerase chain reaction (e-PCR) are valuable for finding marker and sequence identities. Several of the resources discussed below provide marker and sequence integration. Given the error rates inherent in both map-assembly and sequence-assembly methodology, it is good practice to use both map and sequence information simultaneously for independent verification of regional order for partially sequenced genomes.

∎ GENOMIC MAP ELEMENTS

DNA Markers

A DNA marker is simply a uniquely identifiable segment of DNA. There are several different types of markers, usually ranging in size from 1 to 400 nucleotide bases in size. Markers can be thought of as landmarks, and a set of markers whose relative positions (or order) within a genome are known comprises a map. Markers can be categorized in several ways. Some markers are polymorphic, and others are not (monomorphic). Marker positions can be derived experimentally using a variety of approaches but are usually determined by using PCR or hybridization-based methods. Some markers lie in a sequence of DNA that is expressed, some do not, and for some, their expression status may be unknown.

PCR-based markers are commonly referred to as STSs. An STS is defined as a segment of genomic DNA that can be uniquely amplified by PCR using its primer sequences. STSs commonly are used in the construction of physical maps. STS markers may be developed from any genomic sequence of interest, such as from characterized and sequenced genes, or from ESTs. Alternatively, STSs may be identified randomly from genomic DNA. The UniSTS database at the NCBI stores information on STS markers for many organisms, whereas the Genome Database (GDB) and eGenome have extensive human STS collections.

Polymorphic Markers

Polymorphic markers are those that show sequence variation among individuals. Polymorphic markers are used to construct genetic linkage maps. The number of alleles observed in a population for a given marker, which can vary from two to more than 30, determines the degree of polymorphism. For genetic linkage studies, highly polymorphic markers (more than five alleles) usually are most useful, whereas for high-density genetic association studies, markers with a lower polymorphic rate but that are easier to assay may be more desirable.

Polymorphisms may arise from several types of sequence variations. Two early types of polymorphic markers used for genomic mapping were restriction fragment length polymorphisms (RFLPs) and variable number of tandem repeat units (VNTRs), both of which alter the restriction digestion patterns observed during hybridization-based analysis. A third and more commonly used type of polymorphism is the result of tandem repeats of short sequences that can be detected by PCR-based analysis. These are known variously as microsatellites, short tandem repeats (STRs), STR polymorphisms (STRPs), or short sequence length polymorphisms (SSLPs). These repeat sequences usually consist of 2 to 4 nucleotides and are plentiful in most organisms. All PCR-converted microsatellite markers (those for which a pair of oligonucleotides flanking the polymorphic site suitable for PCR amplification of the locus has been designed) are also STSs.

Another polymorphic type of PCR-based marker is a single nucleotide polymorphism (SNP), which results from a base variation at a single nucleotide position (Chapter 7). Most SNPs have only two alleles (biallelic). Because of their low heterozygosity, maps of SNPs require a much higher marker density than maps of microsatellites. SNPs occur frequently in most genomes, with one SNP occurring on average approximately once in every 100 to 300 bases in humans. SNPs lend themselves to highly automated fluidic or DNA array-based and chip-based analyses and have become the focus of several large-scale development and mapping projects in humans and other organisms.

DNA Clones

The possibility of physically mapping eukaryotic genomes largely was realized with the advent of cloning vehicles that efficiently and reproducibly could propagate large DNA fragments. The current generation of large-insert clones consists of bacterial artificial chromosomes (BACs) and P1-artificial chromosomes (PACs), both of which act as episomes in bacterial cells. Bacterial propagation has several advantages, including high DNA yields, ease of use for sequencing, and high integrity of the insert during propagation. As such, BACs and PACs are now the standard cloning vehicles for large-genome mapping and sequencing projects (Iaonnou et al., 1994; Shizuya et al., 1992). DNA fingerprinting has been applied to BACs and PACs to determine insert overlaps and to construct clone contigs. In this technique, clones are digested with a restriction enzyme, and the resulting fragment patterns are compared between clones to identify those sharing subsets of identically sized fragments. In addition, the ends of BAC and PAC inserts can be sequenced directly; clones whose insert-end sequences have been determined are referred to as sequence-tagged clones (STCs). Both DNA fingerprinting and STC generation can play instrumental roles in physical mapping strategies, as is discussed below.

Genomic Annotations

DNA sequence tracts, as well as biologically defined genomic objects such as genes, repetitive sequences, disease loci, or even literature reports, also can be incorporated into maps or even be made as the primary focus of a map (e.g., a gene promoter map). These genomic element classes typically are included in mapping resources as annotations, where they are aligned and displayed relative to a genomic positional scale, usually DNA sequence position. These annotations generally are not formally considered to be genomic map elements because they do not play a role in map construction. However, they are a critical constituent of genomic maps because they represent the biological principles relevant to map use.

∎ COMPLEXITIES AND PITFALLS OF MAPPING

It is important to realize that the genomic mapping information currently available is a collection of a large number of individual data sets, each of which has unique characteristics. The experimental techniques, methods of data collection, annotation, presentation, and quality of the data differ considerably among these data sets. Although most mapping projects include procedures to detect, eliminate, and correct errors, there are invariably some errors that occur, which often result in the incorrect ordering or labeling of individual markers. Although the error rate is usually very low (5% or less), a marker misplacement obviously can have a great impact on a study. A few mapping Web sites flag and correct (or at least warn) users of some potential errors, but most errors cannot be detected easily. Successful strategies for minimizing the effects of data error include:

► Simultaneously assessing several different maps to maximize redundancy (note that ideally "different"

maps use independently derived data sets or different techniques);

► Increased emphasis on using integrated maps and genomic catalogues that provide access to all available genomic information for the region of interest (while closely monitoring the map resolution and marker placement confidence of the integrated map); and

► If possible, experimentally verifying the most critical marker positions or placements.

In addition to data errors, several other, more subtle complexities are notable. Foremost is the issue of nomenclature, or the naming of genomic markers and elements. Most markers have multiple names, and keeping track of all the names is a major bioinformatics challenge. For example, the polymorphic marker *D1S243* has almost 20 unique identifiers associated with it, including AFM214yg7, which is actually the name of the DNA clone from which this polymorphism was identified; SHGC-428 and stSG729, two examples of genome centers renaming a marker to fit their own nomenclature schemes; and both GDB:201358 and GDB:133491, which are database identifier numbers used to track the polymorphism and STS associated with this marker, respectively, in GDB. Furthermore, most genomic maps display only a subset of the possible names, making comparisons of maps problematic. Mapping groups and Web sites are now addressing these inherent problems, but the difficulty of precisely defining the often overlapping terms "markers," "genes," and "genomic elements" adds to the confusion.

It is important to distinguish between groups of names defining different elements. A gene can have several names, although each gene usually has only one "official" name. In humans, this is assigned by the Human Genome Organization's (HUGO) Genome Nomenclature Committee; similar nomenclature committees assign gene names for mouse and rat (White et al., 1997; Bult et al., 2004). A gene also can be associated with one or more EST clusters, polymorphisms, and STSs, each with their own identifiers. Genes spanning a large genomic stretch can be represented even by several markers that individually map to different positions. Web sites providing genomic cataloging, such as NCBI's Gene and UniGene databases, GeneCards, eGenome, and GDB list most names associated with a given genomic element. Nevertheless, collecting, cross-referencing, and frequently updating one's own sets of names for markers of interest also is a good practice, because even the genomic cataloging sites do not always provide complete nomenclature collections.

Each mapping technique yields its own resolution limits. Cytogenetic banding potentially orders markers separated by 1 to 2 Mb or more, whereas genetic linkage (GL)

and radiation hybrid (RH) analyses yield long-range resolutions of 0.5 to 1 Mb or more, although localized ordering can achieve higher resolutions. The confidence level with which markers are ordered on statistically based maps often is overlooked, but this is crucial for assessing map quality. For genomes with abundant mapping data such as human or mouse, the number of markers used for mapping often far exceeds the ability of the technique to order all markers with high confidence; often, confidence levels of 1000:1 are used as a cutoff, which means that a marker is 1000 or more times more likely to be in the given position than in any other. Mappers have taken two approaches to address this issue. One is to order all markers in the best possible linear order, regardless of the confidence for map position of each marker. Alternatively, the high confidence linear order of a subset of markers is determined, and the remaining markers are then placed in high confidence "intervals," or regional positions. The advantage of the first approach is that resolution is maximized, but it is important to pay attention to the odds for placement of individual markers, because alternative local orders often are almost equally likely. Thus, when extended beyond the effective resolving power of a mapping technique, increased resolution may yield decreased accuracy.

Each mapping technique also yields very different measures of distance. Cytogenetic approaches, with the exception of high-resolution fiber fluorescence in situ hybridization (FISH), provide only rough distance estimates, GL and STS content mapping provide marker orientation but only relative distances, and RH mapping yields distances roughly proportional to true physical distance. For GL analysis, unit measurements are in centimorgans, with 1 cM equivalent to a 1% chance of recombination between two linked markers. A conversion factor of 1 cM $\sim$ 1 Mb often is cited for the human genome but is, in reality, overstated, because this is only the average ratio genome-wide, and many chromosomal regions have recombination hotspots and coldspots in which the cM-to-Mb ratio varies as much as 10-fold (Matise et al., 2002; McVean et al., 2004). In general, cytogenetic maps provide subband marker regionalization but limited localized ordering, GL and STS content maps provide excellent ordering and limited-to-moderate distance information, and RH maps potentially provide the best combination of localized ordering and distance estimates.

Finally, there are various levels at which genomic information can be presented. Single-resource maps such as the Généthon GL maps use a single experimental technique and analyze a homogeneous set of markers. Strictly comparative maps make comparisons between two or more different single-dimension maps either within or between species but without combining data sets for integration. NCBI's Map Viewer can display multiple maps in this fashion. Integrated maps recalculate or completely integrate multiple data sets to display the map position of all genomic elements relative to a single scale; the Genetic Location Database is an example of such integration (Ke et al., 2001).

TYPES OF MAPS

Cytogenetic Maps

Cytogenetic maps are those in which the markers are localized to chromosomes in a manner that can be visualized in a microscope. Traditional cytogenetic mapping hybridizes a radioactively or fluorescently labeled DNA probe to a chromosome preparation, usually in parallel with a chromosomal stain such as Giemsa, which produces a banded karyotype of each chromosome (Pinkel et al., 1986). This allows assignment of the probe to a specific chromosomal band or region. Assignment of cytogenetic positions in this manner is dependent on some subjective criteria (variability in technology, methodology, interpretation, reproducibility, and definition of band boundaries). Inferred cytogenetic positions often are fairly large and occasionally are overinterpreted, and some independent verification of cytogenetic position determinations is warranted for crucial genes, markers, or regions. Probes used for cytogenetic mapping are usually large-insert clones containing a gene or polymorphic marker of interest. Despite the subjective aspects of cytogenetic methodology, karyotype analysis is an important and accessible clinical genetic tool; thus, cytogenetic positioning remains an important parameter for defining genes, disease loci, and chromosomal rearrangements.

Additional cytogenetic technical advances such as interphase FISH (Lawrence et al., 1990) and fiber FISH (Parra and Windle, 1993) instead examine chromosomal preparations in which the DNA is either naturally or mechanically extended. Studies of such extended chromatin have demonstrated a directly proportional relationship between the distances measured on the image and the actual physical distance for short stretches, so that a physical distance between two closely linked probes can be determined with some precision (van den Engh et al., 1992). However, these techniques have a limited ordering range ($\leq$1–2 Mb) and are not well-suited for high-throughput mapping.

Most recently, microarray-based comparative genomic hybridization (or array CGH) has been introduced for parallel cytogenetic analysis of chromosomes and even whole genomes (Pinkel et al., 1998). Array CGH makes use of an ordered array of large-insert clones that are hybridized against a target genome. Although not strictly a mapping technique because the clone positions are predetermined, this produces a map of the target genome, in the sense that large-scale, unbalanced re-arrangements and breakpoints can be identified. Array CGH also is amenable to high-throughput analysis, a promising and well-needed advance in this field. This work builds on previous advances such as DNA-based CGH and spectral karyotyping, which provide more indirect and low-resolution ways, respectively, to survey cytogenetically visible breakpoints of individual samples.

Cytogenetic-based methodologies are instrumental in defining inherited and acquired chromosome abnormalities, and (especially gene-based) chromosomal mapping data often is expressed in cytogenetic terms. However, because cytogenetic markers are not sequence based and the technique is less straightforward and usually more subjective than GL, RH, or physical mapping, caution should be taken in equating band assignments with physical or GL positions. Several groups have used large sets of human data to construct computational models equating sequence positions with cytogenetic band boundaries; these models perform well overall. However, it is unclear whether a visible chromosome retains the same order as a stretched DNA strand, and there appears to be variability in compaction ratios between different bands. Accordingly, cytogenetic assignments

are variable in their accuracies and should be confirmed with other information if possible.

Cytogenetic Mapping Resources

Useful human resources can be divided into displays of primary cytogenetic mapping data, efficient methods of integrating cytogenetic and other mapping data, and resources pertaining to specific chromosomal aberrations.

There are currently two important and nonoverlapping repositories for human cytogenetic mapping information. The first of these is the Human BAC Resource, hosted by the NCBI. This resource consists of a series of over 10,000 large-insert clones that have been assigned by FISH to a cytogenetic band or range. Most of these clones also have associated STSs, determined full-insert or clone-end DNA sequences, and integration into the human clone and sequence build. This resource was generated by a consortium of seven high-volume cytogenetic laboratories (Cheung et al., 2001). Clones are shown by chromosome and display information about the source, distributor, localization, associated sequences, and STSs contained within the insert (Figure 2.1). Clones are available for experimental use, and this dataset has been used to integrate cytogenetic band

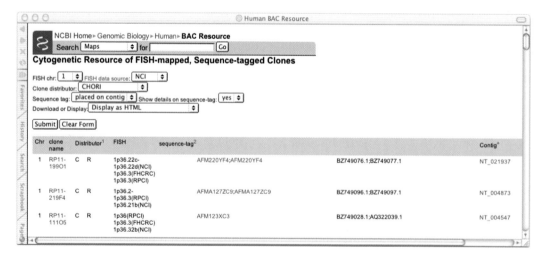

FIGURE 2.1   NCI/NCBI BAC Resource Consortium. The figure shows a partial list of DNA clones that have been mapped to chromosome 1 by FISH and that also have some DNA sequence-based association, either through sequence determination of the insert or insert ends (STCs), or via one or more STSs contained within the clone insert. At the top are a list of search parameters for refining the search, including the chromosome (chromosome 1 is selected), source of the FISH mapping data (NCI), distributor where clones can be obtained (Children's Hospital Oakland Research Institute), and type of sequence association (placed in sequence contig). The table lists the assigned chromosome, clone name, clone distributor(s), FISH-derived cytogenetic location(s), sequence accession number(s) associated with the clone, and genomic sequence contig. Text in light blue hyperlinks to related data records in other NCBI resources. To view this figure from the BAC Resource Consortium home page, click on the "FISH-mapped" clone total for chromosome 1 in Table 1.

positions with genomic sequence for several integrated mapping resources, including UCSC, NCBI, Ensembl, the Genetic Location Database (LDB2000), and eGenome. Another repository for human cytogenetic information is GDB, which centrally collects and disseminates cytogenetic positional information from laboratories worldwide.

Many data repositories and groups creating integrated genome maps list cytogenetic localizations for mapped genomic elements. These include GDB, NCBI, UCSC, Ensembl GeneLoc, LDB2000, and eGenome, all of which infer approximate band assignments to many or all genomic elements in their databases. These assignments rely on determination of the approximate boundaries of each band using subsets of their marker sets for which accurate cytogenetic mapping data are available. An important distinction is whether a cytogenetic position has been determined directly by experimental means, or whether it has been inferred by interpolation based on some other mapping information. Most of the major human resources make this distinction, because they provide tracks or sections showing direct determinations as well as an overall band positioning that is layered on top of the chromosome being represented. This information can be used to determine quickly the cytogenetic position of a gene or localized region and to map cytogenetic observation such as a tumor-specific chromosomal rearrangement.

The National Cancer Institute's (NCI's) Cancer Chromosome Aberration Project, Infobiogen, the Southeastern Regional Genetics Group, the Developmental Genome Anatomy Project, and the Coriell Cell Repositories (among many others) all have Web sites that display cytogenetic maps or descriptions of characterized chromosomal rearrangements (Huret et al., 2003; Wheeler et al., 2004). These sites are useful resources for determining whether a specific genomic region is disrupted frequently in a particular disease or malignancy and for finding chromosomal cell lines and reagents for regional mapping. However, most of these rearrangements have been mapped only at the cytogenetic level.

Nonhuman resources are limited primarily to displays or simple integrations of chromosome ideograms. ArkDB is an advanced resource for displaying chromosomes and other mapping data of many amniotes (Hu et al., 2001), whereas MGI, the Rat Genome Database (RGD), and the resources outlined in Chapter 4 incorporate mouse or chromosome band assignments or both into queries of their databases.

Genetic Linkage Maps

Even now, in the "sequence era," GL maps (also called meiotic maps) remain a valuable and widely used genome mapping resource. GL maps are the starting point for many disease-gene mapping projects and have served as the backbone of many physical mapping efforts. GL maps rely on the naturally occurring process of recombination for determination of the relative order of, and map distances between, polymorphic markers. Crossover and recombination events take place during meiosis and allow rearrangement of genetic material between homologous chromosomes. The likelihood of recombination between markers is evaluated using genotypes observed in multigenerational families. Markers between which only a few recombination events occur are said to be linked, and such markers are usually located close to each other on the same chromosome. Markers between which many recombinations take place are unlinked and usually lie far apart, either at opposite ends of the same chromosome or on different chromosomes.

Because the recombination events cannot be quantified easily, a statistical method of maximum likelihood usually is applied in which the likelihood of two markers being linked is compared with the likelihood of being unlinked. This likelihood ratio is called a lod score (for "logarithm of the odds"), and a lod score of more than 3 (corresponding to odds of 1000:1 or more) usually is taken as evidence that markers are linked. The lod score is computed at a range of recombination fraction values between markers (from 0 to 0.5), and the recombination fraction at which the lod score is maximized provides an estimate of the distance between markers. A map function (usually either Haldane or Kosambi) then is used to convert the recombination fraction into an additive unit of distance measured in centimorgans (cM), with 1 cM representing a 1% probability that a recombination has occurred between two markers on a single chromosome. As mentioned previously, recombination events are not distributed randomly, and map distances on linkage maps are not directly proportional to physical distances.

Most linkage maps are constructed using multipoint linkage analysis, although multiple pairwise linkage analysis and minimization of recombination also are valid approaches. Commonly used and publicly available computer programs for building linkage maps, which are cataloged on the Genetic Analysis Software Web site, include LINKAGE, CRI-MAP, MultiMap, MAPMAKER, and MAP. The MAP-O-MAT Web server is available for estimation of map distances and for evaluation of statistical support for order (see additional discussion below).

Because linkage mapping is based on statistical methods, linkage maps are not guaranteed to show the correct order of markers. Therefore, it is important to be critical of the various available maps and to be aware of the statistical criteria that were used in map construction.

Typically, only a subset of markers (framework or index markers) is mapped with high statistical support. The remainder are either placed into well-supported intervals or are placed into unique map positions but with low statistical support for order (see additional discussion below).

To facilitate global coordination of human linkage mapping, DNAs from a set of reference pedigrees collected for map construction were prepared and distributed by the Centre d'Etude du Polymorphism Humain (CEPH; Dausset et al., 1990). Nearly all human linkage maps are based on genotypes from the CEPH reference pedigrees, and genotypes for more than 14,000 markers scored in the CEPH pedigrees are deposited in a public database (CEPHdb). Most recent maps have been composed almost entirely of highly polymorphic microsatellite or SNP markers. Linkage mapping also is an important tool in experimental animals, with many maps already produced at high resolution and others still under development.

Genetic Linkage Mapping Resources

The number of genome-wide linkage maps that have been produced are too numerous to allow a comprehensive discussion in this chapter. We focus here on those that have been used most widely.

The most commonly used set of human maps was produced at the Center for Medical Genetics at the Marshfield Medical Research Foundation (Broman et al., 1998). This group identified more than 300 dinucleotide repeats and constructed high-density maps using more than 8000 markers. These maps have an average resolution of 2.3 cM per map interval. Markers developed at the Marshfield Foundation have a "Marshfield identifier" (MFD) at the beginning of their names. As the Marshfield staff themselves state, because only eight of the CEPH families were used for the map construction, the orders of some of the markers are not well determined. The Marshfield Web site also provides a useful utility for displaying custom maps that contain user-specified subsets of markers.

Another set of genome-wide linkage maps was produced in 1996 by the group at Généthon (Dib et al., 1996). This group identified and genotyped more than 7800 dinucleotide microsatellite markers and produced maps containing only these Généthon markers. These markers also have unique identifiers; each marker name has the symbols "AFM" at the beginning of the name. The Généthon map contains 5264 markers genotyped in 8 to 20 CEPH pedigrees. These markers have been placed into 2032 well-supported map positions, with an average map resolution of 2.2 cM. Because of homogeneity of their marker and linkage data and the RH and

clone-based mapping efforts at Généthon that incorporated many of their polymorphic markers, the Généthon map is also a widely used human linkage map.

A third genome-wide set of maps was produced by the Cooperative Human Linkage Center (CHLC; Murray et al., 1994). Last updated in 1997, CHLC identified, genotyped, and mapped more than 3300 microsatellite repeat markers. The CHLC Web site currently holds many linkage maps, including maps comprised solely of CHLC-derived markers and maps combining CHLC markers with those from other sources. CHLC markers can be recognized by unique identifiers that contain the nucleotide code for the trinucleotide or tetranucleotide repeat units. For example, CHLC.GATA49A06 (D1S1608) contains a repeat unit of GATA, whereas CHLC.ATA28C07 (D1S1630) contains an ATA repeat. There are more than 10,000 markers on the various linkage maps at CHLC, and most CHLC markers were genotyped in 15 CEPH pedigrees. The highest resolution CHLC maps have an average map distance of 1 to 2 cM between markers. Some of the maps contain markers in well-supported unique positions along with other markers placed at intervals.

A polynomial transformation approach was used subsequently by researchers at the Psychiatric University Hospital of Zurich to collect and integrate the Marshfield, Généthon, CHLC, and several other human linkage maps (Stassen and Scharfetter, 2000). Their Web site provides easy tabular access to several genetic linkage maps as well as their integrated map that combines six of these maps into a single resource.

In 2003, a linkage map and screening set of SNPs was produced to facilitate genome scanning using new high-throughput genotyping technologies (Matise et al., 2003). The map consists of 2771 markers genotyped in 56 CEPH pedigrees and has an average map resolution of 3.9 cM. Almost 70% of the map loci consist of close clusters of 1 to 4 SNPs, whereas the remainder are single SNPs. The average size of the SNP clusters is 53 kb. This SNP-based screening set was estimated to be at least as informative as another commonly used microsatellite-based screening set.

In 2002, a linkage map was constructed using genotype data from 146 Icelandic families (2002). This map contains 5136 markers, and the pedigrees contain 1257 meiotic events—several times more meioses than are in the 8 to 20 CEPH pedigrees used to create the first three linkage maps described here—which has led to a map with a very high average resolution, approximately 1 cM between markers. This map was used to create a modified version of the August 2001 sequence assembly.

Most recently, a unique linkage map containing 15,700 markers was constructed by researchers at Rutgers University (Kong et al., 2003). This map used the

NCBI Build 34 genome assembly to determine an initial order for more than 12,600 PCR-based markers. Support for this order was then confirmed by linkage analysis using genotype data from the CEPH and deCODE pedigrees. Markers whose most likely linkage map positions were inconsistent with their physical position were not included in the final map. The resulting linkage and physical combined map contains more than 11,800 polymorphic markers with an average intermarker distance of less than 0.5 cM. The 3000 markers for which physical map positions are not available were localized onto this map into lod 3 intervals.

Although each of these maps is extremely valuable, it can be very difficult to determine marker order and intermarker distance between markers that are not all represented on the same linkage map. The MAP-O-MAT Web site is a marker-based linkage map server that provides several map-specific queries. The server uses genotypes for more than 16,000 markers obtained from the CEPH database, the Marshfield Foundation, the SNP Consortium, and the deCODE linkage maps. The CRI-MAP computer program estimates map distances, assesses statistical support for order for user-specified maps, and localizes markers onto the deCODE linkage map. Thus, rather than attempting to integrate markers from multiple maps by rough interpolation, likelihood analyses can be performed easily on any subset of markers from these sources. This process facilitates the construction of customized linkage maps containing specific sets of markers used in genetic studies.

Four microsatellite-based linkage screening sets have been developed primarily for use in performing efficient large-scale or genome-wide genotyping, or both. The Applied Biosystems (ABI, Foster City, CA) PRISM linkage mapping sets are composed of dinucleotide repeat markers derived from the Généthon linkage map. The ABI marker sets are available at two different map resolutions (5 and 10 cM), containing 811 and 400 markers, respectively. The Center for Inherited Disease Research (CIDR) provides a genotyping service that uses 392 highly polymorphic trinucleotide and tetranucleotide repeat markers spaced at an average resolution of 9 cM. The CIDR set is derived from the Marshfield version 8 marker set, with improved reverse primers and some additional markers added to fill gaps. Marshfield has developed numerous screening sets that are used by its Mammalian Genotyping Service. The current sets (as of March 2004) consist of 410 (set 13) and 367 (set 53) microsatellite markers, almost entirely comprised of trinucleotide and tetranucleotide repeats. Marker set 13 gives a linkage map of 9.3 cM resolution, and when the set 53 is added in, the average map resolution is approximately 5 cM (Ghebranious et al., 2003). Work is underway at Marshfield to increase further the screening map resolution by adding

a set of diallelic insert and deletion (indel) markers. deCODE Genetics performs genotyping using sets of 500, 1000, or 2000 markers with average resolutions of approximately 8, 4, and 2 cM, respectively, based in part on markers selected from the ABI and Marshfield maps. Some of these groups intend to offer SNP-based genotyping in the future. In addition to these STR-based sets, SNP-based linkage screening sets have been developed by Illumina (San Diego, CA) and Affymetrix (Foster City, CA). The Illumina SNP-based Linkage III Panel consists of approximately 4700 SNPs, with an average spacing of 0.78 cM and 600 kb. The Affymetrix Mapping10K Array provides a microarray for genotyping of over 10,000 SNPs, with an average spacing of 0.31 cM and 210 kb.

High-resolution linkage maps also have been constructed for many other species. These maps are often the most well-developed resource for animal species' whose genome projects are in early stages. The mouse and rat both have multiple genome-wide linkage maps (see MGI and RGD below); other species with well-developed linkage maps include zebrafish, cat, dog, cow, pig, horse, sheep, goat, and chicken (O'Brien et al., 1999).

Physical Maps

Physical maps include maps that either provide directly measured distances between genomic elements or that order cloned DNA fragments known to contain specific genomic elements. Many straightforward and innovative techniques have been created to develop physical maps. Genome-wide physical mapping increasingly occurs through complete or partial sequencing, but other methods often are used as an initial or permanent step, depending on resource availability for that organism. Here we discuss the four most widely used strategies: STS content determination, clone alignments, radiation hybrid mapping, and using available sequence.

STS Content Maps

A widely adopted methodology that is particularly adaptable to compact genomes, largely because of its relative simplicity, is STS content mapping (Green and Olson, 1990). This technique can resolve regions much larger than 1 Mb and has the advantage of using convenient PCR-based positional markers. In STS content maps, STS markers are assayed by PCR or hybridization against a set or array of large-insert clones. If two or more STSs are found to be contained in the same clone, chances are very high that those markers are located close together. The STS content mapping technique builds a series of contigs (i.e., overlapping clusters of clones joined together by shared STSs). The resolution and coverage of such a map are determined by a number of factors, including the density of STSs, the size of the clones, and the depth of the clone set that is screened against. Although it is generally possible to deduce the relative order of markers on STS content maps, the distances between adjacent markers cannot be measured with accuracy without further experimentation, such as by restriction mapping or sequencing. However, STS content maps have the advantage of being associated with a clone resource that can be used for further studies, including subcloning, DNA sequencing, or transfection.

Of particular interest to researchers chasing disease genes are maps of transcribed sequences, which can be readily created by STS content mapping if the STSs represent genes. Projects for creating large numbers of ESTs (Adams et al., 1992; Houlgatte et al., 1995; Hillier et al., 1996) have made tens of thousands of unique expressed sequences suitable for STS creation available to mapping laboratories, and EST cataloging is a resource that often is pursued to characterize a genome initially. An early and widely successful human transcript map was GeneMap '99 (Deloukas et al., 1998), and this model has since been applied successfully to other organisms, using either STS content or RH mapping.

Clone-Based Maps

Clone maps rely on techniques other than STS content to determine the adjacency of clones. Fingerprinting is used commonly by sequencing centers to assemble and BAC and PAC contigs before clones are chosen for sequencing, to select new clones for sequencing that can extend existing contigs, and to help order genomic sequence tracts generated in whole-genome sequencing projects (Chumakov et al., 1995; Marra et al., 1997). Sequencing of large-insert clone ends (STC generation), when applied to a whole-genome clone library of adequate coverage, is very effective for whole-genome mapping when used in combination with fingerprinting of the same library. The UCSC Genome Brower includes tracks to visualize both fingerprinting and STC data in human and several other organisms. The most comprehensive human physical mapping project is the collection of overlapping BAC and PAC clones identified for the human DNA sequencing project, along with the now complete sequence of the human genome. This information was generated by many different labs using a variety of physical mapping techniques, including STS content, fingerprinting, and STC generation to assemble the clones.

Several complete and draft sequence assemblies have been determined from BAC libraries that have been whole-scale DNA fingerprinted and end sequenced. Washington University's Genome Sequencing Center (WUGSC) and the British Columbia Genome Sequence Centre (BCGSC) have fingerprinted collectively seven vertebrate genomes (human, mouse, rat, cow, chimp, dog, chicken, and stickleback) with a clone coverage sufficient to assemble large contigs spanning almost the entire euchromatin of these organisms. Fingerprinting data for each can be viewed and queried online or can be downloaded as a clone database and analyzed in detail using the Unix platform software tools IMAGE (for fingerprint data) and FPC (for contig assembly), which are available from the Sanger Institute.

Radiation Hybrid Maps

RH mapping is very similar to linkage mapping, except that in the construction of radiation hybrids, breaks are induced by the application of lethal doses of radiation rather than occurring naturally as a result of meiotic recombination (Cox et al., 1990). The resolution of a radiation hybrid map is proportional to the amount of irradiation to which the donor cell line was exposed, and like other physical maps, RH map distances are directly proportional to physical distance. A comprehensive discussion of both statistical and laboratory protocols for constructing and evaluating radiation hybrids is presented elsewhere (Matise et al., 1999).

RH maps provide an intermediate level of resolution between linkage and physical maps. They provide a relatively rapid method for surveying a new genome and can serve as an intermediate mapping resource during the sequencing of a genome. After sequencing is complete, their usefulness becomes greatly diminished. For humans, several high-resolution genome-wide RH maps were constructed using three RH panels (Deloukas et al., 1998; Olivier et al., 2001; Hudson et al., 1995; Gyapay et al., 1996; Stewart et al., 1997). Many RH mapping efforts have been completed or are underway in other species. Genome-wide RH maps have been published for mouse, rat, cat, dog, zebrafish, pig, and horse, and chromosome-specific RH maps have been constructed in several other species, including cow and chicken.

Sequence-Based Maps

As mentioned above, the existing complete and draft genomic sequences for a growing number of species are excellent sources for confirming mapping information, positioning and orienting localized markers, and bottom-up mapping of interesting genomic regions. Sequence alignment tools such as NCBI's BLAST (Chapter 12), UCSC's BLAT (Chapter 11), and e-PCR can be very powerful tools for finding marker–sequence links. NCBI's Gene resource lists all homologous sequences, including genomic sequences, for each known human gene (Maglott et al., 2000). e-PCR results showing all sequences containing a specific marker are available at the

UniSTS, GDB, and eGenome Web sites, where each sequence and the exact base pair position of the marker in the sequence are listed. Large sequence contigs also can be viewed schematically by several resources, including NCBI's Map Viewer, the UCSC Genome Browser, and Oakridge National Laboratory's Genome Channel Web tool (Wheeler et al., 2004; Mural et al., 1999; Karolchik et al., 2003).

As eukaryotic sequencing projects progress, a "sequence first" approach to mapping becomes more feasible. As an example (see also Chapter 4), a researcher can go to the NCBI's human Map Viewer home page and click on the ideogram of the chromosome number of interest. Clicking on the ideogram shows an expanded ideogram graphically depicting, among other features, all sequence contigs relative to the chromosome. These contigs can then be viewed further for clone, sequence, and marker content, and links to the relevant GenBank and UniSTS records are provided.

GENOMIC MAPPING RESOURCES

Genomic resources available on the Internet are quite varied and overlapping, providing a bewildering multitude of data sets, reanalyses, entry points, mechanisms for integration, and interfaces. This section concentrates on a subset of resources with a focus on themes that each resource generally provides. Resources may function as portals. Portals are resources that are well integrated and networked with other data sources and resources beyond what their own database contains. Portals are useful for entering a genome in some way (e.g., cytogenetic position or gene), obtaining a summary of a specific genomic element, and then traversing to more detail stored elsewhere through element-specific links. Almost all genomic resources have some interaction with other sites, but resources such as GeneLynx concentrate almost entirely on this function. Genomic repositories such as GDB actively seek out submissions of certain data types from many or all possible sources. Repositories provide more complete coverage of genomic elements, but the data cannot easily be standardized in terms of experimental design and quality control. Genomic catalogs tend to concentrate on one or a few data sets considered to be the most useful, complete, or accurate, or a combination thereof, within a specific genomic domain, such as NCBI's reliance on the Généthon, Marshfield, and deCODE GL maps to represent GL markers in its Map Viewer utility. Catalogs provide a "one-stop shopping" solution to collecting and analyzing genomic data and are recommended as a maximum-impact means to begin a regional analysis. However, individual data sets provide the highest quality

localizations and annotations and ultimately may be the most useful for region definition and refinement. Some resources, such as GeneLoc, serve mainly to redistribute data gathered from other resources and groups. Other resources, such as LDB2000 and eGenome, partially or completely reanalyze data from other sources. Sites that reanalyze data often do so to integrate different mapping scales relative to each other, which is commonly done to equate cytogenetic band and sequence positions, for example.

Because of the large number of primary data sources available for human genome mapping, ensuring that the data collected for a specific region of interest are both current and all-inclusive is a significant task. Genomic resources help in this regard, both to provide a single initial source containing most of the publicly available genomic information for a region and to make the task of monitoring new information easier. Three of the most comprehensive resources for mapping information derived from humans and other sequenced eukaryotic genomes, the NCBI, UCSC Genome Bioinformatics, and the Ensembl project, have genomic data interfaces that are covered more completely in Chapter 4. Each of these resources includes some representation of DNA sequence, cytogenetic bands, clones and clone contigs, transcripts, markers, and polymorphic elements.

As a central data collective for many genomic mapping and sequencing projects, the NCBI in particular supports many other tools and databases that are useful for gene mapping projects. These include GenBank (Chapter 1); Gene, OMIM, UniSTS, and UniGene (Chapter 3); dbSNP (Chapter 7); BLAST (Chapter 11), and e-PCR (Murphy et al., 2004; Schuler, 1997). e-PCR and BLAST in particular are valuable tools to search DNA sequences for the presence of genomic elements and to confirm and refine map localizations. NCBI Gene, OMIM, and UniGene are good starting points for genome catalog information about genes and gene-based markers. NCBI Gene (Pruitt et al., 2000) presents information on official nomenclature, aliases, DNA sequences, phenotypes, Enzyme Commission (EC) numbers, Mendelian Inheritance in Man (MIM) numbers, UniGene clusters, homology, map locations, and related Web sites. The dbSNP database stores population-specific information on variation in humans, primarily for single nucleotide repeats but also for other types of polymorphisms. In addition, the NCBI's Genomic Biology page provides genomic resource home pages for many other organisms, including mouse, rat, *Drosophila*, and zebrafish.

Integrated Mapping Resources

Map integration provides interconnectivity between mapping data generated from two or more different experimental techniques. However, achieving accurate and useful integration is a difficult task. All of the genomic resources discussed in this section provide some measure of integration, and they have created truly integrated maps by placing genomic elements mapped by differing techniques relative to a single map scale. These resources also provide both some level of genomic cataloging, where considerable effort is made to collect, organize, and map substantial available positional information for a given genome.

Most groups use a common integrator approach choosing map data derived from one technique, usually the technique that has the most accurate or greatest number of localizations, or both, and then aligning other maps to it. Increasingly, DNA sequence is used as the common integrator, because it provides the most precise localizations as well as allowing any sequence-based marker with additional mapping information potentially to be aligned. In some cases, there are only a limited number of markers shared between two maps, or some markers on one map do not have associated sequence (e.g., many RFLPs) or localization information used in the other map (e.g., nonpolymorphic markers aligned to a GL map). In these cases, approaches lose precision or their level of integration. GDB and LDB2000 rely on algorithms that transform map positions from single maps onto a standard map and then merge multiple localizations into a single position with some calculated variance in the positional range. This approach maximizes ordering but at the expense of some variability in order confidence for particular markers. eGenome instead determines sequence positions for all possible markers and calculates confidence intervals, based on the mapping technique used for a particular marker, for the non–sequence-aligned markers. This approach maximizes confidence of ordering at the expense of providing linear ordering of all markers. The MGI and the Rat Genome Database have aligned the GL and RH maps for the respective species in a comparative manner. Each of these approaches are valuable for equating GL, RH, and cytogenetic maps, especially in organisms for which sequence data is limited. However, positional estimates that have not actually been experimentally derived for particular markers serve better as initial localization guides and as supportive ordering information rather than as a primary ordering mechanism. For instance, a researcher who has localized a disease locus to a chromosome band or between two flanking markers can use these databases quickly to collect virtually all mapped elements in the defined region, and the inferred physical positions serve as an approximate order of the markers. This information then would be supplanted by more precise ordering information present in single-dimension maps, DNA sequence, from the

researcher's own experimental data, or a combination thereof.

The Genome Database

GDB, hosted by RTI International, is a public repository for human genomic data with particular concentration on cytogenetic localizations and individual maps generated by other groups (Pearson, 1991; Cuticchia, 2000). Its inclusion of most genomic maps provides a useful mechanism to collect information about a defined region. The database holds a vast quantity of data submitted by hundreds of investigators. Furthermore, the site exists as a moderated, open-source project, in that any investigator can edit their own submissions and provide annotated comments to others directly online. Therefore, like other large public databases, the data quality is variable, although significant curation is provided by internal and external scientists.

GDB comprises descriptions of three types of objects from humans: genomic segments (genes, clones, amplimers, breakpoints, cytogenetic markers, fragile sites, ESTs, syndromic regions, contigs, and repeats), maps (including cytogenetic, GL, RH, STS content, and integrated), and variations (primarily relating to polymorphisms).

A simple search is available on the home page of the GDB Web site. This query is used when searching for information on a specific genomic segment, such as a gene or STS (amplimer, in GDB terminology) and can be implemented by entering the segment name or GDB accession number. Depending on the type of segment queried and the available data, many different types of segment-specific information may be returned, such as alternate names (aliases), primer sequences, positions in various maps, related segments, polymorphism details, contributor contact information, citations, and relevant external links. An example of a marker record displayed in GDB as a result of a keyword search for marker D1S2 is shown in Figure 2.2.

At the bottom of the GDB home page is a link to "Other Search Options." From the Other Search Options page, there are links to three customized search forms (Markers and Genes within a Region, Maps within a Region, and Genes by Name or Symbol), sequence-based searches, specific search forms for subclasses of GDB elements, and precompiled lists of data (Genetic Diseases by Chromosome, Lists of Genes by Chromosome, and Lists of Genes by Symbol Name). The Maps within a Region search allows retrieval and display of all maps stored in GDB that span a defined chromosomal region. Among the extensive set of maps is GDB's own Comprehensive Map, which assigns a composite sequence-based position to all GDB elements. Maps are graphically displayed

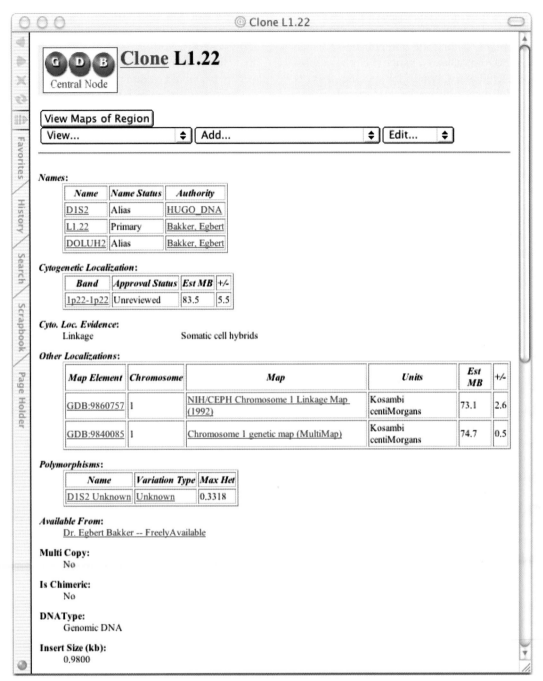

FIGURE 2.2 **The Genome Database.** Shown is a portion of the **GDB** record for L1.22, which is a clone representing **DNA** marker **D1S2.** At top are a number of buttons and pop-up windows allowing a user to view any maps at **GDB** containing this genomic element (**View Maps of Region**), to view an expanded database record or history of the record's editing process (**View...**), to add new genomic objects or annotations to the database (**Add...**), and to edit the record currently viewed (**Edit...**). Below this, each section represents a subset of available information known about L1.22, including element names and aliases, cytogenetic position(s) and evidence for localization, other genomic localizations, associated polymorphisms, contact information, and clone details. Underlined blue text indicates hyperlinks to related **GDB** records or external data resource records. To view this figure, from the **GDB** home page, type "L1.22" into the Simple Search box with "Genomic Elements" and "Name/GDB ID" selected.

in an interactive Java applet called Mapview. This utility allows users to zoom in and out of maps, highlight markers across maps, color code different tiers, display markers using different aliases, change the relative position of the displayed maps, search for specific markers, and retrieve additional information on a marker from any of the maps (by double clicking on marker names to perform a simple search). In addition, if multiple maps are loaded simultaneously, markers in common between maps will be displayed with connecting lines. This provides a unique feature to allow simultaneous representational comparison of marker positions.

GDB has not yet completely integrated its vast set of data with the human genomic sequence. However, the tool GDB e-PCR, available from the Other Search Options page, enables users to associate genomic sequence with GDB elements. GDB's e-PCR finds which of its many amplimers are contained within user-supplied DNA sequences and is thereby a quick means to determine or refine gene or marker localization. In addition, the GDB has many useful genome resource Web links on its *Resources* page.

eGenome

The eGenome project, hosted by The Children's Hospital of Philadelphia, provides a DNA sequence-based approach to integrate human mapping information (White et al., 1999). eGenome is structured both as a portal and a catalog. eGenome concentrates on genomic markers, genes, polymorphisms, and DNA clones. Genomic elements are assigned to DNA sequence positions whenever possible. In addition, subsets of markers that have GL, cytogenetic, RH mapping coordinates, or a combination thereof are used to build maps of each experimental type independently. eGenome attempts to maximize the set of data for each of these categories, making eGenome maps more inclusive than single-resource maps. eGenome maps use a high confidence ordering strategy and thus are conservative in their localizations for nonframeworked markers. Additionally, eGenome also integrates UniGene EST clusters, large-insert clones, SNPs, and DNA sequences associated with mapped elements, and it also infers cytogenetic positions for all markers. In this sense, eGenome can be used as a mapping catalog and then as a portal to related genomic and biological resources.

eGenome search interfaces allow querying by element name or GenBank accession ID or by defining a region with cytogenetic band or flanking marker coordinates. The marker displays include any DNA sequence, GL, cytogenetic, and RH positions, large-insert clones containing the marker, representative DNA sequences, and UniGene clusters. Figure 2.3 shows the results of

a search for the polymorphism D1S2845. The Chromoscape Java applet, a modification of GDB's Mapview, allows users to view and manipulate interactively a specified chromosome or genomic region, with displayed objects hyperlinked to their corresponding text records.

One useful eGenome feature is its convenient tabular layout for genomic elements, arranged in chromosomal order, comprising a user-specified region of interest. A section specifies the genomic markers and SNPs closest to an element being viewed currently. Users can specify the size of the window, as in "show me all SNPs mapped to within 10 kb of D1S2845." Other useful features include the ability to view regions graphically using a graphical browser, systematic management of marker names, an extensive collection of marker-specific hypertext links to related database sites, and direct access to large datasets through an associated FTP site.

LDB2000

LDB2000, hosted by the University of Southampton, provides extensive integration of human GL and cytogenetic positions relative to the DNA sequence (Ke et al., 2001). Somewhat similar to GDB's approach, this is performed by calculating or inferring GL, cytogenetic, and, for those elements without sequence correlates, DNA sequence positions to all genomic markers and polymorphisms in their database. The Web site has a query interface where a map region specified by sequence coordinates, flanking markers, or a sequence range around a marker can be selected based on sequence or coordinates. The query results show a text-based ordered map of markers in the region along with actual or estimated sequence, centimorgan, and cytogenetic band coordinates. Markers and their name aliases are hyperlinked in an object-specific manner to several external databases. Additional features include the ability to search for primer sequences within the genomic sequence, and to retrieve a genomic sequence for a specified region. Moreover, the authors have calculated linkage disequilibrium (LD) rates for their polymorphic data; this information can be viewed as a graph of LD plotted against a specifiable genomic region. A strength of LDB2000 is the rich and thorough approach used to integrate GL mapping information with other mapping data.

Gene Integration Resources

Gene integration resources concentrate more closely on known and putative gene sets, generally without providing surrounding genomic context. Therefore, they play an important complementary approach to integrated mapping resources, because they focus more on specific features of a genome than on ways to identify what features are in a genome. Almost all genomic resources

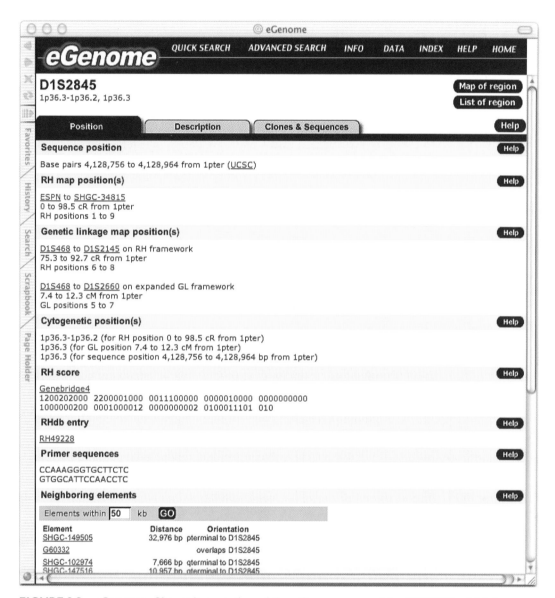

FIGURE 2.3 **eGenome. Shown is a portion of the eGenome record for D1S2845, which is a Généthon microsatellite marker. The "Map of region" and "List of region" buttons generate text and graphical views of the region surrounding the element. Below this, the "Description" and "Clones & Sequences" tabs lead to additional information about D1S2845. The main record is divided into sections representing subsets of available information known about D1S2845, including genomic DNA sequence, RH, GL, and cytogenetic positions; additional RH mapping information; associated primer sequences; and other elements in close sequence proximity to D1S2845. Underlined blue text indicates hyperlinks to related eGenome records or external data resource records. To view this figure from the eGenome home page, type "D1S2845" in the Quick Search box.**

of any type include some gene-specific information. Several gene-inclusive resources are mentioned elsewhere, including the genomic databases at NCBI, Ensembl, and UCSC (Chapter 4), OMIM and NCBI Gene (Chapter 3), and model organism databases (Chapters 3 and 15). Four gene-centric Web resources that provide convenient and

extensive summaries of various organismal gene sets are described below. The resources listed below are in no way inclusive of all such resources, because there are similar Web sites too numerous to mention here. Rather, a few well-known sites that together represent the different approaches taken and informational types

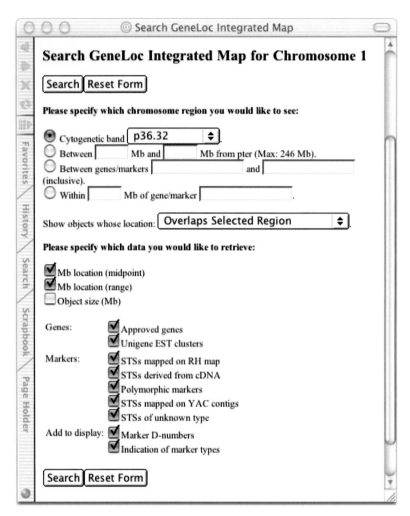

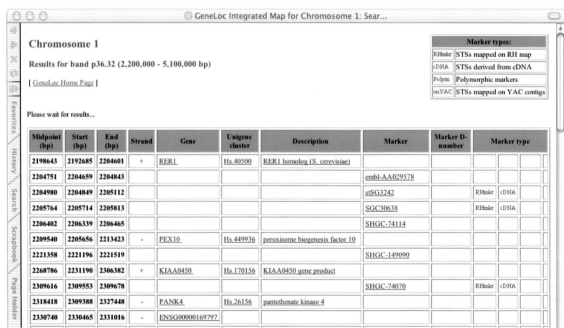

FIGURE 2.4

represented have been chosen. These are especially useful for researchers who have identified a particular gene or set of genes associated with a biological parameter and would like to learn as much about the gene(s) as possible in a rapid manner.

GeneCards and GeneLoc

The dual resources GeneCards and GeneLoc, hosted by the Weizmann Institute of Science, together provide gene and genomic mapping summaries of human genes (GeneCards) and also genomic markers (GeneLoc; Safran et al., 2003; Rosen et al., 2003). The GeneCards model is to create a simple "card" or concise visual representation of a virtual database record for a gene entry. The query entry into GeneCards is by keyword, gene name, or alias, whereas GeneLoc can be queried in this way or by chromosomal position (via sequence position, cytogenetic band, or flanking markers) or sequence ID. An added feature of GeneLoc is that the query result display is parameterized, so users can specify the database elements they wish to see (Figure 2.4 and Worked Example).

GeneCards records display a large number of gene attributes, many of which are hyperlinked to other databases. These include gene name aliases; cytogenetic and DNA sequence build position; DNA sequences; RNA expression data; proteins, protein domains, protein families, and Gene Ontology (GO) terms; gene orthologs and paralogs; gene SNPs and variants; associated disorders and gene mutations; related medical news; and research articles mentioning the gene of interest. GeneLoc records include (if known) certain DNA sequence, RH, GL, and physical map positions, name aliases, and associated DNA sequences. As such, the information displayed is quite broad in scope. GeneCards and GeneLoc operate

almost exclusively as data redistribution sites, relying on mapping and gene annotation data from other projects.

GeneLynx

Hosted by the Karolinska Institute, GeneLynx further extends the GeneCards model to provide a completely portalized view of genes for human, mouse, and rat (Lenhard et al., 2001). The philosophy behind the resource is to create a single summary page of hyperlinks to a large number of data sources for a particular gene. GeneLynx has two simple query interfaces: a simple term search and a DNA sequence-based search that can accommodate raw sequence, accession IDs, or uploaded sequence files. Gene records do not display any genomic or gene annotation data themselves, but instead display object-specific hyperlinked database IDs to a large number of external databases. Genomic links include mRNA and genomic sequences containing the gene, GDB records, comparative genomic sequence alignments, AceView (see below), and views in the UCSC and Ensembl map viewers. Annotation data is classified into the groups "summary page" (other resources displaying similar gene summaries), transcripts, EST and clone libraries, homologs, protein sequences, protein structure and domains, protein function and disease links, networks and pathways, and literature links. As with GeneCards, the depth and scope of linked information is extensive, making GeneLynx a good starting point for obtaining information about genes.

euGenes

euGenes is hosted by the University of Indiana Center for Genomics and Bioinformatics (Gilbert, 2002). This resource currently represents gene sets for nine species: human, mouse, rat, zebrafish, *Arabidopsis*, *Drosophila*,

---

FIGURE 2.4   GeneLoc. (a) GeneLoc Integrated Map search interface. Several ways in which to search the map are shown at the top of the interface, including selecting by cytogenetic band (1p36.32 is selected); by entering a genomic sequence range; by entering flanking genes, markers, or both; and by specifying a sequence window surrounding a given gene or marker. Elements either overlapping (selected) or exactly matching a region can be displayed. Below this, users can specify what types of information they wish to see displayed, including genomic location and several categories of genes, markers, and element names. (b) Results of a GeneLoc Integrated Map search. Shown is a portion of the Integrated Map for 1p36.32. Each element is displayed, in order of genomic position from pter to qter, as a row in a table. Table cells are populated if information corresponding to the element category are known. Categories include the midpoint, start, and end position in the genomic DNA sequence for the element; the DNA strand in which the element is encoded; the gene symbol; associated UniGene clusters; element description; marker name; marker D-number; and marker type. Underlined blue text indicates hyperlinks to related GeneCards records or external data resource records. To view Figure 2.4(a) from the GeneLoc home page, select "1" under "Search GeneLoc integrated map–specify chromosome" within the "Search GeneLoc" box. To view Figure2.4(b), from Figure 2.4(a) select "p36.32" for cytogenetic band, "Overlaps Selected Region" for "Show objects whose location," and click the Search button.

mosquito, *Caenorhabditis elegans*, and yeast. This makes euGenes a particularly powerful comparative gene resource. euGenes has a rich query interface, allowing term searches across multiple or restricted to individual species, or restricted to genomic, functional, or phenotypic subsets. Because GO terms have been incorporated into all entries, euGenes provides a GO vocabulary query selector to allow browsing based on biological function or process. Furthermore, query results can be iteratively field restricted and also can be downloaded via a variety of file formats. Another nice feature is that predicted genes can be excluded in text searches.

As with many resources, queries identifying multiple database records return summary tables displaying key features for each record. Genomic features included in individual records include a graphic of all known transcript structures relative to the genomic sequence (if determined) and any cytogenetic position. Also displayed are mapped GO terms, reference DNA and protein sequences, known orthologs within the other species included in euGenes, and often a text summary of the gene function.

AceView

AceView is an experimental project being conducted at the NCBI. Currently, this resource is focused on mapping transcripts to the human, *C. elegans*, and *Arabidopsis* genomes. AceView is integrated with other NCBI resources. AceView allows term searching within a species. It also provides protein structural and functional term searching, such as linked GO terms, through Pfam (Chapter 8), and DNA sequence-based searches through a BLAST implementation. The latter feature allows the possibility of retrieving all known transcript alignments in a graphical interface for a genomic region of interest.

As with the other described gene-based resources, AceView provides cataloging of genomic and functional elements, with an emphasis on structural attributes of gene products. The position of each gene in the finished genomic sequence is displayed, along with the cytogenetic position. Other attributes include genomic structures, gene and gene family text summaries, associated phenotypes from Online Mendelian Inheritance in Man (OMIM), GO annotations, expression levels deduced from EST libraries, and supporting literature records. The major unique contribution of AceView, however, is in its extensive categorization and display of transcripts and transcript variants for each gene. Tables listing each mRNA-supported transcript variant, which exons it includes or excludes, and the precise genomic position of each exon and alternative exon are included. This is also shown graphically, where all mRNAs, cDNAs, and ESTs are mapped relative to the genomic sequence (Figure 2.5); the graphical interface is particularly useful in that it can be zoomed in and out and scrolled up or down a chromosome to allow users to move to adjacent transcripts. This makes AceView a particularly good tool for researchers focusing on a specific gene or short genomic stretch, especially where numerous existing transcribed sequences, complex alternative splicing mechanisms, or both may be present.

Other Portals and Resources

Although consolidated, whole-genome mapping resources are convenient for initial collection and characterization of a region of interest, data generated for only a single chromosome or a subchromosomal region are often important for fine mapping. In many cases, these regional maps contain more detailed, better integrated, and higher resolution data than the whole-genome maps can provide. The data sets, databases, and maps available for each human chromosome are too numerous to detail here. Most published human chromosome maps are listed and can be viewed at GDB's Web site (see above). The major genome sequencing centers often include detailed mapping and sequence annotation for particular chromosomes at their sites. The Sanger Institute in particular has advanced collections of chromosome-specific genomic data, informatics tools, and resources for human chromosomes 1, 6, 9, 10, 13, 20, 22, and X. For many other species, especially those without finished or draft genomes, the efforts of individual laboratories focused on a genomic region, or providing a preliminary survey of a genome using a single experimental technique, are the only available data sets. Use of these resources requires more effort by the user, and supplementary experiments often are necessary.

COMPARATIVE MAPS

Comparative mapping is the process of identifying conserved chromosome segments across different species. Because of the relatively small number of chromosomal breaks that have occurred during mammalian radiation, the order of genes usually is preserved over large chromosomal segments between related species. Orthologous genes (copies of the same genes from different species) can be identified through DNA sequence homology, and sets of orthologous genes sharing an identical linear order within a chromosomal region in two or more species are used to identify conserved segments and ancestral chromosomal breakpoints.

Knowledge about which chromosomal segments are shared and how they have become rearranged over time greatly increases our understanding of the evolution of

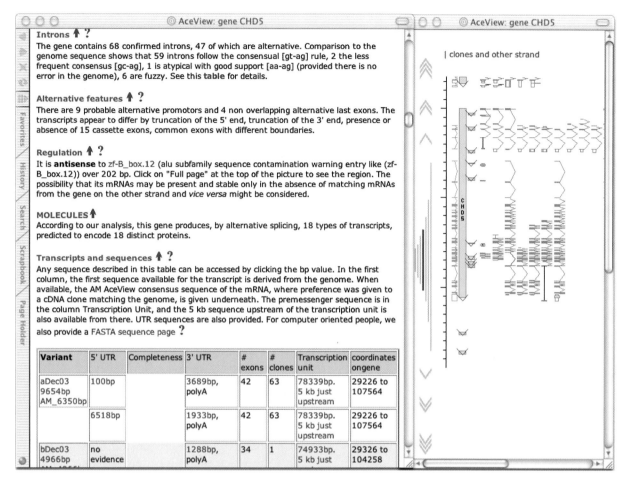

FIGURE 2.5   AceView. A portion of the record for gene CHD5 is displayed. At left are shown several sections with text-centric descriptions of various CHD5 features, including intron information, genomic features generated through alternative splicing, putative mRNA regulation, and alternative mRNA forms. At bottom left is shown a portion of a table displaying various features of predicted alternative transcript forms, including an assigned variant name, the 5′ and 3′ UTR lengths, number of exons, number of supporting cDNA and EST clones, and the position relative to the genomic sequence. At right is a depiction of the genomic region surrounding CHD5. In this inset, navigation bars are at the left (arrows move up and down, with the ability to move to adjacent genomic regions and genes; the vertical lines allow zooming in or out). Known and predicted genes are depicted in blue, and mRNAs, cDNAs, and EST clones are depicted in pink. Blue text and all graphical objects link to associated data at other NCBI resources. To view this figure from the AceView home page, type "CHD5" into the Search box with "AceView" selected as the Query and the latest available Human build also selected. Click the Go button, then select "CHD5" from the resulting list of matching records.

different plant and animal lineages. One of the most valuable applications of comparative maps is to use an established gene map of one species to predict positions of orthologous genes in another species. Many animal models exist for diseases observed in humans. In some cases, it is easier to identify the responsible genes in an animal model than in humans, and the availability of a good comparative map can simplify the process of identifying the responsible genes in humans. In other cases, more may be known about the gene(s) responsible in

humans, and the same comparative map could be used to help identify the gene(s) responsible in the model species. There are several successful examples of comparative candidate gene mapping (O'Brien et al., 1999).

As mapping and sequencing efforts progress in many species, it is becoming possible to identify smaller homologous chromosome segments, and detailed comparative maps are being developed between many different species. Fairly dense gene-based comparative maps now exist between the human, mouse, and rat genomes and also between several agriculturally important mammalian species. Sequence-based and protein-based comparative maps also are under development for several lower organisms for which complete sequence is available (Chapter 5). A comparative map typically is presented either graphically or in tabular format, with one species designated as the index species and one or more others as comparison species. Homologous regions are presented graphically with nonconsecutive segments from the comparison species shown aligned with their corresponding segments along the map of the index species.

Comparative Mapping Resources

Comparative maps provide extremely valuable tools for studying the evolution and relatedness of genes between species and finding disease genes through position-based orthology. There are several multispecies comparative mapping resources available that include various combinations of most animal species for which linkage maps are available. In addition, there are also many sequence-based comparative analysis resources discussed more fully in Chapter 15. Each resource has different coverage and features. Presently, it is necessary to search multiple resources, because no single site contains all of the currently available homology information. Only the most notable resources will be described here.

Mouse Genome Informatics Database

The MGI database is the primary public mouse genomic catalog resource (Bult et al., 2004). Located at The Jackson Laboratory, the MGI encompasses the component Mouse Genome Database (MGD), along with data resources for gene expression, genomic sequence, and tumor biology. The integration between different MGI resources allows cross-resource searches, including vocabulary browsers for GO, anatomical, and phenotypic standardized terms. In all, MGI is arguably the most comprehensive single-organism biological resource.

The MGD component of MGI itself has evolved from a mapping and genetics resource to include sequence and genome information and details on the functions and roles of genes and alleles (Bult et al., 2004). MGD includes information on mouse polymorphisms and genetic markers; QTLs; genes; molecular segments (probes, primers, and clones); phenotypes; comparative genomic alignments; graphical displays of linkage, cytogenetic, and physical maps; experimental mapping data; and strain distribution patterns for recombinant inbred strains (RIs) and cross haplotypes. As of March 2004, there were more than 55,000 genetic markers alone in MGD, with 92% of these placed onto the mouse genetic map.

General MGI searches can be performed via a field-restrictable term query interface, the vocabulary browsers, or a BLAST utility that allows a user to enter a DNA sequence to find database matches. MGI also provides advanced genomic-based query pages for genes and markers; alleles and phenotypes; strains and polymorphisms; linkage, cytogenetic, and physical maps; probes and clones; and comparative maps. Each of these query pages provide extensive parameterization. Results pages contain summary information such as element type, official symbol, name, chromosome, map positions, MGI accession ID, references, and history (Figure 2.6 and Worked Example). Additional element-specific information also may be displayed, including links to outside resources. A thumbnail linkage map of the region is shown to the right, which can be clicked on for an expanded view.

MGI contains many different types of maps and mapping data, including linkage data from 24 different inbred and four congenic strains. Cytogenetic band positions are available for some markers. MGI also computes a linkage map that integrates markers mapped on the various panels. A very useful feature is the ability to build customized maps of specific regions using subsets of available data, incorporating private data, and showing homology information where available. For example, this feature can be used to make comparative genomic maps that simplify the task of studying conserved chromosome segments. Comparative data are included for mouse, human, rat, and 15 additional species. Comparative information can be obtained in one of four manners: searching for orthologous genes, building a comparative linkage map, viewing an Oxford Grid, or using their whole-genome mouse–human or mouse–rat orthology map views. The simple search returns detailed information about orthologous genes in other species, including map positions and codes for how the orthology was identified, links to the relevant references, and links for viewing comparative maps of the surrounding regions in any two species. For example, a search for orthologs of the *Pmp22* gene returns a table listing orthologous genes in cattle, dog, human, mouse, and rat. A comparative map also can be obtained by using the linkage map-building tool to specify a region of the mouse as the index map and to select a second, comparison, species. The resulting display is similar to that shown in Figure 2.7 (refer also to the Worked Example). An Oxford Grid can also be used to view a genome-wide matrix in which the number of gene homologies between each pair of chromosomes between two species is shown along with links to local graphical comparative views. The Oxford Grid view is currently available for seven species. The mouse–human and mouse–rat orthology maps provide a genome-wide graphical view of human or rat homologies

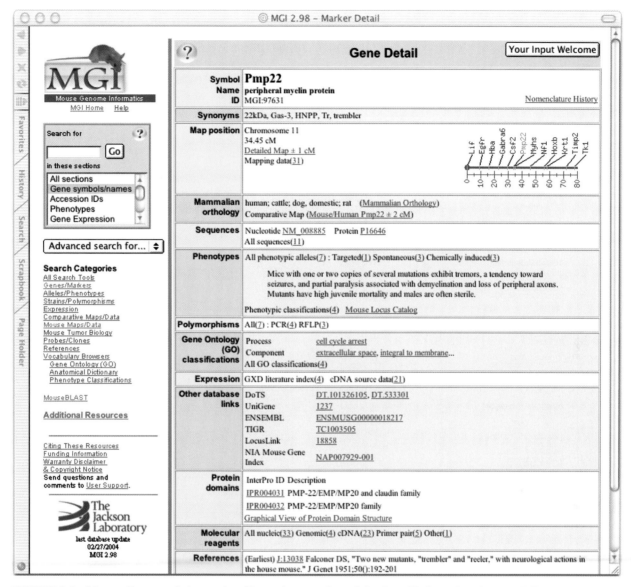

FIGURE 2.6 Mouse Genome Informatics. Shown is a portion of the Pmp22 Gene Detail record. The main record is divided into sections representing subsets of available information known about Pmp22, including gene names and synonyms; map position, with a graphical depiction of the surrounding GL map; known orthologs; associated DNA sequences; associated phenotypes; polymorphisms; GO terms; links to gene expression data; and protein domains. Underlined blue text indicates hyperlinks to related MGI records or external data resource records. To view this figure from the MGI home page, type "Pmp22" into the Search box at right, click the Search button, and then select "Pmp22" from the resulting list of matching records.

on the mouse map with links to detailed tables of gene homology.

Rat Genome Database

The Rat Genome Database, hosted by the Medical College of Wisconsin, has emerged as the rat counterpart to MGI (Twigger et al., 2002). RGD's holdings include genomic maps, markers and polymorphisms, DNA sequences, genes, ESTs, quantitative trait loci (QTLs), strains, and ontologies. RGD's Web site is organized in a manner similar to how researchers interested in identifying disease-associated loci would approach a task: starting with a phenotypic model in a rat strain, proceeding through QTL refinement, genomic localization, gene identification, gene characterization, and genomic comparison with human and other relevant species.

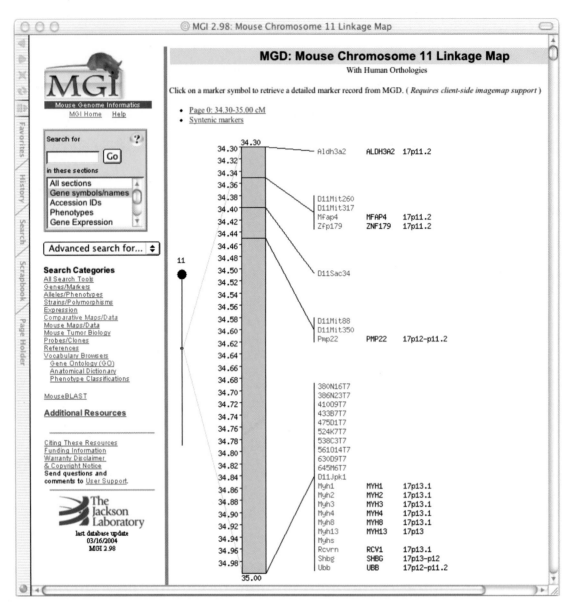

FIGURE 2.7 **Mouse Genome Database at MGI. Shown is the MGD mouse–human comparative map of the region surrounding the Pmp22 gene. At far left is shown where the map lies in relation to the entire chromosome. In the center is displayed the mouse GL map for this region. At right are shown known human orthologs and their cytogenetic positions for particular mouse genes within the GL map. As shown by the human genes displayed on the right, a segment of human chromosome 17 is homologous to this mouse region. Blue text indicates hyperlinks to related MGI records. To view this figure from the MGI home page, click on "Mammalian Orthology and Comparative Maps," then on "Searches: Comparative Maps." In the query form, select Chromosome 11 and input "34.3" and "35" as flanking cM positions under "Restrict map to a chromosomal region."**

RGD provides several query and browser interface components. A simple term query is available at the top of each page, whereas parameter-rich query interfaces are available for several subsets of data (e.g., genes, QTLs, markers). A recently released gene annotation tool acts as an advanced search page for various annotation terms associated with genes, where users can select subsets of RGD, Swiss-Prot, NCBI Gene, the Kyoto Encyclopedia of Genes and Genomes (KEGG), and other databases to include in their query returns. Other integrated tools allow users to BLAST or BLAT sequences against the database. The Genome Scanner utility is designed to allow users to select suitable polymorphic markers for a strain cross, which it calculates using allele characterization data generated for 8000 markers each in 48 strains. The GBrowse implementation allows genes and their genomic structures to be viewed relative to DNA sequence position.

RGD provides one RH and two cross-strain GL maps, each of which can be queried or browsed directly by chromosomal position. Clicking on a particular map and then selecting a chromosome yields a map graphic showing specific markers and map regions, both of which are hyperlinked to text descriptions of the represented objects. Individual marker records include information about the marker's physical properties (e.g., amplimer size, primer sequences, sequence context) as well as mapping data and any strain-specific variations. Gene reports follow the GeneCards model, where a single page describes various structural and functional gene annotations, with hyperlinks to several external databases provided.

Finally, VCMap is a Java applet based on GDB's Mapview that allows users to view comparative maps between rat, human, and mouse graphically, and in an interactive fashion. Currently, sequence, GL, cytogenetic, RH, and QTL-based comparative maps can be displayed, either within or between species. Whole chromosome or regional maps can be created, and the clickable maps can be manipulated directly by the user.

Additional Comparative Mapping Resources

Another resource for homology information is NCBI's HomoloGene database (Chapters 3 and 15). HomoloGene is a resource of curated and computed (*in silico*) cross-species gene homologies for a number of plant and animal species (Wheeler et al., 2004). The availability of both curated and computed homology makes this a unique resource.

The ARKdb database stores and presents curated genome mapping data for cat, chicken, cow, deer, horse, pig, salmon, sheep, tilapia, and turkey. These data include details of loci and markers, references and papers, authors, genetic linkage map assignments, cytogenetic map assignments, experimental techniques, as well as PCR primers and conditions.

Comparative maps will be created for most organisms with genome projects. However, we have found that the Internet resources for most other projects are often still in early development or may focus only on a single or small subset of genomic elements. In addition to the ARKdb resource, the NCBI Genomic Biology section has home pages for several organisms, including dog, cow, pig, and chicken, and these serve as good start-ing point for finding map and comparative resources. The U.S. Meat Animal Research Center has genome maps for cow, pig and sheep. In 2003, the journal *Cytogenetic and Genome Research* published a single-topic volume devoted to animal genetics that included a number of articles presenting cross-species comparative maps (Chowdhary, 2003). Finally, *in silico* mapping is proving to be a very valuable tool for comparative mapping. The Comparative Mapping by Annotation and Sequence Similarity (COMPASS) approach has been used by researchers studying the cattle genome to construct several cattle–human comparative maps. Recently, a COMPASS database tool has been developed and used to construct comparative maps among human, cattle, pig, mouse, and rat (Liu et al., 2004).

▌PRACTICAL USES OF MAPPING RESOURCES

Potential applications of genomic data are numerous and, to a certain extent, depend on the creativity and imagination of the researcher. However, most researchers use genomic information in one of three ways: to find out what genomic elements—usually transcribed elements—are contained within a genomic region, to determine the order of defined elements within a region, or to determine the chromosomal position of a particular element. Each of these goals can be accomplished by various means, and the probability of efficient success often is enhanced by familiarity with many of the resources discussed in this chapter. It is prudent to follow a logical course when using genomic data, especially when there is not an underlying completed genomic sequence available. During the initial data acquisition step, in which genomic data either are generated experimentally or are retrieved from publicly available data sources, simultaneous evaluation of multiple data sets will ensure both higher resolution and greater confidence, subsequently increasing the likelihood that the genomic elements of interest are represented. Second, the interrelationships and limitations of the data sets must be understood sufficiently, because it is easy to overinterpret or underrepresent the data. Finally, it is important to verify critical assignments independently, especially when using mapping data that are not ordered with high confidence. Below are some brief suggestions on how to approach specific map-related tasks, but many modifications or alternative approaches also are viable. The section is organized in a manner similar to a disease locus search, starting with definition of the region's boundaries, determining the content and order of elements in the region, and defining a precise map position of the targeted element.

Defining a Genomic Region

A genomic region of interest is best defined by two flanking markers that have direct DNA sequence coordinates if possible, and which are used commonly for mapping purposes, such as polymorphic Généthon markers in humans or MIT microsatellites in mice. Starting with a cytogenetically defined region is more difficult because of the subjective nature of defining chromosomal band boundaries. For humans, conversion of cytogenetic boundaries to representative markers can be approximated by viewing the inferred cytogenetic positions of markers in comprehensive maps such as at UCSC or LDB2000. Because these cytogenetic positions are inferred and approximate, a conservative approach is recommended when using cytogenetic positions for region definition. The choice of flanking markers will impact how precisely a region's size and exact boundary locations can be defined. Commonly used markers often are present on multiple, independently derived maps, so their "position" on the chromosome provides greater confidence for anchoring a regional endpoint. In contrast, the exact location of less commonly used markers often is locally ambiguous. These markers sometimes can be tethered physically to other markers if a large sequence tract that contains multiple markers can be found. This can be performed by BLASTing marker sequences against GenBank or via e-PCR, online at NCBI and available for downloading at eGenome (Murphy et al., 2004; Schuler, 1997).

Determining, Ordering, and Characterizing the Contents of a Defined Region

Once a region has been defined, there are a number of resources available for determining what lies within the region. A good way to start is to identify a map that contains both flanking markers, either from a genome-wide map from the sources listed above, from a genomic catalog, or from a local map that has been generated by a laboratory interested in this particular region. For humans, any of the various genome browsers, including NCBI's Map Viewer, UCSC's Genome Browser, Ensembl, or eGenome are adequate for this task, whereas MGI and RGD provide such functions in mouse and rat, respectively. For less characterized genomes, localized maps are usually physically based and often more accurate than their computationally derived, whole-genome counterparts. For these species, the number of maps to choose from is usually limited, so it is useful first to define flanking markers known to be contained in the available maps.

The map or maps containing the flanking markers can then be used to create a consensus integrated map of the region. This is often an inexact and tedious process. To begin, it is useful to identify from the available maps a common integrator, or index, map that contains many markers, high map resolution, and good reliability. Integration of markers from additional maps relative to the index map proceeds by comparing the positions of markers placed on each map. For example, if an index map contains markers in the order A-B-C-D and a second map has markers in the order B-E-D, then marker E can be localized to the interval between markers B and D on the index map. Importantly, however, the relative position of marker E with respect to marker C usually cannot be accurately determined by this method. Repeated iterations of this process should allow localization of all markers from multiple maps relative to the index map. This process, of course, is significantly reinforced by experimental verification, such as with STS content mapping of large-insert clones identified for the region-specific markers or, ideally, by sequence-determined order.

Each marker represents some type of genomic element: a gene, an EST, a polymorphism, a large-insert clone end, or a random stretch of genomic DNA. In humans, identifying what a marker represents is relatively straightforward. Simply search for the marker name in GDB or eGenome, and, in most cases, the resulting Web display will provide a summary of what the marker represents, usually along with hyperlinks to relevant functional information. For mice and rat, MGI and RGD provide similar functions. For other organisms, the best source usually is either UniSTS or, if present, Web sites or publications associated with the underlying maps. GenBank and UniSTS are alternatives for finding markers. If a marker is known to be expressed, the NCBI resources UniGene and Gene are excellent sources of additional information.

Many genes and some polymorphisms have been discovered independently and have been developed as markers multiple times, so creating a nonredundant set from a collection of markers is often challenging. GDB, GeneLoc, eGenome, MGI, and (for genes) UniGene (or any of the gene-based resources detailed above) are good sources to use for finding whether two markers are considered equivalent. Even more reliable is a DNA sequence or sequence contig containing both markers' primers. BLAST and the related BLAST2 are efficient for quickly determining sequence relatedness (Chapter 11).

Obviously, the most reliable tool for marker ordering is a DNA sequence or sequence contig. For many markers, searching with the marker name in NCBI Gene or UniSTS returns a page stating where (or if) the marker has been mapped in maps, a list of mRNA, genomic, and EST sequences, and often a link to a Map Viewer-based graphical depiction of the maps, sequence-ready contigs, and available sequence of the region.

Similarly for humans, GDB, GeneLoc, and eGenome show which DNA sequences contain each displayed marker. For other markers, the sequence from which the marker is derived, or alternatively one of the primer sequences, may be used to perform a BLAST search that can identify completely or nearly homologous sequences. For gene-based markers, this can be performed for various species at GeneLynx, euGenes, and AceView. The nonredundant, EST, GSS, and HTGS divisions of GenBank (Box 1.1) all are potentially relevant sources of matching sequence, depending on the aim of the project. Only long sequences are likely to have useful marker-ordering capabilities. Finished genomic sequence tracts have at least some degree of annotation, and scanning the GenBank record for the sequence stretch of interest often will yield annotations of what markers lie within the sequence and where they are. Keep in mind that such annotations vary considerably in their thoroughness and most are fixed in time; that is, they only recognize markers that were known at the time of the annotation. BLAST, BLAST2, and other sequence-alignment programs are helpful in identification or confirmation of what may lie in a large sequence. Also, the NCBI e-PCR Web interface can be used to identify all markers in UniSTS contained within a given sequence, and this program can be installed locally to query customized marker sets with DNA sequences (Murphy et al., 2004; Schuler, 1997).

For genomes in which DNA sequencing is complete or is substantially underway, it may be possible to construct local clone or sequence contigs. Although individual clone sequences can be found in GenBank, larger sequence contigs—sequence tracts comprising more than one BAC or PAC—are more accessible using the Entrez Genome, Ensembl, or UCSC Web sites. For example, by entering a marker or DNA accession number into the Entrez Genome text search box, researchers can identify sequence contigs containing that marker or element. Identified contigs link directly to Map Viewer to provide a graphical view of all other markers contained in that sequence, the base pair position of the markers in the sequence, and display of clone orders within the contig. This process also can be performed using BLAST or e-PCR, although it is somewhat more laborious.

As soon as a sequence has been identified for markers in a given region, DNA fingerprinting and clone contig assemblies and STC data can be used to bridge gaps. For several species, the UCSC Genome Browser identifies STCs from DNA sequence or BAC clones. To use this information, researchers with a sequence tract can go to the UCSC site, enter a sequence accession ID, and view STCs contained in the sequence. Any listed STC represents the end of a BAC clone whose insert contains a

portion of the input sequence (Venter et al., 1996). An STC search tool for human, rat, and mouse BACs at The Institute for Genomic Research (TIGR) is complementary to the UCSC search, because the TIGR site requires input of a large-insert clone name, which yields STC sequences. STCs represent large-insert clones that potentially extend a contig or link two adjacent, nonoverlapping contigs. Similarly, the large numbers of BAC clones that have been fingerprinted for rapid identification of overlapping clones in many species (Marra et al., 1997) are available for searching at WUGSC and BCGSC. Combined use of Entrez, BLAST, the STC resources, and the BAC fingerprinting data can often provide quick and reliable contig assembly by *in silico* sequence and clone walking.

As soon as a region has been defined, the next step is to determine what genomic elements of interest are in the region. Completely and partially sequenced genomes have considerable available online resources for this task. Especially with the dramatic recent advances in gene prediction software, these resources are increasingly inclusive and accurate. Any of the gene integration resources mentioned in this chapter, along with UCSC, NCBI, and Ensembl resources, can assist with this process. In general, characterized genes and those with multiple solid lines of evidence for expression, prediction, and multispecies conservation can be investigated as known commodities. For genomes that have not been sequenced thoroughly, some of the markers mapped to within a defined region may represent transcripts and could be investigated further. In these cases, some experimental studies, such as contig building, STS content mapping, DNA sequencing, and validation of transcripts identified by the use of gene prediction algorithms (Chapter 5) are usually necessary.

Defining a Map Position from a Clone or DNA Sequence

Expressing the chromosomal position of a gene or genomic element in GL (physical) or RH (cytogenetic) terms is not always straightforward. The first approach is to determine whether the element of interest has already been localized. The great majority of transcripts for human, rat, mouse, and other higher eukaryotes with ongoing genome projects are mapped precisely, and many genes have been well localized in other organisms as well. For species with advanced DNA sequencing projects, it is helpful to identify a large DNA sequence tract containing the genomic element of interest and then to determine what markers it contains by looking at the sequence annotation record in GenBank or by e-PCR. Any identified genes will have localizations of various types listed in the integrated mapping and gene integration resources detailed above. Here again, nomenclature difficulties impede such searches, making it necessary to search databases with one or more alternate names in some cases. Another alternative is to determine if the genomic element is contained in a genomic sequence by a simple BLAST search. Many large genomic sequences have been localized cytogenetically, and this information is contained in the sequence annotation record (usually in the title).

If gene-specific or closely linked markers have been used previously for mapping, a position usually can be described in terms specific to the mapping method that was used. For example, if an unknown gene is found to map very close to a Généthon marker, then the gene position can be reported relative to the Généthon GL centimorgan coordinates. Many human markers and many maps have been placed in GDB, so this is a good first step in determining whether a marker has been mapped. Simply search for the relevant marker and see where it has been placed on one or several maps listed under "cytogenetic localizations" and "other localizations." Inferred cytogenetic positions of human genes and markers usually are listed in GDB, UCSC, and eGenome if the elements have been mapped previously. If not, band or band range assignments usually can be approximated by finding the cytogenetic positions of flanking or closely linked markers and genes. Many sequenced large-insert clones have been assigned by FISH to a cytogenetic position; this information usually can be found in the sequence annotation or at the clone originator's Web site. The process of determining whether a transcript or genomic element from another organism has been mapped varies somewhat because of the lack of extensive genomic catalogs, making it usually necessary to cross-reference a marker with the GL or RH maps, or both, available for the species.

If no previous localization exists for a genomic element, some experimental work must be undertaken. For markers where DNA sequence exists or can be quickly generated, simply aligning the sequence with available genomic sequence tracts is an effective strategy for sequence-characterized genomes, as the sequence contigs usually have some chromosome localization assignments. For other species with limited sequence data but where an available RH panel exists, an efficient and precise way to map a sequence-based element is to develop and map an STS derived from the element by RH analysis. A set of primers should be designed that uniquely amplify a product in the species of interest, but not in the RH panel background genome. Suitable primers then can be used to type an appropriate RH panel. For other species, isolation and FISH of a large-insert clone or GL mapping with an identified or known flanking polymorphism may be necessary.

SUMMARY

Genomic mapping is a process that provides different results depending on the research objective. To genomic scientists investigating a new genome, mapping provides a structured way to characterize, organize, and manage genomes for more efficient use by biologists. Used in this way, mapping is largely a technical process, where a set of defined landmarks (or some component thereof) is ordered in respect to a genome. The techniques can provide either an absolute (for physical mapping strategies) or approximate (e.g., cytogenetic, GL) ordering of these landmarks. As such, attention to technical and procedural process, as well as a global understanding of the theory behind the mapping process used, becomes most important. Map users who are interested in looking at large regions of chromosomes or genomes should be well versed in these details, including knowing the strengths and limitations of each approach, the effective resolutions and how well different maps compare with each other.

To molecular biologists interested in specific genome-related research questions, mapping provides a way to annotate more completely a genomic region of interest and to find elements of particular relevance. Usually, the focus is on a specific small region of a genome. Here, integration of various existing mapping data sets and genomic annotations becomes paramount. The available data sets and resources are central to this task. Key issues here include determining what different resources and data sets are available, how to maximize the usefulness of each resource and dataset, how data objects can be associated, and how a comprehensive summation of all available knowledge within a particular region can be compiled.

As researchers continue to gather structural and functional knowledge of genomes, additional classes of biological objects will be able to be associated with particular genomic locations. This will include known genomic features that continue to be defined more precisely, such as gene regulatory elements, sites of epigenetic modification, and chromatin regulation motifs. In addition, classes representing biological functionality also will begin to be mapped, including organismal phenotypes, disease susceptibilities, literature reports, and clinically measurable features. In this sense, genomic mapping is still in its infancy as a discipline.

WORKED EXAMPLE

A. What genes map within cytogenetic band p36.32 of chromosome 1?

One way to answer this question is to use the GeneLoc gene integration resource. From the GeneLoc home page, select "1" under "Search GeneLoc integrated map" and specify "chromosome" within the "Search GeneLoc" box. The resulting screen is shown in Figure 2.4(a). From this screen, select "p36.32" for the cytogenetic band, select "Overlaps Selected Region" for the "Show objects whose location" pull-down menu, and deselect all map elements except for "Approved Genes" and click the Search button. The resulting screen is similar to that shown in Figure 2.4(b). As of March 2004, genes that are mapped to 1p36.32 include: *RER1*, *PEX10*, *KIAA0450*, *PANK4*, *TNFRSF14*, *MGC26818*, *MMEL2*, *ARPM2*, *DKFZp761G0122*, *LOC148872*, *PRDM16*, *ARHGEF16*, *EGFL3*, *LOC127262*, *WDR8*, *TP73*, *FLJ32825*, *KIAA1185*, *KIAA0562*, *DFFB*, *LOC339448*, *SHREW1*, and *LOC126772* (excluding those without a UniGene cluster, and noting that several of these have provisional gene names).

B. How can you learn about the mouse Pmp22 gene, including its map position, orthologous genes in other species, and associated phenotypes?

From the MGI home page, type "Pmp22" into the Search box at right, click the Search button, and then select "Pmp22" from the resulting list of matching records. The resulting screen is shown in Figure 2.6. Here you can easily see that mouse Pmp22 maps to position 34.45 cM on the linkage map of mouse chromosome 11 and that there are homologous genes in human, cattle, dog, and rat. A description of the associated mouse phenotype also is provided. There is additional information available on phenotypic alleles, the corresponding Gene Ontology categories, and expression data. A stylized map showing the position of the mouse Pmp22 gene is shown in the Map Position block, and a detailed map can be obtained by clicking on the Detailed Map link. A map comparing the region containing the Pmp22 gene in mouse with the corresponding human gene map can be obtained by clicking on the link next to Comparative Map, in the Mammalian Orthology block. This produces a map similar to that shown in Figure 2.7 (the image shown in Figure 2.7 is a slightly longer map and was obtained after the path described in the Figure 2.7 legend). Extensive conserved synteny can be observed between mouse chromosome 11 and human chromosome 17. To learn more about the homologous human PMP22 gene, follow the Mammalian Orthology link to the human Gene entry at NCBI.

PROBLEM SET

You have performed a human genome-wide search for the gene for the inherited disorder *Bioinformatosis*. Your initial analyses have identified one region with significant results, flanked by the polymorphic markers D21S260 and D21S262. There are many genes mapping within this region, one of which is particularly interesting, superoxide dismutase 1 (*SOD1*).

1. What is the cytogenetic location of this gene (and hence, at least part of the region of interest)?
2. How large is the region between D21S260 and D21S262 in cM units (i.e., on a genetic linkage map)?
3. How large is the region between D21S260 and D21S262 in physical (base pair) units?
4. What other genes are in this region?
5. What is a previously known disease phenotype associated with *SOD1*?
6. Have any SNP markers been identified within *SOD1* (YES or NO)? If yes, list the dbSNP rs (reference sequence) IDs of 3 SNP markers for *SOD1*.
7. What other species have been identified as having a gene that is orthologous to human *SOD1*?
8. What are the genetic linkage and DNA sequence coordinates for the mouse ortholog of *SOD1*?

INTERNET RESOURCES

Cytogenetic

Cancer Chromosome Aberration Project	http://cgap.nci.nih.gov/Chromosomes/Mitelman/
Coriell Cell Repositories somatic hybrids	http://locus.umdnj.edu/nigms/ideograms/ideograms.html
Developmental Genome Anatomy Project Infobiogen	http://www.bwhpathology.org/dgap/ http://www.infobiogen.fr/services/chromcancer/
NCBI: BAC Resource Consortium	http://www.ncbi.nlm.nih.gov/genome/cyto/hbrc.shtml
Southeastern Regional Genetics Group	http://www.ir.miami.edu/genetics/sergg/chromosome.html

Genetic Linkage

Affymetrix	http://www.affymetrix.com/products/arrays/specific/10k.affx
Applied Biosystems	http://www.appliedbiosystems.com
CEPH Genotype Database	http://www.cephb.fr/cephdb/
Center for Inherited Disease Research	http://www.cidr.jhmi.edu/markerset.html
Cooperative Human Linkage Center	http://gai.nci.nih.gov/CHLC/
deCODE Genetics: Genetic maps	http://www.nature.com/ng/journal/v31/n3/suppinfo/ng917_S1.html
deCODE Genetics: Genotyping sets	http://www.decode.com
Généthon Linkage Maps	http://www.bli.unizh.ch/BLI/Projects/genetics/maps/gthon.html
Genetic Analysis Software	http://linkage.rockefeller.edu/soft/
Illumina	http://www.illumina.com/snp_linkage.htm
MAP-O-MAT	http://compgen.rutgers.edu/mapomat/
Marshfield genetic maps	http://research.marshfieldclinic.org/genetics/Map_Markers/maps/IndexMapFrames.html
Psy. U. Hosp. Zurich GL map integration	http://www.bli.unizh.ch/BLI/Projects/genetics/K225.html
Rutgers U. linkage-physical maps	http://compgen.rutgers.edu/maps/
The SNP Consortium GL maps	http://snp.cshl.org/linkage_maps/

Physical

BC Genome Sequencing Centre	http://www.bcgsc.ca/lab/mapping/
TIGR STC database	http://www.tigr.org/tdb/humgen/bac_end_search/bac_end_intro.shtml
NCBI: UniSTS	http://www.ncbi.nlm.nih.gov/entrez/query.fcgi?db=unists
Sanger Institute: Image/FPC tools	http://www.sanger.ac.uk/HGP/mapping.shtml
Washington U. Genome Sequencing Center	http://genome.wustl.edu

Integrated

eGenome	http://genome.chop.edu
project Ensembl	http://www.ensembl.org
Genome Database	http://www.gdb.org
LDB2000	http://cedar.genetics.soton.ac.uk/public_html/LDBmain.html
NCBI: Entrez Genomes	http://www.ncbi.nlm.nih.gov/entrez/query.fcgi?db=Genome
NCBI: Map Viewer	http://www.ncbi.nlm.nih.gov/mapview/
ORNL Genome Channel	http://compbio.ornl.gov/channel/
Sanger Institute: Human Chromosome Data	http://www.sanger.ac.uk/HGP/
UCSC Genome Browser	http://genome.ucsc.edu/cgi-bin/hgGateway/

Gene Integration and Nomenclature

euGenes	http://iubio.bio.indiana.edu:8089
GeneCards	http://bioinformatics.weizmann.ac.il/cards/
GeneLoc	http://genecards.weizmann.ac.il/geneloc/
Genelynx Genome Portals	http://www.genelynx.org
NCBI: AceView	http://www.ncbi.nih.gov/IEB/Research/Acembly/
NCBI: Gene	http://www.ncbi.nlm.nih.gov:80/entrez/query.fcgi?db=gene
NCBI: Online Mendelian Inheritance in Man	http://www.ncbi.nlm.nih.gov/entrez/query.fcgi?db=OMIM
Human Genome Nomenclature Committee	http://www.gene.ucl.ac.uk/nomenclature/
Mouse Nomenclature Home Page	http://www.informatics.jax.org/mgihome/nomen/
NCBI: UniGene	http://www.ncbi.nlm.nih.gov/entrez/query.fcgi?db=unigene

Comparative

ARKdb	http://www.thearkdb.org
COMPASS comparative mapping resources	http://titan.biotec.uiuc.edu/COMPASS/index.html
Mouse Genome Informatics (MGD/MGI)	http://www.informatics.jax.org
NCBI: Genomic Biology	http://www.ncbi.nlm.nih.gov/Genomes/index.html
NCBI: HomoloGene	http://www.ncbi.nlm.nih.gov/HomoloGene/

Rat Genome Database	http://rgd.mcw.edu
U.S. Meat Animal Research Center	http://www.marc.usda.gov/genome/genome.html

Mapping Tools

Electronic PCR application	http://genome.chop.edu/mePCR/
Electronic PCR Web interface	http://www.ncbi.nih.gov/genome/sts/epcr.cgi/
NCBI: GenBank	http://www.ncbi.nih.gov/Genbank/
NCBI: Online BLAST	http://www.ncbi.nlm.nih.gov/BLAST/

▌ FURTHER READING

DUNHAM, I. (2003). *Genome Mapping and Sequencing.* (Horizon Scientific Press, Norfolk). Covers many aspects of genomic mapping in great detail, including cytogenetic, physical, and radiation hybrid map construction.

RANGEL, P., AND GIOVANNETTI, J. (2002). *Genomes and Databases on the Internet: A Practical Guide to Functions and Applications.* (Horizon Scientific Press, Norfolk). Describes a large number of genomic databases useful for genomic mapping and gene discovery.

STRACHAN, T., AND READ, A. P. (2003). Genetic mapping of Mendelian characters. In: *Human Molecular Genetics* (Strachan, T., and Read, A. P., eds.). (Garland Science Publishing, New York), p. 397–414. Provides an in-depth discussion of genetic linkage analysis, especially as it pertains to identifying disease genes.

▌ REFERENCES

ADAMS, M. D., DUBNICK, M., KERLAVAGE, A. R., MORENO, R., KELLEY, J. M., UTTERBACK, T. R., NAGLE, J. W., FIELDS, C., AND VENTER, J. C. (1992). Sequence identification of 2,375 human brain genes. *Nature* 355, 632–634.

BROMAN, K. W., MURRAY, J. C., SHEFFIELD, V. C., WHITE, R. L., AND WEBER, J. L. (1998). Comprehensive human genetic maps: individual and sex-specific variation in recombination. *Am. J. Hum. Genet.* 63, 861–869.

BULT, C. J., BLAKE, J. A., RICHARDSON, J. E., KADIN, J. A., EPPIG, J. T., BALDARELLI, R. M., BARSANTI, K., BAYA, M., BEAL, J. S., BODDY, W. J., et al. (2004). The Mouse Genome Database (MGD): integrating biology with the genome. *Nucl. Acids Res.* 32 (Database issue), D476–D481.

CHEUNG, V. G., NOWAK, N., JANG, W., KIRSCH, I. R., ZHAO, S., CHEN, X. N., FUREY, T. S., KIM, U. J., KUO, W. L., OLIVIER, M., et al. (2001). Integration of cytogenetic landmarks into the draft sequence of the human genome. *Nature* 409, 953–958.

CHOWDHARY, B. (2003). *Animal Genomics* (Karger, Basel).

CHUMAKOV, I. M., RIGAULT, P., LE GALL, I., BELLANNE-CHANTELOT, C., BILLAULT, A., GUILLOU, S., SOULARUE, P., GUASCONI, G., POULLIER, E.,

AND GROS, I. (1995). A YAC contig map of the human genome. *Nature* 377, 175–297.

COX, D. R., BURMEISTER, M., PRICE, E. R., KIM, S., AND MYERS, R. M. (1990). Radiation hybrid mapping: a somatic cell genetic method for constructing high-resolution maps of mammalian chromosomes. *Science* 250, 245–250.

CUTICCHIA, A. J. (2000). High performance computing and medical research. *Cmaj* 162, 1148–1149.

DAUSSET, J., CANN, H., COHEN, D., LATHROP, M., LALOUEL, J. M., AND WHITE, R. (1990). Centre d'etude du polymorphisme humain (CEPH): collaborative genetic mapping of the human genome. *Genomics* 6, 575–577.

DELOUKAS, P., SCHULER, G. D., GYAPAY, G., BEASLEY, E. M., SODERLUND, C., RODRIGUEZ-TOME, P., HUI, L., MATISE, T. C., MCKUSICK, K. B., BECKMANN, J. S., et al. (1998). A physical map of 30,000 human genes. *Science* 282, 744–746.

DIB, C., FAURE, S., FIZAMES, C., SAMSON, D., DROUOT, N., VIGNAL, A., MILLASSEAU, P., MARC, S., HAZAN, J., SEBOUN, E., et al. (1996). A comprehensive genetic map of the human genome based on 5,264 microsatellites. *Nature* 380, 152–154.

GHEBRANIOUS, N., VASKE, D., YU, A., ZHAO, C., MARTH, G., AND WEBER, J. L. (2003). STRP screening sets for the human genome at 5 cM density. *BMC Genomics* 4, 6.

GILBERT, D. G. (2002). euGenes: a eukaryote genome information system. *Nucl. Acids Res.* 30, 145–148.

GREEN, E. D., AND OLSON, M. V. (1990). Chromosomal region of the cystic fibrosis gene in yeast artificial chromosomes: a model for human genome mapping. *Science* 250, 94–98.

GYAPAY, G., SCHMITT, K., FIZAMES, C., JONES, H., VEGA-CZARNY, N., SPILLETT, D., MUSELET, D., PRUD'HOMME, J. F., DIB, C., AUFFRAY, C., et al. (1996). A radiation hybrid map of the human genome. *Hum. Mol. Genet.* 5, 339–346.

HILLIER, L. D., LENNON, G., BECKER, M., BONALDO, M. F., CHIAPELLI, B., CHISSOE, S., DIETRICH, N., DuBUQUE, T., FAVELLO, A., GISH, W., et al. (1996). Generation and analysis of 280,000 human expressed sequence tags. *Genome Res.* 6, 807–828.

HOULGATTE, R., MARIAGE-SAMSON, R., DUPRAT, S., TESSIER, A., BENTOLILA, S., LAMY, B., AND AUFFRAY, C. (1995). The Genexpress Index: a resource for gene discovery and the genetic map of the human genome. *Genome Res.* 5, 272–304.

HU, J., MUNGALL, C., LAW, A., PAPWORTH, R., NELSON, J. P., BROWN, A., SIMPSON, I., LECKIE, S., BURT, D. W., HILLYARD, A. L., et al. (2001). The ARKdb: genome databases for farmed and other animals. *Nucl. Acids Res.* 29, 106–110.

HUDSON, T. J., STEIN, L. D., GERETY, S. S., MA, J., CASTLE, A. B., SILVA, J., SLONIM, D. K., BAPTISTA, R., KRUGLYAK, L., AND XU, S. H. (1995). An STS-based map of the human genome. *Science* 270, 1945–1954.

HURET, J. L., DESSEN, P., AND BERNHEIM, A. (2003). Atlas of genetics and cytogenetics in oncology and haematology, 2003. *Nucl. Acids Res.* 31, 272–274.

IAONNOU, P. A., AMEMIYA, C. T., GARNES, J., KROISEL, P. M., SHIZUYA, H., CHEN, C., BATZER, M. A., AND DE JONG, P. J. (1994). A new bacteriophage P1-derived vector for the propagation of large human DNA fragments. *Nat. Genet.* 6, 84–89.

KAROLCHIK, D., BAERTSCH, R., DIEKHANS, M., FUREY, T. S., HINRICHS, A., LU, Y. T., ROSKIN, K. M., SCHWARTZ, M., SUGNET, C. W,, THOMAS, D. J., et al. (2003). The UCSC Genome Browser Database. *Nucl. Acids Res.* 31, 51–54.

KE, X., TAPPER, W., AND COLLINS, A. 2001. LDB2000: sequence-based integrated maps of the human genome. *Bioinformatics* 17, 581–586.

KONG, A., GUDBJARTSSON, D. F., SAINZ, J., JONSDOTTIR, G. M., GUDJONSSON, S. A., RICHARDSSON, B., SIGURDADOTTIR, S., BARNARDA, J., HALLBECK, B., MASSON, G., et al. (2002). A high-resolution recombination map of the humangenome. *Nat. Genet.* 31, 241–247.

KONG, X., MURPHY, K., RAJ, T., HE, C., WHITE, P. S., AND MATISE, T. C. (2003). A combined linkage-physical map of the human genome. *Am. J. Hum. Genet.* 73S, 196.

LAWRENCE, J. B., SINGER, R. H., AND NCNEIL, J. A. (1990). Interphase and metaphase resolution of different distances within the human dystrophin gene. *Science* 249, 928–932.

LENHARD, B., HAYES, W. S., AND WASSERMAN, W. W. (2001). GeneLynx: a gene-centric portal to the human genome. *Genome Res.* 11, 2151–2157.

LIU, L., GONG, G., LIU, Y., NATARAJAN, S., LARKIN, D. M., EVERTS-VAN DER WIND, A., REBEIZ, M., AND BEEVER, J. E. (2004). Multi-species comparative mapping *in silico* using the COMPASS strategy. *Bioinformatics* 20, 148–154.

MAGLOTT, D. R., KATZ, K. S., SICOTTE, H., AND PRUITT, K. D. (2000). NCBI's LocusLink and RefSeq. *Nucl. Acids Res.* 28, 126–128.

MARRA, M. A., KUCABA, T. A., DIETRICH, N. L., GREEN, E. D., BROWNSTEIN, B., WILSON, R. K., MCDONALD, K. M., HILLIER, L. W., MCPHERSON, J. D., AND WATERSTON, R. H. (1997). High throughput fingerprint analysis of large-insert clones. *Genome Res.* 7, 1072–1084.

MATISE, T. C., PORTER, C. J., BUYSKE, S., CUTICCHIA, A. J., SULMAN, E. P., AND WHITE, P. S. (2002). Systematic evaluation of map quality: human chromosome 22. *Am. J. Hum. Genet.* 70, 1398–1410.

MATISE, T. C., SACHIDANANDAM, R., CLARK, A. G., KRUGLYAK, L., WIJSMAN, E., KAKOL, J., BUYSKE, S., CHUI, B., COHEN, P., DE TOMA, C., et al. (2003). A 3.9-centimorgan-resolution human single-nucleotide polymorphism linkage map and screening set. *Am. J. Hum. Genet.* 73, 271–284.

MATISE, T. C., WASMUTH, J., MYERS, R. M., AND MCPHERSON, J. (1999). Somatic cell genetics and radiation hybrid mapping. In: *Genome Analysis: A Laboratory Manual* (Birren, B., Green, E., Hieter, P., Klapholz, S., and Myers, R., eds.). (Cold Spring Harbor Laboratory Press, Cold Spring Harbor) p. 259–302.

MCVEAN, G. A., MYERS, S. R., HUNT, S., DELOUKAS, P., BENTLEY, D. R., AND DONNELLY, P. (2004). The fine-scale structure of recombination rate variation in the human genome. *Science* 304, 581–584.

MURAL, R. J., PARANG, M., SHAH, M., SNODDY, J., AND UBERBACHER, E. C. (1999). The Genome Channel: a browser to a uniform first-pass annotation of genomic DNA. *Trends Genet.* 15, 38–39.

MURRAY, J. C., BUETOW, K. H., WEBER, J. L., LUDWIGSEN, S., SCHERPBIER-HEDDEMA, T., MANION, F., QUILLEN, J., SHEFFIELD, V. C., SUNDEN, S., AND DUYK, G. M. (1994). A comprehensive human linkage map with centimorgan density. Cooperative Human Linkage Center (CHLC). *Science* 265, 2049–2054.

MURPHY, K., RAJ, T., WINTERS, R. S., AND WHITE, P. S. (2004). me-PCR: a refined ultrafast algorithm for identifying sequence-defined genomic elements. *Bioinformatics* 20, 588–590.

O'BRIEN, S. J., Eisenberg, J. F., Miyamoto, M., Hedges, S. B., Kumar, S., Wilson, D. E., Menotti-Raymond, M., Murphy, W. J., Nash, W. G., Lyons, L. A., et al. (1999). Genome maps 10. Comparative genomics. Mammalian radiations. Wall chart. *Science* 286, 463–478.

OLIVIER, M., Aggarwal, A., Allen, J., Almendras, A. A., Bajorek, E. S., Beasley, E. M., Brady, S. D., Bushard, J. M., Bustos, V. I., Chu, A., et al. (2001). A high-resolution radiation hybrid map of the human genome draft sequence. *Science* 291, 1298–1302.

PARRA, I., and Windle, B. (1993). High resolution visual mapping of stretched DNA by fluorescent hybridization. *Nat. Genet.* 5, 17–21.

PEARSON, P. L. (1991). The genome data base (GDB)—a human gene mapping repository. *Nucl. Acids Res.* 19 (Suppl), 2237–2239.

PINKEL, D., Straume, T., and Gray, J. W. (1986). Cytogenetic analysis using quantitative, high-sensitivity, fluorescence hybridization. *Proc. Natl. Acad. Sci. U. S. A.* 83, 2934–2938.

PINKEL, D., Segraves, R., Sudar, D., Clark, S., et al. (1998). High resolution analysis of DNA copy number variation using comparative genomic hybridization to microarrays. *Nat. Genet.* 20, 207–211.

PRUITT, K., Katz, K., Sicotte, H., and Maglott, D. (2000). Introducing RefSeq and LocusLink: curated human genome resources at the NCBI. *Trends Genet.* 16, 44–47.

ROSEN, N., CHALIFA-CASPI, V., SHMUELI, O., ADATO, A., LAPIDOT, M., STAMPNITZKY, J., SAFRAN, M., AND LANCET, D. (2003). GeneLoc: exon-based integration of human genome maps. *Bioinformatics* 19 (Suppl 1), I222–I224.

SAFRAN, M., CHALIFA-CASPI, V., SHMUELI, O., OLENDER, T., LAPIDOT, M., ROSEN, N., SHMOISH, M., PETER, Y., GLUSMAN, G., FELDMESSER, E., et al. (2003). Human gene-centric databases at the Weizmann Institute of Science: GeneCards, UDB, CroW 21 and HORDE. *Nucl. Acids Res.* 31, 142–146.

SCHULER, G. D. (1997). Sequence mapping by electronic PCR. *Genome Res.* 7, 541–550.

SHIZUYA, H., BIRREN, B., KIM, U. J., MANCINO, V., SLEPAK, T., TACHIIRI, Y., AND SIMON, M. (1992). Cloning and stable maintenance of 300-kilobase-pair fragments of human DNA in Escherichia coli using an F-factor-based vector. *Proc. Natl. Acad. Sci. U. S. A.* 89, 8794–8797.

STASSEN, H. H., AND SCHARFETTER, C. (2000). Integration of genetic maps by polynomial transformations. *Am. J. Med. Genet.* 96, 108–113.

STEWART, E. A., McKUSICK, K. B., AGGARWAL, A., BAJOREK, E., BRADY, S., CHU, A., FANG, N., HADLEY, D., HARRIS, M., HUSSAIN, S., et al. (1997). An STS-based radiation hybrid map of the human genome. *Genome Res.* 7, 422–433.

TWIGGER, S., LU, J., SHIMOYAMA, M., CHEN, D., PASKO, D., LONG, H., GINSTER, J., CHEN, C. F., NIGAM, R., KWITEK, A., et al. (2002). Rat Genome Database (RGD): mapping disease onto the genome. *Nucl. Acids Res.* 30, 125–128.

VAN DEN ENGH, G., SACHS, R., AND TRASK, B. J. (1992). Estimating genomic distance from DNA sequence location in cell nuclei by a random walk model. *Science* 257, 1410–1412.

VENTER, J. C., SMITH, H. O., AND HOOD, L. (1996). A new strategy for genome sequencing. *Nature* 381, 364–366.

WHEELER, D. L., CHURCH, D. M., EDGAR, R., FEDERHEN, S., et al. (2004). Database resources of the National Center for Biotechnology Information: update. *Nucl. Acids Res.* 32 (Database issue), D35–D40.

WHITE, J. A., McALPINE, P. J., ANTONARAKIS, S., CANN, H., et al. (1997). Guidelines for human gene nomenclature. *Genomics* 45, 468–471.

WHITE, P. S., SULMAN, E. P., PORTER, C. J., AND MATISE, T. C. (1999). A comprehensive view of human chromosome 1. *Genome Res.* 9, 978–988.

KEY TERMS

candidate gene

comparative map

cytogenetic

cytogenetic map

DNA clone

fluorescence in situ hybridization (FISH)

genetic linkage

genetic map

genomic database

genomic map

lod score

marker

microsatellite

physical map

polymorphism

positional cloning

sequence-tagged clone (STC)

sequence-tagged site (STS)

single nucleotide polymorphism (SNP)

## CHAPTER THREE

Information Retrieval from Biological Databases

ANDREAS D. BAXEVANIS

Bioinformatics: A Practical Guide to the Analysis of Genes and Proteins, Third Edition, edited by
Andreas D. Baxevanis and B.F. Francis Ouellette.
ISBN 0-471-47878-4 Copyright © 2005 John Wiley & Sons, Inc.

▌INTRODUCTION

In April 2003, the biological community celebrated the completion of the Human Genome Project's major goal: the complete, accurate, and high-quality sequencing of the human genome. The attainment of this goal, which many have compared with landing a man on the moon, already has had a profound effect on how biological and biomedical research is being conducted. The free availability of not only human genome data, but also human sequence variation data, model organism sequence data, and information on gene structure and function, provides fertile ground for the biologist to better design and interpret their experiments in the laboratory, fulfilling the promise of bioinformatics in advancing and accelerating biological discovery.

The completion of sequencing of a number of model organisms, along with the continued sequencing of others, underscores the necessity for all biologists to learn how to make their way effectively through this sequence space. GenBank, or any other biological database for that matter, serves little purpose unless the database can be easily searched and entries can be retrieved in a usable, meaningful format. Otherwise, sequencing efforts have no useful end, because the biological community as a whole cannot make use of the information hidden within these millions of bases and amino acids. Much effort has gone into making such data accessible to the average user, and the programs and interfaces resulting from these efforts are the focus of this chapter. The discussion centers on querying databases at the National Center for Biotechnology Information (NCBI) because these more "general" repositories are far and away the ones most often accessed by biologists, but attention is also given to a specialized databases that provide information not necessarily found through Entrez.

▌INTEGRATED INFORMATION RETRIEVAL: THE ENTREZ SYSTEM

One of the most widely used interfaces for the retrieval of information from biological databases is the NCBI Entrez system. Entrez capitalizes on the fact that there are pre-existing, logical relationships between the individual entries found in numerous public databases. For example, a paper in MEDLINE (or, more properly, PubMed; Box 3.1) may describe the sequencing of a gene whose sequence appears in GenBank. The nucleotide sequence, in turn, may code for a protein product whose sequence is stored in the protein databases. The three-dimensional structure of that protein may be known, and the coordinates for that structure may appear in the structure database. Finally, the gene may have been mapped to a specific region of a given chromosome, with that information being stored in a mapping database. The existence of such natural connections, mostly biological in nature, argued for the development of a method through which all the information about a particular biological entity could be found without having sequentially to visit and query disparate databases.

Entrez, to be clear, is not a database itself, but rather is the interface through which all of its component databases can be accessed and traversed—an integrated information retrieval system. The Entrez information space includes PubMed records, nucleotide and protein sequence data, three-dimensional structure information, and mapping information. The strength of Entrez lies in the fact that *all* of this information, across numerous component databases, can be accessed by issuing one and only one query. Entrez is able to offer integrated information retrieval through the use of two types of connection between database entries: neighboring and hard links.

Relationships Between Database Entries: Neighboring

The concept of neighboring allows for entries within a given database to be connected to one another. If a user is looking at a particular PubMed entry, the user can ask Entrez to find all of the other papers in PubMed that are similar in subject matter to the original paper. Similarly, if a user is looking at a sequence entry, Entrez can return a list of all other sequences that bear similarity to the original sequence. The establishment of neighboring relationships within a database is based on statistical measures of similarity, as follows. Although the term *neighboring* traditionally is used to describe these connections, the terminology used on the Entrez Web site will describe neighbors as *related papers*, *related sequences*, and so forth.

BLAST. Sequence data are compared with one another using the Basic Local Alignment Search Tool, or BLAST (Altschul et al., 1990). This algorithm attempts to find high-scoring segment pairs, which are pairs of sequences that can be aligned with one another and, when aligned, meet certain scoring and statistical criteria. Chapter 11 discusses the family of BLAST algorithms and their application at length.

VAST. Sets of coordinate data are compared using a vector-based method known as VAST, for Vector Alignment Search Tool (Madej et al., 1995; Gibrat et al., 1996).

BOX 3.1 | PubMed and MEDLINE

Because a significant portion of this chapter deals with searching PubMed, it is important for the reader to understand the distinction between PubMed and MEDLINE. MEDLINE is the National Library of Medicine's database of journal citations from 1966 to the present; updates to MEDLINE are made on a weekly basis. The scope of journals included in MEDLINE roughly covers the general areas of biomedicine and health, encompassing most (but not all) journals that those working in the biomedical sciences routinely access. Although this broad definition brings the contents of approximately 4600 journals into MEDLINE, most records are from English-language publications; the inclusion of non-English publications usually is limited to journals providing abstracts translated into English. Although the MEDLINE database as a whole contains entries going back to 1966, a given journal's entries will be present only from the point when that journal was chosen for inclusion in MEDLINE; this means that a user cannot necessarily be assured that results of a MEDLINE search actually return the most complete set of results.

PubMed, the resource available through Entrez, attempts to broaden the scope of MEDLINE slightly and to address some of its shortfalls by including life sciences citations from general science and chemistry journals, adding roughly one million more entries to the MEDLINE set. PubMed also attempts to index journals completely back to 1966, regard-

less of the date of the journal's inclusion in MEDLINE. For papers published before 1966, the user will need to access OLD-MEDLINE, which must be done through a different search engine, called the NLM Gateway. Strictly speaking, this means that two searches would need to be performed to assure that the complete literature fitting a particular search has been obtained. In the vast majority of cases, though, users are looking for much more "recent" literature, so a search of OLD-MEDLINE seldom is necessary. Both MEDLINE and OLD-MEDLINE can be searched simultaneously using the NLM Gateway, but its Web-based interface is not nearly as user friendly or powerful as that of Entrez, nor do Gateway results pages provide the myriad of links to other databases and resources that Entrez provides.

One final, yet important, historical distinction lies in the number of authors actually indexed for any given paper. From 1966 to 1983, any author whose name was listed on the title page of the article was indexed. From 1984 to 1995, the author list was limited to the first ten authors, possibly omitting the senior author from the list. From 1996 to 1999, the author list was expanded to include the first 25 authors; in the case of large, consortium-based studies, the senior author(s) still might have been omitted, even with the longer list. Finally, from 2000 on, all authors' names were indexed, regardless of the length of the author list.

There are three major steps that take place in the course of a VAST comparison:

▶ First, based on known three-dimensional coordinate data, all of the α-helices and β-sheets that comprise the core of the protein are identified. Straight-line vectors then are calculated based on the position of these secondary structure elements. VAST keeps track of how one vector is connected to the next (that is, how the C-terminal end of one vector connects to the N-terminal end of the next vector), as well as whether a particular vector represents an α-helix or a β-sheet. Subsequent steps use *only* these vectors in making comparisons with other proteins. In effect, most of the coordinate data are discarded at this step. The reason for this apparent oversimplification is simply the scale of the problem at hand: with more than 24,000 structures in PDB that need to be considered, the time that it would take to perform an in-depth comparison of each and every structure to all of the other structures in the database would make the calculations both impractical and intractable. The user should keep this simplification in mind when making

biological inferences based on the results presented in a VAST table.

▶ Next, the algorithm attempts to align these sets of vectors optimally, looking for pairs of structural elements that are of the same type and relative orientation, with consistent connectivity between the individual elements. The object is to identify highly similar core substructures, that is, pairs that represent a statistically significant match above that which would be obtained by comparing randomly chosen proteins to one another.

▶ Finally, a refinement is performed using Monte Carlo methods at each residue position in an attempt to optimize the structural alignment.

Through this method, it is possible to find structural (and, presumably, functional) relationships between proteins in cases that may lack overt sequence similarity. The resultant alignment need not be global; matches may be between individual domains of different proteins.

It is important to note here that VAST is not the best method for determining structural similarities. More robust methods, such as homology model building, provide much greater resolving power in determining such relationships, because the raw information within the three-dimensional coordinate file is used to perform more advanced calculations regarding the positions of side chains and the thermodynamic nature of the interactions between side chains. Reducing a structure to a series of vectors necessarily results in a loss of information. However, considering the magnitude of the problem here—again, the number of pairwise comparisons that need to be made—and both the computing power and time needed to use any of the more advanced methods, VAST provides a simple and fast first answer to the question of structural similarity. More information on other structure prediction methods based on X-ray or nuclear magnetic resonance (NMR) coordinate data can be found in Chapter 9.

Weighted Key Terms. The problem of comparing sequence data somewhat pales next to that of comparing PubMed entries, free text whose rules of syntax are not necessarily fixed. Given that no two individuals' writing styles are exactly the same, finding a way to compare seemingly disparate blocks of text poses a substantial problem. Entrez uses a method known as the *relevance pairs model of retrieval* to make such comparisons, relying on what are known as weighted key terms (Wilbur and Coffee, 1994; Wilbur and Yang, 1996). This concept is best described by example. Consider two manuscripts with the following titles: *BRCA1 as a Genetic Marker for Breast Cancer* and *Genetic Factors in the Familial Transmission of the Breast Cancer BRCA1 Gene*. Both titles contain the terms *BRCA1*, *breast*, and *cancer*, and the presence of these common terms may indicate that the manuscripts are similar in their subject matter. The proximity between the words is also taken into account, so that words common to two records that are closer together are scored higher than common words that are further apart. In the current example, the terms *breast* and *cancer* would score higher based on proximity than either of those words would against *BRCA1*, because the words are next to each other. Common words found in a title are scored higher than those found in an abstract, because title words are presumed to have more importance than those found in the body of an abstract. Overall weighting depends on the frequency of a given word among all the entries in PubMed, with words that occur infrequently in the database as a whole carrying a higher weight.

Hard Links

The hard link concept is much easier conceptually than is neighboring. Hard links are applied between entries in different databases and exist everywhere there is a logical connection between entries. For instance, if a PubMed entry talks about the sequencing of a cosmid, a hard link is established between the PubMed entry and the corresponding nucleotide entry. If an open reading frame in that cosmid codes for a known protein, a hard link is established between the nucleotide entry and the protein entry. If, by sheer luck, the protein entry has an experimentally deduced structure, a hard link would be placed between the protein entry and the structural entry. The hard link relationships between databases are illustrated in Figure 3.1.

Searches can, in essence, begin anywhere within Entrez—the user has no constraints with respect to where the foray into this information space must begin. However, depending on which database is used as the jumping-off point, different fields are available for searching. This stands to reason, inasmuch as the entries in databases of different types are necessarily organized differently, reflecting the biological nature of the entity they are trying to catalog.

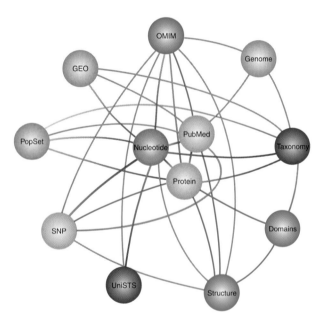

FIGURE 3.1 **An overview of the relationships in the Entrez integrated information retrieval system. Each sphere represents one of the elements that can be accessed through Entrez, and the lines represent how each component database connects to the others. Entrez is under continuous evolution, with both new components being added and the interrelationships between the elements changing dynamically. (Reprinted from Ostell, 2003.)**

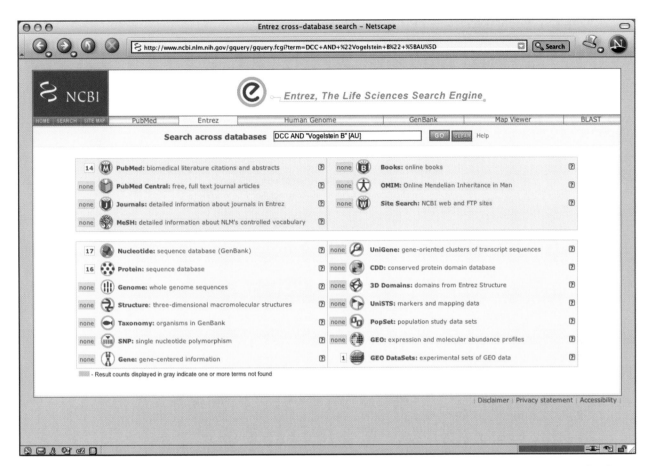

FIGURE 3.2   The Entrez unified results page, showing the number of hits to each of Entrez's component databases fitting the query. Clicking on any of the numbers to the left of the database name takes the user to the results found in that particular database.

The Entrez Discovery Pathway

Navigating the Entrez Search Space. The best way to illustrate the integrated nature of the Entrez system and to drive home the power of neighboring is by considering some biological examples. The simplest way to query Entrez is through the use of individual search terms, coupled together by Boolean operators such as *and*, *or*, or *not*. Consider the case in which one wants to retrieve all available information on a gene named *DCC* (deleted in colorectal cancer), limiting the returned information on entries to those in which Bert Vogelstein at The Johns Hopkins University is the author. Beginning at the NCBI home page, Entrez should appear automatically in the search pull-down menu; within the text box to the right, the user would type DCC AND "Vogelstein B" [AU]. The [AU] qualifying the second term indicates to Entrez that this is an *author* term, so only the author field in entries should be considered when evaluating this part of the search statement. The result

of the query is shown in Figure 3.2. Entrez does a query of all of the available databases, and the number of hits to each database are shown to the left of the name of the database. Here, 14 entries matching the query were found in PubMed, 17 entries were found in GenBank, and 16 entries were found in the protein database. The user can narrow down the query further by adding additional terms, if the user is interested in a more specific aspect of this gene or if there are quite simply too many entries returned by the initial query. A list of all available qualifiers is given in Table 3.1.

At this point, to look at the list of papers found that fit the query, the user would click on the 14 next to PubMed, taking them to the screen shown in Figure 3.3. For each of the found papers in PubMed, the user is presented with the authors on the paper, the name of the paper, and the citation. To look at one of the actual papers resulting from the search, the user can click on any of the hyperlinked author lists. For this example, consider the

TABLE 3.1 ■ Entrez Boolean Search Statements

General syntax:

```
search term [tag] Boolean operator search term [tag] ...
```

where **[tag]** =

Tag	Description
[ACCN]	Accession
[AD]	Affiliation
[ALL]	All fields
[AU]	Author name

> `O'Brien J [AU]` *yields all of* O'Brien JA, O'Brien JB, etc.
> `"O'Brien J" [AU]` *yields only* O'Brien J

Tag	Description
[ECNO]	Enzyme Commission or Chemical Abstract Service numbers
[EDAT]	Entrez date

> `YYYY/MM/DD, YYYY/MM,` or `YYYY`

Tag	Description
[FDAT]	Feature key (nucleotide only)
[GENE]	Gene name
[ISS]	Issue of journal
[JOUR]	Journal title, official abbreviation, or ISSN number

> ```
> Journal of Biological Chemistry
> J Biol Chem
> 0021-9258
> ```

Tag	Description
[LA]	Language
[MAJR]	MeSH Major Topic

> *One of the **major** topics discussed in the article*

Tag	Description
[MH]	MeSH Terms

> *Controlled vocabulary of biomedical terms (**subject**)*

Tag	Description
[ORGN]	Organism
[PS]	Personal name as subject

> *Use when name is subject of article*, e.g., `Varmus H [PS]`

Tag	Description
[PDAT]	Publication date

> `YYYY/MM/DD, YYYY/MM,` or `YYYY`

Tag	Description
[PROT]	Protein name (not available in Structure database)
[PT]	Publication type

> ```
> Review
> Clinical Trial
> Lectures
> Letter
> Technical Publication
> ```

Tag	Description
[SH]	Subheading

> *Used to modify MeSH Terms*
> `hypertension [MH] AND toxicity [SH]`

Tag	Description
[SUBS]	Substance name

> *Name of chemical discussed in article*

Tag	Description
[SI]	Secondary source ID

> *Names of secondary source databanks and/or accession numbers of sequences discussed in article*

Tag	Description
[WORD]	Text words

> *All words and numbers in the title and abstract, MeSH terms, subheadings, chemical substance names, personal name as subject, and MEDLINE secondary sources*

Tag	Description
[TITL]	Title word

> *Only words in the definition line (not available in Structure database)*

Tag	Description
[UID]	Unique Identifiers (PMID/MEDLINE numbers)
[VOL]	Volume of journal

Boolean operator = AND, OR, or NOT

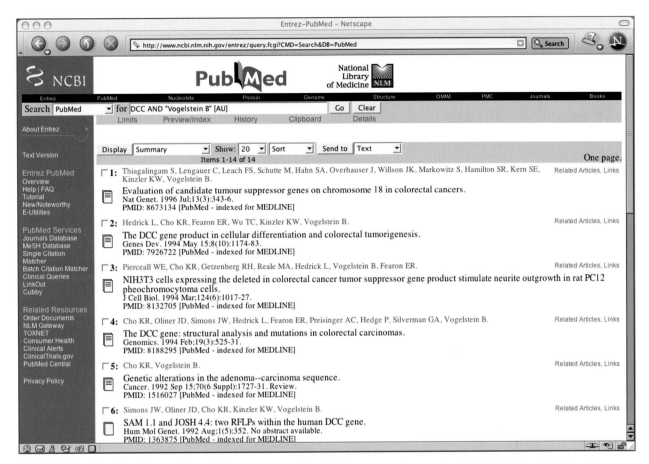

FIGURE 3.3 **Results of a text-based Entrez query using Boolean operators against PubMed. The initial query (from Figure 3.1) is shown in the search box near the top of the window. Each entry gives the names of the authors, the title of the paper, and the citation information. The actual record can be retrieved by clicking on the author list.**

fourth reference in the list, by Kathy Cho et al. Clicking on the list of authors for that paper takes the user to the Abstract view, shown in Figure 3.4. The Abstract view presents the name of the paper, the list of authors, their institutional affiliation, and the abstract itself, in standard format. A number of alternative formats are available for displaying this information, and these various formats can be selected using the pull-down menu next to the Display button. Switching to Citation format would produce a very similar-looking entry, the difference being the cataloging information such as MeSH terms (*medical subject headings*) and indexed substances relating to the entry are shown below the abstract. MEDLINE format produces the MEDLINE/MEDLARS layout, with two-letter codes corresponding to the contents of each field going down the left-hand side of the entry (e.g., the author field is denoted by the code AU). Entries in this format can be saved and easily imported into third-party bibliography management programs, such as EndNote or Reference Manager.

At the top right of the entry are two links that are worth mentioning. First is a hyperlink labeled Related Articles. This is one of the entry points from which the user can take advantage of the neighboring and hard link relationships described earlier. If the user clicks on Related Articles, Entrez will indicate that there are 160 papers related to the original Cho et al. reference—that is, 160 references of similar subject matter—and the first six of these papers are shown in Figure 3.5. The first reference in the list is the same Cho et al. paper because, by definition, it is most related to itself (the parent entry). The order in which the related papers follow is from most statistically similar downward. Thus, the entry closest to the parent is deemed to be the closest in subject matter to the parent. By scanning the titles, the user easily can find related information on other studies as well as can amass quickly a bibliography of relevant references. This is a particularly useful and time-saving function when one is writing grants or papers, because abstracts easily can be scanned and papers of real interest

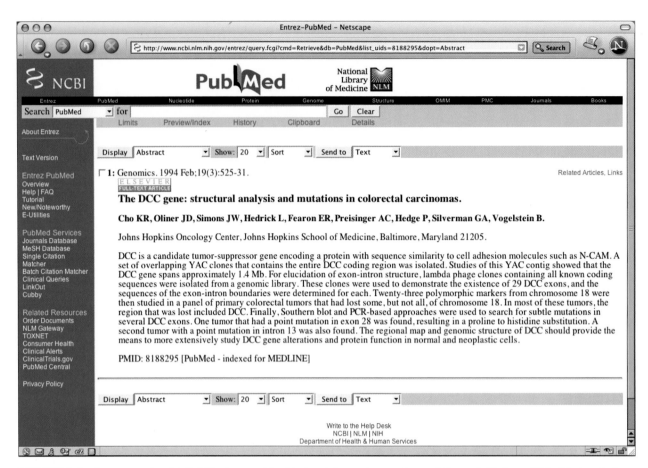

FIGURE 3.4 An example of a PubMed record in Abstract format, as returned through Entrez. This Abstract view is for the fourth reference shown in Figure 3.2. This view provides connections to related articles, sequence information, and the actual, full-text journal article. See text for details.

can be identified before one heads off for the library stacks.

In the view presented in Figure 3.5, if the user clicks now on the Links hyperlink next to the Cho et al. entry, a pop-up menu appears. The pop-up menu provides a new series of links, representing hard link connections to other databases within the Entrez system. The first link (Gene) takes the user to Entrez Gene, a new feature of Entrez that provides information about the gene in question; the data is gathered from a variety of sources, including RefSeq; the Entrez Gene page for *DCC* is shown in Figure 3.6. The screen shows that this is a protein-coding gene at map location 18q21.3, and information on the genomic context of *DCC*, as well as alternative gene names and information on the encoded protein is provided. The next two links in the pop-up menu are for Nucleotide and Protein entries, taking the user to the GenBank or GenPept entries corresponding to *DCC*; if one were to follow the Protein link, the view in Figure 3.7 would appear, and clicking on any of the hyperlinked ac-

cession numbers would take the user to the actual entry for that protein, which includes the protein's sequence.

The next link in the series is labeled OMIM, which would take the user to the entry within Online Mendelian Inheritance in Man describing *DCC* in detail; the reader is referred to the discussion of OMIM at the end of this chapter for more information.

Continuing down the list of links in the pop-up shown in Figure 3.5, the next link is labeled Cited in PMC. If clicked, this would take the user to papers that have referenced the Cho et al. paper that are available through PubMed Central. The penultimate link is labeled Books, and clicking on that link will take the user to a heavily hyperlinked version of the original citation. The highlighted words in this view correspond to keywords that can take the user to full-text books that are available through NCBI. One of these books is *Molecular Biology of the Cell* (Alberts et al., 1994). After the Cho et al. example, if the user were to click on the hyperlinked words cell adhesion molecules, they eventually

FIGURE 3.5   Neighbors to an entry found in PubMed. The original entry from Figure 3.3 (Cho et al., 1994) is at the top of the list, indicating that this is the parent entry. Clicking the Links button to the left of any of the entries produces a pop-up menu, providing links to related entries outside PubMed. See text for details.

would be taken to the relevant part of the textbook, a section devoted to cell–cell adhesion (Figure 3.8). From this page, the user can navigate through this particular section of the book, gathering more general information on cell adherence and anchoring junctions.

The final link in the series is LinkOut. This feature provides a list of third-party Web sites and resources related to the Entrez query being viewed, such as the full text of articles that can be displayed directly through the Web browser, or the capability of ordering the document through online services. Another way of obtaining to the full text of an article is by following a direct link to the publisher's Web site. In the Abstract view for the Cho et al. example (Figure 3.4), a button directly under the citation is marked Elsevier Full-Text Article, and clicking this button indeed would take the user to the full text of the article, as well as would provide the ability to download the article in PDF format. Accessing full-text articles depends on the individual or institutional privileges of the user. Through LinkOut, the user also can obtain information that is particularly useful to

patients or clinicians. From the LinkOut page, clicking on MEDLINEplus takes the user to a page devoted to information on *DCC* for both laymen and physicians and disorders related to *DCC* (Figure 3.9). The information available through this page often is much more appropriate to provide to patients, because the level of writing is geared toward nonprofessionals; there are also interactive tutorials for various procedures related to *DCC* along the right-hand side of the page. If the user were to click on one of the links in the Clinical Trials section, they would leave MEDLINEplus and be taken to the National Institutes of Health's central information source for clinical trials, aptly called clinicaltrials.gov (Figure 3.10). The listing shown in the figure shows the first nine of the 111 clinical trials actively recruiting for patients with *DCC*-related disorders. Although we, as scientists, tend to focus on the types of information discussed throughout this chapter, the clinical trials site is, unarguably, the most important of the sites covered in this chapter, because it provides a means through which patients with a given genetic or metabolic disorder can receive the

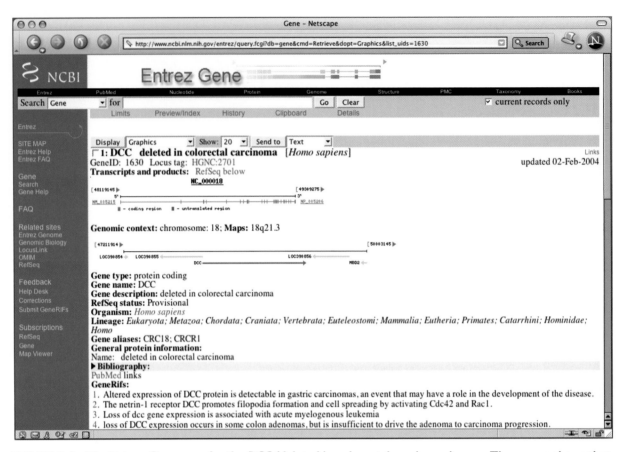

FIGURE 3.6 The Entrez Gene page for the *DCC* (deleted in colorectal carcinoma) gene. The screen shows that this is a protein-coding gene at map location 18q21.3, and information on the genomic context of DCC, as well as alternative gene names and information on the encoded protein, is provided.

latest, cutting-edge treatment, treatment that may make a substantial difference in their quality of life.

Cubby. A storage service called Cubby is provided to save searches and their corresponding results. The advantage of the Cubby system is that it can recall the searches that were saved and can update them with the click of a mouse, rather than reentering the query each time the user wishes to view the most recent results. Although the searches can be stored, links to related articles cannot be stored. The maximum number of stored searches is 100 per user.

Continuing with the *DCC* example, to store the 14 papers found as a result of the search, the user would return to the page shown in Figure 3.3. There is a link to Cubby in the blue sidebar running along the left-hand side of the page. Clicking on that link would take the user to the Cubby registration and login page; new users should follow the instructions for creating their free Cubby account, whereas returning users should log in with their username and password. After logging in, the user would see a screen such as the one shown in Figure 3.11. The

search terms for this search (DCC and "Vogelstein B" [AU]) are shown at the top of the Cubby page, and the user can modify the search, if desired, before clicking the Store in Cubby button. After being stored, the search would appear in the lower portion of the window, under Cubby Stored Searches. To look for new papers that may have been published since the search was last performed, the user simply would check the box next to the stored search of interest, then click What's New for Selected. If there are no new papers, 0 new would be displayed; if there were new papers, the user would see # new (e.g., 6 new), and clicking on these words would produce a new screen with the new papers, in summary format.

Limits and History. There is another way to perform an Entrez query that involves some built-in features of the system. Consider an example in which one is attempting to find all genes coding for DNA-binding proteins in *Methanothermobacter*. In this case, starting from the NCBI home page, the search would begin by setting the Search pull-down menu to Nucleotide and then

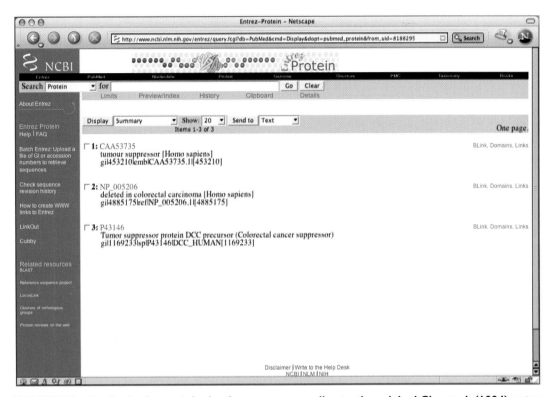

FIGURE 3.7 Entries in the protein databases corresponding to the original Cho et al. (1994) entry shown in Figure 3.2. Entries can be accessed by clicking on any of the accession numbers. See text for details.

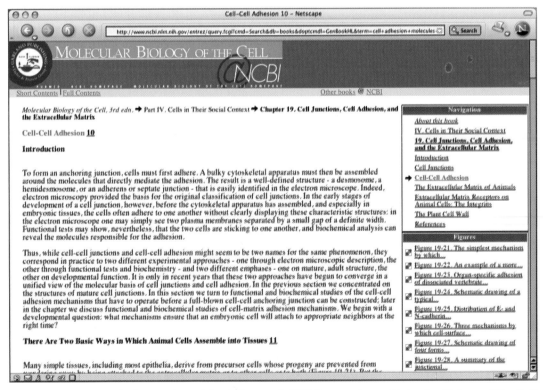

FIGURE 3.8 Text relating to the original Cho et al. (1994) entry from *Molecular Biology of the Cell* (Alberts et al., 1994). This is part of the NCBI Bookshelf, which offers electronic version of many commonly used textbooks. See text for details.

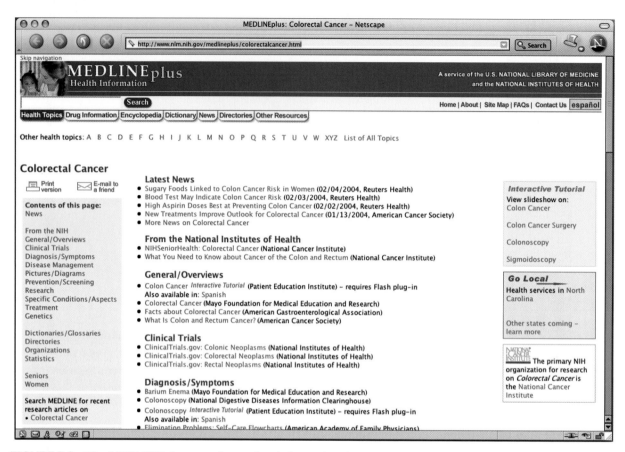

FIGURE 3.9 The **MEDLINE**plus page devoted to information for both laymen and physicians on *DCC* and disorders related to *DCC*. The information available through this page often is much more appropriate to provide to patients, because the level of writing is geared toward nonprofessionals; there also are interactive tutorials for various procedures related to *DCC* along the right-hand side of the page.

typing the term DNA-binding into the text box. The search returns 31,809 entries in which the search term appears (Figure 3.12). At this point, to narrow down the search, the user can click on the Limits hyperlink, directly below the text box. This brings the user to a new page that allows the search to be refined or limited, as implied by the name of the hyperlink. Here, the search will be limited by organism, so the Limited To pulldown is changed to Organism, and the word methanothermobacter is typed into the search box (Figure 3.13). Clicking Go will now return all of the entries in which *Methanothermobacter* is the organism (282 entries). What has happened at this point is that two independent searches have been performed. The results from the first search now can be combined with those from the second by clicking on the History hyperlink below the text box, resulting in a list of recent queries (Figure 3.14). The list shows the individual queries, whether those queries were field limited, the time at which the queries were performed, and how many entries each individual query returned. To combine two separate queries into

one, the user simply combines the query by search number; in this case, because the queries are numbered #38 and #39, the syntax would be #38 AND #39. Clicking Go from this view shows the user the three entries that are common to the two queries, in the now-familiar nucleotide summary format (Figure 3.15).

Structures. The last part of Entrez to be discussed here deals with three-dimensional structures. Structure queries can be performed directly by specifying Structure in the Search pull-down menu. For example, suppose that one wishes to find out information about the structure of the high mobility group (HMG) box B from rat, whose PDB accession number is 1HMF. Typing 1HMF into the query box leads the user to the structure summary page for 1HMG, which has a decidedly different format from any of the pages seen so far (Figure 3.16). This page shows details from the header of the source MMDB document (which is derived from PDB) and links to PubMed and to the taxonomy of the source organism.

FIGURE 3.10   The ClinicalTrials.gov page showing all actively recruiting clinical trials relating to colorectal neoplasms. Information on each trial, including the principal investigator of the trial and qualification criteria, can be found by clicking on the name of the trial.

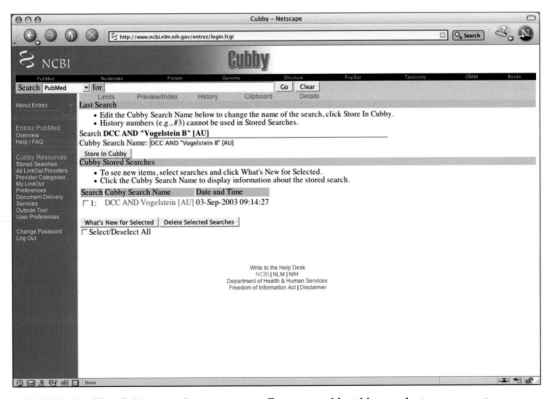

FIGURE 3.11   The Cubby search storage area. Entrez provides this search storage area to save queries, allowing them to be recalled and updated without having to perform the query again. See text for details.

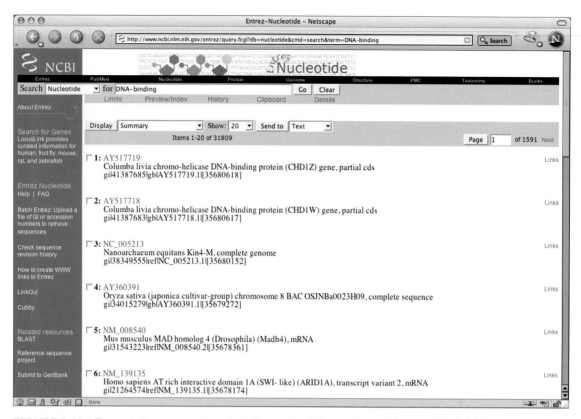

FIGURE 3.12 Formulating a search against the nucleotide portion of Entrez. The initial query is shown in the text box near the top of the window (DNA-binding), and the nucleotide entries matching the query are displayed below. See text for details.

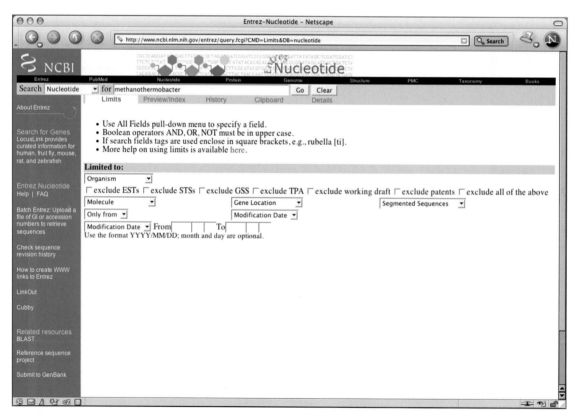

FIGURE 3.13 Using the Limits feature of Entrez to limit a search to a particular organism. See text for details.

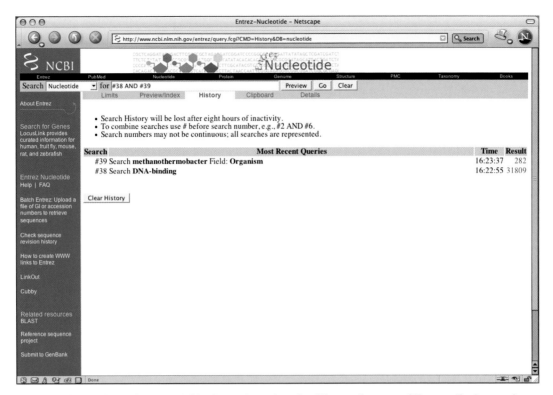

FIGURE 3.14 Combining individual queries using the History feature of Entrez. Each search performed in the last hour is given a number, and the searches can be combined using the search numbers and the Boolean operators *and, or,* or *not.* See text for details.

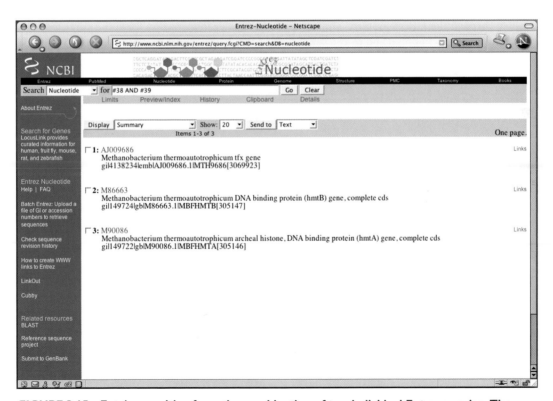

FIGURE 3.15 Entries resulting from the combination of two individual Entrez queries. The command producing the results is shown in the text box near the top of the window (#38 AND #39). The numbers correspond to those assigned to the previously performed searches listed in Figure 3.13. See text for details.

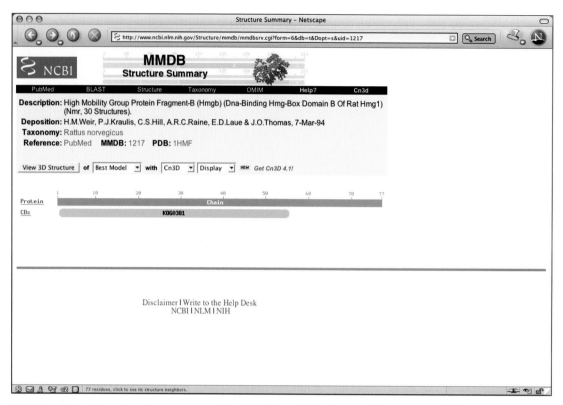

FIGURE 3.16 **The structure summary for 1HMF, resulting from a direct query of the structures accessible through the Entrez system. The entry shows header information from the corresponding MMDB entry, links to PubMed and to the taxonomy of the source organism. Structure neighbors, as assessed by VAST, can be found by clicking on the long purple bar next to the Protein key. The structure itself can be viewed by clicking on the View 3D Structure button, spawning the Cn3D viewer.**

The long, purple bar next to the Protein label would take the user to related structures, as assessed by VAST. For a user interested in gleaning initial impressions about the shape of a protein, the Cn3D plug-in, invoked by clicking the View 3D Structure button, provides a powerful interface (Figure 3.17), giving far more information than anyone could deduce from simply examining a string of letters (the sequence of the protein). The protein may be rotated freely by clicking and holding down the mouse key while the cursor is within the structure window and then dragging. Users are able to zoom in on particular parts of the structure or to change the coloring of the figure, to identify specific structural features of the protein. For instance, in Figure 3.17, the Spacefilling rendering option and the Charge color option have been chosen. Positive charges are in blue and negative charges are in red, and one can see "blue residues" poking into the concave space; this is the space into which DNA docks, and one can surmise that the blue, positively charged residues are involved in binding to the negatively charged backbone of the DNA molecule.

Finally, at any point along the way in using Entrez, if there are partial or complete search results that the user wishes to retain while moving on to a new query, the user can take advantage of an electronic "clipboard," accessible through the Send To pull-down at the top of all Entrez pages. This stores the results of the current query, which the user can return to by again clicking on the Clipboard link. The clipboard holds a maximum of 500 items, and the items are held in memory for one hour.

GENE-CENTRIC INFORMATION RETRIEVAL: LOCUSLINK

The Entrez system revolves necessarily around the individual entries making up the various component databases that are part of the Entrez search space. Another way to think about this search space is to organize it around discrete genetic loci. NCBI LocusLink does just this, providing a single query interface to various types of information regarding a given genetic locus, such as

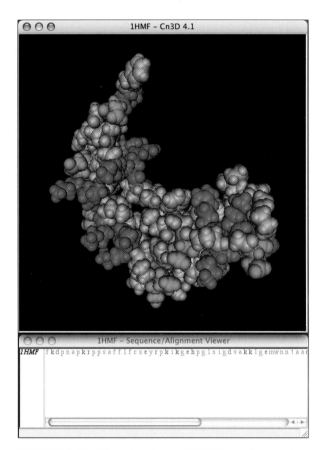

FIGURE 3.17 **The structure of 1HMF rendered using Cn3D version 3.1, an interactive molecular viewer that acts as a plug-in to Web Entrez. Cn3D can also be used as a stand-alone application. In the upper window, the structure is shown in spacefilling style, with the coloring being indicated by charge (red, negative; blue, positive). The lower window shows the sequence of 1HMF, with the coloring scheme mirroring that in the structure window. See text for details.**

phenotypes, map locations, and homologies to other genes. The LocusLink search space currently includes information from a number of organisms, including humans, mice, rats, fruit flies, and zebrafish.

LocusLink queries are very easy to perform, requiring only the name of the gene of interest or the gene symbol. Using the gene for multiple endocrine neoplasia as an example, a LocusLink query begins by the user simply typing the name of the gene into the query box appearing at the top of the LocusLink home page. Alternatively, the user could select the gene of interest from an alphabetical list. The query on MEN1 returns six LocusLink entries, from human, mouse, rat, and *Drosophila* (Figure 3.18). In this view, the user is given the Locus ID in the first column; the Locus ID is intended to be a unique, stable identifier that is associated with this gene locus. Clicking on the Locus ID for the human MEN1

entry (4221) produces the LocusLink report view, as shown in Figure 3.19. The report view begins with links to external sources of information, shown as colored buttons at the top of the page. The links available will change from entry to entry, depending on what information is available for the gene of interest. A complete list of connected data sources is given in the LocusLink online documentation. Continuing down the report view is a section marked Overview, where the user is presented with some basic information about the gene, the official gene symbol and name, as well as a brief summary of the function of the gene. The section immediately following is marked Function and shows the results of an effort called GeneRIF, for "Gene References into Function." GeneRIF is a public, curated annotation effort intended to provide additional information on genes of interest in LocusLink; clicking on the GeneRIF number takes the user to the corresponding PubMed citation. Scrolling down would bring the user to additional sections devoted to mapping information, relationships to other organisms, and associated RefSeq entries.

Returning to the view in Figure 3.18, note that there are rows of colored alphabet blocks to the right of each entry. These blocks are hyperlinked and allow the user to find all available information on the particular gene of interest. In turn, these links connect to the following NCBI resources:

▸ **P**, for PubMed bibliographic entries corresponding to the locus

▸ **O**, for the OMIM summary on this locus

▸ **R**, for the RefSeq entry corresponding to the locus

▸ **G**, for the individual GenBank entries related to the locus; these entries correspond to the RefSeq entry, as shown in the LocusLink report view

▸ **H**, for HomoloGene. HomoloGene includes curated and calculated orthologs and homologs for genes from human, mouse, rat, and zebrafish. The curated orthologs come from the Mouse Genome Database (MGD; Bult et al., 2004), the Zebrafish Information Resource (ZFIN; Sprague et al., 2003), and published reports in the literature. Calculated homologs and orthologs are derived from direct nucleotide sequence comparisons between all UniGene clusters from each pair of organisms.

▸ **U**, if this locus is part of a UniGene cluster

▸ **V**, for variation data on this locus contained within dbSNP (Chapter 7).

When following either the PubMed or GenBank links, the user is, in essence, returned to the Entrez search space, enabling the user to take advantage of Entrez's navigational features once again. Although all

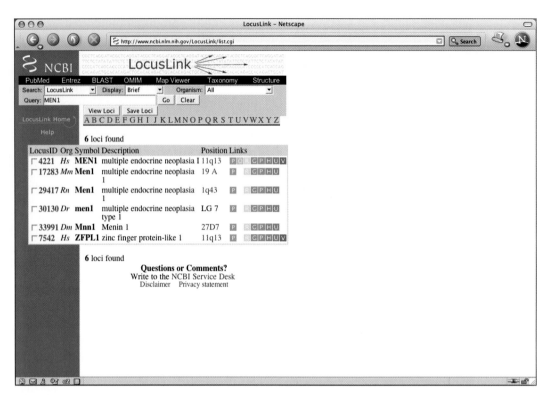

FIGURE 3.18 Results of a LocusLink query, using MEN1 as the search term. The report shows five entries corresponding to MEN1 in human (*Hs*), mouse (*Mm*), rat (*Rn*), zebrafish (*Dr*), and *Drosophila* (*Dm*). The sixth entry is for a human zinc finger protein-like 1 locus that is related to MEN1. A series of colored alphabet blocks is found to the right of each entry, providing a jumping-off point to numerous other sources of data; these links are described in the main text.

of these component resources can be accessed through a LocusLink search, each one of these databases can be queried individually, and the URLs for all of these resources are provided in the list at the end of this chapter.

SEQUENCE DATABASES BEYOND NCBI

Although it may seem from this discussion that NCBI is the center of the sequence universe, many specialized sequence databases throughout the world serve specific groups in the scientific community. Often, these databases provide additional information not available elsewhere, such as phenotypes, experimental conditions, strain crosses, and map features. These data are of great importance to these groups within the greater scientific community, inasmuch as they can influence rational experimental design, but such types of data do not always fit neatly within the confines of the NCBI data model. Development of specialized databases necessarily ensued, but these specialized databases are intended to be used as an adjunct to GenBank, not in place of it. It is impossible to discuss all of these kinds of databases here; however, to emphasize the sheer num-

ber of such databases that exist, *Nucleic Acids Research* devotes its first issue every year to papers describing these databases.

An excellent representative example of a specialized organismal database is the Mouse Genome Database (MGD). Housed at the Jackson Laboratory, MGD provides a curated, comprehensive knowledgebase on the laboratory mouse and is an integral part of their overall Mouse Genome Informatics (MGI) resource. MGD entries provide information on genes, genetic markers, mutant phenotypes, and homologies to other organisms, as well as extensive linkage, cytogenetic, genetic, and physical mapping data. Examples of the types of information available through MGD can be found in Chapter 2.

Another widely used organismal database is FlyBase, which is devoted to *Drosophila* genetic, genomic, and molecular data. FlyBase, which is overseen by the FlyBase Consortium, provides information on genes, genomic clones, mutant alleles, chromosomal aberrations, and gene products. Genetic, cytological, and physical mapping information is available, as well as extensive functional, developmental, and expression data. One of the most valuable aspects of FlyBase is the information available regarding the *Drosophila*

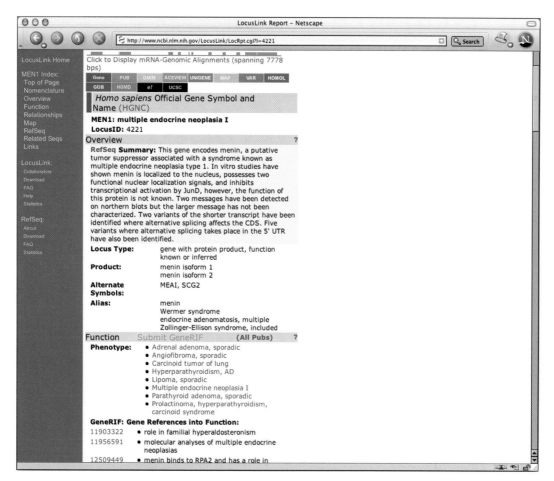

FIGURE 3.19 The LocusLink report for human MEN1. The report is divided into sections devoted to an overview of basic information, functional information, mapping information, relationships to other organisms, and associated RefSeq entries. See text for details.

community itself; for example, there is an address book of *Drosophila* researchers, a comprehensive bibliography of *Drosophila* publications, and information on *Drosophila* stocks that can be obtained through various sources. Data can be searched directly through a Web interface or can be downloaded as flatfiles via FTP. For example, searching by gene symbol and using `capu` as the search term brings up a record for a gene named cappuccino, which is required for the proper polarity of the developing *Drosophila* oocyte (Emmons et al., 1995). Calling up the gene region map view generates a map showing the location of cappuccino and other genes in that immediate area, and users can click on any of the elements in the map to bring up detailed information (Figure 3.20). The view can be changed to display or hide various genomic features through the use of the Display Settings check-off boxes found below the map (not shown). Tiling bacterial artificial chromosome (BAC) in situ images are also provided, corresponding to tiling BACs shown in the map view.

Another long-standing resource devoted to a specific organism in the *Saccharomyces* Genome Database (SGD), housed at the Stanford Human Genome Center. The database provides a very simple search interface that allows text-based searches by gene name, gene information, clone, protein information, sequence name, author name, or full text. For example, using `hho1` as the name of the gene to be searched for produces a window showing all known information on locus HHO1 (Figure 3.21). In addition to providing basic information on this gene in yeast, links also are provided to other databases, such as GenBank, the Munich Information Center for Protein Sequences (MIPS), and Swiss-Prot. Pull-down menus along the right-hand side of the window allow the user to retrieve information such as relevant references from the literature, protein sequence and structure data, various maps and displays, and data on any known interactions. Clicking on the map in the upper right-hand corner produces a graphical view of the area surrounding the locus of interest (Figure 3.22). Note the thick

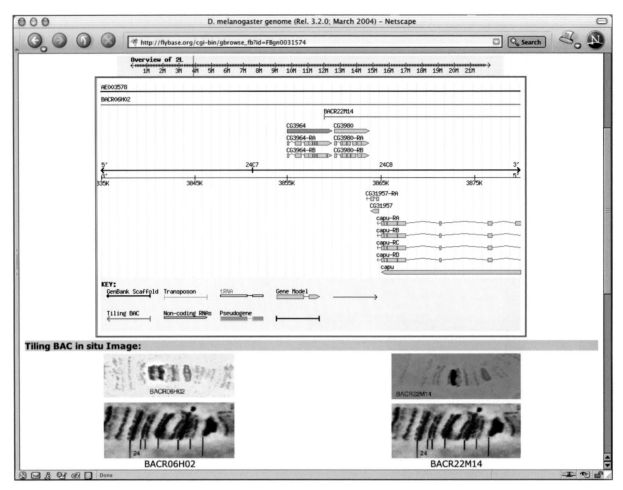

FIGURE 3.20 Genomic map view resulting from querying FlyBase for the cappuccino gene (capu in the figure, at the bottom of the map). Information on any of the map elements shown can be obtained by clicking directly on the map element. The tiling **BAC** in situ images correspond to the tiling BACs shown at the top of the map window (second and third lines).

bar at the top of the figure, which gives the position of the current view with respect to the centromere. Clicking on that bar allows the user to move along the chromosome, and clicking on any individual map element gives more detailed information about that particular entity.

MEDICAL DATABASES

Although the focus of this chapter (and the book in general) is on sequences, databases cataloging and organizing sequence information are not the only kinds of databases useful to the biologist. An example of such a non–sequence-based information resource that is tremendously useful in genomics is Online Mendelian Inheritance in Man (OMIM), the electronic version of the catalog of human genes and genetic disorders founded

by Victor McKusick at The Johns Hopkins University (McKusick, 1998; Hamosh et al., 2002; Baxevanis, 2003). OMIM provides concise textual information from the published literature on most human conditions having a genetic basis, as well as pictures illustrating the condition or disorder (where appropriate) and full citation information. Because the online version of OMIM is housed at NCBI, links to Entrez are provided from all references cited within each OMIM entry.

OMIM has a defined numbering system in which each entry is assigned a unique number, similar to an accession number, but certain positions within that number indicate information about the genetic disorder itself. For example, the first digit represents the mode of inheritance of the disorder: 1 stands for autosomal dominant, 2 for autosomal recessive, 3 for X-linked locus or phenotype, 4 for Y-linked locus or phenotype, 5 for mitochondrial, and 6 for autosomal locus or phenotype. (The

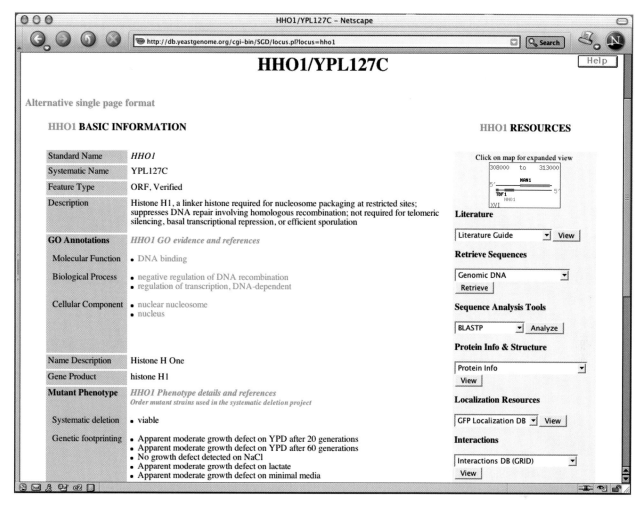

FIGURE 3.21 Basic information on the *HHO1* gene resulting from a simple SGD query. The information returned includes the name of the gene product, a brief description, Gene Ontology annotations, and information on mutant phenotypes. The pull-down menus to the right provide access to citations from the literature, sequence data, structural data, and additional information about the gene product's structure and function. Any available interaction data is available through the Interactions pull-down menu.

distinction between 1 or 2 and 6 is that entries cataloged before May 1994 were assigned either a 1 or 2, whereas entries after that date were assigned a 6 regardless of whether the mode of inheritance was dominant or recessive.) An asterisk preceding a number indicates that the phenotype caused by the gene at this locus is not influenced by genes at other loci; however, the disorder itself may be caused by mutations at multiple loci. Disorders for which no mode of inheritance has been determined do not carry asterisks. Finally, a pound sign (#) indicates that the phenotype is caused by two or more genetic mutations.

OMIM searches are very easy to perform. The search engine executes a simple query based on one or more words typed into a search window. A list of documents containing the query word is returned, and users can select one or more disorders from this list and look at the full text for that OMIM entry. The entries include information such as the gene symbol, alternate names for the disease, a description of the disease (including mapping information), a clinical synopsis, and references. A particularly useful feature is lists of allelic variants; a short description is given after each allelic variant of the clinical or biochemical outcome of that particular mutation. There are currently more than 1000 gene entries containing at least one allelic variant that either causes or is associated with a discrete phenotype in humans. Figure 3.23 shows an example of an allelic variant list, in this case for mutations observed in patients with McKusick-Kaufman syndrome (MKKS).

Features around YPL127C on chromosome XVI

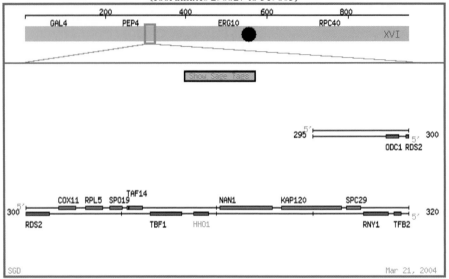

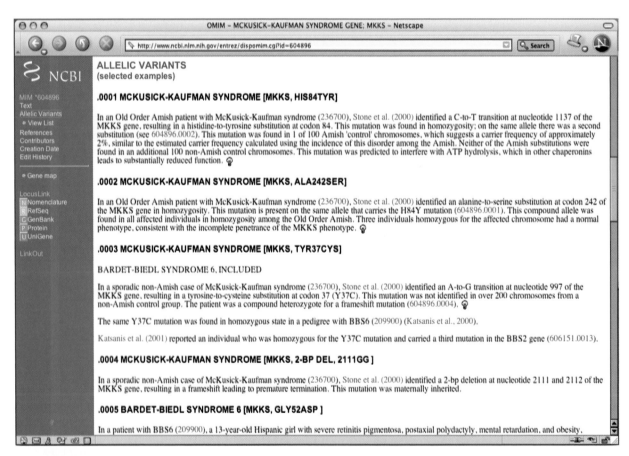

FIGURE 3.22 A chromosomal features map, which is obtained by clicking on the map shown in the upper right of Figure 3.20. Chromosome **XVI** is shown at the top of the figure, with the exploded region highlighted by a box. Most items are clickable, returning detailed information about that particular map element.

FIGURE 3.23 An example of a list of allelic variants that can be obtained through **OMIM**. The figure shows the list of allelic variants for **MKKS** (OMIM 604896).

▌SUMMARY

As alluded to in the introduction to this chapter, the sequence information space available to investigators will continue to expand at breakneck speed, with the size of GenBank doubling roughly once per year. Although the sheer magnitude of data can present a conundrum to the inexperienced user, mastery of the techniques covered in this chapter will allow researchers in all biological disciplines to make the best use of these data. The movement of modern science to more sequence-based approaches underscores the idea that both laboratory-based and computationally based strategies will be absolutely necessary to carry out cutting-edge research. In the same way that investigators are trained in basic biochemistry and molecular biology techniques, a basic understanding of bioinformatic techniques as part of the biologist's arsenal will be absolutely indispensable in the future. As is undoubtedly apparent by this point, there is no substitute for actually placing one's hands on the keyboard to learn how to search and use genomic sequence data effectively. Readers are strongly encouraged to take advantage of the resources presented here, to grow in confidence and capability by working with the available tools, and to begin to apply bioinformatic methods and strategies toward advancing their own research interests.

▌WORKED EXAMPLE

This Worked Example centers on a fictitious scenario, where a story on the evening news relayed recent developments on the genetics of colorectal cancer. The news story was short on specifics, but did relay that the principal investigator was (once again) Bert Vogelstein at The Johns Hopkins University School of Medicine. In considering each part of the Worked Example, use the results from the preceding part to answer the question; issue a query *only* for part 1.

1. How many of the papers that Dr. Vogelstein has written on the subject of colorectal neoplasms are available through PubMed?

   To answer this question, issue a query against PubMed from the NCBI Home Page. Change the Search pull-down to PubMed, and use `"Vogelstein B" [AU] AND "colorectal neoplasms" [MH]` as the search query. The `[AU]` restricts the search to where Dr. Vogelstein is an author (rather than cited or mentioned in the text), and the `[MH]` limits the search by subject. The search returned 161 entries at the time of this writing.

2. A paper by Hedrick et al. describes the role of the DCC gene product in cellular differentiation and colorectal tumorigenesis. Based on *this* study, what is the chromosomal location of the DCC gene?

   From the results list returned in question 1, look for the paper where Hedrick is the first author. This will require moving

through several pages of the output. The paper in question was published in *Genes and Development* in 1994 and is entitled "The DCC Gene Product in Cellular Differentiation and Colorectal Tumorigenesis." Clicking on the author list produces the Abstract view, and the abstract indicates that *DCC* is on the long arm of chromosome 18 (18q).

3. *DCC* codes for a cell-surface localized protein involved in tumor suppression. Based on the Swiss-Prot entry for the *DCC precursor*, which residues comprise the signal sequence?

   Clicking on the Links hyperlink to the right of this entry produces the Links pop-up menu. Clicking on Protein takes the user to four protein entries that have been linked to the Hedrick paper. The question specifically asks for information from the Swiss-Prot entry for the *DCC* precursor; the only entry from Swiss-Prot in this list is P43136, and examination of the definition line shows that this entry does describe the *DCC* precursor. Clicking on the accession number brings the user to the protein entry. Information on particular parts of the protein can be found by scrolling down to the feature table, denoted by the `FEATURES` key in the left-hand column. Within the first several lines is a feature key marked `Region`, with a location `1..25` and a region name of `Signal`. This means that the signal sequence, which is cleaved off in the mature protein, is made up of the first 25 residues of the precursor.

▌PROBLEM SET

1. The OMIM indicates that the gene *SRY* encodes a transcription factor that is a member of the high-mobility group-box family of DNA binding proteins. Mutations in this gene give rise to XY females with gonadal dysgenesis, as well as translocation of part of the Y chromosome containing this gene to the X chromosome in XX males.

   a. An allelic variant of *SRY* causing sex reversal with partial ovarian function has been cataloged in OMIM. What was the mutation at the amino acid level, and what is observed in XY mice carrying this mutation?

   b. Follow the Gene Map link in the left sidebar to access the MIM gene map. Based on the MIM gene map, one other gene is found at the same cytogenetic map location. What is the name of this gene, and what methods were used to map the gene to this location?

   c. From the OMIM entry, follow the link in the left sidebar to UniGene, then continue on to HomoloGene. Curated orthologs exist for human *SRY* and are cataloged in the Mouse Genome Database at the Jackson Laboratory. A paper published by Bowles in 2000 documents orthology through amino acid sequence comparison between *SRY* in the human, mouse, and what other organisms?

   d. Following the MGI:98660 link brings the user to a detail page for the *SRY* gene in the mouse. The page catalogs one spontaneous phenotypic allele. What is the name of the allele, and what is significant about the observed deletion?

2. A very active area of commercial research involves the identification and development of new sweeteners for use by the food industry. Although traditional sweeteners such as table

sugar (sucrose) are carbohydrates, most current research instead is focusing on proteins that have an intrinsically sweet taste. Because these sweet-tasting proteins are much sweeter than their carbohydrate counterparts, they are, in essence, calorie free, because so little is used to achieve a sweet taste in food. The most successful example of such a protein is aspartame; however, aspartame is synthetic and does not occur in nature. Alternate, natural protein sources are being investigated, including a sweet-tasting protein called monellin.

a. According to Ogata et al., how much sweeter than ordinary sugar is monellin on both a molar and a weight basis?
b. Based on the Swiss-Prot entry for monellin chain B from serendipity berry (P02882), how many α-helices and β-strands does this protein possess?
c. What residue (amino acid and position), when blocked, abolishes monellin's sweet taste?

INTERNET RESOURCES

BLAST	http://www.ncbi.nlm.nih.gov/BLAST
Clinical Trials	http://clinicaltrials.gov
Cn3D	http://www.ncbi.nlm.nih.gov/Structure/CN3D/cn3d.shtml
Cubby	http://www.ncbi.nlm.nih.gov/entrez/query/static/help/pmhelp.html#Cubby
dbSNP	http://www.ncbi.nlm.nih.gov/SNP
DDBJ	http://www.ddbj.nig.ac.jp
EMBL	http://www.ebi.ac.uk/embl/index.html
Entrez	http://www.ncbi.nlm.nih.gov/Entrez
FlyBase	http://www.flybase.org
GenBank	http://www.ncbi.nlm.nih.gov
HomoloGene	http://www.ncbi.nlm.nih.gov/HomoloGene
InterPro	http://www.ebi.ac.uk/interpro
LocusLink	http://www.ncbi.nlm.nih.gov/LocusLink
MEDLINEplus	http://www.nlm.nih.gov/medlineplus
MGD	http://www.informatics.jax.org
MIPS	http://mips.gsf.de
NAR Database Issue	http://nar.oupjournals.org
NCBI Bookshelf	http://www.ncbi.nlm.nih.gov/entrez/query.fcgi?db=books
NHGRI	http://www.genome.gov
NLM Gateway	http://gateway.nlm.nih.gov
OMIM	http://www.ncbi.nlm.nih.gov/Omim
PDB	http://www.rcsb.org/pdb/
RefSeq	http://www.ncbi.nlm.nih.gov/RefSeq
SGD	http://www.yeastgenome.org
UniGene	http://www.ncbi.nlm.nih.gov/UniGene
ZFIN	http://zfin.org

FURTHER READING

BAXEVANIS, A. D. (2003). Searching Online Mendelian Inheritance in Man (OMIM) for information on genetic loci involved in human disease. *Curr Topics Bioinformatics* 1.2.1–1.2.15. A protocol-driven description of how to perform OMIM searches, including discussion of external resources such as MEDLINEplus and actively-recruiting clinical trials.

OSTELL, J. (2003). The Entrez search and retrieval system. In: *The NCBI Handbook* Chapter 15. (Available electronically at http://www.ncbi.nlm.nih.gov/books/bv.fcgi?rid=handbook.chapter.588.) A description of the design principles underlying Entrez and how disparate data types are integrated for seamless navigation.

REFERENCES

ALBERTS, B., BRAY, D., LEWIS, J., RAFF, M., ROBERTS, K., AND WATSON, J. D. (1994). *Molecular Biology of the Cell* (Garland Publishing, New York).

ALTSCHUL, S., GISH, W., MILLER, W., MYERS, E., AND LIPMAN, D. (1990). Basic local alignment search tool. *J. Mol. Biol.* 215, 403–410.

BAXEVANIS, A. D. (2003). Searching Online Mendelian Inheritance in Man (OMIM) for information on genetic loci involved in human disease. *Curr Topics Bioinformatics* 1.2.1–1.2.15.

BULT, C. J., BLAKE, J. A., RICHARDSON, J. E., KADIN, J. A., EPPIG, J. T., BALDARELLI, R. M., BARSANTI, K., BAYA, M., BEAL, J. S., BODDY, W. J., et al. (2004). The Mouse Genome Database (MGD): integrating biology with the genome. *Nucleic Acids Res.* 32, D476–D481.

CHO, K. R., OLINER, J. D., SIMONS, J. W., HEDRICK, L., FEARON, E. R., PREISINGER, A. C., HEDGE, P., SILVERMAN, G. A., AND VOGELSTEIN, B. (1994). The DCC gene: structural analysis and mutations in colorectal carcinomas. *Genomics* 19, 525–531.

EMMONS, S., PHAN, H., CALLEY, J., CHEN, W., JAMES, B., AND MANSEAU, L. (1995). Cappucino, a *Drosophila* maternal effect gene required for polarity of the egg and embryo, is related to the vertebrate limb deformity locus. *Genes Dev.* 9, 2484–2494.

GIBRAT, J.-F., MADEJ, T., AND BRYANT, S. (1996). Surprising similarities instructure comparison. *Curr. Opin. Struct. Biol.* 6, 377–385.

HAMOSH, A., SCOTT, A.F., AMBERGER, J., BOCCHINI, C., VALLE, D., AND MCKUSICK, V.A. Online Mendelian Inheritance in Man (OMIM), a knowledgebase of human genes and genetic disorders. *Nucleic Acids Res.* 30, 52–55.

MADEJ, T., GIBRAT, J.-F., AND BRYANT, S. (1995). Threading a database of protein cores. *Proteins* 23, 356–369.

MCKUSICK, V. A. (1998). *Online Mendelian Inheritance in Man: A Catalog of Human Genes and Genetic Disorders*, 12th ed. (The Johns Hopkins University Press, Baltimore).

SPRAGUE, J., CLEMENTS, D., CONLIN, T., EDWARDS, P., FRAZER, K., SCHAPER, K., SEGERDELL, E., SONG, P., SPRUNGER, B., AND WESTERFIELD, M. (2003). The Zebrafish Information Network (ZFIN): the zebrafish model organism database. *Nucl. Acids Res.* 31, 241–243.

WILBUR, W., AND COFFEE, L. (1994). The effectiveness of document neighboring in search enhancement. *Process Manage.* 30, 253–266.

WILBUR, W., AND YANG, Y. (1996). An analysis of statistical term strength and its use in the indexing and retrieval of molecular biology texts. *Comput. Biol. Med.* 26, 209–222.

▌ KEY TERMS

BLAST
Cn3D
Cubby
DDBJ
dbSNP
EMBL
Entrez
GenBank
HomoloGene
InterPro
LocusLink
MEDLINEplus
MGD
NCBI Bookshelf
neighboring
OMIM
PDB
RefSeq
synteny
UniGene
VAST

This chapter was written by Dr. Andreas D. Baxevanis in his private capacity. No official support or endorsement by the National Institutes of Health or the United States Department of Health and Human Services is intended or should be inferred.

Genomic Databases

TYRA G. WOLFSBERG

Bioinformatics: A Practical Guide to the Analysis of Genes and Proteins, Third Edition, edited by
Andreas D. Baxevanis and B.F. Francis Ouellette.
ISBN 0-471-47878-4 Copyright © 2005 John Wiley & Sons, Inc.

▮ INTRODUCTION

The first complete sequence of a eukaryotic genome, that of *Saccharomyces cerevisiae*, was published in 1996 (Goffeau et al., 1996). The chromosomes of this organism, which range in size from 270 to 1500 Kb, presented an immediate challenge in data management, because the upper limit for single database entries in Gen-Bank at the time was 350 Kb. As a response to this yeast sequence, as well as to other chromosome and genome-length sequences being deposited into GenBank around that time, the National Center for Biotechnology Information (NCBI) established the Genomes division of Entrez (Benson et al., 1997). Entries in this division were organized around a reference sequence onto which all other sequences from that organism were aligned. Because these reference sequences have no size limit, virtual reference sequences of large genomes or chromosomes could be assembled from shorter GenBank sequences. For partially sequenced chromosomes, NCBI developed methods to integrate genetic, physical, and cytogenetic maps onto the framework of the whole chromosome. Thus, Entrez Genomes was able to provide the first graphical views of genomic sequence data.

The finishing of the working draft of the human genome in February 2001 (Lander et al., 2001) provided a new data management challenge because, for the first time, virtual reference sequences could be created for each human chromosome, ranging in size from 46 to 246 Mb. In response to this challenge, the NCBI created the first version of the human Map Viewer. Around the same time, the University of California at Santa Cruz (UCSC) was developing its own human Genome Browser, based on software originally designed for displaying the much smaller *Caenorhabditis elegans* genome (Kent & Zahler, 2000), and Ensembl was producing a system to annotate automatically the human genome sequence as well as to store and visualize the data. The three genome browsers all came online at approximately the same time, and researchers began using them to help navigate the human genome (Wolfsberg et al., 2003; Wolfsberg et al., 2002). Today, each site provides free access not only to human sequence data, but also to other assembled genomic sequences, including mouse and rat.

The backbone of each browser is an assembled genomic sequence. The human genome was sequenced in a clone-by-clone shotgun sequencing strategy (Green, 2001) and was declared complete in April 2003. First, a bacterial artificial chromosome (BAC) tiling map was constructed for each human chromosome. Then each BAC was sequenced by a shotgun sequencing approach. The sequences of individual BACs were deposited into the high-throughput genomic (HTG) division of GenBank as they became available. First UCSC, beginning in May 2000 (Kent & Haussler, 2001), and then NCBI (Kitts, 2003) assembled these BAC sequences into longer contigs. These contigs, which contained gaps and regions of uncertain order, became the basis of the three original genome browsers. Over time, as the genome sequence was finished, the human genome assembly was updated every few months. UCSC stopped producing assemblies in December 2001, and it is the NCBI assembly that is now displayed by all three browsers. Now that the sequence has been declared complete, the human genome will be reassembled, or built, by NCBI approximately once per year to take into account sequence updates and improvements in the assembly algorithms. The sequence is known by its build number at NCBI, and by a date at UCSC.

The National Human Genome Research Institute at the National Institutes of Health funds genome sequencing projects for a number of other organisms in addition to human. The mouse (Waterston et al., 2002) and rat (Gibbs et al., 2004) genomes are being sequenced by a hybrid clone-by-clone shotgun sequencing and whole-genome shotgun sequencing approach. BAC clones are available in the HTG division of Gen-Bank, whereas shotgun sequences are in the NCBI or Ensembl Trace Archives. NCBI has been assembling the mouse genomic sequence, whereas the rat sequence assembly is provided by the Atlas group at the Baylor Human Genome Sequencing Center, as part of the Rat Genome Sequencing Consortium. These two genomes, as well as many others, even in their draft state, are available from the three genome browsers. However, not all genomes are available on all browsers. For example, at the time of this writing, *Anopheles gambiae* is available only at NCBI and Ensembl, whereas *Gallus gallus* is displayed at UCSC and on the preview Ensembl browser.

Each of the three genome browsers provides their own annotation of the common assembled sequence. Because these annotation pipelines require different amounts of time to complete, the three browsers may not always be displaying the same version of the genome assembly. In general, UCSC is the first to display a new assembly with annotations, followed by NCBI and then Ensembl. At present, UCSC is the only one of the three sites to provide a graphical interface to older versions of the assembly. Because the assemblies of unfinished genomes may change frequently and without notice, users must take note of the assembly version before comparing data between browsers.

The browsers all provide the same types of information. One main focus of each browser is to display the location of genes, both known and predicted. However, the three browsers may use different sources of mRNA for their known genes, different methods to align the mRNAs to the genome to determine gene locations, as well as different gene prediction tools. The browsers also provide alignments of other sequence data with the genome, such as ESTs and SNPs, the location of STS markers (see Box 1.1), as well as homologous sequences from other organisms. All three browsers provide a Web interface to query the data and navigate within it. The most common way to view the data is in graphical format. Sequences and annotations also can be retrieved in text format for those wishing to carry out their own calculations. Each browser also provides a sequence search tool for accessing the data.

This chapter presents general guidelines for accessing the genome sequence and annotations using the three genome browsers. The examples center on the genomic context around the human *ACHE* gene at all three sites, although we come to that region using different types of queries. Although the same analysis could be carried out with each browser, we have chosen to use different examples at the three sites to illustrate different types of questions that a researcher may want to ask.

UCSC

The UCSC Genome Browser is produced by the University of California, Santa Cruz Genome Bioinformatics Group (Karolchik et al., 2004 Kent et al., 2002; Karolchik & Kent, 2003). The group has developed browsers for 10 eukaryotes and one virus, as well as for a set of sequences derived from the same targeted genomic regions in multiple vertebrates. The UCSC Genome Browser presents genomic annotation in the form of tracks. Each track provides a different type of feature, from genes to CpG islands (regions with high density of CpG nucleotides) to SNPs to predicted gene regulatory regions. Some tracks are created by the UCSC Genome Bioinformatics team, whereas others are provided by outside members of the bioinformatics community. Although all browsers include at least one gene or gene prediction track, other tracks are specific to individual species. The UCSC team announces new genome assemblies and annotation tracks on their genome mailing list. Users also submit questions to this list, and most queries are answered within a day.

The UCSC Genome Bioinformatics home page provides a lengthy News section that details new tools and highlights new genome sequence assemblies. A frequently updated Help page describes the tracks and provides navigation tips. All sequence and annotation data can be downloaded in text format by following the Downloads link. The Table Browser provides an alternate form of access to data in the Genome Browser, because it retrieves DNA sequence data or annotation data for individual tracks, or for intersections or unions of tracks, over specified regions of the genome (Karolchik et al., 2004). UCSC provides two main entry points into the Genome Browser itself. Users starting with a nucleotide or protein sequence would use an alignment program developed at UCSC called BLAT (Chapter 11). Text-based queries are formulated by following the Genome Browser link to the Genome Browser Gateway (Figure 4.1).

On the Gateway page, users select the genome and assembly version to be searched. For most organisms, the two or three most recent assemblies are available from this page; older assemblies are at the UCSC archive Web site. The version of the assembly displayed on the Gateway page defaults to the last one viewed on that computer. In the position box, the user enters a text query, such as an accession number, gene symbol, or chromosome position. If the query maps to a unique position in the genome, such as a query for a particular chromosome and band number, the Submit button links directly to the Genome Browser. If the system finds more than one hit for the query, such as when the gene symbol ACHE is searched for on the July 2003 version of the human genome assembly, the resulting page will contain a list of results (Figure 4.2). The results are grouped by category. The Known Genes, RefSeq Genes, and Human Aligned mRNAs represent the results of using BLAT to align mRNA sequences from different databases to the assembled human genome.

Figure 4.3 shows the genomic context of one of the *ACHE* transcripts, the RefSeq NM_000665. Across the top of the display are the navigation controls. The arrows move the display to the left and right, whereas the other buttons zoom in and out on the chromosome. The *base* button zooms in so far that individual nucleotides are displayed, whereas the zoom out 10 × button will show the entire chromosome if it is selected a few times. The position box indicates the current genomic region and also serves as a search box into which a new query can be entered. The links on the upper blue bar provide access to commonly used tools. To convert the coordinates of the displayed region to coordinates on a different assembly of that genome, click the Convert button. The PDF/PS link provides PostScript or PDF versions of the browser window. The Ensembl and Map View links provide the Ensembl and NCBI view of this genomic region, whereas Tables goes to the Table Browser. The DNA link is described below. Detailed documentation is provided through the Guide link.

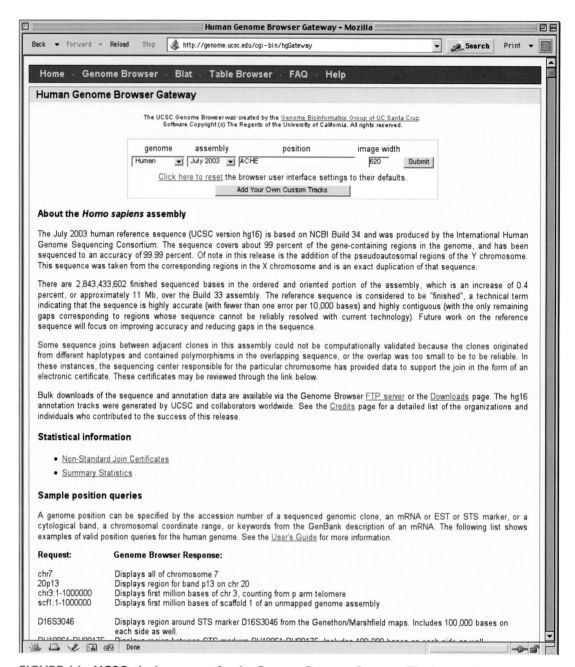

FIGURE 4.1   UCSC: the home page for the Genome Browser Gateway. The browser is set to query for the term *ACHE* in the July 2003 assembly of the human genome.

Each annotation track is depicted horizontally. The view in Figure 4.3 shows the default tracks, but other tracks can be added or removed by selecting from the list at the bottom of the window. The tracks on the July 2003 human assembly can be divided into seven categories: mapping and sequencing, genes and gene predictions, mRNA and ESTs, expression and regulation, comparative genomics, data from the Encyclopedia of DNA Elements (ENCODE) project, and variation and repeats.

Because many of these tracks represent the results of active research programs, other organisms, and even other assemblies of the same genome, have different tracks. Tracks can be hidden in hide mode, shown in detail in full mode, or condensed for ease of viewing in dense, squish, or pack mode. Clicking on a track name links to a description of the track. To change the display, select a different set of tracks and click the Refresh button. To restore the default settings, click Reset All. Hiding

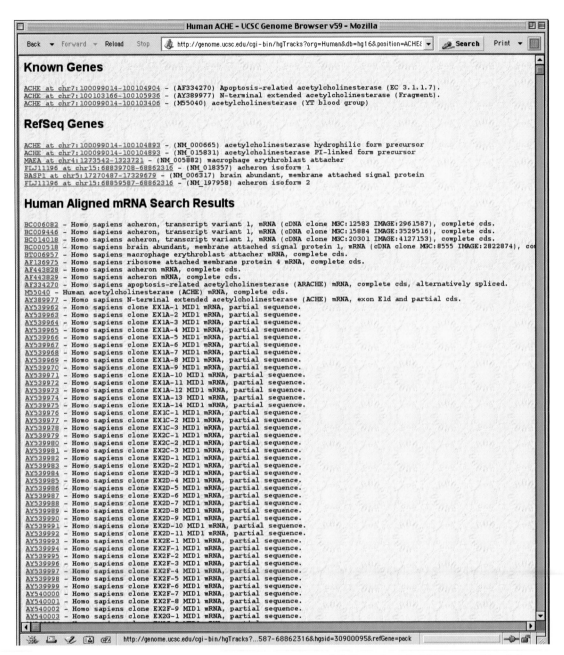

FIGURE 4.2   UCSC: the results of querying for the term *ACHE* on the July 2003 assembly of the human genome. Known Genes are protein coding genes based on proteins from Swiss-Prot, TrEMBL, and TrEMBL-New and their corresponding mRNAs from GenBank. RefSeq Genes are protein-coding genes from NCBI's mRNA reference sequences. Human aligned mRNAs are other mRNAs from GenBank.

unneeded tracks will reduce the time it takes to load the graphic into the Web browser. Track settings persist from session to session on the same Web browser. If the default settings are not reset, the display may appear differently from that shown in Figure 4.3.

In this default view, the first two horizontal tracks display the position of view, in chromosomal (Base Position)

and cytogenetic (Chromosome Band) coordinates. STS markers are shown next in dense mode, all packed onto one line of the display. Gaps in the assembly, if present, are shown in the fourth track. The next two tracks show the position of known genes, the top one from proteins in Swiss-Prot, TrEMBL, and TrEMBL-New, and the bottom one from RefSeq mRNAs. Aligning regions (most likely

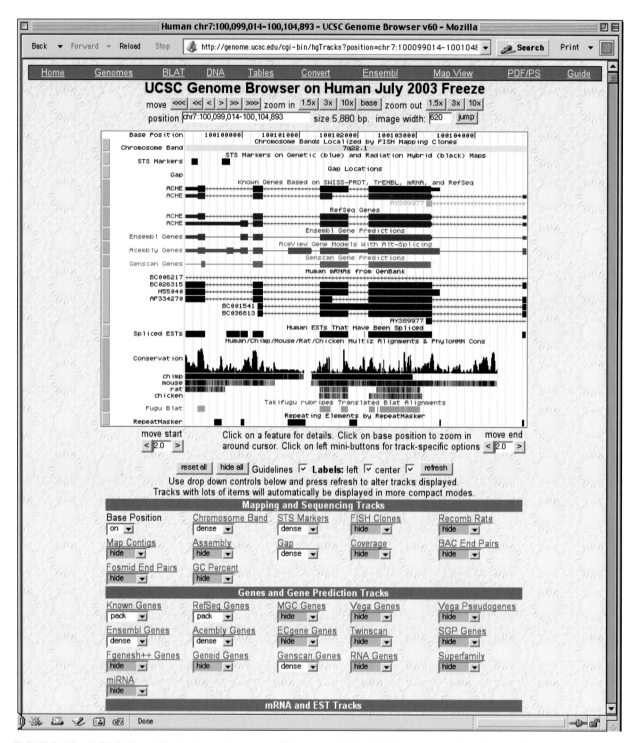

FIGURE 4.3   UCSC: the default view when the RefSeq gene NM_000665 is selected in Figure 4.2.

exons) are represented by boxes, whereas the lines represent gaps in the alignment (likely introns), with hatch marks showing the direction of transcription. Coding region exons are taller than untranslated regions. The RefSeq Genes track shows two alternatively spliced variants of *ACHE* that differ in their fifth exon, which is composed of coding sequence and a 3′ untranslated region. The next three tracks show Ensembl, Acembly, and GENSCAN gene predictions for this region of the genome. Other human mRNAs from GenBank are aligned to the genome in the tenth track. The EST track also is shown in dense mode with all aligning ESTs schematized on a single line. The degree of shading in the block corresponds to the number of ESTs that share that alignment. The Human/Mouse/Rat/Chicken track shows evolutionary conservation based on a phylogenetic hidden Markov model. Conservation scores are shown as a histogram whose height represents the degree of conservation between the four species. The next track shows regions where the *Takifugu rubripes* shotgun assembly can be aligned with the human genome, and the final track shows repetitive regions as annotated by Repeat-Masker. All tracks are described more detail by clicking on the track name at the bottom of Figure 4.3.

Details about a particular aligned item are obtained by clicking on the accession number of the item. The nature of the details depends on the track. For example, for mRNA and EST sequences, the resulting link contains information from GenBank, as well as a link to a sequence alignment between the transcript and the genome. The Known Genes track links to a gene description page that summarizes information from a number of outside sources. Figure 4.4a shows the upper portion of the gene description page for *ACHE*, including links to the mRNA sequence in GenBank, the protein sequence in Swiss-Prot, a summary provided by the NCBI Reference Sequence Project (Chapter 1), and an index of other data sources provided on the page. Figure 4.4b shows the results of viewing the Protein Structure portion of the page

One potential use for a Genome Browser is to see in graphical format any potential alternatively spliced transcripts. In Figure 4.3, the Spliced ESTs track is displayed in dense mode, with all EST alignments schematized on one line. The results of expanding this track to full mode are shown in Figure 4.5a. Each EST is shown as a separate line, with the boxes representing regions of alignment with the genome (likely exons), and a thin line representing a gap. Potential alternatively spliced transcripts (for example, ESTs CD014071 and CD014075) are evident when this track is compared with the RefSeq Genes track. In such a display, it can be difficult to know which ESTs may represent legitimate alternative splices, and which are artifacts of the cloning procedure. Certainly, a splicing pattern that appears in a single EST is more suspect than one that is shared by a few ESTs. In addition, the Alt-Splicing track, shown in Figure 4.5b, attempts to summarize splicing information by showing only exons and splice junctions that have an orthologous exon or splice junction in mouse, or that are present three or more times.

Other tracks highlight other interesting features of the human genome. Many of the genes and gene prediction tracks are contributed by groups outside of UCSC that are developing gene prediction algorithms. The comparative genomics section illustrates comparisons between

the human, mouse, rat, chicken, or chimp genomes, or a combination thereof. Experimental tracks designed by UCSC and outside researchers, which are still under development, may be viewed on a special site.

The Browser also provides several points from which to download sequence. Transcript sequence can be downloaded by clicking on a gene in the Known Genes or RefSeq Genes track. Annotations also can be highlighted directly on the genomic sequence by following the DNA link in the upper blue bar of the browser. By default, the currently viewed genomic region will be exported, but other regions can be entered as well. For example, one can, on Extended case/color options, make the default case Lower, can check the Underline box next to RefSeq Genes, and can check the Toggle Case box next to Human mRNAs (Figure 4.6a). The resulting page (Figure 4.6b) shows RefSeq exons in uppercase and other human mRNAs in underline. Some, but not all, of the exons between these two tracks have the same start and end points. Annotation tracks also can be colored by following the instructions below the selection boxes in Figure 4.6a.

All the annotation data can also be retrieved in text format by following the Tables link in the top blue bar from any Browser page. Biologists wanting to know the length of a gene or the exact size of an intron then can manipulate these files on their desktop computers. For the computationally savvy user, UCSC provides an FTP site through which sequences and annotations can be downloaded in bulk. The Genome Browser also allows researchers to display their data in the context of existing annotation. Data saved in a standard format can be uploaded into the Browser by following the Add Your Own Custom Tracks button in Figure 4.1. Uploaded annotations can be shared with colleagues who know the URL of the files.

NCBI

At the time of this writing, the Map Viewer of the NCBI at the National Institutes of Health provides maps for a total of 23 organisms, including six mammals (Wheeler et al., 2004; Wolfsberg, 2003). Although UCSC and Ensembl provide browsers only for organisms with a finished or working draft genomic sequence assembly, NCBI has created browsers not only for organisms with a genome assembly, but also for species for which little or no genomic sequence is available. For example, all of the plant browsers, except those from thale cress and rice, are based on genetic maps. Although the available maps are different for the different organisms, the navigation principles are the same. The browsers are linked tightly to other NCBI resources, such as sequences in Entrez,

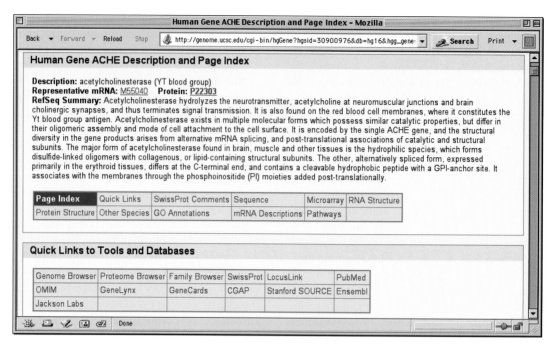

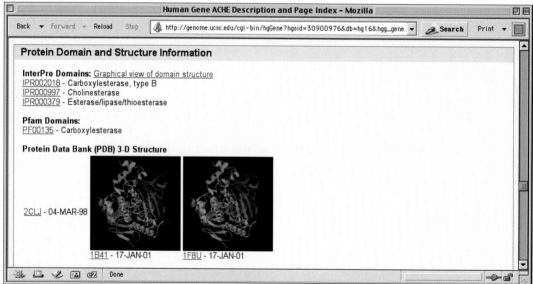

FIGURE 4.4 **UCSC: the details page for the first *ACHE* gene in the Known Genes track shown in Figure 4.3. (a) A summary of gene function, taken from RefSeq, as well as an index of links present on this page. (b) The Protein Structure information for *ACHE*.**

UniGene, Online Mendelian Inheritance in Man (OMIM), dbSNP, and dbSTS.

From the NCBI Map Viewer home page (Figure 4.7), clicking on an organism name opens up the main search page for that organism, whereas links labeled with an orange B go to an organism-specific BLAST page on which genomic sequences, mRNA sequences, protein sequences, or a combination thereof for that organism have been collected. (BLAST is described in detail in Chapter 11.) The search box at the top of the page allows for text-based entries into each organism. The query can be for anything that is mapped in that particular organism, such as gene symbol, nucleotide accession number, or protein domain.

The example followed at NCBI focuses on the same region shown in the UCSC examples, namely, the region around the human *ACHE* gene. However, rather than search for the *ACHE* gene symbol, this example

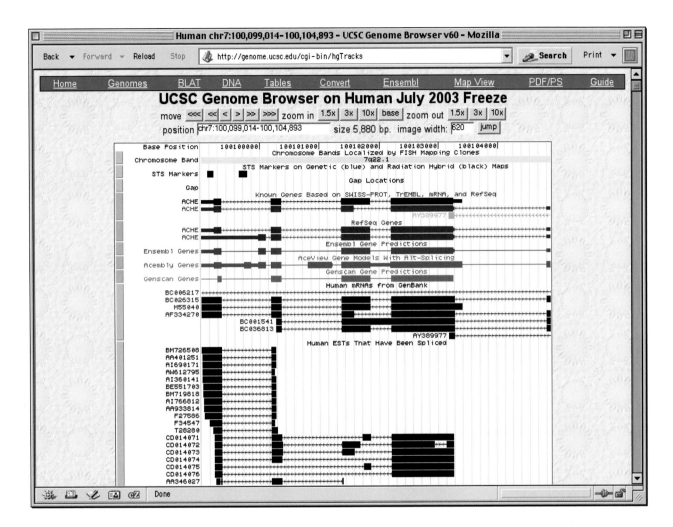

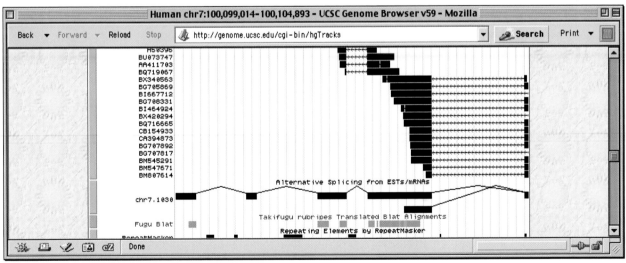

FIGURE 4.5 **UCSC: the view of *ACHE* when the Spliced ESTs track is displayed in its full mode. (a) The 3′ ESTs for** *ACHE*, some showing alternate splicing compared with the Known and RefSeq genes. (b) The 5′ ESTs for ACHE, some showing alternate splicing compared with the Known and RefSeq genes. The Alt-Splicing track summarizes the alternative splicing seen in the mRNA and EST tracks.

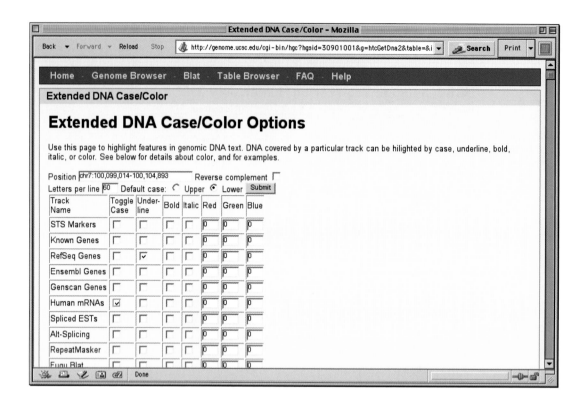

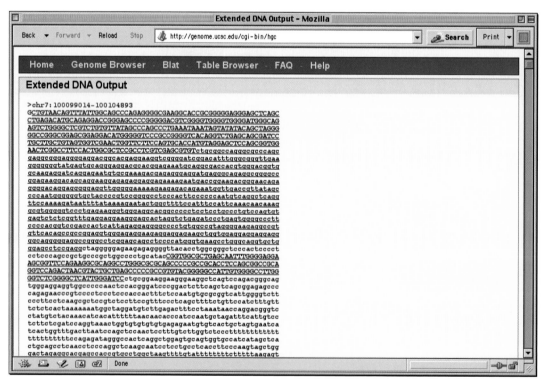

FIGURE 4.6 **UCSC: the option to download genomic sequence, reached by clicking on DNA in the top blue bar of Figures 4.3 and 4.5. (a) Choose how to mark up the genomic sequence based on the annotated features. As indicated here, the DNA will be returned in lower case, with RefSeq gene exons underlined, and Human mRNA exons in uppercase. (b) The exported DNA, formatted as selected in Figure 4.6a.**

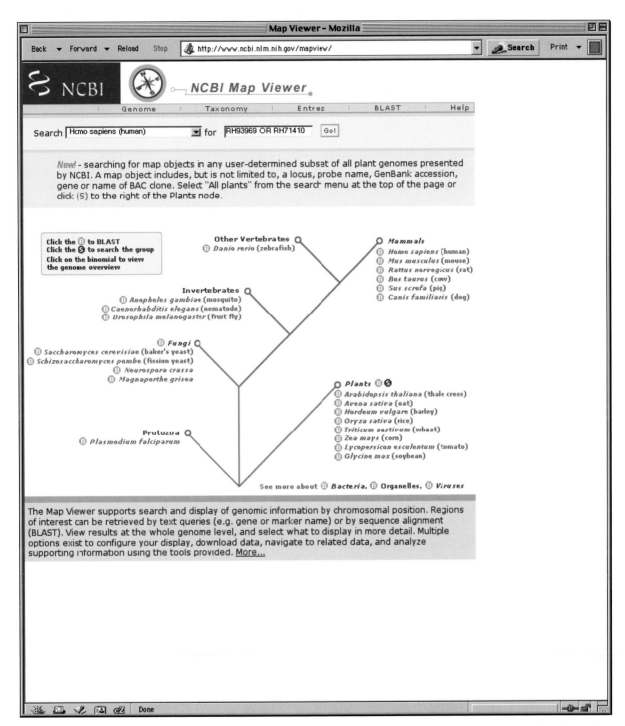

FIGURE 4.7 **NCBI: the Map Viewer home page. The browser is set to query the human genome for the region between the STS markers RH93969 and RH71410.**

illustrates how to explore a region of a genome between two features. Say, for example, that one is carrying out a positional cloning project and has determined that the gene of interest is located between two STS markers, RH93969 and RH71410. In the search box in Figure 4.7, enter the term RH93969 OR RH71410 and set the

organism search to *Homo sapiens*. The resulting page, shown in Figure 4.8, displays a summary of the results. The naming convention for human genome assemblies is different at NCBI than at UCSC. Build 34 is the thirty-fourth assembly of the genome entered at NCBI and corresponds to the July 2003 assembly at UCSC. Although these reference human genome assemblies are recreated approximately yearly, NCBI updates their annotations based on new data and algorithms every few months. The figures shown here represent data from the third version of the annotation on this assembly. In addition to the reference assembly, NCBI also offers assemblies called DR51, a reference sequence for the DR51 haplotype in the major histocompatibility complex on chromosome 6, and HSC_TCAG, an assembly of chromosome 7 from The Center for Applied Genomics.

In Figure 4.8, the red lines on the chromosome overview indicate that the query finds four closely-placed hits on the long arm of chromosome 7. The table at the bottom summarizes the four hits. There are two hits for each marker, one on the reference NCBI genome assembly, and one on the HSC_TCAG assembly. The Maps column links to a view with the individual maps to which the marker has been assigned. The Map element column provides a view with all available maps. To follow this example, click on the "all matches" link to show both STS markers on the reference assembly. The resulting page displays a 121-Mb region of chromosome 7 that contains both STS markers. To narrow down the region displayed to include only the region between the two STS markers, enter one marker name into each of the Region shown boxes in the left blue sidebar, and click Go. In principal, the region shown can be the region between any two mapped features, such as chromosomal coordinates or even genes. Depending on the amount of data being displayed, the maps may be compressed horizontally to save space. To uncompress the maps as shown in Figure 4.9, uncheck the Compress Maps box in the left blue sidebar.

The resulting view in Figure 4.9a highlights the region between the two STS markers. The blue sidebar on the left provides commonly used links. There are two help documents, one for the Map Viewer in general, and one specific to the human data. The NCBI FTP site provides for bulk downloads of Map Viewer data. The subset of information presented on a single page can be retrieved in text format by using the Data As Table View. The red bar on the ideogram on the left blue sidebar indicates the region of chromosome 7 displayed, in the context of the chromosomal banding patterns. To move up or down along the chromosome, click on the arrow at the top or bottom of the right-hand map. To zoom in or out in the display, use the zoom box above the ideogram. The long line at the top of the zoom box shows the entire chromosome, whereas the shortest line at the bottom shows 1/10,000th of the chromosome. The markers themselves are highlighted in pink in the right-hand map. Red dots show where these markers would be on the other four maps. The map on the right of the display is termed the master map, and the viewer provides more information

for it than for the other maps. In this view, the master map is the STS map, which shows STSs from a variety of sources placed onto the genomic sequence using electronic polymerase chain reaction (e-PCR; Schuler, 1998). To the right of the STS name, dots indicate the other maps on which the STS has been placed. The columns on the far right (not shown) are used to indicate if the STS has been used to detect a polymorphism and whether it is in a gene.

Three other maps are shown by default in Figure 4.9a. Any of them can be made the master map by clicking the arrow next to its name. Alternatively, remove a map by clicking on the X next to the name. The map on the left, HsUniG, shows the alignment of ESTs to the genomic sequence. The gray histogram shows the density of ESTs and mRNAs aligned to the genome, along with the UniGene cluster to which they belong. The blue lines indicate the exons (thick line) and introns (thin lines) of the transcripts. The Genes_seq map, also called Genes_sequence, shows the location of known and putative genes. Gene models are colored by the type of evidence used to construct them, such as confirmed, EST-only, or *ab initio* prediction. GM99_GB4 shows STS markers mapped onto the GB4 RH panel by the International Radiation Hybrid Consortium. Additional detail about these and other maps is available by clicking the Human Maps Help in the left blue sidebar. If a large region of a chromosome is displayed, only a subset of the data is displayed in the vertical direction. The View Summary at the bottom of the page provides the details. For example, the region shown in Figure 4.9b contains 82 STS markers, but only 30 of them are shown by name. This section also provides links to download sequence, as well as to view the data as a table instead of a graphic.

Although some navigation can be carried out directly on the search results page as described above, better control, including the addition of other maps, is provided in the Maps & Options window (Figure 4.10), opened by clicking on one of the two yellow links shown in Figure 4.9a. In the top section of the window, the chromosome and position can be changed. Maps are added to the view by highlighting their name in the left Available Maps box and clicking Add. Alternatively, to remove a map, highlight its name in the right Maps Displayed box and click Remove. To make a map the master, highlight its name in the right box, and click Make Master/Move to Bottom. The map listed on top will be on the left in the graphical display. To change the order of maps, highlight a map and Move UP or Move DOWN. The Ruler provides coordinates to the left of a map. Other parts of the display that can be changed include whether to show lines between common elements on different maps (Show Connections), whether to display additional details for

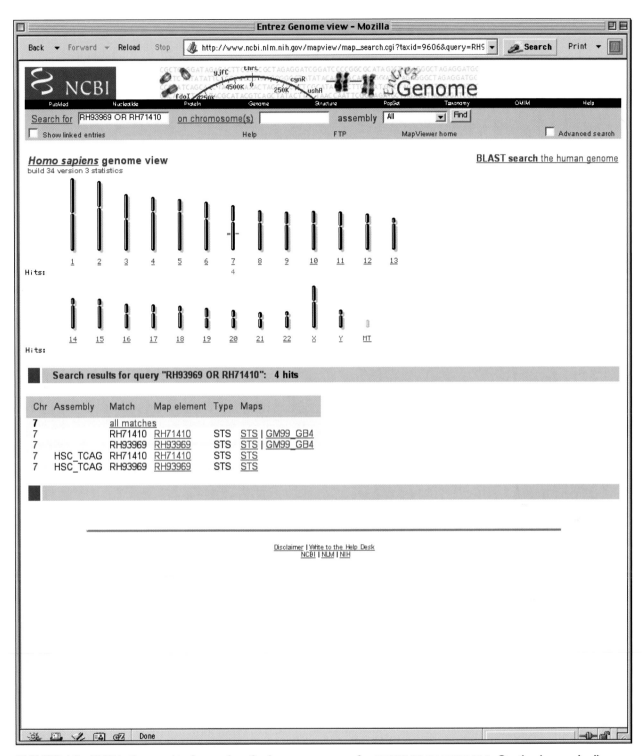

FIGURE 4.8   NCBI: the result of querying the human genome for RH93969 OR RH71410**. On the (unmarked) reference genome assembly from NCBI, both STS markers have been placed on two maps, STS and GM99-GB4. On the HSC-TCAG assembly of chromosome 7 from The Center for Applied Genomics, the markers have been placed on the STS map.**

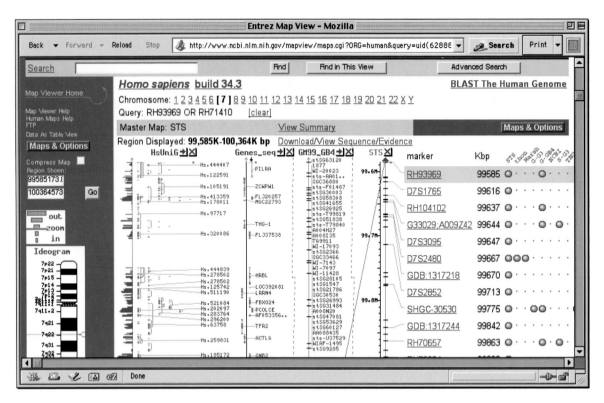

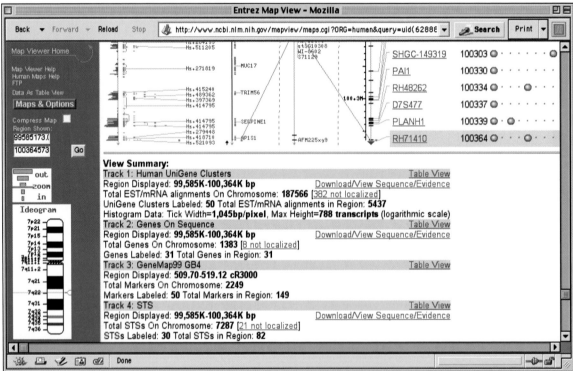

FIGURE 4.9   NCBI: the region of human chromosome 7 between STS markers RH93969 and RH71410. This view was generated by clicking on the all matches link in Figure 4.8 and then narrowing down the region displayed by entering the STS marker names in the Region Shown boxes in the left blue sidebar as well as unchecking the Compress Maps box in the blue sidebar. (a) The top of the page, showing the region around STS marker RH93969. (b) The bottom of the page, showing the region around STS marker RH71410, as well a summary of the information presented on each map.

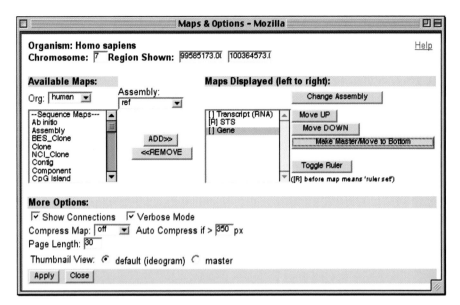

FIGURE 4.10   NCBI: the Maps & Options box. The controls have been set so the browser will display the Transcript, STS, and Genes_Sequence (Gene) map. Because it is at the bottom of the list, the Genes_Sequence map will be the master map and will appear on the right side of the browser with specialized links.

the master map (Verbose Mode), whether to compress the maps horizontally, the page length (a larger number in the text box represents a longer screen), and whether to show the ideogram or master map in the left blue sidebar. Org. allows the user to add maps from other organisms into the viewer (see below), and Assembly selects the genome assembly. The Maps & Options box in Figure 4.10 will result in only the Transcript (RNA), STS, and Genes_sequence (Gene) maps being displayed, with Genes_sequence being the master map.

Hit Apply in the Maps & Options box in Figure 4.10 to continue with the example. The resulting page shows the result of the Genes_sequence map being the master. This view shows 30 of the 31 genes in between the two STS markers RH93969 and RH71410. To zoom in on the *ACHE* gene, hold the mouse over blue graphic to which the *ACHE* text points, and click Zoom in x8. At this resolution, boxes represent exons, and lines represent the connecting introns (Figure 4.11). The direction of transcription is indicated by an arrow to the right of the gene name, as well as by whether the cartoon gene model is to the left or right of the black line. Note that the Genes_sequence map depicts a flattened view of all exons for a particular gene model, and that *ACHE* is shown as a single set of boxes and lines. In the Transcript (RNA) map, transcripts are displayed individually, and the two splice variants of *ACHE*, identified by their mRNA Reference Sequence accession numbers, are shown as two separate graphics.

When the Genes_sequence map is the master map, up to seven additional links are visible. Some of these links provide additional background information on how the gene model was constructed.

▶ The gene symbol itself links to NCBI's Gene database with more information on that gene.

▶ OMIM links to any information about that record described in NCBI's Online Mendelian Inheritance in Man.

▶ sv, or sequence viewer, provides a graphical representation of the position of the gene within the sequence region, including annotated features like coding region (CDS), RNA, gene, and SNP. The sequence is displayed as a graphic and cannot be copied and pasted from this view.

▶ pr, or protein, links to the NCBI Reference protein sequences for that gene.

▶ dl, or download, allows the user to retrieve the genomic sequence or annotation of a region in text format. By default, dl retrieves the region corresponding to the entire gene annotated on the Genes_sequence map. To retrieve a different region, change the coordinates listed in the text box. The region can be returned either as sequence in FASTA format, or in GenBank format. The GenBank format shows all the features that have been annotated on the selected region, like genes, STSs, and SNPs. Note that at the top

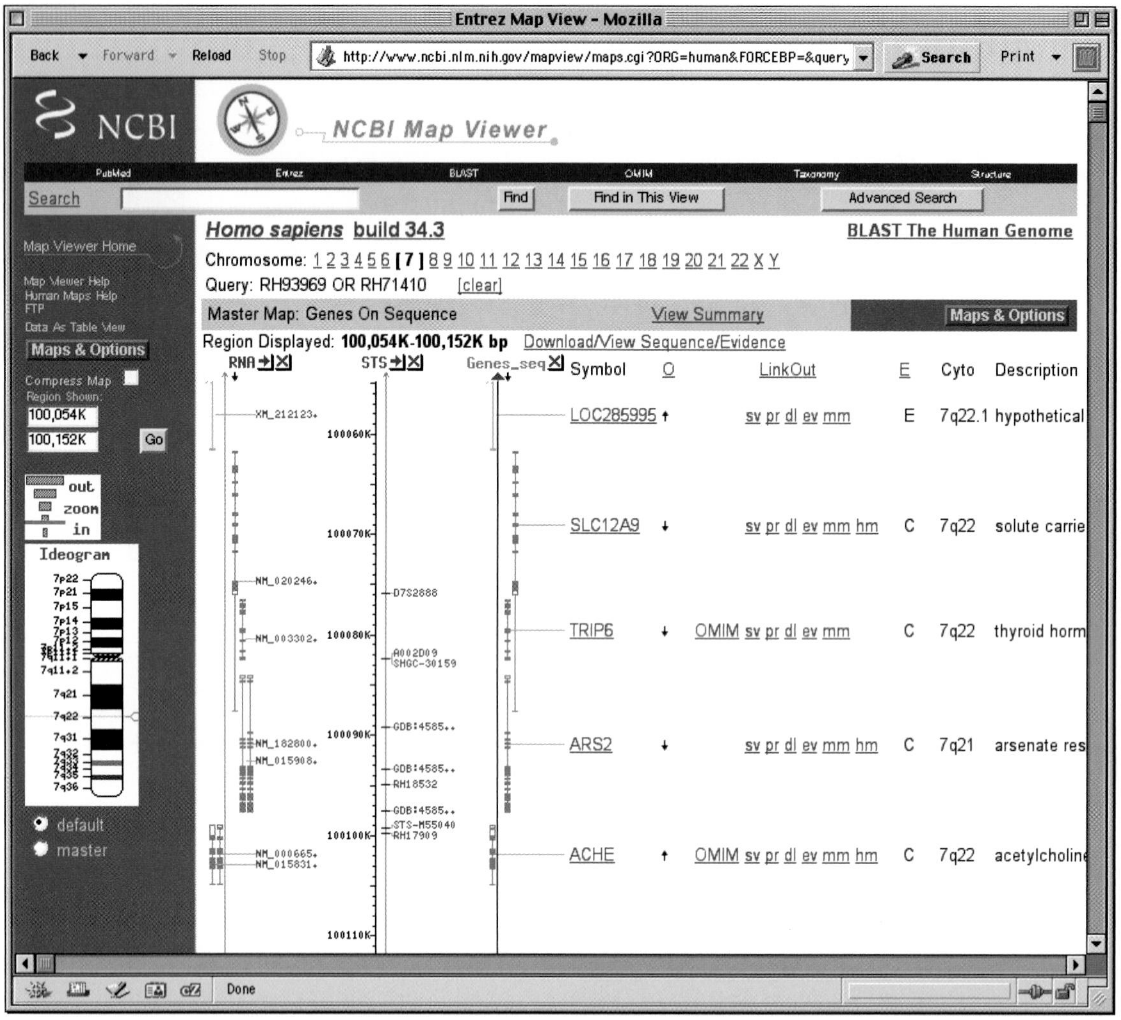

FIGURE 4.11 NCBI: the genomic context of the human *ACHE* gene. The STS map shows STS markers. The Transcript (RNA) map depicts individual transcripts, including all known splice variants. The master Genes_sequence map shows a flattened view of each gene, with each exon appearing once.

of the dl page, the location of the region is shown in chromosomal coordinates. Further down, the location is shown on the coordinates of the NT_###### contig that spans this region. The returned sequence or GenBank file will be annotated in the contig coordinates.

▶ ev, or evidence viewer, displays the biological evidence supporting a particular gene model. This view shows all GenBank and RefSeq mRNAs, ESTs, and model exons in graphical fashion, and also displays alignments of the mRNAs with the genomic sequence. For additional information, click on Evidence Viewer Help on any ev page. Sequences in the alignment can be copied and pasted into other computer applications.

▶ mm links to the Model Maker, which shows the exons that result when GenBank mRNAs and gene predictions are aligned to the genomic sequence. ESTs can be added as well. The user can then select individual exons to create a custom model of the gene.

▶ hm links to NCBI's HomoloGene, which shows automatically calculated homologs of the gene in up to eleven other organisms.

The Model Maker can be a useful tool to explore alternative splicing. The two alternatively spliced mRNA Reference Sequences for *ACHE*, NM_000665.2 and NM_015831.1, are shown in the Model Maker for *ACHE*, along with other mRNAs for *ACHE* (Figure 4.12). An overview of all exons from all transcripts is shown

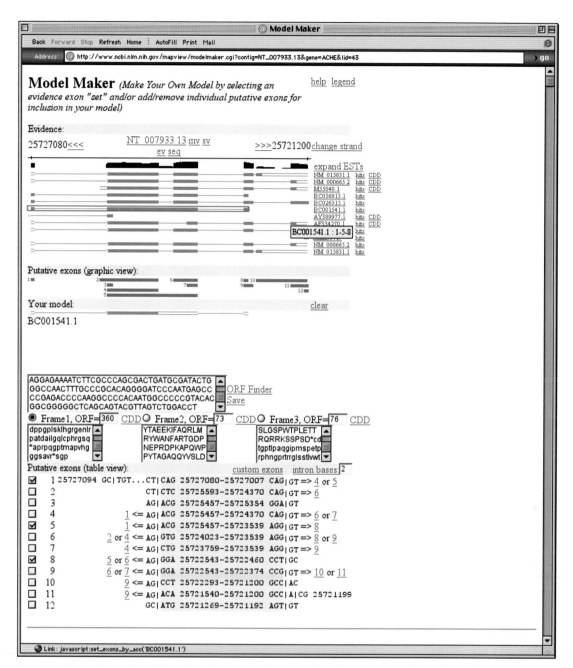

FIGURE 4.12 **NCBI: the Model Maker for the human *ACHE* gene. The mRNA BC001541 has been selected, and its transcript sequence and resulting three-frame translation are shown.**

in green in the putative exons section. To view the details of a particular transcript, click on its blue intron and exon structure. The appropriate exons then are displayed in red in the Your model section, and the transcript appears below the schematic. Alternatively, click on exons in the Putative exons section to create a novel transcript. The three boxes below the transcript sequence show translations of the sequence in all three reading frames, and splice junctions are shown at the bottom of the page. Further exploration

of this view indicates that the long second exon of mRNA BC001541.1 does not encode an open reading frame, beyond where it shares sequence with the other transcripts.

Now it is also possible to see maps from more than one organism displayed together in the Map Viewer. The correspondences between the maps are made through NCBI's HomoloGene. Figure 4.13 demonstrates the result of adding the mouse Genes_sequence map to the human genome display. To reach this view, one must

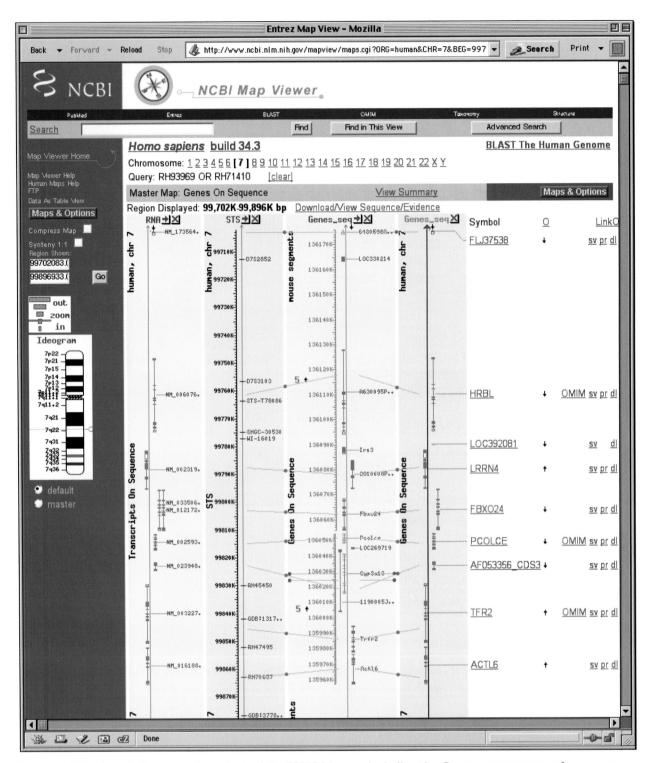

FIGURE 4.13 NCBI: the genomic context of the FBXO24 gene, including the Genes_sequence map for mouse.
This figure was generated from the view in Figure 4.9a by making the Genes_sequence the master map, clicking on the graphic of the FBXO24 gene and selecting Zoom in ×4, and then using the Maps & Options box (Figure 4.10) to display the human RNA, STS, and Genes_sequence maps, along with the mouse Genes_sequence map.

return to the display (not shown) just before zooming in on *ACHE* in Figure 4.11, where the entire region between the two STS markers is shown, and Genes_sequence is the master map. In this view, hold the mouse over the FBXO24 gene schematic, and zoom in 4×. From this display, use the Maps & Options window to view the available mouse maps by selecting mouse as the Org., and then add the Genes_sequence (Gene) map to the display. Figure 4.13 shows syntenic regions of mouse chromosome 5 and human chromosome 7.

ENSEMBL

Project Ensembl is a joint venture between the European Bioinformatics Institute (EBI) and the Sanger Institute and is funded primarily by the Wellcome Trust (Birney et al., 2004). The main browser currently provides a set of gene, transcript, and protein predictions for the genomes of nine organisms. Because optimizing this annotation pipeline requires a few months per genome, Ensembl provides a preview browser for organisms whose genomes are in the pipeline. All data produced by Ensembl, as well the software used for its analysis and presentation, is available free of charge.

The data at Ensembl are presented on pages called Views, with each View showing a different level of detail. Although the searches described at UCSC and NCBI could be performed at Ensembl, in this example, we take a different approach for viewing a portion of the human genome to take advantage of some of the views that are unique to this browser. For this example, imagine a scientist who has mapped a candidate human gene to a specific chromosomal band and who is interested in identifying the genes and SNPs in that band. Start at the Ensembl home page (Figure 4.14), which provides links to news, documentation, and specialized services such as sequence similarity searching, as well as a list of the available genomes. Users can search for terms, such as gene names, across all genomes by entering text into the search box at the top of the page. For this example, however, a more practical search is an organism-specific one, initiated by following the link labeled Human that goes to the Human Ensembl home page (Figure 4.15).

The home page for each organism provides information about the genomic sequence assembly, as well as the date on which the annotations were last updated. At the time of this writing, Ensembl is displaying release v20.34c.1 of the human genome. The second number (34) refers to the version of the genomic sequence assembly, in this case, build 34 from NCBI. From the human genome browser page, one can, among other things, perform text queries, go directly to a region of the genome based on chromosomal coordinates, or download sequence and annotation data. Clicking on the icon

of human chromosome 7 leads to the MapView, shown in Figure 4.16. The top of the MapView page, like the top of many types of Ensembl View pages, provides links to commonly accessed tools. A context-sensitive help document for this view is reached by clicking the red Help button at the top of the page. The TextSearch is a text-based interface to Ensembl where users can enter complex queries based on keywords and database identifiers indexed by Ensembl. BlastSearch is for a sequence-based interface to the database, whereas the Disease Browser provides an interface to diseases listed in OMIM. Ensembl provides three tools for exporting data. The MartSearch links to EnsMart, a data retrieval tool that returns genes, SNPs, or other features of interest from a region defined by the user (Kasprzyk et al., 2004). EnsMart supports various output types, including tabulated lists and sequences. Export Data goes to the ExportView, which returns sequence, annotations, or images from data in a defined region. Finally, Download links to an FTP site with access to all Ensembl data and software.

This MapView illustrates some interesting features of chromosome 7. On the left, histograms depict gene, GC content, repetitive sequence, and SNP density along the chromosome. On the right are statistics, such as chromosome length, number of genes, known genes (those with confirmed protein sequences), and SNPs. Navigate to the ContigView for a particular region of chromosome 7 by clicking on a region in a feature histogram or by entering marker names in the Jump to Contigview section. In this example, navigate to a region contained in band 7q22.1 by placing the computer mouse over that section of the ideogram and clicking.

The ContigView (Figures 4.17–4.19) provides a telescoping graphical view of a chromosomal region, from chromosome band down to sequence. The upper portion of the ContigView is a schematic of the chromosome 7 banding pattern, with the selected region of q22.1 boxed in red (Figure 4.17). The Overview shows in more detail the features in that box, which spans approximately 1 Mb of sequence. The contigs that were sequenced during the course of the genome project are in blue near the top. Markers and genes are shown below the contigs, and syntenic regions from other genomes are shown above. Ensembl gene predictions are marked in red and black, whereas manually curated genes from the Vega database (see below) are in blue. Click on the *ACHE* gene symbol, on the right side of the Ensembl genes section, to recenter the display on *ACHE*. The features in the red-boxed region of the ContigView are shown at higher resolution in the Detailed View, which appears on the page under the Overview. By default, the Detailed View shows 100 Kb, although this region can be changed using the navigation bar (Figure 4.18a). The arrows move the display to the left and right, and the zoom changes the amount of data being displayed.

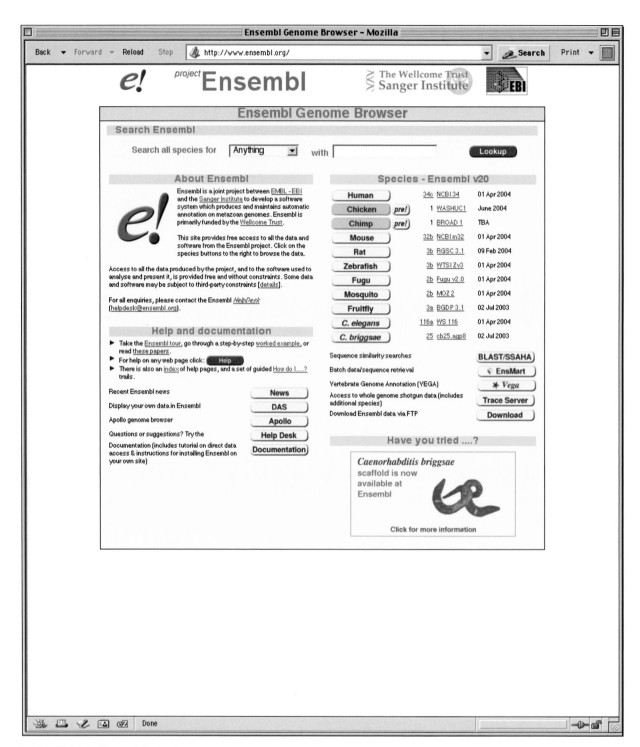

FIGURE 4.14 Ensembl: the home page.

The DNA sequence assembly, in blue, divides the features on the page. Those above the blue bars are on the forward strand, and those below, on the reverse.

Below the sequence assembly bar in Figure 4.18b are schematics of the individual transcripts encoded on the reverse strand. Exons are marked as vertical bars, and each alternatively spliced transcript is shown separately.

By default, Ensembl displays four types of transcripts. Ensembl transcripts are those predicted by Ensembl. The two splice variants of *ACHE* are both visible in this view. Known transcripts, those for which a near–full-length species-specific cDNA sequence, protein sequence, or both are available, are colored red, whereas novel transcripts that cannot be matched with confidence to

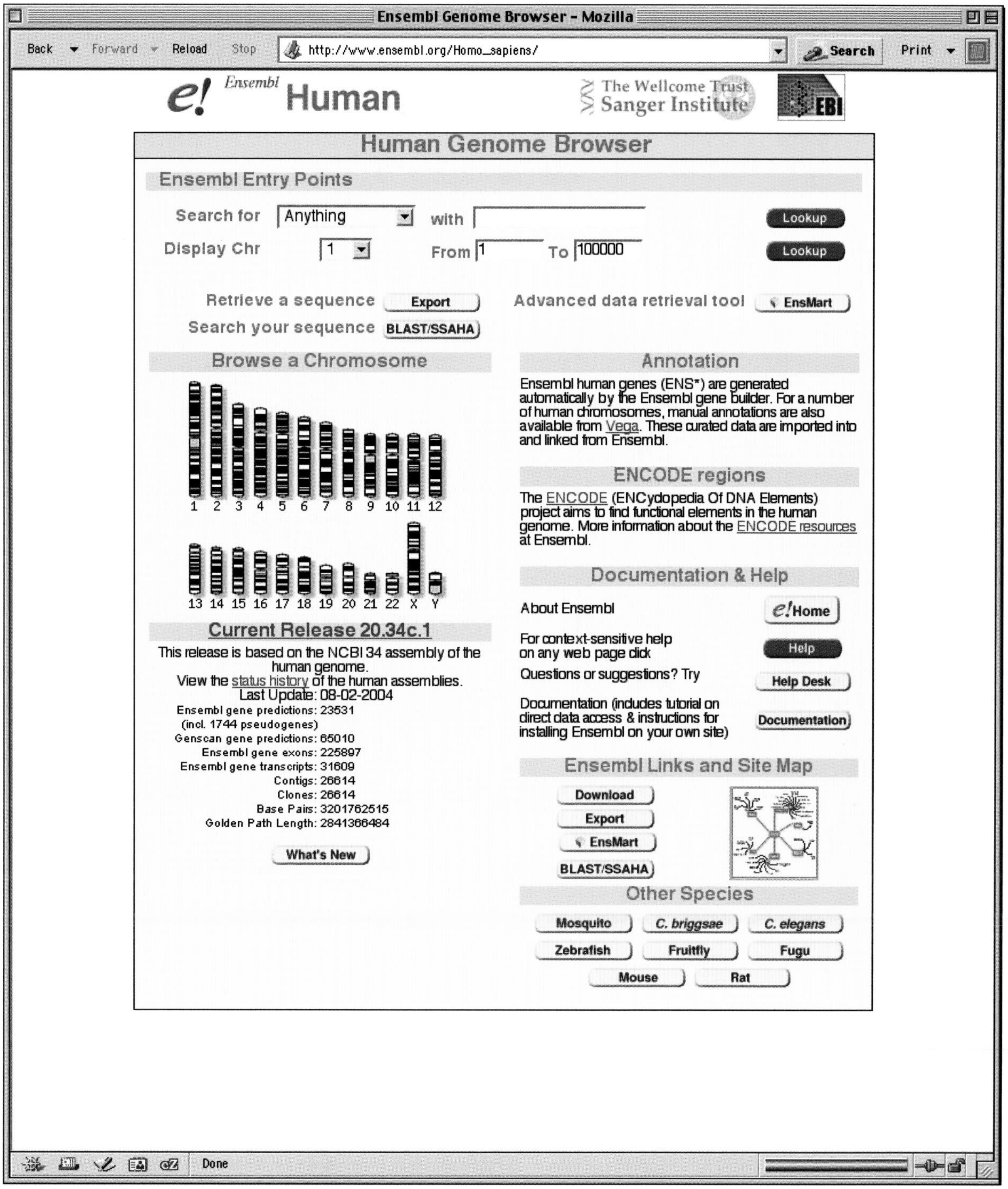

FIGURE 4.15 **Ensembl: the home page for the human genome browser.**

specific database entries are black. Vega transcripts come from the Vertebrate Genome Annotation (VEGA) database, a central repository for manual annotation of finished vertebrate genomes. EST transcripts are predictions made by Ensembl that are based on EST evidence only. Finally, Genscans are transcripts produced by the gene prediction program GENSCAN.

All Ensembl transcripts, both known and novel, are supported by biological evidence. This evidence, which can be either protein or mRNA, is shown below the transcripts (Figure 4.18b). Proteins come from Swiss-Prot and TrEMBL, whereas mRNAs are from UniGene and the EMBL nucleotide sequence database. Using the mouse to move the pointer over the evidence graphic

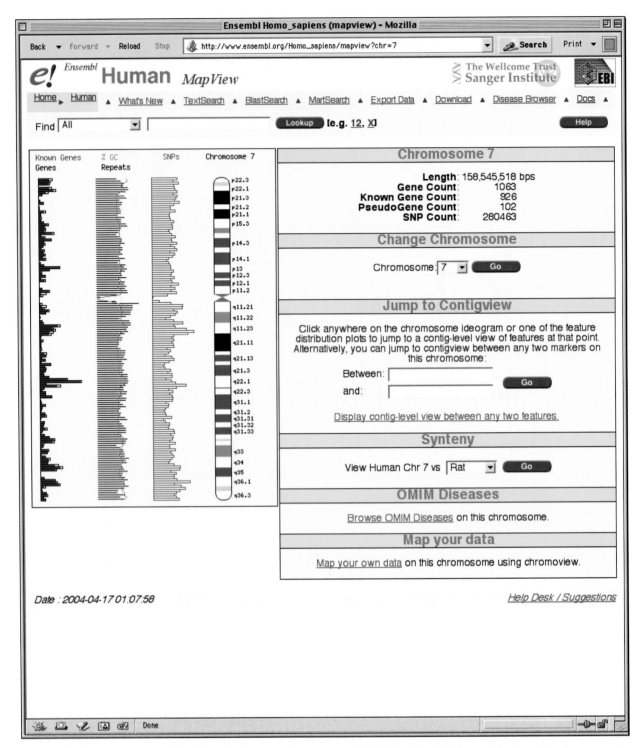

FIGURE 4.16   Ensembl: the MapView for human chromosome 7, obtained by clicking on the icon for chromosome 7 in Figure 4.15.

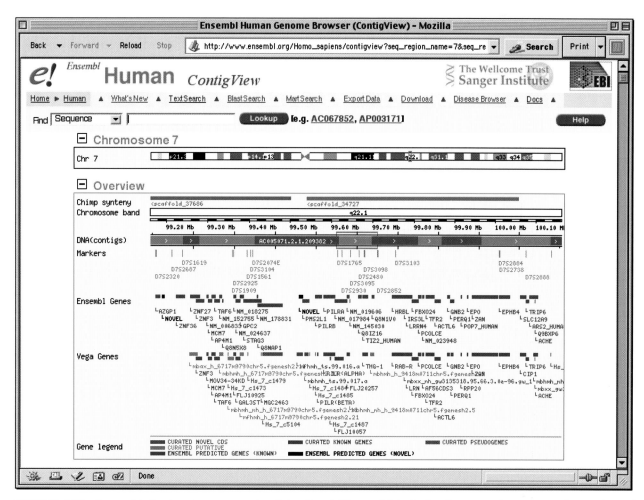

FIGURE 4.17 Ensembl: the top two segments of the ContigView, which depict the genomic context of a portion of band 7q22.1, obtained by clicking near the bottom of the 7q22.1 band in Figure 4.16.

brings up its database identifier. The sequences are displayed if they share at least one exon with an Ensembl or Genscan transcript. Evaluating this evidence may help a user to make an informed choice on whether to believe an Ensembl gene prediction, especially a novel one.

The last section of the Detailed View shows markers, as well as the tiling path of sequence entries used to build the current genome assembly (not shown). Below the Detailed View, at the very bottom of the ContigView page, is the Basepair View (Figure 4.19). By default, the central 101 bp of the Detailed View is shown here. The genomic sequence itself is central to the page, with the forward strand on top and the reverse on the bottom. A six-frame translation of the sequence is shown as well. Individual nucleotides and amino acids are color coded. Finally, the recognition sites of restriction endonucleases are shown at the bottom.

Just above the Detailed View is a gold toolbar that is used to change the display (Figure 4.18a). The Features and Repeats pull-downs provide lists of features

that can be hidden or displayed. For example, to display only the Ensembl transcripts and SNPs in this region of chromosome 7, configure the menu as shown in Figure 4.20 and click on Close Menu. To view all the SNPs and predicted transcripts on 7p22.1, one also would need to zoom out using the controls on the navigation bar, because the view in Figure 4.18b shows only a portion of the band. Other items on the gold bar include the Compara menu, which provides access to whole genome sequence comparisons, and the DAS Sources menu, which provides access to additional sources of genome annotation that have been provided in DAS, or Distributed Annotation System, format. The DAS data available by default is from the Sanger Institute, although data from other sources is available as well. In addition, individual users can display their own data in the context of the Ensembl annotations, and even share this data with collaborators, as long as it is formatted properly. Instructions are provided in the DAS Sources link under Help. Also in the gold bar, Decorations and Image size allow

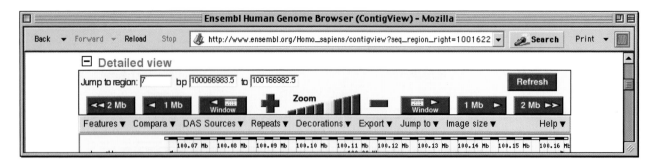

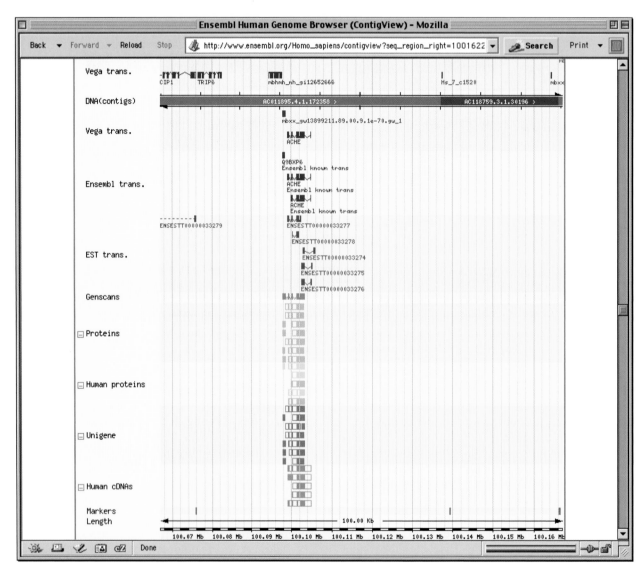

FIGURE 4.18   Ensembl: the Detailed View section of the ContigView. The display was centered around the *ACHE* gene by clicking on its symbol in the Overview in Figure 4.17. (a) The navigation toolbar is used to move the display to the left or right, or to zoom in or out to change the level of detail. The gold bar provides for customization of the display by adding or removing maps. (b) The genomic context of *ACHE*. Genes on the negative strand are shown under the blue DNA (contigs) graphic.

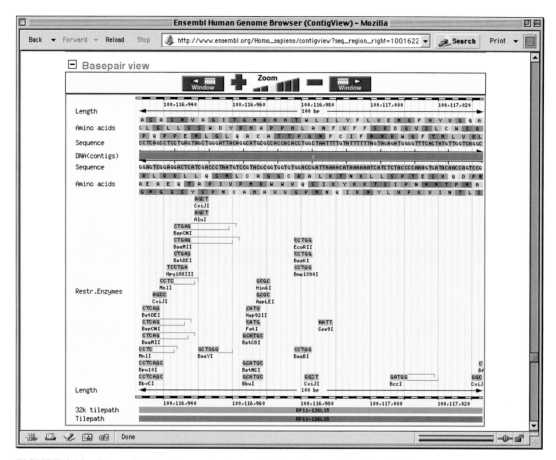

FIGURE 4.19   Ensembl: the Basepair view at the bottom of the ContigView.

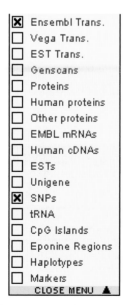

FIGURE 4.20   Ensembl: The Features pull-down menu from the gold bar in Figure 4.18a. The controls have been set so the browser will display the Ensembl Transcript and SNP maps.

for customization of the display. Choosing Reset options in the Decorate menu resets all customizations back to their "factory default." Finally, Export links to EnsMart or ExportView.

Using the mouse to place the pointer over any of the items in the Detailed View or Basepair View brings up a pop-up menu from which more information about that item can be obtained. Text marked in gray is informative, whereas colored text is a link. For example, mousing over an SNP within a coding region of *ACHE* brings up details about it, such as its position (Figure 4.21). Clicking on the SNP Properties link leads to the SNPView (Figure 4.22). The SNP in question, number 8286, has two alleles, A or T, which correspond to ambiguity code W. The SNP Neighborhood section of the Report includes a graphic showing all SNPS in a 20-Kb region, color-coded by class. The W for SNP 8286 is highlighted in black. Its red coloring indicates that it is a coding SNP.

Using the mouse to place the pointer over a transcript on the Detailed View provides links to the GeneView, TransView, and ProteinView. The GeneView for Ensembl transcript *ACHE*, shown in Figure 4.23a, is a collection of information about that gene, including its

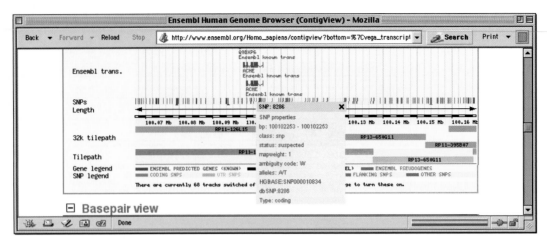

FIGURE 4.21 Ensembl: the Detailed View around *ACHE*, after the features in Figure 4.20 were selected. The mouse has been placed over **SNP 8286** to highlight its properties.

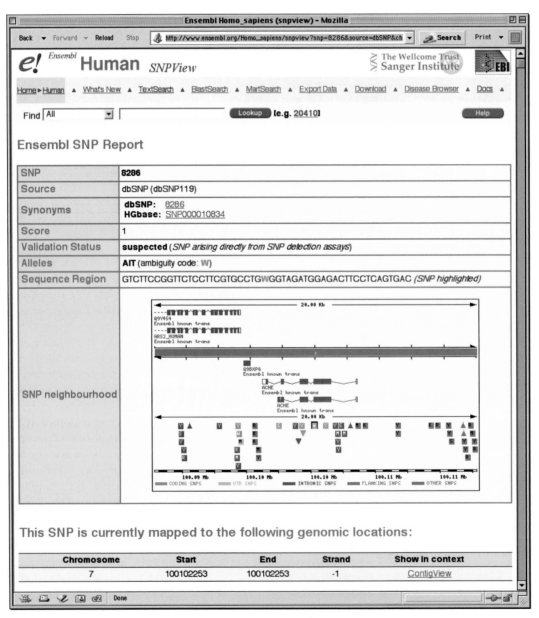

FIGURE 4.22 Ensembl: the **SNPView** of **SNP 8286**. This view was created by following the **SNP** properties link in Figure 4.21.

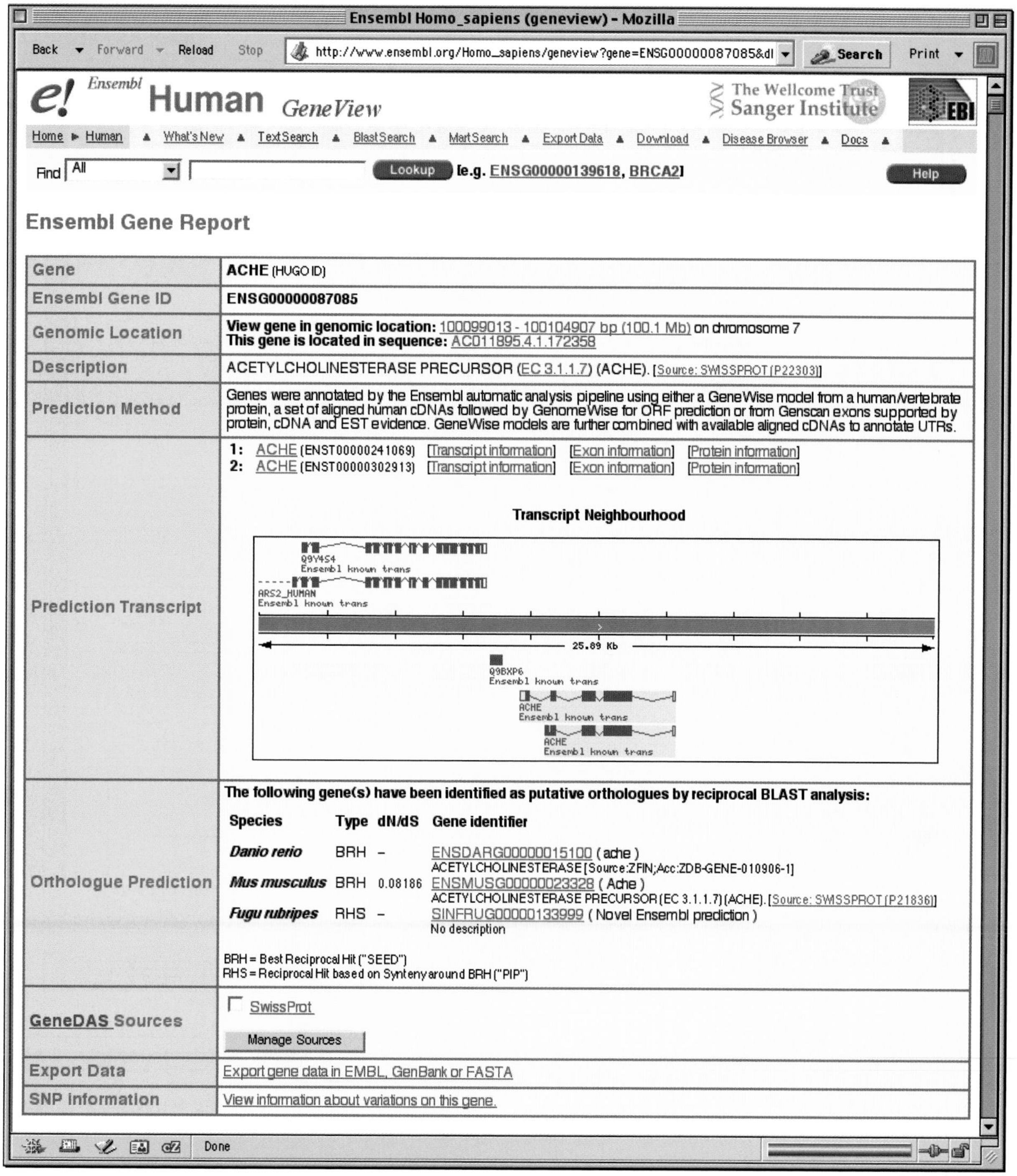

FIGURE 4.23 Ensembl: the GeneView for *ACHE*. This page was created by moving the mouse over the *ACHE* gene in Figure 4.21 and selecting the Gene link. (a) The Gene Report on the top part of the page provides general information about the gene. (b) One of the two Transcript/Translation Summary reports, one for each of the two alternatively spliced transcripts.

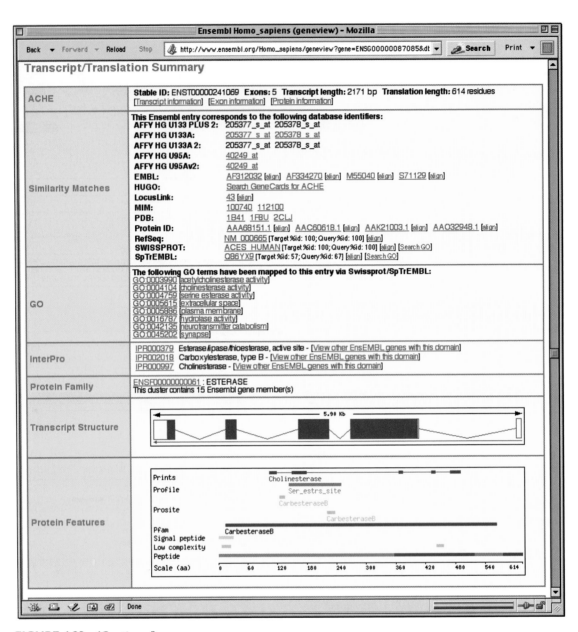

FIGURE 4.23 *(Continued)*

location and putative orthologs. There is a separate Transcript/Translation Summary at the bottom of the GeneView for each alternatively spliced transcript. Figure 4.23b shows the summary for the longer of the two *ACHE* transcripts. This information is an abridged version of what is shown in the TransView and ProteinView and includes links to outside databases, sequence alignments, and protein domains.

SUMMARY

The genomic sequence assemblies that form the basis of the three browsers are works in progress, and updates will continue, even for the finished human genome.

Depending on the state of the sequencing project, genomic coordinates along the chromosome may change dramatically from assembly to assembly. Furthermore, changes in sequence data or algorithm implementation can sometimes cause large changes in the assembly—genes can move around, within, or even between chromosomes. In some cases, the assembly provided may not be correct because of errors in the build process or in the underlying data. If a region of the assembly is suspect, it may be worth reviewing older versions of the genome assembly at UCSC. The examples in this chapter were all illustrated using build 34, or the July 2003 assembly of the human genome. Although users working on later human genome builds will not be able to recreate the exact figures shown here, the queries themselves will remain valid.

The user also should keep in mind that the annotations on the sequence, especially the genes, are only as good as the software that predicts their locations, and that this software is being continuously refined. Thus, is always important to gather as much information as possible when evaluating any putative gene, especially one predicted ab initio. For example, the UCSC Human Genome Browser presents two "known gene" tracks: one is based on mRNAs that have a corresponding protein in Swiss-Prot, TrEMBL, and TrEMBL-New, whereas the other shows protein-coding genes from the NCBI Reference Sequence Project. *Ab initio* gene predictions are depicted separate tracks, as are other aligning mRNAs from GenBank and ESTs. The Comparative Genomics tracks also may help to pinpoint functional regions that have been conserved through evolution. Novel exons that appear only once in a single track are less likely to be correct than those that appear frequently. In the NCBI Map Viewer for human, the Genes_Sequence track shows all gene models, both with and without mRNA evidence. Colors indicate the type of evidence supporting each gene. Additionally, the *ab initio*, Transcript, and EST maps, as well as the model maker or evidence viewer, may help users in their evaluations. Ensembl predictions can be evaluated in the GeneView and TransView for individual genes and transcripts, as well as by adding additional transcript and protein Features to the ContigView.

All of the data presented in the genome browsers are also available for download from the respective FTP sites. At present, UCSC provides flat text files, as well as mySQL tables. NCBI provides only text files. Ensembl provides flat text files, as well as database tables ready for loading into mySQL. Furthermore, all Ensembl software, including the code used to generate the Web site, is freely available.

Each browser presents only one view of a given genome. In many cases, especially if one wants to see all predicted genes in a region, it may be useful to look at the same region of the genome in more than one browser. Because the three sites use different methods to align mRNAs and ESTs to the genome, as well as different gene prediction algorithms, the positions or numbers of predicted genes may vary. When making such comparisons, however, one must be careful to check that the same assembly of the genome is being viewed at each site. The user also may discover that different sites are better for different types of queries. Query results often load more quickly in the UCSC Genome Browser than in either the Map Viewer or Ensembl, making UCSC more efficient for fast searches. At both NCBI and Ensembl, sequence comparisons against the genome are performed with BLAST. UCSC provides the BLAT program, which,

although sometimes not as sensitive as BLAST, often is much faster. Both UCSC and Ensembl allow users to display their own data in the context of the publicly available annotations, a tool that NCBI does not yet provide. However, NCBI provides more non–sequence-based maps, such as the Mitelman Breakpoint, deCODE, and Stanford G3. In short, to make the most of the human genome data, users should learn to use all three sites.

WORKED EXAMPLE

1. Suppose that one wants to explore the transcriptional regulation of human *ADAM10*, a gene that was identified as particularly interesting during a microarray experiment. As a first step, one would need to obtain 10 Kb of sequence upstream of the transcription start site. How would this sequence be obtained using the UCSC Genome Browser?

Query the July 2003 human genome assembly at UCSC for *ADAM10*. On the page with the list of results, select the *ADAM10* RefSeq link for NM_001110. The resulting graphic shows the alignment of the RefSeq mRNA to the genome. Note that the 5′ end of the gene is on the right side of the display. All of the exons, except the first and last, are the same height. These tall segments indicate coding regions, whereas the short segments on the first and last exons are untranslated.

To obtain the actual sequence, click on the gene symbol *ADAM10* in the RefSeq Gene track. On the resulting RefSeq Gene page, scroll down to the section entitled Links to sequence and select Genomic Sequence. This sequence retrieval page allows you to download sequence upstream and downstream of the gene, as well as exons and introns. To obtain the 10-Kb promoter, select Promoter/Upstream by 10000 bases, as well as 5′ UTR Exons and CDS Exons. Also toggle on the One FASTA record per region, as well as CDS in upper case, UTR in lower case. On the resulting page, there are 14 files that contain only sequence in uppercase; these are the coding exons. The second file on the page contains a mix of upper and lower case; the lower case is the 5′ untranslated region, and the uppercase, starting with an ATG, is the coding sequence. The first file contains sequence 10-Kb upstream of the transcription start site.

2. How many members of the *ADAM* gene family have been named in human? Answer this question using the NCBI MapViewer, without performing a BLAST search.

Begin by searching the human genome with the text term ADAM. This returns only one hit. Try again with ADAM*, using the wildcard * to represent any combination of text after the *ADAM* gene symbol. This query returns 56 hits, most of which are correct; however, some unnecessary hits, like "similar to ADAM 25" are included. Querying for ADAM* [sym] limits the search for the term in the gene symbols and is almost correct, but the list of 54 hits includes genes that are members of the *ADAM*, *ADAMTS*, and *ADAMDEC* families. To eliminate the *ADAMTS* and *ADAMDEC* family members, add the term NOT ADAMTS* [sym] NOT ADAMDEC* [sym] to the query. The results of the final query, ADAM* [sym] NOT ADAMTS* [sym] NOT ADAMDEC* [sym], generates 31 hits on two assemblies, the reference assembly from NCBI, as well as the chromosome 7 assembly from TCAG. To limit the search to the reference assembly, select it instead of the default All. The final search returns the 25 members of the *ADAM* gene family that have been named in humans. Additional unnamed members of the *ADAM* gene family may be found in a BLAST search.

3. A laboratory recently undertook work on the human protein single-stranded DNA binding protein 4, or SSBP4. It is thought that the putative mouse ortholog may be informative. How can one find the mouse ortholog at Ensembl, without doing a BLAST search?

   From the Ensembl human genome browser home page, search for the SSBP4 gene by entering SSBP4 in the text box, and selecting *Gene* from the pull-down menu. Ensembl returns a single hit, to gene *ENSG00000130511* (NCBI RefSeq NM_032627). Follow the link to the GeneView. In the Orthologue Prediction section are the results of sequence comparisons between the human gene and genes from other organisms. The mouse gene ENSMUSG00000007887 is a best reciprocal hit to the human, meaning that it is the best hit to the human gene in the mouse genome, and vice versa. This mouse gene, which is a putative ortholog of the human SSBP4, corresponds to the mouse NCBI RefSeq NM_133772.

PROBLEM SET

1. Use the UCSC Genome Browser to explore the genomic context of the region on chromosome 3 around 120,564,000–120,610,000.
   a. What is the gene symbol of the RefSeq gene that has been mapped to this region of the genome?
   b. What is the accession number of the BAC clone that was used in this region to create the genome assembly? (Hint: You will need to view an additional track in order to answer this question.)
   c. Zoom out a bit until you can see the graphic for the full length of this known gene. What are the accession numbers of the two human spliced ESTs that encode the 1st–3rd exons of the gene?
   d. What RefSeq Genes are immediately upstream and downstream of this gene in the UCSC browser?
   e. Looking only at the Human mRNAs from GenBank track (Human mRNAs), you see that one of these neighboring genes may have alternatively spliced forms. What is the accession number of the GenBank mRNA(s) that is spliced differently from the known gene? Look for an mRNA with a potential alternate coding sequence, not just more or less 5′ or 3′ untranslated (UTR) sequence.
2. You have identified a human family with congenital cataracts. You've narrowed down the critical region for the gene to the region between the two STS markers, D21S1869 and D21S1989.
   a. Use the NCBI Map Viewer to view this region of the genome. What chromosome number and band are shown in the default view?
   b. Does the default view that you are looking at show you all the STSs that have been mapped to this region of the chromosome?
   c. To narrow down the view to see only the region between STS markers D21S1869 and D21S1989, type their names into the Region Shown boxes in the left blue sidebar and click Go. After you have narrowed down the region, what are the chromosomal coordinates, in bp, that you are looking at?
   d. The gene that you are interested in is likely between these two STS markers. List the symbols for ALL the genes that NCBI has annotated in this region. (Hint: To make it easier to answer this question, change the master map.)
   e. One of the genes in this region has been shown to be involved in cataract formation in the eye. Use the links from the MapViewer to OMIM to find the gene.
   f. Are there any SNPs in this gene that may affect the protein sequence? (Hint: To answer this question, you will need to add a new map and make it the master map.)
3. Use Ensembl to look at the region of the mouse EGFR gene.
   a. What is the Ensembl accession number for the gene (the accession number will start with ENSMUSG)?
   b. How many transcripts (starts with ENSMUST) has Ensembl predicted for this gene?
   c. What are the lengths of these predicted transcripts, in bp? How long is the corresponding genomic sequence interval, in Kb?
   d. Go to the ContigView for the mouse EGFR gene by clicking on a link in the Genomic Location section. In the Detailed view, these two transcripts are labeled Ensembl trans. and shown in red. Is there any EST evidence for either of the transcripts?
   e. As far as you can see in the Detailed View, is there any EMBL mRNA evidence for either of the transcripts? (Hint: You may need to add an additional Feature to answer this.)
   f. What is the Ensembl accession number of the human gene that is the likely ortholog of EGFR (the accession number will start with ENSG)? (Hint: You don't need to do a BLAST search to answer this question.)

INTERNET RESOURCES

NCBI

NCBI Map Viewer	http://www.ncbi.nlm.nih.gov/mapview/
NCBI Map Viewer Help	http://www.ncbi.nlm.nih.gov/mapview/static/MapViewerHelp.html
NCBI Map Viewer Human Maps Help	http://www.ncbi.nlm.nih.gov/mapview/static/humansearch.html

UCSC

UCSC Genome Browser	http://genome.ucsc.edu/
UCSC Genome Browser Archive	http://genome-archive.cse.ucsc.edu/
UCSC Genome Browser Experimental Tracks	http://genome-test.cse.ucsc.edu/

UCSC Genome Browser Custom Tracks	http://genome.ucsc.edu/goldenPath/help/customTrack.html
Genome Browser User's Guide	http://genome.ucsc.edu/goldenPath/help/hgTracksHelp.html
UCSC Genome Browser Mailing List	http://genome.ucsc.edu/contacts.html

Ensembl

Project Ensembl	http://www.ensembl.org/
Project Ensembl Preview Browser	http://pre.ensembl.org/

Other

Genome Sequencing Projects Funded by NHGRI	http://www.genome.gov/11007951
The Vertebrate Genome Annotation (VEGA) database	http://vega.sanger.ac.uk/

▮ FURTHER READING

Detailed descriptions of how to use the three genome browsers are presented in the publications below:

KAROLCHIK, D., BAERTSCH, R., DIEKHANS, M., FUREY, T. S., HINRICHS, A., LU, Y. T., ROSKIN, K. M., SCHWARTZ, M., SUGNET, C. W., THOMAS, D. J., et al. (2003). The UCSC Genome Browser Database. *Nucl. Acids Res.* 31, 51–54.

DOMBROWSKI, S. M., AND MAGLOTT, D. (2003). Using the Map Viewer to explore genomes. In *The NCBI Handbook*, eds. http://www.ncbi.nlm.nih.gov/books/bv.fcgi?rid=handbook.chapter.1562.

BIRNEY, E., ANDREWS, D., BEVAN, P., CACCAMO, M., CAMERON, G., CHEN, Y., CLARKE, L., COATES, G., COX, T., CUFF, J., et al. (2004). Ensembl 2004. *Nucl. Acids Res.* 32 (Database issue), D468–D470.

The User's Guide to the Genome is a hands-on manual for browsing and analyzing genomic data. The majority of the supplement shows a series of examples from Ensembl, the NCBI Map Viewer, and the UCSC Genome Browser that provides answers to the most common types of questions in sequence-based biology.

WOLFSBERG, T. G., WETTERSTRAND, K. A., GUYER, M. S., COLLINS, F. S., AND BAXEVANIS, A. D. (2002). A user's guide to the human genome. *Nat. Genet.* 32 (Suppl), 1–79.

WOLFSBERG, T. G., WETTERSTRAND, K. A., GUYER, M. S., COLLINS, F. S., AND BAXEVANIS, A. D. (2003). A user's guide to the human genome. *Nat. Genet.* 35 (Suppl 1), 4. Also available directly from *http://www.nature.com/cgi-taf/DynaPage.taf?file=/ng/journal/v35/n1s/index.html*.

▮ REFERENCES

BENSON, D. A., BOGUSKI, M. S., LIPMAN, D. J., AND OSTELL, J. (1997). GenBank. *Nucl. Acids Res.* 25, 1–6.

BIRNEY, E., ANDREWS, D., BEVAN, P., CACCAMO, M., CAMERON, G., CHEN, Y., CLARKE, L., COATES, G., COX, T., CUFF, J., et al. (2004). Ensembl 2004. *Nucl. Acids Res.* 32 (Database issue), D468–D470.

GIBBS, R. A., WEINSTOCK, G. M., METZKER, M. L., MUZNY, D. M., SODERGREN, E. J., SCHERER, S., SCOTT, G., STEFFEN, D., WORLEY, K. C., BURCH, P. E., et al. (2004). Genome sequence of the Brown Norway rat yields insights into mammalian evolution. *Nature* 428, 493–521.

GOFFEAU, A., BARRELL, B. G., BUSSEY, H., DAVIS, R. W., DUJON, B., FELDMANN, H., GALIBERT, F., HOHEISEL, J. D., JACQ, C., JOHNSTON, M.. (1996). Life with 6000 genes. *Science* 274, 546, 563–7.

GREEN, E. D. (2001). Strategies for the systematic sequencing of complex genomes. *Nat. Rev. Genet.* 2, 573–83.

KAROLCHIK, D., HINRICHS, A. S., FUREY, T. S., ROSKIN, K. M., SUGNET, C. W., HAUSSLER, D., AND KENT, W. J. (2004). The UCSC Table Browser data retrieval tool. *Nucl. Acids Res.* 32 (Database issue), D493–D496.

KAROLCHIK, D., AND KENT, W. J. (2003). The UCSC Genome Browser. *Curr. Protocols Bioinformatics* 1.4.1–1.4.23.

KASPRZYK, A., KEEFE, D., SMEDLEY, D., LONDON, D., SPOONER, W., MELSOPP, C., HAMMOND, M., ROCCA-SERRA, P., COX, T., AND BIRNEY, E. (2004). EnsMart: a generic system for fast and flexible access to biological data. *Genome Res.* 14, 160–169.

KENT, W. J., AND HAUSSLER, D. (2001). Assembly of the working draft of the human genome with GigAssembler. *Genome Res.* 11, 1541–1548.

KENT, W. J., SUGNET, C. W., FUREY, T. S., ROSKIN, K. M., PRINGLE, T. H., ZAHLER, A. M., AND HAUSSLER, D. (2002). The human genome browser at UCSC. *Genome Res.* 12, 996–1006.

KENT, W. J., AND ZAHLER, A. M. (2000). The intronerator: exploring introns and alternative splicing in Caenorhabditis elegans. *Nucl. Acids Res.* 28, 91–93.

KITTS, P. (2003). Genome assembly and annotation process. In *The NCBI Handbook* (eds.). http://www.ncbi.nlm.nih.gov/books/bv.fcgi?rid=handbook.chapter.1440.

LANDER, E. S., LINTON, L. M., BIRREN, B., NUSBAUM, C., ZODY, M. C., BALDWIN, J., DEVON, K., DEWAR, K., DOYLE, M., FITZHUGH, W., et al. (2001). Initial sequencing and analysis of the human genome. *Nature* 409, 860–921.

SCHULER, G. D. (1998). Electronic PCR: bridging the gap between genome mapping and genome sequencing. *Trends Biotechnol.* 16, 456–459.

WATERSTON, R. H., LINDBLAD-TOH, K., BIRNEY, E., ROGERS, J., ABRIL, J. F., AGARWAL, P., AGARWALA, R., AINSCOUGH, R., ALEXANDERSSON,

M., AN, P., et al. (2002). Initial sequencing and comparative analysis of the mouse genome. *Nature* 420, 520–562.

WHEELER, D. L., CHURCH, D. M., EDGAR, R., FEDERHEN, S., HELMBERG, W., MADDEN, T. L., PONTIUS, J. U., SCHULER, G. D., SCHRIML, L. M., SEQUEIRA, E., (2004). Database resources of the National Center for Biotechnology Information: update. *Nucl. Acids Res.* 32 (Database issue), D35–D40.

WOLFSBERG, T. G. (2003). Using the NCBI Map Viewer to browse genomic sequence Data. Curr Protocols Bioinformatics 1.5.1–1.5.22.

WOLFSBERG, T. G., WETTERSTRAND, K. A., GUYER, M. S., COLLINS, F. S., AND BAXEVANIS, A. D. (2002). A user's guide to the human genome. *Nat. Genet.* 32 (Suppl), 1–79.

■ KEY TERMS

e-PCR
Ensembl
genome browser
genome assembly
gene prediction
NCBI
UCSC

This chapter was written by Dr. Tyra G. Wolfsberg in her private capacity. No official support or endorsement by the National Institutes of Health or the United States Department of Health and Human Services is intended or should be inferred.

## PART TWO

ANALYSIS AT THE NUCLEOTIDE LEVEL

CHAPTER FIVE

Predictive Methods Using DNA Sequences

ENRIQUE BLANCO

RODERIC GUIGÓ

Bioinformatics: A Practical Guide to the Analysis of Genes and Proteins, Third Edition, edited by
Andreas D. Baxevanis and B.F. Francis Ouellette.
ISBN 0-471-47878-4 Copyright © 2005 John Wiley & Sons, Inc.

▌INTRODUCTION

As soon as the genome of an organism is sequenced and assembled, one of the first ensuing tasks is to locate all of the protein-coding genes hidden within the genomic sequence. This is a necessary step toward understanding better the functional content of the genome. The identification of genes is more difficult in eukaryotes than it is in prokaryotes, primarily because of the split nature of eukaryotic genes and because of the often large spacers found between adjacent genes. It is currently thought that less than 2% of vertebrate genomes code for proteins (Venter et al., 2001; Mouse Genome Sequencing Consortium, 2001). Apparently, the cellular machinery is able to recognize and process, with high precision, sequence signals within the primary DNA sequence or within the intermediate RNA molecules in the pathway leading from DNA to protein (Figure 5.1). However, our understanding of the molecular mechanisms through which these sequence signals are recognized and processed is still limited (Pennisi, 2003). Currently available computational methods for identifying sequence

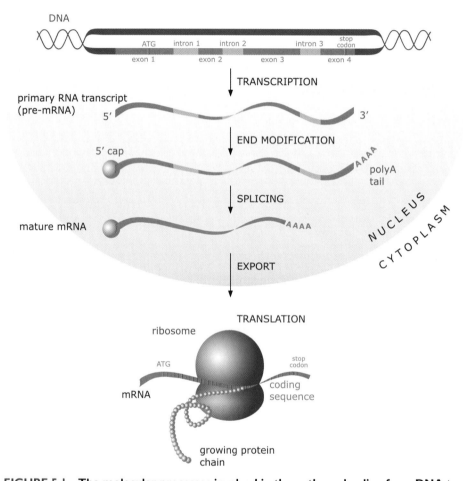

FIGURE 5.1 **The molecular processes involved in the pathway leading from DNA to protein. First, the DNA fragment encoding a single gene is transcribed to RNA. The termini of the resulting RNA molecule are processed to prevent degradation. Next, intervening, noncoding sequences (introns) are eliminated during splicing to produce the messenger RNA (mRNA). The mRNA is exported to the cytoplasm, were it is finally translated into protein. Sequence patterns are recognized and processed by the cellular machinery during all theses processes: promoter elements in the genomic DNA that trigger and control transcription, splice sites in the RNA molecule that identify the intron boundaries, and the start and termination codons that delimit the boundaries of the mRNA sequence that will be translated into protein. (Picture kindly provided by Sanja Rogic and Novak Rogic.)**

signals involved in gene specification are not yet powerful enough to elucidate precisely the gene structure from a large-scale genomic sequence. Therefore, gene prediction programs rely on factors such as compositional bias found in protein-coding regions, as well as similarity with known coding sequences. Even when all of this information is integrated, currently available gene prediction methods are not accurate enough to produce an entirely reliable annotation of genomic sequence from higher eukaryotes in an automated fashion; in the absence of additional information (e.g., cDNA sequence data), one should assume that predictions are highly hypothetical. Indeed, even with the completion of human genome sequencing, the actual number of genes encoded within the human genome is still unknown (Pennisi, 2003).

This chapter briefly reviews some of the computational methods underlying most computational gene finders, then focuses on a number of the most commonly used publicly available methods. There is a veritable plethora of such methods available (see Zhang, 2002, for a review). Here, particular focus is given to methods that have been used to annotate the human genome; results from applying these methods are available through the major human genome browsers, such as the University of California, Santa Cruz (UCSC) Genome Browser (Kent et al., 2002), Ensembl (Birney et al., 2004), and the National Center for Biotechnology Information (NCBI)'s Map Viewer (Chapter 4).

GENE PREDICTION METHODS

Gene-finding methods predict the location of genes in genomic sequences through a combination of one or more of the following approaches:

▶ *Searching by signal:* the analysis of sequence signals that are potentially involved in gene specification

▶ *Searching by content:* the analysis of regions showing compositional bias that has been correlated with coding regions

▶ *Homology-based gene prediction:* comparing sequences of interest against known coding sequences

▶ *Comparative gene prediction:* comparing sequences of interest against anonymous genomic sequences.

The so-called *ab initio* gene prediction approaches include searching by signal and by content, allowing gene structure to be predicted without direct comparison to other sequences. For this reason, these methods often are referred to as either "intrinsic" or "template" gene

prediction. In contrast, "extrinsic" or "look-up" gene prediction involves both homology-based and comparative approaches, in which gene structure is predicted through comparison with other sequences whose characteristics are already known.

As alluded to above, gene prediction is different (and more difficult) in eukaryotes as compared with prokaryotes. Although prokaryotic genes are characterized by single open reading frames (ORFs), usually found adjacent to one another, eukaryotic genes are separated by long stretches of intergenic DNA; their coding sequences (the exons) are interrupted by large, noncoding introns. Typically, computational gene prediction in eukaryotes involves each of the following:

▶ Identifying and scoring suitable splice sites and start and stop signals along the query sequence.

▶ Predicting candidate exons, as deduced through the detection of these signals.

▶ Scoring these exons as a function of both the signals used to detect the exons, as well as on coding statistics computed on the putative exon sequence itself. In homology-based and comparative methods, exon scores factor in the quality of the alignment between the query sequence and either known coding sequences or anonymous genomic sequences.

▶ Assembling a subset of these exon candidates into a predicted gene structure. The assembly is produced in a way that maximizes a particular scoring function; this scoring function is dependent on the score of each of the individual exon candidates that comprise the overall predicted gene structure.

The way in which each of these tasks is actually implemented varies from method to method, so it is important to understand the biological factors underlying these tasks.

Prediction of Exon-Defining Signals

Here, sequence signals are defined as short, functional DNA elements involved in gene specification. There are four basic signals involved in defining coding exons: the translational start site, the 5' (or donor) splice site, the 3' (or acceptor) splice site, and the translational stop codon. Typically, these sequence signals are detected through the use of position weight matrices (PWMs). These matrices are calculated from a set of known functional signals and are used to compute, across a sequence of interest, the position of any putative functional signals.

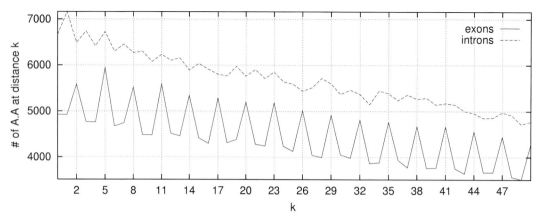

FIGURE 5.2   The absolute frequency of the pair A...A with k (from 0 to 50) nucleotides between the two As in the 200 first base pairs in a set of 1761 human exons and 1753 introns. A clear triplet pattern appears in coding regions; this is not seen in noncoding regions. This periodic pattern is a reflection of the characteristic codon usage seen in coding regions. (Adapted from Guigó, 1999).

Prediction and Scoring of Exons

In addition to sequence signals, the accurate prediction of exons also depends on content-based features. Exons can be divided into three basic types:

▶ *Initial exons:* ORFs delimited by a start site and a 5′ (donor) site

▶ *Internal exons:* ORFs delimited by a 3′ (acceptor) site and a 5′ (donor) site.

▶ *Terminal exons:* ORFs delimited by a 3′ (acceptor) site and a stop codon.

Zhang (2002) provides a comprehensive discussion of these types of eukaryotic exons.

Protein-coding regions are known to exhibit characteristic compositional bias when compared with non-coding regions (Figure 5.2). The observed bias results from the uneven distribution of amino acids in proteins, as well as the uneven use of synonymous codons. To discriminate protein-coding regions from noncoding regions, a number of content-based measures can be used (Fickett & Tung, 1992; Gelfand, 1995; Guigó, 1999). These content measures, which are also referred to as *coding statistics*, reflect the likelihood that a given DNA sequence codes for a protein or protein fragment. Many methods for the computation of content-based measures have been published over the years. Hexamer frequencies, usually in the form of codon position-dependent fifth-order Markov models (Box 5.1; Borodovsky & McIninch, 1993) seem to offer maximal discriminative power; these hexamer frequencies are at the core of gene finders currently finding the most widespread use.

BOX 5.1 | Markov Models

A Markov chain, model, or process refers to a series of observations in which the probability of an observation depends on a number of previous observations. The number of observations defines the "order" of the chain. For example, in a first-order Markov model, the probability of an observation depends only on the previous observation. In a Markov chain of order 5, the probability of an observation depends on the five preceding observations. A DNA sequence can be considered to be an example of a Markov model, because the likelihood of observing a particular base at a given position may depend on the bases preceding it. In particular, in coding regions, it is well known that the probability of a given base depends on the five preceding bases, reflecting observed codon biases and dependencies between adjacent codons. In noncoding regions, such dependence is not observed. When scanning an anonymous genomic region, one can compute how well the local nucleotide sequence conforms to the fifth-order dependencies observed in coding regions and assign appropriate coding likelihood scores.

Prediction of Genes Through *Ab Initio* Methods

Predicted exons need to be assembled into some sort of gene structure. Splicing genes together into a putative gene structure can help to eliminate the prediction of false exons by simply examining whether adjacent exons maintain the open reading frame established by the initial exon. The main difficulty in exon assembly lies in simple combinatorics: the number of possible exon assemblies grows exponentially with the number of predicted exons for any given gene. To address this problem, a number of dynamic programming techniques have been developed. In dynamic programming (Bellman, 1957), the solution to a general problem is obtained by the recursive solution of smaller versions of the problem (see Appendix 6.1 for a detailed discussion). Here, for the optimal exon assembly problem, dynamic programming allows one to find the solution efficiently, without having to enumerate or consider each and every possible combination of exons (Gelfand & Roytberg, 1993). GRAIL2 (Xu et al., 1994), FGENESH (Solovyev et al., 1995), and GENEID (Guigó et al., 1992; Guigó, 1998) all use this basic approach.

The application of hidden Markov models (HMMs) marked a significant advance in the area of gene prediction methodologies. The use of HMMs, described in Box 5.2, makes it possible to define highly complex patterns, such as multigenic genes. Very efficient algorithms have been developed to search for such patterns in genomic sequences. A very popular example of an HMM-based gene finder is GENSCAN (Burge & Karlin, 1997), a program that has been widely used to annotate

eukaryotic genomes. Other examples of HMM-based methods include GENIE (Kulp et al., 1996) and HMM-gene (Krogh, 1997).

Sequence Similarity-Based Gene Prediction

When a genomic sequence encodes a known protein, or a protein with a known homolog, methods that are based on the comparison of the genomic sequence with known coding sequences may be preferable. Translated nucleotide searches, such as BLASTX searches (Gish & States, 1993; Chapter 11) constitute one of the simplest homology-based gene prediction approaches. These searches are particularly useful when comparing ORFs in prokaryotic genomes. However, when dealing with the split nature of eukaryotic genes, BLASTX-like searches do not resolve exon splice boundaries particularly well. A novel approach involves the use of both the results of translated nucleotide searches along with those produced through the use of ab initio methods. Examples of this approach include programs such as GenomeScan (Yeh et al., 2001) and GeneID (Blanco et al., 2002), among others.

BOX 5.2 Hidden Markov Models in Gene Prediction

Hidden Markov models (HMMs) are used to provide a statistical representation of real biological processes. They have found widespread use in many areas of bioinformatics, including multiple sequence alignment, the characterization and classification of protein families, the comparison of protein structures, and the prediction of gene structure.

In this chapter, all of the gene-finding methods that are described have two things in common: They use a raw nucleotide sequence as their input, and, for each position in the sequence, they attempt to predict whether a given base is most likely found in an intron, an exon, or within an intergenic region. In making these predictions, the algorithm applied (HMM or otherwise) must take into account what is known about the structure of a gene, showed in a simplified fashion in Figure 5.1.

Working from the 5' to 3' end of the gene, the method must take into account the unique characteristics of promoter regions, TSSs, 5' UTRs, start codons, exons, splice donors, introns, splice acceptors, stop codons, 3' UTRs, and polyA tails. In addition to any conserved sequences or compositional bias that may characterize each of these regions (see Box 5.1), the method also needs to take into account that each of these elements appear with a controlled syntax; for example, the promoter (and its TATA box) must appear before the start codon, an initial exon must follow the start codon, introns must follow exons, introns can only be

followed by internal or terminal exons, stop codons cannot interrupt the coding region, and polyA signals must appear after the stop codon. Finally, an ORF must be maintained throughout actually to produce a protein once all is said and done.

Each of the elements—exons, introns, and so forth—are referred to as *states*. The sequence characteristics and syntactical constraints described above allows a transition probability to be assigned, indicating how likely a change of state is as one moves through the sequence, base by base. Although the user "sees" the nucleotide sequence being analyzed, the user does not actually "see" the states that the individual bases are in—hence the term *hidden*. Put otherwise, each state emits a particular kind of nucleotide sequence, with its own emission probability; the state emitting the nucleotide sequence is hidden, but the sequence itself is visible. The transition and emission probabilities are derived from training sets, sequences for which the correct gene structure is already known. The goal here is to develop a set of parameters that allows the method to be fine tuned, maximizing the chances that a correct prediction is generated on a new sequence of interest. As alluded to in the main text, these parameters differ from organism to organism, and the success of any given HMM-based method depends on how well these parameters have been deduced from the training set.

Expressed sequence tag (EST) sequences are extremely valuable both for identifying genes and for delineating their exonic structure, particularly when there may be alternative splice forms. EST sequences can be mapped quite accurately to a genomic DNA sequence using tools like BLAT (Kent, 2002) or BLASTN (Altschul et al., 1990), especially when stringent parameters are used. However, this technique still may not provide perfect mapping of exon boundaries, meaning that a viable ORF is not identified. Specialized programs such as GRAIL-EXP (Xu & Uberbacher, 1997), which use splice site models, often provide a more clear solution to the problem.

A more sophisticated approach involves aligning the genomic query against a protein (or cDNA) target, presumably homologous to the protein encoded in the genomic sequence. In these alignments, often referred to as *spliced alignments*, large gaps corresponding to introns in the query sequence are only allowed at "legal" splice junctions. Examples of programs using this approach include SIM4 (Florea et al., 1998), EST_GENOME (Mott, 1997), PROCRUSTES (Gelfand et al., 1996), and GENEWISE (Birney & Durbin, 1997).

Comparative Gene Prediction

With a large number of complete genomes now available, a number of strategies have been developed that use a comparative approach in predicting genes. The rationale behind comparative genomics methods is that functional regions (protein-coding regions) tend to be more conserved than non–protein-coding regions. This observation provides the basis for identifying protein-coding regions in newly sequenced genomes. Three comparative gene prediction programs were used in the analysis of both the human and mouse genomes: TWINSCAN (Korf et al., 2001), SGP-2 (Parra et al., 2003), and SLAM (Alexandersson et al., 2003). SLAM is an HMM-based method in which gene predictions and sequence alignments are performed simultaneously. TWINSCAN is an extension of GENSCAN, whereas SGP-2 is an extension of GeneID. The probability scores calculated by each of these programs for putative exons are adjusted based on comparative results. Comparative genomics techniques are discussed in more detail in Chapter 15.

❚ GENE PREDICTION PROGRAMS

This section describes a representative cross-section of all available gene-finding programs; the programs discussed here use most of the theoretical approaches described above. With minor exceptions, all of these programs can be accessed through easy-to-use Web frontends, but also can be downloaded and run locally. All of

the examples presented in this section use the sequence of the human uroporphyrinogen decarboxylate (URO-D) gene (*U30787*) as the query. An SP1 binding site, TATA box, and 10 exons have been annotated to this sequence, whose length is 4514 bases; a graphical representation of the annotated coding exons and resulting prediction from each of the programs discussed below is shown in Figure 5.3. It is immediately obvious that the programs have produced different predictions, a point that is discussed later in this chapter. At this point, however, keep in mind that the results for this particular prediction do not necessarily reflect the overall accuracy of any individual program; indeed, some programs will perform better on some sequences than others, based on numerous factors that will be illustrated below.

GRAIL

The Gene Recognition and Analysis Internet Link (GRAIL) program was one of the first gene-finding programs developed (Uberbacher & Mural, 1991). GRAIL calculates the likelihood that a particular position is within a coding region by computing and integrating seven separate coding statistic measures. This results in a profile along the length of the query sequence, where peaks correspond to coding regions. A later modification of this program, called GRAIL2 (Xu et al., 1994), incorporated information about different splice and translational signals, improving GRAIL's predictive power. Finally, GRAIL-EXP (Xu & Uberbacher, 1997) further advanced the original GRAIL algorithm by incorporating homology information; the inclusion of BLASTN searches (Chapter 11) against a database of partial and complete transcripts (ESTs) significantly improved the predictive power of the method.

The results of the GRAIL prediction on the URO-D sequence are shown in Figure 5.4. Information on each exon predicted is given on a separate line; each line gives the exon number, what strand the exon lies on (+, meaning forward, or −, meaning reverse), the start and stop points for the exon, the exon type, its length, a raw score, and the quality of that particular exon prediction, in qualitative terms. Here, GRAIL correctly predicted five of the ten known exons, as well as part of a sixth internal exon. The missing exons are short and are difficult to predict using only estimations of coding potential. However, incorporating the BLASTN searches through GRAIL-EXP led to a correct prediction (Figure 5.5), as well as the prediction of at least four different alternative forms.

GeneID

GeneID (Guigó et al., 1992; Parra et al., 2000) is a program that predicts genes in genomic sequences using

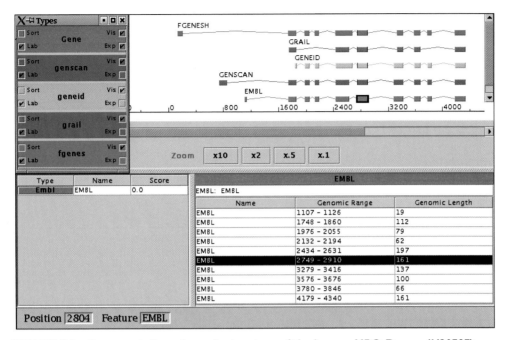

FIGURE 5.3 **Representation of exonic structure of the human URO-D gene (*U30787*),** **displayed using the APOLLO graphical interactive interface. The gene is comprised of 10 coding exons on the forward strand. Predictions by GRAIL, GENSCAN, GeneID, and FGENESH also are displayed.**

a hierarchical approach. In the first step, splice sites and start and stop codons are predicted and scored using position weight matrices. In the second step, exons are built from these identified "defining sites." Exons are scored as the sum of the scores of the defining sites plus the score of their coding potential. In the last step, based on the set of predicted exons, the gene structure is assembled, predicting the most likely gene structure by maximizing the sum of the scores of the assembled exons. The most recent version of GeneID (Blanco

```
# Sequence Name: >gene_grail|PID=18457
# Sequence Length: 4514
# Output_begin: pretty

Sequence:  >gene_grail|PID=18457 (4514 bp)
------------------------------------------------------------
PERCEVAL Exon Candidates (6 predicted)


  Index Std  Begin   End Frm     Type  Len  Scr    Quality

      1   +    1755  1860   0  Internal  106   57   Marginal
      2   +    2434  2631   0  Internal  198  100   Excellent
      3   +    2749  2910   0  Internal  162  100   Excellent
      4   +    3324  3416   0  Internal   93   92   Excellent
      5   +    3576  3676   0  Internal  101  100   Excellent
      6   +    4179  4340   0  Terminal  162  100   Excellent
------------------------------------------------------------

# Output_end: pretty
```

FIGURE 5.4 **GRAIL output in the sequence of the URO-D gene (*U30787*). A detailed explanation of the output is provided in the main text.**

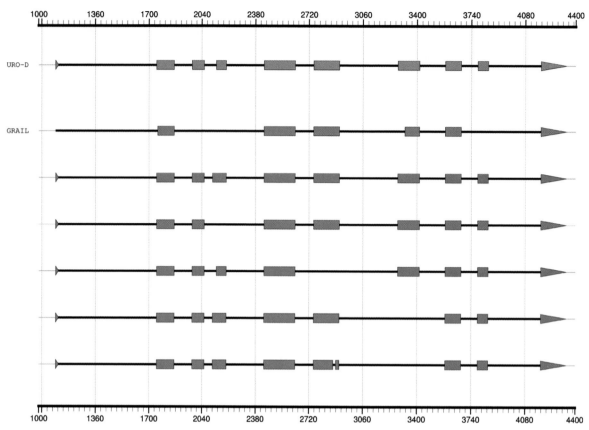

FIGURE 5.5   GRAIL and GRAIL-EXP predictions for the URO-D gene (*U30787*). The top track displays the annotated exonic structure. Below, the GRAIL ab initio prediction is shown. The following tracks display the different alternative forms predicted by GRAIL-EXP using an external EST database.

et al., 2002) incorporates additional information such as sequence similarity, experimental data, or data from other computational predictions.

The results of the GeneID prediction on the URO-D sequence are shown in Figure 5.6. Information on each exon is given on a separate line; the information includes the exon type, its start and stop positions, raw score, strand (+ or −), frame (meaning the number of nucleotides before the first complete codon), remainder (meaning the number of nucleotides after the last complete codon), and a number of scores that contribute to the overall score for this exon. Following the AA: are the coordinates that the exon maps to on the predicted protein product. After the individual exon predictions is the amino acid sequence of the predicted protein product. Here, GeneID predicted two genes. Gene 1 is the initial exon of a gene in the reverse strand, likely to correspond to a real exon from an upstream gene (see Figure 5.10). Gene 2 gives the annotated gene in the forward strand, correctly predicting seven of URO-D's ten exons and partially predicting two. The initial exon was missed, most

likely because of the weakness of the START codon signal and the short length of the coding sequence.

GENSCAN

GENSCAN is a general purpose eukaryotic gene prediction program. For each query sequence, the program determines the most likely gene structure given an underlying hidden Markov model. To model donor splice sites, GENSCAN introduced a new method, called *maximal dependence decomposition*. In this method, a series of weight matrices (instead of just one) are used to capture dependencies between positions in these splice sites. In addition, GENSCAN uses parameters that account for many higher-order properties of genomic sequences (e.g., typical gene density, typical number of exons per gene, and the distribution of exon sizes for different types of exons). Separate sets of gene model parameters can be used to adjust for the differences in gene density and G + C composition seen across genomes. Models also have been developed for use

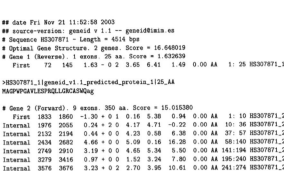
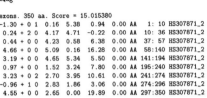
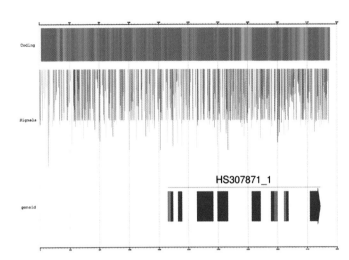

FIGURE 5.6 GeneID output for the URO-D gene. See the main text for a description of the output. GeneID produces graphical output that is highly customizable, through the GFF2PS program. Here, in addition to the predicted gene, included are putative splice sites and coding potential information.

with maize and *Arabidopsis* sequences. GenomeScan (Yeh et al., 2001) is an extension of GENSCAN that incorporates sequence similarity to known proteins using BLASTX (Chapter 11). This leads to higher scores for exons exhibiting similarity to known proteins, but decreased scores for predicted exons having little to no similarity with known proteins.

A typical GENSCAN output is shown in Figure 5.7. Each exon in the prediction is shown in a separate line. The columns, going from left to right, represent the gene and exon number (Gn.Ex), the type of prediction (Type, either the exon type or an identified polyA

signal), the strand on which the prediction was made (+ or −), the beginning and endpoints for the prediction, the length of the predicted exon, its reading frame, several scoring columns, and a probability value (P). GENSCAN exons having a very high probability value ($p > 0.99$) are 97.7% accurate when the prediction matches a true, annotated exon. These high-probability predictions can be used in the rational design of polymerase chain reaction primers for cDNA amplification, or for other purposes where extremely high confidence is necessary. GENSCAN exons that have probabilities in the range 0.50 to 0.99 are deemed to be correct most

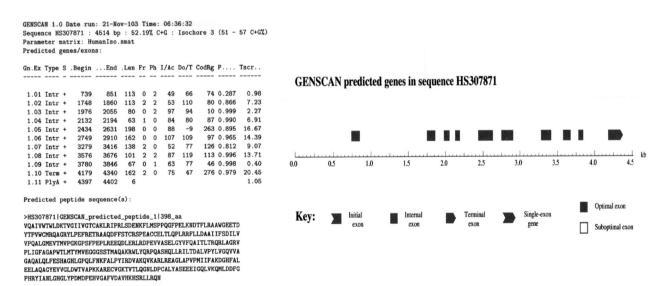

FIGURE 5.7 GENSCAN output for the URO-D gene. See the main text for a description of the output.

of the time; the best-case accuracies for p values higher than 0.90 is on the order of 88%. Any predictions having $p < 0.50$ should be deemed unreliable, and those data are, therefore, not given in the data table. The predicted amino acid sequence is given below the gene predictions. In the example, GENSCAN correctly predicted nine of the ten exons in URO-D, missing the initial exon. The use of GenomeScan did not improve the prediction, because the initial exon was not detected by BLASTX.

FGENES

The first version of FGENES (for "find genes"; Solovyev et al., 1995) was a system using linear discriminant analysis to identify splice sites, exons, and promoter elements (Box 5.3). Filtered exons are assembled using a dynamic programming algorithm that searches paths of compatible exons, with the goal of maximizing the final gene score. FGENESH is an HMM-based variant of FGENES. FGENESH+ and FGENESH-C are two recent extensions that incorporate protein and cDNA sequence homology, respectively (Salamov & Solovyev, 2000). Because these extensions use information from known genes and DNA sequences, predictive power is better than that observed with the purely ab initio FGENESH.

FGENESH predictions on the URO-D sequence are shown in Figure 5.8. The tabular format of the output gives the gene number, the strand (+ or −), the exon number within the gene, the exon type, the start and stop positions for the exon, an exon score, ORF start and stop positions, and exon length. The amino acid sequence of the predicted protein product is given below the gene prediction. The method can also predict TATA boxes and polyA tails. Here, FGENESH correctly predicted seven of the ten exons, two exons were partially detected, and the initial exon was missed altogether. The method detected the presence of a polyA tail as well.

GENEWISE

GENEWISE compares a genomic sequence with a protein sequence or with an HMM representing a protein domain. The comparison is performed at the protein level while maintaining the reading frame, regardless of intervening introns or sequence errors that may cause frameshifts. Put another way, GENEWISE performs both a gene prediction and a homology comparison simultaneously. GENEWISE is computationally expensive, and an accurate prediction requires the presence of a close, homologous protein. Figure 5.9 illustrates the results of GENEWISE predictions when progressively

---

BOX 5.3 Discriminant Analysis in Gene Prediction

Discriminant function analysis is a frequently used technique aimed at determining which variables, if any, can discriminate between two or more naturally occurring groups. In the area of gene prediction, the observables that may be used to try to discriminate whether a particular stretch of DNA is found in either an intron or an exon could include the presence of putative acceptor sites, donor sites, or start and stop codons.

Imagine a case in which two observables (for instance, splice site scores and exon length) are plotted against each other on a simple XY graph, similar to the one in this box. The two different symbols on the graph may represent different groups (here, assume that the X represents an exon, whereas the circle represents an intron). Two different types of discriminant analysis could be applied to try to separate the two states from one another. In linear discriminant analysis, a linear function is used to try to separate the two groups. In quadratic discriminant analysis, a quadratic function is used to separate the two groups.

In cases in which the relationship between the two sets of observables are nonlinear or multivariate, the resulting graph will look like a swarm of points, as they do in this case. Here, a linear function L(x) cannot adequately

separate the two states; an appreciable number of points have been misclassified. However, the quadratic function Q(x) is capable of completely separating the two groups in this case.

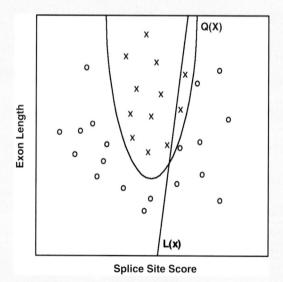

(Figure adapted from Zhang, 1997.)

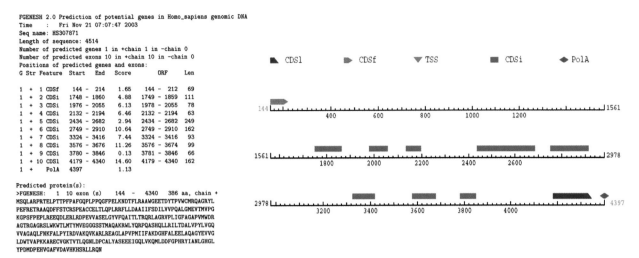

```
FGENESH 2.0 Prediction of potential genes in Homo_sapiens genomic DNA
Time    :  Fri Nov 21 07:07:47 2003
Seq name: HS307871
Length of sequence: 4514
Number of predicted genes 1 in +chain 1 in -chain 0
Number of predicted exons 10 in +chain 10 in -chain 0
Positions of predicted genes and exons:
G Str Feature  Start   End    Score      ORF      Len

1  +  1 CDSf    144 -  214    1.65    144 -  212   69
1  +  2 CDSi   1748 - 1860    4.88   1749 - 1859  111
1  +  3 CDSi   1976 - 2055    6.13   1978 - 2055   78
1  +  4 CDSi   2132 - 2194    6.46   2132 - 2194   63
1  +  5 CDSi   2434 - 2682    2.94   2434 - 2682  249
1  +  6 CDSi   2749 - 2910   10.64   2749 - 2910  162
1  +  7 CDSi   3324 - 3416    7.44   3324 - 3416   93
1  +  8 CDSi   3576 - 3676   11.26   3576 - 3674   99
1  +  9 CDSi   3780 - 3846    0.13   3781 - 3846   66
1  + 10 CDSl   4179 - 4340   14.60   4179 - 4340  162
1  +    PolA   4397           1.13


Predicted protein(s):
>FGENESH:  1  10 exon (s)  144 -  4340   386 aa, chain +
MSQLARPRTELPTTPFPAFGQPLPPQGFPELKNDTFLRAAWGEETDYTPVWCMRQAGRYL
PEFRETRAAQDFFSTCRSPEACCELTLQPLRRFLLDAAIIFSDILVVPQALGMEVTMVPG
KGPSFPEPLREEQDLERLRDPEVVASELGYVFQAITLTRQRLAGRVPLIGFAGAPVMWDR
AGTRGAGRSLWKWTLMTYMVEGGGSSTMAQAKRWLYQRPQASHQLLRILTDALVPYLVGQ
VVAGAQLFNKFALPYIRDVAKQVKARLREAGLAPVPMIIFAKDGHFALEELAQAGYEVVG
LDWTVAPKKARECVGKTVTLQGNLDPCALYASEEEIGQLVKQMLDDFGPHRYIANLGHGL
YPDMDPEHVGAFVDAVHKHSRLLRQN
```

FIGURE 5.8 FGENESH output for the **URO-D** gene. **A detailed explanation of the different fields is provided in the main text.**

distant homologs of the URO-D protein are used. Although the prediction is perfect when mammalian homologs are used, the prediction deteriorates at greater evolutionary distances. Regardless, even with the *Saccharomyces* URO-D protein sequence, the prediction is quite good. Given its predictive power, GENEWISE is at the core of the European Bioinformatics Institute's Ensembl system (Chapter 4). A view of the region containing URO-D is shown in Figure 5.10; note the various gene predictions available in this view.

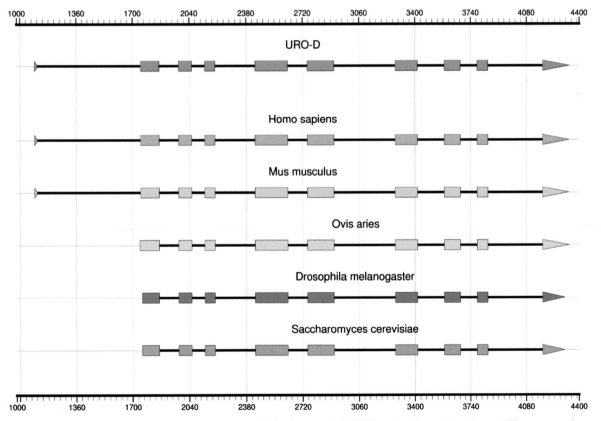

FIGURE 5.9 GENEWISE predictions for the **URO-D** gene (U30787), using homologs from different species as target proteins. The view shown in the figure has been generated using **GFF2PS.**

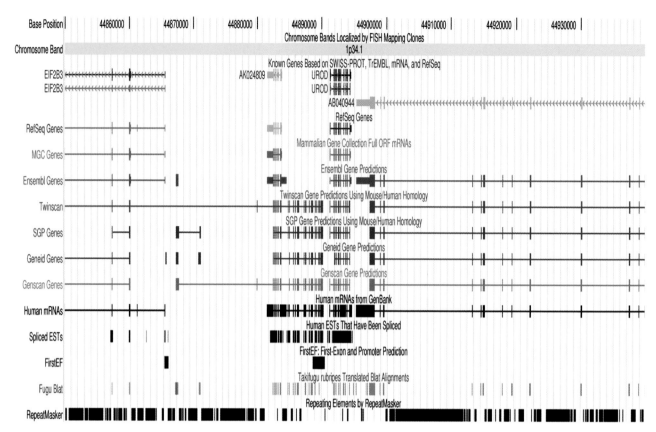

FIGURE 5.10 The **UCSC** browser view of the 100-Kb region centered on human **URO-D.** See text for details.

▌HOW WELL DO THE METHODS WORK?

As seen above, different methods often produce different—and sometimes contradictory—results. A question that naturally arises regards the reliability of any the gene predictions or of the programs themselves. The answer to this question depends on numerous factors, such as the species under consideration, the sequence context, and the existence of experimental evidence. In general, a prediction that is supported by spliced ESTs or that shows strong similarity to known coding sequences is more reliable than one having no supporting evidence. Similarly, consistent predictions on a given genomic region by different methods should bolster confidence in the prediction.

It is useful to be able to measure the overall accuracy of gene prediction methods, and a number of attempts have been made at estimating their performance. The accuracy of gene prediction programs is usually determined using controlled, define data sets, comparing the prediction made by a method with the actual gene structure, determined experimentally (Figure 5.11). Accuracy can be computed at either the nucleotide, exon, or gene level, and each provide different insights into the accuracy of a predictive method. Regardless of the level being examined, two basic measures are used:

▶ Sensitivity (Sn). Sensitivity is defined as the proportion of coding nucleotides, exons, or genes that have been predicted correctly.

▶ Specificity (Sp). Specificity is defined as the proportion of predicted coding nucleotides, exons, or genes that are real (the overall fraction of the prediction that is correct).

Sensitivity and specificity can take on values from zero to one; for a perfect prediction, Sn = 1 and Sp = 1. Neither sensitivity nor specificity alone provide a good measure of global accuracy, because high sensitivity can be achieved with little specificity and vice versa. An easier to understand measure that combines the sensitivity and specificity values is called the *correlation coefficient* (CC). If the four possible outcomes for any prediction are either a true positive (*TP*), a true negative (*TN*), a false positive (*FP*), or a false negative (*FN*), the correlation

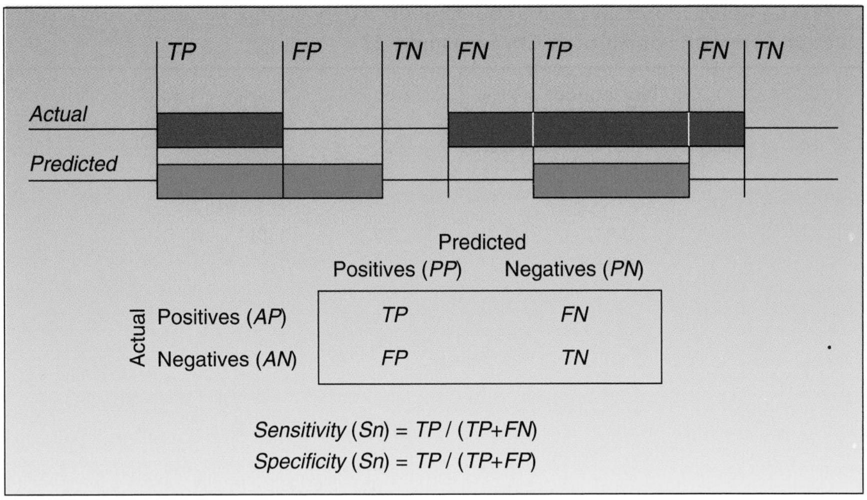

FIGURE 5.11 **Schematic representation of measures of gene prediction accuracy at the nucleotide level. In the upper portion of the figure, the four possible outcomes of a prediction are shown: true positives (TP), true negatives (TN), false positives (FP), and false negatives (FN). The matrix at the bottom of the figure shows how both sensitivity and specificity are determined from these four possible outcomes, giving a tangible measure of the effectiveness of any gene prediction method. (Adapted from Burset & Guigó, 1996; Snyder & Stormo, 1997).**

coefficient is given by the following equation:

$$CC = \frac{(TP \times TN) - (FN \times FP)}{\sqrt{(TP+FN)(TN+FP)(TP+FP)(TN+FN)}}$$

The correlation coefficient ranges from -1 to 1, where a value of 1 corresponds to a perfect prediction; a value of -1 indicates that every coding region has been predicted as noncoding, and vice versa.

Burset and Guigó (1996) published one of the first systematic evaluations of gene finders. This study evaluated seven programs, using a set of 570 vertebrate single-gene sequences. The average CC at the nucleotide level for these programs ranged from 0.65 to 0.80. Later, Rogic et al. (2001) published a new comparative analysis of seven gene prediction programs, using a set of 195 single-gene sequences from human and rodent species. The programs tested in the Rogic et al. study showed substantially higher accuracy than those reported on in the Burset and Guigó study: the average CC at the nucleotide level ranged from 0.66 to 0.91. This increase in the upper part of the range illustrates the significant advances that occurred in the development of gene-finding methods over a relatively short period of time.

The evaluations put forth by Burset and Guigó (1996), Rogic et al. (2001), and others suffered from the same limitation: the gene finders were tested using controlled

data sets comprised of short genomic sequences encoding a single gene, presumably having simple gene structures. These data sets by no means are representative of genomic sequences as a whole; sequences that contain long stretches with low coding density; stretches coding for multiple or incomplete genes, or both; and stretches having very complex or alternative gene structures. The exhaustive scrutiny to which human chromosome 22 was subjected (Dunham et al., 1999) provides an excellent basis for obtaining a more representative estimation of the accuracy of currently available gene finders. Table 5.1 gives the accuracy of a number of ab initio and comparative gene finders when applied to the sequence of human chromosome 22, as compared with curated, manual annotations. Three issues are noteworthy. First, the accuracy of ab initio gene finders substantially suffers when moving up in complexity from single gene sequences to genome-scale sequence data; note that the correlation coefficient of GENSCAN drops from 0.91 from the Rogic et al. study to 0.64 when applied to chromosome 22. Second, dual-genome comparative gene finders, such as SGP-2, provide a level of improvement over their ab initio counterparts. Third, even the more sophisticated gene finders that use known cDNA or RefSeq genes to improve their predictions still fall short of the level needed for the automatic annotation of complex eukaryotic genomes. The reader is referred

TABLE 5.1 ■ **The Relative Accuracy of Sequence Similarity-Based, Ab Initio, and Comparative Gene Prediction Programs on Human Chromosome 22**

Program	Nucleotide			Exon				
	S_n	S_p	CC	S_n	S_p	$\frac{Sn+Sp}{2}$	ME	WE
Sequence similarity based								
ENSEMBL	0.74	0.83	0.78	0.75	0.80	0.77	0.18	0.13
FGENESH++	0.81	0.71	0.75	0.80	0.66	0.73	0.11	0.27
Ab initio								
GENSCAN	0.79	0.53	0.64	0.68	0.41	0.55	0.15	0.48
GENEID	0.73	0.67	0.70	0.65	0.55	0.60	0.21	0.33
Comparative								
SGP2	0.75	0.73	0.73	0.66	0.58	0.62	0.19	0.28

The accuracy measures shown here are, from left to right: sensitivity (Sn), specificity (Sp), and the correlation coefficient (CC) at the nucleotide level; sensitivity (Sn), specificity (Sp), and correlation coefficient (Sn + Sp)/2 at the exon level; and the number of missing and wrong exons in the predictions.

to a recent review on the accuracy of gene prediction programs for an in-depth discussion (Guigó & Wiehe, 2003).

PROMOTER ANALYSIS: CHARACTERIZATION AND PREDICTION

In eukaryotes, gene expression is regulated at different stages; these include the compaction of chromatin, transcriptional initiation, polyadenylation, splicing, mRNA stability, translation initiation, and the control of protein activity. For most genes, the initiation of transcription is considered to be the most important control point, because control at this point ensures that no superfluous intermediates are synthesized. Promoters can be defined as functional regions immediately upstream or downstream of a transcription start site (TSS) that are

intimately involved in the regulation of transcription. Figure 5.12 illustrates the structure of a promoter region, consisting of a specific arrangement of transcription factor binding sites, also called *regulatory* or *promoter elements* (Fickett & Hatzigeorgiou, 1997). The region of the promoter near the TSS where RNA polymerase II binds is known as the *core promoter*. The core promoter is a universal feature that is responsible for basal gene transcription (Zhang, 1998). Transcriptional enhancers are defined as nondirectional promoter regions, and they often are found several thousands of nucleotides away from the regulated gene. Experimental identification of promoter regions at a genomic scale is extremely laborious and expensive, so computational methods may play an important role in the annotation of these sequences (Pennacchio & Rubin, 2001).

There is an intimate relationship between gene finding and promoter prediction. A correct promoter

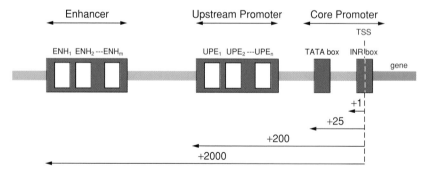

FIGURE 5.12 A schematic representation of a typical promoter. The core of the promoter consists on the TATA box and an initiator sequence. Upstream and downstream promoters (not shown here) are comprised of several binding sites or composites. Enhancers are regulatory regions distant from the regulated gene.

prediction could, in turn, help to improve gene prediction, because it serves as a way to define better the boundaries of a gene. However, correct gene prediction automatically would lead to better predictions of upstream promoter regions. Therefore, the complete annotation of any gene should include both the promoter elements and the protein-coding regions (Pedersen et al., 1999). Two different yet related problems arise in the analysis of promoters: the prediction of promoter regions in genomic sequences (particularly the TSS) and the characterization of promoter regions, which involves the detection of transcription factor binding motifs. The algorithms used to address these problems fall into two basic groups: pattern-driven algorithms and sequence-driven algorithms (Brazma et al., 1998). Pattern-driven algorithms search for known regulatory patterns in genomic sequences, whereas sequence-driven algorithms attempt to "discover" unknown patterns from sets of sequences that are functionally related.

Pattern-Driven Algorithms

Pattern-driven algorithms depend on the availability of collections of experimentally annotated binding sites; examples of these collections include TRANSFAC (Matys et al., 2003) and PROMO (Messeguer et al., 2002). As illustrated in Figure 5.13, general representations or patterns of a given binding site (e.g., consensus sequences or weight matrices) can be constructed from simple sequence alignments of "real" sites. These patterns, in turn, can be used to scan genomic sequences to find "new" occurrences of a binding motif (Bücher, 1990; Stormo, 2000). Pattern-driven searches tend to produce a huge number of false positives for the following reasons (Fickett & Hatzigeorgiou, 1997):

▶ The binding site sequence for a specific transcription factor may be highly variable

▶ The length of the binding sites is very short (typically 5–15 bp)

▶ Interaction between transcription factors may influence binding affinity with the promoter sites

▶ One binding site may be recognized by one or more different transcription factors.

A number of solutions have been proposed to overcome these problems. The context within which the site is predicted is essential: putative sites detected in regions where the concentration of predictions is higher are more reliable than isolated predictions (Werner, 2000). In addition, the probability of a site being a functional site is substantially increased when an annotated TSS is nearby; many of these are cataloged in the Eukaryotic Promoter Database (Praz et al., 2002). However, the correct annotation of the first exon of a gene—whether it codes partially for a protein or does not code at all—still presents a difficult problem (Davuluri et al., 2001). Because cooperation between transcription factors also could play an important role in the regulation of transcription, searching for clusters of associated sites or composites can lead to a substantial improvement in the predictions (Wagner, 1997). However, experimental discovery and classification of new transcription factors can help to develop more complete catalogs of regulatory elements (Pennacchio & Rubin, 2001).

Sequence-Driven Algorithms

Sequence-driven methods rely on the assumption that common functionality can be deduced through underlying sequence conservation (Figure 5.14). Sequence alignments of promoter regions of co-regulated genes, therefore, can highlight regulatory elements involved in co-regulation. Different types of alignment procedures can be applied here. Particularly useful are heuristic techniques such as MEME or AlignAce, which aid in identifying common motifs in sets of unaligned sequences (Bailey & Elkan, 1995; Roth et al., 1998). Two kinds of co-regulated sequences typically are used: orthologous genes from different species and genes that have been experimentally determined to be co-expressed (Pennacchio & Rubin, 2001).

Comparative promoter prediction is based on the hypothesis that patterns of gene regulation are often conserved across species ("phylogenetic footprinting"; Chapter 15); interspecies comparisons therefore could help to identify common regulatory sequences (Wasserman et al., 2000). The selection of appropriate species is always a critical aspect in phylogenetic footprinting (Duret & Bücher, 1997). However, this promising approach does present some problems:

▶ Different genomic regions evolve at different rates, so some genes—and their pattern of regulation—may be more conserved than others

▶ Classical sequence alignments cannot deal with the translocations and inversions in the order of conserved functional elements that are often observed in real promoter regions (Jegga et al., 2002)

▶ If the background conservation of the entire promoter region is very strong, comparative methods are useless

▶ It is unclear to what extent noncoding conserved elements exhibit regulatory functions (Dermitzakis et al., 2002)

▶ There is an important fraction of regulatory elements that are not conserved across species and, therefore, cannot be detected through interspecies comparisons (Pennacchio & Rubin, 2001).

```
AC   M00252
XX
ID   V$TATA_01
XX
DT   25.09.1996 (created); ewi.
DT   25.09.1996 (updated); ewi.
CO   Copyright (C), Biobase GmbH.
XX
NA   TATA
XX
DE   cellular and viral TATA box elements
XX
BF   T00794 TBP; Species: human, Homo sapiens.
BF   T00796 TBP; Species: mouse, Mus musculus.
BF   T00797 TBP; Species: fruit fly, Drosophila melanogaster.
XX
PO      A      C      G      T
01     61    145    152     31    S
02     16     46     18    309    T
03    352      0      2     35    A
04      3     10      2    374    T
05    354      0      5     30    A
06    268      0      0    121    A
07    360      3     20      6    A
08    222      2     44    121    W
09    155     44    157     33    R
10     56    135    150     48    N
11     83    147    128     31    N
12     82    127    128     52    N
13     82    118    128     61    N
14     68    107    139     75    N
15     77    101    140     71    N
XX
BA   389 TATA box elements
XX
CC   selected sequences from 502 promoters of EPD, mainly from vertebrates
XX
RN   [1]
RX   MEDLINE; 90230299.
RA   Bucher P.
RT   Weight matrix descriptions of four eukaryotic RNA polymerase II promoter
RT   elements derived from 502 unrelated promoter sequences
RL   J. Mol. Biol. 212:563-578 (1990).
XX
//
```

FIGURE 5.13   A TRANSFAC matrix entry constructed from a real collection of 389 **TATA** boxes (Bucher, 1990). The field descriptors are located at the beginning of each line. Essentially, the entry contains accession and identification information, a brief description, the transcription factors associated to this entry, the weight matrix corresponding to the promoter element, the number of sites used to build it, and other additional information. Each line in the matrix corresponds to a position in the promoter motif; the last column is the consensus nucleotide at that position. Note the strongly conserved core **TATAAA** in the consensus of the matrix.

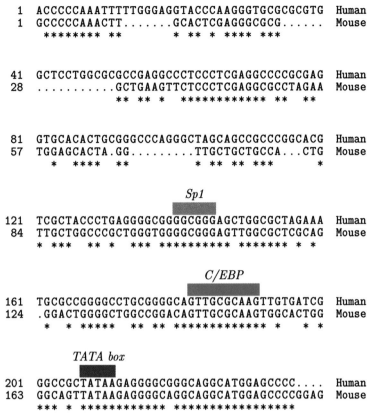

```
  1   ACCCCCAAATTTTTGGGAGGTACCCAAGGGTGCGCGCGTG   Human
  1   GCCCCCAAACTT.......GCACTCGAGGGCGCG......   Mouse
      ******* **       * ** * **** ***
```

```
 41   GCTCCTGGCGCGCCGAGGCCCTCCCTCGAGGCCCCGCGAG   Human
 28   ..........GCTGAAGTTCTCCCTCGAGGCGCCTAGAA   Mouse
                ** ** *  *********** **   **
```

```
 81   GTGCACACTGCGGGCCCAGGGCTAGCAGCCGCCCGGCACG   Human
 57   TGGAGCACTA.GG.........TTGCTGCTGCCA...CTG   Mouse
       *  ****  **         * ** ** ***      *
```

Sp1

```
121   TCGCTACCCTGAGGGGCGGGGCGGGAGCTGGCGCTAGAAA   Human
 84   TTGCTGGCCCGCTGGGTGGGGCGGGAGTTGGCGCTCGCAG   Mouse
      * ***  ** *  *** ********* ******* * *
```

C/EBP

```
161   TGCGCCGGGGCCTGCGGGGCAGTTGCGCAAGTTGTGATCG   Human
124   .GGACTGGGGCTGGCCGGACAGTTGCGCAAGTGGCACTGG   Mouse
       *  * *****  ** ** ************ *   * *
```

TATA box

```
201   GGCCGCTATAAGAGGGGCGGGCAGGCATGGAGCCCC....   Human
163   GGCAGTTATAAGAGGGGCAGGCAGGCATGGAGCCCCGGAG   Mouse
      *** * *********** ****************
```

FIGURE 5.14 Global alignment of the human and mouse obese gene promoters (*U*43589 and U36238, respectively). The alignment shows the fragment of promoter (200 bps) immediately upstream of the TSS. In both sequences, the three known regulatory elements are perfectly conserved: an SP1 element, a C/EBP element, and a TATA box (Mason et al., 1998). Note that the relative order of the elements is conserved as well.

Sequence-driven methods also can be applied after data is obtained from microarray experiments or expression profiling. The co-expression of genes could reflect the existence of common configuration of promoter elements. Promising results have been obtained in yeast (Chu et al., 1998; Tavazoie et al., 1999), but the direct application of these methods to mammalian genomes seems more difficult because of their higher complexity (Pennacchio & Rubin, 2001).

Prediction of Promoter Regions

Gene promoter regions consist of clusters of binding sites and, therefore, can be detected by taking advantage of their biased composition. Basically, weight matrices and oligonucleotide counts (overrepresented words) are used to locate the TSS, as well as the region upstream containing a significant concentration of binding sites. FirstEF (Davuluri et al., 2001) identifies both promoter regions and first exons (including untranslated regions, or UTRs) using a set of discriminant functions such as CpG island detection, donor splice site matrices, and pentamer and hexamer counts. Linear discriminant analysis was also used in methods like TSSG and TSSW (Solovyev & Salamov, 1997). The density of known binding sites and the existence of TATA boxes are used to define promoter regions by PromoterScan (Prestridge, 1995). Promoter Inspector (Scherf et al., 2000) is based on the recognition of the context of promoters by exact pattern matching to a consensus sequence. Artificial neural networks can be used to combine information derived from promoters, exons, and introns; this approach has been implemented in the Dragon Promoter Finder (Bajic et al., 2002). Fickett and Hatzigeorgiou (1997) evaluated the ability of promoter recognition tools to locate the TSS in a set of 24 mammalian promoters that were mapped experimentally. No program was found to be significantly superior to any other, and, in general,

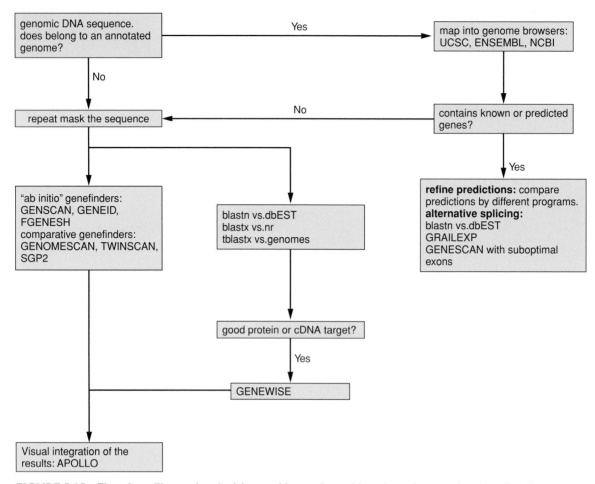

FIGURE 5.15 Flowchart illustrating decision-making and considerations that need to be taken into account when selecting and using gene prediction programs. See main text for discussion.

the quality of the predictions was considered to be quite poor (one false positive per 1000 bp).

STRATEGIES AND CONSIDERATIONS

With the completion of sequencing of a number of eukaryotic genomes, gene prediction has changed substantially, particularly from the user's standpoint. Users may not need to even run gene prediction programs on sequences from completed genomes, because many genome browsers already contain this information. Gene prediction, however, can still be useful, even in completed genomes, because the user may wish to use different parameters, for example, to analyze alternative splicing or to analyze regions apparently devoid of genes. Programs that predict splice signals and suboptimal exons are particularly useful here. Gene prediction techniques obviously are still essential for analyzing the genomes of organisms currently being

sequenced, for which extensive annotations do not exist. In this section, a number of issues that the reader should keep in mind when using computational gene predictors are discussed (Figure 5.15).

Masking the Sequence: Searching for Repeats

One of the first steps that is essential before looking for genes is to identify and locate repetitive elements, discussed in greater detail in Chapter 11. One popular program for finding repetitive elements is Repeat-Masker (Smit & Green, unpublished data). RepeatMasker "masks" the regions containing repeats (that is, substitutes an N for each character in a repetitive element); gene prediction programs ignore such stretches in making their predictions. Because coding exons tend not to overlap or to contain repetitive elements, gene prediction programs tend to predict less false-positive exons when using masked sequences. In Figure 5.10, masking of the URO-D gene sequence does not affect the gene predictions, because this particular gene contains very few repetitive elements. However, approximately 40% of the human genome does contain repetitive elements; when analyzing large genomic sequences, the simple act of masking the sequence can have dramatic effects. For instance, GENSCAN predicts 1128 genes in the unmasked sequence of human chromosome 22, but when the sequence is masked, the number of predicted genes drops to 789. When using GeneID, the number falls from 1119 to 730. Although most of the additional exons predicted using unmasked sequence data are likely to be false positives, there are times where coding regions do occur in repetitive or low-complexity regions (Chapter 11). Aggressive masking of the sequence, then, could lead to missing some actual exons. Given this, it is advisable to run the programs with both masked and unmasked sequences as the input.

Interpreting Gene Predictions

Figure 5.3 illustrates an *ab initio* gene prediction on the URO-D gene by a variety of different programs. Note that the internal exons are predicted consistently across all of the methods, but that there is substantial disagreement in the prediction at the 5′ end. GeneID predicted part of the second exon as the initial exon; GENSCAN did not predict any initial exon, predicting instead a partial gene starting with an internal exon; and FGENESH predicted a wrong exon in a known noncoding region as being the 5′ end of the sequence. In general, gene boundaries are difficult to predict because the coding fraction of the first coding exon often is quite short, yielding a poor coding signal. Thus, programs tend to perform better when examining single gene sequences than with multigenic sequences, where they tend to overpredict exons and genes in intergenic stretches.

In regions containing genes, coding exons tend to be well delineated. However, they are not always assembled in to the correct overall gene structure. Often, programs will split one real gene into gene fragments or predict chimeric genes. However, even in regions apparently devoid of genes, some of the programs still do predict coding exons. Indeed, consistent predictions by different *ab initio* methods can be suggestive of the actual presence of a protein-coding gene, even in the absence of experimental evidence. For instance, all of the programs whose predictions are shown in Figure 5.10 show a significant expansion of the 5′ end of the gene, immediately upstream of the URO-D gene. The existence of a human mRNA confirms that it corresponds to a bona fide exon. Conversely, inconsistent predictions should be taken as indication of a potential false positive, with caution. For example, just downstream of the first known gene shown in Figure 5.10, SGP-2 predicts a gene

with two exons. The first exon is consistently predicted by all of the programs shown, but they are assembled differently by the various programs. The second exon only corresponds to a prediction by GeneID. In the absence of any other information, the prediction would be highly suspicious. However, the two predicted exons are strongly conserved in the pufferfish genome, as determined through a BLAT search (Chapter 11). Conservation between human and *Fugu* is strongly indicative of protein coding function (Roest et al., 2000). Indeed, these are the only two hits in the *Fugu* genome that do not correspond to previously known coding exons. Based on this, one cannot rule out that the SGP-2 prediction actually does correspond to a real gene.

EST Searches

Given the redundancy of EST libraries, a common problem that arises after searching EST databases is in inferring, from the set of EST matches, the minimum number of splice forms to which these ESTs actually correspond. Wheeler (2002) and Eyras et al. (2004) recently have addressed this problem. Because of a relatively large incidence of genomic contamination and unprocessed transcripts in cDNA libraries, similarity to an EST often is considered indicative only of coding function when the alignment of the EST against the query sequence occurs across a splice junction. However, as illustrated in Figure 5.10, not all known genes are supported by EST evidence. It is also important to note that, although 3′ ESTs tend to correspond to the 3′ end of a gene (and may include a substantial fraction of the UTR), 5′ ESTs often are internal to the gene and are mostly coding (Guigó et al., 2000).

Predicting Genes on Top of Previous Annotations

The availability of complete genome sequences and the initial annotation of various eukaryotes is changing the nature of gene prediction. As mentioned earlier, some gene prediction methods have been applied to completed genomes, and the results of these predictions are available through the major genome browsers. In such cases, it makes little sense for users to run the programs again themselves on regions of interest. However, gene prediction programs still can be of use in exploratory data analysis, particularly when the user is interested in alternative splicing of known genes. Programs like GeneID and GENSCAN are particularly useful here. Another potential use of gene finders is to build on previous annotations, specifically targeting regions that are apparently devoid of genes but where experimental evidence may suggest the presence of a protein-coding region. Here, it would make sense to run the programs in a way that "forces" them to include the exon or exons for which experimental evidence exists. Programs like GeneID allow users to provide such information, which is used in making the final prediction (Blanco et al., 2002). The recently developed GAZE system provides a more comprehensive framework, allowing for the integration of gene prediction signals and coding content statistics toward the prediction of complete gene structures (Howe et al., 2002).

The Problem with Pseudogenes

One problem in computational gene prediction is differentiating between predictions identifying "real" genes from those that correspond to nonfunctional pseudogenes. Database searches may not help to provide any clearer picture, because many pseudogenes are similar to functional, paralogous genes. The absence of an EST cannot be used as a criterion either, because ESTs do not always exist for actual genes. In general, intronless gene predictions for which multiexon paralogous genes exist in the same genome are suspicious, because they may indicate sequences that have arisen through retrotransposition. Multiexon predictions, however, also can correspond to pseudogenes arising through a recent gene

duplication. If homologues in another organism exist, one solution is to compute the synonymous versus nonsynonymous substitution rate (K_a/K_s; Fay & Wu, 2003). K_a/K_s values approaching 1 are indicative of neutral evolution, suggesting a pseudogene. Support for multiexon gene predictions can come from conservation of overall gene structure in close homologs. Indeed, the prediction of homologous genes in both human and mouse most likely indicates the presence of actual genes (Guigó et al., 2003).

Using the Right Parameters

Ideally, when using a gene prediction program, one should use parameters that are appropriate for the species or taxonomic group being analyzed. Although this is not always possible, users should be aware that the use of parameters that have been optimized for one organism may produce poor results when used for another organism, especially when the organism is distantly related. Figure 5.16 shows the GeneID prediction for the URO-D gene sequence using parameters that have been optimized for various species. The quality of the prediction is seen to degrade as a function of phylogenetic distance. If no specific parameters are available for a

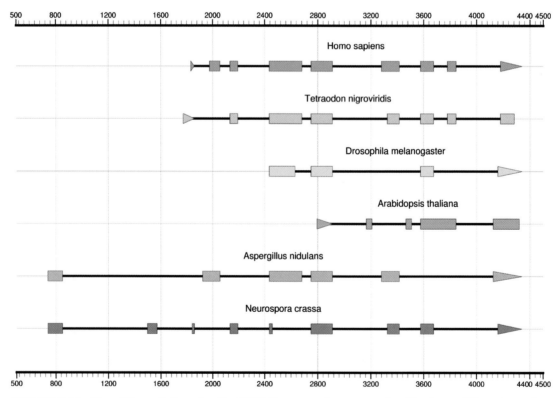

FIGURE 5.16   **GeneID predictions for the URO-D gene, using parameter files from different species. The figure was generated using GFF2PS.**

particular organism of interest, users are encouraged to contact the developers of the program to be used, because they will, more often than not, take an interest in developing such a set of parameters.

Promoter Prediction and Characterization

One of the major problems in the analysis of promoter regions is determining the exact beginning of the TSS. Inaccurate identification of the TSS leads to an obvious misidentification of putative promoter regions. Although there are ongoing efforts to clone and sequence full-length human and other mammalian cDNAs, often times, the 5' end of the gene is not determined accurately. Moreover, there are no full-length cDNAs for a large fraction of mammalian genes, and cDNAs are almost nonexistent for most of the species whose genomes are currently being sequenced. In the absence of full-length cDNAs, a good starting point for identifying genes in human and other vertebrates involves the use of FirstEF (Davuluri et al., 2001). FirstEF predictions can be found within the UCSC Genome Browser or can be obtained by submitting sequences to the FirstEF Web site. As illustrated in Figure 5.10, FirstEF correctly predicted the start of two genes in the URO-D gene region.

As soon as promoter sequences have been extracted from the genome of interest, one could characterize the genome's regulatory elements by performing a blind search against all known transcription factor binding motifs (e.g., those found in TRANSFAC). This usually results in an overwhelming number of predictions; in such cases, comparative genomic techniques may assist in processing the results. Ideally, the alignment of two or more promoter sequences from homologous genes will highlight those common, conserved fragments, fragments that may correspond to functional elements. In the example shown in Figure 5.14, most of the conserved fragments are near the TSS and have TRANS-FAC hits corresponding to actual regulatory elements. To discover potentially novel motifs, programs such as MEME (Bailey & Elkan, 1995) may be used; these programs search for conserved motifs in sets of unaligned, functionally related sequences. Caution should be exerted when identifying "novel" motifs, because they may correspond to statistical artifacts; performing the same analysis in regions within the gene that, obviously, are unlikely to be regulatory provides a good control experiment.

❚ VISUALIZATION AND INTEGRATION TOOLS

When analyzing predictions from different programs or that have resulted from different approaches, it is often useful to use a common visual interface that allows for results to be compared directly. In the course of this chapter, the results generated by a particular program are shown (for the most part) using the graphical tools that are part of that particular prediction program. Figure 5.10, though, provides a good example of how a third-party interface (here, the UCSC Genome Browser) can be used to visualize results generated by multiple programs simultaneously. Both the UCSC Genome Browser and Ensembl provide ways to upload custom tracks containing sequence annotations so that they can be viewed via the browser (Wolfsberg et al., 2001). This provides an easy to use solution for the occasional user.

For more intensive use, local interactive graphical tools provide a better solution. One such solution is the Apollo system (Lewis et al., 2002), which was used to generate the image shown in Figure 5.3. In high-throughput environments, tools such as GFF2PS (Abril & Guigó, 2000) may be particularly useful; Figures 5.5, 5.9, and 5.16 were generated using GFF2PS, as well as the output native to GeneID shown in Figure 5.6. GFF2PS has been used for other applications, such as generating whole-genome content maps for *Drosophila* (Adams et al., 2000), human (Venter et al., 2001), and mosquito (Holt et al., 2002). GFF2PS uses a common file format (the General Feature Format, or GFF), a simple to use format used to document genome annotations; several gene prediction programs can provide their results as GFF files.

❚ WORKED EXAMPLE

Gene Prediction

The ENCODE project aims to identify all of the functional elements within the human genome sequence. During its pilot phase, a number of regions from the human genome (approximately 1% of the genome) were selected for detailed investigation. The ENCODE region ENm012 from chromosome 7, which contains, among others, the *FOXP2* gene, is used here to illustrate gene prediction from a practical standpoint. The sequence can be found on the book's Web site.

Open the GeneID Web server. Paste the sequence into the text area, select geneid format output, and submit the query. The results received for each exon are in the following format, from left to right: exon type, begin and end coordinates, score, strand, frame, remainder (the complementary measure of the frame), site scores, coding potential, similarity score (not used in this example), and the amino acids range in the corresponding gene product. GeneID predicts five complete and partial genes in this sequence. The first complete predicted gene corresponds to the *FOXP2* gene.

```
## date Tue Apr 20 12:46:31 2004
## source-version: geneid v 1.1 -- geneid@imim.es
# Sequence hg16_dna - Length = 1000000 bps
# Optimal Gene Structure. 5 genes. Score = 27.136749
# Gene 1  (Reverse).  1 exons. 20 aa. Score = 2.089868
  First     4123     4180     2.09  - 0  1     1.31   6.27   7.60   0.00   AA    1: 20
>hg16_dna_1| geneid_v1.1_predicted_protein_1| 20_AA
MESLKVSKDKRALKFHREKg
# Gene 2  (Forward).   17 exons. 608 aa. Score = 17.704688
   First    133435   133602    2.44  + 0  0    -1.79   6.29  13.11   0.00   AA    1: 56
Internal    173228   173255   -1.08  + 0  1     1.42   5.34   0.92   0.00   AA   57: 66
Internal    208977   208996   -1.09  + 2  0     5.94   0.12   1.93   0.00   AA   66: 72
Internal    241540   241629    0.12  + 0  0     3.04   2.96   5.05   0.00   AA   73:102
Internal    272621   272678   -1.33  + 0  1     3.78   2.94   0.34   0.00   AA  103:122
Internal    297731   297784   -0.42  + 2  1     5.48   0.78   3.31   0.00   AA  122:140
Internal    335463   335600    1.62  + 2  1     3.61   2.87   8.08   0.00   AA  140:186
Internal    349333   349546    2.65  + 2  2     2.90   3.81  10.31   0.00   AA  186:257
Internal    359126   359213    1.10  + 1  0     4.42   0.81   8.66   0.00   AA  257:286
Internal    360849   360932    1.13  + 0  0     4.15   2.02   7.31   0.00   AA  287:314
Internal    364989   365190    2.69  + 0  1     3.45   3.72   9.71   0.00   AA  315:382
Internal    366279   366355    1.31  + 2  0     2.65   6.29   3.61   0.00   AA  382:407
Internal    366495   366596    2.01  + 0  0     4.83   3.37   6.48   0.00   AA  408:441
Internal    368988   369109    2.92  + 0  2     5.09   2.40   9.81   0.00   AA  442:482
Internal    370373   370442    0.07  + 1  0     4.36   2.87   3.09   0.00   AA  482:505
Internal    371196   371359    0.97  + 0  2     2.11   3.50   7.76   0.00   AA  506:560
Terminal    396705   396849    2.60  + 1  0     2.44   0.00  16.58   0.00   AA  560:608
>hg16_dna_2| geneid_v1.1_predicted_protein_2| 608_AA
MMQESATETISNSSMNQNGMSTLSSQLDAGSRDGRSSGDTSSEVSTVELLHLQQQQRLQS
PGFQSGHRHISKALQAARQLLLQQQTSGLKSPKSSDKQRPLQSTPPSSQCCTGLGVCVTK
ERYDHLDKEGKNQTICFNSGACVSGHDDSPGDHPSANAADPSATSPVSSAATSPSPTTAG
CHAAAAGLSPAEIQQLWKEVTGVHSMEDNGIKHGGLDLTTNNSSSTTSSNTSKASPPITH
HSIVNGQSSVLSARRDRHLNNEHALDDRSTAQCRVQMQVVQQLEIQLSKERERLQAMMTH
LHMRPSEPKPSPKPLNLVSSVTMSKNMLETSPQSLPQTPTTPTAPVTPITQGPSVITPAS
VPNVGAIRRRHSDKYNIPMSSEIAPNYEFYKNADVRPPFTYATLIRQAIMESSDRQLTLN
EIYSWFTRTFAYFRRNAATWKNAVRHNLSLHKCFVRVENVKGAVWTVDEVEYQKRRSQKI
TGSPTLVKNIPTSLGYGAALNASLQAALAESSLPLLSNPGLINNASSGLLQAVHEDLNGS
LDHIDSNGNSSPGCSPQPHIHSIHVKEEPVIAEDEDCPMSLVTTANHSPELEDDREIEEE
PLSEDLE*
# Gene 3  (Forward).   6 exons. 188 aa. Score = 1.225280
   First    430299   430379    0.94  + 0  0     2.79   5.48   3.71   0.00   AA    1: 27
Internal    465157   465222   -2.04  + 0  0     3.06  -0.22   4.39   0.00   AA   28: 49
Internal    487368   487440    2.46  + 0  1     4.02   4.65   6.90   0.00   AA   50: 74
Internal    497844   497890   -2.04  + 2  0     2.67   0.88   3.34   0.00   AA   74: 89
Internal    528389   528445    0.50  + 0  0     5.83   3.33   1.25   0.00   AA   90:108
Terminal    558099   558338    1.40  + 0  0     5.79   0.00   8.55   0.00   AA  109:188
>hg16_dna_3| geneid_v1.1_predicted_protein_3| 188_AA
MENLGDLRLPGRVELALDLEGWVGFKKTIIQTMLYFQIGQGMCIGCKENVMLIIENLENG
EKYNENKFNEIPRGMCGPHMMEHQQELLEDTFSRQSFSNLTCLFKLRKAWFSAAYFSPVG
MYFKESILSIIQSPILLRAMKRKINQPFSNEEIICRKSAHKTDHPLCGEIHQLTEGMVFM
AEWEKLA*
# Gene 4  (Forward).   4 exons. 160 aa. Score = 4.414820
   First    629957   630050    1.98  + 0  1     5.52   3.60   3.77   0.00   AA    1: 32
Internal    655595   655642   -1.42  + 2  1     4.87   1.49   0.67   0.00   AA   32: 48
Internal    686429   686704    5.26  + 2  1     4.28   6.11  11.33   0.00   AA   48:140
Terminal    693922   693983   -1.41  + 2  0     3.46   0.00   5.04   0.00   AA  140:160
>hg16_dna_4|geneid_v1.1_predicted_protein_4|160_AA
MSGAGEALAPGPVGPQRVAEAGGGQLGSTAQDVCNPTAYIDIVHQYKAQPQRLPQLQTSA
QVPSGEEIGKIKNGHTGLSNGNGIHHGAKHGSADNRKLSAPVSQKMHRKIQSSLSVNSDI
SKKSKVNAVFSQKTGSSPEDIVVERAGMAEILKGENVKE*
```

```
# Gene 5  (Reverse).    2 exons. 102 aa. Score = 1.702093
Terminal    722539    722724    -0.57  - 0  0    0.00   3.25   7.45   0.00   AA   41:102
Internal    723694    723815     2.27  - 2  0    5.48   3.23   6.38   0.00   AA    1: 40
>hg16_dna_5|geneid_v1.1_predicted_protein_5|102_AA
atLLSLLNLMFLWTGVELYLSPQSEEESPHSRHSESVEQVEKQQQQASEVQMPHDACPRT
MLQRVRNSQNKQARIQWTQQSSFSVMRRPYSEKKEEHKIRVIN*
```

To view the actual annotation for this sequence, go to the ENCODE Web site. From here, select Target Selection Process and Regions, then click on ENCODE Project Target Selection Process and Target Regions. Click on Encode Project Target Regions. Do a search, using ENm012 FOXP2 as the query, using the July 2003 freeze of the human genome. To show all known *FOXP2* isoforms, center the browser using the coordinates chr7:113,250,000-114,400,000.

Compare the GeneID predictions with those generated by other gene-finding programs, as well as with the known forms of the gene. Note the discrepancies between different predictions, as well as between the predictions and the annotated gene. Note also the degree of conservation of the human exons in the *Fugu* genome. Finally, note the presence of a predicted pseudogene within the *FOXP2* gene, which overlaps some of the predictions generated by several of the methods.

Promoter Prediction

The promoter region of the human obese gene (*U43589*) is used here to illustrate the use of a number of promoter prediction programs. For this analysis, 1000 base pairs upstream of the annotated TSS were extracted.

Three regulatory elements have been annotated experimentally in this region: an SP1 site (GGGGCGG), a cEBP box (GTTGCGCAAG), and a TATA box (TATAA). The sequence used here can be found on the book's Web site. The coordinates of the three annotated regulatory elements are shown below in GFF format, with position 1000 corresponding to the TSS:

```
U43589    lab    SP1    904 909    .    .    .    SP1  # GGGCGG
U43589    lab    CEBP   947 956    .    .    .    cEBP # GTTGCGCAAG
U43589    lab    TBP    972 977    .    .    .    TATA # TATAAG
```

The TRANSFAC database (Matys et al., 2003) contains position weight matrices representing the SP1, cEBP, and TATA box sites. To obtain the TATA matrix, follow these steps: go to the TRANSFAC 6.0 database Web server, then choose Search. Select Matrix, enter the name TATA, set Factor Name (FA) as the field to be searched, then submit the query. Two entries will be returned: M00252 and M00216; select M00252. Repeat the procedure to obtain the SP1 (M00008) and c/EBP (M00159) matrices.

The toolkit RSAtools (van Helden, 2003) can be used to scan the promoter sequence with the TRANSFAC matrices obtained above. To perform the analysis, go to the RSA tools Web site. From the left frame, click on Pattern Matching. Paste in the human obese protein gene promoter sequence (1000 bps); be sure to select transfac as the Matrix Format. Then, paste in the Transfac TATA matrix (including the matrix header). Set Origin to start (of the sequence) and press GO. Check the results: one of these two putative TATA sites is the real one (see the annotations). To obtain a graphical representation of the predictions, press Feature Map. Set the Display limits from 0 to 1000 and press GO. Repeat the procedure using the SP1 and cEBP matrices, trying to find the real sites into the predictions. Two TATA box sites are identified, but more than 50 SP1 and cEBP sites are also reported, among them the experimentally verified ones. Of the predictions for the three elements, only those in the 200-bp upstream of the TSS are shown below (columns, from left to right: sequence, feature, program, strand, motif start, motif end, sequence, score, and *p* value):

```
U43589    tata    patser    D    919    933    ggcgCTAGAAATGCGCCGGGgcc     6.04    -7.90
U43589    tata    patser    D    971    985    gccgCTATAAGAGGGGCGGGcag     9.02   -11.60

U43589    sp1     patser    D    810    819    gctcCTGGCGCGCCgagg          3.91    -6.02
U43589    sp1     patser    R    812    821    tcctGGCGCGCCGAggcc          4.48    -6.48
U43589    sp1     patser    R    822    831    ccgaGGCCCTCCCTcgag          4.20    -6.25
U43589    sp1     patser    R    823    832    cgagGCCCTCCCTcgagg          7.11    -9.19
U43589    sp1     patser    D    896    905    ccctGAGGGGCGGGgcgg          3.95    -6.05
U43589    sp1     patser    D    898    907    ctgaGGGGCGGGGCggga         10.50   -14.70
U43589    sp1     patser    D    902    911    ggggCGGGGCGGGAgctg          4.10    -6.18
U43589    sp1     patser    D    903    912    gggcGGGGCGGGAGctgg          5.98    -7.91
U43589    sp1     patser    D    927    936    aaatGCGCCGGGGCctgc          4.83    -6.80
U43589    sp1     patser    D    939    948    gcctGCGGGGCAGTtgcg          4.15    -6.21
U43589    sp1     patser    D    977    986    ataaGAGGGGCGGGcagg          3.95    -6.05
U43589    sp1     patser    D    978    987    taagAGGGGCGGGCaggc          4.35    -6.37
```

U43589	sp1	patser	D	979	988	aagaGGGGCGGGCAggca	9.31	-12.38
U43589	sp1	patser	D	983	992	ggggCGGGCAGGCAtgga	6.63	-8.61
U43589	sp1	patser	D	987	996	cgggCAGGCATGGAgccc	5.60	-7.51
U43589	cebp	patser	D	843	855	ccgcGAGGTGCACACTGcggg	3.25	-4.93
U43589	cebp	patser	R	844	856	cgcgAGGTGCACACTGCgggc	1.81	-3.87
U43589	cebp	patser	D	939	951	gcctGCGGGGCAGTTGCgcaa	1.81	-3.87
U43589	cebp	patser	D	945	957	ggggCAGTTGCGCAAGTtgtg	2.29	-4.19
U43589	cebp	patser	D	954	966	gcgcAAGTTGTGATCGGgccg	1.79	-3.86

The overwhelming number of predictions already illustrates the difficulties of accurately predicting transcription factor binding sites in DNA sequences. The problem, however, is even more complex because often it is unknown beforehand which transcription factors regulate the expression of the gene. Therefore, the problem we actually face is how to discriminate a few real binding sites from a huge amount of predictions. In such situations, preliminary comparison with homologues from other species and the use of algorithms to discover novel motifs are strongly suggested to elucidate common regulatory features.

PROBLEM SET

Gene Prediction

The human uroporphyrinogen decarboxylase (URO-D) gene (*U30787*) is used in this section. An SP1 binding site, a TATA box, and 10 exons in the forward strand have been annotated in this sequence of 4514 bps. The sequence can be found on the book's Web site.

1. Use GeneID to predict splice sites and start and stop codons in the sequence. Identify the real sites among the predictions. Do they tend to show high scores?
2. Now, use GeneID to predict the set of possible exons; compare the exon predictions with the real exons. Why is the initial exon not included in the final gene assembly?
3. The initial exon is not detected by ab initio methods or homology searches. Explain this observation.
4. Use GENSCAN and FGENESH with parameters from other species to predict genes in the URO-D sequence. Discuss the results. Now do the converse, and more realistic, experiment. Locate the region in the *Drosophila* genome encoding the URO-D gene, and use GeneID, GENSCAN, and FGENESH with human parameters to make the predictions. Compare with the predictions using the *Drosophila* parameters. What differences can be noted?

Promoter Prediction

The promoter region of the human obese gene (leptin, *U43589*) used in the worked example section is used in this problem. Three regulatory elements have been annotated in this region: an SP1 site, a cEBP box, and a TATA box. The sequence can be found on the book's Web site.

1. Obtain the TRANSFAC matrix representing the TATA box. Carefully read the content of the record. How many sites were used to build this matrix? Repeat the process with SP1 and cEBP. How many sites were aligned to build their matrices? Is there any relationship between the quality of the predictions and the number of collected binding sites?
2. Using the TRANSFAC programs MATINSPECTOR or MATCH, scan the promoter sequence using the full collection of vertebrate matrices. Identify the real binding sites in the output.
3. Align the human and the mouse promoters (U43589 and U36238). A graphical output can be obtained using BLAST2SEQ at NCBI (Chapter 11). Set a very restrictive mismatch penalty (−5) and a neutral gap extension (0) to recover short very conserved stretches of genomic sequence. Compare the alignment blocks with the annotations. Are the real binding sites conserved in both promoters?
4. Now, do the same using the promoter region of URO-D homologous from as many species as possible. Search for conserved elements, using both CLUSTAL and MEME-like alignment programs. Can conserved elements be identified across all the promoter sequences? Do they correspond to the known binding motifs?

INTERNET RESOURCES

Genome browsers

ENSEMBL	http://www.ensembl.org/
NCBI Map Viewver	http://www.ncbi.nlm.nih.gov/mapview
UCSC Genome Browser	http://genome.ucsc.edu/

Visualization and other genomic tools

APOLLO	http://www.ensembl.org/apollo/
ENCODE	http://www.nhgri.nih.gov/10005107
GFF	http://www.sanger.ac.uk/Software/formats/GFF/GFF_Spec.shtml
GFF2PS	http://genome.imim.es/software/gfftools/GFF2PS.html
RepeatMasker	http://repeatmasker.genome.washington.edu/

Gene prediction servers

FGENES	http://www.softberry.com
GAZE	http://www.sanger.ac.uk/Software/analysis/GAZE/
GENEID	http://genome.imim.es/software/geneid/index.html
GENEWISE	http://www.ebi.ac.uk/Wise2/
GENIE	http://www.fruitfly.org/seq_tools/genie.html

GENSCAN   http://genes.mit.edu/GENSCAN.html

GRAIL   http://compbio.ornl.gov/Grail-1.3/

HMMgene   http://www.cbs.dtu.dk/services/HMMgene/

Dual genome gene prediction servers

SGP-2   http://genome.imim.es/software/sgp2/index.html

SLAM   http://baboon.math.berkeley.edu/~syntenic/slam.html

TWINSCAN   http://genes.cs.wustl.edu/

Metaservers

METAGENE   http://rgd.mcw.edu/METAGENE/

Promoter prediction

Dragon Promoter Finder   http://sdmc.i2r.a-star.edu.sg/promoter/promoter1_4/DPF.htm

FIRSTEF   http://rulai.cshl.org/tools/FirstEF/

PromoterScan   http://bimas.dcrt.nih.gov/molbio/proscan/

Promoter characterization

Alignace   http://atlas.med.harvard.edu/

MEME   http://meme.sdsc.edu/meme/Website/intro.html

Promo   http://www.lsi.upc.es/~alggen/recerca/promo_v2/intro-promo.html

RSA tools   http://rsat.ulb.ac.be/rsat/

TRANSFAC   http://www.gene-regulation.com/

▮ FURTHER READING

GUIGÓ, R., AND WIEHE, T. (2003). Gene prediction accuracy in large DNA sequences. In *Frontiers in Computational Genomics* (Functional Genomics Series, Volume 3), (Caister Academic Press, Norfolk, UK) p. 1–33. This chapter reviews a number of efforts during the past ten years to evaluate the performance of gene prediction programs in standardized data sets.

ZHANG, M. Q. (2002). Computational prediction of eukaryotic protein-coding genes. *Nat. Rev. Genet.* 3, 698–709. A recent review on the current state of art of gene finding, with emphasis on recent developments and in the strengths and weakness of currently available software.

WASSERMAN, W. W., AND SANDELIN, A. (2004). Applied bioinformatics for the identification of regulatory elements. *Nat. Rev. Genet.* 5, 276–287. An up-to-date and very comprehensive review from the users perspective of tools for the characterization and analysis of regulatory elements, with emphasis on transcriptional regulation.

▮ REFERENCES

ABRIL, J. F., AND GUIGÓ, R. (2000). gff2ps: visualizing genomic annotations. *Bioinformatics* 16, 743–744.

ADAMS, M. D., CELNIKER, S. E., HOLT, R. A., EVANS, C. A., GOCAYNE, J. D., AMANATIDES, P. G., SCHERER, S. E., LI, P. W., HOSKINS, R. A.,

GALLE, R. F., et al. (2000). The Genome Sequence of *Drosophila melanogaster*. *Science* 287, 2185–2195.

ALEXANDERSSON, M., CAWLEY, S., AND PATCHER, L. (2003). SLAM: cross-species gene finding and alignment with a generalized pair hidden Markov model. *Genome Res.* 13, 496–502.

ALTSCHUL, S. F., GISH, W., MILLER, W., MYERS, E. W., AND LIPMAN, D. J. (1990). Basic local alignment search tool. *J. Mol. Biol.* 215, 403–410.

BAILEY, T. L., AND ELKAN, C. (1995). The value of prior knowledge in discovering motifs with MEME. In *Proceedings of the Third International Conference on Intelligent Systems for Molecular Biology* (AAAI Press, Menlo Park, CA) 21–29.

BAJIC, V. B., SEAH, S. H., CHONG, A., ZHANG, G., KOH, J. L. Y., AND BRUSIC, V. (2002). Dragon Promoter Finder: recognition of vertebrate RNA polymerase II promoters. *Bioinformatics* 18, 198–199.

BELLMAN, R. E. (1957). *Dynamic Programming* (Princeton University Press, Princeton).

BIRNEY, E., AND DURBIN, R. (1997). Dynamite: a flexible code generating language for dynamic programming methods used in sequence comparison. In *Proceedings of the Fifth International Conference on Intelligent Systems for Molecular biology*, Volume 5 (AAAI Press, Menlo Park, CA), p. 56–64.

BIRNEY, E., ANDREWS, D., BEVAN, P., CACCAMO, M., CAMERON, G., CHEN, Y., CLARKE, L., COATES, G., COX, T., CUFF, J (2004). Ensembl 2004. *Nucl. Acids Res.* 32 (Database issue), D468–D470.

BLANCO, E., PARRA, G., AND GUIGÓ, R. (2002). Using geneid to identify genes. *Curr. Protocols Bioinformatics* 4.3.1–4.3.26.

BORODOVSKY, M., AND MCININCH, J. (1993). GeneMark: parallel gene recognition for both DNA Strands. *Comput. Chemist.* 17, 123–133.

BRAZMA, A., JONASSEN, I., EIDHAMMER, I., AND GILBERT, D. (1998). Approaches to the automatic discovery of patterns in biosequences. *J. Comput. Biol.* 5, 277–304.

BUCHER, P. (1990). Weight matrix descriptions of four eukaryotic RNA polymerase II promoter elements derived from 502 unrelated promoter sequences. *J. Mol. Biol.* 212, 563–578.

BURGE, C., AND KARLIN, S. (1997). Prediction of complete gene structures in human genomic DNA. *J. Mol. Biol.* 268, 78–94.

BURSET, M., AND GUIGÓ, R. (1996). Evaluation of gene structure prediction programs. *Genomics* 34, 353–357.

CHU, S., DERISI, J., EISEN, M., MULHOLLAND, J., BOSTEIN, D., BROWN P. O., AND HERSKOWITZ, I. (1998). The transcriptional program of sporulation in budding yeast. *Science* 282, 699–705.

DAVULURI, R., GROSSE, I., AND ZHANG, M. Q. (2001). Computational identification of promoters and first exons in the human genome. *Nat. Genet.* 29, 412–417.

DERMITZAKIS, E. T., REYMOND, A., LYLE, R., SCAMUFFA, N., UCLA, C., DEUTSCH, S., STEVENSON, B. J., FLEGEL, V., BUCHER, P., JONGENEEL, C. V., et al. (2002). Numerous potentially functional but non-genic conserved sequences on human chromosome 21. *Nature* 420, 578–582.

DUNHAM, I., SHIMIZU, N., ROE, B. A., CHISSOE, S., HUNT, A. R., COLLINS, J. E., BRUSKIEWICH, R., BEARE, D. M., CLAMP, M., SMINK, L. J., (1999). The DNA sequence of human chromosome 22. Nature 402, 489–495.

DURBIN, R., EDDY, S. R., KROGH, A., AND MITCHISON, G. J. (1998). *Biological Sequence Analysis: Probabilistic Models of Proteins and Nucleic Acids* (Cambridge University Press, Cambridge, UK).

DURET, L., AND BUCHER, P. (1997). Searching for regulatory elements in human noncoding sequences. *Curr. Opin. Struct. Biol.* 7, 399–406.

EYRAS, E., CACCAMO, M., CURWEN, V., AND CLAMP, M. (2004). EST-Genes: alternative splicing from ESTs in Ensembl. *Genome Res.* (In press).

FAY, J. C., AND WU, C. (2003). Sequence divergence, functional constraint, and selection in protein evolution. *Ann. Rev. Genomics Hum. Genet.* 4, 213–235.

FICKETT, J. W., AND TUNG, C. S. (1992). An assessment of protein coding measures. *Nucl. Acids Res.* 20, 6441–6450.

FICKETT, J. W., AND HATZIGEORGIOU, A. G. (1997). Eukaryotic promoter recognition. *Genome Res.* 7, 861–878.

FLOREA, L., HARTZELL, G., ZHANG, Z., RUBIN G. M., AND MILLER, W. (1998). A computer program for aligning a cDNA sequence with a genomic DNA Sequence. *Genome Res.* 8, 967–974.

GELFAND, M. S, AND ROYTBERG, M. A. (1993). Prediction of the exon-intron structure by a dynamic programming approach. *Biosystems* 30, 173–182.

GELFAND, M. S. (1995). Prediction of function in DNA sequence analysis. *J. Comput. Biol.* 2, 87–117.

GELFAND, M. S., MIRONOV, A. A., AND PEVNER, P. A. (1996). Gene recognition via spliced sequence alignment. *Proc. Natl. Acad. Sci. U. S. A.* 93, 9061–9066.

GISH, W., AND STATES, D. (1993). Identification of protein coding regions by database similarity search. *Nat. Genet.* 3, 266–272.

GUIGÓ, R., DRAKE, N., KNUDSEN, S., AND SMITH, T. (1992). Prediction of gene structure. *J. Mol. Biol.* 226, 141–157.

GUIGÓ, R. (1998). Assembling genes from predicted exons in linear time with dynamic programming. *J. Comput. Biol.* 5, 681–702.

GUIGÓ, R. (1999). DNA composition, codon usage and exon prediction. In *Genetic Databases* (Academic Press).

GUIGÓ, R., BURSET, M., AGARWAL, P., ABRIL, J. F., BURSET, M., SMITH, R. F., AND FICKETT, J. W. (2000). Sequence Similarity Based Gene Prediction. *In Genomics and Proteomics: Functional and Computational Aspects* (Suhai, S., ed.), Kluwer Academic Publishers, Dordrecht, The Netherlands, p. 95–105.

GUIGÓ, R., DERMITZAKIS, E. T., AGARWAL, P., PONTING, C. P., PARRA, G., REYMOND, A., ABRIL, J. F., KEIBLER, E., LYLE, R., UCLA, C., et al. (2003). Comparison of mouse and human genomes followed by experimental verification yields an estimated 1,019 additional genes. *Proc. Nat. Acad. Sci. U. S. A.* 100, 1140–1145.

GUIGÓ, R., AND WIEHE, T. (2003). Gene prediction accuracy in large DNA sequences. In *Frontiers in Computational Genomics*, Functional Genomics Series, vol. 3 (Caister Academic Press, Norwich, UK) p. 1–33.

HOLT, R. A., SUBRAMANIAN, G. M., HALPERN, A., SUTTON, G. G., CHARLAB, R., NUSSKERN, D. R., WINCKER, P., CLARK, A. G., RIBEIRO, J. M., WIDES, R., et al. (2002). The genome sequence of the malaria mosquito *Anopheles gambiae*. *Science* 298, 129–149.

HOWE, K. L., CHOTHIA, T., AND DURBIN, R. (2002). GAZE: a generic framework for the integration of gene-prediction data by dynamic programming. *Genome Res.* 12, 1418–1427.

JEGGA, A. G., SHERWOOD, S. P., CARMAN, J. W., PINSKI, A. T., PHILIPS J. L., PESTIAN. J. P., AND ARONOW, B. J. (2002). Detection and visualization of compositionally similar cis-regulatory element clusters in orthologous and coordinately controlled genes. *Genome Res.* 12, 1408–1417.

KENT, W. J. (2002). BLAT: the BLAST-like alignment tool. *Genome Res.* 12, 656–664.

KENT, W. J., SUGNET, C. W., FUREY, T. S., ROSKIN, K. M., PRINGLE, T. H., ZAHLER, A. M., AND HAUSSLER, D. (2002). The Human Genome Browser at UCSC. *Genome Res.* 12, 996–1006.

KORF, I., FLICEK, P., DUAN, D., AND BRENT, M. R. (2001). Integrating genomic homology into gene structure prediction. *Bioinformatics* 17, S140–S148.

KROGH, A. (1997). Two methods for improving performance of a HMM and their application for gene finding. In *Proceedings of the Fifth International Conference on Intelligence Systems for Molecular Biology* (AIII Press, Menlo Park, CA), p. 179–186.

KULP, D., HAUSSLER, D., REESE, M. G., AND EECKMAN, F. H. (1996). A generalized hidden Markov model for the recognition of human genes in DNA. *Proc. Intl. Conf. Intell. Syst. Mol. Biol.* 4, 134–142.

LEWIS, S. E., SEARLE, S. M. J., HARRIS, N., GIBSON, M., IYER, V., RICHTER, J., WIEL, C., BAYRAKTAROGLU, L., BIRNEY, E., CROSBY, M. A., et al. (2002). Apollo: a sequence annotation editor. *Genome Biol.* 3, research0082.

MASON, M. M., HE, Y., CHEN, H., QUON, M. J., AND REITMAN, M. (1998). Regulation of leptin promoter function by Sp1, C/EBP, and a novel factor. *Endocrinology* 139, 1013–1022.

MATYS, V., FRICKE, E., GEFFERS, R., GÖßLING, E., HAUBROCK, M., HEHL, R., HORNISCHER, K., KARAS, D., KEL, A. E., KEL-MARGOULIS, O. V., et al. (2003). TRANSFAC: transcriptional regulation from patterns to profiles. *Nucl. Acids Res.* 31, 374–378.

MESSEGUER, X., ESCUDERO, R., FARRÉ, D., NUÑEZ, O., MARTÍNEZ, J., AND ALBÀ, M. M. (2002). PROMO: detection of known transcription regulatory elements using species-tailored searches. *Bioinformatics* 18, 333–334.

MOTT R. (1997). EST_GENOME: a program to align spliced DNA sequences to unspliced genomic DNA. *Comput. Applic.* 13, 477–478.

Mouse Genome Sequencing Consortium. (2001). Initial sequencing and comparative analysis of the mouse genome. *Nature* 420, 520–562.

PARRA, G., BLANCO, E., AND GUIGÓ, R. (2000). Geneid in *Drosophila*. *Genome Res.* 10, 511–515.

PARRA, G., AGARWAL, P., ABRIL, J. F., WIEHE, T., FICKETT J. W., AND R. GUIGÓ. (2003). Comparative gene prediction in human and mouse. *Genome Res.* 13, 108–117.

PEDERSEN, A. G., BALDI, P., CHAUVIN, Y., AND BRUNAK, S. (1999). The biology of eukaryotic promoter prediction: a review. *Comput. Chem.* 23, 191–207.

PENNACCHIO, L. A., AND RUBIN, E. M. (2001). Genomic strategies to identify mammalian regulatory sequences. *Nat. Rev. Genet.* 2, 100–109.

PENNISI, E. (2003). Gene counters struggle to get the right answer. *Science* 301, 1040–1041.

PRAZ, V., PÉRIER, R., BONNARD, C., AND BUCHER, P. (2002). The Eukaryotic Promoter Database, EPD: new entry types and links to gene expression data. *Nucl. Acids Res.* 30, 322–324.

PRESTRIDGE, D. S. (1995). Predicting Pol II promoter sequences using transcription factor binding sites. *J. Mol. Biol.* 249, 923–932.

ROEST CROLLIUS, H., JAILLON, O., BERNOT, A., DASILVA, C., BOUNEAU, L., FISCHER, C., FIZAMES, C., WINCKER, P., BROTTIER, P., QUETIER, F., et al. (2000). Estimate of human gene number provided by genome-wide analysis using Tetraodon nigroviridis DNA sequence. *Nat. Genet.* 25, 235–238.

ROGIC, S., MACKWORTH, A. K., AND OUELLETTE F. B. F. (2001). Evaluation of gene-finding programs on mammalian sequences. *Genome Res.* 11, 817–832.

ROTH, F. R., HUGHES, J. D., ESTEP, P. E., AND CHURCH, G. M. (1998). Finding DNA regulatory motifs within unaligned non-coding sequences clustered by whole-genome mRNA quantitation. *Nat. Biotechnol.* 16, 939–945.

SALAMOV, A. A., AND SOLOVYEV, V. V. (2000). Ab initio gene finding in *Drosophila* genomic DNA. *Genome Res.* 10, 516–522.

SCHERF, N., KLINGENHOFF, A., AND WERNER, T. (2000). Highly specific localization of promoter regions in large genomic sequences by PromoterInspector: a novel context analysis approach. *J. Mol. Biol.* 297, 599–606.

SNYDER, E. E., AND STORMO, G. D. (1993). Identification of coding regions in genomic DNA sequences: an application of dynamic programming and neural networks, *Nucl. Acids Res.* 21, 607–613.

SNYDER, E. E. AND STORMO, G. D. (1997). Identifying genes in genomic DNA sequences. In DNA and Protein Sequence Analysis, M. J. Bishop and C. J. Rawlings, eds. (New York: Oxford University Press), p. 209–224.

SOLOVYEV, V. V., SALAMOV, A. A., AND LAWRENCE, C. B. (1995). Identification of human gene structure using linear discriminant functions and dynamic programming. In *Proceedings of the Third International Conference on Intelligent Systems for Molecular Biology*, vol. 3 (AAAI Press), p. 367–375.

SOLOVYEV, V. V., AND SALAMOV, A. A. (1997). The Gene-Finder computer tools for analysis of human and model organism genome sequences. In *Proceedings of the Fifth International Conference on Intelligent Systems for Molecular biology* (AAAI Press, Menlo Park, CA), p. 294–302.

STORMO, G. D. (2000). DNA binding sites: representation and discovery. *Bioinformatics* 16, 16–23.

TAVAZOIE, S., HUGHES, J., CAMPBELL, M., CHO, R., AND CHURCH, G. (1999). Systematic determination of genetic network architecture. *Nat. Genet.* 22, 281–285.

UBERBACHER, E. C., AND MURAL, R. J. (1991). Locating protein-coding regions in human DNA sequences by a multiple sensor-neural network approach. *Proc. Natl. Acad. Sci. U. S. A.* 88, 11261–11265.

VAN HELDEN, J. (2003). Regulatory sequence analysis tools. *Nucl. Acids Res.* 31, 3593–3596.

VENTER JC, ADAMS MD, MYERS EW, LI PW, MURAL RJ, SUTTON GG, SMITH HO, YANDELL M, EVANS CA, HOLT RA, et al. (2001). The sequence of the human genome. *Science* 291, 1304–1351.

WAGNER, A. (1997). A computational genomics approach to the identification of gene networks. *Nucl. Acids Res.* 25, 3594–3604.

WASSERMAN, W. W., PALUMBO, M., THOMPSON, W., FICKETT, J. W., AND LAWRENCE, C. E. (2000). Human-mouse genome comparisons to locate regulatory sites. *Nat. Genet.* 26, 225–228.

WERNER, T. (2000). Identification and functional modelling of DNA sequence elements of transcription. *Briefings Bioinform.* 4, 372–380.

WHEELER, R. (2002). A method of consolidating and combining EST and mRNA alignments to a genome to enumerate supported splice variants. In *Proceedings of the Second Workshop on Algorithms in Bioinformatics* (Springer-Verlag, Heidelberg, Germany), p. 201–209.

WOLFSBERG, T. G., WETTERSTRAND, K. A., GUYER, M. S., COLLINS, F. S., AND BAXEVANIS, A. D. (2001). A user's guide to the human genome. *Nat. Genet.* 32 suppl., 1–79.

XU, Y., MURAL, R. J., SHAH, M., AND UBERBACHER, E. C. (1994). Recognizing exons in genomic sequence using GRAIL II. In *Genetic Engineering: Principles and Methods* (Setlow, J., ed.), Plenum Press, New York, vol. 16, p. 241–253.

XU, Y., AND UBERBACHER, E. C. (1997). Automated gene identification in large-scale genomic sequences. *J. Comp. Biol.* 4, 325–338.

YEH, R., LIM, L. P., AND BURGE, C. (2001). Computational inference of the homologous gene structures in the human genome. *Genome Res.* 11, 803–816.

ZHANG, M. Q. (1997). Identification of protein coding regions in the human genome by quadratic discriminant analysis. *Proc. Natl. Acad. Sci. U. S. A.* 94, 565–568.

ZHANG, M. Q. (1998). Identification of human gene core promoters *in silico. Genome Res.* 8, 319–326.

ZHANG, M. Q. (2002). Computational prediction of eukaryotic protein coding genes. *Nat. Rev. Genet.* 3, 698–709.

KEY TERMS

coding regions

gene prediction

genome annotation

promoter prediction

## CHAPTER SIX

Predictive Methods Using RNA Sequences

DAVID MATHEWS

MICHAEL ZUKER

Bioinformatics: A Practical Guide to the Analysis of Genes and Proteins, Third Edition, edited by Andreas D. Baxevanis and B.F. Francis Ouellette.
ISBN 0-471-47878-4 Copyright © 2005 John Wiley & Sons, Inc.

▌INTRODUCTION

RNA is a versatile biopolymer that plays many roles beyond simply carrying and recognizing genetic information as messenger RNA (mRNA) and transfer RNA (tRNA). It has been known for two decades that RNA sequences can catalyze phosphodiester bond cleavage and ligation (Doudna & Cech, 2002) and that RNA is an important component in the signal recognition particle (Walter & Blobel, 1982). More recently, other roles have been discovered for RNA, including roles in development (Lagos-Quintana et al., 2001; Lau et al., 2001), the immune system (Cullen, 2002), and peptide bond catalysis (Hansen et al., 2002; Nissen et al., 2000). Furthermore, RNA can be made to evolve *in vitro* to catalyze reactions that do not naturally occur (Bittker et al., 2002). RNA is also an important target and agent for the pharmaceutical industry. In the ribosome, RNA is the target of several classes of antibiotics. mRNA is the target of drugs that work on the antisense principle (Dias & Stein, 2002) or by redirecting alternative splicing (Sazani & Kole, 2003). RNA sequences can also be tailored to catalyze therapeutic reactions, such as gene repair (Long et al., 2003).

To understand fully its mechanism of action or to target an RNA sequence, the structure of RNA needs to be understood. RNA structure has three levels of organization, as shown in Figure 6.1. The first level, primary structure, is the linear sequence of nucleotides. Secondary structure is the collection of canonical base pairs (meaning both Watson-Crick pairs and G-U pairs) in the RNA structure. Finally, tertiary structure is the three-dimensional arrangement of the atoms in the RNA sequence, and hence includes all of the noncanonical contacts.

Often, the secondary structure of an RNA sequence is solved before its tertiary structure because there are accurate methods for determining the secondary structure of an RNA sequence and because the knowledge of the secondary structure often is helpful in designing constructs for tertiary structure determination. A typical RNA secondary structure, illustrated in Figure 6.2, is composed of both helical and loop regions. The helical

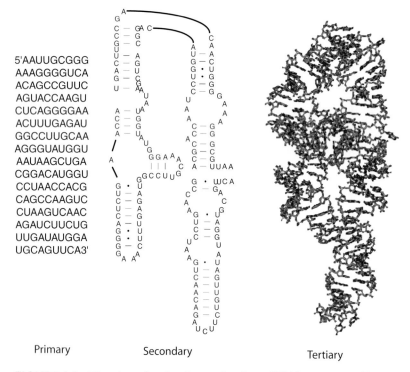

Primary   Secondary   Tertiary

FIGURE 6.1 **The three levels of organization of RNA structure. From left to right are the primary sequence, the secondary structure (Cannone et al., 2002), and the tertiary structure (Cate et al., 1996) of a domain of the group I intron from *Tetrahymena*. The secondary structure illustrates the canonical base pairs, and the tertiary structure is the actual three-dimensional arrangement of atoms.**

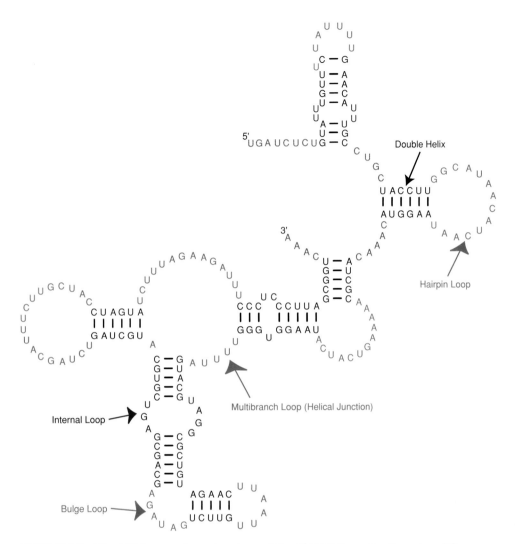

FIGURE 6.2   The RNA secondary structure of the 3′ UTR from the *D. sucinea* R2 element (Lathe & Eickbush, 1997; Mathews et al., 1997). Base pairs in nonhelical regions, known as loops, are colored by type of loop.

regions are held together by canonical base pairs. The loop regions fall into four broad categories: hairpin loops, in which the backbone makes a 180° bend; internal loops, in which the pairing of both strands is interrupted; bulge loops, in which the pairing of one strand is interrupted; and multibranch loops (also called helical junctions), from which more than two helices exit. Although secondary structure diagrams often do not illustrate explicitly the specific nucleotide interactions within the loop regions, these are sites of many noncanonical interactions that stabilize the structure.

The gold standard for predicting the placement of loops and helices, in the absence of a tertiary structure, is comparative sequence analysis, which uses evolutionary evidence found in sequence alignments to determine

base pairs (Pace et al., 1999). Base pairs predicted by comparative sequence analysis for large and small subunit rRNA are 97% accurate when compared with high-resolution crystal structures (Gutell et al., 2002).

This chapter presents current methods for RNA secondary structure prediction, including methods applicable to a single sequence and methods applicable to multiple available sequences. To that end, RNA folding thermodynamics and dynamic programming are introduced. A detailed example for applying secondary structure prediction to a single sequence is drawn from the R2 retrotransposon 3′ untranslated region (UTR) RNA sequences (Eickbush, 2002). This chapter concludes with a brief introduction to the methods used for RNA tertiary structure prediction.

RNA SECONDARY STRUCTURE THERMODYNAMICS

Most methods for RNA secondary structure prediction rely on free energy minimization using nearest-neighbor parameters for predicting the stability of an RNA secondary structure, in terms of Gibbs free energy at 37°C (ΔG_{37}°; Mathews et al., 1999b; Turner, 2000; Xia et al., 1999; Xia et al., 1998). The rules for predicting stability are called *nearest-neighbor parameters* because the stability of each base pair depends only on the most adjacent pairs; the total free energy is the sum of each contribution.

An example of a nearest-neighbor stability calculation is shown in Figure 6.3. Terms for helical stacking, loop initiation, and unpaired nucleotide stacking contribute to the total conformational free energy. Favorable free energy increments are less than zero. The free energy increments of base pairs are counted as stacks of adjacent pairs. The consecutive CG base pairs, for example, are worth −3.3 kcal/mol (Xia et al., 1998). Note that the loop regions have unfavorable increments called *loop initiation energies* that largely reflect an entropic cost for constraining the nucleotides in the loop. For example, the hairpin loop of four nucleotides has an initiation of 5.6 kcal/mol (Mathews et al., 1999b). Unpaired nucleotides in loops can provide favorable energy increments as either stacked nucleotides or as mismatched pairs. The 3′-most G, called a *dangling end*, stacks on the terminal base pair and provides −1.3 kcal/mol of stability. The first mismatch in the hairpin loop with this sequence context is worth −1.1 kcal/mol.

The Gibbs free energy of formation for an RNA structure (ΔG°) quantifies the equilibrium stability of

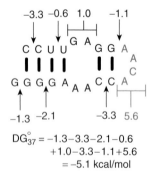

$$DG_{37}^{\circ} = -1.3-3.3-2.1-0.6$$
$$+1.0-3.3-1.1+5.6$$
$$= -5.1 \text{ kcal/mol}$$

FIGURE 6.3 Prediction of conformational free energy for a conformation of rCCUUGAGGAACACCAAAGGGG. Each contributing free energy increment is labeled. The total free energy is the sum of each increment.

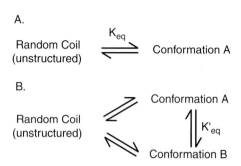

FIGURE 6.4 Equilibria of structures in solution. (a) The equilibrium between conformation A and the random coil structure. K_{eq}, related to the ΔG_{37}°, describes the equilibrium. (b) The equilibrium between two conformations, A and B, and the random coil. K'_{eq}, which is related to the free energy of folding for both A and B, describes the population of conformation A versus conformation B.

that structure at a specific temperature. For example, consider the RNA structure A at equilibrium with the random-coil (i.e., unstructured) conformation. The relative concentration of each conformation is governed by the equilibrium constant, K_{eq}, as illustrated in Figure 6.4a. K_{eq} is related to Gibbs free energy by the relationship shown in Equation 6.1:

$$K_{eq} = \frac{[\text{Conformation } A]}{[\text{Random Coil}]} = e^{-\Delta G^{\circ}/RT}, \qquad (6.1)$$

where R is the universal gas constant and T is the absolute temperature. For the example in Figure 6.3, with a predicted stability of −5.1 kcal/mol, there is a population of 3900 folded strands to every unfolded one (K_{eq} = 3900).

Furthermore, for multiple alternative conformations A and B for which there is an equilibrium distribution of conformations, K'_{eq}, as shown in Figure 6.4b, describes the distribution of strands between the structures. In this case, the free energy of each conformation relative to random coil also describes the population of each conformation, as shown in Equation 6.2:

$$K'_{eq} = \frac{[\text{Conformation } A]}{[\text{Conformation } B]} = e^{-(\Delta G_A^{\circ} - \Delta G_B^{\circ})/RT}. \qquad (6.2)$$

This generalizes to any number of conformations. Therefore, the lowest free energy conformation is the most probable conformation for an RNA at equilibrium.

The nearest-neighbor free energy parameters use sequence-dependent terms for predicting the free energy increments of loop regions (Mathews et al., 1999b) to reflect experimental observations. For example, a symmetric 2×2 internal loop can vary in stability from -2.6 to $+2.8$ kcal/mol, depending on the sequence of the closing pair and mismatches (Schroeder et al., 1999), corresponding to a K_{eq} of 6.4×10^3.

DYNAMIC PROGRAMMING

In the last section, the concept that the lowest free energy structure is the most likely structure for an RNA sequence at equilibrium was introduced. Given that there are nearest-neighbor parameters for predicting the free energy of a given sequence and structure, how, then, is the secondary structure predicted? The naïve approach would be to generate each possible conformation explicitly, to evaluate the free energy of each conformation, and then to choose the conformation that had the lowest free energy.

One estimate is that there are $(1.8)^N$ secondary structures possible for a sequence of N nucleotides (Zuker & Sankoff, 1984). This translates to 3×10^{25} structures for a modest length sequence of 100 nucleotides. Given that a fast computer can calculate the free energy for 10,000 structures in a second, this approach would still require 1.6×10^{14} CPU years! Clearly, a faster solution is needed for this problem.

The most commonly used solution for computationally intensive problems such as this is dynamic programming, which uses recursion to speed the calculation

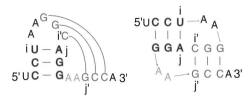

FIGURE 6.5 A simple RNA pseudoknot. This figure illustrates two representations of the same simple, H-type pseudoknot. A pseudoknot is defined by two base pairs such that i—j and i′—j′ are two pairs with ordering i < i′ < j < j′. The base pair between nucleotides i and j defines an enclosed region. The base pair i′ and j′ spans the enclosed region and an adjacent region, making the pseudoknot.

(Nussinov & Jacobson, 1980; Zuker & Stiegler, 1981). Appendix 6.1 describes this method in detail for the interested reader. Modern implementations (Mathews et al., 1999b; Wuchty et al., 1999) of the dynamic programming algorithm for RNA secondary structure prediction also predict structures with free energy greater than the lowest free energy structure. These are called *suboptimal structures* (Zuker, 1989).

The dynamic programming algorithm for secondary structure prediction is $O(N^3)$ in time and $O(N^2)$ in storage when pseudoknots are excluded from the calculation (see Box 6.1). A pseudoknot, illustrated in Figure 6.5, occurs when there are nonnested base pairs. For example, the simplest pseudoknot occurs for which there are two base pairs i—j and i′—j′ such that i < i′ < j < j′. It had been assumed that pseudoknots could not be predicted by a polynomial time dynamic programming until Rivas and Eddy (1999) presented a polynomial time dynamic programming algorithm that can predict structures containing a certain class of pseudoknots that is sufficiently rich to cover all cases of practical importance. Their algorithm, however, is $O(N^6)$ in time and $O(N^4)$ in storage, making the calculation impractical for sequences longer than approximately 300 nucleotides.

ACCURACY OF RNA SECONDARY STRUCTURE PREDICTION

The accuracy of RNA secondary structure can be assessed by predicting structures for RNA sequences with known secondary structures, as determined by comparative sequence analysis. For a collection of structures assembled to test the accuracy of prediction, which included small subunit rRNA (Cannone et al., 2002),

---

BOX 6.1 Algorithm Complexity

Algorithm complexity describes the scaling of a calculation in the worst-case scenario. It is expressed using the "Big-O" notation, which can read as "order." Algorithms that are $O(N)$ in time require a linear increase in time as the size parameter, N, lengthens. $O(N^2)$ and $O(N^3)$ algorithms scale by the square and cube of the parameter N. Therefore, the dynamic programming algorithm for RNA secondary structure prediction, which is $O(N^3)$, where N is the number of nucleotides, requires roughly eight times the execution time for a sequence twice as long. This is a fairly expensive calculation as compared to sorting a list, which can generally be accomplished in $O(N \log(N))$ time.

The Big-O notation also applies to the scaling of memory (also called storage) used by an algorithm. Secondary structure prediction requires two-dimensional arrays of size N × N. Therefore, in storage, the secondary structure prediction algorithm is $O(N^2)$.

large subunit rRNA (Cannone et al., 2002), 5S rRNA (Szymanski et al., 2000), group I introns (Cannone et al., 2002), group II introns (Michel et al., 1989), RNase P RNA (Brown, 1999), SRP RNA (Larsen et al., 1998), and tRNA (Sprinzl et al., 1998), 73% of base pairs in the known structure can, on average, be correctly predicted (Mathews et al., 1999a). For these calculations, the small and large subunit rRNA are divided into domains of fewer than 700 nucleotides, based on the known structure (Mathews et al., 1999b).

It has been demonstrated that the prediction accuracy can be improved by constraining secondary structure prediction with enzymatic constraints. Enzymes are used to determine nucleotides that are single or double stranded (Knapp, 1989). For the 5S rRNA sequence from *Escherichia coli*, which is poorly predicted without experimental constraints, the accuracy improves from 26% to 87% when enzymatic cleavage data are included (Mathews et al., 1999b; Speek & Lind, 1982; Szymanski et al., 2000).

PROGRAMS AVAILABLE FOR RNA SECONDARY STRUCTURE PREDICTION OF A SINGLE SEQUENCE

MFold

Mfold is an RNA secondary structure prediction package available through a Web frontend and as code for compilation on Unix and Linux machines (Mathews et al., 1999b; Zuker, 2003). It uses the current set of nearest neighbor parameters for free energies at 37°C (Mathews et al., 1999b). Minimum free energy and suboptimal secondary structures, sampled heuristically (Zuker, 1989), are predicted. Predicted suboptimal structures represent alternative structures to the lowest free energy structure and reflect both the possibility that an RNA sequence may have more than a single structure (Schultes & Bartel, 2000) and the fact that the energy rules contain some uncertainty (Mathews et al., 1999b). *Mfold* also predicts energy dot plots, which display the lowest free energy conformation possible for each possible base pair (Zuker & Jacobson, 1995). These plots conveniently demonstrate all possible base pairs within a user-specified increment of the lowest free energy structure, and predicted structures can be color annotated to demonstrate regions in the structure for which many folding alternatives exist (Zuker & Jacobson, 1998).

Figure 6.6 shows the input form for the *mfold* RNA server. A separate server for secondary structure prediction of DNA, using DNA folding free energies (SantaLucia, 1998), is available by following the link to the *DNA*

mfold server. A sequence name can be entered in the box labeled *Enter a name for your sequence* and the sequence is typed (or pasted from the clipboard) in the box labeled *Enter the Sequence to be folded in the box*. As the caption explains, blanks and nonalphabetic characters are ignored and do not interfere with sequence interpretation. For example, the form shows the tRNA sequence (Sprinzl et al., 1998), RD1140, pasted into the sequence field. The remainder of the form has default values that can be changed by advanced users. The next box provides the option of constraining structure prediction with auxiliary evidence derived from enzymatic cleavage (Knapp, 1989), comparative sequence analysis (Pace et al., 1999), or intuition. Next, the default is for linear RNA sequence folding, although circular sequences also can be folded by changing the option from linear to circular. Note that the folding temperature is fixed at 37°C using the current parameters. An older, less complete set of parameters allows secondary structure prediction at other temperatures (Jaeger et al., 1989), but it is recommended that the current parameters be used for most applications. The older parameters can be used for folding by following the link at the top of the page to *RNA mfold version 2.3 server* (not shown in Figure 6.6). The percent suboptimality number, 5 by default, is the maximum percent difference in free energy from the lowest free energy structure that is allowed when generating suboptimal secondary structures. The upper bound on the computed foldings (default = 50) is the maximum number of suboptimal secondary structures to be predicted. The window parameter controls how different each suboptimal structure must be from all others. It defaults to a value based on the length of the sequence that is shown by following the link at *Window*. For example, the tRNA used here is 77 nucleotides long and will have a default window of 2. A smaller window allows for more suboptimal structures and a larger window yields greater differences between the predicted structures. The smallest window size allowed is zero. The maximum number of unpaired nucleotides in bulge or internal loops is limited to 30, by default. The maximum asymmetry in internal loops (the difference in length in unpaired nucleotides on each strand) is also 30 by default. The maximum distance allowed between paired nucleotides defaults to no limit. These values can be modified, as appropriate.

The remaining options control the server output. Currently, sequences of 800 or fewer nucleotides can be folded and the results returned as an "immediate job." Longer sequences must be folded as a batch job, requiring that the default option be changed from An immediate to A batch job. Batch jobs also require that

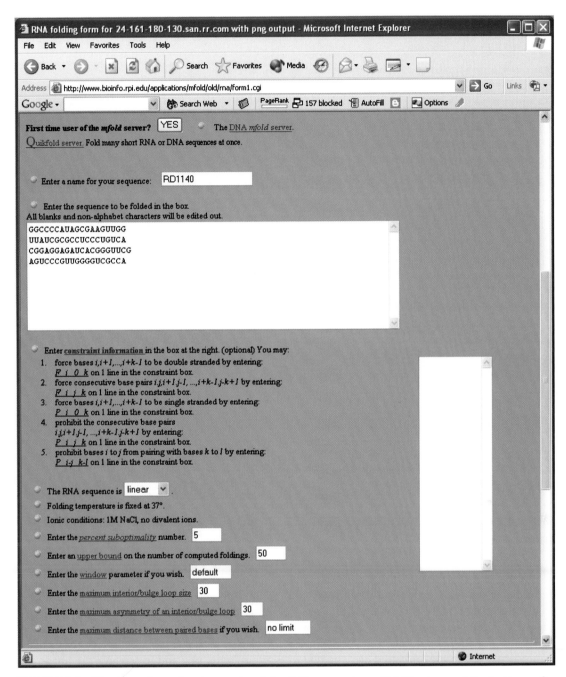

FIGURE 6.6 **The input form for the version 3.1 *mfold* server. (a and b) The top and the bottom of the form, respectively. Default parameters are shown, with the exceptions noted in the text.**

the user enter an E-mail address for receiving notification that the calculation is complete. The tRNA in this example is short, so the default of An immediate job will be used. The remaining options control the way the server generates output. Each of these options has link to a Web page that describes each parameter. For this example, color annotation by p-num is turned on to show

regions in the predicted structure that having alternative low energy base pairs to those in the minimum free energy structure. By default, color annotation is not included. The button labeled *Fold RNA* is clicked to start the calculation.

Figure 6.7 shows the *mfold* server output form for the secondary structure prediction of the RD1140 tRNA.

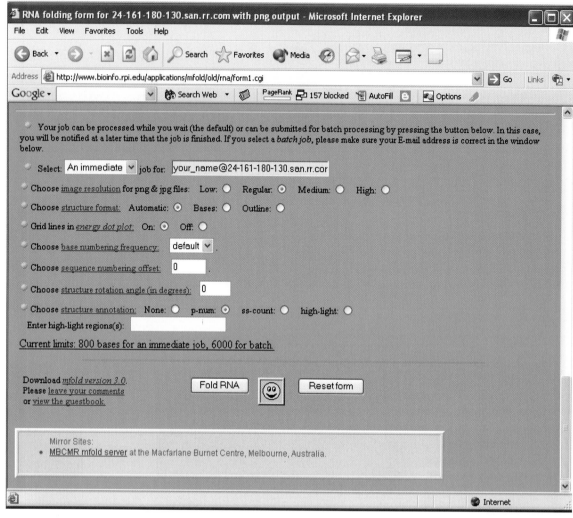

FIGURE 6.6 *Continued*

Results are available on the server for 24 hours after the job has been completed. The first window displays the sequence with nucleotide number. The energy dot plot is available by links to a text-formatted, PostScript-formatted, png-formatted, or jpg-formatted file. The text format is suitable for analysis in other software programs. PostScript is a publication-quality output and is shown in Figure 6.8b. Png and jpg both link to interactive pages that allow the user to zoom to regions, change the energy increment and number of colors, and click on individual base pairs to determine the exact energy. An RNAML-formatted output file is available for exchanging information with other RNAML-compliant programs. This is an xml file format that promises eventually to allow seamless information exchange between RNA analysis programs (Waugh et al., 2002). A diagram of each predicted secondary structure is available in a variety of formats. For this example, only a single structure is predicted

using the default parameters for suboptimal secondary structure prediction. The commonly used formats, available by links adjacent to `Structure 1`, are PostScript, which is a publication-quality output format shown in Figure 6.8A; png and jpg, which are image formats that allow user interaction; and RNAViz CT and XRNAss formats, which are export formats for secondary structure drawing tools, explained below.

Figure 6.8 demonstrates sample output for the *mfold* server using the tRNA sequence for RD1140 (Sprinzl et al., 1998). The predicted secondary structure (Figure 6.8a) is color annotated according to the number of competing pairs in the energy dot plot (Figure 6.8b). Nucleotides outlined in red are in well-defined regions with no competing base pairs. The stem with black outlined pairs is less well-defined than the other stems, according to the dot plot. In the dot plot, each dot represents a base pair between nucleotides indicated on the x-axis

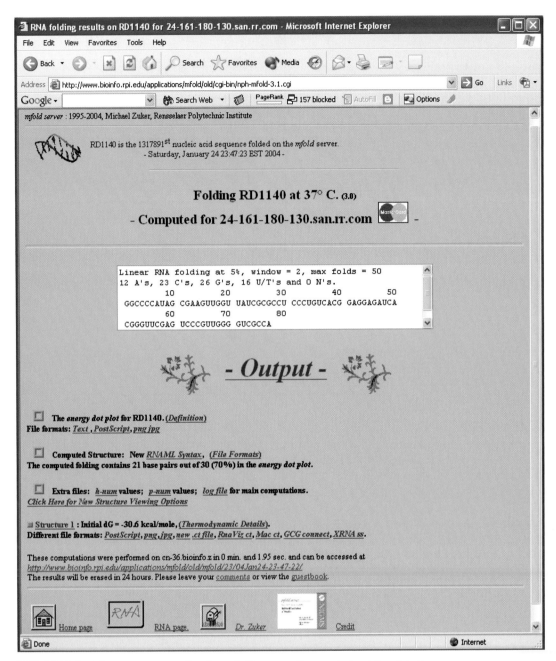

FIGURE 6.7 The output page for the *mfold* server. See main text for details.

and y-axis, and its color indicates the best energy for a structure that contains that pair. The energy dot plot is divided into two triangles. The upper triangle is the energy plot including suboptimal pairs and the lower triangle is the location of base pairs in the predicted minimum free energy structure. The energy dot plot in Figure 6.8 shows that there are alternative base pairs contained in structures with free energies between -29.7 and -30.1 kcal/mol, a separation of less than 0.5 kcal/mol from the lowest free energy structure.

Vienna RNA Package

The Vienna RNA Package can be used to predict RNA secondary structures via either a Web interface or by compilation onto Unix and Linux machines (Hofacker, 2003; Hofacker et al., 1994). It uses a dynamic programming approach and the current set of thermodynamic parameters (Mathews et al., 1999b). The Vienna Package also implements an algorithm that calculates the partition function for RNA folding, which predicts the base

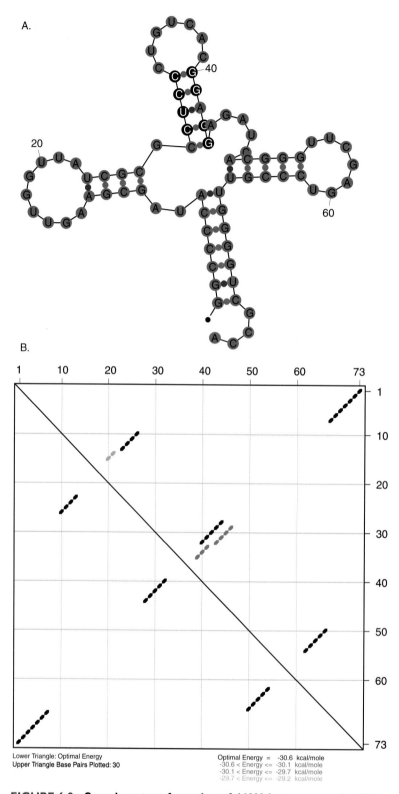

FIGURE 6.8 **Sample output from the** *mfold* **Web server, version 3.1.**
(a) The secondary structure predicted for the tRNA, RD1140 (Sprinzl
et al., 1998). (b) Color annotation based on the energy dot plot.

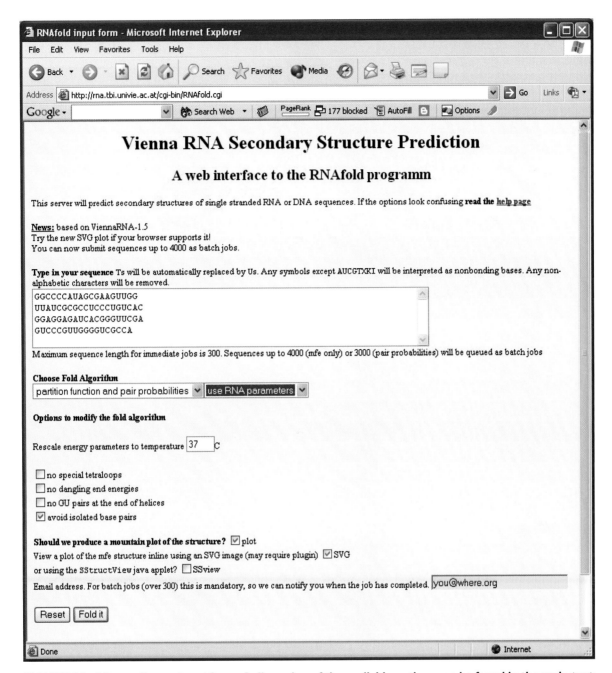

FIGURE 6.9 **Vienna Server input form. A discussion of the available options can be found in the main text.**

pairing probability for each possible base pair in a sequence. The partition function prediction algorithm, first implemented by McCaskill (1990), is also a dynamic programming algorithm. The calculated base pair probabilities are commonly displayed in a probability dot plot, analogous to the energy dot plots from *mfold*. Additionally, the Vienna Package includes software for the generation of all suboptimal secondary structures within a given energy increment of the lowest free energy structure (Wuchty et al., 1999). The number of secondary structures grows exponentially with increasing size of the energy increment.

Figure 6.9 shows the input form for the Vienna Package Web server. The link to the *help page* can be followed for an explanation of the fields. The sequence is typed or pasted from the clipboard in the box below *Type your sequence*. The tRNA sequence, RD1140 (Sprinzl et al., 1998), is shown in the sequence box. Nonalphabetic characters are ignored automatically by the server. The default fold algorithm is partition function and pair probabilities, although the partition function calculation can be turned off by changing to minimum free energy only. The parameter set is chosen on this form as either use RNA parameters, old RNA parameters, or use

A.

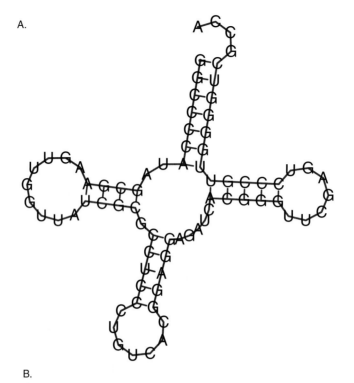

B.

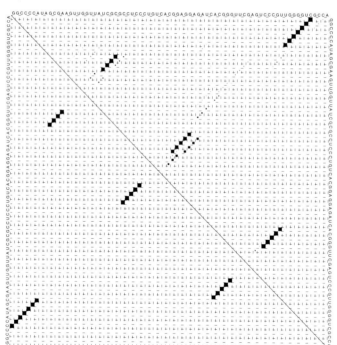

FIGURE 6.10   Sample output from the Vienna Package Web server, version 1.5. (a) The predicted minimum free energy secondary structure for the tRNA RD1140 (Sprinzl et al., 1998). (b) The probability dot plot for the same sequence.

DNA parameters. The old RNA parameters are available (Walter et al., 1994) also, so that previous predictions can be reproduced. The temperature of folding can be changed from the default of 37°C, but for similar temperatures it is recommended that the default be used. Folding at temperatures other than 37°C use an older set of thermodynamic parameters (Jaeger et al., 1989) that are based on fewer experiments than the current set of parameters (Mathews et al., 1999b). The next parameters, *no special tetraloops, no dangling end energies, no GU pairs at the ends of helices,* and *avoid isolated base pairs,* modify the energy rules. The default is to check *avoid isolated pairs,* and this will reproduce the behavior of the *mfold* server. The other choices can be modified by advanced users. The checkboxes at the bottom of the form (*plot, SVG,* and *SSView*) control the output formats. The default options, shown in Figure 6.9, are suitable for most users. Finally, for batch folding (required for sequences longer than 300 nucleotides) the user must enter an E-mail address to receive notification that the calculation is complete. For shorter sequences, an immediate job can be performed without providing an E-mail address. The calculation is started by clicking *Fold it.*

Figure 6.10 demonstrates the output of the Vienna Package Web server, based on the input shown in Figure 6.9. The probability dot plot (Figure 6.10b) is obtained by following the link to PostScript *dot plot* on the output form. The Adobe SVG Viewer, downloaded for free by following the link on the Vienna Package Web server output form, is required to view the predicted structures. Note that the predicted secondary structure (Figure 6.10a) of the RD1140 tRNA sequence (Sprinzl et al., 1998) is identical to that predicted by the *mfold* server (Figure 6.8a). The structure is drawn counterclockwise, with the ends of the sequence at the top of the figure, whereas the *mfold* server draws the structure clockwise, with the ends at the bottom, but the predicted base pairs are identical. The probability dot plot (Figure 6.10b) shows the predicted minimum free energy structure base pairs in the lower triangle. In the upper triangle, the area of a square dot is proportional to the probability of the corresponding base pair, indicated by the nucleotides on the x- and y-axes. The probability dot plot for this sequence also indicates pairs of lower probability competing with those in the stem starting with the pair of nucleotides 28 and 44.

RNAstructure

RNAstructure is a secondary structure prediction dynamic programming algorithm for the Microsoft Windows (Redmond, WA) environment that uses the current set of thermodynamic parameters for RNA secondary structure prediction (Mathews et al., 1999b). Detailed instructions for predicting a secondary structure are available in the online help file and elsewhere (Mathews et al., 2000). OligoWalk (Mathews et al., 1999a) is a component of RNAstructure that uses secondary structure prediction to predict equilibrium binding affinities of complementary DNA or RNA oligonucleotides to an RNA target. OligoWalk considers all $N - L + 1$ fully complementary oligonucleotides of length L to a target of length N. The equilibrium shown in Figure 6.11 is considered by these programs in which a complementary oligomer pairs to the target, but self-structure in both the oligomer and target can reduce the free energy of binding. Oligomers can be either RNA or DNA, where the thermodynamic parameters for DNA oligomers are derived from nearest neighbors for DNA-DNA (SantaLucia, 1998) and DNA-RNA (Sugimoto et al., 1995) base pairing. Predicted free energy parameters for oligomer-target binding correlate with cell-based measures of antisense efficacy (Mathews et al., 1999a; Matveeva et al., 2003). It is likely that this equilibrium also will be important for the design of sequences for RNAi.

Figure 6.12 is a screen shot of the RNAstructure predicted minimum free energy structure for the tRNA sequence RD1140 (Sprinzl et al., 1998), using the default suboptimal structure parameters. This structure is equivalent to that predicted using the programs discussed earlier (Figures 6.8 and 6.10). Figure 6.13 shows a screen shot of the OligoWalk input form for predicting the affinity of complementary oligonucleotides to this sequence. The user clicks the button labeled *CT File* to choose the file that contains the predicted structure of the target. A default output file name, called a report file, is then generated, but the file name can be changed by clicking the *Report File* button. One of three modes is

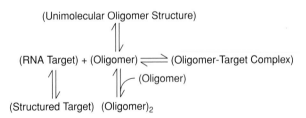

FIGURE 6.11 The equilibrium used by **OligoWalk** for predicting the affinity of an oligomer to an **RNA** target. The oligomer binds by **Watson-Crick** base pairing to the **RNA** target to form the oligomer-target complex. Competing with this basepairing are unimolecular self-structure in the target, unimolecular self-structure in the oligomer, and bimolecular oligomer self-structure (**Mathews et al., 1999a**).

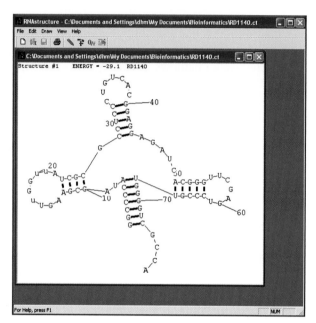

FIGURE 6.12 Screen shot of secondary structure prediction by RNAstructure, version 3.71. This is the predicted minimum free energy structure for the tRNA sequence RD1140 (Sprinzl et al., 1998).

chosen (Mathews et al., 1999a). The *Break Local Structure* mode assumes that the base pairs in the target do not reequilibrate after the oligonucleotide binds and are a suitable default. The user chooses whether to *Include*

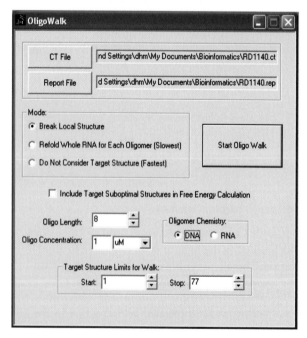

FIGURE 6.13 The input window for an OligoWalk run. The input options are discussed in the main text.

Target Suboptimal Target Structures in the calculation. For the short tRNA target here, not including suboptimal target structures is suitable. For long targets with a large number of suboptimal structures within a small energy increment from the lowest free energy structure, including suboptimal target structures is preferred because this can help overcome some of the drawbacks of limited prediction accuracy. The user then needs to choose the length of the oligonucleotides, whether the oligomers are DNA or RNA, and the concentration of the oligonucleotides. The default is to look at all complementary oligonucleotides from the first to the last nucleotide. This default can be changes by modifying the Start and Stop locations. The calculation is started by clicking *Start OligoWalk*.

Figure 6.14 shows the output of this calculation in the graphical user interface. The target sequence, the tRNA RD1140, is displayed from 5′ to 3′ horizontally along the center of the window with nucleotides predicted to be base paired in the lowest free energy structure in red. The current oligonucleotide, selectable by the user with the right and left arrow keys or by clicking the < or > buttons, is displayed above from 3′ to 5′. The *Go...* button can be used to jump to a specific oligonucleotide or to jump to the highest affinity oligonucleotide. The oligonucleotide predicted to have the highest affinity, at a $\Delta G^\circ_{37overall}$ of −5.7 kcal/mol, is shown on the current display. At the top of the display is cost for opening base pairs in the target (−0.8 kcal/mol), the cost for opening the oligonucleotide bimolecular self structure (−0.6 kcal/mol), and the cost for opening oligonucleotide unimolecular self structure (0 kcal/mol).

Sfold

Sfold is an implementation of the partition function calculation that predicts secondary structures using a stochastic sampling procedure (Ding & Lawrence, 2001; Ding & Lawrence, 1999; Ding & Lawrence, 2003). The sampling procedure guarantees that structures are sampled with true statistical weight. Sfold is available for use through a Web interface.

Sfold has been shown to predict unpaired regions that correlate to regions accessible to antisense oligonucleotide targeting (Ding & Lawrence, 2001). Because the secondary structures are sampled statistically, the fraction of occurrences that a nucleotide is unpaired in a set of sampled structures is the predicted probability for being unpaired.

Figure 6.15 contains sample output from the Sfold Web server for the tRNA sequence RD1140 (Sprinzl et al., 1998). Figure 6.15a shows the predicted most-probable structure, which is the same lowest free energy structure

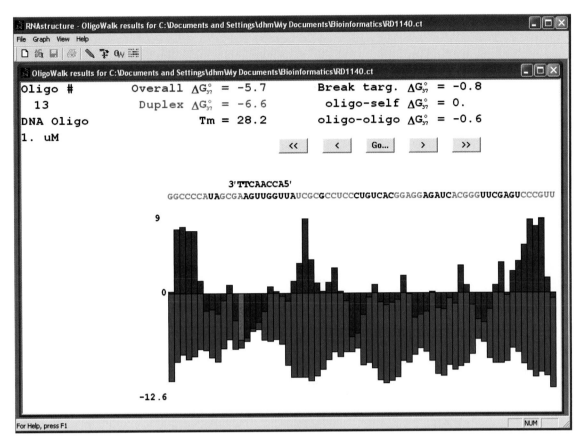

FIGURE 6.14 **A screen shot of OligoWalk from RNAstructure, version 3.71. This screen shot shows the affinity predictions of 8-mer DNA oligomers to the target RNA sequence.**

predicted by the other programs previously discussed. Figure 6.15b shows the probability of pairing, analogous to the probability dot plot produced by the Vienna Package. The areas of the dots correspond to base pairing probability of the nucleotides from the x-axis and y-axis. Figure 6.15c shows the probability profile for the sequence, showing the probability that a single nucleotide in the RNA is unpaired. Nucleotides that have low probability of being base paired are more suitable targets from a thermodynamic perspective.

COMPARISON OF DYNAMIC PROGRAMMING SECONDARY STRUCTURE METHODS

The software packages listed here (*mfold*, the Vienna Package, RNAstructure, and Sfold) each predict secondary structures and alternative secondary structures, and each uses the current set of free energy parameters assembled by Turner et al. (Mathews et al., 1999b). *Mfold*, the Vienna Package, and PFold are freely available through Web interfaces. Additionally, *mfold* and the Vienna Package are available for compilation on Unix and

Linux machines. RNAstructure, however, is a Microsoft Windows program for installation on personal desktop computers. Each package has its own unique features, as described above.

For the example used here, the tRNA sequence of RD1140 (Sprinzl et al., 1998), all of the software packages predicted the same secondary structure. Although all packages are based on the same set of thermodynamic parameters, in general, they do not guarantee identical results. Each program uses a slightly different method for calculating the free energy of multibranch loops. The partition function in the Vienna Package assumes 3′ and 5′ dangling ends at the end of each helix. SFold explicitly checks for 3′ and 5′ dangling ends at the end of each helix, but assumes that a nucleotide will stack preferentially as a 3′ dangling end if both possibilities exist. *Mfold* and RNAstructure explicitly find the optimal stacking of 3′ dangling ends, 5′ dangling ends, or both at the end of each helix in a multibranch loop. Coaxial stacking, the end-to-end stacking of two helices, is included in a second-step calculation that recalculates the free energy of predicted structures, called *efn2*. RNAstructure and *Mfold* differ slightly in the use of

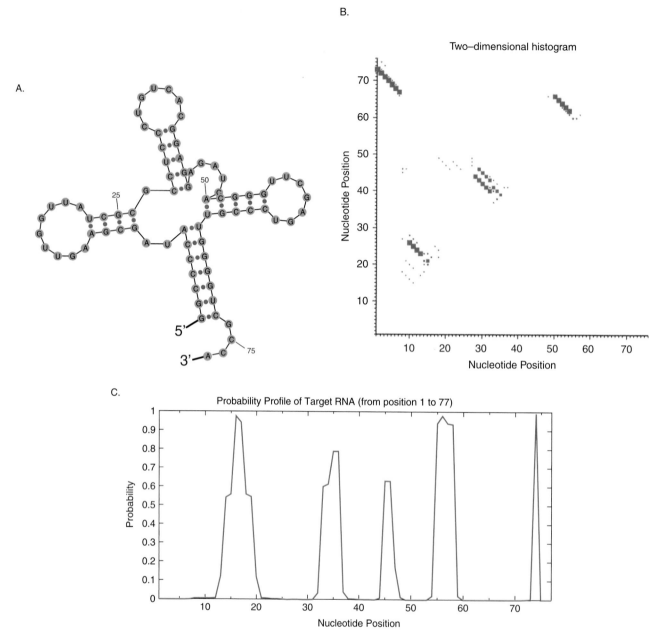

FIGURE 6.15 **Sample output from the SFold server. (a) The most probable secondary structure for the RD1140 tRNA sequence. (b) The probability of pairing for all possible pairs with the largest dots indicating the most probable pairs. (c) The probability profile for a nucleotide being single stranded.**

efn2, creating subtle differences in the predicted structures. Finally, the free energy minimization algorithm from the Vienna Package, RNAfold, explicitly can include the terminal stacking calculations and a subset of the known coaxial stacking interactions in the dynamic programming algorithm. The partition function calculations use the simplified energy rules because of increased computational overhead as compared with free energy minimization programs. Given that there are many secondary structures within a small energy increment of the predicted minimum free energy structure (Wuchty et al., 1999), these subtle differences can result in different structure predictions. Differing structure predictions are more likely the longer the sequence being studied. No systematic studies have been carried out to examine how crucial each of these terms for multibranch loop stability is for the accuracy of secondary structure prediction.

GENETIC ALGORITHM FOR RNA SECONDARY STRUCTURE PREDICTION

Other computational methods have been explored for RNA secondary structure prediction. For example, a genetic algorithm, which uses random mutations of structure and selection of the most fit solutions, is available in STAR (Gultyaev et al., 1995; Van Batenburg et al., 1995). This algorithm determines fitness based on conformational free energy (Mathews et al., 1999b). The algorithm is executed with the sequence lengthening from 5' to 3' end to simulate a pathway of RNA folding. Also, because the algorithm is not based in dynamic programming, it is capable of including pseudoknots explicitly in a computationally reasonable time. However, the drawbacks to simulations like genetic algorithms are that they do not guarantee the optimal solution and that they can provide different results with repeated calculations on the same sequence.

PREDICTING THE SECONDARY STRUCTURE COMMON TO MULTIPLE RNA SEQUENCES

The basis of comparative sequence analysis is the detection of conserved structure, as inferred from sequence differences between species or between sequences discovered by *in vitro* evolution (Pace et al., 1999). The assumption of a conserved secondary structure eliminates from consideration the many possible secondary structures for a single sequence that the ensemble of sequences together cannot adopt. That is, taken together, the multiple sequences constrain the possible secondary structure. These constraints can also be used as auxiliary information in the prediction of secondary structure.

RNA secondary structure prediction algorithms that incorporate information from multiple sequences can be divided between those that are constrained by an initial sequence alignment and those that are not. In general, those methods that are constrained by an initial alignment are not as robust because of the limitations in the alignment, but they are computationally faster.

Algorithms That Are Constrained by an Initial Alignment

Several programs have been developed for finding the secondary structure common to a set of aligned sequences (Hofacker et al., 2002; Juan & Wilson, 1999; Lück et al., 1999; Lück et al., 1996). One approach, called *ConStruct*, uses base pairing probabilities determined by a partition function calculation for each sequence (Lück et al., 1996). These probabilities are then summed according to the alignment to give a consen-

sus probability matrix. The limitations imposed by the sequence alignment are addressed through a user interface in which users can interactively adjust the alignment to improve the consensus probability (Lück et al., 1999; Lück et al., 1996). The source code for ConStruct can be downloaded for compilation.

A second program, called *alifold*, uses a sequence alignment to constrain secondary structure prediction by free energy minimization or to constrain the calculation of the partition function (Hofacker et al., 2002). Additional energy terms are added to the conformational free energy to favor compensating base changes and sequence conservation. This program is available as part of the Vienna Package and through a Web server. Figure 6.16 shows the output for an alifold run for three tRNA sequences; Figure 6.16a shows the consensus secondary structure; and Figure 6.16b shows the probability dot plot. Note that, by including three sequences, the lower-probability base pairs that had competed with one of the stems (e.g., Figure 6.11b) are no longer possible.

A third program for finding a structure common to multiple sequences, called *Pfold*, uses a stochastic context-free grammar (Knudsen & Hein, 1999). The grammar defines rules for emitting a random sequence together with a secondary structure. These rules, encoded as probability parameters, are estimated from a sequence alignment and known, common secondary structures of a number of tRNAs and large ribosomal subunit (LSU) rRNAs. These sequences and structures are referred to as the *training set*. A given sequence is folded using a dynamic programming algorithm that determines a structure with a maximum probability of being emitted by the stochastic context-free grammar. Pfold is available through a Web interface, and sample output for three tRNA sequences is shown in Figure 6.17. The same consensus structure is found as with the alifold server (Figure 6.16).

Algorithms That Are Not Constrained by the Initial Alignment

A genetic algorithm has been developed for finding an alignment and common secondary structure for multiple sequences (Chen et al., 2000). This program makes random mutations on S sequences to make a set of m structures. Alternately, the free energy of conformations and the similarity of conformations are used as fitness criteria for selecting structures for future rounds of mutation and selection. Overall, the algorithm scales as $O(n^2 m^2 S^2)$, where n is the maximum number of stems allowed in a structure. The authors looked at test cases drawn from tRNA, 5S rRNA, and *rev* response elements of human immunodeficiency virus (HIV) and simian immunodeficiency virus (SIV) (Chen et al., 2000).

A.

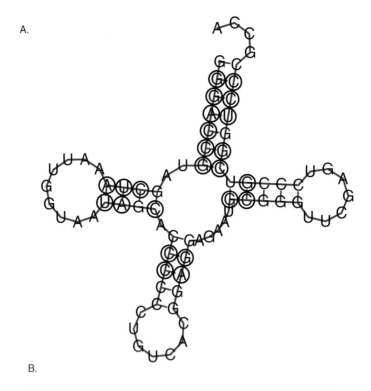

B.

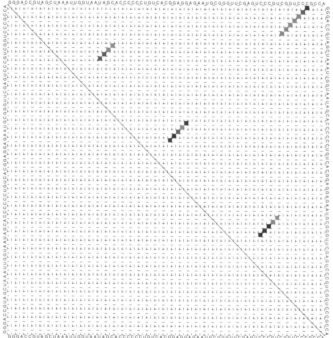

FIGURE 6.16 Sample output from the alifold server. The default parameters were used with three tRNA sequences, RD0260, RD1140, and RD2640, with the alignment taken from the Sprinzl database (Sprinzl et al., 1998). (a) The consensus secondary structure. Circled nucleotides are positions of mutation. (b) The probability dot plot in which dots are color coded to indicate base pair types. Red pairs are conserved, green pairs are positions of more than one compensating base changes, and ochre pairs are positions with a single compensating base change or a neutral change, for example, GC to GU change.

```
                1
Common          ((((((((. . .(  (((. . . . . . . .   . .)))).(((  ((. . . . . . .)
RD0260          GCGACCGGGG  CUGGCUUGGU  AAUGGUACUC  CCCUGUCACG
RD0260          ((((((((. .(  (((. . . . . . .   . .)))).(((  ((. . . . . . .)
RD1140          GGCCCCAUAG  CGAAGUUGGU  UAUCGCGCCU  CCCUGUCACG
RD1140          ((((((((. .(  (((. . . . . . .   . .)))).(((  ((. . . . . . .)
RD2640          GGGAUUGUAG  UUCAAUUGGU  CAGAGCACCG  CCCUGUCAAG
RD2640          ((((((((. .(  (((. . . . . . .   . .)))).(((  ((. . . . . . .)
Reliability     0-1--1--1-0  00-0-00-0  0-0-1--00  00-0-0-0
                1-00-00-0  00-0-0-0  0-0-0-0-0  1-00-00-0
                ...
```

```
                                                               77
Common          )))). . . . . .(  ((((. . . . . . .   . .)))))))))  ))). . . .(
RD0260          GGAGAGAAUG  UGGGUUCAAA  UCCCAUCGGU  CGCGCCA
RD0260          )))). . . . .(  ((((. . . . . .   . .)))))))))  ))). . . .(
RD1140          GAGGAGAUCA  CGGGUUCGAG  UCCCGUUGGG  GUCGCCA
RD1140          )))). . . . .(  ((((. . . . . .   . .)))))))))  ))). . . .(
RD2640          GCGGAAGCUG  CGGGUUCGAG  CCCCGUCAGU  CCCGCCA
RD2640          )))). . . . .(  ((((. . . . . .   . .)))))))))  ))). . . .(
Reliability     0-1--00-0  00-0-0-0  0-0-1--00  00-0-0
                ...
```

FIGURE 6.17 Sample output from the Pfold server. The structures of the three tRNA sequences are shown with bracket notation above each sequence. The parentheses indicate paired nucleotides and the direction of pairing. Every nucleotide with a "(" above is base paired to a downstream nucleotide with a ")" above. The structure predicted for the first sequence, RD0260, is identical to the structure predicted by other methods (e.g., Figure 6.10). Note that base pairing confidences are reported under the structures for each homologous base pair. The input alignment was taken from the Sprinzl database (Sprinzl et al., 1998).

Dynamic programming can be used to predict simultaneously the sequence alignment and common secondary structure for multiple sequences (Sankoff, 1985). In general, this approach is $O(N_1^3 N_2^3 N_3^3 \ldots)$ in time, where N_1 is the length of the first sequence, N_2 is the length of the second sequences, and so on, making it computationally impractical. Two computer programs are available that use dynamic programming, limited to two sequences at most. The first, called FOLDALIGN, finds the local alignment and common structure of two sequences, using a simple scoring scheme (Gorodkin et al., 1997). This scoring scheme favors base pairs, sequence conservation, and compensating base changes. It constructs a multiple sequence alignment from pairwise comparisons using a method similar to that used by ClustalW for building alignments based on sequence matching (Thompson et al., 1994). The algorithm is $O(L^4)$ in time, where L is the maximum motif size. This scaling is achieved by not allowing multibranch loops or pseudoknots. Because multibranch loops are not included, FOLDALIGN is designed to be a screening tool for finding common helices, that is, a first step in comparative sequence analysis.

The second dynamic programming algorithm for simultaneous secondary structure and alignment prediction of two sequences is Dynalign (Mathews & Turner, 2002). It minimizes the sum of the conformational free energy parameters for both sequences, using nearest-neighbor parameters and a term that penalizes the insertion of gaps into the sequence alignment. The gap insertion penalties were calibrated to folding free energies by optimizing the accuracy of pairwise structure predictions for a set of 5S rRNA sequences. Because there are no terms in the optimization for matching sequence in the alignment, Dynalign does not require any sequence similarity in two sequences. Structural bifurcations (i.e., multibranch loops) are allowed. Algorithm scaling is improved by restricting the possible sequence alignments by limiting the maximum separation between nucleotides in the alignment with a parameter M. This results in an algorithm that is $O(N^3 M^3)$ in time and $O(N^2 M^2)$ in storage, where N is the number of nucleotides in the shorter sequence. Dynalign is available as part of the RNAstructure package for Microsoft Windows or as C++ code for local compilation. An application of Dynalign is one of the worked examples at the end of the chapter.

COMPARISON OF METHODS

No single algorithm is yet available that can replace comparative sequence analysis. Each algorithm provides results that are useful for constructing a secondary structure model for multiple sequences. Dynalign can be helpful for aligning sequences that are too dissimilar to be aligned by primary sequence without referring to secondary structure (Mathews & Turner, 2002). Alternatively, FOLDALIGN can be used for sequences too long for Dynalign (Gorodkin et al., 1997). The methods for finding secondary structure in multiple sequence alignments are best used as screening tools to find common helices, which can be used to anchor portions of a sequence alignment when making revisions for further rounds of analysis. The ConStruct tool provides one such convenient user interface for doing the alignment revisions (Lück et al., 1999).

▍INTERACTIVELY DRAWING RNA SECONDARY STRUCTURES

Software packages for secondary structure prediction come with programs to display predicted structures automatically. These diagrams usually are acceptable for looking at results, but generally are not of high enough quality for publication without substantial revision.

Three software packages are available for editing diagrams of RNA secondary structures. The first, xrna, is available from the University of California at Santa Cruz RNA Center. It is written in Java, and therefore should function on any platform that supports the current Java implementation. Figure 6.2 was drawn interactively with xrna on a computer using Microsoft Windows. The second program, RnaViz, is available as executable programs for Windows and Linux (De Rijk et al., 2003). The third program, sir_graph, by D. Stewart and M. Zuker, is written in C and is available, together with source code, for Unix, Linux, Mac OS X (Darwin-Fink-X11 and Darwin-Panther) and Windows (Cygwin and MingW).

▍PREDICTING RNA TERTIARY STRUCTURE

Although there are many automated methods for accurate RNA secondary structure prediction, tertiary structure prediction remains largely a craft that requires user input and insight. One reason for this has been the relative lack of RNA three-dimensional structures compared with secondary structures. Two- and three-dimensional nuclear magnetic resonance (NMR) methods have provided a wealth of information on the solution structure of small loops, but are limited to systems of approximately 50 nucleotides without selective nucleotide labeling. The tRNA crystal structure of yeast phenylalanine tRNA was solved more than 25 years ago (Kim et al., 1974), but few large, nonhelical crystals

of RNA were solved subsequently, until more recent technological breakthroughs culminated in the publication of high-quality crystal structures of the ribosome (Ban et al., 2000; Schluenzen et al., 2000; Wimberly et al., 2000).

Several distinct computational approaches have been used successfully to model RNA tertiary structures. The first is an extension comparative sequence analysis to predict sites of tertiary contacts (Massire et al., 1998; Michel et al., 2000). This approach has its origins in the work by Levitt (1969) on tRNA sequences. In that work, three tertiary contacts, of which two were proven later to be correct, were inferred from an alignment of tRNA sequences (Levitt, 1969; Michel et al., 2000). More recently, Michel and Westhof (1990) modeled the catalytic core of the group I self-splicing intron using high-quality sequence alignment of 86 sequences with well-established secondary structure as the starting point. Nucleotide columns in the alignment not involved in canonical pairing, found to co-vary with statistical significance, are inferred to be involved in tertiary contacts. With a set of tertiary contacts, a model of the catalytic core of the *Tetrahymena* sequence was built (Michel & Westhof, 1990). A model was also built of the tertraloop–tertraloop receptor motif, with an overall orientation that was supported by a later crystal structure (Pley et al., 1994). However, most atomic details of the interaction, such as the locations of hydrogen bonds, were incorrect, suggesting that such models are coarse grained. The Westhof group makes available a computer program called MANIP, for the SGI IRIX operating system, for user assembly of structure motifs into structures (Massire & Westhof, 1998).

A second approach to tertiary structure modeling uses experimentally derived data to constrain model building with a program called MC-SYM (Major et al., 1993; Major et al., 1991). Models are constructed automatically by the stepwise assembly of nucleotides in conformations collected from known structures. Each possible model is stored until it is shown to contradict a constraint, based on experimental data or comparative analysis. The variations between all compatible models can suggest how well-determined the model is with the data used. This approach has been used to construct a model of the hairpin ribozyme using data on secondary structure, hydroxyl radical footprinting, photoaffinity cross-linking, and disulfide cross-linking (Pinard et al., 1999). A later crystal structure verified the existence of a predicted long range GC pair, although a predicted base triple, involving an A at that pair, was not observed (Rupert & Ferré-D'Amaré, 2001). Again, this suggests that the model is coarse grained, that is, many gross features are predicted correctly, although some atomic-level interactions are incorrect. MC-SYM is available for SGI IRIX and Linux.

A third approach is homology model building using a sequence alignment and a reference tertiary structure. Homology modeling is a commonly used method for predicting the structure of proteins (see Chapter 9), but has not been a method available to the RNA community because of the lack of large tertiary structures. With the publication of the crystal structure of the 30S ribosomal subunit (Schluenzen et al., 2000; Wimberly et al., 2000), a template for homology modeling of the 16S rRNA tertiary structure became available. Tung et al. (2002) constructed a model of the 16S rRNA from *E. coli* using the crystal structure of the *Thermus thermophilus* sequence as a template. For regions of the sequence alignment that have no insertions or deletions, a direct substitution of the nucleotides was used. For the more variable regions, entire motifs, borrowed from other regions of the template structure, were inserted into the model structure. The model was found to correlate reasonably with the available cryo-EM map of the *E. coli* structure (Gabashvili et al., 2000). Similarly, a homology model of the tRNA-like domain of the tmRNA was constructed using the tRNA[Phe] (Hingerty et al., 1978) and tRNA[Asp] (Westhof et al., 1988) crystal structures as a reference (Stagg et al., 2001).

Another method applied to RNA tertiary structure modeling is low-resolution molecular mechanics calculations. The Harvey group has developed a reduced representation molecular mechanics software package, called *yammp*, that was used to model the 16 S ribosomal RNA in the context of the small ribosomal subunit (Malhotra & Harvey, 1994). The modeling was started with a representation of the RNA in which one pseudoatom was used for each helix. A random walk was performed to provide a variety of starting structures, followed by simulated annealing and energy minimization. Several possible models were retained for further refinement, starting with simulated annealing and energy minimization on a representation in which each helix was represented with five pseudoatoms. Finally, simulated annealing and energy minimization was performed with each nucleotide represented as a single pseudoatom. Constraints, derived from cross-linking and chemical modification data were modeled as pseudobonds between pseudoatoms. Each ribosomal protein in the small subunit was also considered in the calculation as a single spherical pseudoatom with very soft excluded volume constraints, allowing limited nonspherical behavior. The last step of modeling was to construct a consensus structure from the seven individual models. The regions with large structural differences between these seven models were assumed to be less well defined in the final consensus model. More

recently, yammp was used to help model the tertiary structure of RNase P, constrained with cross-linking data (Chen et al., 1998).

FUTURE OF TERTIARY STRUCTURE PREDICTION

New data are becoming available with which to understand the forces that drive tertiary structure formation in RNA. At the coarse-grained level, recent studies categorized noncanonical pairs based on geometry, providing information needed for improved homology modeling and comparative sequence analysis modeling (Leontis et al., 2002). Newly solved crystal and NMR structures are providing atomic resolution models from which to study RNA structure by example (Ferre-D'Amare & Doudna, 1999; Major & Griffey, 2001; Moore, 2001; Zídek et al., 2001). Computational studies are providing an understanding of the interaction of RNA with metal ions and solvent (Auffinger et al., 2003; Auffinger & Westhof, 2000). New computational methods are also being developed that speed atomic level calculations and improve their accuracy (Kollman et al., 2000; Tsui & Case, 2001).

SUMMARY

RNA secondary structure can be predicted by free energy minimization using dynamic programming, with an average predictive accuracy of 73% for a single sequence (Mathews et al., 1999b). Several software packages, including *mfold* and the Vienna Package, are available to do this calculation (Hofacker, 2003; Zuker, 2003). These packages include algorithms that can help in the identification of base pairs that are not well determined. Secondary structure prediction has been extended to predict regions accessible to oligonucleotide binding in the programs OligoWalk and SFold (Ding & Lawrence, 2001; Mathews et al., 1999a).

Several methods are available to constrain secondary structure prediction using multiple sequences. These are divided among algorithms that are limited to an initial sequence alignment and those that are not limited to an initial alignment. ConStruct, alifold, and PFold all predict a secondary structure common to a set of aligned sequences (Hofacker et al., 2002; Knudsen & Hein, 1999; Lück et al., 1999). Dynalign, FOLDALIGN, and a genetic algorithm are capable of simultaneously predicting a common structure and sequence alignment (Chen et al., 2000; Gorodkin et al., 1997; Mathews & Turner, 2002).

RNA tertiary structure prediction requires user skill and insight. The currently available methods build

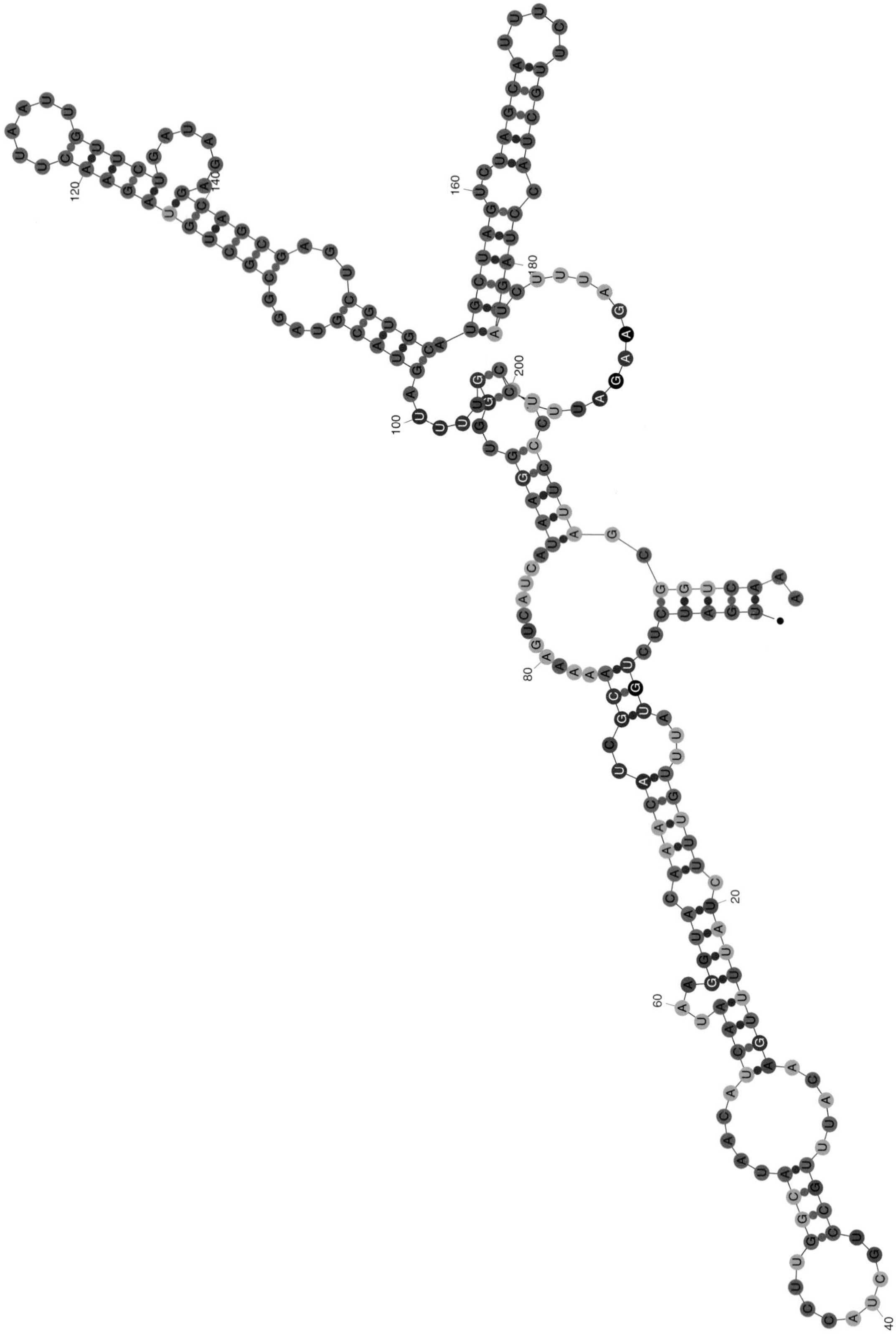

FIGURE 6.18 The predicted, color-annotated structure of the *D. Sucinea* R2 element using the *mfold* server. See Worked Example for details.

coarse-grained structures that can provide an overall sense of the structure, although atomic-scale interactions can be incorrect. Many new experimental and computational results promise to provide insight into the forces that drive tertiary structure formation which should translate to more accurate tertiary structure models.

▋ WORKED EXAMPLE

Two worked examples are presented. The first is the prediction of an RNA secondary structure with color-annotation of "well-definedness" using the *mfold* server. The second example presents the simultaneous prediction of secondary structure and sequence alignment for two sequences using Dynalign.

Mfold Server and Color Annotation

To demonstrate the utility of color annotation on the *mfold* server, predict the secondary structure for the *Drosophila sucinea* R2 3' UTR as shown in Figure 6.2. R2 elements are a class of retrotransposons that are found in most arthropods (Eickbush, 2002). During retrotransposition, the 3' UTR of the message RNA is specifically recognized by the reverse transcriptase during target-primed reverse transcription (Luan & Eickbush, 1995; Luan et al., 1993). The secondary structure of the 3' UTR was predicted for *Drosophila* with comparative sequence analysis of 10 sequences (Mathews et al., 1997). The sequence of the R2 element from *D. sucinea*, which can adopt the comparative analysis structure, was later determined (Lathe & Eickbush, 1997). This sequence has been chosen for this example because it has a known secondary structure and the prediction of this secondary structure by free energy minimization is less accurate than average, so that the usefulness of color annotation is demonstrated (Zuker & Jacobson, 1995; Zuker & Jacobson, 1998).

Download the *D. sucinea* R2 3' UTR sequence from the Book's Web site. Access the *mfold* Web server and paste the *sucinea* R2 element sequence into the large field on the server Web site for the input sequence. Scroll to the bottom of the Web page, to the section marked `Choose color annotation`. Select the button after `p-num` to choose a color annotation that reflects how well determined base pairs are. Keep the default settings for all other fields. Note, however, that there are links to a help page with an explanation of each user definable setting.

Click the *Fold RNA* button at the bottom of the form. This sequence is short enough that the default immediate job can be performed, so the Web browser will move quickly to the results page. The results remain available on the server for 24 hours. Note that the energy dot plot can be viewed by following a hyperlink at the top of the page. Furthermore, a zip or tar file can be downloaded that contains all the predicted structures. On the results page, view the first individual structure by clicking jpg

under `Structure 1`. The jpeg format can be displayed by every graphical Web browser.

Figure 6.18 shows the predicted structure for the *D. sucinea* R2 element, including the p-num color annotation. Five of the predicted helices are identical to helices in the structure based on comparative sequence analysis (Figure 6.2). A sixth helix is predicted that is consistent with, but not included in, the comparative sequence analysis structure. These helices are all between nucleotides U88 and A207. These correctly predicted helices are largely composed of base pairs in which most nucleotides are annotated in red, indicating that there are few competing suboptimal pairs to these base pairs (Zuker & Jacobson, 1998). Most of the remainder of the paired nucleotides, which are not correctly predicted in the lowest free energy structure, are annotated in green, purple, and blue. These colors indicate that there are competing base pairs to these pairs within a small energy increment. The color annotation expresses a measure of confidence in the base pairs where, in this case, 92.3% of base pairs in which both nucleotides are annotated in red are correct. In total, only 54.2% of the predicted pairs are correct.

Dynalign

To demonstrate the usefulness of Dynalign, predict the secondary structures common to the two tRNA sequences RD0260 and RD1140. Download and install RNAstructure on a personal computer using Microsoft Windows. (Alternatively, a text interface version of Dynalign can be used by downloading and compiling onto any Unix or Linux machine with a C++ compiler.) Download the sequence files from the Book's Web site. The sequence file format used by RNAstructure is illustrated by these files. There must be at least one line beginning with a semicolon for comments. The next line must contain a title for the sequence. The following lines contain the sequence, ignoring white space and terminated with a "1." Lower-case nucleotides are forced single stranded.

Start RNAstructure and choose `File|Dynalign` from the menu. Figure 6.19 shows a screen shot of the Dynalign program. Click the `Sequence File 1` button and select the RD0260.seq file with the open file dialog box. Then Click the `Sequence File 2` button and select the RD1140.seq file. The remainder of the fields will fill with default values as shown in Figure 6.19. The output will be saved in three files, `CT File 1`, `CT File 2`, and `Alignment File`. The ct files save the base pairing information and the alignment file is a plain text file with the sequence alignment.

Click the start button to begin the calculation, which will take approximately 6 minutes on a 3.06-GHz Pentium 4 computer. The program then displays the common structure for each sequence in its own window. Click on the window with RD0260 drawn, as illustrated in Figure 6.20. This structure contains all of the correct pairs, as determined by comparative sequence analysis, as does the RD1140 structure. Without the constraints of a second sequence, RD0260 is a tRNA sequence with a poorly

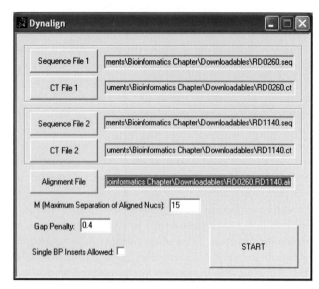

FIGURE 6.19   A screen shot of the Dynalign input form as seen using RNAstructure on Microsoft Windows. See Worked Example for details.

predicted structure. Figure 6.21 shows a screen shot from RNAstructure with the predicted minimum free energy structure for RD0260 when it is predicted alone. This example demonstrates that Dynalign can provide improved accuracy of secondary structure prediction when a second sequence is included to constrain the possible structures.

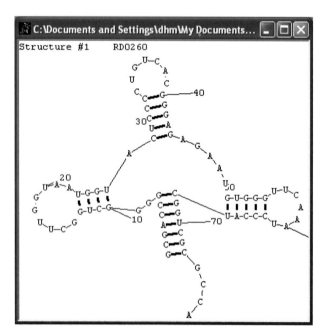

FIGURE 6.20   A screen shot of the RD0260 structure as predicted by Dynalign, in RNAstructure version 3.71. RD1140 was used as the second sequence in the calculation. See Worked Example for details.

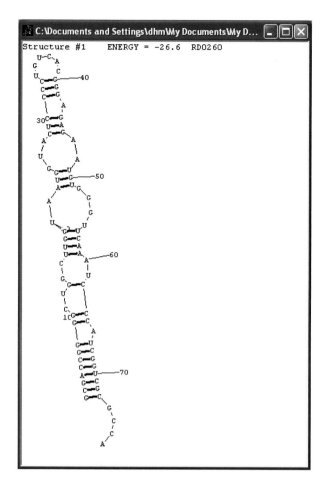

FIGURE 6.21   A screen shot of the RD0260 structure as predicted by free energy minimization of the single sequence in RNAstructure. This tRNA sequence was chosen as an example because its secondary structure is poorly predicted without the constraints provided by a second sequence. See Worked Example for details.

PROBLEM SET

The Book's Web site has a set of four homologous sequences. Predict the secondary structure for each of the sequences using the same program. Determine the consensus secondary structure for these four sequences.

INTERNET RESOURCES

Secondary Structure Drawing Programs

Sir_graph   http://www.bioinfo.rpi.edu/applications/mfold/export/

RnaViz   http://rrna.uia.ac.be/rnaviz/

XRNA   http://rna.ucsc.edu/rnacenter/xrna/xrna_intro.html

Secondary Structure Prediction Programs
for a Single Sequence

mfold server	http://www.bioinfo.rpi.edu/applications/mfold
PKNOTS	http://www.genetics.wustl.edu/eddy/software/
RNAstructure	http://rna.chem.rochester.edu/RNAstructure.html
SFold Server	http://www.bioinfo.rpi.edu/applications/sfold/
STAR	http://wwwbio.leidenuniv.nl/~Batenburg/STROrder.html
Vienna RNA Package	http://www.tbi.univie.ac.at/~ivo/RNA/

Secondary Structure Prediction Programs
for a Multiple Sequence

Construct	http://www.biophys.uni-duesseldorf.de/local/ConStruct/ConStruct.html
FOLDALIGN server	http://www.bioinf.au.dk/FOLDALIGN/
FOLDALIGN server mirror	http://bifrost.wustl.edu/FOLDALIGN/
Genetic Algorithm	ftp://ftp.ncifcrf.gov
PFold server	http://www.daimi.au.dk/~compbio/rnafold/

Tertiary Structure Prediction Software

MANIP	http://www-ibmc.u-strasbg.fr/upr9002/westhof/
MC-SYM	http://www-lbit.iro.umontreal.ca/mcsym/
Yammp	http://rumour.biology.gatech.edu/Programs/YammpWeb/default.html

▌ FURTHER READING

DURBIN, R., EDDY, S., KROGH, A., AND MITCHISON, G. (1998). *Biological Sequence Analysis. Probablistic Models of Proteins and Nucleic Acids* (Cambridge University Press, New York). An excellent primer on probabilistic models for sequence analysis, including hidden Markov models and stochastic context-free grammars.

TURNER, D. H. (2000). Conformational changes. In *Nucleic Acids* (Bloomfield, Crothers, and Tinoco, eds.), (University Science Books, Sausalito, CA), p. 259–334. A thorough review of the free energy nearest neighbor parameters for RNA secondary structure.

▌ REFERENCES

AUFFINGER, P., BEIELECKI, L., AND WESTHOF, E. (2003). The Mg^{2+} binding sites of the 5S rRNA loop E motif as investigated by molecular dynamics simulations. *Chem. Biol.* 10, 551–561.

AUFFINGER, P., AND WESTHOF, E. (2000). Water and ions binding around RNA and DNA (C,G) oligomers. *J. Mol. Biol.* 300, 1113–1131.

BAN, N., NISSEN, P., HANSEN, J., MOORE, P. B., AND STEITZ, T. A. (2000). The complete atomic structure of the large ribosomal subunit at 2.4 Å resolution. *Science* 289, 905–920.

BITTKER, J., PHILLIPS, K., AND LIU, D. (2002). Recent advances in the *in vitro* evolution of nucleic acids. *Curr. Opin. Chem. Biol.* 6, 367–374.

BROWN, J. W. (1999). The ribonuclease P database. *Nucl. Acids Res.* 27, 314.

CANNONE, J. J., SUBRAMANIAN, S., SCHNARE, M. N., COLLETT, J. R., D'SOUZA, L. M., DU, Y., FENG, B., LIN, N., MADABUSI, L.V., MULLER, K.M., et al. (2002). The comparative RNA Web (CRW) site: An online database of comparative sequence and structure information for ribosomal, intron, and other RNAs. *BMC Bioinformatics* 3, Epub 2002 Jan 17.

CATE, J. H., GOODING, A. R., PODELL, E., ZHOU, K., GOLDEN, B. L., KUNDROT, C. E., CECH, T. R., AND DOUDNA, J. A. (1996). Crystal structure of a Group I ribozyme domain: principles of RNA packing. *Science* 273, 1678–1685.

CHEN, J., LE, S., AND MAIZEL, J. V. (2000). Prediction of common secondary structures of RNAs: a genetic algorithm approach. *Nucl. Acids Res.* 28, 991–999.

CHEN, J., NOLAN, J. M., HARRIS, M. E., AND PACE, N. R. (1998). Comparative photocross-linking analysis of the tertiary structures of *Escherichia coli* and *Bacillus subtilis* RNase P RNAs. *EMBO J.* 17, 1515–1525.

CULLEN, B. R. (2002). RNA interference: Antiviral defense and genetic tool. *Nat. Immunol.* 3, 597–599.

DE RIJK, P., WUYTS, J., AND DE WACHTER, R. (2003). RnaViz2: an improved representation of RNA secondary structure. *Bioinformatics* 19, 299–300.

DIAS, N., AND STEIN, C. A. (2002). Antisense oligonucleotides: basic concepts and mechanisms. *Mol. Cancer Ther.* 1, 347–355.

DING, Y., AND LAWRENCE, C. (2001). Statistical prediction of single-stranded regions in RNA secondary structure and application to predicting effective antisense target sites and beyond. *Nucl. Acids Res.* 29, 1034–1046.

DING, Y., AND LAWRENCE, C. E. (1999). A Bayesian statistical algorithm for RNA secondary structure prediction. *Comput. Chem.* 23, 387–400.

DING, Y., AND LAWRENCE, C. E. (2003). A statistical sampling algorithm for RNA secondary structure prediction. *Nucl. Acids Res.* 31, 7280–301.

DOUDNA, J., AND CECH, T. (2002). The chemical repertoire of natural ribozymes. *Nature* 418, 222–228.

EICKBUSH, T. H. (2002). R2 and related site-specific non-long terminal repeat retrotransposons. In *Mobile DNA II* (Craig, N. L., Craigie, R., Gellart, M., and Lambowitz, A. M., eds.), (ASM Press, Washinton, DC) p. 813–835.

FERRE-D'AMARE, A., AND DOUDNA, J. (1999). RNA folds: insights from recent crystal structures. *Annu. Rev. Biophys. Biomol. Struct.* 28, 57–73.

GABASHVILI, I. S., AGRAWAL, R. K., SPAHN, C. M., GRASSUCCI, R. A., SVERGUN, D. I., FRANK, J., AND PENCZEK, P. (2000). Solution structure of the *E. coli* 70S ribsome at 11.5 A resolution. *Cell* 100, 537–549.

GORODKIN, J., HEYER, L. J., AND STORMO, G. D. (1997). Finding the most significant common sequence and structure in a set of RNA sequences. *Nucl. Acids Res.* 25, 3724–3732.

GULTYAEV, A. P., VAN BATENBURG, F. H. D., AND PLEIJ, C. W. A. (1995). The computer simulation of RNA folding pathways using a genetic algorithm. *J. Mol. Biol.* 250, 37–51.

GUTELL, R. R., LEE, J. C., AND CANNONE, J. J. (2002). The accuracy of ribosomal RNA comparative structure models. *Curr. Opin. Struct. Biol.* 12, 301–310.

HANSEN, J. L., SCHMEING, T. M., MOORE, P. B., AND STEITZ, T. A. (2002). Structural insights into peptide bond formation. *Proc. Natl. Acad. Sci. U. S. A.* 99, 11670–11675.

HINGERTY, B., BROWN, R. S., AND JACK, A. (1978). Further refinement of the structure of yeast tRNA^{phe}. *J. Mol. Biol.* 124, 523–534.

HOFACKER, I. L. (2003). Vienna RNA secondary structure server. *Nucl. Acids Res.* 31, 3429–3431.

HOFACKER, I. L., FEKETE, M., AND STADLER, P. F. (2002). Secondary structure prediction for aligned RNA sequences. *J. Mol. Biol.* 319, 1059–1066.

HOFACKER, I. L., FONTANA, W., STADLER, P. F., BONHOEFFER, L. S., TACKER, M., AND SCHUSTER, P. (1994). Fast folding and comparison of RNA secondary structures. *Monatsh. Chem.* 125, 167–168.

JAEGER, J. A., TURNER, D. H., AND ZUKER, M. (1989). Improved predictions of secondary structures for RNA. *Proc. Natl. Acad. Sci. U. S. A.* 86, 7706–7710.

JUAN, V., AND WILSON, C. (1999). RNA secondary structure prediction based on free energy and phylogenetic analysis. *J. Mol. Biol.* 289, 935–947.

KIM, S. H., SUDDATH, F. L., QUIGLEY, G. J., MCPHERSON, A., SUSSMAN, J. L., WANG, A. H. J., SEEMAN, N. C., AND RICH, A. (1974). Three dimensional tertiary structure of yeast phenylalanine transfer RNA. *Science* 185, 435–440.

KNAPP, G. (1989). Enzymatic approaches to probing RNA secondary and tertiary structure. *Methods Enzymol.* 180, 192–212.

KNUDSEN, B., AND HEIN, J. J. (1999). Using stochastic context free grammars and molecular evolution to predict RNA secondary structure. *Bioinformatics* 15, 446–454.

KOLLMAN, P., MASSOVA, I., REYES, C., KUHN, B., HUO, S., CHONG, L., LEE, M., LEE, T., DUAN, Y., WANG, W., et al. (2000). Calculating structures and free energies of complex molecules: combining molecular mechanics and continuum models. *Acc. Chem. Res.* 33, 889–897.

LAGOS-QUINTANA, M., RAUHUT, R., LENDECKEL, W., AND TUSCHL, T. (2001). Identification of novel genes coding for small expressed RNAs. *Science* 294, 853–858.

LARSEN, N., SAMUELSSON, T., AND ZWIEB, C. (1998). The signal recognition particle database (SRPDB). *Nucl. Acids Res.* 26, 177–178.

LATHE, W. C. III, AND EICKBUSH, T. H. (1997). A single lineage of R2 retrotransposable elements is an active, evolutionarily stable component of the Drosophila rDNA locus. *Mol. Biol. Evol.* 14, 1232–1241.

LAU, N. C., LIM, L. P., WEINSTEIN, E. G., AND BARTEL, D. P. (2001). An abundant class of tiny RNAs with probable regulatory roles in *Caenorhabditis elegans*. *Science* 294, 858–862.

LEONTIS, N. B., STOMBAUGH, J., AND WESTHOF, E. (2002). The non-Watson-Crick base pairs and their associated isostericity matrices. *Nucl. Acids Res.* 16, 3497–3531.

LEVITT, M. (1969). Detailed molecular model for transfer ribonucleic acid. *Nature* 224, 759–763.

LONG, M. B., JONES, J. P., SULLENGER, B. A., AND BYUN, J. (2003). Ribozyme-mediated revision of RNA and DNA. *J. Clin. Invest.* 112, 312–486.

LUAN, D. D., AND EICKBUSH, T. H. (1995). RNA template requirements for target primed reverse transcription by the R2 retrotransposable element. *Mol. Cell. Biol.* 15, 3882–3891.

LUAN, D. D., KORMAN, M. H., JAKUBCZAK, J. L., AND EICKBUSH, T. H. (1993). Reverse transcription of R2Bm RNA is primed by a nick at the chromosomal target site: a mechanism for non-LTR retrotransposition. *Cell* 72, 595–605.

LÜCK, R., GRÄF, S., AND STEGER, G. (1999). ConStruct: a tool for thermodynamic controlled prediction of conserved secondary structure. *Nucl. Acids Res.* 27, 4208–4217.

LÜCK, R., STEGER, G., AND RIESNER, D. (1996). Thermodynamic prediction of conserved secondary structure: application to the RRE element of HIV, the tRNA-like element of CMV and the mRNA of prion protein. *J. Mol. Biol.* 258, 813–826.

LYNGSØ, R., ZUKER, M., AND PEDERSON, C. (1999). Fast evaluation of internal loops in RNA secondary structure prediction. *Bioinformatics* 15, 440–445.

MAJOR, F., GAUTHERET, D., AND CEDERGREN, R. (1993). Reproducing the three-dimensional structure of a tRNA molecule from structural constraints. *Proc. Natl. Acad. Sci. U. S. A.* 90, 9408–9412.

MAJOR, F., AND GRIFFEY, R. (2001). Computational methods for RNA structure determination. *Curr. Opin. Struct. Biol.* 11, 282–286.

MAJOR, F., TURCOTTE, M., GAUTHERET, D., LAPALME, G., FILLION, E., AND CEDERGREN, R. (1991). The combination of symbolic and numerical computation for three-dimensional modeling of RNA. *Science* 253, 1255–1260.

MALHOTRA, A., AND HARVEY, S. C. (1994). A quantitative model of the Escherichia coli 16 S RNA in the 30 S ribosomal subunit. *J. Mol. Biol.* 240, 308–340.

MASSIRE, C., JAEGER, L., AND WESTHOF, E. (1998). Derivation of the three-dimensional architecture of bacterial ribonuclease P RNAs from comparative sequence analysis. *J. Mol. Biol.* 279, 773–793.

MASSIRE, C., AND WESTHOF, E. (1998). MANIP: an interactive tool for modelling RNA. *J. Mol. Graph. Model.* 16, 255–257.

MATHEWS, D. H., BANERJEE, A. R., LUAN, D. D., EICKBUSH, T. H., AND TURNER, D. H. (1997). Secondary structure model of the RNA recognized by the reverse transcriptase from the R2 retrotransposable element. *RNA* 3, 1–16.

MATHEWS, D. H., BURKARD, M. E., FREIER, S. M., WYATT, J. R., AND TURNER, D. H. (1999a). Predicting oligonucleotide affinity to nucleic acid targets. *RNA* 5, 1458–1469.

MATHEWS, D. H., SABINA, J., ZUKER, M., AND TURNER, D. H. (1999b). Expanded sequence dependence of thermodynamic parameters provides improved prediction of RNA Secondary Structure. *J. Mol. Biol.* 288, 911–940.

MATHEWS, D. H., AND TURNER, D. H. (2002). Dynalign: an algorithm for finding the secondary structure common to two RNA sequences. *J. Mol. Biol.* 317, 191–203.

MATHEWS, D. H., TURNER, D. H., AND ZUKER, M. (2000). RNA secondary structure prediction. In *Current Protocols in Nucleic Acid Chemistry*, vol. 11 (Beaucage, S. L., Bergstrum, D. E., Glick, G. D., and Jones, R. A., eds.), (John Wiley and Sons, New York), p. 2.1–2.10.

MATVEEVA, O. V., MATHEWS, D. H., TSODIKOV, A. D., SHABALINA, S. A., GESTELAND, R. F., ATKINS, J. F., and Freier, S. M. (2003). Thermodynamic criteria for high hit rate antisense oligonucleotide design. *Nucl. Acids Res.* 31, 4989–4994.

MICHEL, F., COSTA, M., MASSIRE, C., AND WESTHOF, E. (2000). Modeling RNA tertiary structure from patterns of sequence variation. *Meth. Enzymol.* 317, 491–510.

MICHEL, F., UMESONO, K., AND OZEKI, H. (1989). Comparative and functional anatomy of group II catalytic introns—a review. *Gene* 82, 5–30.

MICHEL, F., AND WESTHOF, E. (1990). Modeling of the three-dimensional architecture of group I catalytic introns based on comparative sequence analysis. *J. Mol. Biol.* 216, 585–610.

MOORE, P. B. (2001). The ribosome at atomic resolution. *Biochemistry* 40, 3243–3250.

NISSEN, P., HANSEN, J., BAN, N., MOORE, P. B., AND STEITZ, T. A. (2000). The structural basis of ribosomal activity in peptide bond synthesis. *Science* 289, 920–930.

NUSSINOV, R., AND JACOBSON, A. B. (1980). Fast algorithm for predicting the secondary structure of single-stranded RNA. *Proc. Natl. Acad. Sci. U. S. A.* 77, 6309–6313.

PACE, N. R., THOMAS, B. C., AND WOESE, C. R. (1999). Probing RNA structure, function, and history by comparative analysis. In *The RNA World*, 2nd ed. (Gesteland, R. F., Cech, T. R., and Atkins, J. F., eds.), (Cold Spring Harbor Laboratory Press, Cold Spring Harbor, New York), p. 113–141.

PINARD, R., LAMBERT, D., WALTER, N. G., HECKMAN, J. E., MAJOR, F., AND BURKE, J. M. (1999). Structural basis for the guanosine requirement of the hairpin ribozyme. *Biochemistry* 38, 16035–16039.

PLEY, H. W., FLAHERTY, K. M., AND MCKAY, D. B. (1994). Model for an RNA tertiary interaction from the structure of an intermolecular complex between a GAAA tertraloop and an RNA helix. *Nature* 372, 111–113.

RIVAS, E., AND EDDY, S. R. (1999). A dynamic programming algorithm for RNA structure prediction including pseudoknots. *J. Mol. Biol.* 285, 2053–2068.

RUPERT, P. B., AND FERRÉ-D'AMARÉ, A. R. (2001). Crystal structure of a hairpin ribozyme-inhibitor complex with implications for catalysis. *Nature* 410, 780–786.

SANKOFF, D. (1985). Simultaneous solution of the RNA folding, alignment and protosequence problems. *SIAM J. Appl. Math.* 45, 810–825.

SANTALUCIA, J. JR. (1998). A unified view of polymer, dumbbell, and oligonucleotide DNA nearest-neighbor thermodynamics. *Proc. Natl. Acad. Sci. U. S. A.* 95, 1460–1465.

SAZANI, P., AND KOLE, R. (2003). Therapeutic potential of antisense oligonucleotides as modulators of alternative splicing. *J. Clin. Invest.* 112, 481–486.

SCHLUENZEN, F., A., T., ZARIVACH, R., HARMS, J., GLUEHMANN, M., JANELL, D., BASHAN, A., BARTELS, H., AGMON, I., FRANCESCHI, F., AND YONATH, A. (2000). Structure of functionally activated small ribosomal subunit at 3.3 angstroms resolution. *Cell* 102, 615–623.

SCHROEDER, S. J., BURKARD, M. E., AND TURNER, D. H. (1999). The energetics of small internal loops in RNA. *Biopolymers* 52, 157–167.

SCHULTES, E. A., AND BARTEL, D. P. (2000). One sequence, two ribozymes: implications for emergence of new ribozyme folds. *Science* 289, 448–452.

SPEEK, M., AND LIND, A. (1982). Structural analyses of *E. coli* 5S RNA fragments, their associates and complexes with proteins L18 and L25. *Nucl. Acids Res.* 10, 947–965.

SPRINZL, M., HORN, C., BROWN, M., IOUDOVITCH, A., AND STEINBERG, S. (1998). Compilation of tRNA sequences and sequences of tRNA genes. *Nucl. Acids Res.* 26, 148–153.

STAGG, S. M., FRAZER-ABEL, A. A., HAGERMAN, P. J., AND HARVEY, S. C. (2001). Structural studies of the tRNA domain of tmRNA. *J. Mol. Biol.* 309, 727–735.

SUGIMOTO, N., NAKANO, S., KATOH, M., MATSUMURA, A., NAKAMUTA, H., OHMICHI, T., YONEYAMA, M., AND SASAKI, M. (1995). Thermodynamic parameters to predict stability of RNA/DNA hybrid duplexes. *Biochemistry* 34, 11211–11216.

SZYMANSKI, M., BARCISZEWSKA, M. Z., BARCISZEWSKI, J., AND ERDMANN, V. A. (2000). 5S ribosomal RNA database Y2K. *Nucl. Acids Res.* 28, 166–167.

THOMPSON, J. D., HIGGINS, D. G., AND GIBSON, T. J. (1994). CLUSTAL W: improving the sensitivity of progressive multiple sequence alignment through sequence weighting, position-specific gap penalties and weight matrix choice. *Nucl. Acids Res.* 22, 4673–4680.

TSUI, V., AND CASE, D. A. (2001). Theory and applications of the generalized Born solvation model in macromolecular simulations. *Biopolymers* 56, 275–291.

TURNER, D. H. (2000). Conformational changes. In *Nucleic Acids* (Bloomfield, V., Crothers, D., and Tinoco, I., eds.), (University Science Books, Sausalito, CA), p. 259–334.

TUNG, C. S., JOSEPH, S., AND SANBONMATSU, K. Y. (2002). All-atom homology model of the *Escherichia coli* 30S ribosomal subunit. *Nat. Struct. Biol.* 9, 750–755.

VAN BATENBURG, F. H. D., GULTYAEV, A. P., AND PLEIJ, C. W. A. (1995). An APL-programmed genetic algorithm for the prediction of RNA secondary structure. *J. Theor. Biol.* 174, 269–280.

WALTER, A. E., TURNER, D. H., KIM, J., LYTTLE, M. H., MÜLLER, P., MATHEWS, D. H., AND ZUKER, M. (1994). Coaxial stacking of helixes enhances binding of oligoribonucleotides and improves predictions of RNA folding. *Proc. Natl. Acad. Sci. U. S. A.* 91, 9218–9222.

WALTER, P., AND BLOBEL, G. (1982). Signal recognition particle contains a 7S RNA essential for protein translocation across the endoplasmic reticulum. *Nature* 299, 691–698.

WAUGH, A., GENDRON, P., ALTMAN, R., BROWN, J. W., CASE, D. A., GAUTHERET, D., HARVEY, S. C., LEONTIS, N., WESTBROOK, J., WESTHOF, E., et al. (2002). RNAML: a standard syntax for exchanging RNA information. *RNA* 8, 707–717.

WESTHOF, E., DUMAS, P., AND MORAS, D. (1988). Restrained refinement of two crystalline forms of yeast aspartic acid and phenylalanine transfer RNA crystals. *Acta Crystallog. Sect. A* 44, 112–123.

WIMBERLY, B. T., BRODERSEN, D. E., CLEMONS, W. M., JR., MORGAN-WARREN, R. J., CARTER, A. P., VONRHEIN, C., HARTSCH, T., AND RAMAKRISHNAN, V. (2000). Structure of the 30S ribosomal subunit. *Nature* 407, 327–339.

WUCHTY, S., FONTANA, W., HOFACKER, I. L., AND SCHUSTER, P. (1999). Complete suboptimal folding of RNA and the stability of secondary structures. *Biopolymers* 49, 145–165.

XIA, T., MATHEWS, D. H., AND TURNER, D. H. (1999). Thermodynamics of RNA secondary structure formation. In *Prebiotic Chemistry, Molecular Fossils, Nucleosides, and RNA* (Söll, D. G., Nishimura, S., and Moore, P. B., eds.), (Elsevier, New York), p. 21–47.

XIA, T., SANTALUCIA, J., JR., BURKARD, M. E., KIERZEK, R., SCHROEDER, S. J., JIAO, X., COX, C., AND TURNER, D. H. (1998). Parameters for an expanded nearest-neighbor model for formation of RNA duplexes with Watson-Crick pairs. *Biochemistry* 37, 14719–14735.

ZÍDEK, L., STEFL, R., AND SKLENÁR, V. (2001). NMR methodology for the study of nucleic acids. *Curr. Opin. Struct. Biol.* 11, 275–281.

ZUKER, M. (1989). On finding all suboptimal foldings of an RNA molecule. *Science* 244, 48–52.

ZUKER, M. (2003). Mfold Web server for nucleic acid folding and hybridization prediction. *Nucl. Acids Res.* 31, 3406–3415.

ZUKER, M., AND JACOBSON, A. B. (1995). "Well-determined" regions in RNA secondary structure predictions: applications to small and large subunit rRNA. *Nucl. Acids Res.* 23, 2791–2798.

ZUKER, M., AND JACOBSON, A. B. (1998). Using reliability information to annotate RNA secondary structures. *RNA* 4, 669–679.

ZUKER, M., AND SANKOFF, D. (1984). RNA secondary structures and their prediction. *Bull. Math. Biol.* 46, 591–621.

ZUKER, M., AND STIEGLER, P. (1981). Optimal computer folding of large RNA sequences using thermodynamics and auxiliary information. *Nucl. Acids Res.* 9, 133–148.

▌HEY TERMS

complementary

nucleotide

oligonucleotide

ribozyme

secondary structure

sequence

sequence alignment

tertiary structure

CHAPTER SEVEN

Sequence Polymorphisms

JAMES C. MULLIKIN

STEPHEN T. SHERRY

Bioinformatics: A Practical Guide to the Analysis of Genes and Proteins, Third Edition, edited by
Andreas D. Baxevanis and B.F. Francis Ouellette.
ISBN 0-471-47878-4 Copyright © 2005 John Wiley & Sons, Inc.

INTRODUCTION

Individual variations in genomic sequence arise at an average rate of one nucleotide base difference per 1000 bases. Because these sequence differences, called *polymorphisms*, are, for the most part, inherited, there are many polymorphisms that are quite common in the human population. The particular combination of polymorphisms that an individual carries defines the genetic characteristics of that individual not only in terms of their outward appearance, but also in terms of susceptibility to disease, cancer, genetic disorders, and sensitivity to medications, to name a few. Thus, there is great interest in discovering and cataloging these variations and using them for disease association studies. Polymorphisms also are useful in the functional study of individual genes and simply as positional markers for physical mapping and linkage analysis.

OVERVIEW OF EVOLUTION AND ORIGINS OF POLYMORPHISMS

Mutations: An Evolutionary Process

Mutations fundamentally are produced by errors in DNA replication and are the ultimate source of genetic variation in a population. When a mutation occurs during replication, there exists (at least for one generation) multiple nucleotide states or alleles for that particular location in the genome. Depending on the particular mutational process, these alleles can be as small as a single nucleotide or as large as a multikilobase insertion or deletion. When the scale of the mutational event is sufficiently large, we refer to the mutation as a *chromosomal rearrangement* instead of a mutation. Although there is currently insufficient data in public repositories to specify when the boundary between mutation and chromosomal arrangement has been crossed, model organism genome projects are expected to yield important data on sequence change at this scale.

Coalescent Framework to Model Mutation

The coalescent process is a mathematical framework used to describe the statistical properties of mutations in a sample, as opposed to the entire population (Hudson, 1991). It is used by a medical or population geneticist to model the behavior and ultimate fate of mutations. Conversely, measurements of many polymorphisms in an investigation can be used to constrain estimates of these fundamental evolutionary forces and to assess the significance of specific mutations in affecting a phenotype or clinical disease. The basic equations describe the distribution of mutation events in time and the consequent

frequencies of these mutations in a sample using the expectations of neutral theory, models of selection, models of population subdivision, or a combination thereof (Rosenberg & Nordborg, 2002).

Mutations in Populations

The frequency of alleles depends on the evolutionary forces that have been applied to the population (e.g., genetic drift, selection, migration) and on the age of the mutation itself. Frequencies start as $\frac{1}{2} N$ (for a single individual). Mutations either can be lost in succeeding generations or they ultimately can pass through the population until they become fixed. As a mutation transits the population, it will rise to an appreciable frequency. When the mutant allele exceeds 1% representation in a population, we refer to the mutation as a *polymorphism* (Greek for "many forms"). In subdivided populations, mutations can exhibit quite different allele frequencies. Knowledge about the properties (e.g., size, composition) of the population samples in which the mutation was first found or ascertained and subsequent samples wherein allele frequencies are measured is critical in assessing the usefulness of a polymorphism in other investigations. Public databases consolidate this large set of information about both common polymorphisms and rare mutations of clinical interest.

TYPES OF POLYMORPHISMS

Variations in DNA sequence may be either common or rare in a population, distinguished as polymorphisms in the former case and private polymorphisms (or mutations) in the latter. Databases of human variation exist for both cases, with different organization, content, and functionality to support research in their respective context. Variations also are classified by allelic motif. Nucleotide substitutions, often single nucleotide polymorphisms (SNPs), have alleles that are single-base changes in DNA sequence, occurring at very low rate (mutation frequency $\mu = 1 \le 10^{-8}$ per site per generation) in the human genome. Although restricted to a maximum of only four allelic states, (G, A, C, and T/U), SNPs comprise the largest known class of human genetic variations. Variations also are produced at a higher rate by repetition of specific segments of nucleotide sequence. Short tandem repeats (STR) or microsatellite sequence variation refer to such variation, typically produced by repetition of a unit of two (e.g., CA), three (e.g., GAG), or more nucleotides. STR alleles typically are designated by the characteristic number of repeats in their sequence motif or by the molecular weight of the product.

All variation databases provide some kind of allele-specific information, and most provide some type of sequence context. The former typically is the nucleotide composition of each allele (or repeat size for STRs), and the latter is either a sequence coordinate or specification of flanking sequence that immediately surrounds the variation. Depending on the database, additional information may include:

▶ Population-specific frequencies of alleles, genotypes, or both

▶ Supporting sequence traces (chromatograms) or other assay data used to infer the variation

▶ Statistical tests to measure the general quality of the data and to reveal potential distortions resulting from selection or other evolutionary forces

▶ Genotype data for the variation in reference reagents such as publicly available cell lines (e.g., CEPH and Coriell samples)

▶ Phenotypic effects attributed to a specific allele

▶ Computed functional relationship between the variation and gene based on their common alignment to reference sequence (e.g., if a variation resides in a gene's intron, untranslated region [UTR], or exon; or if a variation in coding sequence has an allele that changes an amino acid in the protein translation)

▶ Database accession numbers for citation in publication.

Database entries range in quality from *in silico* computational predictions to extensively analyzed and validated records that are known to be polymorphic in repeated experiments; some measure of this quality usually is part of the database record. Because variations in the human genome track the complex history of population migration, subdivision, and admixture in addition to the evolutionary forces of selection and genetic drift, the reader should note that no single observation of a variation could guarantee the subsequent observation of the variation in another independent population sample. Rather, evidence for the general applicability of a polymorphism can be inferred from underlying sampling properties such as independent discovery observation of each allele in two or more independent chromosomes or estimation of allele frequency in an appropriately matched population sample.

▌ SNP DISCOVERY METHODS

Pairwise Sequence Comparison

The easiest and most exploited method for discovering SNPs is to align two sequences from different individuals' DNA and to look for high-quality sequence differences.

Most of the data used for SNP discovery by pairwise sequence comparison is available from the National Center for Biotechnology Information (NCBI) TraceArchive. The TraceArchive stores the primary sequencing data from the sequencing machines, and a key aspect of this resource is that not only are the sequence data available, but also the quality values (probability of a base being in error) of each base, ancillary information (like source DNA, size of insert, etc.), and the actual four-channel electrophereogram, if one wishes to look even closer at the raw data. An example of the pairwise sequencing comparison method is shown in Figure 7.1, where the traces are drawn from the TraceArchive. This pairwise method is amenable to many large-scale sequencing projects and was used extensively by The SNP Consortium (TSC; The International SNP Map Working Group, 2001) and more recently by the HapMap Consortium (The International HapMap Consortium, 2003). Together, these two efforts have contributed more than six million huma SNPs to the public archives. Both of these large-scale efforts discovered SNPs by comparing random shotgun sequences from unrelated individuals DNA with the human reference genomic sequence. In addition, TSC also mined SNPs from the BAC sequence where the ends of contiguous BACs overlap each other. It is important to keep in mind that mutations found by this process have frequencies that range from very common to those unique to the genealogical history connecting the two sequences themselves. When evaluating the quality of SNPs in terms of false-positive rates, it is very difficult to distinguish those arising from sequence artifacts from those that arise from a rare allele. TSC resolved this problem by validating the SNP detection method: all 24 DNA samples from which the SNP was detected originally were resequenced, looking for the specific alleles. Their published false-positive rate was confirmed to be less than 5%.

Deep Resequencing

By using polymerase chain reaction (PCR) resequencing of DNA samples, it is possible to discover SNPs in a well-defined region of the genome. For example, the Japanese Millennium Genome Project (Haga et al., 2002) used this approach to identify 174,269 SNPs and 16,293 deletion and insertion polymorphisms (DIPs) within gene regions. DNA from 24 Japanese individuals was pooled into eight samples, each containing three individuals' DNA. Direct sequencing of the PCR products from each of the eight samples in both the sense and antisense directions were processed with PolyPhred to identify SNPs and DIPs. (PolyPhred is a program specifically designed to detect SNPs from directed PCR resequencing of diploid or pooled DNA.) These heterozygous bases are

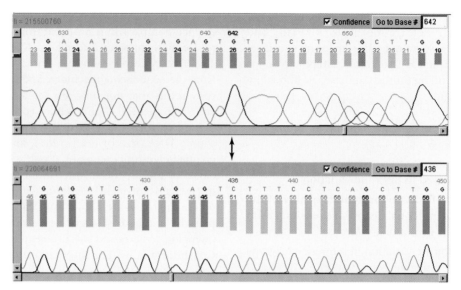

FIGURE 7.1   A large fraction of the SNPs in dbSNP were discovered from traces that are archived in the TraceArchive at NCBI and Ensembl. The chromatograms above show small portions of two traces that are aligned at the same genomic locus. Base calls, base positions, and base call confidence values (Phred scores) are shown above the traces. The G/C SNP at the position of the black arrow is centered in both trace displays, and the dbSNP identifier is rs7936307.

challenging to detect and must be reviewed to insure accuracy. PolyPhred assists the user in reviewing both the homozygous and heterozygous sequence differences relative to the consensus sequence of the assembled data. Many other groups have used this targeted approach as well, with some studies surveying larger numbers of individuals' DNA (for example, The Environmental Genome Project and Innate Immunity Programs for Genomic Applications). These studies are targeting specific genes, first for SNP discovery, followed by case-control studies using these SNPs to find association with disease.

This approach can be taken to include any number of DNA samples, and the cost of this approach scales proportionately with the sample size. However, the number of unique SNPs discovered with an increasing sample size tapers off as the common variants are rediscovered and rarer variants are found at a diminishing rate; Figure 7.2 illustrates this. This figure also illustrates the ascertainment bias associated with SNPs discovered from a limited number of samples.

DHPLC/SSCP

Denaturing high-performance liquid chromatography (DHPLC) and single-strand conformational polymorphism (SSCP) methods reveal differences through viable heteroduplex formation. Although differential migration

rates or disassociation temperatures indicate when pooled sequences contain a variant, these techniques do not indicate the specific sequence change that is responsible for the difference. The techniques are useful as a rapid screening step that identifies reagents for further sequencing. For example, this method was used to discover the *BRAF* oncogene that is associated with some types of cancer, predominately malignant melanomas (Davies et al., 2002).

Discovery methods vary in their ascertainment properties and thus can produce datasets with different proportions of "rare" and "common" polymorphisms. Because more than 90% of the SNPs discovered in the human genome come from random genome shotgun sequence data, at an average depth of approximately fivefold coverage, a technique called *double-hit analysis* (Reich et al., 2003) can filter this large dataset of uncharacterized variations efficiently into rare and common subsets. For a SNP to attain double-hit status, there must be evidence that both alleles are represented at least twice, each arising from unrelated DNAs. At fivefold coverage from TSC and HapMap SNP discovery projects, the six million uniquely mapped SNPs from these combined efforts give rise to 2.7 million double-hit SNPs. SNPs identified as double hit also have a greatly reduced false-positive rate. Under the assumption that erroneous SNP calls are uncorrelated, if the false-positive SNP rate is, for instance, 1 per 30,000 bases examined, then the

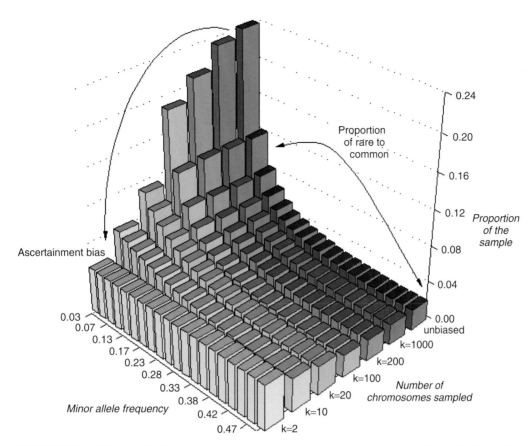

FIGURE 7.2 **Relationship between ascertainment sample size and expected distribution of SNP minor allele frequency. Ascertainment bias describes the overrepresentation of common alleles in small samples relative to the true distribution in the population (e.g., 2 chromosomes, k = 2, vs. unbiased). The distortion of the proportion of rare to common alleles occurs because small sample numbers are less likely to capture rare variations in the population. This bias is clearly seen by comparing the relative mass of rare variants as the number of sequences included in SNP detection decreases to the minimum possible value at k = 2.**

double-hit false-positive SNP rate would be 30,000 times lower.

Although notions of rare and common are properties of a polymorphism's allele frequencies, the usefulness of a polymorphism depends on the investigation. Some experimental designs depend on common variants, whereas others can exploit the unique nature of rare ones. Usefulness and validation should not be confused. The former relates to statistical power and information content and the later expresses confidence in the polymorphism through its observation in subsequent confirming experiments.

▌PUBLIC DATABASES AND BROWSERS

The following section summarizes the large, publicly accessible resources that already are used for variation detection, genotype studies, and haplotype reconstruction. Links are provided at the end of this chapter to Web sites that maintain comprehensive lists of SNP-related resources.

dbSNP

The NCBI dbSNP database of genetic variation currently is the largest public database of sequence polymorphisms and serves as the official repository for public domain SNPs mined by the International Human Genome Sequencing Consortium and collected for the International HapMap project. The 6.1 million nonredundant submissions of human variation submitted between 1998 and 2003 were derived from expressed sequence tag (EST) sequence overlaps, random shotgun sequences used in the TSC and International HapMap projects, deep sequence surveys of individual genes,

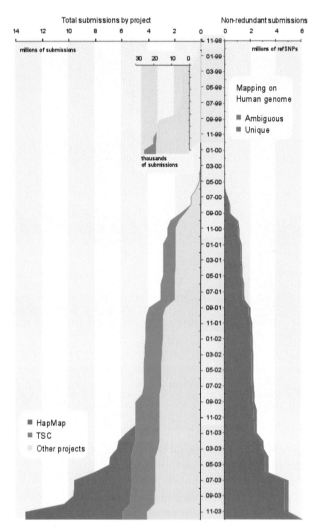

FIGURE 7.3 **Human SNPs deposited in dbSNP through build 118 (November 2003). Total submissions (left) are subdivided by project. Non-redundant submissions (refSNPs, right) are classified as ambiguous either when alignment fails because of repetitive flanking sequence or when they align to more than one location on the genome.**

and overlapping clone sequences used in the Human Genome Project (Figure 7.3). In addition to the large human catalog, dbSNP contains more than 1.1 million submissions for the mosquito, more than 490,000 variations defined between inbred strains of the mouse, 975,000 variations in the dog genome, 42,000 for sugarcane, 31,000 for rat, and an initial set of 2,000 variations in zebrafish to be used as positional landmarks in genome assembly (Figure 7.4). Because dbSNP constantly is receiving SNP submissions, the only way to obtain a current tally of SNPs present in dbSNP is to use the Web site and click on "dbSNP summary."

dbSNP accepts submissions for single nucleotide polymorphisms, microsatellite repeats, and small-scale deletion and insertion polymorphisms. Submissions include the flanking sequence context of variations and a list of their alleles; measures of allele frequency, genotype frequency, observed heterozygosity, or a combination thereof from submitter-defined population samples; individual genotypes for public reagents such as cell lines; pedigree information for family-based samples; and descriptions of common haplotypes.

The dbSNP database group clusters redundant submissions into a non-redundant refSNP collection and computes potential functions and summary metrics for variation, map location, and validation. This group then annotates the data as variation features on the reference human genome sequence, mRNAs and proteins from the NCBI RefSeq project, and three-dimensional protein structures, when possible. dbSNP supports query by term fields in the Entrez retrieval system, sequence similarity via a specialized BLAST service (c.f., Chapter 11), and by map location through most public human genome sequence browsers (e.g., NCBI MapViewer, the European Bioinformatics Institute (EBI)/Sanger Institute Ensembl, and University of California, Santa Cruz [UCSC] Genome Browser; see Chapter 4). Variations retrieved by query can be exported in a variety of structured and human-friendly formats. Public FTP access to the full content of dbSNP is provided through table dumps, FASTA-formatted files, and all supported data formats at dbSNP's FTP site. Detailed descriptions of dbSNP processing steps, encoding values, and mapping algorithms are available online in the NCBI Handbook (Kitts & Sherry, 2002).

Database Content. dbSNP has two major classes of data: the original submitter-supplied data for nucleotide sequence variations and their sequence or diversity properties, or both; and integrated postsubmission content (refSNP clusters, mapping results, functional analysis, average levels of diversity, etc.) generated by NCBI computations on the database in periodic builds. For the submitter-supplied information, each submitted SNP to dbSNP is assigned by dbSNP a unique record number, identified by "ss" followed by a number. These are referred to as ssSNPs. Because more than one submitter may submit information about a SNP, these ssSNP are clustered into reference SNP identifiers, referred to as refSNPs and identified by "rs" followed by a number.

Submitted Data. dbSNP accepts submissions from public laboratories and private organizations. The major data elements of a submission are described below. Complete instructions on preparing a submission to dbSNP can be found online at the dbSNP home page. The submitter

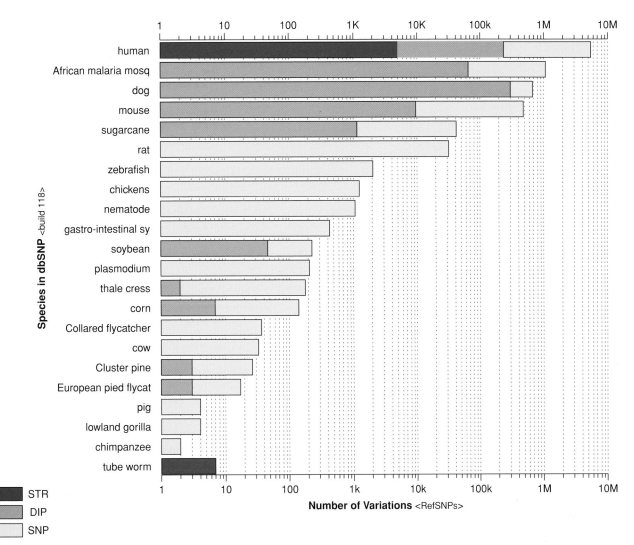

FIGURE 7.4 Submissions of SNP, DIP, and STR to dbSNP by organism, 1998 through 2003.

HANDLE, a short tag or abbreviation that uniquely defines each submitting laboratory in the database, groups submitted content in the database by project. An example submitter SNP record, which has a unique ssSNP identifier of ss4923558, is shown in Figure 7.5. In this example the submitter handle is YUSUKE.

Flanking Sequence Context DNA or cDNA. The essential components of a variation submission include the variant alleles (below) and the flanking nucleotide sequence that specifies a unique location in the genome (Figure 7.6). dbSNP accepts submissions in either genomic DNA or cDNA sequence contexts, with a minimum length requirement of 25 bp per flanking side of the variation and 100 bp total. Within the submission, flanking sequences are tagged to distinguish regions of sequence that were actually surveyed for variation from regions that are supplied (via cut and paste

from a published reference sequence for the region of interest) to satisfy the minimum length requirements. In the example in Figure 7.5, 60 bases per flanking side were submitted.

Alleles. Alleles define the class of the variation from the following allowed classes:

▶ *SNP*: true single nucleotide polymorphism

▶ *in del*: DIPs, deletions represented by "-" in allele string

▶ *het*: variation has unknown sequence composition, but is observed to be heterozygous

▶ *microsat*: microsatellite / simple sequence repeat / short tandem repeat (STR)

▶ *mixed MNP*: multiple nucleotide polymorphism (MNP; all alleles same length, where length is more than 1)

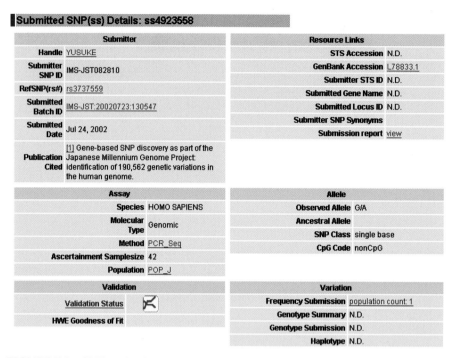

FIGURE 7.5 SNPs submitted to dbSNP are assigned a unique identifier with the format ss number, which in the above example is ss4923558. It is submitted under the Handle YUSUKE, which links to details about the submitter. This SNP is clustered into the reference SNP (refSNP), identified as rs3737559. This SNP is part of a batch of SNPs submitted using the ID given above on July 24, 2002, and is associated with a publication on the Japanese Millennium Genome Project. FASTA sequence around the SNP is provided. Frequency data also is available for this SNP, measured in a group of East Asian DNA samples. The G allele is more common than the A allele in this population.

▶ *named allele*: sequences defined by name tag instead of raw sequence, for example, (Alu)/–

▶ *no variation*: submission reports invariant region in surveyed sequence.

In the dbSNP submission scheme, single nucleotide variants are defined as G, A, T, or C. Ambiguous International Union of Pure and Applied Chemistry (IUPAC) codes such as N are not permitted in the allele definition of a variation. Allele classes are assigned to variations by dbSNP postsubmission processing using rules defined in the NCBI handbook. In the example in Figure 7.5, the observed alleles are G and A.

Method, Population, and Sample Size of Ascertainment. Methods are defined separately by each submitter for techniques used to assay variation and estimate allele frequencies. Methods are grouped by a method class to facilitate query by general experimental technique. All other details are provided by the submitter in a free-text description of the method. In the example in Figure 7.5,

the method is PCR_Seq; this links to additional text describing the method of SNP detection.

Population samples also are defined separately by each submitter for the groups either used to identify variations initially, or subsequently to identify population-specific measures of allele frequencies. Populations are assigned a population class based on geographic provenance of the sample. In the example in Figure 7.5, the population class used for frequency analysis is identified as a link labeled JBIC-allele, which further specifies that these samples are 752 anonymous unrelated Japanese volunteers, Nation:Japan. These are also classified as originating from EAST ASIA.

There are two sample size fields in dbSNP. The first is SNPASSAY SAMPLE SIZE, the number of chromosomes in the sample used to ascertain initially or to discover the variation. The second is the SNPPOPUSE SAMPLE SIZE (allele frequency) that reports the number of chromosomes used as the denominator in computing estimates of allele frequencies. These two measures need not be the same. In the example in Figure 7.5, the ascertainment sample size is 42.

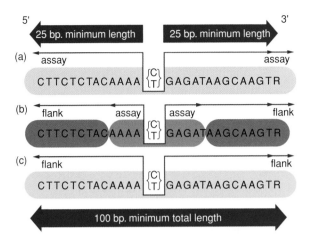

FIGURE 7.6 **Flanking sequence in dbSNP is a composite of bases either assayed for variation or included from published sequence. The minimum sequence length for a variation definition (SNPassay) is 25 bp for both the 5′ and 3′ flanks and 100 bp overall to ensure an adequate sequence for accurate mapping of the variation on reference genome sequence. (a) Flanking sequence tagged as assay indicates complete survey for variation. (b) A partial survey of a flanking sequence can occur when detection methods examine regions of sequence shorter than length rules above. A combination of assay and flank tags are used to construct a record that satisfies the length rules. (c) The flank tag is used alone when variations are captured from published literature and survey conditions are unknown.**

Population-Specific Allele and Genotype Frequencies. Alleles and genotypes typically exist with different frequencies in different populations: Very common alleles in one population may be quite rare in another population. db-SNP thus records allele frequencies for specific population samples defined by each submitter. Frequency data are submitted as allele counts or binned frequency intervals, depending on the precision of the experimental method used to make the measurement.

Individual Genotypes. dbSNP accepts individual genotypes for samples from publicly available repositories such as the Centre d'Etude du Polymorphisme Humain (CEPH) or Coriell. These data are useful for selecting positive and negative control reagents in new experiments and for providing the foundation for individual haplotype estimation.

Validation Information. dbSNP accepts individual assay reports (ss number records) without validation evidence. When possible, however, dbSNP attempts to distinguish high-quality validated data from unconfirmed (usually computational) variation reports. Assays validated directly by the submitter through the VALIDA-

TION section show the type of evidence used to confirm the variation. Additionally, dbSNP will flag an assay as validated when frequency or genotype data are available for the record.

Linkout to Submitter Web Site. dbSNP supports and encourages connections between assay records (ss numbers) and supplementary data on the submitter's Web site. This connection is made using the LINKOUT field in the SNPASSAY batch header. Linkout URLs are base URLs to which dbSNP can append the submitter's ID for the variation to construct a complete URL to the specific data for the record. Linkout pointers are provided in the batch header section of SNP detail reports, and in the refSNP report cluster membership section. Figure 7.7 shows the refSNP cluster containing an example of a linkout for ss4923558 located in the submitter records section under the Handle|Submitter ID column. Clicking on that link will show the JSNP (see "Other SNP Databases" section below) record for this ssSNP.

Postsubmission Computed Data. The dbSNP database is released to the public in periodic "builds" that are synchronized with current genome assemblies and that summarize the current content of variations and their frequencies in a non-redundant set of data.

Resource Integration. The clustered data from dbSNP provides a non-redundant set of variations for each organism in the database. These clusters are maintained in dbSNP in parallel to the underlying submitted data as refSNP clusters. RefSNPs are distinguished from assay submissions by using an rs (refSNP) prefix instead of the ss-prefixed (submitted SNP) accession numbers assigned to submissions; see Figure 7.7 for an example refSNP record for rs3737559.

The refSNP serves as the compact set of identifiers that dbSNP uses to annotate variations on other NCBI resources with summary properties that are computed over all cluster members. The refSNP set is exported in many report formats on the FTP site and, as a result, sets in dbSNP batch query (shown below). Both the refSNP set and the complete set of submissions are maintained as FASTA databases for BLAST searches of dbSNP.

The non-redundant set of variations (refSNP cluster set) is annotated on reference genome sequence contigs, chromosome, mRNAs, and proteins as part of the NCBI RefSeq project. Summary properties are recomputed for each refSNP cluster and are used to build fresh indices for NCBI's Entrez query system and to update variation maps or tracks in genome browsers (e.g., Ensembl, UCSC Genome Browser, NCBI MapViewer; see Integrated Maps section of the refSNP record in Figure 7.7). Finally, links are updated between dbSNP and other NCBI resources such as dbMHC, UniSTS, LocusLink, PubMed

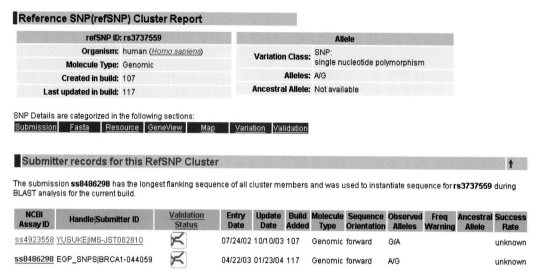

FIGURE 7.7 Submitter SNPs are clustered by dbSNP and assigned unique refSNP identifiers. The example above is rs3737559 and contains the submitter SNP shown in Figure 7.5. The SNP submitted under the handle EGP_SNPS contained more flanking sequence, and thus was used to locate this SNP uniquely on chromosome 17 of the reference genome (see notation under Integrated Maps section). There are links to view this SNP in the three different genome browsers in the Integrated Maps section as well. Under the Variation Summary, observed alleles, frequency information, and genotype information are combined to estimate heterozygosity, Hardy-Weinberg probability, and average allele frequency statistics for this SNP.

and UniGene; these are listed under the NCBI Resource Links section of the refSNP record in Figure 7.7. Public release of a new build involves an update to the public database and the production of a new set of files on the dbSNP FTP site.

Functional Analysis

Variation Function Class. NCBI computes a functional context for sequence variations by inspecting co-located variations and gene features during the contig annotation process. Class is based on the relationship between a variation and any local gene features. When a variation is near a transcript or in a transcript interval but not in the coding region, then the function class is defined by the position of the variation relative to the structure of the aligned transcript. That is, a variation may be near a gene (locus region), in a UTR (mrna-utr), in an intron (intron), or in a splice site (splice site). If the variation is in a coding region, then the functional class of the variation depends on how each allele may affect the translated peptide sequence.

There are four basic outcomes to consider when a variation is in coding sequence:

▶ The allele is the same as the contig (contig reference) and hence causes no change to the translated sequence.

▶ The allele, when substituted for the reference sequence, yields a new codon that encodes the same amino acid. This is commonly termed a *synonymous substitution*.

▶ The allele, when substituted for the reference sequence, yields a new codon that encodes a different amino acid. This is commonly termed a *nonsynonymous substitution*.

▶ A problem with the annotated coding region feature prohibits conceptual translation. In this case, the variation class is noted as coding, based solely on position.

Typically, one allele of a variation will be the same as the contig (contig reference), and the other allele will be either a synonymous change or a nonsynonymous change. In some cases, one allele will be a synonymous change and the other allele will be a nonsynonymous change. If any allele is a nonsynonymous change, then the variation is classified as a nonsynonymous variation. Otherwise, the variation is classified as a synonymous variation.

Because functional classification is defined by positional and sequence parameters, two facts emerge. First, if a gene has multiple transcripts because of alternative splicing, then a variation may have several different functional relationships to a gene. Second, if genes are densely packed in a contig region, then a variation at a single location in the genome can have multiple, potentially different relationships to its local gene neighbors.

Three-Dimensional Structure Neighbors. RefSNPs in protein sequence are projected onto sequence structures when the protein is known to have a structure neighbor. The SNP's nonsynonymous allele and position in the protein sequence defines a corresponding amino acid and position on the three-dimensional structure neighbor. Structure data can be viewed with NCBI's CN3D tool (Chapter 3).

Example Use and Query. The principle user interfaces to dbSNP are Web-based query forms. dbSNP content also is indexed in the NCBI Entrez retrieval system (Chapter 3), so queries can be performed through the respective portals for dbSNP and Entrez SNP.

Entrez Query. Entrez SNP provides a powerful query environment by combining the use of terms and limits. Terms are sets of tags used in Entrez to index the content of dbSNP for fast retrieval (Table 7.1). Querying by tag supports wildcard matching and ranged values. Additionally, tags can be combined in Boolean sets using the *and*, *or*, and *not* operators. For details on issuing complex Entrez queries, see Chapter 3.

The results of an Entrez search can be redisplayed in several formats by using the pull-down menu at the top of the result page next to the `Display` button (Figure 7.8). The graphic summary (Entrez default view) summarizes mapping, function, validation, and variation data for each record as illustrated in the boxed part of Figure 7.8. Additional report formats provide textual data, sequence information, or both using report formats developed for the dbSNP FTP site:

▶ *ASN.1/XML*: provides structured information about each variation from dbSNP regarding gene relationships, flanking sequence, map position(s), and population-specific allele frequencies in two standard provided for variation records

▶ *Flatfile*: a semistructured, human-friendly version of the ASN.1/XML record

▶ *Chromosome Report*: a compact, one-line-per-variation format, ordered by map position.

Other display choices show refSNP cluster contents or related Entrez resources or send the selected list of variation records to the dbSNP batch query service for formatting and delivery by E-mail. Links on the right sidebar connect variations to other NCBI resources (e.g., LocusLink, Entrez Genes, GenBank, and PubMed), as well as to external resources (such as submitter Web sites) through the Entrez LinkOut facility.

dbSNP Query Modules. From the dbSNP home page, users can issue the following types of basic searches:

▶ *Single record query in dbSNP*: The identifiers in dbSNP include submission accessions (ss numbers) that are assigned to each individual submitted variation, local (or submitter) IDs for the same variations, and refSNP cluster IDs (rs numbers).

▶ *dbSNP submission property queries*: Queries can be constructed for submissions by a laboratory (submitter), new data (more recent than a user specified date), queries based on methods used to assay for variation, or populations of interest.

▶ *dbSNP batch query*: A variety of reports can be generated on demand for sets of variation IDs collected from other queries.

▶ *Locus information*: This pointer to the NCBI LocusLink resource permits users to query for records by gene name or symbol. Records in LocusLink will have a pointer back to dbSNP once one or more variations have been associated with a gene feature.

▶ *Free form search (simple and advanced)*: Free form is the most flexible query structure in dbSNP. Modeled on the NCBI Entrez retrieval system, the user can conduct queries by database field values. Multiple terms can be intersected to restrict query to the specific subset of data that is of interest to the user. The easy form ("Simple") query provides the same functionality by the use of pull-down menus of values for the most popular query terms.

▶ *STS markers*: this query approach is appropriate if a user is interested in retrieving variations that have been mapped to a specific region of the genome bounded by two STS markers. Other map-based queries are available through the NCBI MapViewer tool.

Other SNP Databases

ALFRED. The ALFRED (ALlele FREquency Database) is a prototype project intended to document allele frequencies in a broad, anthropological collection of human populations. At the time of this writing, ALFRED contained more than 18,000 individual allele-by-population frequency measures for more than 900 polymorphic sites from more than 400 genes with an average of 19 populations per polymorphic site, or alternatively for more than 350 populations with an average of 51 markers per population. The Kidd laboratory at Yale University and collaborative projects have generated the bulk of ALFRED's data, where variations are defined primarily by their locus, alleles, and a brief description. When possible, variations are linked to other molecular databases (e.g., dbSNP or the Human Genome Variation

TABLE 7.1 ■ Entrez SNP Search Terms

Search Field	Qualifier(s)	Type	Description
Allele	[ALLELE], [VARIATION], [VARI]	IUPAC	Observed allele(s). Ex: R[ALLELE]
Chromosome	[CHR]	Textnum	Mapped chromosome number. Available values [1-22, W-Z, and Un (unknown)]. Ex: 2[CHR] or X[CHR]
Base position	[CHRPOS], [BPOS]	Integer*	Mapped chromosome position; use in conjunction with chromosome field [CHR]. Ex: 7[CHR] AND 88556398:88580839[CHRPOS]
Create build ID	[CREATE_BUILD], [CBID]	Integer*	SNP create build ID. Ex: 103[CBID]
Publication date	[CREATEDATE], [CDAT], [PUBDATE], [PDAT]	Date*	SNP create/publication date. Use the format YYYY/MM/DD; month and day are optional. Ex: 2002/01[CDATE]
Function class	[FXN_CLASS], [FUNC]	Text	Function class: Available values are: locus region, intron, coding nonsynon, mrna, utr, coding synon, reference, exception, and splice site. Ex: "coding synon"[FUNC]
Gene name	[GENE], [GENE_SYMBOL]	Textnum	Entrez genes symbol. Ex: LPL[GENE]
Protein description	[PDSC]	Text	Protein description. Ex: "liver expressed"[PDSC]
Gene description	[GDSC]	Text	Gene description. Ex: "kinase"[Gene Description]
GO terms	[GO]	Text	Gene ontology (GO) terms. Ex: "receptor"[GO term]
Genotype	[GENOTYPE], [GTYPE]	Boolean	Genotype data available in dbSNP. Ex: true[GTYPE]
Heterozygosity	[HET]	Integer*	Avg. heterozygosity exceeds this % value. Ex: 5[HET]
Local SNP ID	[LOC_SNP_ID]	Textnum	Submitter's SNP ID. Ex: "TSC0227737"[LOC_SNP_ID]
LocusLink ID	[LOCUS_ID], [LID]	Integer	LocusLink/Entrez Genes ID number. Ex: 4023[LID]
Map weight	[WEIGHT], [MPWT], [HIT]	Integer*	SNP map weight info—the number of times a SNP map to the genome contig (Available values 1,2,3,10) where: 1 = hit once (annotated set), 2 = hit twice, (annotated with warning), 3 = hit 3–9 times, 10 = hit 10+ times (neither annotated). Ex: 1[WEIGHT]
Method class	[METHOD_CLASS], [METHOD], [MCLS]	Text	Assay method used to identify SNP. Available values are: computed, rflp, dhplc, sequence, hybridize, sscp, other, unknown. Ex: "sequence"[METHOD]
Accession	[ACC]	Textnum	Search by nucleotide or protein accession. Ex: AC000120[ACC]
Contig position	[CTPOS]		Mapped contig position; use in conjunction with contig accession field [ACC] 1000000:2000000[CTPOS] AND NT_034874[ACC]
Reference SNP ID	[RS]	Integer*	dbSNP assigned reference ID (RS). Ex: 709932[RS]
Submitter SNP ID	[SS]	Integer*	dbSNP assigned submitter ID (SS). Ex: 1487247[SS]
Population class	[POP_CLASS], [POP], [PCLS]	Text	Population Classification based on geographic location. Ex: "europe"[POP]
SNP class	[SNP_CLASS], [SCLS]	Text	SNP class/type: available values are: het, mnp, in del, named, microsat, no variation, mixed & snp. Ex: "snp"[SNP_CLASS]
Submitter handle	[HANDLE]	Text	Submitter/Project handle. Ex: "LEE"[HANDLE]
Success rate	[SUCCESS_RATE], [SRATE]	Integer*	Success rate(%) Ex: 95[SRATE]
Organism	[ORGN], [TAX_ID]	Text	Organism name or Taxonomy ID number; use the prefix 'txid' before the Taxonomy ID number. Ex: "human"[ORGN], "mouse"[ORGN], or "txid9606"[ORGN]
Update build ID	[UPD_BUILD], [UBID]	Integer*	SNP update build ID. Ex: 102[UBID]
Modification date	[UDATE], [UDAT], [MODDATE]	Date*	Modification/update date. Use the format YYYY/MM/DD; month and day optional. Ex: 2002/01 [UDATE]
Validation	[VALIDATION]	Text	Validation status: available values are: by cluster, by submitter, by frequency, 2hit 2allele. Ex: "by cluster"[VALIDATION]

* signifies that range searching is available.

182

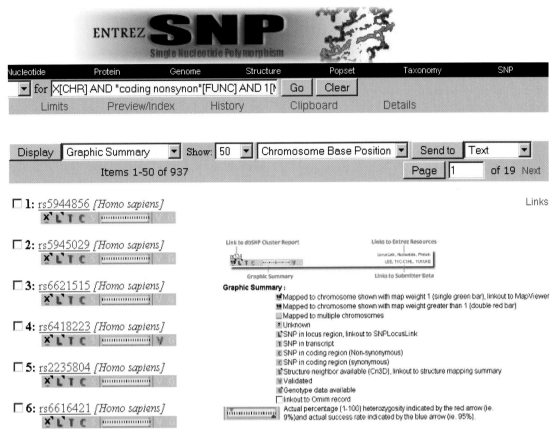

FIGURE 7.8 Query results from Entrez SNP can be displayed or downloaded in a variety of formats, or sent to dbSNP Batch query for additional reports based on the full data for each record. Limits can be applied to a search by clicking the Limits link under the query bar. In this example, the query is to find all **X** chromosome, nonsynonymous coding **SNP** that map once to the genome using the query X[CHR] AND "coding nonsynon" [FUNC] AND 1[MAPWEIGHT]. The default graphic summary is displayed, sorted by chromosome base position. The boxed section of this figure describes the various parts of the graphics displayed for each **SNP**.

database [HGVBase]) for expanded molecular information, populations are linked to Ethnologue for linguistic and geographic information, and all entries to PubMed for relevant citations. Queries start from either the locus or population of interest. Loci and populations are both listed alphabetically and are grouped by chromosome or continent of origin, respectively. Frequency tables can be retrieved either as HTML table structures or as semicolon-delimited text. Public FTP access to the full content of the database is not available.

JSNP. The Japanese SNP (JSNP) database was developed as part of Japan's Millennium Project to identify up to 150,000 sequence variations in gene regions over two years, to make the information related to these SNPs available to the public, and to develop analytical tools for polymorphisms. As of this writing, JSNP contains more than 200,000 records, including more than 85,000 with allele frequency information. Search features support a map-based view of human genomic sequence, with annotated features such as repeat content, known and predicted mRNAs, UniGene (clustered EST) hits, and variations from dbSNP. Lists of JSNPs in a region can be generated in FASTA format for BLAST analysis, and individual records can be browsed for information on flanking sequence, allele frequencies in Japanese populations, assay protocols, and underlying sequence chromatograms. Public FTP access to the JSNP database is available from the JSNP Web page. The downloadable files contain SNPs with flanking sequence available in FASTA format, and allele frequencies are provided as a multicolumn text report. The database contents are covered by copyright protection, and permission is required to reproduce the database and derived documents.

HGVBase. The HGVBase was developed to support genotype–phenotype association analyses that, in turn, explore how common sequence variations may influence phenotypes such as risk of common disease and individual drug response. HGVBase currently serves as the sequence variation companion to the European Ensembl project for genome annotation. Sequence variations are presented with details of how they are physically and functionally related to the closest neighboring gene. Records include SNPs, indels, simple tandem repeats, and other sequence alternatives, regardless of location, allele frequencies, or known effect on phenotype. At this time, HGVBase contains more than 3,000,000 entries and represents approximately 40% of the dbSNP catalog of human sequence variation. The SRS retrieval system supports queries against indexed properties that span gene relationships, allele frequency, medical subject heading (MeSH) terms, citations, and functional classification. Query by chromosomal position and BLAST searches against the database are also supported. Public FTP access to the database is provided with data in XML and FASTA formats.

TSC. The SNP Consortium was formed as a nonprofit corporation in 1999 with the goal of providing public genomic data. Its mission was to develop up to 300,000 SNPs distributed evenly throughout the human genome and to make the information related to these SNPs available to the public without intellectual property restrictions. The effort far surpassed their initial goals: by the end of the project in 2001, 1.8 million SNPs were identified and released to the public through both the TSC Web site and dbSNP. The TSC site supports query by common database identifiers (TSC and dbSNP), by chromosomal location, and by genes, where the query can be restricted to dbSNP functional classifications of interest (nonsynonymous substitutions, mRNA splice sites, intron, UTR, and locus region). Queries by chromosomal location also can be performed with a graphical map viewer that provides annotation tracks for STS, genes, human and mouse mRNAs, ab initio gene predictions, dbSNP refSNP clusters, serial analysis of gene expression (SAGE) tags, and enzyme restriction sites. Specific variation records report flanking sequence context and description of the protocols used in variation detection and allele frequency assays. Screening details provide the sequence chromatograms used to ascertain the variation. All frequency data, genotypes, and linkage data are freely available via public FTP as well as all variation data.

Polymorphism Data and Mutation Data. Many research groups have posted their local polymorphism studies on the Web. The HGVBase site maintains a comprehensive, annotated list of SNP-related databases.

Many clinical studies and research groups also have developed databases or lists of clinical mutations with phenotypic effects. The Human Genome Variation Society (HGVS) compiles and annotates such a list of all active databases.

SNP Integration in Genome Browsers

This section explores how to access and work with SNPs using the three main genome browsers. The same genomic region is used for all the examples that follow so that comparisons can be made among the different systems.

Ensembl. There are, in general, two ways to access SNPs in this browser: via the genomic viewer and using Ens-Mart (Kasprzyk et al., 2004). In the first instance, after a region of interest is located (e.g., the *BRCA1* gene on chromosome 17), a number of tracks appear in the `Detailed View` section of the Ensembl Genome Browser. By default, the SNP track should be visible; if not, it can be activated from the `Features` pull-down menu. With the SNPs track visible, a page like that shown in Figure 7.9 appears by clicking on any of the SNPs in the SNP track. This view shows the SNP selected and a local neighborhood 10 Kb on either side. The different types of SNPs are color coded as to type, for example, coding, intronic, flanking, or other. Deletion and insertion polymorphisms are indicated with a triangle. Links at the top of the page go to other databases that have related or more in-depth information about the selected SNP.

EnsMart. This part of the Ensembl browser system allows users to generate complex queries to the Ensembl database using a series of straightforward Web pages. The two main parts of this system are the FILTER and OUTPUT stages. Continuing with the *BRCA1* gene example, in the FILTER section of EnsMart, the human genome is filtered using a specific transcript for the *BRCA1* gene. If the Ensembl gene ID were used instead, then SNPs for all transcripts would be reported, so limiting the query to one transcript simplifies the results for this example (see Figure 7.10). At the OUTPUT stage, there are four tabs identifying the four broad types of output, and this example uses the SNPs tab. The `Gene Associated SNPs` section allows for selection of many SNP attributes to be reported (Figure 7.11). After clicking on the export button, a summary page is generated, as shown in Figure 7.12.

UCSC. Using the search box for the UCSC Human Genome Browser with `BRCA1` as the query returns a list of matches to that string. Selecting the *BRCA1* gene generates a new browser page, with the gene filling

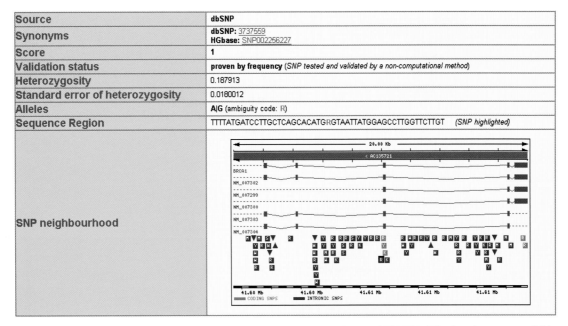

Source	dbSNP
Synonyms	**dbSNP:** 3737559 **HGbase:** SNP002256227
Score	1
Validation status	**proven by frequency** (*SNP tested and validated by a non-computational method*)
Heterozygosity	0.187913
Standard error of heterozygosity	0.0180012
Alleles	A|G (ambiguity code: R)
Sequence Region	TTTTATGATCCTTGCTCAGCACATGRGTAATTATGGAGCCTTGGTTCTTGT (*SNP highlighted*)
SNP neighbourhood	

FIGURE 7.9   This is an example Ensembl **SNP** report for dbSNP rs3737559. The local context within 10 Kb on either side of the **SNP** is shown. The different types of **SNPs** are color coded as to type (e.g., coding, intronic, flanking, or other). DIPs are indicated with a triangle. The letters inside the **SNP** squares indicate the type of **SNP** using **IUPAC** ambiguity codes (Appendix A2).

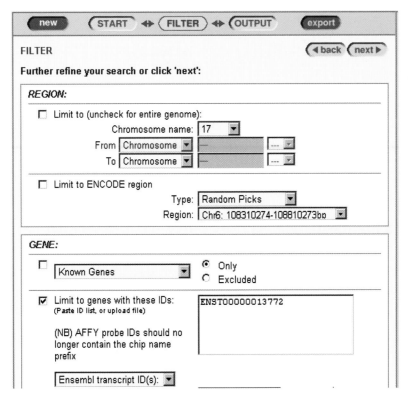

FIGURE 7.10   The EnsMart database query interface allows for filters to be placed on regions of the genome. Here, the selection is limited to a single Ensembl transcript shown in the `list` box.

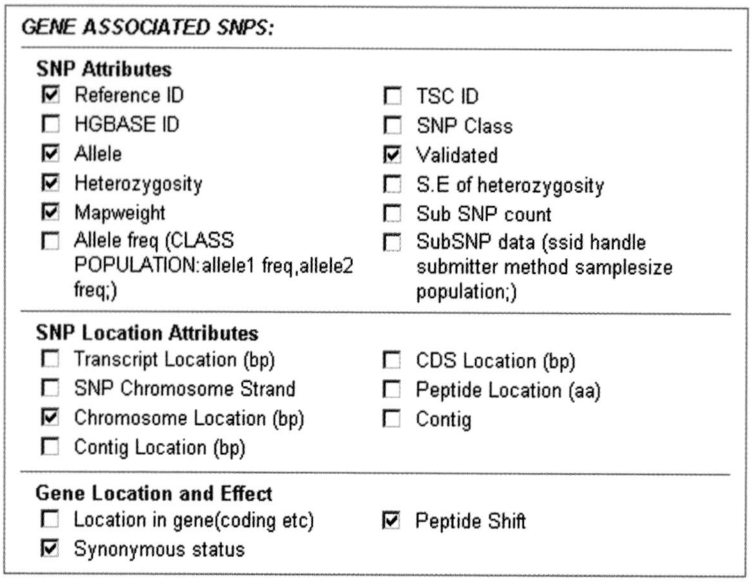

FIGURE 7.11 For this example, the desired output is focused on SNPs, thus the SNP tab is selected. The GENE ASSOCIATED SNPS box is used to indicate which SNP attributes are reported.

the width of the genome display window. Zooming out by 1.5× will give some additional sequence on either side of the gene, as shown in Figure 7.13. Using the Tables button at the top of the screen produces a "table browser" page (Karolchik et al., 2004). On that page, selecting random SNPs under the Choose a table:

drop-down menu and clicking on the get all fields button produces a list of all "random SNPs" within the selected range. To obtain "Overlap SNPs," the user would return to the table browser page and select that table, as described above. (Overlap SNPs are those detected by comparing overlapping clone sequences, and random

Reference ID	Allele	Validated	Heterozygosity	Mapweight	Chromosome Location (bp)	Peptide Shift	Synonymous status
8176099	A/G	no-info	0.0112994	1	41640928	-	yes
16942	A/G	by-cluster	0.409461	1	41617165	K|R	no
2227945	A/G	by-frequency	0.033509	1	41617295	S|G	no
4986852	A/G	by-frequency	0.0454979	1	41617594	N|S	no
16941	A/G	by-frequency	0.38834	1	41617600	E|G	no
1800704	A/G	by-cluster	0	1	41617689	I|M	no
4986848	C/T	by-frequency	0.011735	1	41617747	S|F	no
4986847	A/C	no-info	0.0117876	1	41617940	I|L	no
1800740	A/G	by-cluster	0	1	41617980	-	yes
799917	C/T	by-frequency	0.482381	1	41618101	P|L	no
1800709	C/T	by-cluster	0	1	41618192	R|W	no
7502059	A/G	no-info	0	1	41618332	V|A	no
16940	C/T	by-cluster	0.441639	1	41618402	-	yes
4986846	C/T	by-frequency	0.0117703	1	41618481	-	yes
4986845	A/G	by-frequency	0.0355853	1	41618546	N|D	no
4986844	A/G	by-frequency	0.0355853	1	41618604	-	yes
1799949	C/T	by-cluster	0.456503	1	41618631	-	yes
4986850	A/G	by-frequency	0.0586651	1	41618636	N|D	no
8176154	A/G	no-info	0.0542593	1	41618835	-	yes
1799950	A/G	by-cluster	0.0811928	1	41619646	Q|R	no
8176153	A/G	no-info	0.0954939	1	41619890	S|G	no
4986849	A/G	by-frequency	0.0357053	1	41607615	Q|R	no
8176184	C/T	by-frequency	0.472346	1	41607635	-	yes
1800707	G/T	by-cluster	0	1	41607725	K|N	no
1799967	A/G	by-frequency	0.0348546	1	41596140	I|M	no
4986854	C/T	by-frequency	0.0117367	1	41596213	T|M	no
8176219	A/G	no-info	0.0110494	1	41596238	T|A	no
1799966	A/G	by-cluster	0.417841	1	41596259	S|G	no
4438367	A/G	no-info	0	1	41572859	-	yes

FIGURE 7.12 Output generated from the Ensembl database using the EnsMart filters and output parameters defined in Figures 7.10 and 7.11. The reference ID column contains the dbSNP refSNP identifiers that are hyperlinked to Ensembl SNP report pages, as shown in Figure 7.9. The chromosome location column is hyperlinked to generate an Ensembl ContigView page.

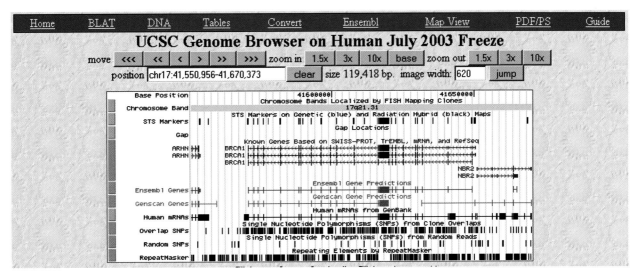

FIGURE 7.13 The **UCSC** Genome Browser centered on the *BRCA1* gene on chromosome 17. Two tracks show the locations of SNPs across this region. Overlap SNPs are those detected by comparing overlapping clone sequences, and random SNPs are those detected by comparing sequence reads from whole genome shotgun from diverse pools of human **DNA**.

SNPs are those detected by comparing sequence reads from whole genome shotgun from diverse pools of human DNA.)

NCBI LocusLink. Using the LocusLink interface (Chapter 3) and entering `BRCA1` as the query produces a summary page describing this gene. Clicking on the `VAR` button generates a SNP-focused page. For viewing the reference SNPs (rsIDs), there are five radio buttons to choose from. The default shows all rsIDs in the gene region. Other options are `cSNP` to show all coding SNPs; `has frequency`, for all rsID with genotype frequency information; `double hit`, for rsIDs where both alleles are detected at least twice in different DNAs; and `haplotype tagged`, for rsIDs that are identified as the minimum set needed to detect the local haplotype structure. Shown in Figure 7.14 are the first few coding SNPs in the *BRCA1* gene. Those that do not change the amino acid, and thus called *synonymous*, are identified in green; those that result in a different amino acid, a *nonsynonymous change*, are identified in red.

∎ GENOTYPING

Typically, genotyping refers to the process of determining the allele states of selected polymorphisms in selected groups of individuals. For example, to genotype a known STR, PCR primers are designed on either side of the STR, and the amplified product from a DNA sample is size-fractionated by electrophoresis to determine the number of copies present. An individual who is homozygous for one of the allele states will show a single predominant band; those who are heterozygous will show two distinct bands. Note that, for STR polymorphisms (STRPs), there can be many different copy numbers present in the population, so the copy number(s) is important to record for each sample. There are many STRPs already reduced to working assays (i.e., with designed primers end expected product sizes). From the dbSNP Entrez search page, these can be found by querying for `microsat [SNP_CLASS]`; note that microsatellite (`microsat`) is synonymous for STR.

There are many technologies available for genotyping SNPs. The advantage of working with SNPs, as opposed to STRPs, is that SNPs are available at much higher densities; the dbSNP build 119 average has one uniquely mapped SNP per 500 bases in the genome, as opposed to one uniquely mapped STRP per one million bases. Therefore, for studies that need to work at higher genomic resolution (say, at the resolution of genes), SNP-based genotyping is required.

Types of projects that need large numbers of genotypes include the HapMap Project (described in the next section), population genetics, and association studies. For association studies, a group of individuals are selected as "cases" and another as "controls." The cases group are individuals that are diagnosed with some disease (e.g., cystic fibrosis), react to some type of medicine (e.g., allergic to penicillin), or are even especially healthy (e.g., in good health and more than 100 years old). The controls group are individuals that do not exhibit the

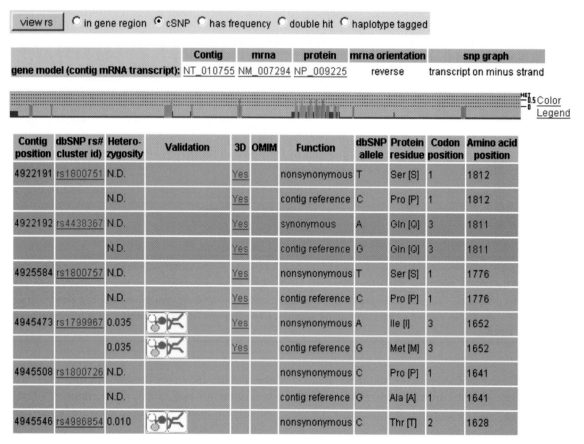

FIGURE 7.14 The *BRCA1* gene LocusLink Variations page. In this example, only the coding **SNPs** are shown. The vertical bars shown on the gene section are color coded as to synonymous (green) and nonsynonymous (red), and the height of the bars indicate the heterosygosity. Note, however, that some of these values are not actually determined. The table below the gene section lists each **SNP** along the gene region and color coded as described above.

feature selected for the cases group. For case-control studies, a selection of SNPs is genotyped in both the case and control groups, and those alleles that exhibit a higher incidence in the case group as opposed to the control group are potential markers for the observed phenotype.

THE INTERNATIONAL HAPLOTYPE MAP PROJECT

The stated goal of the International Haplotype Map Project (The International HapMap Consortium, 2003) is to develop a haplotype map of the human genome. The "HapMap," which will describe the common patterns of human DNA sequence variation, is expected to be a key resource for researchers to use to find genes affecting health, disease, and responses to drugs and environmental factors. A *haplotype* is defined as a specific set of alleles observed on a chromosome. When comparing

haplotypes from many individuals, shared patterns are seen that occur with much greater likelihood than would be estimated by assuming each allele state was independent of the others. This nonrandom association is called *linkage disequilibrium* (LD), a phenomenon that has been measured and applied in many studies (Gabriel et al., 2002, Dawson et al., 2002, Taillon-Miller et al., 2000, Eaves et al., 2000, Abecasis et al., 2001, Reich et al., 2001, Daly et al., 2001, Jeffreys et al., 2001, Patil et al., 2001). The length of a shared haplotype segment is called a *haplotype block*. There is substantial variation in block sizes across the genome; however, current data support a mean haplotype block length in the order of a few tens of kilobases.

The HapMap group is working on detecting the locations of these haplotype blocks by genotyping a set of SNPs (initially 600,000 SNPs, or approximately one every 5 Kb across the genome) in 270 different individuals from four distinct ethnic groups. As soon as these blocks are identified, only three or four SNPs within a block will be necessary to characterize the haplotype of that entire segment of the genome. These are called *haplotype tag SNPs* (Johnson et al., 2001, Ke & Cardon, 2003, Carlson et al., 2004). Across the entire genome, which may contain up to 10 million common SNPs, it is anticipated that only 500,000 tag SNPs will be necessary to identify more than 90% of the haplotype blocks. Thus, instead of typing every SNP across a region, only 1 in 20 will be required for association studies, greatly reducing the costs of these studies.

The genome browser located at the HapMap Web site, called GBrowse, is an interface to access HapMap information (e.g., genotypes and haplotypes). Like other browsers, there are numerous ways to locate a region of interest. Figure 7.15 shows a 500-Kb region located on chromosome 2, and details are given at both the chromosome level, such as gene density and genotyped SNP density, as well as a detailed view of the region of interest showing more precisely where the genotyped SNPs are and their relationship to known genes. There are a

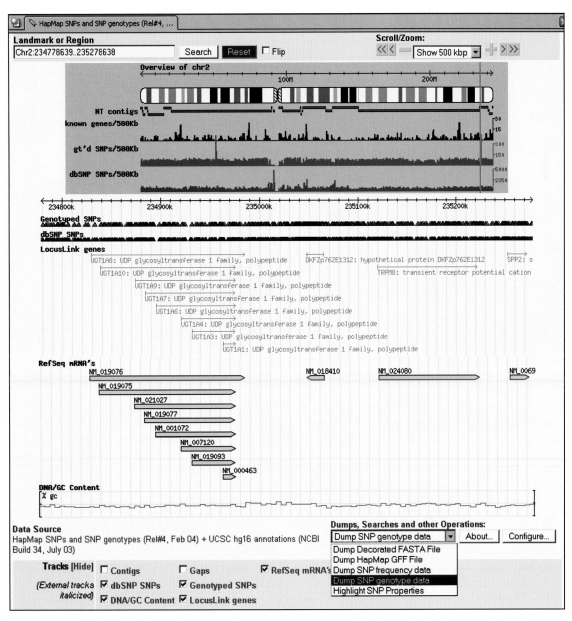

FIGURE 7.15 Overall information about human chromosome 2 is shown in the top panel of this GBrowse page, with the zoomed-in region identified by the tall rectangle. The zoomed-in region shows the positions of genotyped SNPs and positions of genes. Moving the pointer over these features and clicking will give more detailed information.

number of ways to extract data for a given region: as a decorated FASTA file, by SNP frequency, and by SNP genotypes. The SNP genotypes output gives the alleles associated with individual DNAs used in this study. With this information, it is possible construct SNP associations and to construct haplotype maps, and this is illustrated in the Worked Example accompanying this chapter.

▌SUMMARY

The reference sequence for the human genome should not be viewed as just one long string of static characters. Instead, it is riddled with variable sites all along the sequence. In fact, given that the number of people on this planet exceeds the number of bases in the genome, one may imagine that every base in the genome has had its chance to be different. To date, the survey of sequence polymorphisms in the human genome amounts to more than seven million. Studies of these variations and associated genotypes are leading to new insights into population histories (for a review, see Rosenberg & Nordborg, 2002).

Polymorphism data are cataloged in many databases along with auxiliary information describing, for example, how they have been used in experimental studies, which populations may favor one allele over another, and how polymorphisms can be linked together into larger groups called haplotypes; a growing number are linked to specific diseases. Sequence polymorphisms are one of the key resources used to study the genetic aspects of diseases such as cancer, heart disease, diabetes, and neural disorders, to name a few. Specially designed databases and query services are available to assist researchers in narrowing down the millions of variable sites in the genome to a smaller set, and some of the resources that are available for working with polymorphisms (for example, locating coding polymorphisms in a particular gene) have been described in this chapter.

The International Haplotype Map Project, underway now with a target completion date of the end of 2005, has the goal of refining the ever-increasing number of polymorphisms in the human genome to a more manageable set that still captures the underlying variation information, allowing the design of more cost effective association studies.

Polymorphism data are, obviously, not limited to the human genome. Second in number to the human genome are 1.1 million polymorphisms identified to date in the mosquito genome. The 490,000 variations detected among various strains of inbred mice are a rich resource for associating genotypes with phenotypes (Wade et al., 2002). The dog genome, with ~1 million variations available, shows great promise to find genes

responsible for ailments that are similar to ailments in man (Kirkness et al., 2003). Along with the increasing throughput of large-scale genome sequencing centers producing genome assemblies of many more species, so, too, will follow polymorphism discovery, thus allowing researchers easy access to genetic landmarks. Given this ever-increasing amount of variation data, it becomes quite important that the reader is familiar with how to use the resources described in this chapter in an intelligent fashion.

▌WORKED EXAMPLE

The HapMap project is being applied to the entire human genome, with the goal of determining the common patterns of variation across the genome. As a test to see how well the main project is reaching its goals, 10 ENCODE Project regions, 500 Kb in size, were selected for genotyping from the HapMap Project samples. At this time, only CEPH family trio genotypes were available, so this Worked Example focuses on the third of the samples that will be available in the future. This example uses the GBrowse interface to view one of these ENCODE regions, to download the genotypes, and to process the data with HaploView version 2.04. HaploView calculates associations between SNPs, builds haplotypes, and identifies tagSNPs.

From the HapMap Web site, go to the HapMap Project Data page and scroll down to ENCODE region ENr131, located at chr2:234778639..235278638 (in NCBI Build 34 coordinates). Clicking on the `chr2` position hyperlink produces a GBrowse page like that shown in Figure 7.15. In the drop-down list box, select `Dump SNP Genotype Data` and click `Go`. The list of genotype data for this region appears, and the text results can be saved as a file called, for example, `hapmapEncode.txt`.

For the next stage of analysis, install the Java program HaploView. The figures accompanying this text have been generated using HaploView version 2.03 for Windows (Microsoft, Redmond, WA). HaploView initially comes up with an `Open New Data` button box. Clicking on the `Browse HapMap data from DCC` allows the user to load the file that was previously saved (`hapmapEncode.txt`). As soon as the data loads and is processed, one of three tabs can be selected: `Check Markers`, `Haplotypes`, and `D Prime Plot`. Using the `Check Markers` tab, markers can be selected or deselected manually, and thresholds can be set for a number of parameters. In this example, the default values for the minimum minor allele frequency have been changed to 0.05. Click `rescore markers` if any values are changed. Clicking on the `Haplotypes` tab will show the first few haplotype blocks for this region (Figure 7.16). The markers are arranged along the top; directly beneath each marker is a triangle if this is determined to be a tagSNP for the haplotype block, and beneath that are the alleles associated with each haplotype. Clicking on the `D Prime Plot` tab visually shows the association between markers in D-Prime space (Figure 7.17). The markers are arranged along the top and, in this example, show

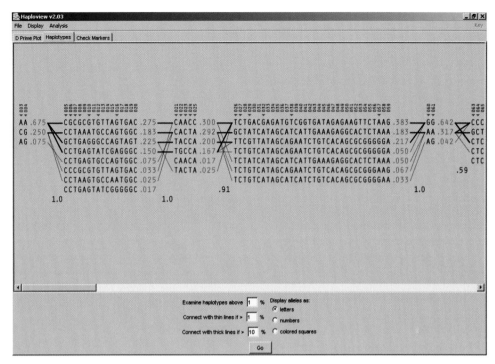

FIGURE 7.16 A representative HaploView screen. The haplotypes are grouped in clusters, with marker numbers along the top. The triangles beneath these numbers indicate which markers could be used as tag SNPs. Each block shows the fraction of cases that particular block is observed in the set. The lines between blocks show the more common transitions with bold lines and less common with thin lines. Factions beneath the lines are a multialleleic D' statistic between blocks.

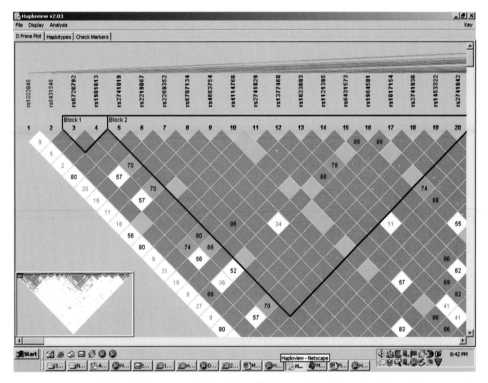

FIGURE 7.17 A HaploView graph showing all the markers in order along the genomic segment being analyzed. The grey scale level is darker for higher D' values between pairs of markers.

the refSNP number for each of the SNPs included. The small rectangle in the lower left shows the entire region with a black rectangle to identify where the main display is located. There are additional pages at the HaploView download Web site describing the package and all of its features in greater detail.

PROBLEM SET

Access the two traces shown in Figure 7.1 from the NBCI TraceArchive by entering their `ti` numbers into the search box (i.e., 215500760 and 220064691). Use the returned FASTA sequence and one of the search tools to find where these sequences align to the human genome.

1. Find the SNP shown in the figure. Which one has the same allele as the reference sequence?
2. From the base location in the trace that agrees with the reference sequence in 1, find the first base that does not agree. Would this be called a SNP, or not? Explain.
3. Do the same for the other trace, starting from the SNP location. Would this be called a SNP, or not? Explain.

INTERNET RESOURCES

Alfred	http://alfred.med.yale.edu/
dbSNP	http://www.ncbi.nlm.nih.gov/SNP/
ENCODE Project Project	http://www.genome.gov/10506161
Ensembl Genome Browser	http://www.ensembl.org/
Entrez SNP	http://www.ncbi.nlm.nih.gov/entrez/query.fcgi?db=snp
HapMap	http://www.hapmap.org/
HGVBase	http://hgvbase.cgb.ki.se/
HGVBase FTP site	ftp://ftp.ebi.ac.uk/pub/databases/variantdbs/hgbase/
HGVBase SNP Related Databases	http://hgvbase.cgb.ki.se/databases.htm
HGVS SNP Related Databases	http://www.genomic.unimelb.edu.au/mdi/dblist/dblist.html
Innate Immunity PGA	http://innateimmunity.net/IIPGA2
JSNP	http://snp.ims.u-tokyo.ac.jp
Map Viewer	http://www.ncbi.nih.gov/mapview/
The NCBI Handbook: SNPs	http://www.ncbi.nlm.nih.gov/books/bookres.fcgi/handbook/ch5d1.pdf
NCBI HomePage	http://www.ncbi.nlm.nih.gov/
NIEHS SNPs	http://egp.gs.washington.edu/welcome.html
OMIM	http://www.ncbi.nlm.nih.gov/entrez/query.fcgi?db=OMIM
PolyPhred	http://droog.mbt.washington.edu/PolyPhred.html
The SNP Consortium (TSC)	http://snp.cshl.org/
TraceArchive	http://www.ncbi.nlm.nih.gov/Traces/trace.fcgi? or http://trace.ensembl.org/
TSC FTP site	http://snp.cshl.org/downloads/
UCSC Genome Browser	http://genome.ucsc.edu/

FURTHER READING

HARTL, D. L., AND CLARK, A. G. (1997). *Principles of Population Genetics*, 3rd ed (Sinauer Associates, Inc., Sunderland, MA). This book introduces the principles of genetics and statistics that are relevant to population studies. In particular, Chapter 5 presents the sources of variation arising from mutation and redistributed through a population through linkage and recombination.

THE INTERNATIONAL HAPMAP CONSORTIUM. (2003). The International HapMap Project. *Nature* 426, 789–796. This paper describes the goals of the HapMap project, with a description of why this project is important for future disease and drug response association studies. It also describes the DNA samples in which a selected set of SNPs will be genotyped in order to develop the haplotype map of the human genome.

REFERENCES

ABECASIS, G. R., NOGUCHI, E., HEINZMANN, A., TRAHERNE, J. A., BHATTACHARYYA, S., LEAVES, N. I., ANDERSON, G. G., ZHANG, Y., LENCH, N. J., CAREY, A., et al. (2001). Extent and distribution of linkage disequilibrium in three genomic regions. *Am. J. Hum. Genet.* 68, 191–197.

CARLSON, C. S., EBERLE, M. A., RIEDER, M. J., YI, Q., KRUGLYAK, L., AND NICKERSON, D. A. (2004). Selecting a maximally informative set of single-nucleotide polymorphisms for association analyses using linkage disequilibrium. *Am. J. Hum. Genet.* 74, 106–120.

DALY, M. J., RIOUX, J. D., SCHAFFNER, S. F., HUDSON, T. J., AND LANDER, E. S. (2001). High-resolution haplotype structure in the human genome. *Nat. Genet.* 29, 229–232.

DAVIES, H., BIGNELL, G. R., COX, C., STEPHENS, P., EDKINS, S., CLEGG, S., TEAGUE, J., WOFFENDIN, H., GARNETT, M. J., BOTTOMLEY, W., et al. (2002). Mutations of the BRAF gene in human cancer. *Nature* 417, 949–954.

DAWSON, E., ABECASIS, G. R., BUMPSTEAD, S., CHEN, Y., HUNT, S., BEARE, D. M., PABIAL, J., DIBLING, T., TINSLEY, E., KIRBY, S., et al. (2002). A first-generation linkage disequilibrium map of human chromosome 22. *Nature* 418, 544–548.

EAVES, I. A., MERRIMAN, T. R., BARBER, R. A., NUTLAND, S., TUOMILEHTO-WOLF, E., TUOMILEHTO, J., CUCCA, F., AND TODD, J. A. (2000). The genetically isolated populations of Finland and Sardinia may not be a panacea for linkage disequilibrium mapping of common disease genes. *Nat. Genet.* 25, 320–323.

GABRIEL, S. B., SCHAFFNER, S. F., NGUYEN, H., MOORE, J. M., ROY, J., BLUMENSTIEL, B., HIGGINS, J., DEFELICE, M., LOCHNER, A., FAGGART, M., et al. (2002). The structure of haplotype blocks in the human genome. *Science* 296, 2225–2229.

HAGA, H., YAMADA, R., OHNISHI, Y., NAKAMURA, Y., AND TANAKA, T. (2002) Gene-based SNP discovery as part of the Japanese Millennium Genome Project: identification of 190,562 genetic variations in the human genome. Single-nucleotide polymorphism. *J. Hum. Genet.* 47, 605–610.

HUDSON, R. R. (1991). Gene genealogies and the coalescent process. In *Oxford Surveys in Evolutionary Biology* (Futuyama, D., and Antonovics, J., eds.), Oxford University Press, Oxford, UK, p. 1–44.

The International HapMap Consortium. (2003). The International HapMap Project. *Nature* 426, 789–796.

The International SNP Map Working Group. (2001). A map of human genome sequence variation containing 1.4 million single nucleotide polymorphisms. *Nature* 409, 928–933.

JEFFREYS, A. J., KAUPPI, L., AND NEUMANN, R. (2001). Intensely punctate meiotic recombination in the class II region of the major histocompatibility complex. *Nat Genet.* 29, 217–222.

JOHNSON, G. C., ESPOSITO, L., BARRATT, B. J., SMITH, A.N., HEWARD, J., DI GENOVA, G., UEDA, H., CORDELL, H. J., EAVES, I. A., DUDBRIDGE, F., et al. (2001). Haplotype tagging for the identification of common disease genes. *Nat Genet.* 29, 233–237.

KAROLCHIK, D., HINRICHS, A. S., FUREY, T. S., ROSKIN, K. M., SUGNET, C. W., HAUSSLER, D. AND KENT, W.J. The UCSC Table Browser data retrieval tool. (2004). *Nucl. Acids Res.* 32, D493–D496.

KASPRZYK, A., KEEFE, D., SMEDLEY, D., LONDON, D., SPOONER, W., MELSOPP, C., HAMMOND, M., ROCCA-SERRA, P., COX, T., AND BIRNEY, E. (2004). EnsMart: a generic system for fast and flexible access to biological data. *Genome Res.* 14, 160–169.

KE, X., AND CARDON, L. R. (2003). Efficient selective screening of haplotype tag SNPs. *Bioinformatics* 19, 287–288.

KIRKNESS, E. F., BAFNA, V., HALPERN, A. L., LEVY, S., REMINGTON, K., RUSCH, D. B., DELCHER, A. L., POP, M., WANG, W., FRASER, C. M., et al. (2003). The dog genome: survey sequencing and comparative analysis. *Science* 301, 1898–1903.

KITTS, A., AND SHERRY, S. T. (2002). The Single Nucleotide Polymorphism Database (dbSNP) of Nucleotide Sequence Variation. In *The NCBI Handbook* (McEntyre, J., ed.), (National Library of Medicine, National Center for Biotechnology Information, Bethesda, MD). Available at: http://ncbi.nlm.nih.gov/entrez/query.fcgi?db=Books.

PATIL, N., BERNO, A. J., HINDS, D. A., BARRETT, W. A., DOSHI, J. M., HACKER, C. R., KAUTZER, C. R., LEE, D. H., MARJORIBANKS, C., MCDONOUGH, D. P., et al. (2001). Blocks of limited haplotype diversity revealed by high-resolution scanning of human chromosome 21. *Science* 294, 1719–1723.

REICH, D. E., GABRIEL, S. B., AND ALTSHULER, D. (2003). Quality and completeness of SNP databases. *Nat. Genet.* 33, 457–458.

REICH, D. E., CARGILL, M., BOLK, S., IRELAND, J., SABETI, P. C., RICHTER, D. J., LAVERY, T., KOUYOUMJIAN, R., FARHADIAN, S. F., WARD, R., et al. (2001). Linkage disequilibrium in the human genome. *Nature* 411, 199–204.

ROSENBERG, N. A., AND NORDBORG, M. (2002). Genealogical trees, coalescent theory and the analysis of genetic polymorphisms. *Nat. Rev. Genet.* 3, 380–390.

TAILLON-MILLER, P., BAUER-SARDINA, I., SACCONE, N. L., PUTZEL, J., LAITINEN, T., CAO, A., KERE, J., PILIA, G., RICE, J. P., AND KWOK, P. Y. (2000). Juxtaposed regions of extensive and minimal linkage disequilibrium in human Xq25 and Xq28. *Nat. Genet.* 25, 324–328.

WADE, C. M., KULBOKAS, E. J., 3RD, KIRBY, A. W., ZODY, M. C., MULLIKIN, J. C., LANDER, E. S., LINDBLAD-TOH, K., AND DALY, M. J. (2002). The mosaic structure of variation in the laboratory mouse genome. *Nature* 420, 574–578.

KEY TERMS

allele frequency
flanking sequence
genotype
haplotype
insertion and deletion polymorphism
linkage disequilibrium
microsatellite
reference SNP
sequence mutation
sequence polymorphisms
short tandem repeat polymorphism
single nucleotide polymorphism

This chapter was written by Dr. James C. Mullikin in his private capacity. No official support or endorsement by the National Institutes of Health or the United States Department of Health and Human Services is intended or should be inferred.

## PART THREE

ANALYSIS AT THE PROTEIN LEVEL

## CHAPTER EIGHT

Predictive Methods Using Protein Sequences

YANAY OFRAN

BURKHARD ROST

Bioinformatics: A Practical Guide to the Analysis of Genes and Proteins, Third Edition, edited by
Andreas D. Baxevanis and B.F. Francis Ouellette.
ISBN 0-471-47878-4 Copyright © 2005 John Wiley & Sons, Inc.

INTRODUCTION

The article entitled "The Central Dogma of Molecular Biology" (Crick, 1958) revolutionized biology by describing life and all its process as, essentially, a linear flow of information. DNA, with its four-letter language, constitutes a *de facto* blueprint for an organism. Pieces of this information are transcribed from the central repository (the DNA) and are dispatched to different destinations, in the form of RNA molecules. The information from the RNA molecule is then converted into a protein, away from a "four-letter language" (the nucleotide bases) and into a "20-letter language" (amino acid residues). This amino acid sequence determines the eventual three-dimensional structure of the protein (Anfinsen, 1973), its ultimate subcellular localization, what other molecules with which it will interact, what biochemical and physiological tasks it will be able to carry out, and eventually, when and how it will be broken down into its component building blocks. In short, the function (or in a case of a disease, the malfunction) of each protein is encrypted in its amino acid sequence. Although it is rather simple to determine protein sequences experimentally, it remains quite difficult (and sometimes even impossible) to determine protein structure and function experimentally.

The relative simplicity of determining sequences led to the launching of several large-scale genome-sequencing projects. Combined with thousands of individual sequencing laboratories all over the world, these projects produce tremendous amounts of sequence data, as alluded to in earlier chapters. Almost 200 organisms have been sequenced over the last decade; in turn, the putative proteomes of these organisms increasingly contribute to the body of known protein sequences (approximately one million as of early 2004). The pace at which these sequences accumulate far exceeds the ability of experimental biologists to process them and to decipher their biochemical traits and biological functions. The growth of sequence databases is so rapid that it even outpaces that of integrated circuits for computers, often considered the most rapidly advancing technological domain. In fact, for most protein sequences, there are no experimental annotations (see UniProt, Chapter 1). The goal of bioinformatics, in this context, is to develop computational tools that will enable us to decipher the information encoded in protein sequences, thus enabling us to predict their structure and function.

Chapters 5 and 6 survey the computational tools that have been designed to deal with DNA and RNA. This chapter elaborates on approaches and tools dedicated to deciphering the biological information that is encoded in protein sequences.

A key underpinning of the central dogma of molecular biology is the hierarchical flow of biological information. Although DNA and RNA sequences hold all the information that eventually is translated into protein sequences, the converse is not true; DNA sequences include additional information that could not be extracted from the corresponding protein sequence, such as instructions for the control and regulation of protein expression. Why should one elaborate on analyzing the protein sequence when the DNA sequence, in principle, could offer the same information and much more? If we were capable of deciphering all the information of interest from DNA, there would be no need to design special methods for the analysis of protein sequences, but this is not the case. Computational methods still are being developed to learn which part of the DNA sequence of an organism ends up being translated into a protein sequence (Chapter 5) and which parts have other possible roles. The magnitude of the problem is illustrated best by the fact that, three years after the publication of the first version of the human genome, we still have no reliable estimate of the number of human proteins encoded by the human genome. Similarly, the number of putative fly proteins rose from approximately 13,000 at the time of publishing the "completed genome" (in 2000) to more than 19,000. By studying protein sequences, one can bypass the problems inherent in analyzing only nucleotide sequences. Focusing on known protein sequences guarantees that one is analyzing the information relating directly to a protein's structure and function. In the following sections, some of the research approaches and computational tools that attempt to predict aspects of the structure and function of a protein from its amino acid sequence are surveyed.

The subsections of this chapter are fairly disproportionate in relation to the activity of the underlying research being performed. For instance, more than 300 different methods have been published that predict secondary structure, whereas only a very few are geared toward predicting functional classes. Although this chapter cannot review every single predictive method available, the most commonly used methods and approaches are discussed.

PREDICTING FEATURES OF INDIVIDUAL RESIDUES

Each protein begins its life as a shapeless string of amino acids. The individual amino acids in this chain are referred to as *residues*, joined through *peptide bonds* to form a chain. Then, in a process that is not fully understood, the protein folds into its native three-dimensional structure. The function of a protein is believed to depend largely on the particulars of this three-dimensional structure. It has been shown that many proteins fold into their native structures in isolation: Structure is determined, for the most part, by sequence alone (Anfinsen, 1973). However, over the last decade, it has become evident that many proteins do not fold properly in the test tube; they require additional information that is not available in the sequence or require assistance from other proteins (e.g., chaperonins) to adopt their native structures. Nevertheless, it is still assumed that the native three-dimensional structure is in some energetic minimum. Because of this, the first forays into the realm of prediction focused on structure.

The early, pioneering structure prediction methods that were developed focused on the structural characteristics of individual residues. Looking at one residue at a time rather than at the whole protein sequence serves two purposes. First, it breaks the problem of structure prediction down into smaller elements that are simpler and easier to handle. Satisfactory results at the residue level may be combined later to give rise to a more comprehensive prediction of the entire structure. Second, identifying residues with certain features, such as membrane- or solvent-accessible residues, could help experimentalists focus their attention to parts of the sequence that are more likely to be relevant for their study. Therefore, these methods, first introduced in the 1960s, have been used widely by both experimental and computational biologists.

Secondary Structure Prediction

The sequence of a protein is sometimes referred to as its *primary structure*. The overall three-dimensional structure of a protein chain commonly is known as its *tertiary structure*. The overall three-dimensional structure is a topological organization of smaller local structures. Short stretches of residues tend to form these local structures, known as *secondary structures* (Figure 8.1). The final three-dimensional structure of the chain could be thought of as the spatial packing of these local structural elements. Physically, the driving force behind the formation of secondary structures is a complex combination of local and global forces. Locally, forces that act between residues, or between the residue and the backbone of the protein, can effect the formation of secondary structures. These local effects include the repulsion between hydrophobic side chains of some amino acids and the hydrophilic backbone of the protein chain, as well as the interaction between side chains and the surrounding solvent (Pauling et al., 1951). Hence, the subcellular environment of the protein surrounding also can affect its secondary structure. Among the global effects that come into play are forces exerted by other, more distant parts of the structure, which may be repulsing or attracting each other. The complex manner in which these forces combine make the task of secondary structure prediction from just the sequence itself a great challenge.

The different types of secondary structures can be grouped into three categories: helices, strands, and "other" (often referred to as nonregular or loop regions). A helix is a corkscrew-like spiral of the backbone with the side chains projecting outward in different angles. The most common type of helix is the α-helix, which also is the most common regular secondary structure. In α-helices, there are almost four residues in each turn of the spiral (more precisely, 3.6). The helical structure itself is stabilized by hydrogen bonds between the carbonyl (CO) group of one amino acid and the amino (NH) group of the amino acid that is four positions C-terminal to it. Strands are structures in which the backbone zigzags to create an extended structure. The most common among these is the β-strand. Two or more stretches of β-strands often interact with each other, through hydrogen bonds formed between them, to create a planar structure known as a β-sheet. Finally, loops are defined as the local structures that do not fall into one of the two previous categories. Biochemists further distinguish between several subtypes of helices, at least two different types of strands, and a few types of loops. Although most of the methods try to predict into which of the three major categories every residue folds, some methods attempt to match the more fine-grained distinctions.

Early analysis of secondary structure showed that different amino acids tend to "prefer" being contained in different secondary structures. Prediction of secondary structure from these amino acid propensities had been attempted even before the first experimentally determined high-resolution three-dimensional structure of a protein existed (Szent-Györgyi & Cohen, 1957). Relating secondary structure to amino acid propensities reemphasizes the importance of local sequence environment in the formation of secondary structures. In fact, most prediction methods rely predominantly on local sequence information in making their determinations. However, nonlocal forces can be crucial; an extreme example is the chameleon protein (Minor & Kim, 1996), in which a stretch of 11 consecutive amino acid residues adopts a helical structure in one region and a strand at another. If prediction methods were to use only local information, they could not predict the difference between the one macroenvironment that induces helix formation and the other that induces strand formation.

Hundreds of ideas, approaches, and methods for secondary structure prediction have been suggested over the last four decades. They are based on various biochemical insights and a wide range of computational techniques. Each has its own strengths and weaknesses, and clearly they result in different levels of predictive success. In presenting an overview of the methods below, their popularity and success is discussed, as well as the nature of the approach employed by the developers.

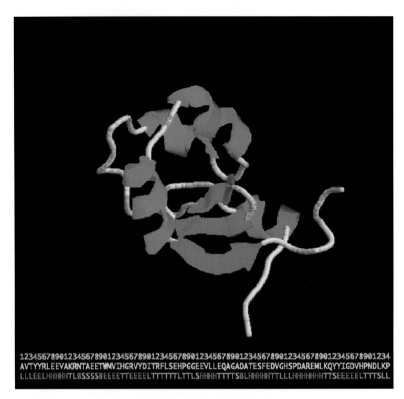

1234567890123456789012345678901234567890123456789012345678901234567890123456789012345678901234
AVTYYRLEEVAKRNTAEETWNVIHGRVYDITRFLSEHPGGEEVLLEQAGADATESFEDVGHSPDAREMLKQYYIGDVHPNDLKP
LLLEELHHHHHTLBSSSSBEEEETTEEEELTTTTTTLTTLSHHHHTTTTSBLHHHHHTTLLLHHHHHHHTTSEEEEELTTTSLL

FIGURE 8.1   **The three-dimensional structure of rat mitochondrial membrane cytochrome B5, highlighting its secondary structure. The green spirals are α-helices and the turquoise arrows are β-strands. The three strands in this structure interact with one another to form a β-sheet. The three-dimensional structure of the protein as a whole can be described as the spatial organization of the secondary structure elements. Each amino acid in the sequence is part of a secondary structure element. In the linear representation of the sequence at the bottom of the figure, every residue is marked according to its secondary structure. The letters H, G, and I (green) denote different types of helices; E and B are strands, and L, S, and T denote different types of loops. The methods for the prediction of secondary structure attempt to give this kind of annotation to proteins whose structures have not yet been determined experimentally.**

Prediction Methods

PHDsec and PROFsec. PHDsec (Rost et al., 1994; Rost et al., 1996) and PROFsec (Rost et al., 2003) are part of the PredictProtein (Rost et al., 2003) service for sequence analysis and structure prediction. Both methods share the same basic approach. Because PROFsec is an improved and overly complicated version of PHDsec, the explanation here focuses on PHDsec. As with almost all prediction methods, the heart of PHDsec is based on the computational concept of machine learning, in which algorithms are designed to "learn" from a large set of examples (the "training set") what the implicit rules and principles underlying a certain phenomenon are. In the

case of secondary structure prediction, the attempt is to learn from the training set which secondary structure a residue in a sequence of interest not included in the training set is most likely to adopt. The success of machine-learning algorithms depends on the careful choice of the biologically based features used for training. For example, the residues surrounding a particular residue i (i.e., the residues $i - n, \ldots, i + n$) are believed to have a tremendous effect on the secondary structure of residue i. Hence, information on surrounding residues should be included as part of the input so as to enable the program to learn how different amino acids affect the probability of their neighbors to form, say, an α-helix. The key to successful prediction methods is the intelligent choice of all biologically relevant input features and a sufficiently large and accurate training set that enables the program to infer accurately any given residue's probability of adopting a particular type of secondary structure.

The machine learning algorithm used by PHDsec is a feed-forward artificial neural network (Box 8.1). When a sequence is submitted to PredictProtein, the server searches for known homologous proteins that are assumed to have similar structures as the query. Then, an algorithm called MaxHom (Sander & Schneider, 1991) is used to produce a multiple sequence alignment of all these putative homologs. By doing so, MaxHom provides a profile of the evolutionary history of the sequence. The profile and alignment that it produces includes detailed information about each residue, revealing its evolutionary conservation and to what extent it can be replaced by other amino acids without

changing its structure. The inclusion of evolutionary information was the single most important contribution advancing the predictive power of secondary structure prediction methods over the last decade. The output of MaxHom then is fed into a system of neural networks, which assigns one of the three secondary states to each amino acid in the input sequence (Figure 8.2).

PSIPRED. PSIPRED (McGuffin et al., 2000) is based on a similar concept as PHD. For each submitted sequence, PSIPRED performs a PSI-BLAST search (Chapter 11) and composes a profile that conveys the evolutionary record of each position. This information then is fed into a system of neural networks that predicts secondary structure in three states. Recently, the developers of PSIPRED explored the option of replacing the neural networks in their system by a support vector machine-based method (Ward et al., 2003), another

---

BOX 8.1 Neural Networks

Neural networks are finding increasing applicability to questions in biology, particularly in the area of secondary structure prediction. Neural networks are a way to achieve machine learning, mimicking the way the human brain processes information when trying to make a meaningful conclusion based on previously seen patterns.

All neural networks are made up of an input layer, one or more hidden layers, and an output layer. A simple neural network with one hidden layer can be represented as follows:

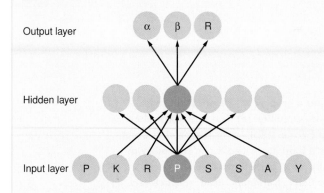

Here, the input layer is a protein sequence, and the output layer is one of the possible outcomes: whether a particular amino acid lies within an α-helix, a β-strand, or an unstructured (random) region. The neural network receives its signals from the input layer and passes information to the hidden layer through a neuron, similar to how a neuron would fire across a synapse. A representative subset of the neurons are shown here by arrows.

In the figure, a proline residue is highlighted in the input layer; it influences a number of nodes in the hidden layer, the

strength or weight of the input being controlled by the neurons. In the hidden layer, one of the nodes is shown in dark blue; many of the positions in the sequence may influence that node, with the neurons again controlling the degree to which those inputs influence the node. The figure illustrates a feed-forward neural network, where the flow of information is in one direction. Recurrent neural networks, where neurons connect back to earlier neurons, are not widely used for biological predictions.

Why use a neural network? If the direct relationship between the input and output layer was perfectly understood, such a complicated approach would not be necessary, because one could write cause-and-effect rules that would make the intermediate, hidden layers unnecessary. In the absence of this direct relationship, neural networks can be used to deduce the probable relationship between the input and output layers; the only requirement is the knowledge that the input and output layers are, indeed, related. Here, there is an obvious relationship between the input and output layers, because the individual amino acids found within a protein must adopt one of three given conformations.

To start to deduce the relationship between the input and output layers, a supervised learning approach is used, based on training sets where the answer is known in advance. For example, in the realm of secondary structure prediction, one would construct data sets based on known three-dimensional structures, noting not only the secondary structure in which a particular residue is found, but other factors influencing structural conformation as well. Based on these training data, the network attempts to "learn" the relationship between the input and output layers, adjusting the strength of each of the interconnected neurons to fine tune the predictive power of the network.

powerful machine-learning algorithm that has been gaining popularity in bioinformatics. They concluded that, as a stand-alone prediction method, the support vector machine (SVM)-based system achieves similar accuracy to that of the neural network-based system. They also found that combining predictions generated by the two algorithms yields significantly better predictions than either of them alone.

SAM-T99. Like the two approaches described above, SAM-T99 (Karplus et al., 1998) is based on a two-stage process of producing an evolutionary profile; then, this profile is used as the input to a machine-learning program that predicts the secondary structure. To produce the alignment, SAM-T99 uses a hidden Markov model

(HMM) approach (Box 8.2). The major strength of this algorithm is in finding remote homologs to the query protein; that is, proteins that are evolutionarily related to that sequence, but for which this relation is difficult to detect because of their ostensible sequence divergence. Incorporating these sequences in the profile improves the quality of predictions. An example of the output produced by SAM-T99 is shown in Figure 8.3.

How the Methods Perform. The automated methods that are surveyed in this chapter typically serve as the basis for more refined predictions by experts. However, these automatic methods also can generate large numbers of predictions in a very short time, thus enabling

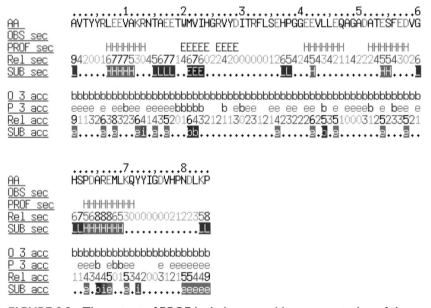

PROF results (normal)

FIGURE 8.2   The output of PROF includes a graphic representation of the query sequence, the predictions, and their reliability. (a) The line marked AA is the amino acid sequence, in single-letter code. PROFsec is the prediction: H for a helix, E for a strand, and a space for a loop. Rel sec is the reliability of the prediction (1–9; see main text). Finally, SUB sec shows only the most reliable of the predictions (H, E, and L for helix, stand, and loop, respectively, and a dot for predictions with low reliability). The next three lines are the solvent accessibility predictions (PROFaac). P 3 acc is the solvent accessibility in a three-state scheme—b for buried, e for exposed, and i for intermediate. Rel acc and SUB acc are the reliability index and the reliable predictions, similar to those in PROFsec. (b) A graphical representation of the score each position received for each prediction. PROF assigns three separate scores for each position representing the likelihood of this position to be in a helix, a strand, or a loop. Another score predicts its exposure. Note that, sometimes, one position could obtain positive scores in more than one state. Looking at this graph can help explain discrepancies between different prediction methods.

PROF results (detail)

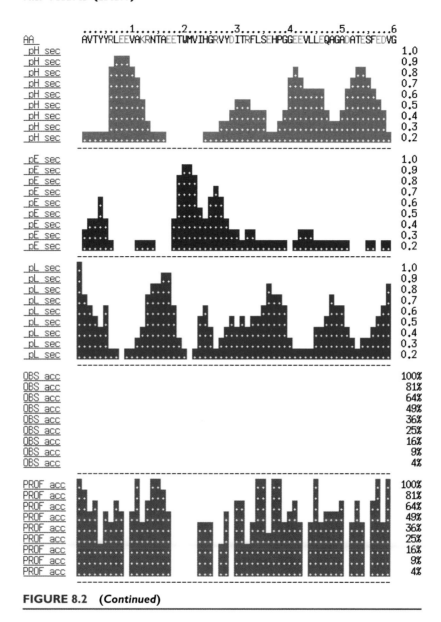

FIGURE 8.2 *(Continued)*

the high-throughput analysis of entire proteomes (see UniProt, Chapter 1). For either approach, it is very important to have an accurate, standardized assessment of the performance of each method. Traditionally, when a new method is published, the developers assess its performance and compare it with that of other available methods. However, when attempting to compare the performance of different methods, one needs to treat these self-reported figures with caution. One critical distinction for appropriately estimating performance is a rigorous split between the data sets used for training and testing. Another common mistake made by developers is not to provide the standard deviations of their estimates. Overall, the correct evaluation of performance

for prediction methods is an art in itself; only a handful of methods turned out over time to not have been overestimated by their developers.

Even when relying on the assessment reported by the developers themselves, comparing different methods is very complicated. Some researchers report their success levels in terms of accuracy and coverage, in terms of positive predictive power or negative predictive power, or through measures of sensitivity and specificity. Still others adhere to more obscure measurements popular within the field of machine learning, such as Matthews coefficients and the like. Although all these measures attempt to measure similar things, comparing their numerical values with each other is nearly impossible and

BOX 8.2 | HMMs in Protein Analysis

As described in Box 5.3, HMMs are used to provide a statistical representation of real biological processes. In the context of gene prediction, the generation of HMMs is needed to take into account the controlled syntax describing the structure of a gene. In the context of protein analysis, there are no syntactical rules *per se*; rather, the application of HMMs at the protein level is aimed at generating the best possible multiple sequence alignment for a given protein family.

Consider a simple multiple sequence alignment of length six:

```
Q - W K P G
Q - W K P G
Q - W R P G
Q I W K - G
Q - W R P G
Q - W R P G
```

Some of the positions are absolutely conserved (shown in red), and position 4 is occupied only by positively charged residues. Position 2 shows a gap introduced by an insertion in one sequence; position 5 shows a gap introduced by a deletion in the same sequence.

Each of these observations can be represented by different states in the HMM. The match state represents the most probable amino acid(s) found at each position of the alignment; *match* is a bit of a misnomer, because the match state takes into account the probability of finding a given amino acid at that position of the alignment. If the position is not absolutely conserved, the probabilities are adjusted accordingly, given the residues found in that column. The insert state represents the case where an additional amino acid needs to be accommodated, as it is in sequence 4. The delete state represents the case where an amino acid is "missing" and where the sequence (here, sequence 4) has to jump over a position to continue the alignment.

Each of these states, as well as the relationship between the states, can be illustrated graphically using a commonly used representation originally introduced by Anders Krogh:

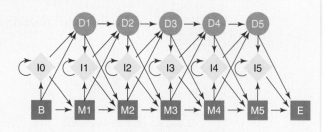

Here, the lower row represents the match states, with B representing the beginning of the alignment and E the end of the alignment. Each of the diamonds represent the insert states, and each of the circles represent the delete states. Each of the arrows represents a movement from state to state, and each is associated with the probability of moving from state to state.

Returning to the alignment, M1 would require a glutamine, M2 a tryptophan, M3 either a lysine or an arginine (50% of the time for either), M4 a proline, and M5 a glycine. Given this, to represent the sequence EWRPG, the movement through the model would take the form B → M1 → M2 → M3 → M4 → M5 → E, because the sequence does not require an insertion or a deletion to align with the rest of the sequences in the group, with the exception of sequence 4. The path for sequence 4 obviously would be different than for most of the sequences; it would take the form B → M1 → I1 → M2 → M3 → D4 → M5 → E. The movement from M1 to I1 accounts for the insertion at position 2, and the movement from M3 to D4 accounts for the deletion at position 6.

The usefulness and elegance of this model comes from the ability to train the model. Returning to the original sequences, imagine that they were fed into the model one by one, without knowing the alignment in advance. For each sequence, the most probable path through the model is determined. As soon as this is carried out for all the sequences, the transition probabilities and probabilities for each match state are determined. This, in turn, can be used to generate the best alignment of the sequences. Knowledge of these probabilities also allows for new sequences to be aligned to the original set. As with the gene prediction models discussed in Box 5.3, the sequences once again are hidden, hence the word *hidden* in hidden Markov model.

Using the collective characteristics of the input sequences allows these profile HMMs to be used to either scan databases for new sequences belonging to the set, or individual sequences can be scanned against a series of HMMs to see whether a new sequence of interest belongs to a previously characterized family.

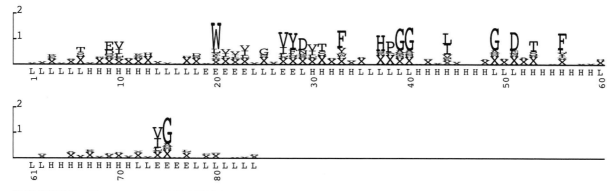

FIGURE 8.3 **The output of SAM-T99 includes the predictions and a graphic representation of the sequence alignment that underlies these predictions. Relying on an evolutionary profile derived from sequence alignment has been shown to improve the predictions. In this figure, the size of the letters in each position reflects relative degree of conservation of that position throughout evolution. Below the profile is the three-state secondary structure prediction.**

is ill-advised. The problem becomes even more complicated when examining how the different methods define a successful prediction. Although some methods measure their success per residue, others may be measuring it per secondary structure element or per protein. Some attempt to predict the state of every residue in the query sequence, whereas others make predictions only about those in which they are confident, leaving some residues unpredicted. These differences make the comparison of different methods even more difficult. A valid and reliable comparison of different methods must be based on a benchmark analysis that uses the same measurements, the same standards, and most importantly, the same sequences to all methods. To this end, the EVA server (Rost & Eyrich, 2001) continuously assesses the predictions of automatic servers (many more than the selected few presented here). Every week, the operators of EVA receive a list of sequences of proteins whose structures have just been determined by experimentalists. EVA automatically submits these sequences as queries to all participating servers and stores the results until the release of the solved structures. As soon as the experimentally solved structure is released, EVA assesses the predictions received from each server and scores them accordingly. Thus, the assessment is continuous over a long period and is highly standardized. This approach enables users to compare methods and allows developers to learn more about the strengths and weaknesses of their method. The best secondary structure prediction methods now reach levels of three-state-per-residue accuracy (percentage of residues predicted accurately as being in a helix, strand, or random-coil conformation) of slightly more than 76% (Rost, 2001). EVA's Web site presents a very detailed statistical analysis of the performance of each server, as well as useful links to many

methods and servers that are available for public use; this is an excellent starting point for anyone interested in exploring the details of secondary structure prediction.

The predictions illustrated in Figures 8.2, 8.3, and 8.4 are based on the same input sequence: a fragment of rat cytochrome C5 whose three-dimensional structure is shown in Figure 8.1. (The prediction shown in Figure 8.4 uses JPred, a program discussed later in this chapter.) Often, it is interesting and extremely useful to compare the predictions of different methods for the same protein. A comparison of the results in Figures 8.2, 8.3, and 8.4 shows that the results obtained using their different methods is quite similar. Furthermore, they are very similar to the experimentally determined secondary structures for this protein (Figure 8.1). When different methods, specifically methods that are based on different algorithms, give similar results, the reliability of these results is higher. In fact, metaservers, which are servers that submit the same query to many different prediction servers and use the results to generate consensus or jury-based metapredictions, have been shown to perform better than any single underlying method they use. Therefore, comparing different prediction methods and choosing those positions about which they agree most often guarantees better results.

What about cases in which the different prediction methods disagree? Sometimes, the differences also can be very revealing. Let us consider positions 24 through 26 of the rat cytochrome C5 sequence. PROFsec predicted His 24 to be a strand (E), the next position (Gly 25) to be part of a loop, and the Arg 26 to be a strand. SAM-T99 predicted all three as loops (L). A closer look reveals that PROFsec assigns a rather low level of confidence to its prediction in this case (the dots on the

```
                     : 1---------11--------21--------31--------41--------51--------61--------71--------81-- :
           OrigSeq   : AVTYYRLEEVAKRNTAEETWMVIHGRVYDITRFLSEHPGGEEVLLEQAGADATESFEDVGHSPDAREMLKQYYIGDVHPNDLKP : OrigSeq

           jalign    : --------------------EEEE--EEEEEEEE------------------------EEE---------------------- : jalign
           jfreq     : -----HHHHHH-------EEEEE-EEEEEEEEE-------EEEEE--------HHHH----HHHHHHH---HE----------- : jfreq
           jhmm      : ----HHHHHHHH-----EEEEE---EE--H-HH------HHHHHHH----HHHHH------HHHHHHHH-------------- : jhmm
           jnet      : ------HHHHHHH----EEEEEEEEEEE-HHHH-----HHHHHHH----HHHHH-----HHHHHH---------------- : jnet
           jpssm     : ------HHHHHHH----EEEEE---EEE----HH-----HHHHHHH----HHHHH------HHHHHH-------------- : jpssm

           jpred     : -----HHHHHHH----EEEEE--EEEE-HHHH-----HHHHHHH----HHHHH-----HHHHHH---------------- : jpred

           Lupas 14  : ----------------------------------------------------------------------------------- : Lupas 14
           Lupas 21  : ----------------------------------------------------------------------------------- : Lupas 21
           Lupas 28  : ----------------------------------------------------------------------------------- : Lupas 28

           Jnet_25   : BB--BBB--B--------BBBBBB-BBBBBBB-BB--B--B--BBB-BBB-BBB-BB--B-BB--B--BB--BBBB-B-----B : Jnet_25
           Jnet_5    : ----------------BBBBB------B-------------B-------B---B--------B--BB--B----B-------- : Jnet_5
           Jnet_0    : ----------B----------BB---------------------------B---------------B---------------- : Jnet_0
           Jnet Rel  : 98415699998638999959998282252111433379993899870785037888318998699999707821313799999 : Jnet Rel
```

FIGURE 8.4 Jpred returns both secondary structure predictions and predictions of solvent accessibility. The line denoted `OrigSeq` shows the query sequence. The line marked `jpred` represents the consensus prediction, based on the different secondary structure methods used. The lines marked `Mcoil` and `Lupas` provide predictions of coiled coils (here, none are predicted). Finally, the bottom section describes the predicted solvent accessibilities (`Jnet_25`, residues predicted to be less than 25% exposed; `Jnet_5`, residues predicted to be less than 5% exposed; `Jnet_0`, residues predicted to be 100% buried; and `Jnet Rel`, reliability of solvent accessibility predictions, on a scale from zero to nine, nine being best).

`SUB sec` line). From the experimentally solved structure (Figure 8.1), one can learn the correct answer. The first two positions (24 and 25) are, according to the experimental evidence, turns (T), a state which most often is considered to be a loop. Position 26 is located at the beginning of a strand. Therefore, SAM-T99 was correct for His 24, whereas PROFsec was correct for Gly 26. These differences may be attributed to differences in the accuracy of different methods, but sometimes disagreement between predictions of different methods stems from genuine ambiguity in the definition of secondary structure states. Even when an experimental structure is available, it sometimes is unclear where one secondary structure element ends and where another one begins. It comes as little surprise, then, that it is more difficult to predict the dubious positions lying at the edges of secondary structure elements. Therefore, in many cases, the disagreement between different methods may indicate that the position under discussion is one of those hard-to-define cases. Another interesting real-life example is the region in the prion protein that is assumed to be responsible for aggregation through a local flip from helix to strand in diseased individuals (e.g., in bovine spongiform encephalopathy, scrapie, and Creutzfeld-Jakob disease (Prusiner, 1998)). The best secondary structure prediction methods all fail to predict this region as helical; instead, they all predict the strand that is believed to cause the disease, even though it has never been observed experimentally. Given that, keep in mind that most deviations of secondary structure prediction methods from the experimental structure simply are mistakes, despite all of the significant advances made in this field over the last decade.

Solvent Accessibility

Background. Another property of proteins that can be predicted from its sequence is solvent accessibility, the area of a protein's surface that is exposed to the surrounding solvent. These accessible regions have the potential to interact with other proteins, peptides, metal atoms, or ions. Residues that are buried in the interior of a protein structure may play an important role in stabilizing its structure, yet they could not be part of an active site of an enzyme, a binding site of a DNA-biding protein, or an interaction site in a signal transduction component, all of which require spatial accessibility of the residue to the solvent. Because the identification of those active residues is at the heart of functional studies, methods identifying them computationally are very useful. Similar to the prediction of secondary structures, most recent methods predicting solvent accessibility combine sequence profiles and machine learning algorithms.

Measuring Solvent Accessibility. Typically, solvent accessibility is measured in square Ångstrøms ($Å^2$); values range from 0 $Å^2$ for entirely buried residues to approximately 300 $Å^2$ for residues on the surface of a protein. In fact, two entirely exposed residues may have very different accessible areas, based simply on the chemical structure of the amino acid at that position; as one would assume, residues with long side chains expose a larger area to solvent than residues with short side chains. Dividing the actual accessibility by the maximum observed for a particular amino acid, one can describe solvent accessibility as the percentage of the surface of a particular residue that is accessible to solvent. This number depends less on the amino acid type than the square Ångstrøms value. When comparing the conservation of accessibility for proteins with similar structures, levels of accessibility in the 0% to 10% range seem to be much more conserved than levels between 60% and 100% (Rost & Sander, 1994). That is, it is more important to distinguish between two residues that are 5% or 10% accessible than between two residues that are 60% or 100% accessible. Earlier prediction methods simplified the task even further by introducing thresholds that divided the 0% to 100% scale into two states, namely, buried and exposed. There is no good biophysical reason for choosing any particular threshold; thresholds of 7%, 9%, 16%, or 25% often are used. When using the 25% threshold, approximately half of all residues in a typical protein will be higher than this threshold (i.e., one half of the residues are exposed, the other half are buried).

Prediction Methods

PHDacc and PROFacc. As in the case of secondary structure prediction, these two sister methods (Rost et al., 1996), which are part of the PredictProtein service, are based on the same basic concept. The sequence alignment and the construction of the profile are carried out using MaxHom, as described above. The neural network then assigns 1 of 10 possible levels of accessibility to each residue in the query sequence. Here, the square of the returned result (the state number) indicates the percent accessibility of the residue (e.g., 1 = 0%-1%, 2 = 2%-4%, etc.). Alternatively, the 10 states could be grouped into a two-state scheme: if more than 16% of the surface area is accessible to solvent, it is defined as exposed; otherwise, the residue is considered to be buried. The 10-state scheme also could be used to predict solvent accessibility in terms of square Ångstrøms.

Jpred. Jpred (Cuff & Barton, 2000) is a prediction service that predicts both secondary structure and solvent accessibility. For the latter, the service uses profiles that are produced by HMMs and by PSI-BLAST. A neural network uses these profiles to predict one of three categories of exposure: 0%, 5%, and 25%. The output of predictions from two different networks is combined to give an average relative solvent accessibility. Figure 8.4 shows the output of a Jpred run, which includes secondary structure prediction and solvent accessibility data. The output from Jpred is described in greater detail below.

How the Methods Perform. Although EVA continuously assesses secondary structure prediction methods using identical data sets, no such large-scale continuous system

evaluates solvent accessibility predictions. Although local sequence information often is sufficient to determine secondary structure with high accuracy, accessibility to the surrounding solvent seems to be influenced to a large extent by nonlocal effects. Therefore, predictions of solvent accessibility from sequence often are less accurate. For two-state accessibility predictions (either exposed or buried), the accuracy of JPred, PHDacc, and PROFacc is between 75% and 85%. For the more detailed definitions, namely predictions of exposed surface area or the percentage of exposure, accuracy is more difficult to measure because the assessment of such value is not binary (either correct or incorrect). One possible way to assess these nonbinary predictions is by calculating a correlation coefficient relating the predicted values and the actual solvent accessibility over a large dataset. For PHDacc, this value is 0.53. Compared with a purely random correlation (a value of zero), this number is rather high. However, there is another way to predict solvent accessibility that achieves a correlation coefficient of 0.66, and that is homology modeling, a method for the direct prediction of tertiary structure (see Chapter 9). The problem is that homology modeling is applicable only if there is a very close sequence homolog with an experimentally determined structure. In those cases, one may prefer to use homology modeling. In other cases where known structures are not available, methods like Jpred and PROFacc are the best solution. Figure 8.4 shows the output of a Jpred run, which includes secondary structure prediction and solvent accessibility data. Comparing these results with the solvent accessibility predictions of PROFacc (Figure 8.2) is illustrative. In contrast to the case of secondary structure, here the differences between the methods seem substantial. Note, however, that some of these differences should be attributed to difference in defining exposure. Although PROFacc defines a residue that has 16% of its surface area accessible to solvent as exposed, the cutoff for Jpred is 25%, and this difference in definition is partially responsible for the variance seen in the results produced by different methods.

There seems to be an apparently significant mismatch in the predictions made by the two methods for the first segment of the protein. Jpred predicts that 6 of the 10 first residues are buried to some extent. PROFacc predicts most of this stretch to be exposed or very exposed. However, both methods are fairly unconfident regarding most of the predictions in this stretch, as shown in the `Jnet Rel` line in JPred and `SUB acc` line in PROFacc. Curiously, both methods are rather confident about the their respective predictions for the first residue; however, one of them predicts that it is completely exposed (PROFacc), whereas the other predicts that it is partly buried (Jpred). Checking the actual, experimentally determined structure reveals that this residue is 100% exposed. It is interesting to note, however, that the first residue about which the two methods agree (Val 10) is predicted to be buried by both methods; it is indeed one of the most buried residues in this protein, with 0% solvent accessibility. This case demonstrates once again the value of comparing different methods and contemplating not only the predictions, but also the reliability that each method assigns to each prediction.

Transmembrane Segments

The communication between a cell and its surroundings, be it a unicellular cell sensing its medium or an animal or plant cell interacting with other cells in its vicinity, is based almost exclusively on proteins that are embedded in the cell's membrane. These proteins interact with molecules on both the intracellular and extracellular sides of the membrane. Approximately one fourth of all proteins are estimated to contain regions that pass through cellular membranes (Melen et al., 2003). Identifying these transmembrane proteins and deciphering their molecular mechanisms, then, is of great importance, particularly as applied to biomedicine.

There are two broad classes of transmembrane proteins: those that insert helices into the lipid bilayer and those that insert strands. It is reasonable to assume that the transmembrane segments of proteins share common biophysical features. These common features undoubtedly are inherent in the kinds of sequence that are able to incorporate themselves into an environment very different from that found within most cellular compartments and serve as the basis for the development of methods that identify transmembrane segments *in silico*. The basic biophysical requirement for a residue to be buried in the membrane is hydrophobicity. High degrees of hydrophobicity enable most transmembrane segments of a protein actually to remain within the membrane, avoiding the solvent on either side. Hence, the first and most basic of the predictive methods focused searching for long hydrophobic stretches of sequence. Kyte and Doolittle (1982) proposed a simple method to identify transmembrane segments based simply on residue hydrophobicity. Many groups have since suggested improvements to Kyte and Doolittle's original idea, as well as novel approaches to the problem. Some methods also predict what is sometime referred to as the topology of the transmembrane protein, the orientation of membrane segments with respect to the N-terminus of a protein; proteins that begin on the outside are classified as having topology out, whereas those that begin on the inside are classified as having topology in. The fact that it is difficult to decipher the structure of transmembrane segments experimentally makes *in silico* prediction

both a greater challenge and a more valuable analytical tool.

Prediction Methods

TopPred. Combining hydrophobicity analysis with the analysis of electrical charges, TopPred (von Heijne, 1992) was one of the first methods developed for the prediction of transmembrane segments and topology. When a protein sequence is submitted to TopPred, the program calculates its hydrophobicity profile. Sequence stretches that are found to be rich in hydrophobic residues are marked as transmembrane helices. Stretches that are hydrophobic but fail to exceed a predefined cutoff of hydrophobicity are considered "putative transmembrane helices." Finally, based on various rules, the most important of which is the distribution of positively charged residues between the transmembrane helices, the overall topology of the protein is predicted, with and without the putative helices. This idea follows the discovery of von Heijne and his collaborators that positively charged residues are more abundant on the inside of membrane (the positive-in rule). The results of a TopPred query using the sequence of the muscarinic acetylcholine receptor are shown in Figure 8.5.

PHDhtm. PHDhtm (Rost et al., 1996) is the part of the PredictProtein service and is geared toward the prediction of transmembrane helices. As in the cases of secondary structure and solvent accessibility prediction, the method first constructs a profile from a multiple sequence alignment. Then, a neural network predicts whether each residue is likely to be part of a transmembrane helix. Another neural network then is used to decide whether the protein as a whole is a putative helix bundle integral membrane protein. Finally, the system predicts the topology of the protein by applying the von Heijne positive-inside rule to the network predictions.

ProfTMB. Specializing in the prediction of transmembrane β-strands, this method (Bigelow et al., 2004 uses multiple sequence alignments to produce a profile that is fed into an HMM. The HMM is trained on examples from one specific group of membrane proteins known as β-barrels, proteins that reside in the outer membrane of gram-negative bacteria, mitochondria, and chloroplasts, making this method particularly useful in finding sequences that belong to this structural family. The program predicts whether the query sequence belongs to this class, and if it does, it identifies the transmembrane β-strands.

SOSUI. This program (Hirokawa et al., 1998) bases its predictions on four main parameters. First, it calculates the hydropathy of residues, based on the

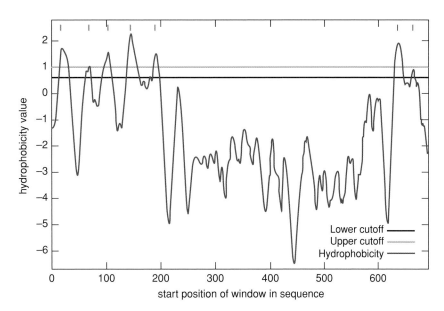

anonymous
Structure no. 1
Segments included: 1   2   3   4   5   6   7

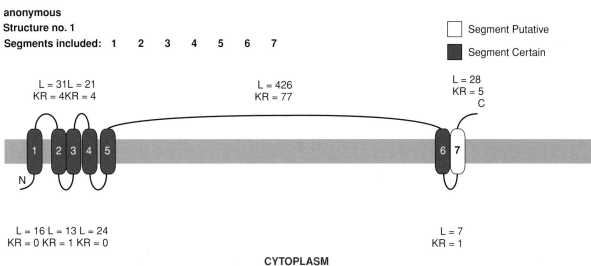

FIGURE 8.5   Output from TopPred. (a) Hydrophobicity values for each position in the query sequence. The prediction is based on the assumption that sequence stretches within a certain range of hydrophobicity values, marked by the green and red lines on the plot, are likely to be embedded in the membrane. (b) The predicted topology of the protein. Note that the first six transmembrane helices are colored gray, indicating high confidence, and that the last one is colored white, indicating a lower reliability. These predictions were made for the sequence of muscarinic acetylcholine receptor (accession Q18007).

Kyle-Doolittle index. Then, it calculates the charges of each of the residues and their amphiphilicity (the distribution of electric charges around the helix). Finally, the length of the sequence is incorporated into the calculation. The output of the program includes a graph with the hydropathy profile of the query sequence and a "helical wheel" diagram illustrating the predicted transmembrane segments. This representation shows the different features of the helix residues and enables visualization of the biophysical traits of the helix as a whole.

TMHMM. TMHMM uses HMMs to predict transmembrane segments and the topology of the transmembrane proteins (Krogh et al., 2001). Many machine-learning algorithms are designed to identify patterns in ostensibly irregular sequences. Among these, HMMs are particularly useful in matching a sequence to a predefined "grammar." Transmembrane proteins tend to obey a relatively strict grammar of alternating segments of membrane and nonmembrane segments and a well-defined organization of positively charged residues. TMHMM

TMHMM result

<u>HELP</u> with output formats

```
# Sequence Length: 713
# Sequence Number of predicted TMHs:  7
# Sequence Exp number of AAs in TMHs: 156.64806
# Sequence Exp number, first 60 AAs:  22.90459
# Sequence Total prob of N-in:        0.00001
# Sequence POSSIBLE N-term signal sequence
Sequence     TMHMM2.0     outside     1    19
Sequence     TMHMM2.0     TMhelix     20   42
Sequence     TMHMM2.0     inside      43   62
Sequence     TMHMM2.0     TMhelix     63   85
Sequence     TMHMM2.0     outside     86   99
Sequence     TMHMM2.0     TMhelix     100  122
Sequence     TMHMM2.0     inside      123  142
Sequence     TMHMM2.0     TMhelix     143  165
Sequence     TMHMM2.0     outside     166  191
Sequence     TMHMM2.0     TMhelix     192  214
Sequence     TMHMM2.0     inside      215  633
Sequence     TMHMM2.0     TMhelix     634  656
Sequence     TMHMM2.0     outside     657  670
Sequence     TMHMM2.0     TMhelix     671  693
Sequence     TMHMM2.0     inside      694  713
```

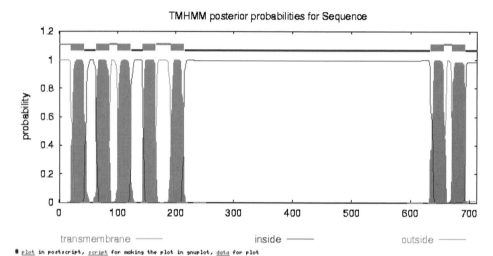

plot in postscript, script for making the plot in gnuplot, data for plot

FIGURE 8.6 **This graph, taken from the output of TMHMM, describes the location of predicted transmembrane segments, their predicted topology, and the reliability of the prediction. The pink line is the probability that a certain position is outside of the cell, the blue line is the probability it resides in the cytoplasmic side of the membrane, and the red line is the probability that this residue is in the membrane. These predictions were made for the sequence of muscarinic acetylcholine receptor (accession Q18007).**

tries to match the query sequence to this grammar, which is derived from a set of well-characterized transmembrane proteins. By searching for known transmembrane grammars matching the query sequence, TMHMM predicts the segments that are most likely to traverse the membrane and the most likely topology of the whole protein (Figure 8.6).

DAS. The dense alignment surface (DAS) method assesses sequence similarities between segments of the query protein and known transmembrane segments (Cserzo et al., 1997). Thus, it identifies those sequence stretches in the query sequence that are likely to be transmembrane by virtue of their biophysical similarity

to stretches that were shown experimentally to be integrated within the membrane.

How the Methods Perform. As in the case of solvent accessibility, there is no continuous, large-scale system that assesses and compares the performance of different membrane prediction methods. The developers of all the methods surveyed here report levels of accuracy of 75% to 95%; however, based on recent reports, these values are likely to be somewhat overoptimistic (Chen & Rost, 2002, Chen et al., 2002). As emphasized above, these numbers are not sufficient to determine the respective strengths and weaknesses of each method, nor are they sufficient to determine which method performs best. However, these numbers can serve as a general estimate of the expected performance of these prediction methods.

Figures 8.5 and 8.6 show the output from TopPred and TMHMM, respectively. As before, the power inherent in comparing results from different methods can be seen immediately, because there are striking similarities between the results. Both methods predict that, along the first 200 residues, the protein crosses the membrane five times. Both methods predict that the protein does not cross the membrane at all over the next 400 residues, and finally, they both agree that, in last 200 residues, there are two transmembrane segments. The same exact segments are predicted by both methods, demonstrating the power of these methods in identifying transmembrane stretches. However, this comparison also reveals some informative differences between the predictions. Both methods predicted that the long, central stretch of the protein, between positions 200 and 600, does not cross the membrane, but on which side of the membrane does this stretch lie? Each method gives a different answer. TopPred predicts this long stretch to be extracellular, whereas TMHMM predicts its location on the cytoplasmic side of the membrane. Although the very similar predictions of the transmembrane segments are reassuring, the different predicted topologies reveal a weaker side of these methods, where success in predicting topologies usually is more limited than that of predicting the transmembrane segments. How should one decide between these two conflicting topologies? Probably the simplest way would be to submit the same sequence to yet another server, preferably one that uses a different algorithm than these two, and hope that the result supports one or the other, in a majority rule fashion.

▌PREDICTING FUNCTION

The attempt to extract biologically important information from a protein sequence has been dominated in the last few decades by structure prediction. In addition to predicting secondary structure, solvent accessibility, and transmembrane helices, this effort includes the attempt to predict the tertiary structure of a protein, the subject of the next chapter. As the fruits of these efforts became available, many people attempted to capitalize on them, using them along with other tools and findings to predict the function of proteins from their sequence. Most attempts at predicting function are single-case studies in which experts combine different tools with their biological knowledge and intuition to guess the function of a newly discovered protein. Naturally, these case-specific attempts did not result in automated tools for function

prediction. However, some researchers have attempted to develop more generally applicable prediction methods for predicting protein function from sequence.

Annotation Transfer

Thousands of proteins have been characterized experimentally in the lab, and their functions have been recorded in various protein databases. It long has been assumed that similarity at the sequence level implies similarity of function; thus, if a newly discovered protein bears high similarity to another, well-characterized one, it is reasonable to assume that they have a similar function. However, there are some notable exceptions to this general rule, such as proteins that are known to have different functions depending on their ceullular location; these proteins, termed *moonlighting proteins*, are discussed in an article by Jeffery (2003). Thus, transferring annotation from an experimentally characterized sequence to its newly discovered homolog may constitute a simple method for predicting function. However, this approach needs to address several important points before it can serve as a basis for automated prediction. Among these difficulties is the need to define a statistical threshold of sequence similarity that permits the annotation transfer. It has been shown that this threshold differs from one biological function to another and needs to be determined ad hoc for each protein family and each biological function (see Rost et al. (2003) for a review).

Motifs and Patterns

The attempt to develop automated tools for the prediction of biological function includes the development of various methods to identify functionally important residues based on their conservation throughout evolution (Casari et al., 1995; see also Chapter 11). If a residue is highly conserved, it is likely to be important functionally. However, this logic cannot lead to any insight with regard to what this putative function may be. A more elaborate version of this same idea is to attempt to identify sequence elements, rather than individual residues, that are conserved throughout evolution and seem to have specific functional importance. Sometimes, the divergence between the sequence of a newly discovered protein and any other previously annotated protein is too wide to establish relatedness based on a simple pairwise sequence alignment. Yet, the existence of a relatively short sequence motif that is highly conserved evolutionarily and highly specific functionally within this newly discovered sequence may help reveal the putative function of this new protein. For example, if we find in a newly sequenced protein, a sequence element that appears in many known DNA-binding proteins, we can predict that the function of our new protein probably involves some sort of interaction with DNA. Several databases offer large libraries of these characterized sequence motifs that have been collected either manually by experts or automatically by pattern-searching algorithms. Many of these libraries include a searching tool, allowing users to submit a sequence of interest to determine whether an interesting motif is contained within their protein. Finding one of these well-characterized motifs in a newly discovered sequence could offer some important insight into its structure and function.

Before discussing the methods that capitalize on such an approach, several terms need to be defined. The first is *profiles*. Profiles are, quite simply, a numerical representation of a multiple sequence alignment, much like the multiple sequence alignments derived from the methods discussed in Chapter 12. Imbedded within a multiple sequence alignment is intrinsic sequence information that represents the common characteristics of that particular collection of sequences, frequently a protein family. By using a profile, one is able to find similarities between sequences with little or no absolute sequence identity, allowing for the identification of distantly related proteins. A more extensive discussion of profiles can be found in Chapter 11.

The second term requiring definition is *pattern* or *signature*. A pattern also represents the common characteristics of a protein family (or a multiple sequence alignment), simply providing a shorthand notation for what residues can be present at any given position. For example, the pattern

```
[IV] - G - x - G - T - [LIVMF] - x(2) - [GS]
```

would be read as follows: The first position could contain either an isoleucine or a valine, the second position could contain only a glycine, and so on. An x means that any residue can appear at that position. The x(2) simply means that two positions can be occupied by any amino acid, the number reflecting simply the length of the nonspecific run.

Methods

PROSITE. The PROSITE database catalogs biologically significant sites through the use of motif and sequence profiles and patterns (Falquet et al., 2002; Hulo et al., 2004). Each of the entries in PROSITE is linked to an "annotation document" that provides detailed information on the protein family that is characterized by the profile or pattern in question. Annotations include information on the taxonomic range where the profile or pattern is found, domain architecture views, known

biological functions, any experimentally determined three-dimensional structures, and relevant references from the literature. Most entries also contain information about how well the pattern or profile characterizes the protein family being described (that is, the number of true and false positives, as well as false negatives), which allows the user to determine the specificity of a given profile or pattern. Finally, one of the most useful features of PROSITE entries is the inclusion of a complete list of Swiss-Prot sequences matching the profile or pattern. An example of a representative PROSITE entry is shown in Figure 8.7; this view is the result of a search using the sequence of the muscarinic acetylcholine receptor (Q18007) as the query. Several search engines are available for searching PROSITE, including ScanPro, which allows for a given sequence to be scanned against all of the entries in the database.

Pfam. Pfam is a collection of protein domain families (Sonnhammer et al., 1997; Bateman et al., 2004). Each Pfam entry is, in essence, a multiple sequence alignment of a protein domain or conserved region of interest. There are actually two Pfam databases: Pfam-A and Pfam-B. Pfam-A differs from most such collections in that the initial alignment of the protein alignments is carried out by hand, rather than by depending on automated methods. Pfam-B is generated through an automatic clustering of the ProDom database. Taken together, more than 80% of all Swiss-Prot and TrEMBL entries are associated with a Pfam entry. Profile HMMs derived from the multiple sequence alignments associated with each entry can be used to deduce whether a new sequence of interest can be assigned to an already-characterized family; this approach is particularly useful when similarity cannot be deduced through the use of simple BLAST or FASTA searches (see Chapter 11). The results of a Pfam search, using the sequence of the muscarinic acetylcholine receptor (Q18007) as the query, are shown in Figure 8.8. Searches of the Pfam database can be carried out in a variety of fashions, including keyword-based and sequence-based queries.

InterPro. InterPro is an integrated resource for information about protein families, domains, and functional sites, bringing together information from a number of protein domain-based resources, such as PROSITE, PRINTS, Pfam, and ProDom (Apweiler et al., 2000). InterPro is intended to provide a unified launching point from which users can explore protein families further, moving from the InterPro entry to any of the sources from which InterPro entries are derived.

The InterPro simple search engine can be accessed directly from the InterPro home page; searches can be

>PDOC00008 PS00008 **MYRISTYL** N-myristoylation site [pattern] [Warning: pattern with a high probability of occurrence].

```
170 - 175   GQstSM
177 - 182   GAecSA
193 - 198   GMyvAY
212 - 217   GIhqAA
241 - 246   GTqvGV
306 - 311   GSlnTE
364 - 369   GVpsTR
416 - 421   GSvlNF
527 - 532   GSssNS
685 - 690   GNpfAY
```

>PDOC00009 PS00009 **AMIDATION** Amidation site [pattern] [Warning: pattern with a high probability of occurrence].

```
620 - 623   rGRK
```

>PDOC00210 PS00237 **G_PROTEIN_RECEP_F1_1** G-protein coupled receptors family 1 signature [pattern].

```
112 - 128   VSIltVllITADRYlsV
```

>PDOC00210 PS50262 **G_PROTEIN_RECEP_F1_2** G-protein coupled receptors family 1 [profile].

```
41 - 690   GNAMVVMAYRIERNIsKQVSNRYIVSLAISDLIIGIEGFpFFTVYVLNGDRWPLGWVACQ
           TWLFLDYTLCLVSILTVLLITADRYLSVCHTAKYLKWQSPTKTQLLIVMSWLLPAIIFGI
           MIYGwqAMTGQSTSMSGAECSAPFL-----SNPYVNMGMYVAYYWTTLVAMLILYKGIHQ
           AAKNLEKKAKAKerrhialilsqrlgtqvgvslmlqskaekekaeeaqkdsgytsnqagd
           annlrrfgfsepetsqfrvdpnsnnnlnvegslntendqnlgvieeersgflsrresnes
           yypgphptaansrrcsemekvsllsesdgvpstrpaksygrlslrsrysasesittthen
           dekevekadslqklfaddelgsvlnfkeeklkntdsnndsdttsvilqrsrkykknkrpr
           ssrrsehstprqiakvkqaegtaaqlieesvpdddqtetievkrtdrwvvsmkkriaral
           irrrsttrpergsssnsddsssevegeekpevrnnglkipqltvnnenrgetssqpgrdr
           lappnktdtflsasgvsrkististvitrekvissifapiavfnrgrKQTKAEKRAHKAF
           RTITFIVGFFAILWSPYYIMATVYGF---CKGECIPSFLYTLSYYNCYLNSSGNPFAY
```

Graphical summary of hits (java applet)

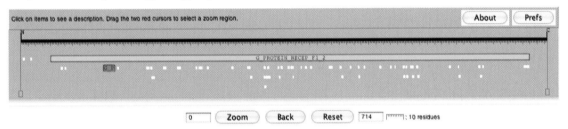

FIGURE 8.7   Output of a PROSITE search, using the muscarinic acetylcholine receptor (accession Q18007) as the query. The gray box at the bottom is an applet that includes a graphical representation of the motifs and patterns that were found, aligned against the query sequence. Using the red markers, the user can zoom in on areas of interest. The top of the page includes a detailed description of the hits and the functional characteristics of each of them. The yellow bar represents a motif characteristic of G-proteins, a family of transmembrane receptors.

either text based or sequence based. Figure 8.9 shows the InterPro entry for the rhodopsin-like GPCR superfamily; this page was obtained by clicking the InterPro link in the PROSITE entry shown in Figure 8.8. This InterPro summary page provides information on the function, intracellular localization, and most importantly, the metabolic role of this protein within the cell. References are provided at the bottom of the summary page for users who wish for more in-depth information about the domain. Users also can retrieve all of the full-length sequences containing the domain; the reader is referred to the InterPro documentation for more details.

BLOCKS. The BLOCKS database uses the concept of blocks to identify a family of proteins, rather than relying on the individual sequences themselves (Pietrovsky et al., 1996). The idea of a block is derived from the more familiar notion of a motif, which usually refers to a conserved stretch of amino acids that confer a specific function or structure to a protein. When these individual motifs from proteins in the same family are aligned without introducing gaps, the result is a block, with the term *block* referring to the alignment, not the individual sequences themselves. Obviously, an individual protein can contain one or more blocks, corresponding to each of its functional or structural motifs.

The BLOCKS database itself is derived from the entries in InterPro. When a BLOCKS search is performed using a sequence of interest, the query sequence is aligned against all blocks in the database at all possible positions. For each alignment, a score is calculated using a position-specific scoring matrix, and results of the best matches

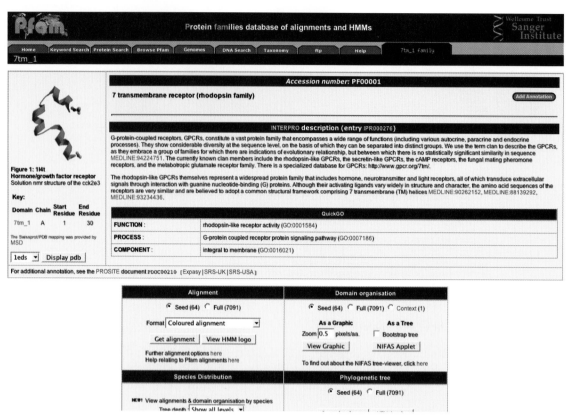

FIGURE 8.8 A representative Pfam summary page, using the muscarinic acetylcholine receptor (accession Q18007) as the query. Pfam identified a long motif that corresponds to a family of transmembrane receptors, to which the query protein belongs. A brief executive summary from InterPro is given, along with links to the InterPro summary page (Figure 8.9). The lower portion of the figure provides links to full alignments of members of this family, information on domain organization, species distribution, and a phylogenetic tree giving the taxonomic range in which members of this protein family are observed.

are returned to the user. Searches can be performed optionally against the PRINTS database, which includes information on more than 300 families that do not have corresponding entries in BLOCKS. To ensure complete coverage, it is recommended that both databases be searched. Finally, a Block Maker is available on the BLOCKS Web site. This tool is the same one used to construct the BLOCKS database; users can submit a set of unaligned, related protein sequences to the Block Maker to detect conserved blocks within the sequence set.

How the Methods Perform. Because these tools offer means for analyzing sequences rather than predicting some measurable trait, it is impossible to assess their performance the way other tools are assessed. Accuracy and predictive power are irrelevant here. The servers described here should be viewed in the same way as the information retrieval tools discussed in Chapter 3: as

reference tools that find elements of interest within the query sequence. Therefore, they are all complementary to each other, and their output could be integrated more straightforwardly.

Figures 8.7 and 8.8 demonstrate this with the output of Pfam and PROSITE, respectively, using the same query sequence. Pfam found a few long motifs that can help associate the query sequence with a well-characterized family and predict its function. PROSITE, however, found many short sequence signatures that imply some functional aspects, such as interaction sites, phosphorilation sites, and the like. PROSITE also found one long hit that corresponds to a well-characterized domain. It is interesting, though not surprising, that this longer motif corresponds to the most trusted match of Pfam. Combining these tools yields many hints that would be very instrumental in the attempt to predict the function of a protein.

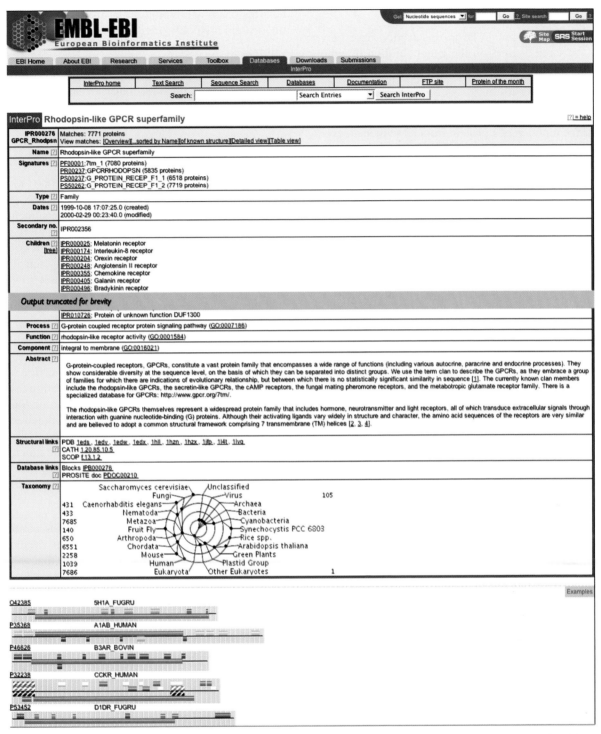

FIGURE 8.9 An InterPro summary page for the rhodopsin-like GPCR superfamily. This view is obtained by clicking on the InterPro link shown in Figure 8.8 (IPR00276). All InterPro pages give the name of the family, links to signatures that characterize members of the family, information on "children" of this protein family (used to indicate protein family and subfamily relationships), any functional information, and a short executive summary of what is known about the family. Links to other databases, such as **PDB**, **CATH**, **SCOP**, **BLOCKS**, and **PROSITE**, also are provided. The radial taxonomy display is intended to provide a quick overview of the taxonomic range in which members of this protein family are observed. Finally, at the bottom of the figure is a graphical view indicating the presence of discrete motifs in proteins belonging to this family.

Subcellular Localization

The methods covered so far in this section have been based, to some degree, on the general notion of annotation transfer: finding similarities between a query sequence and other proteins that have been thoroughly characterized experimentally. However, in recent years, attempts have been made to develop tools that will decipher the function of a protein from its sequence, even when the most sophisticated tools for annotation transfer yield no results.

When the pioneers of structure prediction launched their enterprise, one of their first steps was to break down the somewhat fuzzy concept of "structure" into well-defined structural features such as secondary structures or topologies (discussed above), as well as concepts such as structural families or folds, which are discussed in the next chapter. If structure is a fuzzy concept that requires a more meticulous set of subcategories, then function is even more so. What we usually refer to as the function of a protein could be biochemical (such as phosphorylation), cellular (e.g., cytoskeletal protein), physiological, or pertaining to the organism as a whole (e.g., developmental). Each of these implied functions depends on different biophysical and biochemical features of the proteins, and hence is probably encoded differently within its sequence. Therefore, if one wants to predict function from sequence, a first step would be to define which aspect of function one is attempting to predict. The eukaryotic cell has many compartments, each of which house very different biochemical and biological processes that are carried out by different proteins. Identifying the subcellular localization of a newly discovered sequence is a crucial step in narrowing down its putative function. Some groundbreaking work performed in recent years has shown that, in many cases, it is possible to predict the subcellular localization of a protein from its sequence.

Prediction Methods

PSORT. PSORT (Nakai & Horton, 1999) uses the amino acid sequence of a protein and the type of organism from which it was obtained (Gram-positive bacteria, Gram-negative bacteria, yeast, animal, or plant) as the input. Based on the taxonomic origin of the protein, the system searches for features characterizing that taxonomic group that may help deduce the subcellular localization of the protein. For instance, it has been found that the trafficking of proteins to some subcellular compartments is dictated by short signal peptides at the N- or C-terminal of the protein. PSORT uses a library of known signal peptides and searches for them in the query sequence. It also checks predicted structural features (such as topology) that may indicate whether the protein is soluble or embedded in a membrane.

SUBLOC. Using the amino acid composition alone, SUBLOC (Hua & Sun, 2001) applies support vector machines to predict the subcellular locale of a protein. It predicts one of three localizations for prokaryotes (extracellular, periplasmic, or cytoplasmic) and four for eukaryotes (extracellular, mitochondrial, cytoplasmic, or nuclear).

TargetP. TargetP (Emanuelsson et al., 2000) focuses on signal peptides at the N-terminal end of a protein. It uses a series of machine-learning algorithms, including neural networks and SVMs, to identify signal peptides of three types: chloroplast transit peptides, mitochondrial targeting peptides, and secretory pathway signal peptides. The TargetP interface enables the user to define the desired specificity of the prediction.

LOC3D. LOC3D (Nair & Rost, 2003) is a database of predicted subcellular localizations for eukaryotic proteins of known three-dimensional structure. It is based on three underlying methods: predicNLS, which searches for a known nuclear localization signal; LOChom, which uses homology to determine localization; and LOC3D, which is a neural network-based prediction method. LOCkey, a related service, uses keywords in Swiss-Prot annotation to predict the subcellular localization. Altogether, this suite offers comprehensive coverage of the methods and approaches available for the prediction of subcellular localization.

How the Methods Perform. As in the cases of solvent accessibility and transmembrane segment prediction, there is no continuous, large-scale system that assesses and compares the performance of the different available methods. Using a large test set and applying the same statistical analysis to all the methods, Nair and Rost (2003) found a large variability in the accuracy of the methods. The best methods predicted extracellular proteins with an accuracy of more than 80%, cytoplasmic proteins with an accuracy of more than 50%, nuclear proteins with an accuracy of more than 70%, and mitochondrial proteins with an accuracy of more than 60%.

Functional Class

The prediction of subcellular localization is part of the process of reducing the ambiguous term *function* to one that is better defined. Another, more ambitious, enterprise in this direction is the attempt to break down the notion of function into a series of well-defined categories. It is facilitated by the definition of a set of

Predictive Methods Using Protein Sequences

functional classes to which a protein can be assigned. As soon as the set of functional classes is defined, software can be developed with the goal of assigning proteins to each one of the functional classes. In 1993, a scheme of functional classes to annotate *Escherichia coli* was introduced (Riley, 1993). Some genome projects adopted this general scheme, eventually making this the most widely used terminology for the assignment of functional class.

Prediction Methods

EUCLID. This method uses the keywords in Swiss-Prot to assign a protein to one of Riley's functional classes (Tamames et al., 1998). The algorithm at the heart of this method is a basic machine-learning algorithm that learns, based on a manually curated training set, which combination of keywords is most likely to indicate that the protein belongs to a certain functional type. The developers report that, in more than 90% of the cases, the functional type that was determined by the automated method was identical to the one that was assigned to it by a human expert. However, EUCLID requires that some annotation (namely Swiss-Prot keywords) already be assigned to the sequence. Thus, it is not really a method for prediction strictly from sequence.

ProtFun. ProtFun represents a recent and promising step toward the prediction of function from sequence (Jensen et al., 2003). To define a functional type, ProtFun uses the Gene Ontology (GO; Ashburner et al., 2000) in an attempt to build a controlled vocabulary to describe genes and gene products. Each protein could be assigned to a certain molecular function, a certain biological process, and a certain cellular component. GO attempts to assign a number to each protein that represents these three levels of functional "description." Currently, there are hundreds of GO categories; ProtFun focuses on 347 of them and uses complex systems of neural networks to predict the GO functional classification of a protein from its sequence. The developers report an impressive accuracy—in most cases, more then 90% of their predictions are correct. However, current coverage is only partial, and many of the query proteins are returned without any prediction at all.

∎ SUMMARY

The early discoveries in the 1960s indicating that protein sequences bear information about their ultimate structure and function, combined with the relative simplicity with which these sequences could be obtained in the lab, led to the bold enterprise of trying to predict structure and function from sequence using computerized methods. Different methods use different algorithms to attain this goal, but the logic behind them is fairly similar. As discussed above, most of these algorithms belong to a class of approaches that is called *machine-learning algorithms*, which offer different ways to learn what the characteristic features of the entity of interest are, based on a large number of examples. In the case of secondary structure predictions, for example, a large data set of experimentally determined structures is used to learn the sequence parameters that characterize each secondary structure. Different kinds of machine-learning algorithms are used by the different methods, the predominant among them being artificial neural networks and HMMs. However, it is crucial to remember that learning in this context merely means adjusting and fine tuning parameters. The developers of each method decide in advance what biological features they believe may be the most important in making an accurate prediction, and the algorithms use the data to assign a weight to each of those parameters. When the algorithm is applied to a query sequence, it uses these weights to compute the likelihood of each residue to fold into a certain structure. Therefore, even the best machine-learning algorithm cannot perform well if the training set is not large enough to determine appropriate values for each of the parameters. More importantly, the algorithm cannot find the relevant parameters on its own; it can determine only how important each of the parameters is. Hence, the key to success not only is a good algorithm and a large training set, but also intelligent choice of relevant parameters. Most of the secondary structure prediction methods discussed here dominantly use local sequence and evolutionary information in reaching their conclusions. The same is true for the methods that attempt to predict solvent accessibility and some of the tools for identifying motifs and patterns. The tools for the prediction of more complicated functional aspects, namely subcellular localization and functional class, rely both on local and on nonlocal features.

In the general realm of structure prediction, recent decades have seen a maturation of these methods, specifically, those that are aimed at predicting particular structural features such as secondary structure and solvent accessibility. It is now possible, in a few seconds, to predict these structural features with stunning accuracy. In the past, obtaining this kind of information required laborious and expansive laboratory experiments. However, as illustrated in this chapter, even though the performance of these methods is very impressive, particularly in light of the severity of the problem they attempt to solve, they are not perfect and often fail. Comparing predictions from different methods and looking for consensus between them has been shown to yield better predictions than any single method.

Even more ambitious attempts to predict function—attempts that, until recently, were less successful—also are slowly achieving more reliability. The simplest and most general tools for function prediction are those that look for known motifs and patterns in the query sequence. Although not offering a concrete prediction, they enable the user to make a more educated guess about the function of the protein. The next generation of function prediction methods necessarily will focus on tools that attempt to give a comprehensive functional description of a protein based on its sequence. Methods like ProtFun currently may be of limited applicability, but for computational biologists and bioinformaticians, they are very promising. They demonstrate that high-throughput computerized annotation of newly discovered sequences indeed may be an achievable goal. The coming few years likely will see significant improvement of tools of this kind, making *in silico* function prediction a powerful, swift, and inexpensive means for deciphering the information encoded within the sequence of proteins.

WORKED EXAMPLE

The following worked example is intended to bring together some of the concepts presented in this Chapter, along with some of those presented in Chapter 3. This Worked Example will concentrate on a protein called rhodopsin.

Rhodopsin is formed when a protein called opsin is chemically linked to a specialized form of Vitamin A. Rhodopsin resides almost exclusively in the outer segments of rod photoreceptor cells and can only be formed in the dark. When light strikes, the rhodopsin molecule changes shape, generating the initial signal in the visual process. Ultimately, the vitamin A splits off from the opsin protein but can be reattached in the dark. This series of reactions in light and dark is called the visual cycle.

(a)   The Swiss-Prot entry for rhodopsin can be found by performing an Entrez search, using P08100 as the query. Based simply on the Swiss-Prot record, how many transmembrane regions does rhodopsin possess?

   The feature table within the Swiss-Prot table contains seven incidences of a feature key indicating a transmembrane region (`/region_name="Transmembrane region"`). Therefore, according to the Swiss-Prot record, rhodopsin possesses seven transmembrane regions.

(b)   Using TopPred, determine the number and relative orientation of these predicted transmembrane segments. Is the N-terminus predicted to lie in the extracellular space or in

the cytoplasm? How long is the N-terminal tail preceding the first transmembrane region? Does this region show an excess of positive charges?

To perform the TopPred prediction, take the FASTA-formatted sequence for Swiss-Prot found in the last part of this question and paste it into the query box on the Top-Pred query page. Below the box for the sequence are two options that should be checked off: one to produce the hydrophobicity graph image, and one to produce an image of each topology. Clicking the Run toppred button submits the query to the TopPred server.

A number of files are returned to the user. The file named `P08100.png` contains the hydrophobicity profile for this protein. The file named `P08100-1.png` contains a schematic showing how the rhodopsin protein potentially threads through the membrane. In this case, seven transmembrane regions are predicted; the *number* of transmembrane regions is consistent with the Swiss-Prot entry for rhodopsin. Notice that, for each loop, two values are given: L1, which is the length of the loop between the transmembrane segments, and KR, which gives the number of lysines (K) and arginines (R) in the loop. Notice that all of the transmembrane segments are grey; according to the key in the upper right, these are considered "segment certain," meaning a high probability that the prediction is accurate. Also notice that the N-terminus of the protein is in the extracellular space, while the C-terminus lies in the cytoplasm.

The N-terminal tail has a length of 34 (L1 = 34). There is only one positive charge in this loop (KR = 1), so one would not conclude that there is an excess of positive charges in the N-terminal tail.

(c)   The Swiss-Prot record gives the following information for the first transmembrane helix. Is this consistent with the TopPred prediction? Explain.

```
Region   37..61
         /gene="RHO"
         /region_name="Transmembrane region"
         /note="1 (Potential)."
```

The Swiss-Prot entry indicates that the first transmembrane region consists of residues 37-61 of the rhodopsin protein. One of the other files that is produced by TopPred (`toppred.out`) gives the position of each of the predicted transmembrane regions. The first predicted TopPred helix consists of positions 35-55. The boundaries for the first transmembrane helix are obviously different, leaving to question what the actual boundaries of the transmembrane helices actually are. The purpose of this question was to illustrate that various predictive methods may (and often do) give inconsistent results; it would be incumbent upon the user to consult the literature to see if any of the papers listed in the Swiss-Prot record (or elsewhere) provide actual experimental data that could shed light on the correct solution.

Can any protein domains be identified by submitting the rhodopsin sequence to InterPro?

From the InterPro home page, select the Sequence Search link on the left-hand side of the page. The Sequence Search query page provides a very simple interface for detecting putative domains within a protein. Paste the rhodopsin sequence into the query box, and leave all the default values set as is; then submit the request. The InterPro server returns a graphic overview of any found protein domains within the rhodopsin sequence. The left-hand column of the graphic overview indicates that the found domains belong to three separate InterPro families: IPR000276,

the rhodopsin-like GPCR superfamily; IPR000732, the rhodopsin family; and IPR001760, the opsin family. Clicking on any of the IPR numbers would take the user to detailed information on that protein family, as described earlier in this chapter. The right-hand column gives a graphical representation of where each of the found domains lie along the length of the rhodopsin protein. In order to determine which residues within the rhodopsin protein comprise each one of the found domains, click on the Table View button above the graphic. Consider the found opsin domains (IRP001760), towards the bottom of the figure. The following corresponding entry appears in the Table View:

```
PRINTS PR00238 OPSIN 5.8E-20 [60-72]T 5.8E-20 [174-186]T 5.8E-20 [285-297]T
```

Here, the found domains correspond to the PRINTS domain PR00238, for opsin; the three domains found (as shown in the first line of the graphic for this family) consist of positions 60-72, 174-186, and 285-297. Similar text appears for each of the lines in the graphical overview.

PROBLEM SET

Using the sequence found on the Book's Web site, answer the following questions.

1. Use TopPred to determine whether this sequence contains helices that may be embedded within a membrane. If so, give the positions of these helices in the sequence.

2. Would one expect secondary structure prediction methods intended for soluble proteins to identify membrane helices as helices? Explain.

3. For the same sequence, run a secondary structure prediction, using PROFsec and PSIPRED. Do the results of these two methods agree with each other? Do they agree with TopPred? Can any conclusions be drawn?

4. Run Pfam on this sequence. Discuss the relationship between Pfam results and those of TopPred. Can the function of the query protein now be predicted?

5. Run ProtFun on the same sequence. Do the ProtFun results confirm the predicted function deduced above?

INTERNET RESOURCES

Blocks	http://www.blocks.fhcrc.org/
DAS	http://www.sbc.su.se/~miklos/DAS/
EUCLID	http://www.pdg.cnb.uam.es/EUCLID/Full_Paper/homepage.html
EVA	http://cubic.bioc.columbia.edu/eva/
Jpred	http://www.compbio.dundee.ac.uk/~www-jpred/submit.html
LOC3D	http://cubic.bioc.columbia.edu/db/LOC3d/
Pfam	http://www.sanger.ac.uk/Software/Pfam/
PredictProtein	http://www.predictprotein.org/
ProfTMB	http://cubic.bioc.columbia.edu/services/proftmb/index.html
PROSITE	http://us.expasy.org/prosite/
ProtFun	http://www.cbs.dtu.dk/services/ProtFun/
PSIPRED	http://bioinf.cs.ucl.ac.uk/psiform.html
PSORT	http://psort.ims.u-tokyo.ac.jp/
SAM-T99	http://www.cse.ucsc.edu/research/compbio/HMM-apps/T99-query.html
SOSUI	http://sosui.proteome.bio.tuat.ac.jp/sosuiframe0.html
SUBLOC	http://www.bioinfo.tsinghua.edu.cn/SubLoc/
TargetP	http://www.cbs.dtu.dk/services/TargetP/
TMHMM	http://www.cbs.dtu.dk/services/TMHMM/
TopPred	http://bioWeb.pasteur.fr/seqanal/interfaces/toppred

FURTHER READING

Apweiler, R., Attwood, T. K., Bairoch, A., Bateman, A., Birney, E., Biswas, M., Bucher, P., Cerutti, L., Corpet, F., Croning, M. D., et al. (2000). InterPro—an integrated documentation resource for protein families, domains and functional sites. *Bioinformatics* 16, 1145–1150. Describes an attempt to integrate several databases of motifs and patterns (including Pfam and PROSITE) to one comprehensive system.

Baldi, P., Brunak, S., and Brunak, S. (2001). *Bioinformatics: The Machine Learning Approach*, 2nd ed. (Adaptive Computation and Machine Learning), (MIT Press, Cambridge, MA). A book that deals with the application of machine learning to bioinformatics and elaborates on the computational aspects of some algorithms and their suitability for biological problems.

Bourne, P., and Weissig, H. (eds.). (2003). *Structural Bioinformatics* (Wiley & Sons, Inc., New York, New York). A comprehensive book about the theoretical and applied aspects of computational analysis of protein structure and function. Section IV, Structure and Functional Assignment, addresses many of the topics covered in this chapter.

Rost, J. L., Nair, R., Wrzeszczynski, K. O., and Ofran, Y. (2003). Automatic prediction of protein function. *CMLS Cell. Mol. Life*

Sci. 60 1–14. More about automatic function prediction, with details about prediction of other spects of functions and discussion of more methods, approaches, and prediction services.

REFERENCES

Anfinsen, C. B. (1973). Principles that govern the folding of protein chains. *Science* 181, 223–230.

Apweiler, R., Attwood, T. K., Bairoch, A., Bateman, A., Birney, E., Biswas, M., Bucher, P., Cerutti, L., Corpet, F., Croning, M. D., et al. (2000). InterPro—an integrated documentation resource for protein families, domains and functional sites. *Bioinformatics* 16, 1145–1150.

Ashburner, M., Blake, J. A., Botstein, D., Butler, H., Cherry, J. M., Davis, A. P., Dolinski, K., Dwight, S. S., and Eppig, J. T. (2000). Gene Ontology: tool for the unification of biology. The Gene Ontology Consortium. *Nat. Genet.* 25, 25–29.

Bateman, A., Coin, L., Durbin, R., Finn, R. D., Hollich, V., Griffiths-Jones, S., Khanna, A., Marshall, M., Moxon, S., Sonnhammer, E. L., Studholme, D. J., Yeats, C., Eddy, S. R. (2004). The Pfam protein families database. *Nucl. Acids Res.* 32, D138–D141.

Bigelow, H., Petery, D., Liu, J., Przybylski, D., and Rost, B. (2004). ProfTMB: a profile HMM for two-state residue and whole-protein prediction of transmembrane beta-barrels. *Proteins Struct. Funct. Genet.* In press.

Casari, G., Sander, C., and Valencia, A. (1995). A method to predict functional residues in proteins. *Nat Struct. Biol.* 2, 171–178.

Chen, C. P. and Rost, B. (2002). State-of-the-art in membrane protein prediction. Appl. Bioinformatics 1: 21–35.

Chen, C. P., Kernytsky, A., and Rost, B. (2002). Transmembrane helix predictions, revisited. Protein Sci. 11: 2774–2791.

Crick, F. (1958). The biological replication of biomolecules. *Symp. Soc. Exp. Biol.* 12: 138–163.

Cserzo, M., Wallin, E., Simon, I., von Heijne, G., and Elofsson, A. (1997). Prediction of transmembrane alpha-helices in prokaryotic membrane proteins: the dense alignment surface method. *Protein Eng.* 10, 673–676.

Cuff, J. A., and Barton, G. J. (2000). Application of multiple sequence alignment profiles to improve protein secondary structure prediction. *Proteins Struct. Funct. Genet.* 40, 502–511.

Emanuelsson, O., Nielsen, H., Brunak, S., and von Heijne, G. (2000). Predicting subcellular localization of proteins based on their N-terminal amino acid sequence. *J. Mol. Biol.* 300, 1005–1016.

Falquet, L., Pagni, M., Bucher, P., Hulo, N., Sigrist, C. J., Hofmann, K., and Bairoch, A. (2002). The PROSITE database: its status in 2002. *Nucl. Acids Res.* 30, 235–238.

Hirokawa, T., Boon-Chieng, S., and Mitaku, S. (1998). SOSUI: classification and secondary structure prediction system for membrane proteins. *Bioinformatics* 14, 378–379.

Hua, S., and Sun, Z. (2001). Support vector machine approach for protein subcellular localization prediction. *Bioinformatics* 17, 721–728.

Hulo, N., Sigrist, C. J. A., Le Saux, V., Langenijk-Genevaux, P. S., Bordoli, L., Gattiker, A., De Castro, E., Bucher, P., and Bairoch, A. (2004). Recent improvements to the PROSITE database. *Nucl. Acids Res.* 32, D134–D137.

Jeffery, C. J. (2003). Moonlighting proteins: old proteins learning new tricks. *Trends Genet.* 19, 415–417.

Jensen, L. J., Ussery, D. W., and Brunak, S. (2003). Functionality of system components: conservation of protein function in protein feature space. *Genome Res.* 14, 14.

Karplus, K., Barrett, C., and Hughey, R. (1998). Hidden Markov models for detecting remote protein homologies. *Bioinformatics* 14, 846–856.

Krogh, A., Larsson, B., von Heijne, G., and Sonnhammer, E. L. (2001). Predicting transmembrane protein topology with a hidden Markov model: application to complete genomes. *J. Mol. Biol.* 305, 567–580.

Kyte, J., and Doolittle, R. F. (1982). A simple method for displaying the hydrophathic character of a protein. *J. Mol. Biol.* 157, 105–132.

McGuffin, L. J., Bryson, K., and Jones, D. T. (2000). The PSIPRED protein structure prediction server. *Bioinformatics* 16, 404–405.

Melen, K., Krogh, A., and von Heijne, G. (2003). Reliability measures for membrane protein topology prediction algorithms. *J. Mol. Biol.* 327, 735–744.

Minor, D. L. J., and Kim, P. S. (1996). Context-dependent secondary structure formation of a designed protein sequence. *Nature* 380, 730–734.

Nair, R., and Rost, B. (2003). Better prediction of sub-cellular localization by combining evolutionary and structural information. *Proteins* 53, 917–930.

Nakai, K., and Horton, P. (1999). PSORT: a program for detecting sorting signals in proteins and predicting their subcellular localization. *Trends Biochem. Sci.* 24, 34–36.

Pauling, L., Corey, R. B., and Branson, H. R. (1951). The structure of proteins: two hydrogen-bonded helical configurations of the polypeptide chain. *Proc. Natl. Acad. Sci. U. S. A.* 37, 205–234.

Pietrokovski, S., Henikoff, J. G., and Henikoff, S. (1996). The Blocks database: a system for protein classification. *Nucl. Acids Res.* 24, 197–201.

Prusiner, S. B. (1998). Prions. Proc. Natl. Acad. Sci. USA 95: 13363–13383.

Riley, M. (1993). Function of the gene products in *Escherichia coli*. *Microbiol. Rev.* 57, 862–952.

Rost, B., Casadio, R., and Fariselli, P. (1996). Refining neural network predictions for helical transmembrane proteins by dynamic programming. In *Fourth International Conference on Intelligent Systems for Molecular Biology (States, D.J. Agarwal, P.,*

Gaasterland, T., Hunter, L., Smith, R., eds.), AAAI, St. Louis, MO, p. 192–200.

Rost, B., and Eyrich, V. (2001). EVA: large-scale analysis of secondary structure prediction. Proteins Struct. Funct. Genet. 45(Suppl 5), S192–S199.

Rost, B., Liu, J., Nair, R., Wrzeszczynski, K. O., and Ofran, Y. (2003). Automatic prediction of protein function. Cell Mol Life Sci 60, 2637–2650.

Rost, B., and Sander, C. (1994). 1D secondary structure prediction through evolutionary profiles. Proteins 20: 216–226.

Rost, B., Sander, C., and Schneider, R. (1994). PHD—an automatic server for protein secondary structure prediction. CABIOS 10, 53–60.

Sander, C., and Schneider, R. (1991). Database of homology-derived structures and the structural meaning of sequence alignment. Proteins Struct. Funct. Genet. 9, 56–68.

Sonnhammer, E. L., Eddy, S. R., and Durbin, R. (1997). Pfam: a comprehensive database of protein domain families based on seed alignments. Proteins Struct. Funct. Genet. 28, 405–420.

Szent-Györgyi, A. G., and Cohen, C. (1957). Role of proline in polypeptide chain configuration of proteins. Science 126, 697.

Tamames, J., Ouzounis, C., Casari, G., Sander, C., and Valencia, A. (1998). EUCLID: automatic classification of proteins in functional classes by their database annotations. Bioinformatics 14, 542–543.

von Heijne, G. (1992). Membrane protein structure prediction. J. Mol. Biol. 225, 487–494.

Ward, J. J., McGuffin, L. J., Buxton, B. F., and Jones, D. T. (2003). Secondary structure prediction with support vector machines. Bioinformatics 19 1650–1655.

KEY TERMS

hidden Markov model

neural network

protein function prediction

protein structure prediction

subcellular localization

## CHAPTER NINE

Protein Structure Prediction and Analysis

DAVID WISHART

Bioinformatics: A Practical Guide to the Analysis of Genes and Proteins, Third Edition, edited by
Andreas D. Baxevanis and B.F. Francis Ouellette.
ISBN 0-471-47878-4 Copyright © 2005 John Wiley & Sons, Inc.

▌INTRODUCTION

Over the last several chapters, proteins conveniently have been represented and analyzed as character strings (sequences). Indeed, much of what is called bioinformatics today is based on using computers to manipulate, store, and compare sequences or character strings. However, it is important to remember that bioinformatics is more than just sequence analysis and that many of the most interesting and exciting applications in bioinformatics today actually are concerned with structure analysis or, as it is sometimes called, structural bioinformatics. In fact, the origins of bioinformatics actually lie in the field of structural biology, because many of the first bioinformatics programs and databases were developed to store, compare, and analyze protein structures (Hagen, 2000; Bernstein et al., 1977). This chapter explores some of the tools and techniques that bioinformaticians have developed to analyze, archive, visualize, predict, and evaluate protein structures. Interestingly, many of the concepts used in sequence analysis (including alignment, archiving, and visualization) actually have close parallels in structure analysis. However, protein structure analysis also has an added layer of challenges and complications.

Proteins are perhaps the most complex chemical entities in nature. No other class of molecule exhibits the variety and irregularity in shape, size, texture, and mobility that can be found in proteins. Because protein structures are so inherently complex, scientists have gone to great efforts to try to simplify their description and to look for underlying structural commonalities. Today, the preferred approach to describing protein structures is known as the *hierarchical method*. In this schema, a protein is viewed as having different levels of structure with progressively greater complexity. The simplest level is called the *primary structure*. By definition, the primary structure of a protein is simply its amino acid sequence. Of course, proteins are not just letters printed on a page. In reality, they are made of different combinations of amino acids covalently connected together by peptide bonds. The resulting polymer exhibits much of the chain-like flexibility and behavior as most other polymers. However, the partial-double bond character of each peptide bond, the varying chemical nature of the different amino acid side chains, and the steric restrictions imposed by the presence of these side chains means that proteins do not (or can not) exist as an extended string of amino acids. In other words, proteins have a natural proclivity to form more complex structures.

The next level up in the structural hierarchy is called *secondary structure*. Secondary structures are defined as the repetitive hydrogen-bonded shapes or substructures that make up sequentially proximal components of proteins. Some of the most common protein secondary structures are helices (approximately 35% of all residues) and β-pleated sheets (approximately 25% of all residues). Both kinds of secondary structures were originally predicted by Linus Pauling in the 1950s (Corey & Pauling, 1953). These structures are characterized by regular hydrogen bonding patterns that persist over three or more consecutive residues. In addition to these two very abundant forms of secondary structure, there also several other kinds of less abundant, but important, secondary structures, including β-turns (sharp chain reversals), Ω loops (characterized by loops having a shape resembling the Greek letter Ω), and 3/10 helices. Together, these five general classes of secondary structure can be assigned routinely (either manually or automatically) to approximately 65% to 75% of all the amino acids in proteins (Willard et al., 2003). The remaining unclassified or unclassifiable substructures are typically called *random coil* or, more properly, *unstructured regions*.

By assembling different pieces of secondary structure together, it is possible to create a complete protein structure. This assemblage of different secondary structural components is called the *tertiary structure*. Tertiary structure is just another name for the three-dimensional structure of a protein. Unlike secondary structure, tertiary structure primarily is determined or mediated by hydrophobic interactions between distal parts of the polypeptide chain. Just as with secondary structures, there are several different classes or groupings of tertiary structures. These classes have been identified by careful inspection of thousands of X-ray and nuclear magnetic resonance (NMR) structures by skilled structural biologists and bioinformaticians. The simplest tertiary structure classification scheme refers to the relative content of different secondary structure elements. These include the following structural classes:

▶ All α (>50% helix; <10% β sheet);

▶ All β (>30% β sheet; <5% helix); and

▶ Mixed or α/β (everything else).

More refined tertiary classification schemes exist that take into account common topologies, motifs, or folds that seem to be found in a large number of nonhomologous proteins. Common tertiary folds include the α/β barrel (super oxide dismutase); the four helix bundle (cytochrome C550); the Greek key (immunoglobulin); the E-F hand (calcium binding proteins), the zinc finger, and so on. Among the 20,000 protein structures that have been solved so far, approximately 500 common folds have been identified. What is particularly intriguing (and exciting) is that many structural biologists believe that the vast majority of all protein structures (or domains) found in nature can, or will, eventually be classified into just approximately 1,000 different folds (Koonin et al., 2002). This suggests that the creation of a kind of periodic table of protein structures or substructures may be possible.

Beyond the tertiary structure level is something called *quaternary structure*. Quaternary structure refers to the assemblage of two or more independent tertiary structures into a larger superstructure, such as the two chains of insulin, the four chains of hemoglobin, or the 50+ peptide chains in bacterial ribosomes. Many proteins need to form quaternary complexes to function, and so understanding or identifying quaternary structure is key to understanding protein–protein interactions (Chapter 10).

HOW PROTEIN STRUCTURES ARE DETERMINED

There are only two known experimental techniques that can yield comprehensive structural information about proteins at atomic resolution: X-ray crystallography and NMR spectroscopy. Both techniques have their advantages and disadvantages. X-ray crystallography is the older (and more precise) method. In X-ray crystallography, small protein crystals (measuring less than 1 mm) are exposed to an intense beam of X-rays. The X-rays, which have a wavelength approximately the size of an atom (1–2 Å), are scattered or diffracted by the protein atoms in the crystal. The diffraction pattern arising from this typically appears as tens of thousands of tiny spots arrayed in complex circular patterns. These diffraction patterns are recorded on X-ray film or a digital camera. The positions of the diffraction spots along with their intensity (and some phase information) actually is sufficient for a computer to calculate the x, y, and z coordinates of all the heavy atoms (carbon, nitrogen, oxygen, sulfur) in the diffracting protein. Note that, in X-ray crystallography, even though the diffraction pattern arises from trillions of proteins contained in the crystal, the result is a structure for just a single "average" protein.

Protein crystallography is an experimentally challenging and computationally difficult process, so the brief synopsis given here does not do it justice. An excellent overview of protein crystallography can be found on the Lawrence Livermore National Laboratory Web site. The first X-ray structure of a protein (myoglobin) was determined in the late 1950s (Kendrew et al., 1958) and, since that time, more than 20,000 protein structures have been determined by X-ray techniques. X-ray crystallography permits the determination of very large macromolecular structures (hundreds of kilodaltons, including ribosomes and viruses), allowing for the solution of both cytoplasmic and membrane-bound proteins. Recent computational and instrumental advances have made X-ray crystallography even more powerful and have accelerated greatly the structure determination process. As a result, many laboratories around the world are undertaking major structural genomics projects (i.e., solving all the "unknown" protein structures from a selected single organism) using X-ray methods almost exclusively (Sali, 1998).

Nevertheless, X-ray crystallography is not infallible. Crystallography, as the name implies, requires that proteins be studied in an "artificial" solid-state (crystalline) environment that does not resemble the normal physiological (liquid) environment of the cell or body. As a result, the structures generated by X-ray crystallography often are altered by crystal packing and solvent exclusion effects. Likewise, not all parts of a protein (especially highly mobile regions) can be seen in an X-ray structure. Consequently, these "fuzzy" regions can be open to interpretation—or misinterpretation. It is also important to remember that X-ray structures of proteins typically are underdetermined, especially compared with X-ray structures of small molecules. The R factor (a measure of the agreement between the calculated structure and the experimental data) for "good" protein structures is typically 0.25, whereas for small molecules it is 0.05. Given that the highest R factor possible is 0.59 (for a completely wrong structure), one is led to the conclusion that even good protein structures are not without their faults. Indeed, it is not unusual for many protein structures to have some errors, ambiguities, or inaccuracies in their atomic positions (± 0.5 Å). Likewise, it is not unusual for a structure to be missing atoms and residues.

Compared with X-ray crystallography, NMR spectroscopy is a much newer (the first protein was "solved" in 1983) and somewhat more complicated technique. NMR is unique in that allows one to study the structure and dynamics of molecules in a liquid state or near-physiological environment. In NMR spectroscopy, one determines protein structures not by measuring how X-rays are diffracted by atoms, but by measuring how radio waves are absorbed by atomic nuclei. This absorption measurement allows one to determine how much nuclear magnetism is transferred from one atom (or nucleus) to another. In NMR, this magnetization transfer is measured through chemical shifts, J-couplings, and nuclear Overhauser effects. These parameters, which can be best observed for individual hydrogen atoms, have to be determined for as many protein atoms as possible using complex multidimensional NMR experiments. Once measured, these parameters define a set of approximate structural constraints that can be fed into a computer-based constraint minimization calculation (distance geometry or simulated annealing). The result is a series (15–50) of similar protein structures that satisfy the experimental constraints. Therefore, unlike X-ray methods that yield just one structure, NMR methods generate multiple structures, all of which are overlaid or superimposed on each other to produce so-called "blurrograms." Interestingly, the NMR result is probably more reflective of the true solution behavior of proteins, because most proteins seem to exist in an ensemble of slightly different configurations.

Because there is no requirement for crystals, NMR is inherently a quicker technique than X-ray crystallography, which suggests that the number of NMR structures generated per year may soon exceed the number of X-ray structures produced per year. However, NMR often is limited by the size of the molecule being studied (the practical upper limit is 30 kD), the solubility of the molecule (membrane proteins cannot be studied), and the requirement for special isotopically labeled molecules (expensive). Furthermore, NMR structures are inherently less precise than X-ray structures. Regardless of which structure determination method is chosen, the one certainty in all of these approaches is that the structure eventually will end up in a protein structure database.

▮ PROTEIN STRUCTURE DATABASES

Just as sequence databases serve as the foundation to most elements of conventional bioinformatics, structural databases are the foundation to all structural bioinformatics. Indeed, the very first electronic database in bioinformatics was a protein structure database—the Protein Data Bank (PDB). The PDB originally was set up at the Brookhaven National Laboratory by Walter Hamilton in 1971 (Westbrook et al., 2003). When it started, there were just seven protein structures, and their coordinates were stored and distributed on punch cards and computer tape. Since then, the database has grown to more than 20,000 structures. Furthermore, coordinate distribution and deposition is no longer stored on punch cards; it, like most deposition processes, is distributed on the Web. To cope with these changes and the rapid expansion of the database, the management of PDB was moved from Brookhaven to the Research Collaboratory for Structural Bioinformatics (RCSB) in 1998. RCSB is a multilaboratory effort involving scientists at Rutgers University, the San Diego Supercomputing Center, and the National Institute of Standards and Technology. PDB is the primary archival center for all publicly available, experimentally determined three-dimensional structures of proteins, nucleic acids, carbohydrates, and

their complexes. PDB also contains a separate repository of theoretical models generated through homology modeling.

Just like GenBank and the European Molecular Biology Laboratory (EMBL) Web site, the PDB Web site supports a number of services for submitting, searching, retrieving, and viewing data. It is mirrored in Japan, Singapore, Brazil, the United Kingdom, and Germany to facilitate rapid submission, search, and retrieval of structural data. The PDB equivalent of GenBank's Sequin (for DNA sequence submission) is known as ADIT (AutoDep Input Tool). ADIT is a Web entry system that allows structural biologists directly to deposit their structural data and to have both the format checked (PRECHECK) and the structural data automatically validated using the ADIT Validation Suite. The Validation Suite, which includes NUCheck (for nucleic acids), PROCHECK (Laskowski et al. 1993), and SFCHECK (for structure factors; Vaguine et al., 1999), provides a comprehensive diagnostic report assessing the quality or correctness of the newly deposited structure in terms of atom labels, bond distances, bond angles, torsion angles, and packing quality. Inconsistencies, format problems, or questionable data are reported to the submitters, and it is up to the submitters to make the requested corrections.

Before the introduction of structure validation tools, there were a number of examples of seriously flawed structures deposited into the PDB. Unlike the situation for DNA sequencing, where a sequencing ambiguity can be sorted out by resequencing in a matter of hours or days, problems with structures can take months or years to resolve. Hence, structural validation is a particularly important service for structural biologists and one in which bioinformaticians have played a crucial role.

Of course, most PDB users are not interested in depositing data, but rather in accessing it. RCSB offers a number of utilities for searching and retrieving data through its SearchLite and SearchFields Web forms. Through SearchLite, a user may query the PDB for matching PDB ID codes. The PDB ID code is the equivalent to the GenBank accession number. It is a four-character identifier in which the first character is always a number between one and nine. Users also may search the PDB using keywords, protein names, authors, or any Boolean (*and*, *or*, or *not*) combination. SearchLite is the default query interface for the PDB and it is certainly the PDB's most frequently used query tool. However, it is not necessarily the best way of accessing the PDB. Through the more comprehensive SearchFields search engine, users may construct a customized query form that allows one to search the PDB on the basis of many more search terms, including text, titles, authors, headers, release

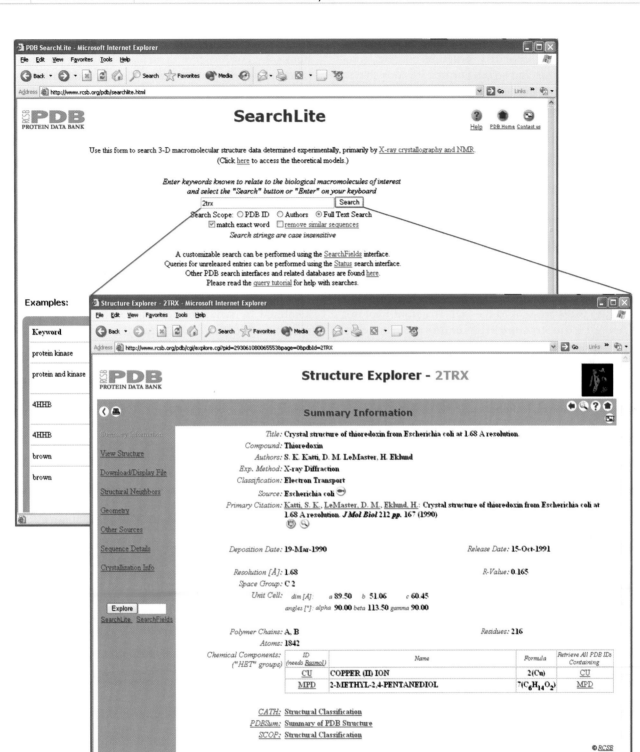

FIGURE 9.1 Screen shot of PDB's SearchLite tool showing the result from typing 2TRX (*E. coli* thioredoxin) into the search field. The query launches the Structure Explorer window (bottom), which allows users to access dozens of other links concerning this protein's sequence and structure.

dates, Enzyme Classification (EC) numbers, sequences (in FASTA format), secondary structure content, resolution, space group, and so on. Further, it is possible to customize the resulting display in terms of what is shown and how it is ordered. The ability to search the PDB on the basis of a sequence query is particularly important, and this is why SearchFields generally is preferable to SearchLite. Nevertheless, it is unfortunate that the PDB does not support sequence queries in a more visible or accessible fashion. Indeed, most users perform sequence queries against the PDB using NCBI's BLASTP because of its faster speed and more convenient interface.

Results from a SearchLite or SearchFields query are displayed in the PDB Query Result Browser. The Browser is a hyperlinked table that lists matches to the query and provides a brief synopsis of each structure. By clicking on the EXPLORE hyperlink (located on the right of the table) users are sent to the PDB Structure Explorer (Figure 9.1). The Structure Explorer provides a more detailed summary of the protein (sometimes called the PDB header), including information on the protein name, authors, resolution, space group, classification, source, and EC number, along with a thumbnail image of the structure. It also is through the Structure Explorer that users are able to view their structure in more detail, to download files, to identify structural neighbors, to inspect secondary structure assignments, to find crystallization information, to view sequence details, and to link to other reports, files, or databases concerning the protein of interest (Figure 9.2). The Structure Explorer is really the heart of the PDB.

Through the View Structure link in the Structure Explorer, users can access almost a dozen different macromolecular viewing packages, including VRML, Protein Explorer, RasMol, Swiss-PDB Viewer, and MICE. Many of these have to be downloaded or installed as Web plug-ins; some of these tools are discussed later in this chapter. However, there is one simple Java applet called QuickPDB that lets users interactively view, rotate, color, and label wire-frame models without any need for downloading (Figure 9.3). It is fast, easy to use, and very convenient. Additionally, PDB provides a number of high-quality still images showing both the asymmetric unit (the structure as it appears in the crystal) and the assumed biological unit (the active version of the molecule, including its quaternary structure). These still images use a rainbow color gradient to help identify the N-terminus (blue) from the C-terminus (red).

In addition to the visualization tools, PDB also provides precalculated lists and links to structural homologues through the Structural Neighbors link (also found in the Structure Explorer; see Figure 9.4). As is discussed later in this chapter, the identification of structural homologs is a much more computationally complicated and time-consuming process than finding sequence homologs. Furthermore, structural similarities are much more ambiguous and difficult to discern or describe than sequence similarities. As a result, PDB provides neighbor assessments using five different packages; CATH (Pearl et al., 2000), SCOP (Murzin et al., 1995), FSSP/DALI (Dietmann et al., 2001), the Vector Alignment Search Tool (VAST; Gibrat et al., 1996), and CE (Shindyalov & Bourne, 2001). Each program provides a slightly different perspective of what is structurally similar to a given protein. Although the results provided by all five are almost identical for trivially obvious similarities, they can differ substantially for less obvious cases. Nevertheless, important and unexpected relationships can be found by inspecting the PDB Structure Neighbor lists. This is because structure is far more conserved than sequence. That is, very remote evolutionary relationships can be identified by structure comparison that would otherwise be unidentifiable via sequence comparison alone. Examples of such unexpected and intriguing relationships include the remarkable similarity between the bacterial toxin colicin A and eukaryotic globins, as well as similarities between the eukaryotic POU-specific DNA-binding domain and the bacterial λ repressor (Dietmann et al., 2001).

The primary purpose of PDB is to store and distribute macromolecular structure files. Hence, through the Structure Explorer, users also can download and display coordinate files. The standard format for protein structure files is called PDB format (Figure 9.5). This is a machine- and human-readable format that allows information about the protein, the depositors, the sequence, the secondary structure, and the x, y, and z coordinates to be stored and read. The PDB format is quite archaic and it reflects the state of computation in the early 1970s, when PDB was established. As a result, each line in a PDB entry must have a seven-letter (or less) tag, followed by an exact number of spaces, which in turn is followed by the information (all in upper case) relevant to that tag. Each PDB file is structured almost identically with the first few lines (labeled HEADER, CMPND, SOURCE, AUTHOR, or JRNL) indicating the PDB ID, deposition date, protein, source organism, author, and journal where the structure was published. The next set of lines (labeled REMARK) provide additional details on the resolution, R factor, methods used to solve the structure, number of molecules in the asymmetric unit, and so on, mostly in free text format. The sequence (labeled SEQRES) is presented using the now-archaic three-letter amino code, followed by HET and FORMUL labels indicating the names and chemical formulae of heteroatoms (non-amino acid moieties found in the structure). The secondary structure, as identified by the depositor, is indicated by HELIX, SHEET, TURN, and SSBOND tags.

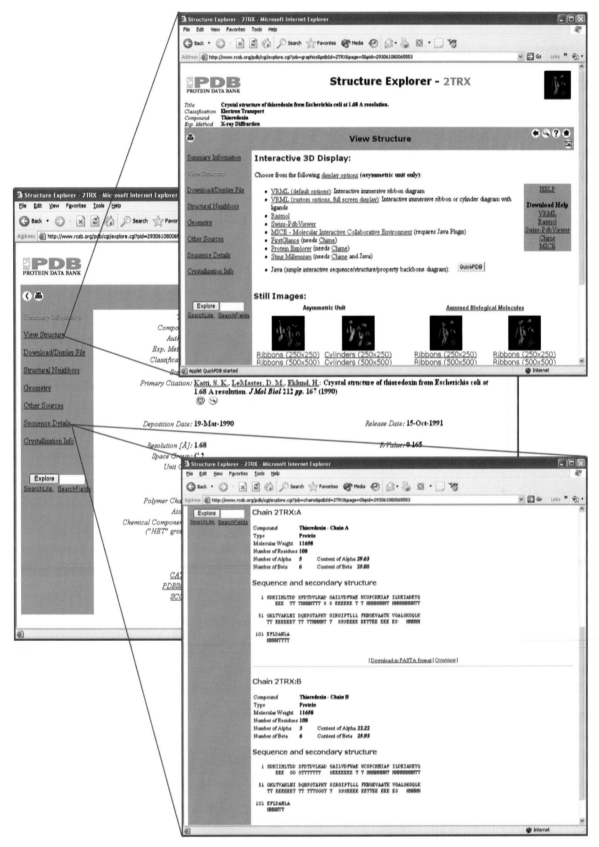

FIGURE 9.2 **Examples of the type of information that can be obtained from the Structure Explorer window, including three-dimensional structure views, sequence details, geometry, and coordinates.**

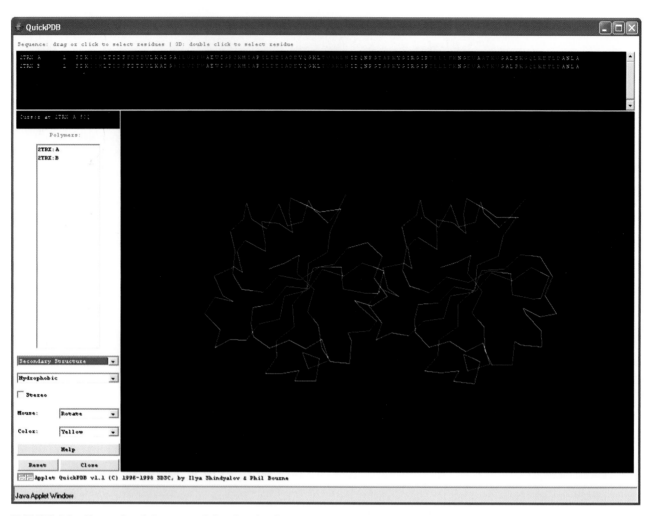

FIGURE 9.3 Example of the type of simple wire frame structure generated by the QuickPDB applet for 2TRX. Both the A and B chains are shown, with the A chain being colored according to its secondary structure.

These first 100 or so lines constitute the "header" in a PDB file and provide a useful overview of the protein and the quality of the structure. The next set of lines in a PDB file provide the atomic coordinates. These are always labeled by the ATOM tag. Up to 10 columns of text and numbers follow each ATOM tag, including the atom number, atom label (e.g., CA = α carbon, C = carbonyl carbon), residue name (three-letter code), chain number or letter, residue number, X coordinate (in Angstroms), Y coordinate (in Angstroms), Z coordinate (in Angstroms), occupancy (usually 1.00), and thermal B factor (a measure of mobility).

PDB format, although generally easy for a human to read, can be quite confounding for a computer to read. For instance, there are frequent exceptions and variations in the labeling, numbering, and formatting of many PDB files, particularly those deposited before 1995. Furthermore, the programs that read PDB-formatted files

must have certain chemical knowledge built into them; that is, the connections and bonds between atoms must be known (or inferred), because this connectivity information is not provided in the PDB file. Additionally, there is no formal data dictionary that describes all the rules for writing or reading a PDB file. This makes writing programs to handle, analyze, and view PDB files quite a challenge.

Because of the inconsistencies, informality, and archaic nature of the PDB format, there have been a number of efforts to correct or migrate PDB files to a more consistent and modern file format. Currently, the PDB is storing its files (internally) in a format called mmCIF (for macromolecular Crystallographic Information File), which is based on the CIF format used by small molecule crystallographers (Hall et al., 1991). The mmCIF format is a simple and consistent data representation for exchanging and archiving structural data that is

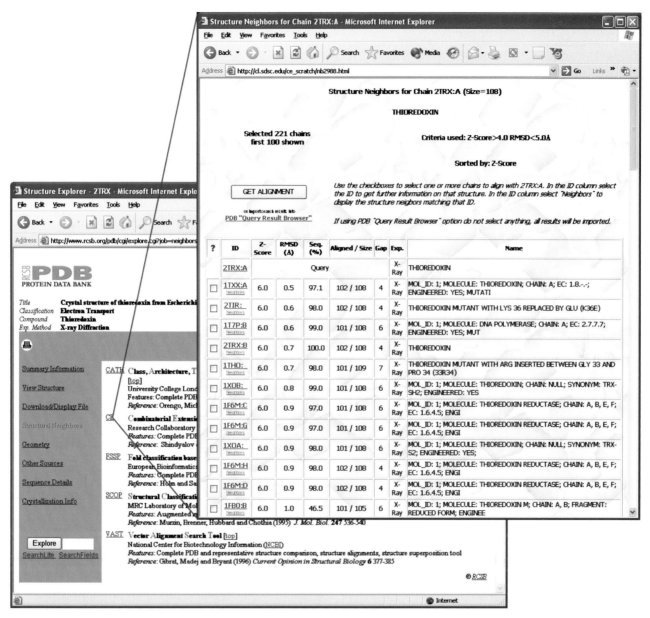

FIGURE 9.4 **A screen shot illustrating the structural neighbors of *E. coli* thioredoxin as determined using the CE (combinatorial extension) search tool. The list includes several dozen proteins with detectable (<5 Å RMSD) similarity.**

endorsed by a number of international agencies. By coupling the mmCIF format with the STAR (Self-defining Text Archival and Retrieval) method of encoding rules, PDB now has a modern file format and a robust ontology (Westbrook and Bourne, 2000). Other groups have worked on converting the PDB format to ASN.1 (Abstract Syntax Notation) or a range of eXtensible Markup Language (XML/BioML/PROXiML) variations, all of which are modern, robust file formats. However, because so many software packages have already been written to

handle PDB-formatted files and relatively few have been written to handle mmCIF/STAR, ASN.1, or XML, it is likely that the PDB format will be around for a long time.

▌OTHER STRUCTURE DATABASES

PDB is not the only repository of structural data. In fact, there are a growing number of secondary or curated structure databases that take the raw data from PDB and

```
HEADER      ELECTRON TRANSPORT                    19-MAR-90   2TRX       2TRXA   1
COMPND      THIOREDOXIN                                                  2TRXA   2
SOURCE      (ESCHERICHIA $COLI)                                          2TRX    4
AUTHOR      S.K.KATTI,D.M.LE*MASTER,H.EKLUND                             2TRX    5
JRNL        AUTH   S.K.KATTI,D.M.LE*MASTER,H.EKLUND                      2TRX    7
JRNL        TITL   CRYSTAL STRUCTURE OF THIOREDOXIN FROM ESCHERICHIA     2TRX    8
JRNL        TITL 2 $COLI AT 1.68 ANGSTROMS RESOLUTION                    2TRX    9
JRNL        REF    J.MOL.BIOL.                    V. 212   167 1990      2TRX   10
JRNL        REFN   ASTM JMOBAK   UK ISSN 0022-2836                 070   2TRX   11
REMARK   2                                                               2TRX   31
REMARK   2 RESOLUTION. 1.68 ANGSTROMS.                                   2TRX   32
REMARK   3                                                               2TRX   33
REMARK   3 REFINEMENT. BY THE RESTRAINED LEAST-SQUARES PROCEDURE OF J.   2TRX   34
REMARK   3  KONNERT AND W. HENDRICKSON AS MODIFIED BY B. FINZEL          2TRX   35
REMARK   3  (PROGRAM *PROFFT*).  THE R VALUE IS 0.165 FOR 25969          2TRX   36
REMARK   3  REFLECTIONS IN THE RESOLUTION RANGE 8.0 TO 1.68 ANGSTROMS    2TRX   37
REMARK   3  WITH FOBS .GT. 3.0*SIGMA(FOBS)                               2TRX   38
REMARK   3                                                               2TRX   39
SEQRES   1 A  108  SER ASP LYS ILE ILE HIS LEU THR ASP ASP SER PHE ASP   2TRX   74
SEQRES   2 A  108  THR ASP VAL LEU LYS ALA ASP GLY ALA ILE LEU VAL ASP   2TRX   75
SEQRES   3 A  108  PHE TRP ALA GLU TRP CYS GLY PRO CYS LYS MET ILE ALA   2TRX   76
SEQRES   4 A  108  PRO ILE LEU ASP GLU ILE ALA ASP GLU TYR GLN GLY LYS   2TRX   77
SEQRES   5 A  108  LEU THR VAL ALA LYS LEU ASN ILE ASP GLN ASN PRO GLY   2TRX   78
SEQRES   6 A  108  THR ALA PRO LYS TYR GLY ILE ARG GLY ILE PRO THR LEU   2TRX   79
SEQRES   7 A  108  LEU LEU PHE LYS ASN GLY GLU VAL ALA ALA THR LYS VAL   2TRX   80
SEQRES   8 A  108  GLY ALA LEU SER LYS GLY GLN LEU LYS GLU PHE LEU ASP   2TRX   81
SEQRES   9 A  108  ALA ASN LEU ALA                                       2TRX   82
HET    MPD  606       8       2-METHYL-2,4-PENTANEDIOL                   2TRX  107
HET    MPD  607       8       2-METHYL-2,4-PENTANEDIOL                   2TRX  108
HET    MPD  608       8       2-METHYL-2,4-PENTANEDIOL                   2TRX  109
FORMUL   3   CU    2(CU1 ++)                                             2TRX  110
FORMUL   4   MPD   8(C6 H14 O2)                                          2TRX  111
FORMUL   5   HOH   *140(H2 O1)                                           2TRX  112
HELIX    1 A1A SER A   11  LEU A   17  1 DISORDERED IN MOLECULE B        2TRX  113
HELIX    2 A2A CYS A   32  TYR A   49  1 BENT BY 30 DEGREES AT RES 39    2TRX  114
HELIX    3 A3A ASN A   59  ASN A   63  1                                 2TRX  115
HELIX    4 31A THR A   66  TYR A   70  5 DISTORTED H-BONDING C-TERMINS   2TRX  116
HELIX    5 A4A SER A   95  LEU A  107  1                                 2TRX  117
HELIX    6 A1B SER B   11  LEU B   17  1 DISORDERED IN MOLECULE B        2TRX  118
SSBOND   1 CYS A   32    CYS A   35                                      2TRX  143
ATOM     1  N   SER A   1      21.389  25.406  -4.628  1.00 23.22        2TRX  152
ATOM     2  CA  SER A   1      21.628  26.691  -3.983  1.00 24.42        2TRX  153
ATOM     3  C   SER A   1      20.937  26.944  -2.679  1.00 24.21        2TRX  154
ATOM     4  O   SER A   1      21.072  28.079  -2.093  1.00 24.97        2TRX  155
ATOM     5  CB  SER A   1      21.117  27.770  -5.002  1.00 28.27        2TRX  156
ATOM     6  OG  SER A   1      22.276  27.925  -5.861  1.00 32.61        2TRX  157
ATOM     7  N   ASP A   2      20.173  26.028  -2.163  1.00 21.39        2TRX  158
ATOM     8  CA  ASP A   2      19.395  26.125  -0.949  1.00 21.57        2TRX  159
ATOM     9  C   ASP A   2      20.264  26.214   0.297  1.00 20.89        2TRX  160
ATOM    10  O   ASP A   2      19.760  26.575   1.371  1.00 21.49        2TRX  161
ATOM    11  CB  ASP A   2      18.439  24.914  -0.856  1.00 22.14        2TRX  162
ATOM    22  CE  LYS A   3      21.620  21.104   2.844  1.00 25.84        2TRX  173
ATOM    23  NZ  LYS A   3      20.830  20.757   1.615  1.00 25.55        2TRX  174
```

FIGURE 9.5 A sample listing of a PDB formatted file for 2TRX. Certain parts of the file have been removed for brevity.

massage or combine it with other data to create some very useful resources. Some of these databases are discussed below.

MSD

The Macromolecular Structure Database (MSD) is the European equivalent to PDB and contains all of the structures found in the American version of PDB. It is maintained at the European Bioinformatics Institute (EBI) and is closely linked with RCSB. MSD allows researchers to deposit structures to the Electron Microscopy Database (EMDB) using EMDep (the European equivalent of ADIT). These structures are then forwarded to RCSB. MSD supports a very broad array of queries and specialized structure databases, with a major emphasis on ligands, binding sites, and protein interactions. MSD also maintains a large database of quaternary structure data that can be accessed through its Protein Quaternary Structure (PQS) query form. MSD's general structure browser, called OCA (one letter removed from PDB, as HAL is from IBM) is a much more comprehensive and user-friendly than PDB's SearchLite or SearchFields. More importantly, OCA supports facile FASTA sequence queries.

MMDB

The Molecular Modeling Database (MMDB) at the National Center for Biotechnology Information (NCBI) is Entrez's three-dimensional structure database (Chen et al., 2003). MMDB is fully integrated into Entrez's PubMed database, with links to the NCBI taxonomy database, Conserved Domain Database (CCDB), precomputed BLAST sequence neighbors, precomputed VAST structural neighbors, and a Cn3D visualization tool. Structural information about a given molecule can be accessed through Entrez's Structure Summary page, which in turn links to MMDB. The data stored in MMDB is uploaded from PDB, checked for exact agreement between coordinate and sequence data, corrected (if necessary), and then mapped to NCBI's ASN.1 format. MMDB is a wonderful example of how structural data can be integrated into a variety of other biomedical data to enrich the content mutually.

PDBSum

The PDBSum database (Laskowski, 2001), which is maintained in the United Kingdom, is a kind of PDBlite database that contains both summary information and derived data from existing PDB entries. The summary information contained in PDBSum is intended to provide a quick overview of the contents of each PDB entry in terms of numbers of protein chains, ligands, metal ions, and the like. The derived data include PROMOTIF analyses, PROCHECK and WHATCHECK statistics, as well as extensive links to CATH, SCOP, OCA, IMB, and other databases.

TargetDB

TargetDB is maintained at RCSB and is a centralized target registry for sequences from structural genomics projects being conducted worldwide (Westbrook et al., 2003). Because structural genomics and proteomics projects are tasked with solving many structures very quickly and because there are so many (>15) structural genomics initiatives, the intent of TargetDB is to ensure that structural biologists are not duplicating their efforts in selecting proteins and solving their structures. TargetDB reports the state or progress a particular genomics center has made on the cloning, production, labeling, crystallization, structure determination, and deposition of proteins and protein structures. Information in TargetDB is updated weekly from many sources, and the database may be searched using keywords (name, project, organism, etc.) or by sequence (using FASTA). Although TargetDB is not strictly a structure database, it is a vital resource for structural biologists and an excellent example how bioinformatics methods can be used to facilitate and coordinate structural biology.

▌ VISUALIZING PROTEINS

As we have seen from the previous section, protein coordinate files are relatively dull looking. They are simply lists of x, y, and z coordinates and provide no visual cues as to what the molecule or molecules actually look like. Before the advent of computer visualization software, structural biologists had to build physical models of protein structures from wood, metal, or plastic components to obtain a "picture" of the structure they had just determined. This obviously proved very challenging—and limiting. To solve these problems, a number of structural biologists developed ingenious ideas to easily visualize or conveniently understand protein structures. One particular approach that is still widely used today was developed by G.N. Ramachandran et al. in 1963 and it is called the Ramachandran plot. Ramachandran's approach was to convert protein x, y, and z (or absolute) coordinates into "internal" coordinates. Internal coordinates are coordinates that do not need or are not defined by an origin. Specifically, Ramachandran realized proteins could be described by a series of torsion or dihedral angles that describe the relative orientation of adjacent peptide bonds. The backbone torsion angles are known as ϕ (phi) and ψ (psi) angles. The ϕ angle is defined as the dihedral angle along the N—Ca bond, whereas the ψ angle is defined as the dihedral angle along the Ca—C bond. Each residue in a protein can be defined by one ϕ and one ψ angle. By plotting the backbone torsion and dihedral angles of each residue in a simple two-dimensional scatter plot, with the ϕ angles on the x-axis and the ψ angles on the y-axis, it is possible to create a very compact and informative representation of a protein structure (Figure 9.6). As seen in this Ramachandran plot, certain residues cluster in the upper left of this plot with a center around the ϕ, ψ coordinates ($-120°$, $120°$). This cluster corresponds to residues in β sheets. Another cluster is seen around ($-60°$, $-40°$). This cluster corresponds to the residues found in helices. Most (approximately 75%) of the rest of the Ramachandran plot is empty because side chain clashes prevent the folded protein from accessing these "disallowed" dihedral angles.

Ramachandran plots occasionally are used to estimate the quantity of a particular secondary structure in a protein by simple inspection. However, their greatest utility is in assessing the quality of protein structures. By studying a large number of high-quality structures and looking at their Ramachandran plots, it has been discovered that very good structures exhibit very tight clustering patterns and that relatively few residues are found to lie outside these tight clusters or "allowed" dihedral regions (Laskowski et al., 1993). Protein structures that are found to have a high percentage (>15%) of nonglycine residues in disallowed regions inevitably are found to be poor-quality structures. Because of their usefulness and simplicity, many software packages now offer Ramachandran plots as part of their structure visualization and evaluation tools (Laskowski et al., 1993; Willard et al., 2003).

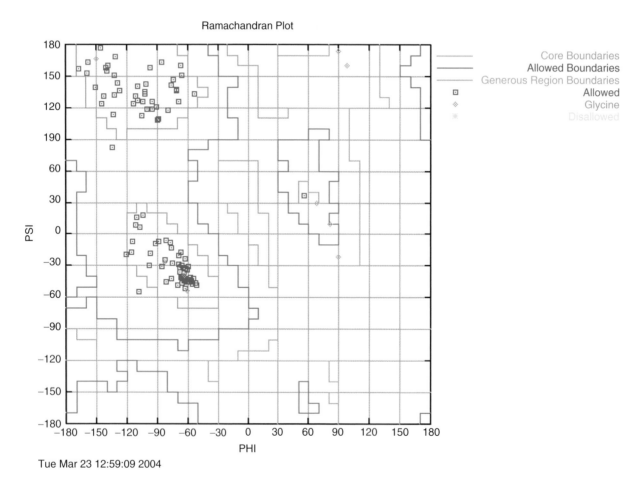

Tue Mar 23 12:59:09 2004

FIGURE 9.6 A Ramachandran plot for the protein **2TRX** as generated using the program **VADAR**. Each point in the plot corresponds to a single residue in the protein. The "Core Boundaries" or red line on the plot delineate the region in the Ramachandran plot where approximately 85% of residues should be found in good quality structures. The "Allowed Boundaries" (green line) delineate the region where approximately 10% of residues should be found. Residues falling in the "Generously Allowed Boundaries" (yellow line) or outside this region indicate residues that may have serious steric problems. Glycine residues are the exception as they can appear anywhere in the plot.

THREE-DIMENSIONAL VISUALIZATION PACKAGES

Of course, with today's high-speed computers and high-end graphics cards, we are not restricted to viewing protein structures through simple scatter plots. Three-dimensional structure visualization using a computer is now commonplace, and we no longer need thread and sealing wax to create a high-quality protein model. Indeed, as can be seen in Figures 9.4 and 9.5, it is actually quite simple to create a virtual protein model that looks every bit as real as the protein molecule itself. These new and powerful three-dimensional visualization packages offer an appealing array of options to represent, manipulate, and render protein structures. Macromolecules can

now be colored, shadowed, tinted, textured, and illuminated in thousands of different ways to create very compelling and very impressive molecular art. Furthermore, molecules can be seamlessly zoomed, rotated, shrunk, and expanded at the touch of a mouse button.

Although the possibilities are almost limitless in the ways we can render, color, and manipulate structures, we still are quite limited in the way in which proteins can be represented in a manner that is understandable. Typically, protein structures can be drawn in just four standard ways: as wire-frame models, as ball-and-stick representations, as CPK (Corey, Pauling, and Koltun) or space-filling models, and as ribbon diagrams (first suggested by Jane Richardson). These representations are shown in Figure 9.7 for the protein ubiquitin (1UBQ). Depending on what feature one may want to be

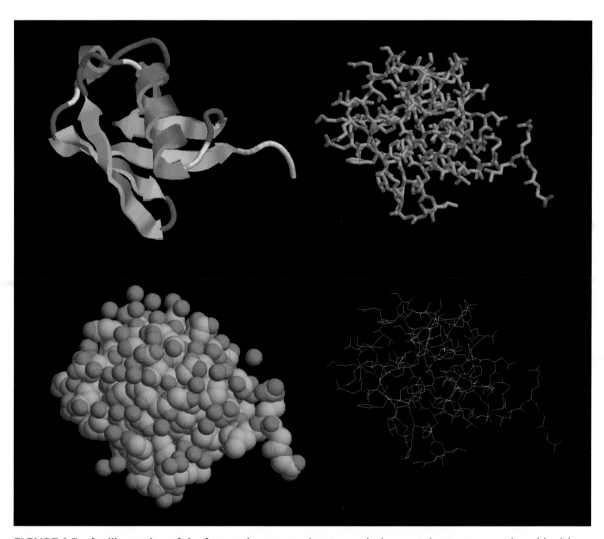

FIGURE 9.7 **An illustration of the four major approaches to rendering protein structures using ubiquitin (1UBQ) as an example. In the upper left is a ribbon diagram that accentuates secondary structure. In the upper right is a ball and stick diagram. In the lower left is the space-filling CPK model, and on the lower right is a wire-frame model.**

highlighted or shown (e.g., secondary structure, active site, atomic packing, etc.), different rendering methods must be chosen. Interestingly, many of these visualization options actually are throwbacks to the way proteins were modeled from wood, metal, and plastic in the 1960s or painted by artists in the 1970s. Nevertheless, these old-fashioned approaches to representing proteins are still very revealing.

Historically, protein visualization software was very expensive and could be run only on very specialized computers operated by highly trained experts. Today, just about anyone can model proteins. Much of this change has come about through major improvements in computer hardware, but also through the introduction and source code release of a software package called RasMol (Sayle & Milner-White, 1995). Originally introduced in 1993, RasMol (for RASter MOLecule) represented a major breakthrough in software-driven three-dimensional rendering. Its innovative code design and remarkably fast ray-tracing algorithms make even the slowest desktop computers appear to have ultrafast graphics engines. Because RasMol was coded in C and because the source code was made public, more than a dozen other visualization packages have been built based on RasMol's powerful rendering engine. Because RasMol was built during a period when the PDB file formats were quite inconsistent, the program uses a very cautious PDB parser and often recomputes information to determine bond existence or bond location. The last release of RasMol in 1999 (version 2.7.1) supported a number of features designed to handle mmCIF files, to display correlated disorder, to select different NMR models from an NMR ensemble, and to work with PostScript (MolScript; Kraulis, 1991) files. Because RasMol does not depend on a system-specific graphics library, it is able to run on just about any platform and operating system. This near-universality has made RasMol very popular. In fact, it is estimated that RasMol has more than one million users. Perhaps RasMol's biggest drawback is the fact that users must master RasMol's relatively awkward command-line language to fully tap into its remarkable capabilities.

With the appearance of the Internet and the desire to view molecules over the Web, a number of groups took advantage of RasMol's freely available source code to make more sophisticated, more user-friendly rendering packages. In 1997, MDL Information Systems converted a large portion of RasMol's C code to C++ and added new functionality, including surface rendering and animation to create a Netscape plug-in called Chime (for CHemical mIME, where MIME stands for Multipart Internet Mail Extension). Like RasMol, Chime was made freely available, leading to the development of even more freeware, with progressively more sophisticated user interfaces.

Now, most of today's visualization software has migrated completely away from mixed command-line interfaces found in RasMol toward intuitive graphical user interfaces with pull-down menus and mouse click-and-dragging operations to make the coloring, manipulation, and labeling of protein structures intuitive and simple.

Examples of these Chime-based packages include Protein Explorer, Sting Millenium, and FirstGlance. All are available at the RCSB Web site for downloading and all require the Chime plug-in. All three packages are compatible with most modern Web browsers on Mac OS or Windows platforms. Protein Explorer is particularly user friendly and feature rich, with context-sensitive help, a large selection of pull-down menus, support for display and animation of NMR ensembles, support for general animation, coloring by multiple sequence alignment, contact surface display, non-covalent bond finding, sequence to three-dimensional mapping, and a large selection of rendering or coloring options. Unfortunately, because Chime was built before the release of RasMol 2.7.1 (i.e., without any capability to read mmCIF files), neither Protein Explorer nor any of the other Chime-based packages is able to handle mmCIF files.

WebMol (Walther, 1997) is another example of a package built from RasMol, but in this case, the source code was converted from C to Java. Because most Web browsers support Java Virtual Machines (a Java interpreter), WebMol can be run directly on a browser as an applet or can be run separately as an application. As an applet, users do not have to worry about installing a plug-in or reconfiguring their browser. WebMol offers a broad selection of menu-driven operations that makes it very easy to learn and use.

Another particularly good macromolecular visualization package is called Cn3D ("see in 3D"). Cn3D (Hogue, 1997) is a visualization freeware package or helper application that allows users to view three-dimensional structures from MMDB via NCBI's Entrez retrieval service. Cn3D (version 4.1) is an open source package written in C++ that uses the OpenGL (Open Graphics Library) to render images. It is compatible with Windows, Mac OS, and Unix operating systems, but it must be downloaded and installed before it can be run. Cn3D offers superb, publication-quality graphics that generally are much better than what can be generated with Chime or RasMol-based packages. Cn3D has an impressive sequence-to-structure interface, a sophisticated alignment editing system, well-developed structure and alignment annotation features, and a close connectivity to VAST (the structure alignment tool from NCBI; see Chapter 3). Cn3D's primary limitation is that it only accepts coordinate files in ASN.1 format, meaning that only files from MMDB can be viewed with Cn3D. The use of ASN.1 formatted files allows Cn3D to avoid some of the pitfalls and complications of handling PDB files (such as parsing, validation, and exception handling). However, it also means that users cannot exchange files easily or move between other visualization packages. Likewise, users generally cannot view a newly released structure from PDB until it has been converted to ASN.1 and deposited in the MMDB, which may take several weeks.

Another important and popular visualization package is known as SwissPDB-Viewer or DeepView (Kaplan & Littlejohn, 2001). This is probably the most powerful, freely available molecular modeling and visualization system available. DeepView is a closed-source program from GlaxoWellcome that is compatible with Windows, Mac OS, SGI, and Linux operating systems. Like Cn3D, it uses OpenGL for its graphics handling routines, allowing for some impressive images to be generated. DeepView supports a range of capabilities, including surface rendering, homology modeling, structure quality (threading) evaluation, energy minimization, site-directed mutagenesis, loop rebuilding, electrostatic field calculation, structure superposition, Ramachandran plot generation, and sequence-structure viewing. Because DeepView offers so much, it is not the most user-friendly package, especially for novices. Nevertheless, an excellent tutorial prepared by Gale Rhodes at the University of Southern Maine offers a fine starting point that allows even beginners to learn how to use this superb visualization and modeling package. A particularly appealing feature of DeepView is its capacity to export files that are compatible with the freeware ray-tracing package called POV-Ray (for Persistence Of Vision–Ray Tracing). POV-Ray allows the more artistically inclined modelers to create stunning images of proteins and protein complexes that are suitable for an art gallery or even a journal cover (Figure 9.8).

There are perhaps more than two dozen freely available macromolecular visualization programs that can be found on the Web. Selecting the best one is very much an individual decision, not unlike choosing a computer or buying a stereo system. Ease of use, stability, platform compatibility, and function are important considerations. Regardless of the program chosen, it is important to remember that the role of visualization software ultimately is to create an image that can convey important scientific information in a visually pleasing manner. Taking the time to create a high-quality image and using the right program for the right kind of task can make a tremendous difference to the message one is trying to deliver. In this regard, there are a number of excellent macromolecular "photo galleries" listed at the end of this chapter. It is highly recommended that readers take the time to study the images contained in these sites. These examples nicely demonstrate the rendering capabilities of several software packages and beautifully

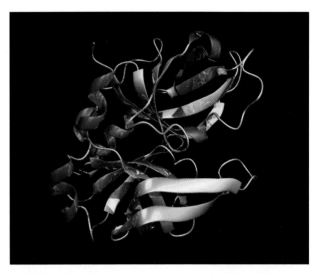

FIGURE 9.8   An example of the high-quality images that can be created using advanced ray tracing methods found in POV-Ray. This image, derived from the coordinates of HAV-3C protease, was prepared by Dr. Alan Gibbs.

illustrate some of the more compelling ways of presenting protein structure data. As the old Chinese proverb says, a picture can be worth a thousand words.

PROTEIN STRUCTURE PREDICTION

Ever since the first protein structure was determined, computational biologists and computational chemists have attempted to develop software that could predict the three-dimensional structure of proteins, using only their sequence as input. Indeed, many of the first bioinformatics programs ever written were directed at trying to solve the "protein folding problem." Even though the field is more than 40 years old, protein structure prediction continues to be one of the most active areas in all of bioinformatics research, with hundreds of papers being published on the subject each year. Encouragingly, some progress has been made and it is now possible to predict or model the three-dimensional structure of proteins using at least three different methods: homology (or comparative) modeling, threading, or ab initio methods. All three methods are fundamentally predictive, meaning that the structures generated are models and are not based on raw experimental data derived from X-ray diffraction or NMR experiments. Rather, each of these predictive approaches attempts to build on prior knowledge about protein structure and to extrapolate these principles towards the generation of new structures.

Homology Modeling

Of the three predictive methods that are currently available, the most powerful and accurate approach is homology modeling. Homology (or comparative) modeling is a robust technique for "predicting" or generating detailed three-dimensional structures of proteins based on the coordinates of known homologs found in PDB. In homology modeling, the quality of the model strongly depends on the degree of similarity between the query sequence and the matching database sequence, with proteins sharing the highest degree of similarity being modeled best. As a general rule, the average coordinate agreement between the modeled structure and the actual structure drops by approximately 0.3 Å for each 10% reduction in sequence identity. Furthermore, homology modeling generally cannot be used for predicting structures of proteins having less than 30% sequence identity to a target protein already in PDB. However, in certain rare cases, homology modeling can be used to generate a reliable three-dimensional structural model of a protein with much less than 20% sequence identity.

Homology modeling is a multistep process that makes use of sequence alignment, structure modification, database searches, energy minimization, and structure evaluation to generate a structure. More specifically, homology modeling can be decomposed into five different steps:

1. Aligning the query or unknown protein sequence to the sequence of a known structure

2. Using the alignment to select and replace backbone segments (usually loops that are contained in a special loop library) that need to altered because of insertions or deletions

3. Replacing side chains that have been changed due to the alignment or loop insertion and deletion process

4. Refining the model using energy minimization to relieve collisions or steric strains

5. Validating the model using visual inspection and software validation tools.

The most critical step to homology modeling is the first step—alignment. An incorrect alignment will have a domino-like effect by increasingly disrupting the remaining steps, eventually leading to a seriously flawed model. To reduce the problems of a single pairwise alignment error, many homology modeling packages generate alignments from multiple database homologs (if they exist) to improve the reliability of the all-important alignment step.

Originally, homology modeling was a very interactive, manually intensive process that depended critically on the expertise of the user and the availability of specialized three-dimensional visualization software

and hardware. Fortunately, many of these complex, time-consuming steps have been automated, and now homology modeling can be carried out by just about anyone on just about any computer. In addition to several high-quality commercial packages, there are now a number of excellent, freely available homology modeling packages, including Modeller (Sali, 1998), DeepView, and WHATIF (Krieger et al., 2003) that can be downloaded and installed on the Unix and Windows platforms. More recently, homology modeling has become available on the Web. These Web-accessible services include the SWISS-MODEL server (Schwede et al., 2003), the CPH Models server, and the SDSC1 server (their Web site addresses are listed at the end of this chapter). Typically, all one has to do is type or paste in the sequence of the protein of interest and press the Submit button. A three-dimensional structure will be returned to the user, via E-mail, within a few minutes. SWISS-MODEL is particularly popular (more than 120,000 requests per year) because it is very accurate, is constantly updated, provides a comprehensive report on the modeled structure quality, and allows various levels of user interactivity. An example of a homology model generated for *Escherichia coli* thioredoxin (generated from a template with just 26% sequence identity) is shown in Figure 9.9.

Most published homology modeling programs and servers are tested rigorously, and so the results from any one package or server generally can be trusted. The Evaluation of Structure Prediction Servers (EVA) Web site (Chapter 8) maintains a continuously updated list and ranking of at least five homology and comparative modeling servers. Currently, SDSC1 and SWISS-MODEL seem to provide the best performance of the participating homology modeling servers.

Threading

Threading (or fold recognition) is a method for predicting the structure, or recognizing a common fold in proteins having essentially no sequence homology, to any protein in PDB. That is, threading is a structure prediction technique that picks up where homology modeling leaves off. Unlike homology modeling, which strives for accurate models, threading is limited to generating very approximate models or (more usually) suggesting very approximate folds (approximately 5 Å RMSD). Threading received its name because it superficially resembles the method used to thread a thin tube down or through a plumbing pipe system. In the course of threading the tube or probe (called a *snake*) through the pipe, the wire takes on the shape of the surrounding pipe (Figure 9.10). If one views the backbone structure of a protein as being very similar to a highly contorted hollow pipe (like an elaborate plumbing system), one could ask, "What

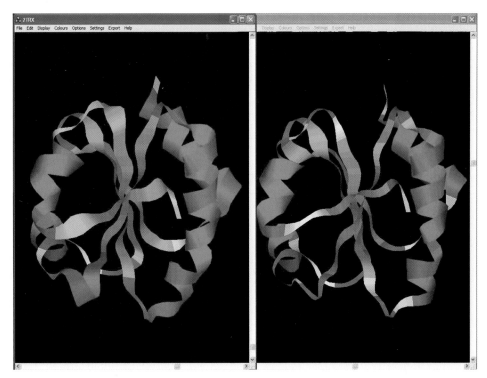

FIGURE 9.9 An illustration of a homology model (on right) of *E. coli* thioredoxin generated using human thioredoxin (3TRX; 26% sequence identity) as a template. The actual X-ray structure of *E. coli* thioredoxin is shown on the left. Note the very good overall similarity.

Fold Database (PDB)

THREADINGSEQNCEECNQESGNI
ERHTHREADINGSEQNCETHREAD
GSEQNCEQCQESGIDAERTHR...

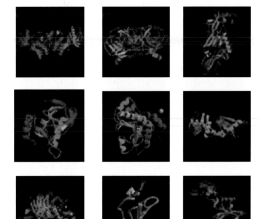

FIGURE 9.10 A schematic illustration of how threading is performed. A query protein with the sequence **THREADINGSE** .... (see top left) is passed through, one residue at a time, the three-dimensional structure of each protein in a fold database (shown by the structures on the right). The energy or quality of the fit is evaluated each time, with the highest scoring match being the most likely fold.

would happen if we threaded a completely different protein sequence through this backbone pipe?" Intuitively, one would expect that if the "probe" sequence resembled the sequence belonging to the original "pipe," then the fit would be rather good (with the amino acid side chains packing closely against one another). If, however, the probe sequence was very different than the pipe sequence, then one might find that when the probe sequence is finally fed through the pipe, it would fit rather poorly, with side chains smashing into each other or pointing in the wrong direction.

If one were to take this threading procedure one step further and automate the process, then it would be possible to run hundreds or thousands of different probe sequences through this protein backbone pipe, one at a time. As each sequence is fed through, the fit is evaluated to determine which sequence fits best with the given template pipe or backbone fold. This evaluation may be carried out quickly using some empirical energy term or some measure of packing efficiency (more on this later). In this way, it is possible to assess which protein sequences are compatible with the given backbone fold. Clearly, one would expect that those sequences that are highly homologous to the original template sequence should fit best. However, it has also been found that this simple-minded approach occasionally can reveal that some completely unrelated sequences also can fit into this fold. When these kinds of sequences are discovered, you are, in effect, predicting the tertiary fold of an unknown protein (i.e., three-dimensional structure prediction).

Two approaches to threading exist. One is called *three-dimensional threading*, which is classified as a distance-based method (DBM). The other is called *two-dimensional threading*, which is classified as a prediction-based method (PBM). Three-dimensional threading was first described in the early 1980s (Novotny et al., 1984) and later "rediscovered" approximately 10 years later (Jones et al., 1992; Sippl & Weitckus; 1992, Bryant & Lawrence, 1993) when the concept of heuristic potential functions matured. Three-dimensional threading uses distance-based or profile-based (Bowie et al., 1991) energy functions and technically resembles the pipe threading description given earlier. In three-dimensional threading, coordinates corresponding to the hypothesized protein fold actually are calculated, and the pseudoenergy functions are evaluated on the basis of these three-dimensional coordinates. Three-dimensional threading is a powerful approach not only to predicting the structure of unknown proteins, but also for evaluating the structural quality of known proteins.

Just like three-dimensional threading, two-dimensional threading was first described in mid 1980s (Sheridan et al., 1985) and then was rediscovered in the mid 1990s (Fischer & Eisenberg, 1996; Rost et al., 1997) when the reliability of secondary structure predictions started improving. Rather than relying on three-dimensional coordinates to evaluate the quality of a fold, two-dimensional threading actually uses secondary structure as the primary evaluation criterion. Indeed, two-dimensional threading is based on the simple observation that secondary structure is more conserved than primary structure (sequence). Therefore, proteins that have lost detectable similarity at the sequence level still could be expected to maintain some similarity at the secondary structure level.

Over the past few years, two-dimensional threading has matured so that secondary structure, solvent accessibility, and sequence information can now be used in the evaluation process. The advantage that two-dimensional threading has over three-dimensional threading is that all this structural information can be encoded into a one-dimensional string of symbols (i.e., a pseudosequence). This allows one to use standard sequence comparison tools, like dynamic programming, to compare a query sequence or secondary structure rapidly with a database of sequences and secondary structures. Consequently, two-dimensional threading is ten to 100 times faster than distance-based three-dimensional threading approaches. Furthermore, two-dimensional threading seems to give comparable (and in some cases, even better) results than three-dimensional threading in terms of fold recognition.

Three-dimensional structures or folds predicted from threading techniques are not generally of high quality (RMSD > 3 Å). However, they can and do reveal the approximate shape and overall fold of proteins that seem to have no known structural homologs. One of the more high-profile and successful examples of threading occurred several years ago when it was used to model the approximate structure of leptin, a protein that plays an important role in obesity, for which no known sequence or structural homolog was previously known (Madej et al., 1995). The threading model suggested a general mechanism for the protein's activity that eventually was found to be quite accurate.

There are a large number of threading services (mostly two-dimensional threading variants) available over the Web. Web site addresses for some of the more popular ones are listed at the end of this chapter. Just as with homology and comparative modeling, the EVA Web site maintains a continuously updated list and ranking of almost a dozen different threading servers, including BLAST and PSI-BLAST (which are not strictly threading servers, just very good alignment servers). Currently, SAMt99, three-dimensional-PSSM, and FUGUE seem to provide the best performance of the participating threading servers. More recently, the use of multiple threading servers (so-called metaservers), which combine the results of several predictions, seems to be yielding the best results.

Ab Initio Structure Prediction

Ab initio prediction literally means "predicting from the beginning." In other words, this approach attempts to predict protein structures without prior knowledge of any related three-dimensional structure. *Ab initio* prediction is generally aimed at identifying "new" folds or folds for which there is no sequence similarity whatsoever to existing structures. The methods are still very experimental and quite unreliable, because the protein folding problem has not yet been solved. Therefore, unless it is in the hands of experts, models generated through ab initio methods generally are too unreliable to be used. Nevertheless, the computational approaches being developed by *ab initio* structure prediction experts are having an impact both in threading and homology modeling. Similarly, the models generated by these approaches can, in some cases, provide useful hypotheses or starting points for further experiments. Every two years, a friendly competition is held among protein structure predictors called the Critical Assessment of Structure Prediction, or CASP. The purpose of CASP is to provide an independent, unbiased, or "blind" assessment of different programs or methods in *ab initio* structure prediction. The organizers of CASP work with crystallographers and NMR spectroscopists, who provide coordinates of newly determined protein structures. The sequences for these structures are then sent to registered CASP predictors, who typically have six to eight weeks to generate structures and to deposit their predictions with the CASP organizers. After the competition closes, all the submitted structures are evaluated using a variety of structure comparison techniques (see next section). Based on the results of the most recent CASP competitions (CASP4, held in 2002, and CASP5, held in 2002), there is good evidence of significant improvement over the past ten years in the quality of these prediction methods. Among the best methods (the clear winner in the CASP4 contest and among the top six in CASP5) is a program called ROSETTA, developed by David Baker's lab (Bonneau et al., 2001). Although not yet publicly available, the concepts embodied in ROSETTA have proven to be very useful and are now in many other *ab initio* structure prediction programs and routines.

▍PROTEIN STRUCTURE EVALUATION

Whether the coordinates for a protein structure have been obtained experimentally (NMR or X-ray) or by modeling (homology or threading), it is always important to ask this one very important question: How good is this structure? A poor structure, like a poor model, can lead to misinterpretation of how a protein works, how it is related to other proteins, or where a potential ligand may or may not bind. However, a high-quality structure can reveal a tremendous amount of biologically important information and can serve as the basis to test new hypotheses on folding or function, to design and construct mutants, or to design new drugs. A large majority of the experimentally-determined structures in PDB are really quite excellent, and certainly most structural biologists strive to generate the best structures they can. However, there are at least a dozen examples of protein structures in PDB that have been found to be so seriously flawed that they had to be withdrawn (Hooft et al., 1996). There also are dozens of protein structures that are poorly resolved (>3 Å resolution), have mislabeled residues or atoms, are missing lengthy tracts of sequence, or provide only Cα coordinates. With the advent of NMR spectroscopy as an alternative to X-ray crystallography, we are now seeing that many protein structures or parts of protein structures actually differ quite substantially between solution and solid (crystal) state conditions. Even among different crystal forms of the same protein, it is quite normal see an average difference of ± 0.5 Å in atomic displacement or $\pm 7°$ in backbone dihedral angle variation. These structural variations are not restricted to experimentally determined structures. For instance, homology models invariably exhibit differences between themselves and the real structure (once determined), with the extent of the differences increasing by approximately 0.3 Å for each 10% drop in sequence identity. In addition, homology models frequently are found to have at least one or two regions that are modeled incorrectly (either because of sequence alignment errors, loop insertion errors, or energy refinement errors). Although these comments may seem to cast doubt on the reliability and usefulness of many protein structures, their intent primarily is to inject an appropriate degree of caution or skepticism with which all scientific data should be treated. These comments also are intended to underline the importance of always trying to answer the question we began with: How good is this protein structure?

Protein structures are remarkably complex and highly variable. This complexity makes it almost impossible simply to look at a protein structure and to assess its quality or correctness. However, by studying large numbers of protein structures and by focusing on those structures that exhibit particularly good resolution, structural biologists have realized that there are some near-universal characteristics to high-quality structures. In particular, good protein structures (here we are primarily referring to water-soluble proteins) should:

1. Minimize the number of torsion angles in disallowed regions of the Ramachandran plot

2. Maximize the number of hydrogen bonds

3. Minimize the number of exposed hydrophobic residues

4. Maximize the number of exposed polar or charged residues

5. Minimize the number of interstitial cavities or packing defects

6. Minimize the number of number of nonbonded atoms within 2.6 Å

7. Minimize the standard deviation in hydrogen bond energies

8. Minimize the standard deviation in dihedral angles for helices

9. Have a low R factor (<0.20 for X-ray structures) or a low backbone RMSD value (<0.8 Å for NMR structure ensembles).

Some of these characteristics or features also seem to represent underlying rules of protein folding. Therefore, it is not surprising that they should be reiterated in the structural features of most proteins. Interestingly, many of these characteristics also can be quantified or measured directly from protein coordinate data. These observations have led to the development of a number of excellent software programs for automatically evaluating protein structures and protein models, including the Dictionary of Secondary Structure for Proteins (DSSP; Kabsch & Sander, 1983), PROCHECK (Laskowski et al., 1993), VADAR (Willard et al., 2003), and Verify3D (Bowie et al., 1991).

DSSP

Originally described in 1983, DSSP has become one of the standard tools that structural biologists and bioinformaticians routinely use to evaluate and annotate protein structures. DSSP is an open-source program, written in Pascal and designed to produce a compact, sequence-centric summary of local protein structure features. It is also available through a Web server. DSSP uses a very stringent method to identify hydrogen bonds and hydrogen bonding patterns, which in turn are used to identify and label seven different kinds of secondary structures (α helices [H], 3/10 helices [G], π helices [I], β bridges [B], extended β strands [E], hydrogen bonded turns [T], and bends [S]). DSSP's definition of secondary structure has become the *de facto* standard for secondary structure annotation in PDB and the reference set for most secondary structure prediction schemes. In addition to performing automated secondary structure identification and assignment, DSSP also determines the accessible surface area of individual residues using the ANAREA algorithm. The results are presented in a simple digital scale (0–9), with 0 corresponding to fully buried and 9 being fully exposed. DSSP does not provide any formal assessment of an input structure per se, but its output can be (and is) used by other programs or by structural biologists to evaluate structures.

PROCHECK

This was perhaps the first quantitative protein structure evaluation program and is still one of the best available. It is used routinely by PDB in screening and evaluating newly deposited structures. PROCHECK may be downloaded and installed locally (it is compatible with the VAX and Unix platforms), or it may be accessed over the Web through the PDB Verification suite. PROCHECK accepts PDB coordinate files as input and uses DSSP to identify secondary structure and to calculate accessible surface area. It also calculates torsion angles (backbone and side chain), bond angles, interatomic distances, and other properties. By comparing these values with those observed for very high-resolution or high-quality structures, PROCHECK is able to provide an estimate of the quality or equivalent resolution for any given query structure. One of PROCHECK's most appealing features is its colorful graphical reports that are generated automatically (including PostScript formatted Ramachandran plots, secondary structure mark-ups, and scatter plots), along with tables, explanations, and references (Figure 9.11). Inspection of these graphs or tables allows users to identify problem areas quickly or to zero-in on suspicious and unusual structural features. More recently, PROCHECK has been expanded to evaluate NMR structures quantitatively through a package called PROCHECK NMR (Laskowski et al., 1996).

VADAR

The Volume, Area, Dihedral Angle Reporter (VADAR) is a fully Web-enabled protein structure evaluation tool that accepts either PDB coordinates or PDB ID codes as input. Like the other programs already mentioned, VADAR measures dihedral angles, identifies hydrogen bonds, and measures interatomic distances to help evaluate protein structures. Unlike the other programs, however, VADAR uses a more comprehensive approach to identifying secondary structures (three methods are used to generate a consensus secondary structure). It also identifies and classifies β-turns, identifies side-chain hydrogen bonds, or salt-bridges, calculates packing volume (in Å^3), determines exact accessible surface areas (in Å^2), performs packing "defect" checks, performs buried charge evaluation, calculates threading and surface free energies, determines residue disposition, and compares many of these values with those that would be expected among high-quality structures. A variety of tables are generated for different parts of the protein (main chain and side chain), as well as a summary table describing

PROCIDICK

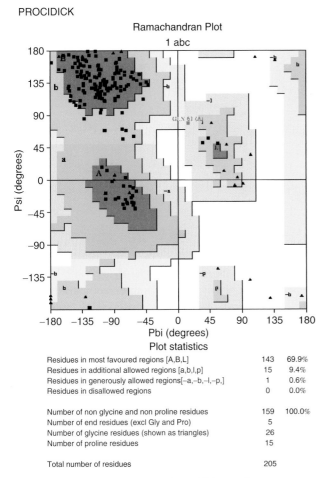

Ramachandran Plot

1 abc

FIGURE 9.11 **An example of the high-quality postscript output data from PROCHECK.**

and identifying suspicious features found in the protein. Ramachandran plots (with outliers marked) and structure quality graphs (JPG or PNG) also are automatically created. VADAR generates a huge amount of numerical output, which can intimidate many first-time users. However, as soon as one becomes familiar with the output, VADAR offers a very comprehensive and highly informative picture of protein structure.

Verify3D

Verify3D uses a form of three-dimensional threading to evaluate protein structure quality. Verify3D is based on the three-dimensional profile method developed by David Eisenberg and his students, James Bowie and Roland Lüthy. This technique originally was developed as a fold recognition technique that attempted to match hydrophobicity and solvent accessibility patterns of query sequences with those of known protein structures. It later evolved into a protein evaluation method. Verify3D

uses a matrix scoring method in which the secondary structure and solvent exposure propensity of each of the 20 amino acids was determined statistically (from high-quality PDB structures). These propensities were determined for each of 18 different structure and accessibility categories, creating a 20×18 three-dimensional profile scoring matrix. Residues that are rarely found in one category are given a low (or negative) score, whereas residues that are found frequently in another category receive a high score. Verify3D takes the three-dimensional coordinates of a query protein and classifies every residue into one of these 18 "profile" categories; these categories then are converted into a numerical score by looking up the three-dimensional profile scoring matrix. The result is a simple line graph with the residue number on the x-axis and the "folding quality" on the y-axis. Low values (<0.3) indicate a problem, whereas high values (>0.5) indicate that the structure is good.

▌PROTEIN STRUCTURE COMPARISON

Like sequence comparison, structure comparison lies at the heart of structural bioinformatics. In the same way that sequence comparisons can provide tremendous insight into the origins, function, location, interactions, and activity of a protein, so, too, can structure comparison. In fact, because structure is actually much more conserved than sequence, structure comparisons allow us to look even further back into Earth's prehistory to track the origins and evolution of many key enzymes and proteins. Unfortunately, structure comparison is a much more computationally difficult process than sequence comparison. In sequence comparison, it is possible to use character string matching or dynamic programming methods to generate alignments easily and rapidly and to identify regions of sequence similarity. In structure comparison, a completely different scheme must be used. This is because one is comparing or aligning complex three-dimensional shapes, not simple character strings. Although computers are very good at handling strings, they are not particularly good at identifying or comparing three-dimensional objects. Indeed, humans still outperform even the fastest computer in recognizing or comparing modestly dissimilar three-dimensional objects.

Nevertheless, there are tools and techniques that make it possible to compare near-identical or relatively similar three-dimensional structures. The most common method is called *structure superposition*. Superposition or superimposition is simply the process of rotating or orienting an object until it can be superimposed on top of a similar object. This is very similar to the process humans normally perform when putting the last piece of a jigsaw puzzle into place, where they rotate and translate the puzzle piece around until it finally fits. The simplest route to three-dimensional superposition is to identify a minimum of two sets of three common reference points, one set for the object to be superimposed and another set on the reference object that is being overlaid. As soon as these points are identified, the object to be superimposed can be rotated and translated until the two sets of reference points are almost matching (i.e., minimally different). The problem, of course, is knowing which three reference points are most appropriate. Humans are very good at this, computers are not. The problem with proteins is further complicated because we typically want to superimpose not just three points but literally hundreds of points (or atoms) at the same time.

Fortunately, there are mathematical approaches that allow this superposition process to be carried out as long as the reference points are identified and as long as the two objects have the same number of identified points. These approaches include Lagrangian multipliers, Quaternion methods, and matrix diagnolization techniques. It is beyond the scope of this chapter to explain the details of these methods, but suffice it to say that all these approaches are very fast and mathematically robust, and a number of them have been coded into readily available computer programs. It is possible to use the same techniques to superimpose more than two structures (as is frequently done for NMR structure ensembles). In this case, an iterative approach is taken where the first two superimposed structures are averaged to create a single structure, which is then used as a template to superimpose the third structure. The process of averaging and adding is repeated until all the structures have been superimposed. Typically, the two most similar structures are superimposed first, with the least similar structure being superimposed last, much as is done in multiple sequence alignment.

Two protein visualization programs, DeepView (Kaplan & Littlejohn, 2001) and MolMol (Koradi et al., 1996), are particularly good at performing and visualizing molecular superpositions (Figure 9.12). There also are at least two Web servers, SuperPose and ProSup, that allow users to superimpose two structures (either through PDB IDs, SCOP IDs, or through uploaded files) and, in the case of SuperPose, to superimpose two or more structures. These servers use initial sequence alignments to help identify reference points (so-called equivalent resides) so that superpositions can be carried out against proteins with different numbers of amino acids. The output for these Web servers include PDB coordinate lists, which can be viewed by any number of visualization tools, images, difference distance matrices

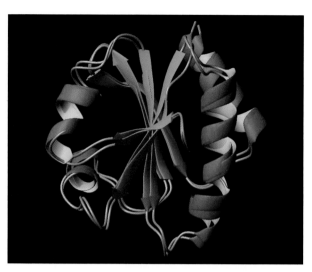

FIGURE 9.12 Illustration of how structural superposition allows structures to be compared more easily. The above diagram (generated using MolMol) illustrates the superposition of a homology model of *E. coli* thioredoxin with the actual X-ray structure. The RMSD between the two structures is 0.7 Å. Compare this figure with the side-by-side comparison of the same two structures in Figure 9.9. The differences between the two structures are made far more obvious through a direct superposition.

(in the case of SuperPose), as well as information on the alignment, number of equivalent residues and, root mean square deviation (RMSD).

As already shown, protein sequence alignments are evaluated either in terms of an Expect (E) value, a bit score, or percent identity. In the case of structure comparisons or structure alignments, these are scored using RMSD (in Ångstroms). RMSD actually is an archaic term for standard deviation. In other words, RMSD is calculated the same way a standard deviation is calculated. After two structures are superimposed, the sum of the square of the differences in distance (in Ångstroms) between Ca atoms or equivalent Ca atoms is calculated and divided by the number of atoms compared. The square root of this number is the RMSD. When more than two structures are superimposed (as is the case with NMR structure ensembles), an average structure for the ensemble is calculated first. The sum of the distance differences then are calculated relative to this hypothetical average structure. RMSD values are used frequently by NMR spectroscopists, structure modelers, and X-ray crystallographers when comparing structure ensembles, looking at related structures, or characterizing structure families. The first column of Table 9.1 provides a rough guideline in terms of what a given RMSD value corresponds to in terms of structure quality for an NMR

TABLE 9.1 ■ Relationship Between Backbone RMSD (Root Mean Square Deviation) in Å and Structure Quality for NMR Structure Ensembles and for Protein Structure Comparisons

RMSD (Å)	NMR Comment	Structure Comparision Comment
>12	Random coil	Completely unrelated
7.0	Major problems	Dubious relationship
5.0	Not quite converging	May be structurally related
4.0	Poor fit	Good structural relationship
2.0	Converging	Closely related
1.5	Barely acceptable	Very closely related
0.8	Typical NMR structure	Differences are not obvious
0.4	Best case NMR structure	Essentially indistinguishable

structure. The second column in the table provides a similar qualitative guideline for what RMSD values mean in terms of structure similarity.

The establishment of methods and criteria to compare moderately similar protein structures quantitatively led to the establishment of a number of databases containing common protein folds. This is the equivalent of grouping sequence families together to identify common sequence motifs, as is the case with the Pfam, Prosite, and InterPro databases. The equivalent databases, in terms of structure, are Class, Architecture, Topology, Homology (CATH; Pearl et al., 2000) and Structural Classification Of Proteins (SCOP; Murzin et al., 1995). Using these kinds of databases, it is possible to discover unexpected or undiscovered relationships between distantly relative proteins or to find fascinating examples of convergent structural evolution. CATH is a database that groups proteins into a taxonomy based on their secondary structure content, fold, and sequence similarity (Figure 9.13). The result is a hierarchical domain classification schema that allows protein structures to be grouped logically and compared. CATH entries are derived from higher resolution (<3.0 Å) protein structures in PDB, with multidomain proteins being partitioned into their constituent domains before classification. At the top of the hierarchy is the Class level, which is determined automatically by the secondary structure content. There are three broad classes: mainly α, mainly β, and α/β (see above). At the Architecture level, protein structures are divided further according to the overall domain shape and orientation of the secondary structures. This is performed manually using naming conventions found in the literature. Third in the hierarchy is the Topology level, where common architectures can be divided further into groups according to their secondary structure connectivity and general shape. This partitioning is carried out automatically using the SSAP algorithm. At the lowest level of the hierarchy, proteins are grouped according to their sequence identity ($>35\%$) and length

of sequence match ($>60\%$). The CATH database can be searched by typing in a PDB accession number to see the Class, Architecture, Topology, and Homologous superfamily to which a protein belongs. Because CATH is maintained manually, there is always a lag between when a new structure is released and when it is formally classified by CATH.

The SCOP database is a similar hierarchically structured database providing a slightly different taxonomic partitioning. Like CATH, the SCOP database aims to provide a comprehensive description of the structural and evolutionary relationships between essentially all protein structures in PDB. Unlike CATH, the SCOP database is constructed primarily through visual comparison and manual grouping. This process is aided, but not guided, by a number of computational tools. SCOP uses a four-part hierarchy (Class, Family, Superfamily, and Fold), with the top of the taxonomic chain being Class. SCOP has seven classes (with four specialty classes for nonconforming proteins) that are based on secondary structure content and size. The next level in the SCOP hierarchy is Fold. Structures are defined as having a common Fold if they have the same major secondary structures in the same arrangement and with the same topological connection. Being grouped in the same Fold does not mean the proteins arose from a common ancestor, just that they look similar topologically. Proteins clustered in the next level, Superfamily, are suspected of having a common evolutionary origin, as assessed by either sequence or structural similarity. At the lowest level in the hierarchy is the Family. Proteins in the same Family are considered to have a clear evolutionary relationship, either on the basis of common structure, common function, or sequence identity ($>30\%$). The CATH database is browsed easily (progressing down the hierarchy through hyperlinks) and also can be searched by keywords. Each entry is full of hyperlinked documents and figures (e.g., Chime, RasMol, static image) that allow facile navigation and exploration of structural and

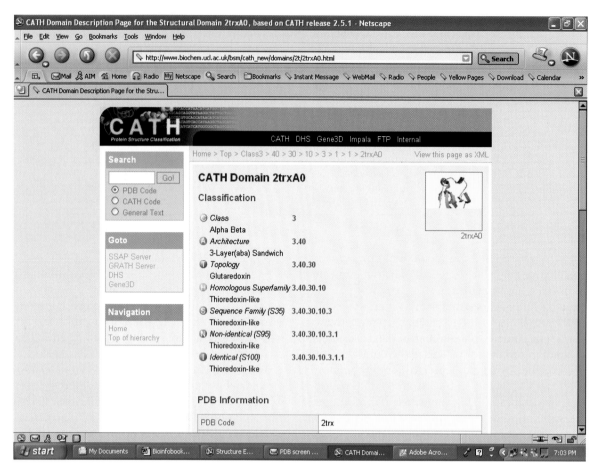

FIGURE 9.13 An example of the CATH database description of *E. coli* thioredoxin, indicating its Class, Architecture, Topology, and Homology to other related structures.

evolutionary relationships. SCOP updates are released approximately every six months, with the last release containing nearly 19,000 proteins and 50,000 domains. Both CATH and SCOP are accessible from the PDB Structure Explorer page, under the Structure Neighbors page.

Because the time and expense of manually classifying protein structures is growing and because many structural and molecular biologists want to identify structural relationships on their own, there are now a number of Web-based services that automatically perform structural classifications. These servers include DALI (Dietmann et al., 2001), CE (Shindyalov and Bourne, 2001), and VAST (Gibrat et al., 1996). Rather than developing a nomenclature or constructing a hierarchical taxonomy as CATH and SCOP have done, these servers simply perform structure comparisons and automatically group structure families using well-defined mathematical criteria. To accelerate the structure comparison process, DALI, CE, and VAST precalculate structure neighbors on

a regular basis so that queries against existing proteins will yield a quick result. As a result, DALI, CE, and VAST have developed structural databases that are equivalent (although not hierarchically ordered) to CATH and SCOP. Because the classification carried out by DALI, CE, and VAST is fully automatic, these databases generally are more current than CATH or SCOP. The main advantage to the DALI, CE, and VAST over CATH and SCOP lies not in their databases, but in their servers. By accessing any of these structure comparison servers directly, it is possible to determine if a newly determined structure (not yet deposited in PDB) is a representative of a new fold or belongs to an existing fold. Such a determination can have profound implications for understanding the function and origin of a protein. In this regard, DALI, CE, and VAST are the structural biologist's equivalent to BLAST.

Essentially, what DALI, CE, and VAST do is to perform a structure superposition of a query structure against every structure in the PDB. Arguably, such a comparison between obviously similar objects is relatively trivial. However, to identify nonobvious structural relationships, more sophisticated approaches are needed. As discussed previously, the identification of remote structural similarities in three-dimensional objects is computationally very difficult and something that humans still do better than machines, one of the main reasons why CATH and SCOP are (mostly) manually curated. However, DALI, CE, and VAST have hit on roughly similar concepts for fishing out remote structural similarities. These approaches seem to work almost as well as manually derived classifications. Essentially, DALI, CE, and VAST look for similar groups of small substructures or supersecondary structures in proteins. The identification of substructures varies between the methods, with DALI using distance matrices (measurements of the pairwise distance between each Ca atom in the protein) to describe elementary contact patterns, whereas CE and VAST use vector representations of secondary structure elements. All three methods have important advantages over simple structure superposition because they accommodate gaps of almost any length, chain reversals, geometrical distortions, and altered topological connectivity of aligned segments.

VAST builds from the concepts developed in BLAST. BLAST scores pairs of text blocks, words, or k-tuples (see Chapter 11). In VAST, the program scores pairs of secondary structure elements (SSEs) that have similar type, relative orientation, and connectivity. The equivalent of high scoring segment pairs (HSPs) in BLAST are called pairs of SSEs in VAST. BLAST pursues alignment extensions only if the HSPs are statistically significant or "surprising" relative to random matches. In VAST, the pairs of SSE matches are pursued or extended only if they exhibit unusual statistical significance relative to random substructure alignments. The use of BLAST-like statistical approaches along with BLAST-like search strategies and the decomposition of larger tertiary structures into smaller, local secondary structure segments allows VAST rapidly to seek out and evaluate quantitatively remote or unexpected structural similarities.

The output from a DALI, CE, or VAST search includes information on both the level of sequence identity, the number of residues aligned, the level of significance of the match (a Z score), and the RMSD of the superimposed structures. Typically, structures with less than 5 Å RMSD or a Z score of more than 4.0 indicate a plausible match or a reasonable degree of structural similarity. If a structure of unknown function exhibits significant structural similarity to a structure of known function, it often is possible to make an assertion about the unknown protein's function. As always, it is particularly interesting and informative to identify those structures where the

RMSD is <2 Å, yet the sequence identity is <15%. These are examples of either very ancient homologs or potentially interesting cases of convergent evolution.

▌ SUMMARY

Many of the concepts and ideas currently used in bioinformatics (sequence comparison, structure and sequence visualization, structure prediction, electronic databases, and evolutionary analysis) can trace their origins to structural biology and the computationally inclined structural biologists who developed many of the earliest bioinformatic tools. Without these important contributions from structural biology and structural biologists, bioinformatics would not be what it is today. More recently, the tables have begun to turn, and now structural biologists are looking to bioinformaticians to help solve emerging problems in pattern finding, remote structure comparison, and large-scale, distributed data management. This give and take between structural biologists and bioinformaticians is vital to sustaining both fields. No doubt this exchange of expertise and insight will continue for some time. This chapter has illustrated how at least some of these interactions have evolved and how structural bioinformatics continues to be integral to gaining a detailed understanding of the engines of life: proteins and enzymes.

▌ WORKED EXAMPLE

Aminoacyl-tRNA synthetases are the enzymes responsible for adding amino acids to their corresponding tRNA molecule. There are 20 different tRNA synthetases for the 20 amino acids. Each is quite different, some being small, others large, some being monomers, others being dimers or tetramers. All bind to their respective tRNAs with very high specificity. TrpRS (tryptophanyl tRNA synthetase) and TyrRS (tyrosyl tRNA synthetase) are both monomeric members of the Class I aminoacyl-tRNA synthetases. They also are very interesting examples of convergent evolution. For this example, the sequences of *Bacillus stearothermophilus* TrpRS (gi: 135187) and *Bacillus stearothermophilus* TyrRS (gi: 230779) are used.

1. Go to the NCBI BLAST Web site. Go to the "Special" section at the bottom of the page and click on the Align two sequences (bl2seq) hyperlink. We are attempting to align TyrRS with TrpRS. Select the "blastp" option at the top of the page and then type in the TyrRS accession numbers (230779) in the appropriate box for "Sequence 1" and the TrpRS accession number (135187) in the other text box for "Sequence 2." Press the "Align" button at the bottom. The program should return the following output:

BLAST 2 SEQUENCES RESULTS VERSION BLASTP 2.2.6 [Apr-09-2003]

Matrix [▼] gap open: [11] gap extension: [1]

x_dropoff: [50] expect: [10.0] wordsize: [3] Filter [✓] [Align]

Sequence 1   gi [230779]   **Length** 419

Sequence 2   gi [135187]   Tryptophanyl-tRNA synthetase (Tryptophan--tRNA ligase) (TrpRS).   **Length** 328

No significant similarity was found

2. Now, go to the PDB Web site. The three-dimensional structure for *Bacillus stearothermophilus* TrpRS has the PDB accession number one-dimensional2R. Using the PDB "Search the Archive" tool, type in this accession number and press "Search." Scroll down to the entry with one-dimensional2R and press the "Explore" hyperlink on the right. Once in PDB Explorer, press the "View Structure" hyperlink, on the left side of the page. Click on the QuickPDB button (or select any other viewing tool) to view the structure. There are several chains in the crystal structure. Select the "A" chain and study its structure. Now launch a new browser window and go to the PDB Web site again. The three-dimensional structure for *Bacillus stearothermophilus* TyrRS has the PDB accession number 2TS1. Using the PDB "Search the Archive" tool, type in this accession number and press "Search." Scroll down to the entry with 2TS1 and press the "Explore" hyperlink on the right. Once in the PDB Explorer, press the "View Structure" hyperlink on the left side. Click on the QuickPDB button (or select any other

viewing tool) to view the structure and compare this structure with the one-dimensional2R structure. Some similarity between the two molecules should be noted.

3. Go to the Structure Explorer view of one-dimensional2R and select "Structural Neighbors" on the left. Scroll down and click on the CE "Combinatorial Extension" hyperlink. The CE home page should appear. Click the "Search database" button. Do not change any of the default values. A list of structurally similar proteins should be returned in approximately 5 seconds. Scroll down to the 2TS1 entry. The CE search has found that one-dimensional2R and 2TS1 share only 10.1% sequence identity, yet they share a substantial degree of structural similarity over 250 of 419 residues. The RMSD value over these 250 residues is just 3.7 Å. To see how the two molecules would be aligned structurally, click on the 2TS1 box (left side) and go the top of the page and click "Get Alignment." The structural alignment should be returned in approximately 5 seconds and should appear as follows:

```
one-dimensional2R:A   1/2     MKTIFSGIQPS--GVITIGNYIGALRQFVELQH-EYNCYFCIVDQHAIT---------V
2TS1:_    30/31    RVTLYCGFDPTADSLHIGHL--ATILTMRRFQQAGHRPIALVGGATGLIGDPSGKKSERT

one-dimensional2R:A   48/49    WQDPHELRQNIRRLAALYLAVGIDPT---QATLFIQSEVPAHAQ---AAWMLQCIVYIGE
2TS1:_    88/89    LNAKETVEAWSARIKEQLGRFLDFEADGNPAKIKNNYDWIGPLDVITFLRDVGKHFSVNY

one-dimensional2R:A   102/103   LERMTQFKEKSAGAAAAAAGLLTYPPLMAADILLYN----TDIVPVGEDQKQHIELTRDL
2TS1:_    148/149   MMAKESVQSRIETG--ISFTEFSYMMLQAYDFLRLYETEGCRLQIGGSDQWGNITAGLEL

one-dimensional2R:A   158/159   AERFNKRYGELFTIPEARIPKVGARIMSLVDPTKKMSKSDPNPKAYITLL---DDAKTIE
2TS1:_    206/207   IRKTKGEA-----RAFGLTI---PLVTK--ADGTKFG---KTESGTIWLDKEKTSPYEFY

one-dimensional2R:A   215/216   KKIKSAVTDSEGTIRYDKEAKPGISNLLNIYS--TLSG-QSIEELERQYEGKGYGVFKAD
2TS1:_    253/254   QFWINTD--------------DRDVIRYLKYFTFLSKEEIEALEQELREAPEKRA--A

one-dimensional2R:A   272/273   LAQVVIETLRPIQE
2TS1:_    295/296   QKTLAEEVTKLVHG
```

4. Several iterations of PSI-BLAST also can be used to extract the very remote sequence relationship between TyrRS and TrpRS. Try using the SuperPose Web site to see how the one-dimensional 2R_A chain superimposes with the 2TSI chain.

PROBLEM SET

1. Proteins can be very flexible, and often X-ray structures of proteins represent only a "snapshot" of a structure under very specific conditions. One of the most flexible proteins is calmodulin, a calcium-dependent protein that is involved in many protein–protein and protein–peptide interactions. Its structure can vary with the amount of calcium and the type of protein–peptide with which it is interacting. Use PDB SearchFields to find how many different structures of calmodulin exist. Use DeepView or Protein Explorer to compare two calmodulin structures: 1CLL and 1A29. How are they different? How are they similar? Try superimposing these structures using SuperPose or DeepView. What is their RMSD?

2. Using 1CLL as a starting point, click on the Structural Neighbors link and find out what structures are most similar to this protein. One protein that is quite similar to calmodulin is troponin C. What does troponin do? Try comparing 1CLL with 1NCX using the visualization program of your choice. How are the two structures similar? How are they different?

3. The 1CLL and 1NCX structures are very extended. Do you believe these extended forms are their natural or preferred shapes? Try evaluating these structures using VADAR. What features are quantitatively different than expected for normal globular proteins?

4. Go to the RasMol image gallery (http://www.umass.edu/microbio/rasmol/sayle1.htm) and study the image shown at this link. Using the PDB file 1HTF, try to generate an image similar to this example using RasMol. Provide a list of commands describing how this image was generated.

INTERNET RESOURCES

123D Server	http://123d.ncifcrf.gov/run123D+.html
3DPSSM	http://www.bmm.icnet.uk/~3dpssm/
CATH	http://www.biochem.ucl.ac.uk/bsm/cath/
CE	http://cl.sdsc.edu/ce.html
Cn3D	http://www.ncbi.nlm.nih.gov/Structure/CN3D/cn3d.shtml
CPH Models	http://www.cbs.dtu.dk/services/CPHmodels/
DALI	http://www.ebi.ac.uk/dali/
DeepView	http://us.expasy.org/spdbv/
DeepView Tutorial	http://www.usm.maine.edu/~rhodes/SPVTut/
DSSP program	http://www.sander.ebi.ac.uk/dssp/
DSSP server	http://bioWeb.pasteur.fr/seqanal/interfaces/dssp-simple.html
EVA (evaluation)	http://cubic.bioc.columbia.edu/eva/
General Structure Links	http://salilab.org/tools/

GenThreader Server	http://insulin.brunel.ac.uk/psipred/
History of Imaging	http://www.umass.edu/microbio/rasmol/history.htm
Image Galleries	http://www.umass.edu/microbio/rasmol/gallery.htm
MMDB	http://www.biochem.ucl.ac.uk/~roman/procheck/procheck.html
MolMol	http://www.mol.biol.ethz.ch/wuthrich/software/molmol/
MSD	http://www.ebi.ac.uk/msd/
PDB	http://www.rcsb.org/pdb/
PDBsum	http://www.biochem.ucl.ac.uk/bsm/pdbsum/
POV-Ray	http://www.povray.org
PredictProtein (TOPITS)	http://dodo.cpmc.columbia.edu/predictprotein/
PROCHECK	http://www.biochem.ucl.ac.uk/~roman/procheck/procheck.html
Prosup Superposition Server	http://lore.came.sbg.ac.at:8080/CAME/CAME_EXTERN/PROSUP/start_html
RasMol/ProteinExplorer	http://www.umass.edu/microbio/rasmol/
SAMt99	http://www.cse.ucsc.edu/research/compbio/HMM-apps/T99-model-library-search.html
SCOP	http://scop.mrc-lmb.cam.ac.uk/scop/
SDSC1	http://cl.sdsc.edu/hm.html
SuperPose Server	http://wishart.biology.ualberta.ca/SuperPose/
Swiss-Model	http://www.expasy.org/swissmod/SWISS-MODEL.html
TargetDB	http://targetdb.pdb.org/
VADAR	http://redpoll.pharmacy.ualberta.ca/vadar/
Validation Server	http://pdb.rutgers.edu/validate/
VAST	http://www.ncbi.nlm.nih.gov/Structure/VAST/vastsearch.html
Verify3D	http://www.doe-mbi.ucla.edu/Services/Verify_3D/
X-ray primer	http://www-structure.llnl.gov/Xray/xrayprimer.html

FURTHER READING

MARTZ, E., AND FRANCOEUR, E. (2002). *History of Visualization of Biological Macromolecules* (Available at: http://www.umass.edu/microbio/rasmol/history.htm). A wonderful hypertext description of the history of protein visualization and modeling. Many interesting nuggets of information to entertain protein chemists and science history buffs alike.

BRANDEN, C., AND TOOZE, J. (1999). *Introduction to Protein Structure*, 2nd ed. (Garland Science Publishing, New York, New York). A superb, easy-to-read reference with excellent coverage and many useful color diagrams. This book covers the field very nicely; just about every practicing structural biologist has a copy of either the first or second edition.

LESK, A. M. (2000). *Introduction to Protein Architecture: The Structural Biology of Proteins* (Oxford University Press, Oxford, UK). Beautifully illustrated and very accessible to readers of all backgrounds. Provides many interesting problems and Web-based exercises.

▌REFERENCES

BERNSTEIN, F. C., KOETZLE, T. F., WILLIAMS, G. J. B., MEYER, E. F., BRICE, M. D., RODGERS, J. R., KENNARD, O., SHIMANOUCHI, T., AND TASUMI, M. (1977). The Protein Data Bank. *J. Mol. Biol.* 112, 535–542.

BONNEAU, R., TSAI, J., RUCZINSKI, I., CHIVIAN, D., ROHL, C., STRAUSS, C. E., AND BAKER, D. (2001). Rosetta in CASP4: progress in ab initio protein structure prediction. *Proteins* (Suppl 5), 119–126

BOWIE, J. U., LUTHY, R., AND EISENBERG, D. (1991). A method to identify protein sequences that fold into a known 3-dimensional structure. *Science* 253, 164–170.

BRYANT, S. H., AND LAWRENCE, C. E. (1993). An empirical energy function for threading a protein sequence through a folding motif. *Proteins* 5, 92–112.

CHEN, J., ANDERSON, J. B., DEWEESE-SCOTT, C., FEDOROVA, N. D., GEER, L. Y., HE, S., HURWITZ, D. I., JACKSON, J. D., JACOBS, A. R., LANCZYCKI, C. J., (2003). MMDB: Entrez's 3D-structure database. *Nucl. Acids Res.* 31, 474–477.

COREY, R. B., AND PAULING, L. (1953). Molecular models of amino acids, peptides, and proteins. *Rev. Scientific Instrum.* 24, 621–627.

DIETMANN, S., PARK, J., NOTREDAME, C., HEGER, A., LAPPE, M., AND HOLM, L. (2001). A fully automatic evolutionary classification of protein folds: Dali Domain Dictionary version 3. *Nucl. Acids Res.* 29, 55–57.

FISCHER, D., AND EISENBERG, D. (1996). Protein fold recognition using sequence-derived predictions. *Protein Sci.* 5, 947–955.

GIBRAT, J. F., MADEJ, T., AND BRYANT, S. H. (1996). Surprising similarities in structure comparison. *Curr. Opin. Struct. Biol.* 6, 377–385.

HAGEN, J. B. (2000). The origins of bioinformatics. *Nat. Rev. Genet.* 1, 231–236.

HALL, S. R., ALLEN, A. H., AND BROWN, I. D. (1991). The crystallographic information file (CIF): a new standard archive file for crystallography. *Acta Crystallogr. Sec. A* 47, 655–685.

HOGUE, C. W. V. (1997). Cn3D: a new generation of three-dimensional molecular structure viewer. *Trends. Biochem. Sci.* 22, 314–316.

HOOFT, R. W., VRIEND, G., SANDER, C., AND ABOLA, E. E. (1996). Errors in protein structures. *Nature* 381, 272.

JONES, D. T., TAYLOR, W. R., AND THORNTON, J. M. (1992). A new approach to protein fold recognition. *Nature* 358, 86–89.

KAPLAN, W., AND LITTLEJOHN, T. G. (2001). Swiss-PDB Viewer (Deep View). *Brief Bioinform.* 2, 195–197.

KABSCH, W., AND SANDER, C. (1983). Dictionary of protein secondary structure: pattern recognition of hydrogen-bonded and geometrical features. *Biopolymers* 22, 2577–2637.

KENDREW, J. C., BODO, G., DINTZIS, H.M., PARRISH, R.G., WYCKOFF, H., AND PHILLIPS, D.C. (1958). A three dimensional model of the myoglobin molecule obtained by x-ray analysis. *Nature* 181, 662–666.

KOONIN, E. V., WOLF, Y. I., KAREV, G. P. (2002). The structure of the protein universe and genome evolution. *Nature* 420, 218–223.

KORADI, R., BILLETER, M., AND WUTHRICH, K. (1996). MOLMOL: a program for display and analysis of macromolecular structures. *J. Mol. Graph.* 14, 29–32.

KRAULIS, P. J. (1991). MOLSCRIPT: a program to produce both detailed and schematic plots of protein structures. *J. Appl. Crystallogr.* 24, 946–950.

KRIEGER, E., NABUURS, S. B., AND VRIEND, G. (2003). Homology modeling. *Methods Biochem. Anal.* 44, 509–523.

LASKOWSKI, R. A. (2001). PDBsum: summaries and analyses of PDB structures. *Nucl. Acids Res.* 29, 221–222.

LASKOWSKI, R. A., RULLMANNN, J. A., MACARTHUR, M. W., KAPTEIN, R., AND THORNTON, J. M. (1996). AQUA and PROCHECK-NMR: programs for checking the quality of protein structures solved by NMR. *J. Biomol. NMR.* 8, 477–478.

LASKOWSKI, R. A., MACARTHUR, M. W., MOSS D. S., AND THORNTON, J. M. (1993). PROCHECK: a program to check the stereochemical quality of protein structures. *J. Appl. Cryst.* 26, 283–291.

MADEJ, T., BOGUSKI, M. S., AND BRYANT, S. H. (1995). Threading analysis suggests that the obese gene product may be a helical cytokine. *FEBS Lett.* 373, 13–18.

MURZIN, A. G., BRENNER, S. E., HUBBARD, T., AND CHOTHIA, C. (1995). SCOP: a structural classification of proteins database for the investigation of sequences and structures. *J. Mol. Biol.* 247, 536–540.

NOVOTNY, J, BRUCCOLERI, R., AND KARPLUS, M. (1984). An analysis of incorrectly folded protein models. Implications for structure predictions. *J. Mol. Biol.* 177, 787–818.

PEARL, F. M. G, LEE, D., BRAY, J. E, SILLITOE, I., TODD, A. E., HARRISON, A. P., THORNTON, J. M., AND ORENGO, C. A. (2000). Assigning genomic sequences to CATH *Nucl. Acids Res.* 28, 277–282.

ROST, B., SCHNEIDER, R., AND SANDER, C. (1997). Protein fold recognition by prediction-based threading. *J. Mol. Biol.* 270, 471–480.

SALI, A. (1998). 100,000 protein structures for the biologist. *Nat. Struct. Biol.* 5, 1029–1032.

SAYLE, R. A., AND MILNER-WHITE, E. J. (1995). RASMOL: biomolecular graphics for all. *Trends. Biochem. Sci.* 20, 374–376.

SCHWEDE, T., KOPP, J, GUEX, N., PEITSCH, M. C. (2003). SWISS-MODEL: an automated protein homology-modeling server. *Nucl. Acids Res.* 31, 3381–3385.

SHERIDAN, R. P., DIXON, J. S., AND VENKATARAGHAVAN, R. (1985). Generating plausible protein folds by secondary structure similarity. *Int. J. Pept. Protein Res.* 25, 132–143.

SHINDYALOV, I. N., AND BOURNE, P. E. (2001). A database and tools for 3-D protein structure comparison and alignment using the Combinatorial Extension (CE) algorithm. *Nucl. Acids Res.* 29, 228–229.

SIPPL, M. J., AND WEITCKUS, S. (1992). Detection of native-like models for amino acid sequences of unknown 3D structure. *Proteins* 13, 258–271.

VAGUINE, A. A., RICHELLE, J., AND WODAK, S. J. (1999). SFCHECK: a unified set of procedures for evaluating the quality of macromolecular structure-factor data and their agreement with the atomic model. *Acta Crystallogr. D Biol. Crystallogr.* 55, 191–205.

WALTHER, D. (1997). WebMol: a Java based PDB viewer. *Trends Biochem. Sci.* 22, 274–275.

WESTBROOK, J. D., AND BOURNE, P. E. (2000). STAR/mmCIF: an ontology for macromolecular structure. *Bioinformatics* 16, 159–168.

WESTBROOK, J. D., FENG, Z., CHEN, L., YANG, H., AND BERMAN, H. M. (2003). The Protein Data Bank and structural genomics. *Nucl. Acids. Res.* 31, 489–491.

WILLARD, L., RANJAN, A., ZHANG, H., MONZAVI, H., BOYKO, R. F., SYKES, B. D., AND WISHART, D. S. (2003). VADAR: a Web server for quantitative evaluation of protein structure quality. *Nucl. Acids Res.* 31, 3316–3319.

HEY TERMS

Ab initio

Accessible surface area

ASN.1

Boolean

Energy minimization

Expect value

Homology modeling

Primary structure

Quaternary structure

R factor

Ramachandran plot

RMSD

Secondary structure

Tertiary structure

Threading

Topology

XML

Z score or Z value

## CHAPTER TEN

Intermolecular Interactions and Biological Pathways

GARY D. BADER

ANTON J. ENRIGHT

Bioinformatics: A Practical Guide to the Analysis of Genes and Proteins, Third Edition, edited by Andreas D. Baxevanis and B.F. Francis Ouellette.
ISBN 0-471-47878-4 Copyright © 2005 John Wiley & Sons, Inc.

∎ INTRODUCTION

A major challenge for biologists today is to gain an understanding of the workings of the cell by integrating available information from the various fields of molecular and cellular biology into an accurate cellular model that can be used to generate hypotheses for testing. New subfields of biology, such as functional genomics and proteomics, take advantage of the availability of completely sequenced genomes to enable large-scale mapping of cellular molecular networks through new experimental methods. These methods are being developed faster than ever before and are creating a tidal wave of new information about cellular processes (Bader et al., 2003b). Bioinformatics will play a vital role in overcoming this data integration and modeling challenge, because databases, visualization software, and analysis software must be built to enable data assimilation and to make the results accessible and useful for answering biological questions.

As experimental methods become more sensitive, more of the cell is being mapped. Decades ago, many metabolic pathways in organisms from bacteria to mammals were mapped because early biochemical methods could detect their abundant enzyme and small molecule components. Today, experimental methods, such as protein identification by mass spectrometry (Chapter 17), are sensitive enough to detect molecules at only a few copies per cell. This allows biologists to "map" cellular metabolism further and, importantly, to see many regulatory, or cell signaling, networks for the first time. Cell signaling network mapping is particularly interesting because of its role in diseases with a high prevalence in the population, such as cancer, diabetes, and Alzheimer's disease.

Molecular interaction networks generated by some of these experimental cell mapping methods provide a convenient and practical scaffold for integrating other types of data, because they represent the intricate connections that are a hallmark of cellular processes. A molecule's interacting and reacting partners define its function in a biological system. Thus, gene expression data derived from a cDNA microarray, when integrated with a molecular interaction network, place the data into a coherent functional context. The opportunity for gaining further understanding of biological systems from large amounts of new and existing data through intelligent data integration has driven biomolecular interaction and pathway analysis in bioinformatics.

Interestingly, the availability of new types of biological data has enabled new computational methods in pathway informatics that, in turn, enables new discoveries at the bench. Computational pathway and network analysis should be considered early on in the conception of cell mapping experiments to quicken the discovery cycle. For example, the computational reconstruction of metabolic pathways from a recently sequenced bacteria allowed investigators to discover that the organism could not synthesize specific amino acids and required an environmental source to live. This allowed the bacteria, which causes a gastrointestinal disease, to be cultured in a lab and studied, something that was previously not possible (Renesto et al., 2003).

The pathway informatics field is relatively new and is changing rapidly, in part because of the large amount of cell map data now available. Initial work in this area involved the computational representation of metabolic pathways; more recently, it has focused on designing cellular signaling pathway databases. The available databases and tools in this area are evolving quickly, much like some other quickly developing areas of bioinformatics. For instance, only recently have the main protein–protein interaction database efforts developed common data exchange formats that make the data more accessible; pathway data exchange formats are only starting this process. Because of this rapid pace of change, this chapter covers a number of existing tools, but also focuses on fundamental theory that should be applicable to many new databases and tools as they become available. Specifically, a number of useful pathway and network resources are covered, focusing on freely available or very accessible tools, or both. Pathway and molecular interaction databases and emerging common data exchange formats that multiple databases and tools are starting to support are covered first. Algorithms for predicting protein–protein interactions and metabolic pathway reconstruction then are described, along with a guide to various Web resources that implement these algorithms in a user-friendly manner. Next, a description of pathway and network visualization tools and important underlying concepts and algorithms for these tools are described. Finally, a special focus section is included that examines some of the emerging analyses that are possible when integrating gene expression data with pathway and network information. This is meant to illustrate the interesting biological questions that can be answered and new hypotheses that can be generated by integrating existing data in the network context. Not all resources can be covered in depth, so the largest databases and most commonly used data analysis tools are featured here; pointers to online descriptions and lists of other pathway and network-related databases and software are provided at the end of the chapter.

Before delving into databases, it is interesting to know where the data come from. What would an ideal cell biological experiment be able to tell us? The answer is no less than everything: what molecules are in the cell at what time and at what place, how many molecules are there, what molecules they interact with, and the specifics of their interaction dynamics. Ideally, one would want this information not only over the course of the cell cycle, but also in all important environmental conditions and under all known disease states. In relation to this huge amount of information, current experimental methods, although incredibly useful and growing better by orders of magnitude every decade, only scratch the surface. A wide range of biochemical, molecular biological, and genetic experiments have been invented to help elucidate cellular systems and to determine which cellular parts are involved and how they fit together.

Enzymatic reactions have been studied for centuries, initially with some easy-to-observe processes such as fermentation. The basic principle of experimentally mapping metabolism, composed mainly of protein enzymes, is to identify an enzymatic process (e.g., the conversion of glucose to ethanol in yeast) and progressively purifying cellular extracts to find the enzymes involved. Validation involves checking to see if the purified enzyme can convert the given substrate to a product. Thus, the process requires protein separation and purification technology, as well as molecule identification methods to identify the enzyme, any cofactors, substrates, and products involved in the reaction.

Major advances in this area have been made using various forms of chromatography, gel-based separation techniques, nuclear magnetic resonance (NMR), and mass spectrometry. Chromatography and gel separation work on the basic principle that a molecular mixture can be decomposed based on component physiochemical properties, such as size or charge. NMR and mass spectrometry can be used to identify small molecules and proteins directly based on atomic distance measurements and mass, respectively. Enzymologists further characterize the reaction rates of enzymes (kinetics) and the detailed enzymatic mechanism involved in catalysis (Voet & Voet, 2004).

Signaling pathways, which involve many more direct protein–protein relationships, such as phosphorylation of one protein by another protein (kinase), can be mapped using protein–protein interaction detection methods. Many other types of molecules are involved in signaling, so protein interactions tell only part of the story. Many techniques for determining protein–protein interactions have been developed over the past few decades. One popular class of experiments depends on co-purification, using the methods described above. It is reasoned that proteins that strongly interact will purify as a complex that can be degraded further using harsher purification conditions finally to separate and identify the complex components. Importantly, this means that the definition of a protein complex depends

on the purification conditions used, which measure a continuum of protein–protein interaction strengths. An example of a modern biochemical co-purification uses affinity chromatography to purify a protein complex from a cellular extract, then identifies the resulting complex components using mass spectrometry. Yeast two-hybrid methods often are used to determine if two proteins are interacting. An activation and DNA binding domain of a transcription factor are attached to each protein, respectively. If the two proteins of interest interact, the activation and DNA binding domains also will interact, forming a functional transcription factor that will express an engineered reporter gene. Presence of the reporter gene thus indicates binding. Another often-used method is molecular cross-linking, an experimental method in which a linear molecule of defined length having two reactive ends is added to a mixture containing a potential complex to cross-link proteins that are close together; the distance over which an interaction can be detected is determined by the length of the cross-linker being used. Subsequent purification and definition of the complex is easier, because the protein complex is tied together covalently instead of just being electrostatically bound. Many other protein–protein interaction-determining experimental methods exist (Voet & Voet, 2004), but almost all current experiments suffer from observer effect, whereby the conditions of the experiment disturb the natural biological process. Because each experiment has its own strengths and weaknesses in this regard, it is only after multiple types of experiments have been performed that one can really be sure of the result.

PATHWAY AND MOLECULAR INTERACTION DATABASES

Given the breadth and depth of pathway and molecular interaction network information already available in the literature, as well as that being generated from large-scale experiments, it is no surprise that a number of databases have been built to try to represent and store this information. In fact, there are more than 100 pathway and molecular interaction-related database resources that are available via the Internet. These range widely in form and content and include full-featured pathway databases, ones that focus on protein–protein interactions, and organism- or disease-specific pathway databases. Some databases contain molecular interaction information, although they are not primarily focused on interactions. For instance, the DNA Databank of Japan (DDBJ)/European Molecular Biology Laboratory (EMBL)/GenBank feature table, originally designed for annotating nucleic acid sequences (Chapter 1), contains some information about binding sites of gene expression and translation control elements, such as ribosome binding sites (specified using the RBS key). This information is not widely used, however. This section focuses on the largest published or freely available database resources, or both, that are considered to be the most generally useful (Table 10.1). It is likely that certain specialist pathway and molecular interaction databases will be better-suited to answering certain types of queries; URLs to these are provided at the end of this chapter.

The cell is a large, complex, and very dynamic connected network of molecules. Because of its complexity, biologists think of the cell as having substructures and subsystems such as organelles, pathways, and complexes, so as to aid in understanding the overall picture. Although organelles and complexes are structures that often can be seen under a microscope, pathways (obviously) are not, so it is important to realize that pathways are human constructs and are just parts of a larger, fully connected molecular interaction network. A working definition of a pathway is a series of molecular interactions and reactions, often forming a network. Sometimes, human pathway organization is based on recognized biochemical or information-processing phenomena. For instance, a series of metabolic reactions could start with the intake of a metabolite from the environment that is converted quickly and irreversibly to something else, such as the glycolysis pathway breaking down glucose to generate energy ATP. Also, signal propagation in a series of signaling pathway steps could be shown to follow a specific pathway, such as when a ligand binds to a cell surface receptor, which results in signal propagation through a kinase cascade to the nucleus where transcription is activated. Often in these cases, the start and end points of a pathway are defined by observation of some readily detectable phenotype after stimulation or perturbation, such as observing gene expression after stimulating the cell with a peptide growth hormone. In other instances, pathway organization is based on the order that components of a pathway are discovered. In this case, it is possible for existing pathways

TABLE 10.1 ■ An Overview of Selected Pathway and Interaction Databases

Database	Scope	Data Model	Special Feature	License
BIND	Many species	Binary molecular and genetic interactions, complexes and pathways created from interactions	BLAST search, protein domain view, graphical view	Public domain
DIP	Many species	Binary protein–protein interactions	BLAST search, graphical view	Free for academic research, commercial license required
GRID	Budding yeast, fruit fly, worm	Binary protein–protein and genetic interactions	Osprey network analysis tool	Free Web-based access
HPRD	Human	Binary protein–protein interactions	Curated protein records	Free for academic research, commercial license required
IntAct	Many species	Sets of interacting proteins	Graphical view	Freely available
MINT	Many species	Sets of interacting proteins	Java viewer provides useful information	Freely available
BioCyc	Many species	Metabolic pathway-based ontology	High quality metabolic pathways and full featured software	Free for academic research, commercial license required
KEGG PATHWAY, LIGAND	Many species	Metabolic pathways	Pathway diagrams, database of compounds that include 2D structure	Freely available, no redistribution rights

2D, two-dimensional.

to be merged if enough "cross-talk" between the existing pathways is found. Not only have biologists organized the cell into pathways and modules, but they have classified the pathways themselves into different types, and each of the main types generally has a different computational representation in the various existing pathway databases.

The main types of biochemical- and biophysical-based pathway representations model metabolic, signal transduction (also called cell signaling) and gene regulation pathways. Metabolic pathways generally are defined by a series of chemical actions and the chemical results of those actions, for the purpose of changing one molecular species into another. Glycolysis is a typical example of a metabolic pathway that converts glucose to pyruvate. Signal transduction pathways usually are defined by binding events, sometimes involving chemical actions (e.g., phosphorylation events), for the purpose of communicating information from one place in the cell to another. Often the binding events are protein–protein interactions. The mitogen-activated protein (MAP) kinase cascade is a common example of a signal transduction pathway that conveys information from an externally activated cell surface receptor to the nucleus to effect change in gene expression in response to the external signal. Gene regulation networks involve transcription factors activating or repressing expression of genes, a simple case being activation of expression of a set of genes. If one or more of the set of genes being activated is itself a transcription factor that can act independently, then a more complex network results. Another type of pathway that is not generally biochemically or biophysically defined but is mapped classically is a genetic pathway, which is a series of genetic interactions. Genetic interactions are not physical binding events, but rather are defined by a change in phenotype caused by a change in genotype. A simple type of genetic interaction is called *synthetic lethal*, where two genes that are genetically altered (for instance, knocked out) do not cause a phenotype change on their own, but when altered together, cause death of the organism. The implication of such a relationship, in a simple case, is that the genes are part of linear parallel pathways such that both can carry out the same vital biological process where one pathway can compensate for the other if one is damaged. An example of this may be two parallel metabolic pathways that both build an essential amino acid from precursor molecules (Figure 10.1). Genetic interactions and pathways always have been important in biology, because most early knowledge of biological processes was defined genetically before the advent of molecular biology techniques starting in the 1950s. The completion of genomes of various model organisms has

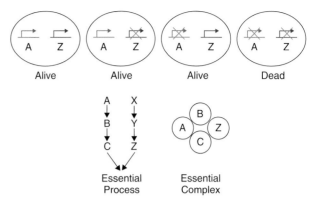

FIGURE 10.1 Biochemical meaning of a synthetic lethal genetic interaction. A genetic interaction occurs when two or more genes affect a phenotype when mutated together. In this case, a synthetic lethal interaction is shown. When genes A or Z, or both, are expressed, the cell is alive, but when both A and Z are not expressed (shown here) or mutated, the cell dies. In the simple biochemical case, this may be the consequence of genes A and Z being in parallel pathways that impinge on a common essential metabolite or process, or perhaps genes A and Z are both part of a molecular complex that can not assemble without both gene products. For the parallel pathways shown here, synthetic lethal interactions between all combinations of genes (A, B, C) and genes (X, Y, Z) would be expected, not just the A–Z interaction shown here. Synthetic lethal interactions may have more complex relationships to the underlying biochemical network and many other types of genetic interactions exist.

led to an increase in the use of genetics to examine certain biological processes and gene function more quickly or easily than some current biochemical techniques allow.

The distinction between these types of pathways here is related to human representation, and so is purely virtual and does not relate to any intrinsic structure in the cell or organism. In fact, many pathways or regions of the molecular interaction network can be classified into multiple categories and can be represented in different ways, depending on the context. For instance, a metabolic pathway database may call a specific pathway metabolic and represent it one way, and a signaling database may classify it as a signaling pathway and represent it in a different way. This can lead to difficulties when trying to integrate these pathways into the same system. Thus, it is important to understand how a database represents the information it stores to be able to query it and to understand its advantages and limitations.

A representation system (also called a *data model* or *abstraction*) is an invention that can be used to describe and organize a set of observations. Often, many different representation schemes are possible for the same type of information, and two different people given the task to invent an abstraction independently can create different systems, especially for complex and partially undefined biological information. A single representation scheme must be agreed on before it can be useful for data communication, although such a decision involves considering a number of trade-offs. An ideal representation system compactly and efficiently describes exactly the information useful to the users of the system. Very compact and efficient representation often results when communicating among people with the same extensive common knowledge, such as scientists in a specific subfield who all understand the jargon and concepts of their field. Compactness can be achieved because common knowledge can be taken for granted, and thus does not have to be represented explicitly each time information is communicated. This compactness can reduce communication time and effort enormously, making it very useful. Unfortunately, using a compact representation to communicate between people who do not share the same common knowledge does not work as well. These people will have trouble understanding each other unless common knowledge is represented explicitly. This frequently happens when people in different subfields in science communicate. Similarly, computer programs that are not programmed with extensive rules defining common knowledge generally can not "understand" properly a very compact representation and require explicit coding of extra information and logic to perform actions such as querying the compact data. If enough information about data relationships is encoded, whether in software or in the data exchange format, a computer may be able to draw new conclusions using logical inference. This is a major basis for the field of artificial intelligence. For example, if the computer program knows that a kinase catalyzes the addition of a phosphate group, it can easily that infer protein X is a kinase if it adds a phosphate group to another protein in the molecular interaction network.

Another related tradeoff is between simplicity and complexity of representation. The advantage of having a simple model that captures the basic properties of the data is that it is easily created, understood, and used, but it can not represent all detail that may be known about a system. The complex model may be able to represent everything that is known, but may be too unwieldy to be useful in some cases. Many aspects of biological systems that may be useful to represent can add significantly to the complexity of a representation scheme. Examples are level of detail, context, and scope and what is

sometimes called provenance in the database community. Each of these are dealt with individually below.

Adding levels of detail in data modeling is useful for representing data at varying levels of knowledge or understanding, down to the limit of detail that is of interest. Certain types of biological information are understood in much more detail than others. When detail is known, a detailed data model should be able to represent it. With a model that includes multiple levels of detail, there is a choice between representing the same information at low, intermediate, or high detail. Depending on the use-case, more or less detail may be required. (Use-case, a technical term from the field of software engineering, describes how a user interacts with a software system from the point of view of different types of users). For instance, if the mechanism of a protein phosphorylation event by a tyrosine kinase is understood down to the movement of electrons in the chemical reaction, it may be useful to capture all of the known information for someone studying electron dynamics. Alternatively, someone studying the global properties of protein interaction networks may be interested only in the fact that one protein interacts with another and would find information on electron dynamics distracting. Adding to the complexity of biological knowledge representation, levels of detail in the cell map can be considered across large ranges (scales) of time and space where each level of the organizational hierarchy may require its own abstraction system. As an example across spatial scales, the molecular parts of the cell have widely established representation systems, such as the 20-letter amino acid code for protein sequence and the atoms, bonds, and connectivity of atoms in a three-dimensional protein structure. Also, atomic bonds are measured in picometers (10^{-18} m). Neither of these abstractions work well in describing larger substructures of the cell. For instance, an organelle like the nucleus simply would be too difficult to examine if it was completely described by three-dimensional molecular structures. An average cell is measured in micrometers (10^{-6} m), and neuron length in large organisms can extend well into the meter range. Similarly, across temporal scales, ultrafast electron flow in a biochemical reaction, measured at attoseconds (10^{-18} s), can be described when it is known, but any useful abstraction to describe electron flow would not be useful for describing events on the time scales of the cell cycle, measured at minutes or hours.

Context and scope of biological network information also can add complexity to a representation scheme because molecular interactions and reactions depend on the presence of the participating molecules at permissive conditions, such as being in the same place at the same time at a normal temperature. Thus, it may not suffice to record that a reaction occurs among participating molecules, because that reaction may or may not occur with the same participants in different cells, in different developmental stages, or in different organisms. Similarly, if the experimental methods used and observations that were made to discover pathway knowledge are of interest, it may be useful to model all different types of experiments that were performed as well as who performed them and when. It also may be useful to track information that was inferred from a similar pathway to the one of interest. This knowledge-tracking information sometimes is referred to as *provenance*, which simply means proof of origin and authenticity, and can be used to track error propagation in a database. Provenance also can add significant complexity to any data model.

These fundamental tradeoffs and issues in knowledge representation are important, because the multiple representation schemes present for pathways make it difficult to integrate information from multiple different pathway sources into a single system. A universal language for pathways has not yet been developed. Such a language may not actually be efficient to use for day-to-day work because it would be too verbose, although it would be useful as a data model for a universal pathway repository and could be mapped to a user-preferred representation scheme for practical purposes. Development of a universal pathway language is difficult, especially when many aspects of biology are poorly understood. Paradigm shifts that significantly change our thinking about an aspect of biology could occur that call for fundamentally different ways of representing the data.

In summary, the preferred representation of a pathway depends heavily on what the information will be used for (the use-case). Different representation schemes and the definition of different types of pathways have evolved in pathway informatics because different sets of common knowledge and different use-cases exist within different communities (different subfields of biology).

Apart from understanding the representation used by a database and why it was chosen, a few things should be kept in mind when using a pathway database. These include scope, data quality, freshness of data, data quantity, availability, and technical architecture, each of which is addressed herein. The scope of a database is important to know when searching for information. Pathway and interaction databases are springing up to collect information from the literature, but this is a difficult task because of the data complexity, thus databases often focus on a specific area. Knowledge of database scope can prevent wasted time searching for information of interest in the wrong database or otherwise misusing the database. For example, the General Repository for Interaction Datasets (GRID) database contains information about protein–protein interactions and genetic interactions, two related data types with very different properties. It is possible for a user to search for protein interaction, only to find genetic interactions and to misinterpret them as protein interactions if they are not aware of the scope of GRID.

The data quality of a database depends heavily on level of curation and validation and can be difficult to assess independently, unless one is already an expert. Pathway databases can range in quality from those that store computed information with little or no validation to those resources with large teams of experienced biologists and complex validation systems. Although expert-curated databases are the gold standard, collections of lower-quality information are still useful, but generally require that the user be an expert and have the time to sort through it. For instance, databases of protein-protein interactions created automatically by literature extraction techniques (text mining) may be only 70% accurate, but may have some correct information that no other database contains. Importantly, many protein-protein interaction databases contain a large amount of information derived from relatively few large-scale or high-throughput experimental methods such as comprehensive yeast two-hybrid or large-scale biochemical purifications. It is known that these techniques can generate a large number of false-positive interactions as well as miss correct information (false negatives); thus, in search results, it is important to determine which records of interest come from large-scale methods versus which ones are curated.

Data freshness also is important, and databases that are well maintained and store current information can indicate higher data quality. Some pathway and network databases, along with many other biological databases, are not being actively maintained, even though the Web site and database may still be available. Old data sets can be very useful, but it is important to be aware of the data set age. Users should make a point of looking for dates on the homepage of the database as well as in the records or creation times of datasets available on FTP sites, if available, to find out how recent the data are.

Another measure of the usefulness of a database is data quantity. Certain databases have been built and published without much data. Possible reasons for this include data model research or showcasing new technology. If a user is interested in the data contained in a database, then the statistics page, more than any other aspect, if available, should be examined before using the resource. Additionally, the user should never assume completeness of a data set, because most of the data in pathway and interaction databases are derived from the literature, and it is difficult to guarantee that all known data about a subject are collected.

Another issue to be aware of before using a database is availability. This comes in two forms: download restrictions and intellectual property (IP) restrictions. Obviously, a database cannot used if it cannot be accessed. Download or electronic availability is simply whether the data can be accessed via some electronic medium (e.g., via the Web or by FTP). It is possible that a database exists only in paper form, in which case it is not very accessible (or useful). Both academic and corporate databases can be advertised on a Web site, but may not actually be accessible either because they are sold or possibly because they are under construction. IP restrictions are copyright statements and licensing terms that must be adhered to when using a given database. For pathway databases, this is generally "freely available to all," "free for academics only," or "restricted use for all users." Also, some licensing terms of corporate databases reach through to cover inventions made using the data in the database (Greenbaum & Gerstein, 2003).

Finally, the technical architecture of a biological network database should be considered if the user is planning to work with the data in a more technical manner, such as writing a program to extract some information of interest. As with other biological databases, pathway databases come in a wide range of formats ranging from simple text files to custom object-oriented databases. For technical work, the ease of access to the data from a program defines another type of data availability. Some databases simplify programmatic access by providing application programming interfaces in multiple programming languages. Discovering the technical aspects of a pathway resource generally is more difficult than for simple user query access because fewer people are interested in the underlying software architecture than the data contained therein. Databases that are published often describe the architecture. If this is not the case, the database creators must be contacted directly.

In summary, to obtain the most value out of pathway and network databases, it is important to know the data, scope, and representation scheme. The following section gives an overview of the most widely used interaction and pathway databases in alphabetical order within categories.

Primarily Molecular Interaction Databases

BIND BIND, the Biomolecular Interaction Network Database (Bader et al., 2003a), currently is the largest collection of freely available information about pairwise molecular interactions and complexes. A small number of pathways also are available through BIND. At the time of this writing, BIND contains mainly yeast (*Saccharomyces cerevisiae*) protein–protein, protein–DNA, and genetic interactions, as well as protein complex data.

Also contained are fruit fly (*Drosophila melanogaster*) and worm (*Caenorhabditis elegans*) protein–protein interactions from large-scale experiments, and a fair amount of curated information from these and more than 800 other species as well. BIND also has the largest staff of curators of any public interaction database and currently is adding records to the database on a regular basis. A subproject of BIND is MMDBBIND (Salama et al., 2002), which stores all of the molecular interactions automatically extracted from the Protein Data Bank (PDB) in BIND format. The biopolymer interaction subset of this was recently made available via BIND's Web interface.

There are three main types of data objects in the BIND data model: interaction, molecular complex, and pathway. Interactions occur between two objects, which can be RNA, DNA, protein, small molecule, molecular complex, photon, and gene (for genetic interactions). Each object contains a description of its origin, whether organismal or chemical, and references a more complete description of the object in a primary database for that object. For instance, a protein may be described further in databases such as Swiss-Prot or GenPept. Importantly, each interaction record is supported by at least one publication. Publications in BIND can describe the publication opinion, whether supporting or disputing, with respect to the information to which they are attached. An interaction record may contain further description (all are optional), such as:

1. A short description of the record.

2. The cellular location of each object and a description of where the interaction takes place; both a start and an end location can be stored.

3. The experimental conditions under which the interaction was observed to occur. This is only a description of the experiments that were performed to show the interaction. Experimental data, such as gel images, are not stored in BIND.

4. A conserved sequence comment containing any potential conserved sequence that is known and that is functionally relevant (for instance, a conserved binding site). Although potentially useful, this field currently is used rarely in BIND.

5. A list of binding sites on each object in the interaction and a list of pairings between these sites. For instance, an SH3 domain can be defined on one protein partner and can be described as binding a proline-rich region defined on the other protein partner.

6. A list of chemical actions and chemical states that describe any chemical reactions that occur while the objects are interacting. For instance, protein A may

phosphorylate protein B to change the state of B from inactive to active.

7. An intramolecular interaction flag to store whether the interaction is occurring within a single molecule. For instance, calmodulin is found in both an extended calcium bound mode and a collapsed noncalcium bound mode where the N and C termini bind to each other.

BIND defines a molecular complex as two or more molecules that interact to form a stable complex and function as a unit. An example is the ribosome. A complex is defined as a collection of interactions that are already part of BIND along with some other information, such as assembly order, stoichiometry, and complex topology.

Similar to complexes, a pathway in BIND is a collection of at least one interaction, but whose molecules form an ordered network and generally are free from each other. Examples of pathways are glycolysis and a MAP kinase cascade.

BIND accepts user-submitted records through either a Web-based form interface or through an import service, if the number of submitted interactions is large. The main searching interface is a full-text search of all text fields in any BIND record, but there is also a BLAST versus BIND tool that allows querying BIND for protein sequences similar to the one of interest. The main BIND browse interface is a list of the records in the database, although there is also an interaction viewer Java applet that allows a user to traverse the molecular interaction network starting from a record of interest. A typical BIND record is shown in Figure 10.2. BIND is available for browsing and querying via the Web and can be downloaded freely without restrictions by FTP in the BIND format (Bader et al., 2001).

DIP. DIP, or the Database of Interacting Proteins (Xenarios et al., 2002), contains only experimentally derived protein–protein interaction data. It is one of the largest collections of publicly accessible protein–protein interaction information, containing data from more than 100 organisms. The data are collected from large-scale protein interaction mapping experiments, as well as from expert curators. The DIP data model consists of binary protein interactions along with information on each protein, the method used to determine the interaction, and a set of publication references to support the record.

DIP allows queries by proteins (called nodes), BLAST, protein sequence motifs, and by journal article. An analysis of the confidence level of interactions in the DIP database has been published (Deane et al., 2002), and two types of confidence of interaction scores are available:

▶ PVM, or paralogous verification method, assigns a higher reliability score to an interaction whose paralogs are also seen to interact in DIP.

▶ EPR, or expression profile reliability, deems a set of protein–protein interactions more reliable if it has a similar expression profile as a high-quality subset of DIP.

These scores can be calculated only for budding yeast (*Saccharomyces cerevisiae*) protein interactions because they depend on the existence of a large amount of external information currently only available for budding yeast.

A few satellite services are available as extensions to DIP. LiveDIP extends the DIP data model to describe protein-protein interaction processes using states and state transitions. Users can search for states or interactions as well as find paths through LiveDIP from one protein of interest to another. DLRP, or the Database of Ligand-Receptor Partners, contains a small set of ligand-receptor interactions for download, but does not provide search services. A BLAST query interface for DIP also is available. DIP is available via the Web for browsing, querying, and downloading by academic users. Commercial users must acquire a license for use. A typical DIP record is shown in Figure 10.3.

GRID. GRID, or the General Repository for Interaction Datasets (Breitkreutz et al., 2003a), contains protein–protein and genetic interactions currently for budding yeast (*Saccharomyces cerevisiae*) as YeastGRID, for the fruit fly (*Drosophila melanogaster*) as FlyGRID, and for *Caenorhabditis elegans* as WormGRID. GRID is being expanded actively, and other species may be available in the near future. GRID provides a simple summary of each interaction along with gene names, Gene Ontology (GO) annotation, and the experimental system that was used to determine the interaction. A network visualization tool called Osprey also is available to visualize, browse, and analyze the interaction networks in the various GRIDs.

HPRD. HPRD, or the Human Protein Reference Database (Peri et al., 2003), is a recently released database of human proteins, but also contains a significant amount of protein-protein interactions. Information about the domain and region of interaction, if available, is present as well as the type of experiment performed to detect the interaction. Expression, domain architecture, and post-translational modifications also are curated for each protein. A number of curated pathways created from the interaction data are available as images. A typical HPRD record is shown in Figure 10.4.

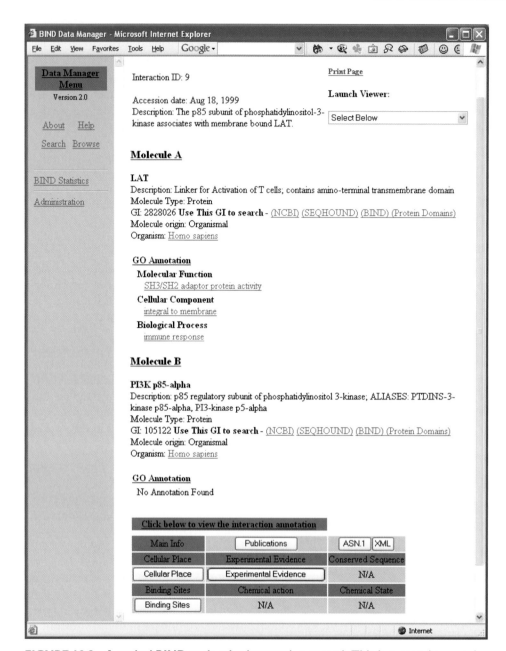

FIGURE 10.2   A typical **BIND** molecular interaction record. This is a protein–protein interaction that contains extra annotation information about the cellular place and experimental evidence for and binding sites involved in the interaction. More information about this protein interaction can be found by clicking the various links. For instance, the Launch Viewer section at the top right of the figure can be used to launch a Java applet that allows visual navigation of the interaction network starting at the molecules in this record. The links within the molecule section (e.g., Molecule A) can be used to access the protein sequence (**NCBI** and **SeqHound**), what other **BIND** records contain this molecule (**BIND**), and what domains are on this protein (**Protein Domains**).

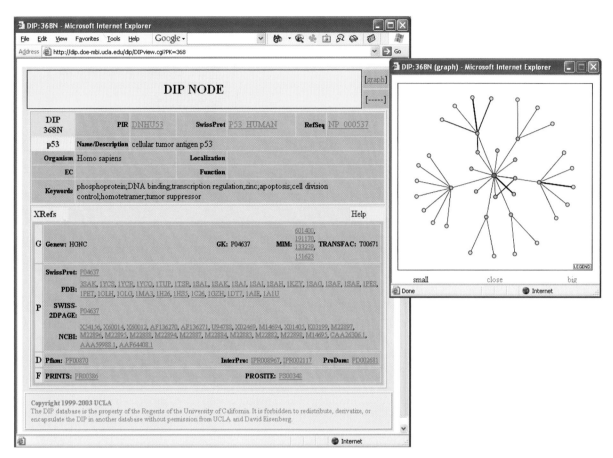

FIGURE 10.3 **A DIP human protein–protein interaction is shown with associated protein interaction network static visualization diagram. The protein shown is p53, involved in a number of cancers. This is the protein-centric viewing mode of DIP, which contains links to find more information about the protein in standard protein databases. The DIP network browser shows a static, clickable image of the neighborhood of the given protein. This view can be accessed using the graph link at the top right hand side of the view. An edge-centric view is also available in DIP (not shown) that additionally shows the evidence for the interaction.**

HPRD data can be browsed and searched by a number of common database fields as well as by BLAST over the Web. Data are freely available to academics in the PSI-MI format, and commercial entities require a license.

IntAct. IntAct is a relatively new database of freely available protein interactions maintained by the European Bioinformatics Institute. An initial implementation available from mid-2003 focuses on protein–protein interactions collected from large-scale published studies and some literature curation and allows searching by protein name and browsing using a graphical network interface. One difference in the IntAct data model compared with many other protein–protein interaction databases is that interactions are not necessarily binary, but rather are sets. The advantage of using sets to store interactions is that they can represent certain types of protein complex

data where information is not known about the exact physical interactions in the complex, but only that the set of proteins co-purifies. Representing information in this way has become more important since the release of large-scale biochemical co-purification studies (Gavin et al., 2002; Ho et al., 2002). Data is available in the PSI-MI XML format. A graphical visualization of a set of IntAct records is shown in Figure 10.5.

MINT. MINT, or the Molecular INTeraction database (Zanzoni et al., 2002), contains data on the functional interactions between proteins. This consists mainly of direct protein–protein interactions, but also includes indirect and genetic interactions for more than a dozen organisms. MINT can store enzymatic modifications and information on binding domains and kinetics. It has a similar data model to IntAct and is searchable by

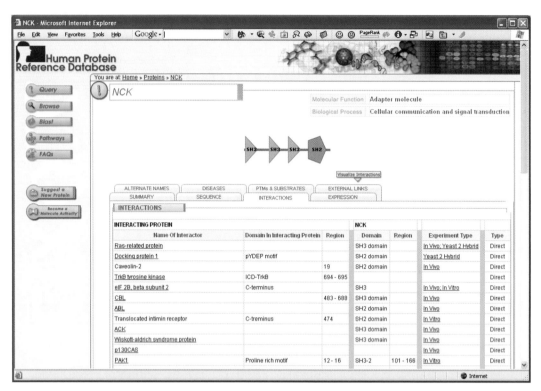

FIGURE 10.4 An **HPRD** protein information record showing a number of protein–protein interactions for **NCK**, the selected protein. **NCK** is involved in the regulation of actin cytoskeleton rearrangement. **HPRD** has many other curated fields, and interactions are just a subset of the information provided. These other fields are accessed using the tabs shown under the domain view of the protein (graphic at the top of the record). The left part of the screen contains links to the main operations on the database. The query button leads to a form that allows searching by a number of database fields, such as protein name, post-translational modifications, and diseases. Other buttons allow browsing, allow querying using **BLAST**, and show pathway diagrams using **HPRD** information.

protein information, domain, and PubMed identifier. Once viewing an interaction record, the user can launch the MintViewer Java application, which allows visual browsing of the database starting from a protein of interest. This viewer is unique in that it shows the sizes of proteins as well as if a protein can be phosphorylated and the number of interactions per edge. Users can submit their own data, and the entire database is freely available for download in PSI-MI format. A typical MINT record is shown in Figure 10.6.

Primarily Metabolic Pathway Databases

EcoCyc EcoCyc (Karp et al., 2002b) is a literature-derived curated encyclopedia of the *Escherichia coli* bacteria metabolism (strain K12). It contains among the highest quality annotation of metabolic pathways of any species. MetaCyc (Karp et al., 2002a) is another literature-derived database that uses the same Pathway Tools software as EcoCyc, thus having the same user interface; it contains information about pathways in more than 150 species, mainly microorganisms, with *E. coli* having the largest representation. BioCyc is a collection of pathway databases containing EcoCyc and MetaCyc and additionally contains metabolic pathway reconstructions for a number of organisms with sequenced genomes, including human, using the pathologic system.

EcoCyc (or, more generally, the Pathway Tools software) uses a hierarchical class structure to define an ontology of metabolic pathways and their components. An ontology is a specification that describes the concepts and their relationships from a specific knowledge domain. It can contain a list of terms and their definitions, a taxonomy of those terms, constraints, attributes, and values. An example of a constraint is a value-type constraint, where a field in a database record is limited to a specific data type, like a floating point number instead of being any data type. The presence of a class hierarchy allows a computer program to "understand" more about the classification of data into a set of types. For instance,

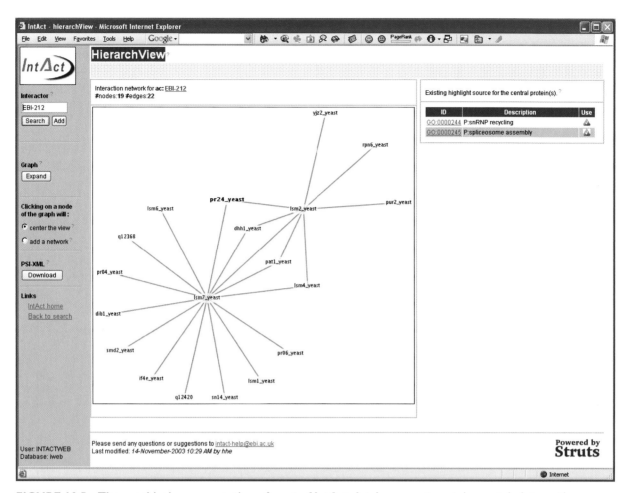

FIGURE 10.5 **The graphical representation of a set of IntAct database yeast protein–protein interaction records. Lines represent protein–protein interactions. IntAct can be queried by protein name or database identifier. The interactions that result from a query are displayed in a table, and selected interactions from this table can be graphed using the Graph button at the bottom of the table to yield this network view. The user can click on the network to link to navigate to the corresponding IntAct record. A summary of network statistics is shown above the network.**

if a ribosomal RNA (rRNA) was classified as such, but the rRNA class is a subclass of RNA, which has children snRNA and tRNA, then a computer program automatically would know by very simple logical inference, in this case, that anything labeled as rRNA, tRNA, or snRNA is also of type RNA. This allows certain complex queries to be made more easily, such as a search for all RNAs, even though nothing in the database is annotated specifically as RNA. Although this kind of search can be implemented on a case-by-case basis in software, the presence of a defined ontology for the data allows it to be carried out automatically. EcoCyc has classes for chemicals, anatomical structures, enzymatic reactions, and generalized reactions, among other things. Chemicals and generalized reactions are the most complex class hierarchies. The top part of the chemicals class hierarchy is shown in Figure 10.7.

EcoCyc models many aspects of metabolism. Instances of classes exist for reactions indexed by the Enzyme Commission and any others that have been added. Enzymes and the biochemical reactions they catalyze are represented, as well as information on transcriptional regulation of gene expression and molecular transport processes and binding reactions. The network of *E. coli* metabolism is organized into pathways and superpathways. The underlying Pathway Tools software is among the more feature-rich tools for metabolic pathway informatics and allows querying and browsing in numerous ways. A user can query by any number and combination of fields and values using Web-based forms, can choose from a list of pathways, can browse the ontology, and can choose specific classes to see instances of those classes and view a metabolic overview (Figure 10.8) that allows gene expression data to be viewed along with

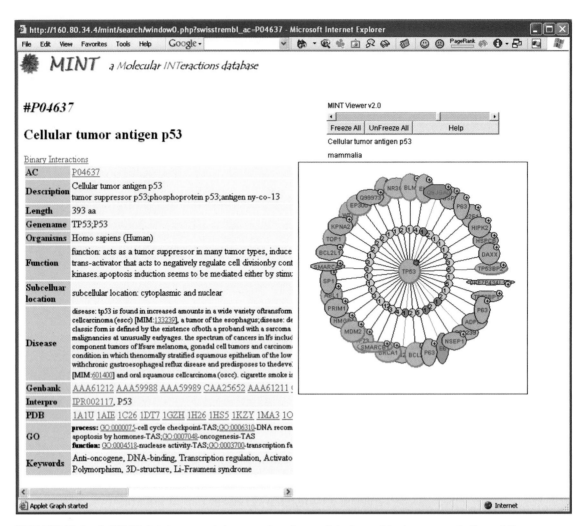

FIGURE 10.6   A MINT database protein record and associated graphical representation of the protein–protein interactions in which this protein is involved. Larger circles in the graphical view indicate larger proteins, whereas small plus symbols indicate that more interactions can be viewed if that node is clicked on. The number of experiments in the database that describe an interaction is shown in the small circles in the middle of the lines that represent interactions.

selected pathways. Users also can search for sequences in EcoCyc similar to one of interest using BLAST. Pathways, reactions, compounds, and genes all have their own record views with links that allow easy traversal from one part of *E. coli* metabolism to another. Pathways, reactions, compounds, transcriptional units, and gene regulation schematics, among other types of data, are visualized as simple diagrams to aid understanding of these relationships. Users also can click on many parts of these images to obtain more information about what they clicked on. Practically, Pathway Tools databases can be downloaded for local installation and can be accessed using Lisp, Perl, or Java. Lisp is the native language of Pathway Tools. Flatfiles also can be accessed for custom parsing.

Generally, all BioCyc databases that use the Pathway Tools software can be accessed in the same manner. EcoCyc, MetaCyc, and some of the other BioCyc databases are freely available only to academics for research purposes, but some databases have used the Pathway Tools to curate their own organism-specific pathway databases, which are made available freely. An example is TAIR, The Arabidopsis Information Resource (Rhee et al., 2003), which makes the AraCyc database available.

KEGG. The Kyoto Encyclopedia of Genes and Genomes (KEGG; Kanehisa et al., 2002) pathway database contains curated metabolic and signaling pathways. Information on enzymatic reactions, enzymes, small molecules, and genes also is available from KEGG. Pathways are

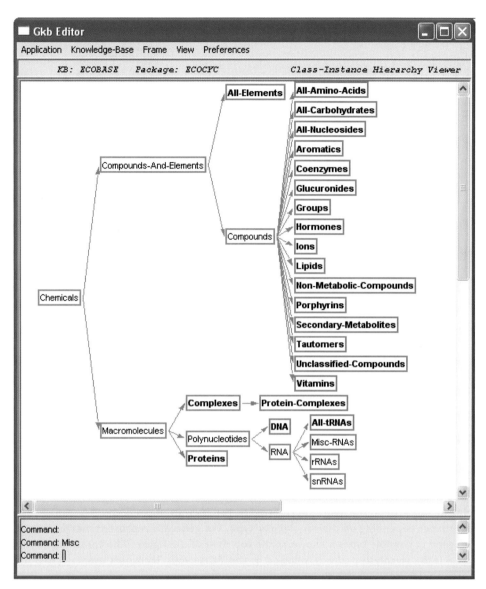

FIGURE 10.7 **A portion of the chemicals class hierarchy is shown for EcoCyc, which is similar across the BioCyc family of databases. Each red box represents a class of data. Classes are organized from most general at the top of the tree to most specific at the bottom of the tree. Bold font names for some classes indicate that subclasses exists that currently are not expanded. Each class contains a number of slots (also called fields) to hold data, which are not shown. Note the specialization of data types from the left (root) to the right (leaves) of the class hierarchy.**

available as searchable and clickable images called *maps*. Pathway maps can depict metabolism, regulatory pathways, and large complexes, such as the ribosome. Each type of these maps has its own graphical representation style. Most metabolic pathway maps are reference maps that depict generalized pathways. Generalized pathways are not species specific, thus they may never be found in their entirety in a single species. The user can select to highlight the enzymes on the generalized map that are

present in an organism of interest. Some pathway maps, such as a subset of the regulatory maps, are truly species specific.

Pathway maps in KEGG link to the underlying LIG-AND database comprising three main types of information: enzymes, reactions, and compounds. Recently, a glycan database was added to KEGG to store information about carbohydrates and their structures. Enzymes that are present in a pathway map are stored in the ENZYME

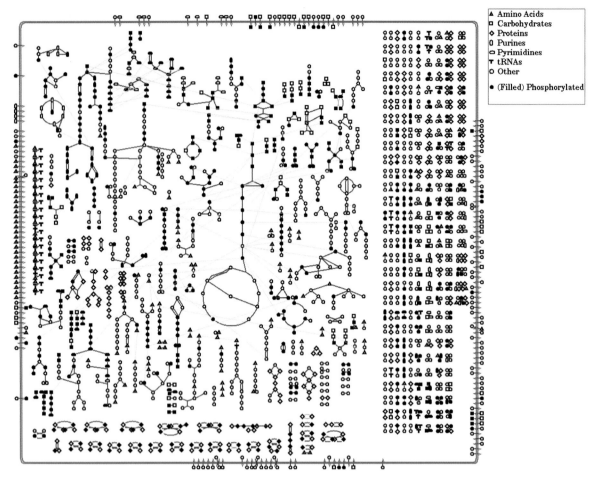

FIGURE 10.8 **An automatically generated overview of all of the pathways and reactions in EcoCyc. The brown double-line box around the figure represents the cell membrane of E. coli. The nodes of the network have different shapes depending on their molecular type, but generally represent metabolites, not enzymes. A legend of possible types is shown at the top right of the figure. The central network that contains a cycle is the glycolysis pathway followed by the TCA cycle. Transport events across the membrane are represented by arrows.**

table along with further information about them, which can link to other parts of KEGG. For instance, the reaction field in the enzyme record links to the REACTION table in KEGG, which stores information about each reaction. Individual compounds in the substrate and product fields link to the COMPOUND table. An enzyme record also links to all of the genes that encode that enzyme in the various species stored in the GENES table in KEGG. A typical enzyme record is shown in Figure 10.9.

Pathways can be searched and browsed via the KEGG Web site. Enzymes, reactions, and compounds also can be searched. The various interlinked KEGG databases are available via the Web and for download by FTP. The COMPOUND database maintains a list of curated chemical structures for most of the compounds available,

although only two-dimensional structures are available on the FTP site.

Strategies for Navigating Interaction Databases

The number and various types of interaction databases can be bewildering. From a very general and practical perspective, users searching for the latest molecular interactions from large-scale studies and the literature should search BIND and DIP, because they are the largest resources of this type of information. If a protein name of interest is not found directly in either of these databases, use the BLAST search functionality with the protein sequence of interest. Users interested in

```
ENTRY         EC 5.4.2.2
NAME          phosphoglucomutase
              glucose phosphomutase
              phosphoglucose mutase
CLASS         Isomerases
              Intramolecular transferases (mutases)
              Phosphotransferases (phosphomutases)
SYSNAME       alpha-D-glucose 1,6-phosphomutase
REACTION      alpha-D-glucose 1-phosphate = alpha-D-glucose 6-phosphate
SUBSTRATE     alpha-D-glucose 1-phosphate
PRODUCT       alpha-D-glucose 6-phosphate
COMMENT       Maximum activity is only obtained in the presence of
              alpha-D-glucose 1,6-bisphosphate. This bisphosphate is an
              intermediate in the reaction, being formed by transfer of a
              phosphate residue from the enzyme to the substrate, but the
              dissociation of bisphosphate from the enzyme complex is much slower
              than the overall isomerization. The enzyme also catalyses (more
              slowly) the interconversion of 1-phosphate and 6-phosphate isomers
              of many other alpha-D-hexoses, and the interconversion of
              alpha-D-ribose 1-phosphate and 5-phosphate. Formerly EC 2.7.5.1.
REFERENCE     1
              Joshi, J.G. and Handler, P. Phosphoglucomutase. I. Purification and
              properties of phosphoglucomutase from Escherichia coli. J. Biol.
              Chem. 239 (1964) 2741-2751.
              2
              Najjar, V.A. Phosphoglucomutase, in Boyer, P.D., Lardy, H. and
              Myrback, K. (Eds.), The Enzymes, 2nd edn., vol. 6, Academic Press,
              New York, 1962, pp. 161-178.
              3
              Ray, W.J. and Roscelli, G.A. A kinetic study of the
              phosphoglucomutase pathway. J. Biol. Chem. 239 (1964) 1228-1236.
              4
              Ray, W.J., Jr. and Peck, E.J., Jr. Phosphomutases, in Boyer, P.D.
              (Ed.), The Enzymes, 3rd edn., vol. 6, Academic Press, New York ,
              1972, pp. 407-477.
              5
              Sutherland, E.W., Cohn, M., Posternak, T. and Cori, C.F. The
              mechanism of the phosphoglucomutase reaction. J. Biol. Chem. 180
              (1949) 1285-1295.
PATHWAY       PATH: MAP00010  Glycolysis / Gluconeogenesis
              PATH: MAP00030  Pentose phosphate pathway
              PATH: MAP00052  Galactose metabolism
              PATH: MAP00500  Starch and sucrose metabolism
              PATH: MAP00521  Streptomycin biosynthesis
              PATH: MAP00522  Erythromycin biosynthesis
              PATH: MAP00530  Aminosugars metabolism
ORTHOLOG      KO: K01835  phosphoglucomutase
GENES         HSA: 5236(PGM1)
              RNO: 24645(Pgm1)
              DME: CG5165-PA(CG5165)
              CEL: R05F9.6

<output truncated for brevity>

TMA: TM0184
              MMA: MM0301 MM1521
DISEASE       MIM: 171900  Phosphoglucomutase-1
MOTIF         PS: PS00710  [GSA]-[LIVMF]-x-[LIVM]-[ST]-[PGA]-S-H-[NIC]-P
STRUCTURES    PDB: 1JDY  1KFI  1KFQ  1LXT  1VKL  3PMG
DBLINKS       IUBMB Enzyme Nomenclature: 5.4.2.2
              ExPASy - ENZYME nomenclature database: 5.4.2.2
              ERGO genome analysis and discovery system: 5.4.2.2
              BRENDA, the Enzyme Database: 5.4.2.2
              CAS: 9001
///
```

FIGURE 10.9   A KEGG ENZYME database record is shown. A number of fields are present, including the name, class, reactions, and curated annotation, links to **KEGG** pathway maps and other external resources. Importantly, the enzyme record is for the general **EC** reaction EC 5.4.2.2, which is for phosphoglucomutase reactions, not any specific enzyme in an organism. The genes that encode this type of enzyme in a number of species are shown in the **GENES** field, some of which are removed here for brevity. The "*///*" string terminates the record to aid in parsing.

human protein–protein interactions should search HPRD as well. Other interaction databases mentioned above also should be searched for completeness. Users interested in well-known metabolic pathways should try searching the BioCyc and KEGG databases. One useful tip is to browse the pathway hierarchy available in the BioCyc pathways to obtain a sense of the type of information available. Those curious about signal transduction pathways can obtain a great deal of useful information from the BioCarta Web site even though the information is not in a computer-readable form. These resources are likely the most widely used freely accessible interaction and pathway databases, although there are many specialized resources available.

Database Standards

Recently, the pathway informatics community has started to develop common data exchange formats. The Proteomics Standards Initiative (PSI) has developed the first version of an XML-based format for exchanging protein–protein interactions, called PSI-MI (PSI Molecular Interactions; Hermjakob et al., 2004). The data model of the format is simple, containing an "interaction" record comprised of a set of proteins that interact, an experimental conditions controlled vocabulary, and information about publication references and protein features, such as binding sites and post-translational modification sites. Figure 10.10 shows the top level

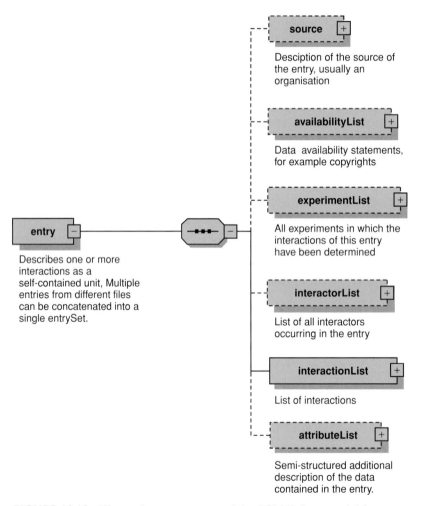

FIGURE 10.10 **The main components of the PSI-MI data model for describing protein–protein interactions. Boxes represent defined XML data types. Dashed lines represent optional elements. The octagonal box represents a collection of elements that are below it. Minus and plus symbols in small boxes represent expanded and collapsed views of each element, respectively. Collapsed boxes have more elements inside them that are not shown. The full schema for PSI-MI is on the PSI-MI Web site.**

of a PSI-MI record. The BIND, DIP, HPRD, MINT, and IntAct databases make their data available for download as PSI-MI files. Also, network visualization tools, such as Cytoscape, can read and write PSI-MI-formatted XML files.

Notably, two data exchange formats for exchanging mathematical pathway simulation models are available, Systems Biology Markup Language (SBML; Hucka et al., 2003) and Cell Markup Language (CellML). An example of a mathematical pathway model is a system of ordinary differential equations that describe the rates of all of the reactions in a pathway. With the right parameters (for example, initial concentrations and kinetic constants), the computer can calculate the concentration of the various molecular species in a pathway over time. A number of simulation tools support these formats. SBML and CellML generally do not contain information relevant to databases, such as accession numbers for proteins and small molecules involved in the reactions. The scope of each data exchange format is shown in Figure 10.11.

PREDICTION ALGORITHMS FOR PATHWAYS AND INTERACTIONS

A number of prediction algorithms for molecular interactions and pathways are available. This section focuses on the most generally accepted types of these algorithms, which attempt to predict protein–protein interactions and to reconstruct metabolic pathways from genome sequences. A summary of the main methods is shown in Figure 10.12.

Methods to Predict Protein–Protein Interactions

The recently available large number of complete genome sequences has allowed researchers to find sequence-based patterns that correlate with protein–protein interactions. Importantly, many of these protein interaction prediction methods predict functional relationships between proteins, which may or may not represent a direct protein–protein interaction. For instance, two proteins

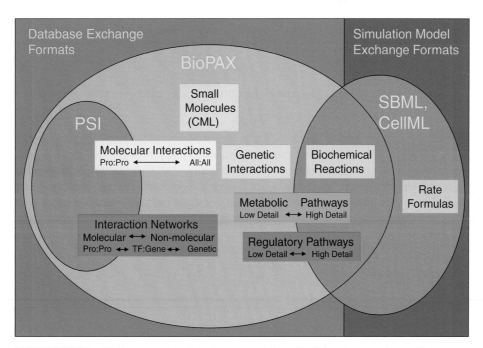

FIGURE 10.11 **A diagram showing the scope of each of the data exchange formats discussed in this chapter. Pro:Pro indicates protein–protein interactions, All:All indicates interactions between many different types of molecules. TF stands for transcription factor. CML stands for chemical markup language, which is an XML format for storing chemicals, generally small molecules. Database exchange formats are those that are suited primarily for data exchange and integration and include data elements like database identifiers. Simulation and model exchange formats primarily are suited for describing mathematical models of biological processes. BioPAX is a pathway data exchange formar. BioPAX Level 1 can represent metabolic pathways, but subsequent levels will be able to also represent molecular interactions and regulatory and genetic pathways.**

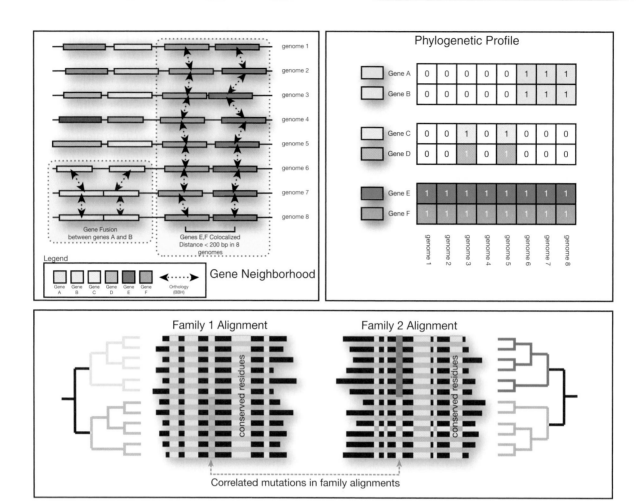

FIGURE 10.12 **(Top left) Co-localization or gene neighborhood plots for eight complete genomes, showing a pair of genes (red and blue) that are in close physical proximity in all eight genomes. A gene fusion event between two genes (yellow and light blue) in two genomes is also shown. (Top right) Example phylogenetic profiles of selected genes from the previous panel. These three pairs of genes have the same patterns of co-occurrence in all eight genomes and may physically interact based on this evidence. (Bottom) Two protein family alignments are shown with conserved regions highlighted (yellow and blue). Correlated mutations (orange) are present in two identical subtrees for each family, which indicates that these sites may have co-evolved and thus may be involved in mediating interactions between proteins from each family.**

may be predicted to interact, but in reality they are only part of the same biological process, pathway, or complex. Thus, these predictions have an associated confidence and must be validated experimentally. At the end of this section, a number of online resources that implement these methods and make available the predictions are discussed.

Gene Neighborhood

Genome co-localization or gene neighborhood approaches were some of the first methods for predicting protein–protein interactions from the genomic context of genes. Such methods exploit the observation that genes whose protein products physically interact (or

are functionally associated) are sometimes maintained in close physical chromosomal proximity to each other (Tamames et al., 1997; Dandekar et al., 1998; Overbeek et al., 1999). The most obvious case of this phenomenon are operons in bacteria and archaea, where genes whose protein products function in the same biological process are transcribed on the same polycistronic mRNA.

Operons are rare in eukaryotic species (Zorio et al., 1994; Blumenthal 1998); however, genes involved in the same biological process or pathway frequently are physically proximal on the chromosome (Dandekar et al., 1998). Thus, it is possible to predict functional or physical interaction between proteins encoded by genes that are repeatedly observed in close proximity (e.g., within

500 bp) across many genomes. This method has been used successfully to identify new members of metabolic pathways (Overbeek et al., 1999). This method is able to predict more functional associations with a larger set of complete genomes.

To assess whether pairs of orthologous genes share a common gene neighborhood across multiple genomes, one needs protein sequences and their genomic locations and an orthology mapping between proteins from the various genomes. Orthology mappings are generated by searching for pairs of close bidirectional best hits (PCBBHs). A bidirectional best hit is defined as the best BLAST hit for protein 1 in genome X is protein 1' in genome Y, and the best BLAST hit for protein 2 in genome X is protein 2' in genome Y. PCBBHs extend this definition to those genes where proteins 1 and 2 are situated within 300 bp in genome X and the genes of proteins 1' and 2' are situated within 300 bp in genome Y. Genes that satisfy these criteria can be considered as having a conserved gene neighborhood across two genomes. When this procedure is repeated across multiple genomes, it becomes possible to identify genes that are statistically significantly co-localized across many genomes, and are hence likely either to interact physically or be associated functionally. These criteria are quite strict, and it is also possible to perform the procedure using pairs of close homologs (PCHs). Sets of PCBBHs or PCHs in multiple genomes typically are scored for significance based on the number and phylogenetic distribution of genomes in which they are co-localized. Phylogenetic distance can be estimated by examining a 16S rRNA phylogenetic tree (see Chapter 14). A common score (coupling score) for the likelihood that two genes interact based on summing individual scores from multiple genomes then is calculated. Finally, candidate genes that have significant coupling scores are candidates for either physical interaction or functional association (Figure 10.12, top left).

Phylogenetic Profiles

Two of the main driving forces in genome evolution are gene genesis and gene loss (Snel et al., 2002). The fact that two genes remain paired across many different species often represents an evolutionary requirement to do so, as may be the case if they functioned in the same biological process. This criterion is less strict than gene co-localization, where gene pairs not only must be present, but also must be closely situated on the genome. Phylogenetic profiles show the presence or absence of genes across complete genomes from many species (Ouzounis & Kyrpides 1996; Rivera et al., 1998; Pellegrini et al., 1999). Pairs of genes that have very similar phylogenetic profiles are candidates for physical interaction or functional association. This method has

been used to infer physical interaction (Pellegrini et al., 1999) and also to predict the cellular localization of gene products (Marcotte et al., 2000), because genes involved in the same biological processes are often co-localized. Disadvantages of this method include heavy dependence on the number and distribution of genomes used to build the profile. A pair of genes with similar profiles across many bacterial, archaeal, and eukaryotic genomes is much more likely to interact than genes found to co-occur in a small number of closely related species. Another weakness is that evolutionary processes such as lineage-specific gene loss, horizontal gene transfer, nonorthologous gene displacement (Galperin & Koonin, 2000), and the extensive expansion of many eukaryotic gene families can make orthology assignment across genomes very difficult. However, given the increasing number of completely sequenced genomes, the accuracy of these predictions is expected to improve over time.

Phylogenetic profile based prediction of protein interactions has been shown to be an accurate and widely applicable method. One of the easiest ways to use this information for prediction of protein interaction is to use precomputed phylogenetic profiles for proteins of interest. The Clusters of Orthologous Groups (COGs) resource at the National Center for Biotechnology Information (NCBI) contains large numbers of profiles for various genomes (Tatusov et al., 2003). To construct a phylogenetic profile, an ortholog mapping must be made for all of the proteins in the genomes of interest. Orthologs can be defined using the bidirectional best hit approach. A phylogenetic profile for a protein then can be constructed by representing the presence or absence of an ortholog for that protein across all genomes analyzed. This can be represented efficiently as a simple binary vector with 1 indicating presence and 0 representing absence of a gene in each genome. A score of the expectation of presence of a homolog in a genome can be used instead of a binary value. All profiles are compared with all other profiles using a clustering procedure. A distance measure (such as Pearson correlation coefficient or Euclidean distance) between each profile (vector) and all other profiles is used to group profiles according to how similar they are. This correlation calculation easily can be performed using the PEARSON function in Microsoft Excel (Microsoft, Seattle, WA). Protein profiles that are highly similar or identical to each other represent candidate proteins that physically or functionally interact (Figure 10.12, top right).

Gene Fusion

A gene fusion event represents the physical fusion of two separate parent genes into a single multifunctional gene. This is the ultimate form of gene co-localization:

Interacting genes are not just kept in close proximity on the genome, but are joined physically as a single entity. It has been suggested that the driving force behind these events is to lower the regulational load of multiple interacting gene products (Enright et al., 1999). Gene fusion events hence provide an elegant way to detect functional and physical interactions computationally between proteins (Enright et al., 1999; Marcotte et al., 1999). This method is complementary to both co-localization of genes and phylogenetic profiles and uses both genome location and phylogenetic analysis to infer function or interaction.

Gene fusion events are detected by cross-species sequence comparison. Fused (composite) proteins in a given reference genome are detected by searching for unfused component protein sequences that are homologous to the reference protein, but not to each other. These unfused query sequences align to different regions of the reference protein, indicating that it is a composite protein resulting from a gene fusion event. A number of issues can complicate this analysis, the largest of which is the presence of promiscuous domains. These domains (such as helix-turn-helix and DnaJ) are highly abundant in eukaryotic organisms. The domain complexity of eukaryotic proteins coupled with the presence of promiscuous domains and large degrees of paralogy can hamper the accurate detection of gene fusion events. Although the method is not generally applicable to all genes (i.e., it requires that an observable fusion event can be detected between gene pairs), it has been applied successfully to a large number of genomes, including eukaryotic genomes (Enright & Ouzounis, 2001b; Figure 10.12, top left).

In Silico Two-Hybrid

It has been shown that a mutation in the sequence of one protein in a pair of interacting proteins frequently is mirrored by a compensatory mutation in its interacting partner. The detection of such correlated mutations can be used to predict protein–protein interactions and also has the potential to identify specific residues involved at the interaction sites (Pazos & Valencia, 2002). Previous analyses (Gobel et al., 1994) involved searching for correlation of residue mutations between sequences in the same protein family alignment (intrafamily). The in silico two-hybrid method extends this approach by searching for such mutations across different protein families (interfamily). Prediction of protein–protein interactions using this approach is achieved by taking pairs of protein family alignments and concatenating these alignments into a single cross-family alignment. A position-specific scoring matrix then is built from this alignment, and a correlation function then is applied to detect residues that are correlated both

within and across families. Correlated sites that potentially indicate protein interaction are scored. Disadvantages of this method include the computational complexity of constructing the large numbers of multiple sequence alignments required. Poor-quality alignments can increase noise in the procedure dramatically. One advantage is that a single accurate prediction of an interaction between two proteins can infer interaction between all members of both families used directly from the sequence alignment (Figure 10.12, bottom).

A related method, called *mirror tree*, predicts that two proteins functionally interact if the phylogenetic trees constructed from the multiple sequence alignments of each protein are similar (Pazos & Valencia, 2001). Phylogenetic trees will be similar for proteins that co-evolve, thus this method is similar to phylogenetic profiles.

Other Biological Context Approaches

A common inductive step in biology involves transferring the function from a known gene to an unknown gene that is similar, where similarity can be defined in many ways. This should be treated as a hypothesis that requires experimental validation or falsification. For example, gene functions often are transferred on the basis of sequence similarity (Chapter 1). Because the molecular interactions involving a protein define its function, protein interactions may correlate among similar genes (again with similarity being defined in possibly many ways). Gene expression microarrays (Chapter 16) often are used to detect genes that have similar expression patterns, which therefore may have similar functions. It has been shown that many interacting proteins are co-expressed, based on microarray analyses (Ge et al., 2001; Grigoriev, 2001; Jansen et al., 2002). Although these methods cannot be used to determine whether two proteins interact directly, a number of computational approaches have been developed that use the correlation between correlated gene expression and interaction for protein–protein interaction or functional linkage prediction. This analysis becomes much more reliable with more expression data, and genes that have high correlation across ten experiments are much more likely to be related functionally than genes correlating across two experiments, for instance.

Another biological context-based protein interaction prediction approach uses interologs, or orthologous interactions. If an interaction between two proteins is known in one organism, it may be possible to predict that their orthologs bind in another organism. This relationship has not been very well studied because of a lack of comprehensive interaction datasets across species, but it has been shown to be useful in some examples (Matthews et al., 2001; Tien et al., 2004).

Integrating Existing Datasets

A useful approach to protein interaction prediction would be to use the best predictions of each existing method and ignore the worst predictions. Without experimental validation, how is it possible to know which predictions are good? A recently described interaction prediction method combines information from multiple biological datasets that are known to be correlated noisily to protein–protein interaction to minimize the noise associated with each set to predict protein co-complex interactions reliably (both proteins are present in the same complex) in the budding yeast (Jansen et al., 2003). This method uses Bayesian networks to compare each source of interaction evidence against samples of known positive (proteins in the same complex) and negative (proteins in different cellular locations) interactions, allowing a statistical reliability score of interaction prediction to be calculated for each data source. A probability value for a protein interaction can be calculated given the set of noisy datasets in which it is present and the confidence in each dataset. The noisy data sources included large-scale protein interaction datasets, gene co-expression, and similar biological functional annotation. Protein interactions predicted in this way have been shown to be as reliable as pure experimental techniques and to cover a larger proportion of genes.

Summary

Each of the methods covered in this section has strengths and weaknesses. Gene neighborhood, phylogenetic, and *in silico* two-hybrid profiles give better predictions when applied to a larger set of completed genomes. The gene fusion method predicts well, but is not general, because the actual number of detected fusion events is small in existing genomes. All of these methods currently are better suited for prokaryotic proteins, because there are few completely sequenced eukaryotic genomes available. Co-expression analysis is limited by a low correlation to known protein interactions, although a great deal of eukaryotic microarray data are available. With all of these complications to protein interaction prediction, where should one start? The next section addresses this question.

▌RESOURCES FOR INTERACTION PREDICTION

A number of resources make available precomputed results using some of the methods described above for a number of genomes in a user-friendly manner. These should be queried first when the user is interested in predicted functional linkages among proteins. The STRING resource (von Mering et al., 2003) makes available precomputed gene neighborhood, gene fusion, phylogenetic profile, co-expression, and co-mentioned in PubMed abstract-based protein–protein functional associations, combined with collected experimental and database evidence information for more than 110 genomes in a very graphical and user-friendly manner. Phylogenetic profiles are derived from the COG database, and protein sequences are updated from Swiss-Prot. STRING allows searching by gene name, accession number, and sequence of interest (as long as it is already present in the database). Results are displayed graphically and are scored using a STRING-specific scoring scheme that correlates with validated protein–protein functional associations. Predictions can be filtered by a user-defined threshold score. Figure 10.13 shows a screenshot of STRING results. All STRING predictions can be downloaded for local use.

Predictome (Mellor et al., 2002) is a Web-based tool for visualizing predicted and experimentally determined interactions between proteins. Computational methods include gene fusion, gene neighborhood, and phylogenetic profiles, whereas experimental methods are yeast two-hybrid, biochemical copurification, and correlated gene expression. The precomputed analysis is available for more than 40 genomes with some genomes, like budding yeast, containing more experimental information than others. Predictome can be searched using gene names or key words and information is visualized graphically using a Java applet that allows browsing the network of stored interactions. All Predictome predictions can be downloaded for local use.

The AllFuse database (Enright & Ouzounis, 2001b) provides a comprehensive set of inferred protein–protein interactions from gene fusions in 24 complete genomes (both prokaryotic and eukaryotic). This information can also be downloaded by FTP for local use. Finally, the GeneCensus site provides the results of the Bayesian network data integration protein interaction predictions in a searchable and graphical form for budding yeast. A user can search by yeast gene name and can select a score cutoff to retrieve the predictions as a graphical network, centered around the gene of interest.

Metabolic Pathway Reconstruction

Given a newly sequenced genome and a list of conserved metabolic pathways from a closely related species, it should be possible to predict metabolic pathways in the new genome. A few software systems attempt to carry out this metabolic pathway reconstruction from complete and almost complete genomes. Signaling pathways currently cannot be reconstructed in this manner because they seem to be much less conserved than metabolic pathways. Starting with a list of predicted open reading frames (ORFs), enzymatic function

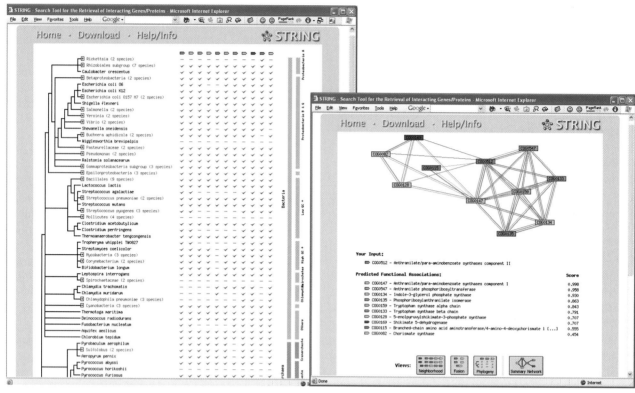

FIGURE 10.13 Two aspects of the **STRING** resource are shown. On the left, an overview of the phylogenetic profiling predictions results is shown. A phylogenetic tree is shown on the left side, with a general phylogenetic grouping shown on the right side of the columns. Each column represents a protein shown in the results (different-colored pointed boxes as column headings). Green check boxes indicate the protein is present in the corresponding organism, and red minus signs mean the protein is not present. Similar columns indicate functional interactions according to the prediction method (see text). The right screenshot shows the results summary view, with different colored lines indicating which method predicted each link. This view is useful to study directly after a query to obtain an idea of the types and strengths of the results. Red, gene fusion; green, gene neighborhood; blue, phylogenetic profiling.

is assigned in an iterative manner from a list of known enzymes (Figure 10.14). Enzymatic functions generally are assigned by sequence similarity, but also could use any other technique for defining gene function until as many links as possible to known pathways have been made. Confidence that a pathway is present in a given organism can be calculated from the number of enzymes that are unique to that pathway that are seen in the new genome. Enzymes that are part of multiple pathways cannot be considered to indicate unambiguously the presence of a pathway. Pathways are then validated by checking that they balance (that is, input compounds equal output compounds). If they do not balance because of missing enzymes, these enzymes can be searched more thoroughly in the genome being annotated. This process is termed *hole filling* and can become quite complex. Results for the reconstruction will improve when the experimentally known pathways being used are from a species that is closely-related to the one being annotated.

Results will suffer when this is not the case. Additionally, biochemical activity may be observed and characterized in a reference pathway without identifying the enzyme involved. For these pathway steps, no reconstruction can take place. Interestingly, metabolic reconstruction can be performed on gapped, or unfinished, genomes, as long as there is enough sequence to make functional enzyme assignments (Selkov et al., 2000). The final stages of metabolic pathway reconstruction can include manual curation of all functional assignments up to and including wet lab experiments to validate the results.

Two tools that are available for metabolic pathway reconstruction are the Pathologic and WIT systems. Pathologic is a component of the Pathway Tools software of the BioCyc project, discussed above. Pathologic takes as input a sequenced genome in GenBank flatfile format as well as information on the ORFs and predicted enzyme commission (EC) numbers for each possible enzyme and uses the MetaCyc database to reconstruct probable

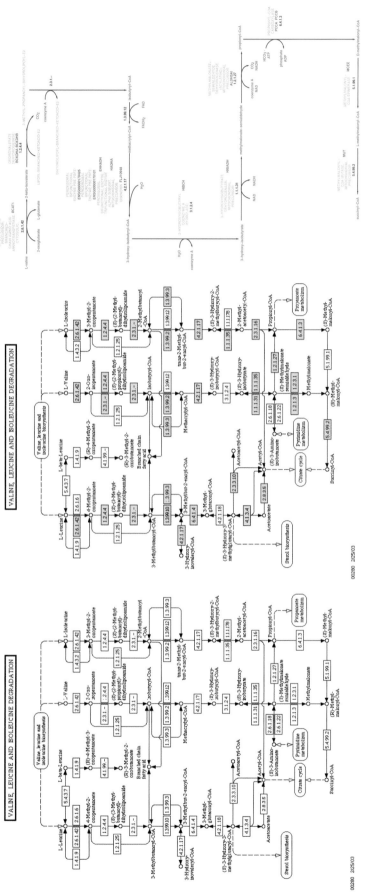

FIGURE 10.14 An example of metabolic pathway reconstruction from KEGG and BioCyc. The valine degradation pathway reconstructed in human. The left panel shows the reference valine degradation pathway in KEGG. The KEGG reference pathway is a superset of all known valine degradation pathway components from all organisms. The middle panel shows enzymes that KEGG has found to be present in the sequenced human genome highlighted in green. In KEGG, the enzymes are represented by their EC number (e.g., 2.6.1.42), which defines the enzyme function. The EC system is a hierarchy of enzyme functions similar to the GO molecular function controlled vocabulary, but much older. Note that not all enzymes from the reference pathway are highlighted in green. This is because KEGG was not able to find these enzymes in the human genome. A good example of this is the 3-hydroxyisobutyryl coenzyme A hydrolase (EC 3.1.2.4) that should exist in the human valine degradation pathway because there are no other enzymes from the reference pathway that can replace its function. Thus, this missing enzyme represents a "hole" in the pathway. This does not mean that the enzyme does not exist in the human genome. It may not be recognized easily because of sequence divergence over evolution or because of inaccurate gene finding. The HumanCyc pathway reconstruction from the BioCyc family of databases is able to fill the hole (right panel). Note that the EC 3.1.2.4 enzyme is present and linked to the *HIBCH* gene. Clicking on this gene in HumanCyc links to various sequence databases that contain this gene, as well as to publications that provide evidence that the *HIBCH* gene is an EC 3.1.2.4 enzyme. The extra computational and curatorial effort by HumanCyc is able to fill pathway holes.

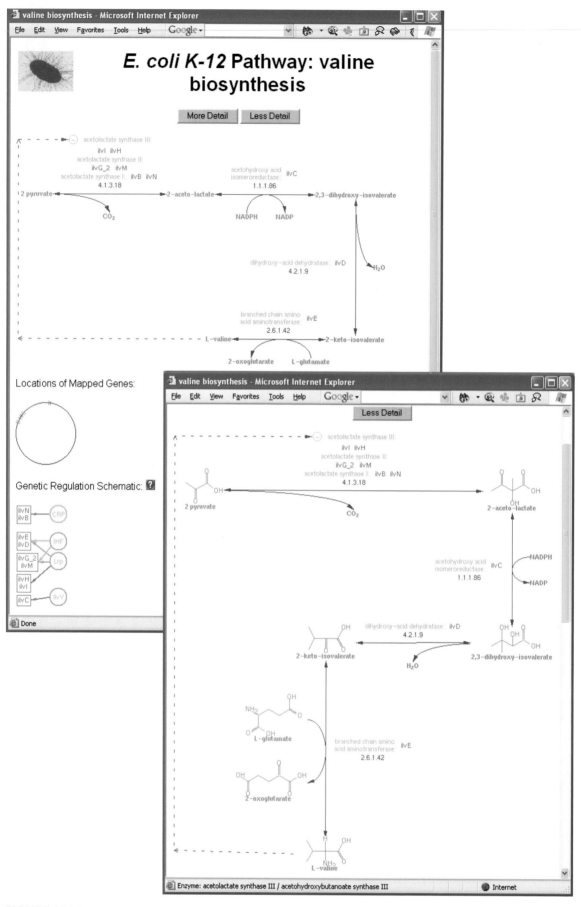

FIGURE 10.15

metabolic pathways. A number of reconstructions for sequenced genomes are available on the BioCyc Web site.

WIT (for What Is There?) is another metabolic pathway reconstruction tool whose results are stored in the WIT database. WIT uses the database of enzyme and metabolic pathways that is available on the same Web site for pathway reconstruction given a genome of interest. Pathway reconstructions in WIT start from raw genomic sequence; functional annotation tools (Chapter 1) are used directly to infer enzymatic functions for predicted ORFs. Finally, each reconstruction is curated by an expert biologist. Currently, WIT contains pathway reconstruction information on 39 completely or partially sequenced genomes and can be searched and can be browsed via the Web. Reconstructed pathways can be visualized as static clickable images.

NETWORK AND PATHWAY VISUALIZATION TOOLS

Biologists are very visually oriented people and often prefer studying diagrams rather than tables. For this reason, it is common to see biologists sketch networks of molecular interactions, although this activity is only practical with small networks. Network and pathway visualization tools are computer programs that automate this task and can draw a diagram of a network or pathway. Often, these tools offer much more than just a pretty picture, and can incorporate data integration features and powerful data analysis modules. This section describes the basic types of tools available, gives some background on how they work, and focuses on newly developed tools for network visualization and analysis.

Pathway visualization tools, especially for browsing metabolic pathways, have been around since shortly after the first metabolic databases were built. For instance, a pathway drawing tool is present in the ACeDB database (Eeckman & Durbin, 1995) and in EcoCyc (Karp et al., 2002b). Many of these tools display static pictures that are "clickable," so a user could use their mouse to click on a component of the pathway, such as an enzyme or small molecule, to obtain more information about it from a database. Examples of static clickable pathway images can be found on the KEGG (Kanehisa et al., 2002; Figure 10.14) or BioCarta Web sites. More advanced tools are able to generate pathway diagrams dynamically from an underlying database that allow the user to change how the pathway is viewed. For instance, the EcoCyc database contains a pathway visualization tool that can display varying levels of detail about a pathway, from an overview to a detailed view showing all chemical structures of small molecules in the pathway (Figure 10.15). The WIT database (Overbeek et al., 2000) also contains a dynamic pathway diagram generator. Pathway tools view data in manageable chunks, the pathways. Although this is very useful for browsing and reference, because a database curator generally predefines each pathway, it is not as amenable to the analysis of large data sets. To map and study new pathways, biologists must possess tools that allow them easily to add their own novel data and to expand beyond previously defined knowledge. Very recently, within the past one to two years, a number of biomolecular network visualization tools have been created and have been made available, fulfilling a need to analyze the large amount of molecular interaction data being generated by proteomics and other high-throughput or large-scale studies (see above and Chapter 17). Although new and often still under development, network visualization tools can be very useful for understanding relationships within large interconnected data sets. They also provide a practical framework for integrating other types of biological data, such as gene expression values (see below).

All network tools rely on concepts from the computer science field of graph theory, so a brief discussion of basic graph theory concepts is in order (Box 10.1). Graph theory is based on the notion of a graph as a representation of connected data as a set of nodes (or vertices) and a set of connecting edges (Figure 10.16). Edges may be directed, in which case they may be called arcs. Nodes and edges may have associated weights or other data values. Different classes of graphs exist; for instance, a graph that does not contain any cycles is called acyclic

FIGURE 10.15 The valine biosynthesis pathway dynamically drawn by the **Pathway Tools** software that supports the **BioCyc** family of databases. The advantage of automatic pathway diagram layout is that the diagram can be drawn according to user preference. Here, two views of the same pathway are shown, the bottom one in more detail than the top. Note the presence of small molecule structures in the bottom view. The pathway diagram uses the same representation as **KEGG**, with nodes being metabolites and edges representing enzymes. The lower left side of the left window graphically shows the locations of the genes involved in the pathway on the E. coli chromosome. Note that many of the genes for this pathway are located very close together on the chromosome. This type of information is used by the gene neighborhood protein interaction approach to predict protein functional relationships (see text). The lower diagram shows the genetic regulatory network for transcription factors (circles) that regulate the genes in this pathway (purple squares).

BOX 10.1 Advanced Graph Theory Applications

Interestingly, any graph can be represented as an N × N matrix, called an *adjacency matrix*, where the rows and columns represent the nodes in a graph and a I is placed in the matrix at position (i, j) if node i connects with node j. If the edges in the graph are weighted, the weight can be recorded at position (i, j) instead of a I. Because many types of matrices in bioinformatics are N × N, or square, they can be represented as a graph, and it is sometimes useful to make this conversion to visualize the matrix. One interesting example is a protein sequence similarity matrix, which records the sequence similarity (e.g., as calculated by BLAST [Chapter 11]), of a set of sequences in an all-against-all fashion. The rows and columns of a similarity matrix represent the set of things being compared; in this case, protein sequences and matrix position (i, j) records the similarity score of protein i compared with protein j. By visualizing this data as a network instead of a matrix, the connections between clusters of similar proteins are more visually apparent.

Mathematicians also may convert a graph to the adjacency matrix to apply algebraic matrix operations to the matrix to solve specific graph problems. Sometimes the matrix operations are faster than the same operations performed directly on a graph. For instance, the entries (i, j) in the square of an adjacency matrix correspond to the number of paths of length two that exist in the graph between nodes i and j. This can be extended to higher powers of the adjacency matrix. Squaring the matrix quickly gives this answer if the matrix is sparse (filled with many zeros), but not as quickly if the graph is dense. Fortunately, many problems in biology translate to sparse graphs. One algorithm in bioinformatics that uses this mathematical problem solving tactic to cluster a similarity matrix is a Markov cluster algorithm (MCL; Enright et al., 2002). Through a series of adjacency matrix multiplications of the similarity graph and other mathematical operations, clusters of similar proteins are detected. Proteins in a similarity cluster have more paths between them than to proteins in other clusters. The matrix squaring operations are involved in counting the number of paths from one protein to another.

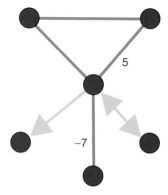

FIGURE 10.16 An introduction to terminology and visual notation in the computer science field of graph theory. Blue circles are nodes or vertices (singular is vertex), undirected lines are called edges (red, green), directed lines are called arcs (cyan). Nodes or edges can have associated attributes, such as weights. Here, two edge weights are shown, 5 and –7. A series of edges that form a closed loop is called a cycle (red lines). The colors are present in this figure solely to annotate the graph and are not part of normal visual notation. A graph is an abstract mathematical concept. Edge direction, weights, and other attributes do not mean anything until mapped to a specific problem.

(also called a *tree*). Tree graphs have a root node and leaf nodes, and a collection of trees is termed a *forest*. An example of a directed acyclic graph in bioinformatics is Gene Ontology, in which the most general annotation term is the root and the most specific terms are leaf nodes. The number of edges connected to a node is called the *degree* for an undirected graph. For a directed graph, *in degree* and *out degree* are the number of arcs input and output, respectively, from a node. Note that a graph is a completely abstract mathematical concept

and can be mapped to any problem where a mapping can be imagined; thus, direction, weight, and connectivity do not have any biologically (or other domain) specific meaning until a mapping is made.

Intuitively, biomolecular interaction networks can be mapped to a graph, where biomolecules are represented as nodes and interaction information can be represented as edges. Other information also could be mapped; for instance, edge direction may be mapped from cell signaling and chemical action information, and edge weight may be derived from reaction kinetics, publication opinion, experimental system type, or statistically derived confidence values for the data. Some types of biological interaction information can not be mapped to a graph faithfully, or there may be multiple ambiguous mappings or mappings that cause loss of information. For example, protein complexes larger than two molecules detected in a co-immunoprecipitation experiment cannot be described easily using the binary relationships in a graph; rather, they can be accurately represented only as a set, because the direct physical connections between the proteins in the complex are not known from the experiment.

The reason graph theory is used to represent biological networks, is that it can be used to answer many interesting biological questions. For instance, if one wants to find out if one protein connects to another protein in a protein interaction network, an algorithm (called a *breadth-first search*) can be run that is guaranteed by a mathematical proof to find the shortest path between the two nodes, if it exists. Many other useful graph algorithms exist to manipulate, query, analyze, and visualize graphs. In a social network, where nodes represent people and edges their friendships, the shortest path between people on average is six, hence the famous saying that everyone on Earth is connected by six degrees of separation. Although shortest path is a relatively quick query, some graph algorithms are notoriously difficult to compute. For example, the traveling salesperson problem aims to find the optimal path (e.g., the least expensive) for a salesperson to travel along to visit all cities and return to the starting point, given a number of cities and the cost between each pair. As more cities are considered, the number of possible cycles that visit all of them grows exponentially, and finding the cycle of minimum cost using an exhaustive search quickly becomes unfeasible. Often, though, it is possible to approximate the optimal solution in a practical amount of time. More information about graph theory can be found in several well-written graph theory algorithm books (Bollobâas, 1998; Mehlhorn & Nèaher, 1999; Cormen, 2001).

Network visualization tools additionally rely on algorithms from the computer science field of graph layout. Typically, graph layout algorithms try to make a graph look aesthetically pleasing; that is, they try to minimize the overlapping of nodes and edges so that as much of the graph as possible is clearly visible. Graph layout is practical and generally works well on small to medium graphs, such as those up to approximately 500 nodes for a typically sized viewing area, such as a computer monitor. Larger networks than this require larger than normal viewing areas, such as a multiple monitor desktop or large format printers.

There are many types of graph layout algorithms, such as arranging nodes hierarchically, in a circular fashion, or in less structured formats. Importantly, the type of graph layout algorithm that will work best depends heavily on the type of network that is input. For instance, a highly connected network will not display well when laid out hierarchically; only a truly hierarchical graph, like a tree, will lay out well in this case. Thus, the most useful network visualization tools contain multiple layout methods that should all be tried to see which one generates the most aesthetically pleasing layout.

One of the most commonly used types of layout is called a *spring-embedded algorithm*, from the general class of force-directed layout algorithms, which contain many variations on a theme. In a typical case, the graph is modeled as a physical system where edges are springs and nodes are like-charged particles. The layout starts by placing all nodes randomly and then calculates the position of each node, given that long edges are like stretched springs and will pull the connected nodes close together, whereas nodes will repel each other the closer they are. By iterating over time, the graph can stabilize on the final layout, which will have relatively short edges and relatively nonoverlapping nodes. Think of this as taking a number of like-charged beads (nodes) connected by springs (edges), throwing them up in the air, and seeing what pattern they are in when they land.

BioLayout

BioLayout is a Java-based general network visualization tool with a custom layout algorithm that preferentially places functionally similar nodes together (Enright & Ouzounis, 2001a), so that biologically relevant functional clustering is seen more easily. For the BioLayout algorithm to function properly, a network has to be loaded with associated functional classes for the nodes. The BioLayout file format supports node classes and edge weights. BioLayout edges are directed by default, but this can be changed in the properties dialog box. A number of useful selection features are available to select nodes based on functional annotation and network topology properties, including a feature to select nodes by edge weight using a slider bar.

Cytoscape

Cytoscape is a freely available, open-source Java-based network visualization and analysis tool. Cytoscape's main strengths compared with other network visualization tools are its ability to analyze network data in the context of other types of data, a range of layout algorithms, and the ability to add new features using plug-ins. For instance, gene expression values for specific genes can be mapped as node colors for a network. Cytoscape networks can be edited and nodes can be selected, dragged, and rotated using the mouse. Also, complex node and edge selections can be made based on user-defined combinations of loaded attributes and graph topology using "filter" functionality.

Cytoscape uses the concepts of network attributes and visual attributes when integrating and visualizing information on the network. There are two types of network attributes: node and edge attributes.

A node attribute is simply a data value that is loaded onto a node. If the node represents a protein, a node attribute could be the name of the protein, a term that describes the functional classification of that protein, perhaps from the gene ontology, or a protein abundance measurement. Similarly, an edge attribute is a data value that is loaded onto an edge. If the edge represents an interaction among two proteins, an edge attribute could be the strength of the interaction or the type of experimental method that was used to detect the interaction. Multiple types of node and edge attributes can be loaded simultaneously, as long as each type has a different name. Either attribute can be discrete or continuous. An example of a discrete attribute is a list of interaction detection experimental methods that could be edge attributes. An example of a continuous attribute is a set of gene expression values that ranges from 0.0 to 1.0. Cytoscape allows all numbers to be continuous and all numbers and strings to be discrete.

Visual attributes in Cytoscape are aspects of a network diagram that could be displayed in different ways (Figure 10.17). The seven types of node visual attributes in Cytoscape currently are node shape, size, label, font, color, border color, and border type. The six types of edge visual attributes currently are edge label, font, color, line type (line, dashed line, etc.), target arrow, and source arrow. The last two types represent the arrow type at each side of an edge. Other types of visual attributes can be imagined, such as transparency and ones that display multidimensional data.

After a network is loaded into Cytoscape, any attributes that are loaded onto edges or nodes can be mapped to visual attributes using the Cytoscape visualization mapper. Multiple visual mappings, called *visual styles* by Cytoscape, can be created, and all are saved automatically in a preferences file whenever any changes are made. A specific example of a mapping for a protein interaction network would be to load in normalized gene expression values, which range from 0.0 to 1.0, with 1.0 being the highest gene expression values in the set, then creating a visual style that maps this to node color, with 0.0 being green and 1.0 being red. Cytoscape then colors all nodes continuously according to the style, and an expression value of 0.5 will be colored midway between green and red.

Another strength of Cytoscape is the ability to add features by loading external plug-ins. Plug-ins can be written in Java and can add any type of feature, such as a new layout algorithm or analysis technique. The source code for Cytoscape is freely available, because it is an open-source program; thus, any interested software developers can write new plug-ins to extend the functionality of Cytoscape for their own purposes. If these are published, it is hoped that they also would be made freely available to the community, although the availability of a plug-in is decided by the plug-in's creator.

Types of plug-ins that are currently available for Cytoscape include ActiveModules, which finds regions of a molecular interaction network that are correlated across multiple gene expression experiments; PathBLAST, which find regions of two protein interaction networks where the protein sequences and connectivity are conserved (possibly with gaps); Biomodules, which is a network clustering application for finding loose functional associations of connected molecules in a network. Plug-ins that add input functionality include a reader for PSI-MI and SBML files. The list of available plug-ins can be found on the Cytoscape Web page.

Cytoscape also makes available a number of network layout algorithms. Useful layouts include circular, hierarchical, organic, and embedded. Circular and hierarchical algorithms try to lay out the network, as their names suggest. Organic and embedded are two versions of a force-directed layout algorithm.

Osprey

Osprey is a Java-based network visualization and analysis tool for protein–protein and genetic interaction networks (Breitkreutz et al., 2003b). Traditionally, Osprey has been yeast focused, but because it connects to the GRID database, other species that GRID supports are available to it. Currently, Osprey connects to yeast, worm, fly, and human versions of GRID. Osprey has a very user-friendly interface and a number of custom graph layouts that have been designed to represent complex biological networks better. Osprey supports visualizing a network and assigning colors to the nodes based on function and edges by experimental interaction detection type. A small set of visual attributes can be custom defined for nodes and edges. These are label font and font type, node size, edge width, and edge arrow size. Networks can be edited to add new nodes and edges. When a new node is added, it requires a name, which is searched in the selected GRID database. Any database match for that protein name automatically imports the biological annotation for that protein. If no match is found, the node is added to the graph without annotation. The network analysis features of Osprey are filters for various types of information present as node and edge attributes (network filters) and topology properties (connection filters). For instance, using a network filter, the user can select to show only nodes that match specific GO process terms or edges that were determined using a given experimental system. Connection filters allow selected viewing of a node by minimum degree and depth from a selected set of nodes of interest. Networks that are built in Osprey can be saved and loaded in the Osprey file format.

VisANT

VisANT (Hu et al., 2004) is a Web-based Java applet for visualizing and analyzing biomolecular interaction data. Like the other tools discussed here, networks can be loaded and visualized with a number of layout schemes. VisANT is interesting in that it connects directly to the Predictome database, which makes it very easy to load

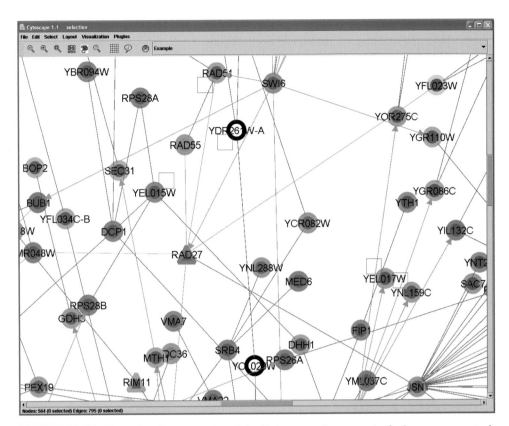

FIGURE 10.17 **Zooming in on a network in Cytoscape shows part of a large, connected network of protein and genetic interactions from budding yeast. This view is meant to emphasize the visual customization available in Cytoscape. Different color edges represent different types of interactions (blue, protein–protein; green, genetic synthetic lethal; cyan, genetic synthetic slow growth; and red, protein–DNA). Arrows point from protein transcription factor to the genes they bind upstream of, potentially regulating them. Nodes represent genes and are colored blue to red by most significant to least significant gene expression fold change from a gene knock-out condition (Gal4 KO) compared with wild-type control. These are statistically processed gene expression values indicating significance of fold change between two conditions (Chapter 16). Node border color ranges from purple to yellow by least gene expression fold change to most gene expression fold change from a gene knock-out condition (Gal4 KO) compared with wild-type control. These are the raw gene expression values from a cDNA comparative hybridization chip (Chapter 16). The shape of each node corresponds to functional annotation of interest, with triangle as either meiosis, PolIII transcription, mating response, or DNA repair. Circles are unassigned categories (other annotation). Importantly, this view in Cytoscape is not standard, but was derived by the user by selecting data attributes to map to visual attributes. For instance, the user could have chosen to represent protein–DNA interactions as yellow dashed-line arrows instead of red arrows simply by changing options in Cytoscape's visual mapper.**

and view a wide range of existing interaction datasets, either by searching for a gene of interest or by experimental method. For instance, all of the known synthetic lethal interactions can be loaded directly using the Method table in the View menu. VisANT also provides many hyperlinks to Web pages that have more information about a particular protein (through a context-sensitive menu). Loading data into VisANT is

species specific, and more than 40 species are supported, although most of them are prokaryotic. Interestingly, VisANT includes the ability to search the graph for feedback or feedforward loops and other cycles that may be involved in interesting regulatory processes in signaling pathways. The user also can answer the question, "How are my selected proteins connected?," using the Find Shortest Path feature. Even though VisANT runs through a Web browser, it allows the user to upload and save their own data as well as to make specific datasets available on the server for others to share (although this requires the user to register with the system and to log in at the beginning of each session).

Summary

BioLayout is useful for laying out large networks in a biologically meaningful way by keeping proteins with similar attributes together. Cytoscape excels at visualizing multiple data types and by performing plug-in analyses. Osprey is tailored for the biologist at the bench and is recommended for this user group. VisANT connects directly to Predictome, and so has direct access to many predicted and experimental interactions, although VisANT currently only runs as a Java applet through a Web page.

SPECIAL FOCUS: INTEGRATING GENE EXPRESSION DATA WITH PATHWAY INFORMATION

As already mentioned in this chapter, many types of biological data can be integrated with biological pathways or networks for the purpose of gaining biological context. Gene co-expression is correlated with protein interactions and pathways and the two types of information can be used together to help define gene function and to understand further the dynamics of cellular pathways. This section showcases some of the free tools that are available for analyzing gene expression in the context of networks and pathways.

There are currently three main categories of tools available that integrate pathway and gene expression information:

▶ Tools that visualize expression on a pathway diagram

▶ Tools that perform overrepresentation analysis (ORA) using pathways

▶ Tools that co-cluster expression and pathway data.

Many tools are available to visualize gene expression information on a pathway diagram. Both Pathway Tools and Pathway Processor (Grosu et al., 2002) allow gene expression data to be visualized on predefined pathways from EcoCyc and KEGG, respectively. GenMAPP (Dahlquist et al., 2002) adds the ability to define pathways using basic drawing tools (Figure 10.18). Cytoscape allows visualization of gene expression data on any network (Figure 10.14). Generically, these tools must be able to load pathway information and gene expression data and to match genes from one data set to the other.

The general problem of automatically matching gene identifiers across datasets is an unsolved problem in bioinformatics, so these tools usually require the gene names to match. One tool available that tries to ease the problem of name or identifier matching for gene expression data sets is MatchMiner (Bussey et al., 2003), currently available for human genes. After being matched, gene expression data is mapped as colors on proteins in the pathway diagram, generally with deeper shades of red indicating overexpression, and deeper shades of green indicating underexpression (see Chapter 16). GenMAPP runs only on Windows (Microsoft), but currently supports human, mouse, rat, and budding yeast (new species are supported regularly), whereas Pathway Processor runs on any platform with a recent version of Java installed, but only supports budding yeast and *Bacillus subtilis*.

Overrepresentation analysis is a statistical analysis that determines if a list of items is significantly overrepresented in a sample given the number and types of items that exist. For instance, if a sample has three blue items and three red items and there are known to be 500 blue items and 100 red items in the world, then red is overrepresented and blue is underrepresented in the sample, because it would be expected that there would be five blue items and one red item if items were randomly picked from the set of 600 blue and red items. This can be applied in biology if the samples are, for instance, sets of genes defined by gene expression clustering, by shared GO annotation terms, or the set of genes in a pathway or region of a network. Typically, a hypergeometric distribution to model random sampling without replacement, with an optional multiple hypothesis correction (such as a Bonferroni correction), is used to calculate the probability that a set of genes is overrepresented compared with chance (Robinson et al., 2002). Sometimes, a Fisher's exact test is used to calculate a similar type of probability indicating if there are nonrandom associations between genes in the category of interest and those that are not in that category. The Fisher's exact test is technically better for small values, but both of these statistical methods can not deal with problems of errors and systematic bias perfectly in the sample (Zeeberg et al., 2003), so statistical values indicating overrepresentation should be interpreted carefully before basing further studies on the results.

At least four tools are available that perform ORA on gene lists, which can be derived from gene expression datasets (e.g., overexpressed or underexpressed genes) using a number of possible annotation categories. MAPPFinder (Doniger et al., 2003), from the GenMAPP project, tests whether a given GO term is significantly enriched for genes of interest from a MAPP file, using a hypergeometric distribution. Because MAPP files

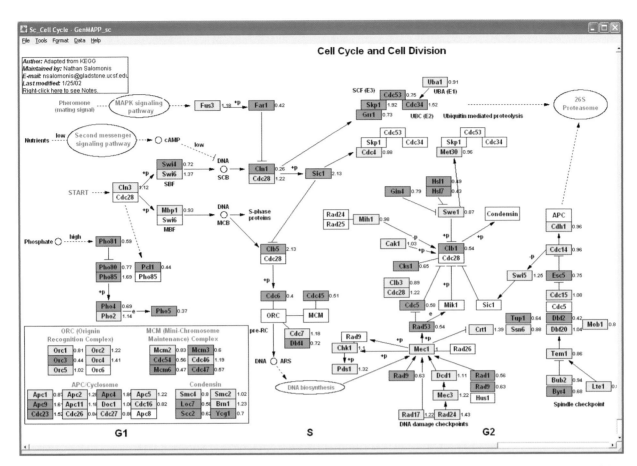

FIGURE 10.18 The GenMAPP program displaying a hand-curated pathway of the yeast cell cycle overlaid with gene expression data from a single experiment. Proteins and genes are represented as boxes, and relationships between them are represented as lines. When creating a pathway diagram, the user can use a number of drawing tools to indicate more than just molecular interactions. For instance, the large ovals on the top left of this diagram represents signaling pathways, and the oval on the top right represents the 26S proteasome, a large protein complex. Both of these are general concepts represented using the same shape and rely on previous biological knowledge to differentiate them. Upregulated genes are colored red, and downregulated genes are colored green according to a gene expression experiment that was loaded in GenMAPP. Information about the maintainer of this pathway is shown on the upper left-hand side of the figure.

can represent any set of genes, including pathways and simple sets of genes with the same GO annotations, MAPPFinder is quite general after a MAPP file is constructed. MAPPFinder conveniently deals with gene expression datasets compatible with GenMAPP. GoMiner (Zeeberg et al., 2003) analyzes two sets of genes, one containing genes of interest (e.g., overexpressed) and the other containing all known genes in a set (e.g., on a microarray) and tests whether a GO annotation term is significantly enriched or depleted in interesting genes, using the Fisher's exact test method. Both MAPPFinder and GoMiner show their results in the context of the GO, but MAPPFinder displays slightly more statistical information for each GO term and GoMiner contains a visualization of a large part of the GO network as a summary,

with terms colored by significant enrichment or depletion of interesting genes (Figure 10.19). EASE (Hosack et al., 2003) is a tool that performs ORA on a given list of genes using an easily customizable set of annotation categories. Predefined categories include GO, KEGG, PFAM, SMART, and a number of others. EASE gene lists support numerous gene identifiers, including Affymetrix IDs for easy analysis of gene expression results. Funspec (Robinson et al., 2002) is another tool that performs ORA, but does so for any given set of budding yeast genes against a number of different types of annotation from GO, MIPS, SMART, and PFAM domains (c.f., Chapter 8) and custom gene sets from large-scale interaction, localization, and protein complex experimental mapping studies.

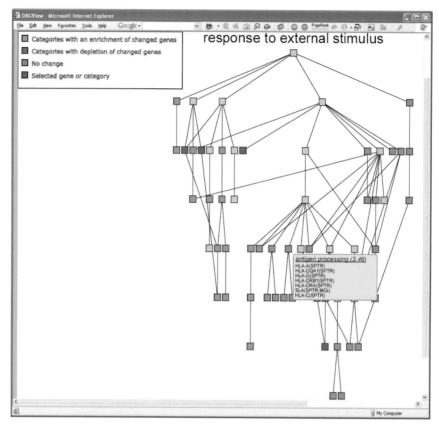

FIGURE 10.19   **The GO DAG** summary view from **GoMiner** showing **GO** annotation terms under the general term "response to external stimulus." **GO** terms are shown as boxes, and lines between the boxes indicate parent–child relationships among terms. Enriched interesting terms (red) and depleted interesting terms (blue) are derived using overrepresentation analysis from the list of interesting genes that were input into **GoMiner** for this analysis. An example of an interesting gene list could be the set of genes that were found to be co-expressed in a microarray gene expression experiment (Chapter 17). Running the mouse over specific categories activates display of a yellow box showing the **GO** term and the genes annotated with that **GO** term. Other views of the data in table form are available from the main **GoMiner** window.

Finally, a Cytoscape plug-in called ActiveModules (Ideker et al., 2002) is available to find regions of a given network that are co-regulated across multiple gene expression conditions. Co-regulated subgraphs are called *active modules* and are hypothesized to represent pathways or biological processes whose components are active at the same time. Gene expression data must be statistically processed to yield p values of significance of fold change between two conditions to use ActiveModules, thus at least two gene expression conditions are required for Affymetrix style gene expression data, one condition of interest and one a control or at least one cDNA differential fluorescence hybridization chip condition; however, ActiveModules was designed to analyze multiple sets of fold change p values at once.

It is interesting to note that although the tools mentioned here for the most part have been designed for studying gene expression information, they also can be used to study other types of data, such as protein expression or other similar data that may be of interest to analyze. Also, gene expression is only mildly correlated with protein abundance; thus, conclusions about the activity of biological processes from gene expression need to be validated further experimentally.

Analysis that integrates transcriptional profiling with pathway information currently is being heavily researched. One example of this is regulatory network reconstruction, where gene expression data sets from multiple conditions as well as a number of known gene expression regulators, such as transcription factors and signal transduction proteins that activate or inactivate those transcription factors, are used to reconstruct portions of the gene regulatory network (Segal et al., 2003). As this research progresses, more advanced tools for this analysis undoubtedly will be created.

∎ SUMMARY

Many other topics about protein–protein interactions and pathways exist beyond what has been covered in this chapter. A sample of these very interesting topics are mathematical pathway modeling (Bower & Bolouri, 2001), molecular docking of proteins with proteins and proteins with small molecules (Ofran & Rost, 2003), genetic interactions (Forsburg, 2001), and molecular interaction network clustering (Bader & Hogue, 2003).

∎ ACKNOWLEDGMENTS

The authors thank Chris Sander for support during the writing of this chapter, Michael Cary for work on the Pathway Resource List, and Debbie Marks for helpful editorial input.

∎ WORKED EXAMPLE

Given a protein sequence, its function, and possible biomolecular interactions are predicted using a number of contextual genomic approaches. This example, although it does not cover all available means, provides a reasonable overview of available methods.

This example uses the yeast tryptophan biosynthesis enzyme TrpCF (Swiss-Prot ID, TRPC_ECOLI). This is a bifunctional enzyme with one domain consisting of an indole-3-glycerol phosphate synthase (EC 4.1.1.48) and the other an isomerase (EC 5.3.1.24). These two domains carry out two enzymatic steps of tryptophan biosynthesis, and the substrate is passed between them. This protein is a typical example of gene fusion in metabolic enzymes.

Although the sequence, structure, and function of the enzyme are well characterized, very little experimental information is available about which proteins this enzyme interacts with (both physical and function interactions). Going to the STRING Web site and typing the identifier of this gene (TRPC_ECOLI) into the identifier search field at the top page results in a summary of predicted interactions displayed from precomputed data.

The initial search returns predicted interaction data from a variety of sources and is shown in Table 10.2. Each row in Table 10.2 indicates a potential interactor based on evidence from a number of sources. Evidence is scored by STRING from 0 to 1. In this case, the threshold is set at 0.40, so only evidence scoring above this threshold is shown. For example, the TrpCF query protein is predicted to interact with TrpB by virtue of high-quality evidence from gene neighborhood, gene fusion, and text mining. Further medium-quality evidence from gene concurrence (phylogenetic profile) adds to this, providing a total evidence score of 1.0. This evidence is obtained across multiple species using ortholog information.

Clicking on the evidence buttons displayed below the results provides details about where the evidence originated from each source. Clicking on the Fusion button hence shows that predicted interactions between the query TrpCF (TRPC_ECOLI) and PabA (PABA_ECOLI) are the result of these genes being fused in two yeast species. Similarly, the interaction predicted with TrpG is the result of these genes being fused in the organism *Archaeoglobus fulgidus*.

Clicking on the Gene Neighborhood button shows that many genes in this pathway are kept together in close proximity on many genomes. The neighborhood plot generated shows that TrpCF often is located in close proximity to many other pathway members (e.g., TrpB and TrpA).

TABLE 10.2 ∎ Initial Predicted Interactions from Worked Example Search

		Neighborhood	Gene fusion	Cooccurence	Homology	Co-expression	Experiments	Databases	Text mining	Score
TRPB_ECOLI	Tryptophan synthase β chain	●	●	●					●	1.00
TRPA_ECOLI	Tryptophan synthase α chain	●		●		○	○	○	●	0.99
TRPE_ECOLI	Anthranilate synthase I	●		●					●	0.99
TRPG_ECOLI	Anthranilate synthase II	●	○	●					●	0.99
PABA_ECOLI	Para-aminobenzoate synthase II	○	●						○	0.90
LPW_ECOLI	Trp operon leader peptide	○							●	0.80
ARGB_ECOLI	Acetylglutamate kinase								●	0.70
PABB_ECOLI	Para-aminobenzoate synthaase I	○					○	○	○	0.60
MOAC_ECOLI	Molybdenum cofactor biosynthesis protein C	○							○	0.54
ILVC_ECOLI	Ketol-acid reductoisomerase					○				0.44

●, high-quality evidence; ◐, medium-quality evidence; ○, low quality evidence.

Finally, if one clicks on the Summary Network button, all of these predictions are overlaid in a graphical representation of this protein's predicted interactions with other proteins. Nodes in this network are connected according to evidence from an interaction prediction source. Evidence from multiple sources is shown as parallel edges connecting the same nodes and allows the highest quality interaction predictions to be located easily in the network.

Proteins involved in biological pathways or in the formation of protein complexes will often form "cliques" (highly connected subnetworks). The resulting graph for TrpCF is one such case. Changing the default network depth parameters to values of more than two expands this network and allows interconnected pathways and biological processes to be visualized. At a network depth of two, one should be able to see connections between these tryptophan biosynthesis genes other biosynthesis pathways, including: aromatic amino acids, arginine, valine, isoleucine, and histidine. An intriguing connection between TrpG (TRPG_ECOLI) and a group of highly connected hypothetical proteins based on gene concurrence (phylogenetic profile) should be visible in this network.

Using the STRING resource hence allows a gene to be placed in a biological context according to a large number of predicted functional associations and protein–protein interactions across many species. Given the large number of poorly characterized or unannotated (hypothetical) genes and proteins in complete genomes, this example shows how useful a resource like STRING is for biological discovery and the guiding of directed experiments.

PROBLEM SET

A protein sequence that was derived as part of a bacterial genome sequencing project is posted on the Book's Web site. Using this sequence, perform the following steps:

► Using the STRING Web server, search using this sequence for genome context links and for the direct function of the protein.

► Build an initial summary network with default parameters to visualize functional links between this protein and other proteins.

► Go to the KEGG Web server and search this sequence against known metabolic pathways. Use BLASTP when searching the KEGG GENES database. Find the corresponding E. coli entry (identifier will start with "eco") for this gene and its KEGG pathway. Remember that, frequently, the same gene may have different identifiers in different databases.

► Click on the KEGG pathway to draw the metabolic map of the pathway in which this gene is involved.

► Go back to the initial STRING network and try to map each member of the functional network to this metabolic pathway.

Based on this analysis, answer the following questions:

1. What is the function of this gene?
2. What is the core metabolic pathway that this gene is involved in?

3. How much of the core KEGG pathway is recovered by functional interactions?
4. What other KEGG pathways are linked to by functional interactions?
5. By varying the *network depth* and *interactors shown* fields of STRING, try to reconstruct a genomic network of pathways and complexes that link to this core pathway. Go to a maximum network depth of 5 and no more than 50 interactors shown.

INTERNET RESOURCES

AllFuse	http://www.ebi.ac.uk/research/cgg/allfuse/
Bayesian network data for yeast	http://bioinfo.mbb.yale.edu/genome/intint/
BIND	http://bind.ca
BioCarta	http://www.biocarta.com
BioCyc	http://biocyc.org/
BioLayout	http://biolayout.org/
BioPAX	http://www.biopax.org
CellML	http://www.cellml.org/
Cytoscape	http://www.cytoscape.org/
DDBJ/EMBL/GenBank Feature Table Definition	http://www.ncbi.nlm.nih.gov/projects/collab/FT/
DIP	http://dip.doe-mbi.ucla.edu/
Funspec	http://funspec.med.utoronto.ca/
GenMAPP and MAPPFinder	http://www.genmapp.org/
GoMiner	http://discover.nci.nih.gov/gominer/
GRID	http://biodata.mshri.on.ca/grid
HPRD	http://www.hprd.org/
IntAct	http://www.ebi.ac.uk/intact
KEGG	http://www.genome.ad.jp/kegg/kegg2.html
MINT	http://160.80.34.4/mint/
Osprey	http://biodata.mshri.on.ca/osprey
Pajek	http://vlado.fmf.uni-lj.si/pub/networks/pajek/
Pathway Resource List	http://www.cbio.mskcc.org/prl
Predictome	http://predictome.bu.edu
PSI-MI	http://psidev.sourceforge.net
SBML	http://sbml.org/
STKE	http://stke.sciencemag.org/
STRING	http://www.bork.embl-heidelberg.de/STRING/
WIT	http://wit.mcs.anl.gov/WIT2/

FURTHER READING

BADER, G. D., HEILBUT, A., ANDREWS, B., TYERS, M., HUGHES, T., AND BOONE, C. (2003). Functional genomics and proteomics: charting a multidimensional map of the yeast cell. *Trends Cell. Biol.* 13, 344–356. Functional genomics and proteomics is producing enormous amounts of data quickly. This review discusses the various types of large-scale data available as of 2003, especially pathway related data, and the possibility of integrating it to better understand the workings of the cell.

KARP, P. D. (2001). Pathway databases: a case study in computational symbolic theories. *Science* 293, 2040–2044. This review discusses pathway databases and knowledge representation, focusing on descriptions of EcoCyc as an example.

PHIZICKY, E. M., AND FIELDS, S. (1995). Protein–protein interactions: methods for detection and analysis. *Microbiol. Rev.* 59, 94–123. This review is one of the best collections of descriptions of experimental methods to detect protein–protein interactions.

UETZ, P. S. B., AND IDEKER, T. (2002). *Visualization and Integration of Protein-Protein Interactions. Protein-Protein Interactions: A Molecular Cloning Manual* (Golemis, E., ed.), (Cold Spring Harbor Laboratory Press, Cold Spring Harbor, NY). This book chapter discusses various ways of visualizing molecular interaction information.

▋REFERENCES

BADER, G. D., BETEL, D., AND HOGUE, C. W. (2003a). BIND: the Biomolecular Interaction Network Database. *Nucl. Acids Res.* 31, 248–250.

BADER, G. D., DONALDSON, I., WOLTING, C., OUELLETTE, B. F., PAWSON, T., AND HOGUE, C. W. (2001). BIND—the Biomolecular Interaction Network Database. *Nucl. Acids Res.* 29, 242–245.

BADER, G. D., HEILBUT, A., ANDREWS, B., TYERS, M., HUGHES, T., AND BOONE, C. (2003b). Functional genomics and proteomics: charting a multidimensional map of the yeast cell. *Trends Cell. Biol.* 13, 344–356.

BADER, G. D., AND HOGUE, C. W. (2003). An automated method for finding molecular complexes in large protein interaction networks. *BMC Bioinformatics* 4, 2.

BLUMENTHAL, T. (1998). Gene clusters and polycistronic transcription in eukaryotes. *Bioessays* 20, 480–487.

BOLLOBÂAS, B. (1998). *Modern Graph Theory* (Springer, New York).

BOWER, J. M., AND BOLOURI, H. (2001). *Computational Modeling of Genetic and Biochemical Networks* (MIT Press, Cambridge, MA).

BREITKREUTZ, B. J., STARK, C., AND TYERS, M. (2003). The GRID: the General Repository for Interaction Datasets. *Genome Biol.* 4, R23.

BREITKREUTZ, B. J., STARK, C., AND TYERS, M. (2003). Osprey: a network visualization system. *Genome Biol.* 4, R22.

BUSSEY, K. J., KANE, D., SUNSHINE, M., NARASIMHAN, S., NISHIZUKA, S., REINHOLD, W. C., ZEEBERG, B., AJAY, W., AND WEINSTEIN, J. N. (2003). MatchMiner: a tool for batch navigation among gene and gene product identifiers. *Genome Biol.* 4, R27.

CORMEN, T. H. (2001). *Introduction to Algorithms* (MIT Press, Cambridge, MA).

DAHLQUIST, K. D., SALOMONIS, N., VRANIZAN, K., LAWLOR, S. C., AND CONKLIN, B. R. (2002). GenMAPP, a new tool for viewing and analyzing microarray data on biological pathways. *Nat. Genet.* 31, 19–20.

DANDEKAR, T., SNEL, B., HUYNEN, M., AND BORK, P. (1998). Conservation of gene order: a fingerprint of proteins that physically interact. *Trends Biochem. Sci.* 23, 324–328.

DEANE, C. M., SALWINSKI, L., XENARIOS, I., AND EISENBERG, D. (2002). Protein interactions: two methods for assessment of the reliability of high throughput observations. *Mol. Cell. Proteomics* 1, 349–356.

DONIGER, S. W., SALOMONIS, N., DAHLQUIST, K. D., VRANIZAN, K., LAWLOR, S. C., AND CONKLIN, B. R. (2003). MAPPFinder: using Gene Ontology and GenMAPP to create a global gene-expression profile from microarray data. *Genome Biol.* 4, R7.

EECKMAN, F. H., AND DURBIN, R. (1995). ACeDB and macace. *Methods Cell. Biol.* 48, 583–605.

ENRIGHT, A. J., ILIOPOULOS, I., KYRPIDES, N. C., AND OUZOUNIS, C. A. (1999). Protein interaction maps for complete genomes based on gene fusion events. *Nature* 402, 86–90.

ENRIGHT, A. J., AND OUZOUNIS, C. A. (2001). BioLayout—an automatic graph layout algorithm for similarity visualization. *Bioinformatics* 17, 853–854.

ENRIGHT, A. J., AND OUZOUNIS, C. A. (2001). Functional associations of proteins in entire genomes by means of exhaustive detection of gene fusions. *Genome Biol.* 2, RESEARCH0034.

ENRIGHT, A. J., VAN DONGEN, S., AND OUZOUNIS, C. A. (2002). An efficient algorithm for large-scale detection of protein families. *Nucl. Acids Res.* 30, 1575–1584.

FORSBURG, S. L. (2001). The art and design of genetic screens: yeast. *Nat. Rev. Genet.* 2, 659–668.

GALPERIN, M. Y., AND KOONIN, E. V. (2000). Who's your neighbor? New computational approaches for functional genomics. *Nat. Biotechnol.* 18, 609–613.

GAVIN, A. C., BOSCHE, M., KRAUSE, R., GRANDI, P., MARZIOCH, M., BAUER, A., SCHULTZ, J., RICK, J. M., MICHON, A. M., CRUCIAT, C. M., et al. (2002). Functional organization of the yeast proteome by systematic analysis of protein complexes. *Nature* 415, 141–147.

GE, H., LIU, Z., CHURCH, G. M., AND VIDAL, M. (2001). Correlation between transcriptome and interactome mapping data from *Saccharomyces cerevisiae*. *Nat. Genet.* 29, 482–486.

GOBEL, U., SANDER, C., SCHNEIDER, R., AND VALENCIA, A. (1994). Correlated mutations and residue contacts in proteins. *Proteins* 18, 309–317.

GREENBAUM, D., AND GERSTEIN, M. (2003). A universal legal framework as a prerequisite for database interoperability. *Nat. Biotechnol.* 21, 979–982.

GRIGORIEV, A. (2001). A relationship between gene expression and protein interactions on the proteome scale: analysis of the bacteriophage T7 and the yeast *Saccharomyces cerevisiae*. *Nucl. Acids Res.* 29, 3513–3519.

Grosu, P., Townsend, J. P., Hartl, D. L., and Cavalieri, D. (2002). Pathway Processor: a tool for integrating whole-genome expression results into metabolic networks. *Genome Res.* 12, 1121–1126.

Hermjakob, H., Montecchi-Palazzi, L., Bader, G., Wojcik, J., Salwinski, L., Ceol, A., Moore, S., Orchard, S., Sarkans, U., von Mering, C., et al. (2004). The HUPO PSI's molecular interaction format—a community standard for the representation of protein interaction data. *Nat. Biotechnol.* 22, 177–183.

Ho, Y., Gruhler, A., Heilbut, A., Bader, G. D., Moore, L., Adams, S. L., Millar, A., Taylor, P., Bennett, K., Boutilier, K., et al. (2002). Systematic identification of protein complexes in *Saccharomyces cerevisiae* by mass spectrometry. *Nature* 415, 180–183.

Hosack, D. A., Dennis, Jr., G., Sherman, B. T., Lane, H. C., and Lempicki, R. A. (2003). Identifying biological themes within lists of genes with EASE. *Genome Biol.* 4, R70.

Hu, Z., Mellor, J., Wu, J., and DeLisi, C. (2004). VisANT: an online visualization and analysis tool for biological interaction data. *BMC Bioinformatics* 5, 17.

Hucka, M., Finney, A., Sauro, H. M., Bolouri, H., Doyle, J. C., Kitano, H., Arkin, A. P., Bornstein, B. J., Bray, D., Cornish-Bowden, A., et al. (2003). The systems biology markup language (SBML): a medium for representation and exchange of biochemical network models. *Bioinformatics* 19, 524–531.

Ideker, T., Ozier, O., Schwikowski, B., and Siegel, A. F. (2002). Discovering regulatory and signalling circuits in molecular interaction networks. *Bioinformatics* 18(Suppl 1), S233–S240.

Jansen, R., Greenbaum, D., and Gerstein, M. (2002). Relating whole-genome expression data with protein-protein interactions. *Genome Res.* 12, 37–46.

Jansen, R., Yu, H., Greenbaum, D., Kluger, Y., Krogan, N. J., Chung, S., Emili, A., Snyder, M., Greenblatt, J. F., and Gerstein, M. (2003). A Bayesian networks approach for predicting protein-protein interactions from genomic data. *Science* 302, 449–453.

Kanehisa, M., Goto, S., Kawashima, S., and Nakaya, A. (2002). The KEGG databases at GenomeNet. *Nucl. Acids Res.* 30, 42–46.

Karp, P. D., Riley, M., Paley, S. M., and Pellegrini-Toole, A. (2002). The MetaCyc Database. *Nucl. Acids Res.* 30, 59–61.

Karp, P. D., Riley, M., Saier, M., Paulsen, I. T., Collado-Vides, J., Paley, S. M., Pellegrini-Toole, A., Bonavides, C., and Gama-Castro, S. (2002). The EcoCyc database. *Nucl. Acids Res.* 30, 56–58.

Marcotte, E. M., Pellegrini, M., Ng, H. L., Rice, D. W., Yeates, T. O., and Eisenberg, D. (1999). Detecting protein function and protein-protein interactions from genome sequences. *Science* 285, 751–753.

Marcotte, E. M., Xenarios, I., van Der Bliek, A. M., and Eisenberg, D. (2000). Localizing proteins in the cell from their phylogenetic profiles. *Proc. Natl. Acad. Sci. U. S. A.* 97, 12115–12120.

Matthews, L. R., Vaglio, P., Reboul, J., Ge, H., Davis, B. P., Garrels, J., Vincent, S., and Vidal, M. (2001). Identification of potential interaction networks using sequence-based searches for conserved protein-protein interactions or interologs. *Genome Res.* 11, 2120–2126.

Mehlhorn, K., and Nèaher, S. (1999). *Leda: A Platform for Combinatorial and Geometric Computing* (Cambridge University Press, New York).

Mellor, J. C., Yanai, I., Clodfelter, K. H., Mintseris, J., and DeLisi, C. (2002). Predictome: a database of putative functional links between proteins. *Nucl. Acids Res.* 30, 306–309.

Ofran, Y., and Rost, B. (2003). Analysing six types of protein-protein interfaces. *J. Mol. Biol.* 325, 377–387.

Ouzounis, C., and Kyrpides, N. (1996). The emergence of major cellular processes in evolution. *FEBS Lett.* 390, 119–123.

Overbeek, R., Fonstein, M., D'Souza, M., Pusch, G. D., and Maltsev, N. (1999). The use of gene clusters to infer functional coupling. *Proc. Natl. Acad. Sci. U. S. A.* 96, 2896–2901.

Overbeek, R., Larsen, N., Pusch, G. D., D'Souza, M., Selkov, Jr., E., Kyrpides, N., Fonstein, M., Maltsev, N., and Selkov, E. (2000). WIT: integrated system for high-throughput genome sequence analysis and metabolic reconstruction. *Nucl. Acids Res.* 28, 123–125.

Pazos, F., and Valencia, A. (2001). Similarity of phylogenetic trees as indicator of protein-protein interaction. *Protein Eng.* 14, 609–614.

Pazos, F., and Valencia, A. (2002). *In silico* two–hybrid system for the selection of physically interacting protein pairs. *Proteins* 47, 219–227.

Pellegrini, M., Marcotte, E. M., Thompson, M. J., Eisenberg, D., and Yeates, T. O. (1999). Assigning protein functions by comparative genome analysis: protein phylogenetic profiles. *Proc. Natl. Acad. Sci. U. S. A.* 96, 4285–4288.

Peri, S., Navarro, J. D., Amanchy, R., Kristiansen, T. Z., Jonnala-gadda, C. K., Surendranath, V., Niranjan, V., Muthusamy, B., Gandhi, T. K., Gronborg, M., et al. (2003). Development of Human Protein Reference Database as an initial platform for approaching systems biology in humans. *Genome Res.* 13, 2363–2371.

Renesto, P., Crapoulet, N., Ogata, H., La Scola, B., Vestris, G., Claverie, J. M., and Raoult, D. (2003). Genome-based design of a cell-free culture medium for *Tropheryma whipplei*. *Lancet* 362, 447–449.

Rhee, S. Y., Beavis, W., Berardini, T. Z., Chen, G., Dixon, D., Doyle, A., Garcia-Hernandez, M., Huala, E., Lander, G., Montoya, M., et al. (2003). The Arabidopsis Information Resource (TAIR): a model organism database providing a centralized, curated gateway to Arabidopsis biology, research materials and community. *Nucl. Acids Res.* 31, 224–228.

Rivera, M. C., Jain, R., Moore, J. E., and Lake, J. A. (1998). Genomic evidence for two functionally distinct gene classes. *Proc. Natl. Acad. Sci. U. S. A.* 95, 6239–6244.

Robinson, M. D., Grigull, J., Mohammad, N., and Hughes, T. R. (2002). FunSpec: a web-based cluster interpreter for yeast. *BMC Bioinformatics* 3, 35.

Salama, J. J., Donaldson, I., and Hogue, C. W. (2002). Automatic annotation of BIND molecular interactions from three-dimensional structures. *Biopolymers* 61, 111–120.

Segal, E., Shapira, M., Regev, A., Pe'er, D., Botstein, D., Koller, D., and Friedman, N. (2003). Module networks: identifying regulatory modules and their condition-specific regulators from gene expression data. *Nat. Genet.* 34, 166–176.

Selkov, E., Overbeek, R., Kogan, Y., Chu, L., Vonstein, V., Holmes, D., Silver, S., Haselkorn, R., and Fonstein, M. (2000). Functional analysis of gapped microbial genomes: amino acid metabolism of *Thiobacillus ferrooxidans*. *Proc. Natl. Acad. Sci. U. S. A.* 97, 3509–3514.

Snel, B., Bork, P., and Huynen, M. A. (2002). Genomes in flux: the evolution of archaeal and proteobacterial gene content. *Genome Res.* 12, 17–25.

Tamames, J., Casari, G., Ouzounis, C., and Valencia, A. (1997). Conserved clusters of functionally related genes in two bacterial genomes. *J. Mol. Evol.* 44, 66–73.

Tatusov, R. L., Fedorova, N. D., Jackson, J. D., Jacobs, A. R., Kiryutin, B., Koonin, E. V., Krylov, D. M., Mazumder, R., Mekhedov, S. L., Nikolskaya, A. N., et al. (2003). The COG database: an updated version includes eukaryotes. *BMC Bioinformatics* 4, 41.

Tien, A. C., Lin, M. H., Su, L. J., Hong, Y. R., Cheng, T. S., Lee, Y. C., Lin, W. J., Still, I. H., and Huang, C. Y. (2004). Identification of the substrates and interaction proteins of aurora kinases from a protein-protein interaction model. *Mol. Cell. Proteomics* 3, 93–104.

Voet, D., and Voet, J. G. (2004). *Biochemistry* (John Wiley & Sons, New York).

von Mering, C., Huynen, M., Jaeggi, D., Schmidt, S., Bork, P., and Snel, B. (2003). STRING: a database of predicted functional associations between proteins. *Nucl. Acids Res.* 31, 258–261.

Xenarios, I., Salwinski, L., Duan, X. J., Higney, P., Kim, S. M., and Eisenberg, D. (2002). DIP, the Database of Interacting Proteins: a research tool for studying cellular networks of protein interactions. *Nucl. Acids Res.* 30, 303–305.

Zanzoni, A., Montecchi-Palazzi, L., Quondam, M., Ausiello, G., Helmer-Citterich, M., and Cesareni, G. (2002). MINT: a Molecular INTeraction database. *FEBS Lett.* 513, 135–140.

Zeeberg, B. R., Feng, W., Wang, G., Wang, M. D., Fojo, A. T., Sunshine, M., Narasimhan, S., Kane, D. W., Reinhold, W. C., Lababidi, S., et al. (2003). GoMiner: a resource for biological interpretation of genomic and proteomic data. *Genome Biol.* 4, R28.

Zorio, D. A., Cheng, N. N., Blumenthal, T., and Spieth, J. (1994). Operons as a common form of chromosomal organization in *C. elegans*. *Nature* 372, 270–272.

KEY TERMS

Bayesian network

Bonferroni correction

data exchange format

graph

interaction

molecular complex

Pathway

Phylogenetic profile

## PART FOUR

INFERRING RELATIONSHIPS

## CHAPTER ELEVEN

Assessing Pairwise Sequence Similarity: BLAST and FASTA

ANDREAS D. BAXEVANIS

Bioinformatics: A Practical Guide to the Analysis of Genes and Proteins, Third Edition, edited by
Andreas D. Baxevanis and B.F. Francis Ouellette.
ISBN 0-471-47878-4 Copyright © 2005 John Wiley & Sons, Inc.

INTRODUCTION

One of the cornerstones of bioinformatics is the process of comparing sequences to deduce whether the sequences are actually related to one another. Through this type of comparative analysis, one can draw inferences regarding whether two proteins have a similar function, contain similar structural motifs, or have a discernible evolutionary relationship. This chapter focuses on pairwise alignments, where two sequences are directly compared, position by position, to deduce these relationships. Another technique, multiple sequence alignment, is used to identify important features common to three or more sequences; this approach, which often is used to predict secondary structure, functional motifs, and residues important to both structure and function, is discussed in the next chapter.

Before entering into any discussion of how relatedness between nucleotide or protein sequences is assessed, two important terms need to be defined: *similarity* and *homology*. These terms tend to be used interchangeably when, in fact, they mean quite different things and imply quite different biological relationships.

Similarity is quantitative measure of how related two sequences are to one another. Similarity is always based on an observable, usually pairwise alignment of two sequences to one another. When two sequences are aligned, one simply can count how many residues line up with one another, and this raw count then can be converted to the most commonly used measure of similarity: percent identity. Measures of similarity are used to quantify changes that occur as two sequences diverge over evolutionary time, taking into account the effect of substitutions, insertions, or deletions. They also can be used to identify residues that are crucial for maintaining a protein's structure or function. In short, high degrees of sequence similarity may imply a common evolutionary history or a possible commonality in biological function.

Homology is the putative conclusion reached based on examining the optimal alignment between two sequences and the assessment of their similarity. Genes (and their protein products) either are or are not homologous; homology is not measured in degrees. The concept of homology implies an evolutionary relationship, and the term *homolog* may apply to two different types of relationships:

▸ If genes are separated by the event of speciation, they are termed *orthologous*. Orthologs are direct descendants of a sequence in a common ancestor, and may have similar domain structure, three-dimensional structure, and biological function.

▸ If genes are separated by the event of genetic duplication, they are termed *paralogous*. The examination of paralogs provides insight into how preexisting genes may have been adapted toward providing a new or modified function within the cell.

The concepts of homology, orthology, and paralogy and methods for determining the evolutionary relationships between sequences are covered in much greater detail in Chapter 14.

GLOBAL VERSUS LOCAL SEQUENCE ALIGNMENTS

The methods used to assess sequence similarity (and, in turn, infer homology) can be grouped into two major types. Global sequence alignment methods take two sequences, compare them along their entire length, and try to come up with the best alignment of the two sequences across their entire length. In general, global sequence alignment methods are most applicable to highly similar sequences of approximately the same length. Although these methods can be applied to any two sequences, as the degree of sequence similarity declines, they will tend to miss important biological relationships between sequences that may not be apparent when looking at the sequences as a whole.

Most biologists depend on the second class of alignment algorithm, which depends on local sequence alignments. In these methods, the sequence comparison is intended to find the most similar regions in the two sequences being aligned rather than finding the best way to align the entire length of the two sequences being compared. As such, they are capable of finding subsequences within the sequences being compared that may have a biological relationship. Often times, these methods will return more than one result for the two sequences being compared, because there may be more than one domain or subsequence common to the two sequences being analyzed. Local sequence alignment methods are best for sequences that share some degree of similarity, or for sequences of different lengths, and the ensuing discussion concentrates mostly on these methods.

DOTPLOTS

One of the most basic ways of comparing two sequences with one another is by a visual method called a *dotplot*. Dotplots allow for the quick identification of regions of local alignment, direct or inverted repeats, insertions, deletions, or low-complexity regions. Although these methods provide an easy to understand, intuitive representation of the local similarity between two sequences, they do not provide a robust statistical measure of the overall quality of the alignment.

In theory, it is quite easy to construct a dotplot, and they can actually be created by hand (even though it would be tedious and time consuming). To demonstrate how a dotplot is constructed, two plain English phrases will be "aligned" with one another: *current topics* and *currently tropical*. To begin, the letters in each phrase are written out across the top and down the side of a square matrix, as shown in Figure 11.1. Now, position by position, a mark (the dot) is placed at each position where there is a match between the two phrases. In column 1, there is a C in "currently tropical" that matches the C in the first row of "current topics," so a mark is placed. There is also another C in the twelfth row of "current topics," so a mark is placed there as well. In the same fashion, the method moves across all the columns, placing a mark anywhere in each of the rows where the characters match. When done, one can identify regions of similarity between the two phrases simply by looking for the diagonals (Figure 11.1, blue). In this example, the method has identified "current" and "opic" as being the two "subsequences" from the input that are similar to one another.

There are a number of publicly available tools that can be used for constructing dotplots, including Dotlet, Dotter, and Dottup. Each of these have certain features making them more appropriate for certain types of analyses; for example, Dottup is best used when comparing entire genomes with one another. The discussion

illustrating the use of dotplots that follows focuses on Dotlet because it arguably is the easiest dotplot tool for the novice user to use; the Dotlet interface is through a Web-based Java applet and does not require the user to install the software on their machine.

Finding Regions of Local Alignment

As with the contrived English example above, two sequences can be aligned to find the domains or subsequences that are similar in both. Consider the example of two proteins that are known to be in the same protein family: human HMGB1 and human SOX-10. In this case, Dotlet produces two major diagonals (Figure 11.2), indicating that there are two separate regions of similarity between these two proteins. The crosshair in the main Dotlet window can be moved to any position within the window. When moved to either of the diagonals, the residues in the region deemed to be similar can be viewed directly in the sequence alignment below the main window, with exact matches highlighted in dark blue and conservative substitutions highlighted in a lighter blue. Because the two similar regions are not found at the same spacing in both proteins, their existence might have been missed if a global alignment method had been applied.

Identifying Repeats

Often, nucleotide or protein sequences will contain large numbers of tandem repeats. An excellent example of this is human mucin, which contains 40 exact tandem repeats of a 20-amino acid stretch and two additional repeats that are slightly different than the others. Here, rather than compare two different sequences with one another, Dotlet is used to compare the sequence of interest with itself (Figure 11.3). This produces a significantly different and more complex type of output as before. Whenever there are tandem repeats in a sequence, the dotplot will look like a square, with numerous diagonals traversing the square. The dotplot is interpreted as follows: The shortest diagonal (at the lower left) yields the beginning and end points of the single repeat; the user can use the crosshair to highlight these points and then observe the "alignment" below the dotplot to see what the sequence of the repeat is. Starting from the shortest diagonal, counting the number of diagonals in the square yields the number of tandem repeats in this region.

Finding Low-Complexity Regions

Low-complexity regions are defined simply as regions of biased composition (Wootton & Federhen, 1993). These

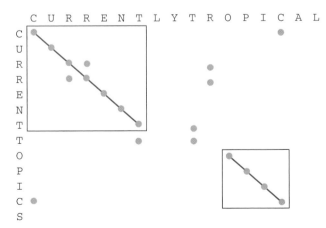

FIGURE 11.1 How dotplots are constructed. In this example, two English phrases ("Current Topics" and "Currently Tropical") are "aligned" with one another. The diagonals (in the boxes) indicate the region of "alignment." See text for details.

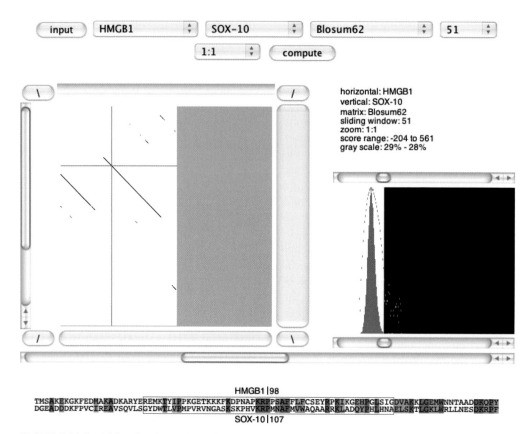

FIGURE 11.2   Using Dotlet to identify regions of local alignment. The sequences of human **HMGB1** (gb|**AAB08987**) and human **SOX-10** (gb|**AAH02824**) are provided as the input, as can be seen at the top of the figure. The sequences have been aligned using a **BLOSUM62** matrix, and the alignment is shown at a zoom of 1:1; the zoom pulldown menu can be used to change the zoom factor of the main dotplot window. The histogram window, to the right of the dotplot window, can be used to adjust the signal-to-noise ratio and, in turn, the contrast within the dotplot window. The alignment at the bottom of the figure shows the area surrounding the intersection of the crosshair in the dotplot window. Additional details can be found in the help documentation on the Dotlet Web site.

may include homopolymeric runs, short-period repeats, or the subtle overrepresentation of several residues in a sequence. The role of these low-complexity regions is not understood; it is thought that they may represent the results of either DNA replication errors or unequal crossing-over events. It is important to determine whether sequences of interest contain low-complexity regions, because they tend to prove problematic when performing sequence analyses and often lead to false-positive results. To find these regions, the same strategy is used as when looking for tandem repeats: the sequence is analyzed against itself. Figure 11.4 shows the Dotlet output when looking for low-complexity regions within the *Drosophila* achaete-scute protein. This protein contains a homopolymeric alanine-glutamine tract (basically, just a run of As and Qs). Because these residues will align position by position with each other, the

low-complexity region is rendered as a solid box in the dotplot.

SCORING MATRICES

Although dotplots are incredibly useful in identifying biologically important or interesting regions, their major drawback is that methods like Dotlet do not provide the user with a measure of statistical similarity when regions of local similarity are found. To do so, numerical methods must be applied that take into account not just the position-by-position overlap between two sequences, but the nature and characteristics of the residues being aligned as well.

To that end, much effort has been devoted to the development of constructs called *scoring matrices*

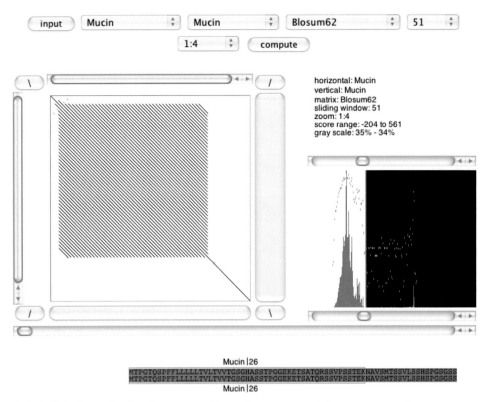

FIGURE 11.3 Using Dotlet to identify tandem repeats. The sequence of human mucin (gb|AAA60019) has been aligned against itself. The dotplot window shows the output characteristic when tandem repeats are present: a series of diagonals that fall within a square bounding box. See text for details.

(c.f., Henikoff & Henikoff (2000) for an excellent review). These matrices are empirical weighting schemes that appear in all analyses involving the comparison of two or more sequences, so it is important to understand how these matrices are constructed and how to choose between matrices. The choice of matrix can (and does) strongly influence the results obtained with most sequence comparison methods.

The most commonly used protein scoring matrices take three major biological factors into account:

▶ *Conservation.* The matrices need to account not only for absolute conservation between proteins, but need to provide a way to assess conservative substitutions as well. The numbers within the scoring matrix provide a way of representing what residues are capable of substituting for other residues while not adversely affecting the function of the native protein. From a physicochemical standpoint, characteristics such as residue charge, size, and hydrophobicity (among others) need to be similar.

▶ *Frequency.* In the same way that amino acid residues cannot freely substitute for one another, the matrices need to reflect how often particular residues occur

among the entire constellation of proteins. Residues that are rare are given more weight than residues that are more common.

▶ *Evolution.* By design, scoring matrices implicitly represent evolutionary patterns, and matrices can be adjusted to favor the detection of closely related or more distantly related proteins. The choice of matrices for different evolutionary distances are discussed below.

There are also subtle nuances that go into constructing a scoring matrix, and these are described in the review by Henikoff and Henikoff (2000).

How these various factors are represented in a scoring matrix can be demonstrated best by deconstructing the most commonly used scoring matrix, called BLOSUM62 (Figure 11.5). Each of the 20 amino acids (as well as the standard ambiguity codes) is shown along the top and down the side of the matrix. The scores in the matrix actually represent the logarithm of an odds ratio (Box 11.1) that takes into account how often a particular residue is observed, in nature, to replace another residue (i.e., How often does tyrosine replace tryptophan?). The odds ratio also takes into account how often a particular residue would be replaced by another if replacements occurred

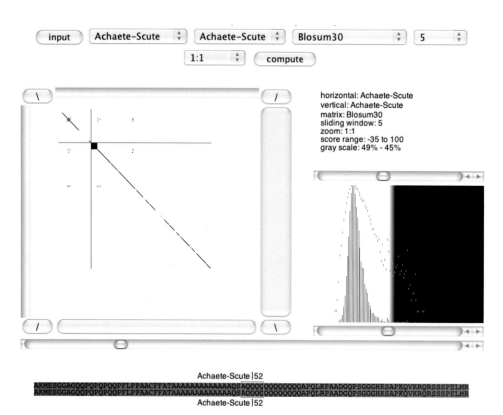

FIGURE 11.4 **Using Dotlet to identify regions of low complexity.** The *Drosophila* achaete-scute protein (sp|P50553) has been aligned against itself. The dotplot window shows the output characteristic when a low-complexity region is present: a solid box. See text for details.

	A	R	N	D	C	Q	E	G	H	I	L	K	M	F	P	S	T	W	Y	V	B	Z	X	*
A	4	-1	-2	-2	0	-1	-1	0	-2	-1	-1	-1	-1	-2	-1	1	0	-3	-2	0	-2	-1	0	-4
R	-1	5	0	-2	-3	1	0	-2	0	-3	-2	2	-1	-3	-2	-1	-1	-3	-2	-3	-1	0	-1	-4
N	-2	0	6	1	-3	0	0	0	1	-3	-3	0	-2	-3	-2	1	0	-4	-2	-3	3	0	-1	-4
D	-2	-2	1	6	-3	0	2	-1	-1	-3	-4	-1	-3	-3	-1	0	-1	-4	-3	-3	4	1	-1	-4
C	0	-3	-3	-3	9	-3	-4	-3	-3	-1	-1	-3	-1	-2	-3	-1	-1	-2	-2	-1	-3	-3	-2	-4
Q	-1	1	0	0	-3	5	2	-2	0	-3	-2	1	0	-3	-1	0	-1	-2	-1	-2	0	3	-1	-4
E	-1	0	0	2	-4	2	5	-2	0	-3	-3	1	-2	-3	-1	0	-1	-3	-2	-2	1	4	-1	-4
G	0	-2	0	-1	-3	-2	-2	6	-2	-4	-4	-2	-3	-3	-2	0	-2	-2	-3	-3	-1	-2	-1	-4
H	-2	0	1	-1	-3	0	0	-2	8	-3	-3	-1	-2	-1	-2	-1	-2	-2	2	-3	0	0	-1	-4
I	-1	-3	-3	-3	-1	-3	-3	-4	-3	4	2	-3	1	0	-3	-2	-1	-3	-1	3	-3	-3	-1	-4
L	-1	-2	-3	-4	-1	-2	-3	-4	-3	2	4	-2	2	0	-3	-2	-1	-2	-1	1	-4	-3	-1	-4
K	-1	2	0	-1	-3	1	1	-2	-1	-3	-2	5	-1	-3	-1	0	-1	-3	-2	-2	0	1	-1	-4
M	-1	-1	-2	-3	-1	0	-2	-3	-2	1	2	-1	5	0	-2	-1	-1	-1	-1	1	-3	-1	-1	-4
F	-2	-3	-3	-3	-2	-3	-3	-3	-1	0	0	-3	0	6	-4	-2	-2	1	3	-1	-3	-3	-1	-4
P	-1	-2	-2	-1	-3	-1	-1	-2	-2	-3	-3	-1	-2	-4	7	-1	-1	-4	-3	-2	-2	-1	-2	-4
S	1	-1	1	0	-1	0	0	0	-1	-2	-2	0	-1	-2	-1	4	1	-3	-2	-2	0	0	0	-4
T	0	-1	0	-1	-1	-1	-1	-2	-2	-1	-1	-1	-1	-2	-1	1	5	-2	-2	0	-1	-1	0	-4
W	-3	-3	-4	-4	-2	-2	-3	-2	-2	-3	-2	-3	-1	1	-4	-3	-2	11	2	-3	-4	-3	-2	-4
Y	-2	-2	-2	-3	-2	-1	-2	-3	2	-1	-1	-2	-1	3	-3	-2	-2	2	7	-1	-3	-2	-1	-4
V	0	-3	-3	-3	-1	-2	-2	-3	-3	3	1	-2	1	-1	-2	-2	0	-3	-1	4	-3	-2	-1	-4
B	-2	-1	3	4	-3	0	1	-1	0	-3	-4	0	-3	-3	-2	0	-1	-4	-3	-3	4	1	-1	-4
Z	-1	0	0	1	-3	3	4	-2	0	-3	-3	1	-1	-3	-1	0	-1	-3	-2	-2	1	4	-1	-4
X	0	-1	-1	-1	-2	-1	-1	-1	-1	-1	-1	-1	-1	-2	0	0	-2	-1	-1	-1	-1	-1	-1	-4
*	-4	-4	-4	-4	-4	-4	-4	-4	-4	-4	-4	-4	-4	-4	-4	-4	-4	-4	-4	-4	-4	-4	-4	1

FIGURE 11.5 **The BLOSUM62 scoring matrix.** BLOSUM62 is the most widely used scoring matrix for protein analysis and provides best coverage for general-use cases. Standard single-letter codes to the left of each row and at the top of each column specify each of the 20 amino acids. The ambiguity codes B (for asparagine or aspartic acid; Asx) and Z (for glutamine or glutamic acid; Glx) also appear. Note that the matrix is a mirror image of itself with respect to the diagonal. See text for details.

in a random fashion (purely by chance). Given this, a positive score indicates two residues that are seen to replace each other more often than by chance, and a negative score indicates two residues that are seen to replace each other less frequently than would be expected by chance. Put more simply, frequently observed substitutions have positive scores and infrequently observed substitutions have negative scores.

To explain the meaning of the numbers in the matrix further, imagine that two sequences have been aligned with one another, and it is now necessary to assess how well the match of a residue in sequence A is to a residue in sequence B at any given position of the alignment. Using the scoring matrix in Figure 11.5:

▶ The values on the diagonal represent the score that would be conferred for an exact match at a given position, and these numbers are always positive. So, if a tryptophan residue (W) in sequence A is aligned with a tryptophan residue in sequence B, this match would be conferred 11 points, the value where the row marked W intersects the column marked W. The alignment of a tryptophan between two sequences scores high because it is a rare amino acid.

▶ Moving off the diagonal, consider the case of a conservative substitution: a tyrosine (Y) for a tryptophan. The intersection of the row marked Y with the column marked W yields a value of two points. Because the value is positive, the substitution is observed to occur more often than would by chance, but the replacement is not as good as if the tryptophan residue had been preserved (2 < 11), or if the tyrosine residue had been preserved (2 < 7).

▶ Finally, consider the case of a nonconservative substitution: a valine (V) for a tryptophan. The intersection of the row marked V with the column marked W yields a value of negative three points. Because the value is negative, the substitution is not observed to occur frequently and may arise more often than not by chance.

Although what the numbers and relationships within the scoring matrices mean seems straightforward enough, some value judgment needs to be made as to what actually constitutes a conservative or nonconservative substitution and how to assess the frequency of either of those events in nature. This is the major factor that differentiates scoring matrices from one another. So that an intelligent choice can be made, a discussion of the approach, advantages, and disadvantages of the various available matrices is in order.

PAM Matrices

The first useful matrices for sequence analysis were developed by Dayhoff et al. (1978). The basis for these matrices was the examination of substitution patterns in a group of proteins that shared more than 85% sequence similarity. The analysis yielded 1572 changes in the 71 groups of closely related proteins that were examined. Using these results, tables were constructed that indicated the frequency of a given amino acid substituting for another amino acid at a single position.

Because the sequences examined shared such a high degree of similarity, the resulting frequencies represent what would be expected over short evolutionary distances. Further, given the close evolutionary relationship between these proteins, one would expect that the observed mutations would not significantly change the function of the protein. This is termed *acceptance*: changes that can be accommodated through natural selection and result in a protein with the same or similar function as the original. Because individual point mutations were considered, the unit of measure resulting from this analysis is the *point accepted mutation*, or PAM unit. One PAM unit corresponds to one amino acid change per 100 residues, or roughly 1% divergence.

Several assumptions went into the construction of the PAM matrices. One of the most important assumptions was that the replacement of an amino acid is independent of previous mutations at the same position. Based on this assumption, the original matrix was extrapolated

---

BOX 11.1   Scoring Matrices and the Log Odds Ratio

Scoring matrices are derived from the observed replacement frequencies of amino acids for one another. Based on these probabilities, the scoring matrices are generated by applying the following equation:

$$S_{i,j} = \log[(q_{i,j})/(p_i \, p_j)],$$

where p_i is the probability with which residue i occurs among all proteins and p_j is the probability with which residue j occurs among all proteins. The quantity $q_{i,j}$ represents how often the two amino acids i and j are seen

to align with one another in multiple sequence alignments of protein families or in sequences that are known to have a biological relationship. Therefore, the log odds ratio $S_{i,j}$ (or lod score) represents the ratio of observed versus random frequency for the substitution of residue i by residue j. For commonly observed substitutions, $S_{i,j}$ will be more than zero. For substitutions that occur less frequently than would be expected by chance, $S_{i,j}$ is less than zero. If the observed frequency and the random frequency are the same, $S_{i,j}$ is zero.

to come up with predicted substitution frequencies at longer evolutionary distances. For example, the PAM1 matrix could be multiplied by itself 100 times to yield the PAM100 matrix, which would represent what one would expect if there were 100 amino acid changes per 100 residues. (This does not imply that each of the 100 residues has changed, only that there were 100 total changes; some positions could conceivably change and then change back to the original residue.) Because the matrices at longer evolutionary distances represent an extrapolation of the original matrix derived from the 1572 observed changes, it is important to remember that these matrices are, indeed, predictions and are not based on direct observation. Any errors in the original matrix would be exaggerated in the extrapolated matrices, because the mere act of multiplication will magnify these errors significantly.

There are additional assumptions that the reader should be aware of regarding the construction of PAM matrices. All sites have been assumed to be equally mutable, replacement has been assumed to be independent of surrounding residues, and there is no consideration of conserved blocks or motifs. The sequences being compared here are of average composition based on the small number of protein sequences available in 1978, so there is a bias toward small, globular proteins, even though efforts have been made to bring in additional sequence data over time (Gonnet et al., 1992; Jones et al., 1992). Finally, there is an implicit assumption that the forces responsible for sequence evolution over shorter time spans are the same as those for longer evolutionary time spans. Although there are significant drawbacks to the PAM matrices, it is important to remember that, given the information available in 1978, the development of these matrices marked an important advance in our ability to quantify the relationships between sequences. Because these matrices are still available for use with numerous bioinformatic tools, the reader should keep their potential drawbacks in mind and use them judiciously.

BLOSUM Matrices

In 1992, Henikoff and Henikoff took a slightly different approach to the one described above, one that addressed many of the drawbacks of the PAM matrices. The groundwork for the development of new matrices was a study aimed at identifying conserved motifs within families of proteins (Henikoff & Henikoff, 1991). This study led to the creation of the BLOCKS database, which uses the concept of a block to identify a family of proteins. The idea of a block is derived from the more familiar notion of a motif, which usually refers to a conserved stretch of amino acids that confer a specific function or structure to a protein. When these individual motifs from proteins in the same family can be aligned without introducing a gap, the result is a block, with the term *block* referring to the alignment, not the individual sequences themselves. Obviously, any given protein can contain one or more blocks, corresponding to each of its functional or structural motifs. With these protein blocks in hand, it was then possible to look for substitution patterns only in the most conserved regions of a protein, the regions that (presumably) were least prone to change. Two thousand blocks representing more than 500 groups of related proteins were examined, and based on the substitution patterns in those conserved blocks, *b*locks *su*bstitution *m*atrices (or BLOSUM, for short) were generated.

Obviously, many more protein sequences were available in 1992 than in 1978, providing for a more robust base set of data from which to derive the matrices. However, the most important distinction between the BLOSUM and PAM matrices is that the BLOSUM matrices are directly calculated across varying evolutionary distances and are not extrapolated, providing a more accurate view of substitution patterns (and, in turn, evolutionary forces) at those various distances. The fact that the BLOSUM matrices are calculated directly based only on conserved regions makes these matrices more sensitive to detecting structural or functional substitutions; because of this, the BLOSUM matrices perform demonstrably better than the PAM matrices for local similarity searches (Henikoff & Henikoff, 1993).

Returning to the point of directly deriving the various matrices, each BLOSUM matrix is assigned a number (BLOSUMn), and that number represents the conservation level of the sequences that were used to derive that particular matrix. For example, the BLOSUM62 matrix is calculated from sequences sharing no more than 62% identity; sequences with more than 62% identity are clustered, and their contribution is weighted to one. The clustering reduces the contribution of closely related sequences, meaning that there is less bias toward substitutions that occur (and may be overrepresented) in the most closely related members of a family. Reducing the value of n yields more distantly related sequences.

What Matrices Should Be Used When?

Although most bioinformatic software will provide users with a default choice of matrix, the default may not necessarily be the most appropriate choice for the biological question being asked. Table 11.1 is intended to provide some guidance as to the proper selection of scoring matrix, based on studies that have examined the effectiveness of these matrices to detect known biological relationships (Altschul, 1991; Henikoff & Henikoff, 1993; Wheeler, 2003). Note that the numbering schemes for the two matrix families move in opposite directions: more divergent sequences are found using higher-numbered PAM matrices and lower-numbered

TABLE 11.1 ■ Selecting an Appropriate Scoring Matrix

Matrix	Best use	Similarity (%)
PAM40	Short alignments that are highly similar	70–90
PAM160	Detecting members of a protein family	50–60
PAM250	Longer alignments of more divergent sequences	~30
BLOSUM90	Short alignments that are highly similar	70–90
BLOSUM80	Detecting members of a protein family	50–60
BLOSUM62	Most effective in finding all potential similarities	30–40
BLOSUM30	Longer alignments of more divergent sequences	<30

The Similarity column gives the range of similarities that the matrix is able to best detect (c.f., Wheeler, 2003).

BLOSUM matrices. The following equivalencies are useful in relating PAM matrices to BLOSUM matrices (Wheeler, 2003):

▶ PAM250 is equivalent to BLOSUM45

▶ PAM160 is equivalent to BLOSUM62

▶ PAM120 is equivalent to BLOSUM80

In addition to the protein matrices discussed here, there are numerous specialized matrices that are either species specific, concentrate on particular classes of proteins (e.g., transmembrane proteins), focus on structural substitutions, or use hydrophobicity measures in attempting to assess similarity (Wheeler, 2003). Given this landscape, the most important message to the reader is that no single matrix is the complete answer for all sequence comparisons. A thorough understanding of what each matrix represents therefore is critical to performing proper sequence-based analyses.

Nucleotide Scoring Matrices

At the nucleotide level, the landscape is much simpler. More often than not, the matrices used simply count matches and mismatches. These matrices also assume that each of the possible four nucleotide bases occur with equal frequency (25% of the time). In some cases, ambiguities or chemical similarities between the bases also are taken into account; an example of this type of matrix is shown in Figure 11.6. The basic differences in the construction of nucleotide scoring matrices and protein scoring matrices should make obvious the fact that protein-based searches are always more powerful than nucleotide-based searches of coding DNA sequences in determining similarity and inferring homology.

Gaps and Gap Penalties

Often times, gaps are introduced into alignments to compensate for insertions and deletions between the sequences being studied. Although gaps are used to improve the alignment between two sequences, they need to be kept to a reasonable number so as not to yield a biologically implausible scenario. The insertion of no more than one gap per 20 residues is a reasonable rule of thumb.

The scoring of gaps in pairwise sequence alignments is different from that discussed to this point, because

```
      A    T    G    C    S    W    R    Y    K    M    B    V    H    D    N
A     5   -4   -4   -4   -4    1    1   -4   -4    1   -4   -1   -1   -1   -2
T    -4    5   -4   -4   -4    1   -4    1    1   -4   -1   -4   -1   -1   -2
G    -4   -4    5   -4    1   -4    1   -4    1   -4   -1   -1   -4   -1   -2
C    -4   -4   -4    5    1   -4   -4    1   -4    1   -1   -1   -1   -4   -2
S    -4   -4    1    1   -1   -4   -2   -2   -2   -2   -1   -1   -3   -3   -1
W     1    1   -4   -4   -4   -1   -2   -2   -2   -2   -3   -3   -1   -1   -1
R     1   -4    1   -4   -2   -2   -1   -4   -2   -2   -3   -1   -3   -1   -1
Y    -4    1   -4    1   -2   -2   -4   -1   -2   -2   -1   -3   -1   -3   -1
K    -4    1    1   -4   -2   -2   -2   -2   -1   -4   -1   -3   -3   -1   -1
M     1   -4   -4    1   -2   -2   -2   -2   -4   -1   -3   -1   -1   -3   -1
B    -4   -1   -1   -1   -1   -3   -3   -1   -1   -3   -1   -2   -2   -2   -1
V    -1   -4   -1   -1   -1   -3   -1   -3   -3   -1   -2   -1   -2   -2   -1
H    -1   -1   -4   -1   -3   -1   -3   -1   -3   -1   -2   -2   -1   -2   -1
D    -1   -1   -1   -4   -3   -1   -1   -3   -1   -3   -2   -2   -2   -1   -1
N    -2   -2   -2   -2   -1   -1   -1   -1   -1   -1   -1   -1   -1   -1   -1
```

FIGURE 11.6 A nucleotide scoring table. The scoring for the four nucleotide bases are shown in the upper left of the figure, with the remaining one-letter codes specifying the IUPAC/UBMB codes for ambiguities or chemical similarities (Appendix 00). Note that the matrix is a mirror image of itself with respect to the diagonal.

no comparison between characters is possible: One sequence has a residue at some position, and the other sequence has nothing. The most widely used method for scoring gaps involves a quantity known as the *affine gap penalty*. Here, a fixed deduction is made for introducing the gap; an additional deduction is made that is proportional to the length of the gap. The formula for the affine gap penalty is $G + Ln$, where G is the gap-opening penalty (the cost of creating the gap), L is the gap-extension penalty, and n is the length of the gap, with $G > L$. Because the gap-opening penalty is larger than the gap-extension penalty, lengthening existing gaps would be favored over creating new ones. The values of G and L can be adjusted manually in most programs to make the insertion of gaps either more or less permissive, but most methods automatically adjust both G and L to the most appropriate values for the scoring matrix being used.

The other major type of gap penalty used is a *non-affine, or linear, gap penalty*. Here, there is no cost for opening the gap; a simple, fixed mismatch penalty is assessed for each position of the gap. It is thought that affine penalties better represent the biology underlying the sequence alignments, because affine gap penalties take into account the fact that most conserved regions are ungapped and that a single mutational event could insert or delete many more than just one residue. In practice, use of the affine gap penalty better enables the detection of more distant homologs.

BLAST

By far, the most widely used technique for detecting similarity between sequences of interest is the Basic Local Alignment Search Tool, or BLAST (Altschul et al., 1991). The widespread adoption of BLAST as a cornerstone technique in sequence analysis lies in its ability to detect similarities accurately between nucleotide or protein sequences quickly, without sacrificing sensitivity. The original, standard family of BLAST programs is shown in Table 11.2, but in the time since its introduction, many variations of the original BLAST program have been developed to address specific needs in the realm of pairwise sequence comparison, many of which are discussed in this chapter.

The Algorithm

BLAST is a local alignment method that is capable of detecting not only the best region of local alignment between a query sequence and its target, but also whether there are other plausible alignments between the query and the target. To find these regions of local alignment in a computationally efficient fashion, the

TABLE 11.2 ■ BLAST Algorithms

Program	Query	Database
BLASTN	Nucleotide	Nucleotide
BLASTP	Protein	Protein
BLASTX	Nucleotide, six-frame translation	Protein
TBLASTN	Protein	Nucleotide, six-frame translation
TBLASTX	Nucleotide, six-frame translation	Nucleotide, six-frame translation

method begins by "seeding" the search with a small subset of letters from the query sequence, known as the *query word*. Using the example shown in Figure 11.7, consider a search where the query word (of default length three) is RDQ. (In practice, all words of length three are considered, so using the sequence in Figure 11.7, the first query word would be TLS, followed by LSH, and so on.) BLAST now needs to find not only the word RDQ in the sequences in the target database, but also related words where conservative substitutions have been introduced, because those matches also may be biologically informative. To determine which words are related to RDQ, scoring matrices are used to develop what is called *the neighborhood*. The center panel of Figure 11.7 shows the collection of words that are related to the original query word, in descending score order, along with their scores using a BLOSUM62 matrix (Figure 11.5). Obviously, some cutoff needs to be applied so that further consideration is given only to words that are indeed closely related to the original query word. The parameter that controls this cutoff is the neighborhood score threshold, or T. The value of T is determined automatically by the BLAST program but can be adjusted by the user. Increasing T would push the search toward more exact matches and would speed up the search, but could lead to overlooking possibly interesting biological relationships. Decreasing T allows for the detection of more distant relationships between sequences. Here, only words with $T \geq 11$ move to the next step.

Focusing now on the lower panel of Figure 11.7, the original query word (RDQ) has been aligned with another word from the neighborhood whose score is more than the score threshold (REQ). The BLAST algorithm now attempts to extend this alignment in both directions, tallying a cumulative score resulting from matches, mismatches, and gaps, until it constructs a local alignment of maximal length. Determining what the maximal length actually is can be best explained by considering the graph in Figure 11.8. Here, the number of residues that have been aligned is plotted against the cumulative score resulting from the alignment. The

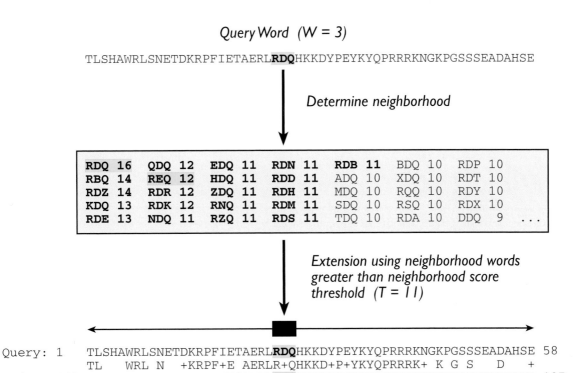

Query Word (W = 3)

TLSHAWRLSNETDKRPFIETAERL**RDQ**HKKDYPEYKYQPRRRKNGKPGSSSEADAHSE

Determine neighborhood

RDQ	16	QDQ	12	EDQ	11	RDN	11	RDB	11	BDQ	10	RDP	10
RBQ	14	REQ	12	HDQ	11	RDD	11	ADQ	10	XDQ	10	RDT	10
RDZ	14	RDR	12	ZDQ	11	RDH	11	MDQ	10	RQQ	10	RDY	10
KDQ	13	RDK	12	RNQ	11	RDM	11	SDQ	10	RSQ	10	RDX	10
RDE	13	NDQ	11	RZQ	11	RDS	11	TDQ	10	RDA	10	DDQ	9 ...

Extension using neighborhood words
greater than neighborhood score
threshold (T = 11)

■

```
Query:    1   TLSHAWRLSNETDKRPFIETAERLRDQHKKDYPEYKYQPRRRKNGKPGSSSEADAHSE  58
              TL   WRL N  +KRPF+E AERLR+QHKKD+P+YKYQPRRRK+ K G S    D   +
Sbjct:  140   TLESGWRLENPGEKRPFVEGAERLREQHKKDHPDYKYQPRRRKSVKNGQSEPEDGSEQ 197
```

FIGURE 11.7 **The initiation of a BLAST search. The search begins with query words of a given length (here, three amino acids) being compared against a scoring matrix to determine additional three-letter words "in the neighborhood" of the original query word. Any occurrences of these neighborhood words in sequences within the target database then are investigated. See text for details.**

left-most point of the graph represents the alignment of the original query word with one of the words from the neighborhood, again having a value of T or more. As the extension proceeds, as long as matches and conservative substitutions outweigh mismatches and gaps, the cumulative score will increase. As soon as the cumulative score breaks the score threshold S, the alignment is reported in the BLAST output. Simply clearing S does not automatically mean that the alignment is biologically significant, a point that is addressed later in this chapter.

As the extension continues, at some point, mismatches and gaps will begin to outweigh the matches and conservative substitutions, accruing negative scores from the scoring matrix. As soon as the curve begins to turn downward, BLAST measures whether the dropoff exceeds a threshold called X. If the curve decays more than is allowed by the value of X, the extension is terminated, and the alignment is trimmed back to the length corresponding to the preceding maximum in the curve. The resulting alignment is called a *high-scoring segment pair*, or HSP. Because the BLAST algorithm systematically marches across the query sequence, using all possible query words, it is possible that more than one HSP may be found for any given sequence pair.

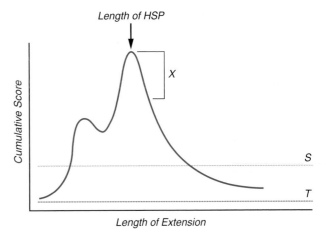

FIGURE 11.8 **BLAST search extension. Length of Extension represents the number of characters that have been aligned in a pairwise sequence comparison. Cumulative Score represents the sum of the position-by-position scores, as determined by the scoring matrix used for the search. T represents the neighborhood score threshold, S is the minimum score required to return a hit in the BLAST output, and X is the significance decay. See text for details.**

BOX 11.2   The Karlin-Altschul Equation

As one may imagine, assessing the putative biological significance of any given BLAST hit based simply on raw scores is difficult, because the scores are dependent on the composition of the query and target sequences, the length of the sequences, the scoring matrix used to compute the raw scores, and numerous other factors. In one of the most important papers on the theory of local sequence alignment statistics, Karlin and Altschul (1990) presented a formula that directly addresses this problem. The formula, which has come to be known as the Karlin-Altschul equation, uses search-specific parameters to calculate an expectation value (E). This value represents the number of high-scoring segment pairs that would be expected purely by chance. The equation and the parameters used to calculate E are as follows:

$$E = kmNe^{-\lambda s},$$

where k is a minor constant, m is the number of letters in the query, N is the total number of letters in the target database, and λ is a constant used to normalize the raw score of the high-scoring segment pair, with the value of λ varying depending on the scoring matrix used, and S is the score of the high-scoring segment pair.

After an HSP is identified, it is important to determine whether the resulting alignment is actually significant. Using the cumulative score from the alignment, along with a number of other parameters, a new value called E is calculated (Box 11.2). For each hit, E gives the number of HSPs having a score of S or more that BLAST would find purely by chance. Put another way, the value of E provides a measure of whether the reported HSP is a false positive. Lower values of E imply greater biological significance.

Running a BLAST Search

Although there are many BLAST servers throughout the world, the most widely used portal for these searches is the BLAST home page at the National Center for Biotechnology Information (NCBI; Figure 11.9). The page is

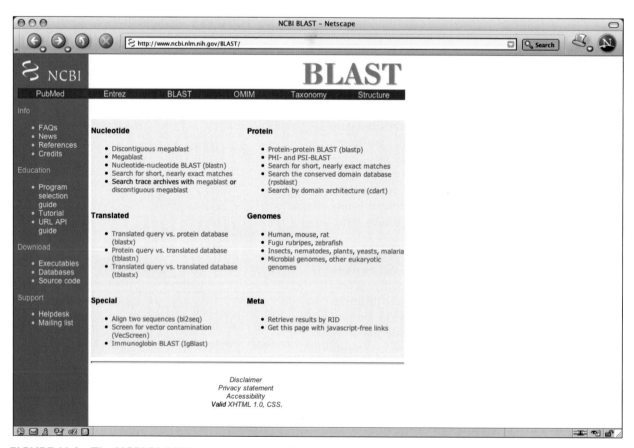

FIGURE 11.9   The NCBI BLAST homepage. Examples of the most useful queries that can be performed using the **BLAST** interface are discussed in the main text.

divided into six sections, corresponding to the many variations of BLAST that are available. To illustrate the relative ease with which one can perform a BLAST search, a protein-based search using BLASTP is discussed. Following the BLASTP hyperlink shown in Figure 11.9 brings users to the BLASTP search page, a portion of which is shown in Figure 11.10. Obviously, a query sequence that is used as the basis for comparison is required, so the sequence of the *Drosophila* homeodomain protein prospero (sp|P29617) has been pasted into the box marked Search. Immediately below, the user can specify whether only a portion of this sequence is to be used; if the whole sequence is to be used, these fields should be left blank. The query sequence needs to be compared against something, and this is specified using the Choose Database pull-down menu; a subset of the databases listed in Table 11.3 can be selected here. The box marked Do CD-Search is checked by default, and when left checked, automatically performs a search of the Conserved Domain Database (CDD) for conserved domains. If the user wishes to use the default settings, the search can be submitted by clicking on the BLAST! button.

The user can exert finer control over how the search is performed by changing the items found in the Options section, in the lower part of Figure 11.10. Users can use the same type of syntax used in issuing Entrez searches (Table 3.1) to limit which entries in the specified database are considered. For example, to consider entries from only mouse and rat, the user would type Mus musculus [ORGN] AND Rattus norvegicus [ORGN] in this field. Single organisms can be selected using the pull-down menu on the same line of the search page. It is recommended that the user leave the Composition-Based Statistics box checked, because this automatically will adjust the resulting BLAST *E* values to take into account the amino acid composition of the sequences being considered (Altschul et al., 1997; Schäffer et al., 1999). Leaving the Low Complexity box checked instructs BLAST automatically to mask-out low-complexity sequences, because they tend to confound BLAST analyses and are best removed from consideration (Wootton & Federhen, 1993). The final three selections are used to control some of the parameters described earlier in this chapter: Expect limits the reporting of

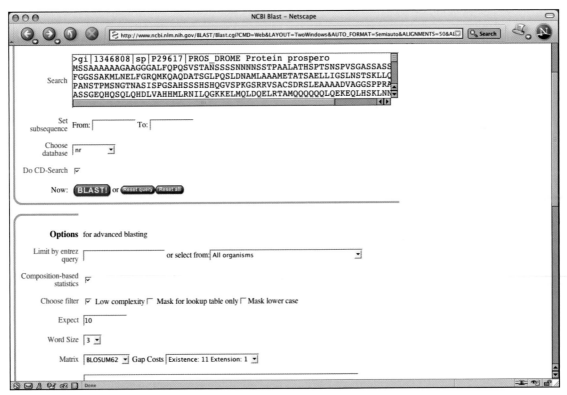

FIGURE 11.10 A portion of the BLASTP query page. The first section in the window is used to specify the sequence of interest, whether only a portion of that sequence should be used in performing the search (Set Subsequence), which database should be searched, and whether the Conserved Domain Database should also be queried (Do CD-Search). The lower portion provides the user the ability to select advanced options that include whether low-complexity regions should be detected and masked-out, the cutoff *E* value for reporting results, the word size, scoring matrix, and associated gap penalties. See text for details.

TABLE 11.3 ■ Main FASTA Algorithms

Program	Query	Database	Corresponding BLAST program
FASTA	Nucleotide	Nucleotide	BLASTN
	Protein	Protein	BLASTP
FASTX/FASTY	DNA	Protein	BLASTX
TFASTYX/TFASTY	Protein	Translated DNA	TBLASTN

results to those having an *E* value lower than the specified value, Word Size changes the size of the query word used to initiate the BLAST search, Matrix allows the user to select an appropriate scoring matrix, and Gap Costs allow the user to specify the magnitude of the affine gap penalties. Changing the matrix automatically changes the gap penalties to values appropriate for that scoring matrix. Again, to initiate the search, the user would click on the BLAST! button at the bottom of the page.

Understanding the BLAST Output

After the BLASTP search is submitted, an intermediate page is presented showing any hits to CDD. The user also can specify formatting options here, but the default values are more than adequate for most uses. To see the BLASTP results, one must request the actual BLASTP report by pressing the Format! button. The first part of the resulting page is shown in Figure 11.11, and this image provides a graphical overview of the BLASTP results. This overview provides a sense of how many sequences were found to have similarity to the query and how they scored against the query. Details of the various features of the graphical display are given in the legend to Figure 11.11.

The list of sequences found as a result of this particular BLASTP search—the hit list—is shown in Figure 11.12. The information included for each hit includes its

Distribution of 55 Blast Hits on the Query Sequence

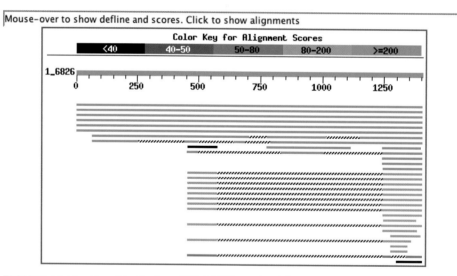

FIGURE 11.11 Graphic display of BLASTP results. The query sequence is represented by the thick red bar (1_6286), with the tick marks indicating residue positions within the query. The thinner bars below the query represent each of the matches detected by the BLAST algorithm. The colors represent the scores for each hit, with the color key for the scores appearing at the top of the display. The length of each line, as well as its position, represents the region of similarity with the query. Hits connected by a cross-hatched line indicate more than one HSP within the same sequence; hits on the same line that are not connected are unrelated. Moving the mouse over any of the lines shows the identity of that hit in the window at the top of the display. Clicking on any of the lines takes the user to detailed information about that hit (Figure 11.13).

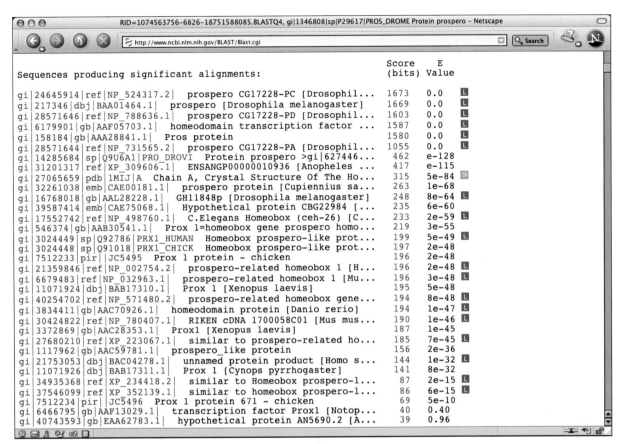

FIGURE 11.12 The **BLASTP** "hit list." For each found sequence, the user is presented with the accession number, a portion of the definition line for the entry, its score, and its *E* value. The colored blocks at the end of some of the hits are links to other **NCBI** resources: **L**, LocusLink; **U**, UniGene; **S**, Structure; and **G**, the Gene Expression Omnibus (GEO). Clicking on any of the hyperlinked score values jumps the user down to the detailed information on that hit (see Figure 11.13).

accession number, as much of the definition line as will fit, its score, and its *E* value. The colored blocks seen at the end of some of the hits take the user to related NCBI resources where more information can be found on that particular sequence. These resources include LocusLink (L), UniGene (U), the structure database (S), and the Gene Expression Omnibus database containing expression data (G). Clicking on the hyperlinked score for any particular hit moves the user down the page to the portion of the output showing the pairwise alignment for that hit (Figure 11.13). The header provides the complete definition line for this particular hit, and each HSP found in that sequence then is shown below the header. In most cases, the user will see only one alignment, but in the case shown in Figure 11.13, there are two, with the hit having the better score shown first. The statistics given for each hit include the *E* value, the number of identities (exact matches), the number of "positives" (exact matches and conservative substitutions), and the number of residues that fell into a gapped region. Note

here that part of the query sequence has been replaced by a series of X characters, denoting a low-complexity region that has been masked.

Suggested BLAST Cutoffs

As was previously alluded to, the listing of a hit in a BLAST report does not automatically mean that the hit is biologically significant. Over time, and based on both the methodical testing and the personal experience of many investigators, many guidelines have been put forward as being appropriate for establishing a boundary that separates meaningful hits from the rest. For nucleotide-based searches, one should look for hits with *E* values of 10^{-6} or less and sequence identity of 70% or more. For protein-based searches, one should look for hits with *E* values of 10^{-3} or less and sequence identity of 25% or more. The reader is cautioned not to use these cutoffs (or any other set of suggested cutoffs) blindly, particularly in the region right around the dividing line. Users should

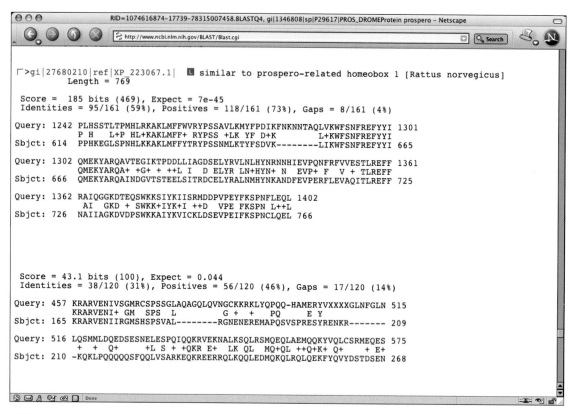

```
>gi|27680210|ref|XP_223067.1|   similar to prospero-related homeobox 1 [Rattus norvegicus]
            Length = 769

 Score =  185 bits (469), Expect = 7e-45
 Identities = 95/161 (59%), Positives = 118/161 (73%), Gaps = 8/161 (4%)

Query: 1242 PLHSSTLTPMHLRKAKLMFFWVRYPSSAVLKMYFPDIKFNKNNTAQLVKWFSNFREFYYI 1301
            P H   L+P HL+KAKLMFF+ RYPSS +LK YF D+K       L+KWFSNFREFYYI
Sbjct: 614  PPHKEGLSPNHLKKAKLMFFYTRYPSSNMLKTYFSDVK--------LIKWFSNFREFYYI 665

Query: 1302 QMEKYARQAVTEGIKTPDDLLIAGDSELYRVLNLHYNRNNHIEVPQNFRFVVESTLREFF 1361
            QMEKYARQA+ +G+ + ++L I   D ELYR LN+HYN+ N  EVP+ F  V + TLREFF
Sbjct: 666  QMEKYARQAINDGVTSTEELSITRDCELYRALNMHYNKANDFEVPERFLEVAQITLREFF 725

Query: 1362 RAIQGGKDTEQSWKKSIYKIISRMDDPVPEYFKSPNFLEQL 1402
            AI  GKD + SWKK+IYK+I ++D  VPE FKSPN L++L
Sbjct: 726  NAIIAGKDVDPSWKKAIYKVICKLDSEVPEIFKSPNCLQEL 766




 Score = 43.1 bits (100), Expect = 0.044
 Identities = 38/120 (31%), Positives = 56/120 (46%), Gaps = 17/120 (14%)

Query: 457  KRARVENIVSGMRCSPSSGLAQAGQLQVNGCKKRKLYQPQQ-HAMERYVXXXXGLNFGLN 515
            KRARVENI+ GM  SPS  L         G + +   PQ      E Y
Sbjct: 165  KRARVENIIRGMSHSPSVAL--------RGNENEREMAPQSVSPRESYRENKR------- 209

Query: 516  LQSMMLDQEDSESNELESPQIQQKRVEKNALKSQLRSMQEQLAEMQQKYVQLCSRMEQES 575
            + + Q+     +LS + +QKR E+  LK QL  MQ+QL ++Q+K+ Q+     + E+
Sbjct: 210  -KQKLPQQQQQSFQQLVSARKEQKREERRQLKQQLEDMQKQLRQLQEKFYQVYDSTDSEN 268
```

FIGURE 11.13 Detailed information on a representative **BLASTP** hit. The header provides the identity of the hit, as well as the score and *E* value. The percent identity indicates exact matches, whereas the percent "positives" takes into account both exact matches and conservative substitutions. The gap figures show how many residues remained unaligned because of the introduction of gaps. Gaps are indicated by dashes (—), whereas masked-out low-complexity regions have been replaced by strings of *X* characters. Note that there is no header preceding the second alignment; this indicates that this is a second **HSP** within the same database entry.

always keep in mind whether the correct scoring matrix was used, should manually inspect the pairwise alignments, and should investigate the biology behind the putative homology by reading the literature to convince themselves whether hits on either side of the suggested cutoffs actually make biological sense.

BLAST Search Artifacts

There are several factors that either can confound BLAST search results or just plainly lead to overinterpretation. The issue of low-complexity regions has already been touched on in the discussion above; these regions potentially can lead to high BLAST scores, even though they do not reflect a meaningful alignment of the two sequences being compared with one another. In the course of nucleotide-based searches, query sequences are masked using a program called DUST, and masked residues are replaced by the character N. Similarly, in the course of

protein-based searches, the masking is performed using a program called SEG (Wootton & Federhen, 1993), and masked residues are replaced by the character X. In nucleotide-based searches, a large number of hits to repetitive elements such as LINE, SINE, and Alu sequences may occur. Automatic masking of these sequences by BLAST currently is under development. In the meantime, programs such as RepeatMasker can be used to mask out these regions effectively and quickly, returning the masked sequences in a format that can be used for database searches. This becomes more important in higher organisms, where low-complexity regions are often seen; these regions are less prevalent in the genomes of lower organisms.

Often, the hit list contains entries that represent hypothetical proteins. These entries result either from gene prediction or the translation of transcripts. Remember that an open reading frame or a prediction of gene structure does not automatically imply translation into a real protein, so these hits should be treated with caution. Finally, although hits to expressed sequence tags (ESTs; Chapter 1) potentially may be informative, they also should be treated with caution. Because ESTs are single-pass sequence reads, their sequencing accuracy is significantly lower than that of "finished" sequences; the EST also may contain vector contaminants that may skew the results.

BLAST2SEQUENCES

A variation of BLAST, called BLAST2Sequences, can be used to find local alignments between any two protein or nucleotide sequences of interest (Tatusova & Madden, 1999). Although the BLAST engine is used to find the best local alignment between the two sequences,

no database search is done. Rather, the two sequences to be compared are specified in advance by the user. The method is particularly useful for comparing sequences that have been determined to be homologous through experimental methods or for making comparisons between the same sequence from different species. BLAST2Sequences can be accessed through the NCBI BLAST homepage (Figure 11.9). The BLAST2Sequences query page allows users to specify the usual array of BLAST-related options, including scoring matrix and gap penalties. A sample set of results from BLAST2Sequences, using the human and mouse McKusick-Kaufman syndrome protein, is shown in Figure 11.14. The major difference between these results and the typical BLAST output is the presentation of the graphic with the diagonal; this is reminiscent of the dot-plot representation described above, and is intended

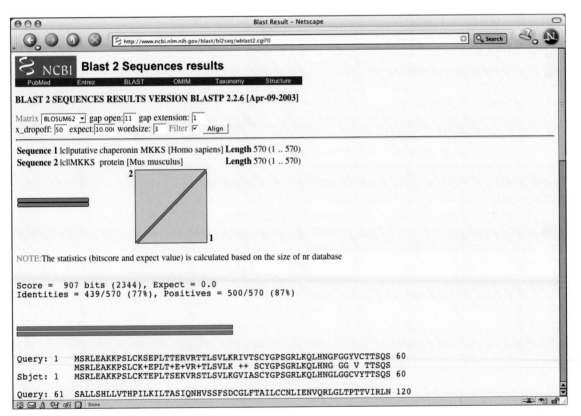

FIGURE 11.14 Typical output from a BLAST2Sequences run. Here, sequences for the human and mouse McKusick-Kaufman syndrome protein were compared. The graphic with the diagonal is similar to the dotplot output described in this chapter, although the orientation of the diagonal is shifted 90° clockwise. The horizontal blue bars represent the two proteins being compared, and any large gaps in the alignment would be shown schematically here. Scoring information for the local alignment is given, in a similar fashion as for routine BLAST searches. Note that the graphic with the diagonal shows a solid bar, even though the two proteins are only 77% identical to one another; this is simply a function of the scale of the graphic. The two sequences can be reanalyzed using different BLAST parameters by changing the settings at the top of this screen.

to convey graphically the degree of similarity between the two sequences being compared. As with all BLAST searches, the user is provided with the score, E value, and percentages for identities, positives, and any gaps that may have been introduced.

MEGABLAST

MegaBLAST is a variation of the BLASTN algorithm that has been optimized specifically for use in aligning either long or highly similar (>95%) sequences and is the method of choice when looking for exact matches in nucleotide databases. The use of a greedy gapped alignment routine allows MegaBLAST to handle longer nucleotide sequences approximately 10 times faster than BLASTN would. MegaBLAST is particularly well suited for finding whether a sequence of interest is part of a larger contig or supercontig, detecting potential sequencing errors, and for comparing large, similar data sets against each other. The run speeds that are achieved using MegaBLAST come from changing two aspects of the traditional BLASTN routine. First, longer default word lengths are used; in BLASTN, the default word length is 11, whereas MegaBLAST uses a default word length of 28. Second, MegaBLAST uses a nonaffine gap penalty scheme, meaning that there is no penalty for opening the gap; there is only a penalty for extending the gap, with a constant charge for each position in the gap. MegaBLAST is capable of accepting batch queries by simply pasting multiple sequences in FASTA format or a list of accession numbers into the query window. The Worked Example at the end of this chapter illustrates how MegaBLAST can be used to determine the position of a cloned contig on a chromosomal map.

There is a second variation of MegaBLAST, called Discontinuous MegaBLAST. This version has been designed for comparing divergent sequences from different organisms, sequences where one would expect there to be low sequence identity. This method uses a discontiguous word approach that is quite different from that used by the rest of the programs in the BLAST suite. Here, rather than looking for query words of a certain length to seed the search, nonconsecutive positions are examined over longer sequence segments (Ma et al., 2002). The approach has been shown to find statistically significant alignments even when the degree of similarity between sequences is very low.

PSI-BLAST

The variation of the BLAST algorithm known as PSI-BLAST (for position-specific-iterated BLAST) is particularly well suited for identifying distantly related proteins,

proteins that may not have been found using the traditional BLASTP method (Altschul & Koonin, 1998). PSI-BLAST relies on the use of position-specific scoring matrices (PSSMs), which are also often called hidden Markov models or profiles (Bucher et al., 1996; Gribskov et al., 1987; Schneider et al., 1986; Staden, 1988; Tatusov et al., 1994). PSSMs are, quite simply, a numerical representation of a multiple sequence alignment, much like the multiple sequence alignments derived from the methods discussed in Chapter 12. Imbedded within a multiple sequence alignment is intrinsic sequence information that represents the common characteristics of that particular collection of sequences, frequently a protein family. By using a PSSM, one is able to use these imbedded, common characteristics to find similarities between sequences with little or no absolute sequence identity, allowing for the identification and analysis of distantly related proteins. PSSMs are constructed by taking a multiple sequence alignment representing a protein family and then asking a series of questions:

▶ What residues are seen at each position of the alignment?

▶ How often does a particular residue appear at each position of the alignment?

▶ Are there positions that show absolute conservation?

▶ Can gaps be introduced anywhere in the alignment?

As soon as those questions are answered, the PSSM is constructed, and the numbers in the table now represent the multiple sequence alignment (Figure 11.15). The numbers within the PSSM reflect the probability of any given amino acid occurring at each position. It also reflects the effect of a conservative or nonconservative substitution at each position in the alignment, much like a PAM or BLOSUM matrix does. This PSSM now can be used for comparison against single sequences, or in an iterative approach where newly found sequences can be incorporated into the original PSSM to find additional sequences that may be of interest.

The Method

Starting with a query sequence of interest, the PSI-BLAST process operates by taking a query protein sequence and performing a standard BLASTP search, as described above. This search produces a number of hits having E values of more than a certain set threshold. These hits, along with the initial, single query sequence, are used to construct a PSSM in an automated fashion. As soon as the PSSM is constructed, the PSSM then serves as the query for researching the target database; PSI-BLAST now is using the collective characteristics of the identified sequences to find new, related sequences. The process continues, round by round, until the search either

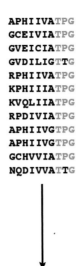

```
APHIIVATPG
GCEIVIATPG
GVEICIATPG
GVDILIGTTG
RPHIIVATPG
KPHIIIATPG
KVQLIIATPG
RPDIVIATPG
APHIIVGTPG
APHIIVGTPG
GCHVVIATPG
NQDIVVATTG
```

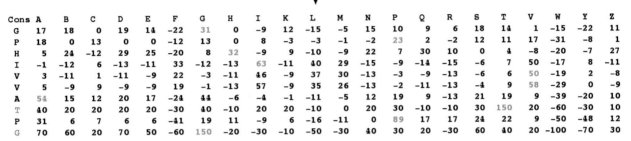

Cons	A	B	C	D	E	F	G	H	I	K	L	M	N	P	Q	R	S	T	V	W	Y	Z
G	17	18	0	19	14	-22	31	0	-9	12	-15	-5	15	10	9	6	18	14	1	-15	-22	11
P	18	0	13	0	0	-12	13	0	8	-3	-1	-2		23	2	-2	12	11	17	-31	-8	1
H	5	24	-12	29	25	-20	8	32	-9	9	-10	-9	22	7	30	10	0	4	-8	-20	-7	27
I	-1	-12	6	-13	-11	33	-12	-13	63	-11	40	29	-15	-9	-14	-15	-6	7	50	-17	8	-11
V	3	-11	1	-11	-9	22	-3	-11	46	-9	37	30	-13	-3	-9	-13	-6	6	50	-19	2	-8
V	5	-9	9	-9	-9	19	-1	-13	57	-9	35	26	-13	-2	-11	-13	-4	9	58	-29	0	-9
A	54	15	12	20	17	-24	44	-6	-4	-1	-11	-5	12	19	9	-13	21	19	9	-39	-20	10
T	40	20	20	20	20	-30	40	-10	20	20	-10	0	20	30	-10	-10	30	150	20	-60	-30	10
P	31	6	7	6	6	-41	19	11	-9	6	-16	-11	0	89	17	17	24	22	9	-50	-48	12
G	70	60	20	70	50	-60	150	-20	-30	-10	-50	-30	40	30	20	-30	60	40	20	-100	-70	30

FIGURE 11.15 Constructing a PSSM. In the upper portion of the figure is a multiple sequence alignment, 10 residues across. Using the criteria described in the main text, the PSSM corresponding to this multiple sequence alignment is shown in the lower portion of the figure. Each row of the PSSM corresponds to each column in the multiple sequence alignment. Note that position 8 of the alignment always has a *T*, whereas position 10 always has a *G*. Looking at the corresponding scores in the matrix, in row 8, the *T* scores 150 points; in row 10, the *G* scores 150 points. These are the highest values in the row, corresponding to the fact that the multiple sequence alignment shows absolute conservation at those positions. Considering position 9, most of the sequences have a *P* at that position; in row 9 of the PSSM. The *P* scores 89 points, still the highest value in the row, but not as high a score as would be assessed if the *P* was absolutely conserved across all the sequences.

converges (meaning that no new sequences have been found) or until the limit on the number of iterations is reached.

Performing a PSI-BLAST Search

PSI-BLAST searches can be initiated by following the PSI-BLAST link on the BLAST homepage (Figure 11.9). The search page is identical to that shown in Figure 11.10, with the exception that certain options have been pres-elected that are specific to PSI-BLAST searches. Scrolling down to the Format section of the page, the PSI-BLAST box already is checked, and a default inclusion value of 0.005 (the default *E* value for moving to the next round) appears. The search is submitted as before, by clicking on the BLAST! button.

The results of a sample search, using the sequence of the sex-determining protein SRY from human, is shown in Figure 11.16. The sequences deemed similar to the query sequence are found in a section marked Sequences with E-value BETTER than threshold. These sequences all have *E* values better than the preset inclusion value. Scrolling down the page, a second set of sequences is listed, with the header Sequences with E-value WORSE than threshold. The sequences in the "better than" set are used to construct a PSSM, as described above, and after the user presses the button marked Run PSI-BLAST Iteration 2, this PSSM serves as the query for finding new sequences related to those in the original set. Note that there is a checkbox next to each of the sequences in the hit list; users can remove sequences manually from the "better than" set or include sequences from the "worse than" set based on other information, such as experimental results or known biological relationships. New relationships are discovered at each iteration, making it possible to identify additional homologs that would not have been found using the standard BLASTP approach.

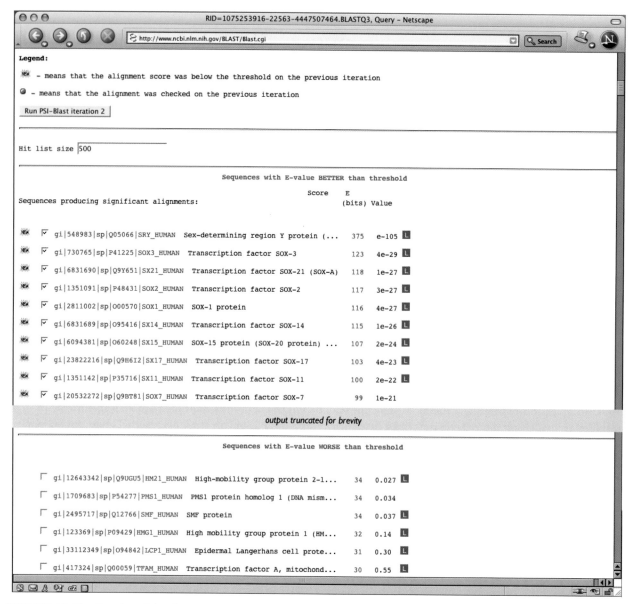

FIGURE 11.16   Results of the first round of a PSI-BLAST search. The initial query sequence is that of the human sex-determining protein SRY (sp|Q05066), using Swiss-Prot as the target database and limiting results to human sequences. The results are grouped into two sets: those above the preset inclusion threshold (default $E = 0.005$; top), and those that fall below the threshold ($E < 0.005$; bottom). The upper portion of the output has been truncated in this figure, for brevity. Sequences that are in the first set are used to calculate a PSSM, and the PSSM then serves as the new "query" as soon as the button for the next iteration is pressed. Individual sequences can be added or excluded by checking the boxes to the left of each sequence. The key denoting newly found and carried-over sequences is shown at the top of the screen.

BLAT

In response to the assembly needs of the Human Genome Project, a new alignment program called BLAT (for BLAST-Like Alignment Tool) was introduced (Kent, 2002). BLAT is most similar to the MegaBLAST version of BLAST in that it is designed rapidly to align longer nucleotide sequences having more than 95% similarity. However, the BLAT algorithm uses a slightly different strategy than does BLAST to achieve faster speeds. Before any searches are performed, the target databases (in this context, genome assemblies) are preindexed, keeping track of all nonoverlapping 11-mers in the assembly; this index then is used to find regions similar to the query

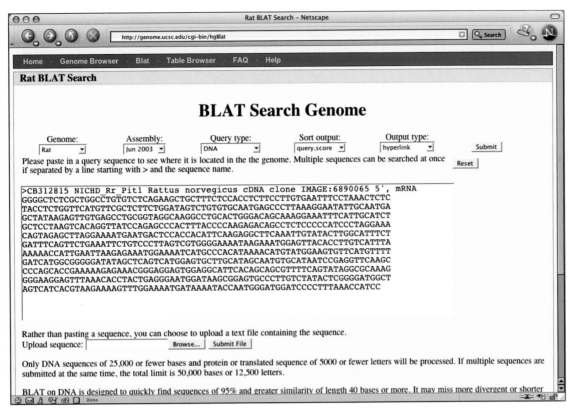

FIGURE 11.17 Submitting a BLAT query. A rat clone from MGC (CB312815) is the query. The pull-down menus at the top of the page can be used to specify which genome should be searched (organism), which assembly should be used (usually, the most recent), and the query type (DNA, protein, translated RNA, or translated DNA).

sequence. BLAT commonly is used to find the position of a sequence of interest in a genome or to perform cross-species analyses.

As an example, consider a case where an investigator wishes to find whether a cDNA clone of interest has been mapped in the rat genome. Here, a rat clone from the Mammalian Gene Collection (MGC) is used as the query. The BLAT query page is shown in Figure 11.17, and the sequence of the clone of interest has been pasted into the sequence box. Above the sequence box are several pull-down menus that can be used to specify which genome should be searched (organism), which assembly should be used (usually, the most recent), and the query type (DNA, protein, translated RNA, or translated DNA). As soon as the appropriate choices have been selected, the search is commenced by pressing the Submit button. The results from the query are shown in the upper panel of Figure 11.18; here, a single match having 98.1% identity with the query sequence has been found. More details on this hit can be found by clicking the details hyperlink, to the left of the entry. A long Web page is then returned, providing information on the original query, the genomic sequence, and an alignment

of the query against the found genomic sequence (Figure 11.18, bottom panel). The genomic sequence here is labeled Chr5, meaning that the query corresponds to a region of rat chromosome 5. Matching bases in the cDNA and genomic sequences are colored in dark blue and are capitalized. Lighter-blue uppercase bases mark the boundaries of aligned regions and often signify splice sites. Gaps and unaligned regions are indicated by lowercase black type. In the side-by-side alignment, exact matches are indicated by the vertical line between the two sequences. Clicking the browser hyperlink in the upper panel of Figure 11.18 would take the user to the UCSC Genome Browser, where detailed information about the genomic assembly in this region of rat chromosome 5 (5q31) can be obtained (c.f., Chapter 4).

FASTA

FASTA was the first widely used program designed for database similarity searching (Lipman & Pearson, 1985; Pearson & Lipman, 1988; Pearson, 2000). Like BLAST, FASTA enables the user to compare a query sequence

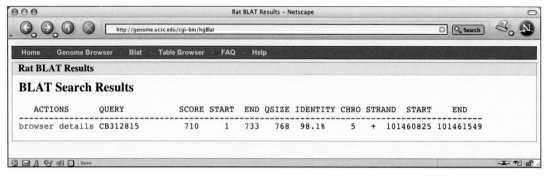

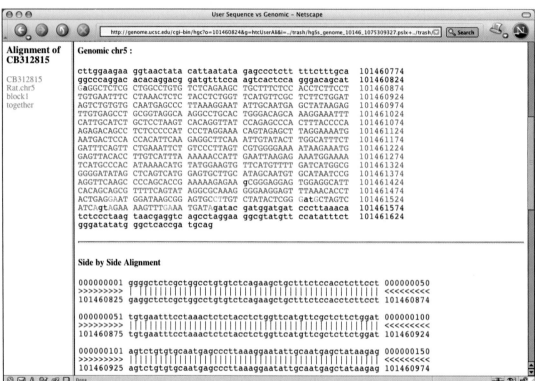

FIGURE 11.18 Results of a BLAT query. Based on the query submitted in Figure 11.17, a single match having 98.1% identity with the query sequence has been found (upper panel). Clicking the details hyperlink brings the user to additional information on the found sequence, shown in the lower panel. Matching bases in the cDNA and genomic sequences are colored in dark blue and capitalized. Lighter-blue uppercase bases mark the boundaries of aligned regions and often signify splice sites. Gaps are indicated by lowercase black type. In the side-by-side alignment, exact matches are indicated by the vertical line between the sequences.

against large databases, and various versions of the program are available (Table 11.3). In addition to the main implementations, a variety of specialized FASTA versions are available, and these versions were described in detail in Pearson (2003).

The Method

The FASTA algorithm can be divided into four major steps. In the first step, FASTA determines all overlapping words of a certain length in both the query sequence and in each of the sequences in the target database, creating two lists in the process. Here, the word length parameter is called *ktup*, which is the equivalent of *W* in BLAST. These lists of overlapping words are compared with one another to identify any words that are common to the two lists. The method then looks for word matches that are in close proximity to one another and connects them to each other (intervening sequence included), without introducing any gaps. This can be represented using the now-familiar dotplot format (Figure 11.19a). After this initial round of connections are made, an

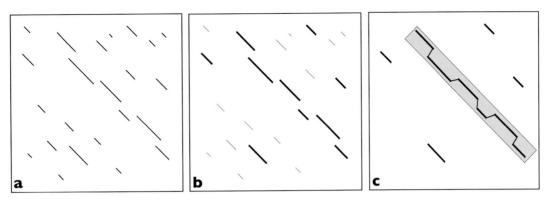

FIGURE 11.19   The FASTA search strategy. (a) As soon as FASTA determines words of length *ktup* common to the query sequence and the target sequence, it connects words that are close to each other, and these are represented by the diagonals. (b) After an initial round of scoring, the top 10 diagonals are selected for further analysis. (c) The Smith-Waterman algorithm is applied to yield the optimal pairwise alignment between the two sequences being considered. See text for details.

initial score (init$_1$) is calculated for each of the regions of similarity.

In step two, only the ten best regions for a given pairwise alignment are considered for further analysis (Figure 11.19b). FASTA now tries to join together regions of similarity that are close to each other in the dotplot, but that do not lie on the same diagonal, with the goal of extending the overall length of the alignment (Figure 11.19c). This means that insertions and deletions are now allowed, but there is a "joining penalty" for each of the diagonals that are connected. The net score for any two diagonals that have been connected is the sum of the score of the original diagonals, less the joining penalty. This new score is referred to as init$_n$.

In step three, FASTA ranks all of the resulting diagonals, and then considers further only the "best" diagonals in the list. For each of the best diagonals, FASTA uses a modification of the Smith-Waterman algorithm (Smith & Waterman, 1981) to come up with the optimal pairwise alignment between the two sequences being considered. A final, optimal score (opt) is calculated on this pairwise alignment.

In the fourth and final step, FASTA assesses the significance of the alignments by estimating what the anticipated distribution of scores would be for randomly generated sequences having the same overall composition (i.e., sequence length and distribution of amino acids or nucleotides). Based on this randomization procedure and on the results from the original query, FASTA calculates an expectation value E that, as before, represents the probability that a reported hit has occurred purely by chance.

Running a FASTA Search

The University of Virginia provides a Web front-end for issuing FASTA queries. Various protein and nucleotide databases are available, and two databases can be selected for use in a single run. From this page, the user also can specify the scoring matrix to be used, gap and extension penalties, and the value for *ktup*. The default values for *ktup* are two for protein-based searches and six for nucleotide-based searches; lowering the value of *ktup* increases the sensitivity of the run, at the expense of speed. The user also can limit the results returned to particular E values.

The results returned by a FASTA query are in a significantly different format than those returned by BLAST. Consider a FASTA search using the sequence of the human homeodomain protein prospero (sp|P29617) as the query, BLOSUM62 as the scoring matrix, and *nr* as the target database. The first part of the FASTA output presents a summary of the search (Figure 11.20), with the results graphed as a histogram. The histogram is intended to convey the distribution of all similarity scores computed in the course of this particular search. The first column represents bins of similarity scores, with the scores increasing as one moves down the page. The second column gives the actual number of sequences observed to fall into each one of these bins. This count is also represented by the length of each of the lines in the histogram, with each of the equal signs representing a certain number of sequences; in the figure, each equal sign corresponds to 3301 sequences from *nr*. The third column of numbers represents how many sequences would be expected to fall into each one of the bins; this is indicated by the asterisks in the histogram. The actual hit list immediately would follow, and a portion of the hit list for this search is shown in Figure 11.21. Here, the accession number and partial definition line for each hit is given, along with its optimal similarity score (opt), a normalized score (bit), and the expectation value E. Not shown here are the individual alignments

```
Query library @ vs %n library searching /slib2/blast/nr.lseg library

  1>>>sp|P29617|PROS_DROME Protein prospero - 1403 aa
 vs  NCBI/Blast non-redundant (nr) proteins library

        opt       E()
 < 20   3193        0:=
   22      0        0:                one = represents 3301 library sequences
   24      2        2:*
   26      2       34:*
   28     12      364:*
   30     52     2210:*
   32    381     8545:= *
   34   2470    23173:=        *
   36  13785    47592:=====              *
   38  46778    78653:===============             *
   40 108094   109713:=================================*
   42 172066   134111:============================================*============
   44 198028   147937:================================================*==============
   46 196864   150678:===============================================*=============
   48 169898   144257:=============================================*========
   50 139063   131635:=========================================*===
   52 114015   115729:====================================*
   54  93277    98853:============================*
   56  72886    82572:======================   *
   58  56471    67790:=================   *
   60  43765    54914:==============   *
   62  34085    44025:==========   *
   64  26851    35013:========= *
   66  20350    27673:======= *
   68  16716    21767:======*
   70  13238    17058:=====*
   72  10518    13329:====*
   74   8600    10392:===*
   76   6829     8089:==*
   78   5517     6287:=*
   80   4502     4882:=*
   82   3809     3735:=*
   84   3274     2958:*
   86   2723     2289:*
   88   2273     1771:*       inset = represents 75 library sequences
   90   2035     1370:*
   92   1793     1060:*      :==============*=========
   94   1396      820:*      :=========*========
   96   1281      635:*      :=======*=========
   98   1097      491:*      :======*========
  100    920      380:*      :=====*=======
  102    914      294:*      :===*=========
  104    737      228:*      :===*======
  106    639      176:*      :==*=====
  108    542      136:*      :=*======
  110    520      105:*      :=*=====
  112    488       82:*      :=*=====
  114    460       63:*      :*======
  116    375       49:*      :*====
  118    363       38:*      :*====
 >120   3701       29:*=     :*===================================
```

FIGURE 11.20 Search summary from a protein–protein **FASTA** search, using the sequence of the human homeodomain protein prospero (sp|P29617) as the query and **BLOSUM62** as the scoring matrix. The header indicates that the query is against the **NCBI** non-redundant (*nr*) protein database. The histogram indicates the distribution of all similarity scores computed for this search. The left-most column provides a normalized similarity score, and the column marked opt gives the number of sequences with that score. The column marked E () gives the number of sequences expected to achieve the score in the first column. In this case, each equal sign in the histogram represents 3301 sequences in *nr*. The asterisks in each row indicate the expected, random distribution of hits. The inset is a magnified version of the histogram in that region.

```
                                                                    opt   bits  E(1607648)
The best scores are:
gi|24645914|ref|NP_524317.2|  prospero CG17228-PC [Drosophila melanoga (1403) 7209 1186.9        0
gi|217346|dbj|BAA01464.1|  prospero [Drosophila melanogaster]         (1403) 7201 1185.6        0
gi|6179901|gb|AAF05703.1|  homeodomain transcription factor Prospero [ (1403) 6942 1143.5        0
gi|158184|gb|AAA28841.1|  Pros protein                                (1407) 6920 1139.9        0
gi|28571646|ref|NP_788636.1|  prospero CG17228-PD [Drosophila melanoga (1374) 6222 1026.4        0
gi|28571644|ref|NP_731565.2|  prospero CG17228-PA [Drosophila melanoga (1535) 4758  788.3        0
gi|31201317|ref|XP_309606.1|  ENSANGP00000010936 [Anopheles gambiae] g (1129) 1124  197.1   1.2e-47
gi|16768018|gb|AAL28228.1|  GH11848p [Drosophila melanogaster]        ( 598) 1088  190.9   4.5e-46
gi|14285684|sp|Q9U6A1|PRO_DROVI Protein prospero gi|6274469|gb|AAF066  (1556)  892  159.5   3.4e-36
gi|27065659|pdb|1MIJ|A Chain A, Crystal Structure Of The Homeo-Prospe  ( 152)  776  139.6   3.2e-31
gi|32261038|emb|CAE00181.1|  prospero protein [Cupiennius salei]       ( 837)  714  130.3   1.2e-27
gi|39587414|emb|CAE75068.1|  Hypothetical protein CBG22984 [Caenorhabd ( 592)  619  114.7   4.1e-23
gi|17552742|ref|NP_498760.1|  C.Elegans Homeobox (ceh-26) [Caenorhabdi ( 586)  610  113.2   1.1e-22
gi|40254702|ref|NP_571480.2|  prospero-related homeobox gene 1 [Danio  ( 739)  571  106.9   1.1e-20
gi|3834411|gb|AAC70926.1|  homeodomain protein [Danio rerio]          ( 739)  571  106.9   1.1e-20
gi|3024449|sp|Q92786|PRX1_HUMAN Homeobox prospero-like protein PROX1   ( 736)  562  105.5   2.9e-20
gi|6679483|ref|NP_032963.1|  prospero-related homeobox 1 [Mus musculus ( 737)  562  105.5   2.9e-20
gi|11071924|dbj|BAB17310.1|  Prox 1 [Xenopus laevis]                   ( 740)  556  104.5   5.8e-20
gi|21359846|ref|NP_002754.2|  prospero-related homeobox 1 [Homo sapien ( 737)  555  104.3   6.5e-20
gi|7512233|pir||JC5495 Prox 1 protein - chicken                       ( 736)  554  104.2   7.2e-20
```

FIGURE 11.21 **Hit list for the protein–protein FASTA search described in Figure 11.19. Only the first 20 hits are shown. For each hit, the accession number and partial definition line for the hit is provided. The column marked** opt **gives the raw similarity score, the column marked** bit **gives a normalized bit score, and the column marked** E **gives the expectation value. See text for details.**

of each hit to the original query sequence, which would be found by further scrolling down in the output. In the pairwise alignments, exact matches are indicated by a colon, whereas conservative substitutions are indicated by a dot.

Statistical Significance of Results

As before, the E values from a FASTA search represent the probability that a hit has occurred purely by chance. Pearson (2003) put forth the following guidelines for inferring homology from protein-based searches, which are slightly different than those previously described for BLAST: An E value of less than 10^{-6} implies homology. When $E < 10^{-3}$, the query and found sequences are probably homologous, but the user should guarantee that the highest-scoring unrelated sequence has an E value near one.

COMPARING FASTA AND BLAST

Because both FASTA and BLAST use rigorous algorithms to find sequences that are statistically (and hopefully biologically) relevant, it is logical to ask which one of the methods is the better choice. There actually is no good answer to the question, because both of the methods bring significant strengths to the table. Summarized below are some of the fine points that distinguish the two methods from one another:

▶ FASTA begins the search by looking for exact matches of words, whereas BLAST allows for conservative substitutions in the first step.

▶ BLAST allows for automatic masking of sequences, whereas FASTA does not.

▶ FASTA will return one and only one alignment for a sequence in the hit list, whereas BLAST can return multiple results for the same sequence, each result representing a distinct HSP.

▶ Because FASTA uses a version of the more rigorous Smith-Waterman alignment method, it generally produces better final alignments and is more apt to find distantly related sequences than BLAST. For highly similar sequences, their performance is fairly similar.

▶ When comparing translated DNA sequences with protein sequences or vice versa, FASTA (specifically, FASTX/FASTY for translated DNA → protein and TFASTX/TFASTY for protein → translated DNA) allows for frameshifts.

▶ BLAST runs faster than FASTA, because FASTA is more computationally intensive.

Several studies have attempted to answer the "Which method is better?" question by performing systematic analyses with test data sets (Pearson, 1995; Agarawal & States, 1998; Chen, 2003). In one such study, Brenner et al. (1998) performed tests using a data set derived from already-known homologies documented in the Structural Classification of Proteins database (SCOP; Chapter 9). They found that FASTA performed better than BLAST in finding relationships between proteins having more than 30% sequence identity, and that the performance of all methods declined to less than 30%. Importantly, although the statistical values reported by BLAST slightly underestimated the true extent of errors when looking for known relationships, they found that BLAST and FASTA (with *ktup* = 2) both were able to detect most known relationships, calling them both "appropriate for rapid initial searches."

▌SUMMARY

The ability to perform pairwise sequence alignments and to interpret the results from such analyses has become commonplace at the bench, no longer being a technique used solely by bioinformaticians. With time, these methods have undergone a continual evolution, keeping pace with the types and scale of data that are being generated both in individual laboratories and by systematic, organismal sequencing projects. As with all computational techniques, the reader should have a firm grasp of the underlying algorithm, always keeping in mind their capabilities and limitations. Intelligent use of the tools presented in this chapter can lead to powerful and interesting biological discoveries, but there also have been many cases documented where improper use of the tools have led to incorrect biological conclusions. By understanding the methods, users can optimize them and end up with a better set of results than if these methods were

treated simply as a "black box." As biology is increasingly undertaken in a sequence-based fashion, using sequence data to underpin the design and interpretation of experiments, it becomes increasingly important that computational results, such as those generated using BLAST and FASTA, are cross-checked in the laboratory, against the literature, and with additional computational analysis to ensure that any conclusions drawn not only make biological sense, but also are correct.

▌WORKED EXAMPLE

This example illustrates the use of MegaBLAST in conjunction with the NCBI Map Browser (Chapter 4) and NCBI Entrez (Chapter 3). The sequence used in the example can be found on the Book's Web page.

Suppose that a human BAC clone in a candidate gene region has just been sequenced, and its position in the human genome needs to be determined. Because the sequence is known to be from human, the most efficient way of running MegaBLAST is to go directly to the BLAST page for analyzing the human genome. The link can be found under the Genomes section of the BLAST homepage, and the search page is shown in Figure 11.22. The sequence of interest is pasted into the query box, in FASTA format. Make sure that the use MegaBLAST box is checked, then click

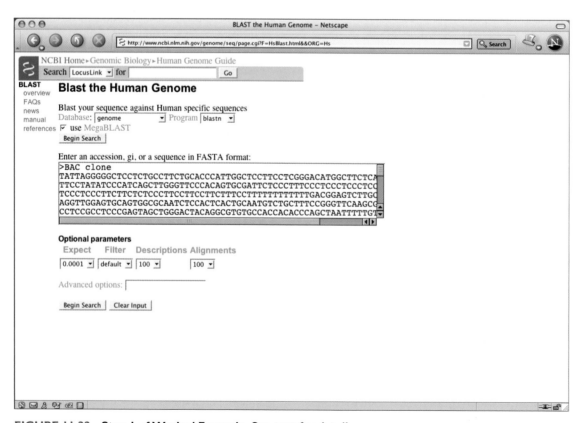

FIGURE 11.22 Step 1 of Worked Example. See text for details.

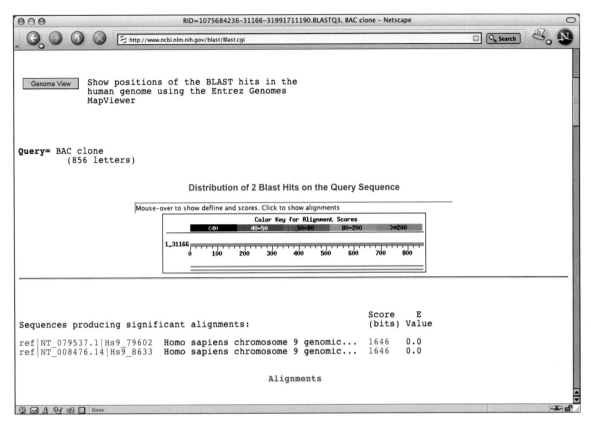

FIGURE 11.23 Step 2 of Worked Example. See text for details.

Begin Search. MegaBLAST returns the familiar BLAST-style output (Figure 11.23), showing two hits with no discontinuities. Both hits map to genomic contigs on chromosome 9, but that is the extent of the mapping information available in the MegaBLAST results. Scrolling down to the individual alignments (not shown) indicates that both hits have 100% identity with the query, and that the query and hits are in the same direction (Strand = Plus/Plus).

It remains to be seen whether the two hits to chromosome 9 actually correspond to two distinct regions of chromosome 9 or whether the two found contigs actually overlap one another, with the BAC clone bridging the region of overlap. Answering this question requires jumping over to the NCBI Map Viewer, which is easily accomplished by following the button labeled Genome View, found directly above the BLAST graphical view.

The two hits from the MegaBLAST search are listed at the bottom of the Map Viewer screen shown in Figure 11.24. Note that, although both have a definition line reading Homo sapiens chromosome 9 genomic contig, only one of the two has been placed definitively onto the map: The ideogram at the top of the window shows one tick mark next to chromosome 9, whereas the other tick mark is on a "chromosome" labeled not placed. The mapped hit corresponds to the second hit from the MegaBLAST results (NT_008476), and the unmapped hit corresponds to the first hit from the MegaBLAST search

(NT_079537). Following the NT_008476 link takes the user to the map view, and the query BAC clone is seen to map to the end of contig NT_008476 (Figure 11.25).

If the nucleotide entry for NT_079537 were looked up using Entrez, the following comment would be found in the entry:

> This DNA sequence is part of the second release of the finished human reference genome. However, it has been included as an unplaced contig rather than being incorporated into one of the chromosomes either because it has not yet reached a finished status or because it is not clear where it should be placed.

So, does the BAC clone of interest actually map to two separate regions of human chromosome 9? It is indeed possible that the unplaced contig maps to another part of chromosome 9. The more likely scenario is that the unplaced contig overlaps with the placed contig or lies totally inside the placed contig; if this is the case, the original BAC clone can be placed uniquely onto chromosome 9. Without having finished sequence for the unplaced contig, the question cannot be answered unequivocally. Under these circumstances, the process described in this example would have to be performed again as soon as new builds become available and until the unplaced contig is finished (and, perhaps, made part of a larger contig).

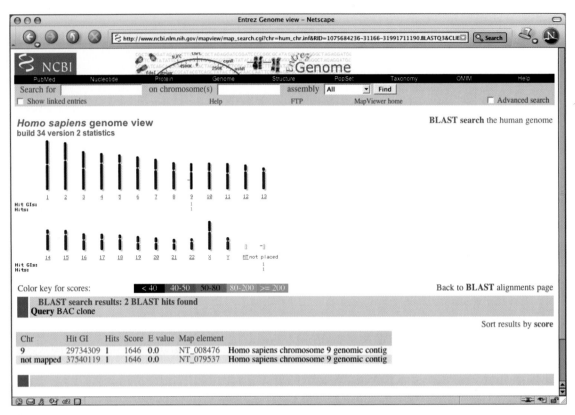

FIGURE 11.24   Step 3 of Worked Example. See text for details.

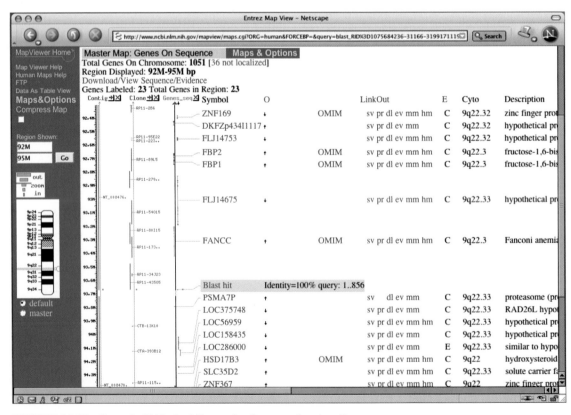

FIGURE 11.25   Step 4 of Worked Example. See text for details.

PROBLEM SET

1. Calculate the score for the DNA sequence alignment shown below, using the scoring matrix shown in Figure 11.6. Use an affine gap penalty to score the gaps, with -11 for opening the gap and -1 for each position in the gap. How would the score change if a non-affine gap penalty was used instead?

```
GACTACGATCCGTATACGCACA---GGTTCAGAC
||||||   ||||||||||||   |||||||||
GACTACAGCTCGTATACGCACACATGGTTCAGAC
```

2. The gene *DCC* (deleted in colorectal cancer), located on human chromosome 18q21.3, encodes for a tumor suppressor protein; expression of the gene is reduced significantly in most colorectal carcinomas. The protein sequence of human DCC can be found by searching NCBI Entrez for RefSeq accession number NP_005206.

   a. Perform a BLASTP search, using this sequence as the query and Swiss-Prot as the target database. Limit the search to mammalian species only, and use BLOSUM62 as the scoring matrix.
      ▶ The DCC protein from human is most closely related to the DCC protein from what other mammal?
      ▶ What percent identity do they share?
      ▶ What is their percent similarity?
      ▶ What is the length of the alignment? Were both proteins aligned along their entire length?

   b. Does the DCC protein contain any low-complexity regions that have been masked-out by BLASTP? If so, where?

   c. Using BLAST2Sequences and BLOSUM62, what percent identity and similarity do the first two hits from mouse in the BLASTP hit list share with one another? How much of the alignment is accounted for by gaps? Does changing the matrix to BLOSUM90 significantly change these numbers?

   d. Perform a FASTA search, using the DCC sequence as the query and Swiss-Prot as the target database. Again, use BLOSUM62 as the scoring matrix, and use *ktup* = 1 for the word size. One of the returned hits is for the Wiskott-Aldrich syndrome protein (sp|Q92558). Does this protein share significant similarity with human DCC?

   e. Based on the BLASTP and FASTA results, can any general observations be made regarding the putative function or cellular role of DCC? Describe what possible functions of this protein may be in the cell, based on all of the significant hits in the BLASTP and FASTA results.

INTERNET RESOURCES

BLAST		
	NCBI	http://www.ncbi.nlm.nih.gov/BLAST
	EBI	http://www.ebi.ac.uk/blastall
BLAT		http://genome.ucsc.edu/cgi-bin/hgBlat
BLOCKS		http://blocks.fhcrc.org
CDD		http://www.ncbi.nlm.nih.gov/Structure/cdd.cdd.shtml
Dotlet		http://www.isrec.isb-sib.ch/java/dotlet/Dotlet.html
Dotter		http://www.cgr.ki.se/cgr/groups/sonnhammer/Dotter.html
Dottup		http://www.emboss.org
FASTA		
	Virginia	http://fasta.bioch.virginia.edu
	EBI	http://www.ebi.ac.uk/fasta33/
MGC		http://mgc.nci.nih.gov
RepeatMasker		http://repeatmasker.genome.washington.edu
SCOP		http://scop.berkeley.edu
SEG		ftp://ncbi.nlm.nih.gov/pub/seg/

FURTHER READING

ALTSCHUL, S. F., BOGUSKI, M. S., GISH, W., AND WOOTTON, J. C. (1994). Issues in searching molecular sequence databases. *Nat. Genet.* 6, 119–129. A review of the issues that are of importance in using sequence similarity search programs, including potential pitfalls.

HENIKOFF, S., AND HENIKOFF, J. G. (2000). Amino acid substitution matrices. *Adv. Protein Chem.* 54, 73–97. A comprehensive review covering the factors critical to the construction of protein scoring matrices.

KORF, I., YANDELL, M., AND BEDELL, J. (2003). BLAST (O'Reilly and Associates, Sebastopol, CA). An in-depth treatment of the BLAST algorithm, its applications, as well as installation, hardware, and software considerations. The book provides "documentation" that is not easily found elsewhere.

PEARSON, W. R. (2003). Finding protein and nucleotide similarities with FASTA. *Curr. Protocols Bioinformatics* 3.9.1–3.9.23. An in-depth discussion of the FASTA algorithm, including worked examples and additional information regarding run options and use scenarios.

WHEELER, D. G. (2003). Selecting the right protein scoring matrix. *Curr. Protocols Bioinformatics* 3.5.1–3.5.6. A discussion of PAM, BLOSUM, and specialized scoring matrices, with guidance regarding the proper choice of matrices for particular types of protein-based analyses.

REFERENCES

AGARAWAL, P., AND STATES, D. J. (1998). Comparative accuracy of methods for protein similarity search. *Bioinformatics* 14, 40–47.

ALTSCHUL, S. F. (1991). Amino acid substitution matrices from an information theoretic perspective. *J. Mol. Biol.* 219, 555–565.

ALTSCHUL, S. F., GISH, W., MILLER, W., MYERS, E. W., AND LIPMAN, D. J. (1991). Basic local alignment search tool. *J. Mol. Biol.* 215, 403–410.

ALTSCHUL, S. F., BOGUSKI, M. S., GISH, W., AND WOOTTON, J. C. (1994). Issues in searching molecular sequence databases. *Nat. Genet.* 6, 119–129.

ALTSCHUL, S. F., MADDEN T. L., SCHÄFFER, A. A., ZHANG, J., ZHANG, Z., MILLER, W., LIPMAN, D. J. (1997). Gapped BLAST and PSI-BLAST: a new generation of protein database search programs. *Nucl. Acids Res.* 25, 3389–3402.

ALTSCHUL, S. F., AND KOONIN, E. V. (1998). Iterated profile searches with PSI-BLAST: a tool for discovery in protein databases. *Trends Biochem. Sci.* 23, 444–447.

BRENNER, S. E., CHOTHIA, C., AND HUBBARD, T. J. P. (1998). Assessing sequence comparison methods with reliable structurally identified evolutionary relationships. *Proc. Natl. Acad. Sci. U. S. A.* 95, 6073–6078.

BÜCHER, P., KARPLUS, K., MOERI, N., AND HOFMANN, K. (1996). A flexible motif search technique based on generalized profiles. *Comput. Chem.* 20, 3–23.

DAYHOFF, M. O., SCHWARTZ, R. M., ORCUTT, B. C. (1978). A model of evolutionary change in proteins. In *Atlas of Protein Sequence and Structure*, vol. 5 (Dayhoff, M. O., ed.), (National Biomedical Research Foundation, Washington, DC) 345–352.

CHEN, Z. (2003). Assessing sequence comparison methods with the average precision criterion. *Bioinformatics* 19, 2456–2460.

GONNET, G. H., COHEN, M. A., AND BENNER, S. A. (1992). Exhaustive matching of the entire protein sequence database. *Proteins* 256, 1443–1445.

GRIBSKOV, M., McLACHLAN, A. D., AND EISENBERG, D. (1987). Profile analysis: detection of distantly-related proteins. *Proc. Natl. Acad. Sci. U. S. A.* 84, 4355–4358.

HENIKOFF, S., AND HENIKOFF, J. G. 1991. Automated assembly of protein blocks for database searching. *Nucl. Acids Res.* 19, 6565–6572.

HENIKOFF, S., AND HENIKOFF, J. G. (1992). Amino acid substitution matrices from protein blocks. *Proc. Natl. Acad. Sci. U. S. A.* 89, 10915–10919.

HENIKOFF, S., AND HENIKOFF, J. G. (1993). Performance evaluation of amino acid substitution matrices. *Proteins Struct. Funct. Genet.* 17, 49–61.

HENIKOFF, S., AND HENIKOFF, J. G. (2000). Amino acid substitution matrices. *Adv. Protein Chem.* 54, 73–97.

JONES, D. T., TAYLOR, W. R., AND THORNTON, J. M. (1992). The rapid generation of mutation data matrices from protein sequences. *Comput. Appl. Biosci.* 8, 275–282.

KARLIN, S., AND ALTSCHUL, S. F. (1990). Methods for assessing the statistical significance of molecular sequence features by using general scoring schemes. *Proc. Natl. Acad. Sci. U. S. A.* 87, 2264–2268.

KENT, W. J. (2002). BLAT: the BLAST-like alignment tool. *Genome Res.* 12, 656–664.

LIPMAN, D. J., AND PEARSON, W. R. (1985). Rapid and sensitive protein similarity searches. *Science* 227, 1435–1441.

MA, B., TROMP, J., AND LI, M. (2002). PatternHunter: faster and more sensitive homology search. *Bioinformatics* 18, 440–445.

PEARSON, W. R. (1995). Comparison of methods for searching protein sequence databases. *Protein Sci.* 4, 1145–1160.

PEARSON, W. R. (2000). Flexible sequence similarity searching with the FASTA3 program package. *Methods Mol. Biol.* 132, 185–219.

PEARSON, W. R. (2003). Finding protein and nucleotide similarities with FASTA. *Curr. Protocols Bioinformatics* 3.9.1–3.9.23.

PEARSON, W. R., AND LIPMAN, D. J. (1988). Improved tools for biological sequence comparison. *Proc. Natl. Acad. Sci. U. S. A.* 85, 2444–2448.

SCHÄFFER, A. A., WOLF, Y. I., PONTING, C. P., KOONIN, E. V., ARAVIND, L., AND ALTSCHUL, S. F. (1999). IMPALA: matching a protein sequence against a collection of PSI-BLAST-constructed position-specific scoring matrices. *Bioinformatics* 15, 1000–1011.

SCHNEIDER, T. D., STORMO, G. D., GOLD, L., AND EHRENFEUCHT, A. (1986). Information content of binding sites on nucleotide sequences. *J. Mol. Biol.* 188, 415–431.

SMITH, T. F., AND WATERMAN, M. S. (1981). Identification of common molecular subsequences. *J. Mol. Biol.* 147, 195–197.

STADEN, R. (1988). Methods to define and locate patterns of motifs in sequences. *Comput. Appl. Biosci.* 4, 53–60.

TATUSOV, R. L., ALTSCHUL, S. F., AND KOONIN, E. V. (1994). Detection of conserved segments in proteins: iterative scanning of sequence databases with alignment blocks. *Proc. Natl. Acad. Sci. U. S. A.* 91, 12091–12095.

TATUSOVA, T. A., AND MADDEN, T. L. (1999). BLAST2Sequences, a new tool for comparing protein and nucleotide sequences. *FEMS Microbiol. Lett.* 174, 247–250.

WHEELER, D. G. (2003). Selecting the right protein scoring matrix. *Curr. Protocols Bioinformatics* 3.5.1–3.5.6.

WOOTTON, J. C., AND FEDERHEN, S. (1993). Statistics of local complexity in amino acid sequences and sequence databases. *Comput. Chem.* 17, 149–163.

▌KEY TERMS

alignment

conservative substitution

dotplot

EST

expressed sequence tag

filtering

gap

homology

identity

low-complexity region

masking

motif

orthology

paralogy

similarity

This chapter was written by Dr. Andreas D. Baxevanis in his private capacity. No official support or endorsement by the National Institutes of Health or the United States Department of Health and Human Services is intended or should be inferred.

## CHAPTER TWELVE

Creation and Analysis of Protein Multiple Sequence Alignments

GEOFFREY J. BARTON

Bioinformatics: A Practical Guide to the Analysis of Genes and Proteins, Third Edition, edited by
Andreas D. Baxevanis and B.F. Francis Ouellette.
ISBN 0-471-47878-4 Copyright © 2005 John Wiley & Sons, Inc.

INTRODUCTION

Genome sequencing projects continue to provide knowledge of a vast number of new protein sequences drawn from dozens of organisms. At the highest level, comparison of genomes to quantify the presence or absence of suspected orthologous genes can suggest differences in biochemical pathways and can give clues about which proteins may interact (e.g., Von Mering et al., 2003). However, any more-detailed investigation of protein function requires comparison at the level of individual amino acids or, ideally, their three–dimensional structures.

Multiple protein sequence alignment is a central tool to aid in inferring function from sequence comparison. Multiple alignments also are the key starting point for the prediction of protein secondary structure, residue accessibility, and the identification of residues important for specificity. Multiple alignments provide the basis for the most sensitive sequence searching algorithms (e.g., see Altschul et al., 1997; Barton & Sternberg, 1990; and Gribskov et al., 1987) and effective analysis of a well-constructed multiple alignment can provide important clues about which residues in the protein are important for stabilizing the secondary and tertiary structure of the protein. In addition, it is often possible to make predictions about which residues confer specificity of function to subsets of the sequences.

Apart from the uses of multiple alignments in inferring structural and functional properties of protein molecules, alignments provide a convenient representation on which to annotate experimental or theoretical features of the protein for publication or presentation.

This chapter provides some guidelines for the generation and analysis of protein multiple sequence alignments. This is not a comprehensive review of techniques; rather, it is a guide based on software that has proven most useful in building alignments and in predicting protein structure and function. A full summary of the software is available at the end of the chapter.

WHAT IS A MULTIPLE ALIGNMENT?

Although proteins are complex macromolecules, they can be represented by a string a of letters coding for the 20 different types of amino acid residue that make up their sequence. A protein sequence alignment is created when the residues in one sequence are lined up with those in at least one other protein sequence. The alignment of the two sequences that optimizes the alignment of amino acids with similar physicochemical properties usually will require the insertion of "gaps" in one or both

sequences. The alignment of two residues implies that those residues are performing similar roles in the two different proteins. This allows for information known about specific residues in one sequence to be potentially tranferred to the residues aligned in the other. For example, if the active site residues of an enzyme have been characterized experimentally, alignment of these residues with similar residues in another protein sequence may suggest that the second protein possesses similar catalytic activity. The validity of such hypotheses depends on the overall similarity of the sequences, which in turn dictates the confidence with which an alignment can be generated. There are typically many millions of different possible alignments for two sequences. The challenge is to find an alignment that best represents the chemical and biological similarities between the two proteins.

A *multiple* sequence alignment is simply an alignment that contains more than two sequences. Even if one is interested in the similarities between only two of the sequences in a set, it is always worth multiply aligning all available sequences. The multiple alignment normally improves the accuracy of alignment between the sequence pairs, as illustrated in Figure 12.1, as well as revealing patterns of conserved residues that are not obvious when only two sequences are studied. Although many computer programs exist that can generate a multiple alignment from unaligned sequences, care must be taken when interpreting their output. An alignment may show perfect matching of a known active-site residue with an identical residue in a well-characterized protein family, but if the alignment is incorrect, then any inference about function also is incorrect.

STRUCTURAL OR EVOLUTIONARY ALIGNMENT?

It is the precise arrangement of the amino acid side chains in the three-dimensional structure of the protein that dictate its function. Comparison of two or more three-dimensional structures highlight which residues are in similar positions in space and, hence, are likely to be performing similar functional roles. Such comparisons can be used to generate a sequence alignment from structure (e.g., Russell & Barton, 1992). The resulting *structural alignment* of two or more protein sequences is the gold standard against which sequence alignment algorithms normally are judged. This is because the extra information available from three-dimensional structures allows for a more reliable alignment of residues that are functionally important.

Unfortunately, structural alignments are possible only when the three-dimensional structures of all the proteins

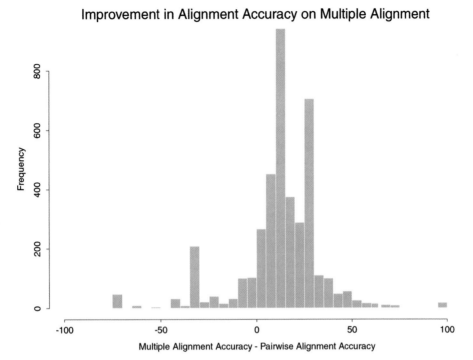

FIGURE 12.1 **Histogram showing the difference in accuracy between the same pairs of sequences aligned as a pair and also as part of a larger multiple sequence alignment. On average, multiple alignments improve the accuracy of alignment which, in this example, is judged as the alignment obtained by comparison of the protein three-dimensional structures rather than just their sequences (Russell & Barton, 1992).**

to be aligned are known. The challenge for sequence alignment methods is to be as close as possible to the structural alignment while having no structural information to work with.

Although the structural alignment is the most important (and useful) type of alignment for the prediction of function, it does not necessarily correspond to the evolutionary alignment implied by divergence from a common ancestor protein. Unfortunately, it rarely, if ever, is possible to determine the evolutionary alignment of two divergent proteins with confidence, because this would require knowledge of the precise history of substitutions, insertions, and deletions that led to present-day proteins from their common ancestor.

HOW TO MULTIPLY ALIGN SEQUENCES

Automatic alignment programs such as ClustalW (Thompson et al., 1994) give good quality alignments for sequences that are significantly similar, as measured by standard criteria (Barton & Sternberg, 1987b; Raghava et al., 2003). However, building good multiple

alignments for sequences that are not substantially similar is an expert task even with the best available alignment tools. This section presents an overview of some of the steps to go through to make alignments that will be useful for structure and function prediction. This is not a universal recipe. Each set of sequences presents its own problems, and only experience can guide the creation of high-quality alignments. Some collections of expertly-created multiple alignments exist (see below), and these should always be consulted when studying sequences that are contained therein.

The key steps in building a multiple alignment include:

▶ Finding the sequences to align by database searching or other means.

▶ Locating the region(s) of each sequence to include in the alignment. Do not try to multiply-align sequences that are very different in length. Most multiple alignment programs are designed to align sequences that are similar over their entire length, so first edit the sequences down to those regions that the sequence database search suggests are similar. Some database search tools automatically do this (e.g., PSI-BLAST; see below).

- Ideally, assessing similarities within the the set of sequences by comparing them pairwise, with randomizations. Select a subset of the sequences to align first that cluster above 6σ (defined below). Automatic alignment of such sequences will likely be accurate (Barton & Sternberg 1987b; Ragahava et al., 2003). An alternative to randomization is to align only sequences that are similar to the query in a database search at some E-value cutoff.

- Running the multiple alignment program.

- Inspecting the alignment for problems. Take particular care over regions that seem to be speckled with gaps. Use an alignment visualization tool (e.g., ALSCRIPT/JalView; see below) to identify positions in the alignment that conserve physicochemical properties across the complete alignment. If there are no such regions, then look at subsets of the sequences.

- Removing sequences that seem to seriously disrupt the alignment and then realigning the subset that is left.

- After identifying key residues in the set of sequences that can be aligned in a straightforward manner, attempting to add the remaining sequences to the alignment so as to preserve the key features of the family.

Assessing the Quality of an Alignment

Multiple alignment programs can align any set of sequences. However, the fact that the program produces an alignment does not mean that the alignment makes any biological sense. Most programs take unrelated protein sequences and align them just as easily as two genuinely related sequences. Even for related sequences, there is no guarantee that the resulting alignment is in any way meaningful. One way of assessing whether an alignment is meaningful is to perform a randomization or Monte Carlo test of significance. To do this, the two sequences first are aligned, and the score (S) for the alignment is recorded. The sequences then are shuffled so that they maintain their length and amino acid composition, but have a randomized order. The shuffled sequences then are compared again, and the score is recorded. The shuffling and realigning process is repeated a number of times (typically 100) and the mean ($\bar{x}$) and standard deviation (σ) for the scores is calculated. The Z-score given by $(S - \bar{x})/\sigma$ provides an indication of the significance of the alignment. If $Z > 6$, then it is highly likely that the two sequences are alignable, and the alignment correctly relates the key functional and structural residues in the proteins (Barton & Sternberg,

1987b). Unfortunately, this is only a rough guide because, although an alignment that gives a $Z < 6$ may be poor, some alignments with low Z-scores are actually correct. This is simply a reflection of the fact that, during the course of evolution, sequence similarity diverges faster than structural or functional similarity. Z-scores are preferable to simple percent identities as a measure of similarity because Z-scores correct for both compositional bias in the sequences and their length. Z-scores also may be converted into probabilities to provide an estimate of the statistical significance of a sequence alignment. Conventional statistical tables overestimate the significance of Z-scores obtained from sequence alignment methods, so alternative tables must be used (e.g., Webber & Barton, 2001).

The Z-score gives an indication of the overall similarity between two sequences. However, it does not help to locate parts of the sequence alignment that are incorrect. As a general rule, if the alignment is between two or more sequences that do indeed share a similar three-dimensional structure, then most of the errors will be concentrated around regions where there are gaps (insertions or deletions.)

Hierarchical Methods

Some of the most accurate practical methods for automatic multiple alignment are hierarchical methods. These work first by finding a guide tree, then following the guide tree to build the alignment. The process is summarized in Figure 12.2. First, all pairs of sequences in the set to be aligned are compared by a pairwise method of sequence comparison. This provides a set of pairwise similarity scores for the sequences that can be fed into a *cluster analaysis*, or tree calculating program. The tree is calculated in a way that places more-similar pairs of sequences closer together on the tree than sequences that are less similar. The multiple alignment then is built by starting with the pair of sequences that is most simlar and aligning them, then aligning the next most similar pair, and so on. Pairs to be aligned need not be single sequences, but can be alignments that have been generated earlier in the tree. If an alignment is compared with a sequence or another alignment, then gaps that exist in the alignment are preserved.

There are many different variations of this basic multiple alignment technique. Because errors in alignment that occur early in the process can become locked in, some methods allow for realignment of the sequences after the initial alignment (e.g., Barton & Sternberg, 1987b; Gotoh, 1996; Katoh et al., 2002 Edgar, 2004). Other refinements include using different similarity scoring matrices at different stages in building up the alignment (e.g., Thompson et al., 1994).

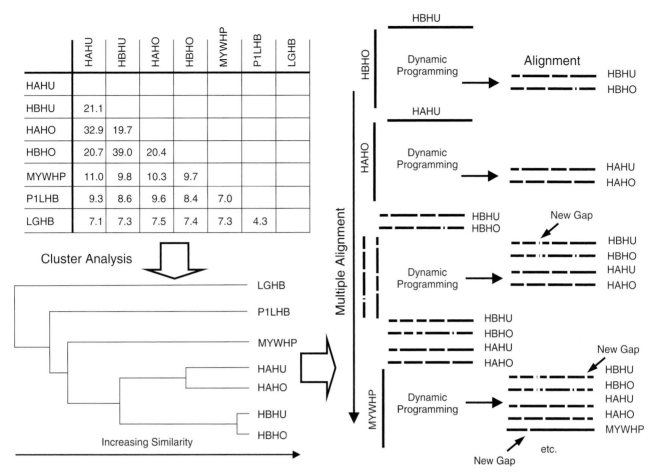

	HAHU	HBHU	HAHO	HBHO	MYWHP	P1LHB	LGHB
HAHU							
HBHU	21.1						
HAHO	32.9	19.7					
HBHO	20.7	39.0	20.4				
MYWHP	11.0	9.8	10.3	9.7			
P1LHB	9.3	8.6	9.6	8.4	7.0		
LGHB	7.1	7.3	7.5	7.4	7.3	4.3	

FIGURE 12.2 **Illustration of the stages in hierarchical multiple alignment of seven sequences with the identifying codes HAHU, HBHU, HAHO, HBHO, MYWHP, P1LHB, and LGHB. The table at the top left of the figure shows the pairwise Z-scores for comparison of each sequence pair. Higher numbers mean greater similarity (see text). Hierarchical cluster analysis of the Z-score table generates the dendrogram or tree shown at the bottom left of the figure. Items joined toward the right of the tree are more similar than those linked at the left. Thus, LGHB is the sequence that is least similar to the other sequences in the set, whereas HBHU and HBHO are the most similar pair. The first four steps in building the multiple alignment are shown on the right of the figure. The first two steps are pairwise alignments. The third step is a comparison of profiles from the two alignments generated in steps 1 and 2. The fourth step adds a single sequence (MYWHP) to the alignment generated at step 3. Further sequences are added in a similar manner.**

Gaps (insertions or deletions) do not occur randomly in protein sequences. The constraints of maintaining a stable, folded protein mean that proteins that have an insertion or deletion in the middle of a secondary structure (α-helix or β-strand) usually are selected against during the course of evolution. As a consequence, present-day proteins show a strong bias toward localizing insertions and deletions to loop regions that link the core secondary structures. This observation can be used to improve the accuracy of multiple sequence alignments when the secondary structure is known for one or more of the proteins by making the penalty for inserting a gap higher in secondary structure regions compared with

loops (Barton & Sternberg, 1987a; Lesk et al., 1986). A further refinement is to bias where gaps are most likely to be inserted in the alignment by examining the growing alignment for regions that are most likely to accommodate gaps (Pascarella & Argos, 1992).

Hierarchical Alignment Software ClustalW is a hierarchical multiple alignment program that combines a robust method for multiple sequence alignment with an easy-to-use interface. ClustalW runs on most computers and incorporates many of the techniques described in the previous section. The program uses a series of different pair-score matrices, biases the location of gaps, and allows one to realign a set of aligned sequences to further refine the alignment. ClustalW can read a secondary structure "mask" which can be used to bias the position of any inserted gaps; the program also can read two preexisting alignments and can align them to each other, or can align a set of sequences to an existing alignment. ClustalW also includes options to calculate neighbor joining trees to use in inferring phylogeny. Although ClustalW does not provide general tools for viewing these trees, the output is compatible with the PHYLIP package (Felsenstein, 1989), which does. ClustalW can read a variety of different common sequence formats and can produce a range of different output formats. The manual for ClustalW is written clearly and explains possible limitations of the alignment process.

A problem with all hierarchical alignment methods, including ClustalW, is the time taken to complete the first, all-against-all set of comparisons that are necessary to calculate the guide tree, as shown in Figure 12.2. For N sequences, $N(N-1)/2$ pairwise comparisons must be performed to work out the guide tree. For example, for 100 sequences, this is 4950 $(100 \times 99/2)$ pairwise comparisons. Clearly, for very large alignments or long sequences, the total number of comparisons required may take an unacceptable time to calculate, even on a fast computer. A number of groups have developed methods that aim to speed up alignment by modifying the way in which the guide tree is calculated. For example, the MAFFT package (Katoh et al., 2002) uses a fast Fourier transform method on amino acid properties to identify regions of similarity between the sequences. These regions then are used to guide dynamic programming alignment of the sequences. MUSCLE (Edgar, 2004) achieves speed by using a fast hashing comparison based on identical matches. The implementation of both MAFFT and MUSCLE makes them straightforward to use, and both claim high accuracy for alignments in standard benchmarks.

Although ClustalW is probably the most widely used multiple alignment program, other software exists that includes functions not present in ClustalW. For example, AMPS (Barton, 1990) provides a pairwise sequence comparison option with randomization, allowing Z-scores to be calculated. The program also can generate alignments without the need to first calculate trees. For large numbers of sequences, this can save a lot of time because it eliminates the need to perform all pairwise comparisons of the sequences. AMPS also has software to visualize trees, which helps in the selection of sequences for alignment. However, the program has no simple menu interface, so it is more difficult for the novice or occasional user to use.

When any of the above methods are combined with JalView (Clamp, 2004), as described below, the process of building and refining a multiple alignment is greatly simplified.

More Rigorous Nonhierarchical Methods

Hierarchical methods do not guarantee to find the mathematically-optimal multiple alignment for a set of sequences. However, in practice, the mathematical optimum rarely makes any more biological sense than the alignment that is found by hierarchical methods. This is probably because a great deal of effort has gone into tuning the parameters used by hierarchical methods to produce alignments that are consistent with those that a human expert or three-dimensional structure comparison may produce. The widespread use of these techniques also has ensured that the parameters are appropriate for a wide range of alignment problems. More rigorous alignment methods that attempt to find the mathematically optimal alignment over a set of sequences (e.g., Lipman et al., 1989) may well be capable of giving better alignments, but in recent benchmarks, they perform worse than the hierarchical methods (Raghava et al., 2003).

T-Coffee

T-Coffee (Notredame et al., 2000) attempts to overcome some of the problems that standard hierarchical methods have in aligning sequences of very different length or that share only local regions of similarity. The program works by building a library of pairwise alignments for the sequences of interest. It then uses this library to inform a hierarchical method to find a multiple alignment that aims to preserve consistency between the pairwise alignments. The algorithm outperforms most other methods in current benchmarks but is rather too time consuming to use for large sequence alignments. Thus, it is worth trying T-Coffee on smaller sequence sets, but it may fail on large alignments.

Since T-Coffee can work from pairwise alignments that originate from any source, it recently has been adapted to include structural alignments and alignments from threading algorithms. This offers the promise of providing better-quality alignments that incorporate structural information when available (Notredame, personal communication, 2004).

Multiple Alignment by PSI-BLAST and *i*SCANPS

Multiple sequence alignments long have been used to accomplish more sensitive searches of protein sequence databases than are possible using only a single sequence as the query. The program PSI-BLAST (Altschul et al., 1997) has made these profile-based methods more easily available (see also Chapter 11). PSI-BLAST searches a database with a single sequence, any high-scoring sequences that are found are built into a multiple alignment, and this multiple alignment is then used to derive a search "profile" for a subsequent search of the database. This process is repeated until no new sequences are added to the profile, or a specified number of iterations have been performed. Iterated SCANPS (*i*SCANPS) works using a similar principle as PSI-BLAST, full dynamic programming made possible by the Smith-Waterman algorithm (Smith & Waterman, 1981) and statistics that taking advantage of account for the differences in each individual database search. The authors claim *i*SCANPS gives improved sensitivity in database searches, with fewer errors than PSI-BLAST in a standard benchmark.

Although both PSI-BLAST and *i*SCANPS produce multiple alignments, the alignments are rather different in style from those made by ClustalW, AMPS, or other traditional multiple alignment tools. In a conventional multiple alignment, all sequences in the set have equal importance. As a consequence, a multiple alignment normally will be longer than any one of the individual sequences, because gaps are inserted to optimize the alignment. In contrast, a PSI-BLAST multiple alignment is always is the length of the query sequence used in the search. If alignment of the query (or query profile) to a database sequence requires an insertion in the query, then the inserted region from the database sequence simply is discarded. The resulting alignment thus highlights the amino acids that may be aligned to each position in the query. Often, this can be the most informative type of alignment when one is focused on understanding a single sequence set. Perhaps for this reason, PSI-BLAST multiple alignments and their associated frequency tables and profiles have proved very effective as input for programs that predict protein secondary structure (Jones, 1999).

HOW TO GENERATE MULTIPLE STRUCTURAL ALIGNMENTS

Technological developments in X-ray and nuclear magnetic resonance (NMR) methods have stimulated a rapid growth in the number of proteins for which all or part of the three-dimensional structure is known. As a consequence, it is now more common for structural data of proteins of interest to be available to the molecular biologist for analysis. Accordingly, it often is necessary to align and interpret the comparison of protein structures in the context of functional studies.

Multiple structure alignments are one way to carry out structural comparisons. This section outlines the broad classes of technique used to compare protein three-dimensional structures and then describes the steps used by one method, STAMP (Russell & Barton, 1992), to generate multiple structure alignments for three or more proteins.

Structural Alignment Methods: STAMP

A common way to compare two protein structures is to superimpose them on each other. In this way, equivalent residues in the three-dimensional structures are placed on top of each other, and similarities and differences may be viewed by inspection using molecular graphics software (see Chapter 9). The problem with superposition is that one needs to know which residues are equivalent in the first place. The normal task of structural alignment programs is to find which residues should be superimposed, yielding both a structural sequence alignment and a three-dimensional superposition of the structures.

A large number of techniques have been developed for structure comparison. Methods often exploit abstract representations of the protein structure that have included intramolecular distance matrices (e.g., Holm & Sander, 1993), graph comparison of vectors through secondary structures (e.g., Grindley et al., 1993), and simultaneous comparison of multiple structural properties (e.g., Taylor & Orengo, 1989; Sali & Blundell, 1990).

STAMP (Russell & Barton, 1992) is one of only a few methods that can align more than two structures simultaneously. STAMP multiple alignments are produced in stages similar to that for protein sequence alignment, using a hierarchical method as described above and illustrated in Figure 12.2. The manual for STAMP includes detailed examples of how to use the program and describes its interfaces to ALSCRIPT and other software for publication-quality output. The basic steps in its use are:

► For two protein structures, an initial alignment of their sequences is produced by some method.

► The structures are superimposed, assuming this alignment is correct.

► A matrix of scores is calculated for the structural similarity of the protein chain between all possible pairs of residues in the two molecules. These scores are key to the algorithm, because they combine both a distance score and a score that takes account of the similarity in local conformation of the chains.

► In a similar manner to protein sequence comparison, a dynamic programming algorithm is applied to the score matrix to find the best score and an alignment of the sequences.

► Given the new alignment, the above process is repeated successively until convergence.

For multiple structure alignments, all pairs of structures are compared and a tree is calculated; then, the tree is followed as for a hierarchical multiple sequence alignment. An important feature of the output of STAMP is the estimate of reliability in the structural alignment that is reported for every aligned position. This allows one to highlight regions of the protein structures that are very different and, therefore, unalignable.

There are many alternative ways of running STAMP. The most important of these affect how the initial alignment is found. The most general way to do this is to scan one structure against another, trying successive alternative starting alignments for the iteration. This method works well for locating domains within a larger structure or for finding alternative valid substructure alignments. The STAMP distribution includes programs to produce input for ALSCRIPT (Barton, 1993) and molscript (Kraulis, 1991) to allow publication-quality output. The distribution also includes extensive example files and documentation.

Which Is the Best Method for Multiple Sequence Alignment?

The straight answer to this question is that there is no best method for multiple sequence alignment. All techniques have their strengths and weaknesses, and the way they are implemented in software for ease of use or otherwise can be the biggest factor that decides which method is eventually selected. In practice, as with most tools in bioinformatics, it is best to run a range of different methods on a sequence set and to compare the results. Regions of alignment that vary dramatically between methods may indicate regions that are aligned less reliably by any of the methods.

Developers of alignment methods also develop benchmarks against which they can test methods to evaluate whether new ideas they try perform better (e.g., (Thompson et al., 1999; Raghava et al., 2003). The most commonly used benchmarks contain a collection of pairwise and multiple alignments that have been derived in some reliable way. Typically, these reference alignments come from comparison of protein three-dimensional structures, followed by human inspection. Given a set of reference alignments, the same sequences are aligned by the method being tested, and then a variety of different scoring schemes are applied to see how well the two alignments agree with each other. For example, every aligned position can be required to be identical in the two alignments, or subregions of the alignments can be compared independently. In this way, the accuracy of alignment for a method can be evaluated and compared.

One weakness of such benchmarks is the reference alignment. If this is incorrect, then alignment methods will be penalized unfairly. An alternative approach to scoring alignment accuracy is to see how similar the two three-dimensional structures of the proteins are after being superimposed using the equivalences from the alignment under test. This type of independent measure alignment provides excellent descrimination between "good" and "bad" alignments, without the need to use a reference alignment (Raghava et al., 2003).

TOOLS TO ASSIST IN THE ANALYSIS OF MULTIPLE ALIGNMENTS

A multiple sequence alignment potentially can consist of several hundred sequences that are 500 or more amino acids long. With such a volume of data, it can be difficult to find key features and to present the alignment in a form that can be analyzed by eye. In the past, the only option was to print out the alignment on many sheets of paper, stick these together, and then study the massive poster with colored highlighter pens. This sort of approach can still be useful, but it is rather inconvenient!

Visualization of the alignment is an important scientific tool, either for analysis or for publication. Appropriate use of color can highlight positions that are either identical in all the aligned sequences or that share common physicochemical properties. Alscript (Barton, 1993) is a program that can assist in this process. Alscript takes a multiple sequence alignment and a file of commands and produces a file (in PostScript format) suitable for printing out or viewing with a utility such as ghostview.

Figure 12.3 illustrates a fragment of Alscript output. In this example, identities across all sequences are shown in white on red and boxed, whereas positions with similar physicochemical properties are shown black on yellow and boxed. Residue numbering according to the bottom sequence is shown underneath the alignment. Green arrows illustrate the location of known β-strands, whereas α-helices are shown as black cylinders. Further symbols highlight specific positions in the alignment for easy cross-referencing to the text. Alscript is extremely flexible and has commands that permit control of font size and type, background coloring, and boxing down to the individual residue. The program automatically splits a large alignment over multiple pages and so permits alignments of any size to be visualized. However, all this flexibility comes at a price. There is no point-and-click interface, and the program requires the user to be familiar with editing files and running programs from the Unix command line. The Alscript distribution includes a

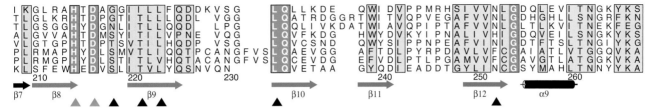

FIGURE 12.3   Example output from the program Alscript (Barton, 1993). See text for details.

comprehensive manual and example files that make the process of making a useful figure a little easier.

Subalignments: AMAS

Alscript provides a few commands for calculating residue conservation across a family of sequences and coloring the alignment accordingly. However, it is really intended as a display tool for multiple alignments, rather than an analysis tool. In contrast, AMAS (Analysis of Multiply Aligned Sequences; Livingstone & Barton, 1993) is a program used for studying the relationships between sequences in a multiple alignment so as to identify possible functional residues. AMAS automatically runs Alscript to provide one output that is a boxed, colored, and annotated multiple alignment.

Why might one want to run AMAS? A common question is, "Which residues in a protein are important for its specificity?" AMAS can help to identify these residues by highlighting similarities and differences between subgroups of sequences in a multiple alignment. For example, given a family of sequences that shows some variation, positions in a multiple alignment that are conserved across the entire family of sequences are likely to be important to stabilize the common fold of the protein, or to preserve common functions. Positions that are conserved within a subset of the sequences but are different in the rest of the family are likely to be important to the specific function or specificity of that subset. AMAS helps identify these positions.

There are a number of subtle types of differences that AMAS searches for, and these are summarized in Figure 12.4. To use AMAS, one first must have an idea of what subgroups of sequences exist in the multiple alignment. One way to do this is to take a tree generated from the multiple alignment and to identify clusters of sequences at some similarity threshold. This is illustrated in Figure 12.4, where three groups have been selected on the basis of the tree at the top left of the figure. Alternatively, if one knows in advance that they are interested in finding common features and differences between, say, sequences 1 through 20 and 21 through 50 in a multiple alignment, these ranges can be specified explicitly.

The output of AMAS is a detailed text summary of the analysis, as well as a colored and shaded multiple sequence alignment. By default, AMAS searches for general features of amino acid physicochemical properties. However, this can be narrowed down just to charge, or any other chosen feature of amino acids. An example of a charge analysis is shown in Figure 12.5 for repeats within the annexin supergene family of proteins (Barton et al., 1991). The analysis highlights a charge swap within two subgroups of the sequences that correctly predicts the presence of a saltbridge in the native folded protein (Huber et al., 1990).

Secondary Structure Prediction and the Prediction of Buried Residues from Multiple Sequence Alignments

When aligning sequences, it is important to think about the protein as a three-dimensional molecule, rather than simply a string of letters. Predicting secondary structure either for the entire collection of sequences or subsets can be used to help in how the protein may fold locally and may guide the alignment of more distantly related sequences. For example, it is common for proteins with similar topologies to have quite different sequences and to be unalignable by an automatic sequence alignment method (e.g., Russell & Barton, 1994; and the SCOP database, Murzin et al., 1995). In these circumstances, the secondary structure may suggest which blocks of sequence should be equivalent.

The prediction of secondary structure (α-helix and β-strand) is enhanced by approximately 6% when performed from a multiple alignment, compared with predictions made using a single sequence (Cuff & Barton, 1999). Two of the best currently-available methods, PSIPRED (Jones, 1999) and JNET (Cuff & Barton, unpublished observations, 2000), give more than 76% accuracy for the prediction of three states (α-helix, β-strand and coil) in rigorous testing. This high accuracy is possible because the prediction algorithms are able to locate regions in the sequences that show patterns of conserved physicochemical properties across the aligned family. These patterns are characteristic of particular secondary

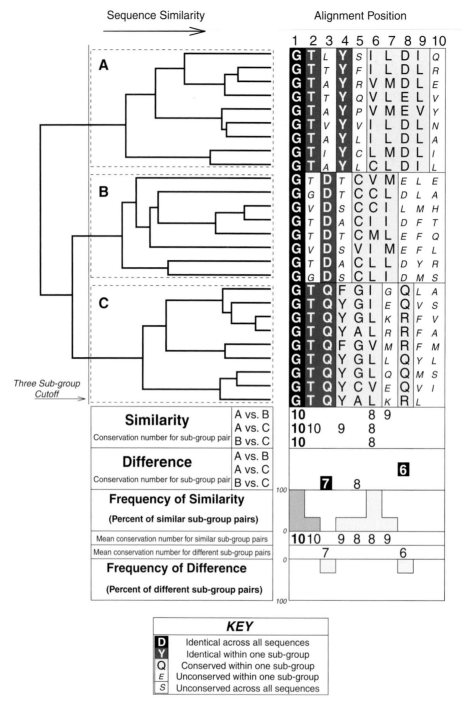

FIGURE 12.4 Stylized output from the program **AMAS** (Livingstone & Barton, 1993). The sequence alignment has been shaded to illustrate similarities within each subgroup of sequences. Conservation numbers (Livingstone & Barton, 1993; Zvelebil et al., 1987) run from 0 to 10 and provide a numerical measure of the similarity in physicochemical properties of each column in the alignment. Below the alignment, the lines "Similar Pairs" show the conservation values obtained when each pair of subgroups is combined and the combined conservation number is not less than a threshold. For example, at position 7, subgroups *A* and *B* combine with a conservation number of 9. The lines "Different Pairs" illustrate positions at which combination of subgroups lowers the conservation number below the threshold. For example, at position 3, there is an identity in subgroup *B* and one in *C*, but when the groups are combined, the identity is lost and the conservation drops below the threshold of 8 to 7. A summary of the similarities and differences is given as a frequency histogram. Each upward bar represents the proportion of subgroup pairs that preserve conservation, whereas each downward bar shows the percentage of differences. For example, at position 6, three of three pairs are conserved (100%), whereas at positions 3 and 8, one of three pairs show differences (33%). With a large alignment, the histogram quickly can draw the eye to regions that are highly conserved or where there are differences in conserved physicochemical properties.

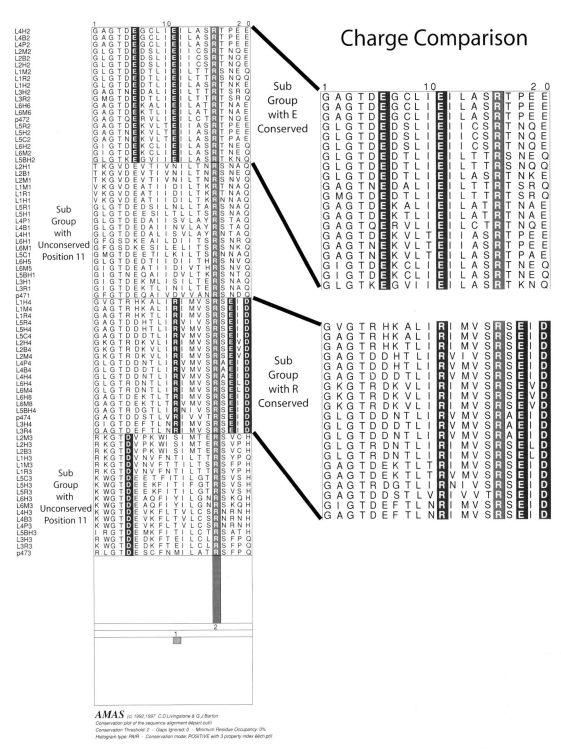

FIGURE 12.5 **Illustration of AMAS output used to find a charge pair in the annexins. There are four groups of sequences in the alignment. The highlighted positions highlight locations where the charge is conserved in each group of sequences, yet different between groups. A change from Glu to Arg is shown at position 11 of the alignment.**

structure types and often can be seen by eye in a multiple sequence alignment, as summarized below:

▶ Short runs of conserved hydrophobic residues suggest a buried β-strand.

▶ An $i, i + 2, i + 4$ pattern of conserved hydrophobic amino acids suggests a surface β-strand, because the alternate residues in a strand point in the same direction. If the alternate residues all conserve similar physicochemical properties, then they are likely to form one face of a β-strand.

▶ $i, i + 3, i + 4, i + 7$ and variations (for example, $i, i + 4, i + 7$) of conserved residues suggest an α-helix, with one surface facing the solvent.

▶ Insertions and deletions normally are tolerated only in regions not associated with the buried core of the protein. Thus, in a good multiple alignment, the location of indels suggests surface loops rather than an α-helix or β-strand.

▶ Conserved glycines and prolines. Although glycines and prolines may be found in all secondary structure types, a glycine or proline that is conserved across a family of sequences is a strong indicator of a loop.

Secondary structure prediction programs such as JNET (Cuff & Barton, unpublished observations, 2000), and PHD (Rost & Sander, 1993) also exploit multiply-aligned sequences to predict the likely exposure to solvent of each residue. Knowledge of a protein's solvent accessibility can help in the identification of residues key to stabilizing the fold of the protein, as well as those that may be involved in binding.

JalView

AMAS and Alscript are not interactive; they run a script or set of commands and produce a PostScript file that can either be viewed on-screen or printed out. Although this provides the maximum number of options and flexibility in display, it is comparatively slow and difficult to learn. In addition, the programs require that a separate program be run to generate the multiple alignment for analysis. If the alignment requires modification, or subsets of the alignment are needed, a difficult cycle of editing and realigning often is required.

JalView (Clamp et al., 2004) overcomes most of these problems. JalView encapsulates many of the most useful features of AMAS and ALSCRIPT in an interactive, mouse-driven program that runs on most computers with a Java interpreter. The core of JalView is an interactive alignment editor. This allows an existing alignment to be read into the program and individual residues or blocks of residues to be moved around. A few mouse clicks permit the the sequences to be "subsetted" into a separate

copy of JalView. JalView can call ClustalW (Thompson et al., 1994), either as a local copy on the same computer that is running JalView or on a remote server. Thus, one also can read in a set of unaligned sequences, align them with ClustalW, edit the alignment, and take subsets with great ease.

Other functions within JalView will calculate a simple or neighbor-joining tree from a multiple alignment or will allow an AMAS-style analysis to be performed on the subgroups of sequences. If the tertiary structure of one of the proteins in the set is available, then the three-dimensional structure may be viewed alongside the alignment in JalView.

Figure 12.6 illustrates a typical JalView session with the alignment editing and tree windows open.

▌ SUMMARY

This chapter has focused on methods for building multiple protein sequence alignments. Although proteins that are clearly similar by the Z-score measure should be straightforward to align by the automatic methods discussed here, for proteins with more remote similarities, obtaining good alignments can be a very time-consuming process. A number of groups have built collections of alignments using a combination of automation and expert curation (e.g., SMART (Schultz et al., 1998), Pfam (Bateman et al., 1999), and PRINTS (Attwood et al., 2000)), and these, together with the tools available at their Web sites, can provide an excellent starting point for further analysis.

▌ WORKED EXAMPLE

The following examples are based on an analysis of the annexin super gene family, as used in the chapter. This family contains a 100-amino acid residue unit that is repeated either four, eight, or 16 times in each protein. The analysis here focuses on the individual repeats, rather than their organization in the protein sequence.

The examples assume that ClustalW and Jalview are correctly installed or that Internet access is available.

File (ann_rep1.fa) contains the sequence of a single annexin domain (the query). This has been used to scan the SWALL protein sequence database with the program SCANPS, and the file ann_rep1_frags.fa contains a subset of the sequence of the segments found to match the query. First, generate a multiple sequence alignment with ClustalW for these sequences, then prune the alignment by editing in JalView.

1. Copy the file ann_rep1_frags.fa to a new directory.
2. Run ClustalW on the file ann_rep1_frags.fa. Accept all defaults, creating an output file called ann_rep1_frags.aln.
3. Read this file into JalView by typing `Jalview ann_rep1_frags.aln CLUSTAL`.

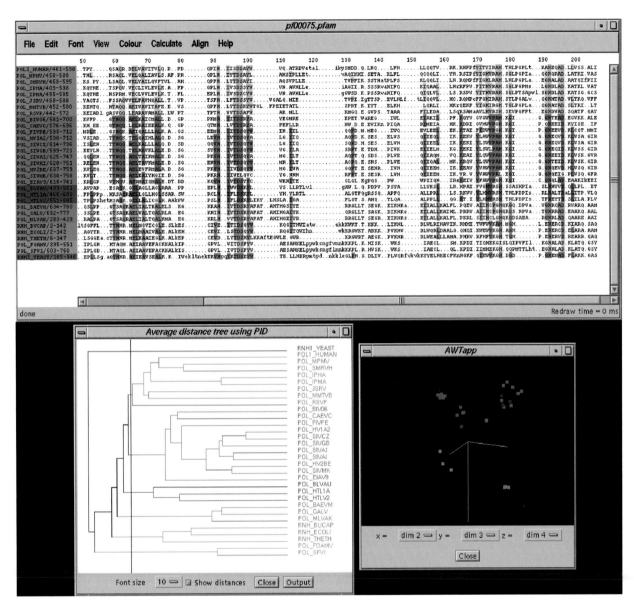

FIGURE 12.6 **A sample JalView alignment editing and analysis session. The top pane contains a multiple alignment, and the bottom left is the similarity tree resulting from that alignment. A vertical line on the tree has separated the sequences into subgroups that have been colored to highlight conservation within each subgroup. The pane at the bottom right illustrates an alternative clustering method.**

4. Select the fragment sequences by clicking on the ID code; then, from the edit menu select "Delete Selected Sequences."

5. Save the modified alignment to a Clustal-format file called ann_rep1_frags_del1.aln.

6. Select "Average Distance Tree" from the Calculate menu. A new window should appear after a few moments with a tree or dendrogram on it. There are three outliers at the top of the tree that will be eliminated.

7. Click on the tree to the left of where the outliers join the tree. A vertical line should appear, and the outliers will be highlighted in a different color to the rest of the tree.

8. Return to the alignment window and delete the outliers from the alignment as in step 4. Save the resulting alignment to the file ann_rep1_frags_del2.aln, as in step 5.

You now have a clean alignment to inspect. Try coloring in different ways to highlight the hydrophobic positions. If you select "Conservation" from the calculate menu, the columns of the alignment will be shaded by how similar the physicochemical properties of the amino acids are in each column. This can be used to spot patterns characteristic of regular secondary structures. For example, look around positions 60 through 70. You should see the pattern of two conserved, two unconserved, two conserved that is typical of an α-helix.

Under the Align menu, try running Jnet. If this works, it will return a secondary structure prediction to your window. You can also try to upload the multiple alignment file to the JPRED server at www.compbio.dundee.ac.uk. To do this, you will need to save the alignment in MSF format (ann_rep1_frags_del2.msf). Either method also should predict the helix in the region between 60 and 70.

By cleaning the alignment, you have thrown away information and sequences. This is why one should save all intermediate steps so that after the easier-to-interpret clean alignment has been studied, you can return to the more difficult alignment to interpret examples.

Subfamily Analysis with Jalview and AMAS

The file ideal_annexins.als has been created to illustrate the sub-family analysis that is possible with both JalView and AMAS.

With JalView

1. Start Jalview and read in the alignment file (`JalView ideal_annexins.blc BLC`).
2. From the Calculate menu, select "Average distance tree." On the tree that appears, you should see four clear clusters with one outlier. Click on the tree at a position to draw a vertical line and highlight the four clusters.
3. Return to the alignment window. From the Calculate menu, select Conservation. The positions most highly conserved within each subgroup of sequences will be colored most brightly. Can you identify the charge pair shown as an example in this chapter? You may find that selecting the Taylor or Zappo color schemes helps.
4. Try subfamily analysis by the AMAS server on the file ideal_annexins.blc. Paste the contents of the file into the alignment window, then paste the contents of the file ideal_annexins.grp into the "Sensible Groups window." The server should run quickly and should provide links to a number of output files. The pretty output file is the PostScript alignment. This is shown in the file ideal_annexins_amas.ps.

PROBLEM SET

Myosin proteins from numerous organisms have been sequenced. A FASTA-formatted sequence file with eight of these sequences can be found on the Book's web site.

Using ClustalW, construct a multiple sequence alignment using the BLOSUM matrices. Use the Jalview applet to answer the following questions.

1. The sequence for MYH3 from mouse is a sequence fragment. Does this fragment align to the N- or C-terminus of MYH3 from rat? What is the percent identity between these two sequences?

2. Which two sequences in the alignment are most similar to one another? (Hint: Select one of the functions available in the Calculate menu.)
3. Construct a neighbor-joining tree for each of the human proteins contained in the alignment. Based on the neighbor-joining tree, is the human MYH6 protein more closely related to human MYH1 or human MYH8? What evidence supports your conclusion?
4. Jalview indicates that there is a highly conserved block of ten amino acids within the first 200 positions of the alignment. What is the sequence of that block?
5. Manually remove the MYH3 sequence from mouse (the sequence fragment). After doing so, how many sequences remain if sequences that are more than 90% related to one another are removed from the alignment?
6. At the C-terminus, a gap of length 23 has been introduced to accommodate one of the remaining sequences. What positions in the alignment comprise the gap?

INTERNET RESOURCES

Alscript	http://www.compbio.dundee.ac.uk/Software/Alscript/alscript.html
AMAS	http://www.compbio.dundee.ac.uk/Software/Amas/amas.html
AMPS	http://www.compbio.dundee.ac.uk/Software/Amps/amps.html
ClustalW	http://www.ebi.ac.uk/clustalW
iSCANPS	http://www.ebi.ac.uk/scanps
JalView	http://www.jalview.org
JPred	http://www.compbio.dundee.ac.uk/Software/JPred/jpred.html
MAFFT	http://www.biophys.kyoto-u.ac.jp/~katoh/programs/align/mafft
MUSCLE	http://www.drive5.com/muscle/
PSI-BLAST	http://www.ncbi.nlm.nih.gov/BLAST/
STAMP	http://www.compbio.dundee.ac.uk/Software/Stamp/stamp.html
T-Coffee	http://igs-server.cnrs-mrs.fr/~cnotred/Projects_home_page/t_coffee_home_page.html

FURTHER READING

SIMOSSIS, V., KLEINJUNG, J., AND HERINGA, J. (2003). An overview of multiple sequence alignment. *Curr. Protocols Bioinformatics* 3.7.1–3.7.26. A comprehensive overview of multiple sequence alignment techniques, including information on scoring functions, alignment strategies, and an extensive range of programs used to generate multiple sequence alignments.

HIGGINS, J. D., GIBSON, T., AND HIGGINS, D. G. (2003). Multiple sequence alignment using ClustalW and ClustalX. *Curr. Protocols Bioinformatics* 2.3.1–2.3.22. A comprehensive description of the most commonly-used package for multiple sequence alignment, including a detailed explanation of the progressive alignment method employed by these algorithms.

NOTREDAME, C. AND SUHRE, K. (2003). Computing multiple sequence/structure alignments with the T-Coffee package. *Curr. Protocols Bioinformatics* 3.8.1–3.8.28. An detailed description of how multiple sequence alignments can be constructed using the T-Coffee package. Examples of cases for performing family or structural modeling are included.

REFERENCES

ALTSCHUL, S. F., MADDEN, T. L., SCHAFFER, A. A., ZHANG, J., ZHANG, Z., MILLER, W., AND LIPMAN. D. J. (1997). Gapped blast and psi-blast: a new generation of protein database search programs. *Nucl. Acids Res.* 25, 3389–3402.

ATTWOOD, T. K., CRONING, M. D. R., FLOWER, D. R., LEWIS, A. P., MABEY, J. E., SCORDIS, P., SELLEY, J., AND WRIGHT, W. (2000). Prints-s: the database formerly known as prints. *Nucl. Acids Res.* 28, 225–227.

BARTON, G. J. (1990). Protein multiple sequence alignment and flexible pattern matching. *Methods Enzymol.* 183, 403–428.

BARTON, G. J. (1993). Alscript: a tool to format multiple sequence alignments. *Protein Eng.* 6, 37–40,

BARTON, G. J., NEWMAN, R. H., FREEMONT, P. F., AND CRUMPTON, M. J. (1991). Amino acid sequence analysis of the annexin super-gene family of proteins. *European J. Biochem.* 198, 749–760.

BARTON, G. J., AND STERNBERG, M. J. E. (1987a). Evaluation and improvements in the automatic alignment of protein sequences. *Protein Eng.* 1, 89–94.

BARTON, G. J., AND STERNBERG, M. J. E. (1987b). A strategy for the rapid multiple alignment of protein sequences: confidence levels from tertiary structure comparisons. *J. Mol. Biol.* 198, 327–337.

BARTON, G. J., AND STERNBERG, M. J. E. (1990). Flexible protein sequence patterns: a sensitive method to detect weak structural similarities. *J. Mol. Biol.* 212, 389–402.

BATEMAN, A., BIRNEY, E., DURBIN, R., EDDY, S. R., FINN, R. D., AND SONNHAMMER, E. L. L. (1999). Pfam 3.1: 1313 multiple alignments match the majority of proteins. *Nucl. Acids Res.* 27, 260–262.

CLAMP, M., CUFF, J., SEARLE, S. M., AND BARTON, G. J. (2004). The jalview java alignment editor. *Bioinformatics* 20, 426–427.

CUFF, J. A., AND BARTON, G. J. (1999). Evaluation and improvement of multiple sequence methods for protein secondary structure prediction. *Proteins* 34, 508–519.

EDGAR, R. C. (2004). Muscle: multiple sequence alignment with high accuracy and high throughput. *Nucl. Acids Res.* 32, 1792–1797.

FELSENSTEIN, J. (1989). Phylip—phylogeny inference package (version 3.2). *Cladistics* 5, 164–166.

MURZIN, A. G., BRENNER, S. E., HUBBARD, T., AND CHOTHIA, C. (1995). Scop: a structural classification of proteins database for the investigation of sequences and structures. *J. Mol. Biol.* 247, 536–540.

GOTOH, O. (1996). Significant improvement in accuracy of multiple protein sequence alignments by iterative refinement as as-

sessed by reference to structural alignments. *J. Mol. Biol.* 264, 823–838.

GRIBSKOV, M., MCLACHLAN, A. D., AND EISENBERG, D. (1987). Profile analysis: detection of distantly related proteins. *Proc. Natl. Acad. Sci. U. S. A.* 84, 4355–4358.

GRINDLEY, H. M., ARTYMIUK, P. J., RICE, D. W., AND WILLETT, P. (1993). Identification of tertiary structure resemblance in proteins using maximal common subgraph isomorphism. *J. Mol. Biol.* 229, 707–721.

HOLM, L., AND SANDER, C. (1993). Protein structure comparison by alignment of distance matrices. *J. Mol. Biol.* 233, 123–128.

HUBER, R., ROMSICH, J., AND PAQUES, E.-P. (1990). The crystal and molecular structure of human annexin v, an anticoagulant protein that binds to calcium and membranes. *EMBO J.* 9, 3867–3874.

JONES, D. T. (1999). Protein secondary structure prediction based on position-specific scoring matrices. *J. Mol. Biol.* 17, 195–202.

KATOH, K., MISAWA, K., KUMA, K., AND MIYATA., T. (2002). Mafft: a novel method for rapid multiple sequence alignment based on fast fourier transform. *Nucl. Acids Res.* 30, 3059–3066.

KRAULIS, P. J. (1991). Molscript: a program to produce both detailed and schematic plots of protein structures. *J. Appl. Cryst.* 24, 964–950.

LESK, A. M., LEVITT, M., AND CHOTHIA, C. (1986). Alignment of the amino acid sequences of distantly related proteins using variable gap penalties. *Protein Eng.* 1, 77–78.

LIPMAN, D. J., ALTSCHUL, S. F., AND KECECIOGLU, J. D. (1989). A tool for multiple sequence alignment. *Proc. Natl. Acad. Sci. U. S. A.* 86, 4412–4415.

LIVINGSTONE, C. D., AND BARTON, G. J. (1993). Protein sequence alignments: a strategy for the hierarchical analysis of residue conservation. *Comp. Appl. Biosci.* 9, 745–756.

NOTREDAME, C., HIGGINS, D. G., AND HERINGA, J. (2000). T-coffee: a novel method for fast and accurate multiple sequence alignment. *J. Mol. Biol.* 302, 205–217.

PASCARELLA, S., AND ARGOS, P. (1992). Analysis of insertions/deletions in protein structures. *J. Mol. Biol.* 224, 461–471.

RAGHAVA, G., SEARLE, S. M., AUDLEY, P. C., BARBER, J. D., AND BARTON, G. J. (2003). OXBench: a benchmark for evaluation of protein multiple sequence alignment accuracy. *BMC Bioinformatics* 4, 47.

ROACH, P. L., CLIFTON, I. J., FULOP, V., HARLOS, K., BARTON, G. J., HAJDU, J., ANDERSSON, I., SCHOFIELD, C. J., AND BALDWIN, J. E. (1995). Crystal structure of isopenicillin n synthase is the first from a new structural family of enzymes. *Nature* 375, 700–704.

ROST, B., AND SANDER, C. (1993). Prediction of protein secondary structure at better than 70% accuracy. *J. Mol. Biol.* 232, 584–599.

RUSSELL, R. B., AND BARTON, G. J. (1992). Multiple protein sequence alignment from tertiary structure comparison: assignment of global and residue confidence levels. *Proteins* 14, 309–323.

RUSSELL, R. B., AND BARTON, G. J. (1994). Structural features can be unconserved in proteins with similar folds. *J. Mol. Biol.* 244, 332–350.

SALI, A., AND BLUNDELL, T. L. (1990). Definition of general topological equivalence in protein structures, a procedure involving comparison of properties and relationships thorugh simulated annealing and dynamic programming. *J. Mol. Biol.* 212, 403–428.

SCHULTZ, J., MILPETZ, F., BORK, P., AND PONTING, C. P. (1998). Smart, a simple modular architecture research tool: identification of signalling domains. *Proc. Natl. Acad. Sci. U. S. A.* 95, 5857–5864.

SMITH, T. F., AND WATERMAN, M. S. (1981). Identification of common molecular subsequences. *J. Mol. Biol.* 147, 195–197.

TAYLOR, W. R., AND ORENGO, C. A. (1989). A holistic approach to protein structre alignment. *Protein Eng.* 2, 505–519.

THOMPSON, J. D., HIGGINS, D. G., AND GIBSON, T. J. (1994). Clustal w: improving the sensitivity of progressive multiple sequence alignment through sequence weighting, position-specific gap penalties and weight matrix choice. *Nucl. Acids Res.* 22, 4673–4680.

THOMPSON, J. D., PLEWNIAK, F., AND POCH, O. (1999). BAliBASE: a benchmark alignment database for the evaluation of multiple sequence alignment programs. *Bioinformatics* 15, 87–88.

VON MERING, C., HUYNEN, M., JAEGGI, D., SCHMIDT, S., BORK, P., AND SNEL, B. (2003). String: a database of predicted functional associations between proteins. *Nucl. Acids Res.* 31, 258–261.

WEBBER, C., AND BARTON, G. J. (2001). Estimation of p-values for global alignments of protein sequences. *Bioinformatics* 17, 1158–1167.

ZVELEBIL, M. J. J. M., BARTON, G. J., TAYLOR, W. R., AND STERNBERG, M. J. E. (1987). Prediction of protein secondary structure and active sites using the alignment of homologous sequences. *J. Mol. Biol.* 195, 957–961.

KEY TERMS

Hierarchical alignment

Multiple sequence alignment

Non-hierarchical alignment

Structural alignment

## CHAPTER THIRTEEN

Sequence Assembly and Finishing Methods

NANCY F. HANSEN

PAMELA JACQUES THOMAS

GERARD G. BOUFFARD

Bioinformatics: A Practical Guide to the Analysis of Genes and Proteins, Third Edition, edited by
Andreas D. Baxevanis and B.F. Francis Ouellette.
ISBN 0-471-47878-4 Copyright © 2005 John Wiley & Sons, Inc.

▌INTRODUCTION

Reasons for Shotgun Sequencing

Some day in the distant future, technology may be available to determine end-to-end nucleotide sequences from large DNA segments, such as chromosomes, in a single reaction process. In the meantime, current DNA sequencing technology, based on the dideoxy terminator technique developed by Sanger et al. in the 1970s (Sanger et al., 1977), limits us to stretches of approximately 1000 bases or fewer. This method, in use by all major sequencing centers, uses specialized DNA polymerase enzymes to extend specially constructed oligonucleotide primers that bind to a single-stranded DNA template. In an approach known as *primer walking*, custom primers designed to be complementary to the known sequence can be used to extend nucleotide sequence data iteratively from the distal ends of known regions into unknown regions of the same molecule. In practice, serial generation of data in this manner is far too time consuming for large-scale sequencing methods. In addition, custom synthesis of so many different oligonucleotide primers would be cost prohibitive. In the shotgun sequencing method, DNA to be sequenced is sheared randomly into appropriately sized fragments that subsequently are ligated into specially designed sequencing vectors. These vectors provide a mechanism for clonal amplification of each fragment by allowing for replication in a suitable host bacteria (*Escherichia coli*). This process also places the fragments adjacent to robust priming sites for which large quantities of matching oligonucleotides can be synthesized in a cost-effective manner. The generation of many of these cloned fragments in parallel lends itself to highly efficient DNA sequence production.

What Assemblers Do

As a consequence of the randomization of DNA fragments, sequence data must be assembled together to derive the nucleotide sequence of the original DNA segment. The process is analogous to the reconstruction of a picture in a common jigsaw puzzle, except that the fragments overlap several layers deep and are linear, rather than two-dimensional. If the starting material used for shotgun sequencing is genomic DNA, the process is referred to as a whole genome shotgun (WGS) assembly (Figure 13.1, right). The alternative hierarchical clone-based shotgun assembly introduces an intermediate layer of cloning, where libraries of large insert clones such as bacterial artificial chromosomes (BACs), yeast artificial chromosomes, cosmids, and fosmids are derived from genomic DNA (Figure 13.1, left). A significant advantage to WGS sequencing is that it reduces dramati-

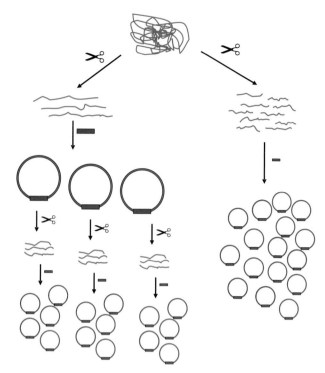

FIGURE 13.1   Shotgun cloning. Genomic DNA sequencing begins with isolated genomic DNA in green at the top of the figure. In the hierarchical clone-based shotgun approach on the left, DNA is sheared and the size is selected for large fragments on the order of 200 Kb, then ligated to a suitable vector, such as a BAC vector shown in blue. Individually isolated clones in turn are sheared independently, generating fragments of approximately 4 Kb, which are then ligated to a small-scale vector, typically a plasmid (red bar) suitable for sequencing reactions. The whole genome shotgun approach bypasses the intermediate large-insert clone and generates large numbers of small fragments, typically 4 Kb and 10 Kb.

cally the cost of generating large quantities of sequence data by eliminating the need to construct and map representative clones of large inserts. Although clone-based shotgun sequencing incurs the initial costs of mapping clones (typically carried out by probe content, restriction fingerprint analysis, or both), the assembly process is much simpler, because it localizes the data and avoids the challenges posed by the large numbers of genomic sequences and the complexities introduced by large genomic duplications. Both approaches, as well as some hybrid strategies, are used widely today. In either case, as described in detail below, assemblers begin by pairwise comparison of individual sequences to identify overlapping sequences; these subsequently are stitched together into longer blocks of contiguous sequences (contigs).

DNA Sequence Finishing

The ultimate goal of DNA sequencing is to determine the entire nucleotide sequence of the source DNA at a desirable level of confidence. Shotgun generation of random fragments is extremely cost effective for obtaining data from most of the starting DNA when the depth of coverage is 8- to 10-fold. That is, each base pair in the original DNA is represented in an average of eight to ten different fragments. The addition of random fragments beyond this level generally is not cost-effective, because the probability of closing remaining gaps or of deepening regions of thin coverage drops dramatically. A directed approach to DNA sequencing, known as *finishing*, is used to determine bases located in sequence gaps and to provide greater depth in low-quality regions. Custom primers on a variety of templates typically are used, as described in greater detail below.

The remainder of this chapter describes the creation of shotgun clone libraries as they typically are used for the sequencing of large insert clones (BACs), the generation of primary sequence data, and its conversion into predicted base calls with associated quality scores. Whole genome shotgun sequencing is described briefly. The process of assembling clone-based shotgun sequence data into contiguous blocks of consensus sequence is detailed. Finishing techniques used to order and orient sequence contigs, to eliminate gaps in sequence data, and to improve regions of low quality are discussed. Finally, the superassembly of large-insert clones to represent a larger genomic segment is described.

▮ SHOTGUN SEQUENCING

Description

Construction of a shotgun library begins with preparation and purification of DNA. For BAC-based shotgun libraries, a single colony grown and isolated on agar containing the appropriate nutrient medium and antibiotic typically is selected and grown to sufficient quantities in liquid media. Host cells then are lysed to separate the BAC DNA from the host cell debris and genomic DNA. Complete exclusion of *E. coli* genomic DNA is practically impossible, but a small percentage can be tolerated. Careful handling of samples is critical because mixture or contamination of DNA here can have catastrophic consequences downstream. An aliquot of the purified DNA can be subjected to restriction fingerprint analysis. A restriction fingerprint is simply the list of DNA fragment sizes that result from the endonuclease digestion of the clone DNA, using a specific enzyme (Figure 13.2). Because these banding patterns for the most part are

unique, comparison of the restriction fingerprint with fingerprints commonly generated in clone mapping provides a powerful means to confirm the identity of each clone, avoiding costly sequencing of undesired clones. DNA then is subjected to one of a variety of treatments, such as nuclease, sonication, or high-pressure hydroshearing, designed to create random fragments of relatively uniform size, typically approximately 4 kb. The purified fragments then are ligated with adaptors to vector DNA that has been cut and purified to form circular plasmids. The ligation mix then is used to transform recipient host bacteria that are plated on the appropriate nutrient agar and selective antibiotic. In a typical high-throughput environment, isolated colonies are picked into 96-well boxes containing 1 to 2 ml of liquid media and grown overnight. In a fashion analogous to BAC DNA preparation, each sample is lysed and plasmid DNA is purified away from host cell debris and genomic DNA. A mixture containing this template DNA, oligonucleotide primer, polymerase, deoxynucleotide triphosphates, and dideoxynucleotide phosphates (ddNTPs) terminators then are subjected to polymerase chain reaction (PCR) thermal cycle sequencing. Low-frequency, random incorporation of ddNTPs causes chain termination, resulting in a mixture of truncated chains whose lengths identify the corresponding terminal base. Either the primers or the ddNTPs are labeled in some cases with a radioactive tag, but much more commonly with a fluorescent tag, making them readily detectable during electrophoretic separation on sequencing instruments. Almost all plasmid sequencing vectors currently in use contain at least two sequence priming sites, one on each side of the insertion site, making it extremely practical to sequence both ends (on opposite strands) of each insert; this reduces the numbers of templates that need to be prepared and provides valuable relative position information for paired end-reads, as discussed in the Assembly section, below.

The Data

A variety of commercial automated DNA sequencing instruments are available to size fractionate DNA fragments, typically using electrophoretic mobility through sieving media (such as polyacrylamide) in capillary arrays, followed by fluorescent or radioisotopic detection. In the brief history of automated DNA sequencing, several proprietary formats (such as ABI and ALF) as well as public formats have been developed to store the raw and ancillary data in files referred to interchangeably as *chromatograms*, *traces*, or *reads*. A graphical view of a sample chromatogram is shown in Figure 13.3. The most popular open format, SCF, was described in 1992 (Dear & Staden, 1992). A relatively new open format known

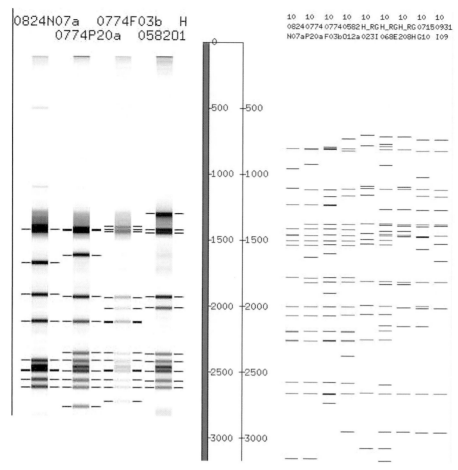

FIGURE 13.2 Clone fingerprinting. Images from four overlapping clone fingerprints as viewed through the FPC program (Soderlund et al., 1997). Fragments identified from gel bands on the left are represented in cartoon fashion on the right. A selected fingerprint (shown in blue) is compared with the banding patterns of other clones, whose shared fragments are shown in red.

as ZTR offers even better compression, access, and extensibility (Bonfield & Staden, 2002). Each of these files is designed to store the data collected from the electrophoresis of a single DNA sample and includes band intensity data of each of the four base types at each position in the sequence, derived base calls, quality scores, position information, and ancillary data such as sequencing chemistry and machine type.

Probably the most widely used program to derive base calls and quality scores is phred (Ewing & Green, 1998; Ewing et al., 1998). Successful basecalling programs rigorously evaluate the geometry of band intensity peaks to yield probability of base call error estimates. Quality value scores then are assigned by multiplying the $\log_{10}$ of the probability of error by -10. That is, a quality value score of 20 (Q20) equates to a 0.01 probability of error, Q30 to a 0.001 probability of error, and so forth. High-throughput sequencing centers commonly measure their production of quality data by tallying the number of bases with scores that are Q20 or more that are generated over a certain period. The phred program also reports stretches of contiguous quality length by defining high-quality start and stop at the ends of a read beyond which the probability of error rises to more than a set threshold. Such a measure is extremely useful in evaluating single-pass reads, such as those generated for expressed sequence tags (ESTs).

Phred output is in the form of text-based phd files that contain ancillary data derived from the original trace file, base calls, quality scores, and peak position information. These phd files are the starting point for phrap and other assembly programs described below. The phd file derived from the chromatogram shown in Figure 13.3 can be seen in Appendix 13.1. The corresponding FASTA file format for the same chromatogram is shown in Appendix 13.2. FASTA files commonly are used by almost

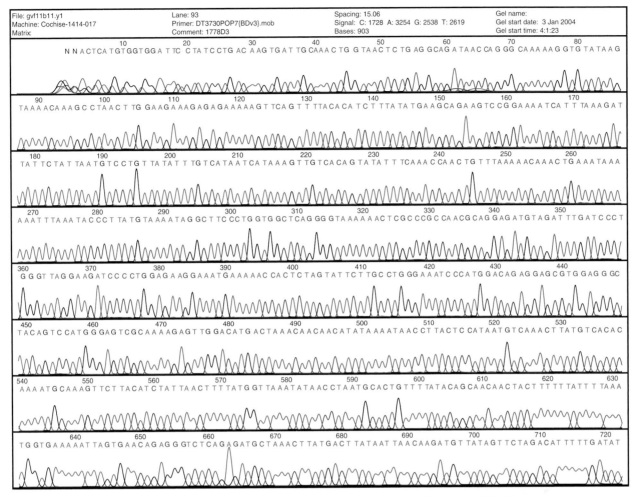

File: gvf11b11.y1	Lane: 93	Spacing: 15.06	Gel name:
Machine: Cochise-1414-017	Primer: DT3730POP7{BDv3}.mob	Signal: C: 1728 A: 3254 G: 2538 T: 2619	Gel start date: 3 Jan 2004
Matrix	Comment: 1778D3	Bases: 903	Gel start time: 4:1:23

FIGURE 13.3   A sample chromatogram, as viewed with the vtrace program (Ewing, 2002). Signal intensities corresponding to fragments ending with A (green), C (blue), G (black), and T (red) are shown out to approximately 722 bases.

all DNA sequence analysis software and begin with a specially formatted definition line (defline) that always begins with the ">" symbol followed by the identifier. Additional information on the same line (in this example, translated from the phd file by the program phd2fasta) communicates information about the read to the assembly program. The lines following the definition line are the nucleotide sequences or basecalls. Multiple FASTA sequences can be concatenated into a single FASTA library file, with each individual sequence introduced by its own defline.

SEQUENCE ASSEMBLY

There are numerous computer programs, called *assemblers*, that are available for assembling shotgun reads into contiguous sequence. In writing these assemblers, programmers have relied on a large array of mathemat-

ical theories and algorithms to solve a problem that is both challenging and computationally intensive: to discover the sequence of the DNA that was the target of a shotgun sequencing experiment (Kececioglu & Myers, 1995). Still, many assemblers share a common roadmap to assembly. Typically, they all perform a pairwise comparison of all the reads, followed by a merging of reads to form contigs, and finally, the assignment of a consensus sequence as the hypothesized actual sequence of the source DNA.

The best assembler for a particular application depends on the size and nature of the shotgun project. For small projects (up to 500 reads), several packages that readily run on desktop computer systems are commercially available. These programs typically provide for the importation of chromatograms and allow editing, assembly, and basic analysis of DNA sequences in a user-friendly environment. For larger projects, several

Unix-based assemblers are available, including the Institute for Genomic Research's TIGR Assembler (Sutton et al., 1995), CAP (Huang et al., 2003), and phrap. Because phrap is perhaps the most widely-used assembler anywhere, it forms the basis of this section's discussion of assembly, but all of the programs mentioned here share parts of phrap's approach.

Assembly with the Phred/Phrap/Consed Suite of Programs

Both the base caller phred and the phrap assembler are parts of a single suite of programs developed and distributed by the research group of Phil Green at the University of Washington. Because this suite of programs was developed together, use of all of them in a unified fashion simplifies many aspects of setup and formatting and allows the use of valuable program features that would be otherwise unavailable; Box 13.1 provides an overview of the typical processing steps. The suite includes a perl script called phredPhrap that performs all the steps necessary to take raw chromatograms to assembled sequences using phred and phrap. It also includes Consed, a sequence editor (Gordon et al., 1998) that reads phrap's output and allows a user easily to perform all the informatics steps necessary to correct assembly errors and to attain a finished sequence.

Phrap requires as its input processed read sequences and qualities in FASTA format. As detailed in the previous section, raw data from a sequencing instrument are processed best with a program like phred to generate a sequence of As, Ts, Gs, Cs, and Ns and to give each base a quality score indicating the base's accuracy. By working within a well-defined directory structure, the phredPhrap script is able to ensure that all the project's chromatograms, deposited in a project subdirectory named `chromat_dir`, have been processed by phred to create the phd files, which are stored in the `phd_dir` subdirectory. This allows the progressive inclusion of new data as it becomes available without unnecessary computation.

Real sequence from real shotgun reads frequently contains contaminants. Often, a read contains small or large segments of cloning or sequencing vector, and in fact, one expects a certain percentage of reads to consist entirely of the cloning vector, because it was fragmented along with the large insert to make the shotgun library. In addition, it is common for some reads to contain the sequence of the cloning host (*E. coli*). Although phrap does make some allowances for small amounts of vector at the beginnings and ends of reads, for the most part, it assumes the sequence fragments it receives as input are free from this kind of contamination, so phredPhrap "cleans up" reads before assembling them with phrap.

To determine whether each read or a portion of it is vector sequence, phredPhrap creates a FASTA file of all the read sequences and compares them using a program called cross_match to a user-created library of sequencing and cloning vectors. When called with the `-screen` option (as it is in phredPhrap), cross_match replaces all bases that have aligned to vector sequence with a score of a predefined threshold score or more with an X character (c.f., Chapter 11). It then writes these new, screened sequences to a FASTA file (with `.screen` appended to its name), which can then be used as the input to phrap.

To facilitate the automated inclusion of various types of information about sequencing reads, phredPhrap calls determineReadTypes.perl, a customizable perl script designed to append to each phd file tags telling how the read was created. Using a read name, determineReadTypes.perl can deduce, either from a specific naming convention or from a call to a local database, specific information about the template, primer, and chemistry used to create the read. This information, now included in a standardized way, is made available to both phrap and Consed.

Phrap Assembly

Phrap, like all other widely used sequence assemblers, begins by performing a pairwise comparison of the read

---

BOX 13.1 Overview of Phred and Phrap Processing Steps

1. The base-calling program phred is run on reads as necessary to create phd-formatted files.

2. The script determineReadTypes.perl appends tags to each phd file containing information about template, primer, and library for the read.

3. The program phd2fasta creates *FASTA*-formatted sequence and quality files from the phd files (one sequence and one quality file for the entire set of reads).

4. The alignment program cross_match is used to screen vector sequence, and optionally, *E. coli* sequence from each read.

5. The *FASTA* and quality files of screened read sequences are used as input to phrap, which attempts to assemble them into contigs.

6. Consensus and read tags from the most recent previous assembly (if there was one) are transferred to the new ace file created by phrap, which is now ready for viewing in Consed.

sequences it has been given as input. The purpose of this comparison is to assess how likely it is that any two shotgun reads resulted from the sequencing of overlapping segments of the original source DNA. By assigning scores to each pair reflecting this likelihood, phrap is setting the stage for when it will merge reads into contigs, beginning with the pairs that it deems most likely to have a true overlap. This will create a read layout, from which it can make a guess at the sequence of the original DNA. Table 13.1 provides a description of optional, useful phrap parameters.

One may imagine choosing a scoring matrix and gap penalties and performing a Smith-Waterman alignment of each and every pair of reads (Chapter 11). The score of the optimal alignment of two reads then could be used as an indicator of the likelihood that they come from overlapping segments of the target DNA. There are two reasons that this approach may not be well advised. First,

a full Smith-Waterman alignment for thousands of reads, and thus millions of unique pairs, is far too time consuming to be practical. Second, such an approach fails to consider the quality scores of the bases it aligns, and thus scores a longer alignment with several high-quality discrepancies more strongly than a shorter exact alignment. To score read pairs more realistically, phrap performs a more approximate alignment only of read pairs that have exact matches of a certain length, then calculates for each pair that aligns with a certain minimum score a likelihood ratio that these reads are actually from the same segment of the target sequence versus two copies of a repeat that are 95% identical.

Phrap begins its comparison of reads by doing something called *word matching*. Even allowing for sequencing errors, two sequencing reads from overlapping segments of the target DNA are likely to share at least some small stretches of exactly matching

TABLE 13.1 ■ Optional Phrap Parameters

Option	Default value	Description
Indexwordsize	10	Length in bases of the "words" phrap catalogs in an effort to find matches between reads
Maxmatch	30	Length of a matching word between two reads that would lead to a banded Smith-Waterman comparison, regardless of the word's base composition
Minmatch	14	Minimum length (when complexity adjusted) of a matching word required to initiate a banded Smith-Waterman comparison of reads
Minscore	30	Minimum alignment score (when complexity adjusted) that a read pair must have to be considered in future assembly steps; if a read matches another read with at least this score, it will be included in the ace file even if it cannot be merged successfully into a contig with another read
Word_raw	OFF	Turns off complexity adjustment of matching word lengths; read pairs with word matches of length −minmatch are always compared in a banded Smith-Waterman alignment when -word_raw is specified
Bandwidth	14	One half the width of the diagonal portion of the Smith-Waterman matrix for two reads that is calculated to align the reads; if multiple word matches are present for two reads at different offsets, this width is expanded to include all matches with at least -bandwidth bases on either side
Repeat_stringency	0.95	Degree of identity of a repeat that will be considered as the alternate hypothesis to the proposition that two reads come from overlapping segments of DNA (see inset)
Forcelevel	0	An integer that roughly specifies the requirements for merging contigs in the final pass; larger integers allow reads with lower log-likelihood ratios to be considered for merging, and for this reason, running phrap with increased values of this parameter can lead to false joins
Maxgap	30	Maximum size of an unmatched portion of a read in a potential contig merge

sequence. Based on this, phrap creates an index containing the locations within all the reads of all occurrences of every possible ATGC "word" of length 10 (this length can be changed using the input parameter `-indexwordsize`). For example, all occurrences of the word AAAAAAAAAA are cataloged, as are all occurrences of the word AAAAAAAAAT, and so on, through all 4^{10} words. This makes it a quick and easy task to look up all occurrences of any given word. Then, each read, as well as its complement (because one read can match the complement of another read), is compared at each of its complete index words with the sequence at every other occurrence of this word. Each match is extended to its maximum exactly matching length and is evaluated to see if it is strong enough to warrant inclusion of the pair of reads it represents in the more accurate alignment calculation to follow. If the match is at least of length 30 (this value can be changed using the `-maxmatch` input parameter), the pair is included without further evaluation. If the length is shorter than 30 bases, its value is adjusted downward depending on its composition with respect to the four nucleotides, so that an exact match consisting of only one or two nucleotides is considered "shorter" than an exact match of the same length with balanced ATGC composition. (This complexity adjustment can be turned off using the input parameter `-word-raw`.) If the complexity-adjusted match is greater than the value of the `-minmatch` input parameter, whose default is 14, the pair of reads is included in the subsequent alignment.

Each of these word matches corresponds to a particular diagonal in the alignment matrix for its two reads (Figure 13.4). Rather than fill the entire matrix with scores, phrap creates a "band" centered on the diagonal indicated by a match, and with width equal to two times the bandwidth plus one, where `bandwidth` is an input parameter whose default is 14. Because large numbers of insertions and deletions in sequencing reads are unlikely, the correct alignment of a pair of reads (assuming one exists) is likely to be contained entirely within a band around the diagonal corresponding to the word match. If different word matches for the same pair of reads point to different diagonals, their bands either are merged (if they overlap) or they are both searched in the next step.

After assuming all the other scores in the Smith-Waterman matrix are zero, phrap calculates scores within this read–read matrix only within the band it is examining. If an alignment is found with complexity-adjusted score of at least 30, phrap also recursively attempts to align the remaining portions of the two reads. All read pairs having alignments of at least the minimum score are included in the next step.

At this point in the assembly, phrap calculates an adjusted quality score for every base of every read. The procedure it uses is complex, but is described in the documentation as assigning each base a score equal to

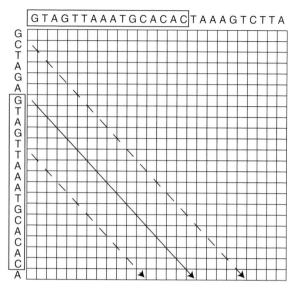

FIGURE 13.4 A portion of the read–read matrix of two different sequence reads. A word match, such as the one between the sequences that are boxed, will initiate a banded Smith-Waterman comparison if the match is sufficiently long. In the comparison, the Smith-Waterman scores are calculated only for matrix elements contained within a certain distance of the solid diagonal determined by the word match. In this case, where the band width is four, the band would include all cells completely contained between the dashed diagonals.

the sum of its original score and the highest score of a matching base in an independent, strongly confirming read. A read is considered strongly confirming if it aligns to the base being considered, is from a different template, and is either from the opposite strand or of a different chemistry than the original read. In addition, unconfirmed ends of reads are assigned an adjusted quality of zero.

Phrap also classifies some of the reads in the assembly as chimeric or deleted. A read is considered chimeric if its confirmed portions separate into two nonoverlapping sets. A "better" segment is chosen, and all matches involving the other segment(s) are ignored. Incorporation of chimeric reads into contigs is delayed until the end of the assembly process, and these reads appear in an assembly editor like Consed as correctly aligned reads with a high-quality portion that is unaligned. If the separated segments are confirmed by the same read and are separated by more than 10 bases, the read is considered "deleted" and is only included in the assembly as a singleton contig.

As was mentioned earlier, this original formation of read pairs by banded Smith-Waterman alignment makes no use of quality scores; thus, the score of a pair with a longer alignment with high-quality mismatches may be larger than a shorter, exact alignment. So, for example, two reads coming from separate copies of a near-exact repeat may have a higher alignment score than two reads that actually come from overlapping locations on the target DNA, but happen to have a shorter overlap length. This is the most common reason for misassemblies in phrap assemblies. Other assemblers like CAP and the TIGR assembler make use of pairs of reads from opposite ends of inserts to sort out repeats that are misassembled this way, but because phrap does not use this informa-tion, it needs to rely on other methods to avoid this type of misassembly.

In an attempt to correct this problem, phrap uses its adjusted quality scores to evaluate a log-likelihood ratio (LLR) for the hypothesis that the reads actually overlap against the hypothesis that the reads are from separate copies of a repeat that is 95% identical (Box 13.2). If this log value is positive (i.e., the likelihood ratio is more than one), then phrap assumes the pair is real. If the log value is negative, it excludes this pair from initial consideration when bringing reads together to form contigs.

BOX 13.2 Log-likelihood Ratio (LLR) Calculations to Differentiate Between Distinct Repetitive Regions and True Overlap

When two reads align in a way that is consistent with their being reads from overlapping sections of the original DNA, an assembler is forced to make a decision: Do these reads really overlap, or do they come from two different copies of a repeat?

Given two reads and an alignment between them, what can be said about the actual source DNA sequence? Sites within the alignment that agree (e.g., an A aligned with an A, or a C aligned with a C) do not give us much information about whether the reads overlap or represent a repeat, but discrepancies can tell us quite a lot, particularly if they are bases with high quality scores (here, the quality scores used by phrap are not the original phred scores, but the adjusted quality scores; see the text). If we consider all positions of an alignment between reads to be independent, then the probability of a particular alignment is simply the product of the probabilities of agreement or discrepancy at each of the individual sites.

Although the information to calculate the actual probability that a given alignment results from an overlap or a repeat is lacking (this would require one to know the prevalence of repeated sequence in the DNA being sequenced), one can calculate the likelihood of the two possibilities or, more simply, their LLR.

Let H_O be the hypothesis that the two reads come from overlapping segments of the original DNA, and let H_R be the hypothesis that they come from two different copies of a repeat that is 95% identical. If the alignment contains n positions, and the values $\{x_1, x_2, x_3, \ldots, x_n\}$ indicate whether the bases match ($x_i = 1$) or are discrepant ($x_i = 0$) at position i, then the conditional probability of observing this alignment if H_O is true is:

$$P\left(\overline{x} \mid H_o\right) = \prod_{\text{all sites } x_i} P_i\left(x_i \mid H_o\right),$$

$$P_i\left(x_i \mid H_o\right) = \begin{cases} (1 - e_{1,i})(1 - e_{2,i}) + \frac{1}{3}e_{1,i}e_{2,i} & \text{if } x_i = 1 \text{ (bases agree)} \\ e_{1,i}(1 - e_{2,i}) + (1 - e_{1,i})e_{2,i} + \frac{2}{3}e_{1,i}e_{2,i} & \text{if } x_i = 0 \text{ (bases disagree)} \end{cases},$$

where H_o is the hypothesis that reads are from overlapping templates and H_R is the hypothesis that reads are from different copies of a 95% identical repeat, and where $e_{1,i} = 10^{-q_{1,i}/10}$ is the probability that the ith base in the first read is a sequencing error. Likewise, the conditional probability of a match or mismatch at a site i if H_R is true is:

$$P_i\left(x_i \mid H_R\right) = \begin{cases} 0.95\left((1 - e_{1,i})(1 - e_{2,i}) + \frac{1}{3}e_{1,i}e_{2,i}\right) \\ \quad + 0.05\left(\frac{1}{3}e_{1,i}(1 - e_{2,i}) + \frac{1}{3}(1 - e_{1,i})e_{2,i} + \frac{2}{9}e_{1,i}e_{2,i}\right) & \text{if } x_i = 1, \\ 0.95\left(e_{1,i}(1 - e_{2,i}) + (1 - e_{1,i})e_{2,i} + \frac{2}{3}e_{1,i}e_{2,i}\right) \\ \quad + 0.05\left((1 - e_{1,i})(1 - e_{2,i}) + \frac{2}{3}e_{1,i}(1 - e_{2,i}) + \frac{2}{3}(1 - e_{1,i})e_{2,i} + \frac{7}{9}e_{1,i}e_{2,i}\right) & \text{if } x_i = 0. \end{cases}$$

When the probabilities of error are small, we can ignore terms of order $e_{m,i}$ or higher, and because the likelihoods are simple products, the LLR becomes:

$$LLR \approx -\sum_{i \, s.t. \, x_i = 1} \log(0.95) + \sum_{i \, s.t. \, x_i = 0} \left\{\log(e_{1,i} + e_{2,i}) - \log\left(0.05 - \frac{0.05}{3}e_{1,i} - \frac{0.05}{3}e_{2,i} + 0.95e_{1,i} + 0.95e_{2,i}\right)\right\}.$$

In practice, phrap simplifies this expression even further, but the effect of the calculation is to penalize pairs with higher quality discrepancies (note that if the sum of $e_{1,i}$ and $e_{2,i}$ is very small, the log will become larger in magnitude but negative, lowering the LLR score). To alter phrap's calculation to consider an H_R for a repeat with a different percentage identity, the phrap parameter −repeat_stringency can be set to a value different from its default, 0.95.

Despite having a measure of the likelihood of any two reads coming from overlapping segments of the target DNA, the merging of these reads into contigs is a challenging problem. Ideally, in addition to pulling together and positioning overlapping reads, phrap would prevent the incorrect positioning of pairs of reads from opposite ends of the same insert, constraining them to be oriented in opposite directions and at a distance from each other consistent with the expected length of the library inserts. This is not currently the case, so a read pair viewer like Orchid (Figure 13.5) or Consed's assembly view module (Figure 13.6) should be used after assembly to check the positioning of these pairs and to correct any errors that have occurred.

What phrap does do is to use a "greedy" algorithm when creating contigs, beginning with each read in its own contig, using pairs beginning with the highest LLR-scoring pair and proceeding to the next highest pair to join contigs together. For each pair, if the two reads are in separate contigs, a possible merging of the two contigs is considered, based on the offset that is implied by the pair. If all other read pairs between reads in the two

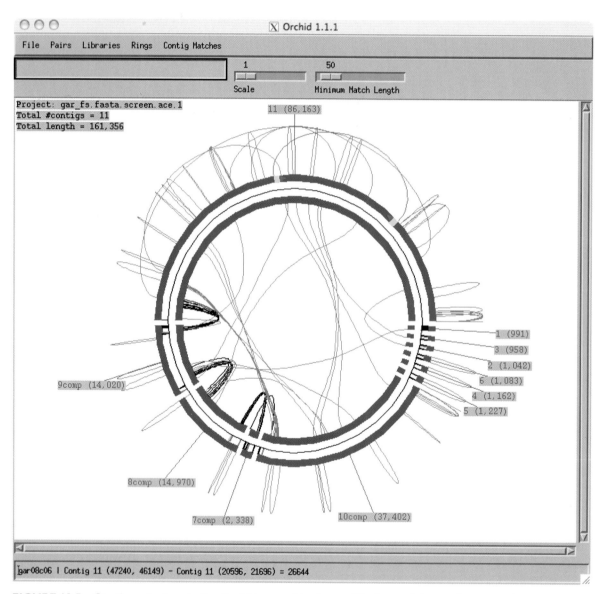

FIGURE 13.5 Contig ordering via the Orchid assembly viewer. Black arcs join consistent read pairs that span gaps. Pink arcs show inconsistent read pairs. The program attempts to order the contigs by using spanning read pairs, but in this case, phrap has misassembled some reads near the end of Contig11 (in the location joined by a pink band to the end of Contig10). The quality scores of the contigs, as well as the location of consensus tags, are displayed between the rings.

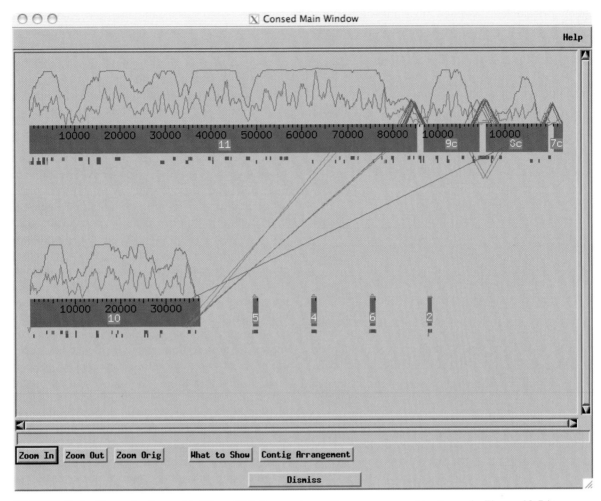

FIGURE 13.6 Consed's Assembly View. This figure shows the same assembly shown in Figure 13.5 in Consed's Assembly View window. The gray ruled bars are contigs, and the V-shaped line shows the locations of read pairs (purple if they are consistent, red if inconsistent). The dark and light green curves show the read depth and forward–reverse read pair depth, respectively. Again, the red lines joining the end of Contig11 to the end of Contig10 indicate a misassembly.

contigs are consistent with this merge, the contigs are joined.

The merging occurs in several passes. In the first pass, pairs involving chimeric and deleted reads are not included, and the pairs of reads involved in merges are required to have a higher LLR. Later, these requirements are relaxed, and in this way, the assembly is guided by the more reliable data, with suspect data still being used at a later point. If a read pair contains a mismatch between two bases that both have quality 99 (a quality never assigned by phred, but that is assigned when a read is edited as high quality within Consed), that pair will never be used in a contig merge, and therefore, these two bases will never be aligned together in an assembly.

Several phrap input parameters allow the user to affect how the merging of contigs is carried out. The -forcelevel parameter affects the stringency of the

final merging pass. By increasing this parameter from its default value of zero to larger integers (with a maximum of 10), the user can relax the requirements for merges to be allowed. Raising the -maxgap parameter from its default of 30 will increase the amount of unmatched sequence allowed when checking other read pairs for the consistency of a potential merge. In practice, changing the values of these parameters can lead to unexpected results.

As soon as phrap has assembled all of the reads that have significant matches into contigs (although some of these still may be in single read contigs), it still needs to report the probable consensus sequence, or its best guess at the true sequence of the original DNA for each contig. The term *consensus* implies that multiple reads influence the base identities (which is, in fact, true for many assemblers), but phrap builds its consensus from the sequence of single reads extending along the contig. One reason it would be difficult for phrap to consider all the base identities at a given position in the contig at this point is that it does not yet have a true multiple alignment of the reads, but rather just a grouping of reads that are aligned to each other in pairs with distinct offsets. Rather than attempt to create a multiple alignment, phrap considers potential paths along reads through the contig, scoring each with the sum of the adjusted qualities of all bases included in the path. Paths can switch only from one read to a paired read at certain strongly aligned positions, and for a defined set of switching positions and base qualities, a maximal weight path can be constructed using graph theory algorithms. As soon as this path has been determined, the consensus takes both its base identity and its quality score from the read used to create the path.

Finally, all of the reads in each contig are aligned against the new consensus sequence to create a multiple pairwise alignment, and all of the information about the assembly, including contig consensus sequence, quality scores, position and alignment of all the reads, identities of consensus-determining reads, and the quality and alignment end points of each read, are written to an `.ace` file suitable for viewing with Consed. Contig consensus sequences and qualities are also written to the `contigs` and `contigs.qual` files, and reads that had no significant match to any other read in the assembly are written to a `singlets` file. The difference between these singlet reads and the reads that appear in the `.ace` file as single read contigs is that the reads included in contigs had significant matches with other reads in the assembly, even though they were not able to be merged consistently with them. In addition, various other statistics and information regarding the assembly are written both to standard out and standard error as the program runs.

Whole Genome Shotgun

Perhaps the most memorable aspect of the recently completed sequencing of the human genome was the colorful debate between proponents of the public consortium's hierarchical approach (Lander et al., 2001) and advocates of the whole genome shotgun approach taken by Celera Genomics (Venter et al., 2001). The hierarchical approach involves an initial step of clone-based physical mapping in an effort to generate a list of overlapping BAC clones to be sequenced (also referred to as a *minimal tiling path*). This is then followed by shotgun sequencing of these individually mapped BAC clones that are roughly 100,000 to 200,000 bases in length. In contrast, the whole genome shotgun sequencing strategy is based on direct sequencing of randomly sheared

genomic DNA; specifically, in the case of Celera's sequencing of the human genome, shotgun libraries of genomic DNA with insert sizes of 2, 10, and 50 Kb. Therefore, because this approach does not require the initial step of creating a clone-based physical map, it can generate sequence data more quickly than the clone-by-clone hierarchical approach. However, without the mapping information, long-range assembly of the genome becomes much more problematic. The whole genome shotgun approach instead relies heavily on sophisticated assembly algorithms to assemble the individual sequencing reads based primarily on the sequence data alone. Before the rough draft of the human genome was published, a number of publications debated the cost and feasibility of obtaining finished sequence by each method (Green, 1997; Weber & Myers, 1997). However, both approaches have advantages, and the current sequencing of the mouse, rat, and zebrafish genomes have used a hybrid approach of both clone-by-clone and whole-genome shotgun sequencing (Green, 2001).

Although shotgun sequencing has been enormously successful at determining the sequence of smaller (on the order of two million base pairs or fewer) segments of DNA, the assembly of shotgun reads from genomes larger than this has presented a formidable challenge. In 1995, the genome of *Haemophilus influenzae*, with 1.8 million base pairs, was the first bacterial genome to be sequenced and assembled using whole-genome shotgun methods (Fleischmann et al., 1995). Since then, more than 100 microbial genomes have been completed, and considerable success has been reported in assembling whole-genome shotgun data sets from the fruit fly *Drosophila melanogaster* with the Celera assembler (Myers et al., 2000) and the mouse with Arachne (Batzoglou et al., 2002) and Phusion (Mullikin & Ning, 2003).

Not surprisingly, repeated sequence presents the greatest difficulty for whole-genome assemblers. The human genome's abundance of interspersed repeats was a strong argument for the "map, then sequence" strategy adopted by the public consortium. Another factor making whole-genome shotgun assembly difficult is the presence in some genomic libraries of two or more copies of each chromosome, leading to reads containing multiple alleles that can be difficult to distinguish from separate copies of a repeat. Most whole-genome assemblers defer consideration of highly repetitive sequences by excluding, in the initial word matching between reads, words that have an extremely high frequency in the data set; even so, it is still crucial for these assemblers to make use of forward and reverse reads from single inserts to prevent the joining of reads based on false overlaps. Large shotgun projects include the sequencing of libraries with a variety of insert sizes to span repeats of different lengths and to ensure correct assembly on both a small and large scale. In addition, some assemblers, like the Baylor College of Medicine's Atlas assembler, allow the inclusion of localized data (e.g., a group of reads from a single BAC clone).

Assemblies of whole-genome shotgun data are evaluated according to the number, size, and accuracy of their supercontigs or scaffolds (sets of contigs ordered by forward–reverse pairs). One often-used measure of assembly quality is the N50 scaffold size. By definition, N50 size of a contig or scaffold is the size for which 50 percent of the consensus nucleotides in the assembly reside in contigs or scaffolds of that size or more.

SEQUENCE FINISHING

Why Finishing Is Needed

As previously mentioned, the random shotgun sequencing method is not cost effective beyond a certain point. Mathematical models that account for the lengths of clones relative to the starting substrate (either BAC or genomic) and the amount of overlap between clones that is required for accurate prediction of overlap have been derived to predict the most effective depth of coverage (Lander & Waterman 1988; Wendl & Waterston, 2002). For most groups sequencing BACs, approximately eightfold coverage results in most full shotgun assemblies having few (0 to 10) gaps. The large contigs resulting from these preliminary assemblies are immediately useful for many investigative purposes, such as detecting the presence of a particular gene or defined sequence of interest. For this reason, the sequencing centers promptly submit this data to GenBank to make it widely available to the research community. The next level of utility is reached when the sequence contigs are ordered and oriented relative to each other, allowing for the study of the relative placement of landmarks of interest. The ultimate sequence utility is reached only when the sequence is completely finished, with no gaps, ambiguities, or misassemblies (Mardis et al., 2002).

Finishing Standards

To ensure a consistent level of sequence quality throughout the human genome, the International Human Genome Consortium met and defined the *Standard Finishing Practices and Annotation of Problem Regions for the Human Genome Project* in 2001. These rules set minimum standards and maximum tolerances for regions such as single-stranded, single-chemistry, and single-plasmid coverage where the ability to represent the source DNA accurately potentially is compromised. Naturally occurring regions of genomic DNA, such as long homopolymeric or short tandem repeat stretches and inverted repeats (hairpins), present extremely difficult or even impossible technical challenges, given currently available DNA sequencing methods. Measures to be taken to address these were detailed. Finally, standard tags and sequence annotations to alert end users to the presence of such features were specified.

Finishing Methods

As a consequence of the multiple contigs that result from a typical BAC assembly at eight times full-shotgun coverage, contigs are not ordered and oriented automatically (sometimes referred to as O&O or OnO). The first step is to identify outermost contigs by identifying those that are adjacent to the BAC cloning vector. Additional contigs can be ordered and oriented by inspecting for the presence of paired subclone end reads. That is, if one subclone end read is near the end of a contig and is oriented toward that end, a search for its mate may locate the other end of that subclone near the end of another contig. If available, multiple pairings across a gap provide greater confidence that the contig ends in question are truly adjacent, because rare chimeric subclones may be misleading. Such cases are referred to as *captured gaps*, because subclones containing the missing sequence are available. These subclones then are subjected to further sequencing attempts, either by repeating end reads with different chemistries to generate longer reads, or by custom primers that can be used to "walk" into the unknown sequences. Contig ends that do not have such paired reads are referred to as *uncaptured gaps*, because there are no known spanning subclones. In these cases, custom primers can be designed to sequence out from the ends of the contigs, using the original BAC as the sequencing template, in hopes of determining additional sequence data that will align with other contig ends. Using BAC DNA as a sequencing template technically is more challenging than using smaller subclone DNA, making it a secondary strategy. Another approach to sequencing uncaptured gaps is to design PCR primers such that each primer at a contig has a compatible mate in each of the potential contig ends to which it may be adjacent. Successful PCR products indicate the correct pairing of PCR primers and hence contig ends. If necessary, these PCR products then can serve as sequencing substrates.

Sequencing gaps can result from secondary structures, particularly high-melting temperature hairpin loops. If these are in captured caps, subclones can be subjected to yet another level of subcloning, such as transposons or "shatter" libraries, where DNA is sheared to very small (hundreds of basepairs) pieces. The goal is to create subclones that disrupt the secondary structures.

An important step in the process of finishing is the inspection of apparent contigs for misassemblies that result from repetitive sequences found in the original DNA. These can be detected by the presence of paired end reads that are not properly oriented toward each other or that are at distances that are not compatible with the expected subclone sizes. The presence of high-quality discrepancies in sequence alignments is another valuable clue that inappropriate alignments have occurred. Typically, such misassemblies are found and corrected through the use of assembly editors, such as Consed.

Consed

Consed is a program commonly used for viewing and editing sequence assemblies. It takes as its input the ace-formatted output of assembly programs like phrap and CAP, displaying the assembled reads aligned to their consensus sequence in graphical format. It also has numerous features that allow finishers to find and correct base errors and misassemblies, to design primers, and to incorporate new finishing reads. Near the end of the finishing process, Consed has tools to help a finisher decide if the sequence has been finished to the standards that have been agreed on for the project.

Although the initial ace file is the output of an assembler, Consed also generates its output in ace format, and when an altered assembly is saved from Consed, an ace file is written with a version number one higher than the highest existing version for that assembly, enabling finishers to keep a history of the finishing process. Because Consed was developed in conjunction with phrap, the ace file format contains information specific to phrap assemblies (e.g., the identity of the read that determines the consensus base at each position, the quality trim points for each read, and the regions of each read that align to the final consensus).

When an ace file is opened in Consed, the main window (Figure 13.7) displays a list of contigs, along with each contig's length in bases and the number of reads it contains, and a read list detailing the exact location of each read in the assembly. The main window also contains buttons allowing the user to search for a particular sequence (either in the contig sequences or within individual reads), to add or remove reads, or to make use of several other features that are detailed later in this section.

Double clicking on any contig in the main window's contig list opens the Aligned Reads window (Figure 13.8), showing the contig's consensus sequence with the read sequences aligned to it. In Consed's default configuration, all base characters in this window have backgrounds of white, gray, or black, depending on their

quality scores, with white indicating a base with quality score of at least 40. Bases in reads are colored red if they disagree with the consensus, but with various selections from the Color menu, Consed can display bases with colors that indicate which read determined the consensus sequence or whether a base has been edited. At the bottom of the Aligned Reads window, navigation buttons allow the user to move forward or backward through the contig or to advance directly to the beginning or end of the contig. Clicking on a read name highlights it and makes it available for pasting into another window. In addition, the consensus sequence of a contig can be written to a file in FASTA format from this window.

Middle clicking on a base in one or more of the aligned reads opens a trace viewer, where multiple traces can be viewed simultaneously to identify compressions or to assess quality (Figure 13.9). It is within the trace viewer, where a trace can be carefully examined, that it is possible to edit its sequence simply by overstriking base characters in the line labeled edt (a base can be deleted by overstriking it with the "pad" character: an asterisk). If a stretch of bases is selected with the middle mouse button, a number of options are given to the user, such as changing these bases to Ns or making them high or low quality. This series of steps also is one way to define "read tags." The ace file format allows for tags to be attached to positions on both the consensus and the reads. These tags can indicate the locations of custom primers, known sequence repeats, or regions that should be ignored by finishers, and are displayed in the aligned reads window with a background color specific to the tag type. In addition, custom tags can be defined to have specific meanings and are displayed in colors the user chooses.

The Navigate menu allows easy navigation through the assembly to view all sites of interest in any of several categories simply by hitting a next button. Regions of low-quality, high-quality bases that do not align to or match the consensus sequence, single-subclone or single-strand and chemistry regions, and even open reading frames can be traversed, and of course, tags of any kind can be viewed as well, including the sites of experiments recommended by autofinish (Gordon et al., 2001). Consed also displays, in green, two types of read tags that phrap writes to its ace file: the matchElsewhere-HighQuality and matchElsewhereLowQuality tags, which can be used to identify a repeat or an area that can be joined.

In addition to information about the assembly contained in the ace file, Consed also reads information about each read from its phd-formatted file. A perl script, determineReadTypes.perl, which should be run before assembly from within the phredPhrap script,

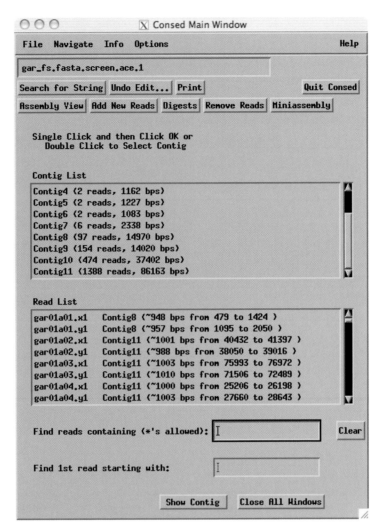

FIGURE 13.7 Consed's main window. From the Contig List, double clicking a contig name displays that contig in an Aligned Reads window, and double clicking a read in the Read List positions the aligned reads window at that read's start. Buttons in the main window open the Assembly View and Miniassembly features or allow users to search for a particular nucleotide sequence, compare computer-generated restriction digests to digests performed in the laboratory, and add reads to or remove them from the assembly. The main window's menus allow the user to save an ace file, to navigate through the assembly based on different criteria, or to change Consed's parameters.

appends tags to each of a project's phd files indicating the library, template, and primer used to create each read; it can be customized to deduce this information from the name of a read using either locally specified naming conventions or a database call. In addition, Consed reads from the phd files the same information about chemistry and direction of reads that is available to phrap via the phd2fasta script. All of this information

about reads enables Consed to order and orient contigs using read pair information and to find regions of the assembly with single-strand, single-chemistry coverage or single-subclone coverage.

One of Consed's most powerful features is the ability to break and join contigs. When an assembler has joined reads incorrectly (or "misassembled" them), a finisher can choose to pull out individual reads or groups

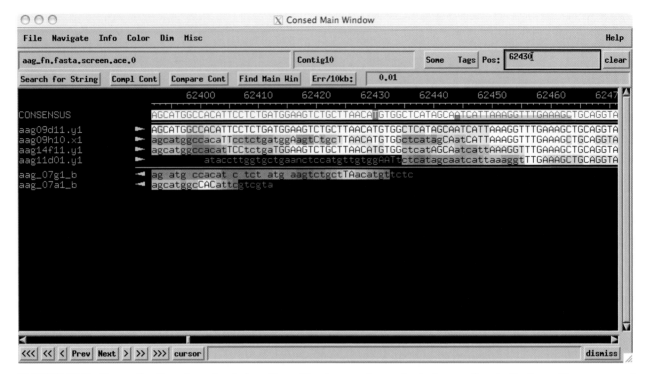

FIGURE 13.8 Consed's aligned reads window. Bases' backgrounds are shaded according to their quality score, and read bases are colored red when they disagree with the contig's consensus sequence. In a Unix environment, right clicking on a readname displays information about the read's template, primer, and chemistry, and middle clicking on a read's sequence opens the trace window. The consensus tag displayed in yellow indicates the location of a custom primer (used to create the two reads on the lower strand).

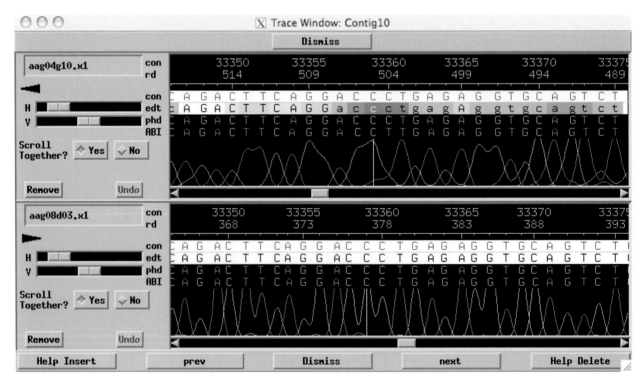

FIGURE 13.9 Consed's trace window. From this window, the actual trace data can be viewed, base calls can be edited, and multiple traces can be compared. The slide bars on the left allow the user to alter the horizontal and vertical scale of the chromatogram.

of reads or to break entire contigs into two separate sets of reads. However, if an assembler has failed to join two contigs that actually overlap, Consed can align the contig sequences and allow the user to view the alignment and then join them. In addition, reads that were not included initially when the assembly program ran can be aligned to existing contigs and then incorporated.

For a more coarse-grained view of contigs and how they may be oriented in the sequenced DNA, Consed has a function called Assembly View. Assembly View displays much of the same information that was formerly available using the phrapview perl script distributed with phrap and cross_match, but because it is run from within Consed, this information is displayed with respect to the contigs in their current state, whereas phrapview allowed this information to be viewed only with respect to the contigs as they were assembled by phrap. Assembly view is accessible from the main window by clicking the Assembly View button.

When opened, Assembly View displays the contigs as ruled bars, with read and forward–reverse read pair depth plotted above them. The *read depth* is simply the number of read bases of quality phred 20 or more aligned at a position in the contig. An especially high read depth could indicate a repeat that has been assembled together incorrectly. The *read pair depth* is the number of consistent forward–reverse read pairs that straddle a contig position. A read pair consists of two reads, one with a forward primer and one with a reverse, from the same subclone template; they are consistent if the reads are oriented toward each other and span a distance within three standard deviations of the mean insert length for that subclone's library. If the read pair depth is smaller than the read depth at a position, a strong possibility of misassembly exists at that position.

Within Assembly View, it also is possible to display the locations of all forward–reverse read pairs, or only the ones that connect two different contigs or are inconsistent. Consed displays these pairs as lines that connect the starting points of their component reads. Consed uses this read pair information to order and orient the contigs, but it is still possible to change this orientation within Assembly View, moving and complementing contigs. In addition to read pairs, Assembly View also can display the alignments that result when the contig sequences are compared with themselves using cross_match, and these alignments can be filtered so that only alignments with a specified minimum length or percent similarity are displayed. Results of filtering on the basis of percent similarity can be misleading, however, because a small alignment with a very high degree of similarity could be contained within a larger one that is less similar. These matches are displayed as orange (uncomplemented) and

black (complemented) bands between regions; it is possible to view the alignment by clicking on it and selecting Show Alignment, which brings up an alignment window that can be used to join the contigs based on that sequence match.

When a set of reads is known to be from the same small region (e.g., reads from a shatter library of a single subclone), it is possible to use phredPhrap to assemble them separately and then to incorporate them into the larger assembly using Consed's Miniassembly option. This feature is also especially useful for correcting misassemblies. Inconsistent read pairs can be pulled out of their contigs and then assembled as a group so that they become consistent.

All of the Consed features described to this point have dealt with tools for "sorting" assemblies, a process that can be loosely defined as rearranging reads to reflect more accurately the true locations of their templates. However, in general, to finish a BAC clone or other region of sequence, experiments must be carried out. Consed provides multiple tools for designing these finishing reactions.

After an assembly for a clone is known to be sorted accurately, Consed can be run in autoFinish mode. In this mode, Consed recommends reactions that it calculates will close gaps or will correct more than some minimum number of expected errors specified by the user. The program can be configured to call only specific types of finishing reads (e.g., only universal primer reactions, custom primer reactions, or whole clone reads). It also has the capability to recommend PCR experiments and the use of shatter libraries. Consed also can be configured not to use certain templates or libraries (if, for example, certain subclones have been discarded and are unavailable). After recommended experiments have been completed and their reads incorporated into an assembly, when autoFinish is run again, it will assess the success rate of the previous set of experiments and will alter its recommendations accordingly.

If a finisher is designing experiments manually, Consed can be used to design custom primers. Each primer is checked for length, melting temperature, false annealing sites on the specified template (be it just the subclone and its vector or the entire BAC clone and its vector), self-complementarity (potential to form primer–dimer pairs), and a specified minimum consensus quality at each base. The maximum number of bases in a mononucleotide repeat within a primer also can be specified. When Consed is asked to find a custom primer for priming on a subclone template or the whole clone, it will display a list of all primers satisfying all the criteria relating to the above-mentioned properties, and the user then can select whichever primer they choose to accept. Primers are written to the ace file as consensus tags, which can be extracted for database tracking and oligonucleotide ordering.

Finally, as a project nears completion, Consed has tools to quantify some of the criteria that are established for a project to be finished. The absence of gaps is obviously apparent, but the overall number of errors per 10,000 bases also is reported. The number of bases in single-strand, single-chemistry regions and the number of bases in single-subclone regions can be quantified, and the virtual restriction digest of the consensus sequence can be computed and compared against an actual digest for numerous different restriction enzymes.

Consed has parameters to customize almost every aspect of its appearance and behavior. Things as trivial as the width of a window or as important as the melting temperature of a primer can be set by changing the values of Consed parameters. Because Consed sets its parameters by examining three separate configuration files, these parameters can be customized to both a user's and a site's preferences. For each parameter, Consed begins by assigning to it its default value. Then, assuming it exists, it reads a user configuration file named `.consedrc` located in the user's home directory. Any parameter assignment located in this file overrides the default parameter value. Next, if the environment variable `CONSEDRC` is set to the name of an existing file, assignments within that file override the current values of their parameters. Finally, if the current working directory (the `edit_dir`) contains a file called .consedrc, the values in that file override the current values of their parameters. Once all three of these files have been examined and their values assigned, the resulting parameters are used by the program.

INTEGRATING CLONE SEQUENCES IN LARGER ASSEMBLIES

Finished Versus Ordered and Oriented Versus Full-Shotgun Sequences

This chapter has covered, in detail, the process of assembling shotgun reads from large insert clones (most commonly BACs) into contiguous sequence, as well as assembling WGS reads. This section discusses how to assemble BAC clones accurately and efficiently into larger assemblies of nonredundant consensus sequence (i.e., supercontigs). The ability to accurately assemble separate overlapping BAC clones into supercontigs not surprisingly is quite dependent on the accuracy of the starting sequence. Therefore, finished BAC sequence is

obviously the best starting product. However, because of the time and cost involved in finishing BAC sequences, this is not practical for all sequencing projects. Some BAC clones currently exist in only the shotgun phase, in which the sequence is comprised of nonordered and nonoriented contigs (Figure 13.10). Although this sequence is useful for many purposes, it is difficult to assemble into larger supercontigs correctly because the order and orientation of the pieces are unknown. Therefore, some sequencing centers generate an intermediate phase of the BAC clone that consists of ordered and oriented contigs that still contains gaps and low-quality regions that are, by definition, not a finished sequence. However, this sequence easily can be used in creating larger assembled data sets. These different stages of BAC clone submissions are available in GenBank and have the following nomenclature:

PHASE 1: Draft sequence; nonordered, nonoriented contigs; contains gaps

PHASE 2: Draft sequence; ordered and oriented contigs; may contain gaps

PHASE 3: Finished sequence; high-quality sequence with no sequencing gaps.

The generation of shotgun (phase 1) and finished (phase 3) sequences was discussed earlier in this chapter. How are the separate contigs of a shotgun BAC clone ordered and oriented to generate a phase 2 sequence? The first step is to determine the BAC ends by analyzing the raw sequence data for the clipped cloning vector. All the remaining contigs then are organized in relation to the end contigs. When sequencing is performed on both ends of the original shotgun sequencing template and paired end reads are generated, it often is possible to use this information to determine the order and orientation of internal contigs using the same finishing software tools described earlier, namely the Assembly View option in Consed. However, the gaps between some contigs are not captured in a single subclone template and can not be ordered or oriented by read pair information alone. In these cases, PCR primers are designed from each end of the contig(s) in question, and combinatorial PCR reactions are performed on the original BAC clone DNA. Any positive result indicates a correct primer pair and orders and orients the contig. In addition, it often is possible to use known, publicly available sequences from the orthologous region of a related organism as a guide to ordering and orienting contigs in another organism. For example, one could use the finished human sequence to help order and orient contigs of a draft sequence baboon BAC clone. There are several alignment programs available to help with this task, one of which

Phase 1: Unfinished; unordered/unoriented contigs with gaps

Phase 2: Unfinished; ordered/oriented contigs with or without gaps

Phase 3: Finished; no gaps

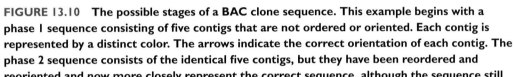

FIGURE 13.10 The possible stages of a **BAC** clone sequence. This example begins with a phase 1 sequence consisting of five contigs that are not ordered or oriented. Each contig is represented by a distinct color. The arrows indicate the correct orientation of each contig. The phase 2 sequence consists of the identical five contigs, but they have been reordered and reoriented and now more closely represent the correct sequence, although the sequence still contains gaps of various lengths and possible low-quality or misassembled regions. The final stage is a phase 3 high-quality sequence that has been finished in accordance with the International Human Genome Consortium finishing standards.

is PipMaker (see Chapter 5). This has a specific OnO option that performs the analysis of the alignment results for the user.

"Targeted" Region Assemblies

Given ordered and oriented (phase 2) or finished (phase 3) BACs, or both, as the starting data, the next step is to order and orient the BAC clones to generate a larger defined target. In many cases, the order of the BAC clones is already known through a preexisting physical map determined either through global genome-wide mapping efforts or specific comparative mapping projects of the "target" region in question (Chapter 3). A comparative BAC-based physical map can be created first by designing probes called *overgos* for a gene or region of interest in a known reference sequence (for example, human) and then using these probes to isolate potentially orthologous BACs in other related species (Thomas et al., 2002). DNA fingerprinting analysis of the BAC clones also can be used to generate potential tiling paths of overlapping clones. The orientation of the clones then can be determined by the sequence overlaps directly if two adjacent BAC clones overlap or, alternatively, if the adjacent clones do not overlap, by PipMaker analysis against

a reference sequence of a different sequenced organism (such as human).

As soon as the order and orientation of the BAC clones is known, the target region can be assembled. Although this would seem to be a straightforward and somewhat simple exercise, DNA sequence variation makes it quite challenging. Fortunately, there are some software tools that greatly aid in this process. Depending on the size and complexity of the target, there are a few different approaches. If only a limited number of BAC sequences need to be assembled, one easily could stitch these overlapping BACs together manually using, for example, BLAST alignments that give the nucleotide spans of the overlapping regions. However, this approach does not take into account the sequence variations that may be present in the overlapping sequence. There may be polymorphisms in the overlapping sequence of the two clones, for example an insertion in one clone. Furthermore, when joining two phase 2 sequences, there may be a sequencing gap(s) in the overlapping sequence in one clone that is not present in the other. For both of these cases, it would be preferable to use the sequence containing the most sequence data, that is, the overlapping sequence with the insertion or the sequence without sequencing gaps, respectively. DNA editing software can assist in this process; for example, the National Center for Biotechnology Information's (NCBI's) sequence submission tool Sequin has a useful Update Sequence feature that generates an alignment of the overlapping sequence that allows one easily to visualize the sequence discrepancies in the overlapping region. Again, if assembling a limited number of clones, Sequin also can be used to create the assembly, most simply by starting at one end of the tiling path and using Update Sequence to append the overlapping clones one by one. If, however, the target region consists of many clones, this manual approach is not practical. Fortunately, there are assembly programs specifically designed to assemble BAC sequences that use tiling path information. The TPF Processor from NCBI uses an ordered list of GenBank accession numbers or user-supplied sequences not present in GenBank, or both, to generate the following output files:

1. A FASTA file of the assembled non-redundant supercontig

2. Quality scores of the nucleotides of the original GenBank submissions used in the assembly, if the quality scores were submitted to GenBank along with the sequence; quality scores are currently required for phase 1 and 2 high-throughput genomic (HTG) submissions, but are optional for finished phase 3 submissions.

3. An .agp file that describes how the supercontig was built (the nucleotide spans of each GenBank submission that were used in the final assembly).

The input must be a Tiling Path Format (TPF) file consisting of three columns. Column 1 contains one of the following: (1) the GenBank accession number of the BAC clone sequence, (2) a reference name for a user-supplied sequence not present in GenBank, or (3) the word *GAP* if the adjacent BACs do not overlap. Column 2 can contain either (1) the clone name of the BAC, (2) "+" or "−" to indicate orientation of the sequence, or (3) the estimated size of a GAP (default is 50,000 bp). Finally, column 3 contains the user-defined output name of the resulting contig (i.e., `Baboon_contig`). The TPF Processor then uses this tiling path of sequences and attempts to generate a single nonredundant supercontig.

Unfortunately, nucleotide differences in the overlapping sequence resulting from either low sequence quality (especially surrounding sequence gaps in phase 2 submissions) or polymorphisms (for example, insertions or deletions) can lead to misassemblies or incorrect joins in the resulting supercontig. Likewise, small overlaps, especially with polymorphisms, sometimes result in alignments too weak to force a join. Therefore, it is always important to perform quality checks of the resulting assembly. Another great benefit of the TPF Processor is that it has a number of allowable user commands that can override the original assembly. They include the ability to add overlaps between two adjacent clones that had an alignment that was either too weak (because of nucleotide discrepancies) or too short for the automated assembler to recognize.

Complete Genome Assemblies Using All Available Data

In the end, the ultimate goal in genomic sequencing is to generate an assembly of the entire genome of a particular organism. There has been much debate over the advantages and disadvantages of shotgun sequencing BAC clones versus whole genome shotgun sequencing. BAC clone sequences are more expensive and time consuming to generate, especially high-quality finished phase 3 sequence. WGS reads are random across the entire genome, and although they in general are more cost effective and are quicker to produce, they also tend to be of lower quality than a finished BAC sequence with a higher number of gaps. WGS reads also are much more difficult to place in an assembly without the accompanying mapping or tiling path information of BAC clones (because of the multitude of repeats in genomic DNA). However, many genomes currently are being sequenced using a combined approach of both BAC-based and whole genome shotgun. For example, the latest mouse genome assembly available from the Mouse Genome Sequencing Consortium/NCBI incorporates both WGS reads and BAC clones for that organism, as well as mapping information that indicates order of specific BAC clones used in the assembly. Two different algorithms were used to create the chromosome sequences for this mouse genome assembly (NCBI build no. 32). Some chromosomes were assembled first by using an assembly of available BAC clones (using a tiling path generated from available mapping data), and then WGS reads were added to that starting assembly to fill in gaps and further improve the quality of the assembly. Alternatively, other chromosomes used the WGS assembly as the starting point and then added BAC clone sequences to complete that sequence. It should be noted that like the Celera (Huson et al., 2001) and euler (Pevzner et al., 2001) genome assemblers, the mouse WGS assembly was generated with additional clone-end sequencing information from clone libraries of sizes ranging from 2 to 40 Kb. The smaller libraries (e.g., 2 Kb) were useful in local assembly, whereas the larger libraries (e.g., 40 Kb) helped with ordering larger intermediate contigs.

▮ SUMMARY

Over the past decade, a variety of approaches to genomic sequencing and assembly have been pioneered and enhanced, and continue to evolve. The powerful techniques of high-throughput clone fingerprinting, BAC-end sequencing, probe-content mapping, hierarchical mapped-clone-based sequencing, and whole-genome shotgun sequencing are being used alone or in a variety of combinations that appropriately match resources available with specific project goals, that in turn catalyze the advancement of genomic studies for large numbers of interesting organisms. Ultimately, the availability of genomic sequences will allow us to compare and contrast, leading to the identification of all genes and elucidating the mechanisms by which their expression is regulated.

▮ WORKED EXAMPLE

A phase I (unordered and unoriented) genomic rabbit sequence contains a gene of interest. However, it would be much easier to annotate this gene and to analyze the remaining sequence for potential regulatory regions if the sequence was ordered and oriented.

The phase I rabbit sequence consists of seven unordered and unoriented contigs:

```
LOCUS              AC124040                208507 bp
DNA          linear        HTG   08-JUN-2002
DEFINITION    Oryctolagus cuniculus clone LB1-18E1, WORKING
DRAFT SEQUENCE,   7
                      unordered pieces.
ACCESSION     AC124040
VERSION        AC124040.1  GI:21358706
KEYWORDS    HTG;   HTGS_PHASE1; HTGS_DRAFT.
SOURCE         Oryctolagus cuniculus (rabbit)
```

As was mentioned in the chapter, the Order and Orient Contigs option of PipMaker can be used in this analysis by aligning the unordered and unoriented rabbit sequence to a human reference of finished sequence that contains the orthologous region. First, download the following files: FASTA files for the rabbit phase I sequence and the human reference sequence, and the human reference masked file (this is an output of RepeatMasker and is used to minimize artificial sequence similarities that result from known repeats). From the PipMaker Web page, select Advanced PipMaker. Then, select Browse for First Sequence Filename and find the human reference sequence. Repeat this for Second Sequence Filename (the rabbit phase I sequence) and First sequence mask (the human reference masked file). Because PipMaker results are returned by E-mail, enter a valid E-mail address in the box entitled Your E-mail Address. Leave the First Sequence Exons, First Sequence Underlay, Annotations, and User Supplied alignment boxes empty. Select the Order and Orient Contigs box and click Submit. Results are sent via E-mail and include the following

OnO table:

```
490869-565055        98.7          >contig7
565938-566795        10.4          >contig2-
566805-583393        41.3          >contig3
583394-633374        83.5          >contig6-
633777-659879        24.8          >contig5-
658617-659825         9.7          >contig1
659880-672482        10.0          >contig4-
```

The first column gives the highest and lowest nucleotide number from the human reference sequence that aligned to each contig of the rabbit phase I sequence. The second column is the normalized score of the contig's highest-scoring local alignment; the higher the score, the better the alignment. The final column lists the original contig number; if it is followed by "–," it indicates the alignment is the reverse complement of the rabbit sequence. Based on this alignment analysis, the predicted order and orientation of the phase I rabbit sequence can be graphically represented as:

```
contig7 (88774bp)   2 (6132bp) 3 (10387bp) 6 (51636bp) 5 (33833bp) 1 (4187bp) 4 (12958bp)
```

(→ + strand; ← – strand)

This rabbit BAC clone also has been submitted to GenBank by the sequencing center as phase 2 (AC124040.2). To confirm the PipMaker prediction, simply perform an alignment of the PipMaker predicted reordered sequence to the phase 2 submission AC124040.2.

▮ PROBLEM SET

A phase I (unordered and unoriented) genomic baboon sequence contains a region of biological interest.

The phase I baboon sequence consists of five unordered and unoriented contigs:

```
LOCUS           AC098645              193186 bp    DNA       linear
HTG   27-OCT-2001
DEFINITION   Papio cynocephalus anubis clone RP41-470J23, WORKING DRAFT
                    SEQUENCE, 5 unordered pieces.
ACCESSION    AC098645
VERSION        AC098645.1    GI:16506407
KEYWORDS    HTG; HTGS_PHASE1; HTGS_DRAFT.
SOURCE           Papio cynocephalus anubis (olive baboon)
```

Predict the order and orientation of all contigs in the phase 1 sequence using PipMaker. Do the results of question 1 agree with the actual order and orientation represented in the phase 2 sequence? What are the major differences between the phase 2 and phase 3 submissions of this BAC clone?

INTERNET RESOURCES

The Atlas Assembler	http://www.hgsc.bcm.tmc.edu/downloads/software/atlas/
Description of Phase 1, 2 and 3 records	http://www.ncbi.nlm.nih.gov/HTGS/
Finishing Standards	http://www.genome.wustl.edu/Overview/g16stand.php
Mouse assembly details	http://www.ncbi.nlm.nih.gov/genome/seq/NCBIContigInfo.html#MGSCV3
phrap	http://www.phrap.org
PipMaker	http://bio.cse.psu.edu/pipmaker/
Sequin	http://www.ncbi.nlm.nih.gov/Sequin/index.html
TPF assembly tool	http://www.ncbi.nlm.nih.gov/projects/zoo_seq/

FURTHER READING

GREEN, E. D. (2001). Strategies for the systematic sequencing of complex genomes. *Nat. Rev. Genet.* 2, 573–583. This paper provides a comprehensive summary and discussion of the various strategies used in sequencing genomes from multiple organisms, including shotgun, whole-genome, and hybrid sequencing approaches.

STEIN, L. (2003). Assembling sequences. In *Current Protocols in Bioinformatics*. This chapter provides additional background information on large-scale sequencing, as well as extensive guidance in the use of the tools described here.

REFERENCES

BATZOGLOU, S., JAFFE, D. B., STANLEY, K., BUTLER, J., GNERRE, S., MAUCELI, E., BERGER, B., MESIROV, J.P., LANDER, E. S. (2002). ARACHNE: a whole-genome shotgun assembler. *Genome Res* 12, 177–189.

BONFIELD, J. K., AND STADEN, R. (2002). ZTR: a new format for DNA sequence trace data. *Bioinformatics* 18, 3–10.

DEAR, S., AND STADEN, R. (1992). A standard file format for data from DNA sequencing instruments. *DNA Seq.* 3, 107–110.

EWING, B. (2002). vtrace chromatogram viewer. Personal communication.

EWING, B., AND GREEN, P. (1998). Base-calling of automated sequencer traces using phred. II. Error probabilities. *Genome Res.* 8, 186–194.

EWING, B., HILLIER, L., et al. (1998). Base-calling of automated sequencer traces using phred. I. Accuracy assessment. *Genome Res.* 8, 175–185.

FLEISCHMANN, R. D., ADAMS, M. D., et al. (1995). Whole-genome random sequencing and assembly of Haemophilus influenzae Rd. *Science* 269, 496–512.

GORDON, D., ABAJIAN, C., et al. (1998). Consed: a graphical tool for sequence finishing. *Genome Res.* 8, 195–202.

GORDON, D., DESMARAIS, C., et al. (2001). Automated finishing with autofinish. *Genome Res.* 11, 614–625.

GREEN, E. D. (2001). Strategies for the systematic sequencing of complex genomes. *Nat. Rev. Genet.* 2, 573–583.

GREEN, P. (1997). Against a whole-genome shotgun. *Genome Res.* 7, 410–417.

HUANG, X., WANG, J., et al. (2003). PCAP: a whole-genome assembly program. *Genome Res.* 13, 2164–2170.

HUSON, D. H., REINERT, K., et al. (2001). Design of a compartmentalized shotgun assembler for the human genome. *Bioinformatics* 17(Suppl 1), S132–S139.

KECECIOGLU, J., AND MYERS, E. (1995). Combinatorial algorithms for DNA sequence assembly. *Algorithmica* 13, 7–51.

LANDER, E. S., LINTON, L. M., et al. (2001). Initial sequencing and analysis of the human genome. *Nature* 409, 860–921.

LANDER, E. S., AND WATERMAN, M. S. (1988). Genomic mapping by fingerprinting random clones: a mathematical analysis. *Genomics* 2, 231–239.

MARDIS, E., MCPHERSON, J., et al. (2002). What is finished, and why does it matter? *Genome Res.* 12, 669–671.

MULLIKIN, J. C., AND NING, Z. (2003). The phusion assembler. *Genome Res.* 13, 81–90.

MYERS, E. W., SUTTON, G. G., et al. (2000). A whole-genome assembly of Drosophila. *Science* 287, 2196–2204.

PEVZNER, P. A., TANG, H., et al. (2001). An Eulerian path approach to DNA fragment assembly. *Proc. Natl. Acad. Sci. U. S. A.* 98, 9748–9753.

SANGER, F., NICKLEN, S., et al. (1977). DNA sequencing with chain-terminating inhibitors. *Proc. Natl. Acad. Sci. U. S. A.* 74, 5463–5467.

SODERLUND, C., LONGDEN, I., et al. (1997). FPC: a system for building contigs from restriction fingerprinted clones. *Comput. Appl. Biosci.* 13, 523–535.

SUTTON, G. G., WHITE, O., et al. (1995). TIGR assembler: a new tool for assembling large shotgun sequencing projects. *Genome Sci. Technol.* 1, 9–19.

THOMAS, J. W., PRASAD, A. B., et al. (2002). Parallel construction of orthologous sequence-ready clone contig maps in multiple species. *Genome Res.* 12, 1277–1285.

VENTER, J. C., ADAMS, M. D., et al. (2001). The sequence of the human genome. *Science* 291, 1304–1351.

WEBER, J. L., AND MYERS, E. W. (1997). Human whole-genome shotgun sequencing. *Genome Res.* 7, 401–409.

WENDL, M. C., AND WATERSTON, R. H. (2002). Generalized gap model for bacterial artificial chromosome clone fingerprint mapping and shotgun sequencing. *Genome Res.* 12, 1943–1949.

▌ KEY TERMS

assembler
BAC (bacterial artificial chromosome)
basecaller
captured gap
chimeric read
chromatogram
complexity adjustment
consensus
contig
Library
OnO (or O&O)
plasmid
primer
restriction fingerprint
supercontig (or scaffold)
tiling path format (TPF)
walking
word matching

This chapter was written by Drs. Hansen, Thomas, and Bouffard in their private capacity. No official support or endorsement by the National Institutes of Health or the United States Department of Health and Human Services is intended or should be inferred.

Phylogenetic Analysis

FIONA S. L. BRINKMAN

Bioinformatics: A Practical Guide to the Analysis of Genes and Proteins, Third Edition, edited by
Andreas D. Baxevanis and B.F. Francis Ouellette.
ISBN 0-471-47878-4 Copyright © 2005 John Wiley & Sons, Inc.

INTRODUCTION

What do BLAST, FASTA, multiple sequence alignment, and protein motif searching have in common? All use evolutionary theory as the basis for their assumptions. An understanding of evolutionary theory, therefore, is critical to appropriate interpretation of bioinformatic results. It is necessary for gene family identification, gene discovery (e.g., inferring gene function, gene annotation), identifying the origins of a genetic disease, characterization of polymorphisms, and more. In many cases, researchers must expand their analyses further to include additional evolutionary analyses. For example, it has been well documented that "the closest BLAST hit is not often the nearest neighbor" (Koski & Golding, 2001); that is, the sequence that is listed first in the BLAST output as being similar to the query sequence is not necessarily the most similar sequence according to a phylogenetic analysis. Knowing how to handle such issues and appreciating the need to perform robust evolutionary analyses is an important component of high-caliber bioinformatics research.

Although evolutionary analysis is not covered in great detail here, this chapter discusses its importance in sequence analysis and reviews the basics of evolutionary analysis, as well as popular phylogenetic analysis methods used for inferring relationships between genes, proteins, or organisms. To this end, the chapter focuses on:

▶ The need to interpret bioinformatics analyses involving sequence alignments in an evolutionary context

▶ The importance of good-quality sequence alignments in any evolutionary analysis

▶ The fundamentals of phylogenetics and interpreting phylogenetic trees (with cautionary notes)

▶ The differences between common phylogenetic methods and software, and their appropriate use.

WHY LEARN MORE ABOUT PHYLOGENETICS AND OTHER EVOLUTIONARY ANALYSES?

High-caliber bioinformatics research requires strong knowledge of the both the algorithms and biological knowledge on which analyses are built. For phylogenetic analysis, there unfortunately is no all-purpose analysis recipe or pipeline that can be used (Hillis et al., 1993). Although numerous phylogenetic algorithms, procedures, and computer programs have been devised, their reliability and practicality are, in all cases, dependent on the structure and size of the data. The merits and pitfalls of various methods are the subject of often acrimonious debates in taxonomic and phylogenetic jour-nals. Some of these debates are summarized in useful reviews of phylogenetics (Saitou, 1996; Li, 1997; Swofford et al., 1996). An especially concise introduction to molecular phylogenetics is provided by Hillis et al. (1993).

The danger of generating incorrect results is inherently greater in computational phylogenetics than in many other fields of science. The events yielding a phylogeny obviously happened in the past and can be only inferred or estimated (with some exceptions; see Hillis et al., 1994). Despite the well-documented limitations of available phylogenetics procedures, current biological literature is replete with examples of conclusions derived from the results of analyses in which data had been simply submitted to one or another phylogenetics program. Occasionally, the limiting factor in phylogenetic analysis is not so much the computational method used; rather, it is often the users' understanding of what the method is doing with the data. Therefore, adequate understanding of evolutionary theory and phylogenetic analysis approaches is critical. This guide to phylogenetic analysis attempts to introduce a conceptual approach that describes some of the most important principles underlying the most widely and easily applied methods of phylogenetic analysis of biological sequences and their interpretation. Practical phylogenetic analysis should be viewed as a search for a correct model, as much as it is a search for the correct tree. In this context, some of the particular models assumed by various popular methods and how these models may affect analysis of particular data sets is considered. Finally, some examples of the application of particular methods to the inferences of evolutionary history are provided. Note that the principles for DNA analysis are discussed initially, although most also apply to protein sequences (except where further description of protein sequences is indicated). Because there is a growing interest in the analysis of protein sequences, the reader is directed to more in-depth descriptions of protein-specific problems, as reviewed by Felsenstein (1996). Remember, critical, conservative inferences in evolutionary analyses (and all bioinformatics analyses having an evolutionary basis) are vital to ensuring appropriate interpretation of results and useful predictions of protein function, gene relationships, and other relationships involving macromolecules.

BACKGROUND TERMINOLOGY AND THE BASICS

Phylogenetics is the study of evolutionary relationships. As alluded to above, phylogenetic analysis is the means of *inferring* or estimating these relationships. The evolutionary history inferred from phylogenetic analysis usually is depicted as branching (treelike) diagrams that represent an estimated pedigree of the inherited relationships among molecules ("gene trees"), organisms, or both. Phylogenetics sometimes is called *cladistics*, because the word *clade*, a set of descendants from a single ancestor, is derived from the Greek word for branch. However, cladistics is a particular method of hypothesizing about evolutionary relationships.

The basic tenet behind cladistics is that members of a group or clade share a common evolutionary history and are more related to each other than to members of another group. A given group is recognized by sharing unique features that were not present in distant ancestors. These shared derived characteristics can be anything from two organisms having developed a spine to two sequences having developed a mutation at a certain base pair of a gene. Usually, cladistic analysis is performed by comparing multiple characteristics, or "characters" at once, either multiple phenotypic characters or multiple base pairs or amino acids in a sequence.

There are three basic assumptions in cladistics:

▶ Any group of organisms are related by descent from a common ancestor (fundamental tenet of evolutionary theory)

▶ There is a bifurcating pattern of cladogenesis.

▶ Change in characteristics occurs in lineages over time (necessary for cladistics to work).

The resulting relationships from cladistic analysis are represented most commonly by a phylogenetic tree, as illustrated in Figure 14.1. Note how trees can be depicted in different visual ways. However, all trees contain the following basic elements:

▶ Clades: a monophyletic taxon; a group of organisms or genes that includes the most recent common ancestor of all of its members and all of the descendants of that most recent common ancestor. From the Greek word *klados*, meaning branch or twig.

▶ Taxons: any named group of organisms; not necessarily a clade.

▶ Branches: for some analyses, branch lengths correspond to the degree of divergence (e.g., in the artificial example in Figure 14.1, the analysis in (b) indicates that mouse is slightly more related to fly than human is to fly, whereas the analysis in (a) does not provide this information). Knowing whether branch lengths are significant requires knowledge of the analysis performed (as is discussed later in this chapter)

▶ nodes: any bifurcating branch point

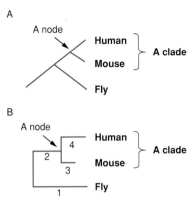

FIGURE 14.1 **Different ways to visualize a tree. In this example, the same tree is presented in both (a) and (b). Taxa are grouped into clades through a tree that comprises of a series of branches and nodes that mark bifurcating points in the branches. (a) Branch lengths are not significant (i.e., they do not indicate the degree of divergence, only what the branching order is). A clue indicating that a tree is illustrating only branching order is the equal length of branches and how they align flush with the name of each taxa. (b) The same tree with branch lengths indicating the degree of divergence that has been inferred from the analysis. By adding up branches between each taxa, one can estimated the degree of divergence between them. In this example, adding up branches 1, 2, and 3 indicates the degree of divergence between fly and mouse. Adding up the lengths of branches 1, 2, and 4 indicate the degree of divergence between fly and human. In this artificial example, the differences in branch length would infer that fly and mouse are slightly more related to each other than fly and human. Note that, in cases such as that shown in (b), only the horizontal branches are significant. The vertical branches are used just to separate out the taxa and to make them easier to view.**

Macromolecules, especially sequences, have surpassed morphological and other organismal characters as the most popular form of data for phylogenetic or cladistic analysis. It is this molecular phylogenetic analysis that is primarily introduced here. However, note that essentially all phylogenetic analyses are still bases on the analysis of characters. For morphological data, this can be the presence of hair or a certain shape in a bone. For sequence data analysis, each column of an alignment is considered to be a character, with each residue or base in the column representing the particular state of that character. It is important always to think of data in this way to ensure appreciation of the importance of a good multiple sequence alignment in phylogenetic analysis and of the importance of understanding the algorithms, assumptions, and models being used to analyze a data set. Only through such understanding, and the issues mentioned below, can effective interpretation of phylogenetic analyses be possible.

▌ INTERPRETATION

Know Your Model and Assumptions

Phylogenetic tree-building methods presume particular evolutionary models. For a given data set, these models can be violated because of occurrences such as the transfer of genetic material between organisms. Thus, when interpreting a given analysis, one always should consider the model used and its assumptions and should consider other possible explanations for the observed results. As an example, consider the tree in Figure 14.2. An investigation of organismal relationships in the tree suggests that eukaryote 1 is more related to bacteria than to the other eukaryotes. Because the vast majority of other cladistic analyses, including those based on morphological features, suggest that eukaryote 1 is more related to the other eukaryotes than to bacteria, for this analysis, the assumptions of a bifurcating pattern of evolution are incorrect. Horizontal gene transfer from an ancestor of

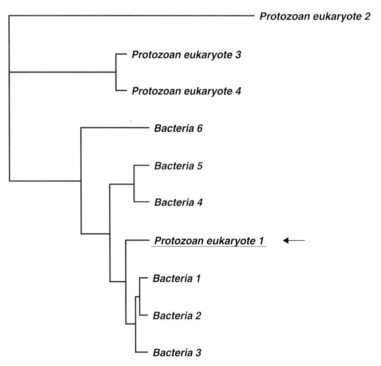

FIGURE 14.2 Example of a phylogenetic tree based on genes that does not match organismal phylogeny, suggesting horizontal gene transfer has occurred. The ancestor of protozoan eukaryote 1 (underlined and marked with an arrow) seems to have obtained the gene from the ancestor of bacteria 1, 2, and 3, because this is the simplest explanation for the results. This unexpected result is not without precedent: There have been a number of reported phylogenetic analyses that suggest that protozoa have taken up genes from bacteria, most probably from bacteria that they have ingested.

the bacterias 1, 2, and 3 to the ancestor of eukaryote 1 may have occurred, because this would most simply explain the results.

Models inherent in phylogenetics methods make additional "default" assumptions:

1. The sequence is correct and originates from the specified source

2. The sequences are homologous (i.e., are all descended in some way from a shared ancestral sequence)

3. Each position in a sequence alignment is homologous with every other in that alignment

4. Each of multiple sequences included in a common analysis has a common phylogenetic history with the others (e.g., there are no mixtures of nuclear and organellar sequences)

5. The sampling of taxa is adequate to resolve the problem of interest

6. Sequence variation among the samples is representative of the broader group of interest

7. The sequence variability in the sample contains phylogenetic signal adequate to resolve the problem of interest.

There are additional assumptions that are default in some methods but can be at least partially corrected for in others:

1. The sequences in the sample evolved according to a single stochastic process

2. All positions in the sequence evolved according to the same stochastic process

3. Each position in the sequence evolved independently.

Errors in published phylogenetic analyses often can be attributed to violations of one of the foregoing assumptions. Every sequence data set must be evaluated in view of these assumptions, and other possible explanations for the observed results must be considered.

The Importance of Differentiating Between Orthologs and Paralogs

As more genomes are sequenced, there is increasing interest in learning about protein or gene evolution (i.e., investigating gene phylogeny, rather than organismal phylogeny). This is primarily because this approach can aid our understanding of the functions of proteins and genes.

Studies of protein and gene evolution involve the comparison of homologs—sequences that have common ancestral origins but may or may not have common ac-

tivity. Such sequences that share an arbitrary threshold level of similarity determined by alignment of matching bases are termed *homologous*. They are inherited from a common ancestor that possessed similar structure, although the structure of the ancestor may be difficult to determine because it has been modified through descent. Again, homology refers to shared ancestry only, not to any level of similarity. *Similarity* is a quantifiable term that refers to a degree of relatedness between sequences, but does not necessarily reflect ancestry. Understanding the difference is important when you are performing evolutionary analysis, and when performing further ortholog analyses, mentioned below, to identify genes or proteins more likely to be similar functionally.

Homologs are most commonly either orthologs, paralogs, or xenologs:

▶ Orthologs: homologs produced by speciation. Orthologs are genes derived from a common ancestor that diverged because of divergence of the organisms with which they are associated. They tend to have similar function.

▶ Paralogs: homologs produced by gene duplication. Paralogs are genes derived from a common ancestral gene that duplicated within an organism and then diverged subsequently. They tend to have differing functions.

▶ Xenologs: homologs resulting from horizontal gene transfer between two organisms. The determination of whether a gene of interest recently was transferred into the current host by horizontal gene transfer often is difficult. Occasionally, the %G + C content may be so vastly different from the average gene in the current host that a conclusion of external origin is nearly inescapable; however, often it is unclear whether a gene has horizontal origins. Function of xenologs can be variable depending on how significant the change in context was for the horizontally moving gene; however, in general, the function tends to be similar.

Therefore, when trying to identify genes that are most functionally similar, aim to identify orthologs. An example of how the identification of orthologs and paralogs can be used to aid prediction of protein function is illustrated in Figure 14.3, and exercises for practice in identifying orthologs and paralogs are presented in Figure 14.4 and are discussed further below.

Examples of Multiple Interpretations

Even if one never constructs a phylogenetic tree, it is more than likely that interpretation of trees made by others will be necessary. Some discussion of detecting phylogenetic relationships therefore is in order.

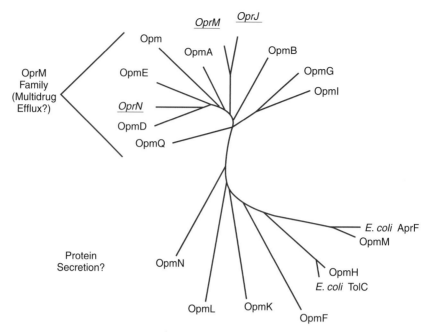

FIGURE 14.3 **An example of insight into protein function from an investigation of paralogs and orthologs.** *P. aeruginosa*, a bacteria that is one of the top three causes of opportunistic infections, is noted for its antimicrobial resistance and resistance to detergents. Three homologous outer membrane proteins, OprJ, OpM, and OprN, were identified as playing a role in this antimicrobial resistance by pumping different antimicrobials out of the cell as they enter. When the genome of this bacterium was sequenced, it was found that there were no fewer than 14 homologs of the genes encoding these three proteins (given names starting with Opm). Phylogenetic analysis showed that this 17-member family was divided into two clades, one containing all three genes with roles in antimicrobial efflux pumps (underlined italics). Two members of the other clade were found to share highest similarity with proteins AprF and TolC from another organism, *E. coli*. AprF and TolC are involved in secreting proteins. This analysis led to the hypothesis that the clade containing OprM, OprJ, and OprN, nicknamed the OprM family, comprises a series of paralogous genes involved in efflux of different antimicrobials or antimicrobial-like compounds. The other cluster, with homologs to AprF and TolC, may be a functionally rated group of paralogs involved in secretion of proteins (of which OpmM seems to be the ortholog of AprF and OpmH is likely the ortholog of TolC, based on the degree of divergence common between *P. aeruginosa* and *E. coli*). Currently, efforts are expanding to characterize *P. aeruginosa* with mutations in these genes to evaluate their ability to efflux antimicrobials. This phylogenetic analysis allowed us to prioritize the analysis of genes in this extended family, analyzing the OprM family genes first because they are more likely to have the functions of interest.

First, keep in mind that the following simple rules apply when identifying orthologs, paralogs, and xenologs: For orthologs, gene phylogeny matches organismal phylogeny. Therefore, if four genes in a tree are related to each other in the same way as the corresponding organisms from which they came, the genes are, most likely, orthologs. For paralogs, the gene phylogeny does not match organismal phylogeny, and there also is further evidence that there has been a gene duplication that has led to the formation of the paralogous genes. Multiple copies of homologs in the same species usually are paralogs. For a xenolog, the gene phylogeny does not match

A

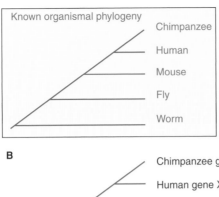

Known organismal phylogeny

Chimpanzee

Human

Mouse

Fly

Worm

Knowing the organismal phylogeny in Panel A, the Fly gene 1 is an ortholog of which genes according to the gene trees in panel B? What are the proposed orthologs of Mouse gene 3, according to the phylogenetic analysis in Panel C?

B

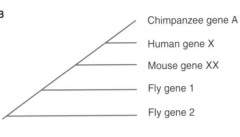

Chimpanzee gene A

Human gene X

Mouse gene XX

Fly gene 1

Fly gene 2

C

Chimpanzee gene y

Human gene W

Mouse gene 3

Worm gene L

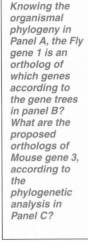

FIGURE 14.4 Identifying orthologs and paralogs. (Note that the following is derived from fabricated data, developed to illustrate this example as simply as possible.) Examine the known organismal phylogeny in (a) and note the relationships between species (branching order and distances in horizontal branches). Now, examine (B), which is the phylogeny inferred from an analysis of the Fly gene 1 gene and its proposed homologs. What are the proposed orthologs of Fly gene 1? What are the paralogs? What are the most likely orthologs and paralogs of Mouse gene 3, according to the analysis in (c)? According to the organismal phylogeny in (a) and the phylogeny of the genes in (b), one would propose that all the genes shown in (b) are orthologs of fly gene 1, except for the fly gene 2 gene. This is because all of the genes seem to match the organismal phylogeny, except for fly gene 2, which is another gene in the same species. Fly gene 2 likely arose as a result of an ancient gene duplication, and so is considered a paralog. In (c), the mouse gene 3 may be an ortholog of chimpanzee gene W and human gene W, because these genes share the same phylogeny as the reported organismal phylogeny. However, the worm gene L is not likely to be an ortholog of mouse gene 3, because it shares more similarity than expected for worm and mouse genes according to the level of divergence observed between the mouse, chimpanzee, and human genes. In both cases, though, note that the number of taxa examined is not enough to make very strong conclusions, and so usually one would propose orthology and then test their proposal by examining more taxa. Also note that in this simplistic case, the level of divergence of the orthologous genes matches the level of divergence of the organismal phylogeny. This does not have to be the case; as long as the divergence between genes is proportional to the relationships between the associated organisms, the proposal of orthology is reasonable.

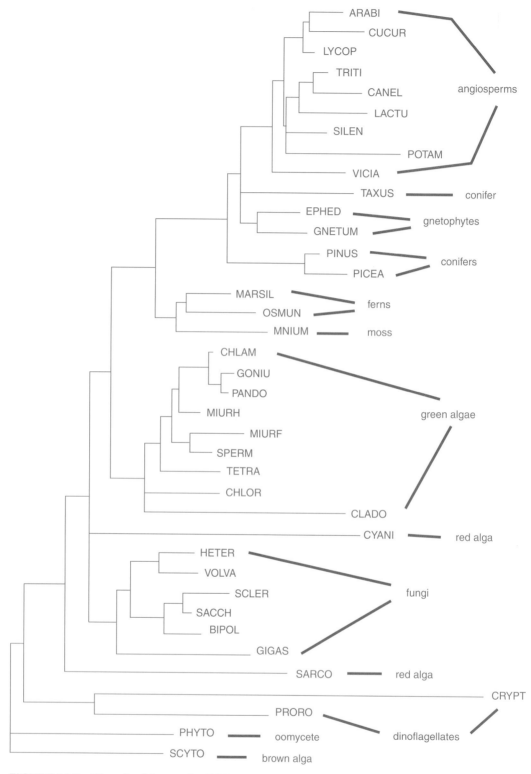

FIGURE 14.5   Clustal guide tree for 5.8S rDNA sequences of selected plants, fungi, and protists. The tree is an NJ (distance) resolution of pairwise sequence similarities determined by pairwise alignment according to specified (in this case, default) gap penalties in Clustal. Similarity is calculated as the proportion of pairwise shared bases, ignoring gap positions in either sequence. The tree can be generated as an end product or as a preliminary step in a multiple alignment

the organismal phylogeny in a tree where most genes do match organismal phylogeny well.

Examine the organismal phylogeny in the tree in Figure 14.4a. Now compare the branching order of these organisms with the gene trees shown in Figure 14.4b and 14.4c. Which genes are orthologs? Which are paralogs? Are there any xenologs? Note again the usefulness of using the criteria that orthologs match organismal phylogeny. This, of course, implies that one must know the organismal phylogeny (i.e., have a good estimate of it) before examining and interpreting any phylogenetic analysis of genes.

■ HOW TO CONSTRUCT A TREE

The Four Steps

A straightforward phylogenetic analysis consists of four steps:

▶ Constructing a multiple sequence alignment

▶ Determining the substitution model

▶ Tree building

▶ Tree evaluation.

Each step is critical for the analysis and should be handled accordingly. For example, a tree is only as good as the alignment it is based on. When performing a phylogenetic analysis, it often is insightful to build trees based on different modifications of the alignment to see how the proposed alignment influences the resulting tree.

Step 1: Alignment and Alignment Editing

Phylogenetic sequence data usually consists of a multiple sequence alignment; that is, the individual, aligned-base positions, commonly referred to as *sites*. These sites are equivalent to *characters* in theoretical phylogenetic

discussions, and the actual base (or gap) occupying a site is the *character state*.

Multiple alignment methods are reviewed in Chapter 12; however, this chapter reviews alignment methods in the context of phylogenetic analysis. Aligned sequence positions subjected to phylogenetic analysis represent a priori phylogenetic conclusions because the sites themselves (not the actual bases) are effectively assumed to be genealogically related or homologous. Sites in which one is confident that they are homologous and contain changes in character states that are useful for the given phylogenetic analysis are often referred to as *informative sites*.

Steps in building the alignment include selection of the alignment procedure(s) and extracting a phylogenetic data set from the alignment. The latter procedure requires determination of how ambiguously aligned regions and insertion–deletions (referred to as indels, or gaps) are treated in the tree-building procedure.

A typical alignment procedure involves the application of a program such as Clustal (ClustalW or ClustalX), followed by manual alignment editing and submission to a tree-building program. This procedure should be performed with the following considerations in mind.

How Much Computer Dependence? Fully computational multiple alignment sometimes is advocated on the grounds that manual editing is inexplicit, unobjective, or both (Gatesy et al., 1993). Usually, however, manual alignment editing is advocated (e.g., Thompson et al., 1994) because alignment algorithms and programs are not optimally adapted for phylogenetic alignment (see example in Figure 14.5).

Phylogenetic Criteria Preferred Some computational multiple alignment methods align sequences strictly based on the order they receive them, without any

---

FIGURE 14.5 *(continued)* procedure. Either way, it is saved to a **PHYLIP**-formatted tree file. For the multiple alignment procedure, the guide tree topology determines the sequence input order (outermost clusters are aligned first), and the branch lengths determine the sequence weights. This tree includes (see Hershkovitz & Lewis, 1996) several groupings that contradict broader evidence (e.g., polyphyly of conifers and red algae; monophyly of ferns plus moss). Such inaccuracies potentially mislead the multiple alignment. This tree was drawn and printed using the tree-drawing feature in the Macintosh version of **PAUP**, followed by aesthetic modification in Macintosh graphics programs. The general tree-viewing and tree-drawing protocol for **PAUP** is as follows: (1) execute a **PAUP** file containing the same taxon names as the tree; (2) import the treefile using the **GETTREES** command, specifying the option to retain the branch lengths in the treefile; (3) draw the tree using the **PRINT TREES** command, again specifying use of input branch lengths; and (4) save the tree to a **PICT** file using the Preview option in the pop-up Print Trees menu. Note that for using the **PAUP** tree-drawing tool, the content of the executed data file (sequences and alignment) is not important, as long as the taxon names are the same. There may even be additional taxa in the data file, as long as these are ignored using the **DELETE TAXA** command.

consideration of their relationship; however, many current methods (e.g., Clustal, PileUp, or ALIGN in ProPack) align according to an explicitly phylogenetic criterion (a *guide tree*), which is generated on the basis of initial pairwise sequence alignments. The theory is that sequences that are more closely related should be aligned first, and then the resulting groups of sequences, which share less relatedness between groups but still have a common ancestor, should share the same ancestral indels and therefore could be more accurately aligned subsequently.

The guide tree (Figure 14.5) from Clustal is formatted as a *Phylogeny Inference Package* (PHYLIP) tree file and can be imported in various tree-drawing programs. Some programs are designed simultaneously (recursively) to optimize an alignment and a phylogenetic tree (e.g., TreeAlign and MALIGN. In theory, an optimal simultaneous solution or set of solutions to an alignment and phylogeny problem exists, but the hazard of the recursive approach lies in the possibility of canalizing the result toward a wrong or incomplete solution (Thorne & Kishino, 1992). Thus, following the tree-building analysis based on the alignment, one should consider whether other evolutionary relationships would be favored using a slightly modified alignment.

Alignment Parameter Estimation The most important parameters in an alignment method are those that determine the placement of indels or gaps in an alignment of length-variable sequences. Alignment parameters should vary dynamically with evolutionary divergence (Thompson et al., 1994), such that base mismatches are more likely as the sequences become more divergent. Alignment parameters also should be adjusted to prevent closely related overrepresented sequences from entraining alignment of underrepresented sequences (Thompson et al., 1994, Hughey et al., 1996). This is accomplished by downweighting the alignment score contribution of the closely related sequences. Both these dynamic parameter adjustments are implemented in Clustal.

Which Alignment Procedure Is Best for Phylogenetic Analysis? The short answer is the method that is closest to understanding the evolutionary relationships between the sequences being examined. Unless phylogenetic relations are known beforehand, there is no clear way to determine which alignment procedure is best for a given phylogenetic analysis. In general, it is inadvisable simply to subject a computer-generated alignment to a tree-building procedure because the latter is blind to errors in the former. However, as long as the entire alignment is scrutinized in view of independent phylogenetic evidence (for example, are there a number of gaps next to each other in the alignment that are more likely to be one gap because, from an evolutionary standpoint, one insertion or deletion is more plausible than many?), methods such as Clustal that use some degree of phylogenetic criteria are some of the best currently available.

Aligning according to secondary or tertiary sequence structure is considered phylogenetically more reliable than sequence-based alignment because confidence in homology assessment is greater in comparisons of complex structures than of simple nucleotides or amino acids characters. More phylogeny-based structural multiple alignment approaches need to be developed.

Should Alignments Be Edited? Alignment "surgery" is sometimes warranted to ensure that unambiguous information relevant to groups of sequences can be retained and that ambiguous information can be removed. An example of alignment surgery is given in Figure 14.6. In gapped regions, one should determine whether alternative alignments seem reasonably plausible and, just as important, whether they may bias the tree-building analysis. When alignment ambiguities are resolved manually, phylogenetic relations, substitution processes, and base composition should be considered. It is perfectly reasonable at this stage to resolve ambiguities in favor of phylogenetic evidence, and in some cases to delete ambiguous regions in the alignment. The advantage of this latter approach is that unambiguous information relevant to particular sequences can be retained over ambiguous data. The disadvantage is that parsimony and likelihood tree-building methods mentioned below can interpret the "missing" information as zero divergence.

Summary The following points should be considered when constructing a multiple sequence alignment for a phylogenetic analysis:

▸ The alignment step in phylogenetic analysis is as important as subsequent steps, if not more important because it produces the dataset on which models of evolution are used.

▸ It is not uncommon to edit the alignment, deleting unambiguously aligned regions and inserting or deleting gaps to reflect more accurately probable evolutionary processes that led to the divergence between sequences.

▸ It is useful to perform the phylogenetic analysis based on a series of slightly modified alignments to determine how ambiguous regions in the alignment affect the results, and what aspects of the results in which one may have more or less confidence.

A

```
          116      122-144               155
           |          |                   |
1  ARABI  GCGCCC  ---CAAGCCTTCT-GGCCG----  AGGGCACGTCT
2  LYCOP  .....C  ---GAAGCCATTT-GGCCG----  A.........
3  triti  .....C  ---GAGGCCACTC-GGCCG----  A......C..
4  LACTU  .....C  ---GAAGCCATCC-GGCTG----  A......C..
5  SILEN  .....C  ---GAAGC--TTC-GGCTG----  A.........
6  vicia  .....C  ---GATGCCATTA-GGTTG----  A.........
7  CANEL  .....C  ---GAGGCCACTA-GGCTG----  A...T..C..
8  potam  .....C  ---TAAGCTTCCG-GGCCG----  A.....A.C..
9  ephed  .-...C  ---GAAGCC--TC-CGCCA----  A.........
10 gnetu  .-...C  TCCG-AGCC--TA-GGCCG----  A.........
11 PINUS  .....C  ---GAGGCC--TC-GGTCG----  A.........
12 PICEA  .....C  ---GAGNCC--TC-GGTCG----  A.........
13 TAXUS  .GC..G  ---GAG-C---TC-GGCCG----  A.........
14 marsi  .-...C  ---GAGGC--TC-GTCCG----   A.........
15 osmun  .-...C  ---GCGGC--TC-GTCCA----   A....T.C..
16 mnium  .....C  ---GAGGC--TC-GTCCG----   A.....TT..C
17 CHLAM  ....TC  ---GAGGC--TTC-GGCCA----  A.A...T....
18 SPERM  ....TC  ---GAGGC--TTC-GGCCG----  A.A...T..T.
19 TETRA  ....TC  ---GAGGC--CTC-GGCCA----  A.A.....C..
20 CHLOR  ....TC  ---GAGAC--CTC-GGTCA----  A.A...T....
21 CLADO  ....TC  ---AAGTC--TAC-GGACT----  T.A...T....
22 HETER  ....C   TTT--GGT-ATT----CCGA---  A.-...C..
23 VOLVA  ....TC  TTT--GGCCATT----CCGA---  A.A...T.C..
24 SCLER  .....C  CTT--GGT-ATT----CCGG---  G.....T.C..
25 sacch  .....C  CTT--GGT-ATT----CCAG---  G.....T.C..
26 BIPOL  .....C  TTT--GGT-ATT----CCAA---  A.....T.C..
27 GLOMU  ....TC  CCT--GGT-ATT----CCGG---  G.A.T.C..
28 CYANI  ....TT  TC--AGGAGAATTTTATTTTCCT  G.A.......
29 SARCO  ....TC  GC---GGTAA-TC--------CT  GCA.--T....
30 PHYTO  .A.TT   CCG--GGTTAGTC---CTG----  G.A.T.T.C..
31 SCYTO  ...-TT  CCG--GGATATGC---CTG----  G.A...T.CT.
32 crypt  .---CT  CC---AGC--TGA---CT-----  ------T...A
33 PRORO  ....TT  TCG--GGATATCC---CTG----  AA....T.C..
```

B

```
          116      122-144               155     [     122'-141'      ]
           |          |                   |
1  ARABI  GCGCCC  ???CAAGCCTTCT?GGCCG????  AGGGCACGTCT  ??????????????????????
2  LYCOP  GCGCCC  ???GAAGCCATTT?GGCCG????  AGGGCACGCTT  ??????????????????????
3  triti  GCGCCC  ???GAGGCCACTC?GGCCG????  AGGGCACGCCT  ??????????????????????
4  LACTU  GCGCCC  ???GAAGCCATCC?GGCTG????  AGGGCACGCCT  ??????????????????????
5  SILEN  GCGCCC  ???GAAGC?-TTC?GGCTG????  AGGGCACGTCT  ??????????????????????
6  vicia  GCGCCC  ???GATGCCATTA?GGTTG????  AGGGCACGTCT  ??????????????????????
7  CANEL  GCGCCC  ???GAGGCCACTA?GGCTG????  AGGGCTCGCCT  ??????????????????????
8  potam  GCGCCC  ???TAAGCTTCCG?GGCCG????  AGGGCAAGCCT  ??????????????????????
9  ephed  GCGCCC  ???GAAGC?-?TC?CGCCA????  AGGGCACGTCT  ??????????????????????
10 gnetu  G-GCCC  TCCG??GC?-?TA?GGCCG????  AGGGCACGTCT  ??????????????????????
11 PINUS  GCGCCC  ???GAGGC?-?TC?GGTCG????  AGGGCACGTCT  ??????????????????????
12 PICEA  GCGCCC  ???GAG?C?-?TC?GGTCG????  AGGGCACGTCT  ??????????????????????
13 TAXUS  GGCCCG  ???GAG-C?-?TC?GGCCG????  AGGGCACGTCT  ??????????????????????
14 marsi  G-GCCC  ???GAGGC??-TC?GTCCG????  AGGGCACGTCT  ??????????????????????
15 osmun  G-GCCC  ???GCGGC??-TC?GTCCA????  AGGGCATGCCT  ??????????????????????
16 mnium  G-GCCC  ???GAGGC??-TC?GTCCG????  AGGGCATTTCC  ??????????????????????
17 CHLAM  GCGCTC  ???GAGGC?-TTC?GGCCA????  AGAGCATGTCT  ??????????????????????
18 SPERM  GCGCTC  ???GAGGC?-TTC?GGCCG????  AGAGCATGTTT  ??????????????????????
19 TETRA  GCGCTC  ???GAGGC?-CTC?GGCCA????  AGAGCACGCCT  ??????????????????????
20 CHLOR  GCGCTC  ???GAGAC?-CTC?GGTCA????  AGAGCATGTCT  ??????????????????????
21 CLADO  GCGCTC  ???AAGTC?-TAC?GGACT????  TGAGCATGTCT  ??????????????????????
22 HETER  GCGCCC  ?????????????????????    AGG-CACGCCT  TTTT??GGT-ATT????CCGA
23 VOLVA  GCGCTC  ?????????????????????    AGAGCACGCCT  TTTT??GGCCATT????CCGG
24 SCLER  GCGCTC  ?????????????????????    GGGGCATGCCT  CTTT??GGT-ATT????CCGG
25 sacch  GCGCCC  ?????????????????????    GGGGCATGCCT  CTTT??GGT-ATT????CCAG
26 BIPOL  GCGCCC  ?????????????????????    GGGGCATGCCT  TTTT??GGT-ATT????CCGG
27 GLOMU  GCACTC  ?????????????????????    GGAGTATGCCT  CCTT??GGT-ATT????CCGG
28 CYANI  GCGCTT  ?????????????????????    GGAGCACGTCT  ??????????????????????
29 SARCO  GCGCTC  ?????????????????????    GCAG-?TGTCT  ??????????????????????
30 PHYTO  GCACTT  ?????????????????????    GGAGTATGCCT  ??????????????????????
31 SCYTO  GCGC-TT ?????????????????????    GGAGCATGCCT  ??????????????????????
32 crypt  G??-CT  ?????????????????????    ?????T?GTCA  ??????????????????????
33 PRORO  GCGCTT  ?????????????????????    AAGGCATGCCT  ??????????????????????
```

FIGURE 14.6 Alignment modification for phylogenetic analysis. (a) Alignment showing a length-variable region (boxed) of 5.8S rDNA for the taxa in the guide tree of Figure 9.1. Taxa 1 through 8 are angiosperms; taxa 9 and 10 are gnetophytes; taxa 11 through 13 are conifers; taxa 14 and 15 are ferns; taxa 16 is moss; taxa 17 through 21 are green algae; taxa 22 through 27 are fungi; and taxa 28 through 33 are protists. The alignment positions correspond to those published elsewhere (Hershkovitz & Lewis, 1996). Each sequence is unique in the shaded region. Taxa represented in the Figure 9.1 tree having the same sequence as any shown here were omitted for brevity. Note that taxa grouped in the guide tree (based on the entire sequence) seem to form alignment groups in the length-variable region. On a pairwise basis, alternative alignments of some of the distantly related taxa seem plausible. For example, if moved two spaces to the left, the **TAC** in the center of the **CLADO** sequence may appear to align better with **YAY** in several angiosperms than the **YYC** in other green algae. Sufficient sampling, however, shows that **YAY** is not universal in the angiosperms, and the guide tree supports the present alignment, which allows no length variability in green algae. In the absence of sufficient sampling, a guide tree, or other prior phylogenetic evidence, no such conclusion could be drawn. Note also that the taxa of the green plant lineage do not align well with the fungi and protists. The variability in the shaded region and the divergences indicated in the guide tree suggest that there is no true alignment between these distantly related groups, that the alignment indicated is arbitrary, and that the actual bases are not likely homologous. (b) The same alignment, modified as follows for phylogenetic analysis: (1) the fungi and protists are rescored as missing for all positions in the shaded region, where alignment with the green plant lineage is ambiguous; (2) the length-variable regions of the fungi were appended to the end of the alignment, because these sequences are alignable among fungi and include phylogenetically useful variation; and (3) multiposition gaps were rescored as one gap position and the rest as missing, so that in **MP** analysis, multiposition gaps are not counted as several independent deletions. The length-variable region of protists was not appended to the end of the alignment because both the alignment and the guide tree indicate that the original alignment is arbitrary.

Step 2: Deciding on a Data Model

The substitution model should be given the same emphasis as alignment and tree building. As implied in the preceding section, the substitution model influences both alignment and tree building; hence, a recursive approach is warranted. At present, two elements of the substitution model can be assessed computationally for nucleotide data but not for amino acid or codon data.

One element is the model of substitution between particular bases; the other is the relative rate of overall substitution among different sites in the sequence. Simple computational procedures have not been developed for assessing more complex variables (e.g., site- or lineage-specific substitution models). An overview of substitution models is presented here; for further information, particularly on models based on calculated matrices, see the sections in this book that deal with matrix development for BLAST (Chapter 11) and other related analyses.

Models of Substitution Rates Between Base In general, substitutions are more frequent between bases or amino acid residues that are more similar biochemically. In the case of DNA, the four types of transition (A → G, G → A, C → T, T → C) usually are more frequent than the eight types of transversion (A → C, A → T, C → G, G → T, and the reverse). Such biases affect the estimated divergence between two sequences.

Specification of relative rates of substitution among particular residues usually takes the form of a square matrix; the number of rows and columns is four in the case of bases, 20 in the case of amino acids (e.g., PAM matrices), and 61 in the case of codons (excluding stop codons). The off-diagonal elements of the matrix correspond to the relative costs of going from one base to another. The diagonal elements represent the cost of having the same base in different sequences.

The cost schedule can be fixed a priori to ensure that the tree-building method will tally an exact cost for each substitution incurred. Fixed-cost matrices are character state weight matrices and are applied in maximum parsimony (MP) tree building (Figure 14.7). When such weights are applied, the method is referred to as *weighted parsimony*. For distance and maximum likelihood (ML) tree building, the costs can be derived from instantaneous rate matrices representing ML estimators of the probability that a particular type of substitution will occur (Figure 14.8). Although the MP weight matrix is simple arithmetic, application of the distance and ML rate matrices can involve complex algebra. To avoid blind application of possibly inappropriate methods, practitioners are advised to familiarize themselves with the underlying theory (see Li, 1997; Swofford et al., 1996).

Character state weight matrices usually have been estimated more or less by eye, but they also can be derived from a rate matrix. For example, if it is presumed that each of the two transitions occurs at double the frequency of each transversion, a weight matrix simply can specify, for example, that the cost of A–G is 1 and the cost of A–T is 2 (Figure 14.7). In the subsequent tree-building step, this set of assumptions minimizes the overall number of transversions and tends to cluster sequences differing mainly by transitions.

A simplified substitution rate matrix used in ML and distance phylogenetic analysis is presented in Figure 14.8. The matrix is analogous to that presented in Figure 14.7, only the actual computation of divergence involves more complex algebra and cannot be determined by simply counting steps between bases.

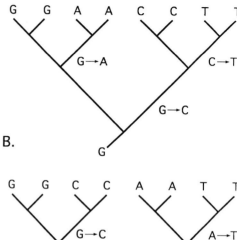

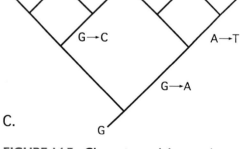

FIGURE 14.7 Character weight matrix and application in MP phylogenetic analysis. (a) Matrix indicating that a transversion substitution costs twice that of a transition. Because MP bases shared between two sequences cannot ever have changed, diagonal elements of the matrix are ignored. (b, c) Two phylogenetic resolutions and reconstructions of the evolution of a hypothetical pattern of aligned bases at a particular site in eight sequences. With unweighted MP, both reconstructions (among several others) have the same cost (three steps), hence they are equally acceptable. With the weight matrix in (a), the reconstruction of (b) requires four steps, and the reconstruction of (c) requires five. Thus, the first reconstruction (b) and others requiring four steps are preferred.

The paralinear, or *log-det*, transformation corrects for nonstationarity (see Swofford et al., 1996). In this method, which is applicable only to distance tree building, the numbers of raw substitutions of each type and

$$
\begin{array}{c}
\begin{array}{cccc}
\ \ A & C & G & T
\end{array} \\
\begin{array}{c} A \\ C \\ G \\ T \end{array}
\left[
\begin{array}{cccc}
-(a_1+a_2+a_3) & a_1 & a_2 & a_3 \\
a_4 & -(a_4+a_5+a_6) & a_5 & a_6 \\
a_7 & a_8 & -(a_7+a_8+a_9) & a_9 \\
a_{10} & a_{11} & a_{12} & -(a_{10}+a_{11}+a_{12})
\end{array}
\right]
\end{array}
$$

FIGURE 14.8 Simplified substitution rate matrix used in ML and distance phylogenetic analysis. The off-diagonal values represent a product of an instantaneous rate of change, a relative rate between the different substitutions, and the frequency of the target base. In practice, the forward rates (upper triangular values) are presumed to equal the reverse rates (corresponding lower triangular values). The diagonal elements are nonzero, which effectively accounts for the possibility that more divergent sequences are more likely to share the same base by chance. In the simplest model of sequence evolution (the Jukes-Cantor model), all values of (a) are the same: All substitution types and base frequencies are presumed equal.

Sclerotinium sclerotiorum

		A	C	G	T	total
	A	340	6	13	4	363
Spinacia	C	10	229	6	36	281
oleracea	G	25	8	229	12	372
	T	5	22	6	312	345
total		380	265	352	364	1361

FIGURE 14.9 Pairwise sequence comparison. The table compares 1361 sites of 18S rDNA aligned between spinach (*Spinacia oleracea*) and a rust fungus (*Sclerotinium sclerotiorum*). The rows indicate the distribution of bases in the fungus aligned to particular bases in spinach. The columns indicate the reverse. The diagonal values are the number of sitewise identities between the sequences. Note the AT bias in the fungus: 83 (10 + 36 + 25 + 12) sites that are G or C in spinach are A or T in the fungus. In contrast, only 47 sites (6 + 22 + 13 + 6) that are G or C in the fungus are A or T in spinach. This bias is muted in simple comparison of base frequencies in the two sequences (the totals) because most sites are the same in both sequences and probably are mutationally constrained. Note also the obviously larger number of transition (13 + 36 + 25 + 22 = 96) versus transversion (6 + 4 + 10 + 6 + 8 + 12 + 5 + 6 = 57) substitutions, and that C–T transitions account for 58 of 153 total differences. The data shown can be generated using the **PAUP** or **MEGA** programs.

in each direction are tallied for each sequence pair in a 4×4 matrix like that shown in Figure 14.9. Each matrix has an algebraic determinant, the log of which becomes a factor in estimating sequence divergence, hence the name log-det. Pairwise comparisons of sequences having various and assorted patterns of base frequencies yield a variety of matrix patterns, hence a variety of determinant values. Thus, each estimated pairwise distance is affected by the determinant peculiar to each pair, which effectively allows the substitution model to be different for each and, hence, to vary along different branches of a phylogenetic tree. Log-det is especially sensitive to among-site rate heterogeneity (see below), because base frequency bias can exist only in sites that are subject to variation.

In addition to variation in substitution patterns, variation in substitution rates among different sites in a sequence has been shown to affect profoundly the results of tree building (Swofford et al., 1996). The most obvious example of among-site rate variation, or heterogeneity, is that evident among the three codon positions in a coding sequence. Because of degeneracy of the genetic code, changes in the third codon position can occur more frequently without affecting the encoded protein sequence. Therefore, this third codon position tends to be much more variable than the first two. For this reason, many phylogenetic analyses of coding DNA sequences exclude the third codon position. In some cases, however, rate variation patterns are more subtle (e.g., those corresponding to conserved regions of proteins or rRNA), and so one should always have as much information as possible about a given gene or sequence

(proposed domains, degree of conservation, coding and noncoding regions, RNA structure if a nonprotein coding gene) before performing any phylogenetic analysis.

Models of Substitution Rates Between Amino Acid. The most widely used models of amino acid substitution include distance-based methods based on matrixes, such as the PAM matrices of Dayhoff et al. (1979) and the BLOSUM matrices. Again, such matrices are described further in other chapters in this book (primarily Chapter 11), and so are not described further here. Although PROTDIST is one of the most widely used programs providing substitution models for calculating protein distances, others that are faster and contain additional matrices such as BLOSUM are becoming increasingly used (i.e., PUZZLE).

Which Substitution Model to Use? Although any of the parameters in a substitution model may prove critical in a given data set, the best model is not always the one with the most parameters. To the contrary, the fewer the parameters, the better. This is because every parameter estimate has an associated variance. As additional parametric dimensions are introduced, the overall variance increases, sometimes prohibitively (see Li, 1997, p. 84, Table 4.1). For a given DNA sequence comparison, a two-parameter model requires that the summed base differences be sorted into two categories, and for a six-parameter model, that the summed based differences be sorted into six categories. Obviously, the number of sites sampled in each of the six categories would be much smaller, and perhaps too small to give a reliable estimate.

A good strategy for substitution model specification for DNA sequences is the "describe tree" feature in the Phylogenetic Analysis using Parsimony (PAUP) package, which uses likelihood to simultaneously estimate the six reversible substitution rates, the α shape parameter of the gamma distribution, and the proportion of invariant sites. These parameters can be estimated by means of equal or specified base frequencies. From the estimated substitution parameters, one can determine whether a simpler model is justified (e.g., whether the six substitution categories can be reduced to two) by comparing likelihood scores estimated for this tree using more or fewer parameters. Parameters for α and the proportion of invariant sites sometimes can substitute for each other, so one should compare likelihoods with each estimated alone versus both together.

For protein sequences, the model used often is dependent on the degree of sequence similarity. For more divergent sequences, the BLOSUM matrices often are better, whereas the PAM matrix is suited for more highly similar sequences. Both parsimony and distance matrix methods (mentioned further below) have benefits and disadvantages, and their use depends on one's philosophy about protein sequence change and its analyses: Is it better to retain information about each character when determining a tree (i.e., parsimony), or is it better to derive distance measures to base the tree (i.e., distance matrix)? Does a matrix based on empirical data present a more accurate reflection of evolutionary change than a matrix based on generated theories about sequence change? Again, although cladistic analysis can be a powerful method for investigating evolutionary relationships, keep in mind that one method is not clearly better than another, each having their own benefits and disadvantages that differ depending on the type of analyses performed and the philosophy of the investigator. (For more information, see the section on scoring matrices in Chapter 11.)

Step 3: Tree Building

Tree-building methods implemented in available software are discussed in detail both in the literature (Saitou, 1996; Swofford et al.,1996; Li, 1997) and on the Internet. This section briefly describes a selection of the most popular methods. Tree-building methods can be sorted into distance-based versus character-based methods. Much of the discussion in molecular phylogenetics dwells on the usefulness of distance- and character-based methods (e.g., Saitou, 1996; Li, 1997). Distance methods compute pairwise distances according to some measure, and then discard the actual data, using only the fixed distances to derive trees. Character-based methods derive trees that optimize the distribution of the actual data patterns for each character. Pairwise distances thus are not fixed, because they are determined by the tree topology. The most commonly applied distance-based methods include NJ and Fitch–Margoliash (FM), whereas the most common character-based methods include maximum parsimony and ML.

Distance-Based Methods. Distance methods use the amount of dissimilarity (the distance) between two aligned sequences to derive trees. A distance method would reconstruct the true tree if all genetic divergence events were recorded accurately in the sequence (Swofford et al., 1996). However, divergence encounters an upper bound as sequences become mutationally saturated. After one sequence of a diverging pair has mutated at a particular site, subsequent mutations in either sequence cannot render the sites any more "different." In fact, subsequent mutations can make them equal again (for example, if a valine mutates to an isoleucine, which mutates back to a valine again). Therefore, most distance-based methods correct for such "unseen" substitutions. In practice, application of the rate matrix effectively presumes that some proportion of observed pairwise base identities actually represents multiple mutations, and that this proportion increases with increasing overall sequence divergence. Some programs implement, at least optionally, calculation of uncorrected distances, whereas, for example, the MEGA program (Kumar et al., 1994) implements only uncorrected distances for codon and amino acid data. Unless overall divergences are very low, the

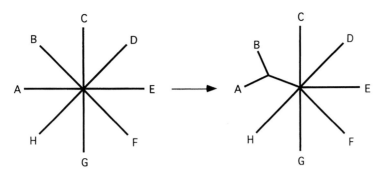

FIGURE 14.10 Star decomposition. This is how tree-building algorithms such as NJ work. The most similar terminals are joined and a branch is inserted between them and the remainder of the star. Subsequently, the new branch is consolidated, so that its value is a mean of the two original values, yielding a star tree with *n* – 1 terminals. The process is repeated until only one terminal remains.

latter approach virtually is guaranteed to give inaccurate results.

Pairwise distance is calculated using ML estimators of substitution rates. The most popular distance tree-building programs have a limited number of substitution models, but PAUP implements a number of models, including the actual model estimated from the data using ML, as well as the log-det distance method.

Distance methods are much less computationally intensive than ML, but can use the same models of sequence evolution. This is their biggest advantage. The disadvantage is that the actual character data are discarded. The most commonly applied distance-based methods are the unweighted pair group method with arithmetic mean (UPGMA), neighbor joining (NJ), and methods that optimize the additivity of a distance tree, including the minimum evolution (ME) method. Several methods are available in more than one phylogenetics software package, but not all implementations allow the same parameter specifications or tree optimization features (e.g., branch swapping—see below).

UPGMA. UPGMA is a clustering or phenetic algorithm; it joins tree branches on the criterion of greatest similarity among pairs and averages of joined pairs. It is not strictly an evolutionary distance method (Li, 1997). UPGMA is expected to generate an accurate topology with true branch lengths only when the divergence is according to a molecular clock (ultrametric; Swofford et al., 1996) or is approximately equal to raw sequence dissimilarity. As mentioned earlier, these conditions rarely are met in practice.

NJ. The NJ algorithm commonly is applied with distance tree building, regardless of the optimization criterion. The fully resolved tree is "decomposed" from a fully unresolved "star" tree by successively inserting branches between a pair of closest (actually, most isolated) neighbors and the remaining terminals in the tree (Figure 14.10). The closest neighbor pair then is consolidated, effectively reforming a star tree, and the process is repeated. The method is comparatively rapid.

FM. The FM method seeks to maximize the fit of the observed pairwise distances to a tree by minimizing the squared deviation of all possible observed distances relative to all possible path lengths on the tree (Felsenstein, 1997). There are several variations that differ in how the error is weighted. The variance estimates are not completely independent, because errors in all the internal tree branches are counted at least twice (Rzhetsky & Nei, 1992).

ME. ME seeks to find the shortest tree that is consistent with the path lengths measured in a manner similar to FM; that is, it works by minimizing the squared deviation of observed to tree-based distances (Rzhetsky & Nei, 1992; Swofford et al., 1996; Felsenstein, 1997). Unlike FM, ME does not use all possible pairwise distances and all possible associated tree-path lengths. Rather, it fixes the location of internal tree nodes based on the distance to external nodes, and then optimizes the internal branch length according to the minimum measured error between these "observed" points. It thus purports to eliminate the nonindependence of FM measurements.

Which Distance-Based Tree-Building Procedure Is Best? ME and FM seem to be the best procedures, and they perform nearly identically in simulation studies (Huelsenbeck, 1995). ME is becoming more widely implemented in computer programs, including METREE (Rzhetsky & Nei, 1994) and PAUP. For protein data, the FM procedure in PHYLIP offers the greatest range of substitution models. The MEGA (Kumar et al.,1994) plus METREE package includes a γ correction for proteins, but only in conjunction with a raw (p distance) divergence model (no distance or bias correction), which is unreliable except for small divergences (Rzhetsky & Nei, 1994). MEGA also computes separate distances for synonymous and nonsynonymous sites, but this method is valid only in the absence of substitution or base frequency bias, and when there is no correction for among-site rate heterogeneity. Thus for most data sets, using the nucleotide data under a more realistic model may be preferable to MEGA's methods.

Simulation studies indicate that UPGMA performs poorly over a broad range of tree-shape space (Huelsenbeck, 1995). The use of this method is not recommended; it is mentioned here only because its application seems to persist, as evidenced by UPGMA gene trees appearing in publications (Huelsenbeck, 1995).

NJ is clearly the fastest procedure and generally yields a tree close to, if not the actual, ME tree (Rzhetsky & Nei, 1992; Li, 1997). However, it yields only one tree. Depending on the structure of the data, numerous different trees may be as good or significantly better than the NJ tree (Swofford et al., 1996). However, the speed of NJ and its ability to produce results very similar to other slower methods ensures that this method continues to be one of the most popular used to date.

Character-Based Methods. The character-based methods have little in common besides the use of the character data at all steps in the analysis. This allows the assessment of the reliability of each base position in an alignment on the basis of all other base positions (Box 14.1).

Maximum Parsimony. Maximum parsimony is an optimality criterion that appeals to the principle that the best explanation of the data is the simplest, which in turn is the one requiring the fewest ad hoc assumptions. In practical terms, the MP tree is the shortest—the one with the fewest changes, which, by definition, is also the one with the fewest parallel changes. There are several variants of MP that differ with regard to the permitted directionality of character state change (Swofford et al.,1996).

BOX 14.1 | Distance, Parsimony, and ML: What Is the Difference?

Distance matrix methods simply count the number of differences between two sequences. This number is referred to as the *evolutionary distance*, and its exact size depends on the evolutionary model used. The actual tree then is computed from the matrix of distance values by running a clustering algorithm that starts with the most similar sequences (i.e., those that have the shortest distance between them) or by trying to minimize the total branch length of the tree. The principle of maximum parsimony searches for a tree that requires the smallest number of changes to explain the differences observed among the taxa under study.

An ML approach to phylogenetic inference evaluates the probability that the chosen evolutionary model has generated the observed data. The evolutionary model simply could mean that one assumes that changes between all nucleotides (or amino acids) are equally probable. The program then assigns all possible nucleotides to the internal nodes of the tree in turn and calculates the probability that each such sequence would have generated the data (if two sister taxa have the nucleotide A, a reconstruction that assumes derivation from a C would be assigned a low probability compared with a derivation that assumes there already was an A). The probabilities for all possible reconstructions (not just the more probable one) are summed up to yield the likelihood for one particular site. The likelihood for the tree is the product of the likelihoods for all alignment positions in the dataset.

To accommodate substitution bias, MP is amenable to weighting; for example, the transformation of a transversion can be weighted relative to a transition (see above). The easiest way to do this is to create a weighting step matrix in which the weights are the reciprocal of the rates estimated using ML as described above. However, step-matrix weighting can slow MP computation greatly.

The MP method performs poorly when there is substantial among-site rate heterogeneity (Huelsenbeck, 1995). There are few good fixes for this problem. One approach is to modify the data set to include only sites that exhibit little or no heterogeneity as determined by likelihood estimation (see above). Another approach is to reweight positions recursively according to their propensity to change as observed in preliminary trees. This successive approximations approach is facilitated automatically in PAUP, but it is prone to error to the degree that the preliminary trees are incorrect.

MP analyses tend to yield numerous (sometimes many thousands of) trees that have the same score. Because each is held to be as optimal as any other, only groupings present in the strict consensus of all trees are considered to be supported by the data. The reason that distance and ML tree methods tend to arrive at a single best tree is that their calculation involves division and decimals, whereas MP merely counts discrete steps. For a given data set, a strict consensus of all ME or ML trees that are not significantly worse than optimal probably would yield resolution more or less comparable with the MP consensus. Unfortunately, although MP users conventionally present strict consensus (and sometimes consensus of trees one or two steps worse), ME and ML users typically do not.

Simulation studies (Huelsenbeck, 1995) have shown that MP performs no better than ME and worse than ML when the amount of sequence evolution since lineages diverged is much greater than the amount of divergence that occurred between lineage splits (i.e., in a tree with very long terminal branches and short internal internodes). This condition produces long branch attraction: The long branches become artificially connected because the number of nonhomologous similarities the sequences have accumulated exceeds the number of homologous similarities they have retained with their true closest relatives (Swofford et al., 1996). Character weighting improves the performance of MP under these conditions (Huelsenbeck, 1995).

ML. ML turns the phylogenetic problem inside out. ML searches for the evolutionary model, including the tree itself, that has the highest likelihood of producing the observed data.

In practice, ML is derived for each base position in an alignment. The likelihood is calculated in terms of the probability that the pattern of variation at a site would be produced by a particular substitution process, given a particular tree and the overall observed base frequencies. The likelihood becomes the sum of the probabilities of each possible reconstruction of substitutions under a particular substitution process. The likelihoods for all the sites are multiplied to give an overall likelihood of the tree (i.e., the probability of the data given the tree and the substitution process). As one can imagine, for one particular tree, the likelihood of the data is low at some sites and high at others. For a "good" tree, many sites will have higher likelihood, so the product of likelihoods is high. For a "poor" tree, the reverse will be true.

The substitution model should be optimized to fit the observed data. For example, if there is a transition bias, evident by an inordinate number of sites that include only purines or pyrimidines, the likelihood of the data under a model that assumes no bias will never be as good as one that does. Likewise, if a substantial proportion of the sites are occupied by a single base, and another substantial proportion have equal base frequencies, the likelihood of the data under a model that assumes that all sites evolve equally will be less than that of a model that allows rate heterogeneity. Modifying the substitution parameters, however, modifies the likelihood of the data associated with particular trees. Thus, the tree yielding the highest likelihood under one substitution model may yield much lower likelihood under another.

Because ML uses great amounts of computation time, it usually is impractical to perform a complete search that simultaneously optimizes the substitution model and the tree for a given data set. An economical, heuristic approach is recommended (Adachi & Hasegawa, 1996; Swofford et al., 1996). Perhaps the best time saver in this regard is preliminary ML estimation of the substitution model (as can be performed using PAUP). This procedure can be applied iteratively, searching for better ML trees, then re-estimating the parameters, then searching for better trees.

As algorithms, computers, and phylogenetic understanding have improved, the ML criterion has become more popular for molecular phylogenetic analysis. In simulation studies, ML consistently has outperformed ME and MP when the data analysis proceeds according to the same model that generates the data (Huelsenbeck, 1995). ML will always be the most computationally intensive method of all, however, so there will always be situations in which it is not practical.

Searching for Trees. The number of unique phylogenetic trees increases exponentially with the number of taxa, becoming astronomical even for, say, 50 sequences (Swofford et al., 1996; Li, 1997). In most cases, computational limitations permit exploration of only a small fraction of possible trees. The exact number depends mainly on the number of taxa, the optimality criterion (e.g., MP is much faster than ML), the parameters (e.g., unweighted MP is much faster than weighted; ML with fewer preset parameters is much faster than with more or simultaneously optimized parameters, or both), computer hardware, and computer software (some algorithms are faster than others; some software allows multiprocessing; some software limits the number and kind of trees that can be stored in memory). The search procedure also is affected by data structure: Poorly resolvable data produces more "nearly optimal" trees that must be evaluated to find the most optimal.

Branch-swapping algorithms successively modify existing trees built by an initial step (Swofford et al., 1996). The algorithms range from those that generate all possible unique trees (exhaustive algorithms) to those that evaluate only minor modifications.

Quartet puzzling is a relatively rapid tree-searching algorithm available for ML tree building (Strimmer & von Haeseler, 1996) and is available in PUZZLE.

One of the best ways to economize search effort is to prune the data set. For example, it may be apparent from the data alone or from preliminary searching that a particular cluster of five terminals is unresolvable, that the arrangement of these terminals does not impact the remainder of the topology, that resolution of these terminals is not the objective of the analysis, or a combination thereof. Removing four of the terminals from the analysis simplifies the search by several orders of magnitude.

Every analysis is unique. The elements that influence the choice of optimal search strategy (amount of data, structure of data, amount of time, hardware, objective of analysis) are too variable to suggest a foolproof recipe. Thus, researchers must be familiar with their data; they also must have specific objectives in mind, understanding the various search procedures as well as the capabilities of their hardware and software.

Rooting Trees. The methods described above produce unrooted trees (i.e., trees having no evolutionary polarity). To evaluate evolutionary hypotheses, it often is necessary to locate the root of the tree. Rooting phylogenetic trees is not a trivial problem (Nixon & Carpenter, 1993).

If one accepts a molecular clock, then the root always will be at the midpoint of the longest span across the tree (Weston, 1994). Whether molecular evolution is indeed clocklike generally remains a contentious issue (Li, 1997), but most gene trees exhibit unclocklike behavior regardless of where the root is placed. Thus, rooting generally is evaluated by extrinsic evidence, that is, by means of determining where the tree would attach to an outgroup, which can be any organism or sequence not descended from the nearest common ancestor of the organisms or sequences analyzed (for example, a bird sequence could be used to root an analysis of mammals). Outgroup rooting, however, creates a dilemma: An outgroup that is closely related to the ingroup may be simply an erroneously excluded member of the ingroup. A clearly distant outgroup (e.g., a fungus for an analysis of plants) can have a sequence so diverged that its attachment to the ingroup is subject to the long branch attraction problem. It is wise to examine the results you obtain for trees both with and without an outgroup.

Another means of rooting involves analysis of a duplicated gene or gene with an internal duplication (Lawson et al., 1996). If all the paralogs from most or all of the organisms are included in the analysis, then one can root the tree logically exactly where the paralog gene trees converge, assuming that there are not long branch problems in all trees.

Step 4: Tree Evaluation

Several procedures are available that evaluate the phylogenetic signal in the data and the robustness of trees (Swofford et al., 1996; Li, 1997). The most popular of the former class are tests of data signal versus randomized data (skewness and permutation tests). The latter class includes tests of tree support from resampling of observed data (nonparametric bootstrap). The likelihood ratio test provides a means of evaluating both the substitution model and the tree.

Randomized Trees (Skewness Test). Simulation studies indicate that the distribution of random MP tree lengths generated using random data sets will be symmetrical, whereas that using data sets with phylogenetic signal will be skewed. The critical value of the g_1 statistic of skewness (a common statistic computed from Fisher's k statistics) will vary with the number of taxa and variable sites in the sequence. The test does not estimate the reliability of a particular topology, and it is sensitive even to very small amounts of signal present in an otherwise random data set. If taxa from groups that are obviously well supported by the data are deleted selectively, the test can be used to determine whether phylogenetic signal remains, provided at least 10 variable characters and five taxa are examined. The procedure is implemented in PAUP.

Randomized Character Data (Permutation Tests)

The randomized data approach determines whether an MP tree or portion thereof derived from the actual data could have arisen by chance. The data is not truly randomized, but rather is permuted within each aligned column, so that covariation in the initial data is removed. The result is an alignment of sequences that are not random sequences; rather, the base at each site in these sequences is drawn randomly from the population of bases occupying that site in the overall alignment. The permutation tail probability test (PTP) compares the score for the MP tree with trees generated by numerous permutations of the data at each site, determining only whether there is phylogenetic signal in the original data. A topology-dependent test (T-PTP) compares the scores for specific trees to determine whether the difference can be attributed to chance. This method does not evaluate whether the tree or any portion thereof is correct (Swofford et al., 1996). In particular, the T-PTP test seems to corroborate groups that are in trees close to the MP tree but not in it. This is because the method is detecting the collective signal that places a taxon even approximately, if not actually, in its correct position. The results can be fine tuned, however, by additional applications using relevant subsets of the data (Faith & Trueman, 1996). The procedure is implemented in PAUP.

Bootstrapping. Bootstrapping is a resampling tree evaluation method that works with distance, parsimony, likelihood, and just about any other tree derivation method. It was invented in 1979 (Efron, 1979) and was introduced as a tree evaluation method in phylogenetic analysis by Felsenstein (1985). The result of bootstrap analysis is typically a number associated with a particular branch in the phylogenetic tree that gives the proportion of bootstrap replicates that support the monophyly of the clade.

How is bootstrapping carried out? Bootstrapping can be considered a two-step process comprising the generation of (many) new data sets from the original set and the computation of a number that gives the proportion of times that a particular branch (e.g., a taxon) appears in the tree. That number is commonly referred to as the *bootstrap value*. New data sets are created from the original data set by sampling columns of characters at random from the original data set with replacement. *With replacement* means that each site can be sampled again with the same probability as any of the other sites. As a consequence, each of the newly created data sets has the same number of total positions as the original data set, but some positions are duplicated or triplicated and others are missing. Therefore, it is possible that some of the newly created data sets are completely identical to the original set—or, on the other extreme, that only one of the sites is replicated, say, 500 times, while the remaining 499 positions in the original data set are dropped.

Although it has become common practice to include bootstrapping as part of a thorough phylogenetic analysis, there is some discussion on what exactly is measured by the method. It was originally suggested that the bootstrap value is a measure of repeatability (Felsenstein, 1985). In more recent interpretations, it has been considered to be a measure of accuracy—a biologically more relevant parameter that gives the probability that the true phylogeny has been recovered. Based on simulation studies, it has been suggested that under favor-

able conditions (roughly equal rates of change, symmetric branches), bootstrap values of more than 70% correspond to a probability of more than 95% that the true phylogeny has been found (Hillis & Bull, 1993). By the same token, under less favorable conditions, bootstrap values of more than 50% are overestimates of accuracy (Hillis & Bull, 1993). Simply put, under certain conditions, high bootstrap values can make the wrong phylogeny look good, so the conditions of the analysis must be considered. Bootstrapping can be used in experiments where trees are recomputed after internal branches are deleted one at a time. The results provide information on branching orders that are ambiguous in the full data set (see example in Leipe et al., 1994). Remember, however, that one always must start a phylogenetic analysis with a good alignment. If one uses a bad alignment, one may generate a tree that seems to be very robust; however, it is just stating robustly the relationships between poorly aligned sequences. Therefore, always examine such measures of tree robustness after generating trees from different variations of a given alignment that allow for any errors in regions of lower confidence within the alignment.

Parametric Bootstrap. The parametric bootstrap differs from the nonparametric in that it uses simulated (nonetheless, actual) replicates, rather than pseudoreplicates. In the case of phylogenetic sequence analysis, replicate data sets of the same size as the original data set are generated according to a specified model of sequence evolution, including the optimal tree topology according to that model (Huelsenbeck et al., 1996). Each data set then is analyzed according to the method of interest. Support for the branches in the test tree can be determined in much the same way as in the nonparametric bootstrap.

Likelihood Ratio Tests. As the name implies, likelihood ratio tests are applicable to ML analyses. A suboptimal likelihood value is evaluated for significance against a normal distribution of the error in the optimal model. In ideal applications, the error curve is presumed to be a χ^2 distribution. Thus, the test statistic is twice the difference between the optimal and test values, and the degree of freedom is the number of parameter differences.

Application of the χ^2 test to alternative phylogenetic trees is problematic, especially because the parameter space is irregular (Yang et al., 1995), but its use has been advocated for evaluating optimality of the substitution model when the number of parameters between models is known.

▌COMMON SOFTWARE

One must first remember that multiple sequence alignment is the first step in any phylogenetic analysis. For this, Clustal has been the leader in terms of being the mostly widely used software. Because multiple sequence alignment software has been discussed elsewhere in this book, it is not mentioned further here. However, do keep in mind that, for phylogenetic analysis, it is important that one uses a multiple sequence alignment method that uses evolutionary theory as its basis, such as Clustal. Other software optimized for other purposes, such as multiple alignment of sequence contigs during genome assembly, do not use evolutionary criteria and are not suitable for this first step of a phylogenetic analysis.

PHYLIP and PAUP compete as the most widely used phylogenetic analysis software for data modeling and tree building, although other newer applications such as PUZZLE are beginning to compete. Herein, PHYLIP and PAUP are described in the most detail, and allusion is made to other available packages that have useful features.

PHYLIP

PHYLIP (for *Phyl*ogeny *I*nference *P*ackage) is a package now comprising approximately 30 programs that cover almost any aspect of phylogenetic analysis. PHYLIP is free and is available for a wide variety of platforms (Mac, DOS, Unix, and others). According to its author, Joe Felsenstein from the University of Washington, PHYLIP is currently the most widely used phylogeny program. PHYLIP version 3.5 has been the most widely used, primarily because it has been the main version available from 1993 through 2000; however, now a new version, 3.6, currently in beta release is now available, and version 4.0 is promised, suggesting that this software will continue to be improved.

PHYLIP is a command line program and does not have a point-and-click interface, as programs like PAUP do. The documentation is well written and very comprehensive, and the interface is straightforward. In addition, a Web-based version of PHYLIP has been constructed, as is described below. Regarding the command-line version, a program within PHYLIP is invoked by typing its name, which automatically causes the data to be read from a file called *infile*, or a file name you specify if no infile exists. This infile must be in PHYLIP format; this data format is described clearly in the documentation. For example, if an alignment is produced using Clustal, or edited using Genedoc, the alignment may be saved in PHYLIP format and then used in PHYLIP programs directly. After the user activates a given PHYLIP program and loads the infile, the user then can choose from an option menu or

can accept the default value, and the program writes its output to a file called *outfile* (and *treefile* where applicable). If the output is to be read by another program, then outfile or treefile must be renamed before execution of the next program, because all files named either outfile or treefile in the current directory will be overwritten at the beginning of any program execution. The treefile generated is a widely used format that can be imported into a variety of tree-drawing programs, including DRAWGRAM and DRAWTREE, which are part of this package. However, these PHYLIP tree-drawing programs use low-resolution graphics, so a more recent program, such as Treeview (described below) is more recommended.

Some of the more commonly used programs within PHYLIP include PROTDIST, a PHYLIP program that computes a distance matrix for an alignment of protein sequences. It allows the user to choose between one of three evolutionary models of amino acid replacements. The simplest, fastest (and least realistic) model assumes that each amino acid has an equal chance of turning into one of the other 19 amino acids. The second is a category model in which the amino acids a redistributed among different groups, and transitions are evaluated differently depending on whether the change would result in an amino acid in the same or in a different group. The third (default) method, which is recommended, uses a table of empirically observed transitions between amino acids, the Dayhoff PAM 001 matrix (Dayhoff, 1979; Chapter 11). More details can be found in the PHYLIP documentation (Felsenstein, 1996).

NEIGHBOR is a tree-generating program that uses the distance matrix data generated from a program such as PROTDIST, and generates a tree using the NJ method (described further above). This is one of the more popular methods because of its high speed of computation.

FITCH is another tree-generating program similar to NEIGHBOR, but it is more robust. It also uses distance matrix data, such as that described in PROTDIST, and generates a tree using the FM method (described above). This method, although more robust than NEIGHBOR, tends to produce a similar answer, yet takes longer to compute, and so is not as frequently used, although it is highly recommended.

PROTPARS is a parsimony program for protein sequences that generates trees using a different method that does not use a distance matrix (i.e., PROTDIST does not need to be run first, as with NEIGHBOR and FITCH). The evolutionary model is different from those used in the PROTDIST program in that it considers the underlying changes in the nucleotide sequence to evaluate the probabilities of the observed amino acid changes. Specifically, it makes the (biologically meaningful) assumption that synonymous changes (e.g., GCA [alanine] → GCC [alanine]) occur more often than nonsynonymous changes. As a consequence, a transition between two amino acids that would require, for example, three non-synonymous changes in the underlying nucleotide sequences is assigned a lower probability than an amino acid change calling for two nonsynonymous changes and one synonymous change. PROTPARS does not have an option that uses empirical values for amino acid changes (e.g., PAM matrices).

DNADIST computes a distance matrix from nucleotide sequences. Trees are generated by running the output through NEIGHBOR or other distance matrix programs in the PHYLIP package (mentioned above). DNADIST allows the user to choose between three models of nucleotide substitution. The older Jukes and Cantor model is similar to the simple model in the PROTDIST program in that it assumes equal probabilities for all changes. The more recent Kimura two-parameter model is very similar but allows the user to weigh transversion more heavily than transitions. PHYLIP also comprises DNAML, an ML program for nucleotide data. Because the program is fairly slow, the use of its faster "sibling," Gary Olsen's fastDNAml program (Olsen et al., 1994), described below, is recommended.

SEQBOOT and CONSENSE are required for bootstrap analysis. SEQBOOT is used to generate x number of replicates of the input data (the user specifies the number of replicates), and then these replicates are used in programs such as PROTDIST then NEIGHBOR, or PROTDIST then FITCH, or PROTPARS (alone) for analysis. The resulting tree file contains, essentially, x trees, and so this file needs to be run through CONSENSE to generate the consensus tree from the analysis. As an example, the steps involved in building a bootstrapped NJ tree for protein sequences are outlined in Figure 14.11.

PAUP

The objective of the development of PAUP is to provide a phylogenetics program that includes as many functions (including tree graphics) as possible in a single, platform-independent program with a menu interface. However, originally PAUP stood for "phylogenetic analysis using parsimony" and still contains one of the most sophisticated parsimony programs available. Version 3 performed only MP-associated tree-building and analytical functions. PAUP version 4 includes distance and ML functions for nucleotide data and other new features.

Current tree-building functions in PAUP include MP and, for nucleotide data, distance and ML functions using the fastDNAml algorithm. In addition, PAUP performs Lake's method of invariants (Swofford et al., 1996; Li, 1997). Each tree-building program permits a variety of options. The MP options include specification of any character-weighting scheme. Distance options

include choice of NJ, ME, FM (see PAUP release notes re: PHYLIP), and UPGMA procedures. The full range of options and their current values can be examined using the menu or by typing pse[ttings] ? dse[ttings] ? and lse[ttings] ? for parsimony, distance, and likelihood, respectively. Both distance likelihood and ML allow detailed specification of the substitution model (values of substitution, γ, and invariant-site parameters assuming equal, specified, or empirical base frequencies), and these can be estimated for any tree by setting the parameter values to est[imate] and applying the des[cribe tree] command with a desired tree in memory.

According to the release notes accompanying PAUP test version 4, "PAUP* usually finds trees with likelihoods as high or higher (i.e., better) than PHYLIP" (both because PAUP*'s tree rearrangements are more extensive and because its convergence criterion for branch length iteration is stricter).

With any tree-building method, PAUP allows a variety of tree search options. These include algorithm specification for generating the initial tree (starting tree): NJ, stepwise addition, or input tree(s). The stepwise-addition algorithm allows numerous options, including addition of taxa "as is" (taxa added in file order): closest, furthest, or random with any number of replicates. All the stepwise options allow for any maximal number of partial trees to be retained and built on during taxon addition. Increasing this number to, say, 100, is another means of increasing the diversity of starting topologies, although these are not random.

A random addition strategy provides a useful complement to the default search strategy (closest addition, tree bisection-reconnection (TBR) swapping, saving all best trees). In the random search, a large number of replicates can be combined with the faster nearest-neighbor interchange (NNI) swapping algorithm. For MP analysis, in which a large number of equal-length trees may exist, the search should specify saving from each replicate only a few trees that match or should better the score of the slower search. In addition, the number of suboptimal trees (the trees that are swapped on to find better trees) should be limited by setting MAXTREES to a low number (e.g., 10). By using this strategy to explore areas of "tree space" possibly missed in the slow search, one sometimes finds better trees, additional unique optimal trees, or both.

PAUP performs the nonparametric bootstrap for distance, MP, and ML using all options available for tree building with these methods. When a bootstrap or jackknife with MP is underway, MAXTREES should be set between 10 and no more than 100. This is because poorly resolvable portions of an MP tree usually are even less resolvable with resampled data; hence, a replicate could find astronomical numbers of equal-length trees.

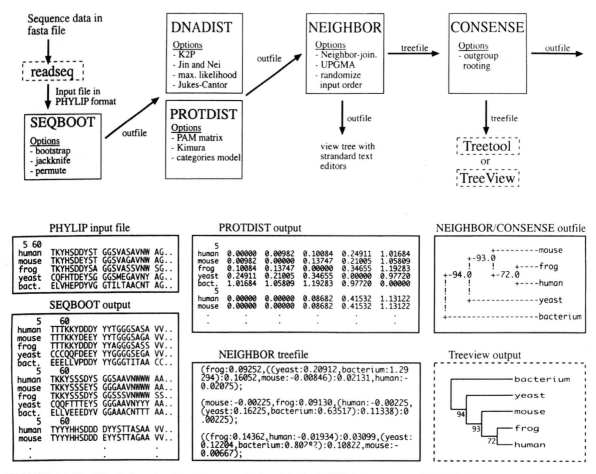

FIGURE 14.11 Work flow for bootstrap analysis with the **PHYLIP** program. SEQBOOT accepts a file in **PHYLIP** format as input and multiplies it a user-specified number of times (e.g., 1000). The resulting outfile can be used to calculate 1000 distance matrices for **DNA** (DNADIST) or protein (PROTDIST) data. In this step, the actual data (nucleotides, amino acids) are discarded and are replaced by a figure that is a measure for the amount of divergence between two sequences. The **NEIGHBOR** program creates 1000 trees from these matrices. The **CONSENSE** program reduces the 1000 trees to a single one and indicates the bootstrap values as numbers on the branches. The topology of the **CONSENSE** tree can be viewed with any text editor in the outfile, whereas the tree file can be processed further for publication purposes. Treetool and **TREEVIEW** allow the user to manipulate the tree (rerooting, branch rearrangements, conversions from dendrograms to phylograms, etc.) and to save the file in commonly used graphic formats (like **PICT**). Although these are not part of the **PHYLIP** package (indicated by boxes with dashed lines), they are freely available (see end-of-chapter list). The figure also shows the different file formats used during date processing through the stages of bootstrap analysis. Periods to the right and at the bottom of a box indicate files that were truncated to save space.

Because tree branches weakly supported by the full data set will not have high bootstrap or jackknife values, limiting MAXTREES will have little, if any, bearing on the results, especially if the number of replicates is increased to, say, 1000.

In addition, PAUP performs the Kishino–Hasegawa test to compare MP or ML trees, computes four types of consensus of multiple trees (usually used for multiple equal-length MP trees), computes stepwise differences between MP trees, and evaluates signal conflict between specified partitions of sites (e.g., nuclear and organellar sequence data in a combined analysis).

Other Programs

In addition to PAUP and PHYLIP, there are phylogenetics programs that have some unique capabilities but generally are more limited in their procedures and portability. These include FastDNAml, PUZZLE, MacClade, MOLPHY, and programs that are developed primarily for another function but do include phylogenetic tree construction methods (for example, Clustal).

FastDNAml. FastDNAml (Olsen et al., 1994) is a freestanding ML tree-building program. Although it currently is not part of the PHYLIP package, it uses largely the same input and output conventions, and the results of fastDNAml and PHYLIP's DNAML should be very similar or identical. FastDNAml can be run on parallel processors, and it comes with a number of useful scripts (in particular for bootstrapping and jumbling the sequence input order). To take full advantage of the program, knowledge of Unix is beneficial. The source code for Unix systems is publicly available from the RDP Web site, and a Macintosh version is available by FTP.

PUZZLE or TREE-PUZZLE. PUZZLE, or TREE-PUZZLE as it is now called (Strimmer & von Haeseler, 1996), is an ML-based program that implements a fast tree search algorithm, quartet puzzling, that allows analysis of large data sets and automatically assigns estimations of support to each internal branch. PUZZLE also computes pairwise ML distances as well as branch lengths for user-specified trees. PUZZLE also offers a novel method, likelihood mapping, to investigate the support of a hypothesized internal branch without computing an overall tree and to visualize the phylogenetic content of a sequence alignment. It conducts a number of statistical tests (χ^2 test for homogeneity of base composition, likelihood ratio clock test, Kishino-Hasegawa test) and includes a large range of models of substitution. Rate heterogeneity is modeled by a discrete γ distribution and by allowing invariable sites.

MacClade. MacClade (Maddison & Maddison, 1992) is an interactive Macintosh program for manipulating trees and data and for studying the phylogenetic behavior of characters. It uses the NEXUS format and reads PAUP data and tree files. Some information in PAUP files are ignored in MacClade (e.g., gapmode), but information in a PAUP "assumptions" block are imported, including character weightings and character and taxon sets. Several subtle differences exist between PAUP and MacClade files. Thus, PAUP files edited with MacClade and vice versa should be saved under new names and the unedited file maintained. PHYLIP, *National Biomedical Research Foundation-Protein Information Resource* (NBRF-PIR), and text files also are readable by MacClade. Any method can be used to generate the trees, but MacClade's functions are based strictly on parsimony. For example, the program allows one to trace the evolution of each individual character on any tree. The MP and ML reconstruction functions differ, however, and the ML function is considered more realistic (Swofford et al., 1996). Tree topologies can be manipulated by dragging branches, and flipping branches can produce aesthetic modifications in tree symmetry.

MacClade includes additional features relevant to sequence analysis, including a chart of character number versus number of changes in a tree, which is useful for visualizing among-site rate heterogeneity, and a chart of the overall numbers of changes from one base to another over an MP tree (state changes and stasis chart: the values are sometimes reported erroneously in the literature as substitution rates, but there is no correction for branch lengths or among-site rate heterogeneity).

MOLPHY. MOLPHY (Adachi & Hasegawa, 1996) is a shareware package of programs and utilities for ML analysis and statistics of nucleotide or amino acid sequences. Practical application requires some knowledge of Unix file management. The ML procedures are similar to those in PHYLIP, but there is a wider range of amino acid substitution models and options for faster, heuristic searches, including an option to use local bootstrap analyses (i.e., a bootstrap on subtrees under the assumption that the remainder of the tree is correct) to search for better ML trees. The output includes branch length estimates and standard error. Analysis of separate codon positions is possible. MOLPHY uses a subset of the nucleotide substitution models available in PAUP, although it allows user-specified parameter values. The current MOLPHY lacks a bootstrap option and also has no accommodation for among-site rate heterogeneity.

Clustal. Clustal is probably the most popular multiple sequence alignment program. ClustalW is the command-line–based version and ClustalX contains a few updates (see ClustalX documentation), although the latter functions only via a graphical user interface. Both are examples of programs primarily developed for multiple sequence alignment generation, but also include the ability to generate simple phylogenetic trees. In Clustal, NJ is the method offered with the option to perform additional common analyses such as bootstrapping. Although not as flexible as other programs, Clustal can be a useful program when one wishes quickly to generate a multiple sequence alignment and associated tree to examine any obvious phylogenetic relationships that would tend to be independent of the method used. Clustal is discussed in more detail in Chapter 12.

Internet-Accessible Software

Currently, there are few Web-based applications that will permit one to perform phylogenetic analyses; however, they are appearing in increasing numbers, and presumably as Internet bandwidth increases and servers have faster central processing units (CPUs), this may become more common. Highlighted here are three Internet-based applications that provide phylogenetic analysis capability (WEBPHYLIP, PhyloBLAST, and the Blast2 & Orthologue Search Server) to illustrate the variety of applications available. Although all use PHYLIP programs, the latter two combine phylogenetic analysis with BLAST to aid the user in retrieving sequences for analysis.

WEBPHYLIP is based on CGI/Perl programming to produce a Web-based cut and paste interface to the PHYLIP programs. Unfortunately, the programs are not linked together, so to generate an NJ tree, for example, the user must run multiple analyses (PROTDIST and NEIGHBOR in this case). Analyses may time out if too intensive an analysis is performed. Also, the trees can not be viewed easily; for example, if the user has a PC, they must have ghostview or another such postscript viewer installed. However, the Web site provides excellent flowcharts and other helpful documentation about running the programs; an extensive collection of the PHYLIP programs is available, unlike the other Internet-based applications described below.

PhyloBLAST is also based on CGI/Perl programming. Its source code is freely available, although it is not maintained further because the project involving its generation was a short-term project that has ended. It is hoped, however, that by releasing the code, others may still use it, improve it, or customize it according to their needs. PhyloBLAST compares a user's protein sequence with a Swiss-Prot/TrEMBL database using BLAST2 and then allows user-defined phylogenetic analyses to be performed on selected sequences from the BLAST output. NJ and parsimony analyses may be performed, either with or without bootstrapping, using PHYLIP programs. Flexible features, such as the ability to input a multiple sequence alignment and to use all options in the PHYLIP programs, provide additional Web-based phylogenetic analysis functionality that goes beyond the simple analysis of a BLAST result. Because PHYLIP programs needed to generate trees are linked, there is less input required by the user than for WEBPHYLIP; however, DNA analysis and analysis using other programs such as FITCH, are not currently available. PhyloBLAST's ability to generate trees containing hyperlinks to further protein sequence information, or to generate JPEG graphics of trees that may be viewed over the Internet or downloaded, are considerable advantages. Also, the program is set up to handle Web page timeouts, so analyses requiring significant computational time are not a problem.

Blast2 & Orthologue Search Server is provided by the Bork group at Heidelberg. This is a fairly specialized application of phylogenetic analysis of a BLAST output for the identification of orthologs verses paralogs. This tool performs a BLAST analysis and then performs a phylogenetic analysis on user-selected sequences based on a ClustalW alignment and PHYLIP's NJ methods. This resulting NJ tree (or gene tree) is compared with a predicted species tree, and the reconciled tree is viewed for analysis. The philosophy is that whenever the phylogeny of the species matches the phylogeny of the gene tree, these genes will be deemed orthologous.

Although a useful tool, users should be cautioned that this does not represent a comprehensive phylogenetic analysis because of the automated nature of the application. Its use should be primarily as intended: to gain insight into what homologous sequences are orthologous in an automated fashion. Further analysis should be performed for any particularly in-depth investigation using less automated alignment and phylogenetic analysis that suits the sequences being investigated.

Tree-Drawing Software

There are a number of tree-drawing programs available now, such as TREEVIEW (Macintosh, Microsoft Windows, Linux, UNIX), TreeTool (Xwindows), Tree-Draw (Macintosh), PHYLODENDRON (Macintosh), or the tree-drawing tool in PAUP. All handle standard tree files. These programs facilitate not only the generation of trees suitable for publication or other presentation, but also facilitate viewing of the data in general. For example, programs such as the freely available Treeview (Web page link provided below) enable the user to manipulate the view of branching order and to root the tree, in addition to other graphical manipulations that aid the user.

SUMMARY

Paradoxical as it may sound, by far the most important factor in inferring phylogenies is not the method of phylogenetic inference but the quality of the input data. The importance of data selection and in particular of the alignment process cannot be overestimated. Even the most sophisticated phylogenetic inference methods are not able to correct for biased or erroneous input data.

Often underappreciated, the multiple sequence alignment step also is critical to effective phylogenetic analysis. The results are only as good as the original alignment, and one should examine the alignment to ensure that the columns of characters in their alignment likely originate from a common ancestor.

Look at the data from as many angles as possible. Use each of the three main methods (distance, maximum parsimony, and ML), and compare the resulting trees for consistency. At the same time, be aware that one cannot rely on having arrived at a good estimate for the true phylogeny just because all three methods produce the same tree. Unfortunately, consistency among results obtained by different methods does not necessarily mean that the result is statistically significant (or represents the true phylogeny), because there can be several reasons for such correspondence.

The choice of outgroup taxa can have as much influence on the analysis as the choice of ingroup taxa. Complications occur in particular when the outgroup shares an unusual property (e.g., composition bias or clock rate) with one or several in-group taxa. It therefore is advisable to compute every analysis with several outgroups and to check for congruency of the in-group topologies.

Be aware that programs can give different answers (trees) depending on the order in which the sequences appear in the input file. PHYLIP, PAUP, and other phylogenetic software provide a "jumble" option that reruns the analysis with different (jumbled) input orders. If, for whatever reason, the tree must be computed in a single run, sequences that are suspected of being "problematic" should be placed toward the end of the input file to lower the probability that tree rearrangement methods will be influenced negatively by a poor initial topology stemming from any problematic sequences.

In general, one always should consider any bioinformatic analysis in an evolutionary context when it is based on evolutionary assumptions. For example, when performing a BLAST analysis, is the selected substitution matrix suitable, based on the level of sequence similarity observed? Which of the hits in the BLAST analysis are orthologs? Which are paralogs? Which may be similar to the query sequence purely by chance and, therefore, may share no similar ancestry or similar function? It is often relevant to follow-up many bioinformatic analyses with subsequent evolutionary analyses, such as performing a phylogenetic analysis of BLAST results, to gain a better appreciation of the relationships between the similar sequences. For such reasons, it is critical for researchers performing bioinformatic analyses to gain familiarity with evolutionary methods and assumptions and to consider their results in an evolutionary context.

ACKNOWLEDGMENTS

The author thanks D. D. Leipe for helpful work on an earlier edition of this book chapter and J. L. Gardy for some text from the worked example.

WORKED EXAMPLE

In this exercise, an automatically generated alignment is created and is used to perform a simple phylogenetic analysis on a set of proteins using the NJ algorithm of the ClustalX program. Normally, one would perform a more thorough analysis of the alignment, but to determine the analysis has been performed correctly and to allow for comparison of the results with those expected, an automated analysis is used in this example.

The bacterium *Pseudomonas aeruginosa* is noted for its resistance to the antimicrobial compound impenem. One of the proteins that mediates this resistance is OprD, an outer membrane protein involved in uptake of the basic amino acid arginine. If OprD is not expressed by the cell, the cell will become resistant to imipenem, because imipenem resembles the basic amino acid arginine and is taken up by cell through OprD. Another protein in the OprD family is OpdT, which (in this contrived example) is thought to be involved in uptake of the neutral amino acid leucine. In some *P. aeruginosa* strains, the OpdT gene is lost, and the bacterium therefore does not take up the antibiotic neutripenem (which resembles the amino acid leucine), and thus is resistant to this drug. OpdQ also has been studied from this family and seems to increase in expression when exposed to the aeromatic compound toluene.

Recently, a genome project was undertaken for the highly pathogenic bacterium *Bioinformaticus examinus*, which is related to *P. aeruginosa*. Some strains of *B. examinus* also are resistant to impenem and neutripenem; however, it has been difficult to study the organism, because it cannot be cultured easily in the laboratory. However, through the genome project, several genes related to OprD were identified via BLAST analysis, and it is hoped that by analyzing these sequences, more insight can be gained regarding what proteins are involved in resistance to imipenem and neutripenem in *B. examinus*. This exercise focuses on determining whether *B. examinus* has orthologs of the OprD family of proteins in its genome, and also on determining whether what is known about the *P. aeruginosa* OprD family can be used to hypothesize about the function of the related genes in *B. examinus*.

ClustalX can be downloaded freely from the Clustal site listed in the Internet Resources for this chapter. Treeview can be downloaded in a similar fashion. It is recommended that, because of a bug in ClustalX, the program be placed in a directory that has no spaces in the directory name. For example, on a Windows-based system, do not place this program in My Documents or Program Files, but rather place it in another directory that has no spaces in its name (i.e., Programs).

Automated Alignment of Sequences with Clustal

Download the file named phylo-example.txt from the Book's Web site. Save the file locally, start ClustalX, and load the sequences into this program. Under the alignment menu, choose Do Complete Alignment to create an alignment.

Constructing and Viewing the Tree

Under the Tree menu of ClustalX, with the alignment loaded, select Exclude Positions with Gaps and Correct for Multiple Substitutions (Why? Check the Trees help file in Clustal).

Draw an NJ tree, saving the output file with a .phy extension. Then, in preparation for constructing a bootstrapped tree, change the output format option (under the Tree menu) for bootstrap labels to be on the node rather than branch (this option makes the tree compatible with viewing in Treeview).

Generate a bootstrapped tree, again saving the file with a .phy or .phb extension (be careful not to overwrite other files). The .phy or .phb extension is required to open the files in Treeview, the program used for viewing.

Open the NJ tree in Treeview. Try adjusting the various settings to view the tree in different ways. Note that, because this tree is unrooted (there is no outgroup reference sequence to anchor the base of the tree), the most appropriate display is the unrooted, or radial, tree format (listed under the Tree menu item).

Open the bootstrapped tree in Treeview. This tree also is unrooted, but contains additional information that can be viewed by selecting Show Internal Edge Labels under the Tree menu in Treeview. At the nodes of the tree are numbers that indicate how many times that, of the number of tree replicates made (default is 1000), this particular branching order occurred. Is there a correlation between the length of branches and the size of the bootstrap values? Poorly resolved nodes tend to have small branch lengths between them and small bootstrap values. The latter is not directly related to the former, but does reflect a lack of certainty of the order of the nodes (using that particular phylogenetic analysis algorithm, i.e., NJ). Examine the bootstrapped tree and compare it with the unbootstrapped tree. Is the branching order similar in the two trees? Which branching orders should one trust? Check that your trees resemble the output illustrated in Figure 14.12.

Interpreting the Data

Consider the following questions, using the information provided by the trees. Assuming there has been no horizontal gene transfer, that PaOpdB and BeGene650 have diverged because of speciation, and that the sequences with PaOp names are from *P. aeruginosa* and the sequences with BeGene names are from *B. examinus*:

▶ What is the most related orthologous sequence to Be-Gene160?

▶ What is the most related paralogous sequence to BeGene160?

▶ Referring to the background information given to you in the introduction to this laboratory, what could you hypothesize about the function of BeGene160? Why?

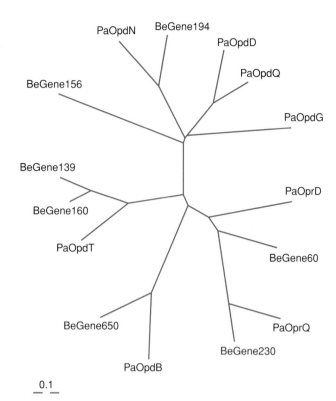

FIGURE 14.12 Phylogenetic trees generated from the Worked Example. (a) Unrooted tree. (b) Unrooted bootstrapped tree (1000 replicates). See text for details.

PROBLEM SET

1. Examine Figure 14.13, which contains a tree depicting organismal phylogeny and a tree depicting a gene phylogeny. Which genes are likely orthologs of the Fly gene *CC2*? Do you have higher confidence in your proposal of orthology for some of the genes verses others?

2. Examine the Worked Example phylogenetic analysis illustrated in Figure 14.12 (see also the Worked Example background text for more information about what genes are from what organisms and what genes have been previously determined to be orthologs). Based on this analysis, which of the following pair of genes would be more likely to have identical functions, PaOpdD and PaOpdQ or PaOprQ and BeGene230? Justify your choice.

3. According to the analysis in the Worked Example, which gene or genes would be prime target(s) for further study of their role in antimicrobial resistance in *B. examinus*?

INTERNET RESOURCES

Bork Group's BLAST2 & Ortholog Search	http://www.Bork. EMBL-Heidelberg.DE/Blast2e/
ClustaL	http://www-igbmc.u-strasbg.fr/BioInfo/
Genedoc	http://www.psc.edu/biomed/genedoc/

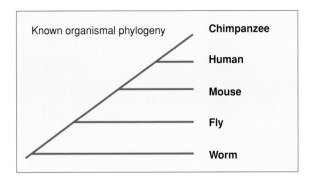

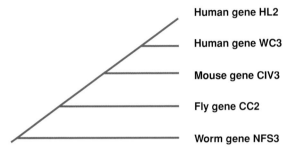

FIGURE 14.13 Trees for use with the Problem Set. See Problem Set for questions.

PHYLIP	http://evolution.genetics.washington.edu/phylip.html
PhyloBLAST	http://www.pathogenomics.bc.ca/phyloBLAST/
Phylogenetic Analysis Computer Programs	http://phylogeny.arizona.edu/tree/programs/programs.html
Phylogenetic Resources	http://www.ucmp.berkeley.edu/subway/phylogen.html
Phylogeny Programs	http://evolution.genetics.washington.edu/phylip/software.html
PUZZLEBOOT	http://www.tree-puzzle.de
ReadSeq	http://dot.imgen.bcm.tmc.edu:9331/seq-util/Options/readseq.html
Ribosomal Database Project II (RDP II)	http://www.cme.msu.edu/RDP/html/
Suggesting a Phylogenetic Placement on the RDP Tree	http://rdp.life.uiuc.edu/RDP/commands/sgtree.html
TreeView	http://taxonomy.zoology.gla.ac.uk/rod/treeview.html
WEBPHYLIP	http://sdmc.krdl.org.sg:8080/~lxzhang/phylip/
WHS – educational material	http://www.cladistics.org/education.html

REFERENCES

ADACHI, J., AND HASEGAWA, M. (1996). *MOLPHY Version 2.3. Programs for Molecular Phylogenetics Based on Maximum Likelihood* (Institute of Statistical Mathematics, Tokyo).

EFRON, B. (1979). Bootstrapping methods: another look at the jackknife. *Ann. Stat.* 7, 1–26.

DAYHOFF, M. O., SCHWARTZ, R. M., AND ORCUTT, B. C. (1978). A model of evolutionary change in proteins. In *Atlas of Protein Sequence and Structure* (Dayhoff, M. O., ed.), (National Biomedical Research Foundation, Washington, DC), p. 345–362.

FAITH, D. P., AND TRUEMAN, J. W. H. (1996). When the topology-dependent permutation test (T-PTP) for monophyly returns significant support for monophyly, should that be equated with (a) rejecting the null hypothesis of nonmonophyly, (b) rejecting the null hypothesis of "no structure," (c) failing to falsify a hypothesis of monophyly, or (d) none of the above? *Syst. Biol.* 45, 580–586.

FELSENSTEIN, J. (1985). Confidence intervals on phylogenies: an approach using the bootstrap. *Evolution* 39, 783–791.

FELSENSTEIN, J. (1996). Inferring phylogenies from protein sequences by parsimony, distance, and likelihood methods. *Methods Enzymol.* 266, 418–427.

FELSENSTEIN, J. (1997). An alternative least-squares approach to inferring phylogenies from pairwise distances. *Syst. Biol.* 46, 101–111.

GATESY, J., DESALLE, R., AND WHEELER, W. (1993). Alignment-ambiguous nucleotide sites and the exclusion of systematic data. *Mol. Phylogenet. Evol.* 2, 152–157.

HILLIS, D. M., AND BULL, J. J. (1993). An empirical test of bootstrapping as a method for assessing confidence in phylogenetic analysis. *Syst. Biol.* 42, 182–192.

HILLIS, D. M., ALLARD, M. W., AND MIYAMOTO, M. M. (1993). Analysis of DNA sequence data: phylogenetic inference. *Methods Enzymol.* 224, 456–487.

HILLIS, D. M., HUELSENBECK, J. P., AND CUNNINGHAM, C. W. (1994). Application and accuracy of molecular phylogenies. *Science* 264, 671–677.

HUELSENBECK, J. P. (1995). Performance of phylogenetic methods in simulation. *Syst. Biol.* 44, 17–48.

HUELSENBECK, J. P., HILLIS, D. M., AND JONES, R. (1996). Parametric bootstrapping in molecular phylogenetics. In *Molecular Zoology: Advances, Strategies, and Protocols* (Ferraris, J. D., and Palumbi, S. R., eds.), (Wiley-Liss, New York) p. 19–45.

HUGHEY, R., KROGH, A., BARRETT, C., AND GRATE, L. (1996). SAM: sequence alignment and modelling software (University of California, Santa Cruz, Baskin Center for Computer Engineering and Information Sciences), available at http://www.cse.ucsc.edu/research/compbio/papers/sam_doc/sam_doc.html.

KOSKI, L. B., AND GOLDING, G. B. (2001). The closest BLAST hit is often not the nearest neighbor. *J. Mol. Evol.* 52, 540–542.

KUMAR, S., TAMURA, K., AND NEI, M. (1994). MEGA: molecular evolutionary genetics analysis software for microcomputers. *Comput. Appl. Biosci.* 10, 189–191.

LAKE, J. A. (1994). Reconstructing evolutionary trees from DNA and protein sequences: -paralinear distances. *Proc. Natl. Acad. Sci. U. S. A.* 91, 1455–1459.

LAWSON, F. S., CHARLEBOIS, R. L., AND DILLON, J. A. (1996). Phylogenetic analysis of carbamoylphosphate synthetase genes: complex evolutionary history includes an internal duplication within a gene which can root the tree of life. *Mol. Biol. Evol.* 13, 970–977.

LEIPE, D. D., WAINRIGHT, P. O., GUNDERSON, J. H., PORTER, D., PATTERSON, D. J., VALOIS, F., HIMMERICH, S., AND SOGIN, M. L. (1994). The Stramenopiles from a molecular perspective: 16S-like rRNA sequences from *Labyrinthuloides minutum* and *Cafeteria roenbergensis*. *Phycologia* 33, 369–377.

LI, W.-H. (1997). *Molecular Evolution* (Sinauer Associates, Sunderland, MA).

MADDISON, W. P., AND MADDISON, D. R. (1992). *MacClade: Analysis of Phylogeny and Character Evolution. Version 3.0* (Sinauer Associates, Sunderland, MA).

NIXON, K. C., AND CARPENTER, J. M. (1993). On outgroups. *Cladistics* 9, 413–426.

OLSEN, G. J., MATSUDA, H., HAGSTROM, R., AND OVERBEEK, R. (1994). fastDNAml: a tool for construction of phylogenetic trees of DNA sequences using maximum likelihood. *Comput. Appl. Biosci.* 10, 41.

RZHETSKY, A., AND NEI, M. (1992). A simple method for estimating and testing minimum evolution trees. *Mol. Biol. Evol.* 9, 945–967.

RZHETSKY, A., AND NEI, M. (1994). METREE: a program package for inferring and testing minimum-evolution trees. *Comput. Appl. Biosci.* 10,409–412.

SAITOU, N. (1996). Reconstruction of gene trees from sequence data. *Methods Enzymol.* 266, 427–449.

STRIMMER, K., AND VON HAESELER, A. (1996). Quartet puzzling: a quartet maximum likelihood method for reconstructing tree topologies. *Mol. Biol. Evol.* 13, 964–969.

SWOFFORD, D. L., OLSEN, G. J., WADDELL, P. J., AND HILLIS, D. M. (1996). Phylogenetic inference. In *Molecular Systematics* (Hillis, D. M., Moritz, C., and Mable, B. K., eds.), (Sinauer Associates, Sunderland, MA) p. 407–514.

THOMPSON, J. D., HIGGINS, D. G., AND GIBSON, T. J. (1994). Clustal W: improving the sensitivity of progressive multiple alignment through sequence weighting. *Nucl. Acids Res.* 22, 4673–4680.

THORNE, J. L., AND KISHINO, H. (1992). Freeing phylogenies from artifacts of alignment. *Mol. Biol. Evol.* 9, 1148–1162.

WESTON, P. H. (1994). Methods for rooting cladistic trees. In *Models in Phylogeny Reconstruction* (Scotland, R. W., Siebert, D. J., and Williams, D. M., eds.), (Systematics Association, Oxford), p. 125–155.

YANG, Z., GOLDMAN, N., AND FRIDAY, A. (1995). Maximum likelihood trees from DNA sequences: a peculiar statistical problem. *Syst. Biol.* 44, 384–399.

KEY TERMS

evolution

evolutionary analysis

ortholog

paralog

phylogenetic tree

phylogenetics

## CHAPTER FIFTEEN

Computational Approaches in Comparative Genomics

ANDREAS D. BAXEVANIS

Bioinformatics: A Practical Guide to the Analysis of Genes and Proteins, Third Edition, edited by
Andreas D. Baxevanis and B.F. Francis Ouellette.
ISBN 0-471-47878-4 Copyright © 2005 John Wiley & Sons, Inc.

INTRODUCTION

Comparing Genomes to Understand Evolution

The preceding chapter was devoted to evolution from the standpoint of phylogenetics, focusing mainly on how to deduce the relationships within gene or protein families. This chapter looks at evolution from a slightly different standpoint, comparing genomes to gain a better understanding of the similarities and differences between genomes over evolutionary time. Because it is generally accepted that genes important to survival have been conserved during evolution and remain common to a large number of organisms, it is critically important to have a firm understanding of how genes in different organisms are related to one another. Often, one can identify the function of a human gene by working on the corresponding gene in a model organism; such comparative studies providing new insight into human biology and gene expression. It also is very important to have a firm understanding of the differences between organisms, because often the differences may be more important than the similarities, particularly with respect to disease susceptibility. For example, it is known that humans and chimpanzees share 98.8% overall sequence identity. Despite this, chimpanzees are not susceptible to a number of diseases that humans are susceptible to, such as malaria and AIDS. Understanding the 1.2% difference may provide clues as to the nature of this species barrier, as well as providing clues to pathways for the prevention of disease.

Most of the efforts in the field of computational comparative genomics focus on detecting conservation within genes and in intergenic regions, the conservation of gene order (synteny), and predicting the presence and pattern of cis-acting regulatory elements. Asking these questions at different evolutionary distances provides different insights as to what the similarities and differences imply. Looking at similarities over short evolutionary distances may indicate the factors making a particular organism unique, whereas looking at similarities over long evolutionary distances may indicate whether generic core sets of genes can be attributed to broad sets of organisms (for a primer, see Hardison, 2003). For example, comparison of the recently completed mouse genome sequence (International Mouse Genome Sequencing Consortium, 2002) indicates that, although the mouse genome is 14% smaller than the human genome, 90% of mouse genes have intact human homologs; further, the comparisons provide clues as to what comprises a generic mammalian gene set. Finally, these similarities, as well as the large degree of synteny between the mouse and human genomes, provide a strong handle for identifying druggable targets for the treatment of disease.

As one may imagine, the main approach for detecting similarities on a genomic scale involves either pairwise or multiple sequence alignments. However, given the unique nature of the problem at hand, the methods described earlier in this book become impractical when applied to such large data sets. This chapter describes new methods that have been developed to facilitate these comparisons. The goal of these new approaches is to capitalize on the information inherent in the ever-increasing number of available genome sequences, with the ultimate goal of understanding human biology better and improving human health.

ALGORITHMS FOR ALIGNING LARGE-SCALE DATA

The basic problem of aligning genomic-scale data sets is, at its most elementary level, no different than the problem posed in Chapter 11. The goal still is to find the best alignment between two sequences of interest. However, using the traditional workhorses for pairwise sequence alignment (BLAST and FASTA) would be inefficient at best, given the computational time it would take actually to align two very long sequences to one another. Recall that two methods presented in Chapter 11 provide a slightly different approach to pairwise sequence alignment: MegaBLAST and BLAT. Both of these methods are optimized rapidly to align longer nucleotide sequences having very high levels of sequence similarity (>95%). As alluded to above, even though both of these methods are incredibly useful, neither of these methods was developed specifically to align entire genomes to one another. Given the availability of an increasing number of complete genome sequences, numerous algorithms for the alignment of two or more genomes have now come to the fore, each allowing questions of evolutionary interest to be addressed.

BLASTZ

BLASTZ (Schwartz et al., 2003b) is a variation on gapped BLAST that is intended to align orthologous regions between two genomes and initially was applied to aligning mouse and human sequences. The method begins with a masking step, identifying regions in the first genome that are found repeatedly in the second genome. The method then proceeds to identify seed sequences from which to begin to build alignments. Recall that, in BLAST, searches begin with the identification of matching or near-matching words of a given length; in BLAST, the default word length is 11, whereas for MegaBLAST, the default word length is 28. Here, a decidedly different approach is taken to determine the initial match.

Rather than look for strings of exact or near-exact matches, BLASTZ looks for stretches of 19 nucleotides in which 12 of the 19 positions fit a strict match–mismatch pattern. The template used takes the form 1110100110010101111, where 1 represents a matched position and 0 represents a mismatched position; this particular template was found to provide the best results when the two sequences being aligned shared more than 60% similarity (Ma et al., 2002). In addition, one of the 12 positions is allowed to undergo a transition (A $\leftrightarrow$ G or C $\leftrightarrow$ T), a subtle change that was found to increase the sensitivity of the method.

As soon as the initial match is determined, a gap-free extension is performed until the cumulative score reaches a certain threshold (default, 3000). If the threshold is met, the extension is redetermined, this time allowing gaps to be included in the pairwise alignment. Only alignments reaching a certain score (default, 5000) move to the next step. The raw scores are derived in a similar fashion to BLASTN, with some subtle differences that confer increased sensitivity. First, the substitution matrices used in BLASTN tend to be simple match–mismatch scoring schemes, whereas the BLASTZ default matrix takes into account the relative frequencies of aligned nucleotides in noncoding, nonrepetitive genomic regions (Chiaromonte et al., 2002). This default matrix, designed specifically for human–mouse comparison, is shown in Figure 15.1. The default affine gap penalty used by BLASTN is $5 + 2L$, whereas the penalty in BLASTZ is $400 + 30L$, with L being the length of the gap.

To extend the contiguity of the alignments, the method now tries to connect individual alignments that are separated by less than 50 Kb of intervening sequence, keeping the proper order and orientation of the flanking alignments when doing so. The steps are the same as before, but rather than using a "12 in 19"

seed in the intervening region, exact 7-mer matches are sought; a threshold of 2200 is used for the gap-free alignment and 2000 is used for the gapped alignment. Final removal of lineage-specific repeats and recursive steps of BLASTZ are performed on adjacent alignments to yield the final alignment. Through this method, BLASTZ was able to align mouse sequences successfully to 40% of the human genome (Schwartz et al., 2003b).

LAGAN

The Limited Area Global Alignment of Nucleotides (LAGAN) algorithm allows for pairwise alignment of genomic-scale sequences (Brudno et al., 2003). As alluded to in its name, LAGAN is a global alignment method, unlike BLASTZ, which is a local alignment method. One of the strengths of the LAGAN algorithm is that it allows for the detection of both closely and distantly related sequences.

The LAGAN algorithm is reminiscent of the FASTA algorithm described in Chapter 11, based on its general approach to performing a global alignment. First, LAGAN determines the best local alignments and assigns a weight to each. The best subset of these alignments is selected to serve as anchors, defining a rough global alignment around which the final global alignment is built. The anchors are used to limit the search space, focusing primarily on aligning the regions between the anchors and, ultimately, connecting them; the Needleman-Wunsch algorithm is applied in these areas. By focusing in on a limited area around the rough global alignment, the computational time needed to generate the final global alignment is reduced greatly.

LAGAN is the basis for Multi-LAGAN, a program that generates multiple genomic sequence alignments. The method is similar to ClustalW (Chapter 12) in that it uses a progressive alignment approach. Here, each pair of sequences is aligned first using LAGAN. As soon as a pair of sequences are aligned, the pair is represented as a single sequence (a multisequence), and a round of alignment of each multisequence is performed. The process continues, merging the closest multisequences to each other, until all of the sequences are represented in the final alignment. The alignment depends on a user-specified phylogenetic tree, further improving the quality of the multiple genomic sequence alignment. To illustrate the speed of Multi-LAGAN, Brudno et al. (2003) used Multi-LAGAN to align sequences from 12 species corresponding to an approximately 1.5-Mb region of human chromosome 7 containing the *CFTR* gene (Thomas et al., 2003); the alignment took 75 minutes to complete on a personal computer. When benchmarked against other alignment algorithms, again using the *CFTR* data set, LAGAN, Multi-LAGAN, and BLASTZ were seen to give the

	A	C	T	G			A	C	T	G
A	1	-3	-3	-3		A	91	-114	-31	-123
C	-3	1	-3	-3		C	-114	100	-125	-31
T	-3	-3	1	-3		T	-31	-125	100	-114
G	-3	-3	-3	1		G	-123	-31	-114	91

FIGURE 15.1 **Default substitution matrices used by BLASTN (left) and BLASTZ (right). The default BLASTN matrix uses a simple match–mismatch approach, whereas the BLASTZ matrix is based on observed substitutions in aligned, conserved regions of mouse and human.**

best results for closely related organisms, with LAGAN and Multi LAGAN performing best for more distantly related organisms.

AVID

The AVID program (Bray et al., 2003) also takes a global approach to the question of genomic alignments. The algorithm is able to align DNA sequences of any length quickly and is able to detect weak homologies. Like LAGAN, AVID relies on the use of anchors, selected using a variation of the Smith-Waterman algorithm (Chapter 11); anchors are required to be nonoverlapping, a deviation from the standard Smith-Waterman approach. As soon as the initial set of anchors is identified, the method focuses on the regions between the anchors; these regions are realigned and new anchors are selected. The process continues in a recursive fashion until the original input sequences have been aligned completely.

■ VIEWING PRECOMPUTED GENOMIC ALIGNMENTS

Both BLASTZ and LAGAN and Multi-LAGAN have been used to generate genomic alignments on selected organisms, and these precomputed alignments can be viewed using one of several browsers. There are several sources for precomputed alignments, summarized briefly in Table 15.1. Two of these will be illustrated here; for both, the region containing the human *SOX10* gene is used as the query.

The University of California Santa Cruz (UCSC) Genome Browser, discussed in detail in Chapter 4, can be used to retrieve pairwise alignments between human and selected model organisms, as well as a multiple

TABLE 15.1 ■ Selected Sources for Precomputed Whole-Genome Alignments

Source	Organisms
Ensembl	Human, *C. briggsae, C. elegans,* chicken, chimpanzee, *Drosophila, Fugu,* mouse, rat, zebrafish
EnteriX	Several *E. coli, Klebsiella, Pseudomonas, Salmonella,* and *Yersinia* strains
GALA	Human, mouse, rat
UCSC Genome Browser	Human, chicken, chimpanzee, *Fugu,* mouse, rat
VISTA Browser	Human, chicken, chimpanzee, mouse, rat
WormBase	*C. briggsae, C. elegans*

genomic sequence alignment between five organisms. The browser window for the area around human *SOX10* is shown in Figure 15.2. Most of the tracks usually displayed have been hidden to focus on the comparative data available through the Browser. Focusing first on the tracks labeled *chimp, mouse, rat,* and *chicken,* each of these represents the BLASTZ pairwise alignment of that organism's sequence with the human sequence. Rather than showing a traditional pairwise alignment, the Browser shows what is, in essence, a histogram, indicating the conservation between the model organism and human across the aligned area. In this region, the chimp sequence shows the greatest conservation across the entire region; the chicken sequence is most divergent from human in this region. Directly above the individual tracks is a track labeled *Conservation;* this track represents a multiple sequence alignment of human, chimp, mouse, rat, and chicken sequences in this region. The multiple alignment is built by applying a method called MULTIZ to the individual BLASTZ alignments (Blanchette et al., 2004); on generation of the multiple genomic sequence alignment, conservation scores were calculated using a phylogenetic hidden Markov model (HMM; Siepel & Haussler, 2003). Note that the greatest overall conservation is in regions corresponding to known *SOX10* exons, as indicated by the thick blue bars in the SOX10 track; it is interesting that part of the left-most exon is "missing" in the *chimp* track. Clicking on any portion of the histograms returns the actual, letter-by-letter multiple sequence alignment.

The VISTA Browser, an interactive Java applet, also can be used to view precomputed alignments between human, chicken, chimpanzee, rat, and mouse (Figure 15.3). Beginning at the top of the main window, the human *SOX10* gene is depicted as a straight line; the arrow on the left end, above the gene name, shows the directionality of the gene. Exons are shown as blue bars, and 5′ and 3′ untranslated regions (UTRs) are in light green. Directly under the line representing the *SOX10* gene is a line showing the position of repeats, the colors corresponding to the key in the lower left of the applet window. The graphs themselves represent the alignments, generated either by LAGAN or Multi-LAGAN. Each graph is numbered, with the key appearing at the bottom of the window, and the order of the curves can be changed using the Up and Down buttons next to the key. The graphs indicate percent conservation across the region; the value itself is an averaged identity score using a variable-sized window, and the scale is given at the right of the curves (here, 0%–100%). Various parts of the curves have been colored in, indicating a region of high conservation; the region is colored blue if it corresponds to a known human exon, pink if it lies within a noncoding region, and light green if it lies in a UTR.

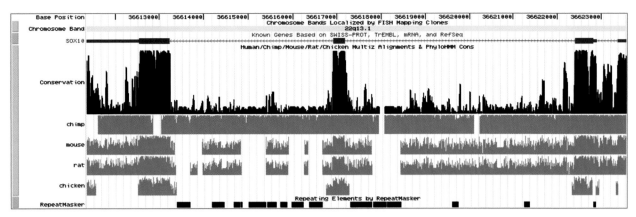

FIGURE 15.2 **UCSC Genome Browser** view of the region containing the human *SOX10* gene. The Chromosome Band track shows that the gene is located at 22q13.1. The *SOX10* track gives the known structure of the gene, based on **Swiss-Prot, TrEMBL,** and **mRNAs** from **GenBank;** thick blue bars represent the coding exons, medium-sized blue bars represent the 5' and 3' UTRs, and the thin blue line represents introns, with the arrows indicating the direction of transcription. The set of conservation tracks show the degree of evolutionary conservation in human, chimpanzee, mouse, rat, and chicken; each track is, in essence, a histogram showing the degree of conservation between the individual organism and human, or between the organisms as a group (Conservation track). Repeat regions identified by RepeatMasker are shown at the bottom of the window.

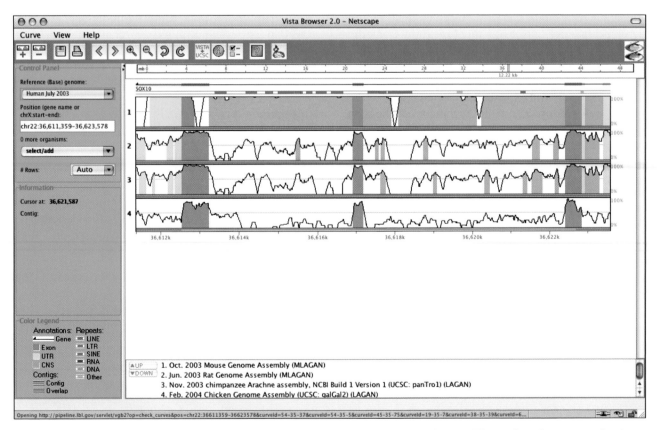

FIGURE 15.3 **VISTA Browser** view of the region containing the human *SOX10* gene. The various features and color keys are described in detail in the text.

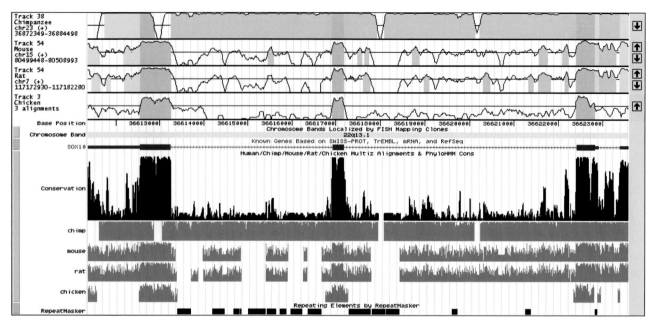

FIGURE 15.4 Superimposition of VISTA Browser results on the UCSC Genome Browser. Clicking the VISTA + UCSC button at the top of the VISTA Browser (Figure 15.3) spawns a new window, automatically retrieving the corresponding region in the UCSC Browser. The user can select and modify which tracks are displayed in the usual fashion.

Scaling and thresholds can be adjusted easily using the curve parameters button (at the top, third from the right). The buttons along the top allow one to scroll along the region or to zoom in or out; alternatively, a region can be highlighted with the mouse, and the applet automatically will expand the selected region to the width of the window. The actual alignments can be seen by highlighting a curve, then clicking the information button at the top of the window (fourth from the right, with the universal information icon). Finally, the information displayed within the VISTA Browser can be overlaid onto the UCSC Browser, providing a unified view of all of the alignments generated by both BLASTZ and LAGAN (Figure 15.4); note that the coloring scheme from the VISTA Browser persists in the UCSC window.

▌GENERATING GENOMIC ALIGNMENTS

As should be evident by the information in Table 15.1, only a small subset of all possible genomic alignments is available in a precomputed fashion. There obviously will be times when one would want to align a different combination of finished genomes or to use large-scale data from an unfinished genome to generate an alignment. The results of such an analysis can be used to deduce whether the presence and order of genomic features has been conserved across organisms, to investigate the structure of gene clusters and other repetitive regions,

or to analyze intergenic regions where sequence conservation is still significant. Two Web-based tools to accomplish this task are described below. In both cases, a 200-Kb region centered on the mouse and rat *Wnt5a* genes were used as the input, for alignment.

PipMaker

PipMaker uses the BLASTZ program to align two very long genomic DNA sequences to one another and is available through both a Web front-end and a downloadable executable. The Web server does not impose a maximum length on the sequences submitted, but does tend to time out for sequences of more than 2 Mb in length. The input to PipMaker consists of two sequences in FASTA format, along with a number of optional files:

▶ A repeats file, giving the position of the repeats in the first sequence

▶ An exon file, giving the position of each known exon

▶ An underlay file, to shade certain portions of the sequence

▶ An annotation file, which allows hyperlinks to online annotations to be included as part of the output.

Because these files can be cumbersome to generate, a set of PipTools have been developed to make the task easier to accomplish. The genomic sequences can be aligned in the forward direction, or the first sequence can be aligned with both directions of the second sequence. The alignment can be performed using one of three modes:

▶ Show All Matches, where the first sequence is allowed to align with more than one region in the second sequence; the output will be reminiscent of a dotplot and can be used to identify multiple repeats or gene clusters

▶ Chaining, where the alignment is constrained to preserving the order of the regions in the two sequences

▶ Single Coverage, where only the highest-scoring alignments are reported, with each region of the first sequence being used only once.

The authors report that chaining should be used over single coverage when the second sequence is contiguous, when the second sequence is being compared only in one direction, and when the order of conserved regions is thought to be the same in the two sequences (Elnitski et al., 2003).

After being submitted, the PipMaker server will return a pip (for "percent identity plot") in PDF or PostScript format, as well as any text-based alignments or output requested on the PipMaker submission form. The first part of the pip is a compact overview of the alignment (Figure 15.5). Here, the green bars indicate regions within an alignment, and strongly aligned regions (defined as ungapped regions >100 in length with >70% identity) are shown in red. The second part of the pip is a series of "graphs" showing the percent identity across the alignment (Figure 15.6). Above the pips are symbols showing the positions of exons, UTRs, or repeats, if the optional repeat and exon files were provided; also noted are CpG-rich regions (CpG islands), which are calculated by PipMaker. A variation of PipMaker, MultiPipMaker, can be used to perform alignments of more than two sequences to one another, producing a stacked set of pips (Schwartz et al., 2003a). MultiPipMaker is illustrated in the Worked Example accompanying this chapter.

mVISTA

mVISTA allows for two or more large-scale sequences of interest to be aligned in a straightforward fashion, using the AVID algorithm described above to perform the alignments. The input to mVISTA are two or more sequences in FASTA format and an optional gene annotation file, indicating the positions of known exons; these are noted in the output but are not used in the alignment. A number of parameters can be set, including the sliding window length to be used in calculating percent identities (default of 100 bp) and the minimum conservation level to show on the plot (default, 50%). The sequences are aligned in the forward direction, as specified in the FASTA input files, but any set of sequences can be selected to align the reverse complement instead. Finally, for shorter sequences (>20 Kb), a box can be checked to invoke rVISTA, a program that attempts to identify potential transcription factor binding sites. After being submitted, the results are returned to the user as a PDF file, and an example of an mVISTA output file is shown in Figure 15.7. Above each line in the plot are colored boxes, indicating the position of identified repeats, with the color key for the repeats given to the left of the plots; unlike PipMaker, mVISTA detects these repeats and does not depend on an auxiliary repeats file. Areas under the curve that have been colored meet the criteria for being conserved regions; in Figure 15.7, the colored regions all share 75% identity over 100 bases. If information regarding the positions of exons had been included in the optional gene annotation file, those regions would be colored in the same way as in the VISTA Browser (Figure 15.3).

Although the view in Figure 15.7 highlights conserved regions, sometimes it is useful to look at nonconserved regions, particularly when the organisms are closely related. In this case, mVISTA can be run in complement mode. When submitting the sequences for alignment, clicking on the radio button marked *cVISTA mode* produces a graph that plots percent difference rather than percent similarity (Figure 15.8). As before, the positions of repeats are noted above the graph, and the peaks in the graph now indicate the most dissimilar regions of the two aligned sequences. Additional features are available as part of the VISTA suite, including GenomeVISTA, which allows a query sequence to be compared with a number of whole-genome assemblies, and PhyloVISTA, which provides an interactive interface for analyzing multiple genomic alignments using a phylogenetic framework (Shah et al., 2003).

FIGURE 15.5   Compact overview of a PipMaker alignment. Green bars indicate regions that have been aligned, and red bars indicate strongly aligned regions (defined as ungapped regions >100 in length having >70% identity).

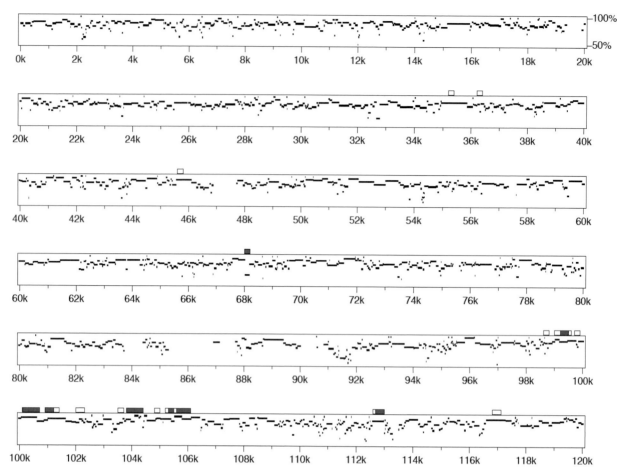

FIGURE 15.6   PipMaker percent identity plots, or pips. The dots across the graph indicate the percent identity of the two sequences aligned over a sliding window. Any symbols above the plots indicate the positions of exons, UTRs, or repeats; these appear if optional repeat and exon files were submitted with the sequences (see text). CpG islands automatically are calculated by PipMaker, and several are denoted in the figure; the unshaded rectangles are areas where the CpG-to-GpC ratio is more than 0.60, and filled-in rectangles are areas where the ratio is more than 0.75.

APPLYING GENE PREDICTIONS TO COMPARATIVE ANALYSES

Up to this point, the methods described in this chapter concentrate on aligning as many regions of two (or more) genomes as possible. Because genes that are important to the survival of most organisms are conserved over evolutionary time, methods have been developed that concentrate primarily on the coding regions of the genome. Although some of the methods discussed in Chapter 5 have been applied to questions in comparative genomics (e.g., GenomeScan, SGP-2, and TwinScan), the methods that are described here perform, in essence, two simultaneous sets of gene predictions on sequences assumed to be related to one another.

Before discussing these methods, it is important to make a distinction between two major types of mutations: those that would have some phenotypic effect (either adaptive or detrimental) and those that do not. Mutations that fall into the former category are called *nonneutral*, and those that fall into the latter category are termed *neutral* (Fay et al., 2001). One way in which neutral mutations can arise are a direct result of the degeneracy in the genetic code. Many amino acids can be coded for by more than one codon, the wobble occurring in the third position of the codon. Because the amino acid coded for by these degenerate codons are the same, no change is seen at the protein level, often making mutations in this third codon position neutral in nature. Methods used specifically for comparative gene

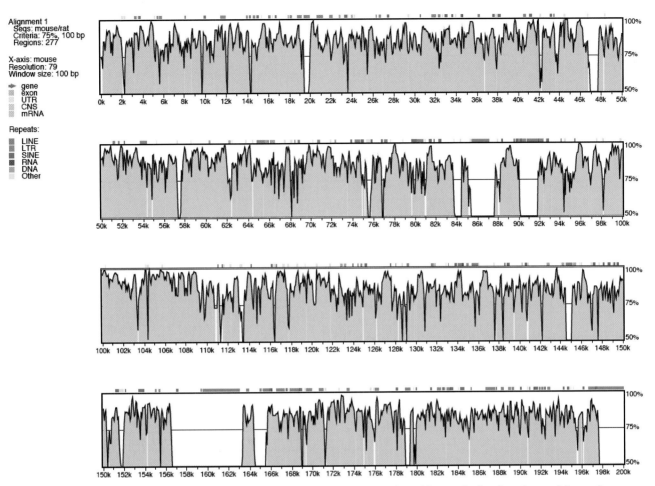

FIGURE 15.7   Results of an mVISTA alignment. Above each line are colored boxes, indicating the positions of identified repeats in the first sequence, and the color key for deciphering the symbols is located in the left part of the window. Rather than use dots to represent the percent identity, as in PipMaker, the results are presented as a continuous graph. Areas under the curve meet the criteria for being conserved regions (75% identity over 100 bases).

prediction take neutral mutations into account, a phenomenon that strict sequence alignment methods would penalize (sometimes strongly) and, perhaps, fail to recognize a biological relationship between two regions in different organisms.

These methods also introduce a new variation on HMMs, called *pair HMMs*. The concept of pair HMMs has been refined over the last several years (Kent & Zahler, 2000; Batzoglou et al., 2000; Korf et al., 2001), but the basic idea here is to look for the similarities between two sequences of interest, using no other comparative information in the course of the prediction; as with the methods discussed in Chapter 5, information on start signals, stop signals, codon bias, splice sites, and the like are used. The methods also distinguish between conserved coding regions and conserved noncoding regions. The first of these methods, DoubleScan (Meyer & Durbin, 2002), was applied to a test set containing 80 pairs of

unmasked, orthologous mouse and human sequences to determine how well it performed as compared with GENSCAN, the ab initio method on which GenomeScan is based (see Chapter 5). Briefly, the use of the pair HMM led to a 10% increase in sensitivity and 4% increase in specificity when compared with GENSCAN. The second such method, SLAM (Alexandersson et al., 2003), was tested using the human genome (NCBI Build 30, June 2002) and mouse genome (MGSC version 3, February 2002); here, a syntenic map was provided as part of the input. In this test, SLAM identified 79.8% of RefSeq human exons and 77.5% of the exons contained in the Ensembl human gene set, fewer than were identified by either GENSCAN or TwinScan.

Another approach that has been used to perform a cross-species prediction relies on looking only at the exons, rather than gene structure in general. A method called ExoFish has been developed to find alignments

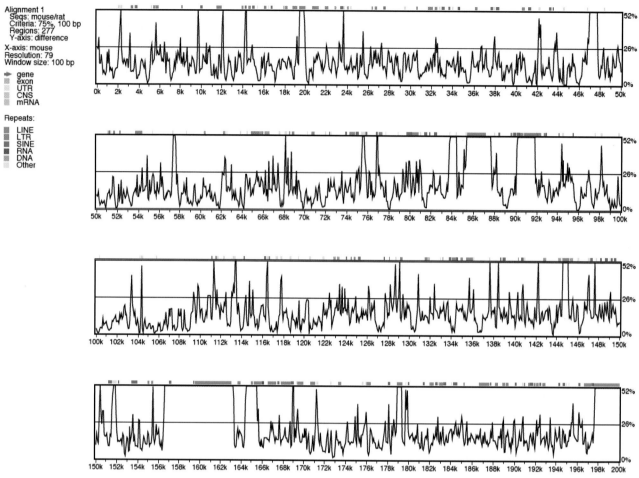

FIGURE 15.8 **Results of a cVISTA alignment. Here, percent difference is plotted, rather than percent identity. Peaks are areas where the greatest difference exists between the two aligned sequences.**

of coding regions between pufferfish and human (Crollius et al., 2000). The method simply fine tunes the parameters used by both BLASTN and TBLASTX (Chapter 11) to identify evolutionarily conserved regions (ecores). When applied to the December 1999 human working draft sequence, ExoFish placed the number of genes in the human genome somewhere between 28,000 and 34,000, one of the first indications that preliminary estimates of the number of genes in the human genome were too high.

PHYLOGENETIC FOOTPRINTING

In the same way that the pair HMM methods described in the previous section concentrate on the coding regions of the genome, other methods concentrate on putative regulatory elements that are conserved across related sequences. These methods, called *phylogenetic footprinting methods*, are particularly well suited for identifying transcription factor binding sites, *cis*-regulatory regions, and other overrepresented patterns. The underlying biological rationale is the same as before: because mutations in these regions potentially are deleterious, there is evolutionary pressure to keep these regions conserved. Commonality in the presence and pattern of regulatory regions may argue that the same gene in different organisms (or even different genes, for that matter) are regulated in the same fashion, so understanding how a gene is regulated in a model organism may provide clues as to how the same gene is regulated in humans.

One of the most widely used methods for phylogenetic footprinting is named simply FootPrinter (Blanchette & Tompa, 2003). The FootPrinter algorithm uses an approach optimized for finding short motifs in the sequences of interest, taking into account known phylogenetic relationships between the species being analyzed. The method also corrects for the fact that many regulatory regions are not completely conserved. Foot-Printer uses a single FASTA file of the sequences to be analyzed as its input, along with a phylogenetic tree; in most cases, a default phylogenetic tree covering many eukaryotes can be used. The sequences must be aligned before submitting them to the server: if submitting upstream sequences, the 3′ end is assumed to be aligned; if submitting 5′ sequences, the 5′ ends are assumed to be aligned. Several parameters regarding allowed gain or loss of regulatory elements and the allowed number of mutations per branch can be adjusted, allowing for different evolutionary models to be tested. The output comes in the form of a simple graphical representation of the motifs found by the method, followed by the input sequences, in which each found motif is highlighted (Figure 15.9). Clicking on any of the highlighted motifs in the sequences changes the coloring in the graphical overview, showing the presence of that particular motif in all of the sequences. The right-hand window in the display gives the position of the motif in each of the sequences, along with a significance score; higher significance scores indicate greater degrees of conservation.

▌SUMMARY

The availability of an increasing number of completed genomes has already opened up new avenues for understanding genome evolution. In the future, more precomputed alignments certainly will become available online, but an understanding of the methods presented here will allow for more detailed analysis of well-defined regions of interest, and several studies already have demonstrated the power of the computational approaches described in this chapter. In the study by Thomas et al. (2002) mentioned above, in which the sequences from 12 species corresponding to an approximately 1.5-Mb region of human chromosome 7 containing the *CFTR* gene were generated, the use of programs such as MultiPipMaker have revealed some interesting patterns of sequence conservation. Although the order of genes is consistent, the amount of noncoding sequence varies; the observations are thought to arise from an increased rate of insertion of interspersed repeats rather than deletions. This study also indicated that rodent genomes have a higher evolutionary rate than primates, carnivores, and

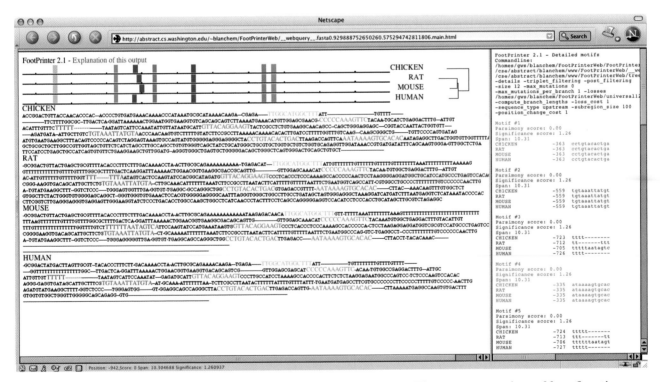

FIGURE 15.9 Results of a FootPrinter phylogenetic footprinting analysis. The upstream regions of four β-actin genes were used in this example. Before submitting to FootPrinter, sequences were aligned using ClustalW. Motif size was set to 12, maximum number of mutations was zero, regulatory element losses were allowed, and the spanned tree significance level was set to very significant. Each identified motif is indicated in the overview (upper left) by a colored bar; the position of each of the identified elements is indicated in the sequence itself, using the same color scheme. Detailed information about the identified motifs, including significance scores, are found in the right-hand window.

artiodactyls. In addition, Margulies et al. (2003) used comparative computational approaches to identify multispecies conserved sequences (MCSs), sequences that are conserved across multiple species. Approximately 70% of these MCSs are found in noncoding regions, meaning that these sequences have no known function. Many of these MCSs lie in regions containing transcription factor binding sites, noncoding RNA transcripts, and other putative functional elements.

Although the popular press often uses the term *junk DNA* to describe the large amount of our genome to which we cannot currently ascribe any function, the following quote, attributed to Sydney Brenner, presents a more biologically insightful angle: "Garbage you throw out; junk is what you store in the attic in case it might be useful one day." It is hoped that the availability of such methods finally will shed light on the significant portion of the human genome that do not lie in coding regions but have been propagated from generation to generation.

▌ WORKED EXAMPLE

This example illustrates the use of MultiPipMaker in generating a multispecies alignment, as well as introducing the use of an auxiliary file to annotate the output. The data that is used originates from a systematic study that was performed by the National Institutes of Health (NIH) Intramural Sequencing Center, focusing on a 1.8-Mb region of human chromosome 7 centered on the gene for cystic fibrosis (Thomas et al., 2003). More than 12 Mb of orthologous sequence was derived from 12 species across a wide taxonomic range. Here, a three-species comparison is performed between human, chimpanzee, and baboon. The files for this example can be found on the Book's Web site.

Before beginning the alignment, the position of any repeats are found in the human sequence. To accomplish this, RepeatMasker is used. The RepeatMasker Web site provides an easy-to-use form for submitting sequences to be masked. Under Basic Options, upload the file with the human sequence (human_T1.txt) using the Browse button. (The file is quite large, so upload the file rather than trying to cut and paste it into the sequence box.) Select HTML for both the return format and return method, input a valid E-mail address, and then click Submit Sequences. The Advanced Options are left in their default position for this example, but do note that the search can be limited to certain types of repeats and can specify the organism from which the sequence was derived. The RepeatMasker server sends an E-mail to the address specified on the form after the run is completed. The E-mail contains a link to a Web page containing the results. The upper portion of the Web page contains a section documenting the position and nature of any matches found in the repeat database. The first few lines are shown below.

```
6321   9.2  1.3  0.0  human_T1  4015  5253  (1872173)  C  L1PA10  LINE/L1        (3)   6165  4922  1
1336  11.2  0.6  0.0  human_T1  5335  5512  (1871914)  C  AluSp   SINE/Alu      (50)    263    85  2
 234  19.2  0.0  0.0  human_T1  5513  5564  (1871862)  C  L1M4    LINE/L1     (1110)   5036  4985  3
 352  35.7  5.7  0.0  human_T1  6434  6573  (1870853)  C  MIRb    SINE/MIR     (100)    168    21  4
 245  35.0  0.0  2.0  human_T1  6863  6964  (1870462)  C  MER5B   DNA/MER1_type (73)    105     6  5
```

For purposes of this example, the most important columns are the ones indicating the start and stop positions of the match (columns 6 and 7), whether the match is with the complement of the consensus sequence in the database (denoted by a C in column 8), the name of the matching interspersed repeat (column 9), and the class of the repeat (column 10). More detailed information about the RepeatMasker output format can be found in the RepeatMasker online documentation. To use this output with MultiPipMaker, the lines containing the repeat information need to be copied from the Web page and into a text file; do not include the masked sequence in the new text file. Name this file repeats_file.txt. (This file also is available on the Book Web site, but readers should go through this exercise themselves.)

The MultiPipMaker run now can be submitted. From the MultiPipMaker page, indicate that three sequences are to be aligned. This generates a new page, as shown in Figure 15.10. Input a valid E-mail address to which the results can be sent, and select the options as shown in the figure. For the first sequence, use Human as the label, upload the sequence file (human_T1.txt), then upload the RepeatMasker file (repeats_file.txt). For the second sequence, use Chimp as the label and upload the file containing the chimpanzee sequence (chimp_T1.txt). For the third sequence, use Baboon as the label and upload the file containing the baboon sequence (baboon_T1.txt). For both the second and third sequence, search only one strand, with chaining. When finished, click Submit.

When the MultiPipMaker alignment is complete, an E-mail is received. In the E-mail is a link to a PDF-formatted file containing the pip (blastz output, PIP). Clicking the link will launch a PDF viewer (e.g., Adobe Acrobat or Macintosh Preview). The first page of the PDF file contains the compact overview of the alignment (Figure 15.11). Again, strongly aligned regions (defined as ungapped regions >100 in length with >70% identity) are shown in red. In this case, no green bars indicating alignment are seen, meaning that all of the aligned regions are considered to be strongly aligned. The following pages show the calculated pip across all 1,877,426 positions in the alignment, and a subset of the results is shown in Figure 15.12. First, note that, unlike the PipMaker example shown in the main text, the output here is decorated with various symbols above the plots; these symbols represent

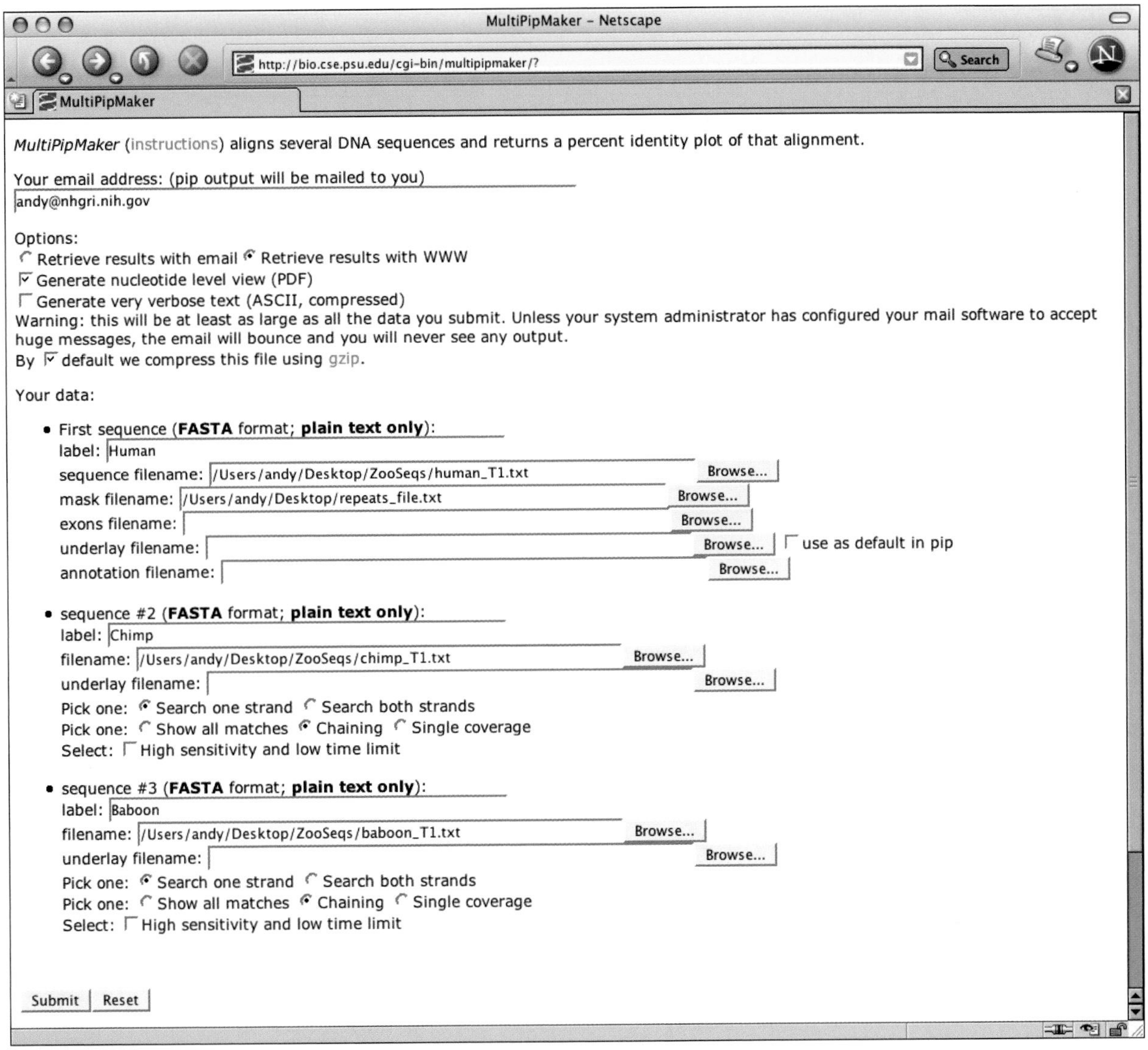

MultiPipMaker – Netscape

http://bio.cse.psu.edu/cgi-bin/multipipmaker/? | Search

MultiPipMaker

MultiPipMaker (instructions) aligns several DNA sequences and returns a percent identity plot of that alignment.

Your email address: (pip output will be mailed to you)
andy@nhgri.nih.gov

Options:
⊙ Retrieve results with email ⊙ Retrieve results with WWW
☑ Generate nucleotide level view (PDF)
☐ Generate very verbose text (ASCII, compressed)
Warning: this will be at least as large as all the data you submit. Unless your system administrator has configured your mail software to accept huge messages, the email will bounce and you will never see any output.
By ☑ default we compress this file using gzip.

Your data:
- First sequence (**FASTA** format; **plain text only**):
  label: Human
  sequence filename: /Users/andy/Desktop/ZooSeqs/human_T1.txt   Browse...
  mask filename: /Users/andy/Desktop/repeats_file.txt   Browse...
  exons filename: | Browse...
  underlay filename: | Browse... ☐ use as default in pip
  annotation filename: | Browse...

- sequence #2 (**FASTA** format; **plain text only**):
  label: Chimp
  filename: /Users/andy/Desktop/ZooSeqs/chimp_T1.txt   Browse...
  underlay filename: | Browse...
  Pick one: ⊙ Search one strand ⊙ Search both strands
  Pick one: ⊙ Show all matches ⊙ Chaining ⊙ Single coverage
  Select: ☐ High sensitivity and low time limit

- sequence #3 (**FASTA** format; **plain text only**):
  label: Baboon
  filename: /Users/andy/Desktop/ZooSeqs/baboon_T1.txt   Browse...
  underlay filename: | Browse...
  Pick one: ⊙ Search one strand ⊙ Search both strands
  Pick one: ⊙ Show all matches ⊙ Chaining ⊙ Single coverage
  Select: ☐ High sensitivity and low time limit

Submit | Reset

FIGURE 15.10   The MultiPipMaker input page. See Worked Example for details.

each of the repeats found by RepeatMasker and are interpreted as follows:

▶ White pointed boxes: L1 repeats

▶ Light gray triangles: SINEs other than MIR

▶ Black triangles: MIRs

▶ Black pointed boxes: LINE2s

▶ Dark gray triangles and pointed boxes: other kinds of interspersed repeats, such as LTR elements and DNA transposons

▶ Short dark gray boxes: CpG islands in which the CpG-to-GpC ratio is more than 0.75

▶ Short white boxes: CpG islands in which the CpG-to-GpC ratio is more than 0.60.

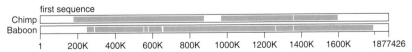

FIGURE 15.11   The compact overview produced by MultiPipMaker for the alignment of human, chimpanzee, and baboon sequences used in the Worked Example. See Worked Example for details.

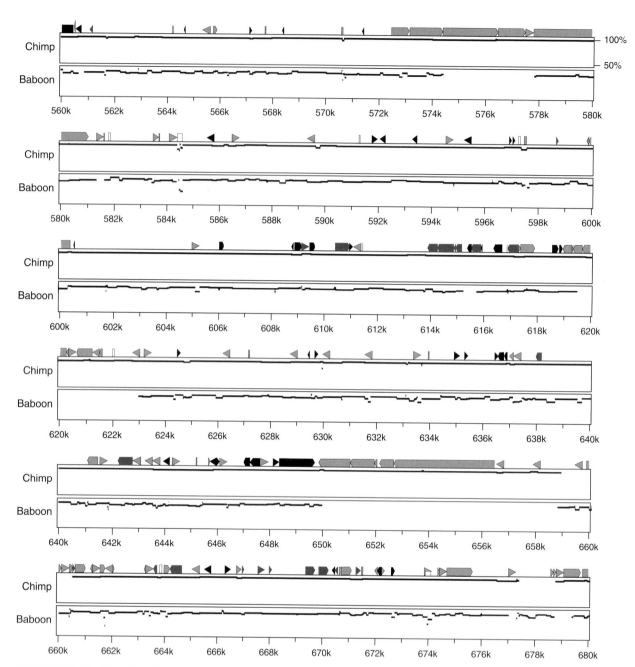

FIGURE 15.12 The MultiPipMaker percent identity plots (pips) for the alignment of human, chimpanzee, and baboon sequences used in the Worked Example. See Worked Example for details.

In the region of the pip shown in Figure 15.12, note that the chimpanzee percent identity is very high throughout. The human–baboon identity also is high, but not as high as that for human–chimpanzee, with more variance across the region. Also note that there are several significant gaps in the human–baboon alignment in this region; a large number of repeats are seen in this area, possibly confounding the alignment. It would be interesting to repeat the analysis, now including an exons file documenting the position of each known human exon and UTR to see whether the gaps fall into coding or intergenic regions; the reader is encouraged to read Elnitski et al. (2003) for more information on how to include additional annotation tracks that may be useful in identifying orthologous regions. The reader also is encouraged to rework the example using more divergent sequences; to that end, additional sequences are available from cat (`cat_T1.txt`), cow (`cow_T1.txt`), *Fugu* (`fugu_T1.txt`), mouse (`mouse_T1.txt`), rat (`rat_T1.txt`), and zebrafish (`zfish_T1.txt`).

PROBLEM SET

1. Data from the NIH Intramural Sequencing Center's ZooSeq project (Thomas et al., 2003) are available through the UCSC Genome Browser. From the Genome Browser home page, select Zoo from the list of available organisms, then click Submit. For purposes of this question, hide all of the tracks except for the following: set Base Position to on, RefSeq genes to full, ZooSeq to full, and RepeatMasker to dense.

   a. What genes are found in this region, moving from 5′ to 3′ across the region? Do any of these genes overlap?

   b. When examining the BLASTZ alignment of chimpanzee versus human, there is a significant gap in the middle of the region. Which gene falls in this region? What is the product of this gene?

   c. Follow the Stanford Source link for this gene. Does this gene lie within a disease susceptibility locus? If so, for what disease?

   d. Examining the chimpanzee and baboon tracks, are the intergenic regions generally conserved?

   e. Based on the BLASTZ alignments, would the rodent species be considered closely related to human?

2. A sequence from human chromosome 4 can be found in a file named `GenomeVISTA.txt` on the Book's Web site. Using this sequence, run GenomeVISTA, a program that facilitates the detection of orthologous regions in other organisms. To run GenomeVISTA, upload the sequence file and set the base genome to `Human` (use the latest release available). Type in a valid E-mail address to receive notification once the run is completed. Name the request `Unknown`, and select `Human` as the organism. When finished, click on the Submit Query button. When the results are available, open the Vista Browser and use the Select/Add pull-down menu to add all available tracks to the display

   a. What human genes lie within the region of the unknown human sequence? Do these genes all have the same orientation?

   b. To which other genome does the unknown sequence have overwhelming similarity?

   c. Is significant conservation observed in intergenic regions?

INTERNET RESOURCES

BLASTZ	http://bio.cse.psu.edu
BLAT	http://genome.ucsc.edu/cgi-bin/hgBlat
ClustalW	http://www.ebi.ac.uk/clustalw
Ensembl	http://www.ensembl.org
EnteriX	http://bio.cse.psu.edu
ExoFish	http://www.genoscope.cns.fr/proxy/cgi-bin/exofish.cgi
DoubleScan	http://www.sanger.ac.uk/Software/analysis/doublescan
FootPrinter	http://bio.cs.washington.edu/software.html
GALA	http://bio.cse.psu.edu
GenomeScan	http://genes.mit.edu/genomescan
GenomeVISTA	http://pipeline.lbl.gov
LAGAN/MLAGAN	http://lagan.stanford.edu
MegaBLAST	http://www.ncbi.nlm.nih.gov/BLAST/
PipMaker	http://bio.cse.psu.edu/pipmaker
RepeatMasker	http://www.repeatmasker.org
SLAM	http://baboon.math.berkeley.edu/~syntenic/slam.html
SGP-2	http://www1.imim.es/software/sgp2/
TWINSCAN	http://genes.cs.wustl.edu
UCSC	http://genome.ucsc.edu
VISTA	http://www-gsd.lbl.gov/vista/
VISTA Browser	http://pipeline.lbl.gov
WormBase	http://www.wormbase.org

FURTHER READING

ELNITSKI, L., RIEMER, C., SCHWARTZ, S., HARDISON, R., and MILLER, W. (2003). PipMaker: a World Wide Web server for genomic sequence alignments. *Curr. Protocols Bioinformatics* 10.2.1–10.2.23. A step-by-step guide to the use of PipMaker in generating large-scale alignments and identifying conserved segments.

HARDISON, R. (2003). Comparative genomics. *PLoS Biology* 1, 156–160. A primer on the importance of comparative genomics, including a brief review of preliminary observations resulting from the sequencing of the mouse genome.

REFERENCES

ALEXANDERSSON, M., CAWLEY, S., AND PACHTER, L. (2003). SLAM: cross-species gene finding and alignment with a generalized pair hidden Markov model. *Genome Res.* 13, 496–502.

BATZOGLOU, S., PACHTER, L., MESIROV, J., BERGER, B., AND LANDER E. (2000). Human and mouse gene structure: comparative analysis and application to exon prediction. *Genome Res.* 10, 950–958.

BLANCHETTE, M. AND TOMPA, M. (2003). FootPrinter: a program designed for phylogenetic footprinting. *Nucl. Acids Res.* 31, 3840–3842.

BLANCHETTE, M., KENT, W. J., RIEMER, C., ELNITSKI, L., SMIT, A. F. A., ROSKIN, K. M., BAERTSCH, R., ROSENBLOOM, K., CLAWSON, H., GREEN, E. D., et al. (2004). Aligning multiple genomic sequences with the threaded blockset aligner. *Genome Res.* 14, 708–715.

BRAY, N., DUBCHAK, I., AND PACHTER, L. (2003). AVID: a global alignment program. *Genome Res.* 13, 97–102.

Brudno, M., Do, C. B., Cooper, G. M., Kim, M. F., Davydov, E., NISC Comparative Sequencing Program, Green, E. D., Sidow, A., and Batzoglou, S. (2003). LAGAN and Multi-LAGAN: efficient tools for large-scale multiple alignment of genomic DNA. *Genome Res.* 13, 721–731.

Chiaromonte, F., Yap, V. B., and Miller, W. (2002). Scoring pairwise genomic sequence alignments. *Pac. Symp. Biocomput.* 115–126.

Crollius, H. R., Jaillon, O., Bernot, A., Dasilva, C., Bouneau, L., Fischer, C., Fizames, C., Wincker, P., Brottier, P., Quétier, F., et al. (2000). Estimate of human gene number provided by genome-wide analysis using *Tetraodon nigroviridis* DNA sequence. *Nat. Genet.* 25, 235–238.

Elnitski, L., Riemer, C., Schwartz, S., Hardison, R., and Miller, W. (2003). PipMaker: a World Wide Web server for genomic sequence alignments. *Curr. Protocols Bioinformatics* 10.2.1–10.2.23.

Fay, J. C., Wyckoff, G. J., and Wu, C. I. (2001). Positive and negative selection on the human genome. *Genetics* 158, 1227–1234.

Hardison, R. (2003). Comparative genomics. *PLoS Biology* 1, 156–160.

International Mouse Genome Sequencing Consortium. (2002). Initial sequencing and comparative analysis of the mouse genome. *Nature* 420, 520–562.

Kent, W., and Zahler, A. (2000). Conservation, regulation, synteny, and introns in a large-scale *C. briggsae*–*C. elegans* genomic alignment. *Genome Res.* 10, 1115–1125.

Korf, I., Flicek, P., Duan, D., and Brent, M. R. (2001). Integrating genomic homology into gene structure prediction. *Bioinformatics* 1, 1–9.

Ma, B., Tromp, J., and Li, M. (2002). PatternHunter: faster and more sensitive homology search. *Bioinformatics* 18, 440–445.

Margulies, E. H., Blanchette, M., Haussler, D., Green, E. D., and the NISC Comparative Sequencing Program. (2003). Identification of multi-species conserved sequences. *Genome Res.* 13, 2507–2518.

Meyer, I. M., and Durbin, R. (2002). Comparative *ab initio* prediction of gene structures using pair HMMs. *Bioinformatics* 18, 1309–1318.

Schwartz, S., Elnitski, L., Li, M., Weirauch, M., Riemer, C., Smit, A., NISC Comparative Sequencing Program, Green, E. D., Hardison, R. C., and Miller, W. (2003a). MultiPipMaker and supporting tools: alignments and analysis of multiple genomic DNA sequences. *Nucl. Acids Res.* 31, 3518–3524.

Schwartz, S., Kent, W. J., Smit, A., Zhang, Z., Baertsch, R., Hardison, R. C., Haussler, D., and Miller, W. (2003b). Human-mouse alignments with BLASTZ. *Genome Res.* 13, 103–107.

Shah, N., Couronne, O., Pennacchio, L. A., Brudno, M., Batzoglou, S., Bethel, E. W., Rubin, E. M., Hamman, B., and Dubchak, I. (2003). Phylo-VISTA: interactive visualization of multiple DNA sequence alignments. *Bioinformatics* 20, 636–643.

Siepel, A., and Haussler, D. (2003). Combining phylogenetic and hidden Markov models in biosequence analysis. In *Proceedings of the Seventh Annual International Conference on Computational Molecular Biology (RECOMB 2003) Berlin, Germany*, p. 277–286.

Thomas, J. W., Touchman, J. W., Blakesley, R. W., Bouffard, G. G., Beckstrom-Sternberg, S. M., Margulies, E. H., Blanchette, M., Siepel, A. C., Thomas, P. J., McDowell, J. C., et al. (2003). Comparative analyses of multi-species sequences from targeted genomic regions. *Nature* 424, 788–793.

KEY TERMS

comparative genomics
BLASTZ
PipMaker
VISTA
Phylo-VISTA
LAGAN
Multi-LAGAN
AVID
DoubleScan
SLAM
ExoFish
FootPrinter

This chapter was written by Dr. Andreas D. Baxevanis in his private capacity. No official support or endorsement by the National Institutes of Health or the United States Department of Health and Human Services is intended or should be inferred.

## CHAPTER SIXTEEN

Using DNA Microarrays to Assay Gene Expression

JOHN QUACKENBUSH

Bioinformatics: A Practical Guide to the Analysis of Genes and Proteins, Third Edition, edited by
Andreas D. Baxevanis and B.F. Francis Ouellette.
ISBN 0-471-47878-4 Copyright © 2005 John Wiley & Sons, Inc.

INTRODUCTION

With the completion of draft genome sequences for human, mouse, rat, *Drosophila*, *Arabidopsis*, and an increasing number of other species, including hundreds of microbial species, a preliminary gene catalog for many organisms of medical and scientific interest now is available. However, interpreting these gene lists, in light of the organism's underlying biology, remains an ongoing challenge.

DNA microarrays are one of a number of technologies that use the information and reagents arising from genome projects that have allowed for the exploration of patterns of gene expression on a global scale. As microarrays and other technologies have become more commonplace, the challenges associated with collecting, managing, and analyzing the data from each experiment have increased substantially. Increasingly robust laboratory protocols, falling prices for commercial platforms, and an improved understanding of the intricacies of experimental design all have combined to drive the field to more complex experiments, generating enormous amounts of data. Just a few years ago, microarray studies typically included on the order of 10 hybridization assays; now, studies tend to have 100 or more such assays. The goal of this chapter is to present an overview of some of the issues associated with analyzing such data to extract meaningful biological results.

THE STARTING POINT: ANNOTATING ARRAY PROBES

There are a growing number of approaches used to construct DNA microarrays. These include those used to manufacture Affymetrix (Santa Clara, CA) GeneChip arrays, in situ synthesized long oligonucleotide arrays, randomly assembled bead-based arrays, and mechanically spotted arrays in which the spotted material may be an oligonucleotide, a cDNA clone, a polymerase chain reaction (PCR) amplicon, or some other material. Despite the differences in these platforms, they share an underlying design: each produces an array with unique, addressable positions at which there are distinct, distinguishable probes, typically representing individual genes that are used to assay expression. Having selected an array technology, RNA is extracted from the tissues, states, or conditions of interest and is used to generate a labeled "target" nucleic acid pool that then is hybridized to the array. In a typical experiment, spanning a large number of hybridizations, the underlying question is, ultimately, "Which of the genes surveyed in this experiment correlate with some relevant biological state?" To answer that question effectively, it is essential that one understand what the probes on our arrays represent.

This understanding actually can be a greater challenge than one may anticipate. With the annotation and prediction of gene structure on genomic sequences undergoing a continuous evolution, the functional annotation attached to array probes can become "stale," requiring that they be updated regularly. For widely used mammalian array platforms, there are publicly available annotation resources, including SOURCE (Diehn et al., 2003), DAVID (Diehn et al., 2003), DRAGON (Bouton & Pevsner, 2002), and RESOURCERER (Tsai et al., 2001). Each of these databases provides a variety of information about the array probes for a large number of microarray platforms and resources; RESOURCERER also identifies links across platforms and species based on the TIGR Gene Indices and EGO databases.

Each piece of annotation can provide crucial information for the interpretation of array results. Although one tends to think of gene names as being the primary source of information about a gene, other information can be equally (or more) useful. The Gene Ontology (GO) project is attempting to classify gene products, assigning proteins to groups specifying their molecular function, the biological process to which they contribute, and their cellular component. GO terms in each class form a hierarchy of increasing specificity (formally, a directed acyclic graph), so that the broadest classifications provide a general picture of the functional class to which a gene belongs (for example, a kinase); more precise terms specify precisely what a particular gene does (such as specifying the substrate on which a kinase acts). Because not all genes have a complete functional classification, increasing specificity reduces the sensitivity for placing genes into a particular functional class. Because the functions of many genes have not been explored fully, there are some advantages to using the less specific classes, which often are assigned based on sequence homology searches for some analyses. Similarly, using Enzyme Commission (EC) numbers, genes can be mapped to metabolic and signaling pathway databases such as the Kyoto Encyclopedia of Genes and Genomes (KEGG) (Kanehisa, 2002). An approach as simple as linking array elements to relevant PubMed abstracts can provide insight to some final significant gene list.

DESIGNING THE EXPERIMENT

The next and, in many ways, most crucial step in a microarray study is to design an experiment that allows a relevant experimental question to be addressed directly. For two-color microarray experiments, this can be a challenging problem, because one must decide what the most appropriate comparison is to be made with each array hybridization. Even for single-color Affymetrix GeneChip assays, where each sample is hybridized to a single array, one has to ask whether a study includes a sufficient number of samples to make statistically significant measures of gene expression (Box 16.1).

Two-Color Microarray Experiments

There have been many published discussions of approaches to the design of two-color microarray experiments (Kerr & Churchill, 2001; Churchill, 2002; Dobbin et al., 2003a; Dobbin et al., 2003b; Simon & Dobbin, 2003), and many complex designs have been proposed, but the simplest comparisons can be separated into four general classes as shown in Figure 16.1: direct comparisons, balanced block designs, reference

designs, and loop designs. In the figure, the boxes represent the individual samples to be compared, and the arrows represent hybridization assays, with the "tail" of each arrow representing one dye and the "head" representing the other used in two-color assays.

In many ways, direct comparisons are the simplest conceptually; they are used when two distinct classes of experimental samples are to be compared, such as a treated sample and its untreated control, or a mutant gene and its corresponding wild-type gene. On each array, representatives of the two classes are paired and cohybridized together such that the relative expression levels are measured directly on each array. The choice of appropriate pairing depends on the experimental

Direct Comparison with Dye Swap:

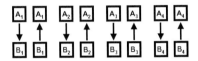

• RNA sample is *not* limiting (i.e. plenty of sample)
• Flip dye pairs account for any gene-dye effects

Balanced Block Design:

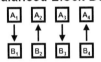

• RNA sample is limiting
• Balanced blocking accounts for any gene-dye effects

Reference Design:

• More than two samples are compared (e.g. tumor classification, time course)
• Flip dye pairs are not necessary but can be used to increase precision
• Ratio values are inferred (indirect)
• Requires a common reference RNA for all hybridizations

Loop Design:

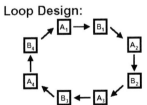

• Two or more sample classes
• Flip dye pairs can be used to increase precision, as can alternate loops
• Analysis requires ANOVA to estimate $\log_2$(expression)
• Results are not immediately intuitive
• Bad hybridizations must be repeated, requiring more RNA

FIGURE 16.1 **Experimental design paradigms for two-color DNA microarrays. Samples are represented in as boxes and the arrows represent hybridization assays, with the "tail" of each arrow representing the first dye and the "head" representing the second.**

BOX 16.1 Replication, Power, and Pooling

One question that arises in the discussion of microarray experiments, regardless of platform, is the level of replication needed to make an accurate measurement. To address this question, one must realize that there are two types of replication: technical and biological. Technical replicates repeat a measurement using the same RNA samples and include using multiple probes for each gene on a single array (within-slide replicates) or repeating hybridizations on separate arrays (between-slide replicates). Biological replication uses independent RNA sources to repeat the measurements made in an experiment. Although both technical and biological replicates are useful, technical replicates only increase the precision with which one measures expression in a single sample. Within-slide replicates provide a better measure on any given array, but do not take into account variation between arrays or in sample preparation and handling, whereas between-slide replicates do.

The problem with using only technical replicates is that one has no way of knowing whether the particular biological sample chosen is representative of the group from which it is selected or if it is an outlier. For example, in a cage of six male mice, there is always a dominant male, and depending on the tissue chosen, there are likely to be distinct patterns of gene expression that distinguish him from the other mice. If we compare a nondominant mouse from a treatment group with the dominant mouse in a control group, we may conclude mistakenly that differences exist because of a particular treatment, when in fact they are caused by something else altogether. Biological replication increases the accuracy of any measurement, providing a better estimate of the characteristic expression level of any gene in a particular class of sample.

What is the difference between precision and accuracy? Imagine an archery target. A precise archer would group all of his shots close together on the target, although he may or may not place the arrows close to the center of the target. An accurate archer may place his arrows more widely across the face of the target, but these would, on average, be centered on the bull's-eye. Biological replication is obviously preferable to the alternatives, but any level of replication can help improve the quality of the data that come from an array assay.

What level of biological replication is necessary? One simple method is to assess the degrees of freedom (df) represented in an experiment (Churchill, 2002). This is accomplished by counting the number of independent biological samples and subtracting from it the number of distinct treatments (counting all combinations if there are multiple treatment factors, such as time and dose). If $df = 0$, then there

may be no information in the experiment that allows an accurate estimate of the biological variation between groups; a good rule of thumb is that an experiment should have $df \geq 5$.

Simon et al. (2002) described a relatively simple power calculation for the analysis of single-color microarray or two-color array reference designs for the comparison of two classes. Assume that some measures of gene expression, such as the $\log_2(\text{ratio})$ values for each gene, are normally distributed in each class. Let σ denote the standard deviation of the expression level among samples within the each class and suppose that the means of the two classes differ by δ. For example, for $\log_2(\text{ratio})$ values, a $\delta = 1$ represents a two-fold difference between classes. Assume that some statistical test, such as a t test, is used to identify genes that have a statistically significant difference between the experimental classes at significance level α (with α set stringently to avoid false-positive identification of genes). The power for detecting statistical significance when the true difference in mean expression levels between the classes is δ is denoted by $1 - \beta$. This requires n total tissue samples, where

$$ n = \frac{4(z_{\frac{\alpha}{2}} + z_\beta)^2}{\left(\frac{\delta}{\sigma}\right)^2} $$

and $z_{\alpha/2}$ and z_β denote the corresponding percentiles of the standard normal distribution (Desu & Raghavarao, 2003). If the ratio of sample sizes in the two groups is $k:1$ rather than $1:1$, the total sample size increases by a factor of $(k + 1)^2 / (4k)$. The fact that expression levels for many genes will be examined indicates that the size of α and β should be smaller than for experiments where the focus is on a single gene, so as to limit the false-positive and false-negative rates, respectively. A good general guideline is to choose $\alpha \leq 0.001$ and $\beta \leq 0.05$ (Simon et al., 2002).

There also are questions regarding the acceptability of pooling samples for hybridization. Although there have been some arguments presented against pooling, it is best to take a pragmatic approach. There are instances where one has many more biological samples than can be profiled easily, or situation may arise where RNA samples are too limited to allow individual samples to be profiled. Pooling RNAs essential produces a biological average across the samples, but cannot reduce variability because of sample handling and measurement error. The best approach is to treat pools as individual samples and consequently to create as many independent pools as possible, assaying individual pools rather than performing multiple technical replicates on a smaller number of pools (Churchill, 2002).

question under study. For example, one can pair diseased and normal tissue from the same patient or randomly selected animals from mutant and wild-type groups. Because experimentalists do express concern about potential dye bias affecting some subset of the genes such that these genes always seem to be labeled preferentially by one of the two fluorescent markers, a common approach is to use dye-reversal replicates (flip-dye pairs), where the resultant expression levels are averaged between replicates or are used in an analysis of variance (ANOVA) model that estimates the relative dye bias for each gene.

If direct comparisons are desired, but the quantity of available RNA from the samples is limiting and there is some concern about the effects of potential dye biases, then a good alternative is to use a balanced block design. Here, samples are selected as for a direct comparison, but rather than using dye-reversal pairs, the labeling chosen for each array comparison is swapped between groups in subsequent hybridizations. Here, any gene suffering from preferential labeling with one dye appears in both samples and, in any statistical analysis, should not appear to distinguish the classes significantly.

A third alternative is to compare all of the samples with a common reference RNA source. This approach is very useful if there are multiple classes of sample to be analyzed, such as in the classification of tumor samples or in a time-course experiment. The challenge here is to select an appropriate reference RNA sample. The most generally useful reference RNA samples are those that are closely related to experimental samples; a common approach is to use a pool of all of the experimental samples. Alternatives may include RNA from a "time zero" sample in a time course, a wild-type animal for comparison with a number of mutant animal strains, or a "universal" RNA pool derived from a renewable source, such as tissue culture cell lines.

Reference comparisons are particularly well suited to cluster analysis, but any direct comparison between the experimental classes must be inferred through comparisons to a common reference. Statistical tests such as *t* tests or ANOVAs are very useful for identifying genes that distinguish between classes. One advantage of the reference design is that, if a laboratory uses a single reference RNA sample for all array assays, even for those from different experiments, then all of their expression profiles can be compared. For example, this allows expression profiles from different tissues studied in different experiments to be compared with a great degree of sensitivity. This advantage can extend to comparisons of expression profiles made by different laboratories using reference designs with the same reference sample. The one disadvantage of a reference design is that it requires many more array assays for a fixed number of samples than do other approaches.

The final alternative in widespread use is the loop design. In this approach, random samples representing the various classes are selected sequentially, class by class, and are compared directly, with the final sample compared back with the first. In this design, the dye selection is unbiased, because each sample from one class is compared with two representatives of the other class, with the dyes reversed between comparisons. If more than two classes are to be analyzed, additional comparisons can be added and dye-reversal hybridizations can be added to increase precision. The results that emerge from these analyses are not immediately obvious, but ANOVA techniques have been developed that allow the $\log_2$(expression) values to be estimated for each sample (Kerr & Churchill, 2001). One drawback of this approach is that bad hybridizations have to be reperformed to provide the necessary constraints for analysis, requiring more RNA from each of the samples used in that assay; this can be a problem when RNA quantities are limited. Further, loop designs require all of the samples to be available as the experiment is designed, which makes this approach impractical for prospective clinical studies that collect samples from patients as they present in the clinic.

There is good deal of discussion regarding what is the best strategy for any given case. As with many such questions, the definition of "best" is influenced by a wide range of factors, including the availability of samples, the quantity of RNA that can be obtained, the size of the study, and logistical constraints in the laboratory. The starting point in selecting an experimental design is to ask what biological difference needs to be measured, then choose a design that allows the comparisons to be made most easily.

There are two broad categories of experiments involving microarrays. The first investigates the response of a biological system to some perturbation to determine which genes correspond to a particular physical state. For example, one may want to compare treated and untreated cell lines to gauge their response to a particular compound or to compare tumor and normal samples from the same patient to identify genes that are associated with the disease state. For such studies, direct comparisons or a balanced block approach are the simplest if there are only two classes. If there are more than two classes of samples, then a reference design is a better alternative. For both of these sample cases, loop designs can be used as well.

The second category of microarray experiments includes class discovery and classification experiments. In class discovery experiments, one compares a large number of samples to discover distinct expression types within the samples. For example, one may profile tumors to look for previously unrecognized subtypes of the disease. In classification experiments, one uses knowledge of the groups represented in the samples to look for expression fingerprints that can distinguish between them and then develops an approach to use these fingerprints to classify new samples. For both class discovery and classification experiments, reference designs generally are most appropriate.

DATA COLLECTION AND MANAGEMENT

Having selected an appropriate array platform and having designed an experiment that allows a biological question to be addressed, one is ready to begin the process of collecting data and extracting biological insight. This process actually can require a substantial investment in data management. Although many have drawn parallels between functional genomics experiments and genome sequencing projects, data management issues are somewhat more complex for functional assays. Although genome sequencing does generate a great deal of data, detailed information about the source of the DNA, such as its age, source tissue, or treatment, generally is not of great importance. However, for any method that surveys expression, these and other factors are essential for proper interpretation of the data.

Realizing that these issues needed to be addressed, and with the goal of developing public repositories for expression data, a group representing the major DNA sequence databases, large-scale practitioners of microarray analysis, and a number of companies developing microarray hardware, reagents, and software tools began discussing the issues relevant to archiving microarray data effectively. What emerged from those discussions was the Microarray Gene Expression Data Society (MGED). MGED took on the task of developing standards for describing microarray experiments with one simple question in mind: "What is the minimum information necessary for an independent scientist to perform an independent analysis of the data?" Based on feedback received through numerous discussions and a series of public meetings and workshops, a new standard called MIAME (for minimal information about a microarray experiment) emerged (Brazma et al., 2001). The publication of this new standard met with general enthusiasm from the scientific community, and it has evolved over time with continued input from scientists actively performing microarray studies. To facilitate usage of this new standard, brief guidelines and a MIAME checklist were developed and provided to scientific journals for their use when considering manuscripts presenting microarray data (Ball et al., 2002a; Ball et al., 2002b). The MIAME standard also has been adopted and supported by the European Bioinformatics Institute's (EBI) ArrayExpress database (Brazma et al., 2003), as well as National Center for Biotechnology Information's Gene Expression Omnibus (Edgar et al., 2002) and the CIBEX

database at the DNA Databank of Japan (DDBJ). Following the same model as that used for sequence data (Chapter 1), data exchange protocols currently are being developed to link expression data found in each of these three major repositories.

Although MIAME can be thought of as a set of guidelines for describing an experiment, it is clear that these guidelines must be translated into protocols enabling the electronic exchange of data in a standard format. To meet that challenge, a collaborative effort by members of MGED and a group at Rosetta Inpharmatics led to the development of the microarray gene expression object model (MAGE-OM), as well as its implementation as an XML-based extensible markup language (MAGE-ML; Spellman et al., 2002). The adoption of MAGE by the Object Management Group has promoted it to the status of an "official" industry standard. MAGE is now being built into a wide range of freely available microarray software, including BASE (Saal et al., 2002), BioConductor (Dudoit et al., 2003), and TM4 (Saeed et al., 2003). MIAME and MAGE are also being adopted by an increasing number of companies as essential components of their products.

There are elements of a microarray experiment that are not addressed in MIAME, particularly those associated with the management of laboratory resources and reagents. For small-scale experiments, this may not be a significant issue, but for larger microarray projects, implementing a full-scale laboratory information management system similar to BASE, TM4, or one of the commercial solutions is essential (Figure 16.2). Regardless, the requirement for submission of microarray data to a public data repository necessitates that everyone become familiar with these standards and develop means of collecting the necessary data while conducting the experiment; the MIAME checklist is a good place to start in developing a protocol for collecting the requisite ancillary data.

IMAGE PROCESSING: EXTRACTING ESTIMATES OF EXPRESSION

The first step in extracting information from an array experiment is image processing. This is carried out to identify the relative fluorescence intensity of each of the features on the array, because these are used to infer expression levels. Most commercially available microarray scanners provide software to handle image processing, and a range of additional third-party programs also is available. Although these applications are fairly straightforward, it is important to understand how information is extracted from the images, because they represent the primary data collected from each experiment; all downstream analysis directly depends on the extracted intensities.

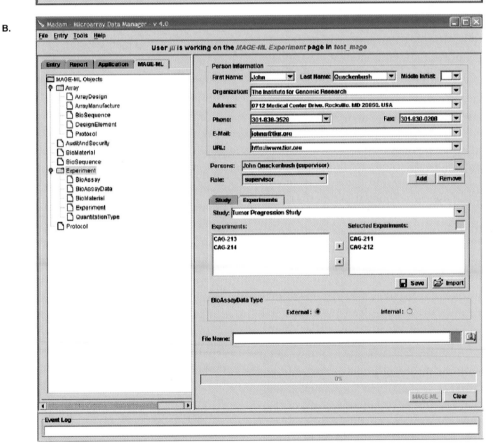

FIGURE 16.2 Analysis of microarray data requires the collection of a large body of ancillary data and databases, and data entry tools like **MADAM** help to facilitate the process of collecting, managing, analyzing, and publishing the results of a microarray experiment. **(a)** For data entry, **MADAM** uses a graphical representation of the microarray process in the left-hand window to bring up data entry screens. Red fields are mandatory because they are required by **MIAME** or for internal quality control and data management. **(b)** **MADAM** also allows **MAGE-ML** export so that experiments can be submitted directly to expression databases such as **ArrayExpress**.

The first step in image processing is identifying the features on the arrays, but this problem is somewhat simplified by the fact that the features are arranged in a regular format during array manufacture. For mechanically spotted arrays, the features are typically arranged in subarrays or pen groups representing each of the spotting pens used to deposit the features, with most arrays using a rectangular arrangement of features.

Most microarray image processing software packages require the user to specify approximately where each subgrid lies and to supply some critical parameters, such as the number of rows and columns in each subgrid, the number and arrangement of subgrids, and the approximate spot size and separation. This information then is used to place the grids roughly over the arrayed spots, to adjust them dynamically to represent the features best (often using a center-of-mass calculation for each spot), and to determine both the approximate spot area to be surveyed and a local area that can be used to estimate background.

After the grid has been placed, areas within each cell are selected to determine the spot signal and to provide an estimate of background. There are two widely used approaches for determining the spot area. The first is simply to use a fixed region that is centered on the spot; for spotted arrays, this is typically a circle of predetermined area. Although this is computationally simple, it has the disadvantage of possibly leading to a misestimate of the spot signal and local background if there is a great deal of variability in the spotted features. A second approach is to identify the spot boundaries and to include only those pixels within the boundary in any calculation of the hybridization intensity. Although computationally more difficult, this allows a more precise identification of the array feature and can provide a better estimate of the intensity and the background.

As soon as the features on the array have been identified, the image analysis software measures the intensities in each channel for each pixel comprising each feature and reports a variety of summary statistics; these include the total intensity for each feature, the mean, median, and mode of the pixel intensity distribution; an estimate of each of these for the local background, and statistics such as the standard deviation of both the signal and background. The most widely used estimates of expression rely on using background-subtracted median values or background-subtracted total intensity for each feature. The median, which is the value of the intensity with exactly half of the measurements at greater intensity and half at lower intensity, has the advantage of being relatively insensitive to outlying, high-intensity pixels in the spot image that can be caused by dust, unincorporated label, or other artifacts that cause a small number of saturated pixels within the spot. However, the

median is sensitive to misidentification of the spot area, and an overestimation of the region of the spot that includes too many of the background pixels can skew the median and any quantities calculated from it. This is because the area of the spot, and consequently the number of pixels assessed in calculating the median, grows quickly as the radius of the spot boundary increases beyond its actual area.

The total intensity, however, is relatively insensitive to misidentification of the spot boundary, because adding background pixels with intensities near or equal to zero after background subtraction has little effect on either the final sum or the final ratio. The total intensity does have the disadvantage that it can be skewed by a few anomalous highly fluorescent pixels that greatly inflate the sum. The mean intensity, which also is used widely, is simply the integrated intensity divided by the spot area.

Estimating Background

There are a number of schools of thought regarding the estimation of background for DNA microarrays. The first is simply not to calculate a background value, but rather to try to estimate it using statistical techniques. The argument here is that subtracting background introduces significant variance into the estimate of hybridization intensity, decreasing the reliability of any measurements. Although this may not produce any significant changes in relative expression levels between conditions for highly expressed genes (assuming the background is much smaller than the signal), it can have a profound effect on estimates for genes expressed at low to moderate levels.

If one chooses to subtract background, then there are a number of choices for background measurements. The first is simply to use the fluorescence of the area surrounding each feature on the array. This estimates the background of the substrate on which the array is printed and local variations in the overall background, but it may not provide an accurate estimate because it uses the "naked" substrate (where no DNA is spotted) to estimate the background for features that contain DNA, and as such neglects contributions from nonspecific hybridization. An alternative is to use negative control features printed on the array. Although these may provide an estimate of nonspecific hybridization, there are rarely enough elements on any array to provide an estimate of local background variations.

MEASURES OF EXPRESSION

Most microarray experiments investigate relationships between related biological samples based on patterns of expression, and the simplest approach looks for genes that are expressed differentially. For spotted arrays, this has an impact on experimental design, and as noted, the simplest comparisons are those comparing a query and reference sample on the same array in a co-hybridization assay.

For an array containing N_{array} distinct elements, we assume our goal is to compare a query and reference sample, which for convenience we call, respectively, R and G (or "red" and "green" for the "colors" commonly used to represent array data), then the ratio for the ith gene on the array (where i is an index running over all the arrayed genes from 1 to N_{array}) can be written as

$$T_i = \frac{R_i}{G_i}.$$

Note that this definition does not limit us to any specific array technology; the measures R_i and G_i can be made either on a single array or on two replicate arrays. Further, all of the transformations described below can be applied to data from any microarray platform.

Although ratios provide an intuitive measure of expression changes, they have the disadvantage of treating upregulated and downregulated genes differently and making mathematical operations involving the data difficult. Consequently, expression data most often are represented as the logarithm base 2 of the expression ratio. This has the advantages that it produces a continuous spectrum of values and that it treats upregulated and downregulated genes in a similar fashion. Recall that logarithms treat numbers and their reciprocals symmetrically: $\log_2(1) = 0, \log_2(2) = 1, \log_2(1/2) = -1, \log_2(4) = 2, \log_2(1/4) = -2$, and so forth. When one takes the logarithm of the expression ratio, these also are treated symmetrically so that a gene that is upregulated by a factor of two has a $\log_2(\text{ratio})$ of one, a gene downregulated by a factor of 2 has a $\log_2(\text{ratio})$ of -1, and a gene expressed at a constant level (with a ratio of 1) has a $\log_2(\text{ratio})$ equal to zero. Consequently, the $\log_2(\text{ratio})$ will be used as the measure of expression.

▮ NORMALIZING EXPRESSION MEASUREMENTS

Progressing through the analysis of microarray data, the first step is typically a "normalization" of the measured expression levels or $\log_2(\text{ratio})$ values. Normalization adjusts the individual hybridization intensities to balance them appropriately so that meaningful biological comparisons can be made. There are a number of reasons why data must be normalized, including unequal quantities of starting RNA, differences in labelling or detection efficiencies between the fluorescence dyes used, or systematic biases in the measured expression levels. Conceptually, this is similar to what is done in Northern

analysis or quantitative reverse-transcriptase PCR (qRT-PCR), where measured expression levels are adjusted relative to expression of one or more reference genes whose levels are assumed to be constant between samples.

There are many approaches to normalizing expression levels. Some, such as total intensity normalization, are based on rather simple assumptions. First, assume that one is starting with equal quantities of RNA for the two samples that will be compared. Given that there are millions of individual RNA molecules in each sample, assume that the average mass of each molecule is approximately the same and, consequently, that the number of molecules in each sample is also the same. Second, assume that the arrayed elements represent a random sampling of the genes in the organism. This point is important because it also will be assumed that the arrayed elements randomly interrogate the two RNA samples. If the arrayed genes are selected to represent only those known to change, then one will likely oversample or undersample the genes in one of the biological samples being compared. If the array contains a large enough assortment of random genes, one does not expect to see such bias. This is because, for a finite RNA sample where representation of one RNA species increases, representation of the other species must decrease. Consequently, approximately the same number of labeled molecules from each sample should hybridize to the arrays, and therefore, the total hybridization intensities summed over all elements in the arrays should be the same for each sample.

Using this approach, a normalization factor is calculated by summing the measured intensities in both channels:

$$N_{\text{total}} = \frac{\sum\limits_{i=1}^{N_{\text{array}}} R_i}{\sum\limits_{i=1}^{N_{\text{array}}} G_i},$$

where G_i and R_i are the measured intensities for the ith array element (for example, the green and red intensities in a two-color microarray assay) and N_{array} is the total number of elements represented in the microarray. One or both intensities are scaled appropriately, for example (there are other alternatives), as

$$G'_k = N_{\text{total}} G_k \quad \text{and} \quad R'_k = R_k,$$

so that the normalized expression ratio for each element becomes

$$T'_i = \frac{R'_i}{G'_i} = \frac{1}{N_{\text{total}}} \frac{R_i}{G_i},$$

which adjusts each ratio such that the mean ratio across the array is equal to one. Regardless of the normalization point, total intensity normalization is equivalent to subtracting a constant from the logarithm of the expression ratio

$$\log_2(T_i') = \log_2(T_i) - \log_2(N_{\text{total}}),$$

which results in a mean $\log_2$(ratio) equal to zero.

There are many variations on this type of normalization, including scaling the individual intensities so that the mean or median intensities are the same within a single array or across all arrays, or using a selected subset of the arrayed genes rather than the entire collection.

Although total intensity normalization is attractive because of its simplicity, it suffers from being insensitive to systematic variations that may occur in the data. For that reason, the most widely used approach for spotted array normalization is "lowess," a locally weighted linear regression used to estimate systematic biases in the data. In particular, there have been a number of reports of systematic variation in the $\log_2$(ratio) values (Yang et al., 2002a; Yang et al., 2002b), which most commonly appears as a deviation from zero for low-intensity spots. This systematic error is visualized most easily using a ratio-intensity (R-I) plot (also called an MA plot by Yang et al., 2002a and Yang et al., 2002b). Here, the $\log_2$(ratio) for each spot, $[\log_2(R/G)]$, is plotted as a function of one half the logarithm of the product of the measured intensity $[\frac{1}{2}\log_2(R^*G)]$ which is equivalent to the logarithm of the geometric mean of the intensity for that gene, a measure of the relative expression level of a particular gene. An example is shown in Figure 16.3a.

Lowess detects systematic deviations in the R-I plot and corrects them by performing a local weighted linear regression as a function of the $\log_2$(intensity) and subtracting the calculated best-fit average $\log_2$(ratio) from the experimentally observed ratio for each data point. Lowess uses a weight function that deemphasises the contributions of data from array elements that are far (on the R-I plot) from each point.

If one sets

$$x_i = \frac{1}{2}\log_2(R_i^* G_i) = \log_2(I_i) \quad \text{and} \quad y_i = \log_2\left(\frac{R_i}{G_i}\right)$$
$$= \log_2(T_i),$$

lowess first estimates $y(x_i)$, the dependence of the $\log_2$(ratio) on the $\log_2$(intensity), and then uses this function, point by point, to correct the measured $\log_2$(ratio) values, so that

$$\log_2(T_i') = \log_2(T_i) - y(x_i) = \log_2(T_i) - \log_2(2^{y(x_i)}),$$

or equivalently,

$$\log_2(T_i') = \log_2\left(T_i^* \frac{1}{2^{y(x_i)}}\right) = \log_2\left(\frac{R_i^*}{G_i}\frac{1}{2^{y(x_i)}}\right).$$

As with the other normalization methods, this can be made equivalent to a transformation on the intensities,

$$\log_2(R_i') = \frac{1}{2}[2^* \log_2(I_i) + \log_2(T_i')] \quad \text{and} \quad \log_2(G_i')$$
$$= \frac{1}{2}[2^* \log_2(I_i) - \log_2(T_i')].$$

The results of applying such a lowess correction can be seen in Figure 16.3b.

Global Versus Local Normalization

Most normalization algorithms, including lowess, can be applied either globally (to the entire dataset) or locally (to some physical subset of the data). For spotted arrays, local normalization often is applied to each group of array elements deposited by a single spotting pen (a pen group or subgrid). Local normalization has the advantage of being able to correct for systematic spatial variations in the array, including inconsistencies between the spotting pens used to make the array, variability in the slide surface, and slight local differences in hybridization conditions across the array. However, if one applies a particular normalization algorithm locally, all of the conditions and assumptions that underlie the validity of the approach must be satisfied. For example, one must assume that the elements in any pen group are not selected preferentially to represent differentially expressed genes and that a sufficiently large number of elements are included in each pen group for the approach to be valid.

Variance Regularization

Although normalization adjusts the mean of the $\log_2$(ratio) measurements, stochastic processes can cause the variance of the measured $\log_2$(ratio) values to differ from one region of an array to another or between arrays themselves. One approach to dealing with this problem is to adjust the $\log_2$(ratio) measures so that the variance is the same (Huber et al., 2002; Yang et al., 2002b). If one considers a single array with distinct subgrids for which local normalization has been performed, then what is needed is a factor for each subgrid that can be used to scale all of the measurements within that subgrid.

An appropriate scaling factor is the variance for a particular subgrid, divided by the geometric mean of the variances for all subgrids. If one assumes that each subgrid has M elements, then because the mean of the $\log_2$(ratio) values in each subgrid has been adjusted to zero, their variance in the nth subgrid is

$$\sigma_n^2 = \sum_{j=1}^{M}[\log_2(T_j)]^2,$$

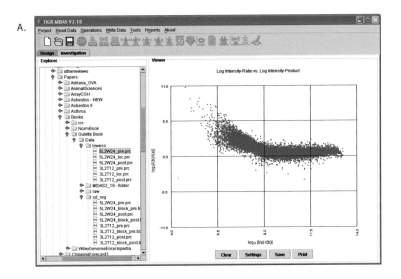

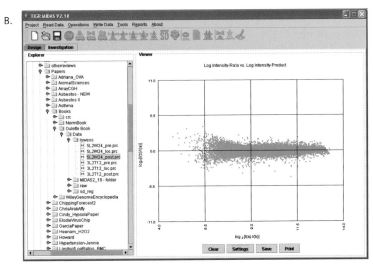

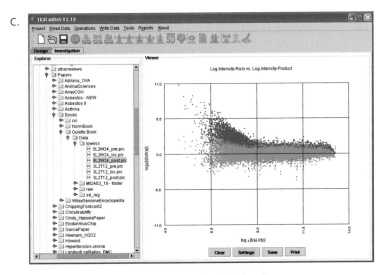

FIGURE 16.3   R-I plots for a two-color DNA microarray hybridization. (a) Raw background-subtracted data. (b) The same hybridization data following lowess normalization. (c) An overlay of the prenormalization and postnormalization data. All data were normalized and displayed using the TIGR MIDAS software tool.

where the summation runs over all the elements in that subgrid. If the number of subgrids in the array is N_{grids}, then the appropriate scaling factor for the elements of the kth subgrid on the array is

$$a_k = \frac{\sigma_k^2}{\left[\prod_{n=1}^{N_{grids}} \sigma_n^2\right]^{\frac{1}{N_{grids}}}}.$$

Scaling all of the elements within the kth subgrid by dividing by the same value a_k computed for that subgrid,

$$\log_2(T_i') = \frac{\log_2(T_i)}{a_k}.$$

This is equivalent to taking the a_kth root of the individual intensities in the kth subgrid,

$$G_i' = [G_i]^{\frac{1}{a_k}} \quad \text{and} \quad R_i' = [R_i]^{\frac{1}{a_k}}.$$

It should be noted that other variance regularization factors have been suggested (Yang et al., 2002b) and that, obviously, a similar process can be used to regularize the variance between normalized arrays.

Filtering Low-Intensity Data

If one examines several representative R-I plots, it becomes obvious that the variability in the measured $\log_2$(ratio) values increases as the measured hybridization intensity decreases. This is not surprising, because relative error increases at lower intensities, where the signal approaches background. A commonly used approach to address this problem is to use only array elements with intensities that are statistically significantly different from background. If one measures the average local background near each array element and its standard deviation, at 95.5% confidence, one would expect that good elements would have intensities more than two standard deviations above background. By keeping only array elements where

$$G_i^{spot} > G_i^{background} + 2^*\sigma\left(G_i^{background}\right) \quad \text{and}$$

$$R_i^{spot} > R_i^{background} + 2^*\sigma\left(R_i^{background}\right),$$

one can increase the reliability of measurements. Other approaches include the use of absolute lower thresholds for acceptable array elements (sometimes referred to as "floors") or percentage-based cutoffs in which some fixed fraction of elements is discarded.

A different problem can occur at the high end of the intensity spectrum, where the array elements saturate the detector used to measure fluorescence intensity. As soon as the intensity approaches its maximum value

(typically, $2^{16} - 1 = 65,535$/pixel for a 16-bit scanner), comparisons are no longer are meaningful, because the array elements become saturated and intensity measurements cannot go higher. Again, there are a variety of approaches to dealing with this problem as well, including eliminating saturated pixels in the image-processing step or setting a maximum acceptable value (often referred to as a *ceiling*) for each array element.

Limits of $\log_2$(ratio) (and Other Microarray) Measurements

The quality of any microarray analysis depends on the quality of the input data, and the effects of the high-intensity and low-intensity thresholds can have important but subtle effects on the final analysis. In many cases, no computational tools or statistical filtering can solve the problem of poor quality data. The R-I plot is quite useful for understanding some of these effects; the shape of the distribution one observes depends in a fundamental way on the experimental design one chooses, because that defines the comparisons that are made. For closely related samples where one expects gene expression to be highly similar, the distribution of log-ratio values is broad at lower intensities, reflecting greater relative uncertainties as one approaches the detection limits in one or both channels, although it narrows at higher expression levels (Figure 16.4a,b). For biologically diverse samples, the R-I plot can present a very different profile (Figure 16.4c–f). If one closely examines the R-I plots for diverse samples with many high-intensity elements on the array, it is often possible to detect a slight "arrowhead" shape at high average intensities. In many assays, the effects are subtle, but these effects can have an impact on the conclusions that are drawn.

As noted previously, the 16-bit scanners in wide use for array analysis limit the maximum intensity that can be measured in both red and green channels such that both $\log_2(R)$ and $\log_2(G)$ values range independently between a minimum of 0 and a maximum of 16. One can visualize this as a square box in the a plot of $\log_2(R)$ versus $\log_2(G)$, or as a diamond-shaped area in an R-I plot (Figure 16.5a); this relationship is because the R-I plot is essentially a 45° ($\pi/4$) rotation (and slight rescaling) of the log-intensity plot, where the square represents the limits defined by each of the two independent fluorescence measurements (Figure 16.5b). This relationship is reflected in an upper limit on the dynamic range of the measurable $\log_2$(ratio) values (or the equivalent fold-change measurements) on arrays, particularly as the intensities approach either the minimum or maximum detectable levels accessible on a particular array scanner. Furthermore, it is important to note that these limits are not unique to dual-color detection techniques. Comparisons

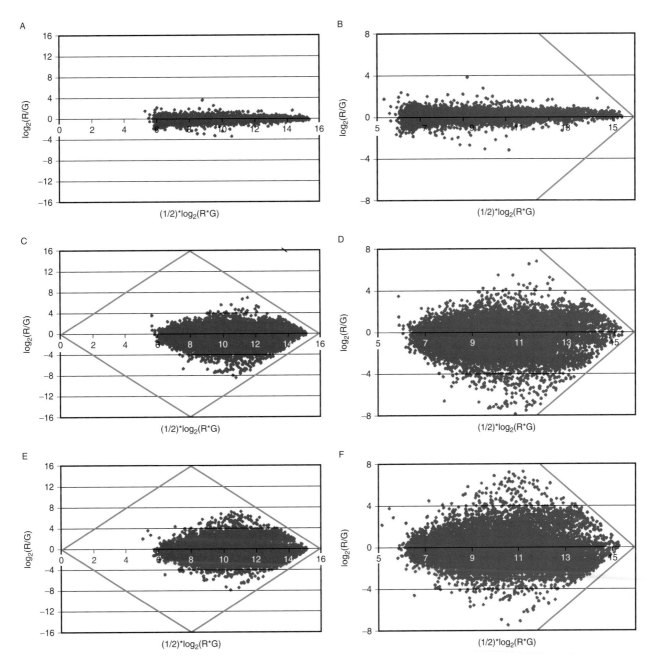

FIGURE 16.4 R-I plots for microarray expression data exhibit the limits of log-ratio measurements obtained on arrays. As the measured intensity on the arrays approaches its upper and lower limits, the dynamic range for accurately estimating fold-change measurements also is limited. Shown here are R-I plots for three different data sets showing the entire range (a, c, e) and a close-up of the upper end of the end of the effective range for array measurements (b, d, and f, respectively). The diamond delimits the range of measurements obtainable on microarrays.

made using single-color microarrays also are limited by the dynamic range of the individual measurements; fold-change estimates in comparisons demonstrate exactly the same type of artifact.

Most people generating microarray data are interested in obtaining "pretty" microarray images, consequently tuning the scanner parameters on the array to achieve this goal. The limitations placed by the dynamic range of the scanners suggests that, rather than try to maximize signal on the fluorescent images from the array, a better approach would be to target background-subtracted fluorescent intensities to the middle of the range where

---

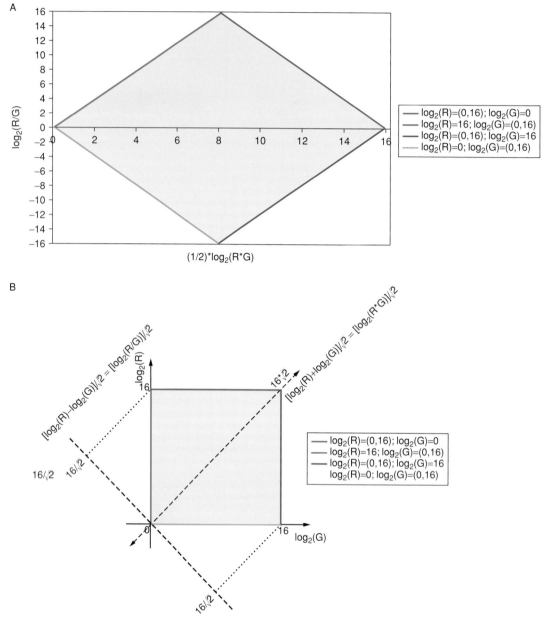

FIGURE 16.5 The limitation on the dynamic range of log-ratio measurements. (a) The diamond-shaped gray-shaded box between the colored lines on an R-I plot reflects the limited range of values that can be obtained from existing microarray technology that typically uses 16-bit array scanners that allow each channel on the array to produce measurements ranging in $\log_2$ values from 0 through 16. (b) The diamond area represents a rotation of the original axes, $x = \log_2(G)$ and $y = \log_2(R)$ to new axes $x' = [\log_2(R) + \log_2(G)]/\sqrt{2}$ and $y' = [\log_2(R) + \log_2(G)]/\sqrt{2}$, followed by a simple rescaling to $x'' = [\log_2(R) + \log_2(G)]/2$ and $y'' = [\log_2(R) - \log_2(G)]$.

the dynamic range for fold change measurements is maximized, or a $\left[\frac{1}{2}\log_2(R * G)\right]$ of 8. However, this corresponds to an average expression measurement of only 256 relative fluorescence units, which on most arrays is uncomfortably close to background. In practice, an average $\left[\frac{1}{2}\log_2(R * G)\right]$ of 10 to 12 (1024 to 4096) strikes

a good balance between intensities that are too close to background and those that approach the limits of the dynamic range of the assay. Although the raw images from these arrays may not provide as pretty a picture of they hybridization assay, they are more likely to provide useful data that can be validated.

FINDING SIGNIFICANT GENES

After the data are normalized, the next step in any experiment typically is to search for genes that distinguish the various biological classes in any experiment. Even if data mining analysis is going to be performed using one or more of the widely used clustering methods (Eisen et al., 1998; Wen et al., 1998; Tamayo et al., 1999), it is still extremely useful to reduce the dataset to those genes that are best distinguish between the sample classes. The earliest microarray papers used a simple fold-change approach to find differences, using the assumption that changes above some threshold, typically twofold, were biologically significant. The problem with this, of course, is that it does not take into account the variability inherent in the data. If one is performing a two-color array assay in which two classes of interest in each array are compared directly, a twofold cutoff is equivalent to setting a threshold $|\text{Log}_2(T_i)| \geq 1$; such criteria would be represented as parallel horizontal lines in an R-I plot so that genes outside of those lines would be called "differentially expressed." Clearly, this ignores the structure that exists even in the normalized data, where there is a greater variability in the measured $\log_2(\text{ratio})$ values at lower intensities.

As noted earlier, any good experimental design has multiple replicate measurements of the expression levels within each class, and as a result, one can represent the measurements not as a single value, but rather as a distribution of values centered on a mean. For the measurements made for each gene, one can calculate its variation using the standard deviation of the mean, sometimes also called the standard error. If one considers an experiment in which all of the samples are compared with a common reference RNA, a fixed fold-change cutoff is equivalent to specifying a minimum separation between the average peaks for all of the expression measurements for a particular gene among our two classes, as shown in Figure 16.6. Here, the two distributions reflect the variation in the measurements for any particular gene and the separation of the difference in the average $\log_2(\text{ratio})$ between conditions. With this view, the obvious question is whether a given difference is significant. If both measures have relatively low variability, then the difference likely is significant, but if the variability is large relative to the difference in $\log_2(\text{ratio})$ values, then the difference likely is not significant.

To test whether a difference is significant, one can use a relatively simple statistical test, the Student's t test. The basis of this test is the t statistic, which is an assessment of signal-to-noise ratio for the particular gene in question, comparing its expression measure for the two conditions under study. Consider two conditions, A and B. If we use X_i^A to denote the $\log_2(\text{ratio})$ that we measure in

assay i in condition A, then its average value across N_A measurements is simply

$$\langle X_A \rangle = \frac{1}{N_A} \sum_{i-1}^{N_A} X_{Ai},$$

and the standard deviation of the mean is

$$\sigma_A = \sqrt{\frac{\sum\limits_{i-1}^{N_A} [X_{Ai} - \langle X_A \rangle]^2}{N_A}}.$$

With these definitions, one can define the t statistic as

$$t = \frac{\text{signal}}{\text{noise}} = \frac{\text{difference between groups}}{\text{variability of groups}} = \frac{\langle X_A \rangle - \langle X_B \rangle}{\sqrt{\sigma_A^2 + \sigma_B^2}}.$$

Clearly, a large value for the t statistic indicates that the populations representing measurements of a gene for conditions A and B are well separated and, consequently, that the gene is differentially expressed between those conditions. The converse is true for a small value of t. But what actually is meant by "large" and "small," and can t be used to estimate how likely that a gene is differentially expressed between conditions?

There are a number of approaches to addressing these questions. The first is to use well-established properties of the t distribution for normally distributed random variables. This allows for the calculation of a probability, or p value that the two distributions of the expression measures for a gene under conditions A and B overlap for a given value of t. Although the t statistic is based on the assumption that variability in these measurements follows a normal distribution and there is evidence to suggest that this is not necessarily the case for gene expression, the t test is well known to be quite robust to violations of the assumption of normality. The second approach is to use the properties of the expression measures themselves to estimate the significance of a given value of t by performing a permutation test. Permutation testing randomly swaps expression level measurements between groups A and B, up to the total number of unique permutations that can be made. Each time, a value for t is calculated. One then asks how often, by chance, a value for t occurs that is equal to or more than that measured for the real data, which allows an estimate to be made of the probability that our dataset shows a significant separation between the classes.

In biological studies, it is common to use a p value cutoff of $p \leq 0.05$, which means that there is a 95% or more chance that a gene's expression levels can distinguish between groups. Although this seems like a reasonable approach, there can be problems with using strict p value cutoffs. In most biological experiments, one measures a small number of parameters across a relatively large number of samples. However, in most

BOX 16.2 Distance: A Mathematical Definition of "Similar"

Euclidean Distance Metrics

This is the most familiar distance measure; it is the straight-line distance between two points in Euclidean space. In a three-dimensional space, the Euclidean distance, d_{12}, between two points, (x_1, x_2, x_3) and (y_1, y_2, y_3) is given by

$$d_{12} = \sqrt{(x_1 - y_1)^2 + (x_2 - y_2)^2 + (x_3 - y_3)^2}.$$

This is just a generalization of the familiar Pythagorean theorem, and (x_1, x_2, x_3) are the usual (x, y, z) Cartesian coordinates. The generalization of this to higher-dimensional expression spaces is straightforward. Generalizing to n-dimensional expression vectors,

$$d = \sqrt{\sum_{i=1}^{n}(x_i - y_i)^2},$$

where x_i and y_i are the measured expression values, respectively, for genes X and Y in hybridization i, and the summation runs over the n hybridizations under analysis.

Non-Euclidean Metrics

Other distance measures can be defined consistently that are distinct from the straight-line Euclidean distance. Any distance d_{ij} between two vectors, i and j, must still obey a number of rules:

1. The distance must be positive definite, $d_{ij} \geq 0$ (i.e., it must be zero or positive).

2. The distance must be symmetric, $d_{ij} = d_{ji}$, so that the distance from i to j is the same as the distance from j to i.

3. An object is zero distance from itself, $d_{ii} = 0$.

4. When considering three objects, i, j, and k, the distance from i to the k is always less than or equal to the sum of the distance from the i to j and the distance from j to k, $d_{ik} \leq d_{ij} + d_{jk}$. This is sometimes called the "triangle" rule.

The Manhattan (or city block) distance is an example of a non-Euclidean distance metric. The Manhattan distance is simply calculated as the sum of the absolute distances between the components of each expression vector,

$$d = \sum_{i=1}^{n} |x_i - y_i|.$$

Semimetric Distances

Distance measures that obey the first three consistency rules, but fail to maintain the triangle rule, are referred to as semimetric. There are a large number of semimetric distance measures, and these are used often in expression analysis. Many of these are distance measures based on similarity measures. It should be noted that similarity and distance

are inversely correlated—a high degree of similarity implies a small distance. The most widely used similarity measure is the Pearson correlation coefficient (typically the centered Pearson correlation coefficient), r, given by

$$r = \frac{\sum_{i=1}^{n}(x_i - \bar{x})(y_i - \bar{y})}{\sqrt{\sum_{i=1}^{n}(x_i - \bar{x})^2}\sqrt{\sum_{i=1}^{n}(y_i - \bar{y})^2}},$$

where $\bar{x}$ and $\bar{y}$ are the mean expression values for genes X and Y, respectively.

The values of the Pearson correlation coefficient ranges between -1 and $+1$, with $r = 1$ when the two vectors are identical (perfect correlation), $r = -1$ when the two vectors are exact opposites (perfect anticorrelation), and $r = 0$ when the two vectors are completely independent (uncorrelated or orthogonal vectors).

The Pearson correlation coefficient is very useful if the "shape" of the expression vector is more important than its magnitude. If, however, the relative expression level is important, it is better to use the uncentered Pearson correlation coefficient:

$$r_{u,n} = \frac{\sum_{i=1}^{n} x_i y_i}{\sqrt{\sum_{i=1}^{n}(x_i - \bar{x})^2}\sqrt{\sum_{i=1}^{n}(y_i - \bar{y})^2}}.$$

For curves of the same shape, but different relative magnitudes, $|r_{un}| < 1$.

The centered and uncentered Pearson correlation coefficients are useful for examining correlations in the data, but are not useful for identifying genes whose expression levels are anticorrelated. One may imagine an instance, for example, in which the same transcription factor can cause both enhancement and repression of expression. In this case, a better alternative is the squared Pearson correlation coefficient:

$$r_{sq} \left\{ \frac{\sum_{i=1}^{n}(x_i - \bar{x})(y_i - \bar{y})}{\sqrt{\sum_{i=1}^{n} x_i^2}\sqrt{\sum_{i=1}^{n} y_i^2}} \right\}^2.$$

Although the Pearson correlation coefficient takes on values $-1 \leq r \leq 1$, the squared Pearson correlation coefficient takes values in the range $0 \leq r_{sq} \leq 1$, where uncorrelated vectors have $r_{sq} = 0$, whereas both perfectly correlated and anticorrelated expression vectors have $r_{sq} = 1$.

It should be noted that these correlation coefficients are measures of similarity and that similarity and distance have a reciprocal relationship: A high degree of similarity implies a small distance and vice versa. Consequently, $d = 1 - r$ typically is used as a measure of distance.

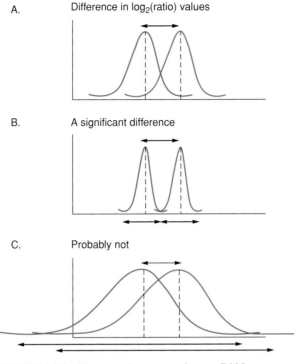

A. Difference in log$_2$(ratio) values

B. A significant difference

C. Probably not

FIGURE 16.6 Many early approaches to DNA microarray analysis focused on (a) finding genes with specific differences in the log$_2$(ratio) values between biological classes, although differences in the mean between states (b) may or (c) may not be significant, depending on the distribution of expression values in each class.

microarray experiments, one is measuring thousands of parameters (the expression levels of the genes) across a relatively small number of samples, and this can lead to the misidentification of genes being differentially expressed even when they are not—the problem of false positives. As an example of this phenomenon, known as the *multiple testing problem*, consider the case where 10,000 distinct gene-specific probes are on a given array. If a cutoff for differential expression of $p \leq 0.05$ (95% confidence) is used, one would expect, by chance, that 5% of the genes represented on the array, or 500 of them, would be identified as being significant.

Fortunately, there are a number of approaches that have been developed to deal with the multiple testing problem, the simplest of which is the Bonferroni correction. The Bonferroni correction adjusts the way in which one calculates acceptable p values. If the p value threshold nominally is some value, say, α, then for an array with N_{array} elements, the actual p value we accept is reduced to $p \leq (\alpha/N_{array})$. For a 10,000-element array, a Bonferroni-corrected $p \leq 0.05$ corresponds to an uncorrected cutoff of $p \leq 0.000005$. For this reason, many consider the Bonferroni correction to be too severe, because it often leads to few (if any) genes being identified

as being differentially expressed. There are, however, many less severe corrections that can be applied, including adjusted Bonferroni corrections that first rank genes by their t statistic and then apply increasingly less stringent criteria to subsequent genes in the list until an appropriate threshold p value is reached. The Westphal and Young stepdown p values rely on permutation testing to select appropriate significance cutoffs. Significance analysis of microarrays (SAM; Tusher et al., 2001) uses an adjusted t statistic, modified to correct for overestimates arising from small values in the denominator, along with permutation testing to estimate the false discovery rate in any selected significant gene set.

The t test is only one of many tools that are available for analysis of expression data. As described, the unpaired t test is a good approach for the analysis of a microarray experiment conducted using a reference design in which two classes of RNA are compared with a common reference RNA in each hybridization, or for a single-color assay such as that performed on an Affymetrix GeneChip. A one sample t test, or a variant such as one-sample SAM, is a good approach for two-color microarray hybridizations when using a block design in which paired classes are co-hybridized together on a single array, and the primary question is whether the $\log_2$(ratio) values are consistently significantly different from zero. ANOVA and related techniques are good if there are three or more nonoverlapping classes in the data, and the question is whether there are genes that can distinguish all of the classes represented. A two-factor ANOVA analysis, however, is appropriate if there are overlapping classes, such as two strains of mouse in which two treatments are applied in both strains, and the goal is to find genes that correlate with each of the factors as well as their interactions.

Although each of these techniques could be described in detail, the important thing to remember is that what they provide are methods for prioritizing genes for further analysis. Typically, some statistical filtering of the data is a key first step in any further data mining that will be used to search for biological patterns in the data. Although statistical significance is not the same as biological significance, the genes that have the best chance of being validated as differentially expressed between experimental classes are those with the smallest p values. However, many genes that fail to pass an unbiased cutoff for statistical significance may well prove to be of biological importance in distinguishing the biological classes represented in the data. And at the end of the day, independent biological validation of the results is the ultimate judge of the true significance of any apparent correlation.

EXPRESSION VECTORS

The ultimate goal of a microarray experiment is to compare patterns of expression across multiple samples hybridized to a particular array. One typically is looking for patterns of gene expression that correlate with the biological states of the system being analyzed or is searching for genes that have "similar" patterns of expression across multiple samples. For each gene, the process begins by defining an expression vector that represents its location in expression space. In this view of gene expression, each hybridization represents a separate distinct axis in space, and the $\log_2$(ratio) measured for that gene in that particular hybridization represents its geometric coordinate. For example, for three hybridizations, the $\log_2$(ratio) for a given gene in hybridization 1 is its x coordinate, the $\log_2$(ratio) in hybridization 2 is its y coordinate, and the $\log_2$(ratio) in hybridization 3 its z coordinate. In this way, all of the information about this gene can be represented by a point in x, y, z expression space. A second gene with nearly the same $\log_2$(ratio) values for each hybridization is represented by a (spatially) nearby point in expression space; a gene with a very different pattern of expression is far from

our original gene. An example is shown in Figure 16.7. The generalization to a greater number of hybridizations is straightforward, although harder to draw; the dimensionality of expression space grows to be equal to the number of hybridizations. In this way, expression data can be represented in m-dimensional expression space, where m is the number of hybridizations and where each gene expression vector is represented as a single point in that space. It should be noted that one can use a similar approach to representing each hybridization assay using a sample vector consisting of the expression values for each gene; these define a sample space whose dimension is equal to the number of genes assayed in each array.

Although these representations provide an intuitive picture of similarity, to define a computational method for analyzing the data, a mathematical formulation is needed for calculating the "distance" between two expression vectors, because this is what will be used to organize these into groups. There are a variety of methods for measuring distance, typically falling into three general classes: Euclidean, non-Euclidean, and semimetric.

To interpret the results from any analysis of multiple hybridizations, it is helpful to have an intuitive visual representation. A commonly used approach relies on the creation of an expression matrix in which each column of the matrix represents a single sample and each row represents the expression vector for each gene across all of the hybridizations. Coloring each of the matrix elements based on its expression value creates a visual representation of gene expression patterns across the collection of hybridizations. There are countless ways in which the expression matrix can be colored and presented. The most common approach colors genes based on their $\log_2$(ratio) in each hybridization, with $\log_2$(ratio) values close to zero colored black, those with $\log_2$(ratio) values of more than zero colored red, and those with negative values colored green. For each element in the matrix, the relative intensity represents the relative expression, with brighter elements being more highly differentially expressed. For any particular group of samples, the expression matrix generally appears without any apparent pattern or order. Programs designed to perform clustering generally reorder the rows, columns, or both such that patterns of expression become visually apparent when presented in this fashion.

CLUSTERING APPROACHES

A useful first approach to the analysis of microarray data is to use an unsupervised method to explore the expression patterns that exist in the data. Three of the

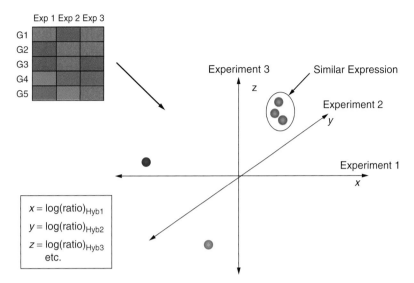

FIGURE 16.7 **Much of microarray data mining involves looking for "similar" patterns of expression between genes or experiments. If three hybridization assays are considered, the expression vector for each gene can be represented as a point in three-dimensional space, where the expression measure in hybridization 1 is its x coordinate, the expression measure in hybridization 2 is its y coordinate, and that in hybridization 3 is its z coordinate. In such a geometric representation, the definition of "similar" is intuitive.**

most widely used methods are hierarchical clustering, k-means clustering, and self-organizing maps. Although each of these approaches works with any dataset, in practice they often do not work well for large datasets in which many of the genes do not vary between samples. Consequently, it is useful first to apply a statistical filter to the data to exclude genes that simply are not varying between experimental classes. If there are no predetermined classes in the data, a useful alternative simply is to eliminate those genes that have minimal variance across the collection of samples because those genes are not changing significantly in the dataset and are therefore the least likely to shed any light on subclasses that exist in the sample collection.

Hierarchical Clustering

Hierarchical clustering has become one of the most widely used techniques for the analysis of gene expression data; it has the advantage that it is simple and the result can be visualized easily (Eisen et al., 1998; Michaels et al., 1998; Wen et al., 1998). Initially, one starts with N clusters, where N is the number of genes (or samples) to be in the target dataset. Hierarchical clustering is an agglomerative approach in which single expression profiles are joined to form nodes, which are further joined until the process has been carried to completion, form-

ing a single hierarchical tree. The algorithm proceeds in a straightforward manner:

1. Calculate the pairwise distance matrix for all of the genes to be clustered.

2. Search the distance matrix for the two most similar genes or clusters; initially each cluster consists of a single gene. This is the true first stage in the clustering process. If several pairs share the same similarity, a predetermined rule is used to decide between alternatives.

3. The two selected clusters are merged to produce a new cluster that now contains two or more objects.

4. The distances are calculated between this new cluster and all other clusters. There is no need to calculate all distances because only those involving the new cluster have changed.

5. Steps 2 through 4 are repeated until all objects are grouped in one cluster.

There are a number of variants of hierarchical clustering that reflect different approaches to calculating distances between the newly defined clusters and the other genes or clusters:

▶ Single linkage clustering uses the shortest distance between one cluster and any other

- complete linkage clustering takes the largest distance between any two clusters
- average linkage clustering uses the average distance between two clusters.

Typically, the relationship between samples is represented using a dendrogram, where branches in the tree are built based on the connections determined between clusters as the algorithm progresses. To visualize the relationships between samples, the dendrogram is used to rearrange the rows (or columns as appropriate) in the expression matrix to visualize patterns in the dataset.

Hierarchical clustering often is misused to partition data into some number of clusters without the application of any objective criteria. Fortunately, there are a number of approaches that can be used to identify subgroups in the clustering dendrograms. One method simply is to use the distances calculated in building the clusters as a measure of the connectivity of the individual clusters. As one moves up the dendrogram from the individual elements, the distance between clusters increases. Consequently, as one increases the distance threshold, the effective number of clusters decreases. An alternative approach is to use bootstrapping or jack-knifing techniques to measure the stability of relationships in the dendrogram, using this stability as a measure of the number of clusters represented. In bootstrapping, there are a number of approaches that can be used, but the simplest is to use sampling of the dataset with replacement, each time calculating a new hierarchical clustering dendrogram and simply counting how often each branch in the dendrogram is recovered; a percentage cutoff on the dendrogram sets the number of clusters. In making a bootstrap estimate for gene cluster stability, it is appropriate to resample the collection of biological samples, whereas in estimating the number of clusters in the biological samples, one bootstraps the gene expression vectors. Jack-knifing is similar, but instead of resampling, the appropriate vectors are left out sequentially as new dendrograms are calculated until all vectors have been considered. Again, the stability of each cluster is estimated based on how often a given relationship in the dendrogram is recovered.

One potential problem with many hierarchical clustering methods is that, as clusters grow, the expression vector that represents the cluster when calculating distance no longer may represent any of the genes within the cluster. Consequently, as clustering progresses, the actual expression patterns of the genes themselves become less relevant. Furthermore, if a bad assignment is made early in the process, it cannot be corrected. An alternative that can avoid these artifacts is to use a divisive clustering approach, such as k-means, to partition data (either genes or samples) into groups having similar expression patterns.

k-Means Clustering

If there is advanced knowledge regarding the number of clusters that should be represented in the data, k-means clustering is a good alternative to hierarchical methods (Soukas et al., 2000; Aronow et al., 2001). In k-means, objects are partitioned into a fixed number (k) of clusters such that the clusters internally are similar but externally are dissimilar. No dendrograms are produced, but one could use hierarchical techniques on each of the data partitions after they are constructed. The process involved in k-means clustering is conceptually simple, but can be computationally intensive:

1. All initial objects are randomly assigned to one of k clusters (where k is specified by the user).

2. An average expression vector then is calculated for each cluster, and this is used to compute the distances between clusters.

3. Using an iterative method, objects are moved between clusters, and intracluster and intercluster distances are measured with each move. Objects are allowed to remain in the new cluster only if they are closer to it than to their previous cluster.

4. After each move, the expression vectors for each cluster are recalculated.

5. The shuffling proceeds until moving any more objects would make the clusters more variable, increasing intracluster distances and decreasing intercluster dissimilarity.

Some implementations of k-means clustering allow not only the number of clusters to be specified, but also seed cases for each cluster. This has the potential to allow one to use prior knowledge of the system to help define the cluster output, such as a typical profile for a few key genes known to distinguish classes of patients. Of course, the "means" in k-means refers to the use of a mean expression vector for each emerging cluster. As one may imagine, there are variations also use other measures, such as k-medians clustering.

Self-Organizing Maps

A self-organizing map (SOM) is a neural network-based divisive clustering approach (Tamayo et al., 1999; Toronen et al., 1999; Wang et al., 2002). An SOM assigns genes to a series of partitions based on the similarity of their expression vectors to reference vectors that are defined for each partition. It is the process of defining these reference vectors that distinguishes SOMs from *k*-means clustering. Before initiating the analysis, the user defines a geometric configuration for the partitions, typically a two-dimensional rectangular or hexagonal grid. Random vectors are generated for each partition, but before genes can be assigned to partitions, the vectors are first "trained" using an iterative process that continues until convergence so that the data are most effectively separated:

1. Random vectors are constructed and assigned to each partition.

2. A gene is picked at random and, using a selected distance metric, the reference vector that is closest to the gene is identified.

3. This reference vector then is adjusted so that it is more similar to the randomly picked gene. The other reference vectors that are nearby on the two-dimensional grid also are adjusted so that they, too, are more similar to the randomly selected gene.

4. Steps 2 and 3 are iterated several thousand times, decreasing the amount by which the reference vectors are adjusted and increasing the stringency used to define closeness in each step. As the process continues, the reference vectors converge to fixed values.

5. Finally, the genes are mapped to the relevant partitions, depending on the reference vector to which they are most similar.

In choosing the geometric configuration for the clusters, the user effectively is specifying the number of partitions into which the data are to be divided. As with *k*-means clustering, the user has to rely on some other sources of information, such as principal component analysis (PCA), to determine the number of clusters that best represents the available data.

There are many additional approaches to partitioning the data, including self-organizing trees (Herrero et al., 2001), relevance networks (Butte & Kohane, 1999), force-directed layouts (Kim et al., 2001), principal component analysis (Raychaudhuri et al., 2000), and others. Fundamentally, each of these approaches uses some feature of the data and a rule for determining relationships to group genes (or samples) that share similar patterns of expression.

BEYOND STATISTICAL SIGNIFICANCE AND CLUSTERING

Many analyses of microarray data reach the stage where some collection of genes that share similar patterns of expression has been identified. The challenge, then, is to attach some biological meaning to the gene sets identified through this process. Some approaches use relationships identified based on linking genes to PubMed abstracts or associated medical subject heading (MeSH) terms (Jenssen et al., 2001; Masys et al., 2001; Doniger et al., 2003; Fink et al., 2003; Zeeberg et al., 2003). Others use constraints from the biological system under analysis, such as using genetic linkage or quantitative trait locus maps to narrow down the set of significant genes to those mapping to regions of the genome associated with appropriate trait (Kwitek-Black & Jacob, 2001; Doerge, 2002; Cook et al., 2004; Schadt et al., 2003). In solid tumor studies, one may look for correlations with genome deletions or amplifications as determined by comparative genomic hybridization on arrays (Gray & Collins, 2000; Cheung et al., 2002). Finally, in developmental imprinting studies, gene expression may be compared with patterns of methylation (Chen et al., 2001; Ehrlich, 2002).

Another very attractive approach is to use the properties of the data and the construction of the array to look for significant functional associations. Recall that one of the key elements in establishing an array platform is the annotation of the arrayed probe elements. For example, imagine that 20% of the genes on the array are annotated as belonging to GO categories representing energy metabolism. If this is the case, randomly selecting a collection of "significant" genes most likely would yield approximately 20% of its elements as belonging to the same energy metabolism class. In fact, it would not be surprising to find that 30% of the genes in the "significant" set were energy metabolism genes; however, if the fraction were 80%, it may suggest that the experiment affected energy metabolism with a much higher frequency than would be expected by chance. Such insight indeed may provide clues as to the mechanisms at work in the biological system under study.

An obvious question is whether the probability that a given functional class is overrepresented in our significant gene set can be estimated. This can be determined using the Fisher exact test, and the mathematics behind the approach are described in Box 16.3.

THE CLASSIFICATION PROBLEM

As mentioned earlier, some microarray experiments do not focus on identifying function, but rather on finding genes that can be used to group samples into biologically or clinically relevant classes and supervised approaches to data analysis are particularly useful for these studies. One typically begins with a priori knowledge of the groups represented in the data, although

BOX 16.3 Using the Fisher Exact Test to Assess Significance

Imagine that there are n total elements on a microarray and, of those, n_{sig} were selected as members of a significant (or interesting) cluster by some method—a statistical test, a clustering approach, or a combination of these. Now, assume that the array contains m total elements that have been assigned to a particular functional class and that, of these, m_{sig} fall into the significant set. Obviously, the relationships $m \leq n$ and $m_{sig} \leq n_{sig}$ must hold true.

Now, a "contingency" matrix that shows the status of all of the array elements in terms of their representation in the significant cluster can be constructed in a class of interest, or for the array as a whole:

		Cluster		
		In	out	
Class	in	a	b	$a+b=m$
	out	c	d	
		$a+c=n_{sig}$		$a+b+c+d=n$

Here, $a = m_{sig}$ is the number of significant genes that are also in the class of interest, whereas b is the number of genes in the significant cluster that are not within the class. Further, c is the number of elements within the cluster, but not belonging to the class of interest, and d is the remainder—those elements belonging neither to the cluster nor to the class of interest. The following constraints must hold true: that $a + b = m$, the total number of elements on the array within our class; that $a + c = n_{sig}$, the total number of significant genes in our cluster; and that $a + b + c + d = n$, the total number of elements on the array.

One then can calculate the probability of finding precisely a of m elements of the class of interest within the cluster. As specified by the Fisher exact test, the probability of obtaining exactly a significant elements within the class is given a the hypergeometric distribution:

$$p_a = \frac{\frac{(a+c)!}{a!c!} \times \frac{(b+d)!}{b!d!}}{\frac{n!}{(a+b)!(c+d)!}} = \frac{(a+b)!(c+d)!(a+c)!(b+d)!}{n!a!b!c!d!}.$$

Now, in fact, for any value of a, the probability of finding precisely that number of elements on that array is going to be a small number, because the sum of p_a values over all possible values of a, with $0 \leq a \leq m$, has to add to one,

reflecting the fact that the total probability of either finding either something or nothing that meets the criteria of being in the class and being found significant has to be one. Consequently, the probability that one wants to use in estimating the likelihood of finding a significant elements coming from the class is the probability of finding a or more:

$$p = \sum_{i=a}^{m} p_i,$$

where p_i is calculated from a contingency table where a is incremented while keeping the total number of significant elements (n_{sig}) constant; this is subject to the constraint that the sums of the rows and columns in the relevant contingency tables are constant as well.

Although calculating this for any particular class is a relatively straightforward, applying this method to a large collection of assigned classes such as KEGG pathways or GO terms can be a huge challenge. For GO, the object is to consider all possible terms in the GO hierarchy. Fortunately, there are some software tools, including MAPPFinder (Doniger et al., 2003), GOMiner (Zeeberg et al., 2003), and EASE (Hosack et al., 2003) that calculate p values for GO, KEGG, GenMAPP, PFAM, and SMART protein domain assignments, promoter elements, and a range of other classification systems.

The advantage of this approach is that it can provide a high-level view of functional classes or pathways that may be affected significantly in an experiment. However, remember that these are functional classes, not functions, and deciphering the underlying functions requires significant additional effort. It also should be noted that the only genes that can be analyzed using this approach are those for which functional assignments have been made. In any given experiment, one often finds a number of unknown expressed sequence tags (ESTs) and predicted genes that significantly correlate with biological groups, and these drop out of any functionally based analysis. One widely used approach that can be applied to study genes of unknown function is to look for functional classes that pass a significance test and then to look for unknowns that group with these in a hierarchical clustering or other analysis; this provides a testable hypothesis that the unknown genes belong to the same functional class.

any hypothesis along these lines can be explored further using clustering techniques and other information. With those groups, one then asks whether there are genes that can be used to separate the relevant classes. For two groups of samples, a t test or unpaired two-class SAM

are useful tools, whereas for a larger number of classes, ANOVA or multiclass SAM are appropriate. Having identified a set of genes that show significant differences, one then builds a classification algorithm that can be used to assign a new sample to one of the classes.

There are a wide range of algorithms that have been used for classification, including weighted voting (Tamayo et al., 1999), artificial neural networks (Ellis et al., 2002; Bloom et al., 2004), discriminant analysis (Nguyen & Rocke, 2002; Orr & Scherf, 2002; Antoniadis et al., 2003; Le et al., 2003), classification and regression trees (Boulesteix et al., 2003), support vector machines (Furey et al., 2000; Ramaswamy et al., 2001), k-nearest neighbors (kNN; Theilhaber et al., 2002), and a host of others. Essentially, each of these uses an original set of samples—a training set—to develop a rule that takes a new test sample from a test set and uses its expression vector, trimmed to a previously identified set of classification genes, to place this test sample into the context of the original sample set, thus identifying its class.

In many ways, kNN is the simplest approach to carrying out classification. First, one must assemble a collection of expression vectors for the samples and must assign the samples to various experimental classes. We refer to these samples, about which we have prior knowledge, as our *training set*. Next, genes are selected that separate the various classes using an appropriate statistical test to identify good classification candidate genes, thus reducing the size of the sample classification vectors. This represents a first-pass collection of classification genes. The next step is to identify and eliminate samples that seem to be outliers. These may be important because they may represent new subclasses in our original sample classification set; alternatively, they simply may represent poor-quality data. The outlying samples are identified by applying a correlation filter to the reduced sample expression vectors, as follows:

1. The Pearson correlation coefficient (r) is computed between a given vector and each member of the training set; the maximum r identified is called the r_{max} for that vector.
2. The vector is randomized a user-specified number of times. Each time, an r_{max} is calculated using the randomized vector (called r^*_{max}), just as in step 1.
3. The fraction of times r^*_{max} exceeds r_{max} over all randomizations is used to calculate a p value for that vector.
4. If the p value for a vector is less than a user-specified threshold (meaning it is well correlated with other samples), that vector is retained for further analysis. Otherwise, it is discarded.
5. Steps 1 through 4 are repeated for every sample vector in the set.

At this point, the training set has led to the generation of a collection of sample vectors that represent prior knowledge regarding the biological classes represented in the data. The next step in the analysis involves assigning new samples from the test set to classes, based on their expression vectors.

For each sample in the test set, its expression vector is reduced to include only those genes previously identified as being significant for classification. The distance between this reduced expression vector and the reduced expression vectors then is computed for each and every sample in the training set. As the name kNN implies, some number k of nearest neighbors is chosen from the training set—those k vectors that have the smallest distances from the test sample. The new test vector then is assigned to the class most highly represented in its k nearest neighbors. If there is a tie, the new sample remains unclassified.

Validation

Ideally, to validate a classification method, it is most useful to have a set of samples in the test set that is independent of those used in the training set. In practice, microarray studies often have a limited number of samples, and these are needed for building and training the algorithm. An alternative to using an independent test set is to perform leave k out cross-validation (LKOCV; Simon et al., 2003). As one may guess, this approach leaves out some subset of the initial collection of N samples, develops a classifier using the $(N - k)$ samples that remain, and applies it to k samples in the test set. This process then is repeated, choosing a new set of k vectors to be left out and classified, and the process repeats itself. The simplest approach is simply to perform leave one out cross-validation (LOOCV).

Although this approach can be extremely useful when lacking an independent test set, it often is applied inappropriately as a partial rather than a full cross-validation. The distinction is the stage in the process where one leaves k out. Many published studies have used their entire dataset to select a set of classification genes and then have divided the samples into k and $(N - k)$ sample test and training sets. In fact, this has the potential to bias the results because the test and training sets are not independent, because all of the samples were used to select the classification gene set. In particular, the presence of all of the samples in the initial gene selection process may bias favorably the ultimate success of any classifier that is constructed.

In full LKOCV, the data is divided into k and $(N - k)$ sample test and training sets and the $(N - k)$ training set is used to select a classification gene set and then to apply it to creating a classification algorithm and using it to classifying the k test samples. One then can estimate the accuracy of the classification system simply by averaging over the complete set of classifiers.

Developing a biological interpretation for any classification experiment can be difficult, because very often the genes providing the best discriminating power between classes may be difficult to link casually or mechanistically to the underlying disease. LKOCV approaches present the further challenge that each iteration may produce a unique set of classification genes with a very small number in common to all of these (although further insight may come from using genes appearing in most iterations or by taking the union of all iterations). Analyzing these gene lists generally follows the same approach we use in a discovery experiment, and the most effective approaches come from linking these gene lists to ancillary information such as polymorphism data or functional roles. Regardless, it may be that the classification gene set cannot be linked to the disease. In this context, it is useful to note that there are many examples of biomarkers of unknown function in the context of the disease that are extremely useful as diagnostic or prognostic markers for various diseases. In some sense, the gene lists emerging from classification experiments can be thought of as sets of biomarkers that potentially have important applications in a clinical setting, and if these have some biological relevance, this is a significant bonus.

▌ SUMMARY

During the past few years, there have been many discussions in the literature on "noise" in microarray assays: disparate results arising from the use of different platforms, questions regarding the validity of microarray results, and the need to validate the findings. If one closely examines the underlying issues, it is clear that microarrays are no different than any other approach to assaying levels of gene expression—each method has its own biases and limitations. Microarrays simply provide much more data than do techniques such as quantitative RT-PCR or Northern blots, and the likelihood of false positives and false negatives increases as the number of genes assayed increases—a manifestation of the multiple testing problem. What is underlying all of these issues is trying to understand what can be done with the data that emerges. Although there are no absolute answers, there are some overarching generalizations that can be made that will help guide the follow-on experiments.

First, whether one is doing a mechanistic study or trying to identify genes that can be used for sample classification, what microarray assays generally give us are lists of genes that can be significantly correlated with some classes in our experiments. These should be treated not as truths, but rather as hypotheses that can be tested.

Second, statistical significance is fine, but biological significance is better. Statistics provides very powerful tools for identifying candidate genes, for prioritizing them in the lack of any other evidence, and in helping to resolve features in the data. For example, if 30 of the top 50 genes in a list are "energy metabolism" genes, a likely working hypothesis is that the experimental system under study involves changes in energy metabolism, regardless of where these 30 fall in the list.

Third, it is very important to note that any change in how one carries out the analysis is likely to change what is identified as significant in any experiment. This obviously includes changing microarray platform, but even subtle changes in the analysis performed on a single platform can change what is identified as significant. Starting from the laboratory protocols to parameters for slide scanning, image processing, data normalization, and the choice of the analysis tools all contribute significantly to outcome of any analysis. One way to approach this problem is to apply multiple approaches and then to look for a common set of high-confidence genes. Another way that may be more useful is to look at pathways and functional classes to identify common biological themes that overlie all of the analyses. It is these functional classes and pathways in which we are ultimately interested.

Fourth, in confirming any microarray result often it is useful to use an alternate technique to assay gene expression levels. At this stage, it is useful to define two approaches: verification and validation. Verification involves using another technique with the same RNA samples used for array profiling. Verification confirms the observed patterns of expression in the sample set under analysis and addresses questions related to the bias in the technique. Validation, however, uses independent RNA sources to assay the individual genes and their patterns of expression. This can confirm the results independent of biases in the sample selection and in the choice of a particular technique. Validation also includes LKOCV and LOOCV approaches to classification algorithms. Validation is a much more powerful statement than verification.

Finally, all microarrays provide are correlations between a particular pattern of expression and some biological class. The real biology is not on the array, but back in the laboratory. Microarray experiments can be powerful tools for developing testable hypotheses and even can play a significant role in conducting such tests. The value of functional genomics experiments is that they provide unbiased surveys of large numbers of genes, and this can be extremely powerful for discovering potential new mechanisms and new subgroups within classes.

Ultimately, microarrays remain a tool for discovery, and bioinformatics is simply a filter that can increase the power of any array experiment.

█ WORKED EXAMPLE

As noted previously, the approach used to analyze any dataset depends on the underlying experimental design, which depends fundamentally on the questions one wants to ask of the data. This Worked Example looks at a single microarray study, with the goal of understanding possible approaches to extracting meaning from microarray data. To accomplish this, software tools developed at TIGR as part of the TM4 software package (Saeed et al., 2003), which is available with source code, are used. There are a number of other available free and commercial software packages that would allow similar analyses to be performed.

The dataset under consideration comes from an experiment recently described by Larkin et al. (2004) in which mice were exposed to acute and chronic treatments of angiotensin II (Ang II). Ang II is produced through the renin-angiotensin-aldosterone system and is a major contributor to hypertension and resulting target organ damage, including cardiac hypertrophy, inflammation, and myocardial necrosis and fibrosis; some of the most effective antihypertensive treatments are those that antagonize Ang II. The goal of this study was to identify genes induced by short-term (24 hours) and long-term (2 weeks) exposure to Ang II. Although the focus of the published analysis was heart tissue, four different tissues were profiled: heart, liver, kidney, and brain. All data are available from ArrayExpress (accession IDs E-TIGR-11 HTA1 and E-TIGR-12 HTA2).

This dataset allows one to look at a number of different questions regarding Ang II exposure. First, because all of the hybridizations involve a direct comparison between animals treated with Ang II and control animals, we can examine the general effects of Ang II treatment, the general differences between short-term and long-term exposure, the factors that distinguish tissue-specific response, and the effects of multiple factors such as tissue and time of exposure.

The experimental design in this study was straightforward: for each target tissue, expression in a treated animal was compared with that of a randomly selected control animal using spotted cDNA arrays containing approximately 27,000 mouse cDNA clones from the Trans-NIH Brain Molecular Anatomy Project (BMAP) and National Institute of Aging (NIA) clone sets (the TIGR 25-k mouse set); all hybridizations were performed with dye-reversal replicates. Using MIDAS (Saeed et al., 2003), the data were subjected to lowess normalization followed by variance regularization, and the geometric mean of the $\log_2$(ratio) values (treated versus control) were calculated for each gene in each set of paired samples and loaded into the TIGR Multiexperiment Viewer (MeV) (Saeed et al., 2003). GO terms and metabolic pathway assignments provided by RESORUCERER (Tsai et al., 2001) were assigned to each gene using the version of EASE (Hosack et al., 2003) integrated in MeV. Figure 16.8a shows the data loaded into MeV represented as a heat map, where a blue-yellow (rather than a green-red) color scale is displayed, ranging from $\log_2$(ratios) of -2 (-4-fold downregulation) to $+2$ ($+4$-fold upregulation); annotation for the individual arrayed elements can be displayed by clicking on an array element. Figure 16.8b shows the GO term annotation loaded using the EASE module.

The first question that is asked of the data is whether genes that respond to the administration of Ang II independent of the period of administration can be identified. Because the data all represent $\log_2$(ratio) values of the expression in treated animals relative to control, the question really being asked is which genes have $\log_2$(ratio) values that are significantly different from zero, because these are the genes that are significantly upregulated or downregulated. The tools that are appropriate for addressing this question are the one-class t test or one-class SAM. For this example, the t test with adjusted Bonferroni-corrected p values determined by 1000 random permutations for each gene and a significance level set at $p < 0.05$ are used. This identified 45 significant genes that are generally responsive to Ang II. Figure 16.9a shows a hierarchical clustering dendrogram (average linkage, Euclidean distance) for both genes and samples using this significant gene subset. One can then ask whether these genes represent any particular functional classes and analysis. EASE suggests that both acute and chronic Ang II treatments cause decreased expression of mitochondrial metabolic genes, notably those for the electron transport chain (Figure 16.9b). When viewed in the context of reports linking hypertension and mitochondrial dysfunction (Ramachandran et al., 2002; Watson, 2003; Doroshchuk et al., 2004), this suggests that Ang II may be involved causatively as an inhibitor of mitochondrial function.

The next question is to determine which genes best distinguish acute and chronic response to Ang II exposure. Here, rather than comparing expression levels with a fixed value, expression between two groups is compared to find significant differences between them. In this case, the appropriate techniques for identification of differentially expressed genes are the between-subjects t test or between-groups SAM. If SAM is applied, with s_0 calculated using the method described by Tuscher et al. (2001), 100 random permutations, and a false discovery rate of zero (Figure 16.10a), 26 genes that separate the samples based on duration of treatment are found. Using EASE to examine the functional classes represented shows a significant representation of stress-response genes, with heat-shock proteins upregulated in acute treatment and cold-inducible proteins upregulated in response to chronic treatments. This is consistent with a number of reports, including suggestions that Hsp90, which is among those genes seen here upregulated in response to chronic exposure to Ang II, both may be a marker and therapeutic target for hypertension and atherosclerosis (Ai et al., 2003; Pockley et al., 2003; Chen et al., 2004).

One also can investigate which genes best distinguish the four tissues under study: heart, kidney, liver, and brain. A one-way ANOVA with four groups (with the data from each tissue placed into its own group) and a p value cutoff of $p \leq 0.01$ identifies 271 significant genes (Figure 16.11a). Grouping these using average

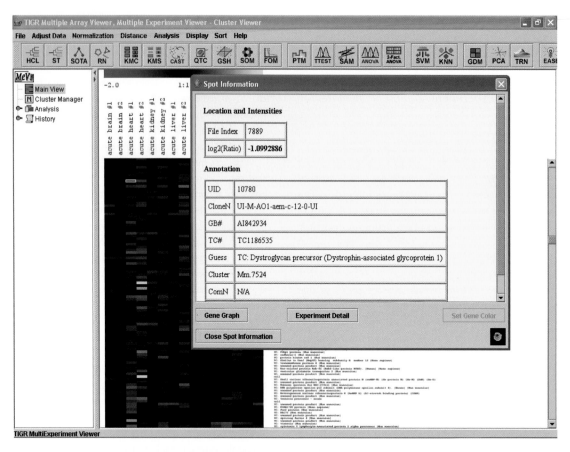

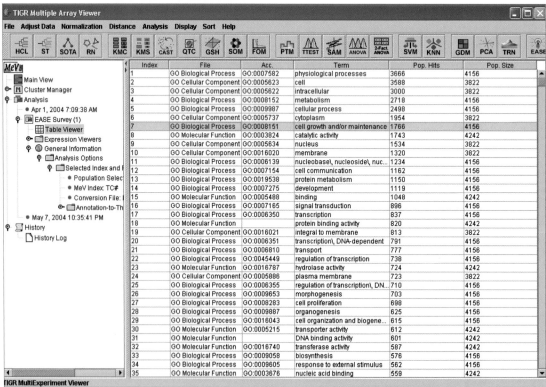

FIGURE 16.8 Worked Example. (a) Spot information from MeV showing the loaded data represented as a "heat map," using a blue-yellow color scale ranging from $\log_2$(ratios) of -2 to $+2$. (b) A text view of annotation for the individual arrayed elements showing the GO term annotation loaded using the EASE module. See text for details.

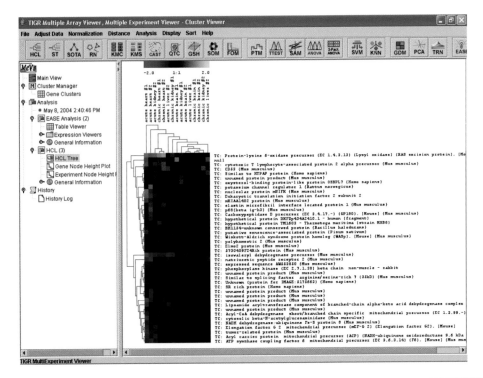

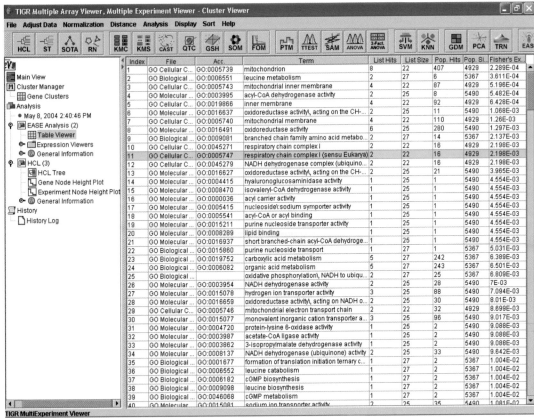

FIGURE 16.9 Worked Example for genes which respond to Ang II treatment independent of duration. (a) Hierarchical clustering dendrogram from MeV for both genes and samples using this significant gene subset. (b) Table view of (a) showing decreased expression of mitochondrial metabolic genes, notably those for the electron transport chain. See text for details.

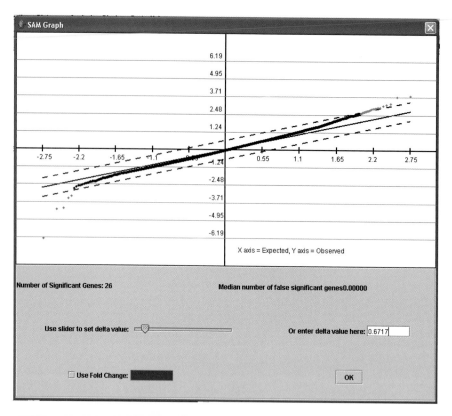

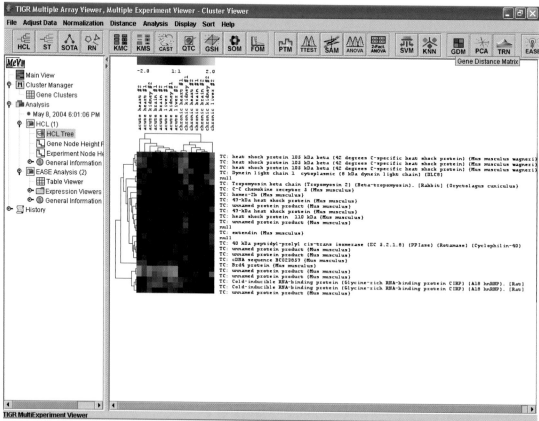

FIGURE 16.10 **Worked Example. Genes selected as significant for separating short- and long-term Ang II treatment. (a) SAM** graph from the **TIGR MeV** program. **(b)** Heat map from the same clustering. See text for details.

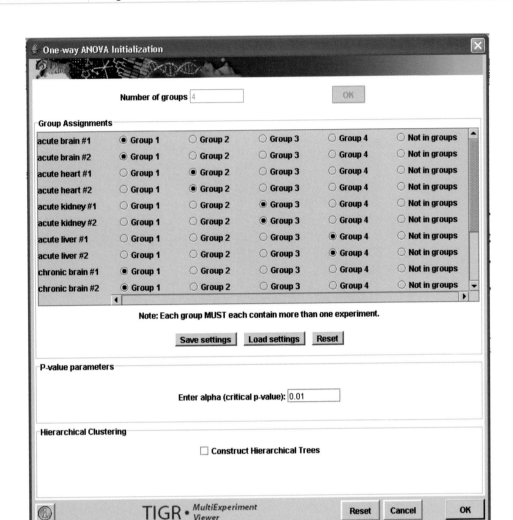

FIGURE 16.11 Worked Example. (a) One-way **ANOVA** initialization with four groups (with the data from each tissue placed into its own group) and a p value cutoff of $p \leq$ 0.01. (b) Hierarchical cluster view with a **Pearson correlation coefficient distance** measure. (c) Upregulated genes in the heart relative to other tissues using **MeV** filters. See text for details.

linkage hierarchical clustering with a Pearson correlation coefficient distance measure clearly separates the various tissues and shows that heart, which Larkin et al. (2004) described as being the most responsive tissue, stands out as an independent clade in the tissue sample dendrogram (Figure 16.11b). MeV contains a template matching algorithm (Pavlidis & Noble, 2001) that allows one to focus on genes that upregulated in the heart relative to other tissues (Figure 16.11c); many of these are muscle-specific genes. This may not be surprising, but it illustrates the power of microarray assays to uncover relevant biology.

Finally, because this data set involves two factors, the various tissues and the time of exposure to Ang II (acute and chronic), a two-factor ANOVA (TFA) can be performed. With respect to time, there are two classes; for tissues, there are four. However,

there is only one chronic liver sample in this dataset, and the implementation of TFA in MeV requires two or more examples of each composite class. Consequently, the number of tissue classes will be reduced to three, and the liver samples will be assigned to "not in group" (Figure 16.12a). Using the F distribution to calculate p values and requiring $p \leq 0.01$, 446 genes that separate samples based on time of exposure are found, 500 genes that distinguish heart, kidney, and brain are found; and 136 that represent interactions between time and tissue (Figure 16.12b) are found. In many ways, the most interesting are the interaction terms, and an analysis of the GO categories significantly represented include "organogenesis," (GO: 0009887) "morphogenesis," (GO: 0009653), "cytoskeleton organization and biogenesis" (GO: 0007010), and other related processes.

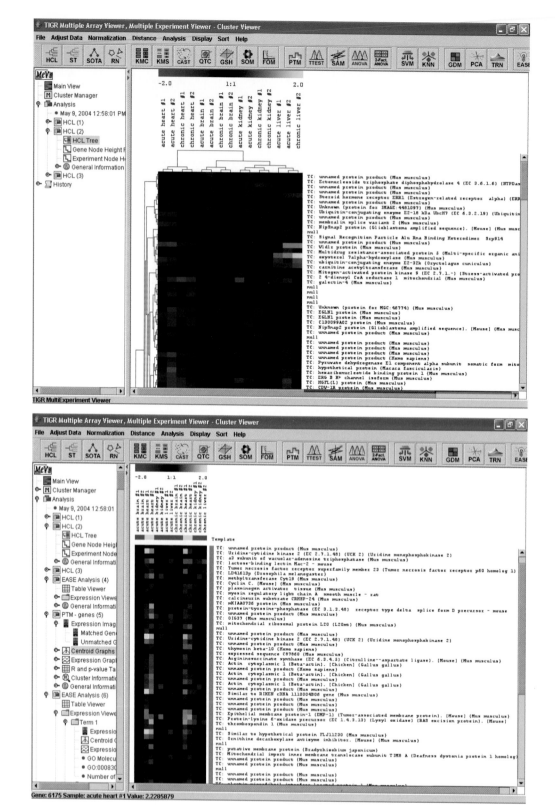

FIGURE 16.11

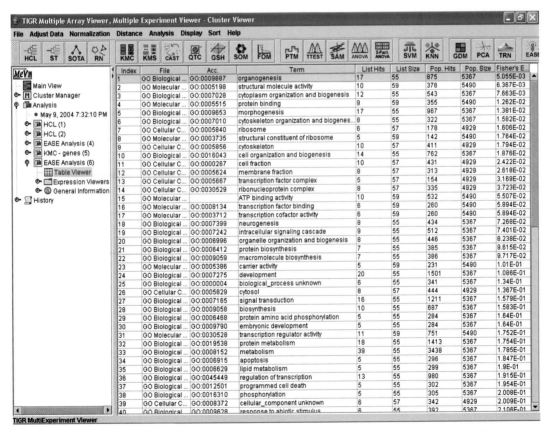

FIGURE 16.12 **Worked Example.** The structure of this dataset allows multiple factors (tissue and exposure time) to be analyzed. (a) Group assignment dialog window in MeV used to select a two-factor **ANOVA** (TFA). (b) **EASE** analysis of the significant gene set identifies "organogenesis" genes as the most significant subset for separating tissues. See text for details.

The key element here is that one has to design an experiment to address a particular question. The design dictates the how the data should be analyzed and with the same data set, we often can ask a number of questions that help shed light on the biology of the processes being studied. As soon as a set of genes are found that correlate with the biology we are investigating, placing these genes into a biological context requires additional work.

PROBLEM SET

1. Discuss the relative advantages and disadvantages of one-color and two-color microarray platforms with respect to experimental design.
2. There are two general classes of microarray experiments. The first attempts to deduce gene function based on patterns of expression, whereas the second uses patterns of expression as a form of biomarker to classify samples. Describe some of the differences between these approaches and the potential for overlap between them, if any.
3. What is the goal of data normalization in a microarray experiment?
4. Discuss the differences between supervised and unsupervised approaches to data analysis, focusing on where these may be applicable.
5. In a study in the Netherlands, van't Veer et al. (2002) used DNA microarrays to identify 70 genes whose expression profiles separate patients based on their long-term prognosis. In a follow-up study, an additional 295 patients were profiled (van de Vijver et al., 2002) to validate the original signatures. The follow-up expression data are available online at http://www.rii.com/publications/2002/nejm.htm. In Table 16.1, the expression ratios for 32 patients are provided along with a classification of their five-year survival (more or less than five years). Using Welsh's t test (which does not assume equal variance between groups), identify the genes on this array (based on the annotation and data available) that, at 95% confidence, distinguish between survival groups.

INTERNET RESOURCES

Expression Databases
ArrayExpress — http://www.ebi.ac.uk/arrayexpress
CIBEX — http://cibex.nig.ac.jp
Gene Expression Omnibus — http://www.ncbi.nlm.nih.gov/geo

Expression Software
BASE — http://base.thep.lu.se
BioConductor — http://www.bioconductor.org
TM4 Software — http://www.tigr.org/software/tm4

Annotation Resources
DAVID — http://david.niaid.nih.gov
The Gene Ontology Project — http://www.geneontology.org
Kyoto Encyclopedia of Genes and Genomes — http://www.genome.ad.jp/kegg

RESOURCERER — http://pga.tigr.org/tigr-scripts/magic/r1.pl
The Source Database — http://source.stanford.edu

Professional Groups
Microarray Gene Expression Data Society — http://www.mged.org
Object Management Group — http://www.omg.org

REFERENCES

Ai, J. H., Yang, Z., Qiu, F. Z., and Zhu, T. (2003). Heat shock protein 90 is responsible for hyperdynamic circulation in portal hypertensive rats. World J. Gastroenterol. 9, 2544–2547.

Antoniadis, A., Lambert-Lacroix, S., and Leblanc, F. (2003). Effective dimension reduction methods for tumor classification using gene expression data. Bioinformatics 19, 563–570.

Aronow, B. J., Toyokawa, T., Canning, A., Haghighi, K., Delling, U., Kranias, E., Molkentin, J. D., and Dorn, G. W. 2nd. (2001). Divergent transcriptional responses to independent genetic causes of cardiac hypertrophy. Physiol. Genomics 6, 19–28.

Ball, C. A., Sherlock, G., Parkinson, H., Rocca-Sera, P., Brooksbank, C., Causton, H. C., Cavalieri, D., Gaasterland, T., Hingamp, P., Holstege, F., et al. (2002a). The underlying principles of scientific publication. Bioinformatics 18, 1409.

Ball, C. A., Sherlock, G., Parkinson, H., Rocca-Sera, P., Brooksbank, C., Causton, H. C., Cavalieri, D., Gaasterland, T., Hingamp, P., Holstege, F., et al. (2002b). Standards for microarray data. Science 298, 539.

Bloom, G., Yang, I. V., Boulware, D., Kwong, K. Y., Coppola, D., Eschrich, S., Quackenbush, J., and Yeatman, T. J. (2004). Multi-platform, multi-site, microarray-based human tumor classification. Am. J. Pathol. 164, 9–16.

Boulesteix, A. L., Tutz, G., and Strimmer, K. (2003). A cart-based approach to discover emerging patterns in microarray data. Bioinformatics 19, 2465–2472.

Bouton, C. M., and Pevsner, J. (2002). Dragon view: information visualization for annotated microarray data. Bioinformatics 18, 323–324.

Brazma, A., Hingamp, P., Quackenbush, J., Sherlock, G., Spellman, P., Stoeckert, C., Aach, J., Ansorge, W., Ball, C. A., Causton, H. C., et al. (2001). Minimum information about a microarray experiment (miame)-toward standards for microarray data. Nat. Genet. 29, 365–371.

Brazma, A., Parkinson, H., Sarkans, U., Shojatalab, M., Vilo, J., Abeygunawardena, N., Holloway, E., Kapushesky, M., Kemmeren, P., Lara, G. G., et al. (2003). Arrayexpress—a public repository for microarray gene expression data at the ebi. Nucl. Acids Res. 31, 68–71.

Butte, A. J., and Kohane, I. S. (1999). Unsupervised knowledge discovery in medical databases using relevance networks. Proc. AMIA Symp. 711–715.

TABLE 16.1 ■

Systematic Sequence Name	Gene Name	Absolute t Value	Degrees of Freedom	p Value
Contig48328_RC		4.105754	26	3.55×10^{-04}
AL080059		4.048125	26	4.12×10^{-04}
NM_003862	FGF18	4.0567994	24	4.56×10^{-04}
AF201951	CFFM4	3.7266428	29	8.36×10^{-04}
AL080079	DKFZP564D0462	3.7335453	27	8.92×10^{-04}
AF257175	PECI	3.6435118	29	1.04×10^{-03}
NM_003748	ALDH4	3.6571686	28	1.05×10^{-03}
AB037863	KIAA1442	3.6543376	26	1.14×10^{-03}
Contig2399_RC	SM-20	3.5123057	29	1.48×10^{-03}
Contig32125_RC		3.4875245	25	1.82×10^{-03}
NM_006117	PECI	3.3243823	29	2.41×10^{-03}
Contig46223_RC		3.2819667	29	2.69×10^{-03}
NM_006681	NMU	3.2795556	19	3.94×10^{-03}
NM_003882	WISPI	3.14374	27	4.03×10^{-03}
NM_000849	GSTM3	2.9302838	29	6.54×10^{-03}
NM_015984	UCH37	2.924327	29	6.64×10^{-03}
NM_016448	L2DTL	2.9094033	26	7.32×10^{-03}
NM_003981	PRCI	2.853291	29	7.90×10^{-03}
U82987	BBC3	2.7786508	29	9.48×10^{-03}
Contig63649_RC		2.7560925	23	1.12×10^{-02}
NM_004702	CCNE2	2.6825519	27	1.23×10^{-02}
NM_020974	CEGPI	2.6737323	28	1.24×10^{-02}
NM_016359	LOC51203	2.6388283	29	1.32×10^{-02}
NM_014321	ORC6L	2.6364782	29	1.33×10^{-02}
Contig38288_RC		2.60632	24	1.55×10^{-02}
NM_018401	HSA250839	2.4955266	28	1.87×10^{-02}
AF073519	SERF1A	2.5612595	19	1.91×10^{-02}
NM_020188	DC13	2.4749522	29	1.94×10^{-02}
Contig55725_RC		2.4509566	28	2.08×10^{-02}
Contig40831_RC		2.4605196	25	2.11×10^{-02}
NM_003239	TGFB3	2.4351125	29	2.13×10^{-02}
NM_002916	RFC4	2.391319	24	2.50×10^{-02}
NM_018354	FLJ11190	2.3679094	27	2.53×10^{-02}
AL137718		2.3765066	24	2.58×10^{-02}
NM_014791	KIAA0175	2.3200622	24	2.92×10^{-02}
Contig32185_RC		2.349117	20	2.92×10^{-02}
NM_014889	MPI	2.3225565	23	2.94×10^{-02}
NM_006931	SLC2A3	2.3165574	23	2.98×10^{-02}
NM_003607	PK428	2.2883475	28	2.99×10^{-02}
NM_020386	LOC57110	2.280264	29	3.01×10^{-02}
Contig55377_RC		2.290061	24	3.11×10^{-02}
NM_005915	MCM6	2.2115324	26	3.60×10^{-02}
NM_002073	GNAZ	2.2194262	23	3.66×10^{-02}
NM_001282	AP2B1	2.1662617	29	3.87×10^{-02}
AK000745	KIAA1067	2.1654806	28	3.90×10^{-02}
Contig25991	ECT2	2.1836183	21	4.05×10^{-02}
NM_007036	ESM1	2.1380804	28	4.14×10^{-02}
NM_006101	HEC	2.1038282	28	4.45×10^{-02}
Contig20217_RC		2.1026435	28	4.46×10^{-02}
NM_000788	DCK	2.0970812	29	4.48×10^{-02}
Contig46218_RC		2.0984237	25	4.61×10^{-02}
NM_002019	FLT1	2.0489104	29	4.96×10^{-02}

CHEN, H., LIU, J., ZHAO, C. Q., DIWAN, B. A., MERRICK, B. A., AND WAALKES, M. P. (2001). Association of c-myc overexpression and hyperproliferation with arsenite-induced malignant transformation. *Toxicol. Appl. Pharmacol.* 175, 260–268.

CHEN, Y., ARRIGO, A. P., AND CURRIE, R. W. (2004). Heat shock treatment suppresses angiotensin ii-induced activation of nf-{kappa}b pathway and heart inflammation: a role for ikk depletion by heat shock? *Am. J. Physiol. Heart Circ. Physiol.*

CHEUNG, S. T., CHEN, X., GUAN, X. Y., WONG, S. Y., TAI, L. S., NG, I. O., SO, S., AND FAN, S. T. (2002). Identify metastasis-associated genes in hepatocellular carcinoma through clonality delineation for multinodular tumor. *Cancer Res.* 62, 4711–4721.

CHURCHILL, G. A. (2002). Fundamentals of experimental design for cDNA microarrays. *Nat. Genet.* 32(Suppl), 490–495.

COOK, D. N., WANG, S., WANG, Y., HOWLES, G. P., WHITEHEAD, G. S., BERMAN, K. G., CHURCH, T. D., FRANK, B. C., GASPARD, R. M., YU, Y., et al. (2004). Genetic regulation of endotoxin-induced airway disease. *Genomics* 83, 961–967.

DESU, M. M., AND RAGHAVARAO, D. (2003). *Nonparametric Statistical Methods for Complete and Censored Data* (Chapman & Hall/CRC Press, Boca Raton, FL).

DIEHN, M., SHERLOCK, G., BINKLEY, G., JIN, H., MATESE, J. C., HERNANDEZ-BOUSSARD, T., REES, C. A., CHERRY, J. M., BOTSTEIN, D., BROWN, P. O., et al. (2003). Source: a unified genomic resource of functional annotations, ontologies, and gene expression data. *Nucl. Acids Res.* 31, 219–223.

DOBBIN, K., SHIH, J. H., AND SIMON, R. (2003a). Questions and answers on design of dual-label microarrays for identifying differentially expressed genes. *J. Natl. Cancer Inst.* 95, 1362–1369.

DOBBIN, K., SHIH, J. H., AND SIMON, R. (2003b). Statistical design of reverse dye microarrays. *Bioinformatics* 19, 803–810.

DOERGE, R. W. (2002). Mapping and analysis of quantitative trait loci in experimental populations. *Nat. Rev. Genet.* 3, 43–52.

DONIGER, S. W., SALOMONIS, N., DAHLQUIST, K. D., VRANIZAN, K., LAWLOR, S. C., AND CONKLIN, B. R. (2003). Mappfinder: using gene ontology and genmapp to create a global gene-expression profile from microarray data. *Genome Biol.* 4, R7.

DUDOIT, S., GENTLEMAN, R. C., AND QUACKENBUSH, J. (2003). Open source software for the analysis of microarray data. *Biotechniques* 34(Suppl), S45–S51.

EDGAR, R., DOMRACHEV, M., AND LASH, A. E. (2002). Gene expression omnibus: NCBI gene expression and hybridization array data repository. *Nucl. Acids Res.* 30, 207–210.

DOROSHCHUK, A. D., POSTNOV, A. U., AFANAS'EVA, G. V., BUDNIKOV, E. U., AND POSTNOV, U. V. (2004). Decreased atp-synthesis ability of brain mitochondria in spontaneously hypertensive rats. *Kardiologiia* 44, 64–65.

EHRLICH, M. (2002). DNA hypomethylation, cancer, the immunodeficiency, centromeric region instability, facial anomalies syndrome and chromosomal rearrangements. *J. Nutr.* 132, 2424S–2429S.

EISEN, M. B., SPELLMAN, P. T., BROWN, P. O., AND BOTSTEIN, D. (1998). Cluster analysis and display of genome-wide expression patterns. *Proc. Natl. Acad. Sci. U. S. A.* 95, 14863–14868.

ELLIS, M., DAVIS, N., COOP, A., LIU, M., SCHUMAKER, L., LEE, R. Y., SRIKANCHANA, R., RUSSELL, C. G., SINGH, B., MILLER, et al. (2002). Development and validation of a method for using breast core needle biopsies for gene expression microarray analyses. *Clin. Cancer Res.* 8, 1155–1166.

FINK, J. L., DREWES, S., PATEL, H., WELSH, J. B., MASYS, D. R., CORBEIL, J., AND GRIBSKOV, M. (2003). 2hapi: a microarray data analysis system. *Bioinformatics* 19, 1443–1445.

FUREY, T. S., CRISTIANINI, N., DUFFY, N., BEDNARSKI, D. W., SCHUMMER, M., AND HAUSSLER, D. (2000). Support vector machine classification and validation of cancer tissue samples using microarray expression data. *Bioinformatics* 16, 906–914.

GRAY, J. W., AND COLLINS, C. (2000). Genome changes and gene expression in human solid tumors. *Carcinogenesis* 21, 443–452.

HERRERO, J., VALENCIA, A., AND DOPAZO, J. (2001). A hierarchical unsupervised growing neural network for clustering gene expression patterns. *Bioinformatics* 17, 126–136.

HOSACK, D. A., DENNIS, G., Jr., SHERMAN, B. T., LANE, H. C., AND LEMPICKI, R. A. (2003). Identifying biological themes within lists of genes with ease. *Genome Biol.* 4, R70.

HUBER, W., VON HEYDEBRECK, A., SULTMANN, H., POUSTKA, A., AND VINGRON, M. (2002). Variance stabilization applied to microarray data calibration and to the quantification of differential expression. *Bioinformatics* 18(Suppl 1), S96–S104.

IRIZARRY, R. A., BOLSTAD, B. M., COLLIN, F., COPE, L. M., HOBBS, B., AND SPEED, T. P. (2003). Summaries of affymetrix genechip probe level data. *Nucl. Acids Res.* 31, e15.

JENSSEN, T. K., LAEGREID, A., KOMOROWSKI, J., AND HOVIG, E. (2001) A literature network of human genes for high-throughput analysis of gene expression. *Nat. Genet.* 28, 21–28.

KANEHISA, M. (2002). The KEGG database. *Novartis Found. Symp.* 247, 91–101; discussion 101–103, 119–128, 244–152.

KERR, M. K., AND CHURCHILL, G. A. (2001). Statistical design and the analysis of gene expression microarray data. *Genet. Res.* 77, 123–128.

KIM, S. K., LUND, J., KIRALY, M., DUKE, K., JIANG, M., STUART, J. M., EIZINGER, A., WYLIE, B. N., AND DAVIDSON, G. S. (2001). A gene expression map for caenorhabditis elegans. *Science* 293, 2087–2092.

KWITEK-BLACK, A. E., AND JACOB, H. J. (2001). The use of designer rats in the genetic dissection of hypertension. *Curr. Hypertens. Rep.* 3, 12–18.

LARKIN, J. E., FRANK, B. C., GASPARD, R. M., DUKA, I., GAVRAS, H., AND QUACKENBUSH, J. (2004). Cardiac transcriptional response to acute and chronic angiotensin ii treatments. *Physiol. Genomics* 18, 152-166.

LE, Q. T., SUTPHIN, P. D., RAYCHAUDHURI, S., YU, S. C., TERRIS, D. J., LIN, H. S., LUM, B., PINTO, H. A., KOONG, A. C., AND GIACCIA, A. J. (2003). Identification of osteopontin as a prognostic plasma marker for head and neck squamous cell carcinomas. *Clin. Cancer Res.* 9, 59–67.

MASYS, D. R., WELSH, J. B., LYNN FINK, J., GRIBSKOV, M., KLACANSKY, I., AND CORBEIL, J. (2001). Use of keyword hierarchies to interpret gene expression patterns. *Bioinformatics* 17, 319–326.

MICHAELS, G. S., CARR, D. B., ASKENAZI, M., FUHRMAN, S., WEN, X., AND SOMOGYI, R. (1998). Cluster analysis and data visualization of large-scale gene expression data. In *Pacific Symposium in Biocomputing* 42–53.

NGUYEN, D. V., AND ROCKE, D. M. (2002). Tumor classification by partial least squares using microarray gene expression data. *Bioinformatics* 18, 39–50.

ORR, M. S., AND SCHERF, U. (2002). Large-scale gene expression analysis in molecular target discovery. *Leukemia* 16, 473–477.

PAVLIDIS, P., AND NOBLE, W. S. (2001). Analysis of strain and regional variation in gene expression in mouse brain. *Genome Biol.* 2, RESEARCH0042.

POCKLEY, A. G., GEORGIADES, A., THULIN, T., DE FAIRE, U., AND FROSTEGARD, J. (2003). Serum heat shock protein 70 levels predict the development of atherosclerosis in subjects with established hypertension. *Hypertension* 42, 235–238.

RAMACHANDRAN, A., LEVONEN, A. L., BROOKES, P. S., CEASER, E., SHIVA, S., BARONE, M. C., AND DARLEY-USMAR, V. (2002). Mitochondria, nitric oxide, and cardiovascular dysfunction. *Free Radic. Biol. Med.* 33, 1465–1474.

RAMASWAMY, S., TAMAYO, P., RIFKIN, R., MUKHERJEE, S., YEANG, C. H., ANGELO, M., LADD, C., REICH, M., LATULIPPE, E., MESIROV, J. P., et al. (2001) Multiclass cancer diagnosis using tumor gene expression signatures. *Proc. Natl. Acad. Sci. U. S. A.* 98, 15149–15154.

RAYCHAUDHURI, S., STUART, J. M., AND ALTMAN, R. B. (2000). Principal components analysis to summarize microarray experiments: Application to sporulation time series. In *Pacific Symposium in Biocomputing* 455–466.

SAAL, L. H., TROEIN, C., VALLON-CHRISTERSSON, J., GRUVBERGER, S., BORG, A., AND PETERSON, C. (2002). Bioarray software environment (base): a platform for comprehensive management and analysis of microarray data. *Genome Biol.* 3, SOFTWARE0003.

SAEED, A. I., SHAROV, V., WHITE, J., LI, J., LIANG, W., BHAGABATI, N., BRAISTED, J., KLAPA, M., CURRIER, T., THIAGARAJAN, M., et al. (2003) Tm4: a free, open-source system for microarray data management and analysis. *Biotechniques* 34, 374–378.

SCHADT, E. E., MONKS, S. A., DRAKE, T. A., LUSIS, A. J., CHE, N., COLINAYO, V., RUFF, T. G., MILLIGAN, S. B., LAMB, J. R., CAVET, G., et al. (2003) Genetics of gene expression surveyed in maize, mouse and man. *Nature* 422, 297–302.

SIMON, R., RADMACHER, M. D., AND DOBBIN, K. (2002). Design of studies using DNA microarrays. *Genet. Epidemiol.* 23, 21–36.

SIMON, R., RADMACHER, M. D., DOBBIN, K., AND MCSHANE, L. M. (2003). Pitfalls in the use of DNA microarray data for diagnostic and prognostic classification. *J. Natl. Cancer Inst.* 95, 14–18.

SIMON, R. M., AND DOBBIN, K. (2003). Experimental design of DNA microarray experiments. *Biotechniques* 34(Suppl), S16–S21.

SOUKAS, A., COHEN, P., SOCCI, N. D., AND FRIEDMAN, J. M. (2000). Leptin-specific patterns of gene expression in white adipose tissue. *Genes Dev.* 14, 963–980.

SPELLMAN, P. T., MILLER, M., STEWART, J., TROUP, C., SARKANS, U., CHERVITZ, S., BERNHART, D., SHERLOCK, G., BALL, C., LEPAGE, M., et al. (2002). Design and implementation of microarray gene expression markup language (mage-ml). *Genome Biol.* 3, RESEARCH0046.

TAMAYO, P., SLONIM, D., MESIROV, J., ZHU, Q., KITAREEWAN, S., DMITROVSKY, E., LANDER, E. S., AND GOLUMB, T. R. (1999). Interpreting patterns of gene expression with self-organizing maps: methods and application to hematopoietic differentiation. *Proc. Natl. Acad. Sci. U. S. A.* 96, 2907–2912.

THEILHABER, J., CONNOLLY, T., ROMAN-ROMAN, S., BUSHNELL, S., JACKSON, A., CALL, K., GARCIA, T., AND BARON, R. (2002). Finding genes in the c2c12 osteogenic pathway by k-nearest-neighbor classification of expression data. *Genome Res.* 12, 165–176.

TORONEN, P., KOLEHMAINEN, M., WONG, G., AND CASTREN, E. (1999). Analysis of gene expression data using self-organizing maps. *FEBS Lett.* 451, 142–146.

TSAI, J., SULTANA, R., LEE, Y., PERTEA, G., KARAMYCHEVA, K., ANTONESCU, V., CHO, J., PARVIZI, B., CHEUNG, F., AND QUACKENBUSH, J. (2001). Resourcerer: a database for annotating and linking microarray resources within and across species. *Genome Biol.* 2, software0002.0001-0002.0004.

TUSHER, V. G., TIBSHIRANI, R., AND CHU, G. (2001). Significance analysis of microarrays applied to the ionizing radiation response. *Proc. Natl. Acad. Sci. U. S. A.* 98, 5116–5121.

VAN DE VIJVER, M. J., HE, Y. D., VAN'T VEER, L. J., DAI, H., HART, A. A., VOSKUIL, D. W., SCHREIBER, G. J., PETERSE, J. L., ROBERTS, C., MARTON, et al. (2002). A gene-expression signature as a predictor of survival in breast cancer. *N. Engl. J. Med.* 347, 1999–2009.

VAN'T VEER, L. J., DAI, H., VAN DE VIJVER, M. J., HE, Y. D., HART, A. A., MAO, M., PETERSE, H. L., VAN DER KOOY, K., MARTON, M. J., WITTEVEEN, A. T., et al. (2002) Gene expression profiling predicts clinical outcome of breast cancer. *Nature* 415, 530–536.

WANG, J., DELABIE, J., AASHEIM, H., SMELAND, E., AND MYKLEBOST, O. (2002). Clustering of the SOM easily reveals distinct gene expression patterns: results of a reanalysis of lymphoma study. *BMC Bioinformatics* 3, 36.

WATSON, B., Jr. (2003). Genetics of the kidney and hypertension. *Curr. Hypertens. Rep.* 5, 273–276.

WEN, X., FUHRMAN, S., MICHAELS, G. S., CARR, D. B., SMITH, S., BARKER, J. L., AND SOMOGYI, R. (1998) Large-scale temporal gene expression mapping of central nervous system development. *Proc. Natl. Acad. Sci. U. S. A.* 95, 334–339.

YANG, I. V., CHEN, E., HASSEMAN, J. P., LIANG, W., FRANK, B. C., WANG, S., SHAROV, V., SAEED, A. I., WHITE, J., LI, J., et al. (2002a). Within the fold: assessing differential expression measures and reproducibility in microarray assays. *Genome Biol.* 3, research0062.

YANG, Y. H., DUDOIT, S., LUU, P., LIN, D. M., PENG, V., Ngai, J., AND SPEED, T. P. (2002b). Normalization for cDNA microarray data: a robust composite method addressing single and multiple slide systematic variation. *Nucl. Acids Res.* 30, e15.

ZEEBERG, B. R., FENG, W., WANG, G., WANG, M. D., FOJO, A. T., SUNSHINE, M., NARASIMHAN, S., KANE, D. W., REINHOLD, W. C., LABABIDI, S., et al. (2003). Gominer: a resource for biological interpretation of genomic and proteomic data. *Genome Biol.* 4, R28.

▌ KEY TERMS

analysis of variance

clustering

experimental design

gene expression

microarrays

minimal information about a microarray experiment (MIAME)

## CHAPTER SEVENTEEN

Proteomics and Protein Identification

MARK R. HOLMES

KEVIN R. RAMKISSOON

MORGAN C. GIDDINGS

Bioinformatics: A Practical Guide to the Analysis of Genes and Proteins, Third Edition, edited by
Andreas D. Baxevanis and B.F. Francis Ouellette.
ISBN 0-471-47878-4 Copyright © 2005 John Wiley & Sons, Inc.

▌INTRODUCTION

Since the beginning of modern biology, researchers have sought ways to better elucidate the relationships among protein sequence, structure, and function. The central dogma of biology holds that DNA sequence encodes the protein sequence, which in turn determines the three-dimensional structure of the protein, and hence, its function. Although much attention has been paid to the sequencing aspects of genome projects, the eventual end goal of these projects actually is to determine how the genome builds life through proteins. DNA has been the focus of attention because the tools for studying it are more advanced and because it is at the heart of the cell, carrying all the information—the blueprint—for life. However, a blueprint without a builder is not very useful, and the proteins are the primary builders within the cell. As more and more genome sequences are completed and DNA analysis technologies mature, attention is turning to new ways to study proteins in the same kind of rapid and automatic way in which DNA is now examined.

Proteins are more difficult to analyze than DNA for several reasons. For DNA and RNA research, the polymerase chain reaction (PCR) provides the ability to make nearly unlimited copies of a target nucleic acid sequence, which greatly benefits its study. In the protein world, there is no analogous process. Research techniques used to study proteins must analyze the relatively small number of molecules that are produced *in vivo*, and therefore must be exquisitely sensitive and accurate.

Currently, there are several major realms of protein study: structural studies using X-ray crystallography, nuclear magnetic resonance (NMR), or both to determine the final three-dimensional shape that proteins assume in the cell; functional studies, using mass spectrometry (MS) to examine the regulation, timing, and location of protein expression; and interaction studies, which examine how proteins pair between themselves and other cellular components to form more complex molecular machines (Chapter 10). Although each of these approaches has been labeled *proteomics*, the term actually was coined by Marc Wilkins in 1994 in referring to the functional study of proteins using MS. This chapter focuses on this original definition of proteomics and, in particular, on the critical role that computing and informatics play in the ability to analyze MS data and relate it to the rapidly accumulating information from systematic large-scale sequencing projects.

Proteomic study generally proceeds from the starting point of proteins from cell lysate that are separated and visualized using an approach such as two-dimensional polyacrylamide gel electrophoresis (2D-PAGE; see Box 17.1). By examining multiple 2D gels, protein expression under different biological conditions can be compared. Although this kind of separation and visualization has been used for many years, the ability to identify and to examine further the proteins in those spots was limited until the advent of new methods in MS in the late 1980s (Fenn et al., 1989; Tanaka et al., 1988). This led to an explosion of interest in protein study through a related set of approaches all grouped under the label proteomics.

On the surface, there are many similarities between this type of proteomic study and microarray analysis (Chapter 16). Both aim to evaluate the mechanisms present in the cell that upregulate or downregulate the products of genes. There are some important differences between the two approaches, however. One is that, in a microarray study, the identity of the probes (target sequences) is known beforehand, whereas with proteins it is only after analysis (using MS) that the identity of the responsible gene is revealed. Also, the lack of amplification methods for proteins requires that the methods used in studying them be extremely sensitive. A third difference is subcellular location. Proteins often are localized functionally and are used in only one particular part of the cell; determining this specificity is another goal of proteomic research. However, the greatest difference lies in the simple although not widely appreciated fact that multiple, distinct proteins can result from one gene. The best known mechanisms for this are alternative splicing of RNA transcripts and covalent modification of proteins after expression, but protein diversity is not confined to these. There are known mechanisms at each step in the protein expression process that can lead to an unexpected result, in turn leading to significant proteomic diversity (Figure 17.1). For example, recoding, or the dynamic reprogramming of translation, alters the protein resulting from a messenger RNA molecule (Gesteland & Atkins, 1996). Thus, in studying proteomes, it becomes important not only to identify what gene a protein came from, but also what particular form the protein has taken on in the particular biological circumstances. This often is called *protein characterization*.

Proteomic techniques are being used increasingly to help decipher complex diseases. The most common approach compares proteins expressed in diseased versus normal tissues to determine proteins whose expression levels or forms are significantly changed, thus indicating a potential role in the causation of the disease. Examples of proteomic techniques being used this way include a study identifying some of the important regulatory gene clusters controlling glucose responsiveness in a key metabolic pathway affecting diabetes (Schuit et al., 2002), or the discovery of the genes producing many abnormal regulatory proteins found in Alzheimer's disease (recently reviewed in Butterfield et al., (2003)).

BOX 17.1   Mass Spectrometry

Time-of-Flight MS

MALDI ion source

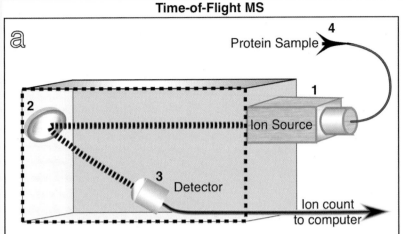

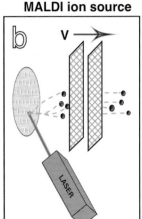

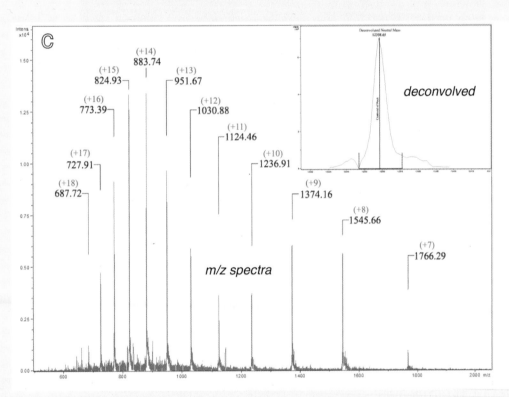

FIGURE 17B.1   **(a) Schematic of a TOF mass spectrometer. The main components are (1) an ion source, (2) an ion reflector, and (3) a detector. Sample peptides or proteins are ionized in the source, either by ESI (4) via injection through a capillary or (b) by MALDI. In either case, after being charged, they are accelerated by a voltage gradient. The lighter ions and those with more charge gain more speed during acceleration. The ions travel across the flight path to the ion reflector and concentrator, where they are directed to the detector. The fastest ions arrive at the detector first: Given two ions with different masses and the same charge state, the lighter one will be faster. The detector measures the time of flight of each ion, and the time signal is converted to a mass-to-charge (m/z) ratio by the computer. Because ions can have multiple charges, there are typically several peaks for the same protein or peptide species, each at a multiple of the +1 charge state (or −1 for negative-ion mode). This is illustrated by the mass spectrum for a single protein in (c). The acquisition and analysis software then deconvolves (combines) these multiple peaks into their equivalent intensity at +1 charge state and subtracts the ions' proton masses to yield a single peak for each molecule. The process of mass calling then determines the precise mass for each peak, using one of several methods such as a centroid, Gaussian fit, or center of width at half-maximum height. The result is a mass list (or peak list) and, for peptide digests, forms the PMF such as that used in the Worked Example.**

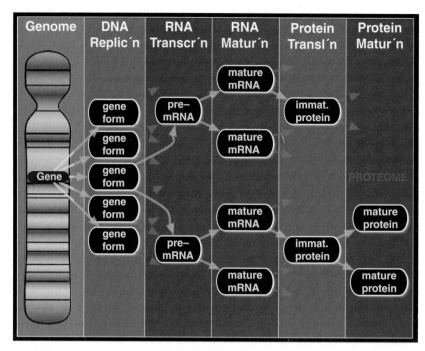

FIGURE 17.1 **The complexity of protein expression. The figure represents the diversity of proteins in a proteome resulting from alternative means of protein expression. At each step of the process from genes to proteins, alternative mechanisms can occur that produce nonstandard or unexpected products compared with a static database sequence. During DNA replication, polymorphism can occur, resulting in various gene forms. During RNA transcription, polymerase slippage can occur, producing multiple different transcripts. In eukaryotes, the RNA maturation process, involving RNA splicing, can produce variable results (alternative splicing). Also, RNA can be edited further enzymatically, potentially changing its translation. In protein translation, recoding can occur that produces, for example, frameshift fusion proteins. During RNA maturation, signal peptides can be removed to activate a protein, and varying numbers of other chemical modifications can be added. The combination of these possible variations results in an enormous potential for complexity in the resulting proteome.**

MS FOR PROTEIN ANALYSIS

As its name implies, MS is about measuring molecules based on mass. MS ionizes sample molecules such as proteins or peptides, introducing a positive or negative charge that allows them to be manipulated using electric or magnetic fields in the instrument. There are two main parts to a mass spectrometer: the ionizer and the mass analyzer. The ionizer forms gaseous ions from a sample whose mass properties then are measured by the mass analyzer. There is a wide array of both ionizer and analyzer types, and deciphering the terminology of all the possible permutations is challenging. The most common ionizers for protein analysis are matrix-assisted laser desorption ionization (MALDI) and electrospray ionization (ESI). MALDI uses a laser to blast and ionize sample molecules, which are embedded in a chemical matrix, off a target plate. ESI works by forming tiny charged droplets containing sample molecules. The solvent in the droplets is evaporated away, leaving ions. Ions produced by either method can then be measured by methods such as time of flight (TOF), quadrupole, or Fourier transform MS (FT/MS). The technical details are not important here, except to note that these methods vary greatly in their accuracy, cost, and sensitivity. Each of these methods will produce a mass spectrum, the x-axis representing the mass range of the analyzer and the y-axis representing the number of ions detected.

Analyzing a complex mixture of proteins or peptides requires some type of chemical separation before MS is performed; ionization is not as efficient with many different molecular species present, making analysis more difficult. The most common separation approaches are two-dimensional electrophoretic gel separation and liquid chromatography. Each of these methods produces samples for the mass spectrometer containing a simplified mixture of molecules. Whole protein molecules are more difficult to ionize and analyze in a mass spectrometer, and measuring the mass of a whole protein provides only limited information to aid its identification. Therefore, most proteomic approaches involve a process of fragmenting the proteins into many smaller pieces, which are analyzed to identify the protein (Figure 17.2). Commonly, proteins are digested chemically using an enzyme, such as trypsin, into peptides. Trypsin cleaves a protein after lysine or arginine residues, producing peptides that are typically from three to 20 or more amino acids.

Peptides are analyzed on a mass spectrometer to determine their masses. The entire set of masses observed typically is unique to a specific protein. Any single peptide mass may be produced by many different proteins, because many different combinations of residues can add up to the same mass. For example, the peptides IQVMVYR and QVVYMIR have the same mass but

(obviously) different sequences. The key to identifying proteins from their constituent peptide masses then lies in the specific combination of masses observed. The process of measuring a set of peptide masses from a protein and matching these against a database is called *peptide mass fingerprinting* (PMF). The common software approach to the matching problem is to use a protein database, and for each protein sequence to calculate all the peptides it may produce. This theoretical list is matched to the actual mass spectrometer data, within a certain error range called the *tolerance*, which reflects inherent inaccuracy of the particular mass spectrometer. After matches are found, many of the programs perform what is called a *significance assessment*, which calculates a probability that the resulting match was a chance occurrence, meaning that it would be a false positive. Programs that perform peptide mass fingerprinting include Mascot, PeptIdent, Profound, and Genome Fingerprint Scanning (GFS). Each is described below.

Another increasingly popular approach for analyzing peptides is tandem MS, or MS/MS. This method uses a special type of mass spectrometer that performs several sequential MS analyses. In the first stage, peptides are analyzed and a mass spectrum is produced, just as previously described. After this first step, a few peptides are selected, one at a time, for a second stage of MS

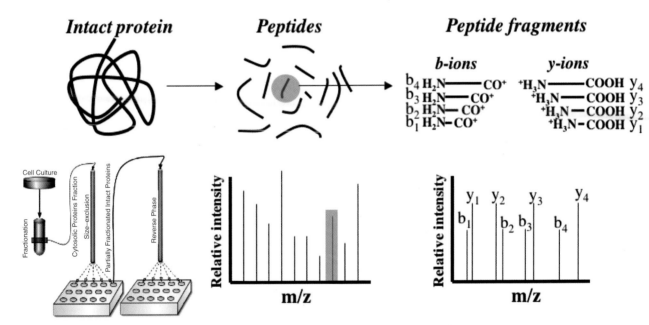

FIGURE 17.2 Breaking proteins down for MS analysis. The process of breaking proteins down into constituent components for identification. An intact protein is digested to peptides by an enzyme such as trypsin (center panel), and MS of the peptides produces a peptide mass fingerprint. In tandem MS, one or more peptides are selected (while still in the mass spectrometer) and degraded further by collisional induced dissociation, producing a spectra of subions (b-ions, y-ions, and sometimes a-ions) that can be used to identify the sequence of the peptide.

analysis. These peptides can be selected based on mass, peak intensity, or more complex criteria. The selected peptides are broken down into even smaller pieces by a process of bombarding them with fast-moving atoms that collide and cause the peptide bond to break; this is called *collision-induced dissociation* (CID). The product of these collisions is a set of charged peptides with one or more amino acids removed from either the C- or N-terminus of the peptide that produce a second mass spectrum. The ions produced by removal of residues from the C-terminus are called *b-ions* and those produced by removal of N-terminal residues are termed *y-ions* (Figure 17.2).

The resulting spectrum can be used to help identify the peptides present by one of two methods. The *de novo* approach interprets the mass spectrum data to determine the amino acid sequence of the selected peptides, which can be used (for example) in a BLAST search. This approach works by constructing a sequence graph, in which each peak in the MS/MS spectrum is assumed to be all possible ion types. Then, a set of amino acid sequences are generated that is consistent with the mass of the intact peptide. These sequences (often in the tens of thousands) are narrowed down by a variety of criteria based on their fit to the MS/MS spectrum. However, if chemical modifications are present on the peptide, or if the signal is weak, the *de novo* approach can have difficulty. Two prominent examples of the *de novo* method include Lutefisk (Taylor & Johnson, 2001) and PEAKS (Ma et al., 2003).

Another and perhaps more commonly used approach is uninterpreted MS/MS spectral matching. This method uses a protein or DNA sequence database to produce hypothetical spectra, which are compared with the actual experimental spectrum for similarity. The match score indicates how likely it is that the spectrum was produced by each possible peptide in the database. Sequest (Eng et al., 1994) is the primary package using this approach. Because of the computationally intensive nature of cross-correlating the real versus the hypothetical, this method is difficult to apply to full-genome scans without access to a lot of computing power.

Fortunately, a choice does not necessarily have to be made between these two different approaches to MS/MS interpretation, because they easily can complement each other. The *de novo* method can be used to generate a number of partial sequence tags (only one of which is the correct sequence), and then spectrum cross-correlation can be applied for all matching sequence regions to narrow the choice down to the best match. This combined strategy was used successfully by the creators of the Lutefisk program (Taylor & Johnson, 2001).

THE MAJOR PROTEOMIC APPROACHES

There are several approaches to analyzing proteins on a cell-wide basis. The most common is to separate the proteins extracted from a cell sample using 2D gels and then to select spots from the gel for MS analysis. Spots often are selected based on comparisons between gels from different cell types (for example, cancerous versus normal cells). Usually, the spots that change the most from one gel to the next are selected for identification. When a spot from a gel is analyzed, it is digested using an enzyme like trypsin, which cuts the protein backbone following lysine or arginine residues. The resulting set of peptide masses then can be analyzed, usually with the assumption that only one protein is present. Sometimes, tandem MS is performed on individual peptides, which provides even more precise information about the protein present.

Recently, several alternatives to this method have arisen that promise to provide new and perhaps more sensitive information about the proteins in a sample. Because they can impact the data processing significantly, they are mentioned here briefly. Bottom-up, or shotgun, proteomics is an approach in which all the proteins in a sample are digested enzymatically before separation; the resulting peptides are separated by chromatography and then are analyzed by tandem MS. The advantage of this method is that peptide analysis is very sensitive, so more proteins can be found. This approach also can be used to compare expression level differences using a labeling technology such as isotope coded affinity tags (ICAT). From an informatics perspective, the challenge in this approach is that peptide data are produced in essentially random order and are not correlated to one another or to a single protein. Protein identification must rely solely on matching of MS/MS spectra from the peptides to the databases. Doing so gives little information about what the intact protein looked like.

Another even newer method is top-down proteomics. Although there are a variety of methods, the top-down moniker comes from the idea that protein analysis begins using a mass spectrometer to measure the intact protein, directly, before any fragmentation or digestion is performed. After measuring an intact mass, the protein is fragmented further, by one of several approaches, into peptides that can then be measured to provide additional identifying information about the protein. The computational goal then is to put these measurements back together into a picture of both the protein's identity as well as its chemical state in the cell. However, in the top-down method, the separation and MS both are more challenging than for peptides, and the informatics tools for analyzing these data currently are not very mature.

DATA PREPROCESSING

Before data from a mass spectrometer can be used to identify a protein or peptide, data preprocessing typically is applied. Most commercial instruments will have included software that can perform the preprocessing, although its use can be tricky. There are several steps that always must be performed. The most important of these is necessitated by the fact that mass spectrometers do not measure ion mass; rather, they measure the mass-to-charge ratio (m/z). Contrasting two ions of the same mass, one of which has a +1 charge and the other with a +2 charge, the second ion will have a lower m/z (by half) because the expression divides the mass by the charge. For most purposes, it is useful to transform the m/z spectrum directly to a mass spectrum that is independent of the charge state. When using MALDI, this can be an easy task, because it usually produces ions with low charge states (+1 predominating). However, ESI can produce ions with a variety of charge states. The process of reducing these to a single mass measurement is called *charge state deconvolution*. All of the algorithms for performing this process are heuristically based, meaning that they do not produce the "correct" or "perfect" answer every time. Thus, they must be applied with caution and (over time) with the benefit of experience.

Some modern mass spectrometers have high enough resolution that they can display distinct isotopic peaks for peptides. For example, a peptide that happens to contain one ^{13}C (in place of a ^{12}C) will be measured as approximately 1 Dalton (Da) heavier than its nonisotopic counterpart. In practice, all biologically derived molecules display this type of isotopic variation, meaning that multiple isotope peaks are observed for each molecule measured, and these are based on the mass of the molecules being close to 1 Da apart. Mass spectrometers typically can produce data in one of two forms: average or monoisotopic mass. The average mass is simply the average of the masses of each of the common isotopes. This is how data are reported for low-resolution machines, or large molecules, where individual isotopes cannot be resolved. For higher-resolution data, the spectrum is often deisotoped, meaning that the isotope pattern is used to calculate the monoisotopic mass. This is the mass of the peak containing only the most abundant isotopes and generally is more accurate than the average mass calculation. The fact that the isotope peaks are close to 1 Da apart sometimes can be used to help the charge state deconvolution process. For example, if a molecule has a charge of +2, its isotope peaks will be seen on the m/z spectrum as being approximately 0.5 Da apart. If it is +3, they will be approximately 0.33 apart, and so on.

Before discussing some of the major tools used for protein analysis and identification, we mention several difficulties that can arise in processing these kinds of data. One is ion suppression. This is the case where some ions grab a charge more readily than others, and in any typical MS experiment involving multiple peptides, some of them will not become ionized and thus will not be observed in the spectrum. These missing peptides make the search process more difficult, but fortunately, modern software packages are sensitive enough that they can tolerate some missing peptides. Another issue is that peptides can have chemical modifications that can arise both *in vivo* and from the experimental procedure. For example, during 2D gel analysis, it is common that methionine residues become oxidized, which adds approximately 16 Da of mass for each oxidation, and the number of oxidations can vary. Many of the available search algorithms can accommodate some common modifications; however, the search space for peptides grows exponentially as more types of modifications are considered, and the specificity of the programs can be reduced drastically (meaning more false positives can arise). Therefore, it is particularly important that these kinds of modifications are minimized by selecting the appropriate laboratory protocols during experimental analysis.

The other complication is the presence of multiple proteins in a sample. As mentioned before, proteins typically are separated before they are analyzed by peptide mass fingerprinting, either by 2D gels, liquid chromatography, or similar approaches. However, none of the separation methods is perfect, and occasionally a sample (such as a spot from a gel) is selected that contains two or more proteins. This means that, after digesting the protein sample, peptides will be present from different proteins, confounding the search process. In some cases, depending on the search engine and the complexity of the proteins present, this may not have a major impact on identification, but in other cases, it can prevent a proper identification altogether. This issue arises even more frequently with proteins separated by liquid chromatography. A related but distinct issue is when there are homologous genes, either in the same organism or other organisms, to the target. This means that multiple hits will arise with the peptide set.

Another consideration for proteomic research is the database against which the MS data are compared. The most common approach is to use a large database like Swiss-Prot or GenBank. Protein and gene entries from the database are matched up individually against the MS data to determine how well the particular gene or protein entry corresponds with the mass spectrum being considered. This process works well when an entry is present for the protein being analyzed, but will fail if the protein being analyzed is not represented in the database, which can occur for several reasons. The most common is that gene finding (see Chapter 5) is a difficult process, and for complex genomes, not all genes have been identified yet (Harrison et al., 2002). Also, gene or protein entries sometimes can be incorrect because intron and exon boundaries have not been identified properly. As a result, interest in both *de novo* interpretation of MS/MS spectra, as well as in approaches that match up the MS data directly against the genome, is increasing. Methods have been developed that match peptide mass fingerprints, MS/MS data, or both, directly against genome sequence information. GFS compares MS data directly against raw genomic sequence, whereas Mascot allows comparison of MS data against EST databases, both of which are described below.

THE MAJOR PROTEIN IDENTIFICATION PROGRAMS

Some of the major applications for protein identification are described in this section. Each of the programs performs a match between experimentally collected MS data and protein or nucleotide sequence databases to identify the protein sample in the mass spectrometer. Each program has essentially two major steps:

1. Calculate the potential ion products that each protein or nucleotide sequence from the database could generate

2. Match the calculated ions from the database to the observed ions from MS and score the match.

There are several ways that the described programs differ from one another that are worth noting. A fundamental difference comes from the databases used to make the comparisons. Several use the National Center for Biotechnology Information (NCBI) databases, one (PeptIdent) uses Swiss-Prot, and one uses raw genome sequence databases (GFS). The choice of database significantly impacts the results, depending on whether the proteins of interest are actually in the database being searched. Another difference among the programs is the type of input data they will accept. Some accept peptide fingerprint data, some work solely with MS/MS data, and others can use a combination of both. The other major difference is the scoring used to assess the match between the calculated ions and the real mass spectra. A number of different scoring approaches are used, and this also can impact the results significantly. The parameters the programs will accept also can vary, with some allowing much more flexibility than others.

Mascot

Mascot, developed and maintained by Matrix Science, is one of the more popular search engines used for the identification of proteins from mass spectral data. Based on the Molecular Weight Search (MOWSE) scoring algorithm, it provides flexible searching with several functions that can be used in combination or individually. It is available through a Web-based interface for limited research use; for high-throughput operation, it is available commercially.

Mascot can perform searches based on a peptide mass fingerprint (PMF), MS/MS peptide ions, or partial amino acid sequences (PMF query; Figure 17.3). Mascot can use factors such as approximate mass of the parent protein and isoelectric point (pI) of the parent protein to constrain the search. It can use a number of different databases in its search, including Swiss-Prot, NCBI, and MSDB. It can also search MS/MS and sequence query data against GenBank's EST database if the protein in question is missing from the other databases.

Query data (e.g., peptide masses) are submitted to Mascot either as an uploaded file or as typed text and pasted text in the appropriate browser field. The data required and the search parameters used depend on the query type. With a PMF query, the input data is a list of peptide masses from either MALDI or ESI MS. Standard adjustable parameters include the enzyme used for cleavage, the number of missed cleavages accounted for in the calculated peptides to be matched, the search tolerance (in Daltons, parts per million [ppm], percent, or millimass unit [mmu]), and the search database. Mass data can be input as single positively charged ion masses (MH+) or as neutral ion masses, and either monoisotopic or average isotopic peptide mass can be used. Mascot also allows refinement of the search through specification of taxonomy and selection of possible fixed and variable protein modifications.

Mascot's many search options have advantages and disadvantages associated with them, usually involving a tradeoff between sensitivity (the rate of missed identifications) and specificity (the rate of false-positive identifications). It generally is useful to select parameters that help narrow the search, such as specifying the protein's parent mass and the smallest peptide match tolerance possible for the instrument being used (100–200 ppm often is a good starting point). However, it is crucial to be careful with the variable modifications feature, which can expand the search greatly. An example is methionine oxidation. When this feature is turned on, the program considers that each methionine present can either have an oxygen or not, which changes the peptide mass by approximately 16 Da. If a peptide has multiple methionine residues, this means that there are many possible

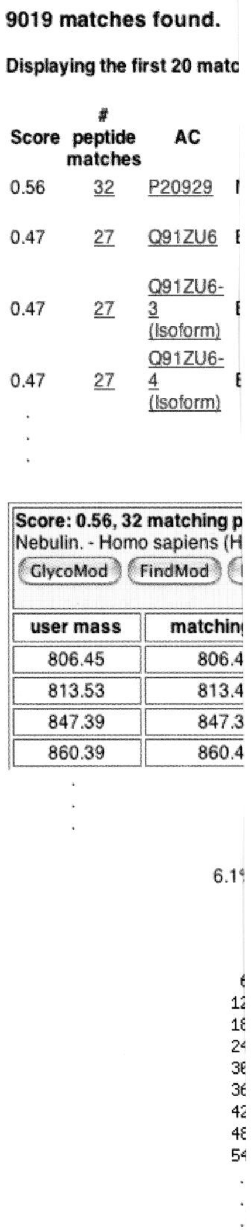

9019 matches found.

Displaying the first 20 matc

Score	# peptide matches	AC
0.56	32	P20929
0.47	27	Q91ZU6
0.47	27	Q91ZU6-3 (Isoform)
0.47	27	Q91ZU6-4 (Isoform)

·
·
·

Score: 0.56, 32 matching p
Nebulin. - Homo sapiens (H

(GlycoMod) (FindMod)

user mass	matchin
806.45	806.4
813.53	813.4
847.39	847.3
860.39	860.4

·
·
·

6.1

6
12
18
24
36
36
42
48
54

·
·
·

FIGURE 17.6 A c
is an extract from
as the ratio of the
Hyperlinks are pro
(as shown), it is use
panel shows a port
buttons in the cent
simulated spectrun
displays a portion o

measurements, one per line. In
fied using the "Data Format" pa
ther "m/z Charge," "m/z Intensit
plorer Spec Peak List." ProteinI
both singly and multiply charged
and negative ion mode experime
The mass tolerance should reflec
the machine from which the da
typically will be 50 to 200 ppm f

result in a less than 0.05 chance of a match happening by chance. For example, if Mascot sets this threshold to 72 and a result score is 105, it is a very strong result, being three orders of magnitude (approximately 33 points) more significant than the 0.05 confidence level.

As with all of the tools, the less complex the sample the mass data represents, the greater the likelihood that accurate identifications will be made. A PMF query using Mascot 1.9 and higher automatically looks for mixtures of up to six components and returns those that are statistically significant, but in both Mascot and GFS (which also has this feature), the presence of multiple proteins reduces the significance of protein matches.

An MS/MS ion query submission consists of paired mass and intensity data in a peak list. This search mode is especially useful for analyzing liquid chromatography MS/MS runs containing data from multiple peptides. For a sequence query, one or more of the peptide molecular masses is combined with sequence, composition, and fragment ion data. The usual source of sequence information is a partial interpretation of an MS/MS spectrum. This general approach was pioneered by Mann et al. at the European Molecular Biology Laboratory (EMBL), who used the term *sequence tag* for the combination of a few residues of sequence data combined with molecular weight information (Mann & Wilm, 1994). The sequence query mode of Mascot differs from a sequence tag search in that fragment ion mass data and sequence data can be supplied in any combination, as opposed to the slightly more stringent format required for a sequence tag query.

Matrix Science also offers a number of other applications not available from the publicly accessible Web site, such as Mascot Distiller, Mascot Parser, and the MassLynx set of MS preprocessing utilities. A Mascot daemon also allows automated analysis of mass lists after the MS software processes them. Mascot Distiller (Matrix Science, Boston, MA) is a commercial application that reads and processes raw data from mass spectrometers, be it in the form of single MS, multiple MS/MS, or liquid chromatography MS/MS spectral data, among others. It allows for the automation of peak list output and provides support for data files created by most of the current spectral analysis applications, including Analyst, Data Explorer, Data Analysis, MassLynx, and XMass. Mascot Parser (for use with Mascot 2.0) is a toolkit that assists in the export of Mascot Results files by enabling a programmer full access to Mascot results for input into a database or for customization of output.

PeptIdent

PeptIdent is one of the many proteomics and sequence analysis tools available on the Expert Protein Analysis System (ExPASy) server. ExPASy is maintained by

the Swiss Institute of Bioinformatics (SIB), a not-for-profit academic foundation dedicated to promoting research and computer technology in the bioinformatics field. PeptIdent compares experimental peptide masses against a precomputed index of theoretical peptide masses generated from proteins in the Swiss-Prot or TrEMBL databases, both of which also are maintained by SIB.

Experimental masses from MS can be entered into a browser text field (Figure 17.5) or can be uploaded as either a plain text file, .pkm (PE Biosystems, Boston, MA) file, or .dta (Sequest) file. Users of the Web interface have only a few parameters from which to choose, such as the type of masses (average or monoisotopic), the cleavage enzyme, how many missed cleavages are allowed, and which common modifications to consider. Database queries against Swiss-Prot consider all alternative protein isoforms resulting from alternative splicing that are available from the Swiss-Prot feature table (although it is important to realize that this may be an incomplete listing of isoforms for many proteins). PeptIdent also can consider covalent protein modifications that are noted in Swiss-Prot as either observed or potential, although it does not perform *de novo* post-translational modification (PTM) predictions. The program also considers documented signal peptides, which are sequences at one terminus of the protein removed by an enzyme in the cell reducing the mature protein mass.

PeptIdent's scoring function is simply the ratio of theoretical peptides matched to the protein to the total number of peptide masses submitted. As a general guide (which also applies to many of the other programs), the strength of a result can be gauged roughly by the percent coverage obtained and the difference between the top and subsequent hits. If there are a lot of hits with approximately the same score, this indicates several possibilities: either there are multiple proteins in the sample, there are a number of homologous proteins in the database matching the query, or the reported matches are all random. It takes experience to help distinguish the above cases, although understanding the type and origin of the protein sample can help.

PeptIdent results are displayed online (Figure 17.6) and also may be E-mailed to the user. Results include a summary of the search parameters; basic information about the proteins matched, such as the Swiss-Prot/TrEMBL accession number; the protein sequence; matched modifications; the percent coverage; and the score. The output also provides convenient links to other ExPASy programs for each protein hit; these include GlycoMod, which provides prediction of possible oligosaccharide structures, FindMod, which predicts potential PTMs and amino acid substitutions, FindPept, for the identification of peptides resulting from

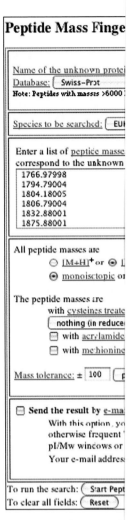

FIGURE 17.5 PeptIde[...] peptide mass fingerpri[...] in the bottom half, sea[...] tolerance.

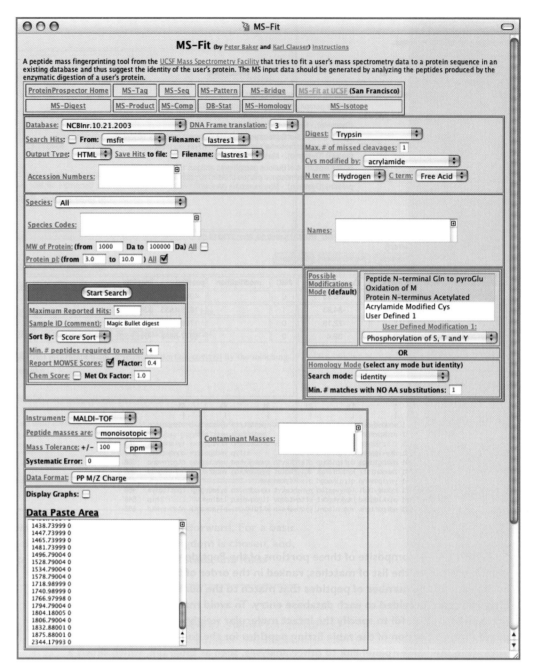

FIGURE 17.7 ProteinProspector submission screen. ProteinProspector has a large variety of options, but for a standard search, most can be left at the default values. The number of missed cleavages is adjusted in the upper right, and the mass tolerance is set on the lower left. Note that there is no way to set the charge state for all peptides together—it must be specified individually for each peptide unless they are +1 (the default). The contaminant masses field (lower right) allows filtering of trypsin, keratin, and so forth.

unspecific cleavage and proteas[...] Mass, which predicts the peptid[...] protease cleavage of a protein [...] a Java applet that graphically [...] spectrum for the matching pro[...]

ProteinProspector

Developed at the University of [...] (UCSF) by Peter Baker and Carl[...] tor is a collection of Web-based[...] ysis and protein identification [...] Here we briefly describe some [...] protein identification process. [...]

ProteinProspector program[...] sequence databases (Figure 17[...]

locations of this information within the FASTA definition line can be a source of problems.

The constraints related to intact protein characteristics also need to be used with care, because the programs follow strict rules for calculating their characteristics (for

example, assuming that parent protein masses are reported as the average isotopic mass and that cystines are unmodified). Applying these rules incorrectly or improperly can result in no matches. Sequences database entries for proteins and genes can be stored in a variety of forms. Sometimes entries represent the mature protein and sometimes an immature protein, and isoforms can be represented in various ways (or may not be present at all). If an intact molecular weight is specified, it may not match the sequence database if the mature protein form is not represented in that database (e.g., with a transit peptide removed).

Matches are scored either on the MOWSE algorithm, which is also the basis of Mascot (Pappin et al., 1993), or by a simple hit-count scheme (Figure 17.8). If MOWSE score reporting is chosen, a modified version of the algorithm is used in which the final score is based on the frequency of a peptide molecular weight's presence in a protein of a given weight range. Peptides with no missed cleavages are weighted as more than those containing missed cleavages in this score. The Pfactor setting determines the weighting given to partially cleaved peptides (0.1 ≡ 10% of the score of a peptide of identical molecular weight with no missed cleavages). Some experience is required to know what setting works best to maximize correct matches while minimizing the influence of spurious hits. The type of digest (limited/complete) also should be considered. Although the MOWSE score can differ over several orders, one also can gauge the quality of hits using other information provided, such as percent coverage and mean parts per million error. Without MOWSE scoring, the database hits are listed simply with the ones having the least number of unmatched masses being ranked higher. In the case where the rank is equal, they are sorted further by increasing index number.

The output from a PMF query returns a summary of the search parameters and information about the number of entries that fit the filter parameters set, along with the top proteins matched. The MOWSE score also can be reported, which may be handy for comparing results with Mascot searches. Detailed information for each protein is available through hyperlinks to the corresponding database entry. Useful quick links to searches for cystine-linked fragments (MS-Bridge) or nonspecific cleavage fragments (MS-NonSpecific) also are provided for each protein hit that had unmatched masses. These tools assume that only a single protein is present in a sample. If more than one protein is present, these tools are likely to provide false matches for both of the above cases.

The ProteinProspector software may be licensed for local installation on Microsoft Windows NT 4.0, Windows 2000, and IBM AIX platforms. Using a licensed copy has advantages, because administrators change many of the default parameters not openly adjustable through the Web interface. For example, one may change enzyme cleavage rules or add new ones, may modify dissociation constant (pK) values used to calculate the isoelectric point (pI), or may write automated scripts for high throughput searches, making the programs amenable to suit a laboratory's particular research interest.

GFS

The GFS method was developed by Giddings and colleagues and is maintained at the University of North Carolina. It represents a different approach to protein identification from previously discussed programs. GFS compares experimental mass spectral directly against a *de novo* theoretical translation and digest of an entire genome sequence, rather than against theoretical digests of protein sequences stored in a database, as in the other programs. By comparing against the theoretical translation and digest of an entire genome, GFS avoids problems faced by other methods, such as lacking or incorrect protein annotations and the need for predefined open reading frames (ORFs). This method also makes GFS a potentially useful tool to assist in the annotation of new genomes or in the identification of proteins for which annotation is incorrect or not available. Using the genome as a reference (instead of annotated proteins) also allows GFS to detect protein products generated by alternative splicing (Black, 2000), transcriptional slippage, and recoding (Gesteland & Atkins, 1996).

The theoretical genome translation and proteolytic digestion is carried out in all forward and reverse frames that, depending on genome size, easily can generate tens of millions of theoretical peptides. When matching MS data, the program scores matches in fixed-sized windows along the genomic sequence; a commonly used window size is 500 nucleotides, although this can be adjusted if the approximate mass of the parent protein is known. For example, a 38-kDa protein equates to approximately 380 amino acids, estimating the average amino acid weight at 100 Da. Multiplied by three to account for three nucleotides per amino acid, this becomes an optimal window size of approximately 1140 nucleotides; because GFS requires setting the window size in increments of 50, 1150 could be used as an appropriate window size.

The calculated window peptide match score takes into account the number of peptides matched, any missed cleavages, duplicate matches, the number of in-frame stop codons, and the adjacency between peptides. More recently, a function was implemented that scores matching windows with a probability score that has a similar interpretation to that of Mascot, although its derivation is different. This enables comparison of results from the two programs. In doing so, it is important to realize that the programs are using different databases, so the threshold at which a result is considered significant can be different.

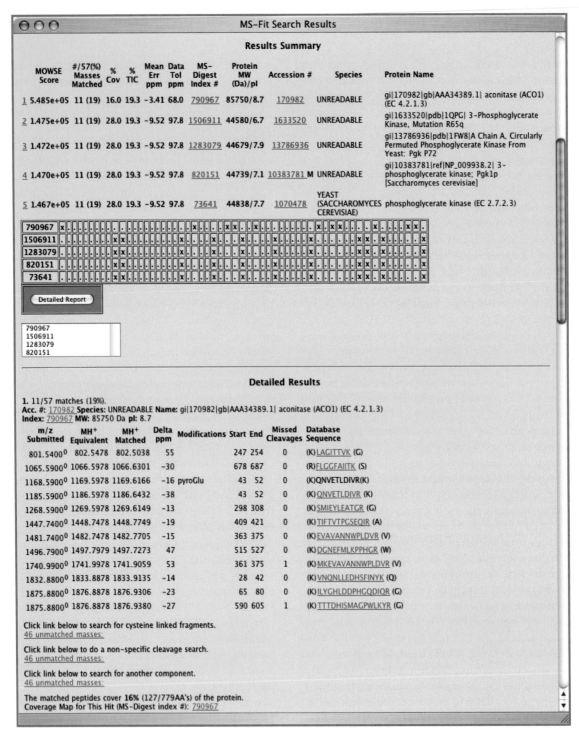

FIGURE 17.8 Two portions of the ProteinProspector output screen. The top half displays the list of best hits achieved, with the **MOWSE** score on the left, followed by other match parameters, including a hyperlink to the matching database entry. Note that, for many of the matches, the database format issue has prevented listing of the species. Right below the list, a map of all the peptides entered, and the subset that matched (**Xs**) is shown. This is useful to determine whether the protein matches are overlapping, as illustrated by the second through fifth hit, which matches have an identical pattern of matching masses (and happen to be the same protein), whereas the first match has an orthogonal set. The lower panel shows a portion of the detailed results for the best hit. This provides a peptide list, along with options for resubmitting the unmatched masses for additional searches such as cystine cross-linked peptides, nonspecific cleavages, or searching for additional protein hits.

GFS is capable of handling both MS and MS/MS data from peptide mass fingerprints, although the MS/MS functionality is not available presently on the GFS Web site because of licensing issues. A new MS/MS functionality is being implemented to address this issue so that it can be made available publicly. The MS/MS matching is designed for use in conjunction with peptide mass fingerprints and presently cannot be used for shotgun data.

Input data may be uploaded as a plain text file of uncharged or charged masses or entered directly into the browser submission window (Figure 17.9). In addition to selecting the genome to use in the analysis, users of the Web interface set options similar to those in other PMF analysis programs, such as the cleavage enzyme, number of missed cleavages, and mass matching tolerance. Currently, the only variable peptide modification

available in GFS is methionine oxidation. As mentioned, one important parameter for GFS is scan window size. Links to explanations of all input parameters are provided. Currently, the GFS Web server provides access to the genomes of *Escherichia coli* and *Saccharomyces cerevisiae*, with plans for several additions in the near future. Users also can obtain the code for installation on a local system, supplying their own genomic sequence. The system runs on Mac OS X at the Unix command line, and there also has been a port to Linux (not presently maintained).

The output from GFS is displayed online (Figure 17.10) and is E-mailed to the user. The HTML-formatted results page is quite rich in information. This information is shown in the form of numerical values indicating the scores and locations in the genome of the

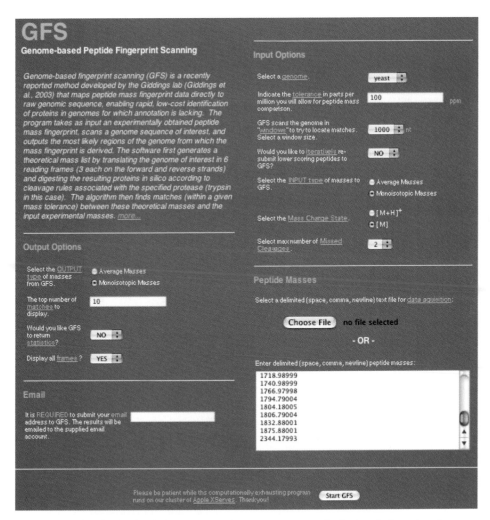

FIGURE 17.9 **GFS submission screen. Input parameters include window size, in nucleotides, that is used to scan across the genome, and many of the other parameters are common with the other programs, including mass tolerance, charge state, and number of missed cleavages.**

LEGEND

Frame 0 1 2

Overlapping 0/1 1/2 0/2

TGGIMATCHINFRAME#1CCA

Best 20 hit regions

Hit Region	Sequence name	Score	PScor
1	>Escherichia coli K-12 MG1655 rev-comp	116.8946	142.61
2	>Escherichia coli O157:H7 rev-comp	78.6107	104.53
3	>Escherichia coli O157:H7 EDL933 rev-comp	77.6829	105.68
4	>Escherichia coli CFT073 rev-comp	63.2855	74.145
5	>dbj|BA000033| Staphylococcus aureus MW2, complete genome rev-comp	53.4990	58.800

.
.
.

HIT REGION: 1

Sequence:>Escherichia coli K-12 MG1655 rev-comp

Frame: 0

	Score	Start	End	Length	# Hits
Window	116.8946	585121	584121	1000	12
Region	86.6341	585571	583471	2100	12
ProbWindow	142.6157	585121	584121	1000	12
ProbRegion	134.3464	585571	583471	2100	12

Back To Hit List   Next Hit

ORFs:

Start	Stop	Length	Frame	Fragm
584856	583905	954	0	0.4686
584616	583905	714	0	0.4454
584556	583905	654	0	0.4404
584538	583905	636	0	0.4528
584406	583905	504	0	0.3929
584265	583905	363	0	0.3471

Results of Annotation search:

583903..584856 317 Rev:1 ompT/b0565 16128548 outer membrane protein 3b (a), protease VII 35562.348

SEQUENCE:

584871 GAATGGAGAACTTTT*ATGC*GGGCGAAACTTCTGGGAATAGTCCTGACAAC 584822

584821 CCCTATTGCGATCAGCTCTTTTGCTTCTACCGAGACTTTATCGTTTACTC 584772

584771 CTGACAACATAAATGCGGACATTAGTCTTGGAACTCTGAGCGGAAAAACA 584722

584721 AAA*GAGCGTGTTTATCTAGCCGAAGAAGGAGGCCGA*AAAGTCAGTCAACT 584672

584671 CGACTGGAAATTCAATAACGCTGCAATTATTAAAGGTGCAATTAATTGGG 584622

584621 ATTTGATGCCCCAGATATCTATCGGGGCTGCTGGCTGGACAACTCTCGGC 584572

584571 AGCCGAGGTGGCAATATGGTCGATCAGGACTGGATGGATTCCAGTAACCC 584522

584521 CGGAACCTGGACGGATGAAAGTAGACACCCTGATACACAACTCAATTATG 584472

584471 CCAACGAATTTGATCTGAATATCAAAGGCTGGCTCCTCAACGAACCCAAT 584422

584421 TACCGCCTGGGACTCATGGCCGGATATCAGGAAAGCCGTTATAGCTTTAC 584372

584371 AGCCAGAGGTGGTTCCTATATCTACAGTTCTGAGGAGGGATTCAGAGATG 584322

584321 ATATCGGCTCCTTCCCGAATGGAGAAAGAGCAATCGGCTACAAACAACGT 584272

584271 TTTAAAATGCCCTACATTGGCTTGACTGGAAGTTATCGTTATGAAGATTT 584222

FIGURE 17.10 This shows several parts of the GFS output summary for a search of the *E. coli* protein against multiple genomes. In the top panel, a list of the best-scoring hits is shown, with both the original GFS score, and the new probability-based score (P-score). Also specified are the genome and positions within the genome where the match occurred. This is followed by the top-ranked hit, which shows both the new and old scores for the best scoring window of the specified size (1000), and then the score for the entire region found. The genome sequence is shown, color coded by frame, with potential ORFs underlined (and also listed in tabular format within the inset box, which is normally below). At the bottom, the list of matching peptides is shown.

top hit regions, with text showing the nucleotide sequence of the hit regions, and color coding of this text to indicate the location and frame of fragment matches, as well as location and frame of potential ORFs and annotated proteins. The layout of the page includes a header consisting of the overall statistics on the hit regions found (if the statistics option is turned on), a list of user parameters, a legend explaining the color scheme of the output, and a clickable table of all the resulting hit regions. This table contains the number of the hit region, the name of the sequence in which the region is found, the maximum window score within the region, the start and stop position of the hit region, and the number of peptide hits in the region. Clicking on the number of the hit region takes the user directly to the detailed view on that particular region. After this table, each hit region is listed, rank ordered by maximum window score. The hit region section contains information on the fragment matches in a single frame, as well as a subsequent, optional All Frames version of the same region that is useful to detect cases where frameshift or sequencing errors have occurred. These outputs contain the location and score of the hit region, the text of the region sequence color coded for various features, a description of the matching fragments in that region, and potential ORFs and annotated proteins associated with the sequence. The statistical significance of each score is also included, facilitating easier interpretation of the results.

OTHER IDENTIFICATION TOOLS

There are a number of other MS data analysis tools for protein identification that are available for use both freely on the Web and commercially. One that falls into the latter category is Sequest, developed at the University of Washington by Eng, Yates, and colleagues. It currently is available through Thermo Finnigan (San Jose, CA), makers of mass spectrometers and other analytical equipment such as spectrometers and high-performance liquid chromatography systems. Sequest is capable of searching against multiple databases and correlating uninterpreted tandem mass spectra to known sequences by identifying amino acid sequences in the database that match the measured mass of the peptide and comparing the fragment ions against the MS/MS spectrum. A preliminary score for each sequence is generated and used in a cross-correlation analysis step where the top 500 peptides are used to correlate theoretically constructed spectra against the experimental spectrum.

Other software tools available for protein identification using MS data include ProFound, PeptideSearch, Sherpa, MassSearch, PepMapper, and Lutefisk.

CHARACTERIZATION TOOLS

Although the tools for protein identification are relatively mature, the potential exists to use MS data to provide further information about the state of a protein in the cell. For example, chemical modifications such as lipids or carbohydrates on a protein may be identified, or products from alternative splicing may be determined. The process of using MS data for this purpose is called *characterization*. Protein characterization is the newest method for such purposes, and the tools in this area are not yet as mature as those discussed earlier in this chapter. Development in this area centers on new MS methods that can provide increasing sensitivity and mass accuracy for large, intact proteins, as well as new informatics tools that can use this new MS information.

One of the first tasks of characterization is to classify the co-translational or post-translational modifications to a protein. Processes that modify proteins during or after translation include covalent chemical modifications such as phosphorylation; proteolysis (such as the cleavage of an intracellular localization tag); and the addition of special purpose, variable chains (such as carbohydrates and lipids). Identifying any of these events is a computational challenge and, to date, no single program attempts to determine them all comprehensively.

There are a variety of tools, each of which usually focuses on one or two specific types of characterizations. Importantly, all PTM analysis tools require the investigator to know the sequence of the unmodified precursor protein or have a reference to it. This generally is obtained by one of the identification tools described previously. Some of those identification utilities offer preliminary checks for well-known PTMs that occur on peptides, but these work well only if the user can narrow the expected set of modifications they expect to find. This process easily can be confounded if multiple proteins are present in the sample, yielding extra peptides that may be matched falsely as PTMs, or if a peptide containing a modification is not observed by the MS. One characterization tool, FindMod, uses sequence context information to assign likely modifications to peptides that help match up those experimental masses that did not result in matches on the first pass. This context-specific search is very helpful for reducing false positives, but the trade-off is that it is unlikely to identify novel modifications.

A limitation of peptide-based modification analyses is that they have difficulty identifying lost signal peptides. Also called *sorting* or *processing signals*, these peptides are like baggage tags that are removed after a protein has reached its destination. A good introduction to signal peptides is the press release and illustrated presentation at the Nobel Foundation Web site for the 1999 Prize in Physiology or Medicine, awarded to Günter

Blobel for his role in this area. More thorough characterization is performed by analysis of the protein's intact mass. For this, there are two recently published tools: ProSight PTM (Taylor et al., 2003), which uses fragment-ion masses from on-line top-down MS protein analysis, and PROCLAME (Holmes & Giddings, 2004), which uses the mature mass along with the gene identification from one of the identification methods.

Many utilities for prediction of post-translational events are specialized, such as NMT (Eisenhaber et al., 2003) for prediction of N-terminal N-myristoylation, and NetOglyc (Hansen et al., 1998) for prediction of mucin type O-glycosylation. Glycomod (Cooper et al., 2001) looks for N-linked polysaccharide modifications based on a database of the known moieties (forms). For identifying transit peptides, there are tools such as SignalP (Nielsen et al., 1999) and PSORT (Gardy et al., 2003), which operate by predicting signal peptide cleavage sites. NetPhos (Blom et al., 1999) is available for prediction of phosphorylation sites in eukaryotic proteins. The ExPASy Proteomics Tools section provides an excellent jumping-off point to proteomic software, linking to approximately 20 of these utilities. To our knowledge, there is currently no public tool to determine lipid modifications comprehensively, such as those found on many membrane proteins. This may be the result of the challenge of analyzing lipid-modified proteins using MS, combined with the complexity of analyzing data for which of a large variety of lipid forms may be present.

COMPARATIVE PROTEOMICS METHODS

This section presents an overview of the processing steps commonly taken in comparative proteomics studies using 2D-PAGE (Box 17.2), as well as a brief review of some of the alternative technologies that show promise for automation. Because many good reviews exist and the process is complicated, the focus here is on what the various problems are, as well as what some of the products and algorithms do, rather than on the specifics of how they work. Note that many utilities are available and only a few arbitrarily selected applications are discussed in this section.

A common goal of many laboratories is the identification of proteins that are differentially expressed under specific sets of biological conditions. This can involve diseased versus healthy cells, immature versus mature cell types, or environmental stresses such as heat shock and nutrient deprivation. Analysis of two or more gels for differences in spot location and intensity, followed by MS-based protein identification, is a keystone of many such efforts, causing many to equate 2D gel comparison erroneously with the entire field of comparative proteomics.

Limitations and variations inherent in 2D gel methodology make fully automated differential expression analysis challenging at present. The gel protocol itself is poorly suited to low-abundance proteins and to those with very high or low molecular weight, and without special adjustments, it is difficult to separate membrane or other hydrophobic proteins. Even when performed correctly, the procedure can yield gels of variable shape, thickness, and staining, whose spots are variably separated because of such factors as shrinkage along the gel edges. Those limitations aside, the postprocessing of the gel images presents complications that are addressed through time-consuming expert adjustment of the software parameters. These and other issues make 2D gel preparation and processing a craft in itself. Despite its limitations, 2D-PAGE remains the separation method of choice for many laboratories.

Computational Analysis

There is a complex constellation of computational steps that face an application whose task is to compare multiple 2D gels. Typical of the problems is the equitable balancing of brightness and contrast and uniform background subtraction so that true spots are not lost and background artifacts are not treated as spots. A second obstacle is protein quantification: spot density is not related to protein quantity linearly, and it changes under various conditions such as when the protein carries a naturally occurring chemical modification. Yet another major challenge is the warping and registration of images for overlaying. There are two major processes: The first is the analysis of one gel (a singleton) to identify spots and to quantify proteins, and the second is the comparison of two or more resultant images to determine the expression differences.

Processing of any single gel begins with scanning it and performing several normalization steps. The intensity of both the spots and the background must be equalized relative to the entire gel, to account for such factors as current leakage. The image usually is cropped, and visual noise and streaking may need removal. Then, spot detection and quantification is performed, usually by numerical fitting of mathematical functions such as a Gaussian or Laplacian (often both) to each spot on the gel.

Multiple Gels

Identifying the spot changes in different cellular states begins with image registration. The gels are landmarked through user selection of several spots common to each. This step cannot be automated reliably because software cannot confirm definitively which spots are common to both gels. The comparison image is then warped to align

Two-Dimensional Polyacrylamide Gel Electrophoresis

2D-PAGE has many monikers, including 2-DE, 2D-PAGE, and 2DGE, but in practice, the product of this method usually is called a 2D gel. It is popular in part because it yields with relative ease a good initial overview of whole-cell protein expression. Using a large format, approximately 10,000 proteins have been detected on a single gel.

The technique involves passing a mixture of proteins, sometimes whole-cell lysates, through a gel in two dimensions. The first phase applies current across a pH gradient to separate individual polypeptides by charge (isoelectric point, or pI). Then, in the perpendicular direction, molecules are separated by size (molecular weight, or MW) through standard sodium dodecyl sulfate (SDS) electrophoresis. The resulting gel then is stained to reveal the spots whose location, size, and density give a rough idea not only of pI and MW, but also of protein quantity. The entire process takes approximately one day but is often carrried out over several days for practical reasons.

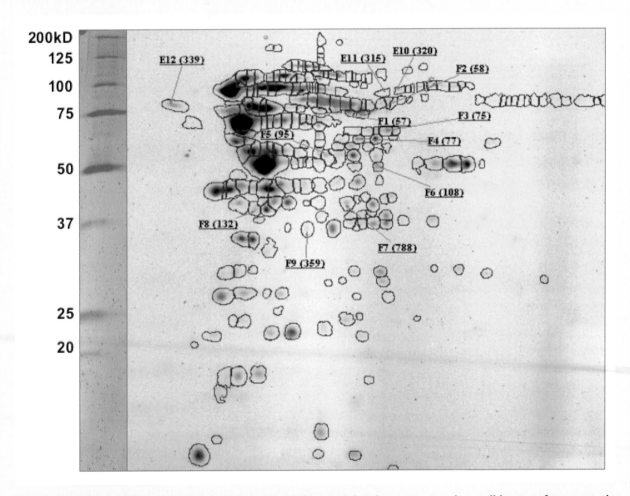

FIGURE 17B.2 **A DIGE** image of a recently sequenced bacterial pathogen, comparing a wild-type reference strain with one undergoing a stress-response to hydrogen peroxide. Molecular weight markers are on the left. Spots in green and purple are proteins that were upregulated or downregulated, respectively, in the antibiotic-resistant strain. For clarity, the annotated spots are just a few of the many differential expressions that were identified from the relative quantification lists that can be produced by all the commercial image analysis programs. Such a list (Table 17B.1) is shown for the colored spots with their relative density changes. Note the background variation; this is a serious challenge when comparing multiple gels because imbalances can lead to improper spot quantification and other problems. (Courtesy of Ed Collins, UNC-Chapel Hill.)

BOX 17.2 Continued

TABLE 17B.1

| MALDI-MS spot no. | Gel exciser spot no. | Normalized spot volume | |
		H$_2$O$_2$-treated Cy3-labeled proteins	Macrophage-passed Cy5-labeled proteins
F1	57	—	−2.847
F2	58	−6.49	−2.093
F3	75	−2.834	1.046
F4	77	2.026	−8.254
F5	95	2.188	−2.338
F6	108	−4.251	1.013
F8	132	1.742	1.252
E11	315	1.569	—
E10	320	1.24	—
E12	339	1.177	—
F9	359	1.342	—
F6	788	2.166	−7.933

First developed in 1975, 2D-PAGE developed an increasing following, becoming a central proteomics method in the late 1990s because of numerous advances in both gel technology and mass spectrometry. Immobilized pH gradients (IPGs), introduced in 1988, magnify the entire IEF separation across a small pH range usually of approximately one point. This technique dramatically improves spot separation of protein species that are concentrated in a region, but it requires a larger protein sample. Low-abundance proteins also can be found much more easily, requiring only a few hundred copies of a protein rather than approximately 1000. Other developments include alternative stains and detergents for separating specialized types of protein. A good review of some of these developments can be found in Lilley et al. (2002), which includes an annotated bibliography.

DIGE, or difference gel expression, is a promising technique from the late 1990s that sidesteps the major problem of registering two gels so that spots are aligned properly. Two samples are labeled with different fluorescent cyanine dyes, mixed, and then run together on the same gel. The gel then is scanned at each dye wavelength; calibration protein mixture may be included, possibly with a third dye. The resulting images can be overlaid perfectly without any warping or registration, making differential expression analysis much easier and quantifiable. An important advantage is that the cyanine dyes allow for subsequent in-gel protein digestion and are only minimally intrusive on MS processing.

the reference spots, and the rest of the spots are paired automatically. Finally, differential analysis of spot clusters is performed, and the nonmatching spots are highlighted in a viewer. Typically, differing spots then are cut from the gel, often by a gel excision robot guided by the annotations made in the previous step; these spots are then digested and put through MS to yield an identification by peptide mass fingerprinting or MS/MS peptide sequencing. Image preparation and comparison is computationally intensive and is well suited to cluster computing. Differential clustering among many gels also is possible with many of the analysis tools to identify and quantify the spot changes occurring under a multiplicity of biological conditions.

Some of the commercial analysis tools include ImageMaster (Amersham Biosciences, Piscataway, NJ), Z3 (CompuGen, Richmond Hill, Ontario, Canada), and PDQuest (Bio-Rad, Hercules, CA). Melanie (*M*edical *E*lectrophoresis *A*nalysis *I*nteractive *E*xpert; Geneva Bioinformatics, Geneva, Switzerland) was a mature and popular tool for soup-to-nuts image preparation and comparison that has now been integrated into ImageMaster. A good free utility that offers many analysis options is Flicker, based on algorithms used in GELLAB II, one of the first programs offered in the early 1990s. For a thorough treatment of the mathematics typically used in each step, readers are directed to the review by Dowsey et al. (2003), developers of the comprehensive ProTurbo image analysis framework that currently is under development, and authors of the MIR (Multiregistration Image Registration) algorithm and program.

2D Gel Databases

The effective population, cross-linking, and use of 2D gel databases is limited, in large part because of the unavailability of data standards. To address this, the Human Proteome Organization has begun a data standards initiative that may enhance data interchange significantly in the future (Orchard et al., 2003). The most well-known existing database, SWISS-2DPAGE, currently contains approximately 1000 proteins annotated on 34 master gel images from six organisms. As when dealing with many other proteomic problems, there is no one location where gel comparisons can be made against a single metadatabase, although hyperlinking to other resources often is provided. The 2DWG Image Meta-Database maintained by the National Cancer Institute provides a good search interface for locating reference gels by species, tissue type, and other factors for subsequent spot comparison;

that site currently links to approximately 30 databases of 2D gels. Most users' images are added to a locally created database after comparison; a tool for personal database creation, Make2D-DB II, is available from the SWISS-2DPAGE site.

Although 2D-PAGE is an effective method for separating high-abundance proteins, it is time consuming, labor intensive, and inherently bound to only rough quantification and relative expression identification. The technique of difference gel electrophoresis (DIGE) obviates many of these problems by allowing two samples to be run on one gel. Alternatively, two emerging technologies, capillary isoelectric focusing (IEF) with MS and protein arrays, offer promise for full automation. A good review and annotated bibliography of these technologies is the humorous and circumspect "2D or Not 2D" by Fey and Larsen (2001). Capillary IEF is a relatively mature technology, is extremely precise, and can model the protein separation process in many of the same ways as 2D electrophoresis. Most importantly, sample separation and basic analysis already can be automated. A thorough metastudy directly comparing 2D electrophoresis with IEF is in Hille et al. (2001).

Protein Arrays

Protein arrays present many more challenges than those involved with DNA and other nucleotide microarrays, currently this technology is best suited to specialized studies. As mentioned at the start of this chapter, proteins cannot be directly "amplified" as can DNA. One may want to use mRNA as an indicator of protein expression, but its presence and content are not correlated with protein quantity. Thus, protein arrays commonly use indirect protocols in which identity and function are inferred through interaction of the array substrate with the analyte, either of which can contain the actual proteins. These methods use both analytical arrays, in which protein mixtures are selectively bound after passing over an array of identifying ligands such as antibodies or antigens, and functional arrays, in which large numbers of purified proteins are arrayed before being washed with functional analytes such as enzymes, liposomes, or specific drugs. In either case, the specialized growth and purification steps are the current factors limiting widespread high-throughput use of protein arrays. Reviews of the technology are in Zhu and Snyder (2003) and Cutler (2003).

▌SUMMARY

As in many areas of bioinformatics, the algorithms used for proteomic analysis are complex, many of them are based on heuristics, and the parameters chosen and the data submitted by the user greatly impact the results.

In a practical sense, what this means is that no software works perfectly in all circumstances, and some work better than others in particular instances. The most important consideration is the source and quality of the input data. It is critically important that the user have good knowledge of the sample. Factors that are important to understand include:

▶ What is the mass accuracy expected from the instrument used?

▶ What modifications have been introduced by the laboratory handling (e.g., Met oxidation)?

▶ Are contaminant peptide masses present from sources such as trypsin autolysis or keratin?

▶ Is it possible that multiple proteins are present?

▶ What charge state and isotopic state are the data in?

▶ Was there a good signal-to-noise ratio for the measured spectrum?

The answers to these questions must be known and translated into proper parameter adjustment and interpretation to maximize the possibility of success. A related issue that holds true for all applications is the importance of familiarity with the various available search parameters, how they affect the scope of the search, and, ultimately, the quality of the results.

There are two general procedures that can assist in analysis with any of the programs. One is to vary search parameters systematically if a satisfactory result is not achieved initially. For example, if an initial mass tolerance of 100 ppm is specified and does not yield any hits, it can be loosened to 200 ppm to account for the possibility that the mass spectrometer has drifted out of calibration. Or, if a taxonomy-specific database does not yield a match, one can broaden the search to include more organisms in the hopes of finding a homologous protein elsewhere. This is also a case in which GFS can be applied to bypass the limitations inherent in the available genome annotations.

The second procedure that is of use is to apply multiple programs to the search and analysis task. Because several of the programs are freely available on the Web, this is relatively easy to do. For example, Mascot and GFS often produce similar results, but occasionally one of the two programs finds a strong match that the other did not, even for well-studied genomes like *E. coli*. This is because each program uses a different scoring method that takes into account differing features of the input data. However, one must be careful of false positives when using multiple search engines, particularly if the hits are only marginally significant.

When comparing multiple gels, several considerations arise. One is that it is important to maximize the consistency with which they are produced. If an image registration program is used, one must look out for the possibility that real differences in the proteome are removed accidentally by aligning spots that are truly different. It is also important to keep in mind that not only do spots on a gel vary in intensity, but they can move around because of biochemical changes to the proteins themselves (a substantial difference from microarray data analysis). For example, in different cellular states, different modifications may be present on a protein, or samples from different individuals may have different polymorphisms present that affect the proteins produced. One situation frequently seen is that different spots on a gel identify as the same protein. This often is the result of chemical differences in proteins that are expressed by the same gene, although it also can be the result of the presence of homologous proteins on the gel. It is important to realize that the p values produced by programs like Mascot and GFS do not eliminate false positives because of homologous hits; they only eliminate those that are the result of random chance.

In cases where multiple proteins identify to the same gene, the process known as *characterization* would be useful, consisting of separating the protein(s) in question, analyzing them by one of the high-mass accuracy methods such as FT/MS, and then submitting the data to one or more of the available tools. There are numerous ways by which this protein purification can be carried out; for example, custom antibodies may be produced to precipitate the target protein, or a genetic tagging approach may be used to affinity-purify the resulting protein. Unfortunately, it is difficult to use proteins directly from a gel spot for high-mass accuracy analysis, because the ionization method of choice—ESI—is inhibited by the sodium dodecyl sulfate (SDS) typically used during electrophoresis.

In all, the two major considerations are to know one's data and to be mindful that protein identification is only a first step, one that can be misleading if a protein exists in multiple forms or has close homologs.

WORKED EXAMPLE

The following peptide mass lists were submitted as PMF queries. The peptide mass lists were generated from mass spectrometric analysis of a trypsin-digested, 2D-PAGE–separated fraction of *E. coli* cellular extract and an *S. cerevisiae* protein extract on a MALDI-TOF and an ESI-quadrupole, respectively.

E. coli (average masses, neutral charge):

```
744.09, 993.28, 1003.27, 1093.38, 1240.49,
1257, 1261.62, 1278.48, 1296.61, 1305.61,
1320.23, 1451.35, 1533.08, 1783.49,
1930.19, 1986.15, 2032.34, 2058.54,
2085.14, 2153.46, 2194.84, 2241.29,
2273.7, 2464.94, 2481.82, 2515.93,
```

```
2531.81, 2545.7, 2585.46, 2601.47,
2640.12, 2680.08, 2820.2, 2836.11,
3387.94, 3695.77, 3754.69, 3824.47,
3971.02, 4599.6, 4615.57, 4631.73,
5042.46
```

S. cerevisiae (monoisotopic masses, neutral charge, may contain several proteins):

```
801.53, 806.45, 813.53, 828.59, 847.39,
860.39, 886.04, 893.39, 917.59, 920.39,
924.59, 947.39, 967.59, 973.39, 983.39,
989.64, 1017.49, 1024.59, 1027.89,
1042.39, 1049.49, 1050.59, 1065.59,
1077.59, 1081.59, 1102.59, 1129.59,
1168.59, 1185.59, 1188.59, 1247.59,
1268.59, 1275.59, 1287.24, 1300.79,
1321.59, 1354.68, 1394.79, 1426.79,
1430.79, 1438.74, 1447.74, 1465.74,
1481.74, 1496.79, 1528.79, 1534.79,
1578.79, 1718.99, 1740.99, 1766.98,
1794.79, 1804.18, 1806.79, 1832.88,
1875.88, 2344.18
```

With the knowledge of the organism of origin already in hand, at first glance it would seem sensible to limit the search species. However, in keeping with previous suggestions the search is kept as broad as possible, because this increases the likelihood of finding a match, even if it is only a homologous protein in a related species. It generally is better to start with a broad search, then narrow it down later if necessary. Although the sample's origination is known, there is always the chance that contaminant masses (trypsin autolysis fragments, keratin, etc.) are included the list. The masses listed are neutral charge, and although methionines may have been oxidized during electrophoresis in the *E. coli* sample, assume they are not for this example (see Problem Set for a further exploration).

Search Parameters

Database, Swiss-Prot; species, all; missed cleavages, 2; 100 ppm. (Parameters not listed were not altered from their default settings.)

Mascot

Note that Mascot requires the mass list entered with one mass per line; otherwise, the search will not operate properly. The top hit for the *E. coli* PMF was (OMPT_ECOLI) Protease VII precursor (EC 3.4.21.87; Omptin; outer membrane protein, 3B) accession number P09169, with 11 peptides matching and a calculated score of 114. This can be compared with the score at which Mascot results become significant, that is, 65, based on the database search size and the mass list size. The comparison in scores ($114 - 65 = 49$) means that the chance of this being a false positive is close to 10^5 smaller than the significance value, which translates into an error expectation of 10^{-7}. The next best hit, and the only other significant score returned, also was for the same *E. coli* protein. We can have strong confidence that this is a correct identification, especially considering that the search was performed against all species. For the yeast sample and at these settings, Mascot identified an isoform of the yeast phosphoglycerate kinase (PGK1) as the top hit, but the score was considered barely significant (65, with 65 being significant). Changing only the missed cleavages parameter to one was enough to increase the score to 71. There were a number of other yeast proteins returned in the list, albeit with nonsignificant scores. One of these was the fourth-best hit, a mitochondrial aconitate hydratase precursor (ACO1). This is interesting, considering our sample is enriched for mitochondrial proteins, and deserves closer inspection even though the score was not significant at these search parameters.

PeptIdent

For the *E. coli* sample, the two top scoring hits were human proteins, with the third matching the *E. coli* top hit returned by Mascot. This is a good case to illustrate the importance of being familiar with the program being used. The observed result is because, for any search, PeptIdent scores are based on the number of peptides matched. It therefore is not surprising that a human protein was matched higher than the *E. coli*, because there is a greater chance for random peptide match on the much larger human gene. Luckily, and of utmost importance, PeptIdent also returns information on percent coverage, from which it is easy to determine what the true match is. The higher scored human genes with 13 peptide matches each only had 4.3% coverage, versus 12 peptides matched and 58.6% coverage for the *E. coli* protease precursor. For the yeast data, no yeast proteins were returned in a search against all species in the Swiss-Prot database. The 20-protein hit list returned by PeptIdent had the highest-scoring hits from human and mouse, but none was significant, ranging between only 3% and 5% coverage.

ProteinProspector

In protein prospector, each mass is listed one per line, followed by white space, then a 0 for the charge state (DNA frame, 3; Cys modification, unmodified). This is necessary because if the charge of each peptide is not specified, ProteinProspector assumes they are [Mr + H$^+$] masses. There is no global setting to change the charge state. MOWSE scoring is specified because it is a measure related to how likely each hit was by chance, so it generally has much better specificity than the hit-count scheme. A Prospector run at 100 ppm yielded the *E. coli* outer membrane protein protease VII precursor, as with the previous searches. For the yeast masses, ProteinProspector identified three yeast proteins in the top 10 hits, with ACO1 coming out on top, and then several entries all related to PGK1 are scored in second to fifth place, agreeing with Mascot. As an experiment to illustrate the effect of the scoring method, if MOWSE scoring is turned off, similar results to PeptIdent are obtained: A human protein is at the top of the list, with the first yeast hit being PGK at fifth place—not

a very satisfactory result. This experiment illustrates how useful the proper scoring function can be to distinguish real hits. The main difference between the MOWSE scores reported here and Mascot is that Mascot translates them into a probability-based measure (Perkins et al., 1999).

GFS

GFS queries (window size, 1000) against one or more genome sequences, rather than a database of proteins. For the *E. coli* data, just the *E. coli* strain K-12 genome was selected (although multiple bacterial genomes can now be searched), and hence all potential matches are to sequence regions in that genome. GFS has a flexible input format, so the peptide masses can be specified with or without commas. GFS identified a sequence region that is annotated as the same outer membrane protein as the top Mascot/ProteinProspector hit, with a P-score of 143. This score is a new feature of GFS[a] that is interpreted in a similar way to scores from Mascot, meaning that this hit has a 1 in 10^{14} probability of being accidental. Based on calculations, a score of 70 is at the significant ($p < 0.05$) level, so this match is very good because the OMP score is 70 ($p < 10^{-7}$) better. Notably, it was the only significant match, although in a separate multigenome search, we also match the same gene in three other sequenced strains of *E. coli*. With the yeast data, GFS identified PGK1 as the top-scoring hit, with a P-score of 65, and ACO1 as the second-best P-score of 48. Neither of these scores is considered significant because we calculate the threshold for the yeast genome, based on its size, in the high 70s. However, the P-score function presently is designed for MALDI peptides, and these yeast data are from ESI, which produces lower scores. One good way to differentiate a real hit versus false positive for any of the programs is to note the difference between the best hit and the next top scoring hit. Given that PGK1 is 17 points—nearly two orders of magnitude—better than the next best hit, this top identification is a safe bet. On the flip side, the ACO1 identification may not be reliable, because it scores only four points better than the next hit.

The goal here was not to obtain the exact same protein identifications from each of the PMF tools, but to illustrate how significantly the parameters can affect the outcome, and also the importance of being methodical. The *E. coli* example leads to an easy identification, whereas the yeast sample illustrates a more difficult and ambiguous case because of the presence of multiple proteins and possibly contaminants. The latter is particularly important because it illustrates that with PMF queries, it is not always simple to obtain a confident identification. In cases where one does not achieve anticipated results, such as proteins from another organism other than the organism of origin coming out as the best hits in a search against all species, it is useful to start with parameter adjustment, but may be necessary to add data from tandem MS or to use a tool such as GFS in case the protein is missing from the database. Changing the tolerance and the

---

[a]The feature is still being fine tuned at the time of writing, so the scores may be different in the GFS version available when this book is published.

number of missed cleavages considered is a good first consideration in such situations. These parameters can be altered before one begins to consider potential modifications that may have occurred as a result of the sample preparation protocol used. An effective approach may be to use multiple programs in a query.

PROBLEM SET

1. The *E. coli* data that was presented in the Worked Example may contain peptides where one or more methionine residues have been oxidized.
   a. What indicators can be used to tell that methionine oxidation may be present?
   b. Submit the peptide list to Mascot, GFS, and ProteinProspector, each with oxidized methionines turned on as a variable modification. How many additional peptide masses are matched by each of the engines? Discuss the differences, if any, in the results compared with those in the Worked Example.
2. It is believed that at least two proteins are present in the peptide mass fingerprint from the Worked Example for yeast. One method that can be used to deal with a sample containing multiple proteins is to find the top-scoring match, subtract its peptide masses out of the list, and then resubmit the smaller list for another search. Try this approach with the yeast mass list from the Worked Example. Submit the list to Mascot, GFS, or ProteinProspector, then subtract the peptides from the top-scoring match and resubmit (in Mascot this can be carried out by hitting the Search Unmatched button on the first results page). Aside from the top hit, PGK, are any other proteins found in both the original match set and the subtracted set? If so, name the protein then explain the results.
3. Download the sample1.pkl from the Book's Web site. This is a peak-list file from a tandem MS run that analyzed two peptides from one protein. The file lists the peptide mass, intensity, and charge, followed by a list of b- and y-ions, and their intensities. The sample masses are monoisotopic. Use one or more of the discussed tools to identify the protein.
4. The following mass list represents the combined isotopic envelopes for three different peptides, each in the +1 charge state. Determine the monoisotopic neutral mass for each one (H mass is approximately 1.008): 833.2, 834.2, 835.2, 836.2, 1056.3, 1057.3, 1058.3, 2204.2, 2205.2, 2206.2, 2207.2.
5. The following mass list contains three different peptides, in various charge and isotopic states. Determine the neutral charge, monoisotopic mass for each of the three: 262.75, 263.09, 263.42, 263.76, 735.29, 735.79, 736.30, 736.80, 898.13, 899.14, 900.14, 901.15

INTERNET RESOURCES

2DWG Meta-database of 2D-gels	http://www.lecb.ncifcrf.gov/2dwgDB
ExPASy	http://www.expasy.org
Flicker 2D gel analysis software	http://www.lecb.ncifcrf.gov/flicker/
GFS	http://gfs.unc.edu
HUPO proteomics standards initiative	http://psidev.sourceforge.net/
Lutefisk	http://www.hairyfatguy.com/Lutefisk/
MASCOT	http://www.matrixscience.com
MassSearch	http://cbrg.inf.ethz.ch/Server/MassSearch.html
MSDB	http://csc-fserve.hh.med.ic.ac.uk/msdb.html
NCBI (nr)	ftp://ftp.ncbi.nih.gov/blast/db/nr.tar.gz
Nobel Prize in Physiology or Medicine 1999	http://www.nobel.se/medicine/laureates/1999/
PepMapper	http://wolf.bms.umist.ac.uk/mapper/
PeptIdent & other ExPASy tools	http://www.expasy.org/tools
PEPTIDESEARCH	http://www.narrador.embl-heidelberg.de
PROCLAME	http://proclame.unc.edu
ProteinProspector	http://prospector.ucsf.edu
Sequest	http://fields.scripps.edu/sequest
Sherpa	http://www.hairyfatguy.com/Sherpa/info.html
SWISS-2DPAGE	http://www.expasy.org/ch2d
Swiss-Prot	http://www.expasy.org/sprot/
Unimod	http://www.unimod.org

FURTHER READING

MANN, M., HENDRICKSON, R. C., AND PANDEY, A. (2001). Analysis of proteins and proteomes by mass spectrometry. *Annu. Rev. Biochem.* 70, 437–473. An in-depth review article covering important aspects of mass spectrometry and proteomics.

DOWSEY, A. W., DUNN, M. J., AND YANG, G. Z. (2003). The role of bioinformatics in two-dimensional gel electrophoresis. *Proteomics* 3, 1567–1596. Very thorough and comprehensive treatment of the issues involved and mathematics used in 2D gel image processing and comparison.

GESTELAND, R. F., AND ATKINS, J. F. (1996). Recoding: dynamic reprogramming of translation. *Annu. Rev. Biochem.* 65, 741–768. This review article discusses one of the major phenomena that can result in multiple or unexpected proteins from a transcript.

REFERENCES

BLACK, D. L. (2000). Protein diversity from alternative splicing: a challenge for bioinformatics and post-genome biology. *Cell* 103, 367–370.

BLOM, N., GAMMELTOFT, S., AND BRUNAK, S. (1999). Sequence and structure-based prediction of eukaryotic protein phosphorylation sites. *J. Mol. Biol.* 294, 1351–1362.

BUTTERFIELD, D. A., BOYD-KIMBALL, D., AND CASTEGNA, A. (2003). Proteomics in Alzheimer's disease: insights into potential mechanisms of neurodegeneration. *J. Neurochem.* 86, 1313–1327.

COOPER, C. A., GASTEIGER, E., AND PACKER, N. H. (2001). GlycoMod—a software tool for determining glycosylation compositions from mass spectrometric data. *Proteomics* 1, 340–349.

CUTLER, P. (2003). Protein arrays: the current state-of-the-art. *Proteomics* 3, 3–18.

DOWSEY, A. W., DUNN, M. J., AND YANG, G. Z. (2003). The role of bioinformatics in two-dimensional gel electrophoresis. *Proteomics* 3, 1567–1596.

EISENHABER, F., EISENHABER, B., KUBINA, W., MAURER-STROH, S., NEUBERGER, G., SCHNEIDER, G., AND WILDPANER, M. (2003). Prediction of lipid posttranslational modifications and localization signals from protein sequences: big-Pi, NMT and PTS1. *Nucl. Acids Res.* 31, 3631–3634.

ENG, J. K., MCCORMACK, A. L., AND YATES, J. R. I. (1994). An approach to correlate tandem mass spectral data of peptides with amino acid sequences in a protein database. *J. Am. Soc. Mass Spectrom.* 5, 976–989.

FENN, J. B., MANN, M., MENG, C. K., WONG, S. F., AND WHITEHOUSE, C. M. (1989). Electrospray ionization for mass spectrometry of large biomolecules. *Science* 246, 64–71.

FEY, S. J., AND LARSEN, P. M. (2001). 2D or not 2D. Two-dimensional gel electrophoresis. *Curr. Opin. Chem. Biol.* 5, 26–33.

GARDY, J. L., SPENCER, C., WANG, K., ESTER, M., TUSNADY, G. E., SIMON, I., HUA, S., DEFAYS, K., LAMBERT, C., NAKAI, K., et al. (2003). PSORT-B: improving protein subcellular localization prediction for Gram-negative bacteria. *Nucl. Acids Res.* 31, 3613–3617.

GESTELAND, R. F., AND ATKINS, J. F. (1996). Recoding: dynamic reprogramming of translation. *Annu. Rev. Biochem.* 65, 741–768.

HANSEN, J. E., LUND, O., TOLSTRUP, N., GOOLEY, A. A., WILLIAMS, K. L., AND BRUNAK, S. (1998). NetOglyc: prediction of mucin type O-glycosylation sites based on sequence context and surface accessibility. *Glycoconj. J.* 15, 115–130.

HARRISON, P. M., KUMAR, A., LANG, N., SNYDER, M., AND GERSTEIN, M. (2002). A question of size: the eukaryotic proteome and the problems in defining it. *Nucl. Acids Res.* 30, 1083–1090.

HILLE, J. M., FREED, A. L., AND WATZIG, H. (2001). Possibilities to improve automation, speed and precision of proteome analysis: a comparison of two-dimensional electrophoresis and alternatives. *Electrophoresis* 22, 4035–4052.

HOLMES, M. R., AND GIDDINGS, M. C. 2004. Prediction of posttranslational modifications using intact-protein mass spectrometric data. *Anal. Chem.* 76, 276–282.

LILLEY, K. S., RAZZAQ, A., AND DUPREE, P. (2002). Two-dimensional gel electrophoresis: recent advances in sample preparation, detection and quantitation. *Curr. Opin. Chem. Biol.* 6, 46–50.

MA, B., ZHANG, K., HENDRIE, C., LIANG, C., LI, M., DOHERTY-KIRBY, A., AND LAJOIE, G. (2003). PEAKS: powerful software for peptide *de novo* sequencing by tandem mass spectrometry. *Rapid Commun. Mass Spectrometry* 17, 2337–2342.

MANN, M., AND WILM, M. (1994). Error-tolerant identification of peptides in sequence databases by peptide sequence tags. *Anal. Chem.* 66, 4390–4399.

NIELSEN, H., BRUNAK, S., AND VON HEIJNE, G. (1999). Machine learning approaches for the prediction of signal peptides and other protein sorting signals. *Protein Eng.* 12, 3–9.

ORCHARD, S., HERMJAKOB, H., AND APWEILER, R. (2003). The proteomics standards initiative. *Proteomics* 3, 1374–1376.

PAPPIN, D. J. C., HOJRUP, P., AND BLEASBY, A. J. (1993). Rapid identification of proteins by peptide-mass fingerprinting. *Curr. Biol.* 3, 327–332.

PERKINS, D. N., PAPPIN, D. J., CREASY, D. M., AND COTTRELL, J. S. (1999). Probability-based protein identification by searching sequence databases using mass spectrometry data. *Electrophoresis* 20, 3551–3567.

SCHUIT, F., FLAMEZ, D., DE VOS, A., AND PIPELEERS, D. (2002). Glucose-regulated gene expression maintaining the glucose-responsive state of beta-cells. *Diabetes* 51(Suppl 3), S326–S332.

TANAKA, K., WAKI, H., IDO, Y., AKITA, S., YOSHIDA, Y., YOSHIDA, T. (1988). Protein and polymer analysis up to m/z 100.000 by laser ionisation time-of-flight mass spectrometry. *Rapid Commun. Mass Spectrometry* 2, 151–153.

TAYLOR, G. K., KIM, Y. B., FORBES, A. J., MENG, F., MCCARTHY, R., AND KELLEHER, N. L. (2003). Web and database software for identification of intact proteins using "top down" mass spectrometry. *Anal. Chem.* 75, 4081–4086.

TAYLOR, J. A., AND JOHNSON, R. S. (2001). Implementation and uses of automated *de novo* peptide sequencing by tandem mass spectrometry. *Analyt. Chem.* 73, 2594–2604.

ZHU, H., AND SNYDER, M. (2003). Protein chip technology. *Curr. Opin. Chem. Biol.* 7, 55–63.

▌ KEY TERMS

amu

average mass

bottom up

comparative proteomics

dalton

deconvolution

DIGE

electrospray ionization

FTICR or FT/MS

isoelectric point

isotope coded affinity tagging

liquid chromatography

MALDI

mass spectrometry

mmu

monoisotopic mass

neutral mass

open reading frame

peptide mass fingerprint

pI

ppm

protein identification

proteomics

shotgun proteomics

tandem mass spectrometry

time-of-flight mass spectrometer

top-down proteomics

2D gel electrophoresis

## PART FIVE

DEVELOPING TOOLS

CHAPTER EIGHTEEN

Using Perl to Facilitate Biological Analysis

LINCOLN D. STEIN

Bioinformatics: A Practical Guide to the Analysis of Genes and Proteins, Third Edition, edited by
Andreas D. Baxevanis and B.F. Francis Ouellette.
ISBN 0-471-47878-4 Copyright © 2005 John Wiley & Sons, Inc.

INTRODUCTION

Consider a situation in which an investigator is studying genes that affect neuronal signaling in *C. elegans*, with a primary interest in identifying those whose gene products may be secreted. A Web site that reports the results of a large systematic study of predicted *C. elegans* genes using the RNA-induced inhibition of gene expression (RNAi) technique is available, and the investigator can download a summary file based on a few thousand experiments. The latest release of WormPep, which reports the peptide sequences of more than 19,000 known and predicted worm genes, also is available. What is needed now is the ability to search the RNAi results file for those genes that affect worm movement in some way (e.g., a common phenotype for genes affecting neuronal activity) and to extract the sequence of those genes from WormPep. The ultimate plan is to submit these sequences of interest to SignalP, an E-mail–based signal peptide cleavage site predictor based at the Technical University of Denmark.

How would one accomplish this? Obviously, one way is by hand. First, one would need to read the RNAi summary file into a word processing program, cull it for experiments that affected locomotion in some way, and then assemble a list of all of the genes that produce relevant phenotypes. Next, one would open WormPep, search for the corresponding sequence for each of these genes, and cut and paste these sequences into another file. The last step would be to reformat the entries into the format required by the SignalP server, pasting all of the entries into an E-mail message.

It should be apparent immediately that there are some problems with this approach. If there are more than just a few genes of interest to analyze, the job quickly becomes rather tedious, if not overly time consuming. Worse yet, the next time that new RNAi results are released, the whole process will need to be repeated, determining which RNAi entries are new. The step involving loading WormPep into a word processor may not even be tenable because of the sheer size of the database, well more than 10 megabases.

This is the type of problem that a Perl script can help with. The Perl programming language excels at slicing, dicing, and integrating data files, and is the language of choice for the many bioinformatics researchers. This chapter provides a gentle introduction to Perl, with examples designed to illustrate the usefulness of learning this language.

GETTING STARTED

As this chapter progresses, a solution is developed for the data integration problem introduced in the first paragraph of this chapter. Before attacking this problem, however, some very simple scripts that illustrate the basics of Perl programming are discussed. In considering these examples, the reader is strongly encouraged to follow along by typing the examples into a Perl interpreter to develop a better sense for what these short scripts actually do. Modifying and experimenting with the scripts for individual use also is encouraged.

Perl interpreters are available for the Macintosh, Windows, and Unix operating systems. Perl usually is not pre-installed on Microsoft Windows systems, but the ActiveState company provides a good Windows version of Perl as a free download.

Users of Mac OS X, Unix, or Linux systems often find that Perl is already installed. If one types "perl -v" on the command line and Perl is installed, its version number and copyright information appears. Alternatively, for those with login access to a departmental Unix or Linux server and some comfort in creating and editing text files, it may be wise to try out Perl from within that account before installing it on a desktop machine.

Perl consists of two essential parts:

▶ the interpreter, called *perl* on Unix and Mac OS X systems, and *perl.exe* on Windows machines; and

▶ *scripts*, text files that are written by the user describing a discrete set of steps to be performed by the interpreter. The scripts are actually computer programs, and the words *script* and *program* can be used interchangeably.

The process of writing and running a Perl script is similar on Windows, Mac OS X, and Unix systems. The basic steps are described below.

Create a text-only file containing the following lines:

```
#!/usr/bin/perl
print "My first Perl script.";
```

Any word processing program may be used, as long as the file is saved as `text only`. The Windows Notepad program is good for this task, because it saves its files in text-only format by default. On Macintosh OS X systems, use the TextEdit application (located in the Applications folder) and create a plain text document using Format → Make Plain Text. The script then can be typed in and saved in the usual way. Name the file `first.pl`.

This newly created file contains two lines. The first line is a comment that identifies the file as a true Perl script (indicated by the `#!` symbol at the beginning of the line). The second line is a print statement that tells Perl to print out the following text:

```
My first Perl script.
```

The name of the file ends in the extension **.pl**, which is a standard naming convention for Perl scripts.

To run this command, open a command-line window (the DOS window on Windows systems, a shell window on Unix, or the Terminal window in Mac OS X), change to the directory that contains the file, and type the command:

```
% perl first.pl
My first Perl script.
```

where % represents the command-line prompts, and boldface type represents input typed by the user at the keyboard.

What this particular command does is invokes the Perl command interpreter, passing to it the name of the file that should be run. The interpreter dutifully processes the script line by line, sees the single print command, and executes it. The output of the script appears in the command window.

If Perl is installed in the standard way on the computer, the perl command does not have to be typed explicitly. On Unix systems, the script file can be marked as being directly executable using the chmod command:

```
% chmod +x first.pl
```

On Windows systems, the file does not have to be marked explicitly as executable, because Perl usually is installed in such a way that any file ending in the .pl extension is associated with the Perl interpreter. Simply typing in the name of the program will run it:

```
% first.pl
My first Perl script.
```

HOW SCRIPTS WORK

A script consists a series of commands, more formally called *statements*, that are meaningful to the Perl interpreter. Unless told otherwise, the interpreter starts at the top of the script file and works its way down to the bottom, executing each statement in turn.

Consider this new script:

```
#!/usr/bin/perl
# preamble...
print "I can do math!\n";

# do some calculations
$sum = 3 + 4;

# print the result
print "The sum of 3+4 is ",$sum,".\n";
```

This script consists of three statements; the first one (print "I can do math!\n") tells the interpreter to print out the indicated text. As will be discussed in more detail later, the special character sequence \n is not interpreted literally, but instead prints out as a newline character. The second statement, $sum = 3 + 4, adds the numbers three and four together and stores the result in a variable named $sum. The last statement prints the text The sum of 3+4 is, followed by the contents of the variable $sum, followed by a period and a newline (a carriage return).

Note that each statement ends with a semicolon. The semicolon tells Perl where one statement ends and another begins. Blank lines and other white space can help make the script more readable, but are ignored by the interpreter. Any line that begins with a number sign (#) is a comment. When Perl sees a hash mark it simply ignores everything between it and the end of the line. The use of comments is strongly encouraged, because it allows other users to understand better what the programmer was trying to accomplish in a particular block of code, as well as reminding the programmer themselves of the same when reexamining code written long before.

The topmost line also is a Perl comment, but on Mac OS X and Unix systems, it serves double duty as a directive to the Unix shell to tell it to execute the command /usr/bin/perl when the script file is executed. On Windows systems, this line is extraneous, but it is better to include it to maintain portability with Unix machines and as a matter of good form.

Unless otherwise instructed, the Perl interpreter starts at the first statement and works its way to the last. When this script is run, the following output is produced:

```
I can do math!
The sum of 3+4 is 7.
```

Note that the user only sees the output from the two print statements. The statement that performs the addition acts silently, behind the scenes.

STRINGS, NUMBERS, AND VARIABLES

Perl can deal with an astonishing number of data types, including, but not limited to, text, integers, floating point numbers, complex numbers, and binary numbers.

Following a long computer science tradition of using obscure terms for simple concepts, the Perl term for text is *string*. Strings are surrounded by single or double quotation marks:

```
'I am a string.'
"I am another string."
```

Having two types of quotation marks available makes it easier to create strings that contain embedded quotation marks:

```
'"Anna," she wailed "come quickly! The
  parakeet's gone!"'
```

There also are some more substantial differences between the two types of quotes that are discussed later in this chapter under Variable Interpolation.

Numbers are written just as one would expect:

```
1
49
28.2
-109
6.04E23
```

The last example shows how one represents scientific notation. The E means exponent, and the number should be interpreted as 6.02×10^{23}.

If you want strings to contain special characters, such as tabs or new lines, Perl provides special escape sequences to represent them. These escape sequences consist of a backslash followed by a single character. The two most commonly used are \n, which begins a new line, and \t, which inserts a tab. For example,

```
print "There is a newline\nhere and a tab
   \t there.\n";
```

produces the following output:

```
There is a newline
here and a tab     there.
```

Perl interprets escape sequences only when they occur in double-quoted strings. In single-quoted strings, the backslash and the character that follows it are interpreted literally.

Variables provide temporary storage for strings, numbers, and other values. In Perl, variables are arbitrary names preceded by a dollar sign. Examples of valid variable names are shown below.

```
$x
$X
$i_am_a_variable
$LongVariableName
```

Perl variables are case sensitive. In the list above, $x is one variable, and $X is a different one entirely.

When first created, variables are empty, or undefined. Values are assigned to variables using the = sign, also known as the *assignment operator*:

```
$x = 42;
print 'The value of $x is ',$x,"\n";
```

Assignment works from right to left. In the example above, the number 42 is assigned to the variable $x. Once assigned, the variable can be used in the place of a value, as the print statement above shows. The same variable can be used multiple times, using the assignment operator to change its contents.

```
print 'The value of $x is still',$x, "\n";
$x = 'Mary had a little lamb';
print 'But now the value of $x is',
   $x, "\n";
```

This code fragment now prints out the following:

```
The value of $x is still 42
But now the value of $x is Mary had a
little lamb
```

Note that there is no restriction on the type of data a variable can hold. In this example, $x initially contained an integer and then held a string. Unlike some programming languages, Perl does not require the user to declare (formally describe) variables before using them, although this type of checking can be activated if desired. Perl actually has several types of variables. In addition to variables that hold a single value, which are technically called *scalar* variables, there are arrays and hashes, two types of variables that are capable of holding multiple values. These are discussed in an upcoming example.

ARITHMETIC

Perl knows basic arithmetic. Symbols known as *operators* are responsible for the various arithmetic operations:

+	addition
−	subtraction
*	multiplication
/	division
**	exponentiation
()	grouping

The following example does a little math and prints out the result:

```
$x = 4;
$y = 2;
$z = 3 + $x * $y;
print $z,"\n";
```

The result that is printed out is 11. However, a more succinct way to express this would be to combine the first three lines into a single expression passed to print:

```
print 3+4*2,"\n";
```

Note that the arithmetic expression is processed as 3+(4*2) rather than (3+4)*2. When evaluating numeric expressions, Perl uses the standard rules of precedence. The precedence can be changed by explicitly using parentheses:

```
print (3+4)*2,"\n";
```

▌VARIABLE INTERPOLATION

Another interesting difference between double- and single-quoted strings is what happens when a variable is embedded inside a string. In double-quoted strings, the variable is expanded to its contents, a process known as *string interpolation*. This can aid readability considerably:

```
print "The value of $x is $x\n";
```

Assuming that $x again contains "Mary had a little lamb," the above statement outputs:

```
The value of Mary had a little lamb is
Mary had a little lamb
```

Single-quoted strings do not work in this fashion. If the print statement used a single-quoted string instead, it would print:

```
The value of $x is $x\n
```

The user can precisely control whether variable interpolation occurs in double-quoted strings by placing a backslash in front of variables that should not be interpolated:

```
print "The value of \$x is $x\n";
```

In this statement, the first occurrence of the $x variable is protected against interpolation because of the backslash, but the second is not.

```
The value of $x is Mary had
a little lamb
```

The backslash character also can be used to embed a double-quote character inside a double-quoted string. Consider how the following may be different from the outputs shown above, either by hand or through the Perl interpreter:

```
print "The value of \$x is \"$x\"\n";
```

Variable interpolation extends only to the contents of the variable itself. Perl will not try to evaluate arithmetic expressions or other programming statements that are embedded in double-quoted strings. For example, the statements

```
$y = 19;
print "The result is $y+3\n";
```

produces the output

```
The result is 19+3
```

To evaluate the expression, put it outside the double quotes. Perl carries out the arithmetic, and the print statement outputs the result.

```
print "The result is ",$y+3,"\n";
```

▌BASIC INPUT AND OUTPUT

Input, in programming parlance, is how data "gets into" a script. Output is, of course, what comes out of the script. Most scripts do both, inputting data from one source and outputting it to another.

The main method of producing output is to use the print function. Print takes a list of one or more arguments separated by commas and sends them to the current output device, which by default is the computer's screen. As has already been shown, print can deal equally well with text, numbers, and variables:

```
$sidekick = 100;
print "Maxwell Smart's sidekick is ",
  $sidekick-1,".\n";
print "If she had a twin, her twin might
  be called",
2*($sidekick-1),".\n";
```

The result of this script is:

```
Maxwell Smart's sidekick is 99.
If she had a twin, her twin might be
called 198.
```

The main way to read input data is to use the angle bracket operator <>, which reads a line of input from the current input device. This operator is usually called in conjunction with the assignment operator to save the returned information into a variable:

```
$line = <>;
print "Got $line";
```

With these two operations, one can now write a fully interactive program named "dog years" that converts your age in human years to your age in dog years:

```
#!/usr/bin/perl
print "Enter your age: ";
$age = <>;
print "Your age in dog years is ",
  $age/7, "\n";
```

When this program is run, the result looks like this:

```
% dog_years.pl
Enter your age: 42
Your age in dog years is 6
```

where the 42 is typed in at the keyboard. Another tiny program illustrates one of the idiosyncrasies of the <> operator:

```
#!/usr/bin/perl
print "Enter your name: ";
$name = <>;
print "Hello $name, happy to meet you!\n";
```

Running this program produces output that may not be what is expected:

```
% hello.pl
Enter your name: Lincoln
Hello Lincoln
, happy to meet you!
```

What's going on? In fact, when the <> operator reads a line of input, the newline character at the end of the input data is still there! More often than not, the newline character must be removed. Obligingly, Perl provides a function named *chomp* that does exactly that, removing the terminal new line from a string. The rewritten program looks like this:

```
#!/usr/bin/perl
print "Enter your name: ";
$name = <>;
chomp $name;
print "Hello $name, happy to meet you!\n";
```

With the new line removed, the output looks the way it should:

```
% hello.pl
Enter your name: Lincoln
Hello Lincoln, happy to meet you!
```

The program still can be made a bit shorter by combining the input and chomp statements into a single statement, at the risk of making the program slightly harder to understand:

```
#!/usr/bin/perl
print "Enter your name: ";
chomp($name = <>);
print "Hello $name, happy to meet you!\n";
```

The parentheses control the precedence of the operation so that Perl performs the input first, and then passes $name to the chomp function.

FILEHANDLES

When lines of input are read, the data comes from the keyboard by default. When the script writes lines of output, the output goes to the screen by default. What if one wants to change these defaults so that input comes from a file, or output goes into one?

There are several ways to do this, but the most straightforward is to use filehandles. A filehandle is the connection between a script and a file. Scripts can read from a filehandle to obtain the contents of the file a line at a time and can print to a filehandle to add data to a file.

To open a file for reading, use the open function:

```
open MYFILE,'data.txt';
```

The open function expects exactly two arguments. The first is a name for the filehandle (MYFILE). This is an arbitrary name that the user chooses, with the convention being to use all uppercase letters. The second argument is the name of the file to open. If just the file name is provided, as shown in the example, Perl attempts to open a file by that name in the current directory (on Windows and Unix systems, the directory in which the command to run the script was given; on Macintoshes, the folder that the script is located in). The full path, explicitly giving the location of the file, also can be given.

Unfortunately, the way one specifies a file path is different on the three different operating systems. On Mac OS X and Unix systems, a path begins with a forward slash and each directory is separated by additional slashes. On Windows systems, a path begins with the drive letter (e.g., C:) and uses backslashes to separate directories. Examples of fully-qualified path names on Unix, Windows, and Macintosh systems are shown below.

```
Unix       /usr/local/blast/data/cosmids.txt
Windows    C:\Documents\Blast\Data\Cosmids.txt
Macintosh  usr/local/blast/data/cosmids.txt
```

The open command may not be able to open a file for reading if, for instance, the file does not actually exist. Ways to detect and handle this kind of error are discussed in the next section.

As soon as a filehandle is open, it can be read from using the <> operator:

```
$line = <MYFILE>;
chomp $line;
$next_line = <MYFILE>;
chomp $next_line;
```

The only difference between reading from the keyboard and reading from a file is that, instead of using an empty pair of angle brackets (<>), the open filehandle is placed between them (<MYFILE>).

Each time you call <MYFILE>, a new line of data is read from the file. When the last line has been read, the operation returns the undefined value; again, detecting this type of error is discussed later. When a filehandle is no longer needed, it can be closed using the close function:

```
close MYFILE;
```

Writing to a file works in much the same way. The main difference is that, when the file is opened, Perl is instructed to write to the file by placing a > sign before the filename:

```
open MYFILE,'>data.txt';
```

If the file does not already exist, Perl creates it and opens it for writing. If the file already exists, then Perl empties out its existing contents before opening it. This ensures that the new data that is written to the file replaces anything that was already there. To add data to the end of the file without disrupting its current contents, the file can be opened for appending using the >> sign:

```
open MYFILE,'>>data.txt';
```

Data written to the file is now be appended to the end of its current contents rather than writing over the file. If the file does not already exist, then an empty one is created automatically.

ERROR HANDLING

As before, open may fail when opening a file for writing if the specified path is incorrect, or if the user does not have write permission for the indicated directory. This section discusses how to deal with these errors.

As soon as a filehandle is opened for writing, data can be sent to it, using the filehandle as the print command's first argument:

```
print MYFILE "Your age in dog years is ",
   $age/7,"\n";
```

This writes the indicated line of text to the file associated with MYFILE. Be sure to note that there is no comma between the filehandle and the list of data arguments! The full, generalized syntax for print is:

```
print [FILEHANDLE] $data1
   [,$data2 [,$data3....]]
```

The square brackets mean an argument is optional. One or more spaces is used to separate the optional filehandle from the first data argument, and commas are used to separate the individual items to be written to the filehandle.

When finished with writing to a filehandle, use the close function to close it as before. If the program ends without explicitly closing the filehandle, Perl closes the file automatically.

Nothing prevents a script from having multiple filehandles open at the same time. This odd little program writes the first two odd-numbered lines of input to the file odd.txt, and even-numbered lines to the file even.txt:

```
#!/usr/bin/perl
open ODD,">odd.txt";
open EVEN,">even.txt";
$line = <>;
print ODD $line;
```

```
$line = <>;
print EVEN $line;
$line = <>
print ODD $line;
$line = <>
print EVEN $line;
close ODD;
close EVEN;
```

There is a certain amount of repetition in this script, for the sake of clarity. This script will be revisited shortly, using a more elegant loop to perform the same function.

Each time <> is called, a new line of input is obtained either from the keyboard or the file. What happens when the end of the file is reached? When this happens, because there are not any more lines to read, <> returns the undefined value.

MAKING DECISIONS

So far, the programs that have been discussed have been very linear (see Figure 18.1). The Perl interpreter starts at the first statement and works its way to the last, executing each of them along the way.

Life is full of decisions, however, and so are Perl scripts. Often, there should be different paths followed if a particular condition is true, another if the condition is false. Considering the dog years calculator shown above, what would happen if the user had entered a negative number for the age, or a number that is unreasonably large? It would be desirable to reject the input outright, rather than produce and output a preposterous answer.

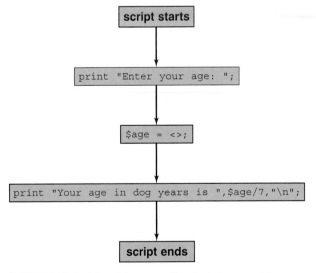

FIGURE 18.1 The "dog years" calculator provides an example of entirely linear program flow.

This simple modification to the original script achieves this goal:

```
#!/usr/bin/perl
print "Enter your age: ";
  $age = <>;
die "Preposterous age" if $age <= 0 or
  $age >= 100;
print "Your age in dog years is ",
  $age/7, "\n";
```

The fourth line is the new one, consisting of two parts. The first part (die "Preposterous age") introduces the die function, which is a lethal form of the print command. It prints out the error message given to it, along with information indicating the current line number. It then immediately terminates the program. It is great for handling those occasions when a fatal, unrecoverable error has occurred. The second part of the line (if $age <= 0 or $age >= 100) tests the $age variable's numeric value. If $age is either zero or less or is 100 or more, then the test is true and the die function is executed. If $age satisfies neither test, then the die function is skipped and the program goes on as before. In plain English, the statement can be read as, "Die if the age is either zero or less or the age is 100 or more." If the age is invalid, the program terminates at the die statement, and the last print statement is never executed. Testing the potential scenarios of the now-modified program,

```
% dog_years.pl
Enter your age:  -20
Preposterous age at dog_years.pl line 4,
<> chunk 1.

% dog_years.pl
Enter your age:  as old as Methuselah
Preposterous age at dog_years.pl line 4,
<> chunk 1.

% dog_years.pl
Enter your age:  42
Your age in dog years is 6
```

Perl has a complete set of comparison operators that work on numbers and strings. To compare numbers, use any of the operators shown in Table 18.1. To compare strings, use any of the operators shown in Table 18.2. The numeric comparison operators are straightforward because they look, for the most part, like conventional expressions used in algebra. The big trap is the == operator that is used to test the equality of two numbers. Two equal signs are used instead of just one.

If the assignment operator (=) is used accidentally, the expected result is not returned:

```
$a == $b; # compare $a to $b, return true if equal
$a = $b; # assign contents of $b to $a
```

TABLE 18.1 ■ Numeric Comparison Operators

Operator	Description	Example
==	Equality	$a == $b
!=	Not equal	$a != $b
<	Less than	$a < $b
>	Greater than	$a > $b
<=	Less than or equal to	$a <= $b
>=	Greater than or equal to	$a >= $b
!	Logical not	$ = !$b

Read the ! operator as *not*. Unlike the other operators, it takes a single argument and reverses its truth. True expressions become false and vice versa. For example,

```
print "the number is not greater than 0"
  if !($a > 0);
```

This statement first compares the current value of $a with zero and returns a true value if $a is more than zero. The ! operator then reverses the test so that the expression as a whole is true only if $a is zero or less.

The string comparison operators are funny two-letter commands. The one used most frequently is eq, for testing whether two strings are the same. Consider this new version of the hello.pl script:

```
#!/usr/bin/perl
print "Enter your name: ";
chomp($name = <>);
print "Hello $name, happy to meet you!\n";
print "Hail great leader!\n" if $name eq
  'Lincoln';
```

The output of the program uses eq to give Lincoln a special greeting:

```
% hello.pl
Enter your name:  George
Hello George, happy to meet you!
% hello.pl
Enter your name:  Lincoln
Hello Lincoln, happy to meet you!
Hail great leader!
```

TABLE 18.2 ■ String Comparison Operators

Operator	Description	Example
eq	Equality	$a eq $b
ne	Not equal	$a ne $b
lt	Less than	$a lt $b
gt	Greater than	$a gt $b
le	Less than or equal to	$a le $b
ge	Greater than or equal to	$a ge $b
=	Pattern match	$a = /gattc/

Other handy string comparison operators are `lt`, which is true if the first string is less than the second string, and `gt` if the first is greater than the second. Perl compares strings alphabetically, but uses different criteria than the telephone book does. Among other subtle (and not-so-subtle) differences, the set of uppercase letters is less than the set of lowercase letters; in Perl, Z is less than a. Be careful not to use == to compare strings, or `eq` to compare numbers. The handiest string comparison operator of them all is `=~`, the pattern matching operator. This is the most powerful of Perl operators, deserving of its own discussion later in this chapter.

Two or more comparison operations can be combined using the operators `and` and `or`. An expression involving `and` is true only if both the right and left sides are true, whereas `or` expressions are true if either side is true. There is also a `not` operator, which reverses the sense of whatever comes to the right, making true expressions false and false ones true, just like Big Brother did in George Orwell's *1984*.

The use of the `if` statement has already been demonstrated, executing a statement only when the condition that follows is true. As always with Perl, the opposite operator exists, called `unless`, executing a statement only when the condition following is false. Returning to the program testing for preposterous ages, the test could be rewritten this way:

```
die "Preposterous age"
   unless 0 < $age and $age < 100;
```

Read the statement this way: "Die unless the age is more than zero and less than 100." The effect is the same. Sometimes it seems more natural to write the conditional with an `if`, sometimes with an `unless`.

▌CONDITIONAL BLOCKS

How would one approach executing several statements conditionally? In this case, the statements can be grouped into a block, using curly braces. The grouped statements then can be executed altogether, using the block form of `if`. Returning again to the dog age calculator,

```
#!/usr/bin/perl
print "Enter your age: ";
$age = <>;
if ($age <= 0 or $age >= 100) {
    print "That age doesn't look
    reasonable to me.\n";
    die "Preposterous age";
    }
print "Your age in dog years is ",
  $age/7, "\n";
```

In this example, `if` controls a block of two statements surrounded by the curly braces. The first statement prints out a warning, and the second one terminates the program with die. If the age does not fall within the range of 0 through 100, then the statements within the block execute and the program ends before reaching the last line of code. If the age does fall within the specified range, the two statements in the `if` block are ignored and the program goes on to print out the calculated result, as before. The effect is to create two alternative paths in the program, one of which leads to termination with an error statement (Figure 18.2).

`If` blocks have this general form:

```
if (TEST) {
    STATEMENT 1;
    STATEMENT 2;
    STATEMENT 3;
    ...
}
```

The test itself must be enclosed by parentheses in the manner shown, but any comparison operation involving numbers or strings is allowed. The indentation is a matter of style; although Perl does not depend on the indentation to interpret the code, indenting code in this fashion is invaluable when debugging a program, because it is easier to see where a given block of code begins and ends.

Perl also can handle situations where one set of statements should be executed if the test condition is true, another set of statements if the test condition is false. To do so, an `else` block is added to the if structure, changing the construct from an if-then statement to an if-then–else statement.

```
#!/usr/bin/perl
print "Enter your age: ";
$age = <>;
if ($age <= 0 or $age >= 100) {
    print "That age doesn't look
    reasonable to me.\n";
} else {
    print "Your age in dog years is",
        $age/7,"\n";
}
```

The if-then-else statement shown above has two blocks, each surrounded by curly braces. The contents of the first block are executed when the test is true. Otherwise, the second block is executed. The result is that, if the entered age falls outside the acceptable range of the program, an error message is printed; if not, it prints the calculated results instead:

```
%  dog_years.pl
Enter your age: eighteen
That age doesn't look reasonable to me.
```

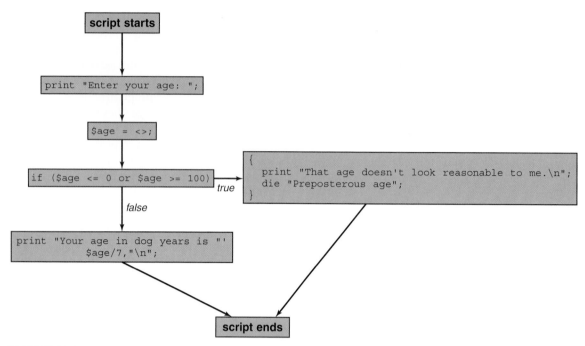

FIGURE 18.2   If blocks can change the flow of execution.

```
%  dog_years.pl
Enter your age:   21
Your age in dog years is 3
```

There happens to be a single statement in each block in this example, but there is no limit in to the number of statements that can be enclosed within a block. Finally, for the sake of completeness, code that specifies what is wrong with bad input data can be included in the program. A handy elsif block can test one string after another:

```
#!/usr/bin/perl
print "Enter your age: ";
$age = <>;
if ($age <= 0) {
    print "You are way too young to
    be using a computer.\n";
} elsif ($age >= 100) {
    print "Not in a dog's life!\n";
} else {
    print "Your age in dog years is",
    $age/7,"\n";
}
```

There are now two $age checks in this program. The first test compares the age with zero and prints out a warning message if it is zero or less. If the test is false, then the program proceeds to the elsif block and tries the second test, which compares $age with 100. If this is true, then the second error message is printed

out. Otherwise, if both tests are false, the program falls through to the else block. The possible outcomes are now as follows:

```
%  dog_years.pl
Enter your age:   -20
You are way too young to be using a
computer.
```

```
%  dog_years.pl
Enter your age:   999
Not in a dog's life!
```

```
%  dog_years.pl
Enter your age:   28
Your age in dog years is 4
```

WHAT IS TRUTH?

The words *true* and *false* have been tossed around rather blithely in this chapter. It is now appropriate to define these terms and answer the question of what truth actually is. Regardless of the meaning of truth in the broader, philosophical sense, truth in Perl boils down to four very simple rules.

▶ Zero (0) is false

▶ The empty string (" ") is false

▶ The undefined value is false

▶ Everything else is true.

The various numeric and string comparison tests that were illustrated in the previous section evaluate to one when true and to the undefined value when false.

LOOPS

Conditional statements allow the flow of a program to be modified so that sections of code can be executed or skipped over as need be. They cannot, however, make the program execute a particular section of code more than once. For this, Perl (and most programming languages) use what are known as *loops*. Perl has a number of different types of loops available to the user, but the most useful one is the while loop. The while loop looks very much like an if block, but instead of executing the contents of the block once if the test is true, it executes the statements repeatedly until the test becomes false (Figure 18.3). An example of this type of loop is illustrated by this simple counting program:

```
#!/usr/bin/perl
$count = 1;
while ($count <= 5) {
    print "$count potato\n";
    $count = $count + 1;
}
```

Before the loop begins, the program creates a variable named $count and sets its value to 1. The while loop test checks whether $count is 10 or less and executes the two statements contained in the curly braces as long as this condition holds true. The first statement prints out the current value of $count, and the second increments the variable by one. The first time the while statement is encountered, $count was set to one, so the block is executed. The second time, $count is two, and the block is executed again. This continues until $count is six, at which point the test is no longer true (because $count is more than five) and the loop terminates. The output for the program is quite simply:

```
% count.pl
1 potato
2 potato
3 potato
4 potato
5 potato
```

In the same way that unless reverses the sense of the if statement, until can be used as an alternative to while. Until loops execute the contents of a block until a certain test becomes true. The counting program then can be rewritten as follows, to yield the same output:

```
#!/usr/bin/perl
$count = 1;
until ($count > 5) {
    print "$count potato\n";
    $count = $count + 1;
}
```

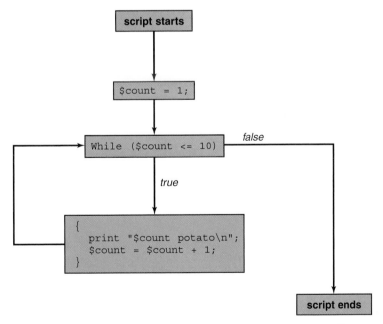

FIGURE 18.3 While loops execute the same block repeatedly, until a defined condition is satisfied.

▌COMBINING LOOPS WITH INPUT

Loops become very powerful when combined with input statements. Consider this simple example:

```
#!/usr/bin/perl
print "Type something> ";
while ( defined($line = <> ) ) {
    chomp $line;
    print "You typed '$line'\n\n";
    print "Type something> ";
}
```

This script prints out the prompt Type something> and immediately enters a while loop. The while loop here is a little different from the ones shown before. Instead of carrying out a comparison, the while loop's test contains the expression defined($line = <>). This expression looks somewhat bizarre, but can be explained very simply. The first thing that happens is that a line of input is read and assigned to the variable $line. Then, $line is passed to a new function named defined, which returns true if the contents of a variable are defined, false otherwise. Recall that <> reads lines from a file (or keyboard) until it reaches the end of the file, at which point it returns undefined. This test is telling the while loop to read input lines one at a time until the end of the file is reached. The parentheses ensure that defined is called after the line is read into $line, not before.

For each line read in this way, the while loop executes three statements. The first statement calls chomp to remove the newline character from the end of $line. The second statement uses variable interpolation to insert the input line into the string "You typed '$line'\n\n" and then prints the resulting string out. The last statement displays the prompt again. The result looks like this:

```
% echo.pl
Type something> hi there
You typed 'hi there'

Type something> this is something
You typed 'this is something'

Type something> ^D
%
```

As you can see, this program echoes back everything typed in, just like a particularly annoying child. Even if nothing were typed in, the program simply would echo back an empty string; this is because the script would read a single newline character, which it would then remove with chomp, yielding an empty string. To stop the program, an end-of-file character would have to be sent. On Unix and Macintosh systems, this is carried out by typing control-D (written ^D for short). On Microsoft Windows systems, this is carried out by typing control-Z (^Z). An alternative is to kill the program by typing control-C (^C). This stops the program dead in its tracks.

Because it can be inconvenient to remember obscure control characters, the program can be made a bit friendlier by allowing the user to type quit to exit the loop:

```
#!/usr/bin/perl
print "Type something. 'quit' to
finish> ";
while ( defined($line = <>) ) {
    chomp $line;
    last if $line eq 'quit';
    print "You typed '$line'\n\n";
    print "Type something> ";
}
print "goodbye!\n";
```

The main change is the line that immediately follows the chomp. This introduces a new function named last, which acts as a loop modifier. It is allowed to occur only within the body of a loop. When executed, last causes the script to exit the loop immediately, even though the loop test still may be true. This statement compares the contents of $line with the string quit. If they match, the last function is executed and the loop finishes. Running the program now, entering the word quit exits the loop so that the last line (which prints goodbye!) can be executed.

Because the process of reading and processing incoming data a line at a time is so common, Perl provides a handy shortcut. If <> appears all alone in the test part of a while statement, Perl reads a line into an automatic variable with the odd-looking name, $_ (which is read as "dollar sign underscore"), and then calls defined on your behalf. Furthermore, many text-processing functions operate on $_ by default, including chomp. Taking advantage of this shortcut, one can rewrite the previous example in this way:

```
#!/usr/bin/perl
print "Type something. 'quit'
  to finish> ";
while (<>) {
    chomp;
    last if $_ eq 'quit';
    print "You typed '$_'\n\n";
    print "Type something> ";
}
print "goodbye!\n";
```

STANDARD INPUT AND OUTPUT

When a Perl script reads a line from <> and prints without using a specified filehandle, it instead uses two automatic filehandles called *STDIN* and *STDOUT*. The statements

```
print "The answer to life is...";
print STDOUT "The answer to life
is...";
```

are exactly equivalent. In the same vein, the statements $line = <>; and $line = <STDIN>; are almost equivalent. The subtle differences between <> and <STDIN> are discussed below.

The names STDIN and STDOUT are derived from "standard input" and "standard output," an idea popularized by the Unix operating system. Standard input and standard output are abstract files from which a script can accept input and send output, respectively. When a script is first launched, standard input corresponds to the keyboard and standard output corresponds to the computer screen. On Windows and Unix systems, standard output appears in the command interpreter window. On Macs, the output appears in a small scrolling window that MacPerl creates specifically for this purpose. When a Perl script is launched, the user has the option of changing where standard input and output come from and go to. The user also can arrange for the standard output of one script to be sent to the standard input of another script in assembly-line fashion. This is actually a very powerful facility, but one that is beyond the scope of this chapter.

To redirect standard input from a file in either Microsoft Windows or Unix systems, use the less than symbol (<) to indicate the file:

```
% count_words.pl <C:\My
Documents\cosmids\11_22_00cosmids.txt
```

To redirect standard output to a file on Windows or Unix systems, use the greater than symbol (>):

```
% reverse_translate.pl > dna.txt
```

Standard input and output can be redirected simultaneously by using both symbols on the same command line:

```
% reverse_translate.pl < protein.txt >
  dna.txt
```

There is actually a third automatic filehandle called STDERR, for "standard error." Perl sends its error messages and other diagnostics to standard error rather than standard output. When die is used to display error messages, the messages go to the STDERR filehandle automatically. STDERR initially is attached to the screen, just like STDOUT. On Unix systems, STDERR can be redirected using >&. The following command sends the standard output of reverse_translate.pl to a file named dna.txt and sends any warnings or errors to a file named errors.out:

```
% reverse_translate.pl > dna.txt >&
  errors.out
```

When using Perl on Windows systems, there is no support for a separate, standard error, so this type of redirection does not work on those systems.

Returning to the idea that <STDIN> and <> are almost—but not exactly—the same, the difference lies in the fact that <> contains some additional magic that makes it easy to process command line arguments. Given a file named unsorted.txt that is to be processed using a file named odd_even.pl, one way to process this file would be to redirect standard input, like so:

```
% odd_even.pl < unsorted.txt
```

However, because odd_even.pl contains a line using <> operator to read from standard input, the command can also be written in the following way:

```
% odd_even.pl unsorted.txt
```

The file name unsorted.txt is now being passed to the script as an argument and not as standard input. When <> is used, it looks for any filenames on the command line, opens them, and reads from them a line at a time. If no files are mentioned on the command line, <> reads from standard input. This feature can be used to process multiple files at once as well, listing them in order on the command line, moving sequentially through the files as each line of each file is read.

FINDING THE LENGTH OF A SEQUENCE FILE

Moving to a biologically based example, consider a text file containing a large DNA sequence in single-letter format. The sequence is of unknown length, and it would be desirable to determine the number of bases in the sequence quickly. Using the file size alone would not be appropriate, because the presence of end-of-line characters at the end of each line would inflate the number artificially. The Perl script that is developed in this section answers the question, as well as counts up the number of lines in the original text file. This short script reads in the file, one line at a time, removing each line's terminal newline character and determining the length of what is left. The length for that line is added to a running total, with a counter tracking the number of lines in the file.

```
#!/usr/bin/perl
# file_size.pl
$length = 0; # set length counter to zero
$lines = 0;   # set number of lines to zero
while (<>) {  # read file one line
                at a time
    chomp;    # remove terminal newline
    $length = $length + length $_;
    $lines = $lines + 1;
}
print "LENGTH = $length\n";
print "LINES = $lines\n";
```

A built-in function named length is invoked to determine the length of the line as soon as the terminal newline is removed. When the script is finished, it prints out the ultimate values of $length and $lines:

```
% file_size.pl dna.txt
LENGTH = 50649
LINES = 1387
```

PATTERN MATCHING

The script from the previous section was useful only for calculating DNA lengths in the unusual case of having a file that contains nothing but raw DNA sequence. More frequently, however, sequence data comes in FASTA format. To tally up the length of all the sequence in a FASTA file, the lines that begin with > must be ignored. Perl's pattern matching operations make this easy to do.

A pattern match is a special type of text comparison. It is something like eq, but instead of testing for an exact match between two strings, it tests a string against a pattern, using a pattern description language known as a *regular expression*. A simple example of a pattern match is:

```
print "EcoRI site found!" if $dna
=~/GAATTC/;
```

This if statement is comparing the contents of the variable $dna against the pattern GAATTC. The funny looking =~ symbol is the pattern match comparison operator; think of it as an approximately equal comparison. If the string to the left of the pattern match operator contains the indicated pattern, it returns true. In the script fragment above, the program prints out EcoRI site found! if the string contains GAATTC anywhere along its length.

Regular expression patterns are delimited by forward slashes. The simplest ones contain a sequence of normal characters that must match somewhere within the body of a string. The EcoRI-site detector is one such example. Regular expressions are much more powerful than

this, however. For example, square brackets can be used to specify a set of alternative characters in the manner shown here:

```
$dna =~ /GGG[GATC]CCC/
```

This pattern matches a sequence of characters beginning with GGG, followed by any of the characters G, A, T, or C, followed by the sequence CCC. That is, this pattern searches for GGGNCCC.

To search for a series of alternative patterns, you can use the | symbol to separate the alternatives. This example searches for either EcoRI sites or HindIII sites:

```
$dna =~ /GAATTC|AAGCTT/;
```

This facility is greatly enhanced by metacharacters and quantifiers. A metacharacter represents a whole class of characters. For example, a single dot (.) matches any character except the end of a line, whereas \d signifies any digit. There also are metacharacters that match the beginning and ending of lines and match the boundaries between one word and the next. Table 18.3 lists some of the more common metacharacters. Note that there are many cases in which a metacharacter representing a character set is paired with its complement. For example, \s matches white space, and \S matches nonwhite space (in other words, printing characters). Another frequently used pair, ^ and $, match the beginning and end of lines, respectively.

For example, to match a "ZIP + 4" format ZIP code, the required regular expression would be written as follows:

```
$address =~ /\d\d\d\d\d-\d\d\d\d/;
```

For a regular expression to match a metacharacter literally, it must be preceded by a backslash. For example, to match DNA sequence IDs of the form M58200.2, where a dot is used literally, the regular expression should be written as:

```
$sequence_id =~ /\w+\.\d+/;
```

TABLE 18.3 ■ Regular Expression Metacharacters

Metacharacter	Description
.	Any character except newline
^	The beginning of a line
$	The end of a line
\w	Any word character (nonpunctuation, nonwhitespace)
\W	Any nonword character
\s	Whitespace (spaces, tabs, carriage returns)
\S	Nonwhitespace
\d	Any digit
\D	Any nondigit

TABLE 18.4 ■ **Quantifiers**

Quantifier	Description
?	0 or 1 occurrence
+	1 or more occurrences
*	0 or more occurrences

By default, any character or metacharacter in a regular expression matches exactly once. By placing a quantifier after the character, Perl can match a character a specific number of times, or a range of times. The simplest type of quantifier is {M}, which tells Perl to match the pattern exactly M times. Using this notation, the ZIP + 4 regular expression could be rewritten as:

```
$address =~ /\d{5}-\d{4}/;
```

Similar quantifiers include the form {M,N}, which match at least M times but no more than N times; {M, }, which matches at least M times; and { ,N}, which matches no more than N times. To bring the examples back into a biological context, an expression that matches the plant mcrBC methylation site Pu-C-X(40-80)-Pu-C is shown, where the center of the recognition site can be anywhere from 40 to 80 nucleotides long:

```
$sequence =~ /[AG]C[GATC]{40,80}[AG]C/;
```

Although the curly braces can be used to describe any quantification, there are some shortcut metacharacters that are used for the frequent cases (Table 18.4).

Parentheses can be used to group parts of a regular expression, and then a quantifier can be applied to the entire group. For example, this regular expression matches normal five-digit ZIP codes as well as the ZIP +4 form:

```
$address =~ /\d{5}(-\d{4})?/;
```

The \d{5} part matches a digit repeated exactly five times. This is followed by an optional section containing -\d{4}, a hyphen followed by four digits. The optional section is completely surrounded by parentheses to group it, and the group is followed by a ? symbol, meaning that it can match at most once, and possibly not at all. Parenthesized groups also can be used to extract portions of regular expressions.

With regular expressions, the DNA length calculator can be rewritten so that it correctly ignores lines that begin with the > sign. The modified program looks like this:

```
#!/usr/bin/perl
# file_size2.pl
$length = 0;
$lines = 0;
while (<>) {
    chomp;
    $length = $length + length $_ if
        $_ =~ / [GATCNgatcn]+$/;
    $lines = $lines + 1;
}
print "LENGTH = $length\n";
print "LINES = $lines\n";
```

The key modification to the original script is the insertion of a conditional test on the statement that tallies the length of each line of text. The script tests $_ for a pattern match with the regular expression /^[GATCNgatcn]+$/, which matches lines containing DNA sequence. The initial ^ character matches the beginning of the line, [GATCNgatcn]+ matches one or more of the characters GATCN or their lowercase equivalents, and the $ matches the end of the line. Other lines in the FASTA file, including blank lines and the description lines, are ignored. Now, the file length that is printed out corresponds to the sequence only.

Before leaving this script, some syntactical tricks can be applied to make the script more concise. If a regular expression appears alone without a =~ operator, then Perl assumes that the variable to be tested for a pattern match is $_. The string length function also behaves this way, returning the length of $_ if no variable is specified explicitly. So, the length-tallying line can be rewritten as:

```
$length = $length + length if
/^ [GATCNgatcn]+$/;
```

A second shortcut is to append an i flag at the end of the regular expression right after the second slash. This puts the regular expression into case insensitive mode and allows the statement to be written as:

```
$length = $length + length if /^[GATCN]+$/i;
```

Finally, because adding a value to a variable and storing the sum back into the same variable is such a common operation, Perl provides the shortcut operator += (read as "plus equals"). This operator takes a numeric value on its right side, adds it to the contents of the variable on its left side, and stores the result back into the same variable, all in one graceful step. Taking advantage of this feature gives statements of the form:

```
$length += length if /^[GATCN]+$/i;
```

Similar assignment shortcuts are summarized in Table 18.5. Putting all these shortcuts together gives the final version of the DNA-length tallying script:

TABLE 18.5 ■ Assignment Shortcut Operators

Operator	Example	Description
+=	$a += 3	Add a number to a variable
-=	$a -= 3	Subtract a number from a variable
*=	$a *= 10	Multiply variable by a number
/=	$a /= 2	Divide a variable by a number
.=	$txt .= "abc"	Append a string to a variable

```perl
#!/usr/bin/perl
# file_size3.pl
$length = 0;
$lines = 0;
while (<>) {
    chomp;
    $length += length if /^[GATCN]+$/i;
    $lines += 1;
}
print "LENGTH = $length\n";
print "LINES = $lines\n";
```

▌EXTRACTING PATTERNS

Not only are regular expressions good for detecting patterns in text, but they can be used to extract matching portions of the text as well. To see how this might be useful, consider a FASTA description line like this one:

```
>M18580 Clone 305A4, complete sequence
```

In addition to the initial >, the description line contains two different fields that we may want to capture. The first is M18580, the mandatory sequence ID. The second is Clone 305A4, complete sequence, an optional human-readable comment. In regular expression terms, the description line looks like this:

```
/^>\S+\s*.*$/
```

Reading from left to right is the beginning of the line (^), a > sign, one or more nonwhite space characters corresponding to the sequence ID; zero or more spaces or other white space; zero or more of any character corresponding to the optional description; and the end of the line ($). This regular expression match can be made to extract the ID and description lines simply by putting parentheses around the parts that should be captured:

```
^>(\S+)\s*(.*)$/;
$id = $1;
$description = $2;
```

When a string successfully matches a regular expression, any portions of the expression that are contained within parentheses are extracted and placed into the automatic variables $1, $2, $3, and so forth. The

extraction works from left to right and happens only if the entire regular expression matches.

This trick can be used to fix a deficiency in the DNA length calculator from the previous section. Previous versions of this script naively treated the entire FASTA file as a single DNA sequence. However, a FASTA file usually contains entries for multiple sequences. With pattern matching, the description lines can be identified and the sequence IDs extracted, allowing for the length of each sequence to be printed out separately:

```perl
#!/usr/bin/perl
$id = '';           # holds sequence
                    ID of current
                    sequence
$length = 0;        # holds length of
                    current sequence
$total_length = 0;  # tallies aggregate
                    length of all seqs
while (<>) {
    chomp;
    if (/^>(\S+)$/) { # found a new
        description line print
        "$id: $length\n" if
        $length > 0;
        $id = $1;
        $length = 0;
    } else {
        $length += length;
        $total_length += length;
    }
}
print "$id: $length\n" if $length > 0;
# last entry
print "TOTAL LENGTH = $total_length\n";
```

After initializing the three variables at the top of the program, the script enters a while loop. As before, it reads a line at a time into $_ and removes the terminating new line. The new feature is an if-else block. The block performs a pattern match on the line, looking for a FASTA description line. If one is found, it signals the beginning of a new sequence. The following then occurs:

▶ If $length is nonzero, the ID and length of the previous sequence is printed. The check on $length prevents the program from printing out an empty line when it hits the very first sequence in the file.

▶ The matched sequence ID is copied into $id.

▶ $length is set to zero.

Otherwise, the program is in the middle of a sequence, in which case the length of the current line is added to the appropriate counters. After the last line is read, the ID and length of the last sequence in the file is printed, as well as the total length of all the sequences:

```
%  fasta_length.pl ests.fasta
D28205: 1105
BCD207F: 402
BCD207R: 332
BCD386F: 192
BCD386R: 362
CDO98F: 374
TOTAL LENGTH = 2767
```

ARRAYS

Previous examples have worked with single-valued scalar variables only. However, Perl has the ability to work with multivalued variables as well. There are two basic multivalued variables, named *arrays* and *hashes*. An array is a list of data values indexed by number. A hash is a list of data values indexed by string. Both are very easy to use and are incredibly handy. To understand arrays, consider how one may keep track of a large number of identifiers, such as clone names. With scalar variables, one approach could be to assign each clone name to a different variable:

```
$clone1 = '192a8';
$clone2 = '18c10';
$clone3 = '327h1';
...
```

The problem with this approach, besides being tedious, is that it does not offer any way to step through the entire list of clones one by one, performing the same operation on each one. Arrays circumvent this problem. An array can be defined as follows:

```
@clones = ('192a8','18c10','327h1','201e4');
```

This new array, named @clones, contains four strings. Array variables begin with an @ sign to distinguish them from scalar variables, which begin with a $. Scalars and array variables are completely separate. In fact, a scalar variable can be named $clones and an array variable can be named @clones within the same program. They do not interact in any way. As alluded to above, operations can be applied to arrays as a whole. For example, the = operator can be used to copy one array into another:

```
@old_clones = @clones;
```

Items can be added to the end of an array using the push function:

```
push @clones,'281e3';
```

After this statement executes, @clones contains five items. The opposite of push is pop, which removes the last item from the array, reducing it in size by one, and returns the removed item as its result. This statement reduces @clones back to a length of four, assigning 281e3 to the scalar variable $last_clone:

```
$last_clone = pop @clones;
```

Two array operations are particularly common: accessing an arbitrary array element by its positions in the array using indexing, and looping over each element of the array in order using the foreach loop. Considering indexing first, to copy the third element of @clones into a variable named $third_clone, the statement would be written as:

```
$third_clone = $clones[2];
```

This does—and should—look strange at first. The numeral in the square brackets, [2], is the index. Perl numbers its arrays starting with zero, so the first item is actually index 0, the second item is index 1, and the third item is index 2. Any expression can be placed within the square brackets, as long as that expression ultimately evaluates to an integer. As an example, if a scalar variable $i contains a number, to address the next element in the series, it could be referred to as $clones[$i+1]. More mystifying, however, is the $ at the beginning of the array name. What happened to @clones?

When one indexes into an array, the symbol at the front refers to the individual array element, not the array as a whole. Because the element itself is a scalar, the symbol at the front should be a $. To clarify, look at the following two examples:

```
@old_clones = @clones;
$first_clone = $clones[0];
```

The first line would copy the entire array, whereas the second line copies just a single element within the array.

Arrays can be extremely long; ones with thousands of elements are not unusual. A common operation is to loop through each member of an array and do something with it. The foreach loop makes this possible. For instance, say that the array @dna contains a list of DNA sequences and that a printout of the length of each element would be helpful. The following small loop would accomplish this:

```
foreach $dna (@dna) {
    print length $dna,"\n";
}
```

The foreach loop has three parts: the name of a scalar variable known as the *loop variable*, an array name enclosed in parentheses, and a block containing the statements to be executed. Foreach steps through the array one element at a time, placing each element in the loop variable and executing the statements within the block. The statements may examine the contents of the loop variable and act on it, or even change the loop variable to change the corresponding array element. After the loop is finished, the loop variable again contains whatever it had before the loop began or is undefined if this is the only time it was used.

To illustrate how assigning to the loop variable changes the contents of the array, below is a fragment of code that treat every element of an array as a DNA sequence, replacing it with its reverse complement:

```
foreach $dna (@dna) {
    $dna = reverse $dna; # reverse it
    $dna =~ tr/gatcGATC/ctagCTAG/; #
    complement it
}
```

The two statements in the block show off a pair of Perl functions that have not yet been discussed. The first of these, reverse, returns the reverse of a scalar variable, turning GGGGTTTT into TTTTGGGG. The reversed sequence is assigned back into the loop variable. The next statement uses the tr function (for "translate") to substitute one set of characters with another. tr has an unusual syntax that is rooted in Perl's historical origins. It uses the slash as a delimiter, replacing the list of characters between the first set of delimiters with the characters in the second set. The replacement occurs on whatever variable tr is bound to using the =~ operator (the syntax should be reminiscent of pattern matching). Characters not mentioned in the list are left unchanged. In the example above, the list gatcGATC is replaced with ctagCTAG. What happens is that "g" is replaced with "c," "a" is replaced with "t," and so forth. So TTTTGGGG becomes AAAACCCC, which is the reverse complement of the original element, GGGGTTTT.

ARRAYS AND LISTS

Perl lists are closely related to arrays. Lists are a set of constants or variables enclosed in parentheses. An example of a list of strings would be ("one", "two", "buckle my shoe"), whereas an example of a list of variables would be ($a, $b, $c). A list that combines variables, constant strings, and constant numbers ay be something like ($a, "the Roman empire", 3.1415926, $ipath). Lists can be thought of as being related to array variables in the same way that the constant 123.4 may be related to the scalar variable $total.

Lists are useful for performing operations in parallel. For example, lists can be assigned to array variables to make the array identical to the list. In fact, one example of this was shown earlier:

```
@clones = ('192a8','18c10','327h1','201e4');
```

Arrays can be assigned to l lists, provided that each element of the list is a variable and is not a constant. For example, to extract the first three elements of an array, one could write:

```
($first,$second,$third) = @clones;
```

After this operation, $first contains 192a8, $second contains 18c10, and so on. Naturally enough, lists can be assigned to lists as well, again provided that the list on the left contains variables only:

```
($one,$two,$three) = (1,2,3);
```

SPLIT AND JOIN

It often is very useful to transform strings into arrays and to join the elements of arrays together into strings. The split and join functions allow for these operations. Split takes two arguments: a delimiter and a string. It splits the string at delimiter boundaries, returning an array consisting of the split elements. The delimiters themselves are discarded. To illustrate this, consider a case requiring the manipulation of a long file containing comma-delimited files, such as the following:

```
192a8,Sanger,GGGTTCCGATTTCCAA,
CCTTAGGCCAAATTAAGGCC
```

Split makes it easy to convert the long string into a more manageable array. To split on the comma, the comma is used as the delimiter:

```
chomp($line = <>);    # read the line into $line
@fields = split ',',$line;
```

@fields now contains the five individual elements, which can now be indexed or looped over. Split often is used with a list on the left side instead of an array, allowing one to go directly to assigning to the list. For example, rather than creating an array named @fields, the result of a split command can assign values to a list of named, scalar variables:

```
($clone,$laboratory,$left_oligo,
$right_oligo) = split ',',$line;
```

The join function has exactly the opposite effect of split, taking a delimiter and an array (or list) and returning a scalar containing each of the elements joined together by the delimiter. So, continuing the earlier example, the @fields array can be turned into a tab-delimited string by joining on the tab character (whose escape symbol is \t):

```
$tab_line = join "\t",@fields;
```

After this operation, `$tab_line` looks like this:

```
192a8 Sanger GGGTTCCGATTTCCAA
CCTTAGGCCAAATTAAGGCC
```

HASHES

The last Perl data type to be considered is the hash. Hashes are similar to arrays in many respects. They hold multiple values, they can be indexed, and hashes can be looped over, one element at a time. What distinguishes hashes from arrays is that the elements of a hash are unordered, and the indexes are not numbers but strings. A few examples will clarify this:

```
%oligos = ();
$oligos{'192a8'} = 'GGGTTCCGATTTCCAA';
$oligos{'18c10'} = 'CTCTCTCTAGAGAGAGCCCC';
$oligos{'327h1'} = 'GGACCTAACCTATTGGC';
```

In this example, an empty hash named `%oligos` is created, and three elements then are added to it. Each element has an index named after the clone from which it was derived and a value containing the sequence of the oligo itself. After the assignments, the values can be accessed by indexing into the hash with curly braces:

```
$s = $oligos{'192a8'};
print "oligo 192a8 is $\n";
print "oligo 192a8 is ",length $oligos
{'192a8'}," base pairs long\n";
print "oligo 18c10 is $oligos
   {'18c10'}\n";
```

This prints out:

```
oligo 192a8 is GGGTTCCGATTTCCAA
oligo 192a8 is 16 base pairs long
oligo 18c10 is CTCTCTCTAGAGAGAGCCCC
```

Just as a variable containing an integer can be used as an index into an array, a variable containing a string can be used as the index into a hash. The following example uses a loop to print out the sequence of each of the three oligos previously defined by `%oligos`:

```
foreach $clone ('327h1','192a8','18c10') {
    print "$clone: $oligos{$clone}\n";
}
```

As with arrays, there is a distinction between the hash as a whole and individual elements of a hash. When referring to an element of a hash using its index surrounded by curly braces, one is referring to the scalar value contained within the hash, so the `$` symbol must be used as a prefix. To refer to the hash variable as a whole, use the `%` symbol as the prefix. This allows for one hash to

be assigned to another, as well as the ability to perform other whole-hash operations.

For historical reasons, the indexes of a hash are called its *keys*. Calling the keys function produces a list of all the keys in the hash. Using a command of the form `@clones = keys %clones;` assigns to the array three string elements (`'327h1'`, `'192a8'`, `'18c10'`), but in no predictable order. The elements of a hash are unordered, and the order in which they are put into a hash has no effect on the order in which they are returned.

To obtain all the values of a hash, use the **values** function:

```
@oligos = values %clones;
```

The `@oligos` array now contains a three-element list consisting of each of the oligo sequences that were placed into the hash. As with keys, the values are returned in an unpredictable order. However, the order of elements retrieved by keys matches the order retrieved by values. Hence, the position of clone 192a8 in the `@clones` array matches the position of its corresponding oligo in `@oligos`.

SUMMARY

Perl has many features that obviously cannot be covered in a single book chapter. For example, subroutines allow one to define customized functions that take arguments and return a result. References allow sophisticated data structures such as lists of lists to be created. Objects allow large, complex programs to be written so that code can be reused in different contexts. Pipes and processes allow for the control of external programs, perhaps to create an automated pipeline invoking commonly used programs.

Last, but not nearly least, there are modules, which are libraries of useful code routines put together by Perl programmers around the world and made available for public use. The `Mail::Send` module is one example, but there are literally thousands more. Other modules allow for the creation of interactive, graphical front ends for programs or the creation of dynamic Web pages. Most relevant for biologists are the modules that form Bioperl, an extremely powerful collection of tools for searching biological databases, manipulating and processing sequences, and analyzing nucleotides and proteins.

WORKED EXAMPLE

At this point in the discussion, all the tools needed to solve the problem posed at the very beginning of this chapter are now at hand. The problem is approached in steps. The first task is to scan through a file of RNAi results, collecting the genes that have anything to do with locomotion. Assume that the contrived input file is named `rnai.txt`, containing lines in the following format (each field is separated by a tab):

```
Gene          Date         Status        Phenotype Summary

B0310.2       2/18/2000    complete      larval arrest
B0379.4       2/18/2000    complete      none
B0496.8       2/19/2000    incomplete
ZK899.6       2/19/2000    complete      uncoordinated, coils and kinks
ZK945.6       2/19/2000    complete      hermaphrodites sterile
M6.1          2/19/2000    complete      flaccid paralysis
...
```

The main challenge here is to search the Phenotype Summary field for results having to do with locomotion. This is a fuzzy sort of problem, best solved using Perl's pattern matching facility. After scanning through the results for a while, we decide to search for any of the following keywords: uncoordinated, paralysis, paralyzed, coils, coiler, movement, kinky, and jerky.

With this decision made, the first part of the script can be written (Figure 18.4, step 1). The script attempts to open the

```perl
#!/usr/bin/perl

# STEP 1: extract RNA inhibition data
open RNAi,"rnai.txt" or die "Couldn't open rnai.txt: $!";
%interesting_genes = ();
while (<RNAi>) {
      chomp;
      ($gene,$date,$status,$phenotype) = split "\t";
      $interesting_genes{$gene} = $phenotype
            if $phenotype =~ /uncoordinated|paraly|coil|movement|kink|jerk/;
}
close RNAi;


# STEP 2: extract protein sequence data
open WP,"WormPep.fasta" or die "Can't open WormPep: $!";
%sequences = ();
while (<WP>) {
      if (/^>(\S+)$/) { # found a new description line
            $id = $1;
      } else {
            $sequences{$id} .= $_ if $interesting_genes{$id};
      }
}
close WP;


# STEP 3: reformat for submission to SignalP
open SIGNALP,">signalP.txt" or die "Couldn't open signalP.txt: $!";
print SIGNALP "euk\n";
print SIGNALP "graphics\n";
foreach $gene (keys %sequences) {
      print SIGNALP ">$gene $interesting_genes{$gene}\n";
      print SIGNALP $sequences{$gene};
}
close SIGNALP;
```

FIGURE 18.4 This script reformats a set of neuron-related C. *elegans* genes for submission to the SignalP signal peptide prediction program.

file `rnai.txt`. If unsuccessful, it dies with an error message. If successful, it initializes the hash `%interesting_genes` to empty. This hash is used to hold the list of locomotion-related genes and is set up so that the keys are gene names and the values are the corresponding phenotypes. The program then steps through the input file, one line at a time. It chomps off the newline from the end of each line, and then uses the split function to split each line into fields, using the tab character as the delimiter. This results in a four-element list, which is assigned to an array containing the variables `$gene`, `$date`, `$status`, and `$phenotype`.

As soon as this is done, the contents of `$phenotype` are compared with a regular expression. The regular expression is a series of alternatives, separated by the | character. Any phenotype that contains any of the strings listed produces a match. Note that some of the keywords have been shortened to reduce the length of the expression, as well as to pull in some terms that may not have been anticipated. For example, `paraly` matches both `paralysis` and `paralyzed`, without much risk of matching something unintended. If the pattern matches, then the corresponding gene is recorded. By the end of the loop, `%interesting_genes` is populated with all of the genes whose phenotypes matched the target list. Because `rnai.txt` is no longer used, its filehandle is closed.

In step 2 of Figure 18.4, the WormPep set of predicted *C. elegans* proteins is stepped through, pulling out all the ones matching the collection of genes identified in step 1. WormPep's format is similar to the standard FASTA format:

```
>2L52.1 CE20433 Zinc finger, C2H2 type (CAMBRIDGE) protein_id:CAA21776.1
MSMVRNVSNQSEKLEILSCKWVGCLKSTEVFKTVEKLLDHVTADHIPEVIVNDDGSEEVV
CQWDCCEMGASRGNLQKKKEWMENHFKTRHVRKAKIFKCLIEDCPVVKSSSQEIETH...
```

The portion of the definition line (def line) that immediately follows the > is the name of the gene. The program needs to step through all of these entries, extracting the gene names and saving the sequences of those contained in the collection of interesting genes. The script begins step 2 by opening the WormPep file using a filehandle named `WP`. If successful, it initializes a hash named `%sequences`. This hash has keys corresponding to the names of the interesting genes, with values consisting of their peptide sequences. The script then enters a loop in which it retrieves each line of the WormPep file, pattern matching it against a regular expression that examines the def lines. If the program detects a def line, meaning the beginning of a new sequence, it puts the gene name into a scalar variable named `$id`, taking advantage of Perl's ability to extract parenthesized portions of regular expressions.

If the current line does not match the regular expression, then the program has hit a sequence line, with the name of the current gene being held in `$id`. The `if` statement tests whether the current gene is an element of `%interesting_genes`, and if so, the sequence is read in, growing one line at a time, until the next def line is reached. At the end of the loop, `%interesting_genes` is fully populated with the sequences of interest. Note that the new line has not been removed from the end of each line of input sequence data; in this case, it is desirable to keep the new lines, to facilitate later parts of the program.

In step 3 of Figure 18.4, the gene sequences are formatted into an E-mail message for submission to the SignalP server. The server expects E-mail submissions in the following format:

```
euk
graphics
>ID1 Comments (ignored)
MLETLCYNYLPLCEQLEPVLNVRDKEDLATSLVRVMYKHNLAKEFLCDLIMKEVEKL...
>ID2 More comments (ignored)
MPARRHLSQPAREGSLRACRSHESLLSSAHSTHMIELNEDNRLHPVHPSIFEVPNCF...
.
```

The first two lines contain information required by SignalP to process the sequences properly; here, the server is being instructed that the sequences are from a eukaryote, and that graphics of the predictions should be returned. After these flags are the sequences, in FASTA format. The sequence ID is required, and anything following it is ignored by the server. A dot follows the last sequence in the file.

The script begins step 3 by attempting to open the file `signalP.txt` for writing. If successful, it writes the top two lines of the outgoing E-mail message to the file. The program then enters a foreach loop, calling the keys function to recover all keys from the `%sequences` hash. This retrieves all of the names of all of the genes for which sequence information has been assembled.

For each gene, a description line containing the gene name and its phenotype is printed to the filehandle. Although the phenotype is ignored by SignalP, the information is retained for future reference. After this, the sequence of the gene is printed, newlines and all. At the end of the loop, the `signalP.txt` filehandle is closed. The final step in the analysis now is to take the newly created `signalP.txt` file and to send it to the SignalP server. The most useful part of this script is that it can be rerun automatically each time WormPep is updated to repeat the analysis.

Finally, just to give you a sense of the power and flexibility of Perl, take a look at Figure 18.5, which shows an alternative ending for the SignalP submission script. In this version, instead of writing the SignalP E-mail file out to disk, it submits it to the SignalP

```
# STEP 3(revised): reformat and submit to SignalP
use Mail::Send;
$msg = Mail::Send->new(Subject=> 'signalP submission',
                       To       => 'signalp@cbs.dtu.dk ');
$signalp = $msg->open;
print $signalp "euk\n";
print $signalp "graphics\n";
foreach $gene (keys %sequences) {
    print $signalp ">$gene $interesting_genes{$gene}\n";
    print $signalp $sequences{$gene};
}
close $signalp;
```

FIGURE 18.5 **Replace the section under step 3 of the previous script to send the request directly to the SignalP server without having to perform a manual mailing step.**

E-mail server directly. The results arrive in your inbox without the intermediate step of manually mailing out the request.

This variant uses an optional Perl module called Mail::Send, which provides Perl with direct access to E-mail. Perl modules are collections of useful code routines written by the worldwide community of developers and made available for free use and redistribution under the same terms as Perl itself. The Mail::Send module uses an object-oriented syntax that is beyond the scope of the chapter, but is not difficult to understand at a basic level:

1. Create a new E-mail message with the subject "signalP submission" and the recipient signalp@cbs.dtu.dk. (This is the current SignalP E-mail server address, but it may change in the future. Always check the documentation for the current address.)
2. Open the message, creating a filehandle to which to print. This filehandle is stored into the variable $signalp. When printed, instead of the text going to a disk file, it goes into the E-mail message directed to the SignalP server.
3. Print the correctly formatted request. This code is identical to what was produced previously, except that the filehandle stored in $signalp was used.
4. Close the filehandle. This completes the E-mail message and posts it.

PROBLEM SET

1. Write a script to read the file example1.fasta, one line at a time. Determine the length of each line, not counting the newline. As soon as the end of the file is reached, print out the total number of lines and the total number of characters in the file. The input file can be found on the Book's Web site.
2. Modify the script written for question 1 to examine the distribution of line lengths. The output should be a two-column list of line lengths and the number of times each line length occurred, sorted by length. (Hint: use a hash and the sort function.)
3. Once again, modify the script to present the distribution data sorted by frequency, rather than by length.
4. Using the file example1.fasta, "unwrap" the contents of the file so that each sequence is printed out as one long line. Print the identifier, followed by a tab, followed by the sequence. (Hint: read up on the input record separator $/ and on the pattern-matching operator.)

INTERNET RESOURCES

BioPerl	http://www.bioperl.org/
Comprehensive Perl Archive Network	http://www.cpan.org/
Perl home page	http://www.perl.com/

FURTHER READING

SCHWARTZ, R. L. (1998). *Learning Perl*, 2nd ed (O'Reilly & Associates Sebastopol, CA). This is the essential introduction to Perl

CHRISTIANSEN, T., AND TORKINGTON, N. (1999). *Perl Cookbook* (O'Reilly & Associates Sebastopol, CA). An extremely useful book of Perl "recipes" written by two of the foremost Perl programmers worldwide.

Appendices

▌APPENDIX 1.1. EXAMPLE OF A NUCLEOTIDE RECORD IN DDBJ FLATFILE FORMAT

```
LOCUS       DMU54469                2881 bp    DNA        linear   INV 22-FEB-1998
DEFINITION  Drosophila melanogaster eukaryotic initiation factor 4E (eIF4E)
            gene, alternative splice products, complete cds.
ACCESSION   U54469
VERSION     U54469.1
KEYWORDS    .
SOURCE      Drosophila melanogaster
  ORGANISM  Drosophila melanogaster
            Eukaryota; Metazoa; Arthropoda; Hexapoda; Insecta; Pterygota;
            Neoptera; Endopterygota; Diptera; Brachycera; Muscomorpha;
            Ephydroidea; Drosophilidae; Drosophila.
REFERENCE   1  (bases 1 to 2881)
  AUTHORS   Lavoie,C.A., Lachance,P.E., Sonenberg,N. and Lasko,P.
  TITLE     Alternatively spliced transcripts from the Drosophila eIF4E gene
            produce two different Cap-binding proteins
  JOURNAL   J. Biol. Chem. 271 (27), 16393-16398 (1996)
  MEDLINE   96279193
   PUBMED   8663200
REFERENCE   2  (bases 1 to 2881)
  AUTHORS   Lasko,P.F.
  TITLE     Direct Submission
  JOURNAL   Submitted (09-APR-1996) Paul F. Lasko, Biology, McGill University,
            1205 Avenue Docteur Penfield, Montreal, QC H3A 1B1, Canada
FEATURES             Location/Qualifiers
     source          1..2881
                     /organism="Drosophila melanogaster"
                     /mol_type="genomic DNA"
                     /db_xref="taxon:7227"
                     /chromosome="3"
                     /map="67A8-B2"
     gene            80..2881
                     /gene="eIF4E"
     mRNA            join(80..224,892..1458,1550..1920,1986..2085,2317..2404,
                     2466..2881)
```

```
                    /gene="eIF4E"
                    /product="eukaryotic initiation factor 4E-I"
      mRNA          join(80..224,1129..1458,1550..1920,1986..2085,2317..2404,
                    2466..2881)
                    /gene="eIF4E"
                    /product="eukaryotic initiation factor 4E-I"
      mRNA          join(80..224,1550..1920,1986..2085,2317..2404,2466..2881)
                    /gene="eIF4E"
                    /product="eukaryotic initiation factor 4E-II"
      CDS           join(201..224,1550..1920,1986..2085,2317..2404,2466..2629)
                    /gene="eIF4E"
                    /note="Method: conceptual translation with partial peptide
                    sequencing"
                    /codon_start=1
                    /product="eukaryotic initiation factor 4E-II"
                    /protein_id="AAC03524.1"
                    /db_xref="GI:1322284"
                    /translation="MVVLETEKTSAPSTEQGRPEPPTSAAAPAEAKDVKPKEDPQETG
                    EPAGNTATTTAPAGDDAVRTEHLYKHPLMNVWTLWYLENDRSKSWEDMQNEITSFDTV
                    EDFWSLYNHIKPPSEIKLGSDYSLFKKNIRPMWEDAANKQGGRWVITLNKSSKTDLDN
                    LWLDVLLCLIGEAFDHSDQICGAVINIRGKSNKISIWTADGNNEEAALEIGHKLRDAL
                    RLGRNNSLQYQLHKDTMVKQGSNVKSIYTL"
      CDS           join(1402..1458,1550..1920,1986..2085,2317..2404,2466..2629)
                    /gene="eIF4E"
                    /note="Method: conceptual translation with partial peptide
                    sequencing; two alternatively spliced transcripts both
                    encode 4E-I"
                    /codon_start=1
                    /product="eukaryotic initiation factor 4E-I"
                    /protein_id="AAC03525.1"
                    /db_xref="GI:1322285"
                    /translation="MQSDFHRMKNFANPKSMFKTSAPSTEQGRPEPPTSAAAPAEAKD
                    VKPKEDPQETGEPAGNTATTTAPAGDDAVRTEHLYKHPLMNVWTLWYLENDRSKSWED
                    MQNEITSFDTVEDFWSLYNHIKPPSEIKLGSDYSLFKKNIRPMWEDAANKQGGRWVIT
                    LNKSSKTDLDNLWLDVLLCLIGEAFDHSDQICGAVINIRGKSNKISIWTADGNNEEAA
                    LEIGHKLRDALRLGRNNSLQYQLHKDTMVKQGSNVKSIYTL"
BASE COUNT          849 a        699 c        585 g        748 t
ORIGIN
        1 cggttgcttg ggttttataa catcagtcag tgacaggcat ttccagagtt gccctgttca
       61 acaatcgata gctgcctttg gccaccaaaa tcccaaactt aattaaagaa ttaaataatt
      121 cgaataataa ttaagcccag taacctacgc agcttgagtg cgtaaccgat atctagtata
      181 catttcgata catcgaaatc atggtagtgt tggagacgga gaaggtaaga cgatgataga
      241 cggcgagccg catgggttcg atttgcgctg agccgtggca gggaacaaca aaaacagggt
      301 tgttgcacaa gagggggggc gatagtcgag cggaaaagag tgcagttggc gtggctacat
      361 catcattgtg ttcaccgatt attttttgca caattgctta atattaattg tacttgcacg
      421 ctattgtcta cgtcatagct atcgctcatc tctgtctgtc tctatcaagc tatctctctt
      481 tcgcggtcac tcgttctctt ttttctctcc tttcgcattt gcatacgcat accacacgtt
      541 ttcagtgttc tcgctctctc tctcttgtca agacatcgcg cgcgtgtgtg tgggtgtgtc
      601 tctagcacat atacataaat aggagagcgg agagacaaat atggaaagaa tgaaaaagag
      661 tgaattactg caattaacca gtcgcgaaca gttaaatcat attttttgtcg gccattgcag
      721 taaataaacc gttggctttc cctccttcac tttccacctc ctttcttgac gttaattttt
      781 tcagttaatc gcgccgctgc tttgaactcg aacacgaatt ttagccgcaa cataaaataa
      841 aatcaagtaa ctctttaact caatataaaa caacaatcca atcttcaaca ggcaatctgt
      901 gttttatgt cagatacgag cgcgtgtgtg tgtgtgctgt aattccatcg cccctttcga
      961 ttccgagttc gttaggaaca gcattagttc gcctatttta gtagtagcct agtccgattt
     1021 taagtgaaac aggacactcc aacaccatat acgcaataat tagttaccac ccactcaacc
     1081 atacagcaac aacaagttta acgagttttt tgtattatca ttacttagtt ttttggttaa
     1141 taatacaaca agtgaagagc gaactgcagg ggagcgagga tatcacgaaa caatccaaaa
     1201 tccacacaca ctcaaacaga aatcaaaagc ttcgctctct cgcacacaca cgcaccaacc
```

```
1261 aactatcaac tatcacaaac accgcgacag agagagagcg gcaagtgaat cacggcgaat
1321 cgaaaccgat ccgaacccac tccggagccg aaaaagaact gatcctacca tcaaacgcat
1381 ccaataaaca cggccgccaa catgcagagc gactttcaca gaatgaagaa ctttgccaat
1441 cccaagtcca tgttcaaagt aatactctca gtgcgcctgt cgctaagcca agccaagcta
1501 atctaatctt ctgattcccc ttcccatcca ttgccatctt ctcccgcaga ccagcgcccc
1561 cagcaccgag cagggtcgtc cggaaccacc aacttcggct gcagcgcccg ccgaggctaa
1621 ggatgtcaag cccaaggagg acccacagga gactggtgaa ccagcaggca acactgcaac
1681 cactactgct cctgccggcg acgatgctgt gcgcaccgag catttataca aacacccgct
1741 catgaatgtc tggacgctgt ggtaccttga aaacgatcgg tccaagtcct gggaggacat
1801 gcaaaacgag atcaccagct tcgataccgt cgaggacttc tggagcctat acaaccacat
1861 caagccccca tcagagatca agctgggtag tgactactcg ctattcaaga agaacattcg
1921 gtgggtttgc tgtttattg caatttctac caagataacc tttactaact gatatctcat
1981 tgcagtccca tgtgggagga tgcagccaac aaacagggcg gtcgttgggt cattacccctt
2041 aacaaaagct ccaagaccga tctggataac ctatggctcg atgtggtaag tgcacaaaga
2101 acgagtggtt agaggatgtc tattatagtg aatgtacatt cttgaaatgc aaaaatatag
2161 aaataggtgt atgatttgc agtataaatt ataacttata gaaaatatca gctaaaaata
2221 cgctagtgtt agcttttgtc ttaggaacat tcaatagtga gcttatatca taaatatctt
2281 tcgcatatga gtaactacaa ctgttttgcc ttccagctgc tctgcctgat tggcgaggcc
2341 ttcgatcact ccgatcagat ctgcggcgct gttataaaca ttcgcggcaa gagcaacaag
2401 atatgtaagt tttcacgcac acccaacttc agcggaattc ctttgtttaa cattaatctt
2461 tccagccatc tggactgccg acggaaacaa cgaggaagct gcccttgaga ttggtcacaa
2521 gctgcgcgat gccttgcgtc tgggacgcaa caactcgctg cagtatcagt tgcacaagga
2581 cacgatggtc aagcagggct ccaacgtgaa atcgatctac actttgtagg cggctaataa
2641 ctggccgctc cttactcggt ccgatcccac acagattagt ttgtctttca tttatttatc
2701 gttataagca acagtagcga ttaatcgtga ctattgtcta agacccgcgt aacgaaaccg
2761 aaacggaacc ccctttgtta tcaaaaatcg gcataatata aaatctatcc gctttttgta
2821 gtcactgtca ataatggatt agacggaaaa gtatattaat aaaaacctac attaaaaccg
2881 g
//
```

▌APPENDIX 1.2. EXAMPLE OF A NUCLEOTIDE RECORD IN GENBANK FLATFILE FORMAT

```
REFERENCE   1  (bases 1 to 2881)
  AUTHORS   Lavoie,C.A., Lachance,P.E., Sonenberg,N. and Lasko,P.
  TITLE     Alternatively spliced transcripts from the Drosophila eIF4E gene
            produce two different Cap-binding proteins
  JOURNAL   J. Biol. Chem. 271 (27), 16393-16398 (1996)
  MEDLINE   96279193
   PUBMED   8663200
REFERENCE   2  (bases 1 to 2881)
  AUTHORS   Lasko,P.F.
  TITLE     Direct Submission
  JOURNAL   Submitted (09-APR-1996) Paul F. Lasko, Biology, McGill University,
            1205 Avenue Docteur Penfield, Montreal, QC H3A 1B1, Canada
FEATURES             Location/Qualifiers
     source          1..2881
                     /organism="Drosophila melanogaster"
                     /mol_type="genomic DNA"
                     /db_xref="taxon:7227"
                     /chromosome="3"
                     /map="67A8-B2"
     gene            80..2881
                     /gene="eIF4E"
     mRNA            join(80..224,892..1458,1550..1920,1986..2085,2317..2404,
                     2466..2881)
                     /gene="eIF4E"
                     /product="eukaryotic initiation factor 4E-I"
```

```
mRNA                join(80..224,1129..1458,1550..1920,1986..2085,2317..2404,
                    2466..2881)
                    /gene="eIF4E"
                    /product="eukaryotic initiation factor 4E-I"
mRNA                join(80..224,1550..1920,1986..2085,2317..2404,2466..2881)
                    /gene="eIF4E"
                    /product="eukaryotic initiation factor 4E-II"
CDS                 join(201..224,1550..1920,1986..2085,2317..2404,2466..2629)
                    /gene="eIF4E"
                    /note="Method: conceptual translation with partial peptide
                    sequencing"
                    /codon_start=1
                    /product="eukaryotic initiation factor 4E-II"
                    /protein_id="AAC03524.1"
                    /db_xref="GI:1322284"
                    /translation="MVVLETEKTSAPSTEQGRPEPPTSAAAPAEAKDVKPKEDPQETG
                    EPAGNTATTTAPAGDDAVRTEHLYKHPLMNVWTLWYLENDRSKSWEDMQNEITSFDTV
                    EDFWSLYNHIKPPSEIKLGSDYSLFKKNIRPMWEDAANKQGGRWVITLNKSSKTDLDN
                    LWLDVLLCLIGEAFDHSDQICGAVINIRGKSNKISIWTADGNNEEAALEIGHKLRDAL
                    RLGRNNSLQYQLHKDTMVKQGSNVKSIYTL"
CDS                 join(1402..1458,1550..1920,1986..2085,2317..2404,
                    2466..2629)
                    /gene="eIF4E"
                    /note="Method: conceptual translation with partial peptide
                    sequencing; two alternatively spliced transcripts both
                    encode 4E-I"
                    /codon_start=1
                    /product="eukaryotic initiation factor 4E-I"
                    /protein_id="AAC03525.1"
                    /db_xref="GI:1322285"
                    /translation="MQSDFHRMKNFANPKSMFKTSAPSTEQGRPEPPTSAAAPAEAKD
                    VKPKEDPQETGEPAGNTATTTAPAGDDAVRTEHLYKHPLMNVWTLWYLENDRSKSWED
                    MQNEITSFDTVEDFWSLYNHIKPPSEIKLGSDYSLFKKNIRPMWEDAANKQGGRWVIT
                    LNKSSKTDLDNLWLDVLLCLIGEAFDHSDQICGAVINIRGKSNKISIWTADGNNEEAA
                    LEIGHKLRDALRLGRNNSLQYQLHKDTMVKQGSNVKSIYTL"
ORIGIN
        1 cggttgcttg ggttttataa catcagtcag tgacaggcat ttccagagtt gccctgttca
       61 acaatcgata gctgcctttg gccaccaaaa tcccaaactt aattaaagaa ttaaataatt
      121 cgaataataa ttaagcccag taacctacgc agcttgagtg cgtaaccgat atctagtata
      181 catttcgata catcgaaatc atggtagtgt tggagacgga gaaggtaaga cgatgataga
      241 cggcgagccg catgggttcg atttgcgctg agccgtggca gggaacaaca aaaacagggt
      301 tgttgcacaa gaggggaggc gatagtcgag cggaaaagag tgcagttggc gtggctacat
      361 catcattgtg ttcaccgatt attttttgca caattgctta atattaattg tacttgcacg
      421 ctattgtcta cgtcatagct atcgctcatc tctgtctgtc tctatcaagc tatctctctt
      481 tcgcggtcac tcgttctctt ttttctctcc tttcgcattt gcatacgcat accacacgtt
      541 ttcagtgttc tcgctctctc tcttgtca agacatcgcg cgcgtgtgtg tgggtgtgtc
      601 tctagcacat atacataaat aggagagcgg agagacaaat atggaaagaa tgaaaaagag
      661 tgaattactg caattaacca gtcgcgaaca gttaaatcat attttgtcg gccattgcag
      721 taaataaacc gttggctttc cctccttcac tttccacctc ctttcttgac gttaattttt
      781 tcagttaatc gcgccgctgc tttgaactcg aacacgaatt ttagccgcaa cataaaataa
      841 aatcaagtaa ctctttaact caatataaaa caacaatcca atcttcaaca ggcaatctgt
      901 gtttttatgt cagatacgag cgcgtgtgtg tgtgtgctgt aattccatcg cccctttcga
      961 ttccgagttc gttaggaaca gcattagttc gcctatttta gtagtagcct agtccgattt
     1021 taagtgaaac aggacactcc aacaccatat acgcaataat tagttaccac ccactcaacc
     1081 atacagcaac aacaagttta acgagttttt tgtattatca ttacttagtt ttttggttaa
     1141 taatacaaca agtgaagagc gaactgcagg ggagcgagga tatcacgaaa caatccaaaa
     1201 tccacacaca ctcaaacaga aatcaaaagc ttcgctctct cgcacacaca cgcaccaacc
     1261 aactatcaac tatcacaaac accgcgacag agagagagcg gcaagtgaat cacggcgaat
```

```
1321 cgaaaccgat ccgaacccac tccggagccg aaaaagaact gatcctacca tcaaacgcat
1381 ccaataaaca cggccgccaa catgcagagc gactttcaca gaatgaagaa ctttgccaat
1441 cccaagtcca tgttcaaagt aatactctca gtgcgcctgt cgctaagcca agccaagcta
1501 atctaatctt ctgattcccc ttcccatcca ttgccatctt ctcccgcaga ccagcgcccc
1561 cagcaccgag cagggtcgtc cggaaccacc aacttcggct gcagcgcccg ccgaggctaa
1621 ggatgtcaag cccaaggagg acccacagga gactggtgaa ccagcaggca acactgcaac
1681 cactactgct cctgccggcg acgatgctgt gcgcaccgag catttataca aacacccgct
1741 catgaatgtc tggacgctgt ggtaccttga aaacgatcgg tccaagtcct gggaggacat
1801 gcaaacgag atcaccagct tcgataccgt cgaggacttc tggagcctat acaaccacat
1861 caagccccca tcagagatca agctgggtag tgactactcg ctattcaaga gaacattcg
1921 gtgggtttgc tgttttattg caatttctac caagataacc tttactaact gatatctcat
1981 tgcagtccca tgtgggagga tgcagccaac aaacagggcg gtcgttgggt cattacccttt
2041 aacaaaagct ccaagaccga tctggataac ctatggctcg atgtggtaag tgcacaaaga
2101 acgagtggtt agaggatgtc tattatagtg aatgtacatt cttgaaatgc aaaaatatag
2161 aaataggtgt atgattttgc agtataaatt ataacttata gaaaatatca gctaaaaata
2221 cgctagtgtt agcttttgtc ttaggaacat tcaatagtga gcttatatca taaatatctt
2281 tcgcatatga gtaactacaa ctgtttttgcc ttccagctgc tctgcctgat tggcgaggcc
2341 ttcgatcact ccgatcagat ctgcggcgct gttataaaca ttcgcggcaa gagcaacaag
2401 atatgtaagt tttcacgcac acccaacttc agcggaattc ctttgtttaa cattaatctt
2461 tccagccatc tggactgccg acggaaacaa cgaggaagct gcccttgaga ttggtcacaa
2521 gctgcgcgat gccttgcgtc tgggacgcaa caactcgctg cagtatcagt tgcacaagga
2581 cacgatggtc aagcagggct ccaacgtgaa atcgatctac actttgtagg cggctaataa
2641 ctggccgctc cttactcggt ccgatcccac acagattagt ttgtctttca tttatttatc
2701 gttataagca acagtagcga ttaatcgtga ctattgtcta agacccgcgt aacgaaaccg
2761 aaacggaacc ccctttgtta tcaaaaatcg gcataatata aaatctatcc gcttttttgta
2821 gtcactgtca ataatggatt agacggaaaa gtatattaat aaaaacctac attaaaaccg
2881 g
//
```

▌APPENDIX 1.3. EXAMPLE OF A NUCLEOTIDE RECORD IN EMBL FLATFILE FORMAT

```
ID   DM54469      standard; genomic DNA; INV; 2881 BP.
XX
AC   U54469;
XX
SV   U54469.1
XX
DT   19-MAY-1996 (Rel. 47, Created)
DT   04-MAR-2000 (Rel. 63, Last updated, Version 3)
XX
DE   Drosophila melanogaster eukaryotic initiation factor 4E (eIF4E) gene,
DE   alternative splice products, complete cds.
XX
KW   .
XX
OS   Drosophila melanogaster (fruit fly)
OC   Eukaryota; Metazoa; Arthropoda; Hexapoda; Insecta; Pterygota; Neoptera;
OC   Endopterygota; Diptera; Brachycera; Muscomorpha; Ephydroidea;
OC   Drosophilidae; Drosophila.
XX
RN   [1]
RP   1-2881
RX   MEDLINE; 96279193.
RX   PUBMED; 8663200.
RA   Lavoie C.A., Lachance P.E.D., Sonenberg N., Lasko P.;
RT   "Alternatively spliced transcripts from the Drosophila eIF4E gene produce
RT   two different Cap-binding proteins";
RL   J. Biol. Chem. 271(27):16393-16398(1996).
```

```
XX
RN   [2]
RP   1-2881
RA   Lasko P.F.;
RT   ;
RL   Submitted (09-APR-1996) to the EMBL/GenBank/DDBJ databases.
RL   Paul F. Lasko, Biology, McGill University, 1205 Avenue Docteur Penfield,
RL   Montreal, QC H3A 1B1, Canada
XX
DR   FLYBASE; FBgn0015218; eIF-4E.
DR   GOA; P48598.
DR   Swiss-Prot; P48598; IF4E_DROME.
XX
FH   Key             Location/Qualifiers
FH
FT   source          1..2881
FT                   /chromosome="3"
FT                   /db_xref="taxon:7227"
FT                   /mol_type="genomic DNA"
FT                   /organism="Drosophila melanogaster"
FT                   /map="67A8-B2"
FT   mRNA            join(80..224,1129..1458,1550..1920,1986..2085,2317..2404,
FT                   2466..2881)
FT                   /product="eukaryotic initiation factor 4E-I"
FT                   /gene="Eif4E"
FT   mRNA            join(80..224,892..1458,1550..1920,1986..2085,2317..2404,
FT                   2466..2881)
FT                   /product="eukaryotic initiation factor 4E-I"
FT                   /gene="Eif4E"
FT   mRNA            join(80..224,1550..1920,1986..2085,2317..2404,2466..2881)
FT                   /product="eukaryotic initiation factor 4E-II"
FT                   /gene="Eif4E"
FT   CDS             join(201..224,1550..1920,1986..2085,2317..2404,2466..2629)
FT                   /codon_start=1
FT                   /db_xref="FLYBASE:FBgn0015218"
FT                   /db_xref="GOA:P48598"
FT                   /db_xref="Swiss-Prot:P48598"
FT                   /note="Method: conceptual translation with partial peptide
FT                   sequencing."
FT                   /product="eukaryotic initiation factor 4E-II"
FT                   /gene="Eif4E"
FT                   /protein_id="AAC03524.1"
FT                   /translation="MVVLETEKTSAPSTEQGRPEPPTSAAAPAEAKDVKPKEDPQETGE
FT                   PAGNTATTTAPAGDDAVRTEHLYKHPLMNVWTLWYLENDRSKSWEDMQNEITSFDTVED
FT                   FWSLYNHIKPPSEIKLGSDYSLFKKNIRPMWEDAANKQGGRWVITLNKSSKTDLDNLWL
FT                   DVLLCLIGEAFDHSDQICGAVINIRGKSNKISIWTADGNNEEAALEIGHKLRDALRLGR
FT                   NNSLQYQLHKDTMVKQGSNVKSIYTL"
FT   CDS             join(1402..1458,1550..1920,1986..2085,2317..2404,
FT                   2466..2629)
FT                   /codon_start=1
FT                   /db_xref="FLYBASE:FBgn0015218"
FT                   /db_xref="GOA:P48598"
FT                   /db_xref="Swiss-Prot:P48598"
FT                   /note="Method: conceptual translation with partial peptide
FT                   sequencing; two alternatively spliced transcripts both
FT                   encode 4E-I"
FT                   /product="eukaryotic initiation factor 4E-I"
```

```
FT                         /gene="Eif4E"
FT                         /protein_id="AAC03525.1"
FT                         /translation="MQSDFHRMKNFANPKSMFKTSAPSTEQGRPEPPTSAAAPAEAKDV
FT                         KPKEDPQETGEPAGNTATTTAPAGDDAVRTEHLYKHPLMNVWTLWYLENDRSKSWEDMQ
FT                         NEITSFDTVEDFWSLYNHIKPPSEIKLGSDYSLFKKNIRPMWEDAANKQGGRWVITLNK
FT                         SSKTDLDNLWLDVLLCLIGEAFDHSDQICGAVINIRGKSNKISIWTADGNNEEAALEIG
FT                         HKLRDALRLGRNNSLQYQLHKDTMVKQGSNVKSIYTL"
XX
SQ      Sequence 2881 BP; 849 A; 699 C; 585 G; 748 T; 0 other;
     cggttgcttg ggttttataa catcagtcag tgacaggcat ttccagagtt gccctgttca        60
     acaatcgata gctgcctttg gccaccaaaa tcccaaactt aattaaagaa ttaaataatt       120
     cgaataataa ttaagcccag taacctacgc agcttgagtg cgtaaccgat atctagtata       180
     catttcgata catcgaaatc atggtagtgt tggagacgga gaaggtaaga cgatgataga       240
     cggcgagccg catgggttcg atttgcgctg agccgtggca gggaacaaca aaaacagggt       300
     tgttgcacaa gaggggaggc gatagtcgag cggaaaagag tgcagttggc gtggctacat       360
     catcattgtg ttcaccgatt attttttgca caattgctta atattaattg tacttgcacg       420
     ctattgtcta cgtcatagct atcgctcatc tctgtctgtc tctatcaagc tatctctctt       480
     tcgcggtcac tcgttctctt ttttctctcc tttcgcattt gcatacgcat accacacgtt       540
     ttcagtgttc tcgctctctc tctcttgtca agacatcgcg cgcgtgtgtg tgggtgtgtc       600
     tctagcacat atacataaat aggagagcgg agagacaaat atggaaagaa tgaaaaagag       660
     tgaattactg caattaacca gtcgcgaaca gttaaatcat attttgtcg gccattgcag        720
     taaataaacc gttggctttc cctccttcac tttccacctc ctttcttgac gttaattttt       780
     tcagttaatc gcgccgctgc tttgaactcg aacacgaatt ttagccgcaa cataaaataa       840
     aatcaagtaa ctctttaact caatataaaa caacaatcca atcttcaaca ggcaatctgt       900
     gttttatgt cagatacgag cgcgtgtgtg tgtgtgctgt aattccatcg cccctttcga        960
     ttccgagttc gttaggaaca gcattagttc gcctatttta gtagtagcct agtccgattt      1020
     taagtgaaac aggacactcc aacaccatat acgcaataat tagttaccac ccactcaacc      1080
     atacagcaac aacaagttta acgagttttt tgtattatca ttacttagtt ttttggttaa      1140
     taatacaaca agtgaagagc gaactgcagg ggagcgagga tatcacgaaa caatccaaaa      1200
     tccacacaca ctcaaacaga aatcaaaagc ttcgctctct cgcacacaca cgcaccaacc      1260
     aactatcaac tatcacaaac accgcgacag agagagagcg gcaagtgaat cacggcgaat      1320
     cgaaaccgat ccgaacccac tccggagccg aaaaagaact gatcctacca tcaaacgcat      1380
     ccaataaaca cggccgccaa catgcagagc gactttcaca gaatgaagaa ctttgccaat      1440
     cccaagtcca tgttcaaagt aatactctca gtgcgcctgt cgctaagcca agccaagcta      1500
     atctaatctt ctgattcccc ttcccatcca ttgccatctt ctcccgcaga ccagcgcccc      1560
     cagcaccgag cagggtcgtc cggaaccacc aacttcggct gcagcgcccg ccgaggctaa      1620
     ggatgtcaag cccaaggagg acccacagga gactggtgaa ccagcaggca acactgcaac      1680
     cactactgct cctgccggcg acgatgctgt gcgcaccgag catttataca aacacccgct      1740
     catgaatgtc tggacgctgt ggtaccttga aaacgatcgg tccaagtcct gggaggacat      1800
     gcaaaacgag atcaccagct tcgataccgt cgaggacttc tggagcctat acaaccacat      1860
     caagcccca tcagagatca agctgggtag tgactactcg ctattcaaga gaacattcg       1920
     gtgggtttgc tgtttttattg caatttctac caagataacc tttactaact gatatctcat     1980
     tgcagtccca tgtgggagga tgcagccaac aaacagggcg gtcgttgggt cattaccctt      2040
     aacaaaagct ccaagaccga tctggataac ctatggctcg atgtggtaag tgcacaaaga      2100
     acgagtggtt agaggatgtc tattatagtg aatgtacatt cttgaaatgc aaaaatatag      2160
     aaataggtgt atgattttgc agtataaatt ataacttata gaaaatatca gctaaaaata      2220
     cgctagtgtt agcttttgtc ttaggaacat tcaatagtga gcttatatca taaatatctt      2280
     tcgcatatga gtaactacaa ctgttttgcc ttccagctgc tctgcctgat tggcgaggcc      2340
     ttcgatcact ccgatcagat ctgcggcgct gttataaaca ttcgcggcaa gagcaacaag      2400
     atatgtaagt tttcacgcac acccaacttc agcggaattc ctttgtttaa cattaatctt      2460
     tccagccatc tggactgccg acggaaacaa cgaggaagct gcccttgaga ttggtcacaa      2520
     gctgcgcgat gccttgcgtc tgggacgcaa caactcgctg cagtatcagt tgcacaagga      2580
     cacgatggtc aagcagggct ccaacgtgaa atcgatctac actttgtagg cggctaataa      2640
     ctggccgctc cttactcggt ccgatcccac acagattagt ttgtctttca tttatttatc      2700
     gttataagca acagtagcga ttaatcgtga ctattgtcta agacccgcgt aacgaaaccg      2760
     aaacggaacc ccctttgtta tcaaaaatcg gcataatata aaatctatcc gcttttttgta     2820
     gtcactgtca ataatggatt agacggaaaa gtatattaat aaaaacctac attaaaaccg      2880
     g                                                                     2881
//
```

APPENDIX 1.4. INITIAL PORTION OF AN EMBL GENOME REVIEWS RECORD

```
ID   U00089_GR   standard; circular genomic DNA; GRV; 816394 BP.
XX
AC   U00089_GR;
XX
SV   U00089_GR.2
XX
DT   18-FEB-2004 (Rel. 0.1, Created)
DT   15-MAR-2004 (Rel. 0.3, Last updated, Version 3)
XX
DE   Mycoplasma pneumoniae ATCC 29342 / M129 chromosome, complete sequence.
XX
KW   complete genome; genome reviews.
XX
OS   Mycoplasma pneumoniae ATCC 29342 / M129
OC   Bacteria; Firmicutes; Mollicutes; Mycoplasmataceae; Mycoplasma.
XX
RN   [1]
RX   PUBMED; 8948633.
RA   Himmelreich R., Hilbert H., Plagens H., Pirkl E., Li B.-C., Herrmann R.
RT   "Complete sequence analysis of the genome of the bacterium Mycoplasma
RT   pneumoniae.";
RL   Nucleic Acids Res. 24:4420-4449(1996).
XX
RN   [2]
RX   PUBMED; 10954595.
RA   Dandekar T., Huynen M., Regula J.T., Ueberle B., Zimmermann C.U., Andrade
RA   M.A., Doerks T., Sanchez-Pulido L., Snel B., Suyama M., Yuan Y.P.,
RA   Herrmann R., Bork P.
RT   "Re-annotating the Mycoplasma pneumoniae genome sequence: adding value,
RT   function and reading frames.";
RL   Nucleic Acids Res. 28:3278-3288(2000).
XX
CC   This Genome Reviews entry was created from entry U00089.2 in the
CC   EMBL/GenBank/DDBJ databases on March 15, 2004.
XX
FH   Key             Location/Qualifiers
FH
FT   source          1..816394
FT                   /chromosome="Chromosome"
FT                   /organism="Mycoplasma pneumoniae"
FT                   /strain="ATCC 29342 = M129"
FT                   /mol_type="genomic DNA"
FT                   /db_xref="taxon:2104"
FT   CDS             692..1834
FT                   /codon_start=1
FT                   /gene="dnaN {Swiss-Prot:Q50313}"
FT                   /synonym="MP153 {Swiss-Prot:Q50313}"
FT                   /locus_tag="MPN001 {Swiss-Prot:Q50313}"
FT                   /product="DNA polymerase III, beta chain
FT                   {Swiss-Prot:Q50313}"
FT                   /EC_number="2.7.7.7 {Swiss-Prot:Q50313}"
FT                   /function="DNA binding {GO:0003677}"
FT                   /function="DNA-directed DNA polymerase activity
FT                   {GO:0003887}"
FT                   /function="3'-5'-exonuclease activity {GO:0008408}"
FT                   /process="DNA replication {GO:0006260}"
```

```
FT                         /protein_id="AAG34739.1"
FT                         /db_xref="EMBL:AAC43645.1 {Swiss-Prot:Q50313}"
FT                         /db_xref="GO:0003677 {GOA:IEA,InterPro,IPR001001}"
FT                         /db_xref="GO:0003887 {GOA:IEA,InterPro,IPR001001;
FT                         GOA:IEA,Swiss-Prot,Q50313; GOA:IEA,Swiss-Prot,Q50313}"
FT                         /db_xref="GO:0006260 {GOA:IEA,InterPro,IPR001001;
FT                         GOA:IEA,Swiss-Prot,Q50313}"
FT                         /db_xref="GO:0008408 {GOA:IEA,InterPro,IPR001001}"
FT                         /db_xref="InterPro:IPR001001 {Swiss-Prot:Q50313}"
FT                         /db_xref="Swiss-Prot:Q50313 {EMBL:U00089}"
FT                         /db_xref="UniParc:UPI0000129701 {UniParc}"
FT                         /transl_table=4
FT                         /translation="MKVLINKNELNKILKKLNNVIVSNNKMKPYHSYLLIEATEKEINF
FT                         YANNEYFSAKCTLAENIDVLEEGEVIVKGKIFSELINGIKEDIITIQEKDQTLLVKTKK
FT                         TNINLNTIDKKEFPRIRFNQNVDLKEFDELKIQHSLLTKGLKKIAHAVSTFRESTRKFN
FT                         GVNFNGSNGKQIFLEASDSYKLSVYEIKQKTDPFNFIVETNLLSFINSFNPEGGDLISI
FT                         FFRKEHKDDLSTELLIKLDNFLINYTSINESFPRVMQLFDFEPETKVTIQKNELKDALQ
FT                         RILTLAQNERFFLCDMQVTNSHLKINSNVQNIGASLEEVTCLKFEGHKLNIAVNALSLL
FT                         EHIDSFDTDEIELYFQGSNKYFLISSNNEPELKEILVPSK"
FT      CDS                1838..2767
FT                         /codon_start=1
FT                         /gene="MP152 {Swiss-Prot:Q50312}"
FT                         /locus_tag="MPN002 {Swiss-Prot:Q50312}"
FT                         /product="DnaJ-like protein MG002 homolog
FT                         {Swiss-Prot:Q50312}"
FT                         /function="chaperone activity {GO:0003754}"
FT                         /process="protein folding {GO:0006457}"
FT                         /protein_id="AAG34740.1"
FT                         /db_xref="EMBL:AAC43644.1 {Swiss-Prot:Q50312}"
FT                         /db_xref="GO:0003754 {GOA:IEA,InterPro,IPR003095;
FT                         GOA:IEA,Swiss-Prot,Q50312}"
FT                         /db_xref="GO:0006457 {GOA:IEA,InterPro,IPR003095}"
FT                         /db_xref="HSSP:P08622 {Swiss-Prot:Q50312}"
FT                         /db_xref="InterPro:IPR001623 {Swiss-Prot:Q50312}"
FT                         /db_xref="InterPro:IPR003095 {Swiss-Prot:Q50312}"
FT                         /db_xref="InterPro:IPR008971 {Swiss-Prot:Q50312}"
FT                         /db_xref="Swiss-Prot:Q50312 {EMBL:U00089}"
FT                         /db_xref="UniParc:UPI000012964D {UniParc}"
FT                         /transl_table=4
FT                         /translation="MTLYDLLELPQTATLQEIKTAYKRLAKRYHPDINKQGADTFVKIN
FT                         NAYAVLSDTTQKAEYDAMLRFSEFEDRVKRLDFSIKWHEQFMEELQFHHNWDFDFIRNR
FT                         EYTQPTPTNNKYSSFLDKDVSLAFYQLYSKGKLDFDLEDTLLRRHSIKQAFLKGKKLND
FT                         VLKEQYNYLGWLEAKRYFNIDVEIELTPKEVREGGVVNLPLKIKVISNNYPGQMWYELN
FT                         KNYSFRLLWDIKNGEVAEFFGKGNRALGWRGDLIVRMRIVDKIKKRLRIFSSHFEQDKT
FT                         KLWFLVPQDKQDNPNKWVFDYKTHEFIV"
FT      CDS                2869..4821
FT                         /codon_start=1
FT                         /gene="gyrB {Swiss-Prot:P22447}"
FT                         /synonym="MP151 {Swiss-Prot:P22447}"
FT                         /locus_tag="MPN003 {Swiss-Prot:P22447}"
FT                         /product="DNA gyrase subunit B {Swiss-Prot:P22447}"
FT                         /EC_number="5.99.1.3 {Swiss-Prot:P22447}"
FT                         /function="DNA binding {GO:0003677}"
FT                         /function="DNA topoisomerase (ATP-hydrolyzing) activity
FT                         {GO:0003918}"
FT                         /function="ATP binding {GO:0005524}"
FT                         /process="DNA topological change {GO:0006265}"
FT                         /process="DNA modification {GO:0006304}"
```

```
FT                      /protein_id="AAB95799.1"
FT                      /db_xref="EMBL:AAC43643.1 {Swiss-Prot:P22447}"
FT                      /db_xref="EMBL:CAA37622.1 {Swiss-Prot:P22447}"
FT                      /db_xref="GO:0003677 {GOA:IEA,InterPro,IPR000565;
FT                      GOA:IEA,InterPro,IPR001241; GOA:IEA,InterPro,IPR002288;
FT                      GOA:IEA,InterPro,IPR002936}"
FT                      /db_xref="GO:0003918 {GOA:IEA,InterPro,IPR000565;
FT                      GOA:IEA,InterPro,IPR001241; GOA:IEA,InterPro,IPR002288;
FT                      GOA:IEA,Swiss-Prot,P22447}"
FT                      /db_xref="GO:0005524 {GOA:IEA,InterPro,IPR000565;
FT                      GOA:IEA,InterPro,IPR001241; GOA:IEA,InterPro,IPR002288;
FT                      GOA:IEA,InterPro,IPR003594; GOA:IEA,Swiss-Prot,P22447}"
FT                      /db_xref="GO:0006265 {GOA:IEA,InterPro,IPR000565;
FT                      GOA:IEA,InterPro,IPR001241; GOA:IEA,InterPro,IPR002288}"
FT                      /db_xref="GO:0006304 {GOA:IEA,InterPro,IPR002936}"
FT                      /db_xref="HSSP:P06982 {Swiss-Prot:P22447}"
FT                      /db_xref="InterPro:IPR000565 {Swiss-Prot:P22447}"
FT                      /db_xref="InterPro:IPR001241 {Swiss-Prot:P22447}"
FT                      /db_xref="InterPro:IPR002288 {Swiss-Prot:P22447}"
FT                      /db_xref="InterPro:IPR003594 {Swiss-Prot:P22447}"
FT                      /db_xref="InterPro:IPR006171 {Swiss-Prot:P22447}"
FT                      /db_xref="Swiss-Prot:P22447 {EMBL:U00089}"
FT                      /db_xref="UniParc:UPI000012BECC {UniParc}"
FT                      /transl_table=4
FT                      /translation="MEDNNKTQAYDSSSIKILEGLEAVRKRPGMYIGSTGEEGLHHMIW
FT                      EIIDNSIDEAMGGFASTVKLTLKDNFVTIVEDDGRGIPVDIHPKTNRSTVETVFTVLHA
FT                      GGKFDNDSYKVSGGLHGVGASVVNALSSSFKVWVAREHQQYFLAFHNGGEVIGDLVNEG
FT                      KCDKEHGTKVEFVPDFTVMEKSDYKQTVIASRLQQLAFLNKGIQIDFVDERRQNPQSFS
FT                      WKYDGGLVQYIHHLNNEKEPLFEDIIFGEKTDTVKSVSRDESYTIKVEVAFQYNKTYNQ
FT                      SIFSFCNNINTTEGGTHVEGFRNALVKIINRFAVENKFLKETDEKITRDDICEGLTAII
FT                      SIKHPNPQYEGQTKKKLGNTEVRPLVNSIVSEIFERFMLENPQEANAIIRKTLLAQEAR
FT                      RRSQEARELTRRKSPFDSGSLPGKLADCTTRDPSISELYIVEGDSAGGTAKTGRDRYFQ
FT                      AILPLRGKILNVEKSHFEQIFNNVEISALVMAVGCGIKPDFELEKLRYNKIIIMTDADV
FT                      DGAHIRTLLLTFFFRFMYPLVEQGNIYIAQPPLYKVSYSNKDLYMQTDVQLEEWKQQHP
FT                      NLKYNLQRYKGLGEMDAIQLWETTMDPKVRTLLKVTVEDASIADKAFSLLMGDEVPPRR
FT                      EFIEQNARNVKNIDI"
FT   CDS              4821..7340
FT                      /codon_start=1
FT                      /gene="gyrA {Swiss-Prot:P22446}"
FT                      /synonym="MP150 {Swiss-Prot:P22446}"
FT                      /locus_tag="MPN004 {Swiss-Prot:P22446}"
FT                      /product="DNA gyrase subunit A {Swiss-Prot:P22446}"
FT                      /EC_number="5.99.1.3 {Swiss-Prot:P22446}"
FT                      /function="DNA binding {GO:0003677}"
FT                      /function="DNA topoisomerase (ATP-hydrolyzing) activity
FT                      {GO:0003918}"
FT                      /function="ATP binding {GO:0005524}"
FT                      /process="DNA topological change {GO:0006265}"
FT                      /process="DNA unwinding {GO:0006268}"
FT                      /cellular_component="chromosome {GO:0005694}"
FT                      /protein_id="AAB95798.1"
FT                      /db_xref="EMBL:CAA37623.1 {Swiss-Prot:P22446}"
FT                      /db_xref="GO:0003677 {GOA:IEA,InterPro,IPR002205;
FT                      GOA:IEA,Swiss-Prot,P22446}"
FT                      /db_xref="GO:0003918 {GOA:IEA,InterPro,IPR002205;
FT                      GOA:IEA,Swiss-Prot,P22446}"
FT                      /db_xref="GO:0005524 {GOA:IEA,InterPro,IPR002205}"
FT                      /db_xref="GO:0005694 {GOA:IEA,InterPro,IPR005743}"
```

```
FT                              /db_xref="GO:0006265 {GOA:IEA,InterPro,IPR002205}"
FT                              /db_xref="GO:0006268 {GOA:IEA,InterPro,IPR005743}"
FT                              /db_xref="HSSP:P09097 {Swiss-Prot:P22446}"
FT                              /db_xref="InterPro:IPR002205 {Swiss-Prot:P22446}"
FT                              /db_xref="InterPro:IPR005743 {Swiss-Prot:P22446}"
FT                              /db_xref="InterPro:IPR006691 {Swiss-Prot:P22446}"
FT                              /db_xref="Swiss-Prot:P22446 {EMBL:U00089}"
FT                              /db_xref="UniParc:UPI000012BE91 {UniParc}"
FT                              /transl_table=4
FT                              /translation="MAKQQDQIDKIRQELAQSAIKNISLSSELERSFMEYAMSVIVARA
FT                              LPDARDGLKPVHRRVLYGAYTGGMHHDRPFKKSARIVGDVMSKFHPHGDMAIYDTMSRM
FT                              AQDFSLRYLLIDGHGNFGSIDGDRPAAQRYTEARLSKLAGELLRDIDKDTVDFVANYDG
FT                              EEQEPTVLPAAFPNLLANGSSGIAVGMSTSIPSHNLSELIQGLILLIDNPDCTINDLLG
FT                              VIKGPDFPTGANIIYTKGIESYFETGKGNVVIRSKVSIEQLPTRAALVVTEIPYMVNKT
FT                              SLIEKIVELVKAEEITGIADIRDESSREGIRLVIEVKRDTVPEVLLNQLFKSTRLQVRF
FT                              PVNMLALVKGAPKLLNMKQALTVYLEHQLDVLIRKTQFNLKKYQERFHILSGLLIAALN
FT                              IDEVIAIIKKSANNQVAMEALHERFGLDEIQARAVLDMRLRSLSVLEVNKLQTEQQELK
FT                              ALIEFCQQVLADKQLQLKLIKEQLTKINEQFGDPRRSEILYGISEDIDDEDLITQENVV
FT                              ITMSTNGYLKRIGVDAYNLQHRGGVGVKGLTTYTDDSISQLLVCSTHSDLLFFTDKGKV
FT                              YRIRAHQIPPGFRTNKGIPAVNLIKIDKDEKICALISVNDYQNGYFFCTKNGTIKRTS
FT                              LSEFANILSIGKRAILFKENDVLFSVIRTSGQDDIFIGSTAGFVVRFHEDTVRPLSRAA
FT                              MGVLGINLNQCEFVNGLSTSSNGSLLLSVGQNGIGKLTSIDKYRLTKRNAKGVKTLRVT
FT                              AKTGPVVTTTTVFGNEDLLMISSAGKIVRISLEQLSEQRKNTSGVKLIKLKEKERLETV
FT                              TIFKKEEAIKTTTATETDDVGSKQITQ"
FT      CDS                     7312..8574
FT                              /codon_start=1
FT                              /gene="serS {Swiss-Prot:P75107}"
FT                              /synonym="MP149 {Swiss-Prot:P75107}"
FT                              /locus_tag="MPN005 {Swiss-Prot:P75107}"
FT                              /product="Seryl-tRNA synthetase {Swiss-Prot:P75107}"
FT                              /EC_number="6.1.1.11 {Swiss-Prot:P75107}"
FT                              /function="serine-tRNA ligase activity {GO:0004828}"
FT                              /function="ATP binding {GO:0005524}"
FT                              /process="seryl-tRNA aminoacylation {GO:0006434}"
FT                              /protein_id="AAB95797.1"
FT                              /db_xref="GO:0004828 {GOA:IEA,InterPro,IPR002317;
FT                              GOA:IEA,InterPro,IPR003364; GOA:IEA,Swiss-Prot,P75107;
FT                              GOA:IEA,Swiss-Prot,P75107}"
FT                              /db_xref="GO:0005524 {GOA:IEA,InterPro,IPR002106;
FT                              GOA:IEA,InterPro,IPR002314; GOA:IEA,InterPro,IPR002317;
FT                              GOA:IEA,InterPro,IPR003364; GOA:IEA,Swiss-Prot,P75107;
FT                              GOA:IEA,Swiss-Prot,P75107}"
FT                              /db_xref="GO:0006434 {GOA:IEA,InterPro,IPR002317;
FT                              GOA:IEA,Swiss-Prot,P75107}"
FT                              /db_xref="HSSP:P34945 {Swiss-Prot:P75107}"
FT                              /db_xref="InterPro:IPR002314 {Swiss-Prot:P75107}"
FT                              /db_xref="InterPro:IPR002317 {Swiss-Prot:P75107}"
FT                              /db_xref="InterPro:IPR006195 {Swiss-Prot:P75107}"
FT                              /db_xref="Swiss-Prot:P75107 {EMBL:U00089}"
FT                              /db_xref="UniParc:UPI0000136689 {UniParc}"
FT                              /transl_table=4
FT                              /translation="MLDRNKLRNNLDFFKKKLVERGVSESQFEAYVQADKAMRKLLHQI
FT                              ELANQKQTLLAQQVAKKKGDPKLLKESKELKQKLEQLNIAFKEAETLSQELLLNLPNIA
FT                              DESVPVGRDETANLELLKEGRKPVFDFTPLPHWELCERLQLVAFDKATKLTGARFVAYT
FT                              DKAAKLLRAIASLMIDLNKNKYQEWNVPVIVNETSLTGTGQLPKFKDDVFKLENTRYYL
FT                              SPTLEVQLANLHANEIFTEGELPKYYTATGVNFRQEAGSAGKQTKGTIRLHQFQKVELV
FT                              KFCKPSEAIHELEEMTRDAEQILLELKIPFRRLLLCSGDMGFSAQKTYDLEVWMAGCNE
FT                              YREVSSCSSCGDFQARRAMIRYKDLTTGKNTYVATLNGTALAIDRIFAAILEHYQTKAG
FT                              EVMIPQALLKYLDFDKITKPK"
```

APPENDIX 1.5. EXAMPLE OF A SWISS-PROT ENTRY

```
ID   ROA1_HUMAN      STANDARD;      PRT;    371 AA.
AC   P09651;
DT   01-MAR-1989 (Rel. 10, Created)
DT   01-AUG-1990 (Rel. 15, Last sequence update)
DT   15-MAR-2004 (Rel. 43, Last annotation update)
DE   Heterogeneous nuclear ribonucleoprotein A1 (Helix-destabilizing
DE   protein) (Single-strand binding protein) (hnRNP core protein A1).
GN   HNRPA1.
OS   Homo sapiens (Human).
OC   Eukaryota; Metazoa; Chordata; Craniata; Vertebrata; Euteleostomi;
OC   Mammalia; Eutheria; Primates; Catarrhini; Hominidae; Homo.
OX   NCBI_TaxID=9606;
RN   [1]
RP   SEQUENCE FROM N.A. (ISOFORM A1-A).
RC   TISSUE=Liver;
RX   MEDLINE=89342435; PubMed=2760922;
RA   Biamonti G., Buvoli M., Bassi M.T., Morandi C., Cobianchi F., Riva S.;
RT   "Isolation of an active gene encoding human hnRNP protein A1.
RT   Evidence for alternative splicing.";
RL   J. Mol. Biol. 207:491-503(1989).
RN   [2]
RP   SEQUENCE FROM N.A. (ISOFORM A1-A).
RC   TISSUE=Fibroblast;
RX   MEDLINE=88233978; PubMed=2836799;
RA   Buvoli M., Biamonti G., Ghetti A., Riva S., Bassi M.T., Horandi C.;
RT   "cDNA cloning of human hnRNP protein A1 reveals the existence of
RT   multiple mRNA isoforms.";
RL   Nucleic Acids Res. 16:3751-3770(1988).
RN   [3]
RP   SEQUENCE FROM N.A. (ISOFORM A1-A).
RC   TISSUE=Lung;
RA   Knudsen S.M., Leffers H.;
RL   Submitted (JUN-1994) to the EMBL/GenBank/DDBJ databases.
RN   [4]
RP   PARTIAL SEQUENCE FROM N.A.
RC   TISSUE=Liver;
RX   MEDLINE=87053868; PubMed=3023065;
RA   Riva S., Morandi C., Tsoulfas P., Pandolfo M., Biamonti G.,
RA   Merrill B., Williams K.R., Multhaup G., Beyreuther K., Werr H.,
RA   Heinrich B., Schaefer K.P.;
RT   "Mammalian single-stranded DNA binding protein UP I is derived from
RT   the hnRNP core protein A1.";
RL   EMBO J. 5:2267-2273(1986).
RN   [5]
RP   SEQUENCE OF 251-302 FROM N.A. (ISOFORM A1-B).
RX   MEDLINE=90214633; PubMed=1691095;
RA   Buvoli M., Cobianchi F., Bestagno M.G., Mangiarotti A., Bassi M.T.,
RA   Biamonti G., Riva S.;
RT   "Alternative splicing in the human gene for the core protein A1
RT   generates another hnRNP protein.";
RL   EMBO J. 9:1229-1235(1990).
RN   [6]
RP   NUCLEAR LOCALIZATION DOMAIN.
RX   MEDLINE=95247808; PubMed=7730395;
RA   Siomi H., Dreyfuss G.;
RT   "A nuclear localization domain in the hnRNP A1 protein.";
RL   J. Cell Biol. 129:551-560(1995).
```

```
RN   [7]
RP   NUCLEAR LOCALIZATION DOMAIN, AND NUCLEAR EXPORT.
RX   MEDLINE=96067639; PubMed=8521471;
RA   Michael W.M., Choi M., Dreyfuss G.;
RT   "A nuclear export signal in hnRNP A1: a signal-mediated, temperature-
RT   dependent nuclear protein export pathway.";
RL   Cell 83:415-422(1995).
RN   [8]
RP   NUCLEAR LOCALIZATION DOMAIN.
RX   MEDLINE=95286702; PubMed=7769000;
RA   Weighardt F., Biamonti G., Riva S.;
RT   "Nucleo-cytoplasmic distribution of human hnRNP proteins: a search
RT   for the targeting domains in hnRNP A1.";
RL   J. Cell Sci. 108:545-555(1995).
RN   [9]
RP   3D-STRUCTURE MODELING OF 106-189.
RX   MEDLINE=91099515; PubMed=2176620;
RA   Ghetti A., Bolognesi M., Cobianchi F., Morandi C.;
RT   "Modeling by homology of RNA binding domain in A1 hnRNP protein.";
RL   FEBS Lett. 277:272-276(1990).
RN   [10]
RP   X-RAY CRYSTALLOGRAPHY (1.75 ANGSTROMS) OF 8-180.
RX   MEDLINE=97307256; PubMed=9164463;
RA   Shamoo Y., Krueger U., Rice L.M., Williams K.R., Steitz T.A.;
RT   "Crystal structure of the two RNA binding domains of human hnRNP A1
RT   at 1.75-A resolution.";
RL   Nat. Struct. Biol. 4:215-222(1997).
RN   [11]
RP   X-RAY CRYSTALLOGRAPHY (1.9 ANGSTROMS) OF 6-181.
RX   MEDLINE=97277240; PubMed=9115444;
RA   Xu R.M., Jokhan L., Cheng X., Mayeda A., Krainer A.R.;
RT   "Crystal structure of human UP1, the domain of hnRNP A1 that contains
RT   two RNA-recognition motifs.";
RL   Structure 5:559-570(1997).
CC   -!- FUNCTION: Involved in the packaging of pre-mRNA into hnRNP
CC       particles, transport of poly(A) mRNA from the nucleus to the
CC       cytoplasm and may modulate splice site selection.
CC   -!- SUBCELLULAR LOCATION: Nuclear. Shuttles continuously between the
CC       nucleus and the cytoplasm along with mRNA. Component of
CC       ribonucleosomes.
CC   -!- ALTERNATIVE PRODUCTS:
CC       Event=Alternative splicing; Named isoforms=2;
CC       Name=A1-B;
CC         IsoId=P09651-1; Sequence=Displayed;
CC       Name=A1-A;
CC         IsoId=P09651-2; Sequence=VSP_005824;
CC         Note=Is twenty times more abundant than isoform A1-B;
CC   -!- SIMILARITY: BELONGS TO THE A/B GROUP OF HNRNP, WHICH ARE BASIC AND
CC       GLY-RICH PROTEINS.
CC   -!- SIMILARITY: Contains 2 RNA recognition motif (RRM) domains.
CC   -----------------------------------------------------------------------
CC   This SWISS-PROT entry is copyright. It is produced through a collaboration
CC   between  the Swiss Institute of Bioinformatics  and the  EMBL outstation -
CC   the European Bioinformatics Institute.  There are no  restrictions on  its
CC   use  by  non-profit  institutions as long  as its content  is  in  no  way
CC   modified and this statement is not removed.  Usage  by  and for commercial
CC   entities requires a license agreement (See http://www.isb-sib.ch/announce/
CC   or send an email to license@isb-sib.ch).
CC   -----------------------------------------------------------------------
```

```
DR    EMBL; X12671; CAA31191.1; -.
DR    EMBL; X06747; CAA29922.1; ALT_SEQ.
DR    EMBL; X04347; CAA27874.1; -.
DR    EMBL; X79536; CAA56072.1; -.
DR    PIR; S02061; S02061.
DR    PDB; 1HA1; 15-MAY-97.
DR    PDB; 1L3K; 17-APR-02.
DR    PDB; 1UP1; 17-SEP-97.
DR    PDB; 2UP1; 22-JUN-99.
DR    SWISS-2DPAGE; P09651; HUMAN.
DR    Aarhus/Ghent-2DPAGE; 207; NEPHGE.
DR    Aarhus/Ghent-2DPAGE; 2114; NEPHGE.
DR    Aarhus/Ghent-2DPAGE; 3612; NEPHGE.
DR    Genew; HGNC:5031; HNRPA1.
DR    GK; P09651; -.
DR    MIM; 164017; -.
DR    GO; GO:0005737; C:cytoplasm; TAS.
DR    GO; GO:0030530; C:heterogeneous nuclear ribonucleoprotein com...; TAS.
DR    GO; GO:0005654; C:nucleoplasm; TAS.
DR    GO; GO:0003723; F:RNA binding; TAS.
DR    GO; GO:0006397; P:mRNA processing; TAS.
DR    GO; GO:0006405; P:RNA-nucleus export; TAS.
DR    InterPro; IPR000504; RNA_rec_mot.
DR    Pfam; PF00076; rrm; 2.
DR    SMART; SM00360; RRM; 2.
DR    PROSITE; PS50102; RRM; 2.
DR    PROSITE; PS00030; RRM_RNP_1; 2.
KW    Nuclear protein; RNA-binding; Repeat; Ribonucleoprotein; Methylation;
KW    Alternative splicing; 3D-structure; Polymorphism.
FT    INIT_MET       0        0
FT    DOMAIN         3       93     GLOBULAR A DOMAIN.
FT    DOMAIN        94      184     GLOBULAR B DOMAIN.
FT    DOMAIN        13       96     RNA-binding (RRM) 1.
FT    DOMAIN       104      183     RNA-binding (RRM) 2.
FT    DOMAIN       217      239     RNA-BINDING RGG-BOX.
FT    DOMAIN       194      371     Gly-rich.
FT    DOMAIN       319      356     NUCLEAR TARGETING SEQUENCE (M9).
FT    MOD_RES      193      193     METHYLATION (BY SIMILARITY).
FT    VARSPLIC     251      302     Missing (in isoform A1-A).
FT                                  /FTId=VSP_005824.
FT    VARIANT       72       72     N -> S (in dbSNP:6533).
FT                                  /FTId=VAR_014711.
FT    MUTAGEN      325      325     G->A: NO NUCLEAR IMPORT NOR EXPORT.
FT    MUTAGEN      326      326     P->A: NO NUCLEAR IMPORT NOR EXPORT.
FT    MUTAGEN      333      334     GG->LL: NORMAL NUCLEAR IMPORT AND EXPORT.
FT    CONFLICT     139      139     R -> P (in Ref. 4).
FT    HELIX         10       13
FT    STRAND        14       18
FT    TURN          22       23
FT    HELIX         26       33
FT    HELIX         34       36
FT    STRAND        39       46
FT    TURN          48       50
FT    STRAND        53       61
FT    HELIX         64       72
FT    TURN          73       73
FT    STRAND        77       78
FT    TURN          79       80
```

```
FT      STRAND          81      82
FT      STRAND          84      87
FT      STRAND          105     112
FT      TURN            113     114
FT      HELIX           117     124
FT      TURN            125     127
FT      STRAND          130     137
FT      TURN            139     141
FT      STRAND          144     152
FT      HELIX           155     162
FT      TURN            163     163
FT      STRAND          168     169
FT      TURN            170     171
FT      STRAND          172     173
FT      STRAND          175     178
SQ      SEQUENCE        371 AA;   38715 MW;   B3EEFA5AE1DB7C26 CRC64;
        SKSESPKEPE  QLRKLFIGGL  SFETTDESLR  SHFEQWGTLT  DCVVMRDPNT  KRSRGFGFVT
        YATVEEVDAA  MNARPHKVDG  RVVEPKRAVS  REDSQRPGAH  LTVKKIFVGG  IKEDTEEHHL
        RDYFEQYGKI  EVIEIMTDRG  SGKKRGFAFV  TFDDHDSVDK  IVIQKYHTVN  GHNCEVRKAL
        SKQEMASASS  SQRGRSGSGN  FGGGRGGGFG  GNDNFGRGGN  FSGRGGFGGS  RGGGGYGGSG
        DGYNGFGNDG  GYGGGGPGYS  GGSRGYGSGG  QGYGNQGSGY  GGSGSYDSYN  NGGGRGFGGG
        SGSNFGGGGS  YNDFGNYNNQ  SSNFGPMKGG  NFGGRSSGPY  GGGGQYFAKP  RNQGGYGGSS
        SSSSYGSGRR  F
//
```

APPENDIX 6.1 FOR DYNAMIC PROGRAMMING

This appendix describes the basic dynamic programming method for RNA secondary structure prediction. An in-depth example is provided for prediction of a structure that uses a simplified energy model, suitable for manual calculation.

The dynamic programming algorithm is divided into two steps. In the first step of the algorithm, called the fill step, the lowest conformational free energy possible for each subfragment of sequence, from nucleotide i to nucleotide j, is calculated. Two arrays are stored, $V(i, j)$ and $W(i, j)$. In $V(i, j)$, the lowest free energy from nucleotide i to nucleotide j, inclusive, is stored with the requirement that i base pair to j. Similarly, $W(i, j)$ is the lowest free energy for the same nucleotide fragment, requiring that $W(i, j)$ will be incorporated into a multibranch loop and there be at least one base pair. These arrays are filled taking advantage of recursions. For example, the free energy of a base pair i and j, stacked on paired nucleotides i + 1 and j − 1 is:

$$\Delta G^{\circ}_{37} = V(i + 1, j - 1) + \Delta G^{\circ}_{37}(\text{base pair stacking}),$$

$$(6A.1)$$

where $V(i + 1, j − 1)$ was calculated previously because it corresponds to a shorter sequence fragment. Once the arrays are filled, the lowest conformational free en-ergy possible for the sequence is determined, but the structure is not yet known. The second step of the dynamic programming algorithm, called traceback, determines the secondary structure that is the lowest free energy conformation.

As an illustration of dynamic programming for secondary structure prediction, consider the folding of rGCGGGUACCGAUCGUCGC, for which the number of hydrogen bonds in canonical pairs will be maximized. This calculation is simpler than energy minimization, but it illustrates the important points of dynamic programming. The following recursions will be used for $1 \leq i < j \leq N$, where N is, as usual, the number of nucleotides in the sequence:

$$V(i, j) = 0 \text{ if i and j cannot pair canonically}$$

$$= \max[V_{\text{hairpin}}(i, j), V_{\text{stack/internal/bulge}}(i, j),$$

$$V_{\text{multibranch}}(i, j)] \text{ if i and j can pair,} \quad (6A.2)$$

$$W(i, j) = \max[V(i, j), W(i + 1, j), W(i, j - 1),$$

$$W(i, k) + W(k + 1, j) \text{ for i} < k < j]. \ (6A.3)$$

$V(i, j)$ is the maximum number of hydrogen bonds for the sequence fragment from nucleotides i to j with i and j paired. So, as shown in Equation 6.4, to fill $V(i, j)$ the possibilities that the pair of i and j can close a hairpin loop, stack on a previous pair, close an internal loop, close a bulge loop, or close a multibranch loop all need consideration. Each term counts the total hydrogen bonds:

$$V_{\text{hairpin}} = \text{\# hydrogen bonds in pair i and j,}$$

$$\text{if } j - i > 3$$

$$= 0, \text{ if } j - i \leq 3, \qquad (6A.4)$$

$$V_{\text{stack/internal/bulge}} = (\text{\# hydrogen bonds in pair i and j})$$

$$+ \max[V(k_1, k_2) \text{ for } i < k_1 < k_2 < j], \qquad (6A.5)$$

$$V_{\text{multibranch}} = (\text{\# hydrogen bonds in pair i and j})$$

$$+ \max[W(i + 1, k) + W(k + 1, j - 1)$$

$$\text{for } i + 1 < k < j - 1]. \qquad (6A.6)$$

$V(i, j)$ is zero when i and j cannot form a canonical pair. Furthermore, hairpin loops that enclose fewer than three unpaired nucleotides are forbidden by assigning those loops 0 hydrogen bonds (Equation A.4). AU and GU pairs have two hydrogen bonds, and a GC pair has three hydrogen bonds. W is the maximum number of hydrogen bonds for the fragment of nucleotides i to j, without the constraint that i and j must be paired. The term, $W(i, k) + W(k + 1, j)$ in equation A.3 allows any number of helical branches in a multibranch loop by recursion. V and W are filled by considering all 5-mers, then 6-mers, then 7-mers, etc of sequence length. Note that V and W for sequences shorter than five nucleotides are zero because of the assumption in equation A.4 that the minimum length of a hairpin is three unpaired nucleotides. Figure A.1 shows the pseudo-computer code for the fill order.

```
L = 4
i = 1
While (L ≤ N) {
    j = i + L
    Calculate V(i,j) according to equation 7.4
    Calculate W(i,j) according to equation 7.5
    If (i+L ≤ N) i = i + 1
    Else {
        i = 1
        L = L + 1
    }
}
```

FIGURE A.1 Pseudo-computer code for the fill order of V (i, j) and W(i, j). This is one representative scheme for the direction the filling of the two dimensional arrays. This scheme calculates V and W for each 1-mer, then 2-mer, then 3-mer, etc starting from the 5' end of the sequence.

Tables 6A.1 and 6A.2 show the filled V and W arrays, respectively. The values of some entries are instructive and the conformations with the maximum hydrogen bonds for those entries are illustrated in Figure A.2. Consider, for example, V(14, 18) = 3. This is the number of hydrogen bonds in the pair of G14 and C18, with G14 and C18 closing a hairpin loop. V(10, 16) = 5 is a stack of G10 and C16 onto the pair of A11 and U15. V(6, 14) = 4 is the pair of U6 and G14 closing a bulge loop, for which a pair between A7 and U12 close the interior end of the loop. Finally, V(2, 17) = 14 is the closure of a multibranch loop by C2 and G17 with the bifurcation of branches represented by W(3, 9) and W(10, 16). W(14, 18) = 3 is equal to V(14, 18). W(8, 18) = 8 is the extension of an unpaired nucleotide on W(9, 18), (which is equal to

TABLE 6A.1 Filled V Array

V	i	1	2	3	4	5	6	7	8	9	10	11	12	13	14	15	16	17	18
j		G	C	G	G	G	U	A	C	C	G	A	U	C	G	U	C	G	C
18	C	17	0	14	11	11	0	0	0	0	6	0	0	0	3	0	0	0	
17	G	0	14	0	0	0	7	0	8	8	0	0	2	3	0	0	0		
16	C	14	0	10	9	8	0	0	0	0	5	0	0	0	0	0			
15	U	13	0	9	7	6	0	5	0	0	2	2	0	0	0				
14	G	0	11	0	0	0	4	0	3	3	0	0	0	0					
13	C	12	0	8	7	5	0	0	0	0	0	0	0						
12	U	11	0	5	5	4	0	2	0	0	0	0							
11	A	0	0	0	0	0	2	0	0	0	0								
10	G	0	9	0	0	0	2	0	0	0									
9	C	6	0	6	3	3	0	0	0										
8	C	3	0	3	3	0	0	0											
7	A	0	0	0	0	0	0												
6	U	2	0	0	0	0													
5	G	0	0	0	0														
4	G	0	0	0															
3	G	0	0																
2	C	0																	
1	G																		

TABLE 6A.2 Filled W Array

W / i		1	2	3	4	5	6	7	8	9	10	11	12	13	14	15	16	17	18
j		G	C	G	G	G	U	A	C	C	G	A	U	C	G	U	C	G	C
18	C	17	14	14	11	11	8	8	8	8	6	3	3	3	3	0	0	0	
17	G	14	14	11	11	8	8	8	8	8	5	3	3	3	0	0	0		
16	C	14	11	11	9	8	5	5	5	5	5	2	0	0	0	0			
15	U	13	11	9	7	6	5	5	3	3	2	2	0	0	0				
14	G	12	11	8	7	5	4	3	3	3	0	0	0	0					
13	C	12	9	8	7	5	2	2	0	0	0	0	0						
12	U	11	9	6	5	4	2	2	0	0	0	0							
11	A	9	9	6	3	3	2	0	0	0	0								
10	G	9	9	6	3	3	2	0	0	0									
9	C	6	6	6	3	3	0	0	0										
8	C	3	3	3	3	0	0	0											
7	A	2	0	0	0	0	0												
6	U	2	0	0	0	0													
5	G	0	0	0	0														
4	G	0	0	0															
3	G	0	0																
2	C	0																	
1	G																		

the extension of an unpaired nucleotide on W(8, 17)). W(4, 17) = 11 is a bifurcation and is the sum of W(4, 8) and W(9, 17).

At this point, it is clear that the maximum number of hydrogen bonds for this sequence is 17 and is represented by V(1, N). To find the structure that has 17 hydrogen bonds, the traceback must be performed as illustrated in Figure A.3. Traceback starts by placing 1, N, and the maximum number of hydrogen bonds on the stack. The stack is a storage device that can expand to accommodate as many sequence fragments as needed for the structure traceback. At each step of the main loop, a triple, consisting of i, j, and the number of hydrogen bonds are taken from the stack. For this sequence, in the first step through the loop, V(1, 18) equals 17, the number of hydrogen bonds. Therefore, nucleotides 1 and 18 are base paired. Following the flowchart, V(1, 18) is not equal to the hairpin term and there is not bifurcation such that V(1, 18) = W(1, k) + W(k+1, 18). Instead, V(1, 18) = V(2, 17) + 3 (the number of hydrogen bonds in the GC pair, so 2, 17, and V(2, 17) = 14 are placed on the stack.

When taking V(2,17) from the stack, again V(2,17) = 14, the number of hydrogen bonds, so nucleotide 2 is paired to 17. V(2,17) does not equal $V_{hairpin}(2,17)$. V(2,17) does equal W(3, 9) + W(10,16), so 3, 9, and W(3, 9) = 6 are placed on the stack, as are 10, 16, and W(10, 16) = 5.

Now, 10, 16, and 5 are taken from the stack. Again, V(10, 16) = 5, so nucleotide 10 is paired to 16. Following down the flowchart, V(10, 16) is found to be V(11, 15) + 3, the number of hydrogen bonds in the air of G10 and C16. Therefore, 11, 15, and V(11, 15) = 2 are placed on

Array:	Representation:
V(14,18) = 3	
V(10,16) = 5	
V(6,14) = 4	
V(2,17) = 14	
W(8,18) = 8	
W(4,17) = 11	

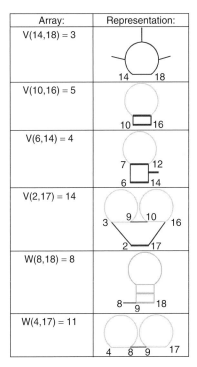

FIGURE A.2 Illustrations of maximum hydrogen bond conformations as found by the recursions. Regions in gray are not required by recursions and the conformation in those regions is unknown as the arrays are filled recursively. For example, V(10, 16) = 5 is a case in which a base pair stacks on a previous pair, 11-15. The recursions utilize V(11, 15), but the structure for the region between nucleotides 11 and 15 is unknown as V(10, 16) was previously calculated and is therefore drawn in gray.

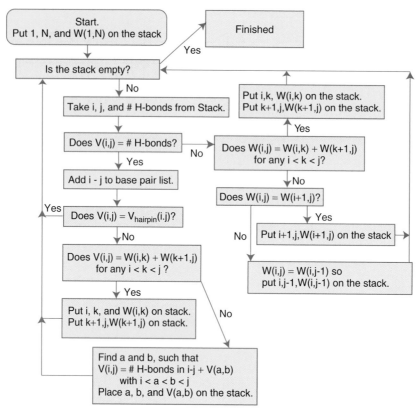

FIGURE A.3 **Flowchart for structure traceback. Traceback starts by placing 1, N, and the maximum number of hydrogen bonds for the sequence onto the stack and proceeds until the stack is empty.**

the stack. Next 11, 15, and 2 are removed from the stack, A11 and U15 are paired and V(11, 15) = V$_{hairpin}$(11, 15), so nothing is placed on the stack as this branch has been followed to its termination in a hairpin loop.

Now, 3, 9, and 6 are taken from the stack. This branch is similar to the branch starting with nucleotides 10 and 16, in that it has two base pairs: G3–C9 and G4–C8. After finding those two pairs, the stack is empty and we have determined the structure with 17 hydrogen bonds as illustrated in Figure A.4.

The scaling of RNA secondary structure is limited by multibranch loop searching which must be done for every subfragment in the sequence, i.e. from nucleotides i to j with i < j ≤ N. The search looks for a bifurcation for which the fragment is divided by k

into two segments with stems, so i < k < j. Therefore, three indices are being searched over N nucleotides in the worst case step, the fragment that stretches the length of the sequence, from 1 to N. This is N^3 steps. Internal loop searching, which would naturally require a search over i < i' < j' < j, and therefore be O(N^4), can be limited in two ways. The first, tradition method is to simply limit the size of internal loops so that i' − i + j − < M, where M is the maximum loop size. A second method has also been cleverly devised that does not limit the size of internal loops, but instead takes advantage of the form of the internal loop nearest neighbor parameters to pre-fill the arrays, splitting the N^4 process into two N^3 steps (Lyngsø *et al.*, 1999).

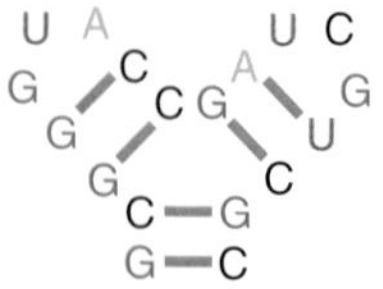

▌ PROBLEM: APPENDIX 6.1

Using the recursions for maximizing hydrogen bonds introduced in this chapter, calculate the maximum number of hydrogen bonds for the sequence 5'rCUACGUUCGC-GAAG3'. Traceback the structure. Now, use a free energy minimization structure prediction program to predict the structure. What minimum free energy structure is predicted for this sequence? Why do the two methods predict different structures?

FIGURE A.4 **The secondary structure of rGCGGGUACCGAUCGUCGC with 17 hydrogen bonds.**

APPENDIX 13.1 PHD FILE FORMAT EXAMPLE

```
BEGIN_SEQUENCE gvf11b11.y1

BEGIN_COMMENT

CHROMAT_FILE: gvf11b11.y1
ABI_THUMBPRINT: 0
PHRED_VERSION: 0.990722.g
CALL_METHOD: phred
QUALITY_LEVELS: 99
TIME: Sat Jan  3 07:41:36 2004
TRACE_ARRAY_MIN_INDEX: 0
TRACE_ARRAY_MAX_INDEX: 10924
TRIM: 26 823 0.0500
CHEM: term
DYE: big

END_COMMENT

BEGIN_DNA
n 0 2
n 0 15
n 0 28
n 0 41
n 0 54
g 4 77
g 6 84
a 6 87
t 8 107
a 8 119
```

```
c 8 129
t 6 142
c 6 148
a 8 158
g 8 178
t 8 194
```

<truncated for brevity>

```
c 13 10828
t 10 10839
a 8 10851
g 8 10865
a 8 10879
g 8 10890
a 7 10906
a 7 10923
END_DNA

END_SEQUENCE

WR{
template determineReadTypes
040103:074252
name: gvf11b11
}

WR{
primer determineReadTypes 040103:074252
type: univ rev
}
```

APPENDIX 13.2 FASTA FORMAT EXAMPLE

```
>gvf11b11.y1 CHROMAT_FILE: gvf11b11.y1 PHD_FILE: gvf11b11.
y1.phd.1CHEM: term DYE: big TIME: Sat Jan  3 07:41:36 2004 TEMPLATE:gvf11b11
DIRECTION: rev
NNNNNGGATACTCAGTGGTGGATTCCTATCCTGACAAGTGATTGCAAACTGGTAACTCTG
AGGCAGATAACCAGGGCAAAAAGGTGTATAAGTAAAACAAAGCCTAACTTGGAAGAAAGA
GAGAAAAAGTTCAGTTTTACACATCTTTATATGAAGCAGAAGTCCGGAAAATCATTTAAA
GATTATTCTATTAATGTCCTGTTATATTTGTCATAATCATAAAGTTGTCACAGTATATTT
CAAACCAACTGTTTAAAAACAAACTGAAATAAAAAATTTAAATACCCTTATGTAAAATAG
GCTTCCCTGGTGGCTCAGGGGTAAAAAACTCGCCCGCCAACGCAGGAGATGTAGATTTGA
TCCCTGGGTTAGGAAGATCCCCTGGAGAAGGAAATGAAAAACCACTCTAGTATTCTTGCC
TGGGAAATCCCATGGACAGAGGAGCGTGGAGGGCTACAGTCCATGGGAGTCGCAAAAGAG
TTGGACATGACTAAACAACAACATATAAAATAACCTTACTCCATAATGTCAAACTTATGT
CACACAAAATGCAAAGTTCTTACATCTATTAACTTTTATGGTTAAATATAACCTAATGCA
CTGTTTTATACAGCAACAACTACTTTTTTATTTTAAATGGTGAAAAATTAGTGAACAGAG
GGTCTCAGAGATGCTAAACTTATGACTTATAATTAACAAGATGTTATAGTTCTAGACATT
TTTGATATATATTAGTGAGTACTCGTTTACTATTTAATTAGAAGCTTTTCTTCACTAAAG
TGCTATAGATTGTTCTGAGGAGTAGTAGATAACTGAGATGTACCATNCATTCAATAGTAA
CTGATTAATTGGTAATTAGGTTTCCACTGGTGATCAATCATCCATNTTGAAGAGGGCTGG
NNACTAGAGAA
```

APPENDIX 18.1 IUPAC/UBMB CODES FOR NUCLEIC ACID BASES

Code	Nucleic Acid Base
A	Adenine
C	Cytosine
G	Guanine
T	Thymine
U	Uracil
R	Guanine or adenine (purine)
Y	Thymine or cytosine (pyrimidine)
K	Guanine or thymine (keto group at similar positions)
M	Adenine or cytosine (amino group at similar positions)
S	Guanine or cytosine (strong interaction: 3 hydrogen bonds)
W	Adenine or thymine (strong interaction: 2 hydrogen bonds)
B	Not adenine
D	Not cytosine
H	Not guanine
V	Not thymine
N	Any nucleic acid base

APPENDIX 18.2 ONE- AND THREE-LETTER CODES FOR AMINO ACIDS

Nonpolar and uncharged

A	Ala	Alanine
F	Phe	Phenylalanine
G	Gly	Glycine
I	Ile	Isoleucine
L	Leu	Leucine
M	Met	Methionine
P	Pro	Proline
V	Val	Valine
W	Trp	Tryptophan

Polar and uncharged

C	Cys	Cysteine
N	Asn	Asparagine
Q	Gln	Glutamine
S	Ser	Serine
T	Thr	Threonine
Y	Tyr	Tyrosine

Positively charged (basic)

H	His	Histidine
K	Lys	Lysine
R	Arg	Arginine

Negatively charged (acidic)

D	Asp	Aspartic acid
E	Glu	Glutamic acid

Ambiguity codes

B	Asx	Asparagine or aspartic acid
Z	Glx	Glutamine or glutamic acid

Glossary

An extensive glossary of genetic terms can be found on the Web site of the National Human Genome Research Institute (http://www.genome.gov/glossary.cfm). The entries in this online glossary provide a brief written definition of the term; the user also can listen to an informative explanation of the term using RealAudio or the Windows Media Player.

2D gel electrophoresis. Two-dimensional polyacrylamide electrophoresis. A technique for separating large numbers of proteins by loading them onto a gel, applying an electric current to separate by isoelectric point (pI), then, in the perpendicular direction, separating them by molecular weight.

accessible surface area. The surface area of a protein or macromolecule that can be contacted by water molecules or other solvent or solute molecules. Accessible surface area is measured in square Ångstroms and often is used to assess the quality of protein structures and the strength of hydrophobic interactions.

algorithm. Any sequence of actions (e.g., computational steps) that perform a particular task.

alignment. Two or more sequences that have been lined up, matching as many identical residues or conservatively substituted positions as possible.

allele. Any of the forms of a gene that may occur at a given locus. In simple Mendelian inheritance, dominant alleles are expressed more than recessive alleles.

analogous. In phylogenetics, characters that have descended in a convergent fashion from unrelated ancestors.

ASN.1. Abstract syntax notation one. ASN.1 is a formal language for abstractly describing messages or information to be exchanged. ASN.1 is used extensively by the National Center for Biotechnology Information in representing sequence, structure, interaction, mapping, and bibliographic records.

assembler. A program used to deduce the sequence of original DNA used to make a shotgun library from a set of shotgun reads.

average mass. The mass of an ion calculated by averaging all common isotope variations. This quantity typically is used when the resolution of the instrumentation is not adequate to distinguish individual isotopes.

BAC. Bacterial artificial chromosome. A vector used to clone segments of DNA roughly 100 to 200 Kb in length.

base caller. A program used to convert raw sequencer output to an ordered list of base identities and quality scores. See also *chromatogram*.

Bayesian network. A method in machine learning used to predict a feature in a dataset given some known but incomplete information. Based on Bayes' rule for conditional probability.

BLOSUM matrix. See *PAM matrix*.

Bonferroni correction. A conservative statistical multiple comparison correction used to correct the significance threshold (α value) of multiple independent statistical tests, which together may have a greater chance of generating false positives than the individual test.

Boolean. Refers to an expression or variable that can have only a true or false value. Named after George Boole, a British mathematician who developed the theory of algebraic logic or Boolean algebra, which now is used in almost all electronic computation.

Bioinformatics: A Practical Guide to the Analysis of Genes and Proteins, Third Edition, edited by Andreas D. Baxevanis and B.F. Francis Ouellette.
ISBN 0-471-47878-4 Copyright © 2005 John Wiley & Sons, Inc.

bottom-up proteomics. Another term for shotgun proteomics, referring to the fact that the analysis begins with the peptide constituents of a sample.

browser. Program used to access sites on the Internet. Using hypertext markup language (HTML), browsers are capable of representing a Web page the same way regardless of computer platform.

candidate gene. A gene that is implicated in the causation of a disease or phenotype. Candidate genes lie in a region that has been identified through genetic mapping. The protein product of a candidate gene may implicate the candidate gene as being the actual disease gene being sought.

captured gap. In sequencing, a gap that is contained within one or more subclones.

cDNA. Complementary DNA. Single-stranded DNA that has been synthesized from an mRNA template by reverse transcriptase.

cDNA library. A collection of double-stranded DNA sequences that are generated by copying mRNA molecules. Because these sequences are derived from mRNAs, they contain only protein-coding DNA.

CDS. Coding sequence. A segment of genomic DNA or mRNA that codes for a protein. This abbreviation is used extensively in sequence database records.

characters and character states. In phylogenetics, characters are homologous features in different organisms. The exact condition of that feature in a particular individual is the character state. As an example, the character "hair color" can have the character states "gold," "red," and "yellow." In molecular biology, the character states can be one of the four nucleotides (A, C, T, G) or one of the 20 amino acids. Please note that some authors define character to mean the character state as defined here.

chimeric read. In sequencing, a read containing sequence from two noncontiguous regions of the target or vector. Chimeric reads can be the result of multiple inserts ligating into the same vector during library construction, or sequence from a mixture of two clones that have regions in which each of the clones is more obvious.

chromatogram. A file containing raw data and ancillary information about a single DNA sample that has been run through an automated DNA sequencing instrument.

client. A computer, or the software running on a computer, that interacts with another computer at a remote site (server). Note the difference between client and user.

cM. Centimorgan. A unit of measure used to indicate the distance between two genes or markers. 1 cM corresponds to approximately 1 million base pairs (1 Mb).

coding statistic. A mathematical function that computes a real number related to the likelihood that a given DNA sequence codes for a protein.

codon. The triplet of bases in either a DNA or RNA sequence that ultimately codes for a specific, single amino acid.

comparative proteomics. The general approach of comparing proteomes from two or more cellular states, then using mass spectrometry to identify the proteins or peptides that differ between them.

complementary. Two sequences that can form an uninterrupted helix of Watson-Crick base pairs.

consensus. In sequencing, the predicted sequence of the original DNA used to create a shotgun library. In alignments, the base or amino acid most likely to occur at any given position; consensus sequences can be used to characterize protein families.

conservative substitution. The replacement of one residue by another residue having similar properties (e.g., size, charge, hydrophobicity).

contig. Short for *contiguous*. Refers to a contiguous set of overlapping DNA sequences in the context of a sequencing project.

cytogenetic map. The representation of a chromosome on staining and examination by microscopy. Visually distinct light and dark bands give each chromosome a unique morphological appearance and allow for the visual tracking of cytogenetic abnormalities such as deletions or inversions.

Dalton. The basic measure of molecular mass used in mass sprectrometry, which is 1/12th of the mass of the carbon atom.

deletion. A mutation in which one or more bases is lost from a given region of a chromosome.

deletion–insertion polymorphism (DIP). Alleles that are represented by one base or more that are present in one sequence and absent in the other.

descriptor. Information about a sequence or set of sequences whose scope depends on its placement in a record. Placed on a set of sequences to reduce the need to save multiple redundant copies of information.

DIGE. Difference gel electrophoresis. A type of two-dimensional polyacrylamide gel electrophoresis (2D-PAGE) in which two samples are run on a single gel.

domain name. Refers to one of the levels of organization of the Internet and used both to classify and to identify host machines. Top-level domain names usually indicate the type of site or the country in which the host is located.

dotplot. A visual technique for comparing two sequences with one another, allowing for the identification of regions of local alignment, direct or inverted repeats, insertions, deletions, or low-complexity regions.

download. The act of transferring a file from a remote host to a local machine via FTP.

dynamic programming. A computational technique used to solve complex problems by decomposing the problem into successively smaller subproblems, then solving them recursively. The solution of a subproblem of given complexity is dependent on the solutions already computed for subproblems of lesser complexity.

electrospray ionization. A method for creating ions in mass spectrometry that consists of forming a spray of charged droplets containing analyte molecules, then desolvating the droplets, leaving charged ions for analysis.

E-mail. Electronic mail. Refers to messages that can be composed on the computer and transmitted via the Internet to a remote location within seconds. [*Ant*: snail mail, postal mail.]

energy minimization. A computational method for reducing the calculated covalent and noncovalent energy of a molecule with a given geometry. Energy minimization uses highly parameterized Newtonian descriptions of molecular bonds and atomic interactions. Energy minimization frequently is used to refine or fix protein structures determined from X-ray, nuclear magnetic resonance (NMR), or homology modeling.

e-PCR. Electronic polymerase chain reaction. A computational method that predicts the location of sequence tagged sites (STSs) in DNA by searching for subsequences that closely match the PCR primers used to make the STS; these subsequences also must have the correct order, orientation, and spacing such that they could prime the amplification of a PCR product of the correct molecular weight.

EST. Expressed sequence tags. These are usually short (300-500 bp), single reads from mRNA (cDNA) that usually are produced in large numbers. They represent a snapshot of what is expressed in a given tissue or at a given developmental stage. They represent tags (some coding, others not) of expression for a given cDNA library.

exon. Within a gene, a region that codes for part of the gene's protein product; the **ex**pressed **region** of a gene.

family trio. DNA samples from mother, father, and child.

FAQ. Frequently asked questions. Exactly what it sounds like: a compiled list of questions and answers intended for new users of any computer-based resource, such as mailing lists or newsgroups.

feature. Annotation on a specific location on a given sequence.

filtering. See *masking*.

firewall. A computer separating a company or organization's internal network from the public part, if any, of the same network. Intended to prevent unauthorized access to private computer systems.

flanking sequence. Sequences 5′ or 3′ of a core sequence of interest.

FTICR or FT/MS. Fourier transform mass spectrometry or Fourier transform ion cyclotron resonance MS. A highly accurate ion measurement used especially for large molecules of up to 1,000,000 Daltons or more. Electromagnetic forces are used to cycle ions in a chamber, which are then measured by the frequency at which they resonate. To convert from frequency to a mass-charge (m/z) spectrum, a Fourier transform is applied.

FTP. File transfer protocol. The method by which files are transferred between hosts.

gap. Used to improve alignments between sequences. Gaps theoretically represent insertions and deletions between sequences being studied.

genetic map. Gives the relative positions of known genes, markers, or both. Markers must have two or more alleles that can be distinguished readily.

genetic marker. A DNA feature whose physical location is known and that can be used to (indirectly) deduce the method of inheritance of a gene.

genome. All of the DNA found within each of the cells of an organism. Eukaryotic genomes can be subdivided into their nuclear genome (chromosomes found within the nucleus) and their mitochondrial genome.

genotype. [1] The alleles present in a given individual's DNA for a particular genetic marker or set of markers. [2] The unique genetic makeup of an organism. See also *phenotype*.

graph. A set of vertices (also called *nodes*) and a set of edges connecting those vertices. Can be visualized as a set of points connected by lines.

GSS. Genome survey sequences. This DDBJ/EMBL/GenBank division is similar in nature to the EST division, except that its sequences are genomic, rather than originating from cDNA (mRNA). The GSS division contains (but is not limited to) the following types of data: random "single-pass read" genome survey sequences, single-pass reads from cosmid/bacterial artificial chromosome (BAC)/yeast artificial chromosome (YAC) ends (these could be chromosome specific, but need not be), exon-trapped genomic sequences, and Alu PCR sequences.

GUI. Graphical user interface. Refers to software front-ends that rely on pictures and icons to direct the interaction of users with the application.

haplotype. A set of closely related genes or genetic markers that tend to be inherited as a single unit.

heuristic algorithm. An economical strategy for deriving a solution to a problem for which an exact solution is computationally impractical or intractable. Consequently, a heuristic approach is not guaranteed to find the optimal or "true" solution.

homologs/homologous. In phylogenetics, particular features in different individuals that are descended genetically from the same feature in a common ancestor are termed *homologous*.

homology. In phylogenetics, particular features in different individuals that are genetically descended from the same feature in a common ancestor are termed *homologous*.

homology modeling. A method for predicting the tertiary structure of a protein by using an existing homologous protein structure as a template.

homoplasy. Similarity that has evolved independently and is not indicative of common phylogenetic origin.

host. Any computer on the Internet that can be addressed directly through a unique IP address.

HTG/HTGS. High-throughput genome sequences. Various genome sequencing centers worldwide are performing large-scale, systematic sequencing of human and other genomes of interest. The databases have deemed it beneficial to put the unfinished sequences that are the result of such sequencing efforts in a separate division. HTG sequence entries undergo a maturation process. In phase 0, the entry contains a single-to-few pass read of a single clone. In phase 1, the entry contains unfinished sequence, which may be unordered and may contain unoriented contigs or a large number of gaps. In phase 2, the entry still contains unfinished sequence, but is ordered, with oriented contigs that may or may not contain gaps. In phase 3, the entry contains finished sequence, with no gaps; at this point, the entry is moved into the appropriate primary DDBJ/EMBL/GenBank division. In all cases, irrespective of phase, these records (sets of sequences) are assigned a single accession number that is maintained throughout the maturation of the DNA sequence in question.

HTML. Hypertext markup language. The standard, text-based language used to specify the format of Internet documents. HTML files are translated and rendered through the use of Web browsers.

haplotype. Sets of alleles that usually are inherited together.

hyperlink. A graphic or text within an Internet document that can be selected using a mouse. Clicking on a hyperlink transports the user to another part of the same Web page or to another Web page, regardless of location.

hypertext. Within a Web page, text that is differentiated either by color or by underlining that functions as a hyperlink.

ICAT. Isotope coded affinity tagging. A method used to compare the quantities of proteins directly from two different cellular states by mass spectrometry analysis of a shotgun digest of a proteome and appropriate isotopic labeling.

identity. A quantitative measure of how related two sequences are to one another, assessed as the total number of exact matches in a pairwise sequence alignment.

indel. Acronym for **in**sertion or **del**etion. Applied to length-variable regions of a multiple alignment when it is not specified whether sequence length differences have been created by insertions or deletions.

insertion. A mutation in which one or more bases are inserted into a region of DNA.

interaction. Any relationship, physical or otherwise, between biological entities (e.g., proteins, cells, amino acids) that can be defined experimentally.

Internet. A system of linked computer networks used for the transmission of files and messages between hosts.

Intranet. A computer network internal to a company or organization. Intranets often are not connected to the Internet or are protected by a firewall.

intron. Within a gene, a noncoding region that is transcribed into RNA but spliced out of the messenger RNA transcript that is translated into a protein.

IP address. The unique, numeric address of a computer host on the Internet.

isoelectric point. The pH value at which the net charge of a protein or peptide is neutral, as determined by isoelectric focusing.

Java. A programming language developed by Sun Microsystems that allows small programs (applets) to be run on any computer. Java applets typically are invoked when a user clicks on a hyperlink on a Web page.

LAN. Local area network. A network that connects computers in a small, defined area, such as the offices in a single wing or a group of buildings.

library. In sequencing, a collection of insert-containing clones. Sequencing libraries are created from a sequencing vector (see *plasmid*) and a set of inserts obtained by fragmentation of a larger piece of DNA.

linkage. Genes or genetic markers that physically are close to one another on a chromosome and that tend to be inherited together.

linkage disequilibrium. A state resulting when alleles at two defined loci are linked more frequently than would be expected, based on the known allele frequencies and recombination rate between the two loci. Linkage disequilibrium indicates that the two alleles being examined are close physically.

liquid chromatography. A method for separating sample proteins or peptides in preparation for mass spectrometry; separations may be based on properties such as hydrophobicity (reverse phase), surface charge (ion exchange), or diffusion rate (size exclusion or gel filtration).

LOD score. For **log od**ds, a statistical estimate of the linkage between two loci on the same chromosome.

low-complexity region. Regions of biased composition, usually homopolymeric runs, short-period repeats, or the subtle overrepresentation of several residues in a sequence.

MALDI. Matrix-assisted laser-desorption ionization. A common method for generating ions from analyte molecules for analysis by mass spectrometry.

masking. The technique by which low-complexity regions are removed from protein sequences, or LINE, SINE, Alu, and similar sequences are removed from nucleotide sequences before database searches.

mass spectrometry. A collection of exquisitely sensitive and accurate analytical techniques that precisely measure molecular masses through a process of ionization and subsequent mass-to-charge measurement.

microsatellite. Same as a short tandem repeat polymorphism.

mmu. one millimass unit, or one thousandth of a Dalton.

molecular clock. The hypothesis that nucleotide or amino acid substitutions occur at a more or less fixed rate over evolutionary time like the slow ticking of a clock. It has been proposed that given a calibration date and a constant molecular clock, the amount of sequence divergence can be used to calculate the time that has elapsed since two molecules diverged.

molecular complex. A stable complex of molecules functioning as a biological unit.

monoisotopic mass. The base mass of a protein or peptide containing none of the rarer, higher-mass isotopes in any of its constituent atoms.

motif. Conserved sequences within proteins that usually correspond to structural or functional regions.

MS. See *mass spectrometry.*

MS/MS. Tandem mass spectrometry. A process whereby a first stage of mass spectrometry is used to select certain components of a sample, which are then broken down for further analysis by a second stage of mass spectrometry. In some instruments, this can be applied repeatedly to yield MS^n separations.

mutation. An irreversible modification to a chromosome. Mutations can involve single bases or entire regions of a chromosome. Mutations can be neutral (have no effect), harmful, or beneficial; as such, mutations drive evolutionary change.

neutral mass. The actual mass, in Daltons, of a measured protein or peptide after deconvolution and subtraction of any associated ion mass. It refers to the neutral (noncharged) state of the analyzed molecule.

noncoding DNA. A region of DNA that does not code for a protein.

nucleotide. The basic component of both DNA and RNA. Nucleotides consist of both a base (adenine, cytosine, guanine, or cytosine), a sugar molecule, and a phosphoric acid molecule.

oligo. For oligonucleotide, a short, single-stranded DNA or RNA.

OnO (or O&O). Ordered and oriented. The particular order and direction (complemented or uncomplemented) of each contig from an assembly that is known and specified.

ORF. Open reading frame. A DNA sequence that has the potential to encode a protein sequence.

orthologs/orthologous. Homologous sequences are said to be orthologous when they are direct descendants of a sequence in the common ancestor, that is, without having undergone a gene duplication event. See also *homologs* and *paralogs*.

PAM matrix. PAM (percent accepted mutation) and BLOSUM (blocks substitution matrix) are matrices that define scores for each of the 210 possible amino acid substitutions. The scores are based on empirical substitution frequencies observed in alignments of database sequences and, in general, reflect similar physicochemical properties (e.g., a substitution of leucine for isoleucine, two amino acids of similar hydrophobicity and size, will score higher than a substitution of leucine for glutamate).

paralogs/paralogous. Homologous sequences in two organisms, A and B, that are descendants of two different copies of a sequence that has been created by a duplication event in the genome of the common ancestor. See also *homologous* and *orthologs*.

pathway. A set of interactions among biological entities; these interactions may or may not be linear or ordered in any way. Usually defined by a perturbation to a biological system whose output can be measured experimentally.

pedigree. A tree representation of a family (cohort) showing the relationships between members and the pattern of inheritance of a given trait.

peptide mass fingerprint. A protein identification method that works by enzymatically digesting a protein to produce a distinctive fingerprint of masses. The fingerprint is matched against putative fingerprints from protein or nucleotide databases to identify the unknown.

phenotype. The outwardly observable characteristics of an organism. See also *genotype*.

phylogenetic profile. A profile capturing the existence of orthologs of a gene across genomes. Genes with similar phylogenetic profiles are hypothesized to interact physically or at least to be linked functionally.

physical map. A genome map showing the exact location of genes and markers. The highest-resolution physical map is the DNA sequence itself.

pI. See *isoelectric point*.

plasmid. A circular, self-replicating piece of bacterial DNA. Numerous artificially designed plasmids contain priming sites, making them suitable for cloning and

sequencing segments of DNA that range from 2000 to 10,000 bases in length.

platform. Properly, the operating system running software on a computer, for example, UNIX or Windows. More often used to refer to the type of computer, such as a Macintosh or PC.

PMF. See *peptide mass fingerprint*.

polymorphism. Common differences in DNA sequence among individuals that can be used as markers for linkage analysis.

positional cloning. Relies on the identification of a gene through pedigree analysis, genetic and physical mapping, and mutation analysis. Does not require extensive knowledge of the biochemistry of the disease to determine the gene responsible for the disease. [*Ant:* functional cloning.]

primary structure. The amino acid sequence of a protein or polypeptide.

primary transcript. The RNA molecule resulting from the transcription of the DNA sequence encoding a gene.

primer. An oligonucleotide used to initiate polymerase-mediated replication of a strand of DNA.

promoter. The region upstream of a gene where transcription is initiated.

pseudogene. DNA that is similar to a normal, coding gene but that is not functional (may or may not be expressed). Pseudogenes are incapable of producing functional gene products.

quaternary structure. The arrangement or positioning of multiple polypeptide chains (with defined tertiary structures) in larger protein complexes.

R factor. Residual disagreement. Used in X-ray crystallography as a measure of agreement between the experimentally measured diffraction amplitudes and those calculated using the protein coordinates. Perfect agreement corresponds to an R factor of 0.0. Total disagreement corresponds to an R factor of 0.59. Most good-quality protein structures have R factors between 0.15 and 0.20.

Ramachandran plot. A scatterplot showing the disposition of backbone. Phi (ϕ) and psi (φ) torsion angles for each residue in a protein or set of proteins. Certain combinations of ϕ and φ angles are preferred strongly or are repeated over a series of residues, and these patterns can be detected easily in a Ramachandran plot.

reference SNP. Reference single nucleotide polymorphism. Curated dbSNP records that define a nonredundant set of markers used for annotation of reference genome sequence and integration with other National Center for Biotechnology Information resources. Each refSNP record provides a summary list of submitter records in dbSNP and a list of external resource and database links.

repetitive DNA. DNA sequences of variable length that occur in multiple copies in the human and other eukaryotic genomes.

restriction fingerprint. The sizes of the DNA fragments resulting from an endonuclease digestion of the piece of DNA of interest.

ribozyme. A catalytic RNA sequence.

RMSD. Root mean square deviation. An archaic term for standard deviation. RMSD is still used in the quantification of the atomic position differences between protein structures. Very similar structures have RMSD values between 0 and 1.5 Å; moderately similar structures have RMSD values between 1.5 and 3.0 Å.

secondary structure. In proteins, the local, regular backbone structures found in folded proteins (α-helices and β-strands). In RNA, secondary structure is the set of canonical base pairs.

sequence polymorphisms. A divergent allele that exceeds 1% representation in a population.

server. A computer that processes requests issued from remote locations by client machines.

shotgun proteomics. An approach to proteome analysis where all components of a sample are first enzymatically digested into peptides, then separated by liquid chromatography, and finally analyzed by MS/MS to identify them.

shotgun sequencing. A sequencing method in which the DNA to be sequenced is broken into many small fragments. The fragments in turn are sequenced individually; based on overlaps between the individual sequences, the pieces can be reassembled and the original sequence can be deduced.

similarity. A quantitative measure of how related two sequences are to one another, usually assessed as the total number of identities and conservative substitutions in a pairwise sequence alignment. Similarity does not imply homology.

single nucleotide polymorphism (SNP). Alleles that are represented by single-base changes in DNA sequence.

site. An individual column of residues in an amino acid or nucleotide alignment. The residues at a site are presumed to be homologous.

STS. Sequenced tagged sites. An operationally unique sequence that identifies the combination of primer pairs used in a PCR assay, generating a reagent that maps to a single position within the genome. STS sequences usually are on the order of 200 to 500 bases in length. STS is a division of GenBank devoted to STS sequences; it is intended to facilitate cross-comparison of STSs with sequences in other divisions for the purpose of correlating map positions of anonymous sequences with known genes.

supercontig, scaffold. A stretch of DNA sequence composed of one or more contigs known to be ordered and oriented in the same direction.

synteny. In comparative mapping, the observation that the order of loci in a chromosomal region of one organism is conserved in a chromosomal region of a second organism.

tertiary structure. The arrangement or positioning of secondary structure elements into compact, nonoverlapping globules or domains. Tertiary structures are the three-dimensional structures of proteins. In RNA, tertiary structure is the three-dimensional arrangement of atoms.

threading. A method for predicting the most likely fold or topology of a protein by assessing the likelihood that its sequence "fits" into a known three-dimensional fold or a known arrangement of secondary structure.

tiling path format (TPF). Format indicating the identities and order of sequences to be included in a targeted region assembly.

top-down proteomics. A newer method of proteomics that begins with mass spectrometry of intact proteins, followed by subsequent analysis of their constituents via MS degradation methods or peptide mass fingerprinting.

topology. The map or plan of a physical system or set of connected objects. The topology of proteins generally is described by their backbone tertiary (three-dimensional) structure.

URL. Uniform resource locator. Used within Web browsers, URLs specify both the type of site being accessed (FTP, Gopher, or Web) and the address of the Web site.

user. The person using client-server or other types of software.

walking. In sequencing, the extension of nucleotide sequence by generating reads using custom primers designed to be complementary to a known sequence.

word matching. Computer-based search for small segments ("words") of identical DNA sequence.

World wide Web. A document delivery system capable of handling various types of non–text-based media.

YAC. Yeast artificial chromosome. A vector used to clone segments of DNA up to 1 million bases in length.

Z-score, z-value. This measures the distance of a value from the mean of a normal or Gaussian distribution in standard deviation units. A z-score of one means the value is one standard deviation away from the mean. A z-score of four indicates the value is four standard deviations away from the mean (indicating the value has less than a 99.9% chance of occurring randomly).

Index

NOTE: Page numbers followed by f refer to figures, page numbers followed by t refer to tables.